Welcome to the exciting 1ˢᵗ edition of
Forensic Science: An Introduction

A Classic Adapted
for the
High School
Course

Richard Saferstein has carefully adapted his classic **Criminalistics text** to create a comprehensive program **designed specifically for high school students and teachers.**

High School Design

Accessible Text and Motivational 4-Color Presentation

Reader-friendly font and format make science content easy-to-read and exciting.

Students live in a visual world, and the functional use of full color conveys forensic science to today's students.

Over 150 full-color photos and 4-color presentation motivate students to read.

Chapter Openers

A stunning visual element starts off each chapter, bringing the topic to life.

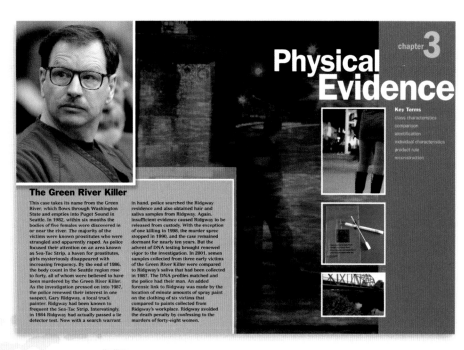

Dimensional Illustrations

Full-color art program helps students better understand key forensics concepts.

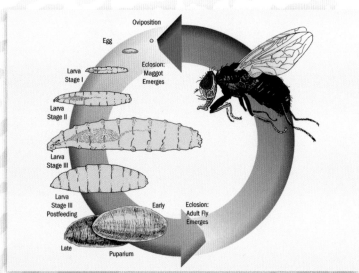

Open & Accessible Design

Every design detail has been carefully thought out—even the text font and open space.

Learning Tools

Learning Objectives

Learning Objectives

After studying this chapter you should be able to:

■ Review the common types of physical evidence encountered at crime scenes

■ Explain the difference between the identification and comparison of physical evidence

■ Define and contrast individual and class characteristics of physical evidence

■ Appreciate the value of class evidence as it relates to a criminal investigation

■ List and explain the function of national databases available to forensic scientists

■ Explain the purpose physical evidence plays in reconstructing the events surrounding the commission of a crime

This feature highlights the key concepts of the chapter.

Key Terms

Forensic-specific vocabulary is explained in the margins.

created, different in its physical and chemical properties from its elemental components. This new material is called a compound. Compounds contain at least two elements. Considering that there are eighty-nine natural elements, it is easy to imagine the large number of possible elemental combinations that may form compounds. Not surprisingly, more than 16 million known compounds have already been identified.

Just as the atom is the basic unit of an element, the molecule is the smallest unit of a compound. Thus, a molecule of carbon dioxide is represented by the symbol CO_2, and a molecule of table salt is symbolized by NaCl, representing the combination of one atom of the element sodium (Na) with one atom of the element chlorine (Cl).

States of Matter

As we look around us and view the materials that make up the earth, it becomes an awesome task even to attempt to estimate the number of different kinds of matter. A much more logical approach is to classify matter according to the physical form it takes. These forms are called physical states. There are three such states: solid, liquid, and gas (vapor).

In the solid state, molecules of matter are held closely together by strong attractive forces. This tightly packed molecular arrangement makes solid matter rigid and gives it a definite shape and volume. In a liquid, the attractive forces between molecules are weaker. The molecules are in contact with one another, but are not held as rigidly in place. Like a solid, a liquid also occupies a specific volume, but its fluidity causes it to take the

compound
A pure substance composed of two or more elements.

physical state
The physical form taken by matter: solid, liquid, or gas.

solid
A state of matter in which molecules are held closely together by strong attractive forces.

liquid
A state of matter in which the attractive forces are strong enough to allow molecules to be contact with one another but too weak to hold them rigidly in place.

Web Links

With a click of the mouse, the power of the Web brings forensic principles to life.

WebExtra 2.1
Making a Photographic Record of the Crime Scene
www.prenhall.com/hsforensics

Forensics at Work

Liquid Explosives

Of the hundreds of types of explosives, most are solid. Only about a dozen are liquid. But some of those liquid explosives can be readily purchased and others can be made from hundreds of different kinds of chemicals that are not difficult to blow up ten international planes to obtain. A memo issued by federal security officials about the plot, highlighted a type of liquid explosive based on peroxide.

The most common peroxide explosive is triacetone triperoxide, or TATP, which is made from two liquids: acetone, the primary ingredient of most nail polish removers, and hydrogen peroxide, commonly used in diluted form as an antiseptic. TATP, which can be used as a detonator or a primary explosive, has been used in Qaeda-related bomb plots and by Palestinian suicide bombers.

TATP itself is a white powder made up of crystals that form when acetone and

hydrogen peroxide are mixed together, usually with a catalyst added to speed the chemical reactions. But there is no need to wait for the crystals. Acetone and peroxide form is an "exceedingly reactive mixture" that can be easily detonated by an electrical spark, said Neal Langerman, president of Advanced Chemical Safety, a consulting company in San Diego.

Acetone is easy to obtain; hydrogen peroxide is somewhat more difficult to obtain. The hydrogen peroxide solution sold in pharmacies is too dilute—only 3 percent—to be used in an explosive. Stronger hydrogen peroxide of 30 percent concentration can be ordered from chemical supply companies, but concentrations strong enough to generate a powerful explosion—about 70 percent—are not readily available, Dr. Langerman said.

Liquids and gels discarded by airline passengers before boarding.

"Forensics at Work" Boxes

Forensic applications provide students with examples from the real world.

Forensic Brief

The Crash of TWA Flight 800

Although the crash of TWA Flight 800 was ultimately not proven to be an act of terrorism, the initial investigation revealed the difficulties investigators can expect to encounter in recovering explosive residues at bombing scenes. For example, in spite of the large quantities of explosive used, investigators encountered extreme difficulties in recovering explosive residues at both the World Trade Center (1993) and Oklahoma federal building bombing sites.

The Search: The TWA Plane Crash

Three weeks after the Atlantic Ocean swallowed a flaming Boeing 747, investigators continue to explore a prevailing theory that the downfall of Trans World Airlines Flight 800 was caused by a bomb. But their complicated mission is made all the more complex by the very water in which much of the plane rests.

Investigators say they are still concerned that the extended submersion in saltwater might have an effect on telltale chemical traces that a bomb would have left on airplane aluminum, plastic containers, luggage—and anything else from the jumbo jet's front end, where, investigators theorize, the explosion that downed the

FBI agents and New York State Police guard the reconstruction of TWA Flight 800.

(continued)

"Forensic Brief" Boxes

Linked to the chapter material, these boxes provide students with quick and pertinent facts about forensic cases.

Case Readings

End-of-chapter in-depth cases that further explore the world of forensic science.

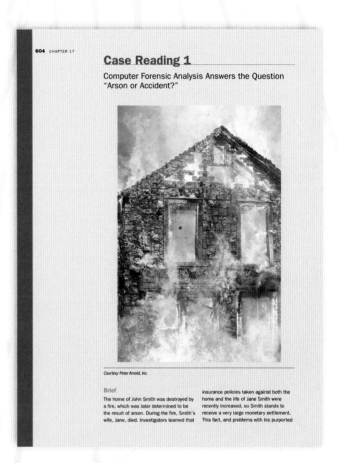

604 CHAPTER 17

Case Reading 1

Computer Forensic Analysis Answers the Question "Arson or Accident?"

Courtesy Peter Arnold, Inc.

Brief

The home of John Smith was destroyed by a fire, which was later determined to be the result of arson. During the fire, Smith's wife, Jane, died. Investigators learned that insurance policies taken against both the home and the life of Jane Smith were recently increased, so Smith stands to receive a very large monetary settlement. This fact, and problems with his purported

Engaging Forensic Cases

Each chapter begins with a gripping forensic case, showing students how that chapter relates to the real world.

chapter **15**

Firearms, Tool Marks, and Other Impressions

Key Terms
bore
breechblock
caliber
choke
distance determination
ejector
extractor
firearms identification
gauge
Greiss test
grooves
lands
rifling

The Beltway Snipers

During a three-week period in October 2002, ten people were killed and three others were wounded as two snipers terrorized the region in and around the Baltimore-Washington metropolitan area. The arrest of John Allen Muhammad, 41, and Lee Boyd Malvo, 17, ended the ordeal. The semiautomatic .223-caliber rifle seized from them was ultimately linked by ballistic tests to eight of the ten killings. The car that Muhammad and Malvo were driving had been specially configured with one hole in the trunk through which a rifle barrel could protrude, so that a sniper could shoot from inside a slightly ajar trunk.

The major break in the case came when a friend of Muhammad's called police suggesting that Muhammad and his friend Malvo were the likely snipers. Muhammad's automobile records revealed numerous traffic stops in the Beltway area during the time of the shootings. Another break in the case came when Malvo called a priest to boast of a killing weeks before in Montgomery, Alabama. Investigators traced the claim to a recent liquor store holdup that left one person dead. Fortunately, the perpetrator of this crime left a latent fingerprint at the murder scene. Authorities quickly tracked the print to Malvo, a Jamaican citizen, through his fingerprints on file with the Immigration and Naturalization Service. A description of Muhammad's car was released to the media, leading to tips from alert citizens who noticed the car parked in a rest area with both occupants asleep.

The motive for the shooting spree was believed to be a planned plot to extort $10 million from local and state governments. Muhammad was sentenced to death and Malvo is currently serving life imprisonment without parole.

Computer Forensics

Chapter 17 shows students how computers are playing an increasingly significant role in criminal activity and the collection of forensic evidence.

From Input to Output: How Does the Computer Work?

Hardware Versus Software

Before we get into the nuts and bolts of computers, we must establish the important distinction between hardware and software. Hardware comprises the physical components of the computer: the computer chassis, monitor, keyboard, mouse, hard disk drive, random-access memory (RAM), central processing unit (CPU), and so on (see Figure 17–1). The list is much more extensive but, generally speaking, if it is a computer component or peripheral that you can see, feel, and touch, it is hardware.

Software, conversely, is a set of instructions compiled into a program that performs a particular task. Software consists of programs and applications that carry out a set of instructions on the hardware. Operating systems (Windows, Mac OS, Linux, Unix), word-processing programs (Microsoft Word, WordPerfect), web-browsing applications (Internet Explorer, Netscape Navigator, Firefox), and accounting applications (Quicken, QuickBooks, Microsoft Money) are all examples of software.

It is important not to confuse software with the physical media that it comes on. When you buy an application such as Microsoft Office, it comes

hardware
The physical components of a computer: case, keyboard, monitor, motherboard, RAM, HDD, mouse, and so on. Generally speaking, if it is a computer component you can touch, it is hardware.

software
A set of instructions compiled into a program that performs a particular task.

FIGURE 17–1 **Cutaway diagram of a personal computer.** *Courtesy Tim Downs*

WebExtras

Interactive activities and in-depth information are just a click away. Hand-picked by the author, WebExtras deliver bonus Internet-related information.

Forensic Science and the Internet

A full chapter on the role the Web plays in modern forensic science.

Student Supplements

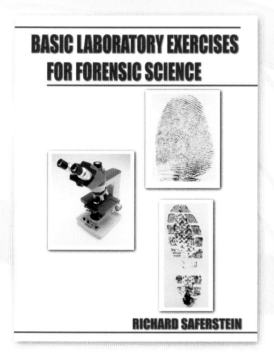

Basic Laboratory Exercises for Forensic Science
0-13-196143-8

The Basic Laboratory Exercises workbook brings the real world of forensic science into the classroom with hands-on activities from fingerprinting, to blood stain analysis, to forensic entomology, to forensic anthropology.

Companion Web Site

www.prenhall.com/hsforensics

Instructor Supplements

Annotated Instructor's Edition
0-13-196142-X

INSTRUCTOR'S MANUAL & LESSON PLANS
FORENSIC SCIENCE
AN INTRODUCTION
RICHARD SAFERSTEIN

Instructor's Manual & Lesson Plans
0-13-225294-5
Includes Aids, Helpful Hints, and Answers to the *Basic Laboratory Exercises for Forensic Science*

TestGen
0-13-196145-4

Test Item File
0-13-225295-3

PowerPoints and Instructor's Resources
0-13-196144-6

DNA Typing

D N A

- Portions of the DNA molecule contain sequences of bases that are repeated numerous times, known as tandem repeats.
- To a forensic scientist, these tandem repeats offer a means of distinguishing one individual from another through DNA typing.
- Tandem repeats seem to act as filler or spacers between the coding regions of DNA.
- What is important to understand is that all humans have the same type of repeats, but there is tremendous variation in the number of repeats each of us have.

FORENSIC SCIENCE

An Introduction

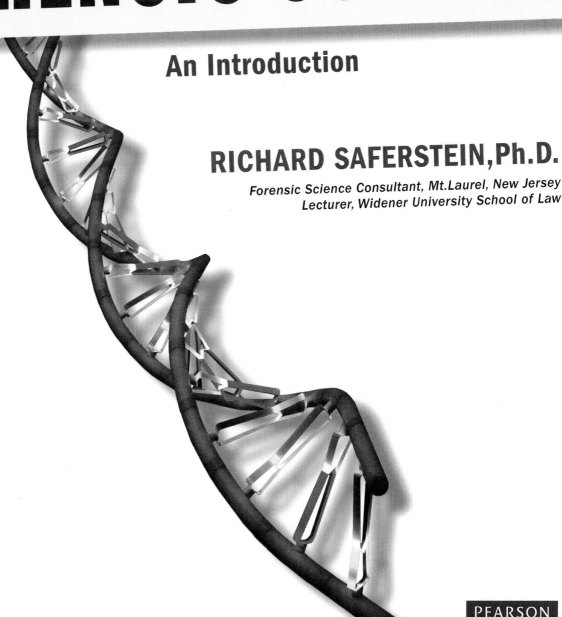

RICHARD SAFERSTEIN, Ph.D.

Forensic Science Consultant, Mt. Laurel, New Jersey
Lecturer, Widener University School of Law

PEARSON

Prentice
Hall

Upper Saddle River, New Jersey 07458

Library of Congress Cataloging-in-Publication Data
Saferstein, Richard, (date)
    Forensic science: an introduction/Richard Saferstein.
    p. cm.
    Includes index.
    ISBN 0-13-196141-1
    1. Forensic sciences. I. Title.

    HV8073.S213 2007
    363.25—dc22

Editor-in-Chief: Vernon R. Anthony
Senior Acquisitions Editor: Tim Peyton
Assistant Editor: Mayda Bosco
Marketing Manager: Adam Kloza
Editorial Assistant: Jillian Allison
Production Editor: Linda Zuk
Production Liaison: Barbara Marttine Cappuccio
Managing Editor: Mary Carnis
Manufacturing Manager: Ilene Sanford
Manufacturing Buyer: Cathleen Petersen
Senior Design Coordinator: Mary Siener
Interior Design: Pronk and Associates
Cover Designer: Jonathan Boylan
Cover Images: DNA strand: Fritz Goro, Getty Images; Footprints: Alan Polansky;
    Broken glass: K Hackenberg/zefa/Corbis; Crime scene: Sirchie Finger Print
    Laboratories, Inc., Youngsville, N.C.
Director, Image Resource Center: Melinda Patelli
Manager, Rights and Permissions: Zina Arabia
Manager, Visual Research: Beth Brenzel
Manager, Cover Visual Research & Permissions: Karen Sanatar
Image Permissions Coordinator: Richard Rodrigues
Media Editor: John J. Jordan
Media Production Project Manager: Lisa Rinaldi
Formatting: Carlisle Publishing Services
Printing and Binding: R.R. Donnelley & Sons, Willard, Ohio
Cover Printer: Lehigh Press

This book is adapted from *Criminalistics: An Introduction to Forensic Science,* 9th edition, © 2007 by Pearson
Education, Inc.

Pearson Education Ltd.   Pearson Education Australia PTY, Limited
Pearson Education Singapore, Pte. Ltd.   Pearson Education North Asia Ltd.
Pearson Education, Canada, Ltd.   Pearson Educación de Mexico, S.A. de C.V.
Pearson Education—Japan   Pearson Education Malaysia, Pte. Ltd.

10 9 8 7 6 5 4 3 2 1
ISBN: 0-13-196141-1
ISBN: 0-13-196142-X

To my wife Gail, the pillar of my life

CONTENTS

Chapter 6

Forensic Toxicology   200

Chapter 7

The Microscope   236

Chapter 8

Forensic Serology   266

Chapter 9

DNA: The Indispensable Forensic Science Tool 306

Chapter 10

Trace Evidence I: Hairs and Fibers 354

Chapter 17
Computer Forensics   578

Andrew W. Donofrio

Chapter 18
Forensic Science and the Internet   610

Andrew W. Donofrio and Richard Saferstein

Chapter 19

Careers in Forensic Science 632

PREFACE

The level of sophistication that forensic science has brought to criminal investigations is awesome. But one cannot lose sight of the fact that, once all the drama of a forensic science case is put aside, what remains is an academic subject emphasizing science and technology. It is to this end that this first edition of *Forensic Science: An Introduction* is dedicated.

This first edition follows the tradition, philosophy, and objectives of my introductory college text, *Criminalistics: An Introduction to Forensic Science*, which is in its ninth edition. In creating this introductory text, every chapter of the college text was examined to improve the clarity of the narrative. This improvement has been accomplished by presenting the science of forensics in a very straightforward and student-friendly format. Topics have been rearranged to better integrate scientific methodology with actual forensic application. The reader is offered the option of delving into the more difficult technical aspects of the book by going into the "Closer Analysis" sections in each chapter, an option that can be bypassed without detracting from a basic comprehension of the subject of forensic science.

Only the most relevant scientific and technological concepts are presented to the reader, so that the subject is not watered down with superfluous discussions that are of no real significance to current forensic science practices. It is the author's belief that, by learning in an interactive environment using the Internet, the reader will be a more motivated and active participant in the learning process. The text is accompanied by a companion website (www.prenhall.com/hsforensics) that provides additional exercises, text information, and WebExtras. The latter serve to expand the coverage of the book through video presentations and graphic displays that enhance the reader's understanding of the subject's more difficult concepts.

One of the constants of forensic science is how frequently its applications become front-page news. Whether the story is sniper shootings or the tragic consequences of the terrorist attacks of 9/11/01, forensic science is at the forefront of the public response. In order to merge theory with practice, a significant number of actual forensic case histories are included in the text. In fact, eleven cases that do not appear in the college edition have been included in this introductory edition. The intent is for all the case illustrations to capture the interest of the reader and to move forensic science from the domain of the abstract into the real world of criminal investigation.

At the end of each chapter, the student will encounter a chapter summary that recaps all of the major points of the chapter. This summary is followed by review questions and, in some chapters, virtual crime scene exercises that enable the reader to move through various types of crime scenes while identifying and collecting physical evidence. Finally, Web resources are suggested for the reader who would like to pursue the chapter's subjects in more detail.

Acknowledgments

I am most appreciative of the contribution that Detective Sergeant Andrew (Drew) Donofrio of New Jersey's Bergen County Prosecutor's Office made to *Forensic Science*. I was fortunate to find in Drew a contributor who not only possesses extraordinary skill, knowledge, and hands-on experience with computer forensics, but who was able to combine those attributes with sophisticated communication skills.

Sarah A. Skorupsky-Borg, MSFS, invested an extraordinary amount of time and effort in preparing an accompanying supplement to this text: *Basic Laboratory Exercises for Forensic Science*. Her skills and tenacity in carrying out this task are acknowledged and greatly appreciated.

Many people provided assistance and advice in the preparation of this book. Many faculty members, colleagues, and friends have read and commented on various portions of the text. I would like to acknowledge the contributions of Jeffrey C. Kercheval, Robert Thompson, Roger Ely, Jose R. Almirall, Darlene Brezinski, Gavin Edmonstone, and Michael Malone.

The following reviewers provided insightful and helpful critiques of the manuscript: Craig Anderson, Galt High School, Galt, California; Margaret Barthel, Ph.D., Freedom High School, Orlando, Florida; Thomas J. Costello, High Point Regional High School, Sussex, New Jersey; Thomas Donley, The Hotchkiss School, Lakeville, Connecticut; Shelly Duk, Walled Lake Central High School, Commerce, Michigan; Mark Feil, Glasgow High School, Wilmington, Delaware; Myra Frank, Marjory Stoneman Douglas High School, Parkland, Florida; Jim Hurley, Waverly-Shell Rock Community Schools, Waverly, Iowa; Lisa Kiann, River Valley High School, Caledonia, Ohio; Mary Monte, Eastern Technical High School, Baltimore, Maryland; Mary J. Monte, Woodlawn High School, Timonium, Maryland; Kevin Mugridge, Bishop Timon St. Jude High School, Buffalo, New York; Barbara Olsen, Rocky Hill High School, Rocky Hill, Connecticut; Bruce Parce, Albert Einstein High School, Kensington, Maryland; Tod Suttle, Mayfair Middle/High School, Lakewood, California; Danielle DuChesne Thompson, Mariner High School, Everett, Washington; and Penny Wolkow, Oakland Mills High School, Columbia, Maryland.

The assistance of Pamela Cook and Gonul Turhan, whose research efforts are an integral part of this text, was invaluable. I am also appreciative of the time and talent given by development editor Mayda Bosco and production editor Linda Zuk. The transformation of *Criminalistics* from a college text into this edition is the result in large part of the editorial skills of John Haley, who reorganized substantial portions of the text and rewrote end-of-chapter questions.

Finally, I am grateful to those law enforcement agencies, government agencies, private individuals, and equipment manufacturers cited in the text for contributing their photographs and illustrations.

ABOUT THE AUTHOR

Richard Saferstein, Ph.D., retired in 1991 after serving twenty-one years as the Chief Forensic Scientist of the New Jersey State Police Laboratory, one of the largest crime laboratories in the United States. He currently acts as a consultant for attorneys and the media in the area of forensic science. During the O. J. Simpson criminal trial, Dr. Saferstein provided extensive commentary on forensic aspects of the case for the *Rivera Live* show, the E! television network, ABC radio, and various radio talk shows. Dr. Saferstein holds degrees from the City College of New York and earned his doctorate degree in chemistry in 1970 from the City University of New York. From 1972 to 1991, he taught an introductory forensic science course in the criminal justice programs at The College of New Jersey and Ocean County College. These teaching experiences played an influential role in Dr. Saferstein's authorship in 1977 of the widely used introductory textbook *Criminalistics: An Introduction to Forensic Science,* currently in its ninth edition, Saferstein's basic philosophy in writing *Criminalistics* is to make forensic science understandable and meaningful to the nonscience reader while giving the reader an appreciation for the scientific principles that underlie the subject.

Dr. Saferstein currently teaches a course on the role of the expert witness in the courtroom at the law school of Widener University in Wilmington, Delaware. He has authored or co-authored more than forty-four technical papers covering a variety of forensic topics. Dr. Saferstein has authored *Basic Laboratory Exercises for Forensic Science* (Prentice Hall, 2007) and co-authored *Lab Manual for Criminalistics* (Prentice Hall, 2007). He has also edited the widely used professional reference books *Forensic Science Handbook,* Volume 1, 2nd edition (Prentice Hall, 2002), *Forensic Science Handbook,* Volume 2, 2nd edition (Prentice Hall, 2005), and *Forensic Science Handbook,* Volume 3 (Prentice Hall, 1993). Dr. Saferstein is a member of the American Chemical Society, the American Academy of Forensic Sciences, the Forensic Science Society of England, the Canadian Society of Forensic Scientists, the International Association for Identification, the Mid-Atlantic Association of Forensic Scientists, the Northeastern Association of Forensic Scientists, the Northwestern Association of Forensic Scientists, and the Society of Forensic Toxicologists.

In 2006, Dr. Saferstein received the American Academy of Forensic Sciences Paul L. Kirk award for distinguished service and contributions to the field of criminalistics.

INSTRUCTOR'S RESOURCES

To The Instructor

The supplemental materials in this *Annotated Instructor's Edition* have been prepared to facilitate the use of the high school edition of *Forensic Science: An Introduction* by Richard Saferstein. They are intended to help the instructor prepare reading assignments, class lectures, demonstrations, and quizzes, and to help students get the greatest possible benefit from the text. These materials include the following:

Key Terms—An alphabetical listing of all key terms in the chapter, accompanied by the definition of each term drawn from the marginal glossary in the text.

Learning Objectives—Prepared by the text author, the learning objectives outline the most important concepts for students to master in each chapter.

Key Points—A bulleted summary of the basic concepts covered in each chapter.

Supplemental Questions—Ten to twenty review questions drawn from the text and reviewed and approved by the text author. Every question is in a short answer/brief essay format that challenges students to demonstrate a fuller understanding of the concepts in the text than multiple choice or true/false questions. Answers are provided for all questions.

Videos/DVDs—A list of widely available video resources for use in class. Includes description of the material, format, rating (if any), studio, date of publication, and ASIN.

Books—Print resources that can be used to supplement the main text, as sources for case studies, or for outside reading assignments for students. Features a description of the work, format (paperback or hardcover), length, publisher, date of publication, and ISBN.

Advanced Reading—A listing of books and journal articles that take a more in-depth look at topics covered in each chapter. These readings are geared for more advanced students or for instructors who wish to introduce more difficult concepts in their classes.

Demonstrations and Lecture Starters—This section features brief in-class demonstrations and ideas for lecture topics and in-class discussions. These materials are intended to help instructors explore different ways to explain basic concepts in the chapter. All demonstrations are designed to be performed with materials that are readily available or that can be ordered from outside sources whose addresses and URLs are included.

Chapter 1

Introduction

Key Terms

expert witness—An individual whom the court determines to possess knowledge relevant to the trial that is not expected of the average layperson.

Locard's exchange principle—Whenever two objects come into contact with one another, they exchange materials between them.

scientific method—A process that uses strict guidelines to ensure careful and systematic collection, organization, and analysis of information.

Learning Objectives

• Define and distinguish forensic science and criminalistics

• Recognize the major contributors to the development of forensic science

• Account for the rapid growth of forensic laboratories in the past forty years

• Describe the services of a typical comprehensive crime laboratory in the criminal justice system

• Compare and contrast the *Frye* and *Daubert* decisions relating to the admissibility of scientific evidence in the courtroom

• Explain the role and responsibilities of the expert witness

Key Points

• Forensic science is the application of science to criminal and civil laws that are enforced by police agencies in a criminal justice system.

• The development of crime laboratories in the United States has been characterized by rapid growth accompanied by a lack of national and regional planning and coordination.

• The technical support provided by crime laboratories can be assigned to five basic services: the physical science unit, the biology unit, the firearms unit, the document examination unit, and the photography unit.

• Some crime laboratories offer optional services such as toxicology, fingerprint analysis, voiceprint analysis, crime-scene investigation, and polygraph administration.

• A forensic scientist must be skilled in applying the principles and techniques of the physical and natural sciences to the analysis of evidence that may be recovered during a criminal investigation.

• An expert witness evaluates evidence based on specialized training and experience.

• Forensic scientists train law enforcement personnel in the proper recognition, collection, and preservation of physical evidence.

• The *Frye* v. *United States* decision set guidelines for determining the admissibility of scientific evidence into the courtroom. To meet the *Frye* standard, the evidence in question must be "generally accepted" by the scientific community.

• In the case of *Daubert* v. *Merrell Dow Pharmaceuticals, Inc.*, the U.S. Supreme Court ruled that trial judges were responsible for the admissibility and validity of scientific evidence presented in their courts.

Supplemental Questions

1. Why is Mathieu Orfila considered "the father of forensic toxicology"?

2. What was anthropometry and who developed it?

3. Who developed the first definitive study of fingerprints and a methodology of classifying them for filing?

4. How did Calvin Goddard advance the science of firearms examination?

5. What is Locard's exchange principle?

6. What contribution did Sir Alec Jeffreys make to forensic science?

7. What major advance in forensic science did the state of California undertake in 1972?

8. How does the British system of forensic laboratories differ from that of the United States?

9. How has the emergence of the "fee-for-service" system affected the practice of forensic science in Great Britain?

10. List three reasons for the unparalleled growth of crime laboratories in the United States since the 1960s.

11. Describe how the structure of the U.S. federal government has affected the organization of crime labs in the United States.

12. List three main reasons for the wide variation in total services offered by crime labs in different communities.

13. Describe the basic duties of the physical science unit in a crime lab and give three examples of the type of work performed by a physical science unit.

14. In addition to the physical science unit, what four units typically are found in full-service crime labs? List at least one function performed by each of these units.

15. List two optional units found in most crime labs and give at least one example of the type of work done by each.

16. List the main functions of the forensic scientist.

17. What important principle was established in the case of *Frye* v. *United States?*

18. How did the court's ruling in the case of *Daubert* v. *Merrell Dow Pharmaceuticals, Inc.* affect the admissibility of scientific evidence in federal courts?

19. How does the testimony of an expert witness differ from the testimony of a lay witness?

20. List two ways in which a forensic odontologist can assist in criminal investigations.

Answers to Supplemental Questions

1. Orfila published the first scientific treatise on the detection of poisons and their effects on animals.

2. Anthropometry, developed by Alphonse Bertillon, was a system for identifying individuals based on the measurement of various parts of the body.

3. Francis Galton developed the first definitive study of fingerprints and a methodology of classifying them for filing.

4. Goddard was the first to use a comparison microscope to analyze bullets to determine whether they were fired from the same gun.

5. Locard's exchange principle states that when a criminal comes in contact with an object or person, a cross-transfer of evidence occurs that can connect the suspect to his or her victim.

6. Sir Alec Jeffreys developed the first DNA-profiling test.

7. In 1972 California began creating an integrated network of state-operated forensic laboratories consisting of regional and satellite facilities.

8. In contrast to the American system of independent local laboratories, Britain has developed a national system of regional laboratories under the direction of the government's Home Office.

9. The fee-for-service concept has encouraged the creation of private laboratories that make their services available to police and defense alike.

10. First, Supreme Court decisions in the 1960s required police to place greater emphasis on securing scientifically evaluated evidence and all but eliminated confessions as a routine investigative tool. Second, the dramatic increase in U.S. crime rates led to a greater need for scientific examination of criminal evidence. Third, the advent of DNA profiling led to a need for crime labs to expand their staffs and modernize their facilities to meet the demands of DNA technology.

11. The federal system of government emphasizes the importance of retaining local control over important matters such as criminal prosecution. This has led to the growth of many local and state crime laboratories and precluded the creation of a national system. In addition, the federal government has no single law enforcement or investigative agency that has unlimited jurisdiction throughout the country.

12. Three main reasons for the wide variation in total services offered by crime labs are variations in local laws, different capabilities and functions of the organization to which a laboratory is attached, and budget and staffing limitations.

13. The physical science unit applies principles and techniques of chemistry, physics, and geology to the identification and comparison of crime-scene evidence. Three examples of the type of work performed by the physical science unit are drug identification, soil and mineral analysis, and examination of trace physical evidence.

14. The biology unit performs DNA profiling of dried bloodstains and other body fluids, compares hairs and fibers, and identifies and compares botanical materials such as wood and plants. The firearms unit examines firearms and ammunition of all types, examines garments and other objects in order to detect firearms discharge residues, and examines crime-scene evidence to approximate the distance from a target at which a weapon was fired. The document examination unit studies questioned documents to ascertain their authenticity and/or source; analyzes paper and ink; and examines indented writings, obliterations, erasures, and burned or charred documents. The photography unit examines and records physical evidence, uses specialized photographic techniques to make invisible information visible to the naked eye, and helps prepare photographic exhibits for courtroom presentation.

15. The toxicology unit examines body fluids and organs to determine the presence or absence of drugs and poisons, determines the alcoholic consumption of individuals, trains operators in the use of field instruments, and maintains and services such instruments. The latent fingerprint unit processes and examines evidence for latent fingerprints. The polygraph unit administers and interprets the results of polygraph tests. The voiceprint analysis unit analyzes sound recordings to connect voiceprints to particular criminal suspects. The crime-scene investigation unit dispatches specially trained personnel to the crime scene to collect and preserve physical evidence that will later be processed at the crime laboratory.

16. The main functions of the forensic scientist include analyzing physical evidence; providing expert testimony; and furnishing training in the proper recognition, collection, and preservation of physical evidence.

17. *Frye* v. *United States* established the principle that questioned procedures, techniques, or principles must be "generally accepted" by a meaningful segment of the relevant scientific community before they are admissible as evidence at trial.

18. In *Daubert* v. *Merrell Dow Pharmaceuticals, Inc.*, the Supreme Court asserted that "general acceptance" is not an absolute prerequisite to the admissibility of scientific evidence under the Federal Rules of Evidence. According to the Court, the Rules of Evidence assign to the trial judge the task of ensuring that an expert's testimony rests on a reliable foundation and is relevant to the task at hand.

19. A lay witness must give testimony on events or observations that arise from personal knowledge. This testimony must be factual and, with few exceptions, cannot contain the personal opinions of the witness. By contrast, the expert witness evaluates evidence that the court lacks the expertise to do, and thus must express his or her personal opinion as to the significance of the findings. The views expressed

are accepted only as representing the expert's opinion and may later be accepted or ignored in jury deliberations.

20. Forensic odontologists can use dental records such as X-rays, dental casts, and a photograph of a person's smile to compare a set of dental remains and a suspected victim. A forensic odontologist can also compare bite marks left on a victim to the tooth structure of suspects.

Resources

Videos/DVDs

CSI: Crime Scene Investigation

This fictionalized television drama is set in the world of crime-scene investigation and forensic science. The first three seasons of the program are available on DVD. The following information refers to the complete three-season boxed set.

> Format: Color, DVD, Fullscreen
>
> Rated: TV14
>
> Studio: Paramount
>
> DVD Release Date: November 29, 2005
>
> ASIN: B000B9EYIY

Forensics

This six-tape set from the award-winning *NOVA* series discusses the key topic of forensics. The set includes *Hunt for the Serial Arsonist, The Killer's Trail, Anastasia: Dead or Alive?, Mind of a Serial Killer, Return of the Iceman* and *Mystery of the First Americans.*

> Format: Color, VHS
>
> Rated: NR
>
> Studio: WGBH
>
> Video Release Date: October 14, 2000
>
> ASIN: 1578075424

Modern Marvels: Forensic Science

This video traces the development of forensics, demonstrates modern techniques such as DNA fingerprinting and fiber science, and revisits famous cases such as the ballistics evidence that led to the conviction of James Earl Ray and the tiny clues that put investigators of the Lockerbie disaster on the trail of Libyan terrorists.

> Format: Color, VHS
>
> Rated: NR
>
> Studio: A&E Entertainment
>
> Video Release Date: April 22, 1998
>
> ASIN: B000006QZP

Books

Hidden Evidence: 40 True Crimes and How Forensic Science Helped Solve Them

David Owen

This book looks at how forensic science has developed and how techniques have evolved from methods of investigation used in ancient China to computerized DNA analysis. The book highlights forty actual crimes, including explanations of how evidence was investigated, in such cases as the Lindbergh baby kidnapping and the O. J. Simpson murder trial. The author examines detective methods, details the procedures used by police and investigators at the crime scene and forensic lab, and looks at promising developments in forensic science.

> Format: Hardcover, 240 pages
>
> Publisher: Sagebrush Press (2001)
>
> ISBN: 0613339096

Police Lab: How Forensic Science Tracks Down and Convicts Criminals

David Owen

This paperback combines forensics and historical crime review. Owen explains how forensics experts gather, analyze, and assess data on forgery; poisoning; suicides; explosions; and murder by fire, water, suffocation, and various weapons. Descriptions of the forensics process are put into historical context, with famous case studies and historical events.

> Format: Paperback, 128 pages
>
> Publisher: Firefly Books (2002)
>
> ISBN: 155297619X

Written in Blood: A History of Forensic Detection

Colin Wilson

This book charts the progress of criminalistics from the first attempts at detecting arsenic to the development of modern techniques such as ballistics analysis, textile analysis, psychological profiling, and genetic fingerprinting. It includes discussions of notorious cases such as Jack the Ripper; the Black Dahlia; Charles Manson; and Peter Sutcliffe, the so-called Yorkshire Ripper.

> Format: Paperback, 544 pages
>
> Publisher: Carroll and Graf (2003)
>
> ISBN: 078671266X

Advanced Reading

Berg, Stanton O., "Sherlock Holmes: Father of Scientific Crime Detection," *Journal of Criminal Law, Criminology and Police Science* 61, no. 3 (1970): 446–452.

Cohen, Stanley A., "The Role of the Forensic Expert in a Criminal Trial," *Canadian Society of Forensic Science Journal* 12 (1979): 75.

Doyle, Sir Arthur Conan, *The Complete Sherlock Holmes,* Vol. 1. New York: Doubleday, 1956.

Gallop, A. M. C., "Forensic Science Coming of Age," *Science & Justice,* 43 (2003): 55.

Kagan, J. D., "On Being a Good Expert Witness in a Criminal Case," *Journal of Forensic Sciences* 23 (1978): 190.

Lucas, D. M., "North of 49—The Development of Forensic Science in Canada," *Science & Justice* 37 (1997): 47.

Midkiff, C. R., "More Mountebanks," in R. Saferstein, ed., *Forensic Science Handbook,* vol. 2, 2nd ed. Upper Saddle River, N.J.: Prentice Hall, 2005.

Sapir, Gil I., "Legal Aspects of Forensic Science," in R. Saferstein, ed., *Forensic Science Handbook,* vol. l, 2nd ed. Upper Saddle River, N.J.: Prentice Hall, 2002.

Starrs, James E., "Mountebanks among Forensic Scientists," in R. Saferstein, ed., *Forensic Science Handbook,* vol. 2, 2nd ed. Upper Saddle River, N.J.: Prentice Hall, 2005.

Demonstrations and Lecture Starters

Deductive Reasoning Exercise: The Deadly Picnic

This exercise challenges students to critically analyze evidence and emphasizes the importance of thorough observation and note taking at the crime scene.

The Facts of the Case

Centerville police discovered the bodies of a 36-year-old white male (later identified as Gaven Brooks) in a field about twenty miles north of town. Mr. Brooks's body was discovered at 7:30 p.m. on Friday, October 11. He was found lying face up on a yellow, queen-size sheet. According to autopsy reports, one fatal gunshot to the back of the head ended Mr. Brooks's life. Scientists estimate that death occurred at about 4:20 p.m. As investigators scanned the crime scene, they made the following notes:

- Paper plates filled with partially eaten fried chicken, deviled eggs, potato salad, and chocolate cake were located near Mr. Brooks's body.

- An open bottle of red wine and two partially filled glasses of wine were found next to the yellow sheet.

- A recently smoked cigarette butt was found near the sheet.

- Shoeprints from the road to the field were those of a male, size 10, and a female, size 5. The only shoeprints from the field back to the road were those of a female, size 5.

- Car tracks of the same wheel base and tread pattern as Mr. Brooks's automobile were found at the road. The car was not found at the scene.

- Mr. Brooks's car was found abandoned in an empty parking lot in downtown Centerville.

Investigators believe that a female friend of Mr. Brooks was responsible for his demise. After questioning family and friends, it was discovered that the deceased had frequent social outings with six women who live in or near Centerville. The women's names are Rita, Lauren, Gail, Janice, Elaine, and Peggy. Investigators gathered the following information about the six women:

- Janice works full time as a caterer.

- Elaine and Gail are schoolteachers.

- Rita's babysitter says Rita arrived home in her own car at about five p.m.

- Peggy and Elaine live together in a two-bedroom apartment in downtown Centerville.

- Gail lives in a nearby town called Jordan.

- Elaine and Janice are very petite women—they wear size 4 blue jeans.

- Gail and Peggy are smokers.

- Rita's father owns a gun shop.

- Elaine attends a five p.m. step aerobics class in downtown Centerville every Friday afternoon and has not missed a class in two years.

- Peggy is deathly allergic to grapes.

- Lauren works at a chemical supply house.

- Rita lives in a country house about thirty miles west of Centerville.

- Gail is a vegan (she eats no animal products).

- Rita is a florist.

- Janice doesn't know how to drive.

- Elaine and Gail hate the color yellow.

- Lauren played center for a semiprofessional basketball team five years ago. She has red hair and is six feet, one inch tall.

Based on the preceding information, students must determine who murdered Mr. Brooks and the general facts of the case.

The Solution

The general facts of the case are that Mr. Brooks and one of the women took his car on a picnic north of Centerville. After dining, Mr. Brooks was killed by his female companion, who then drove back to town and abandoned his car. Based on the evidence, the murderer is Elaine. At least one piece of evidence eliminates every other suspect. Peggy is deathly allergic to grapes, so she would not have drunk the wine. Lauren is obviously a large woman, so the shoe prints found in the field are too small to be hers. Janice does not know how to drive, so she could not have driven the car back to town by herself. Doubt may fall on Rita, who has no alibi until half an hour after the murder was committed. However, she would not have enough time to drive the twenty miles to Centerville, abandon the car there, then drive an additional thirty miles home and still arrive by 5:00. That leaves Gail and Elaine as possible suspects. Gail might fit the profile because she is a smoker and a cigarette butt was found near the body. However, there is no indication of the sex of the person who smoked the cigarette, so this alone is not sufficient proof. Moreover, Gail is a vegan (she eats no animal products), so she would not have eaten the chicken or deviled eggs. Elaine has the alibi that she was at a 5:00 aerobics class, but the class is in downtown Centerville, where the car was abandoned. This means that she would have had time to commit the murder and still make the class on time. Because all other suspects have been eliminated, Elaine must be the murderer.

Chapter 2

The Crime Scene

Key Terms

algor mortis—Postmortem changes that cause a body to lose heat.

autopsy—The medical dissection and examination of a body in order to determine the cause of death.

buccal swab—A swab of the inner portion of the cheek; cheek cells are usually collected to determine the DNA profile of an individual.

chain of custody—A list of all people who came into possession of an item of evidence.

finished sketch—A precise rendering of the crime scene, usually drawn to scale.

livor mortis—The medical condition that occurs after death and results in the settling of blood in areas of the body closest to the ground.

physical evidence—Any object that can establish that a crime has been committed or can link a crime and its victim or its perpetrator.

rigor mortis—The medical condition that occurs after death and results in the stiffening of body parts in the position they are in when death occurs.

rough sketch—A draft representation of all essential information and measurements at a crime scene. This sketch is drawn at the crime scene.

standard/reference sample—Physical evidence whose origin is known, such as blood or hair from a suspect, that can be compared to crime-scene evidence.

substrate control—Uncontaminated surface material close to an area where physical evidence has been deposited. This sample is to be used to ensure that the surface on which a sample has been deposited does not interfere with laboratory tests.

Learning Objectives

- Define *physical evidence*
- Discuss the responsibilities of the first police officer who arrives at a crime scene
- Explain the steps to be taken to thoroughly record the crime scene
- Describe proper procedures for conducting a systematic search of a crime scene for physical evidence
- Describe proper techniques for packaging common types of physical evidence
- Define and understand the concept of chain of custody

Key Points

- Physical evidence includes any and all objects that can establish that a crime has been committed or can link crime and victim or victim and perpetrator.

- Forensic science begins at the crime scene, where investigators must recognize and properly preserve evidence for laboratory examination.

- The first officer to arrive must secure the crime scene.

- Investigators record the crime scene by using photographs, sketches, and notes and make a preliminary examination of the scene as it was left by the perpetrator.

- The search pattern selected at a crime scene depends on the size and locale of the scene and the number of collectors participating in the search.

- Many items of evidence may be detected only through examination at the crime laboratory. For this reason, it is important to collect possible carriers of trace evidence, such as clothing, vacuum sweepings, and fingernail scrapings, in addition to more discernible items.

- Each item of physical evidence collected at a crime scene must be placed in a separate appropriate container to prevent damage through contact or cross-contamination.

- Investigators must maintain the chain of custody, which is a record for denoting the location of the evidence.

- Proper standard/reference samples, such as hairs, blood, and fibers, must be collected at the crime scene and from appropriate subjects for comparison purposes in the laboratory.

- The removal of any evidence from a person or from the scene of a crime must be done in accordance with appropriate search and seizure protocols.

- Special forensic science services available to the law enforcement community include forensic pathology, forensic anthropology, forensic entomology, forensic psychiatry, forensic odontology, and forensic engineering.

Supplemental Questions

1. How does the textbook define physical evidence?
2. What is the first critical step in crime-scene investigation? Why is this step so important?
3. List the three methods of crime-scene recording.
4. What is the most important prerequisite for photographing a crime scene? Why is this so critical?
5. What is a rough sketch and what information must it accurately reflect?
6. What information must be included in any notes taken at the crime scene?
7. Besides the crime scene itself, what locations must investigators search?
8. What items from deceased victims must be collected and sent to a forensic laboratory?

9. What is the main objective in collecting and packaging physical evidence?

10. What is the best way to maintain the integrity of evidence that is collected and submitted to the crime laboratory?

11. Why is it important to package items of physical evidence in separate containers?

12. Why should ordinary mailing envelopes not be used for packaging physical evidence?

13. Describe a druggist fold and explain why it is a superior way to package small amounts of trace evidence.

14. Why should bloodstained evidence not be stored in airtight containers? What is the best way to store such evidence?

15. Define *chain of custody* and explain why maintaining a proper chain of custody is important. What are the possible consequences of failing to maintain a proper chain of custody?

16. What is a standard/reference sample and why is it important to the criminalist?

17. What is a substrate control and why is it important?

18. Why is it important to include a brief description of the case history on an evidence submission form?

19. List and describe three physical and/or chemical changes that occur in the body that enable a forensic pathologist to determine time of death.

Answers to Supplemental Questions

1. Physical evidence is any object that can establish that a crime has been committed or can link a crime and its victim or a crime and its perpetrator.

2. The first critical step in crime-scene investigation is securing and isolating the crime scene. It is critical because anyone who enters a crime scene potentially could destroy physical evidence important to the investigation.

3. The three methods of crime scene recording are photography, sketches, and notes.

4. The most important prerequisite for photographing a crime scene is for the scene to be in an unaltered condition. If objects at the scene have been removed, been added, or changed positions, the photographs may not be admissible as evidence at a trial, and their intended value will be lost.

5. A rough sketch is a draft representation of all essential information and measurements at a crime scene. A rough sketch must accurately depict the dimensions of the crime scene as well as all recovered items of physical evidence and their exact locations.

6. Crime-scene notes must include a detailed written description of the scene with the location of items of physical evidence recovered. They must also identify the time an item of physical evidence was discovered, by whom, how and by whom it was packaged and marked, and the disposition of the item after it was collected.

7. The areas searched must include all probable points of entry and exit used by the criminal(s).

8. The following items must be sent to the forensic laboratory: the victim's clothing, fingernail scrapings, head and pubic hairs, blood, bullets recovered from the body, hand swabs (from shooting victims), and vaginal/anal/oral swabs (in sex-related crimes).

9. The main objective in collecting and packaging physical evidence is to prevent any change in the evidence between the time it is removed from the crime scene and the time it is received by the crime laboratory.

10. The integrity of evidence is best maintained when the item is kept in its original condition as found at the crime site.

11. Packaging evidence separately prevents damage through contact and cross-contamination.

12. Ordinary mailing envelopes should not be used as evidence containers because powders and fine particles will leak out of their corners.

13. A druggist fold consists of folding one end of a piece of paper over one-third, then folding the other end (one-third) over that, and repeating the process from the other two sides. After the paper is folded in this manner, the outside two edges are tucked into each other. A druggist fold produces a closed container that keeps the specimen from falling out.

14. Bloodstained materials should not be stored in airtight containers because the accumulation of moisture in such containers may encourage the growth of mold, which can destroy the evidential value of blood. In these instances, wrapping paper, manila envelopes, and paper bags are recommended packaging materials.

15. The chain of custody is a list of all people who came into possession of an item of evidence. Maintaining a proper chain of custody is the best guarantee that the evidence will withstand inquiries of what happened to it from the time of its finding to its presentation in court. Failure to substantiate the evidence's chain of custody may lead to serious questions regarding the authenticity and integrity of the evidence and examinations of it.

16. A standard/reference sample is physical evidence whose origin is known, such as blood or hair from a suspect, that can be compared to crime-scene evidence. Standard/reference samples are important because they allow the criminalist to connect evidence found at the scene of a crime to the suspect and/or victim.

17. A substrate control consists of uncontaminated surface material close to an area where physical evidence has been deposited. A substrate control ensures that the surface on which a sample has been

deposited does not interfere with the interpretation of laboratory tests.

18. Providing a case history allows the examiner to analyze specimens in a logical sequence and make the proper comparisons, and it also facilitates the search for trace quantities of evidence.

19. Rigor mortis, or stiffening of the muscles, occurs within twenty-four hours of death and disappears within thirty-six hours. The settling of blood in the parts of the body closest to the ground, known as livor mortis, creates a dark blue or purple appearance immediately and continues for up to twelve hours after death. The cooling of the body after death, or algor mortis, occurs at a predictable rate, enabling the pathologist to estimate time of death from the temperature of the body. Time of death can also be estimated by measuring the concentration of potassium in the victim's eye fluids, because cells in the eyeball release potassium at a predictable rate after death.

Resources

Videos/DVDs

Inside Story: Scene of the Crime

This video follows Baltimore Crime Lab personnel as they collect evidence from various crime scenes in Baltimore. It illustrates crime-scene investigation techniques including photography, fingerprint detection, sketching, and gathering physical evidence.

> Format: Color, VHS
>
> Rated: NR
>
> Studio: A&E Home Video
>
> DVD Release Date: August 13, 2001
>
> ASIN: 0767016459

Von Bulow: Wealth of Evidence

This video about the Klaus and Sunny von Bulow murder case explores the prosecution evidence and the defense challenges to it. It also looks into the legal aspects of evidentiary presentation that influenced the verdict.

> Format: Color, VHS
>
> Rated: NR
>
> Studio: A&E Entertainment
>
> Video Release Date: April 22, 1998
>
> ASIN: B000006QP0

Books

The Complete Idiot's Guide to Criminal Investigation

Alex Axelrod and Guy Antinozzi

This layperson's overview of the necessary steps involved in basic investigation is intended for readers looking to form a working knowledge of the basics of criminal investigation.

> Format: Paperback, 384 pages
>
> Publisher: Alpha (2002)
>
> ISBN: 0028643461

Corpse: Nature, Forensics, and the Struggle to Pinpoint Time of Death: An Exploration of the Haunting Science of Forensic Ecology

Jessica Snyder Sachs

This work explores forensic ecology, entomology, and pathology, including a discussion of techniques and historical cases.

> Format: Hardcover, 240 pages
>
> Publisher: Perseus Publishers (2001)
>
> ISBN: 073820336X

Crime Scene Evidence: A Guide to the Recovery and Collection of Physical Evidence

Mike Byrd

Written by a veteran crime-scene investigator, this guide is designed to be carried in the field and used as a reference in the recovery, collection, and packaging of crime-scene evidence. Categories of evidence covered include impression evidence, forensic biology evidence, trace evidence, firearms evidence, and questioned documents. Topics cover most evidence located at crime scenes, from fingerprints, including fingerprints on human skin, to recovering bullets from inside walls. The book includes an appendix that lists likely evidence found at scenes by type of investigation.

> Format: Spiral Bound, 102 pages
>
> Publisher: Staggs (2001)
>
> ISBN: 0966197054

Evidence Collection

Joseph Vince

This handbook is designed to serve as a quick reference on effective procedures for collecting, preserving, and transmitting evidence for examination, analysis, and presentation at the time of prosecution.

> Format: Paperback, 99 pages
>
> Publisher: Jones and Bartlett (2005)
>
> ISBN: 0763747874

Flesh and Bone: An Introduction to Forensic Anthropology

Myriam Nafte

This layperson's introduction to forensic anthropology begins with a general discussion of forensics and then details the field of anthropology, the process of death, decomposition, and skeletonization. Methods of identifying the human skeleton, DNA analysis, and the reconstruction of identity are highlighted. The final chapter deals with the modern application of forensic anthropology to human rights missions.

> Format: Paperback, 173 pages
>
> Publisher: Carolina Academic Press (2000)
>
> ISBN: 0890896380

A Fly for the Prosecution: How Insect Evidence Helps Solve Crimes

M. Lee Goff

Much of this firsthand account of forensic entomology in the United States deals with estimating the time elapsed between death and discovery of the body by identifying the insects present on the corpse, their stages of development, and their relationships with other insects. The book also covers coping with murder scenes, testifying in court, and publicizing the profession.

> Format: Hardcover, 225 pages
>
> Publisher: Harvard University Press (2000)
>
> ISBN: 0674002202

Hot Zone Forensics: Chemical, Biological, and Radiological Evidence Collection

Steven C. Drielak

This paperback describes procedures for collecting forensic evidence from scenes containing hazardous materials, with an emphasis on examining WMD scenes.

> Format: Paperback, 420 pages
>
> Publisher: Charles C. Thomas (2004)
>
> ISBN: 0398074658

Practical Crime Scene Processing and Investigation

Ross M. Gardner

This guide to basic crime-scene processing and investigation covers procedures such as officer safety, emergency care to the injured, securing and controlling the scene, search methods, scene documentation, and photography. The author introduces a field-tested crime-scene processing methodology based on his experience. The book is accompanied by a CD-ROM edition.

> Format: Hardcover, 360 pages
>
> Publisher: CRC Press (2004)
>
> ISBN: 0849320437

Advanced Reading

Geberth, Vernon J., *Practical Homicide Investigation: Tactics, Procedures, and Forensic Techniques,* 4th ed. Boca Raton, Fla.: Taylor & Francis, 2006.

Nickell, J., and J. F. Fischer, *Crime Scene: Methods of Forensic Detection.* Lexington: University Press of Kentucky, 1999.

Osterburg, James W., and Richard H. Ward, *Criminal Investigation—A Method for Reconstructing the Past,* 3rd ed. Cincinnati, Ohio: Anderson, 2000.

Demonstrations and Lecture Starters

Mock Crime Scene

A mock crime scene can be set up in a classroom. Students are encouraged to become familiar with proper packaging and handling of common types of physical evidence. Emphasize preparation and use of the druggist fold. All pertinent information should be recorded in a notebook. Sketches may be made of the crime scene. A crime-scene sketch kit, which includes an excellent instructional manual on sketching, is available from Sirchie Finger Print Laboratories, 100 Hunter Place, Youngsville, NC 27596 (www.sirchie.com).

Securing and Controlling the Crime Scene

Police officers are typically the first to arrive at a scene, and their actions in securing and controlling the area can greatly help or hinder the subsequent investigation. The scene of a crime can be a dynamic and even chaotic place. Exploring the role of the first responders alerts students to the many ways that evidence can be compromised and highlights the care that all law enforcement personnel must take at a crime scene.

- The first priority at the scene is to preserve life and help any living victims to ensure that they are no longer at risk of harm. This includes treating injuries and moving victims who are in imminent danger. Discuss how a police officer may risk destroying or contaminating evidence while helping victims.

- The second priority is to detain and question any suspects and remove them from the scene. Discuss why it is important to remove suspects immediately, with respect to both preserving evidence and prejudicing eyewitness testimony.

- Potential witnesses should be detained and questioned. Discuss the proper procedure for questioning witnesses (witnesses should be interviewed alone and separate from other witnesses at some distance from the scene) and why following this procedure is important.

- After interviewing witnesses, the police must secure the crime scene to prevent traffic through the area that may destroy evidence. Point out that much activity occurs before the scene can be completely secured, which highlights the need for care and efficiency on the part of police. Discuss the standard procedure for securing and protecting a crime scene.

- Discuss the importance of good record keeping by the investigating officers, including its relevance to chain of custody.

Estimating Time Since Death

One task that often confronts the crime-scene investigator is determining the time of a victim's death. Estimating time of death draws on various skills of the criminalist, including observation, deductive and inductive reasoning, knowledge of bodily processes, and even knowledge of the life cycles of nonhuman animals. A discussion of time of death can introduce topics such as crime-scene processing, evidence collection and interpretation, autopsies and lab procedures, and forensic specialties such as anthropology and entomology. Commonly used indicators of the time of a victim's death include the following:

- *Algor mortis,* or cooling of the body's core temperature. Core temperature falls about 1.5°F (about

0.8°C) per hour after death. Factors such as body size, condition (clothed or unclothed), and location affect the speed of cooling.

- *Livor mortis,* or settling of the blood caused by gravity. This process can take up to twelve hours and is marked by the presence of a dark blue or purple color on the skin.

- *Rigor mortis,* or stiffening of the body. This process, which begins within a few hours of death, is first noticeable in the eyelids and jaw. After about twenty-four hours the body begins to lose its stiffness, which disappears after about thirty-six hours following death. As with algor mortis, temperature and other factors can accelerate or slow the amount and rate of stiffening.

- *Contents of the digestive tract.* The location of food in the digestive tract can indicate when the victim last ate and help fix an approximate interval in which death probably occurred. For example, because food remains in the stomach for about three hours after eating, the presence of undigested food in the stomach would indicate that the victim died within the past three hours. Speed of digestion, however, varies somewhat by the type of food consumed (heavier foods digest more slowly) and external factors such as illness or drug/alcohol use.

- *Clues from the eye.* The lens of the eye clouds over within several hours of the time of death. A more precise measure is obtained by drawing fluid called vitreous humor from the eye. Because potassium rises at a known rate in the eye after death, measuring the amount of potassium in the vitreous humor provides an accurate estimate of time of death.

- *Animal clues.* Some insects lay eggs in a body almost immediately after death and these eggs eventually develop into larvae. Because the life cycles of many species of insects are well-known, the stage of development of insect eggs or larvae on a body can help determine the time of death.

Chapter 3
Physical Evidence

Key Terms

class characteristics—Properties of evidence that can be associated only with a group and never with a single source.

comparison—The process of ascertaining whether two or more objects have a common origin.

identification—The process of determining a substance's physical or chemical identity. Drug analysis, species determination, and explosive residue analysis are typical examples of this undertaking in a forensic setting.

individual characteristics—Properties of evidence that can be attributed to a common source with an extremely high degree of certainty.

product rule—Multiplying together the frequencies of independently occurring genetic markers to obtain an overall frequency of occurrence for a genetic profile.

reconstruction—The method used to support a likely sequence of events by observing and evaluating physical evidence and statements made by those involved with the incident.

Learning Objectives

- Review the common types of physical evidence encountered at crime scenes
- Explain the difference between the identification and comparison of physical evidence
- Define and contrast individual and class characteristics of physical evidence
- Appreciate the value of class evidence as it relates to a criminal investigation
- List and explain the function of national databases available to forensic scientists
- Explain the purpose physical evidence plays in reconstructing the events surrounding the commission of a crime

Key Points

- The object of identification is to determine physical or chemical identity with as near absolute certainty as existing analytical techniques will permit.
- The process of identification requires the use of tests that give characteristic results for specific standard materials.
- The examiner uses an appropriate number of tests to identify a substance and exclude all other substances from consideration.
- The identification process is used to identify drugs, explosives, petroleum products, blood, semen, and hair.

- A comparative analysis determines whether a suspect specimen and a standard/reference specimen have a common origin. Both the standard/reference and the suspect specimen are subject to the same tests.
- Evidence that can be associated with a common source with an extremely high degree of probability is said to possess individual characteristics. Evidence associated only with a group is said to have class characteristics.
- As the number of different objects linking an individual to a crime scene increases, so does the likelihood of that individual's involvement with the crime.
- A person may be exonerated or excluded from suspicion if physical evidence collected at a crime scene is found to be different from standard/reference samples collected from that person.
- The creation of computerized databases for fingerprints, criminal histories, DNA profiles, markings on bullets and cartridges, automotive paints, and shoe marks has dramatically enhanced the role of forensic science in criminal investigation.
- Crime-scene reconstruction relies on the combined efforts of medical examiners, criminalists, and law enforcement personnel to recover physical evidence and to sort out the events surrounding the occurrence of a crime.

Supplemental Questions

1. List six types of physical evidence derived from human or other animal sources that are commonly found at crime scenes.
2. List and define the two methods used by forensic scientists when examining physical evidence.
3. To permit positive identification, testing procedures used by a forensic scientist must meet what two conditions?
4. Describe the two steps in the process of comparison. What question does each step attempt to answer?
5. Define *individual* and *class characteristics*.
6. Define the product rule and explain how it can be used to determine whether two blood samples come from the same source.
7. What is the greatest weakness of class evidence? List two factors that contribute to this weakness.
8. What is the value of class evidence? Why is this important in making a case to a jury?
9. Why are some jurists wary of allowing unconditional use of scientific evidence in court?
10. How can the extreme sensitivity of modern analytical techniques hinder the process of comparing items of physical evidence?

11. What are IAFIS and CODIS? Describe the purpose of each.

12. Define crime-scene reconstruction. What is the foundation of a crime-scene reconstruction?

13. What is the first and most important step in reconstruction? Why is it important?

14. What is the purpose of a walk-through? What are the investigator's main tasks during the walk-through?

15. List three specialized skills that a criminalist can apply during crime-scene reconstruction.

Answers to Supplemental Questions

1. Blood, semen, saliva, hair, fingerprints, organs, and physiological fluids are some types of physical evidence derived from human or other animal sources that are commonly found at crime scenes.

2. The two methods used by forensic scientists when examining physical evidence are identification and comparison. Identification is the process of determining a substance's physical or chemical identity. Comparison is the process of ascertaining whether two or more objects have a common origin.

3. To permit positive identification, testing procedures must give characteristic results for specific standard materials. In addition, the number and type of tests required to positively identify a substance must be sufficient to exclude all other substances.

4. The first step in comparison is determining which properties from the suspect and the standard/reference specimen to compare. This step attempts to determine whether the two samples are the same. The second step is concluding the origins of the specimens. This step attempts to determine how likely it is that two samples came from the same source.

5. Individual characteristics are properties of evidence that can be attributed to a common source with an extremely high degree of certainty. Class characteristics are properties of evidence that can be associated only with a group and never with a single source. Examples include paint and fibers.

6. The product rule states that one can obtain an overall frequency of occurrence for a genetic profile by multiplying together the frequencies of independently occurring genetic markers. If several different factors from two blood samples are found to be identical, a forensic scientist can apply the product rule to calculate how frequently blood containing that combination of factors occurs in the population. The more blood factors that match, the greater the probability that the two blood samples originated from a common source.

7. The greatest weakness of class evidence is that examiners cannot assign exact or even approximate probability values to the comparison of most class evidence. Few statistical data exist from which to derive comparative information for most class evidence, and society is increasingly dependent on mass-produced products that are extremely difficult to distinguish from one another.

8. The value of class evidence lies in its ability to corroborate events with data that are, as nearly as possible, free of human error and bias. This is important because most other types of evidence (such as eyewitness testimony and confessions) are subjective and susceptible to dispute, human error, or bias.

9. Some jurists are wary about scientific evidence because juries often accord scientific evidence greater weight than other evidence, tend to consider it more trustworthy, and often view it with less skepticism. Without proper safeguards, the use of scientific evidence may unfairly prejudice a case against the accused.

10. When measured or examined with extreme precision, no two items—even those originating from the same source—are exactly alike. Thus, using an analytic technique that is too sensitive makes it impossible to meaningfully compare different items of evidence.

11. IAFIS is the Integrated Automated Fingerprint Identification System, a national fingerprint and criminal history database maintained by the FBI. IAFIS allows criminal investigators to compare fingerprints at a crime scene to an index of 500 million known prints. CODIS is the FBI's Combined DNA Index System. It enables federal, state, and local crime laboratories to electronically exchange and compare DNA profiles, linking crimes to each other and to convicted offenders.

12. Crime-scene reconstruction is the method used to support a likely sequence of events by observing and evaluating physical evidence, as well as statements made by those involved with the incident. The collection and documentation of physical evidence is the foundation of a crime-scene reconstruction.

13. The first and most important step in reconstruction is securing and protecting the crime scene. It is important because anyone entering the crime scene can potentially destroy or contaminate important physical evidence.

14. The purpose of the walk-through is to assess the general nature of the crime scene and to hypothesize about what occurred, where it occurred, and when it occurred. During the walk-through the investigator must document observations and determine how the crime scene should be processed.

15. Examples of specialized skills applied during crime-scene reconstruction include determining whether a body was moved after death, determining whether a victim was clothed after death, analyzing bullet trajectory, analyzing blood spatter, determining the direction from which projectiles penetrated glass objects, estimating the distance of a shooter from a target, and locating primer residue on suspects.

Resources

Videos/DVDs

Forensic Firearms Evidence: Elements of Shooting Incident Reconstruction

This two-tape training and reference video for professionals explains the value of firearms evidence, with a thorough introduction to the fundamentals of shooting incident investigations and firearms evidence collection and marking. It discusses class and individual characteristics of firearms evidence such as ammunition identification, bullet characteristics, rifling characteristics, and tool marks on cartridges. It also shows how these elements of evidence can be used in the courtroom. The set is accompanied by a ninety-page written reference text.

> Format: Color, VHS
> Rated: NR
> Studio: Unknown
> Video Release Date: June 1, 1991
> ASIN: B00006JLPN

Books

Crime Scene Investigation and Reconstruction

Robert R. Ogle

Written by a veteran crime-scene investigator, this book is designed to be carried in the field and used as a reference in the recovery, collection, and packaging of crime-scene evidence. Categories of evidence covered include impression evidence, forensic biology evidence, trace evidence, firearms evidence, and questioned documents. Topics cover most evidence located at crime scenes, from fingerprints, including fingerprints on human skin, to recovering bullets from inside walls. The book includes an appendix listing likely evidence found at scenes by type of investigation.

> Format: Paperback, 333 pages
> Publisher: Pearson Education (2004)
> ISBN: 0131119095

Crime Scene Search and Physical Evidence Handbook

Richard Fox and Carl Cunningham

This book spells out legal and scientific standards for processing evidence in solving crimes. Fingerprints, fibers, drug residue, and altered documents involved in fires and murders are just some of the topics covered.

> Format: Paperback, 208 pages
> Publisher: Paladin Press (1987)
> ISBN: 0873644433

Physical Evidence in Forensic Science

Henry C. Lee

This easy-to-understand guide by one of the nation's foremost forensic scientists introduces the basics of collecting, storing, and analyzing all types of physical evidence.

> Format: Hardcover, 328 pages
> Publisher: Lawyers and Judges (2000)
> ISBN: 1930056001

A Practical Guide to the Basics of Physical Evidence: A Reference Text for the Criminalist, Investigator, Student, and Attorney

Claude W. Cook

This book provides an overview of basic issues relating to the collection, use, interpretation, and presentation of physical evidence.

> Format: Hardcover, 271 pages
> Publisher: Charles C. Thomas (2004)
> ISBN: 0398049335

Advanced Reading

Houck, M. M., and J.A. Siegel. *Fundamentals of Forensic Science*. Burlington, Mass.: Elsevier Academic Press, 2006.

Kirk, Paul L., in John I. Thornton, ed., *Crime Investigation*, 2nd ed. New York: Wiley, 1974.

Osterburg, James W., "The Evaluation of Physical Evidence in Criminalistics: Subjective or Objective Process?" *Journal of Criminal Law, Criminology and Police Science* 60 (1969): 97.

Walls, H. J., "What Is Reasonable Doubt? A Forensic Scientist Looks at the Law," in Joseph L. Peterson, ed., *Forensic Science*. New York: AMS Press, 1975.

Demonstrations and Lecture Starters

Crime-Scene Reconstruction

Create a mock crime scene using the setup described in Chapter 2. After students have made observations and taken notes, ask each student to reconstruct the sequence of events and describe in writing what he or she believes happened at the crime scene. The student's description of events must be backed up by reference to the physical evidence found at the scene. Identify any common errors or misperceptions and discuss how these might have occurred and ways to guard against making similar mistakes.

Probability and the Product Rule

Physical evidence often lacks individual characteristics that can tie a suspect conclusively to a crime scene. In such cases, prosecutors must rely on evidence with class characteristics to link the suspect to the crime. The likelihood that the suspect and victim are related depends on the number of pieces of evidence linking them and the uniqueness of the evidence. Present the students with the following three cases in which several pieces of evidence link a suspect and a crime. The lists indicate the evidence found in each case and, for each piece of evidence, the frequency of that characteristic in the population at large. Ask the students to indicate in which case they believe the evidence most strongly suggests the suspect is guilty (note that these percentages are used as examples only and are NOT scientifically accurate):

Case 1	Case 2	Case 3
Blond hair (32%)	Red hair (11%)	Brown hair (51%)
Type O blood (43%)	Type B blood (12%)	Type AB blood (3%)
Arch fingerprints (5%)	Loop fingerprints (65%)	Whorl fingerprints (33%)

After students have guessed, ask the students how they came to their answers, then introduce the product rule and ask the students to apply it to see whether their guesses were correct. (The correct answer should be case 3. The likelihood that two individuals would share the stated characteristics in case 3 is 0.5 percent, compared with 0.69 percent for case 1 and 0.86 percent for case 2.) This demonstration can be used to emphasize the uncertainty inherent in dealing with class evidence and the importance of having multiple pieces of evidence to tie a suspect to a crime.

Drawing Conclusions from Physical Evidence: Forensic Anthropology

Close observation of physical evidence helps forensic experts answer important questions during the investigation of a crime. Forensic anthropologists, who specialize in analyzing evidence of human remains, are sometimes asked to determine the sex of a victim from nothing more than scattered bones. This is typically accomplished by measuring the dimensions of certain bones such as the pelvis, which shows significant differences between the sexes. In this demonstration students are asked to use their observation and reasoning skills to determine the difference between male and female skeletons, then to use that knowledge to determine the sex of three unknown pelvises.

Provide the following information about two typical skeletons—one male and one female. The students will use this information to form conclusions about differences between the skeletons of each sex. (The sacrum is a bone that joins the two halves of the pelvic girdle at the top. Femur spread A is the distance between the upper leg bones about 2 inches below the hip joint. Femur spread B is the distance between the upper leg bones at a point about 2 inches below femur spread A.)

	Pelvic Width	Pelvic Opening	Sacrum Length	Sacrum Width	Femur Spread A	Femur Spread B
Male Pelvis	16″	7″	6″	$6\frac{1}{2}$″	16″	16″
Female Pelvis	17″	9″	4″	$5\frac{3}{4}$″	14″	13″

Following are the measurements of the unknown pelvises:

	Pelvic Width	Pelvic Opening	Sacrum Length	Sacrum Width	Femur Spread A	Femur Spread B
Pelvis A	18″	$9\frac{1}{2}$″	6″	8″	17″	$15\frac{3}{4}$″
Pelvis B	17″	$8\frac{1}{4}$″	7″	$7\frac{3}{4}$″	$16\frac{3}{4}$″	$16\frac{3}{4}$″
Pelvis C	$16\frac{1}{2}$″	$8\frac{1}{2}$″	$5\frac{1}{4}$″	7″	15″	$14\frac{1}{4}$″

The students should draw the following conclusions from studying the "sample" pelvises:

- The pelvic opening in the female is much wider in relation to its width than is the male pelvic opening.
- The female sacrum is very wide in relation to its length; the length and width of the male sacrum are roughly equal.
- The upper leg bones of the female bow inward from point A to B on the femur; the male leg bones do not bow inward.

Based on these observations, the student should conclude that pelvises A and C are female, while pelvis B is male.

Properties of Matter and the Analysis of Glass

Key Terms

amorphous solid—A solid in which the constituent atoms or molecules are arranged in random or disordered positions. There is no regular order in amorphous solids.

atom—The smallest unit of an element; not divisible by ordinary chemical means. Atoms are made up of electrons, protons, and neutrons plus other subatomic particles.

Becke line—A bright halo observed near the border of a particle immersed in a liquid of a different refractive index.

birefringence—A difference in the two indices of refraction exhibited by most crystalline materials.

Celsius scale—The temperature scale using the melting point of ice as 0° and the boiling point of water as 100°, with 100 equal divisions or degrees between.

chemical property—Describes the behavior of a substance when it reacts or combines with another substance.

compound—A pure substance created by combining two or more elements.

concentric fracture—A crack in glass that forms a rough circle around the point of impact.

crystalline solid—A solid in which the constituent atoms have a regular arrangement.

density—A physical property of matter that is equivalent to the mass per unit volume of a substance.

dispersion—The separation of light into its component wavelengths.

electromagnetic spectrum—The entire range of radiation energy from the most energetic cosmic rays to the least energetic radio waves.

element—A fundamental particle of matter. An element cannot be broken down into simpler substances by chemical means.

Fahrenheit scale—The temperature scale using the melting point of ice as 32° and the boiling point of water as 212°, with 180 equal divisions or degrees between.

frequency—The number of waves that pass a given point per second.

gas (vapor)—A state of matter in which the attractive forces between molecules are small enough to permit them to move with complete freedom.

intensive property—A property that is not dependent on the size of an object.

laminated glass—Two sheets of ordinary glass bonded together with a plastic film.

laser—An acronym for light amplification by stimulated emission of radiation; light that has all its waves pulsating in unison.

liquid—A state of matter in which molecules are in contact with one another but are not rigidly held in place.

mass—A constant property of matter that reflects the amount of material present.

matter—All things of substance. Matter is composed of atoms or molecules.

periodic table—A chart of elements arranged in a systematic fashion. Vertical rows are called groups or families; horizontal rows are called series. Elements in a given row have similar properties.

phase—A uniform body of matter; different phases are separated by definite visible boundaries.

photon—A small packet of electromagnetic radiation energy. Each photon contains a unit of energy equal to the product of Planck's constant and the frequency of radiation: $E \times hf$.

physical property—Describes the behavior of a substance without having to alter the substance's composition through a chemical reaction.

physical state—A condition or stage in the form of matter; a solid, liquid, or gas.

radial fracture—A crack in glass that extends outward like the spoke of a wheel from the point at which the glass was struck.

refraction—The bending of a light wave as it passes from one medium to another.

refractive index—The ratio of the speed of light in a vacuum to its speed in a given substance.

solid—A state of matter in which the molecules are held closely together in a rigid state.

sublimation—A physical change from the solid state directly into the gaseous state.

tempered glass—Glass that is strengthened by introducing stress through rapid heating and cooling of the glass surfaces.

visible light—Colored light ranging from red to violet in the electromagnetic spectrum.

wavelength—The distance between crests of adjacent waves.

weight—A property of matter that depends on both the mass of a substance and the effects of gravity on that mass.

X-ray—A high-energy, short-wavelength form of electromagnetic radiation.

Learning Objectives

- Define and distinguish the physical and chemical properties of matter
- Understand how to use the basic units of the metric system
- Define and distinguish elements and compounds
- Contrast the differences between a solid, liquid, and gas
- Define and understand the properties of density and refractive index
- Understand and explain the dispersion of light through a prism

- Describe the electromagnetic spectrum
- Understand the differences between the wave and particle theories of light
- List and explain forensic methods for comparing glass fragments
- Understand how to examine glass fractures to determine the direction of impact for a projectile
- Describe proper collection of glass evidence

Key Points

- Physical properties such as weight, volume, color, boiling point, and melting point describe a substance without reference to any other substance. A chemical property describes the behavior of a substance when it reacts or combines with another substance.
- Temperature is a measure of heat intensity, or the amount of heat in a substance.
- In science, the most commonly used temperature scale is the Celsius scale, which is derived by assigning the freezing point of water a value of 0°C and its boiling point a value of 100°C.
- To compare glass fragments, a forensic scientist evaluates two important physical properties: density and refractive index. Density is defined as the mass per unit volume. Refractive index is the ratio of the velocity of light in a vacuum to that in the medium under examination.
- Crystalline solids have definite geometric forms because of the orderly arrangement of their atoms.
- Crystalline solids refract a beam of light in two different light-ray components, resulting in double refraction. Birefringence is the numerical difference between these two refractive indices.
- Not all solids are crystalline in nature. Glass has a random arrangement of atoms to form an amorphous or noncrystalline solid.
- The immersion method is used to determine a glass fragment's refractive index. It involves immersing a glass particle in a liquid medium whose refractive index is varied until it equals that of the glass particle. At this point, known as the match point, minimum contrast between liquid and particle is observed.
- The flotation method is used to determine a glass fragment's density. It involves immersing a glass particle in a liquid whose density is carefully adjusted by the addition of small amounts of an appropriate liquid until the glass chip remains suspended in the liquid medium. At this point, the glass has the same density as the liquid medium and can be compared to other relevant pieces of glass.
- By analyzing the radial and concentric fracture patterns in glass, the forensic scientist can determine the direction of impact by applying the 3R rule: Radial cracks form a Right angle on the Reverse side of the force.

Supplemental Questions

1. Define *physical property* and *chemical property*.
2. Why is the metric system of measurement easier to use than the "English system"? Which system is used in the United States?
3. List the basic units of length, mass, and volume in the metric system.
4. Define *element* and *compound* and name the smallest unit of each.
5. Name the three forms, or states, of matter and explain how the shape and volume of matter are expressed in each state.
6. What physical change occurs when a substance undergoes the following changes of state: (a) from liquid to solid, and (b) from liquid to gas?
7. Define *sublimation*. What happens to the attractive forces between molecules of a substance that undergo sublimation?
8. What is a phase and how can two different phases be distinguished from one another?
9. What is color? What determines the color of an opaque object?
10. What two models do scientists use to explain the nature of light? Under what conditions does each model best describe the behavior of light?
11. What reference points are most often chosen when constructing a temperature scale?
12. List the two most commonly used temperature scales and their respective reference points.
13. Define *weight* and *mass* and explain the difference between the two concepts.
14. What is density? How does heat affect the density of gases and liquids?
15. Define *refraction* and *refractive index*.
16. What is the difference between a crystalline solid and an amorphous solid? How does this difference affect the refractive index of each of these types of solid?
17. Explain how a prism disperses white light into its constituent colors.
18. Define *intensive property* and name two intensive properties of matter.
19. List two factors that make it difficult for criminalists to compare glass samples.
20. Describe the process of flotation and explain what it is used for.
21. What is the Becke line and how is it used to determine the refractive index of a glass sample?
22. What is the 3R rule and how is it applied to the analysis of glass fractures?
23. How can an investigator determine the order in which several successive penetrations of a glass occurred?

Answers to Supplemental Questions

1. A physical property describes the behavior of a substance without having to alter the substance's composition through a chemical reaction. A chemical property describes the behavior of a substance when it reacts or combines with another substance.

2. The metric system is easier to use because it employs a simple decimal relationship so that any unit of length, volume, or mass can be converted into another unit by multiplying or dividing by a factor of 10. By contrast, no simple numerical relationship exists between the various units of measurement in the English system. The English system is used in the United States.

3. The basic units of length, mass, and volume in the metric system are the meter, the gram, and the liter, respectively.

4. An element is a fundamental particle of matter. A compound is a pure substance composed of two or more elements. The smallest unit of an element is an atom. The smallest unit of a compound is a molecule.

5. The three states of matter are solid, liquid, and gas. A solid has both a specific shape and volume. A liquid has a specific volume, but takes the shape of the container in which it resides. A gas has neither a specific shape nor a specific volume.

6. When a substance undergoes a change of state from liquid to solid, the attractive forces between the molecules increase in strength. When a substance undergoes a change of state from liquid to gas, the attractive forces between the molecules decrease in strength.

7. Sublimation is a physical change from the solid state directly into the gaseous state. Sublimation causes the attractive forces between molecules to decrease in strength.

8. A phase is a uniform piece of matter. Different phases are distinguished from one another by definite visible boundaries.

9. Color is a visual indication of the fact that objects absorb certain portions of visible light and transmit or reflect others. The color of an opaque object is determined by which component color(s) of light it reflects.

10. The first model describes light as a continuous wave; the second depicts it as a stream of discrete energy particles. When light is moving through space, its behavior can best be described as that of a continuous wave. Light as a stream of discrete particles best describes its behavior when light is absorbed by a substance.

11. The most convenient reference points are the melting point of ice and the boiling point of water.

12. The most commonly used temperature scales are the Fahrenheit and Celsius scales. The Fahrenheit scale uses a melting point of 32° and a boiling point of 212°. The Celsius scale uses a melting point of 0° and a boiling point of 100°.

13. Weight is a property of matter that depends on both the mass of a substance and the effects of gravity on that mass. Mass is a constant property of matter that reflects the amount of material present. Because weight depends on the force of gravity, the weight of an object can vary from one location to another. Mass differs from weight because it remains the same regardless of location.

14. Density is a physical property of matter that is equivalent to the mass per unit volume of a substance. As the temperature of a liquid or gas increases, its density decreases.

15. Refraction is the bending of a light wave as it passes from one medium to another. Refractive index is the ratio of the speed of light in a vacuum to its speed in a given substance.

16. The atoms in a crystalline solid have a regular arrangement; the atoms in an amorphous solid have no regular order. Amorphous solids have only one refractive index; crystalline solids have two refractive indices.

17. Because each color component of light has a slightly different frequency, each color passes through the prism at a slightly different speed. This causes each color component to refract at a different angle as it emerges from the prism, thus dispersing the light into its constituent colors.

18. An intensive property is a property that does not depend on the size of an object. Intensive properties include density and refractive index.

19. Most glass evidence presented to the criminalist is either too fragmentary or too minute for the pieces to be physically reassembled or fitted together. In addition, the general chemical composition of various window glasses has so far been found to be relatively uniform among various manufacturers and thus offers no basis for identifying individual samples.

20. Flotation is a process used to compare the densities of glass samples. In flotation, a standard/reference glass particle is immersed in a liquid. The composition of the liquid is carefully adjusted until the glass remains suspended in the liquid. Glass chips of approximately the same size and shape as the standard/reference are then added to the liquid for comparison. If both the unknown and the standard/reference particles remain suspended in the liquid, their densities are equal to each other and to that of the liquid. Particles of different densities either sink or float, depending on whether they are more or less dense than the liquid.

21. The Becke line is a bright halo observed near the border of a particle that is immersed in a liquid with a different refractive index. When the refractive index of the liquid is altered so that it is the same as that of the glass sample immersed in it, the Becke line disappears. This reveals the refractive index of the sample.

22. The 3R rule states that *Radial* cracks form a *Right* angle on the *Reverse* side of the force. This rule enables an examiner to determine readily the side on which a window or pane of glass was broken.

23. It is frequently possible to determine the sequence of impacts in glass by observing the existing fracture lines and their points of termination. Each fracture always terminates at an existing line of fracture. Thus, if fracture line A terminates in fracture line B, fracture line B was made first.

Resources

Videos/DVDs

Temperature and Heat

This video uses animation, humorous skits, and experiments to show heat and temperature as the movement of molecules. It also covers various practical uses of heat such as infrared detection and manufacture of thermometers.

> Format: Color, VHS
>
> Rated: NR
>
> Studio: New Dimension Media
>
> Video Release Date: March 18, 2004
>
> ASIN: B00028G5RW

Understanding the Metric System

This DVD explains basic metric units as well as how to convert from one metric unit to another. In addition, conversion from English units to metric units and proper notation for expressing the metric system are discussed.

> Format: Color, DVD
>
> Rated: NR
>
> Studio: Educational Video Network
>
> DVD Release Date: March 18, 2004
>
> ASIN: B0001YJ4LQ

Books

Forensic Interpretation of Glass Evidence

James Michael Curran, Tacha Natalie Hicks, and John S. Buckleton

This book provides information on glass evidence procedure and analysis, approaches to interpreting glass evidence, application of statistics to forensic science, and presentation of statistical evidence in court. It contains more than 150 illustrations, tables, and equations.

> Format: Hardcover, 200 pages
>
> Publisher: CRC Press (2000)
>
> ISBN: 084930069X

A Guide to the Elements

Robert Stwertka

This introduction to the chemical elements begins with a general introduction to the history, theory, and arrangement of the periodic table, then offers a brief (one- to seven-page) article on each of the 112 elements that details its history, chemical and physical properties, and modern applications.

> Format: Paperback, 248 pages
>
> Publisher: Oxford University Press (2002)
>
> ISBN: 0195150279

Physical Evidence in Forensic Science

Henry C. Lee

This easy-to-understand guide by one of the nation's foremost forensic scientists introduces the basics of collecting, storing, and analyzing all types of physical evidence.

> Format: Hardcover, 328 pages
>
> Publisher: Lawyers and Judges (2000)
>
> ISBN: 1930056001

Advanced Reading

Caddy, B., ed., *Forensic Examination of Glass and Paint.* New York: Taylor & Francis, 2001.

Koons, R. D., J. Buscaglia, M. Bottrell, and E. T. Miller, "Forensic Glass Comparisons," in R. Saferstein, ed., *Forensic Science Handbook,* vol. 1, 2nd ed. Upper Saddle River, N.J.: Prentice Hall, 2002.

Thornton, J. I., "Interpretation of Physical Aspects of Glass Evidence," in B. Caddy, ed., *Forensic Examination of Glass and Paint.* New York: Taylor & Francis, 2001.

Demonstrations and Lecture Starters

Introduction to Balances

The use of the triple-beam, top-loading, and single-pan analytical balances should be demonstrated. An interesting experiment that introduces the student to the concept of density requires determining the density of an aluminum bar. Cylindrical aluminum bars are cut into sections weighing between 3 and 10 grams. The student first weighs the bar on a balance. The volume of a bar is determined by the amount of water it displaces in a graduated cylinder. The student should determine the densities of at least two aluminum bars of different sizes. The density of aluminum is 2.70 g/mL.

Density: The Flotation Technique

The comparative density of two window glass chips can be demonstrated by the flotation technique. The density of a glass particle can be found by placing it in a test tube with a mixture of bromoform and bromobenzene. The particle remains suspended in the solution. A second particle is now added to the test tube and its ability to sink, float, or remain suspended is compared to the first particle. If both chips remain suspended, the closed tube may be heated and cooled to confirm that both sink and rise together. The glass chips must be clean and approximately the same size.

Chapter 5

Drugs

Key Terms

anabolic steroids—Steroids that promote muscle growth.

analgesic—A drug or substance that lessens or eliminates pain.

chromatography—A means of separating and tentatively identifying the components of a mixture.

confirmation—A single test that specifically identifies a substance.

depressant—A substance that depresses the functions of the central nervous system. Depressants calm irritability and anxiety and may induce sleep.

fluoresce—To emit visible light when exposed to light of a shorter wavelength.

hallucinogen—A substance that induces changes in mood, attitude, thought processes, and perceptions.

infrared—Invisible short frequencies of light before red in the visible spectrum.

ion—An atom or molecule bearing a positive or negative charge.

microcrystalline tests—Tests to identify specific substances by the color and morphology of the crystals formed when the substance is mixed with specific reagents.

monochromatic light—Light having a single wavelength frequency.

monochromator—A device used to isolate individual wavelengths or frequencies of light.

narcotic—An analgesic or pain-killing substance that depresses vital body functions such as blood pressure, pulse rate, and breathing rate. Regular administration of narcotics produces physical dependence.

physical dependence—Physiological need for a drug that has been brought about by its regular use. Dependence is characterized by withdrawal sickness when administration of the drug is abruptly stopped.

psychological dependence—Conditioned use of a drug caused by underlying emotional needs.

screening test—A test that is nonspecific and preliminary in nature.

spectrophotometry—An analytical method for identifying a substance by exposing it to a specific type of electromagnetic radiation.

stimulant—A substance taken to increase alertness or activity.

ultraviolet—Invisible long frequencies of light beyond violet in the visible spectrum.

Learning Objectives

- Compare and contrast psychological and physical dependence
- Name and classify the commonly abused drugs
- Describe the laboratory tests normally used to perform a routine drug identification analysis
- Describe and explain the process of chromatography
- List and describe the parts of a gas chromatograph
- Explain the difference between thin-layer chromatography and gas chromatography
- Describe the utility of ultraviolet and infrared spectroscopy for the identification of organic compounds
- Describe the concept and utility of mass spectrometry for identification analysis
- Understand proper collection and preservation of drug evidence

Key Points

- A drug is a natural or synthetic substance that is used to produce physiological or psychological effects in humans or other higher-order animals.
- Narcotic drugs are analgesics, meaning they relieve pain by depressing the central nervous system.
- The most common source for narcotic drugs is opium. Morphine is extracted from opium and used to synthesize heroin.
- Opiates are not derived from opium or morphine, but they have the same physiological effects on the body. Examples of opiates include methadone and OxyContin (oxycodone).
- Hallucinogens cause marked changes in normal thought processes, perceptions, and moods. Marijuana is the most well-known drug in this class. Other hallucinogens include LSD, mescaline, PCP, psilocybin, and MDMA (Ecstasy).
- Depressants decrease the activity of the central nervous system, calm irritability and excitability, and may cause sleep. Depressants include alcohol (ethanol), barbiturates, tranquilizers, and various substances that can be sniffed, such as airplane glue and model cement.
- Stimulants increase the activity of the central nervous system and are taken to increase alertness and activity. Stimulants include amphetamines, sometimes known as "uppers" or "speed," and cocaine, which in its free base form is known as crack.
- Club drugs are synthetic drugs that are used at nightclubs, bars, and raves (all-night dance parties). Some club drugs act as stimulants; others have depressant effects. Substances that are often used as club drugs include, but are not limited to, MDMA (Ecstasy), GHB (gamma hydroxybutyrate), Rohypnol ("roofies"), ketamine, and methamphetamine.
- Anabolic steroids are synthetic compounds that are chemically related to the male sex hormone testosterone. Anabolic steroids are often abused by

individuals who are interested in accelerating muscle growth.

- Federal law establishes five schedules of classification for controlled dangerous substances on the basis of a drug's potential for abuse, potential for physical and psychological dependence, and medical value.

- Analysts employ screening tests to determine the identity of drugs present in a sample. These tests reduce the number of possible drugs to a small and manageable number.

- A series of color tests produce characteristic colors for the more commonly encountered illicit drugs.

- Chromatography is a means of separating and tentatively identifying the components of a mixture.

- Gas chromatography (GC) separates mixtures on the basis of their distribution between a stationary liquid phase and a mobile gas phase.

- TLC uses a solid stationary phase, usually coated onto a glass plate, and a mobile liquid phase to separate the components of the mixture.

- After preliminary testing, forensic chemists employ more specific tests to identify a drug substance to the exclusion of all other known chemical substances. Infrared spectrophotometry and mass spectrometry typically are used to specifically identify a drug substance.

- Spectrophotometry is the study of the absorption of light by chemical substances.

- Most forensic laboratories use ultraviolet (UV) and infrared (IR) spectrophotometers to characterize chemical compounds.

- Infrared (IR) spectrophotometry provides a far more complex pattern than ultraviolet (UV) spectrophotometry. Because different materials have distinctively different infrared spectra, each IR spectrum is equivalent to a "fingerprint" of that substance.

- Mass spectrometry characterizes organic molecules by observing their fragmentation pattern after their collision with a beam of high-energy electrons.

Supplemental Questions

1. Name two physiological factors and two nondrug factors that influence drug dependence.

2. Under what class of drugs is cocaine listed according to U.S. federal drug laws? Explain why this classification is pharmacologically incorrect.

3. What is the source of most narcotic drugs? From what plant is this substance derived?

4. What opium derivative is most widely used by addicts? How is it typically administered? Give two reasons why this route of administration is popular.

5. What is the most widely used illicit drug in the United States? Under what class of drugs is it listed and what are its short-term physical and psychological effects at low to moderate doses?

6. What is the most widely abused drug in the United States? Under what class of drugs is it listed and what are its short-term physical and psychological effects at low to moderate doses?

7. How can excessive use of depressants cause death?

8. Name the two most commonly abused illegal stimulants and the smokable forms of each. Why does smoking provide a more intense drug experience than inhaling, or "snorting," stimulants?

9. Name two club drugs that are associated with drug-facilitated sexual assault, rape, and robbery. Why are these drugs relatively easy to administer to an unsuspecting victim?

10. What is the most popular club drug? Name three negative health effects associated with chronic use of the drug.

11. On what three criteria does the Controlled Substances Act classify dangerous substances?

12. According to the Controlled Substances Act, what is the legal difference between a Schedule I drug and a Schedule II drug?

13. What is a controlled substance analog? Why are such substances considered Schedule I drugs?

14. What is a precursor? How is possession of a precursor treated under the Controlled Substances Act?

15. List and describe the two phases in a criminalist's scheme of action for identifying a drug.

16. What two goals must laboratory testing accomplish to positively identify a drug?

17. How does a color test work? What is the main limitation of a color test for identifying drugs?

18. Describe how a microcrystalline test works. Name two advantages of microcrystalline tests.

19. Briefly describe the basic chromatographic process. Be sure to explain how motion is important to the process.

20. What two chromatographic processes are most applicable for solving analytical problems typically encountered in the crime laboratory? What is the main advantage of each?

21. What is the most important drawback of gas chromatography?

22. What is Beer's law and what analytical technique is based on it?

23. How are ultraviolet spectrophotometry and infrared spectrophotometry used in drug analysis?

24. Briefly describe the basic process of spectrophotometry.

25. What are the main strength and main weakness of ultraviolet spectrophotometry?

26. What major advantage does infrared spectrophotometry enjoy over ultraviolet spectrophotometry?

27. In what area does mass spectrometry currently have its greatest application for forensic scientists?

Answers to Supplemental Questions

1. Physiological factors influencing drug dependence include the nature of the drug, the route of administration, the dose, the frequency of administration, and the individual's rate of metabolism. Nondrug factors that play a role in drug dependence include personal characteristics of the user, his or her expectations about the drug experience, society's attitudes and possible responses, and the setting in which the drug is used.

2. Cocaine is classified as a narcotic under current federal law. However, cocaine is actually a powerful central nervous system stimulant, whereas narcotics are analgesic or pain-killing substances that depress the central nervous system.

3. The source of most analgesic narcotics is opium, which is derived from the poppy.

4. Heroin is the opium derivative most frequently used by addicts. It usually is injected intravenously because by injection its effects are felt almost instantaneously and with maximum sensitivity. In addition, heroin's high solubility in water makes its street preparation for intravenous administration rather simple.

5. Marijuana is the most widely used illicit drug in the United States. It is classified as a hallucinogen. At low doses the user may experience an increased sense of well-being; initial restlessness and hilarity followed by a state of relaxation; alteration of sensory perceptions; a more vivid sense of touch, sight, smell, taste, and sound; feelings of hunger; and subtle changes in thought formation and expression.

6. Alcohol is the most widely abused drug in the United States. It is classified as a depressant. Low doses of alcohol tend to inhibit the mental processes of judgment, memory, and concentration. At low to moderate doses alcohol causes the user to become expansive and exude confidence, reduces coordination substantially, inhibits orderly thought processes and speech patterns, and slows reaction time.

7. Excessive use of depressants can decrease the activity of the central nervous system dramatically, causing the body to cease breathing or circulating blood, which can lead to death.

8. The two most commonly abused illegal stimulants are amphetamines and cocaine. Their smokable forms are ice and crack, respectively. Smoking causes a more intense drug experience than "snorting" because it causes the drug to enter the bloodstream more quickly and to reach the brain faster.

9. GHB and Rohypnol are central nervous system depressants that are often connected with drug-facilitated sexual assault, rape, and robbery. Both drugs are odorless, colorless, and tasteless and remain undetected when slipped into a drink.

10. The most popular club drug is Ecstasy. Health effects associated with chronic use include seizures, muscle breakdown, stroke, kidney failure, cardiovascular system failure, and damage to the areas of the brain responsible for thought and memory.

11. The Controlled Substances Act classifies dangerous substances on the basis of their potential for abuse, their potential for physical and psychological dependence, and their medical value.

12. Schedule I drugs have no accepted medical value in the United States; Schedule II drugs may have medical use with severe restrictions.

13. A controlled substance analog is a chemical substance substantially similar in chemical structure to a controlled substance. They are considered Schedule I drugs to combat the proliferation of "designer drugs"—substances that are chemically related to some controlled drugs but are not listed under Schedule I.

14. A precursor is a chemical compound used by clandestine drug laboratories to synthesize abused drugs. The Controlled Substances Act provides severe penalties for a person who possesses a listed precursor chemical with the intent to manufacture a controlled substance. Precursors to PCP, amphetamines, and methamphetamines are regulated in the same manner as Schedule II substances.

15. The first phase is to run screening tests to reduce the number of possible drugs to a small and manageable number. The second phase of the analysis involves employing specific tests, or confirmations, to pinpoint and confirm the drug's identity.

16. Confirmation tests must produce a combination of results that are characteristic of only one chemical substance—the drug under investigation. Furthermore, experimental evidence must confirm that the probability of any other substance responding in an identical manner to the scheme selected is so small as to be beyond any reasonable scientific certainty.

17. In a color test, a chemical reagent turns a specific color when brought into contact with a particular drug. The main limitation of color tests is that they are useful for screening purposes only and are never taken as conclusive identification of unknown drugs.

18. In a microcrystalline test, a drop of a chemical reagent added to a small quantity of drug on a microscopic slide produces crystals that are highly characteristic of the drug. Two advantages of these tests are that they are rapid and often do not require the isolation of a drug from its diluents.

19. In one form of chromatography, a questioned mixture is dissolved in liquid so that some of its molecules enter the surrounding air as gas molecules, while others remain in the liquid. During this process, the air containing the gas molecules is forced to move continuously in one direction over the liquid. If one component of the mixture has a greater percentage of its molecules in the moving (gas) phase than other components, those molecules travel over the liquid at a faster pace. When the moving phase has advanced a reasonable distance, the molecules of the different components are completely separated from one another. This allows the scientist to identify the various components in the mixture.

20. Gas chromatography and thin-layer chromatography (TLC) are most applicable for solving analytical problems in the crime laboratory. Gas chromatography is widely used because of its ability to resolve a highly complex mixture into its components, usually within minutes. TLC is inexpensive and allows numerous samples to be analyzed simultaneously on one thin-layer plate.

21. The most important drawback of gas chromatography is that a forensic chemist cannot identify an unknown substance based solely on the results of gas chromatography.

22. Beer's law states that the quantity of light absorbed at any frequency is directly proportional to the concentration of material absorbing it; the more material one has, the more radiation it will absorb. Beer's law permits spectrophotometry to be used as a technique for quantification.

23. Ultraviolet spectrophotometry is useful for establishing the probable identity of a drug. Infrared spectrophotometry is one of the few analytical techniques that can specifically identify a substance.

24. In spectrophotometry, a beam of radiation is passed through a tube containing an unknown sample dissolved in a solution. A detector then compares the intensity of radiation passing through the solution to the intensity of a similar beam of radiation that does not pass through the solution. A signal from the detector is then fed into a recorder that produces an absorption spectrum that characterizes the sample being tested.

25. The main strength of UV spectrophotometry is that the spectra it produces are very simple, which makes determining a material's probable identity easier. The main drawback of UV spectrophotometry is that UV spectra of different substances can be similar, so the technique may not provide a definitive result.

26. Because different materials always have distinctively different infrared spectra, the IR spectrum for each substance is unique. Thus, unlike UV spectrophotometry, IR spectrophotometry can reliably identify specific substances.

27. Mass spectrometry currently finds its widest application in areas relating to the identification of drugs.

Resources

Videos/DVDs

Hooked: Illegal Drugs and How They Got That Way

This video takes a historical look at the use of illegal drugs in the United States and the social and legal forces that led to prohibition of today's illicit drugs.

> Format: Color, VHS
> Rated: NR
> Studio: A&E Home Video
> Video Release Date: May 6, 2002
> ASIN: B000065Q94

Thin-Layer Chromatography

This video describes the principles and practice of thin-layer chromatography.

> Format: Color, VHS
> Rated: NR
> Studio: Vision Quest Video
> Video Release Date: March 19, 1999
> ASIN: 6304464363

Books

Alien Vision: Exploring the Electromagnetic Spectrum with Imaging Technology
Austin Richards

This tour of the electromagnetic spectrum beyond the range of human sight explores the many uses of imaging technology to "see" invisible light. Dozens of colorful images and clear descriptions explain the light spectrum, including visible light, and advanced imaging technologies and their applications ranging from firefighting and law enforcement to botany and medicine.

> Format: Paperback, 184 pages
> Publisher: International Society for Optical Engineering (2001)
> ISBN: 0819441422

Buzzed: The Straight Facts about the Most Used and Abused Drugs from Alcohol to Ecstasy
Cynthia Kuhn et al.

Written by professors at the Duke University Medical Center, this book adopts a straight, neutral tone that reflects a commitment to providing unbiased, scientific fact. It is divided into a dozen sections on commonly used drugs: alcohol, caffeine, Ecstasy, hallucinogens, herbal drugs, inhalants, marijuana, nicotine, opiates, sedatives, steroids, and stimulants.

> Format: Paperback, 317 pages
> Publisher: W. W. Norton (1998)
> ISBN: 0393317323

Drug Identification and Investigation for Law Enforcement

Brent Paterline

Written from a criminal justice standpoint, this book discusses the identification and effects of illicit drugs as well as the investigative techniques used by law enforcement to apprehend drug users and traffickers. It covers the physical forms of drugs, methods of use, paraphernalia and packaging, and slang terminology. The book also covers the physiological and psychological effects of drugs and the recognition of the physical indicators and behavior patterns of a person under the influence of drugs.

> Format: Paperback, 94 pages
>
> Publisher: Staggs (2003)
>
> ISBN: 0966197062

Illegal Drugs: A Complete Guide to Their History, Chemistry, Use and Abuse

Paul Gahlinger

This detailed reference covers every aspect of illegal substance use and all 178 drugs outlawed in the United States. It includes a history of drug use, the role of drugs in the workplace, the psychology of addiction, the war on drugs, and the biological effect of drugs on the brain. Each drug listing discusses its history, users, chemical characteristics, long-term health problems, and overdose information.

> Format: Paperback, 480 pages
>
> Publisher: Sagebrush Press (2001)
>
> ISBN: 0970313012

Marijuana Myths, Marijuana Facts: A Review of the Scientific Evidence

Lynn Etta Zimmer and John P. Morgan

This comprehensive work is based on scientific findings about the health and behavioral effects of marijuana. It avoids playing on the myths of either supporters or opponents of marijuana use by looking solely at the conclusions of published, refereed studies. The book also examines the dynamics and implications of the U.S. "war on drugs."

> Format: Paperback, 241 pages
>
> Publisher: Lindesmith Center (1997)
>
> ISBN: 0964156849

On-Site Drug Testing

Amanda J. Jenkins and Bruce A. Goldberger

This book provides a comprehensive discussion of a variety of on-site drug assay devices, their validation studies, and the use of the devices in a variety of settings. It presents an assessment of advantages, disadvantages, uses, and potential uses.

> Format: Hardcover, 276 pages
>
> Publisher: Humana Press (2001)
>
> ISBN: 089603870X

A Primer of Drug Action: A Concise, Nontechnical Guide to the Actions, Uses, and Side Effects of Psychoactive Drugs

Robert M. Julien

This easy-to-read guide to actions, uses, and side effects of psychoactive drugs covers general principles of each class of psychoactive drugs and specific information about each drug within that class. Each of the twenty chapters examines current and future directions in drug research (including drugs not yet available for clinical use).

> Format: Paperback, 512 pages
>
> Publisher: Owl Books (2001)
>
> ISBN: 080507158X

Advanced Reading

Bono, J. P., "Criminalistics—Introduction to Controlled Substances," in S. B. Karch, ed., *Drug Abuse Handbook.* Boca Raton, Fla.: Taylor & Francis, 1998.

Christian, D. R., Jr., "Analysis of Controlled Substances," in S. H. James and J. J. Nordby, eds., *Forensic Science: An Introduction to Scientific and Investigative Techniques,* 2nd ed. Boca Raton, Fla.: Taylor & Francis, 2005.

Northrop, David, "Forensic Applications of High-Performance Liquid Chromatography and Capillary Electrophoresis," in R. Saferstein, ed., *Forensic Science Handbook,* vol. 1, 2nd ed. Upper Saddle River, N.J.: Prentice Hall, 2002.

Saferstein, Richard, "Forensic Applications of Mass Spectrometry," in R. Saferstein, ed., *Forensic Science Handbook,* vol. 1, 2nd ed. Upper Saddle River, N.J.: Prentice Hall, 2002.

Siegel, J. A., "Forensic Identification of Controlled Substances," in R. Saferstein, ed., *Forensic Science Handbook,* vol. 2, 2nd ed. Upper Saddle River, N.J.: Prentice Hall, 2005.

Smith, F., and J. A. Siegel, eds., *Handbook of Forensic Drug Analysis.* Boca Raton, Fla.: Taylor & Francis, 2005.

Demonstrations and Lecture Starters

Drug Identification

A number of alternatives are available for demonstrating laboratory techniques used for drug identification. I would recommend emphasizing the application of color tests and TLC to drug analysis.

Drug standards exempted from Drug Enforcement Administration licensing requirements can be obtained from various suppliers, including Alltech Associates Inc., 2051 Waukegan Road, Deerfield, IL 60015-1899 (www.alltechweb.com) and Sigma-Aldrich Corp., 6050 Spruce Street, St. Louis, MO 63103 (www.sigmaaldrich.com).

Thin-Layer Chromatography

A demonstration of the operation of a gas chromatograph and the infrared spectrophotometer should supplement lecture material relating to these instrumental techniques. During a laboratory session I have had good luck with a prepackaged TLC experiment marketed by Lab-Aids Inc., 17 Colt Court, Ronkonkoma, NY 11779 (www.lab-aids.com). Using the thin-layer chromatography kit, each student runs chromatograms of five different sample dye solutions in order to establish standards and then two chromatograms of two unknowns. This approach gives each student an opportunity to appreciate the usefulness of TLC.

Chapter 6
Forensic Toxicology

Key Terms

absorption—Passage of alcohol across the wall of the stomach and small intestine into the bloodstream.

acid—A compound capable of donating a hydrogen ion (H^+) to another compound.

alveoli—Small sacs in the lungs through whose walls air and other gases are exchanged between the breath and the blood.

anticoagulant—A substance that prevents coagulation or clotting of blood.

artery—A blood vessel that carries blood away from the heart.

base—A compound capable of accepting a hydrogen ion (H^+).

capillary—A tiny blood vessel that receives blood from arteries and carries it to veins, and across whose walls exchange of materials between the blood and the tissues takes place.

catalyst—A substance that accelerates the rate of a chemical reaction but is not itself permanently changed by the reaction.

excretion—Elimination of alcohol from the body in an unchanged state; alcohol is normally excreted in breath and urine.

fuel cell detector—A detector in which a chemical reaction involving alcohol produces electricity.

metabolism—The transformation of a chemical in the body to other chemicals to facilitate its elimination from the body.

oxidation—The combination of oxygen with other substances to produce new products.

pH scale—A scale used to express the basicity or acidity of a substance. A pH of 7 is neutral; lower values are acidic and higher values are basic.

preservative—A substance that stops the growth of microorganisms in blood.

toxicologist—An individual whose job is to detect and identify drugs and poisons in body fluids, tissues, and organs.

vein—A blood vessel that carries blood toward the heart.

Learning Objectives

- Explain how alcohol is absorbed into the bloodstream, transported throughout the body, and eliminated by oxidation and excretion
- Understand the process by which alcohol is excreted in the breath via the lungs
- Understand the concepts of infrared and fuel cell breath-testing devices for alcohol testing
- Describe commonly employed field sobriety tests to assess alcohol impairment
- List and contrast laboratory procedures for measuring the concentration of alcohol in the blood
- Relate the precautions to be taken to properly preserve blood in order to analyze its alcohol content
- Understand the significance of implied-consent laws and the *Schmerber* v. *California* case to traffic enforcement
- Describe techniques that forensic toxicologists use to isolate and identify drugs and poisons
- Appreciate the significance of finding a drug in human tissues and organs to assessing impairment

Key Points

- Toxicologists detect and identify drugs and poisons in body fluids, tissues, and organs.
- Alcohol appears in the blood within minutes after it has been taken by mouth. It slowly increases in concentration while it is being absorbed from the stomach and the small intestine into the bloodstream.
- When all the alcohol has been absorbed, a maximum alcohol level is reached in the blood, and the postabsorption period begins. During postabsorption, the alcohol concentration slowly decreases until a zero level is reached.
- Elimination of alcohol throughout the body is accomplished through oxidation and excretion. Oxidation takes place almost entirely in the liver, while alcohol is excreted unchanged in the breath, urine, and perspiration.
- Many breath testers capture a set volume of breath and expose it to infrared light. The instrument measures blood-alcohol concentration in breath by measuring the degree of the interaction of the light with alcohol in the captured breath sample.
- Breath-testing devices operate on the principle that the ratio between the concentration of alcohol in alveolar breath and its concentration in blood is fixed.
- Law enforcement officers use field sobriety tests to estimate a motorist's degree of physical impairment by alcohol and to determine whether an evidential test for alcohol is justified.
- The horizontal-gaze nystagmus test, walk and turn, and the one-leg stand are all considered reliable and effective psychophysical tests for alcohol impairment.
- Gas chromatography is the most widely used approach for determining blood-alcohol levels in forensic laboratories.
- The forensic toxicologist must devise an analytical scheme to detect, isolate, and identify toxic drug substances extracted from biological fluids, tissues, and organs.
- A screening test gives quick insight into the likelihood that a specimen contains a drug substance.

Positive results from a screening test are tentative at best and must be verified with a confirmation test.

- The most widely used screening tests are thin-layer chromatography, gas chromatography, and immunoassay. Gas chromatography/mass spectrometry is generally accepted as the confirmation test of choice.

- Once a drug is extracted and identified, a toxicologist may be required to judge the drug's effect on an individual's natural performance or physical state.

Supplemental Questions

1. What is the primary duty of a forensic toxicologist?

2. What are the requirements of a suitable test for alcohol intoxication?

3. List at least three factors that determine the rate at which alcohol is absorbed into the bloodstream.

4. Name and describe the process by which most alcohol is eliminated from the body. How is the remaining alcohol eliminated and how is this useful in testing for alcohol?

5. Why is a blood test for alcohol taken shortly after drinking more advantageous for the suspect than one taken thirty minutes or more after drinking?

6. What was the first successful breath-test device and what did it measure to determine blood-alcohol concentration? What is the main difference between this device and the breath-test devices currently in use?

7. Describe how a fuel cell detector measures blood alcohol.

8. What is the key to the accuracy of a breath tester? Describe two steps the operator takes to ensure that this key requirement is met.

9. What is a divided-attention task? Name and describe two divided-attention tasks often administered during field sobriety tests.

10. What is horizontal-gaze nystagmus and how does the test for it reveal blood-alcohol levels?

11. What substances are typically added to blood that is collected from a subject before it is sent to a toxicology lab, and why are they added?

12. Why is it best to collect blood samples from different body sites for postmortem blood-alcohol determination?

13. At what blood-alcohol level is a typical driver in the United States considered legally intoxicated? At what blood-alcohol level is a commercial truck or bus driver in the United States considered legally intoxicated?

14. List two significant challenges a forensic toxicologist faces when attempting to identify drugs present in a body.

15. What is metabolism and how does it complicate the task of the forensic toxicologist?

16. Why is it necessary to follow a positive screening test for drugs with a confirmation test? What is the confirmation test of choice?

17. A body is found at a fire scene but investigators are not sure whether the victim was alive when the fire began. How can measuring the level of carbon monoxide in the victim's blood help determine this?

18. Why is knowledge of an individual's history of drug use important in evaluating drug concentrations?

Answers to Supplemental Questions

1. Forensic toxicologists detect and identify drugs and poisons in body fluids, tissues, and organs.

2. Tests for alcohol intoxication must be rapid and specific; they must be designed to test hundreds of thousands of motorists annually without causing them undue physical harm or unreasonable inconvenience; and they must provide a reliable diagnosis that can be supported and defended within the framework of the legal system.

3. Factors that determine the rate at which alcohol is absorbed into the bloodstream include the total time taken to consume the drink, the alcohol content of the beverage, the amount of beverage consumed, and the quantity and type of food in the stomach at the time of drinking.

4. Nearly all of the alcohol consumed is eventually oxidized to carbon dioxide and water. The remaining alcohol is excreted unchanged in the breath, urine, and perspiration. The fact that the amount of alcohol exhaled in the breath is in direct proportion to the concentration of alcohol in the blood has led to the development of instruments that quickly, easily, and reliably measure breath for its alcohol content.

5. The administration of a blood test for alcohol requires drawing blood from a vein, but alcohol in the veins diffuses very rapidly into body tissues during the early phases of absorption compared to blood in the arteries. Thus, blood from a vein can show a misleadingly low blood-alcohol concentration immediately after drinking. Once absorption is complete, however, the alcohol becomes equally distributed throughout the blood system, so blood taken from a vein a short time after drinking shows a more accurate blood-alcohol concentration.

6. The first successful breath-test device was the Breathalyzer. It measured the concentration of alcohol in alveolar breath. The Breathalyzer used chemical reactions to detect the presence of alcohol, whereas most modern testing devices use infrared radiation.

7. In a fuel cell detector, alcohol in a suspect's breath combines with oxygen in the air to produce acetic acid. This process generates an electrical current that is proportional to the quantity of alcohol present in the breath.

8. The key to the accuracy of a breath tester is to ensure that the device captures the alcohol in the alveolar

(deep-lung) breath of the subject. This is typically accomplished by programming the unit to accept a minimum amount of breath (typically 1.5 liters) from the subject. Also, the subject must blow for a minimum time with a minimum breath flow rate.

9. A divided-attention task tests a subject's ability to comprehend and execute two or more simple instructions at one time. The walk and turn test requires the suspect to walk a straight line, touching heel to toe for nine steps, then turn around on the line and repeat the process. The one-leg stand requires the suspect to stand on one foot while holding the other foot several inches off the ground for thirty seconds and simultaneously counting out loud.

10. Horizontal-gaze nystagmus is an involuntary jerking of the eye as it moves to the side. The subject is asked to follow an object with his or her eye as far to the side as the eye can go. The higher a person's blood-alcohol concentration, the less the eye has to move toward the side before jerking or nystagmus begins.

11. An anticoagulant usually is added to blood collected from a subject to prevent it from clotting. A preservative is also added to inhibit the growth of microorganisms capable of destroying alcohol in the blood.

12. It is best to collect a number of blood samples from different body sites because ethyl alcohol may be generated in a deceased individual as a result of bacterial action. Several samples taken from different sites can then be compared to each other. If the results for all blood samples are similar, the blood-alcohol levels can safely be attributed to alcohol consumption.

13. A typical driver in the United States is considered legally intoxicated at a blood-alcohol level of 0.08 percent. A commercial truck or bus driver in the United States is considered legally intoxicated at a blood-alcohol level of 0.04 percent.

14. The forensic toxicologist often has no clue as to which drug or drugs might be present. Also, by the time a drug specimen reaches the toxicology laboratory, it has been dissipated and distributed throughout the body, so the toxicologist must work with very small amounts of drugs. These small amounts must be carefully extracted from the body before they can be analyzed.

15. Metabolism is the process by which the body changes one chemical to another in order to facilitate its elimination from the body. Because of metabolism, few substances enter and completely leave the body in the same chemical state. Thus, the forensic toxicologist must thoroughly understand how the body alters or metabolizes the chemical structure of a drug in order to detect the presence of that drug.

16. A follow-up test is required after a positive screening test to ensure that the positive result was not caused by a substance with a chemical structure similar to that of an illegal drug. Gas chromatography/mass spectrometry is generally accepted as the confirmation test of choice.

17. The presence of high levels of carbon monoxide in the blood would prove that the victim breathed the combustion products of the fire and was therefore alive when the fire began. Low levels of carbon monoxide would suggest that the victim was dead before the fire started.

18. Knowledge of an individual's history of drug use is very important in evaluating drug concentrations because factors such as age, physical condition, and tolerance of the drug user can affect an individual's response to a drug's effects. For example, long-term users of a drug may be able to tolerate blood-drug concentrations that would normally be fatal to the casual drug user.

Resources

Videos/DVDs

Alcohol: Brain under the Influence

This live-action presentation of how the human brain is affected by alcohol explains why drinking alcohol is pleasurable, how field sobriety tests work, how drinking styles affect blood alcohol levels, and why driving skills become impaired. Two-time Indianapolis 500 winner Arie Luyendyk discusses alcohol and driving safety. The video includes live demonstrations and reenactments and 3D animation.

Format: Color, VHS

Rated: NR

Studio: Tapeworm

Video Release Date: October 22, 1998

ASIN: 6305237050

In the Mix—Alcohol: What You Don't Know

Based on a PBS television series, this thirty-minute anti-drinking-and-driving video aimed at young adult audiences features a segment showing a police sobriety check.

Format: Color, VHS

Rated: NR

Studio: Castle Works

Video Release Date: 1996

ASIN: B00024E4TW

Books

Drugs and the Law: Detection, Recognition, and Investigation

Gary J. Miller

This comprehensive work on legal aspects of drug possession includes sections on drug testing and recognition.

Format: Paperback, 700 pages

Publisher: Gould (1997)

ISBN: 0875263984

Handbook of Forensic Drug Analysis

Fred Smith

This book provides an in-depth, up-to-date review of methods and results of forensic drug analyses. Chapters written by leading researchers in the field discuss the various forms of the drug as well as the origin and nature of samples. How to perform various tests, the use of best practices, and the analysis of results are discussed in detail. Numerous forensic and chemical analytic techniques are covered, including immunoassay, gas chromatography, and mass spectrometry.

Format: Hardcover, 584 pages

Publisher: Academic Press (2004)

ISBN: 0126506418

Principles of Forensic Toxicology

Barry Levine (Ed.)

This basic introduction to the instruments, principles, and theories of forensic toxicology includes sections on illicit drugs, alcohol, postmortem toxicology, and general principles of toxicology.

Format: Paperback, 385 pages

Publisher: AACC Press (2003)

ISBN: 1590186176

The Visual Detection of DWI Motorists

This pamphlet issued by the National Highway Transportation Safety Administration offers guidelines for patrol officers to identify and detect individuals driving while intoxicated.

Format: Paperback

Publisher: NHTSA (2001)

ASIN: B0001150CG

Advanced Reading

Benjamin, David M., "Forensic Pharmacology," in R. Saferstein, ed., *Forensic Science Handbook,* vol. 3. Upper Saddle River, N.J.: Prentice Hall, 1993.

Caplan, Y. H., and J. R. Zettl, "The Determination of Alcohol in Blood and Breath," in R. Saferstein, ed., *Forensic Science Handbook,* vol. 1, 2nd ed. Upper Saddle River, N.J.: Prentice Hall, 2002.

Fenton, John J., *Toxicology: A Case-Oriented Approach.* Boca Raton, Fla.: Taylor & Francis, 2002.

Garriott, James C., ed., *Medicolegal Aspects of Alcohol,* 4th ed. Tucson, Ariz.: Lawyers & Judges, 2004.

Karch, S. B., ed., *Drug Abuse Handbook.* Boca Raton, Fla.: CRC Press, 1998.

Demonstrations and Lecture Starters

Breath Testing

Students should become familiar with the operation of a breath-testing device. One interesting demonstration involving a breath tester requires a student to rinse his or her mouth with some 80–90 proof liquor without swallowing the beverage. The subject is then tested on the breath tester ten, fifteen, and twenty minutes from the time the liquor is removed from the mouth. The breath-test reading of the subject will be zero after twenty minutes. Traces of alcohol in the mouth will produce excessively high readings. It takes twenty minutes for mouth alcohol to dissipate. For this reason, a properly conducted breath test requires that a subject be observed for twenty minutes before the administration of a breath test to verify that no oral intake of alcohol has occurred during this period of time.

Blood-Alcohol Level

A person's blood-alcohol concentration (BAC) depends on several factors, including number of drinks, total elapsed time drinking, body mass, and gender. This demonstration illustrates the fact that one must consider all of these factors when determining when one is legally intoxicated. At the beginning of class, give each student a piece of paper that reads: "Imagine you have been drinking for two hours and in that time you have consumed five beers. Do you believe you are legally intoxicated?" Have each student write his or her name and answer on the paper and turn it in immediately. Before the next class, have students enter this information, along with data about weight and gender, into the BAC calculator at www.rupissed.com to determine whether they were correct. At the beginning of the following class, return the sheets to the students and ask how many guessed incorrectly. This can lead to a discussion of the effects of alcohol and factors that influence drug reactions.

Chapter 7
The Microscope

Key Terms

binocular—Describes a microscope with two eyepieces.

condenser—The lens system under the microscope stage that collects light rays from the base illuminator and focuses them onto the specimen.

depth of focus—The thickness of a specimen that is entirely in focus under a microscope.

eyepiece lens—The upper lens of a compound microscope, into which the viewer looks.

field of view—The area of the specimen that can be seen after it is magnified.

microspectrophotometer—An instrument that links a microscope to a spectrophotometer.

monocular—Describes a microscope with one eyepiece.

objective lens—The lower lens of a compound microscope; it is positioned directly over the specimen.

parfocal—Describes a microscope such that when an image is focused with one objective in position, the other objective can be rotated into place and the field will remain in focus.

plane-polarized light—Light confined to a single plane of vibration.

polarizer—A device that permits the passage of light waves vibrating in only one plane.

real image—An image that can be seen directly by the naked eye.

transmitted illumination—Light that passes up from the condenser and through the specimen; it is used to examine transparent specimens.

vertical or reflected illumination—Illumination of a specimen from above; in it is used to examine opaque specimens.

virtual image—An image that cannot be seen directly, but can be seen only by a viewer looking through a lens.

Learning Objectives

- List and understand the parts of the compound microscope
- Define *magnification, field of view, working distance*, and *depth of focus*
- Contrast the comparison and compound microscopes
- Understand the theory and utility of the stereoscopic microscope
- Appreciate how a polarizing microscope is designed to characterize polarized light
- Appreciate how a microspectrophotometer can be used to examine trace physical evidence
- Compare and contrast the image formation mechanism of a light microscope to that of a scanning electron microscope
- Outline some forensic applications of the scanning electron microscope

Key Points

- A microscope is an optical instrument that uses a lens or a combination of lenses to magnify and resolve the fine details of an object.
- In the basic compound microscope, the object to be magnified is placed under the lower lens, called the objective lens, and the magnified image is viewed through the upper lens, known as the eyepiece lens.
- The comparison microscope consists of two independent objective lenses joined by an optical bridge to a common eyepiece lens. A viewer looking through the eyepiece lens observes the objects under investigation side-by-side in a circular field that is equally divided into two parts.
- Modern firearms examination began with the introduction of the comparison microscope, which gives the examiner a side-by-side magnified view of bullets.
- The stereoscopic microscope consists of two monocular compound microscopes properly spaced and aligned to present a three-dimensional image of a specimen to the viewer, who looks through both eyepiece lenses.
- The large working distance of the stereoscopic microscope makes it ideal for microscopic examination of big, bulky items.
- Light that is confined to a single plane of vibration is said to be plane-polarized.
- The polarizing microscope made possible the examination of the interaction of plane-polarized light with matter.
- Polarizing microscopy is used to study birefringent materials, that is, materials that have a double refraction. Refractive-index data provide information that helps identify minerals present in a soil sample or determine the identity of a synthetic fiber.
- The microspectrophotometer is a spectrophotometer coupled with a light microscope. The device allows an examiner studying a specimen under the microscope to obtain the visible-light or IR spectrum of the material.
- The scanning electron microscope (SEM) bombards a specimen with a beam of electrons instead of light to produce a highly magnified image. This produces X-ray emissions that can be used to characterize elements present in the material.

Supplemental Questions

1. How does a magnifying glass enlarge objects viewed through it?

2. What is the difference between a real image and a virtual image?

3. Why does a compound microscope produce greater magnification than a magnifying glass? How does the eyepiece lens contribute to magnification?

4. What is vertical illumination and under what conditions would a forensic scientist use it to examine a sample? Why is it superior to transmitted illumination under such conditions?

5. How does one calculate the magnification power of a compound microscope?

6. What does numerical aperture (N.A.) measure? What is the difference between a lens with N.A. 1.0 and one with N.A. 0.5?

7. Why might an examiner choose a microscope with a lesser magnification to study a specimen?

8. Briefly describe how a comparison microscope works and what it is used for.

9. How did the comparison microscope make possible modern firearms examination?

10. List two unique characteristics of the stereoscopic microscope.

11. What is the most widely used microscope in the crime laboratory? What features make it particularly suited for examination of physical evidence?

12. What happens to a light beam that passes through a polarizing crystal? What happens when plane-polarized light passes through a second polarizing crystal set perpendicular to the first crystal?

13. What is the main advantage of the microspectrophotometer?

14. Explain how the infrared microspectrophotometer identifies a specimen. What type of physical evidence is the microspectrophotometer typically used to analyze?

15. What is the basic difference between a scanning electron microscope and the other microscopes used in the crime laboratory?

16. How can a scanning electron microscope be used to identify the elements present in a specimen?

17. How can a scanning electron microscope be used to determine whether a suspect has recently fired a gun?

Answers to Supplemental Questions

1. A magnifying glass makes things appear larger by refracting, or bending, light rays as they pass from the air into the glass and back into the air.

2. A real image is an image formed when light rays converge on a surface. An observer can see a real image with the naked eye. A virtual image cannot be seen directly, but can be seen only by an observer looking through a lens.

3. A compound microscope produces greater magnification because it uses two lenses to enlarge the object being viewed instead of just one. The eyepiece lens magnifies the real, enlarged image created by the objective lens, producing a greatly enlarged virtual image of the object.

4. Vertical illumination is illumination of a specimen from above. A forensic scientist would use vertical illumination when studying opaque specimens. Transmitted illumination can be used only with specimens that are transparent. With opaque specimens, the light source must be placed above the specimen and reflected off the specimen's surface and into the lens.

5. The total magnification power of a compound microscope is the product of the magnifying power of each lens.

6. Numerical aperture measures the ability of an objective lens to resolve details into separate images instead of one blurred image. A lens with N.A. 1.0 can separate details at half the distance of a lens with N.A. 0.5.

7. As magnifying power increases, the microscope's field of view—the size of the specimen it can study—decreases. The microscope's depth of focus—the thickness of the specimen it can study—also decreases with increasing magnification. An examiner might first select a lower-magnification microscope to get a good general overall view of the specimen, then switch later to a higher-power microscope to study smaller portions of the specimen in more detail.

8. The comparison microscope is two compound microscopes connected by a bridge that uses mirrors and lenses to combine the images from two objective lenses into a single image. A viewer looking through the eyepiece sees a circular field divided into two equal halves by a fine line. The specimen mounted under the left-hand objective lens appears in the left half of the field, and the specimen under the right-hand objective lens appears in the right half. A comparison microscope is used to make side-by-side comparison of specimens.

9. The comparison microscope enabled firearms examiners to compare a side-by-side magnified view of two bullets and thus to determine whether they were fired by the same gun. Bullets fired through the same barrel display comparable markings, called striations, caused by the rifling of the barrel. If the striations on two bullets viewed through a comparison microscope are alike, the examiner can conclude that both bullets traveled through the same barrel.

10. The stereoscopic microscope presents a three-dimensional image of an object. Also, whereas the image formed by the compound microscope is inverted and reversed, the stereoscopic microscope forms a right-side-up image.

11. The stereoscopic microscope is the most widely used microscope in the crime laboratory. Its wide field of view and great depth of focus make it an ideal instrument for locating trace evidence. Its large working distance (the distance between the objective lens and the specimen) makes it ideal for microscopic examination of big, bulky items.

12. A beam of light passing through a polarizing crystal emerges vibrating in only one plane. When plane-polarized light passes through a second

polarizing crystal set perpendicular to the first crystal, the light is blocked by the second crystal.

13. The microspectrophotometer allows the forensic scientist to view a particle under a microscope while obtaining its absorption spectrum. This provides added information to help characterize trace quantities of evidence.

14. The infrared microspectrophotometer identifies a specimen by obtaining its IR spectrum, which is unique for every chemical substance. The technique is used to analyze fibers and paints.

15. A scanning electron microscope uses a stream of electrons to create an image of the specimen being studied; all other microscopes use light coming off the specimen to create an image.

16. When the electron beam of the scanning electron microscope strikes a specimen, it creates X-rays that can be sorted by an X-ray analyzer. Because each element emits X-rays of characteristic energy values, the analyzer can identify the elements present in the specimen based on the energy values of the X-rays emitted by the specimen.

17. Possible gunshot particles remaining on a shooter's hands are lifted off with a piece of adhesive tape; the tape is then examined under the scanning electron microscope. The X-rays produced by the particles are analyzed and displayed according to their energies. This allows the examiner to detect elements frequently found in bullet primers.

Resources

Videos/DVDs

How to Use a Microscope

This educational DVD describes various types of microscopes and provides detailed instructions on use of the light microscope.

> Format: Color, DVD
>
> Rated: NR
>
> Studio: Educational Video Network
>
> DVD Release Date: July 6, 2000
>
> ASIN: B000063O7JQ

Books

Forensic Microscopy: A Practical Guide

P. D. G. Richards

This handbook outlines procedures and practices in forensic use of the microscope.

> Format: Paperback, 265 pages
>
> Publisher: BIOS Scientific (2001)
>
> ISBN: 0387916164

The Use of the Compound Microscope: A Self-Instructional Unit

Betty Smith

This brief volume discusses the basic operation and care of the compound microscope.

> Format: Paperback, 53 pages
>
> Publisher: Educational Materials for Health Professionals (1997)
>
> ISBN: B0006QS3NY

Advanced Reading

Bartick, E. G., and M. W. Tungol, "Infrared Microscopy and Its Forensic Applications," in R. Saferstein, ed., *Forensic Science Handbook,* vol. 3. Upper Saddle River, N.J.: Prentice Hall, 1993.

De Forest, Peter R., "Foundations of Forensic Microscopy," in R. Saferstein, ed., *Forensic Science Handbook,* vol. 1, 2nd ed. Upper Saddle River, N.J.: Prentice Hall, 2002.

Eyring, Michael B., "Visible Microscopical Spectrophotometry in the Forensic Sciences," in R. Saferstein, ed., *Forensic Science Handbook,* vol. 1, 2nd ed. Upper Saddle River, N.J.: Prentice Hall, 2002.

Palenik, S., and C. Palenik, "Microscopy and Microchemistry of Physical Evidence," in R. Saferstein, ed., *Forensic Science Handbook,* vol. 2, 2nd ed. Upper Saddle River, N.J.: Prentice Hall, 2005.

Petraco, N., and T. Kubic, *Basic Concepts in Optical Microscopy for Criminalists, Chemists, and Conservators.* Boca Raton, Fla.: Taylor & Francis, 2004.

Stoney, D. A., and P. M. Dougherty, "The Microscope in Forensic Science," in S. M. Gerber and R. Saferstein, eds., *More Chemistry and Crime.* Washington, D.C.: American Chemical Society, 1997.

Demonstrations and Lecture Starters

Introduction to Microscopes

Because of the importance of the microscope to the crime laboratory, a criminalistics course must stress the use of these instruments. Each student should have access to compound and stereoscopic microscopes, and possibly a comparison microscope. The proper handling and care of the microscope are to be emphasized in the laboratory. Exercises demonstrating the magnifying power and depth of field of the microscope are suitable for introducing the student to this instrument. Observing specimens such as tea and tobacco under the stereoscopic microscope allows the student to appreciate the stereo's great depth of field. The student must also learn how to prepare dry-mount and wet-mount slides for examination under the compound microscope.

Chapter 8
Forensic Serology

Key Terms

acid phosphatase—An enzyme found in high concentration in semen.

agglutination—The clumping together of red blood cells by the action of an antibody.

allele—Any of several alternative forms of a gene located at the same point on a particular pair of chromosomes.

antibody—A protein in the blood serum that destroys or inactivates a specific antigen.

antigen—A substance, usually a protein, that stimulates the body to produce antibodies against it.

antiserum—Blood serum that contains specific antibodies.

aspermia—The absence of sperm; sterility in males.

chromosome—A threadlike structure in the cell nucleus, along which the genes are located.

deoxyribonucleic acid (DNA)—The molecules that carry the body's genetic information.

egg—The female reproductive cell.

enzyme—A protein that acts as a catalyst for certain specific reactions.

erythrocyte—A red blood cell.

gene—The basic unit of heredity, consisting of a DNA segment located on a chromosome.

genotype—The particular combination of genes present in the cells of an individual.

hemoglobin—A red blood cell protein that transports oxygen in the bloodstream; it is responsible for the red color of blood.

heterozygous—Having two different allelic genes on two corresponding positions of a pair of chromosomes.

homozygous—Having two identical allelic genes on two corresponding positions of a pair of chromosomes.

hybridoma cells—Fused spleen and tumor cells. Used to produce identical monoclonal antibodies in a limitless supply.

locus—The physical location of a gene on a chromosome.

luminol—The most sensitive chemical test that is capable of presumptively detecting bloodstains diluted up to 300,000 times. Its reaction with blood emits light and thus requires that the result be observed in a darkened area.

monoclonal antibodies—A collection of identical antibodies that interact with a single antigen site.

oligospermia—An abnormally low sperm count.

phenotype—The physical manifestation of a genetic trait such as shape, color, or blood type.

plasma—The fluid portion of unclotted blood.

polyclonal antibodies—Antibodies produced by injecting animals with a specific antigen. A series of antibodies is produced responding to a variety of different sites on the antigen.

precipitin—An antibody that reacts with its corresponding antigen to form a precipitate.

serology—The study of antigen–antibody reactions.

serum—The liquid that separates from the blood when a clot is formed.

sperm—The male reproductive cell.

X chromosome—The female sex chromosome.

Y chromosome—The male sex chromosome.

zygote—The cell arising from the union of an egg and a sperm cell.

Learning Objectives

- List the A-B-O antigens and antibodies found in the blood for each of the four blood types: A, B, AB, and O

- Understand and describe how whole blood is typed

- List and describe forensic tests used to characterize a stain as blood

- Understand the concept of antigen–antibody interactions and how it is applied to species identification and drug identification

- Contrast chromosomes and genes

- Learn how the Punnett square is used to determine the genotypes and phenotypes of offspring

- List the laboratory tests necessary to characterize seminal stains

- Explain how suspect blood and semen stains are properly preserved for laboratory examination

- Describe the proper collection of physical evidence in a rape investigation

Key Points

- Serology involves a broad scope of laboratory tests that use specific antigen and serum antibody reactions.

- An antibody reacts or agglutinates only with its specific antigen. The concept of specific antigen–antibody reactions has been applied to techniques for detecting abused drugs in blood and urine.

- When an animal is injected with an antigen, its body produces a series of different antibodies, all of which are designed to attack some particular site on the antigen of interest. These antibodies are known as polyclonal antibodies.

- A more uniform and specific collection of antibodies designed to combine with a single antigen site can be manufactured. Such antibodies are known as monoclonal antibodies.

- The criminalist must answer the following questions when examining dried blood: (1) Is it blood? (2) From what species did the blood originate? (3) If the blood is human, how closely can it be associated with a particular individual?

- The determination of blood is best made with a preliminary color test. A positive result from the Kastle-Meyer color test is highly indicative of blood.

- The luminol test is used to find trace amounts of blood at crime scenes.

- The precipitin test uses antisera normally derived from rabbits that have been injected with the blood of a known animal to determine the species origin of a questioned bloodstain.

- At one time, bloodstains were linked to a source by A-B-O typing and the characterization of polymorphic blood enzymes and proteins. This approach has now been supplanted by newer DNA technology.

- The location, distribution, and appearance of bloodstains and spatters may be useful for interpreting and reconstructing the events that produced the bleeding.

- Surface texture and the stain's shape, size, and location must be considered when determining the direction, dropping distance, and angle of impact of a bloodstain.

- The best way to locate and characterize a seminal stain is to perform the acid phosphatase color test.

- Forensic scientists can link seminal material to an individual by DNA typing.

- A rape victim must undergo a medical examination as soon as possible after the assault. At that time clothing, hairs, and vaginal and rectal swabs can be collected for subsequent laboratory examination.

- If a suspect is apprehended within twenty-four hours of a sexual assault, it may be possible to detect the victim's DNA on the suspect's underwear or on a penile swab of the suspect.

Supplemental Questions

1. What is the A-B-O system? Why is the system no longer used by forensic scientists?
2. What is an antigen and how is it useful in individualizing blood?
3. What is an antibody and what happens when an antibody reacts with its specific antigen?
4. What factor is most whole blood typed for? What is the most common blood type in the United States? Which is least common?
5. For what other application do forensic scientists often use specific antigen–antibody reactions? What is EMIT frequently used for and what is its greatest problem?

6. What is the difference between monoclonal and polyclonal antibodies? Which type are more useful for the forensic scientist and why?
7. What three questions must the criminalist answer when examining dried blood?
8. List two commonly used color tests for blood. How does a luminol test differ from these tests?
9. What is the purpose of a precipitin test? Name three strengths of precipitin tests.
10. How does the texture of a surface affect bloodstain patterns made on that surface?
11. How can a criminalist identify the direction in which blood traveled and the angle at which it struck a flat surface?
12. What is a genotype and how do parents' genotypes affect the blood type of their offspring? In what area of the law does this information have important implications?
13. What is acid phosphatase and how do forensic scientists use it?
14. List three reasons why spermatozoa are often not found in seminal fluid collected at a crime scene.
15. Why is it important for investigators to seek information about when and if voluntary sexual activity last occurred prior to a sexual assault?

Answers to Supplemental Questions

1. The A-B-O system is a system for classifying blood according to general groups or types. Forensic scientists no longer use it because DNA identification has replaced the A-B-O system as the most accurate means of linking blood evidence to an individual.
2. An antigen is a substance, usually a protein, that stimulates the body to produce antibodies against it. The surface of every blood cell contains antigens that can be grouped into systems depending on their relationship to one another. The combination of antigens on blood cells serves as a basis for comparing blood samples.
3. An antibody is a protein that destroys or inactivates a specific antigen. When an antibody reacts with its specific antigen the two immediately combine, causing the antibody to attach itself to the blood cell containing the antigen. Because antibodies can simultaneously be attached to antigens located on two different red blood cells, this creates a vast network of cross-linked cells usually seen as clumping or agglutination.
4. Most whole blood is typed for its A-B-O identity. Type O blood is the most common in the United States; type AB is the least common.
5. Specific antigen–antibody reactions are used to detect drugs in blood and urine. One of the most frequent uses of EMIT in forensic laboratories has been to screen the urine of suspected marijuana smokers. The greatest problem associated with the technique is determining when the individual

actually used marijuana. Some individuals may yield positive urine test results up to ten days after the last use of marijuana.

6. Monoclonal antibodies bind to only one specific antigen site; polyclonal antibodies can bind to a number of different sites on an antigen. Monoclonal antibodies are more useful because they can be used to create antigens for specific substances that the forensic scientist may need to test for, such as illegal drugs.

7. The criminalist must answer the following three questions when examining dried blood: (1) Is it blood? (2) From what species did the blood originate? (3) If the blood is human, how closely can it be associated with a particular individual?

8. Two commonly used color tests for blood are the Kastle-Meyer test and the Hemastix test. Luminol testing differs from these techniques because the reaction of luminol with blood produces light rather than color.

9. A precipitin test is used to determine whether a bloodstain is of human or animal origin. Strengths of the precipitin test include the fact that it is very sensitive, it requires only a small amount of blood for testing, and human bloodstains dried for years may still give a positive reaction.

10. In general, the harder and less porous the surface, the less blood spatter.

11. The direction of travel of blood striking an object can be discerned by the stain's shape. The pointed end of a bloodstain always faces its direction of travel. It is possible to determine the impact angle of blood on a flat surface by measuring the degree of circular distortion of the stain. A drop of blood striking a surface at right angles produces a nearly circular stain; as the angle decreases, the stain elongates.

12. A genotype is the particular combination of genes present in the cells of an individual. Because each parent passes his or her genes to the offspring, and blood type is determined by genes, a child cannot have a gene for a blood type that does not appear in either of his or her parents. This fact has important implications in resolving cases of disputed paternity.

13. Acid phosphatase is an enzyme that is secreted by the prostate gland into seminal fluid. Forensic scientists use it to determine the presence of semen in a stain.

14. Reasons why spermatozoa are not always present in semen stains include the following: spermatozoa bind tightly to cloth materials such as underwear; spermatozoa are extremely brittle when dry and easily disintegrate if the stain is washed or rubbed; and sexual crimes may involve males who have an abnormally low—or even zero—sperm count.

15. If a rape victim has consensual sex prior to the sexual assault, spermatozoa or acid phosphatase from the consensual partner may remain in the victim's vaginal cavity at the time of examination. Information about when the victim last had consensual sex will thus be useful for evaluating the significance of finding these substances in the victim.

Resources

Books

Bloodstain Pattern Analysis: With an Introduction to Crime Scene Reconstruction

Tom Bevel and Ross Gardner

This book covers the analysis of bloodstain evidence with an emphasis on application of scientific method, the use of flow charts, and the interrelationship of crime-scene analysis to criminal profiling. Explains the use of computer programs to create demonstrative evidence for court.

> Format: Hardcover, 424 pages
>
> Publisher: CRC Press (2001)
>
> ISBN: 0849309506

Forensic Serology

A. D. Beveridge (Ed.)

One in a series of brief works featuring case studies in forensic topics, this volume examines forensic blood and semen analysis.

> Format: Paperback, 100 pages
>
> Publisher: Chelsea House (2005)
>
> ISBN: 0791089096

Interpretation of Bloodstain Evidence at Crime Scenes

Stuart James, William Eckert, and Florida Eckert (Eds.)

This book features an introduction to bloodstain interpretation; impact and angle considerations; the significance of partially dried, clotted, aged, and physically altered bloodstains; and detection of blood. It also includes twenty case studies and more than four hundred photographs.

> Format: Hardcover, 324 pages
>
> Publisher: CRC Press (1998)
>
> ISBN: 0849381266

Principles of Bloodstain Pattern Analysis, Theory and Practice

Stuart H. James, Paul Erwin Kish, and T. Paulette Sutton

This in-depth, multidisciplinary investigation of bloodstain analysis explores crime-scene and laboratory examinations in conjunction with forensic pathology, forensic serology, and chemical enhancement techniques. Emphasis is on classification of bloodstains by physical characteristics of size, shape, and distribution, and the specific mechanisms that produce them. Individual chapters analyze case studies, with two chapters specifically discussing the details of legal issues as they pertain to bloodstain pattern analysis.

Format: Hardcover, 542 pages

Publisher: CRC Press (2005)

ISBN: 0849320143

Rape Investigation Handbook

Brent E. Turvey and John Savino

This thorough overview of the investigative and forensic processes related to sex crime investigation takes the reader through investigative and forensic processes in a logical sequence, showing how investigations of rape and sexual assault can and should be conducted from start to finish. Includes extensive illustrations of perpetrators, victims, and other rape case evidence for identification of incidents of rape.

Format: Hardcover, 456 pages

Publisher: Academic Press (2004)

ISBN: 012072832X

Advanced Reading

Jones, E. L., Jr., "The Identification and Individualization of Semen Stains," in R. Saferstein, ed., *Forensic Science Handbook*, vol. 2, 2nd ed. Upper Saddle River, N.J.: Prentice Hall, 2005.

Shaler, R. C., "Modern Forensic Biology," in R. Saferstein, ed., *Forensic Science Handbook*, vol. 1, 2nd ed. Upper Saddle River, N.J.: Prentice Hall, 2002.

Whitehead, P. H., "A Historical Review of the Characterization of Blood and Secretion Stains in the Forensic Laboratory—Part One: Bloodstains," *Forensic Science Review* 5 (1993): 35.

Wonder, A., *Blood Dynamics*. Boca Raton, Fla.: Taylor & Francis, 2002.

Demonstrations and Lecture Starters

Blood Typing and Testing

The typing of whole blood is an experiment that illustrates some important points covered in the chapter. Blood-typing kits that allow each student to safely determine his or her own blood type are available from several scientific supply companies. This kit should include anti-A, anti-B, and anti-D sera.

A presumptive test reagent for blood is prepared by adding phenolphthalein (4 grams), potassium hydroxide (40 grams), and zinc dust (20 grams) to distilled water (200 milliliters). The mixture is boiled until the pink coloration has practically disappeared, cooled, and stored in a refrigerator. Before use, an aliquot of stock solution is diluted with an equal volume of ethyl alcohol. Any suspicious stain is lightly rubbed with dry filter paper. A drop of the phenolphthalein reagent and a drop of hydrogen peroxide (3 percent w/v) is put on the paper. A deep pink color indicates a positive reaction.

Commercially prepared presumptive blood testing reagents and kits can be purchased from Doje's Forensic Supplies., P.O. Box 500, Ocoee, Fla., 407-880-8149 (www.dojes.com).

Blood Drop Analysis

This demonstration, which illustrates one aspect of blood spatter analysis, requires both the students and instructor to prepare materials beforehand outside class.

The Scenario

Mrs. Lipton and her dog, Skipper, walk the neighborhood each evening, and on these outings Skipper often digs up all sorts of interesting objects. Last night, Skipper spotted some sheets of soiled and wrinkled newspaper and began to sniff at them furiously. As Mrs. Lipton bent down to collect the papers and throw them out, she noticed something sticky on them that looked like blood. She immediately took out her cell phone and called the police. A short time later, Detective Bosco arrived to investigate the find. It turns out that a young woman was found that morning beaten to death in the trunk of her car. The evidence suggests that she was killed outside the car and later placed in the trunk. It also provides broad clues that suggest that the crime was committed in one of three places: a parking lot just north of downtown, a nearby park on the banks of a small creek, or a hilly area lying on the far side of the creek. Detective Bosco knows that if the blood on the papers belongs to the young woman, the shape of the bloodstains on the newspaper can provide clues about where the crime was committed.

Instructor Preparation

At the end of the class session before the demonstration, divide the class into a few groups of several students each. For each group, spread a sheet of newspaper on the ground. Choose either a relatively flat surface, a surface with a gentle slope, or a relatively steep slope. Place the papers for all groups on the same slope. Fill a pipette or eyedropper with simulated blood and let a few drops fall on each paper. Measure and record the height from which you dropped the simulated blood. Allow the spots to dry before carefully collecting the papers and bringing them to class.

Supplies

Commercially available simulated blood (available in movie or theatrical supply stores: Star Light & Magic, www.starmgc.com/blood.html, or Reel Creations, www.reelcreations.com/store/store/) or prepare your own.

The following recipes have been proposed*

1. Mix 4 ounces evaporated milk, 2–3 tablespoons tomato paste, and red food coloring. Add water as needed to achieve the approximate consistency of blood. Store in refrigerator for up to two days.

2. Mix dry milk powder, water, and red food coloring to desired thickness. Store in refrigerator.

---

*T. Kubic and N. Patraco, *Forensic Science Laboratory Manual and Workbook*, rev. ed. (Boca Raton, FL.: CRC Press, 2005).

3. Mix white corn syrup and red food coloring. Add water to desired thickness. Store at room temperature.

Student Preparation

Each group should collect the following materials:

- "Blood" (ketchup) in a 100-milliliter beaker
- Aprons
- Newspaper
- Plastic knife
- Yardstick or tape measure

Each team should go outdoors and spread four sheets of newspaper on level ground. Dip the plastic knife in the "blood" and walk across the newspapers holding the knife 12 inches from the ground, allowing the "blood" to drip on the papers. Label the papers as "12 inches/flat surface." Now repeat the process with the other three pieces of newspaper, holding the knife at heights of 24 ", 36 ", and 48 " from the ground. Label the papers with the height at which the knife was held and the words "flat surface." Now place another four sheets of clean newspaper on a gentle slope and repeat the process. These sheets of newspaper should be labeled with the height at which the knife was held and the words "gentle slope." Place the last four sheets of newspaper on a steep slope and repeat the process. These sheets of newspaper should be labeled with the height at which the knife was held and the words "steep slope." Allow the spots to dry before carefully collecting the papers and bringing them to class.

Comparing Bloodstains

In class, the instructor gives each team of students a piece of bloodstained paper that he or she prepared and asks them to compare it to the stains on the papers they prepared and answer the following questions: Was the crime committed on a flat surface, a gentle slope, or a steep slope? Based on this evidence, which of the three locations is the most likely scene of the crime?

Chapter 9

DNA: The Indispensable Forensic Science Tool

Key Terms

amelogenin gene—A genetic locus useful for determining gender.

amino acids—The building blocks of proteins.

buccal cells—Cells from the inner cheek lining.

chromosome—A threadlike structure in the cell nucleus, along which the genes are located.

complementary base pairing—The specific pairing of base *A* with *T* and base *C* with *G* in double-stranded DNA.

deoxyribonucleic acid (DNA)—The molecules that carry the body's genetic information.

electrophoresis—A technique for separating molecules through their migration on a support medium while under the influence of an electrical potential.

epithelial cells—The outer layer of skin cells.

human genome—The order of bases on all twenty-three pairs of human chromosomes.

hybridization—The process of joining two complementary strands of DNA to form a double-stranded molecule.

low copy number—Fewer than eighteen DNA-bearing cells.

mitochondria—Small structures outside the nucleus that supply energy to the cell.

multiplexing—A technique that simultaneously detects more than one DNA marker in a single analysis.

nucleotide—A repeating unit of DNA consisting of one of four bases—adenine, guanine, cytosine, or thymine—attached to a phosphate–sugar group.

picogram—One-trillionth of a gram, or 0.000000000001 gram.

polymer—A substance composed of a large number of atoms. These atoms are usually arranged in repeating units, or monomers.

polymerase chain reaction (PCR)—A technique for replicating or copying a portion of a DNA strand outside a living cell.

primer—A short strand of DNA used to target a region of DNA for replication by PCR.

proteins—Polymers of amino acids that play basic roles in the structures and functions of living things.

replication—The synthesis of new DNA from existing DNA.

restriction enzyme—Chemical that acts as scissors to cut DNA molecules at specific locations.

restriction fragment length polymorphisms (RFLPs)—Different fragment lengths of base pairs that result from cutting a DNA molecule with restriction enzymes.

sequencing—A procedure used to determine the order of the base pairs that constitute DNA.

short tandem repeat (STR)—A region of a DNA molecule that contains short segments of three to seven repeating base pairs.

substrate control—An unstained object adjacent to an area on which biological material has been deposited.

tandem repeat—A region of a chromosome that contains multiple copies of a core DNA sequence that are arranged in a repeating fashion.

Y-STRs—Short tandem repeats located on the human Y chromosome.

Learning Objectives

* Name the parts of a nucleotide and explain how they are linked to form DNA

* Understand the concept of base pairing as it relates to the double-helix structure of DNA

* Contrast DNA strands that code for the production of proteins with strands that contain repeating base sequences

* Explain the technology of polymerase chain reaction (PCR) and how it applies to forensic DNA typing

* Contrast the newest DNA-typing technique, short tandem repeats (STRs), with previous DNA-typing technologies

* Describe the difference between nuclear and mitochondrial DNA

* Understand the use of DNA computerized databases in criminal investigation

* List the necessary procedures for proper preservation of biological evidence for laboratory DNA analysis

Key Points

* Portions of the DNA structure are as unique to each individual as fingerprints.

* The gene is the fundamental unit of heredity. Each gene is composed of DNA specifically designed to control the genetic traits of our cells.

* DNA is constructed as a very large molecule made by linking a series of repeating units called nucleotides.

* Four types of bases are associated with the DNA structure: adenine (*A*), guanine (*G*), cytosine (*C*), and thymine (*T*).

* The bases on each strand of DNA are aligned in a double-helix configuration so that adenine pairs with thymine and guanine pairs with cytosine. This concept is known as base pairing. The order of the bases distinguishes different DNA strands.

* Portions of the DNA molecule contain sequences of bases that are repeated numerous times. These

tandem repeats offer a means of distinguishing one individual from another through DNA typing.

- Length differences associated with relatively long repeating DNA strands—called restriction fragment length polymorphisms (RFLPs)—formed the basis for one of the first DNA-typing procedures.

- In the laboratory, DNA molecules are cut up by a restriction enzyme and the resulting fragments are sorted out by electrophoresis.

- A typical DNA fragment pattern shows two bands (one RFLP from each chromosome). When comparing the DNA fragment patterns of two or more specimens, the analyst looks for a match between the band sets.

- Electrophoresis is an analytical technique in which materials are forced to move across a gel-coated plate under the influence of an electrical potential. Substances such as proteins and DNA can be separated and characterized using electrophoresis.

- Polymerase chain reaction (PCR) can amplify minute quantities of DNA. The technique evolved from an understanding of how DNA strands naturally replicate within a cell.

- PCR technology cannot be applied to RFLP DNA typing because RFLP strands are too long, often numbering in the thousands of bases. PCR is best used with DNA strands that are no longer than a couple of hundred bases.

- Long RFLP strands tend to break apart under the adverse conditions at many crime scenes. The shorter DNA strands used in PCR are more stable and less subject to degradation caused by adverse environmental conditions.

- The latest method of DNA typing, short tandem repeat (STR) analysis, is the most successful and widely used DNA-profiling procedure.

- STRs are locations on the chromosome that contain short sequences that repeat themselves within the DNA molecule. They serve as useful markers for identification because they are found in great abundance throughout the human genome.

- The entire strand of an STR is very short, less than 450 bases long. This makes STRs much less susceptible to degradation and they are often recovered from bodies or stains that have been subjected to extreme decomposition.

- Because of their shortness, STRs are ideal candidates for multiplication by PCR, thus overcoming the limited-sample-size problem often associated with crime-scene evidence.

- Hundreds of different types of STRs are found in human genes.

- The more STRs one can characterize, the smaller the percentage of the population from which a particular combination of STRs can emanate. This gives rise to the concept of multiplexing, in which the

forensic scientist can simultaneously extract and amplify a combination of different STRs.

- With STR, as little as 125 picograms of DNA is required for analysis—1/100 the amount normally required for RFLP analysis.

- Mitochondrial DNA is located outside the cell's nucleus and is inherited from the mother.

- Mitochondrial DNA typing does not approach STR analysis in its discrimination power and thus is best reserved for samples, such as hair, for which STR analysis may not be possible.

- Biological evidence should not be packaged in plastic or airtight containers because the accumulation of residual moisture could contribute to the growth of blood-destroying bacteria and fungi. Each article should be packaged separately in a paper bag or in a well-ventilated box.

Supplemental Questions

1. What is complementary base pairing? What is the importance of the order in which base pairs are arranged?

2. How are proteins formed? What determines the shape and function of a protein?

3. List three advantages gained from decoding the human genome.

4. Describe the process of DNA replication. What is the importance of DNA replication?

5. What is polymerase chain reaction (PCR) and how is it useful to forensic scientists?

6. What is recombinant DNA technology and what is its purpose? How can recombinant DNA be used to increase the production of insulin?

7. What are tandem repeats and how are they useful to the forensic scientist?

8. What is electrophoresis and what is it most widely used for?

9. What are short tandem repeats (STRs) and what are their significance to DNA typing?

10. List two advantages STRs have over restriction fragment length polymorphisms (RFLP).

11. What is multiplexing and why is it used in DNA profiling?

12. What characteristics are revealed by the amelogenin gene and Y-STRs?

13. What are the three main differences between nuclear DNA and mitochondrial DNA?

14. Name two advantages and two disadvantages of mitochondrial DNA analysis compared to nuclear DNA analysis.

15. How should packages containing DNA evidence be stored? Name one common exception and explain why it should be handled differently and how it should be stored.

16. List four steps an investigator should take to prevent contamination of DNA evidence.

Answers to Supplemental Questions

1. Complementary base pairing is the specific pairing of adenine with thymine and cytosine with guanine in DNA. The order in which base pairs are arranged defines the role and function of a DNA molecule.

2. Proteins are formed by linking a combination of amino acids. The sequence of amino acids in a protein chain determines the shape and function of the protein.

3. Decoding the human genome can be useful for diagnosing and treating genetic diseases; it is crucial for understanding the underlying causes of cancer; and comparing the human genome with that of other organisms will help us understand the role and implications of evolution.

4. DNA replication begins with the unwinding of the DNA strands in the double helix. Each strand is then exposed to a collection of free nucleotides. The double helix is re-created as the nucleotides are assembled in the proper order (*A* with *T* and *G* with *C*). The result is the emergence of two identical copies of DNA. DNA replication allows a cell to pass on its genetic identity when it divides.

5. PCR is a technique for replicating or copying a portion of a DNA strand outside a living cell. The ability to multiply small bits of DNA with PCR means that sample size is no longer a limitation for the forensic scientist attempting to characterize DNA recovered from crime-scene evidence.

6. Recombinant DNA technology is a technique by which a fragment of DNA is removed from one organism and replaced by a fragment taken from a different organism. The technology is used to pass specific genetic traits from an organism to another. If the DNA segment that makes human insulin is implanted into bacteria, the bacteria make human insulin. Because bacteria multiply rapidly, this technique could be used to make significant amounts of insulin in a short period of time.

7. Tandem repeats are regions of a chromosome that contain multiple copies of a core DNA sequence arranged in a repeating fashion. Tandem repeats are useful for the forensic scientist because they provide a way to distinguish one individual from another through DNA typing.

8. Electrophoresis is a technique for separating molecules by migration on a support medium while under the influence of an electrical potential. Electrophoresis is widely used to characterize proteins and DNA in dried blood.

9. STRs are locations (loci) on the chromosome that contain a short sequence core that repeats itself within the DNA molecule and that serve as helpful markers for identification. STR analysis has emerged as the most successful and widely used DNA profiling procedure.

10. The shorter DNA strands found in STRs are likely to be more stable and less subject to degradation brought about by adverse environmental conditions than the long RFLP strands. Another distinct advantage is that STRs can be amplified by PCR, thus overcoming the limited-sample-size problem often associated with crime-scene evidence. Amplification of STRs by PCR allows forensic analysts to characterize small quantities of DNA that could never be detected by RFLP.

11. Multiplexing is a technique that simultaneously detects more than one STR in a single DNA analysis. Multiplexing is important to DNA profiling because the more STRs a forensic scientist can characterize, the greater the likelihood that they originated from the same individual.

12. The amelogenin gene can reveal the sex of the person who contributed a DNA sample. Y-STRs are male specific and are useful for characterizing multiple-male DNA mixtures.

13. Nuclear DNA is found only in the nucleus of the cell, is arranged in a continuous strand of bases, and is contributed by both parents. Mitochondrial DNA (mtDNA) is found outside the nucleus of the cell, is arranged in a circular loop of bases, and is contributed only by the mother.

14. Mitochondrial DNA is much more abundant in the body than is nuclear DNA, so it can be more readily recovered for analysis. In addition, a matching sample of a person's mtDNA can be obtained from any maternally related relative. Also, mtDNA analysis is significantly more sensitive than nuclear DNA profiling. Disadvantages include the fact that individuals of the same maternal lineage are indistinguishable by mtDNA analysis, and that even under the best circumstances mtDNA typing does not approach STR analysis in its discrimination power. Thus, mtDNA analysis is best reserved for samples for which nuclear DNA typing is simply not possible.

15. All packages containing DNA evidence should be refrigerated or stored in a cool location out of direct sunlight until delivery to the laboratory. One common exception is blood mixed with soil. Microbes present in soil rapidly degrade DNA, so blood in soil must be stored in a clean glass or plastic container and immediately frozen.

16. To minimize possible contamination of biological evidence, the investigator should change gloves before handling each new piece of evidence, collect a substrate control for possible subsequent laboratory examination, pick up small items of evidence such as cigarette butts and stamps with clean forceps, and always package each item of evidence in its own well-ventilated container.

Resources

Videos/DVDs

DNA: The Secret of Life

This video combines cinematography and animation from the team that won the 2000 Academy Award for special effects in the movie *Gladiator*. The video explores the basics of molecular biology and presents a visually stunning and easily understood explanation of DNA and illustration of the mechanics of the DNA double helix.

> Format: Color, VHS
>
> Rated: NR
>
> Studio: Windfall Films
>
> Video Release Date: May 1, 2003
>
> ASIN: B0000BZLGO

Understanding DNA

This video features computer graphics that guide the viewer through the world of DNA. It examines the importance of DNA composition, structure, and replication.

> Format: Color, VHS
>
> Rated: NR
>
> Studio: Unknown
>
> Video Release Date: August 22, 1997
>
> ASIN: B00004T01W

Books

DNA Analysis

William Hunter

Part of a series of works examining various topics in forensic science, this volume looks at DNA analysis.

> Format: Paperback, 112 pages
>
> Publisher: Mason Crest (2005)
>
> ISBN: 1422200264

DNA Fingerprinting: The Ultimate Identity

Ron Fridell

This book makes the history of DNA technology accessible to readers, covering its somewhat checkered background and science and discussing how it's being used today. Other topics discussed include how the technique is used to identify casualties of war, exonerate incarcerated individuals, and provide accurate answers to historical questions—for example, to determine whether Thomas Jefferson was the father of Sally Hemings's son.

> Format: Hardcover, 112 pages
>
> Publisher: Franklin Watts (2001)
>
> ISBN: 0531118584

Forensic DNA Analysis

Jay Robert Nash

One of a series of brief works examining various topics in forensic science though the use of case studies, this volume explores the basics of DNA analysis.

> Format: Hardcover, 100 pages
>
> Publisher: Chelsea House (2000)
>
> ISBN: 079108910X

Forensic DNA Typing: Biology, Technology, and Genetics of STR Markers

John Butler

This book is a comprehensive and practical guide to current forensic DNA-typing theory and procedures.

> Format: Hardcover, 688 pages
>
> Publisher: Academic Press (2005)
>
> ISBN: 0121479528

Genetic Testimony: A Guide to Forensic DNA Profiling

Charlotte A. Spencer

This brief work explains the subject of modern DNA profiling in straightforward language and is aimed at readers with little background in science or biotechnology. It introduces basic concepts of genetics and biotechnology in the context of modern criminal investigation. This book raises controversial questions about the uses and potential misuses of DNA forensics and illustrates issues by presenting recent criminal cases involving DNA profiling.

> Format: Paperback, 48 pages
>
> Publisher: Prentice Hall (2003)
>
> ISBN: 013142338X

An Introduction to Forensic DNA Analysis, Second Edition

Norah Rudin and Keith Inman

This work presents forensic DNA issues from a scientific and legal perspective and translates new and established concepts into plain English.

> Format: Hardcover, 312 pages
>
> Publisher: CRC Press (2001)
>
> ISBN: 0849302331

Advanced Reading

Isenberg, A. R., "Forensic Mitochondrial DNA Analysis," in R. Saferstein, ed., *Forensic Science Handbook,* vol. 2, 2nd ed. Upper Saddle River, N.J.: Prentice Hall, 2005.

Kobilinsky, L., "Deoxyribonucleic Acid Structure and Function—A Review," in R. Saferstein, ed., *Forensic Science Handbook,* vol. 3. Upper Saddle River, N.J.: Prentice Hall, 1993.

Sensabaugh, G. F., and E. T. Blake, "DNA Analysis in Biological Evidence: Application of the Polymerase Chain Reaction," in R. Saferstein, ed., *Forensic Science Handbook,* vol. 3. Upper Saddle River, N.J.: Prentice Hall, 1993.

Stafford, David T., "Forensic Capillary Gas Chromatography," in R. Saferstein, ed., *Forensic Science Handbook,* vol. 2, 2nd ed. Upper Saddle River, N.J.: Prentice Hall, 2005.

Demonstrations and Lecture Starters

DNA Fingerprinting

Using a kit such as the one supplied by Lab-Aids, Inc., 17 Colt Court, Ronkonkoma, N.Y. 11779 (www.lab-aids.com), the student can build a model of DNA to see what a double-helix structure looks like. The components are made of color-coded plastic and are easily assembled and disassembled. The model is flexible and is twisted to form the double-helix structure. Lab-Aid Kit #1271, "Forensic Science: Introduction to DNA Fingerprinting," simulates a crime scene and instructs students on how to interpret DNA X-ray films. Lab-Aid Kit #75 introduces the concept of PCR and the RFLP analysis of DNA. The kit simulates the gel electrophoresis of DNA. Another interesting experiment is based on the Feulgen reaction, in which DNA in plant cells can be stained purple. With the aid of a microscope, students can view DNA in a plant cell. A DNA-staining kit is available from Lab-Aids, Inc. (Kit #170).

Chapter 10
Trace Evidence I: Hair and Fibers

Key Terms

anagen phase—The initial growth phase during which the hair follicle actively produces hair.

catagen phase—A transition stage between the anagen and telogen phases of hair growth.

cortex—The main body of the hair shaft.

cuticle—The scale structure covering the exterior of the hair.

follicular tag—A translucent piece of tissue surrounding the hair's shaft near the root that contains the richest source of DNA associated with hair.

macromolecule—A molecule with a high molecular mass.

manufactured fibers—Fibers derived from either natural or synthetic polymers.

medulla—A cellular column running through the center of the hair.

mitochondrial DNA—DNA present in small structures (mitochondria) outside the nucleus of a cell. Mitochondria supply energy to the cell. This form of DNA is inherited maternally (from the mother).

molecule—Two or more atoms held together by chemical bonds.

monomer—The basic unit of structure from which a polymer is constructed.

natural fibers—Fibers derived entirely from animal or plant sources.

nuclear DNA—DNA that is present in the nucleus of a cell and is inherited from both parents.

polymer—A substance composed of a large number of atoms that are usually arranged in repeating units.

telogen phase—The final growth phase in which hair naturally falls out of the skin.

Learning Objectives

- Recognize and understand the cuticle, cortex, and medulla areas of hair
- List the three phases of hair growth
- Appreciate the distinction between animal and human hairs
- List hair features that are useful for microscopic comparison of human hairs
- Explain proper collection of forensic hair evidence
- Describe and understand the role of DNA typing in hair comparisons
- Understand the differences between natural and manufactured fibers
- List the properties of fibers that are most useful for forensic comparisons
- Describe proper collection of fiber evidence

Key Points

- Hair is an appendage of the skin that grows from an organ called the hair follicle, continues into a shaft, and terminates at a tip end.
- The hair shaft is composed of three layers called the cuticle, cortex, and medulla and is most intensely examined by the forensic scientist.
- When comparing strands of hair, the criminalist is particularly interested in matching the color, length, and diameter. The comparison microscope is an indispensable tool for comparing these characteristics.
- A careful microscopic examination of hair can distinguish human hair from animal hair.
- Scale structure, medullary index, and medullary shape are particularly important in hair identification. Other important features for comparing hair are the presence or absence of a medulla and the distribution, shape, and color intensity of pigment granules in the cortex.
- The probability of detecting DNA in hair roots is more likely for hair being examined in its anagen or early growth phase as opposed to its catagen or telogen phase.
- The follicular tag, a translucent piece of tissue surrounding the hair's shaft near the root, is a rich source of DNA associated with hair. Mitochondrial DNA can also be extracted from the hair shaft.
- Microscopic hair examinations tend to be subjective and highly dependent on the skills and integrity of the analyst. All positive microscopic hair comparisons must be confirmed by DNA analysis.
- The quality of fiber evidence depends on the ability of the criminalist to identify the origin of the fiber or to narrow the possibilities to a limited number of sources.
- Microscopic comparisons between questioned and standard/reference fibers are initially undertaken for color and diameter characteristics. Other features that could be important in comparing fibers are striations on the surface of the fiber, the presence of delustering particles, and the cross-sectional shape of the fiber.
- The visible-light microspectrophotometer is a convenient way for analysts to compare the colors of fibers through spectral patterns.
- Infrared spectrophotometry and the polarizing microscope are other reliable methods for identifying the generic class of fibers.

Supplemental Questions

1. How is the hair cuticle used to identify different animal species?

2. What aspect of the hair cortex is most important for the criminalist and why?

3. What is the follicular tag and why is it important to forensic scientists studying hair?

4. In comparing two hair samples, what aspects of the hair is the criminalist particularly interested in matching? What other features of hair are important to compare?

5. Which of the following cannot be confidently determined by a microscopic examination of hair: age, sex, racial origin, the part of the body from which the hair came, or whether the hair was pulled out or fell out?

6. Why are most hair specimens collected at crime scenes not good sources of DNA?

7. What types of hair specimens are potentially the richest source of nuclear DNA and why?

8. What is mitochondrial DNA and why is it useful in analyzing hair samples?

9. List three important considerations when submitting hair samples to a crime laboratory.

10. How has mass production limited the value of fiber evidence?

11. What is the first and most important step in the examination of fiber? What physical characteristics of fiber might help an examiner identify it?

12. How can microspectrophotometry and chromatography be used to analyze fiber evidence?

13. Name two analytical devices used by forensic scientists to determine the class of a fiber.

Answers to Supplemental Questions

1. The cuticle is formed by overlapping scales that occur in a variety of patterns in different animal species. The distinctive scale pattern formed by animal hair makes it an important feature for species identification.

2. The cortex derives its major forensic importance from the fact that it is embedded with the pigment granules that impart hair with color. The color, shape, and distribution of these granules provide important points of comparison among the hairs of different individuals.

3. The follicular tag is a translucent piece of tissue surrounding the hair's shaft near the root. It contains the richest source of DNA associated with a hair.

4. In comparing hair, the criminalist is particularly interested in matching the color, length, and diameter. Other important features to compare are the presence or absence of a medulla and the distribution, shape, and color intensity of pigment granules in the cortex.

5. Microscopic examination of hair cannot confidently identify a subject's age or sex.

6. Most hairs collected at crime scenes are naturally shed and thus in the telogen stage of growth. At this stage of growth the hairs have too little nuclear DNA to successfully type.

7. Hairs forcibly removed from the head are the richest potential sources of DNA because they often have a follicular tag attached.

8. Mitochondrial DNA is DNA outside the nucleus of a cell that is inherited only from the mother. It is useful in analyzing hair because there are many more copies of mitochondrial DNA located in samples such as hair cells, which otherwise contain a limited amount of nuclear DNA.

9. Questioned hairs submitted to a crime laboratory for examination must be accompanied by an adequate number of standard/reference samples from the victim and from individuals suspected of being present at the crime scene. Questioned and standard/reference hairs must come from the same area of the body. The collection of standard/reference hairs must be carried out in a way that ensures a representative sampling of hair from any one area of the body.

10. Because of mass production, many goods are made from almost identical fibers, making it difficult to provide individual identification of specific fibers with any degree of certainty.

11. The first and most important step in the examination is a microscopic comparison for color and diameter using a comparison microscope. Other features that could aid in comparison are lengthwise striations on the surface of some fibers and the pitting of the fiber's surface with particles added in the manufacturing process to reduce shine. The cross-sectional shape of a fiber may also help characterize the fiber.

12. Microspectrophotometry can be used to compare the colors of fibers through their spectral patterns. Using chromatography, the forensic scientist can separate the constituents of dyes found in two fabric samples and compare them for similarity.

13. The polarizing microscope and the infrared microspectrophotometer are both used to determine the class of a fiber.

Resources

Books

Forensic Examination of Human Hair
James Robertson (Ed.)

This book includes articles written by experts about various aspects of the forensic examination of hair.

> Format: Hardcover, 288 pages
>
> Publisher: CRC Press (1999)
>
> ISBN: 0748405674

Advanced Reading

Bisbing, R. E., "The Forensic Identification and Association of Human Hair," in R. Saferstein, ed.,

Forensic Science Handbook, vol. 1, 2nd ed. Upper Saddle River, N.J.: Prentice Hall, 2002.

Eyring, M. B., and B. D. Gaudette, "The Forensic Aspects of Textile Fiber Examination," in R. Saferstein, ed., *Forensic Science Handbook,* vol. 2, 2nd ed. Upper Saddle River, N.J.: Prentice Hall, 2005.

Ogle, R. R., Jr., and M. J. Fox, *Atlas of Human Hair: Microscopic Characteristics.* Boca Raton, Fla.: CRC Press, 1999.

Petraco, N., and P. R. De Forest, "A Guide to the Analysis of Forensic Dust Specimens," in R. Saferstein, ed., *Forensic Science Handbook,* vol. 3. Upper Saddle River, N.J.: Prentice Hall, 1993.

Robertson, J., and M. Grieve, eds., *Forensic Examination of Fibres,* 2nd ed. New York: Taylor & Francis, 1999.

Demonstrations and Lecture Starters

Hair Variability

An effective demonstration of the variability of hair over the human scalp is to have your students compare at least six to eight hairs that have been wet-mounted. Upon completion of the examination, the class is asked to estimate the number of individuals that contributed to the hair collection. Of course, the collection consists of hair from only one individual. The instructor should compile at least twenty-four hair mounts from one person for this experiment. Additionally, each student is to examine his or her own scalp hair using a glycerin wet mount. Students should also be encouraged to bring in hair from household pets for examination.

Animal Hair

Instructors should obtain the CD-ROM database for common animal hairs from RJ Lee Group, Inc., 350 Hochberg Road, Monroeville, PA 15146 (www.rjls.com). Students should be given the opportunity to familiarize themselves with the applicability of this database to forensic hair analysis.

Fibers

To demonstrate the difficulty of analyzing fiber evidence, find three or four scraps of different material and snip or pull several fiber samples from each. Each scrap should consist of a different type of fiber. At least some of the scraps should contain several different colors; from those scraps collect samples of at least two different colors. Number the samples and record the scrap from which each sample came (do not reveal this information to the students before the demonstration). Have the students examine the scraps with the naked eye and, if possible, under a microscope. Afterward, ask them to indicate which samples they believe came from the same scraps of material and why.

Chapter 11
Trace Evidence II: Metals, Paint, and Soil

Key Terms

alpha ray—Radiation composed of helium atoms minus their orbiting electrons.

atomic mass—The sum of the number of protons and neutrons in the nucleus of an atom.

atomic number—The number of protons in the nucleus of an atom.

beta ray—Radiation composed of electrons.

continuous spectrum—A type of emission spectrum showing a continuous band of colors all blending into one another.

density-gradient tube—A glass tube filled from bottom to top with liquids of successively lighter densities; used to determine the density distribution of soil.

electron—A negatively charged particle that is one of the fundamental structural units of the atom.

electron orbital—The path of electrons as they move around the nuclei of atoms; each orbital is associated with a particular electronic energy level.

emission spectrum—Light emitted from a source and separated into its component colors or frequencies.

excited state—The state in which an atom absorbs energy and an electron moves from a lower to a higher energy level.

gamma ray—A high-energy form of electromagnetic radiation.

isotope—An atom differing from another atom of the same element in the number of neutrons in its nucleus.

line spectrum—A type of emission spectrum showing a series of lines separated by black areas. Each line represents a definite wavelength or frequency.

mineral—A naturally occurring crystalline solid.

neutron—A particle with no electrical charge that is one of the basic structures in the nucleus of an atom.

nucleus—The core of an atom, consisting of protons and neutrons.

proton—A positively charged particle that is one of the basic structures in the nucleus of an atom.

pyrolysis—The decomposition of organic matter by heat.

radioactivity—The emission of high-energy subatomic particles that accompanies the spontaneous disintegration of unstable nuclei.

Learning Objectives

- Describe the usefulness of trace elements for forensic comparison of various types of physical evidence
- Define and distinguish protons, neutrons, and electrons
- Define and distinguish *atomic number* and *atomic mass number*
- Explain the concept of an isotope

- Understand how elements can be made radioactive
- List the most useful examinations for performing a forensic comparison of paint
- Distinguish continuous and line emission spectra
- Understand the parts of a simple emission spectrograph
- Appreciate the phenomenon of how an atom absorbs and releases energy in the form of light
- Describe proper collection and preservation of forensic paint evidence
- List the important forensic properties of soil
- Describe proper collection of soil evidence

Key Points

- Trace elements are small quantities of elements present in concentrations of less than 1 percent. They provide "invisible" markers that may establish the source of a material or provide additional points for comparison.

- Emission spectroscopy and inductively coupled plasma are techniques available for determining the elemental composition of materials.

- An emission spectrograph vaporizes samples and heats them to a high temperature so that the atoms present in the material achieve an "excited" state in which they emit light that can be separated into its components to create a line spectrum.

- Each element present in a line spectrum can be identified by its characteristic line frequencies.

- In inductively coupled plasma, the sample, in the form of an aerosol, is introduced into a hot plasma. This creates charged particles that emit light of characteristic wavelengths corresponding to the identity of the elements present.

- Neutron activation analysis measures the gamma-ray frequencies of specimens that have been bombarded with neutrons. This method provides a highly sensitive and nondestructive analysis for simultaneously identifying and quantifying twenty to thirty trace elements.

- Paint spread onto a surface dries into a hard film that is best described as consisting of pigments and additives suspended in the binder.

- Some of the most common types of paint examined in the crime laboratory are finishes from automobiles.

- Manufacturers normally apply a variety of coatings to the body of an automobile. This wide diversity of automotive paint contributes to the forensic significance of an automobile paint comparison.

- Questioned and known paint specimens are best compared side by side under a stereoscopic microscope for color, surface texture, and color layer sequence.

- Pyrolysis gas chromatography and infrared spectrophotometry are used to distinguish most paint binder formulations.

- The value of soil as evidence rests with its prevalence at crime scenes and its transferability between the scene and the criminal.

- Most soils can be differentiated by their gross appearance.

- A side-by-side visual comparison of the color and texture of soil specimens provides a way to distinguish soils that originate from different locations.

- Some crime laboratories compare soils by using density-gradient tubes filled with layers of liquids with different density values.

Supplemental Questions

1. What is a trace element and why are trace elements important in analyzing physical evidence?

2. Explain how the analysis of trace elements was important to the investigation of the assassination of President John F. Kennedy.

3. Describe the difference between a continuous spectrum and a line spectrum. Which is most helpful in identifying a particular element and why?

4. Why do forensic scientists often use inductively coupled plasma (ICP) emission spectrophotometry to analyze mutilated bullets?

5. List the three basic subatomic particles and indicate whether each has positive, negative, or no electrical charge.

6. What is the net electrical charge of an atom? What does this indicate about the arrangement of subatomic particles in an atom?

7. What causes an electron to move to a higher energy level? What happens when an electron moves to a lower energy level?

8. What is measured in emission spectroscopy?

9. What is an isotope? List two ways in which isotopes differ from one another.

10. What causes radioactivity? List and define the three types of radiation.

11. How does a nuclear reactor generate radioactive elements?

12. Describe the process of neutron activation analysis. How does the process allow a forensic scientist to identify an isotope?

13. What are the main advantage and the main weakness of neutron activation analysis?

14. What important information about the identity of a sample cannot be determined by emission spectroscopy or neutron activation?

15. How does the way most automobile manufacturers paint their cars help in the forensic comparison of automobile paint?

16. What three features of paint does a forensic scientist compare using a microscope?

17. Why is layer structure important for evaluating the significance of paint evidence? What is the greatest shortcoming in using layer structure to analyze paint evidence?

18. How is pyrolysis gas chromatography used to distinguish one paint binder formulation from another?

19. What is PDQ and how is it used in identifying paint samples?

20. Where is most paint evidence likely to be found?

21. Why should paint evidence from a hit-and-run accident be collected close to the area of the car suspected of being in contact with the victim?

22. How can soil evidence be valuable even if the site of the crime has not been ascertained?

23. What is a mineral and how can minerals be important in the comparison of soil samples?

24. What is the most important consideration when collecting soil samples from a crime scene? At what locations should soil standard/reference samples be collected?

25. Why is soil collected from suspect automobiles left in lump form?

Answers to Supplemental Questions

1. A trace element is an element found in very small quantities. For the criminalist, the presence of trace elements is particularly useful because they provide markers that may establish the source of a material or at least provide additional points for comparison of two items of physical evidence.

2. Bullets recovered from Kennedy's brain, the wrist of Governor John Connally, and the car in which both were riding at the time of the assassination were found to have almost identical concentrations of the trace elements silver and antimony. This supports the conclusion that the bullets that struck Kennedy and Connally were fired by the same shooter.

3. A continuous spectrum shows a continuous band of colors all blending into one another. A line spectrum shows a series of lines separated by black areas in which each line represents a definite wavelength or frequency. A line spectrum is most helpful in identifying a particular element because it serves as a unique "fingerprint" of an element that differs from the spectra of all other elements.

4. Mutilated bullets are often not suitable for traditional microscopic comparisons against an exemplar test-fired bullet. In such situations, ICP emission spectrophotometry can be used to obtain an elemental profile of the questioned bullet fragment for comparison against an unfired bullet generally found in the possession of the suspect.

5. The three basic subatomic particles are the proton (positive charge), electron (negative charge), and neutron (no charge).

6. An atom has a net zero electrical charge, which indicates that it contains the same number of protons and electrons.

7. An electron moves to a higher-energy orbital when it absorbs energy, such as heat or light. When an electron moves to a lower-energy orbital, it emits energy.

8. Emission spectroscopy measures the frequency of light emitted by an atom when one of its electrons moves to a lower orbital.

9. Isotopes are atoms of the same element that have different numbers of neutrons in their respective nuclei. Isotopes have different atomic mass numbers. In addition, some isotopes of an element may be very stable, while others may be quite unstable and decay rapidly.

10. Radioactivity is the emission of radiation that accompanies the spontaneous disintegration of unstable nuclei. The three types of radiation are alpha rays, beta rays, and gamma rays. Alpha rays are a type of radiation composed of helium atoms minus their orbiting electrons. Beta rays are a form of radiation consisting of electrons. Gamma rays are a high-energy form of electromagnetic radiation.

11. In a nuclear reactor, a source of neutrons bombards the atoms of an element to create radioactive isotopes of that element. When the nucleus of an atom captures a bombarding neutron, a new isotope is formed and the nucleus is now said to be activated. Many activated nuclei immediately begin to decompose and emit radioactivity.

12. In neutron activation analysis, a forensic scientist measures the gamma-ray radioactivity produced by a specimen that has been bombarded with neutrons. This allows the forensic scientist to identify the sample because the gamma rays of each element are associated with specific and unique energy values.

13. The major advantage of neutron activation analysis is that it provides a nondestructive method for identifying and quantitating trace elements. A major weakness of the technique is its expense and regulatory requirements. Only a handful of crime laboratories worldwide have access to a nuclear reactor, and sophisticated analyzers are needed to detect and discriminate gamma-ray emissions.

14. Emission spectroscopy and neutron activation analysis do not provide any information as to how the elements are combined into compounds.

15. Manufacturers apply a variety of coatings to the body of an automobile, which adds significant diversity to automobile paint. This diversity makes it easier for the forensic scientist to compare different paint samples.

16. The forensic scientist compares paint specimens under a microscope for color, surface texture, and color layer sequence.

17. When paint specimens possess colored layers that match with respect to number and sequence of colors, the examiner can begin to think confidently in terms of relating the paints to a common origin. The shortcoming of analysis of paint layer structures is that most paint specimens presented to the criminalist do not have a layer structure sufficiently complex to allow individualization to a single source.

18. In pyrolysis gas chromatography, heat is used to break apart the chain of polymers that make up the paint binder. The decomposed products of the polymer are swept through a gas chromatograph, which records a pattern of the separated products of the polymer. This pattern, or pyrogram, is sufficiently detailed to reflect the specific chemical makeup of the binder.

19. PDQ (Paint Data Query) is a computerized database maintained by the Royal Canadian Mounted Police Forensic Laboratories that contains information about automotive paint layer colors, primer colors, and binder composition. PDQ allows an analyst to obtain information on paints related to automobile make, model, and year.

20. Paint evidence is most likely to be found on or near people or objects involved in hit-and-run and burglary incidents.

21. Collected paint should be close to the area of the car suspected of being in contact with the victim because other portions of the car may have faded or been repainted.

22. A geologist may be able to examine soil found on a victim or suspect and direct police to an area or areas where the soil originally may have been picked up. This can make it easier for the police to determine where the crime was committed.

23. A mineral is a naturally occurring crystalline solid that can be identified by its physical properties. The combination of minerals found in different soil or rock samples can be used to compare the samples to determine whether they have the same origin.

24. Establishing the variation of soil at the crime scene is the primary consideration when collecting soil specimens. Standard/reference soil samples should be collected at the site of the crime, at various intervals within a 100-yard radius of the crime scene, and at all possible alibi locations that the suspect may claim.

25. Soil is collected as lumps because lumps preserve a record of the buildup of several layers of soil from different locations over time. This layering effect gives a sample greater variation, and thus makes it easier to compare the sample to soil samples found at the site of an accident.

Resources

Videos/DVDs
The Atom

In this two-part video on atomic theory and structure, part one tells the story of humankind's search for the atom; part two outlines the current state of scientific understanding about atoms.

    Format: Color, VHS

    Rated: NR

    Studio: Hawkhill Associates

    Video Release Date: 2003

    ASIN: B0006OIJJO

Books

Atomic Spectra

T. P. Softley

This book provides a detailed introduction to the spectra and structure of atoms in the gas phase and the principles of spectroscopy. It begins with a review of elementary quantum mechanics and a discussion of electromagnetic radiation properties. Modern applications and techniques such as lasers and cooling of atoms are briefly discussed.

    Format: Paperback, 96 pages

    Publisher: Oxford University Press (1994)

    ISBN: 0198556888

Evidence from the Earth: Forensic Geology and Criminal Investigation

Raymond C. Murray

Written by a well-respected forensic and sedimentary geologist, this book illustrates the basic facts of collecting, preserving, and interpreting mineral and geological evidence. It covers the historical improvement of technology, the nature of geological materials, relevant geological principles, geophysical methods, evidence collection, laboratory examination, and fraud related to the mining industry, gems, and art. Each chapter focuses on one of these topics which is illustrated with actual cases.

    Format: Paperback, 226 pages

    Publisher: Mountain Press (2004)

    ISBN: 0878424989

Forensic Examination of Glass and Paint: Analysis and Interpretation

Brian Caddy (Ed.)

This book examines the analysis of glass and paint as they occur as trace evidence in forensic cases. Each chapter is written by an expert in that particular area. The book is divided into two sections: one referring to paint and one referring to glass. Each section covers an introduction to the composition of these materials and the analytical approach to obtaining information from these types of exhibits, together with an interpretation of that evidence in the context of the forensic cases.

    Format: Hardcover, 288 pages

    Publisher: CRC Press (2001)

    ISBN: 0748405798

Nucleus: A Trip into the Heart of the Matter

Ray Mackintosh, Jim Al-Khalili, Bjorn Jonsen, and Theresa Penae

This book tells the story of the exploration of the nucleus from early experimental work to modern particle accelerators. It examines the protons and neutrons of which the nucleus is made, why some nuclei crumble and are radioactive, and how scientists came up with the "standard model," which shows the nucleus composed of quarks held together by gluons. *Nucleus* is also the tale of the people behind the struggle to understand the atom more fully.

    Format: Hardcover, 160 pages

    Publisher: Johns Hopkins University Press (2001)

    ISBN: 0801868602

Advanced Reading

Demmelmeyer, H., and J. Adam, "Forensic Investigation of Soil and Vegetable Materials," *Forensic Science Review* 7 (1995): 119–142.

Forensic Analysis: Weighing Bullet Lead Evidence. Washington D.C.: National Academies Press, 2004.

Guinn, V. P., "The Elemental Comparison of Bullet-Lead Evidence Specimens," in S. M. Gerber, ed., *Chemistry and Crime.* Washington, D.C.: American Chemical Society, 1983.

Murray, R. C. *Evidence from the Earth: Forensic Geology and Criminal Investigation.* Missoula, Mont.: Mountain Press, 2004.

Murray, R. C., and L. P. Solebello, "Forensic Examination of Soil," in R. Saferstein, ed., *Forensic Science Handbook,* vol. 1, 2nd ed. Upper Saddle River, N.J.: Prentice Hall, 2002.

Saferstein, R., "Forensic Aspects of Analytical Pyrolysis," in S. A. Lieberman and E. J. Levy, eds., *Pyrolysis and GC in Polymer Analysis.* New York: Dekker, 1985.

Thornton, J. L., "Forensic Paint Examination," in R. Saferstein, ed., *Forensic Science Handbook,* vol. 1, 2nd ed. Upper Saddle River, N.J.: Prentice Hall, 2002.

Demonstrations and Lecture Starters

Atomic Emission Spectra

Atomic emission spectra can be demonstrated with the use of a simple diffraction grating spectroscope. The chloride salts of lithium, calcium, strontium, copper, barium, and potassium can produce characteristic line spectra. Dip a loop of a clean nichrome wire into each salt (moistened with a few drops of 6M HCl) and place it in a small blue Bunsen burner flame. Also, the student should use the spectroscope to look at a tungsten filament lamp and a hydrogen discharge tube.

Emission Spectroscopy

Lab-Aids, Inc., 17 Colt Court, Ronkonkoma, N.Y. 11779 (www.lab-aids.com), markets an emission spectroscopy kit (#111) that includes several water-based solutions that can be sprayed into a Bunsen burner flame to produce spectra. The kit includes handheld spectroscopes and provides a basic demonstration of the spectral analysis of unknown substances.

Measuring Soil Density: The Gradient Tube Technique

Comparison of soil specimens by the density-gradient tube technique is a recommended laboratory exercise. Prepare four soil specimens, two of which originate from the same source. Randomly assign each student two soils for comparison. Each student prepares two density-gradient columns using glass tubing approximately 30 centimeters long and 6–10 millimeters in diameter. Five layers are prepared. The heaviest layer is pure tetrabromoethane, while the lightest is a 1:1 mixture of ethanol and tetrabromoethane. The intermediate layers are mixtures of the heavy and light liquids in the ratio of 3:1, 1:1, and 1:3, respectively.

Visual Identification of Soil

This quick demonstration can be used to start a discussion of some basic principles of soil comparison. Fill several small plastic containers with soil samples taken from three different locations, as follows:

Container 1: Dried soil sample from location A

Container 2: Moist soil sample from location A or B

Container 3: Dried soil sample from location B

Container 4: Dried soil sample from location C

Container 5: Dried soil sample from location A

Container 6: Moist soil sample from location C or D

Container 7: Moist soil sample from location A or B

Container 8: Dried soil sample from location C

If possible, each sample should also contain some small amount of plant material. Before class, empty the samples onto paper plates and tell the students that the soils come from three different locations. Ask students to visually examine and take brief notes about each sample. Then have them write down which samples they believe came from the same location and explain how they came to their conclusions. Note that students should show caution in drawing conclusions about the moist samples, because soil should be dried to allow for a valid visual comparison.

Chapter 12
Forensic Aspects of Fire Investigation

Key Terms

accelerant—Any material used to start or sustain a fire.

combustion—Rapid combination of oxygen with another substance, accompanied by production of noticeable heat and light.

endothermic reaction—A chemical transformation in which heat energy is absorbed from the surroundings.

energy—The ability or potential of a system or material to do work.

exothermic reaction—A chemical transformation in which heat energy is liberated.

flammable range—The entire range of possible gas or vapor fuel concentrations in air that are capable of burning.

flash point—The minimum temperature at which a liquid fuel produces enough vapor to burn.

glowing combustion—Combustion on the surface of a solid fuel in the absence of heat high enough to pyrolyze the fuel.

heat of combustion—The heat liberated during combustion.

hydrocarbon—Any compound consisting of only carbon and hydrogen.

ignition temperature—The minimum temperature at which a fuel spontaneously ignites.

modus operandi—An offender's pattern of operation.

oxidation—The combination of oxygen with other substances to produce new substances.

oxidizing agent—A substance that supplies oxygen to a chemical reaction.

pyrolysis—The decomposition of solid organic matter by heat.

spontaneous combustion—A fire caused by a natural heat-producing process in the presence of sufficient air and fuel.

Learning Objectives

- List the conditions necessary to initiate and sustain combustion
- Understand the three mechanisms of heat transfer
- Recognize the telltale signs of an accelerant-initiated fire
- Describe how to collect physical evidence at the scene of a suspected arson
- Describe laboratory procedures used to detect and identify hydrocarbon residues

Key Points

- The arson investigator needs to begin examining a fire scene for signs of arson as soon as the fire has been extinguished. The investigation must focus on finding the fire's origin.

- Telltale signs of arson include evidence of separate and unconnected fires, the use of "streamers" to spread the fire from one area to another, and evidence of severe burning found on the floor as opposed to the ceiling of a structure.

- Porous materials at the suspected point of origin of a fire should be collected and stored in airtight containers.

- Fire occurs when oxygen combines with a fuel to produce noticeable quantities of heat and light (flames).

- To initiate and sustain combustion, (1) a fuel must be present, (2) oxygen must be available, in sufficient quantity to combine with the fuel, and (3) heat must be applied to initiate the combustion, and sufficient heat must be generated to sustain the reaction.

- A fuel achieves a reaction rate with oxygen sufficient to sustain a fire only when it is in the gaseous state.

- Heat tends to move from high-temperature regions to low-temperature regions by combustion, radiation, and convection.

- Most arsons are initiated by petroleum distillates such as gasoline and kerosene.

- The gas chromatograph is the most sensitive and reliable instrument for detecting and characterizing flammable residues. A gas chromatograph separates the hydrocarbon components and produces a chromatographic pattern characteristic of a particular petroleum product.

- By comparing select gas chromatographic peaks recovered from fire-scene debris to known flammable liquids, a forensic analyst may be able to identify the accelerant used to initiate the fire.

Supplemental Questions

1. List three factors that make investigating arson particularly difficult for forensic scientists.

2. What happens to the atoms of a molecule that undergoes a chemical reaction? How is energy consumed in a chemical reaction? How is energy released in a chemical reaction?

3. What is the energy barrier and how does it relate to the concept of ignition temperature?

4. How does the speed of an oxidation reaction affect its ability to produce a flame? What factors influence the speed of the reaction?

5. What physical state must a fuel be in to produce a flame? Why can it produce a flame only in this state?

6. Define and describe the process of pyrolysis.

7. What are oxidizing agents and why are they used in explosives?

8. Why is it important that the arson investigator begin examining a fire scene for signs of arson as soon as the fire has been extinguished?

9. What is the primary focus of a fire-scene search and why? What evidence at a fire site may indicate the possibility of arson?

10. Where will an investigator usually locate the probable point of origin of a fire? What factors can cause a fire to deviate from normal behavior?

11. Why are some traces of the accelerants used in an arson usually found even after intense fires?

12. Why might an investigator conduct laboratory tests on unburned control material collected from a fire scene?

13. Describe the headspace technique for recovering accelerant residues. What instrument is most often used to detect and characterize recovered flammable residues?

Answers to Supplemental Questions

1. Arson incidents are committed at the convenience of a perpetrator who has thoroughly planned the act; the perpetrator has left the scene long before an investigation is launched; and the extensive destruction that frequently dominates the crime scene makes it more difficult to obtain proof of the commission of the offense.

2. In a chemical reaction, the atoms of a molecule are rearranged to form new substances, or products. Energy is consumed in a chemical reaction when the bonds holding the atoms of the original molecules together are broken. Energy is released when the bonds between atoms re-form to create new products as a result of the reaction.

3. The energy barrier is the minimum amount of energy required to initiate a chemical reaction. Ignition temperature is the minimum temperature at which a fuel spontaneously ignites. Thus, the energy barrier for any fuel is directly related to its ignition temperature.

4. The faster an oxidation reaction takes place, the greater the likelihood that it will produce a flame. Factors that influence the speed of the reaction include the physical state of the fuel and the temperature.

5. Fuel must be in a gaseous state to produce a flame, because only in the gaseous state can its molecules collide frequently enough to support a flaming fire.

6. Pyrolysis is the decomposition of organic matter by heat. In pyrolysis, heat causes solid organic matter to decay. This generates gaseous products that can combine with oxygen to produce a fire. The heat from the fire pyrolyzes more solid fuel into volatile gases, which sustains the fire.

7. An oxidizing agent is a substance that supplies oxygen to a chemical reaction. An explosion occurs so rapidly that oxygen in the air cannot participate in the reaction. For this reason, many explosives must have their own source of oxygen in order to produce the chemical reaction necessary to create an explosion.

8. Most arsons are started with petroleum-based accelerants that may evaporate within a matter of days or even hours. Immediate investigation may also be necessary to preserve evidence from intentional or accidental destruction. Safety and health conditions may necessitate that cleanup and salvage operations begin as quickly as possible. Once clean-up efforts begin, it is impossible to conduct a meaningful investigation of the fire scene.

9. A search of the fire scene must focus on finding the fire's origin, for this area will prove most productive in any search for an accelerant or ignition device. Telltale signs of arson include evidence of separate and unconnected fires; use of "streamers"—such as a trail of gasoline or paper—to spread the fire from one area to another; the presence of containers capable of holding an accelerant; finding a potential ignition device; and an irregular-shaped pattern on a floor or on the ground caused by pouring an accelerant onto the surface.

10. The probable origin of a fire will most likely be located closest to the lowest point that shows the most intense characteristics of burning. Factors that can cause a fire to deviate from normal behavior include prevailing drafts and winds; secondary fires due to collapsing floors and roofs; the physical arrangement of the burning structure; stairways and elevator shafts; holes in the floor, wall, or roof; and the effects of the firefighters in suppressing the fire.

11. When an accelerant is poured over a large area, some of it will likely seep into porous surfaces such as cracks in the floor, upholstery, rags, plaster, wallboards, and carpet, where enough of it remains unchanged that it can be detected in the crime laboratory. In addition, when a fire is extinguished with water, volatile fluids may evaporate more slowly as water cools and covers materials through which the fluids may have soaked.

12. Laboratory tests may be made on unburned control material to analyze the breakdown products caused by the material's exposure to intense heat during the fire. Because common materials such as plastic floor tiles, carpet, linoleum, and adhesives can produce volatile hydrocarbons when they are burned, these breakdown products might be mistaken for an accelerant.

13. In the headspace technique, an airtight container holding debris from the fire scene is heated, vaporizing any volatile residue present in the debris and trapping the vapor in the container's enclosed airspace. The vapor, or headspace, is removed with a syringe. A gas chromatograph is usually used to detect and characterize residues in the vapor.

Resources

Books

Arson: Inside the Crime Lab

Gail Stewart

This book looks at crime lab procedures used to investigate of arson cases.

> Format: Hardcover
>
> Publisher: Lucent Books (2005)
>
> ISBN: 1590186176

Arson Investigation: The Step-by-Step Procedure

Thomas J. Bouquard

This book, which takes a systematic approach to arson investigation, begins with an explanation of the nature and behavior of fire, then looks into the techniques of arson investigation.

> Format: Paperback, 313 pages
>
> Publisher: Charles C. Thomas (2004)
>
> ISBN: 0748405674

Explosives and Arson Investigation

Jean Ford

This book provides a layperson's approach to the theory and practice of arson and explosion investigations.

> Format: Hardcover, 112 pages
>
> Publisher: Mason Crest (2005)
>
> ISBN: 1422200345

Forensic Fire Scene Reconstruction

David Icove and John DeHaan

This book describes a new approach to reconstructing fire scenes that blends the principles of fire protection with forensic and behavioral science. It includes information about identifiable fire pattern damage, human factors, physical evidence of human activity, and application of the scientific method based on relevant scientific principles and research.

> Format: Hardcover, 416 pages
>
> Publisher: Prentice Hall (2003)
>
> ISBN: 0130942057

Advanced Reading

Almirall, J. R., and K. G. Furton, eds., *Fire Scene Evidence.* Boca Raton, Fla.: Taylor & Francis, 2004.

DeHaan, John D., *Kirk's Fire Investigation*, 5th ed. Upper Saddle River, N.J.: Prentice Hall, 2002.

Lentini, J., *Scientific Protocols for Fire Investigation*. Boca Raton, Fla.: Taylor & Francis, 2006.

Midkiff, C. R., "Arson and Explosive Investigation," in R. Saferstein, ed., *Forensic Science Handbook*, vol. 1, 2nd ed. Upper Saddle River, N.J.: Prentice Hall, 2002.

Midkiff, C. R., "Laboratory Examination of Arson Evidence," in S. M. Gerber and R. Saferstein, eds., *More Chemistry and Crime.* Washington, D.C.: American Chemical Society, 1997.

NFPA 921 Guide for Fire and Explosion Investigations, Quincy, Mass.: National Fire Protection Association, 2004.

Demonstrations and Lecture Starters

Gas Chromatography of Gasoline

The gas chromatographic analysis of gasoline makes for an interesting demonstration. I recommend using a packed or capillary nonpolar silicone column. Gasoline is placed in a vial covered with a rubber septum. Remove 1–2 milliliters of air above the liquid with a syringe for injection into the GC. Refer to the text for the resultant chromatograms.

Clues to Arson

This brief demonstration touches on evidence that arson is responsible for a fire. Describe the following fire situations to the students and ask them to indicate in which ones the evidence suggests arson:

1. Investigators at a residential fire find much of the roof destroyed and the floor in the living room seriously damaged. However, there is little fire damage to the floors and walls of rooms not adjacent to the living room.

2. A large, multistory warehouse, bordered on the north and south by residential areas, burns to the ground. Residents of both neighborhoods report seeing small fires burning on the ground floor earlier in the evening.

3. The fire in a three-room office is extinguished before a great deal of damage is done. The floors of each room are charred, but there is little damage to the ceiling.

4. Most of the damage from a home fire is confined to two adjacent walls. Neighbors report that the lights in the house went out shortly before the fire started.

Cases 2 and 3 contain the strongest evidence of arson. In case 2, the appearance of fires at separate locations in the warehouse suggests that they were deliberately started. In case 3, the severe burning of the floor and not the ceiling—as well as the fact that the fire spread to the floors in every room in a short period of time—suggests the likelihood of arson. In case 1, the fact that fire damage was confined largely to one room while the roof was destroyed suggests an accidental fire starting in the living room. In case 4, both the loss of power and the fire probably were caused by faulty electrical wiring.

As a follow-up, ask the students what other information they should gather in these cases to confirm or exclude the possibility of arson.

Chapter 13
Forensic Investigation of Explosions

Key Terms

black powder—Normally, a mixture of potassium nitrate, carbon, and sulfur in the ratio 75/15/10.

deflagration—A very rapid oxidation reaction accompanied by the generation of a low-intensity pressure wave that can disrupt the surroundings.

detonating cord—A cordlike explosive containing a core of high-explosive material, usually PETN; also called primacord.

detonation—An extremely rapid oxidation reaction accompanied by a violent disruptive effect and an intense, high-speed shock wave.

explosion—A chemical or mechanical action caused by combustion, accompanied by creation of heat and rapid expansion of gases.

high explosive—An explosive with a velocity of detonation greater than 1,000 meters per second. Examples include dynamite and RDX.

low explosive—An explosive with a velocity of detonation less than 1,000 meters per second. Examples include black powder and smokeless powder.

oxidizing agent—A substance that supplies oxygen to a chemical reaction.

primary explosive—A high explosive that is easily detonated by heat, shock, or friction.

safety fuse—A cord containing a core of black powder, used to carry a flame at a uniform rate to an explosive charge.

secondary explosive—A high explosive that is relatively insensitive to heat, shock, or friction.

smokeless powder (double-base)—An explosive consisting of a mixture of nitrocellulose and nitroglycerin.

smokeless powder (single-base)—An explosive consisting of nitrocellulose.

X-ray diffraction—An analytical technique for identifying crystalline materials.

Learning Objectives

- Understand how explosives are classified
- List some common commercial, homemade, and military explosives
- Describe how to collect physical evidence at the scene of an explosion
- Describe laboratory procedures used to detect and identify explosive residues

Key Points

- Explosives are substances that undergo a rapid oxidation reaction with the production of large quantities of gases. The sudden buildup of gas pressure leads to the explosion.

- The speed at which an explosive decomposes determines whether it is classified as a high or low explosive.

- The most widely used low explosives are black powder and smokeless powder.

- Common high explosives include ammonium nitrate–based explosives (water gels, emulsions, and ANFO explosives).

- Among the high explosives, primary explosives are ultrasensitive to heat, shock, and friction and provide the major ingredients found in blasting caps. Secondary explosives normally constitute the main charge of a high explosive.

- The entire bomb site must be systematically searched to recover any trace of a detonating mechanism or any other item foreign to the explosion site. Objects located at or near the origin of the explosion must be collected for laboratory examination.

- Debris collected at explosion scenes is examined microscopically for unconsumed explosive particles.

- Recovered debris may be thoroughly rinsed with organic solvents and analyzed by testing procedures that include color spot tests, thin-layer chromatography, and gas chromatography/mass spectrometry.

- Intact explosives can be identified by either infrared spectrophotometry or X-ray diffraction.

- X-ray diffraction is used to study solid crystalline materials. As the X-rays penetrate the crystal, a portion of the beam is reflected by each of the atomic planes and the beams combine with one another to form a series of light and dark bands known as a *diffraction pattern*.

- Every compound produces a unique X-ray diffraction pattern, which gives analysts a means for "fingerprinting" compounds often associated with unconsumed explosives.

Supplemental Questions

1. What produces the violent physical disruption of the surrounding environment released in an explosion? Explain how this creates shrapnel when a bomb explodes.

2. What is an oxidizing agent? Why is an oxidizing agent important to an explosion?

3. What characteristic of an explosive determines whether it is classified as a low explosive or a high explosive? How is this reflected in the type of pressure wave produced by the explosive?

4. Name two types of low explosives and list the ingredients of each.

5. Why does black powder not explode unless it is ignited in a confined area? What practical application besides explosives does this make black powder suitable for?

6. What are primary explosives and what are they used for?

7. What is a detonator? What is the most common form of detonator?

8. What role does ammonium nitrate play in water gels, emulsions, and ANFO explosives? In what commercial form can ammonium nitrate be readily obtained?

9. In what liquid does a forensic scientist rinse debris recovered from an explosion site and why?

10. What type of materials can be identified using X-ray diffraction?

11. What are taggants and how are they used to identify explosives?

Answers to Supplemental Questions

1. The sudden buildup of expanding gas pressure at the origin of an explosion produces the violent physical disruption of the surrounding environment. In a bomb, the extremely high pressure caused by the expanding gases pushes on the walls of the bomb, stretching and finally shattering them. The pieces of the walls are shattered and thrown outward in all directions by the force of the explosion, creating shrapnel.

2. An oxidizing agent is a chemical that supplies oxygen to a reaction. Oxidizing agents are important to explosions because detonation occurs so rapidly that oxygen in the air cannot participate in the reaction; thus, many explosives must have their own source of oxygen.

3. The speed at which an explosive decomposes determines its classification as a low or high explosive. Low explosives produce a subsonic pressure wave, while high explosives produce a supersonic pressure wave.

4. Two types of low explosives are black powder and smokeless powder. The ingredients in black powder include potassium nitrate, carbon, and sulfur. The ingredients in smokeless powder are nitrocellulose and either nitroglycerin or nitrated cotton.

5. Black powder does not explode when unconfined because it decomposes too slowly. This makes black powder suitable for use in safety fuses, in which it carries a flame to an explosive charge.

6. A primary explosive is a high explosive that is easily detonated by heat or shock. They are used to detonate the most commonly used high explosives, which are known as secondary explosives. Primary explosives are necessary because secondary explosives are relatively insensitive to heat, shock, or friction and usually burn rather than detonate if ignited in small quantities in the open air.

7. A detonator is a device used to initiate an explosion using high explosives. The most common type of detonator is a blasting cap.

8. Ammonium nitrate is an oxidizing agent—it supplies the oxygen needed to detonate the explosive. Ammonium nitrate is readily available in a commercial form as fertilizer.

9. A forensic scientist rinses debris from an explosion site in acetone because most explosives are highly soluble in acetone. This allows the scientist to quickly remove any traces of explosive from the debris so they can be isolated and identified.

10. X-ray diffraction can be applied only to the study of solid, crystalline materials—that is, solids whose atoms have a definite and orderly arrangement.

11. Taggants are tiny color-coded chips added to commercial explosives during the manufacturing process. Some of these chips would be expected to survive an explosion and be recovered at explosion scenes. The taggants in an explosive are arranged in a color sequence that indicates where the explosive was made and when it was produced, which means the explosive can be traced through its distribution chain to its final legal possessor.

Resources

Videos/DVDs

Deadly Explosives: How and Why They Work

This video examines the different types of high and low explosives and explains how each one works.

Format: Color, VHS

Rated: NR

Studio: Paladin Enterprises

Video Release Date: April 10, 1998

ASIN: 6304967233

Investigative Reports: War on Arson

This video follows Chicago firefighters and police detectives as they try to piece together clues to catch an arsonist.

Format: Color, VHS

Rated: NR

Studio: A&E Home Video

Video Release Date: February 10, 2000

ASIN: 0767014502

Pickett's Primer on Explosives

Individuals and organizations use this video as training for identifying and correctly responding to commercial explosives, military ordnance, homemade bombs, and weapons of mass destruction. It includes instructor and student guides as well as a book on explosive identification.

Format: Color, VHS

Rated: NR

Studio: Unknown

Video Release Date: December 1, 1999

ASIN: 0970193246

Books

Explosives and Arson Investigation

Jean Ford

This book outlines a layperson's approach to the theory and practice of arson and explosion investigations.

> Format: Hardcover, 112 pages
>
> Publisher: Mason Crest (2005)
>
> ISBN: 1422200345

Forensic Investigation of Explosions

A. D. Beveridge (Ed.)

This book includes contributed articles by experts in the field of explosion investigation.

> Format: Hardcover, 300 pages
>
> Publisher: Taylor & Francis (1996)
>
> ISBN: 0133416291

Guide for Explosion and Bombing Scene Investigation

John C. Hitt and Richard Rau

This very brief volume outlines professional procedures to be used in the investigation of explosion and bombing scenes.

> Format: Paperback, 52 pages
>
> Publisher: Diane (2000)
>
> ISBN: 0756709415

Advanced Reading

Midkiff, C. R., "Arson and Explosive Investigation," in R. Saferstein, ed., *Forensic Science Handbook*, vol. 1, 2nd ed. Upper Saddle River, N.J.: Prentice Hall, 2002.

NFPA 921 Guide for Fire and Explosion Investigations, Quincy, Mass.: National Fire Protection Association, 2004.

Thurman, J. T., *Practical Bomb Scene Investigation.* Boca Raton, Fla.: Taylor & Francis, 2006.

Yinon, J., *Forensic and Environmental Detection of Explosives.* West Sussex, England: Wiley, 1999.

Yinon, J, and S. Zitrin, *Modern Methods and Applications in Analysis of Explosives.* West Sussex, England: Wiley, 1993.

Chapter 14

Fingerprints

Key Terms

anthropometry—A system of identification of individuals by measurement of parts of the body, developed by Alphonse Bertillon.

arch—A class of fingerprints characterized by ridge lines that enter the print from one side and flow out the other side.

digital imaging—A process through which a picture is converted into a series of square electronic dots known as pixels.

fluoresce—To emit visible light when exposed to light of a shorter wavelength.

iodine fuming—A technique for visualizing latent fingerprints by exposing them to iodine vapors.

latent fingerprint—A fingerprint made by the deposit of oils and/or perspiration; it is invisible to the naked eye.

livescan—An inkless device that captures digital images of fingerprints and palm prints and electronically transmits them to an AFIS.

loop—A class of fingerprints characterized by ridge lines that enter from one side of the pattern and curve around to exit from the same side of the pattern.

ninhydrin—A chemical reagent used to develop latent fingerprints on porous materials by reacting with amino acids in perspiration.

Physical Developer—A silver nitrate–based reagent formulated to develop latent fingerprints on porous surfaces.

pixel—A square electronic dot that is used to compose a digital image.

plastic print—A fingerprint impressed in a soft surface.

portrait parlé—A verbal description of a perpetrator's physical characteristics and dress provided by an eyewitness.

ridge characteristics (minutiae)—Ridge endings, bifurcations, enclosures, and other ridge details, which must match in two fingerprints to establish their common origin.

sublimation—A physical change from the solid directly into the gaseous state.

Super Glue fuming—A technique for visualizing latent fingerprints on nonporous surfaces by exposing them to cyanoacrylate vapors; named for the commercial product Super Glue.

visible print—A fingerprint made when the finger deposits a visible material such as ink, dirt, or blood onto a surface.

whorl—A class of fingerprints that includes ridge patterns that are generally rounded or circular and have two deltas.

Learning Objectives

- Know the common ridge characteristics of a fingerprint
- List the three major fingerprint patterns and their respective subclasses
- Distinguish visible, plastic, and latent fingerprints
- Describe the concept of an automated fingerprint identification system (AFIS)
- List the techniques for developing latent fingerprints on porous and nonporous objects
- Describe the proper procedures for preserving a developed latent fingerprint

Key Points

- Fingerprints are a reproduction of friction skin ridges found on the palm side of the fingers and thumbs.
- The basic principles underlying the use of fingerprints in criminal investigations are as follows: (1) A fingerprint is an individual characteristic because no two fingers have yet been found to possess identical ridge characteristics; (2) a fingerprint remains unchanged during an individual's lifetime; and (3) fingerprints have general ridge patterns that permit them to be systematically classified.
- All fingerprints are divided into three classes on the basis of their general pattern: loops, whorls, and arches.
- The individuality of a fingerprint is determined not by its general shape or pattern, but by a careful study of its ridge characteristics. The expert must demonstrate a point-by-point comparison in order to prove the identity of an individual.
- The FBI fingerprint database known as AFIS converts the image of a fingerprint into digital minutiae that contain data showing ridges at their points of termination (ridge endings) and their branching into two ridges (bifurcations).
- Visible prints are made when fingers touch a surface after the ridges have been in contact with a colored material such as blood, paint, grease, or ink.
- Plastic prints are ridge impressions left on a soft material, such as putty, wax, soap, or dust.
- When the finger touches a surface, perspiration and oils are transferred onto that surface, leaving a fingerprint. Prints deposited in this manner are invisible to the eye and are commonly referred to as latent or invisible fingerprints.
- Latent prints deposited on hard and nonabsorbent surfaces (such as glass, mirror, tile, and painted wood) are usually developed by the application of a

powder, whereas prints on porous surfaces (such as papers and cardboard) generally require treatment with a chemical.

- Examiners use various chemical methods to visualize latent prints, such as iodine fuming, ninhydrin, and Physical Developer.

- Super Glue fuming develops latent prints on nonporous surfaces, such as metals, electrical tape, leather, and plastic bags. Development occurs when fumes from the glue adhere to the print, usually producing a white latent print.

- Latent fingerprints can also be treated with chemicals that induce fluorescence when exposed to a high-intensity light or an alternate light source.

- Once a latent print has been visualized, it must be permanently preserved for future comparison and for possible use as court evidence. A photograph must be taken before any further attempts at preservation are made.

- If an object containing a fingerprint is small enough to be transported without destroying the print, it should be preserved in its entirety.

- Prints on large immovable objects that have been developed with a powder can best be preserved by "lifting" with a broad adhesive tape.

Supplemental Questions

1. Who published the first book on the science of fingerprinting? What were the book's most important contributions to understanding fingerprints?

2. What major advance in fingerprint technology was pioneered by Juan Vucetich and Sir Richard Henry? What was the importance of this advance?

3. What aspect of a fingerprint determines its individuality?

4. What are the dermal papillae and why are they important in fingerprinting?

5. Why is it almost impossible to obscure one's fingerprints by surgery or mutilation?

6. Describe each of the three classes of fingerprints. Which class is the most common in the population? Which is least common?

7. What aspect of a fingerprint forms the basis for primary classification under the FBI system? What is the main drawback of the FBI system?

8. Briefly describe how the Automated Fingerprint Identification System (AFIS) creates a fingerprint image. What characteristics of the fingerprint does the AFIS record for comparison?

9. What is the final step in fingerprint identification? Why is this step necessary if a computerized database of fingerprints is available to the forensic scientist?

10. List and describe the three types of fingerprints that may be found at a crime scene.

11. List two types of specialized fingerprint powders and name one advantage each has over traditional fingerprint powder.

12. What is the most commonly used chemical method to visualize latent fingerprints on porous materials? If this method is unsuccessful, what other technique typically is used?

13. What phenomenon underlies many of the new chemical techniques used to visualize latent fingerprints? Why is this phenomenon so valuable in fingerprint visualization?

14. When should a fingerprint be "lifted" from a crime scene? Describe how to lift and preserve a fingerprint using adhesive tape.

15. What is digital imaging and how is it used in fingerprint analysis? What is the greatest limitation to digital imaging?

Answers to Supplemental Questions

1. Francis Galton published the first book on the subject of fingerprinting. The book's most important contributions were to demonstrate that no two prints are identical and that an individual's prints remain unchanged from year to year.

2. Vucetich and Henry pioneered the creation of classification systems capable of filing thousands of prints in a logical and searchable sequence. This allowed law enforcement officials to quickly compare prints found at a crime scene to those of known criminals as an aid to identifying potential suspects.

3. The identity, number, and relative location of ridge characteristics impart individuality to a fingerprint.

4. The dermal papillae are a boundary of cells separating the outer portion of the skin (epidermis) and the inner skin (dermis). The shape of the dermal papillae determines the form and pattern of the ridges on the surface of the skin. Because the dermal papillae do not change shape throughout life, the ridge patterns of fingerprints also do not change.

5. To obscure one's fingerprints, an injury or surgery must reach deeply enough into the skin to damage the dermal papillae. Even so, it would be totally impossible to obliterate all of the ridge characteristics on the hand. Any attempt to do so would create deep scars that would provide new characteristics for identifying one's prints.

6. The three classes of fingerprints are loops, whorls, and arches. Loops are characterized by ridge lines that enter from one side of the pattern and curve around to exit from the same side of the pattern. Whorls include ridge patterns that are generally rounded or circular in shape and have two deltas. Arches are characterized by ridge lines that enter the print from one side and flow out the other side. Loops are most common; arches are least common.

7. The presence or absence of the whorl pattern is the basis for determining the primary classification in the FBI system. The main drawback of the FBI system is that it is useful only when a full set of fingerprints is available.

8. AFIS scans fingerprints and converts them into digital images that contain data on the relative location and orientation of ridge characteristics. The system records the points where ridges terminate, the points where they branch into two ridges, and the relative position and orientation of each ridge characteristic.

9. The final step in fingerprint identification is always visual comparison of the prints in question by a trained examiner. A computer database can only produce a list of prints that are similar to the print in question; it cannot make a positive identification.

10. Visible prints are made when a finger deposits a visible material such as ink, dirt, or blood onto a surface. Plastic prints are ridge impressions left on a soft material such as putty, wax, soap, or dust. Latent or invisible prints are caused by the transfer of body perspiration or oils present on finger ridges to the surface of an object.

11. Two specialized fingerprint powders are magnetic-sensitive powder and fluorescent powder. Using magnetic-sensitive powder offers less chance that the print will be destroyed or damaged because the powder is spread using a magnetic brush that has no bristles to come in contact with the surface containing the print. Fluorescent powders reveal a vivid image of a print under ultraviolet light. When the developing print is photographed under UV light, the color of the surface does not obscure the print.

12. The ninhydrin method is most commonly used to visualize latent fingerprints on porous materials. If the ninhydrin method fails, the Physical Developer technique typically is used.

13. The phenomenon of fluorescence serves as the underlying principle of many of the new chemical techniques used to visualize latent fingerprints. Substances that emit light or fluoresce are more readily seen either with the naked eye or through photography as compared to non-light-emitting materials. Thus, techniques based on fluorescence permit better visualization of all prints and allow the visualization of faint prints that other methods may fail to visualize.

14. A print should be "lifted" from a crime scene when it is on a large, immovable object. One method of lifting is to dust the print with fingerprint powder, then cover the print with adhesive tape. When the tape is pulled up, the powder is transferred to the tape. Then the tape is placed on a card that provides a good background contrast with the powder.

15. Digital imaging is a process through which a picture is converted into a series of square electronic dots known as pixels. It is used to compare fingerprints and to enhance poor fingerprint images. The main limitation of digital imaging is that it is only as useful as the images it has to work with. If the images are poor or incomplete, enhancement procedures will not work.

Resources

Videos/DVDs

Hunt: Fingerprinting and Ballistics

This video examines the origins of fingerprinting and looks at important case studies in fingerprinting.

Format: Color, VHS

Rated: NR

Studio: A&E Home Video

Video Release Date: May 6, 2002

ASIN: B000067J6W

Books

Advances in Fingerprint Technology

Henry Lee and R. E. Gaensslen (Eds.)

This book covers major developments in latent fingerprint processing, including physical, chemical, instrumental, and combination techniques. It discusses topics including latent fingerprint chemistry, treatment of AFIS, new procedures that apply nanocrystal technology to latent fingerprint development, and a systematic, statistically based point of view regarding the individuality of fingerprints.

Format: Hardcover, 456 pages

Publisher: CRC Press (2001)

ISBN: 0849309239

Contrast: An Investigator's Basic Reference Guide to Fingerprint Identification Concepts

Craig A. Coppock

This work illustrates the basic concepts involved in the science of fingerprints and fingerprint identification. Major topics include fingerprints in context; friction skin and friction skin classification; exemplar fingerprint impressions; latent fingerprint development and recovery; special development processes and conditions; latent fingerprint quality variations; fingerprint identification; fingerprint fabrication, errors, and evidence; photography, image enhancement, and color; and computerized fingerprint databases.

Format: Hardcover, 131 pages

Publisher: Charles C. Thomas (2001)

ISBN: 0398071306

Fingerprint Science

Clarence Gerald Collins

This paperback presents a comprehensive, easily understood approach to all aspects of fingerprint classification, identification, and filing systems.

Format: Paperback, 192 pages

Publisher: Wadsworth (2001)

ISBN: 0942728181

Fingerprints and Other Ridge Skin Impressions
Chris Lennard et al.

Chapters in this comprehensive guide to modern fingerprint science cover all aspects of the subject, including the formation of friction ridges on the skin, the deposition of latent prints, the detection and enhancement of such marks, recording of fingerprint evidence, and fingerprint identification. Recent advances in statistical interpretation, fingerprint detection techniques, and computer technology are also discussed in detail.

> Format: Hardcover, 496 pages
> Publisher: CRC Press (2004)
> ISBN: 0415271754

Handbook of Fingerprint Recognition
Davide Maltoni et al.

This reference on automatic fingerprint recognition provides in-depth coverage of the most recent advances and practices, including sensing, feature extraction and matching, synthetic fingerprint image generation, indexing, and multimodal systems.

> Format: Hardcover, 348 pages
> Publisher: Springer-Verlag (2005)
> ISBN: 0387954317

Introduction to Fingerprint Comparison
Gary W. Jones

This brief and straightforward introduction to the art and science of comparing fingerprints is written for the layperson.

> Format: Spiral Bound, 87 pages
> Publisher: Staggs (2000)
> ISBN: 0966197038

Suspect Identities: A History of Fingerprinting and Criminal Identification
Simon A. Cole

This comprehensive book traces the roots of fingerprinting technology and explores recent developments, including the controversial certification process for fingerprint examiners, defense attorney attacks on examiner credibility or corruption, and law enforcement reliance on DNA typing and other new forms of biometric identification.

> Format: Paperback, 400 pages
> Publisher: Harvard University Press (2002)
> ISBN: 0674010027

Advanced Reading
Cowger, James E., *Friction Ridge Skin*. Boca Raton, Fla.: Taylor & Francis, 1992.

Komarinski, Peter, *Automated Fingerprint Identification Systems (AFIS)*. Burlington, Mass.: Elsevier Academic Press, 2005.

U.S. Department of Justice, *The Science of Fingerprints*. Washington, D.C.: U.S. Government Printing Office, 1990.

Demonstrations and Lecture Starters
General Fingerprinting
Lab-Aids, Inc., 17 Colt Court, Ronkonkoma, N.Y. 11779 (www.lab-aids.com) produces a lab kit (#1275) covering the science of fingerprinting. Students take fingerprints and establish a fingerprint file. The kit also permits the student to develop and lift fingerprints using different methods.

Latent Prints
Latent fingerprint development always proves to be a fun exercise. The following supplies can be purchased from police equipment suppliers such as Sirchie Finger Print Laboratories, 100 Hunter Place, Youngsville, NC 27596 (www.sirchie.com):

> Brushes
> Black and gray latent powder
> Ninhydrin spray
> Black and white hinge lifters
> Transparent tape

Cyanoacrylate Fuming
Cyanoacrylate fuming can readily be demonstrated through the use of a small handheld fuming wand. This wand is available from Lightning Powder Company 13386 International Parkway, Jacksonville, FL 32218 (www.redwop.com).

Brief History of Biometric Identification
Fingerprints were the first in a series of increasingly sophisticated and accurate biometric identification tools available to police. A brief overview of the development of identification technology can give students an appreciation of how these tools have improved over the past 125 years. The textbook (pp. 428–429) contains a good discussion of anthropometry and the *portrait parlé* system that preceded fingerprinting, and also traces the main developments in fingerprint technology from Fauld and Galton to computerized databases such as AFIS. This can lead to a discussion of emerging modern identification technologies such as finger scans, iris scans, and voice identification. Address issues including the state of the art in each of these technologies; advantages and drawbacks to their use as identification tools; and issues regarding scientific validity, privacy, and civil liberties.

Identifying Fingerprints: Super Glue Fuming
In this demonstration, students will use the Super Glue fuming technique to identify questioned fingerprints. Before class, mount a lightbulb (or place a small lamp) in a clean aquarium. Cover the bulb or lamp with an aluminum can cut in half lengthwise. Seal the opening of the aquarium with a piece of wood or stiff cardboard cut to fit. At the beginning of class, distribute a clean glass slide to each student. Be sure to wear gloves when distributing the slides. Have each student label the slide with his or her name and make an impression of his or

her right index finger on the slide. Collect the slides; remove the name labels from several of them; relabel them A, B, C, and so on; and place the slides in the aquarium. Now drop a little Super Glue on the can and turn on the lamp. In about fifteen minutes you should see white prints begin to form on the slides.

While the slides are fuming, make a fingerprint ID sheet for everyone in the class. To do so, have the students pair up in teams of two. Have one member of each pair turn a pencil sideways and rub a thick spot of graphite onto a piece of clear paper. The student should then roll his or her right index finger firmly from left to right in the graphite. Have the other member of the pair then place a piece of clear tape over the finger, gently remove the tape, and stick it to another clean sheet of paper. Label the print with the name of the student. Now each member of the pair reverses roles, so that you have a record of all of the students' fingerprints.

After the prints on the slides appear, remove the slides from the aquarium and allow students to examine them. Have them compare the prints on the slides to the class fingerprint record and ask them to identify the "suspect" prints on the slides. Also have students indicate whether each of the suspect prints is a loop, whorl, or arch pattern. After identifying the suspect prints, have students classify each of the fingerprints on the student record as either a loop, whorl, or arch, then calculate the percentage of each in the sample. Referring to the text, ask students how the percentages in the student sample compare with the population at large.

Chapter 15

Firearms, Tool Marks, and Other Impressions

Key Terms

bore—The interior of a firearm barrel.

breechblock—The rear part of a firearm barrel.

caliber—The diameter of the bore of a rifled firearm, usually expressed in hundredths of an inch or millimeters—for example, .22 caliber and 9 mm.

choke—An interior constriction placed at or near the muzzle end of a shotgun's barrel to control shot dispersion.

distance determination—The process of determining the distance between the firearm and a target, usually based on the distribution of powder patterns or the spread of a shot pattern.

ejector—The mechanism in a firearm that throws the cartridge or fired case from the firearm.

extractor—The mechanism in a firearm by which a cartridge or fired case is withdrawn from the chamber.

firearms identification—A discipline mainly concerned with determining whether a bullet or cartridge was fired by a particular weapon.

gauge—Size designation of a shotgun, originally the number of lead balls with the same diameter as the barrel that would make a pound. The only exception is the .410 shotgun, in which bore size is 0.41 inch.

Greiss test—A chemical test used to develop patterns of gunpowder residues around bullet holes.

grooves—The cut or low-lying portions between the lands in a rifled bore.

lands—The raised portion between the grooves in a rifled bore.

rifling—The spiral grooves formed in the bore of a firearm barrel that impart spin to the projectile when it is fired.

Learning Objectives

- Describe techniques for rifling a barrel
- Recognize the class and individual characteristics of bullets and cartridge cases
- Understand the use of the comparison microscope to compare bullets and cartridge cases
- Explain the concept of the IBIS database
- Explain the procedure for determining how far a weapon was fired from a target
- Identify the laboratory tests for determining whether an individual has fired a weapon
- Explain the forensic significance of class and individual characteristics to the comparison of tool mark, footwear, and tire impressions
- List some common field reagents used to enhance bloody footprints

Key Points

- Structural variations and irregularities caused by scratches, nicks, breaks, and wear permit the criminalist to relate a bullet to a gun; a scratch or abrasion mark to a single tool; or a tire track to a particular automobile.

- The manufacture of a gun barrel requires impressing its inner surface with spiral grooves, a step known as rifling. The surfaces of the original bore remaining between the grooves are called lands.

- No two rifled barrels have identical striation markings. These striations form the individual characteristics of the barrel. The inner surface of the barrel of a gun leaves its striation markings on a bullet passing through it.

- The number of lands and grooves and their direction of twist are obvious points of comparison during the initial stages of an examination. Any differences in these characteristics eliminate the possibility that both bullets traveled through the same barrel.

- Not only must the lands and grooves of the test and evidence bullet have identical widths, but the longitudinal striations on each also must coincide.

- The comparison microscope is a firearms examiner's most important tool because it allows two bullets to be observed and compared simultaneously.

- The firing pin, breechblock, and ejector and extractor mechanism also offer a highly distinctive signature for individualization of cartridge cases.

- The advent of computerized imaging technology has made possible the storage of bullet and cartridge surface characteristics in a manner analogous to automated fingerprint files.

- The distribution of gunpowder particles and other discharge residues around a bullet hole permits an assessment of the distance from which a handgun or rifle was fired.

- Firing a weapon propels residues toward the target and blows gunpowder and primer residues back toward the shooter. Traces of these residues are often deposited on the firing hand of the shooter, providing valuable information as to whether an individual has recently fired a weapon.

- Examiners measure the amount of barium and antimony on the relevant portion of the suspect's hands or characterize the morphology of particles containing these elements to determine whether a person has fired or handled a weapon or was near a discharged firearm.

- In atomic absorption spectrophotometry, a specimen is heated to a temperature that is hot enough to vaporize its atoms while leaving a substantial number of atoms in an unexcited state. The vaporized atoms are then exposed to radiation emitted from a light source specific for a particular element. If that element is present in the material under investigation, a portion of the light will be absorbed by the substance.

- Atomic absorption spectrophotometry can detect elements characteristic of primer residues at levels that approach one-trillionth of a gram.

- Criminalists can restore serial numbers removed or obliterated by grinding, rifling, or punching. Because the metal crystals in the stamped zone are placed under a permanent strain that extends a short distance beneath the original numbers, the serial number can be restored through chemical etching.

- A tool mark is any impression, cut, gouge, or abrasion caused by a tool coming into contact with another object.

- The presence of minute imperfections on a tool imparts individuality to that tool. The shape and pattern of such imperfections are further modified by damage and wear during the life of the tool.

- The comparison microscope is used to compare crime-scene tool marks with test impressions made with the suspect tool.

- Shoe and tire marks impressed into soft earth at a crime scene are best preserved by photography and casting.

- In areas where a bloody footwear impression is very faint or where the subject has tracked through blood, leaving a trail of bloody impressions, chemical enhancement can visualize latent or nearly invisible blood impressions. A sufficient number of points of comparison or the uniqueness of such points will show that both the questioned and test impressions originated from one and only one source.

Supplemental Questions

1. List three class characteristics of a gun barrel.
2. Describe how a firearms examiner compares two bullets. What characteristic does an examiner most often use to identify bullets and why?
3. List two reasons why striations on bullets fired from the same gun might vary slightly.
4. Besides the barrel, what parts of a firearm may leave distinctive markings on a shell cartridge?
5. Why does a firearms examiner test-fire bullets from a suspect barrel?
6. What is distance determination? Describe two situations in which distance determination can establish the facts of a shooting incident.
7. What evidence does an investigator study to make a distance determination? How can test-firing a suspect weapon help the investigator make a distance determination?
8. List three characteristics of a bullet hole that indicate that the shot was fired at extremely close range.

9. What is the Greiss test and what two pieces of information can it provide to an investigator?
10. How is shot pattern used to make a distance determination for shotgun blasts? What factors other than distance to target can affect the distance determination?
11. What evidence do investigators look for when trying to determine whether a suspect has fired a handgun? Where is such evidence typically found and why?
12. Why does analysis of primer residue from a suspect's hands produce a low rate of positive results? Why is such analysis typically ineffective in locating primer residue from a .22-caliber gun?
13. How does the quantity of light absorbed during atomic absorption spectrophotometry relate to the concentration of the absorbing element? What is the significance of this relationship for primer residue detection?
14. What is the primary drawback to atomic absorption spectrophotometry?
15. What advantage does "flameless" atomic absorption enjoy over standard atomic absorption techniques?
16. Describe how a criminalist restores an obliterated serial number on a weapon.
17. Why would an investigator not pick up a weapon by its barrel with a pencil or stick in order to protect latent fingerprints? How should suspect firearms be handled in such a situation?
18. What characteristics of a suspect firearm should an investigator record before unloading it? Why should the investigator number the chambers and cartridges when unloading a suspect weapon?
19. What is the investigator's primary concern when collecting and handling bullets and cartridge cases? Why must the investigator exercise extreme caution when removing a bullet lodged in a wall or other object?
20. Name two types of marks that impart individuality to a tool and explain how the marks are made.
21. What techniques does an investigator use to analyze tool marks that cannot be removed from a crime scene? What is the disadvantage of this technique?
22. What is the first thing the investigator does before handling or moving any impression at a crime scene? Why is this considered merely a backup or precautionary procedure?
23. What kinds of impression evidence might a forensic odontologist be asked to analyze? How might this help identify a suspect?

Answers to Supplemental Questions

1. Three class characteristics of a gun barrel are its caliber, the number of lands and grooves, and the direction and twist of the lands and grooves.
2. The examiner places both bullets under a comparison microscope, pointing in the same direction, and then rotates one bullet until a well-defined land or groove comes into view. When the examiner locates striation markings on this bullet, the other bullet is rotated until

a matching region is found. When a matching area is located, the two bullets are simultaneously rotated to locate additional matching areas around the periphery of the bullets. The examiner uses the striation markings to identify bullets because no two rifled barrels have identical striation markings.

3. The presence of grit and rust can alter the markings on bullets fired through the same barrel. Striation markings on a barrel are not permanent structures; they are subject to continuing alteration through wear as succeeding bullets traverse the length of the barrel.

4. The firing pin, the breechblock, the extractor, the ejector, the magazine, the clip, and the firing chamber walls may all leave distinctive markings on a shell casing.

5. The examiner must test-fire bullets through the suspect barrel because there is no other practical way to directly compare the markings on the fired bullet and those found within a barrel.

6. Distance determination is the process of determining the distance between the firearm and a target, usually based on the distribution of powder patterns or the spread of a shot pattern. If a suspect pleads self-defense as the motive for a shooting, determining how far apart the suspect and victim were at the time of shooting can establish the facts of the incident. Distance determination can also determine whether a shooting was suicide, which usually involves a very close-range gunshot wound. The absence of characteristics consistent with a close-range shot strongly indicates that the wound was not self-inflicted and signals the possibility of foul play.

7. The distribution of gunpowder particles and other discharge residues around the bullet hole permits an assessment of the distance from which a handgun or rifle was fired. To determine the precise distance from which a gun has been fired requires a comparison of the powder-residue pattern on the victim's clothing or skin against patterns made from test-firing the suspect weapon. By comparing residue patterns from test firings to those found at the crime scene, the examiner may find enough similarity in shape and density on which to base an opinion as to the distance from which the shot was fired.

8. If the weapon is fired less than 1 inch from the target, a heavy concentration of smokelike vaporous lead usually surrounds the bullet entrance hole. Often, loose fibers surrounding a contact hole show scorch marks from the flame discharge of the weapon, and some synthetic fibers show signs of being melted as a result of the heat from the discharge. Furthermore, the blowback of muzzle gases may produce a stellate (star-shape) tear pattern around the hole.

9. The Greiss test is a chemical test used to develop patterns of gunpowder residues around bullet holes. The test results can reveal whether powder residues from a gunshot are present and can also help determine the distance from the shooter to the target.

10. Distance determination for a shotgun blast is made by measuring the spread of the discharged shot—the wider the spread, the farther the shooter was from the target. Other factors include the barrel length, the size and quantity of the pellets fired, the quantity of powder charge used to propel the pellets, and the choke of the gun (the degree of constriction placed at the muzzle end of the barrel).

11. Current efforts to identify a shooter center on the detection of primer residues deposited on the hand of a shooter at the time of firing. Shortly after the weapon is fired, residues are most likely to be deposited on the thumb web and the back of the firing hand of a shooter, because these areas are closest to gases escaping along the side or back of the gun during discharge.

12. Analysis of primer residue from a suspect's hands produces a low rate of positive results because primer residues remain on the hands only for a short time and are easily removed by rubbing or washing. This technique cannot be used to detect firings with most .22-caliber rim-fire ammunition because the primer for this ammunition often does not contain characteristic elements associated with primer residues.

13. In atomic absorption spectrophotometry, the concentration of the absorbing elements associated with primer residues is directly proportional to the quantity of the light absorbed.

14. The primary drawback of atomic absorption spectrophotometry is that it allows the analyst to determine only one element in a sample at a time. The forensic scientist must thus run several tests using different lamps to identify all of the elements in a sample.

15. "Flameless" atomic absorption spectrophotometry is substantially more sensitive, allowing the forensic scientist to detect many elements at levels that approach one-trillionth of a gram.

16. To restore an obliterated serial number, the criminalist applies a suitable etching agent to the area that has been defaced. The metal in this area dissolves at a faster rate than the unaltered metal surrounding it, thus permitting the etched pattern to appear in the form of the original numbers.

17. An investigator would not pick up a weapon by its barrel with a pencil or stick in order to protect fingerprints because this may disturb powder deposits, rust, or dirt lodged in the barrel, and consequently may alter the striation markings on test-fired bullets. If the recovery of latent fingerprints is a primary concern, it is best to hold the weapon by the edge of the trigger guard or by the checkered portion of the grip.

18. The investigator should record the weapon's hammer and safety position as well as the location of all fired and unfired ammunition in the weapon. The chambers and cartridges should be numbered because this information may be useful to determine the sequence of events, particularly in cases in which several shots were fired.

19. The investigator's primary concern is the protection of class and individual markings on bullets and cartridge cases. If the bullet's surface is accidentally scratched when removing it from a wall or other object, valuable striation markings could be obliterated that can help link the bullet to a suspect weapon.

20. The edges of any tool display a series of microscopic irregularities that look like ridges and valleys. These marks are created during the machining processes used to cut and finish the tool. Another type of mark is caused by nicks and breaks in the tool that occur during normal use.

21. When removal of the tool mark is impractical, the area is photographed and marked to scale, and a silicone cast of the mark is made. The disadvantage of this technique is that even under the best conditions, the clarity of many of the tool mark's minute details are lost or obscured in a photograph or cast.

22. Before any impression is moved or otherwise handled, it must be photographed to show all the observable details of the impression. Photography is considered merely a backup procedure in case the impression is damaged before reaching the crime laboratory. The examiner prefers to receive the actual impression for comparison to the suspect object that made the impression.

23. A forensic odontologist might be asked to analyze bite marks on a person or object found at a crime scene. If a sufficient number of points of similarity exist between the test and suspect marks, the forensic odontologist may conclude that the marks were made by one particular individual.

Resources

Videos/DVDs

Forensic Firearms Evidence: Elements of Shooting Incident Reconstruction

This thorough introduction to the fundamentals of the many elements of shooting incident investigation discusses firearms classification, small-arms propellants, ammunition identification, bullet design characteristics, gunshot residue, rifling characteristics, firearms evidence marking, evidence collection, tool marks on cartridges, shotgun ammunition, small-arms functioning, and actual shooting case evidence examples.

> Format: Color, VHS
>
> Rated: NR
>
> Studio: Unknown
>
> Video Release Date: June 1, 1991
>
> ASIN: B00006JLPN

Books

Ballistics

Jay Robert Nash

One in a series of brief works based on case studies in forensic science, this volume explores ballistics and firearms identification.

> Format: Hardcover, 100 pages
>
> Publisher: Chelsea House (2005)
>
> ISBN: 0791089126

Current Methods in Forensic Gunshot Residue Analysis

A. J. Schwoeble and David L. Exline

This work deals with major areas of gunshot residue analysis such as current and future methods of analysis, collection techniques, interpretation of evidence, expert testimony, and report writing. The book presents new research into ammunition formulation, particle formation, and distribution of gunshot residue plumes.

> Format: Hardcover, 192 pages
>
> Publisher: CRC Press (2000)
>
> ISBN: 0849300290

Footwear Impression Evidence: Detection, Recovery and Examination

William J. Bodziak

This book describes the methods used to recover and identify footwear impressions from the scene of a crime. It includes updated and new information on recovery procedures and materials such as lifting, photography, and casting; chemical enhancement; updated information about footwear manufacturing; footwear sizing; and known impression techniques and materials. It also features chapters on barefoot evidence; several cases in which the footwear impression evidence was of primary importance in bringing about a conviction or confession; and a chapter on the footwear impression evidence in the O. J. Simpson criminal and civil cases.

> Format: Hardcover, 528 pages
>
> Publisher: CRC Press (1999)
>
> ISBN: 0849310458

Gunshot Wounds: Practical Aspects of Firearms, Ballistics, and Forensic Techniques

Vincent Di Maio

This book provides information on gunshot wounds and the weapons and ammunition used to inflict them. It describes practical aspects of ballistics; wound ballistics; and the classification of various wounds caused by handguns, bang guns, rifles, and shotguns. The final chapters explain autopsy technique and procedure and laboratory analysis relating to weapons and gunshot evidence.

> Format: Hardcover, 424 pages
>
> Publisher: CRC Press (1998)
>
> ISBN: 0849381630

Handbook of Firearms and Ballistics: Examining and Interpreting Forensic Evidence

Brian J. Heard

This book traces the worldwide use and development of firearms and ammunition and provides information on the specifications and characteristics of common weapons and explains specialist terminology in everyday language. It also includes case studies.

Format: Hardcover, 278 pages

Publisher: Wiley (1997)

ISBN: 0471965634

Silent Evidence: Firearms Forensic Ballistics and Toolmarks—Cases from Forensic Science
Charles Meyers

This work describes several criminal cases that illustrate the influence of firearms and tool mark identification methods in solving crimes. Many of the homicides involve "twists" in the evidence, not usually reported, that will be of interest to the general public. The book also includes an addendum, "A Primer on Firearms and Toolmark Identification," for readers who desire a deeper understanding of the discipline and its scientific foundation.

Format: Paperback, 219 pages

Publisher: Parkway (2004)

ISBN: 1887905391

Tire Imprint Evidence
Peter MacDonald

This book discusses methods for examining, capturing, and recording imprints; outlines standard procedures for identification; shows how to prepare expert testimony; and provides detailed technical information helpful in identifying imprints.

Format: Hardcover, 226 pages

Publisher: CRC Press (1992)

ISBN: 0849395151

Advanced Reading

Di Maio, V. J. M., *Gunshot Wounds: Practical Aspects of Firearms, Ballistics, and Forensic Techniques,* 2nd ed. Boca Raton, Fla.: CRC Press, 1999.

Heard, Brian J., *Handbook of Firearms and Ballistics.* Chichester, England: Wiley, 1997.

Rowe, Walter F., "Firearms Identification," in R. Saferstein, ed., *Forensic Science Handbook,* vol. 2, 2nd ed. Upper Saddle River, N.J.: Prentice Hall, 2005.

Demonstrations and Lecture Starters

Tool Marks

Tool mark casts are easily prepared with liquid silicone rubber or silicone rubber putty. Both of these products are available from Sirchie Finger Print Laboratories, 100 Hunter Place, Youngsville, N.C. 27596 (www.sirchie.com).

Footprint Casting

I always require my class to prepare a cast of a footprint in the laboratory. Each student is asked to bring in a shoe box partially filled with soil. Other supplies required are a can of aerosol hair spray with a lacquer base (spraying the lacquer carefully over the impression hardens it); a 5-pound bag of plaster of Paris; several tongue depressors or a length of wire mesh to serve as reinforcing material; and a mixing bowl.

The following guidelines should be followed when preparing the cast:

1. Spray the lacquer over the impression, being careful not to disturb the details of the impression.

2. Pour the plaster of Paris in two steps. First, add enough plaster to water to make an initial pouring approximately ½ inch thick. The consistency of the mixture should be that of sour cream. Do not pour the material directly onto the impression, but over a tongue depressor or spoon to prevent marring the impression. The cast may then be reinforced with tongue depressors or wire mesh.

3. After reinforcing the cast, prepare another mixture of plaster of Paris for an additional pouring approximately ½ inch thick.

4. Before the plaster completely dries, mark it for identification on the upper surface.

A series of photographs clearly illustrating the steps to be carried out in the casting of an impression with dental stone appears at www.sccja.org/csr-mix.htm. Remember, when casting with dental stone it's not necessary to reinforce the cast.

Other Impressions: Lip Prints

This demonstration shows how various types of impressions can be used to help solve a crime. You will need the following items:

- Six tubes of red lipstick (all the same color)
- Forty-eight pieces of white paper
- Stereomicroscope
- Ruler

The Scenario

Each month the local women's club sponsors a luncheon at which several prospective new members are invited to attend. This month's meeting was held at the home of club president Janet Graves. Ms. Graves asks the prospective members to wait in her sunroom while the regular members hold a brief business meeting. While they wait they are served lemonade in crystal glasses. Later that day, after the luncheon, Ms. Graves notices that a diamond necklace is missing from her bedroom. When the police arrive they notice a crystal glass in the room with red lipstick on the rim. Ms. Graves states that it must have been used by one of the guests, because she does not wear red lipstick. Suspecting that the person who used the glass was probably the one who stole the necklace, police lift lip prints from the glass. After collecting the names of the prospective members, police visit each woman and take her lip prints for comparison to the prints on the glass.

Divide the students into investigative teams. Choose six students at random as "suspects" and give each six pieces of paper and a tube of lipstick. Have each suspect apply the lipstick, fold each sheet of paper in half, and blot her lips on the paper, making sure not to smudge the lip print. This way you will have six lip prints for each suspect. Have each suspect write her name on a piece of notebook paper and attach the papers with the lip prints to the notebook paper. Each suspect gives the prints to the instructor, who will decide which print matches those found at the scene.

Place the print chosen as the crime-scene print under the stereomicroscope. Have one member of each team sketch the print, noting any special characteristics as well as the line patterns in the print. Now have each sus-pect apply lipstick and make a lip print for the class. Write the person's name on the paper containing the print. Now have the teams examine each of these prints under the stereomicroscope, then sketch and make notes on them.

After students have completed sketching and note taking, ask them to answer the following questions: Which suspect left the prints on the glass found in the bedroom? What features of the suspect lip prints led you to this conclusion? Is this enough evidence to convict the suspect of theft? Why or why not?

Chapter 16

Document Examination

Key Terms

charred document—Any document that has become darkened and brittle through exposure to fire or excessive heat.

erasure—The removal of writing, typewriting, or printing from a document, normally accomplished by either chemical means or an abrasive instrument.

exemplar—An authentic sample used for comparison purposes, such as handwriting.

indented writings—Impressions left on paper positioned under a piece of paper that has been written on.

infrared luminescence—A property exhibited by some dyes that emit infrared light when exposed to blue-green light.

natural variations—Normal deviations found between repeated specimens of an individual's handwriting.

obliteration—Blotting out or smearing over writing or printing to make the original unreadable.

questioned document—Any document about which some issue has been raised or that is the subject of an investigation.

Learning Objectives

- Define *questioned document*
- Know what common individual characteristics are associated with handwriting
- List some important guidelines for collecting known writings for comparison to a questioned document
- Recognize some of the class and individual characteristics of printers and photocopiers
- List some of the techniques document examiners use to uncover alterations, erasures, obliterations, and variations in pen inks

Key Points

- Any object with handwriting or print whose source or authenticity is in doubt may be referred to as a questioned document.
- Document examiners gather documents of known authorship or origin and compare them to the individual characteristics of questioned writings.
- Collecting an adequate number of known writings is critical for determining the outcome of a handwriting comparison. Known writing should contain some of the words and combinations of letters in the questioned document.
- The unconscious handwriting of two different individuals can never be identical. However, the writing style of an individual may be altered beyond recognition by the influence of drugs or alcohol.

- The two requests most often made of the examiner in connection with the examination of typewriters and printing devices are to identify the make and model of the typewriter or printing device used to prepare the questioned document, and determine whether a particular suspect typewriter or printing device prepared the questioned document.
- The examiner compares the individual type character's style, shape, and size to a complete reference collection of past and present typefaces.
- Use of a printing device results in wear and damage to the machine's moving parts in a way that is both random and irregular, thereby imparting individual characteristics to it.
- Document examiners deal with evidence that has been changed in several ways, such as through alterations, erasures, and obliterations.
- It may be possible to read indented writing—the impressions left on a paper pad—by applying an electrostatic charge to the surface of a polymer film that has been placed in contact with a questioned document.
- Studying the chemical composition of writing ink present on documents may verify whether known and questioned documents were prepared by the same pen.

Supplemental Questions

1. What activity is critical to the outcome of document examination and why is it so important?
2. List three characteristics of handwriting, as well as three characteristics of writing not related to handwriting, that a examiner compares when studying a questioned document.
3. List three factors that can make it difficult for an examiner to determine the author of a questioned writing.
4. Why might a traced signature be more easily detected as a forgery than one that is copied freehand?
5. List three characteristics of exemplars that should be as alike as possible to the questioned document.
6. What individual characteristics are valuable for proving the identity of a typewriter?
7. What kinds of marks can a document examiner use to identify the machine that produced a photocopy? What information is used to identify the machine that produced a fax copy?
8. What class characteristics can an examiner study to help identify a suspect photocopy machine?
9. What is infrared luminescence? Describe how it can be used to detect alterations or erasures in a document.
10. Describe two methods used to recover writing from charred documents.
11. Describe two methods used to read indented writing.

12. From what substances are most commercial inks made? What technique is used to compare inks? What characteristic provides points of comparison between different inks?

Answers to Supplemental Questions

1. Gathering documents of known authorship or origin is critical to the outcome of document examination because the document examiner's success depends on the ability to recognize the characteristics of known authentic writings and compare them to questioned writings.

2. Handwriting characteristics that an examiner looks for include angularity, slope, speed, pressure, letter and word spacing, relative dimensions of letters, connections, pen movement, writing skill, and finger dexterity. Nonhandwriting characteristics to consider include margins, crowding, insertions, alignment, spelling, punctuation, phraseology, and grammar.

3. Factors that can make it difficult for an examiner to determine the author of a questioned writing include having an insufficient number of known writings; having questioned writing containing only a few, deliberately altered words; and having writing that is unrecognizable because it was made under the influence of alcohol or drugs.

4. There are variations in the writing characteristics of all people. No two specimens of writing prepared by one person are ever identical in every detail. Thus, a signature forged by tracing an authentic signature can often be detected more easily than a freehand copy because no one ever signs two signatures exactly alike.

5. Characteristics of exemplars that should be as alike as possible to the questioned document include the type of writing implement used, the type of paper, whether the paper is ruled or unruled, the presence of some of the same words or letter combinations, and the relative age of the two documents.

6. Individual characteristics valuable for proving the identity of a typewriter are variations in vertical and horizontal alignment (characters are too high or low or too far left or right of their correct position), perpendicular misalignment of characters (characters leaning to the left or to the right), and defects in the typeface.

7. Defect marks originating from the random formation of debris on the glass platen, inner cover, or mechanical portions of a copier themselves produce images. These images can form distinctive patterns that document examiners can study to identify individual photocopy machines. When dealing with questioned faxes, an examiner can study the header known as the transmitting terminal identifier (TTI) that can be read at the top of each fax page.

8. Class characteristics of photocopy machines studied by the examiner include the printing technology, the type of paper, the type of toner or ink used, the chemical composition of the toner, and the type of toner-to-paper fusing method used in producing the document.

9. Infrared luminescence is the emission of infrared light by an object that is exposed to blue-green light. An alteration made to a document with ink differing from the original can sometimes be detected by illuminating the document with blue-green light and using infrared-sensitive film to record infrared light emitted by the different ink. Infrared luminescence can also reveal writing that has been erased because invisible residues of the original ink remain embedded in the paper even after erasure.

10. Infrared photography is sometimes used to reveal the contents of a charred document that has been accidentally or purposely charred. Another way to decipher charred documents involves reflecting light off the paper's surface at different angles in order to contrast the writing against the charred background of the paper.

11. Indented writings are often readable when the paper is studied under oblique or side lighting. Another method involves applying toner powder to a polymer film that is brought into contact with a questioned document. An electrostatic charge is then applied to the surface of the film, causing the powder to adhere to the impressions on the document and revealing the writing.

12. Most commercial inks are mixtures of several organic dyes. Thin-layer chromatography is used to compare inks. The separation pattern of the component dyes is distinctly different for inks with different dye compositions, which provides many points of comparison between a known and a questioned ink.

Resources

Books

Advances in the Forensic Analysis and Dating of Writing Ink

Richard L. Brunelle and Kenneth R. Crawford

This book describes the many advances that have occurred in the field of forensic examination and dating of inks on documents. Actual laboratory procedures for examining and dating inks and other related substances are described, as well as the forensic applications of these techniques in criminal and civil litigations. In addition, the authors discuss theories for each type of chemical analysis that serve as useful guidelines for explaining the science to lay juries.

Format: Hardcover, 215 pages

Publisher: Charles C. Thomas (2003)

ISBN: 0398073465

Detecting Forgery: Forensic Investigation of Documents

Joe Nickell

This paperback covers the arsenal of forensic techniques used to detect forged handwriting and alterations in documents and to identify the authorship of disputed writings. The book looks at famous cases such as Clifford Irving's "autobiography" of Howard Hughes and the Mormon papers of document dealer Mark Hoffman, as well as cases involving works of art.

Format: Paperback, 228 pages

Publisher: University Press of Kentucky (2005)

ISBN: 0813191254

Document Analysis

Elizabeth Bauchner

One in a series of brief works covering various topics in forensic science, this work explores the basics of document analysis.

Format: Hardcover, 112 pages

Publisher: Mason Crest (2005)

ISBN: 1422200299

Forensic Document Examination Techniques

Thomas W. Vastrick

This in-depth look at forgery and fraud, including handwriting, disguises, charred documents, counterfeiting, and anonymous messages, details how examiners conduct their duties and the assistance auditors can provide. It examines problems that arise in investigations and how to effectively reach scientific conclusions, and explores how to prepare a court case, including collection and preservation of evidence as well as testimony and legal issues.

Format: Paperback, 141 pages

Publisher: Institute of Internal Auditors Research Foundation (2004)

ISBN: 0894135414

Forensic Handwriting Identification: Fundamental Concepts and Principles

Ron M. Morris

This book covers basic principles and procedures in handwriting identification.

Format: Hardcover, 238 pages

Publisher: Academic Press (2000)

ISBN: 0125076401

Forensic Signature Examination

Steven A. Slyter and C. C. Thomas

This paperback covers the techniques, problems, and challenges of examining and comparing questioned signatures.

Format: Paperback, 117 pages

Publisher: Charles C. Thomas (1996)

ISBN: 039806542X

Handwriting Identification: Facts and Fundamentals

Jay Robert Nash

This book consolidates pertinent information from published and unpublished sources regarding handwriting identification. Written in a question-and-answer format, it suggests some of the questions that one might ask of an examiner and provides the answers that knowledgeable and competent examiners should be expected to give.

Format: Hardcover, 456 pages

Publisher: CRC Press (1999)

ISBN: 084931285X

Advanced Reading

Brunelle, Richard L., "Questioned Document Examination," in R. Saferstein, ed., *Forensic Science Handbook,* vol. l, 2nd ed. Upper Saddle River, N.J.: Prentice Hall, 2002.

Ellen, David, *The Scientific Examination of Documents—Methods and Techniques,* 3rd ed. Boca Raton, Fla.: Taylor & Francis, 2006.

Hilton, Ordway, "The Evolution of Questioned Document Examination in the Last 50 Years," *Journal of Forensic Sciences* 33 (1987): 1310.

Hilton, Ordway, *Scientific Examination of Questioned Documents,* rev. ed. Boca Raton, Fla.: Taylor & Francis, 1992.

Levinson, Jay, *Questioned Documents—A Lawyer's Handbook.* San Diego: Academic Press, 2001.

Chapter 17
Computer Forensics

Key Terms

bit—Short for *binary digit;* taking the form of either a one or a zero, it is the smallest unit of information on a machine.

byte—A group of eight bits.

central processing unit (CPU)—The main chip within the computer; also referred to as the brain of the computer. This microprocessor chip handles most of the operations (code and instructions) of the computer.

cluster—A group of sectors in multiples of two; typically the minimum space allocated to a file.

file slack—The area that begins at the end of the last sector that contains logical data and terminates at the end of the cluster.

hard disk drive (HDD)—Typically the main storage location within the computer, consisting of magnetic platters contained in a case.

hardware—The physical components of a computer: case, keyboard, monitor, motherboard, RAM, HDD, mouse, and so on. Generally speaking, if it is a computer component you can touch, it is hardware.

latent data—Areas of files and disks that are typically not apparent to the computer user (and often not to the operating system), but contain data nonetheless.

Message Digest 5 (MD5)/Secure Hash Algorithm (SHA)—A software algorithm used to "fingerprint" a file or contents of a disk; used to verify the integrity of data. In forensic analysis it is typically used to verify that an acquired image of suspect data was not altered during the process of imaging.

motherboard—The main system board of a computer (and many other electronic devices) that delivers power, data, and instructions to the computer's components.

operating system (OS)—Software that allows the user to interact with the hardware and manages the file system and applications.

partition—A contiguous set of blocks that are defined and treated as an independent disk.

RAM slack—The area beginning at the end of the logical file and terminating at the end of that sector. In some older operating systems this area is padded with information contained in RAM.

random-access memory (RAM)—The volatile memory of the computer; when power is turned off, its contents are lost. Programs and instructions are loaded into RAM while they are in use.

sector—The smallest unit of data addressable by a hard disk drive, generally consisting of 512 bytes.

software—A set of instructions compiled into a program that performs a particular task.

swap space—A file or defined space on the HDD to which data is written, or swapped, to free RAM for applications that are in use.

temporary files—Files temporarily written by an application to perform a function.

unallocated space—The area of the HDD that the operating system (file system table) sees as empty (containing no logical files) and ready for data. Simply stated, it is the unused portion of the HDD, but is not necessarily empty.

visible data—All data that the operating system is presently aware of, and thus is readily accessible to the user.

Learning Objectives

- List and describe the hardware and software components of a computer
- Understand the difference between read-only memory and random-access memory
- Describe how a hard disk drive is partitioned
- Describe the proper procedure for preserving computer evidence at a crime scene
- Understand the difference between and location of visible and latent data
- List the areas of the computer that will be examined to retrieve forensic data

Key Points

- Computer forensics involves preserving, acquiring, extracting, analyzing, and interpreting computer data.
- The central processing unit (CPU) is the brain of the computer—the main chip responsible for doing the actual computing.
- Random-access memory (RAM) is volatile memory, which is lost when power is turned off. Programs are loaded into RAM because of its faster read speed.
- The hard disk drive (HDD) is typically the primary location of data storage within the computer.
- Different operating systems map out (partition) HDDs in different manners, and examiners must be familiar with the file system they are examining.
- The types of computer evidence can be grouped under two major subheadings: visible and latent data.
- Visible data is data that the operating system is aware of, and thus is easily accessible to the user. It includes any type of user-created data, such as word-processing documents, spreadsheets, accounting records, databases, and pictures.
- Temporary files created by programs as a sort of backup on the fly can prove valuable as evidence. Data in the swap space (used to conserve the valu-

able RAM within the computer system) can also yield evidentiary data.

- Latent data is data that the operating system is not aware of. The constant shuffling of data through deletion, defragmentation, swapping, and so on is one of the ways data is stored in latent areas.

- Latent data can exist in both RAM slack and file slack. RAM slack is the area from the end of the logical file to the end of the sector. File slack is the remaining area from the end of the final sector containing data to the end of the cluster.

- Latent data might be found in unallocated space—space on a HDD that the operating system sees as empty and ready for data.

- When a user deletes files the data typically remains behind, so deleted files are another source of latent data.

Supplemental Questions

1. Describe the difference between software and media and give two examples of each.
2. What is the motherboard and why is it central to the functioning of a computer?
3. Define RAM and ROM and explain the difference between the two.
4. Define *input device* and *output device* and name three examples of each.
5. What is the most common storage device on most computers? Name three other types of storage devices.
6. What type of hardware device do personal computers typically use to communicate with one another? Name two ways this device can send and receive data.
7. What is the role of the operating system in a computer? Name three common operating systems.
8. Name and describe the two processes that must be performed on a hard disk drive (HDD) before it is ready for use.
9. What is a FAT and what is its purpose?
10. What is the forensic examiner's main goal when obtaining data from a HDD? Why is this best accomplished by removing the HDD from the system and placing it in a laboratory forensic computer?
11. Why does a forensic examiner take a "fingerprint" of a drive before and after imaging its contents?
12. What is a swap file and how is it useful for forensic examiners?
13. What is the difference between visible and latent data? How is latent data viewed?
14. What is file slack? How can it be useful to the forensic examiner?
15. What is unallocated space? Name three processes that cause latent data to be stored in unallocated space.

Answers to Supplemental Questions

1. Software programs are applications that carry out a set of instructions. Examples include operating systems, word-processing systems, Web browsers, accounting applications, and games. Media is a container for software and a device to load it onto a hard disk drive (HDD). Examples include CD-ROMs, DVDs, and floppy disks.
2. The motherboard is the main circuit board within a computer. The motherboard is central to the functioning of the computer because all computer peripherals and components—keyboard, mouse, CD-ROM drives, floppy disk drives, monitor, and so on—connect to the motherboard in one way or another.
3. ROM, or read-only memory, is a term used to describe memory chips on the motherboard that store programs that control the boot (start-up) process and configure a computer's components. RAM, or random-access memory, consists of memory chips where the computer temporarily stores data for quick retrieval so that it doesn't have to access the HDD constantly.
4. Input devices are equipment used to get data into the computer or to give the computer instructions. Examples include the keyboard, mouse, joystick, and scanner. Output devices are equipment through which data is obtained from the computer. Examples include the monitor, printer, and speakers.
5. The HDD is the most common storage device on most computers. Other types of storage devices include CDs, DVDs, floppy disks, Zip disks, USB thumb drives, smart media cards, and tapes.
6. Personal computers typically use a network interface card (NIC) to communicate with one another. NICs can send and receive data either through a physical wire connection or via radio waves.
7. The operating system provides the computer user with a working environment and facilitates interaction with the system's components. Three common operating systems are Windows, Macintosh, and Linux.
8. Before a HDD is ready for use, it must be partitioned and formatted. Partitioning consists of dividing the hard disk into logical areas in which data can be stored. Formatting determines how the HDD is divided, and how data is read from or written to it.
9. FAT stands for *file allocation table*. The FAT keeps track of the location of files and folders (data) stored on the HDD.
10. The forensic examiner's main goal when obtaining data from a hard disk drive is to do so without altering even one bit of data. The HDD is often removed from the system because booting (starting up) a HDD to its operating system changes many files and could potentially destroy evidentiary data.
11. The forensic examiner takes a "fingerprint" of the drive before and after imaging its contents to prove that the forensic image obtained from the drive

includes every bit of data and caused no changes (writes) to the HDD.

12. A swap file is a space on the hard disk drive where programs and data not presently being used are temporarily stored. The swap file allows the user to retrieve the stored data quickly without having to search the hard disk drive for it. Data that is swapped back and forth in this fashion is sometimes left behind in the swap file and may be recovered by a forensic examiner.

13. Visible data includes all information that the operating system is presently aware of, and thus is readily accessible to the user. Latent data includes data that are blocked (intentionally or not) from a user's view. It includes areas of files and disks that are typically not apparent to the computer user, but contain data nonetheless. Latent data is viewed with a utility that allows a user to examine the contents of a hard disk drive in the binary language used by the computer.

14. File slack is empty data storage space in a file cluster on a hard disk drive. File slack is useful to the forensic examiner because data from deleted files that once filled the slack space may remain behind on the hard disk drive.

15. Unallocated space is storage space on a hard disk drive that does not contain visible data. Three processes that store latent data in unallocated space are defragmenting a hard disk drive, swapping files, and deleting files.

Resources

Books

Computer Forensics and Cyber Crime: An Introduction

Marjie T. Britz

This book explores the current state of computer crime within the United States, evaluates forensic practices and software in light of government legislation, and analyzes emerging case law in a jurisprudential climate. It offers guidelines for the development of forensic computer laboratories, the creation of computer crime task forces, and search and seizures of electronic equipment.

Format: Paperback, 272 pages

Publisher: Prentice Hall (2004)

ISBN: 0130907588

Computer Forensics: Computer Crime Scene Investigation (with CD-ROM)

John R. Vacca

This book/CD package provides an overview of computer forensics including its definition, crime-scene investigation, seizure of data, determining the "fingerprints" of the crime, and tracking down the criminal. The book focuses on aspects of criminal investigation rather than information security.

Format: Paperback, 600 pages

Publisher: Charles River Media (2002)

ISBN: 1584500182

Cyber Forensics: A Field Manual for Collecting, Examining, and Preserving Evidence of Computer Crimes

Albert J. Marcella, Jr., and Robert S. Greenfield (Eds.)

This comprehensive examination of the issues, tools, and control techniques used to investigate illegal activities perpetuated through the use of information technology introduces the broad field of cyber forensics and presents the various tools and techniques designed to maintain control over electronic data. It includes information on identifying inappropriate uses of corporate IT, examining computing environments to identify and gather electronic evidence of wrongdoing, securing corporate systems from further misuse, and identifying individuals responsible for engaging in inappropriate acts.

Format: Paperback, 464 pages

Publisher: Auerbach (2002)

ISBN: 0849309557

Hacking Exposed: Computer Forensics

Chris Davis, Aaron Philipp, and David Cowen

This book focuses on providing tips on investigating computer crime, corporate malfeasance, and hacker break-ins. It offers expert information on procedures to prosecute violators while avoiding obstacles such as illicit searches, privacy violations, and illegally obtained evidence. The book also covers PDA and cell phone investigation techniques and real-world case studies.

Format: Paperback, 480 pages

Publisher: McGraw-Hill/Osborne Media (2004)

ISBN: 0072256753

Handbook of Computer Crime Investigation: Forensic Tools & Technology

Eoghan Casey

This handbook is a comprehensive introduction to the basic techniques and tools of computer forensics.

Format: Paperback, 448 pages

Publisher: Academic Press (2001)

ISBN: 0894135414

Incident Response and Computer Forensics

Chris Prosise, Kevin Mandia, and Matt Pepe

Written by FBI insiders, this book offers a look at the legal, procedural, and technical steps of incident response and computer forensics. It includes chapters on forensic analysis and remediation and real-world case studies.

Format: Hardcover, 544 pages

Publisher: McGraw-Hill/Osborne Media (2003)

ISBN: 007222696X

Real Digital Forensics: Computer Security and Incident Response (with CD-ROM)

Keith Jones, Richard Bejtlich, and Curtis W. Rose

A team of computer forensics experts walks the reader through six detailed computer investigations with the aid of a DVD that allows the user to follow along and practice. The intrusion data was generated by attacking live systems using the same tools and methods real-world attackers use. The evidence was captured and analyzed using the same tools the authors employ in their own investigations. Scenarios include cases ranging from intellectual property theft to SEC violations. Step-by-step investigation reveals practical techniques for overcoming the challenges forensics professionals face most often.

Format: Paperback, 688 pages

Publisher: Addison-Wesley (2005)

ISBN: 0321240693

Scene of the Cybercrime: Computer Forensics Handbook

Debra Littlejohn Shinder and Ed Tittel

This book introduces IT professionals to the highly structured world of law enforcement, where rules of evidence must be followed closely and crime scenes must not be contaminated. It also provides law enforcement officers with an understanding of the technical aspects of cybercrime and of how technology can be used to help solve crimes that have been committed.

Format: Hardcover, 752 pages

Publisher: Syngress (2002)

ISBN: 1931836655

Advanced Reading

Kruse, W. G., and J. G., Heiser, *Computer Forensics—Incident Response Essentials*. Boston: Addison-Wesley, 2001.

Nelson, B., A. Phillips, F. Enfinger, and C. Steuart, *Guide to Computer Forensics and Investigations*, 2nd ed. Boston: Thomson Course Technology, 2005.

Chapter 18

Forensic Science and the Internet

Key Terms

bookmark—A feature that allows the user to designate favorite Web sites for fast and easy access.

broadband—Describes any kind of Internet connection with a download speed of more than 56 kilobits per second.

browser—A program that allows a computer user to access Web sites.

cookies—Files placed on a computer from a visited Web site; they are used to track visits and usage of that site.

domain—A human-readable name and abbreviation for a Web site.

download—The transfer of a file through an Internet connection from a remote computer to a user's computer.

e-mail—Electronic mail.

firewall—Hardware or software designed to protect against intrusions into an Internet network.

hacking—Slang term for an unauthorized computer or network intrusion.

hypertext—Highlighted text or graphics on a Web page that, when clicked, links to other Web sites.

Internet cache—Portions of visited Web pages placed on the local hard disk drive to facilitate quicker retrieval once revisited.

Internet history—An accounting of Web sites visited. Different browsers store this information in different ways.

Internet protocol (IP)—The set of rules used to transmit packets of data over the Internet and route them to their destination.

Internet service provider (ISP)—A company that provides connections to the Internet.

mailing list—A list of people with a common interest who receive all the e-mails sent to the list.

modem—A device that connects a computer to another computer through a phone line.

newsgroups—Large bulletin board systems that consist of several thousand specialized discussion groups. Messages are posted to a bulletin board for others to read.

router—A device that manages traffic between computers belonging to a network, enabling them to share a connection to the Internet.

search engine—A Web site devoted to searching for information on the Internet using keywords.

uniform resource locator (URL)—A standard method by which Internet sites are addressed.

VoIP (voice over Internet protocol)—Transmission of the human voice over the Internet, usually through a telephone.

Wi-Fi—Technology that uses high-frequency radio signals to transmit and receive data over the Internet. Allows for a wireless connection to the Internet.

Learning Objectives

- Understand how the Internet is structured
- Know how to search for information on the Internet
- Describe information retrieval sources, such as mailing lists and newsgroups, available through the Internet
- Learn how to retrieve information about forensic science on the Internet
- Relate various areas found on the computer where a user's Internet activities can be investigated
- Describe how e-mails, chat, and instant messages on the Internet can be traced and recovered
- List and describe three locations where investigators may pinpoint the origin of a hacker

Key Points

- The major impact of the Internet on forensics will be to bring together forensic scientists from all parts of the world, linking them into one common electronic community.
- A single network consists of two or more computers that are connected to share information. The Internet can be defined as a "network of networks"—it connects thousands of networks so information can be exchanged worldwide.
- Connection to the Internet can be made through a modem, a device that allows computers to exchange and transmit information through telephone lines. Higher-speed broadband connections are available through cable lines or through DSL telephone lines. Computers can be linked or networked through wired or wireless (Wi-Fi) connections.
- Computers that participate in the Internet have a unique numerical Internet protocol (IP) address and usually a name.
- The most popular area of the Internet is the World Wide Web, a collection of pages stored in computers connected to the Internet throughout the world.
- Web browsers allow the user to explore information stored on the Web and to retrieve Web pages the viewer wishes to read.
- Several directories and indexes on the Internet, known as search engines, help users find information on a particular topic from the hundreds of thousands of Web sites located on the Internet. A keyword or phrase entered into a search engine locates sites on the Internet that are relevant to that subject.
- The service that is most commonly used in conjunction with the Internet is electronic mail (e-mail), a communication system that can transport messages across the world in a matter of seconds.
- Extensive information relating to forensic science is available on the Internet. The types of Web pages

range from simple explanations of the different fields of forensics to intricate details of forensic science specialties.

- Investigators seeking a history of an Internet user's destinations can take advantage of the fact that computers store or cache portions of Web pages visited. Also, Web sites often create cookies to track certain information about Web site visitors.

- An investigator tracking the origin of an e-mail seeks out the sender's IP address in the e-mail's header. Chat and instant messages are typically located in a computer's random-access memory (RAM).

- Determining the origin of unauthorized computer intrusions (hacking) requires investigating a computer's log file, RAM, and network traffic.

Supplemental Questions

1. What is a network? Why can the Internet be defined as a "network of networks"?

2. List four ways computers are connected to the Internet. Briefly explain how computers transmit information over each type of connection.

3. What is an IP address and who assigns it? What part does it play in organizing the Internet?

4. What is a domain? List five common domain abbreviations and explain what each represents.

5. What is a search engine and why are search engines useful? Why should you use more than one search engine for the same task?

6. What is the difference between a mailing list and a newsgroup? Which is likely to offer a larger amount of information?

7. What is an Internet cache and why is it of interest to forensic examiners?

8. What are cookies? What is their basic purpose and how are they used by forensic examiners?

9. Name two features in a Web browser that can be sources of information for forensic examiners. How would the examiner use each of these features?

10. What information in an e-mail message allows an investigator to identify the sender? How would the examiner use this information to identify the sender?

11. Why are online conversations conducted using chat and instant messaging more difficult to recover than e-mail messages? Where are files containing such conversations likely to be stored?

12. Why should an investigator not unplug a computer that may contain chat or instant message conversations?

13. What is a log file and how is it used to identify hackers? Name three locations on a computer network that may contain log files.

14. What is volatile data and how can it provide clues to the identity of a hacker?

15. How can network traffic help identify the source of an unwanted network intrusion?

Answers to Supplemental Questions

1. A network consists of two or more computers that are connected in some fashion to share information. The Internet can be defined as a "network of networks" because it connects thousands of networks together so that the information on them can be exchanged worldwide.

2. Four ways to connect a computer to the Internet are via a modem, DSL, a cable modem, and a Wi-Fi connection. A modem converts digital information to analog signals or sound waves that can be passed over a telephone line. DSL carries digital information on your regular telephone line without disturbing voice traffic. A cable modem transmits information over a TV cable line. Wi-Fi connections transmit information via radio waves, without the use of a physical connection between computers.

3. An IP address is a unique number assigned to each computer that is connected to the Internet. The number is assigned by the Internet service provider (ISP) the computer uses to connect to the Internet.

4. A domain is a human-readable name given to a computer connected to the Internet. Five common domain abbreviations are *.gov* (government), *.mil* (military), *.edu* (educational institution), *.com* (commercial Web site), and *.org* (nonprofit organization).

5. Search engines are directories and indexes found on the World Wide Web that help users search the Internet for information on particular topics. They are useful because they save a great deal of time sorting through the enormous amount of information available online. Multiple search engines should be used when researching a subject because each search engine has different capabilities and thus may provide different search results.

6. A mailing list is a discussion group for a selected topic in which related messages are sent directly to your mailbox through e-mail. A newsgroup networks many sites that are set up by local Internet providers that act as a bulletin board where articles (messages) about a particular subject are posted by subscribers. A newsgroup is likely to offer more information because it joins a significantly larger audience compared to a mailing list.

7. An Internet cache is a space on a computer's hard disk drive (HDD) in which information from Web pages is stored (cached) when the user is online. Because much of this information remains in the cache, the Internet cache is a potential source of evidence for the computer investigator. A forensic examiner can reconstruct portions of or even entire Web pages from data in the Internet cache, even after the files have been deleted.

8. Cookies are files placed on a computer's HDD by Web sites the user has visited. A cookie is used by the Web site to track certain information about its

visitors, often for sales and marketing purposes. Cookies are useful for forensic examiners because they can provide a history of the Web sites visited by the user of a particular computer.

9. Two features in a Web browser that can be sources of information for forensic examiners are the Internet history feature and the bookmark (or favorites) feature. Using the Internet history, an examiner can track all of the Web sites the user has visited for periods as long as several weeks. The bookmark feature can help an examiner learn more about a computer user's interests by showing what kinds of Web sites he or she visits frequently.

10. The IP address of the computer from which the message was sent can allow an investigator to identify the sender. To do so, the investigator researches the IP address in the e-mail to determine which Internet service provider was issued the block of IP addresses that included that particular number. The investigator then contacts the ISP to find out the name of the customer to whom it assigned that IP address.

11. These types of conversations are more difficult to recover because most of them are not saved by the parties involved. Files containing chat and instant messaging conversations are most likely to be stored in RAM.

12. Unplugging the computer will cause the data located in RAM to be lost, and RAM is where most chat and instant messaging conversations are likely to be stored.

13. Log files document the IP addresses of computers that connect to a network. These files can provide investigators with a list of potential suspects in hacking cases. Log files are found on the server that connects computers to the network, on the router that directs data to computers connected to the network, and on the firewall that blocks access to the network by unauthorized computers.

14. Volatile data is data stored in RAM. The data in RAM at the time of an intrusion may provide valuable clues into the identity of the intruder, or at the very least the method of attack.

15. Network traffic travels in the form of "data packets" that contain information as well as source and destination IP addresses. If a hacker tries to steal data from a network, the network needs to know the IP address of the hacker's computer to transmit the data to it. The investigation can use this IP information to track down the computer used in the attack.

Resources

Advanced Reading

Carrier, Brian, *File System Forensic Analysis*. Upper Saddle River, N.J.: Addison-Wesley, 2005.

Casad, J., *Sams Teach Yourself TCP/IP in 24 Hours,* 3rd ed. Indianapolis, Ind.: SAMS, 2004.

Chamakura, R. P., "Forensic Science and the Internet—Current Utilization and Future Potential," *Forensic Science Review* 9 (1997): 97.

Leshin, C. B., *Internet Investigations in Criminal Justice*. Upper Saddle River, N.J.: Prentice Hall, 1997.

Prosise, C., K. Mandia, and M. Peppe, *Incident Response and Computer Forensics,* 2nd ed. New York: McGraw-Hill, 2003.

FORENSIC SCIENCE

Ted Bundy, Serial Killer

The name Ted Bundy is synonymous with the term *serial killer*. This handsome, gregarious, and worldly onetime law student is believed to be responsible for forty murders between 1964 and 1978. His reign of terror stretched from the Pacific Northwest down to California and into Utah, Idaho, and Colorado, finally ending in Florida. His victims were typically young women, usually murdered with a blunt instrument or by strangulation, and sexually assaulted before and after death.

First convicted in Utah in 1976 on a charge of kidnapping, Bundy managed to escape after his extradition to Colorado on a murder charge. Ultimately, Bundy found his way to the Tallahassee area of Florida. There he unleashed mayhem, killing two women at a Florida State University sorority house and then murdering a 12-year-old girl three weeks later. Fortunately, future victims were spared when Bundy was arrested while driving a stolen vehicle. As police investigated the sorority murders, they noted that one victim, who had been beaten over the head with a log, raped, and strangled, also had bite marks on her left buttock and breast.

Supremely confident that he could beat the sorority murder charges, the arrogant Bundy insisted on acting as his own attorney. His unfounded optimism was shattered in the courtroom when a forensic odontologist matched the bite mark on the victim's buttock to Bundy's front teeth. Bundy was ultimately executed in 1989.

chapter 1

Introduction

Key Terms

expert witness

Locard's exchange principle

scientific method

Learning Objectives

After studying this chapter you should be able to:

- Define forensic science and list the major disciplines it encompasses.

- Recognize the major contributors to the development of forensic science

- Account for the rapid growth of forensic laboratories in the past forty years

- Describe the services of a typical comprehensive crime laboratory in the criminal justice system

- Compare and contrast the *Frye* and *Daubert* decisions relating to the admissibility of scientific evidence in the courtroom

- Explain the role and responsibilities of the expert witness

- List the specialized forensic services, aside from the crime laboratory, that are generally available to law enforcement personnel.

Definition and Scope of Forensic Science

Forensic science in its broadest definition is the application of science to law. As our society has grown more complex, it has become more dependent on rules of law to regulate the activities of its members. Forensic science applies the knowledge and technology of science to the definition and enforcement of such laws.

Each year, as government finds it increasingly necessary to regulate the activities that most intimately influence our daily lives, science merges more closely with civil and criminal law. Consider, for example, the laws and agencies that regulate the quality of our food, the nature and potency of drugs, the extent of automobile emissions, the kind of fuel oil we burn, the purity of our drinking water, and the pesticides we use on our crops and plants. It would be difficult to conceive of any food and drug regulation or environmental protection act that could be effectively monitored and enforced without the assistance of scientific technology and the skill of the scientific community.

Laws are continually being broadened and revised to counter the alarming increase in crime rates. In response to public concern, law enforcement agencies have expanded their patrol and investigative functions, hoping to stem the rising tide of crime. At the same time they are looking more to the scientific community for advice and technical support for their efforts. Can the technology that put astronauts on the moon, split the atom, and eradicated most dreaded diseases be enlisted in this critical battle?

Unfortunately science cannot offer final and authoritative solutions to problems that stem from a maze of social and psychological factors. However, as the contents of this book attests, science occupies an important and unique role in the criminal justice system—a role that relates to the scientist's ability to supply accurate and objective information that reflects the events that have occurred at a crime scene. A good deal of work remains to be done if the full potential of science as applied to criminal investigations is to be realized.

Considering the vast array of civil and criminal laws that regulate society, forensic science, in its broadest sense, has become so comprehensive a

FIGURE 1–1   **Scene from CSI, a forensic science television show.** *Courtesy Picture Desk, Inc./Kobal Collection*

subject as to make a meaningful introductory textbook treatment of its role and techniques difficult, if not overwhelming. For this reason, we must narrow the scope of the subject. Fortunately, common usage provides us with such a limited definition: **Forensic science is the application of science to the criminal and civil laws that are enforced by police agencies in a criminal justice system.** Forensic science is an umbrella term encompassing a myriad of professions that bring skills to bear to aid law enforcement officials in conducting their investigations.

The diversity of professions practicing forensic science is illustrated by the ten sections of The American Academy of Forensic Science, the largest forensic science organization in the world:

1. Criminalistics

2. Engineering Science

3. General

4. Jurisprudence

5. Odontology

6. Pathology/Biology

7. Physical Anthropology

8. Psychiatry and Behavioral Science

9. Questioned Documents

10. Toxicology

Even this list of professions is not exclusive. It does not encompass skills such as fingerprint examination, firearm and tool mark examination, computer and digital data analysis, and photography.

Obviously, any intent to author a book covering all of the major activities of forensic science as they apply to the enforcement of criminal and civil laws by police agencies would be a major undertaking. Thus, this book will restrict itself to discussions of the subjects of chemistry, biology, physics, geology, and computer technology, which are useful for determining the evidential value of crime-scene and related evidence. Forensic pathology, psychology, anthropology, and odontology encompass important and relevant areas of knowledge and practice in law enforcement, each being an integral part of the total forensic science service that is provided to any up-to-date criminal justice system. However, except for brief discussions, along with pointing the reader to relevent websites, these subjects go beyond the intended scope of this book, and the reader is referred elsewhere for discussions of their applications and techniques.[1] Instead, we will attempt to focus on the services of what has popularly become known as the crime laboratory, where the principles and techniques of the physical and natural sciences are practiced and applied to the analysis of crime-scene evidence.

For many, the term *criminalistics* seems more descriptive than **forensic science** for describing the services of a crime laboratory. Regardless of title—criminalist or forensic scientist—the trend of events has made the scientist in the crime laboratory an active participant in the criminal justice system.

History and Development of Forensic Science

Forensic science owes its origins first to the individuals who developed the principles and techniques needed to identify or compare physical evidence, and second to those who recognized the need to merge these principles into a coherent discipline that could be practically applied to a criminal justice system.

The roots of forensic science reach back many centuries, and history records a number of instances in which individuals used close observation of evidence and applied basic scientific principles to solve crimes. Not until relatively recently, however, did forensic science take on the more careful and systematic approach that characterizes the modern discipline.

Early Developments

One of the earliest records of applying forensics to solve criminal cases comes from third-century China. A manuscript titled *Yi Yu Ji* ("A Collection of Criminal Cases") reports how a coroner solved a case in which a woman was suspected of murdering her husband and burning the body, then claiming that he died in an accidental fire. Noticing that the husband's corpse had no ashes in its mouth, the coroner performed an experiment to test the woman's story. He burned two pigs—one alive and one dead—and then checked for ashes inside the mouth of each. He found ashes in the mouth of the pig that was alive before it was burned, but none in the mouth of the pig that was dead beforehand. The coroner thus concluded that the husband, too, was dead before his body was burned. Confronted with this evidence, the woman admitted her guilt. The Chinese were also among the first to recognize the potential of fingerprints as a means of identification.

While cases such as that of the Chinese coroner are noteworthy, this kind of scientific approach to criminal investigation was for many years the exception rather than the rule. Limited knowledge of anatomy and pathology hampered the development of forensic science until the late seventeeth and early eighteenth centuries. For example, the first recorded notes about fingerprint characteristics were prepared in 1686 by Marcello Malpighi, a professor of anatomy at the University of Bologna in Italy. Malpighi, however, did not acknowledge the value of fingerprints as a method of identification. The first scientific paper about the nature of fingerprints did not appear until more than a century later, but that work also did not recognize their potential as a form of identification.

Initial Scientific Advances

As physicians gained a greater understanding of the workings of the body, the first scientific treatises on forensic science began to appear, such as the 1798 work "A Treatise on Forensic Medicine and Public Health" by the French physician François-Emanuel Fodéré. Breakthroughs in chemistry at this time also helped forensic science take significant strides forward. In 1775, the Swedish chemist Carl Wilhelm Scheele devised the first successful test for detecting the poison arsenic in corpses. By 1806, the German chemist Valentin Ross had discovered a more precise method for detecting small amounts of arsenic in the walls of a victim's stomach. The most significant early figure in this area was Mathieu Orfila, a Spaniard who is considered the father of forensic toxicology. In 1814, Orfila published the first scientific treatise on the detection of poisons and their effects on animals. This treatise established forensic toxicology as a legitimate scientific endeavor.

FIGURE 1-2 Mathieu Orfila.
Courtesy The Granga Collection, New York

The mid-1800s saw a spate of advances in several scientific disciplines that furthered the field of forensic science. In 1828, William Nichol invented the polarizing microscope. Eleven years later, Henri-Louis Bayard formulated the first procedures for microscopic detection of sperm. Other developments during this time included the first microcrystalline test for hemoglobin (1853) and the first presumptive test for blood (1863). Such tests soon found practical applications in criminal trials. Toxicological evidence at trial was first used in 1839, when a Scottish chemist named James Marsh testified on the detection of arsenic in a victim's body. During the 1850s and 1860s, the new science of photography was also used in forensics, recording images of prisoners and crime scenes.

Late Nineteenth-Century Progress

By the late nineteenth-century, public officials were beginning to apply knowledge from virtually all scientific disciplines to the study of crime. Anthropology and morphology (the study of the structure of living organisms) were applied to the first system of personal identification, devised by the French scientist Alphonse Bertillon in 1879. Bertillon's system, which he dubbed *anthropometry,* was a systematic procedure that involved taking a series of body measurements as a means of distinguishing one individual from another. For nearly two decades, this system was considered the most accurate method of personal identification, before being replaced by fingerprinting in the early 1900s. Bertillon's early efforts earned him the distinction of being known as the father of criminal identification.

Bertillon's anthropometry, however, would soon be supplanted by the more reliable method of identification by fingerprinting. Two years before the publication of Bertillon's system, the U.S. microscopist Thomas Taylor suggested that fingerprints could be used as a means of identification, but his ideas were not immediately followed up. Three years later, the Scottish physician Henry Faulds made a similar assertion in a paper published in the journal *Nature.* However, the Englishman Francis Henry Galton undertook the first definitive study of fingerprints and developed a methodology of classifying them for filing. In 1892, Galton published a book titled *Finger Prints,* which contained the first statistical proof supporting the uniqueness of his method of personal identification. His work went on to describe the basic principles that form the present system of identification by fingerprints.

The first treatise describing the application of scientific disciplines to the field of criminal investigation was written by Hans Gross in 1893. Gross, a public prosecutor and judge in Graz, Austria, spent many years studying and developing principles of criminal investigation. In his classic book, *Handbuch für Untersuchungsrichter als System der Kriminalistik* (later published in English under the title *Criminal Investigation*), he detailed the assistance that investigators could expect from the fields of microscopy, chemistry, physics, mineralogy, zoology, botany, anthropometry, and fingerprinting. He later introduced the forensic journal *Archiv für Kriminal Anthropologie und Kriminalistik,* which still reports improved methods of scientific crime detection.

Ironically, the best-known figure in nineteenth-century forensics was not a real person, but a fictional character, the legendary detective Sherlock Holmes. Many people today believe that Holmes's creator, Sir Arthur Conan Doyle, had a considerable influence on popularizing scientific crime-detection methods. In adventures with his partner and biographer, Dr. John Watson, Holmes first applied the newly developing principles of

FIGURE 1–3 **Bertillon's system of bodily measurements as used for the identification of an individual.** *Courtesy Sirchie Finger Print Laboratories, Inc., Youngsville, N.C., www.sirchie.com*

serology (the study of blood and bodily fluids), fingerprinting, firearms identification, and questioned-document examination long before their value was recognized and accepted by real-life criminal investigators. Holmes's feats excited the imagination of an emerging generation of forensic scientists and criminal investigators. Even in the first Sherlock Holmes novel, *A Study in Scarlet,* published in 1887, we find examples of Doyle's uncanny ability to describe scientific methods of detection years before they were actually discovered and implemented. For instance, here Holmes probes and recognizes the potential usefulness of forensic serology to criminal investigation:

> "I've found it. I've found it," he shouted to my companion, running towards us with a test tube in his hand. "I have found a reagent which is precipitated by hemoglobin and by nothing else. . . . Why, man, it is the most practical medico-legal discovery for years. Don't you see that it gives us an infallible test for blood stains? . . . The old guaiacum test was very clumsy and uncertain. So is the microscopic examination for blood corpuscles. The latter is valueless if the stains are a few hours old. Now, this appears to act as well whether the blood is old or new. Had this test been invented, there are hundreds of men now walking the earth who would long ago have paid the penalty of their crimes. . . . Criminal cases are continually hinging upon that one point. A man is suspected of a crime months perhaps after it has been committed. His linen or clothes are examined and brownish stains discovered upon them. Are they blood stains, or rust stains, or fruit stains, or what are they? That is a question which has puzzled many an expert, and why? Because there was no reliable test. Now we have the Sherlock Holmes test, and there will no longer be any difficulty."

Twentieth-Century Breakthroughs

The pace of technological change quickened considerably in the twentieth century, and with it the rate of advancement in the field of forensic science. In 1901, Dr. Karl Landsteiner discovered that blood can be grouped into different categories, now recognized as the blood types A, B, AB, and O. The possibility that blood grouping could be useful in identifying an individual intrigued Dr. Leone Lattes, a professor at the Institute of Forensic Medicine at the University of Turin in Italy. In 1915, Lattes devised a relatively simple procedure for determining the blood group of a dried bloodstain, a technique that he immediately applied to criminal investigations.

At around the same time, Albert S. Osborn was conducting pioneering work in document examination. In 1910, Osborn wrote the first significant text in this field, *Questioned Documents*. This book is still considered a primary reference for document examiners. Osborn's development of the fundamental principles of document examination was responsible for the acceptance of documents as scientific evidence by the courts.

One of the most important contributors to the field in the early twentieth-century was the Frenchman Edmond Locard. Although Hans Gross was a pioneer advocate of the use of the scientific method in criminal investigation, Locard first demonstrated how the principles enunciated by Gross could be incorporated within a workable crime laboratory. Locard's formal education was in both medicine and law. In 1910, he persuaded the Lyons police department to give him two attic rooms and two assistants to start a police laboratory. During Locard's first years of work, the only available instruments were a microscope and a rudimentary spectrometer. However, his enthusiasm quickly overcame the technical and monetary deficiencies he encountered. From these modest beginnings, Locard's research and accomplishments became known throughout the world by forensic scientists and criminal investigators. Eventually he became the founder and director of the Institute of Criminalistics at the University of Lyons; this quickly developed into a leading international center for study and research in forensic science.

Locard asserted that when two objects come into contact with each other, a cross-transfer of materials occurs (Locard's exchange principle). He strongly believed that every criminal can be connected to a crime by dust particles carried from the crime scene. This concept was reinforced by a series of successful and well-publicized investigations. In one case, presented with counterfeit coins and the names of three suspects, Locard urged the police to bring the suspects' clothing to his laboratory. On careful examination, he located small metallic particles in all the garments. Chemical analysis revealed that the particles and coins were composed of exactly the same metallic elements. Confronted with this evidence, the suspects were arrested and soon confessed to the crime. After World War I,

Locard's exchange principle
When two objects come into contact with each other, a cross-transfer of materials occurs.

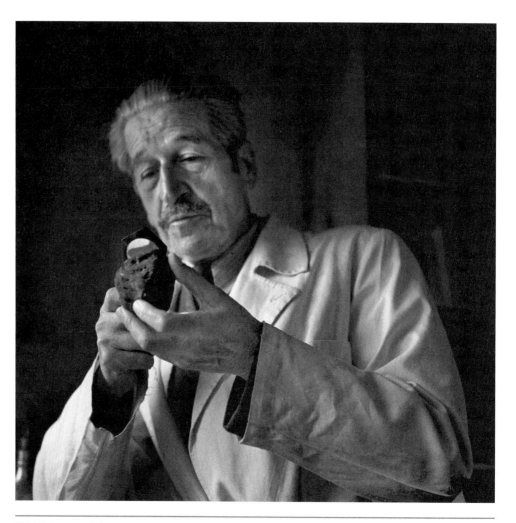

FIGURE 1–5 **Edmond Locard.** *Courtesy Collection of Roger-Viollet, The Image Works*

Locard's successes served as an impetus for the formation of police laboratories in Vienna, Berlin, Sweden, Finland, and Holland.

The microscope came into widespread use in forensic science during the twentieth century, and its applications grew dramatically. Perhaps the leading figure in the field of microscopy was Dr. Walter C. McCrone. During his lifetime, McCrone became the world's preeminent microscopist. Through his books, journal publications, and research institute, he was a tireless advocate for applying microscopy to analytical problems, particularly forensic science cases. McCrone's exceptional communication skills made him a much-sought-after instructor, and he educated thousands of forensic scientists throughout the world in the application of microscopic techniques. Dr. McCrone used microscopy, often in conjunction with other analytical methodologies, to examine evidence in thousands of criminal and civil cases throughout a long and illustrious career.

Another trailblazer in forensic applications of microscopy was U.S. Army Colonel Calvin Goddard, who refined the techniques of firearms examination by using the comparison microscope. Goddard's work allowed investigators to determine whether a particular gun has fired a bullet by comparing the bullet with one that has been test-fired from the suspect's weapon. His expertise established the comparison microscope as the indispensable tool of the modern firearms examiner.

Modern Scientific Advances

Since the mid-twentieth century, a revolution in computer technology has made possible a quantum leap forward in human knowledge. The resulting explosion of scientific advances has dramatically impacted the field of forensic science by introducing a wide array of sophisticated techniques for analyzing evidence related to a crime. Procedures such as chromatography, spectrophotometry, and electrophoresis (all discussed in later chapters) allow the modern forensic scientist to determine with astounding accuracy the identity of a suspect substance, and to connect even tiny fragments of evidence to a particular person and place.

The most significant modern advance in forensic science undoubtedly has been the discovery and refinement of DNA typing in the late twentieth and early twenty-first centuries. Sir Alec Jeffreys developed the first DNA profiling test in 1984, and two years later he applied it for the first time to solve a crime by identifying Colin Pitchfork as the murderer of two young English girls. The same case also marked the first time DNA profiling established the innocence of a criminal suspect. Made possible by scientific breakthroughs in the 1950s and 1960s, DNA typing offers law enforcement officials a powerful tool for establishing the precise identity of a suspect, even when only a small amount of physical evidence is available. Combined with the modern analytical tools mentioned earlier, DNA typing has revolutionized the practice of forensic science.

Another significant recent development in forensics is the establishment of computerized databases on physical evidence such as fingerprints, markings on bullets and shell casings, and DNA. These databases have proven to be invaluable, enabling law enforcement officials to compare evidence found at crime scenes to records of thousands of pieces of similar information. This has significantly reduced the time required to analyze evidence and increased the accuracy of the work done by police and forensic investigators.

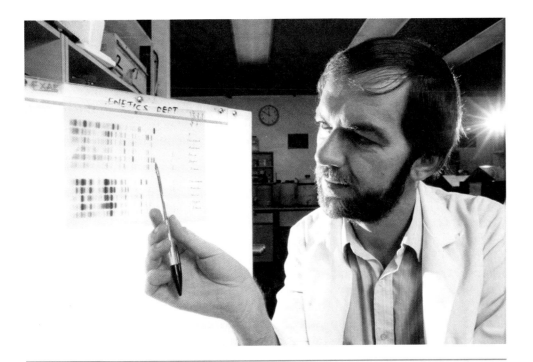

FIGURE 1–6   Sir Alec Jeffreys. *Courtesy Homer Sykes, Alamy Images Royalty Free*

While this brief narrative is by no means a complete summary of historical advances in forensics, it provides an idea of the progress made in the field by dedicated scientists and law enforcement personnel. Even Sherlock Holmes probably couldn't have imagined the lengths to which science today is applied in the service of criminal investigation.

Key Points

- Forensic science is the application of science to criminal and civil laws that are enforced by police agencies in a criminal justice system.

- The first system of personal identification was called anthropometry. It distinguished one individual from another based on a series of body measurements.

- Forensic science owes its origins to individuals such as Bertillon, Galton, Lattes, Goddard, Osborn, and Locard, who developed the principles and techniques needed to identify or compare physical evidence.

- Locard's exchange principle states that when two objects come into contact with each other, a cross-transfer of materials occurs that can connect a criminal suspect to his or her victim.

Crime Laboratories

The steady advance of forensic science technologies during the twentieth century led to the establishment of the first facilities specifically dedicated to forensic analysis of criminal evidence. These crime laboratories are now the centers for both forensic investigation of ongoing criminal cases and research into new techniques and procedures to aid investigators in the future.

History of Crime Labs in the United States

The oldest forensic laboratory in the United States is that of the Los Angeles Police Department, created in 1923 by August Vollmer, a police chief from Berkeley, California. In the 1930s, Vollmer headed the first U.S. university institute for criminology and criminalistics at the University of California at Berkeley. However, this institute lacked any official status in the university until 1948, when a school of criminology was formed. The famous criminalist Paul Kirk was selected to head its criminalistics department. Many graduates of this school have gone on to develop forensic laboratories in other parts of the state and country.

In 1932, the Federal Bureau of Investigation (FBI), under the directorship of J. Edgar Hoover, organized a national laboratory that offered forensic services to all law enforcement agencies in the country. During its formative stages, Hoover consulted extensively with business executives, manufacturers, and scientists whose knowledge and experience guided the new facility through its infancy. The FBI Laboratory is now the world's largest forensic laboratory, performing more than one million examinations every year. Its accomplishments have earned it worldwide recognition, and its structure and organization have served as a model for forensic laboratories formed at the state and local levels in the United States as well as in other countries. Furthermore, the opening of the FBI's Forensic Science Research and Training Center in 1981 gave the United States, for the

(a)   (b)

FIGURE 1–7   (a) Exterior and (b) interior views of the FBI crime laboratory in Quantico, Virginia. *Courtesy AP Wide World Photos*

first time, a facility dedicated to conducting research to develop new and reliable scientific methods that can be applied to forensic science. This facility is also used to train crime laboratory personnel in the latest forensic science techniques and methods.

Despite the existence of the FBI Laboratory, the United States has no national system of forensic laboratories. Instead, many local law enforcement jurisdictions—city, county, and state—around the country each operate their own independent crime labs. California, for example, has numerous federal, state, county, and city crime laboratories, many of which operate independently. However, in 1972 the California Department of Justice created a network of integrated state-operated crime laboratories consisting of regional and satellite facilities. An informal exchange of information and expertise occurs within California's criminalist community through a regional professional society, the California Association of Criminalists. This organization was the forerunner of a number of regional organizations that have developed throughout the United States to foster cooperation among the nation's growing community of criminalists.

Organization of a Crime Laboratory

The development of crime laboratories in the United States has been characterized by rapid growth accompanied by a lack of national and regional planning and coordination. Approximately 350 public crime laboratories operate at various levels of government—federal, state, county, and municipal. The size and diversity of crime laboratories make it impossible to select any one model that best describes a typical crime laboratory. Although most of these facilities function as part of a police department, others operate under the direction of the prosecutor's or district attorney's office; some work with the laboratories of the medical examiner or coroner. Far fewer are affiliated with universities or exist as independent agencies in government. Laboratory staff sizes range from one person to more than 100, and their services may be diverse or specialized, depending on the responsibilities of the agency that houses the laboratory.

The Growth of Crime Laboratories   Crime laboratories have mostly been organized by agencies that either foresaw their potential application to criminal investigation or were pressed by the increasing demands of casework. Several reasons explain the unparalleled growth of crime laboratories during the past forty years. Supreme Court decisions in the 1960s compelled police to place greater emphasis on securing scientifically evaluated evidence. The requirement to advise criminal suspects of their constitutional rights and their right of immediate access to counsel has all but eliminated confessions as a routine investigative tool. Successful prosecution of criminal cases requires a thorough and professional police investigation, frequently incorporating the skills of forensic science experts. Modern technology has provided forensic scientists with many new skills and techniques to meet the challenges accompanying their increased participation in the criminal justice system.

Coinciding with changing judicial requirements has been the staggering increase in crime rates in the United States over the past forty years. This factor alone would probably have accounted for the increased use of crime laboratory services by police agencies, but only a small percentage of police investigations generate evidence requiring scientific examination. There is, however, one important exception to this observation: drug-related arrests. All illicit-drug seizures must be sent to a forensic laboratory for confirmatory chemical analysis before the case can be adjudicated. Since the mid-1960s, drug abuse has accelerated to nearly uncontrollable levels and has resulted in crime laboratories being inundated with drug specimens.

A more recent impetus leading to the growth and maturation of crime laboratories has been the advent of DNA profiling. Since the early 1990s, this technology has progressed to the point at which traces of bloodstains; semen stains; hair; and saliva residues left behind on stamps, cups, bite marks, and so on have made possible the individualization or near-individualization of biological evidence. To meet the demands of DNA technology, crime labs have expanded staff and in many cases modernized their physical plants. While drug cases still far outnumber DNA cases, the labor-intensive demands and sophisticated technology requirements of the latter have affected the structure of the forensic laboratory as has no other technology in the past fifty years. Likewise, DNA profiling has become the dominant factor in explaining how the general public perceives the workings and capabilities of the modern crime laboratory.

In coming years an estimated ten thousand forensic scientists will be added to the rolls of both public and private forensic laboratories to process crime-scene evidence for DNA and to acquire DNA profiles, as mandated by state laws, from the hundreds of thousands of individuals convicted of crimes. This will more than double the number of scientists currently employed by forensic laboratories in the United States. These DNA profiles are continually added to state and national DNA data banks, which have proven to be invaluable investigative resources for law enforcement. The United States has a substantial backlog of samples requiring DNA analysis. Approximately 200,000 to 300,000 convicted-offender samples and more than 540,000 evidentiary samples, for which no suspect has been located, remain to be analyzed nationwide.

Crime Laboratories in the United States   Historically, a federal system of government, combined with a desire to retain local control, has produced a variety of independent laboratories in the United States, precluding the creation of a national system. Crime laboratories to a large extent mirror the fragmented law enforcement structure that exists on the national, state, and local levels. The federal government has no single law enforcement or investigative agency with unlimited jurisdiction.

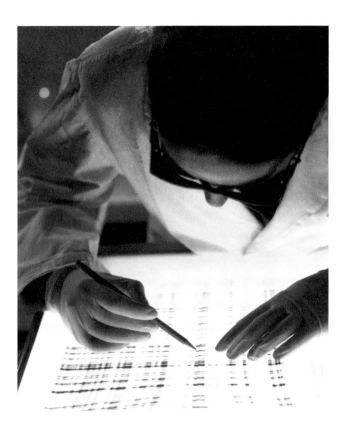

FIGURE 1–8 **A forensic scientist performing DNA analysis.** *Courtesy Mauro Fermariello, Photo Researchers, Inc.*

Four major federal crime laboratories have been created to help investigate and enforce criminal laws that extend beyond the jurisdictional boundaries of state and local forces. The FBI (Department of Justice) maintains the largest crime laboratory in the world. An ultramodern facility housing the FBI's forensic science services is located in Quantico, Virginia. Its expertise and technology support its broad investigative powers. The Drug Enforcement Administration laboratories (Department of Justice) analyze drugs seized in violation of federal laws regulating the production, sale, and transportation of drugs. The laboratories of the Bureau of Alcohol, Tobacco, Firearms and Explosives (Department of Justice) analyze alcoholic beverages and documents relating to alcohol and firearm excise tax law enforcement and examine weapons, explosive devices, and related evidence to enforce the Gun Control Act of 1968 and the Organized Crime Control Act of 1970. The U.S. Postal Inspection Service maintains laboratories concerned with criminal investigations relating to the postal service. Each of these federal facilities offers its expertise to any local agency that requests assistance in relevant investigative matters.

Most state governments maintain a crime laboratory to service state and local law enforcement agencies that do not have ready access to a laboratory. Some states, such as Alabama, California, Illinois, Michigan, New Jersey, Texas, Washington, Oregon, Virginia, and Florida, have developed a comprehensive statewide system of regional or satellite laboratories. These operate under the direction of a central facility and provide forensic services to most areas of the state. The concept of a regional laboratory operating as part of a statewide system has increased the accessibility of many local law enforcement agencies to a crime laboratory, while minimizing duplication of services and ensuring maximum interlaboratory cooperation through the sharing of expertise and equipment.

Local laboratories provide services to county and municipal agencies. Generally, these facilities operate independently of the state crime laboratory and are financed directly by local government. However, as costs have risen, some counties have combined resources and created multicounty laboratories to service their jurisdictions. Many of the larger cities in the United States maintain their own crime laboratories, usually under the direction of the local police department. Frequently, high population and high crime rates combine to make a municipal facility, such as that of New York City, the largest crime laboratory in the state.

Crime Laboratories Abroad   Like the United States, most countries in the world have created and now maintain forensic facilities. In contrast to the American system of independent local laboratories, Great Britain has developed a national system of regional laboratories under the direction of the government's Home Office. England and Wales are serviced by six regional laboratories, including the Metropolitan Police Laboratory (established in 1935), which services London. In the early 1990s, the British Home Office reorganized the country's forensic laboratories into the Forensic Science Service and instituted a system in which police agencies are charged a fee for services rendered by the laboratory. The fees are based on "products," or a set of examinations that are packaged together and designed to be suitable for particular types of physical evidence. The fee-for-service concept has encouraged the creation of a number of private laboratories that provide services to both police and criminal defense attorneys. One such laboratory, Forensic Alliance, has two facilities employing more than one hundred forensic scientists.

In Canada, forensic services are provided by three government-funded institutes: (1) six Royal Canadian Mounted Police regional laboratories, (2) the Centre of Forensic Sciences in Toronto, and (3) the Institute of Legal Medicine and Police Science in Montreal. Altogether, more than a hundred countries throughout the world have at least one laboratory facility offering forensic science services.

Services of the Crime Laboratory

Bearing in mind the independent development of crime laboratories in the United States, the wide variation in total services offered in different communities is not surprising. There are many reasons for this, including (1) variations in local laws, (2) the different capabilities and functions of the organization to which a laboratory is attached, and (3) budgetary and staffing limitations.

In recent years, many local crime laboratories have been created solely to process drug specimens. Often these facilities were staffed with few personnel and operated under limited budgets. Although many have expanded their forensic services, some still primarily perform drug analyses. However, even among crime laboratories providing services beyond drug identification, the diversity and quality of services rendered varies significantly. For the purposes of this text, I have arbitrarily designated the following units as those that should constitute a "full-service" crime laboratory.

Physical science unit. The physical science unit applies principles and techniques of chemistry, physics, and geology to the identification and comparison of crime-scene evidence. It is staffed by criminalists who have the expertise to use chemical tests and modern analytical instrumentation to examine items as diverse as drugs, glass, paint, explosives, and soil. In a laboratory that has a staff large enough to permit specialization, the responsibilities of this unit may be further subdivided into drug identification, soil and mineral analyses, and examination of a variety of trace physical evidence.

Biology unit. The biology unit is staffed with biologists and biochemists who identify and perform DNA profiling on dried bloodstains and other body fluids, compare hairs and fibers, and identify and compare botanical materials such as wood and plants.

Firearms unit. The firearms unit examines firearms, discharged bullets, cartridge cases, shotgun shells, and ammunition of all types. Garments and other objects are also examined to detect firearms discharge residues and to approximate the distance from a target at which a weapon was fired. The basic principles of firearms examination are also applied here to the comparison of marks made by tools.

Document examination unit. The documentation unit studies the handwriting and typewriting on questioned documents to ascertain authenticity and/or source. Related responsibilities include analyzing paper and ink and examining indented writings (the term usually applied to the partially visible depressions appearing on a sheet of paper underneath the one on which the visible writing appears), obliterations, erasures, and burned or charred documents.

Photography unit. A complete photographic laboratory examines and records physical evidence. Its procedures may require the use of highly

FIGURE 1–9 **A forensic analyst examining a firearm.** *Courtesy Mediacolors, Alamy Images*

specialized photographic techniques, such as digital imaging, infrared, ultraviolet, and X-ray photography, to make invisible information visible to the naked eye. This unit also prepares photographic exhibits for courtroom presentation.

Optional Services Provided by Full-Service Crime Laboratories

Toxicology unit. The toxicology group examines body fluids and organs to determine the presence or absence of drugs and poisons. Frequently, such functions are shared with or may be the sole responsibility of a separate laboratory facility placed under the direction of the medical examiner's or coroner's office. In most jurisdictions, field instruments such as the Intoxilyzer are used to determine the alcoholic consumption of individuals. Often the toxicology section also trains operators and maintains and services these instruments.

Latent fingerprint unit. The latent fingerprint unit processes and examines evidence for latent fingerprints when they are submitted in conjunction with other laboratory examinations.

Polygraph unit. The polygraph, or lie detector, has come to be recognized as an essential tool of the criminal investigator rather than the forensic scientist. However, during the formative years of polygraph technology, many police agencies incorporated this unit into the laboratory's administrative structure, where it sometimes remains today. In any case, its functions are handled by people trained in the techniques of criminal investigation and interrogation.

Voiceprint analysis unit. In cases involving telephoned threats or tape-recorded messages, investigators may require the skills of the voiceprint analysis unit to tie the voice to a particular suspect. To this end, a good deal of casework has been performed with the sound spectrograph, an instrument that transforms speech into a visual graphic display called a *voiceprint*. The validity of this technique as a means of personal identification rests on the premise that the sound patterns produced in speech are unique to the individual and that the voiceprint displays this uniqueness.

Crime-scene investigation unit. The concept of incorporating crime-scene evidence collection into the total forensic science service is slowly gaining recognition in the United States. This unit dispatches specially trained personnel (civilian and/or police) to the crime scene to collect and preserve physical evidence that will later be processed at the crime laboratory.

Whatever the organizational structure of a forensic science laboratory may be, specialization must not impede the overall coordination of services demanded by today's criminal investigator. Laboratory administrators need to keep open the lines of communication between analysts (civilian and uniform), crime-scene investigators, and police personnel. Inevitably, forensic investigations require the skills of many individuals. One notoriously high-profile investigation illustrates this process—the search for the source of the anthrax letters mailed shortly after September 11, 2001. Figure 1–10 shows one of the letters and illustrates the multitude of skills required in the investigation—skills possessed by forensic chemists and biologists, fingerprint examiners, and forensic document examiners.

Other Forensic Science Services Even though this textbook is devoted to describing the services normally provided by a crime laboratory, the field of forensic science is by no means limited to the areas covered in this book.

WebExtra 1.1
Take a Virtual Tour of a
Forensic Laboratory
www.prenhall.com/hsforensics

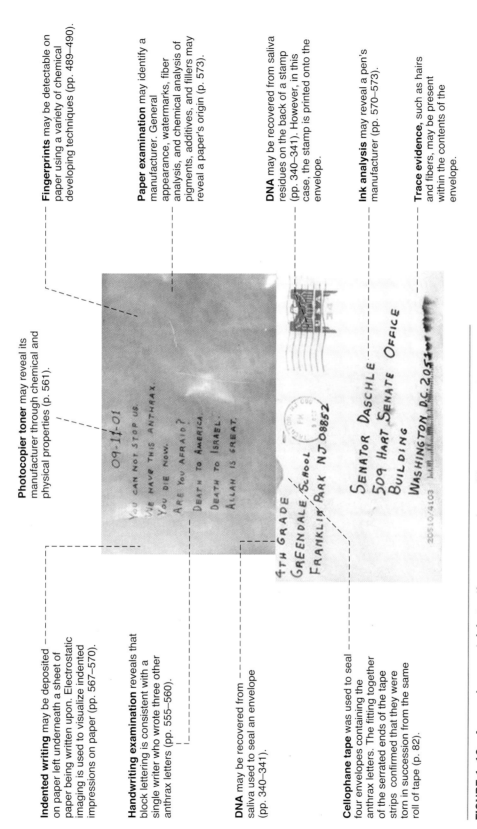

Fingerprints may be detectable on paper using a variety of chemical developing techniques (pp. 489–490).

Paper examination may identify a manufacturer. General appearance, watermarks, fiber analysis, and chemical analysis of pigments, additives, and fillers may reveal a paper's origin (p. 573).

DNA may be recovered from saliva residues on the back of a stamp (pp. 340–341). However, in this case, the stamp is printed onto the envelope.

Ink analysis may reveal a pen's manufacturer (pp. 570–573).

Trace evidence, such as hairs and fibers, may be present within the contents of the envelope.

Photocopier toner may reveal its manufacturer through chemical and physical properties (p. 561).

Indented writing may be deposited on paper left underneath a sheet of paper being written upon. Electrostatic imaging is used to visualize indented impressions on paper (pp. 567–570).

Handwriting examination reveals that block lettering is consistent with a single writer who wrote three other anthrax letters (pp. 555–560).

DNA may be recovered from saliva used to seal an envelope (pp. 340–341).

Cellophane tape was used to seal four envelopes containing the anthrax letters. The fitting together of the serrated ends of the tape strips confirmed that they were torn in succession from the same roll of tape (p. 82).

FIGURE 1–10 An envelope containing anthrax spores along with an anonymous letter was sent to the office of Senator Tom Daschle shortly after the terrorist attacks of September 11, 2001. A variety of forensic skills were used to examine the envelope and letter. Also, bar codes placed on the front and back of the envelope by mail-sorting machines contain address information and information about where the envelope was first processed.

Courtesy Getty Images, Inc.—Liaison

A number of specialized forensic science services outside the crime laboratory are routinely available to law enforcement personnel. These services are important aids to a criminal investigation and require the involvement of individuals who have highly specialized skills.

Three specialized forensic services—forensic pathology, forensic anthropology, and forensic entomology—are frequently employed at a murder scene and will be discussed at greater length when we examine crime-scene procedures in Chapter 2. Other services, such as those discussed next, are used in a wide variety of criminal investigations.

Forensic psychiatry. Forensic psychiatry is a specialized area that examines the relationship between human behavior and legal proceedings. Forensic psychiatrists are retained for both civil and criminal litigations. In civil cases, they typically perform tasks such as determining whether an individual is competent to make decisions about preparing a will, settling property, or refusing medical treatment. In criminal cases, forensic psychologists evaluate behavioral disorders and determine whether defendants are competent to stand trial. Forensic psychiatrists also examine behavior patterns of criminals as an aid in developing a suspect's behavioral profile.

Forensic odontology. Practitioners of forensic odontology help identify victims based on dental evidence when the body is left in an unrecognizable state. Teeth are composed of enamel, the hardest substance in the body. Because of enamel's resilience, the teeth outlast tissues and organs as decomposition begins. The characteristics of teeth, their alignment, and the overall structure of the mouth provide individual evidence for identifying a specific person. With the use of dental records such as X-rays and dental casts or even a photograph of the person's smile, a set of dental remains can be compared to a suspected victim. Another application of forensic odontology to criminal investigations is bite mark analysis. Bite marks are sometimes left on the victim in assault cases. A forensic

(a)

(b)

FIGURE 1–11   (a) Bite mark on victim's body. (b) Comparison to suspect's teeth.
Courtesy David Sweet, DMD, Ph.D., DABFO BOLD Forensic Laboratory, Vancouver, B.C., Canada

odontologist can compare the marks left on a victim and the tooth structure of the suspect.

Forensic engineering. Forensic engineers are concerned with failure analysis, accident reconstruction, and causes and origins of fires or explosions. Forensic engineers answer questions such as these: How did an accident or structural failure occur? Were the parties involved responsible? If so, how were they responsible? Accident scenes are examined, photographs are reviewed, and any mechanical objects involved are inspected.

Forensic computer and digital analysis. Forensic computer science is a new and fast-growing field that involves identifying, collecting, preserving, and examining information derived from computers and other digital devices, such as cell phones. Law enforcement aspects of this work normally involve recovering deleted or overwritten data from a computer's hard drive and tracking hacking activities within a compromised system. This field of forensic computer analysis will be addressed in detail in Chapters 17 and 18.

WebExtra 1.2

Explore Forensic Dentistry
www.prenhall.com/hsforensics

Key Points

- The development of crime laboratories in the United States has been characterized by rapid growth accompanied by a lack of national and regional planning and coordination.

- Four major reasons for the increase in the number of crime laboratories in the United States since the 1960s are as follows: (1) The fact that the requirement to advise criminal suspects of their constitutional rights and their right of immediate access to counsel has all but eliminated confessions as a routine investigative tool; (2) the staggering increase in crime rates in the United States; (3) the fact that all illicit-drug seizures must be sent to a forensic laboratory for confirmatory chemical analysis before the case can be adjudicated in court; and (4) the advent of DNA profiling.

- The technical support provided by crime laboratories can be assigned to five basic services: the physical science unit, the biology unit, the firearms unit, the document examination unit, and the photography unit.

- Some crime laboratories offer optional services such as toxicology, fingerprint analysis, polygraph administration, voiceprint analysis, and crime-scene investigation.

- Special forensic science services available to the law enforcement community include forensic pathology, forensic anthropology, forensic entomology, forensic psychiatry, forensic odontology, forensic engineering, and forensic computer and digital analysis.

The Functions of the Forensic Scientist

Although a forensic scientist relies primarily on scientific knowledge and skill, only half of the job is performed in the laboratory. The other half takes place in the courtroom, where the ultimate significance of the evidence is determined. The forensic scientist must not only analyze physical evidence but also persuade a jury to accept the conclusions derived from that analysis.

Analyzing of Physical Evidence

First and foremost the forensic scientist must be skilled in applying the principles and techniques of the physical and natural sciences to analyze the many types of physical evidence that may be recovered during a criminal investigation. Of the three major avenues available to police investigators for assistance in solving a crime—confessions, eyewitness accounts by victims or witnesses, and the evaluation of physical evidence retrieved from the crime scene—only physical evidence is free of inherent error or bias.

Criminal cases are replete with examples of individuals who were incorrectly charged with and convicted of committing a crime because of faulty memories or lapses in judgment. For example, investigators may be led astray during their preliminary evaluation of the events and circumstances surrounding the commission of a crime. These errors might be compounded by misleading eyewitness statements and inappropriate confessions. These same concerns don't apply to physical evidence.

What about physical evidence allows investigators to sort out facts as they are and not what one wishes they were? The hallmark of physical evidence is that it must undergo scientific inquiry. Science derives its integrity from adherence to strict guidelines that ensure careful and systematic collection, organization, and analysis of information—a process known as the scientific method. The underlying principles of the scientific method provide a safety net to ensure that the outcome of an investigation is not tainted by human emotion or compromised by distorting, belittling, or ignoring contrary evidence.

scientific method
A process that uses strict guidelines to ensure careful and systematic collection, organization, and analysis of information.

The scientific method begins by formulating a question worthy of investigation, such as who committed a particular crime. The investigator next formulates a hypothesis, a reasonable explanation proposed to answer the question. What follows is the basic foundation of scientific inquiry—the testing of the hypothesis through experimentation. The testing process must be thorough and recognized by other scientists as valid. Scientists and investigators must accept the experimental findings even when they wish they were different. Finally, when the hypothesis is validated by experimentation, it becomes suitable as scientific evidence, appropriate for use in a criminal investigation and ultimately available for admission in a court of law.

Determining Admissibility of Evidence   In rejecting the scientific validity of the lie detector (polygraph), the District of Columbia Circuit Court in 1923 set forth what has since become a standard guideline for determining the judicial admissibility of scientific examinations. In *Frye* v. *United States*,[2] the court ruled that in order to be admitted as evidence at trial, the questioned procedure, technique, or principles must be "generally accepted" by a meaningful segment of the relevant scientific community. In practice, this approach requires the proponent of a scientific test to present to the court a collection of experts who can testify that the scientific issue before the court is generally accepted by the relevant members of the scientific community. Furthermore, in determining whether a novel technique meets criteria associated with "general acceptance," courts have frequently taken note of books and papers written on the subject, as well as prior judicial decisions relating to the reliability and general acceptance of the technique.

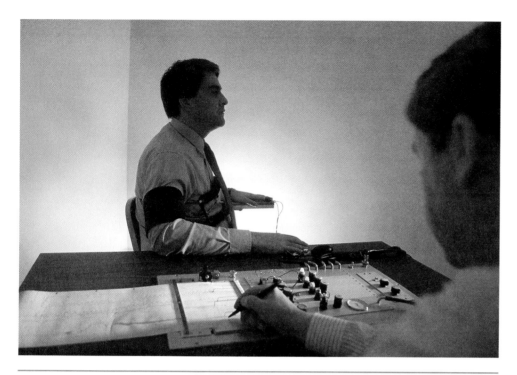

FIGURE 1–12   An individual undergoing a polygraph test. *Courtesy Woodfire Camp & Associates*

In recent years many observers have questioned whether this approach is sufficiently flexible to deal with new scientific issues that may not have gained widespread support within the scientific community.

The Federal Rules of Evidence offer an alternative to the *Frye* standard, one that some courts believe espouses a more flexible standard for admitting scientific evidence. Part of the Federal Rules of Evidence governs the admissibility of all evidence, including expert testimony, in federal courts, and many states have adopted codes similar to those of the Federal Rules. Specifically, Rule 702 of the Federal Rules of Evidence sets a different standard from "general acceptance" for admissibility of expert testimony. Under this standard, a witness "qualified as an expert by knowledge, skill, experience, training, or education" may offer expert testimony on a scientific or technical matter if "(1) the testimony is based upon sufficient facts or data, (2) the testimony is the product of reliable principles and methods, and (3) the witness has applied the principles and methods reliably to the facts of the case."

In a landmark ruling in the 1993 case of *Daubert* v. *Merrell Dow Pharmaceuticals, Inc.,*[3] the U.S. Supreme Court asserted that "general acceptance," or the *Frye* standard, is not an absolute prerequisite to the admissibility of scientific evidence under the Federal Rules of Evidence. According to the Court, the Rules of Evidence—especially Rule 702—assign to the trial judge the task of ensuring that an expert's testimony rests on a reliable foundation and is relevant to the case. Although this ruling applies only to federal courts, many state courts are expected to use this decision as a guideline in setting standards for the admissibility of scientific evidence.

Judging Scientific Evidence   In *Daubert,* the Court advocates that trial judges assume the ultimate responsibility for acting as a "gatekeeper" in judging the admissibility and reliability of scientific evidence presented in their courts. The Court offered some guidelines as to how a judge can gauge the veracity of scientific evidence, emphasizing that the inquiry should be flexible. Suggested areas of inquiry include the following:

1. Whether the scientific technique or theory can be (and has been) tested
2. Whether the technique or theory has been subject to peer review and publication
3. The technique's potential rate of error
4. Existence and maintenance of standards controlling the technique's operation
5. Whether the scientific theory or method has attracted widespread acceptance within a relevant scientific community

Some legal experts have expressed concern that abandoning *Frye*'s general-acceptance test will result in the introduction of absurd and irrational pseudoscientific claims in the courtroom. The Supreme Court rejected these concerns, pointing out the inherent strengths of the American judicial process in identifying unreliable evidence:

> In this regard the respondent seems to us to be overly pessimistic about the capabilities of the jury and of the adversary system generally. Vigorous cross-examination, presentation of contrary evidence, and careful instruction on the burden of proof are the traditional and appropriate means of attacking shaky but admissible evidence.

In a 1999 decision, *Kumho Tire Co., Ltd.* v. *Carmichael,*[4] the Court unanimously ruled that the "gatekeeping" role of the trial judge applied not only to scientific testimony, but to all expert testimony:

> We conclude that *Daubert*'s general holding—setting forth the trial judge's general "gatekeeping" obligation—applies not only to testimony based on "scientific" knowledge, but also to testimony based on "technical" and "other specialized" knowledge. . . . We also conclude that a trial court may consider one or more of the more specific factors that *Daubert* mentioned when doing so will help determine that testimony's reliability. But, as the Court stated in *Daubert,* the test of reliability is "flexible," and *Daubert*'s list of specific factors neither necessarily nor exclusively applies to all experts in every case.

The case of *Coppolino* v. *State*[5] (examined more closely in the following case study) exemplifies the flexibility and wide discretion that the *Daubert* ruling, twenty-five years later, apparently gave to trial judges in matters of scientific inquiry. The issue at question was whether the results of a new procedure that have not been widely accepted in the scientific community are necessarily inadmissible as evidence. The court rejected this argument, recognizing that researchers must devise new scientific tests to solve the special problems that continually arise in the forensic laboratory.

The *Coppolino* ruling acknowledged that even well-established scientific procedures were once new and unproven, and noted the court's duty to protect the public when weighing the admissibility of a new test. In the words of the concurring opinion, "Society need not tolerate homicide until there develops a body of medical literature about some particular lethal agent." The court emphasized, however, that although these tests may be new and unique, they are admissible only if they are based on scientifically valid principles and techniques.

Case Study

Dr. Coppolino's Deadly House Calls

A frantic late-night telephone call to Dr. Juliette Karow brought her to the Longport Key, Florida, home of Drs. Carl and Carmela Coppolino. Carl had called for Dr. Karow's help because he believed Carmela was dying. He said she had complained of chest pains earlier in the evening and he was certain she had suffered a heart attack. Dr. Karow arrived to find Carmela beyond help.

Although Dr. Karow felt that the scene in the room appeared staged, and her own observations of Carmela's body did not support Carl's claim of heart trouble, she agreed to sign 32-year-old Carmela's death certificate. Dr. Karow cited "coronary occlusion" as the cause of death, but reported the death to the local police department. The investigating officer was satisfied that Dr. Karow had correctly listed the cause of death, so he did not apply the law that required that an autopsy be performed. The medical examiner could not order an autopsy without a request from the police or the district attorney, which was not forthcoming. Thus, Carmela Coppolino's body, unexamined by anyone, was buried in her family's plot in her home state of New Jersey.

A little more than a month later, Carl married a moneyed socialite, Mary Gibson. News of Carl's marriage infuriated Marjorie Farber, a former New Jersey neighbor of Dr. Coppolino who had been a having an affair with the good doctor. Soon Marjorie had an interesting story to recount to investigators. Her husband's death two years before, although ruled to be from natural causes, had actually been murder! Carl, an anesthesiologist, had given Marjorie a syringe containing some medication and told her to inject her husband, William, while he was sleeping. Ultimately, Marjorie claimed, she was unable to inject the full dose and called Carl, who finished the job by suffocating William with a pillow.

In a cruel and ironic twist, Carl called his wife, Carmela, to sign William Farber's death certificate. She listed the cause of death, at Carl's insistence, as coronary artery disease. This type of death is common, especially in men in their fifties. Such deaths are rarely questioned, and the Department of Health accepted the certificate without any inquiry.

Marjorie Farber's astonishing story was supported in part by Carl's recent increase in his wife's life insurance. Carmela's $65,000 policy, along with his new wife's fortune, would keep Dr. Coppolino in high society for the rest of his life. Based on this information, authorities in New Jersey and Florida now obtained exhumation orders for both William Farber and Carmela Coppolino. After examination of both bodies, Dr. Coppolino was charged with the murders of William and Carmela.

Officials decided to try Dr. Coppolino first in New Jersey for the murder of William Farber. Coppolino was represented by the famous defense attorney F. Lee Bailey. The Farber autopsy did not reveal any evidence of poisoning, but seemed to show strong evidence of strangulation. The absence of toxicological findings left the jury to deliberate the conflicting medical expert testimony versus the sensational story told by a scorned and embittered woman. In the end, Bailey secured an acquittal for his client.

The Florida trial presented another chance to bring Carl Coppolino to justice. Florida officials called on the experienced New York City medical examiner Dr. Milton Halpern and his colleague, toxicologist Dr. Charles Umberger, to determine how Carl Coppolino had killed his wife. Recalling Dr. Coppolino's career as an anesthesiologist, Halpern theorized that Coppolino had exploited his access to the many potent drugs used during surgery to commit these murders, specifically an injectable paralytic agent called succinylcholine chloride.

(continued)

Case Study

Dr. Coppolino's Deadly House Calls (*continued*)

After having Carmela's body exhumed, Halpern examined her body with a magnifying glass in search of an injection site. He found that Carmela had been injected in her left buttock shortly before her death. Dr. Umberger's mission as the toxicologist in this case was to prove the administration of succinylcholine chloride by chemical analysis of Carmela's tissues.

This presented a serious problem because succinylcholine was purported to be untraceable in human tissue. The drug breaks down in the body to succinic acid and choline, both of which are naturally occurring chemicals in the human body. The chemical method necessary to make this determination did not exist at the time of the murder.

Ultimately, Dr. Umberger developed a completely novel procedure for detecting succinylcholine chloride. He isolated elevated levels of succinic acid in Carmela's brain, which proved that she had received a large dose of the paralytic drug shortly before her death. This evidence, along with the finding of the same drug residues in the injection site on her buttock, was presented in the Florida murder trial of Carl Coppolino, who was convicted of second-degree murder.

On appeal, the defense raised an interesting point of law. Can a defendant be convicted of murder based on a series of tests that were specifically devised for this case? Tests that indirectly showed that Carmela had been injected with succinylcholine chloride had never before been used in a criminal trial. The court ruled that the novelty of a scientific method does not preclude its significance to a criminal prosecution. Just because an otherwise valid method was developed specifically for this trial and had not yet been proven in court did not mean that the murderer should be allowed to get away with the perfect crime. The conviction of Dr. Coppolino was upheld.

Providing Expert Testimony

expert witness
An individual whom the court determines to possess a particular skill or knowledge in a trade or profession that is not expected of the average layperson and that will aid a court in determining the truth of a matter at trial.

Because the results of their work may ultimately be a factor in determining a person's guilt or innocence, forensic scientists may be required to testify about their methods and conclusions at a trial or hearing. Trial courts have broad discretion in accepting an individual as an expert witness on any particular subject. Generally, if a witness can establish to the satisfaction of a trial judge that he or she possesses a particular skill or has knowledge in a trade or profession that will aid the court in determining the truth of the matter at issue, that individual will be accepted as an expert witness. Depending on the subject area in question, the court will usually consider knowledge acquired through experience, training, education, or a combination as sufficient grounds for qualification as an expert witness.

In court, an expert witness may be asked questions intended to demonstrate his or her ability and competence pertaining to the matter at hand. Competency may be established by having the witness cite educational degrees, participation in special courses, membership in professional societies, and any professional articles or books published. Also important

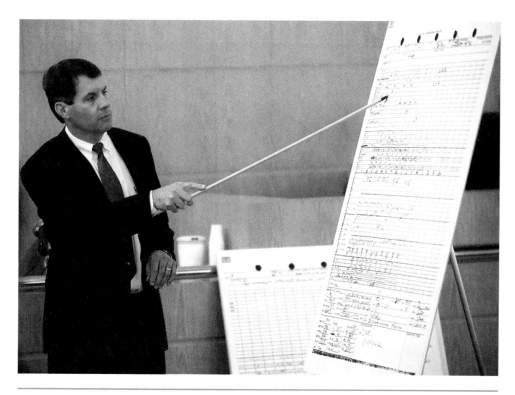

FIGURE 1–13 **An expert witness testifying in court.** *Courtesy Jeff Siner, Corbis/Sygma*

is the number of years of occupational experience the witness has in areas related to the matter before the court.

Unfortunately, few schools confer degrees in forensic science. Most chemists, biologists, geologists, and physicists prepare themselves for careers in forensic science by combining training under an experienced examiner with independent study. Of course, formal education in the physical sciences provides a firm foundation for learning and understanding the principles and techniques of forensic science. Nevertheless, for the most part, courts must rely on training and years of experience as a measurement of the knowledge and ability of the expert.

Before the judge rules on the witness's qualifications, the opposing attorney may cross-examine the witness and point out weaknesses in background and knowledge. Most courts are reluctant to disqualify an individual as an expert even when presented with someone whose background is only remotely associated with the issue at hand. The question of what credentials are suitable for qualification as an expert is ambiguous and highly subjective and one that the courts wisely try to avoid.

The weight that a judge or jury assigns to "expert" testimony in subsequent deliberations is, however, quite another matter. Undoubtedly, education and experience have considerable bearing on the value assigned to the expert's opinions. Just as important may be his or her demeanor and ability to explain scientific data and conclusions clearly, concisely, and logically to a judge and jury composed of nonscientists. The problem of sorting out the strengths and weaknesses of expert testimony falls to prosecution and defense counsel.

The ordinary or lay witness must testify on events or observations that arise from personal knowledge. This testimony must be factual and, with few exceptions, cannot contain the personal opinions of the witness. On the other hand, the expert witness is called on to evaluate evidence when the court lacks the expertise to do so. This expert then expresses an opinion as to the significance of the findings. The views expressed are accepted only as representing the expert's opinion and may later be accepted or ignored in jury deliberations.

The expert cannot render any view with absolute certainty. At best, he or she may only be able to offer an opinion based on a reasonable scientific certainty derived from training and experience. Obviously, the expert is expected to defend vigorously the techniques and conclusions of the analysis, but at the same time must not be reluctant to discuss impartially any findings that could minimize the significance of the analysis. The forensic scientist should not be an advocate of one party's cause, but only an advocate of truth. An adversary system of justice must give the prosecutor and defense ample opportunity to offer expert opinions and to argue the merits of such testimony. Ultimately, the duty of the judge or jury is to weigh the pros and cons of all the information presented in deciding guilt or innocence.

Furnishing Training in the Proper Recognition, Collection, and Preservation of Physical Evidence

The competence of a laboratory staff and the sophistication of its analytical equipment have little or no value if relevant evidence cannot be properly recognized, collected, and preserved at the site of a crime. For this reason, the forensic staff must have responsibilities that will influence the conduct of the crime-scene investigation.

The most direct and effective response to this problem has been to dispatch specially trained evidence-collection technicians to the crime scene. A growing number of crime laboratories and the police agencies they service keep trained "evidence technicians" on 24-hour call to help criminal investigators retrieve evidence. These technicians are trained by the laboratory staff to recognize and gather pertinent physical evidence at the crime scene. They are assigned to the laboratory full-time for continued exposure to forensic techniques and procedures. They have at their disposal all the proper tools and supplies for proper collection and packaging of evidence for future scientific examination.

Unfortunately, many police forces still have not adopted this approach. Often a patrol officer or detective collects the evidence. The individual's effectiveness in this role depends on the extent of his or her training and working relationship with the laboratory. For maximum use of the skills of the crime laboratory, training of the crime-scene investigator must go beyond superficial classroom lectures to involve extensive personal contact with the forensic scientist. Each must become aware of the other's problems, techniques, and limitations.

The training of police officers in evidence collection and their familiarization with the capabilities of a crime laboratory should not be restricted to a select group of personnel on the force. Every officer engaged in fieldwork, whether it be traffic, patrol, investigation, or juvenile control, often must process evidence for laboratory examination. Obviously, it would be difficult and time consuming to give everyone the in-depth training and attention that a qualified criminal investigator requires. However, familiarity with crime laboratory services and capabilities can be gained through periodic lectures, laboratory tours, and dissemination of manuals prepared

WebExtra 1.3
Watch a Forensic Expert
Witness Testify—I
www.prenhall.com/hsforensics

WebExtra 1.4
Watch a Forensic Expert
Witness Testify—II
www.prenhall.com/hsforensics

FIGURE 1–14 Representative evidence-collection guides prepared by various police agencies.

by the laboratory staff that outline the proper methods for collecting and submitting physical evidence to the laboratory.

A brief outline describing the proper collection and packaging of common types of physical evidence is found in Appendix I. The procedures and information summarized in this appendix are discussed in greater detail in forthcoming chapters.

Key Points

- A forensic scientist must be skilled in applying the principles and techniques of the physical and natural sciences to analyzing evidence that may be recovered during a criminal investigation.

- The cases *Frye* v. *United States* and *Daubert* v. *Merrell Dow Pharmaceuticals, Inc.* set guidelines for determining the admissibility of scientific evidence into the courtroom.

- An expert witness evaluates evidence based on specialized training and experience.

- Forensic scientists participate in training law enforcement personnel in the proper recognition, collection, and preservation of physical evidence.

Chapter Summary

In its broadest definition, forensic science is the application of science to criminal and civil laws. This book emphasizes the application of science to the criminal and civil laws that are enforced by police agencies in a criminal justice system. Forensic science owes its origins to a wide variety of individuals who developed the principles and techniques needed to identify or compare physical evidence.

The development of crime laboratories in the United States has been characterized by rapid growth accompanied by a lack of national and regional planning and coordination. Approximately 350 public crime laboratories operate at various levels of government—federal, state, county, and municipal.

The technical support provided by crime laboratories can be assigned to five basic services. The physical science unit uses the principles of chemistry, physics, and geology to identify and compare physical evidence. The biology unit uses knowledge of biological sciences to investigate blood samples, body fluids, hair, and fiber samples. The firearms unit investigates discharged bullets, cartridge cases, shotgun shells, and ammunition. The document examination unit performs handwriting analysis and other questioned-document examination. Finally, the photography unit uses specialized photographic techniques to record and examine physical evidence.

Some crime laboratories offer the optional services of toxicology, fingerprint analysis, polygraph administration, voiceprint analysis, and crime-scene investigation. Several special forensic science services are available to the law enforcement community to augment the services of the crime laboratory. These services include forensic pathology, forensic anthropology, forensic entomology, forensic psychiatry, forensic odontology, forensic engineering, and forensic computer and digital analysis.

A forensic scientist must be skilled in applying the principles and techniques of the physical and natural sciences to analyze the many types of evidence that may be recovered during a criminal investigation. A forensic scientist may also provide expert court testimony. An expert witness evaluates evidence based on specialized training and experience and to express an opinion as to the significance of the findings. Also, forensic scientists participate in training law enforcement personnel in the proper recognition, collection, and preservation of physical evidence.

The *Frye* v. *United States* decision set guidelines for determining the admissibility of scientific evidence into the courtroom. To meet the *Frye* standard, the evidence in question must be "generally accepted" by the scientific community. However, in the 1993 case of *Daubert* v. *Merrell Dow Pharmaceuticals, Inc.,* the U.S. Supreme Court asserted that the *Frye* standard is not an absolute prerequisite to the admissibility of scientific evidence. Trial judges were said to be ultimately responsible as "gatekeepers" for the admissibility and validity of scientific evidence presented in their courts.

Review Questions

Facts and Concepts

1. Define *forensic science*.

2. What was the name of the first system of personal identification? What criteria did it use to distinguish individuals?

3. What was Francis Henry Galton's major contribution to forensic science?

4. Who is known as "the father of forensic toxicology" and why?

5. Name two major contributions to forensic science made by Hans Gross.

6. Which of the following people did *not* make a contribution to forensic toxicology?
   a. Valentin Ross
   b. Alphonse Bertillon
   c. Carl Wilhelm Scheele
   d. Mathieu Orfila

7. With what area of forensic investigation are Karl Landsteiner and Louis Lattes associated?

8. Who was the first person to apply the principles of forensic science to a working crime laboratory?

9. What is Locard's exchange principle?

10. With what instrument did Dr. Walter C. McCrone make significant contributions to forensic science?

11. Which city's police department boasts the oldest forensic laboratory in the United States?

12. What is the world's largest forensic laboratory?

13. List four major reasons for the increase in the number of crime laboratories in the United States since the 1960s.

14. Demand for analysis of what substance is expected to lead to a dramatic increase in the number of crime lab personnel?

15. List four government agencies that offer forensic services at the federal level.

16. The current system of crime laboratories in the United States can best be described as
    a. centralized.
    b. regional.
    c. decentralized.
    d. national.

17. List three advantages of having regional crime laboratories operate as part of a statewide system.

18. How does the organization of Great Britain's forensic laboratories differ from that of the United States?

19. Which of the following is *not* a reason for the wide variation in services offered by crime laboratories in different communities?
    a. variations in local laws
    b. varying local approaches to crime-scene investigation
    c. different capabilities and functions of the organization to which a laboratory is attached
    d. budgetary and staffing limitations

20. Which unit examines body fluids and organs for drugs and poisons?

21. Which unit examines and compares tool marks?

22. What part of the body do forensic odontologists use to identify a victim? Why is this body part particularly useful as a source of identification?

23. List the three basic functions of a forensic scientist.

24. Describe the criteria for admissibility of scientific evidence as laid out in *Frye* v. *United States*.

25. What document offers an alternative to the *Frye* standard that some courts believe espouses a more flexible standard for admitting scientific evidence?

26. In its decision in *Daubert* v. *Merrell Dow Pharmaceuticals, Inc.*, whom did the U.S. Supreme Court charge with ensuring that an expert's testimony rests on a reliable foundation and is relevant to the case?

27. In *Kumho Tire Co., Ltd.* v. *Carmichael*, the U.S. Supreme Court ruled that the "gatekeeping" role of a trial judge
    a. was restricted to scientific testimony.
    b. applied only to cases involving capital crimes.
    c. was subject to appeal by a higher court.
    d. applied to all expert testimony.

28. What is an expert witness?

29. What is the main difference between the testimony given by an expert witness and that given by a lay witness?

Application and Critical Thinking

1. Most crime labs in the United States are funded and operated by the government and provide services free to police and prosecutors. Great Britain, however, uses a quasi-governmental agency that charges fees for its services and keeps any profits it makes. Suggest potential strengths and weaknesses of each system.

2. Police investigating an apparent suicide collect the following items at the scene: a note purportedly written by the victim, a revolver bearing very faint fingerprints, and traces of skin and blood under the victim's fingernails. What units of the crime laboratory will examine each piece of evidence?

3. List at least three advantages of having an evidence-collection unit process a crime scene instead of a patrol officer or detective.

4. What legal issue was raised on appeal by the defense in Carl Coppolino's Florida murder trial? What court ruling is most relevant to the decision to reject the appeal? Explain your answer.

Case Analysis

The prosecution of Dr. Mario Jascalevich for murder turned on issues of both law and forensic science. Favorable resolution of the key legal issue was crucial to the state's ability to present a credible case against Dr. Jascalevich. Once in court, similarly unresolved issues pertaining to forensic science became central to the final verdict.

1. Describe the primary issue of law whose resolution by the court was critical to the state's case against Dr. Jascalevich.

2. How did the court ultimately rule on this issue? Describe the main arguments supporting the court's decision.

3. Describe the primary scientific issue raised during the trial. What were the defense's main challenges to the scientific evidence presented by the prosecution?

Web Resources

Admissibility of Scientific Evidence under *Daubert* (Brief comparison and discussion of the *Frye* and *Daubert* tests)
faculty.ncwc.edu/toconnor/425/425lect02.htm

Autopsy (Step-by-step description of an autopsy written by a pathologist with additional links to articles and videos about autopsies)
www.pathguy.com/autopsy.htm

Forensic Anthropology (Articles, essays, and links to topics in forensic anthropology)
library.med.utah.edu/kw/osteo/forensics/index.html

Forensic Science Resources in a Criminal Fact Investigation Index—Specific Topics (Online bibliography of topics in forensic science)
www.tncrimlaw.com/forensic/fsbindx.htm

History of Forensic Science
www.crimezzz.net/forensic_history/index.htm

Endnotes

1. Two excellent references are André A. Moenssens, Fred E. Inbau, James Starrs, and Carol E. Henderson, *Scientific Evidence in Civil and Criminal Cases,* 4th ed. (Mineola, N.Y.: Foundation Press, 1995); and Werner U. Spitz, ed., *Medicolegal Investigation of Death,* 3rd ed. (Springfield, Ill.: Charles C. Thomas, 1993).

2. 293 Fed. 1013 (D.C. Cir. 1923).

3. 509 U.S. 579 (1993).

4. 526 U.S 137 (1999).

5. 223 So. 2d 68 (Fla. App. 1968), *app. dismissed,* 234 So. 2d (Fla. 1969), *cert. denied,* 399 U.S. 927 (1970).

Case Reading

Detection of Curare in the Jascalevich Murder Trial

Lawrence H. Hall
Star-Ledger, Newark, New Jersey

Roland H. Hirsch
Chemistry Department, Seton Hall University
South Orange, New Jersey

Dr. Mario E. Jascalevich and his wife Nora display the "V for Victory" sign at their attorney's office in Hackensack, NJ. *Courtesy AP Wide World Photos*

The case of *State* v. *Jascalevich* that follows preceded the *Daubert* ruling by fifteen years. Nevertheless, it is interesting to note that the trial judge, after listening to both sides in his "gatekeeping" role, admitted into testimony what in 1978 were rather novel scientific test procedures for the drug curare. The case offers an excellent example of the legal and scientific issues involved in assessing the admissibility and value of scientific evidence in the courtroom. Dr. Jascalevich was accused of murdering several of his patients by administering lethal doses of curare. The issue of whether the curare was detected and identified in the exhumed bodies of the alleged murder victims was central to proving the state's case against the

defendant. What ensued at the trial was a classic illustration of conflicting expert testimony on both sides of a scientific issue. Ultimately, the jury's task was to weigh the data and arguments presented by both sides and to reach a verdict.

The murder trial of Dr. Mario E. Jascalevich was one of the most complicated criminal proceedings ever tried in an American courtroom. The 34-week trial before a Superior Court judge in New Jersey resulted in a not-guilty verdict for the Englewood Cliffs, N.J., surgeon. The questions concerning analytical chemistry raised in the trial will continue to be discussed in years to come.

Not since the controversial trial of Dr. Carl Coppolino—convicted in a Florida courtroom in 1967 of murdering his wife with succinylcholine chloride—have so many forensic experts of national and international stature labored so long over the scientific questions at issue in the case:

What happens to human tissue embalmed and interred for a decade? Assuming lethal doses of a drug such as curare were given to hospital patients, would the drug have changed chemically or have been destroyed entirely over a 10-year period?

Assuming again that the drug had been injected, what analytical techniques could be employed to trace submicrogram amounts of it?

Could components of embalming fluids or bacteria in the earth react chemically, forming substances giving a false positive reading in the analytical procedures used?

Forensic scientists first grappled with these questions during the latter part of 1966. Two of Jascalevich's colleagues at Riverdell Hospital in Oradell, N.J.— Dr. Stanley Harris, a surgeon, and

Dr. Allan Lans, an osteopathic physician—suspected him of murdering their patients with curare. There were no eyewitnesses to the alleged murders, but Drs. Harris and Lans discovered 18 vials of curare in Jascalevich's surgical locker after breaking into it.

They took their suspicions to the Bergen County Prosecutor's office in November 1966, and a brief but unpublicized investigation was launched. Items taken from the surgeon's locker, including the vials of curare and syringes, were sent for analysis at the New York City Medical Examiner's office.

In the interim, Jascalevich told authorities he used the muscle-relaxant drug in animal experiments at the Seton Hall Medical College. The surgeon presented the prosecutor his medical research papers and other documentation to support his contention. In addition, he reviewed the medical charts of the alleged murder victims and told the prosecutor there was no need for the operations the patients received. Malpractice and misdiagnosis were the causes of the deaths, Jascalevich stated at that time. Dr. Milton Helpern, chief of the New York City Medical Examiner's office, and his staff in early 1967 concluded their testing on the items taken from Jascalevich's locker. Dog hair and animal blood were detected on the vials of curare and syringes.

The prosecutor's office terminated its investigation and stated there were more reasons to look into allegations of malpractice than murder at the small osteopathic hospital.

In January 1976 a series of articles about a "Doctor X" suspected of murdering patients at Riverdell Hospital appeared in the *New York Times,* and the Bergen County Prosecutor's office reopened its case.

A month prior to the case being officially reopened, however, New York Deputy Medical Examiner Dr. Michael Baden supplied an affidavit to the Superior Court in Bergen County stating that at least a score of patients who died at Riverdell in 1966 succumbed from other reasons than those stated on death certificates.

A Superior Court judge signed the order in January 1976, granting the prosecutor's office the right to exhume the bodies of Nancy Savino, 4; Emma Arzt, 70; Frank Biggs, 59; Margaret Henderson, 27; and Carl Rohrbeck, 73.

All these patients entered Riverdell Hospital between December 1965 and September 1966 for routine surgical procedures and succumbed days afterward.

In mid-January 1976 the body of the Savino child was exhumed from a gravesite in Bergen County and taken to the medical examiner's office in New York City.

There, Dr. Baden, in the presence of New Jersey State Medical Examiner Dr. Edwin Albano and others, began performing the almost 4-hour examination of the child's body, which was said to be well preserved.

On May 18, 1976, Dr. Jascalevich was indicted for five murders.

A little more than a year later, the state's forensic experts began using radioimmunoassay (RIA) and high-performance liquid chromatography (HPLC) on the tissue specimens. In the fall of 1977, the defense received from Drs. Baden and Dal Cortivo samples of tissues and embalming fluids of the alleged murder victims.

For the remainder of the year, both the defense and the state experts worked to develop analytical procedures to settle the question of detection of curare in human tissue.

In addition, there were numerous pretrial hearings at which time the defense, headed by Jersey City attorney Raymond Brown, requested medical slides, reports, and patient charts relating to the alleged murder victims, as well as the methodologies used in treating the specimens.

On February 28, 1978, a panel of 18 jurors was chosen for what was to become the second longest criminal trial in the nation's history. At the outset, the defense wanted a hearing to ascertain the validity of the scientific procedures employed by the state to reportedly detect curare.

The defense contended that RIA and HPLC were relatively new procedures and could not be used to detect curare in human tissue. RIA, for example, could only be used to detect drugs in blood and body fluids, according to defense experts.

The defense motion for a hearing outside of the presence of the jury was denied by Superior Court Judge William J. Arnold, who maintained the motion could be made later in the trial when the evidence obtained by the analytical techniques would actually be scheduled for presentation to the jury.

The trial got underway with testimony by osteopathic physicians, nurses, and other hospital personnel employed by Riverdell during the time the alleged murders were committed. The physicians told Assistant Prosecutor Sybil Moses that in each instance the patient had been recovering from surgery when he succumbed.

However, on cross-examination, the physicians admitted they had misdiagnosed their patients' conditions and that there was inferior postoperative care. For example, in the case of the Savino child, the defense experts held that the little girl died of acute diffuse peritonitis—the source of her abdominal pain when she was brought into Riverdell after having been diagnosed as having acute appendicitis.

After the prosecution completed presentation of the medical aspects of its case, the defense renewed its request for a special hearing on the admissibility of the evidence obtained by radioimmunoassay, liquid chromatography, and other analytical techniques. This request came as Dr. Baden took the witness stand to explain why he had recommended reautopsy of the bodies. The prosecution was opposed to a hearing:

> The techniques used by the State are not new toxicological methodologies, but are standard methods, used widely throughout the field. These

methodologies include radioimmunoassay and high-pressure liquid chromatography. . . .

> Since the methodologies used to detect the curare are widely accepted in the scientific community, there is no necessity for the Court to conduct a hearing as to their reliability.

Nevertheless, Judge Arnold ruled that a hearing should be held. Arguments began, in the absence of the jury, on June 10. Both sides presented statements by their technical experts and affidavits from other scientists regarding the validity of the analytical methods.

On June 20 the judge ruled that the analytical evidence was admissible. He stated,

> All I'm saying is under the law the evidence is admissible. I'm not going to comment on the value or trustworthiness of the witnesses [who testified]. The ultimate decision must be made by the jury.

Following this decision, the jury began listening to the scientific evidence, with the State's and the defense's witnesses in the process explaining such points as: What is curare, and specifically *d*-tubocurarine? What is radioimmunoassay? What is an antibody, and how is the antibody for *d*-tubocurarine created? What is high-pressure liquid chromatography?

Dr. Richard Coumbis testified about his finding tubocurarine in tissues from four of the five patients: "can only state there is presumptive evidence" that curare was discovered in the fifth patient. Under cross-examination by defense attorney Raymond Brown, Coumbis maintained that the RIA and HPLC procedures were valid methods of detecting curare because "on the basis of my personal experience, I did not find any other substance interfering with curare."

Dr. David Beggs of Hewlett-Packard then testified that he found curare in the Savino lung and liver samples using mass spectrometry. He said the Biggs and Arzt samples contained possible traces of curare; however, he could not be scientifically certain of this. He stated that mass spectrometry "is not an absolute test" for curare, but "just indicated that it is probably there."

Dr. Leo Dal Cortivo then took the witness stand and testified that he had found curare in tissue remains of three of the patients using HPLC. He also had measured curare in vials found in the defendant's locker at Riverdell Hospital in 1966, which the defense contended had been used in animal experiments conducted by Jascalevich at the College of Medicine in Jersey City. It was necessary to use RIA for the detection of curare in the HPLC eluates.

The prosecution then completed its case. At this point Judge Arnold dismissed two counts of murder and stated that the prosecution had not presented scientific evidence for the presence of curare in the bodies of Emma Arzt and Margaret Henderson. The defense then began presentation of its case with testimony about the medical aspects.

In September, attention returned to the analytical data. Drs. Frederick Rieders and Bo Holmstedt testified about the experiments they carried out on the samples provided by the prosecution. The major question they addressed was that of the long-term stability of curare under the conditions to which the bodies were subjected between 1966 and 1976.

Dr. Rieders maintained that, in his opinion, the RIA was not specific enough and "could only raise suspicions that something is there but it might not be there." The only procedure he found specific enough to be confident of identification of curare was mass spectrometry, using the entire spectrum, not just selected ion monitoring.

Rieders tested for the stability of curare and found that both embalming fluids and tissue juices (from the patients) had destructive effects on this compound.

He added curare to these liquids and could detect it by TLC initially, but after a few days could find no trace of it or other nitrogenous bases. These liquids altered curare chemically to the point where it was no longer recognizable as such. He concluded that the rapid rate of decomposition meant that to detect curare in the specimens in 1976 would have required huge, medically impossible amounts to have been present in 1966.

Rieders tested the samples for curare and found it only in the liver specimen of Nancy Savino. He stated that mass spectrometry indicated that the curare in this sample was highly pure and could not have been present in the ground for 10 years. Furthermore, if curare was present in the liver, it should also have been found in the child's muscle tissue. That it was not detected in the latter specimen was a "tremendous inconsistency."

Dr. Bo Holmstedt then stated that curare could not survive in embalmed bodies for 10 years, especially because of the effects of bacteria and repeated fluctuations in temperature of the bodies. He reviewed experiments which showed that curare, upon injection, shows levels of the same order of magnitude in liver and muscle tissues. After 10 minutes, "40 percent of the drug is to be found in the muscle and 3 percent in the liver."

On October 14 the defense rested its case. On October 23, after both sides had presented summations of their cases, Judge Arnold gave his charge to the jury. The next day, October 24, 1978—seven and a half months after the trial had begun—the jury received the case. After just over 2 hours of deliberations, the jury returned a unanimous verdict of not guilty on all three remaining counts of murder. Two years and five months after the indictments against him had been returned, Dr. Mario Jascalevich was free.

JonBenet Ramsey: Who Did It?

Patsy and John Ramsey were in the upper crust of Boulder, Colorado, society. In the span of five short years, John had built his computer company into a billion-dollar corporation. In addition to financial success, the Ramseys also had a beautiful 6-year-old daughter, JonBenet.

Just after five a.m. on December 26, 1996, Patsy Ramsey awoke and walked downstairs to her kitchen. At the foot of the staircase, she found a two-and-a-half-page note saying that JonBenet had been kidnapped. The note contained a ransom demand of $118,000. When the police arrived to investigate, it was quite apparent to all that JonBenet was missing.

In retrospect, some serious mistakes were made in securing the crime scene—the Ramsey household. Initially, the police conducted a cursory search of the house, but failed to find JonBenet. The house was not sealed off; in fact, four friends along with the Ramsey pastor were let into the home and allowed to move about at will. John was permitted to leave the premises unattended for one and a half hours. One hour after his return, John and two of his friends searched the house again. This time John went down into the basement, where he discovered JonBenet's body. He removed a white blanket from JonBenet and carried her upstairs, placing the body on the living room floor.

The murder of JonBenet Ramsey remains as baffling a mystery today as it was on its first day. Ample physical evidence supports the theory that the crime was committed by an outsider, as well as the competing theory that JonBenet was murdered by someone who resided in the Ramsey household. Perhaps better care at securing and processing the crime scene could have resolved some of the crime's outstanding questions.

The Crime Scene

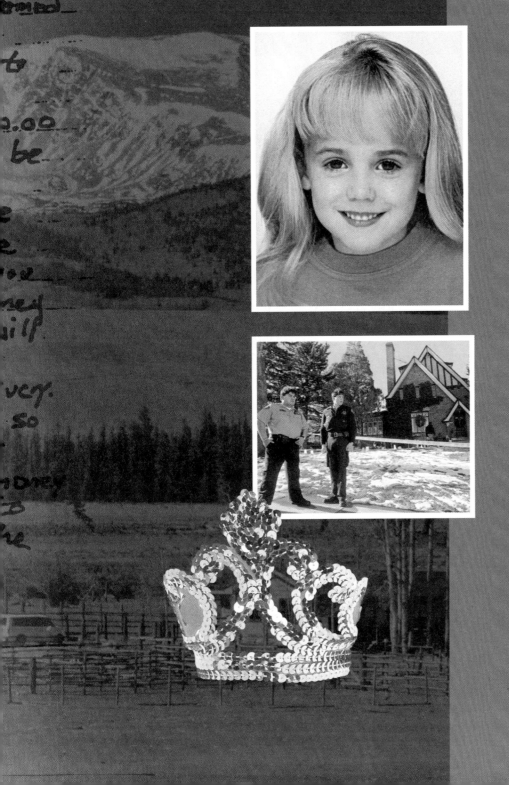

Physical Evidence and the Crime Scene

physical evidence
Any object that can establish that a crime has been committed or can link a crime and its victim or its perpetrator.

As automobiles run on gasoline, crime laboratories "run" on physical evidence. Physical evidence encompasses any and all objects that can establish that a crime has been committed or can link a crime and its victim or its perpetrator. But if physical evidence is to be used effectively to aid the investigator, its presence first must be recognized at the crime scene. If all the natural and commercial objects within a reasonable distance of a crime were gathered so that the scientist could uncover significant clues from them, the deluge of material would quickly immobilize the laboratory facility. Physical evidence achieves its optimum value in criminal investigations only when its collection is performed with a selectivity governed by the collector's thorough knowledge of the crime laboratory's techniques, capabilities, and limitations.

Forthcoming chapters will discuss methods and techniques available to forensic scientists to evaluate physical evidence. Although current technology has given the crime laboratory capabilities far exceeding those of past decades, these advances are no excuse for complacency on the part of criminal investigators. Crime laboratories do not solve crimes; only a thorough and competent investigation conducted by professional police officers will enhance the chances for a successful criminal investigation. Forensic science is, and will continue to be, an important element of the total investigative process, but it is only one aspect of an endeavor that must be a team effort. The investigator who believes the crime laboratory to be a panacea for laxity or ineptness is in for a rude awakening.

Forensic science begins at the crime scene. If the investigator cannot recognize physical evidence or cannot properly preserve it for laboratory examination, no amount of sophisticated laboratory instrumentation or technical expertise can salvage the situation. The know-how for conducting a proper crime-scene search for physical evidence is not beyond the grasp of any police department, regardless of its size. With proper training, police agencies can ensure competent performance at crime scenes. In many jurisdictions, police agencies have delegated this task to a specialized team of technicians. However, the techniques of crime-scene investigation are not difficult to master and certainly lie within the bounds of comprehension of the average police officer.

Not all crime scenes require retrieval of physical evidence, and limited resources and personnel have forced many police agencies to restrict their efforts in this area to crimes of a more serious nature. Once the commitment is made to process a crime site for physical evidence, however, certain fundamental practices must be followed.

Securing and Recording the Crime Scene

In order to be useful to investigators, evidence at a crime scene must be preserved and recorded in its original condition as much as possible. Failure to protect a crime scene properly or record its details accurately may result in the destruction or altering of evidence, or hinder the search for the perpetrator by misleading investigators about the facts of the incident.

Secure and Isolate the Crime Scene

The first officer arriving on the scene of a crime must preserve and protect the area as much as possible. Of course, first priority should be given to obtaining medical assistance for individuals in need of it and to arresting the perpetrator. However, as soon as possible, extensive efforts must be made to exclude all unauthorized personnel from the scene. As additional officers arrive, measures are immediately initiated to isolate the area. (See Figure 2–1.) Ropes or barricades along with strategic positioning of guards will prevent unauthorized access to the area.

Sometimes the exclusion of unauthorized personnel proves more difficult than expected. Violent crimes are especially susceptible to attention from higher-level police officials and members of the press, as well as

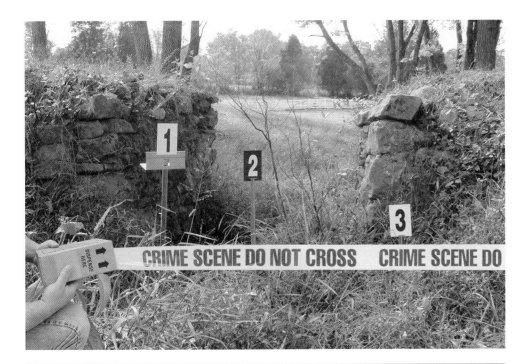

FIGURE 2–1 The first investigators to arrive must secure the crime scene and establish the crime-scene perimeter. *Courtesy Sirchie Finger Print Laboratories, Inc., Youngsville, N.C., www.sirchie.com*

by emotionally charged neighbors and curiosity seekers. Every individual who enters the scene has the potential to destroy physical evidence, even if by unintentional carelessness. To exercise proper control over the crime scene, the officer protecting it must have the authority to exclude everyone, including fellow police officers not directly involved in processing the site or in conducting the investigation. Seasoned criminal investigators are always prepared to relate horror stories about crime scenes where physical evidence was rendered totally valueless by hordes of people who trampled through the site. Securing and isolating the crime scene are critical steps in an investigation, the accomplishment of which is the mark of a trained and professional crime-scene investigative team.

Once the scene has been secured, a lead investigator starts evaluating the area. First, he or she determines the boundaries of the scene, and then establishes the perpetrator's path of entry and exit. Logic dictates that obvious items of crime-scene evidence will first come to the attention of the crime-scene investigator. These items must be documented and photographed. The investigator then proceeds with an initial walk-through of the scene to gain an overview of the situation and develop a strategy for systematically examining and documenting the entire crime scene.

Record the Scene

Investigators have only a limited amount of time to work a crime site in its untouched state. The opportunity to permanently record the scene in its original state must not be lost. Such records not only will prove useful during the subsequent investigation, but also are required for presentation at a trial in order to document the condition of the crime site and to delineate the location of physical evidence. Photography, sketches, and notes are the three methods for crime-scene recording (see Figure 2–2). Ideally all three should be employed; however, personnel and monetary limitations often

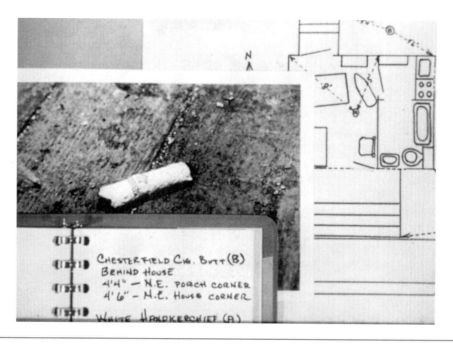

FIGURE 2–2 The finding of an evidential cigarette butt at the crime scene requires photographing it, making a sketch showing its relation to the crime scene, and recording the find in field notes. *Courtesy Police Science Services, Niles, Ill.*

The Crime Scene **45**

prohibit the use of photography at every crime site. Under these circumstances, departmental guidelines will establish priorities for deploying photographic resources. However, there is no reason not to make sketches and notes at the crime scene.

Photography   The most important prerequisite for photographing a crime scene is for it to be unaltered. Unless injured people are involved, objects must not be moved until they have been photographed from all necessary angles. If objects are removed, positions changed, or items added, the photographs may not be admissible as evidence at a trial, and their intended value will be lost. If evidence has been removed or moved prior to photography, the fact should be noted in the report, but the evidence should not be reintroduced into the scene in order to take photographs.

Each crime scene should be photographed as completely as possible. This means that the crime scene should include the area in which the crime actually took place and all adjacent areas where important acts occurred immediately before or after the commission of the crime. Overview photographs of the entire scene and surrounding area, including points of exit and entry, must be taken from various angles. If the crime took place indoors, the entire room should be photographed to show each wall area. Rooms adjacent to the actual crime site must be similarly photographed. If the crime scene includes a body, photographs must be taken to show the body's position and location relative to the entire scene. Close-up photos depicting injuries and weapons lying near the body are also necessary. After the body is removed from the scene, the surface beneath the body should be photographed.

As items of physical evidence are discovered, they are photographed to show their position and location relative to the entire scene. After these overviews are taken, close-ups should be taken to record the details of the object itself. When the size of an item is significant, a ruler or other measuring scale may be inserted near the object and included in the photograph as a point of reference.

The digital revolution promises to bring enhanced photographic capabilities to the crime scene. For example, individual images of the crime scene captured with a digital camera can be stitched together electronically to reveal a near three-dimensional panoramic view of the crime scene (see Figure 2–3). With the aid of a computer, any area of the scene captured digitally can be enhanced and examined in fine detail.

The use of videotape at crime scenes is becoming increasingly popular because the cost of this equipment is decreasing. The same principles used in crime-scene photographs apply to videotaping. As with conventional photography, videotaping should include the entire scene and the immediate surrounding area. Long shots as well as close-ups should be taken in a slow and systematic manner. Furthermore, it is desirable to have one crime-scene investigator narrate the events and scenes being taped while another does the actual shooting.

While videotaping can capture the sounds and scenes of the crime site with relative ease, the technique cannot at this time be used in place of still photography. The still photograph remains unsurpassed in the definition of detail it provides to the human eye.

WebExtra 2.1

Making a Photographic Record of the Crime Scene
www.prenhall.com/hsforensics

Sketches   Once photographs have been taken, the crime-scene investigator sketches the scene. The investigator may have neither the skill nor the time to make a polished sketch of the scene. However, this is not required

FIGURE 2–3 Individual images (*top*) are shown before being electronically stitched together into a single panoramic image (*bottom*). Individual photographs should be taken with about a **30 percent overlap.** *Courtesy Imaging Forensics, Fountain Valley, Calif., www.imagingforensics.com*

rough sketch

A sketch, drawn at the crime scene, that contains an accurate depiction of the dimensions of the scene and shows the location of all objects having a bearing on the case.

during the early phase of the investigation. What is necessary is a rough sketch containing an accurate depiction of the dimensions of the scene and showing the location of all objects having a bearing on the case.

A rough sketch is illustrated in Figure 2–4. It shows all recovered items of physical evidence, as well as other important features of the crime scene. Objects are located in the sketch by distance measurements from two fixed points, such as the walls of a room. It is important that distances shown on the sketch be accurate and not the result of a guess or estimate. For this reason, all measurements are made with a tape measure. The simplest way to designate an item in a sketch is to assign it a number or letter. A legend or list placed below the sketch then correlates the letter to the item's description. The sketch should also show a compass heading designating north.

finished sketch

A precise rendering of the crime scene, usually drawn to scale.

Unlike the rough sketch, the finished sketch in Figure 2–5 is constructed with care and concern for aesthetic appearance. When the finished sketch is completed, it must reflect information contained within the rough sketch in order to be admissible evidence in a courtroom. Computer-aided drafting (CAD) has become the standard method for reconstructing crime scenes from rough sketches. The software, ranging from simple, low-cost programs to complex, expensive ones, contains predrawn intersections, roadways, buildings, and rooms onto which information can be entered (see Figure 2–6). A generous symbol library provides a variety of images that can be used to add intricate details such as blood spatters to a crime-scene sketch. Equipped with a zoom function, computerized sketching can focus on a specific area for a more detailed

CASE: 10-789-96
301 N. CENTRE ST.
OCT. 6, 1996   11:40 PM
HOMICIDE

VICTIM: LESTER W. BROWN
INVESTIGATOR: SGT. L.A. DUFFY
ASS'T BY: PTLM. R.W. HICKS

BOOKCASE
BOOKCASE
DESK
LAMP TABLE
COUCH
TABLE
FIRE PLACE
CHAIR

LEGEND
A = COCKTAIL GLASS
B = TELEPHONE
C = VICTIM
D = BULLET HOLE
E = BLOOD STAINS
F = SHELL CASING
▲ = CAMERA LOCATIONS

* D 3'-4¾" FROM FLOOR

¼" = 1 FOOT

FIGURE 2–4   Rough-sketch diagram of a crime scene. *Courtesy Sirchie Finger Print Laboratories, Inc., Youngsville, N.C., www.sirchie.com*

FIGURE 2–5 **Finished-sketch diagram of a crime scene.** *Courtesy Sirchie Finger Print Laboratories, Inc., Youngsville, N.C., www.sirchie.com*

picture. The CAD programs allow the user to select scale size so that the final product can be produced in a size suitable for courtroom presentation.

Notes Note taking must be a constant activity throughout the processing of the crime scene. These notes must include a detailed written description of the scene with the location of items of physical evidence recovered. They must also identify the time an item of physical evidence was discovered, by whom, how and by whom it was packaged and marked, and the disposition of the item after it was collected. The note taker must keep in mind that

FIGURE 2–6   Construction of a crime-scene diagram with the aid of a computer-aided drafting program. *Courtesy Sirchie Finger Print Laboratories, Inc., Youngsville, N.C., www.sirchie.com*

this written record may be the only source of information for refreshing one's memory months, perhaps years, after a crime has been processed. The notes must be sufficiently detailed to anticipate this need. Tape-recording notes at a scene can be advantageous—detailed notes can be taped much faster than they can be written. Another method of recording notes is to narrate a videotape of the crime scene. This has the advantage of combining note taking with photography. However, at some point the tape must be transcribed into a written document.

Key Points

- Physical evidence includes any and all objects that can establish that a crime has been committed or can link the crime and its victim or its perpetrator.

- Forensic science begins at the crime scene, where investigators must recognize and properly preserve evidence for laboratory examination.

- The first officer to arrive must secure the crime scene.

- Investigators record the crime scene by using photographs, sketches, and notes and make a preliminary examination of the scene as the perpetrator left it.

Dealing with Physical Evidence

After the lead detective has conducted a preliminary walk-through, a more thorough search for physical evidence begins. Once found, physical evidence must be collected and stored in a way that preserves its integrity for forensic comparison and analysis. As a result, law enforcement officials have developed specific procedures for finding, collecting, and transporting physical evidence that preserve its evidentiary value.

Conduct a Systematic Search for Evidence

The search for physical evidence at a crime scene must be thorough and systematic. For a factual, unbiased reconstruction of the crime, the investigator, relying on his or her training and experience, must not overlook any pertinent evidence. Even when suspects are immediately seized and the motives and circumstances of the crime are readily apparent, a thorough search for physical evidence must be conducted at once. Failure in this, even though it may seem unnecessary, can lead to accusations of negligence or charges that the investigative agency knowingly "covered up" evidence that would be detrimental to its case.

The investigator in charge assigns the personnel responsible for searching a crime scene. Except in major crimes, or when the evidence is very complex, a forensic scientist is usually not needed at the crime scene; his or her role appropriately begins with the submission of evidence to the crime laboratory. As has already been observed, some police agencies have trained field evidence technicians to search for physical evidence at the crime scene. They have the equipment and skill to photograph the scene and examine it for the presence of fingerprints, footprints, tool marks, or any other type of evidence that may be relevant to the crime.

Considerations in Searching the Crime Scene   How one conducts a crime-scene search will depend on the locale and size of the area, as well as on the actions of the suspect(s) and victim(s) at the scene. When possible, one person should supervise and coordinate the collection of evidence. Without proper control, the search may be conducted in an atmosphere of confusion with needless duplication of effort. Evidence collectors may subdivide the scene into segments and search each segment individually, or the search may start at some outer point and gradually move toward the center of the scene in a circular fashion (see Figure 2–7). The areas searched must include all probable points of entry and exit used by the criminals.

What to search for will be determined by the particular circumstances of the crime. Obviously, the skill of crime-scene investigators at recognizing evidence and searching relevant locations is paramount to successful processing of the crime scene. While training will impart general knowledge for conducting a proper crime-scene investigation, ultimately the investigator must rely on the experience gained from numerous investigations to formulate a successful strategy for recovering relevant physical evidence at crime scenes. For example, in the case of homicide, the search will center on the weapon and any type of evidence left as a result of contact between the victim and the assailant. The cross-transfer of evidence, such as hairs, fibers, and blood, between individuals involved in the crime is particularly useful for linking suspects to the crime site and for corroborating events that transpired during the commission of the crime. During the investigation of a burglary, efforts will be made to locate tool marks at the point of entry. In most crimes, a thorough and systematic search for latent fingerprints is required.

Vehicle searches must be carefully planned and systematically carried out. The nature of the case determines how detailed the search must be. In hit-and-run cases, the outside and undercarriage of the car must be examined with care. Particular attention is paid to looking for any evidence resulting from a cross-transfer of evidence between the car and the victim—including blood, tissue, hair, fibers, and fabric impressions. Traces of paint or broken glass may be located on the victim. In cases of homicide, burglary, kidnapping, and so on, all areas of the vehicle, inside and outside, are searched with equal care for physical evidence.

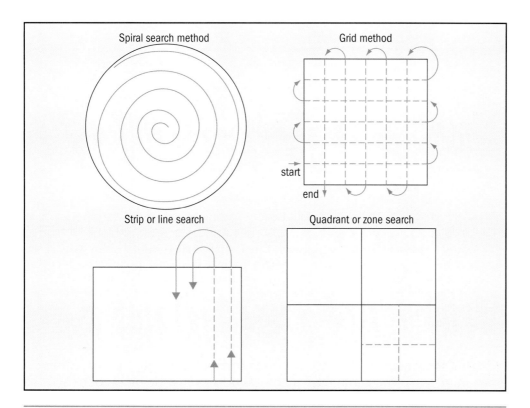

FIGURE 2–7   Several typical examples of crime-scene search patterns. The pattern selected normally depends on the size and locale of the scene and the number of collectors participating in the search.

Collect Physical Evidence

Physical evidence can be anything from massive objects to microscopic traces. Often, many items of evidence are obvious in their presence, but others may be detected only through examination in the crime laboratory. For example, minute traces of blood may be discovered on garments only after a thorough search in the laboratory; the presence of hairs and fibers may be revealed in vacuum sweepings or on garments only after close laboratory scrutiny. For this reason, it is important to collect possible carriers of trace evidence in addition to more discernible items. Hence, it may be necessary to take custody of all clothing worn by the participants in a crime. Each clothing item should be handled carefully and wrapped separately to avoid loss of trace materials.

Critical areas of the crime scene should be vacuumed and the sweepings submitted to the laboratory for analysis. The sweepings from different areas must be collected and packaged separately. A portable vacuum cleaner equipped with a special filter attachment is suitable for this purpose (see Figure 2–8). Additionally, fingernail scrapings from individuals who were in contact with other individuals may contain minute fragments of evidence capable of linking the assailant and victim. The undersurface of each nail is best scraped with a dull object such as a toothpick to avoid cutting the skin. These scrapings will be subjected to microscopic examination in the laboratory.

The search for physical evidence must extend beyond the crime scene to the autopsy room of a deceased victim. Here, the medical examiner or coroner carefully examines the victim to establish a cause and manner of

FIGURE 2–8 Vacuum sweeper attachment, constructed of clear plastic in two pieces that are joined by a threaded joint. A metal screen is mounted in one half to support a filter paper to collect debris. The unit attaches to the hose of the vacuum sweeper. After a designated area of the crime scene is vacuumed, the filter paper is removed and retained for laboratory examination. *Courtesy Sirchie Finger Print Laboratories, Inc., Youngsville, N.C., www.sirchie.com*

death. Tissues and organs are retained for pathological and toxicological examination. At the same time, arrangements must be made between the examiner and investigator to secure a variety of items that may be obtainable from the body for laboratory examination. The following are to be collected and sent to the forensic laboratory:

1. Victim's clothing

2. Fingernail scrapings

3. Head and pubic hairs

4. Blood (for DNA typing)

5. Vaginal, anal, and oral swabs (in sex-related crimes)

6. Recovered bullets from the body

7. Hand swabs from shooting victims (for gunshot residue analysis)

Once the body is buried, efforts at obtaining these items may prove difficult or futile. Furthermore, a lengthy delay in obtaining many of these items will diminish or destroy their forensic value.

Many police departments have recently purchased and equipped "mobile crime laboratories" (see Figure 2–9) for their evidence technicians. However, the term *mobile crime laboratory* is a misnomer. These vehicles carry the necessary supplies to protect the crime scene; photograph, collect, and package physical evidence; and develop latent prints. They are not designed to carry out the functions of a chemical laboratory. *Crime-scene search vehicle* would be a more appropriate but perhaps less dramatic name for such a vehicle.

Procedures for Collecting and Packaging Physical Evidence Physical evidence must be handled and processed in a way that prevents any change from taking place between the time it is removed from the crime scene and the time it is received by the crime laboratory. Changes can arise through contamination, breakage, evaporation, accidental scratching or bending, or loss through improper or careless packaging.

(a)

(b)

FIGURE 2–9 **Inside view of a mobile crime-scene van: (a) driver's side and (b) passenger's side.** *Courtesy Sirchie Finger Print Laboratories, Inc., Youngsville, N.C., www.sirchie.com*

The integrity of evidence is best maintained when the item is kept in its original condition as found at the crime site. Whenever possible, evidence should be submitted to the laboratory intact. Blood, hairs, fibers, soil particles, and other types of trace evidence should not normally be removed from garments, weapons, or other articles that bear them. Instead, the entire object should be sent to the laboratory for processing.

Of course, if evidence is adhering to an object in a precarious manner, good judgment dictates removing and packaging the item. If evidence is found adhering to a large structure, such as a door, wall, or floor, common sense must be used; remove the specimen with a forceps or other appropriate tool. In the case of a bloodstain, one may either scrape the stain off the surface, transfer the stain to a moistened swab, or cut out the area of the object bearing the stain.

Each different item or similar items collected at different locations must be placed in separate containers. Packaging evidence separately prevents damage through contact and prevents cross-contamination.

Tools for Evidence Collection   The well-prepared evidence collector arrives at a crime scene with a large assortment of packaging materials and tools, ready to encounter any type of situation. Forceps and similar tools may be used to pick up small items. Unbreakable plastic pill bottles with pressure lids are excellent containers for hairs, glass, fibers, and various other kinds of small or trace evidence. Alternatively, manila envelopes, screw-cap glass vials, or cardboard pillboxes are adequate containers for most trace evidence encountered at crime sites. Ordinary mailing envelopes should not be used as evidence containers because powders and fine particles will leak out of their corners.

Small amounts of trace evidence can also be conveniently packaged in a carefully folded paper, using what is known as a "druggist fold." This consists of folding one end of the paper over one-third, then folding the other end (one-third) over that, and repeating the process from the other two sides. After the paper is folded in this manner, the outside two edges are tucked into each other to produce a closed container that keeps the specimen from falling out.

Although manila envelopes, pillboxes, or sealable plastic bags (see Figure 2–10) are good universal containers for most trace evidence, two frequent finds at crime scenes warrant special attention. If bloodstained materials are stored in airtight containers, the accumulation of moisture may encourage the growth of mold, which can destroy the evidential value of blood. In these instances, wrapping paper, manila envelopes, or paper bags are recommended packaging materials (see Figure 2–11). All items of clothing must be air-dried and placed individually in separate paper bags to ensure constant circulation of air through them. This will prevent the formation of mold and mildew. On the other hand, charred debris recovered from the scene of a suspicious fire must be sealed in an airtight container to prevent the evaporation of volatile petroleum residues. New paint cans or tightly sealed jars are recommended in such situations.

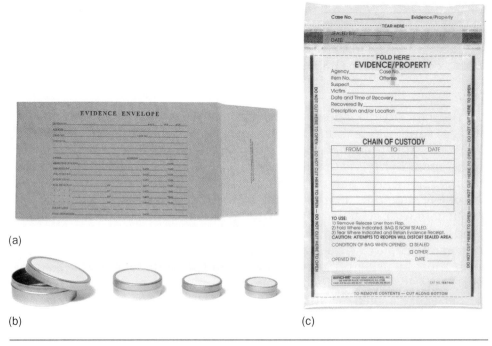

(a)

(b)

(c)

FIGURE 2–10   (a) Manila evidence envelope, (b) metal pillboxes, (c) sealable plastic evidence bag. *Courtesy Sirchie Finger Print Laboratories, Inc., Youngsville, N.C., www.sirchie.com*

FIGURE 2–11 **Paper bags are recommended evidence containers for objects suspected of containing blood and semen stains. Each object should be packaged in a separate bag.**
Courtesy Sirchie Finger Print Laboratories, Inc., Youngsville, N.C., www.sirchie.com

A detailed description of the proper collection and packaging of various types of physical evidence will be discussed in forthcoming chapters; additionally, most of this information is summarized in the evidence guide found in Appendix I.

Maintain the Chain of Custody

Continuity of possession, or the chain of custody, must be established whenever evidence is presented in court as an exhibit. This means that every person who handled or examined the evidence must be accounted for. Failure to substantiate the evidence's chain of custody may lead to serious questions regarding the authenticity and integrity of the evidence and the examinations of it. Adhering to standard procedures in recording the location of evidence, marking it for identification, and properly completing evidence submission forms for laboratory analysis are the best guarantee that the evidence will withstand inquiries of what happened to it from the time of its finding to its presentation in court.

All items of physical evidence should be carefully packaged and marked upon their retrieval at crime sites. This should be done with the utmost care to avoid destroying their evidential value or restricting the number and kind of examinations to which the criminalist may subject them. If at all possible, the evidence itself should be marked for identification. Normally, the collector's initials and the date of collection are inscribed directly on the article. However, if the evidence collector is unsure of the necessity of marking the item itself, or has doubts as to where to mark it, it is best to omit this step. Where appropriate, the evidence is to be tagged for identification.

Once an evidence container is selected for the evidence, whether a box, bag, vial, or can, it also must be marked for identification. A minimum record would show the collector's initials, location of the evidence, and date of collection. If the evidence is turned over to another individual for care or delivery to the laboratory, this transfer must be recorded in notes and other appropriate forms. In fact, every individual who possesses the evidence must maintain a written record of its acquisition and disposition. Frequently, all of the individuals involved in the collection and transportation of the evidence may be requested to testify in court. Thus, to avoid

chain of custody
A list of all people who came into possession of an item of evidence.

confusion and to retain complete control of the evidence at all times, the chain of custody should be kept to a minimum.

Obtain Standard/Reference Samples

standard/reference sample

Physical evidence whose origin is known, such as blood or hair from a suspect, that can be compared to crime-scene evidence.

The examination of evidence, whether soil, blood, glass, hair, fibers, and so on, often requires comparison with a known standard/reference sample. Although most investigators have little difficulty recognizing and collecting relevant crime-scene evidence, few seem aware of the necessity and importance of providing the crime lab with a thorough sampling of standard/reference materials. Such materials may be obtained from the victim, a suspect, or other known sources. For instance, investigation of a hit-and-run incident might require the removal of standard/reference paint from a suspect vehicle. This will permit its comparison to paint recovered at the scene.

The presence of standard/reference samples greatly facilitates the work of the forensic scientist. For example, hair found at a crime scene will be of optimum value only when compared to standard/reference hairs removed from the suspect and victim. Likewise, bloodstained evidence must be accompanied by a whole-blood or buccal swab standard/reference sample obtained from all relevant crime-scene participants. The quality and quantity of standard/reference specimens often determine the evidential value of crime-scene evidence, and these standard/reference specimens must be treated with equal care.

buccal swab

A swab of the inner portion of the cheek, performed to collect cells for use in determining the DNA profile of an individual.

substrate control

Uncontaminated surface material close to an area where physical evidence has been deposited; used to ensure that the surface on which a sample has been deposited does not interfere with laboratory tests.

Some types of evidence must also be accompanied by the collection of substrate controls. These are materials close to areas where physical evidence has been deposited. For example, substrate controls are normally collected at arson scenes. If an investigator suspects that a particular surface has been exposed to gasoline or some other accelerant, the investigator should also collect a piece of the same surface material that is believed *not* to have been exposed to the accelerant. At the laboratory, the substrate control is tested to ensure that the surface on which the accelerant was deposited does not interfere with testing procedures. Another common example of a substrate control is a material on which a bloodstain has been deposited. Unstained areas close to the stain may be sampled to determine whether this material can interfere with the interpretation of laboratory results. Thorough collection and proper packaging of standard/reference specimens and substrate controls are the mark of a skilled investigator.

Submit Evidence to the Laboratory

Evidence is usually submitted to the laboratory either by personal delivery or by mail shipment. The method of transmittal is determined by the distance the submitting agency must travel to the laboratory and the urgency of the case. If the evidence is delivered personally, the deliverer should be familiar with the case, to facilitate any discussions between laboratory personnel and the deliverer concerning specific aspects of the case.

If desired, most evidence can be conveniently shipped by mail. However, postal regulations restrict the shipment of certain chemicals and live ammunition and prohibit the mailing of explosives. In such situations, the laboratory must be consulted to determine the disposition of these substances. Care must also be exercised in the packaging of evidence in order to prevent breakage or other accidental destruction while it is in transit to the laboratory.

Most laboratories require that an evidence submission form accompany all evidence submitted (see Figure 2–12). This form must be properly

CRIME:						COUNTY OF:			
Homicide; Aggravated Sexual Assault						Mercer			

VICTIM:	Age	Sex	Race	SUSPECT:	Age	Sex	Race
Jane Doe (v)	25	F	C	John Doe(s)	30	M	C

SUBMITTING AGENCY: (Address)
Trenton P.D. Central Evidence 225 N. Clinton Avenue, Trenton, N.J. 08609

FORWARD REPLIES TO:	(Name)	(Address)	Telephone Number:
Capt. John Smith, Chief of Detectives	Same as above		609 555-5555

INVESTIGATED BY:
Detective John Jones

DELIVERED BY: (Signature of Person Delivering Evidence)

BRIEF HISTORY OF CASE: (Include Date and Location, if Applicable)
On March 1st, 2001 the victim was found dead in her bedroom. Victim was partially clothed and autopsy revealed that victim was stabbed numerous times and medical examiner stated that there was evidence of sexual assault. Victim was last seen drinking with suspect at a local tavern. Suspect was arrested and item # 23, a folding knife, was found in his pocket.

* Note* Suspect is HIV+

EXAMINATION REQUESTED ON SPECIMENS LISTED BELOW:

Examine items 2, 5, 8-11, 13-15, 18 and 19 for seminal material and compare to controls #'s 12 and 26. Examine #1, 2, 4, 7,13, 14, 15, 18, 20, 21, 22 and 23 for trace evidence transfer. Examine #3 for saliva from suspect. Examine #6 for skin, blood and trace evidence. Examine #'s 20-23 for transfer blood evidence and compare to control #'s 12 and 26.

Item #	* Code	LIST OF SPECIMENS *SOURCE OF EVIDENCE CODE (V-Victim, S-Suspect, SC-Scene)
1	V	Debris collection
2	V	Clothing, white panties
3	V	Dried Secretions/bite marks
4	V	Head Hair Combings
5	V	Oral Specimens
6	V	Fingernail Specimens
7	V	Pubic Hair Combings
8	V	External Genital Specimen
9	V	Vaginal Specimens
10	V	Cervical Specimens

Right margin checkboxes (LABORATORY USE ONLY): DRUG ☐ TRACE ☐ BIO/CHEM ☐ TOX ☐ ABC ☐ EQUINE ☐ BALLISTICS ☐

FOR ADDITIONAL INFORMATION USE FORM 631A AND ATTACH   Page 1 of 2 pages

FIGURE 2–12 **An example of a properly completed evidence submission form.** *Courtesy New Jersey State Police*

completed. Its information will enable the laboratory analyst to make an intelligent and complete examination of the evidence. Particular attention should be paid to providing the laboratory with a brief description of the case history. This information will allow the examiner to analyze the specimens in a logical sequence and make the proper comparisons, and it will also facilitate the search for trace quantities of evidence.

The particular kind of examination requested for each type of evidence should be delineated. However, the analyst will not be bound to adhere strictly to the specific tests requested by the investigator. During the examination new evidence may be uncovered, and as a result the complexity of the case may change. Furthermore, the analyst may find the initial requests incomplete or not totally relevant to the case. Finally, a list of items submitted for examination must be included on the evidence submission form. Each item is to be packaged separately and assigned a number or letter, which should be listed in an orderly and logical sequence on the form.

Key Points

- The search pattern selected at a crime scene depends on the size and locale of the scene and the number of collectors participating in the search.

- Many items of evidence may be detected only through examination at the crime laboratory. For this reason, it is important to collect possible carriers of trace evidence, such as clothing, vacuum sweepings, and fingernail scrapings, in addition to more discernible items.

- Each item of physical evidence collected at a crime scene must be placed in a separate appropriate container to prevent damage through contact or cross-contamination.

- Investigators must maintain the chain of custody, a record for denoting the location of the evidence.

- Proper standard/reference samples, such as hairs, blood, and fibers, must be collected at the crime scene and from appropriate subjects for comparison purposes in the laboratory.

The Murder Scene: Death and Autopsies

Unfortunately, the most important piece of evidence at many crime scenes is the dead body of a victim. When foul play is suspected, a victim's corpse is subjected to the same kind of intense physical analysis as any other piece of evidence. This task falls primarily to a forensic pathologist, often aided by the skills of specialists including forensic anthropologists and forensic entomologists. In its broadest sense, forensic pathology involves the study of medicine as it relates to the application of the law, particularly criminal law. In practice, this most often involves the investigation of sudden, unnatural, unexplained, or violent deaths.

Role of the Forensic Pathologist   Typically, forensic pathologists, in their role as medical examiners or coroners, must answer several basic questions: Who is the victim? What injuries are present? When did the injuries occur? Why and how were the injuries produced? The primary role of the medical examiner is to determine the cause of death. If a cause cannot be found through observation, an **autopsy** is normally performed to establish the cause of death. The manner in which death occurred is classified into five categories: natural, homicide, suicide, accident, or undetermined, based on the circumstances surrounding the incident.

Frequently, medical examiners must perform autopsies if a death is deemed suspicious or unexplained. The cause of death may not always be what it seems at first glance. For example, a decedent with a gunshot wound and a gun in his hand may appear to have committed suicide. However, an autopsy may reveal that the victim actually died of suffocation and

autopsy
The medical dissection and examination of a body in order to determine the cause of death.

the gunshot wound occurred after death to cover up the circumstances surrounding the commission of a crime.

Estimating Time of Death

After a human body expires, it goes through several stages of decomposition. A medical examiner can often estimate the time of death by evaluating the stage of decomposition in which the victim was found. Immediately following death, the muscles relax and then become rigid. This condition, rigor mortis, manifests itself within the first twenty-four hours and disappears within thirty-six hours.

Another condition occurring in the early stages of decomposition is livor mortis. When the human heart stops pumping, the blood begins to settle in the parts of the body closest to the ground. The skin appears dark blue or purple in these areas. The onset of this condition begins immediately and continues for up to twelve hours after death. The skin does not appear discolored in areas where the body is restricted by either clothing or an object pressing against the body. This information can be useful in determining whether the victim's position was changed after death.

Other physical and chemical changes within the body also help approximate the time of death. Algor mortis is the process by which the body temperature continually cools after death until it reaches the ambient or room temperature. The rate of heat loss is influenced by factors such as the location and size of the body, the victim's clothing, and weather conditions. Because of such factors, this method can only estimate the approximate time period since death. As a general rule, beginning about an hour after death, the body loses heat at a rate of approximately $1–1\frac{1}{2}°F$ per hour until the body reaches the environmental temperature.

Another approach helpful for estimating the time of death is to determine potassium levels in the ocular fluid (fluid within the eye, also known as the vitreous humor). After death, cells within the inner surface of the eyeball release potassium into the ocular fluid. By analyzing the amount of potassium present at various intervals after death, the forensic pathologist can determine the rate at which potassium is released into the vitreous humor and use it to approximate the time of death. During the autopsy, other factors may indicate the time period in which death occurred. For example, the amount of food in the stomach can help estimate when a person's last meal was eaten. This information can be valuable when investigating a death.

Forensic Anthropology: Skeletal Detectives

Forensic anthropology is concerned primarily with the identification and examination of human skeletal remains. Bones are remarkably durable and undergo an extremely slow breakdown process that last decades or even centuries. Because of their resistance to rapid decomposition, skeletal remains can provide a multitude of individual characteristics. An examination of bones may reveal their sex, approximate age, race, and skeletal injury (see Figure 2–13). For example, a female's bone structure differs from a male's, especially within the pelvic area because of a woman's childbearing capabilities.

This area of expertise is not limited just to identification, however. A forensic anthropologist may also help create facial reconstructions to identify skeletal remains. With the help of this technique, a composite of the victim can be drawn and advertised in an attempt to identify the victim. Forensic anthropologists are also helpful in identifying victims of a mass disaster such as a plane crash. When such a tragedy occurs, forensic anthropologists can help identify victims through the collection of bone fragments.

WebExtra 2.2

See How an Autopsy Is Performed
www.prenhall.com/hsforensics

rigor mortis
A medical condition that occurs after death and results in the stiffening of muscle mass; the rigidity of the body begins within 24 hours of death and disappears within 36 hours of death.

livor mortis
A medical condition that occurs after death and results in the settling of blood in areas of the body closest to the ground.

algor mortis
A process that occurs after death in which the body temperature continually cools until it reaches the ambient or room temperature.

WebExtra 2.3

Explore Forensic Anthropology
www.prenhall.com/hsforensics

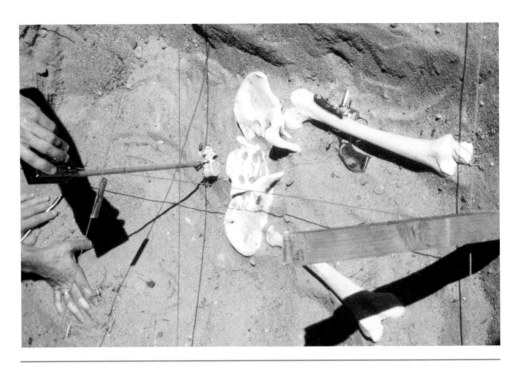

FIGURE 2–13 **Crime-scene site showing a pelvis partly buried in sand and a femur lying across a pistol.** *Courtesy Paul Sledzik*

Case Study

Identifying a Serial Killer's Victims

The worst serial killer in America calmly admitted his guilt as he led investigators to a crawl space under his house. There, John Wayne Gacy had buried twenty-eight young men, after brutally raping and murdering them in cold blood. Because no identification was found with the bodies, the police were forced to examine missing-person reports for leads. However, these boys and men were so alike in age, race, and stature that police were unable to make individual identifications for most of the victims. Clyde Snow, the world-renowned forensic anthropologist from Oklahoma, was asked to help the investigators make these difficult identifications.

Snow began by making a thirty-five-point examination of each skull for comparison to known individuals. By examining each skeleton, he made sure each bone was correctly attributed to an individual. This was crucial to later efforts because some of the victims had been buried on top of older graves, mingling

their remains. Once Snow was sure all the bones were sorted properly, he began his in-depth study. Long bones such as the femur (thigh bone) were used to estimate each individual's height. This helped narrow the search when attempting to match the victims with the descriptions of missing people.

After narrowing the possibilities to missing people fitting the general description, investigators consulted potential victims' hospital and dental records. Evidence of injury, illness, surgery, or other unique skeletal defects were used to make identifications. Snow also pointed out features that gave clues to the victim's behavior and medical history. For example, he discovered that one of Gacy's victims had an old fracture of his left arm, and that his left scapula (shoulder blade) and arm bore the telltale signs of a left-handed individual. These details were matched to a missing-person report and another young victim was identified.

John Wayne Gacy. © *Bettmann/CORBIS. All Rights Reserved*

For the most difficult cases, Snow called in the help of forensic sculptor and facial reconstructionist Betty Pat Gatliff. She used clay and depth markers to put the flesh back on the faces of these forgotten boys in the hopes that someone would recognize them after their photographs were released to the media. Her efforts were successful, but investigators found some families unwilling to accept the idea that their loved ones were among Gacy's victims. Even with Gatliff's help, nine of Gacy's victims remain unidentified.

Forensic Entomology: Testimony from Insects

The study of insects and their relation to a criminal investigation is known as forensic entomology. Such a practice is commonly used to estimate the time of death when the circumstances surrounding the crime are unknown. After decomposition begins, insects such as blowflies are the first to infest the body. Their eggs are laid in the human remains and ultimately hatch into maggots or fly larvae (see Figure 2–14), which consume human organs and tissues. Forensic entomologists can identify the specific insects present in the body and approximate how long a body has been left exposed by examining the stage of development of the fly larvae.

These determinations are not always straightforward, however. The time required for stage development is affected by environmental influences such as geographical location, climate, and weather conditions. For example, cold temperatures hinder the development of fly eggs into adult flies. The forensic entomologist must consider these conditions when estimating the postmortem interval. Knowledge of insects, their life cycles, and their habits make entomological evidence an invaluable tool for an investigation (see Figure 2–15).

Key Points

- An autopsy is normally performed if a death is suspicious or unexplained.

- Rigor mortis occurs after death and results in the stiffening of body parts in the position they are in when death occurs. Livor mortis occurs after death and results in the settling of blood in areas of the body closest to the ground. Algor mortis refers to postmortem changes that cause a body to lose heat.

- Forensic anthropology is concerned primarily with the identification and examination of human skeletal remains.

- A forensic entomologist studies the development of insect larvae in a body to estimate time of death.

WebExtra 2.4
Patricia Cornwell's Challenge
www.prenhall.com/hsforensics

FIGURE 2–14 A scanning electron micrograph of two-hour-old blowfly maggots. *Courtesy Science Photo Library*

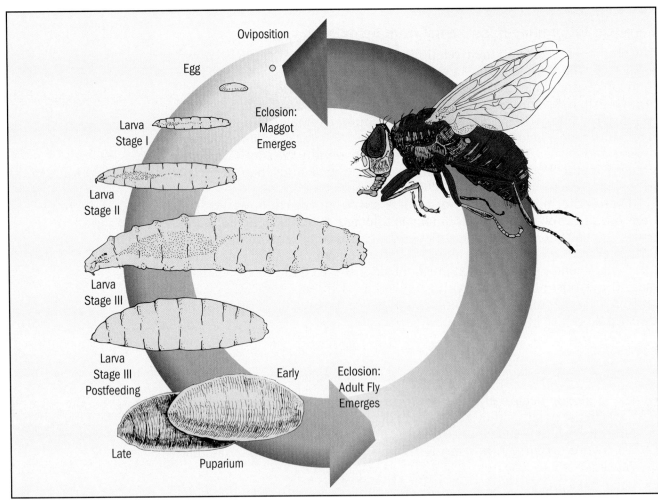

FIGURE 2–15 Typical blowfly life cycle from egg deposition to adult fly emergence. This cycle is representative of any one of the nearly ninety species of blowflies in North America. *Courtesy E. P. Catts, Ph.D., deceased, and Neal H. Haskell, Ph.D., forensic entomology consultant, www. forensic-entomology.com*

Chapter Summary

Physical evidence includes any and all objects that can establish that a crime has been committed or can link a crime and its victim or its perpetrator. Forensic science begins at the crime scene. Here, investigators must recognize and properly preserve evidence for laboratory examination. The first officer to arrive at the scene must secure the crime scene. Once the scene is secured, relevant investigators record the crime scene by using photographs, sketches, and notes. Before processing the crime scene for physical evidence, the investigator should make a preliminary examination of the scene as it was left by the perpetrator. The search for physical evidence at a crime scene must be thorough and systematic. The search pattern selected normally depends on the size and locale of the scene and the number of collectors participating in the search.

Physical evidence can be anything from massive objects to microscopic traces. Often, many items of evidence are clearly visible but others may be detected only through examination at the crime laboratory. For this reason, it is important to collect possible carriers of trace evidence, such as clothing, vacuum sweepings, and fingernail scrapings, in addition to more discernible items. Each different item or similar items collected at different locations must be placed in a separate, appropriate container. Packaging evidence separately prevents damage through contact and cross-contamination.

During the collection of evidence, the chain of custody, a record for denoting the location of the evidence, must be maintained. In addition, proper standard/reference samples, such as hairs, blood, and fibers, must be collected at the crime scene and from appropriate subjects for comparison purposes in the laboratory. The removal of any evidence from a person or from the scene of a crime must be done in accordance with appropriate search and seizure protocols.

Several special forensic science services are available to the law enforcement community to augment the services of the crime laboratory when an investigation involves a sudden, unnatural, unexplained, or violent death. These services include forensic pathology, forensic anthropology, and forensic entomology.

Review Questions

Facts and Concepts

1. What is physical evidence? Give three examples of physical evidence that might be found at a crime scene.

2. What is the first step in processing a crime scene?

3. Why is it important to exclude onlookers from a crime scene?

4. Name three methods for recording a crime scene and list one unique advantage of each.

5. What is the most important prerequisite for photographing a crime scene?

6. If objects have been moved or removed from a crime scene, the investigator should
   a. replace them and photograph them in their original position.
   b. reconstruct the scene in the crime laboratory, then take a photo showing where the moved objects were originally located.
   c. note that the objects were moved, but do not reintroduce them to the crime scene.
   d. exclude those objects as possible pieces of evidence.

7. What areas should be photographed during a crime-scene investigation?

8. Name and describe the two kinds of sketches prepared for a crime scene.

9. What information must be included in written notes made at the crime scene?

10. Name three factors that influence how an investigator conducts a crime scene search.

11. List at least four pieces of evidence from a murder scene that must be collected and sent to the forensic laboratory. Why must these items be collected at the crime scene instead of later?

12. What is the most important consideration when handling and processing physical evidence?

13. What is the best way to maintain the integrity of physical evidence?

14. Describe the best way for an investigator to handle trace evidence found on articles collected at the crime scene. Name two exceptions to this general rule.

15. Describe a "druggist's fold" and explain why it is a better way to store trace evidence than an ordinary mailing envelope.

16. Why should all items of evidence be placed in separate containers?

17. Name one type of evidence that should be stored in an airtight container and one type that should not be stored in such a container. Explain why each type of evidence should be stored (or not stored) in this way.

18. What is chain of custody and why is it important to maintain chain of custody?

19. What is a standard/reference sample? Why is collecting such a sample important to the crime-scene investigator?

20. What is a substrate control and how is it used by the crime-scene investigator?

21. Which of the following is an example of a substrate control?
    a. a fingerprint found on a murder weapon
    b. floorboards from an arson scene that contain no trace of accelerants
    c. pieces of fiber adhering to a body discovered at a crime scene
    d. blood and skin found under the fingernails of a murder suspect

22. In what situations is an autopsy typically performed?

23. Define the terms *rigor mortis, livor mortis,* and *algor mortis* and explain how they are important to a forensic pathologist.

24. Which of the following methods is *not* used to approximate time of death?
    a. temperature of the body
    b. potassium level in the vitreous humor

c. loss of body mass

d. settling of blood in the body

25. What is forensic anthropology? List two ways in which a forensic anthropologist might identify a victim.

26. What does a forensic entomologist study to estimate time of death? Explain why such estimates are not always straightforward.

Application and Critical Thinking

1. Give at least three examples of how evidence might be destroyed by onlookers at a crime scene.

2. What important elements are missing from the following crime-scene sketch?

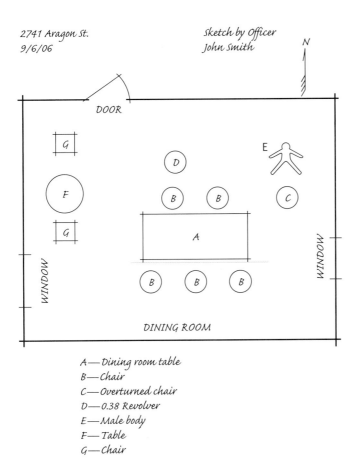

2741 Aragon St.
9/6/06

Sketch by Officer
John Smith

N

DOOR

DINING ROOM

WINDOW

WINDOW

A—Dining room table
B—Chair
C—Overturned chair
D—0.38 Revolver
E—Male body
F—Table
G—Chair

3. An investigator at a murder scene notes signs of a prolonged struggle between the attacker and victim. Name at least three types of physical evidence for which the investigator would likely collect standard/reference samples and explain why he or she would collect them.

4. Rigor mortis, livor mortis, and algor mortis are all used to help determine time of death. However, each method has its limitations. For each method, describe at least one condition that would render that method unsuitable or inaccurate for determining time of death.

5. What kind of forensic expert would most likely be asked to help identify human remains in each of the following conditions?
   a. a body that has been decomposing for a day or two
   b. fragmentary remains of a few arm bones and part of a jaw
   c. a skeleton that is missing the skull

Case Analysis

Investigators looking into the kidnapping and murder of DEA Special Agent Enrique Camarena and DEA source Alfredo Zavala faced several hurdles that threatened to derail their efforts to collect evidence in the case. These hurdles almost prevented forensics experts from determining the facts of the case and threatened to undermine the investigation of the crime. However, despite these obstacles, use of standard forensic techniques eventually enabled investigators to solve the case.

1. What were the main challenges facing investigators who were collecting evidence in the case? Give specific examples of these challenges.

2. Explain how investigators used reference samples to determine that the victims had been held at the residence located at 881 Lope De Vega.

3. Explain how investigators used soil evidence to determine that the victims' bodies had been buried and later moved to the site where they were discovered.

WebExtra 2.5

Virtual Crime Scene 2.1
www.prenhall/hsforensics

Virtual Crime Scene

Search for clues at the scene of a murder. Once you've located the relevant evidence, you will need to collect the evidence for laboratory testing.

Web Resources

Forensic Science Resources (Links to CSI articles and sites; includes CSI bibliography)
www.tncrimlaw.com/forensic/f_crimescene.html

Crime Scene Investigation (Guidelines and articles on response, evidence collection, photography, and other topics)
www.crime-scene-investigator.net

Crime and Clues (Articles on crime-scene protection, processing, and reconstruction)
www.crimeandclues.com/crimescene.htm

Crime Scene Investigation: A Guide for Law Enforcement
www.ncjrs.gov/pdffiles1/nij/178280.pdf

Death Investigation: A Guide for the Scene Investigator
www.ncjrs.gov/pdffiles/167568.pdf

Forensic Entomology (Good general site for information on how entomology is used; includes information on equipment used by entomologists and how to handle and ship specimens)
www.forensic-entomology.com

Case Reading

The Enrique Camarena Case: A Forensic Nightmare

On February 7, 1985, U.S. Drug Enforcement Agency (DEA) Special Agent (SA) Enrique Camarena was abducted near the U.S. Consulate in Guadalajara, Mexico. A short time later, Capt. Alfredo Zavala, a DEA source, was also abducted from a car near the Guadalajara Airport. These two abductions would trigger a series of events leading to one of the largest investigations ever conducted by the DEA and would result in one of the most extensive cases ever received by the FBI Laboratory.

Throughout this lengthy investigation, unusual forensic problems arose that required unusual solutions. Eventually, numerous suspects were arrested, both in the United States and Mexico, which culminated in an 8-week trial held in U.S. District Court in Los Angeles, CA.

The Abduction

On February 7, 1985, SA Camarena left the DEA Resident Office to meet his wife for lunch. On this day, a witness observed a man being forced into the rear seat of a light-colored compact car in front of the Camelot Restaurant and provided descriptions of several of the assailants. After some initial reluctance, Primer Comandante Pavon-Reyes of the Mexican Federal Judicial Police (MFJP) was put in charge of the investigation, and Mexican investigators were assigned to the case. Two known drug traffickers, Rafael Caro-Quintero and Ernesto Fonseca, were quickly developed as suspects. A short time later at the Guadalajara Airport, as Caro-Quintero and his men attempted to flee by private jet, a confrontation developed between Caro-Quintero's men, the MFJP, and DEA Agents. After some discussion, Caro-Quintero and his men were permitted to board and leave. It was later learned that a

6-figure bribe had been paid to Pavon-Reyes to allow this departure.

The Investigation

During February 1985, searches of several residences and ranches throughout Mexico proved fruitless, despite the efforts of the DEA task force assigned to investigate this matter and the tremendous pressure being applied by the U.S. Government to accelerate the investigation. High-level U.S. Government officials, as well as their Mexican counterparts, were becoming directly involved in the case. It is believed that because of this "heat," the Mexican drug traffickers and certain Mexican law enforcement officials fabricated a plan. According to the plan, the MFJP would receive an anonymous letter indicating that SA Camarena and Captain Zavala were being held at the Bravo drug gang's ranch in La Angostura, Michoacan, approximately

Michael P. Malone
Special Agent, Laboratory Division
Federal Bureau of Investigation,
Washington, D.C.

Undated photo of Enrique Camarena.
Courtesy AP Wide World Photos

Reprinted from *FBI Law Enforcement Bulletin,* September 1989.

60 miles southeast of Guadalajara. The MFJP was supposed to raid the ranch, eliminate the drug gang, and eventually discover the bodies of SA Camarena and Captain Zavala buried on the ranch. The DEA would then be notified and the case would be closed. Thus, the Bravo gang would provide an easy scapegoat.

During early March, MFJP officers raided the Bravo ranch before the DEA Agents arrived. In the resulting shootout, all of the gang members, as well as one MFJP officer, were killed. However, due to a mix-up, the bodies of SA Camarena and Captain Zavala were not buried on the Bravo ranch in time to be discovered as planned. The individuals paid to do this job simply left them by the side of a road near the ranch. It was later learned that certain Mexican law enforcement officials were paid a large sum of money to formulate and carry out this plan in order to obstruct and prematurely conclude the investigation.

Shortly after this shootout, a passerby found two partially decomposed bodies, wrapped in plastic bags, along a road near the Bravo ranch. The bodies were removed and transported to a local morgue where they were autopsied. The DEA was then advised of the discovery of the bodies and their subsequent removal to another morgue in Guadalajara, where a second autopsy was performed.

On March 7, 1985, the FBI dispatched a forensic team to Guadalajara. They immediately proceeded to the morgue to identify the bodies and to process any evidence which might be present. After much bureaucratic delay from the local officials, they were finally allowed to proceed. The bodies were identified only as cadavers number 1 and number 2. It was apparent that each body had been autopsied and that both were in an advanced state of decomposition. Cadaver number 1 was quickly identified by the fingerprint expert as that of SA Camarena. Mexican officials would not allow the

second body to be identified at this time; however, it was later identified through dental records as Captain Zavala.

The FBI forensic team requested permission to process the clothing, cordage, and burial sheet found with the bodies but the request was denied. However, they were allowed to cut small, "known" samples from these items and obtain hair samples from both bodies. Soil samples were also removed from the bodies and the clothing items.

A forensic pathologist from the Armed Forces Institute of Pathology was allowed to examine the body of SA Camarena. He concluded that SA Camarena's death was caused by blunt-force injuries. In addition, SA Camarena had a hole in his skull caused by a rod-like instrument. SA Camarena's body was then released to the American officials and immediately flown to the United States.

The next day, both FBI and DEA personnel proceeded to the Bravo ranch where the bodies were initially found. Because this site had been a completely uncontrolled crime scene, contaminated by both police personnel and onlookers, only a limited crime-scene search was conducted. It was immediately noted that there was no grave site in the area and that the color of the soil where the bodies had been deposited differed from the soil that had been removed from the bodies. Therefore, "known" soil samples from the drop site were taken to compare with soil removed from the victims. It was also noted that there were no significant body fluids at the "burial" site. This led the forensic team to conclude that the bodies had been buried elsewhere, exhumed, and transported to this site.

The MFJP officials were later confronted with the evidence that the bodies had been relocated to the Michoacan area. This was one of the factors which led to a new, unilateral MFJP investigation. As a result, several suspects, including State Judicial Police Officers, were arrested and interrogated concerning the kidnapping of SA Camarena. Primer Comandante Pavon-Reyes was fired, and arrest warrants were issued for a number of international drug traffickers, including Rafael Caro-Quintero and Ernesto Fonseca.

In late March 1985, DEA Agents located a black Mercury Gran Marquis which they believed was used in the kidnapping or transportation of SA Camarena. The vehicle had been stored in a garage in Guadalajara, and a brick wall had been constructed at the entrance to conceal it. The vehicle was traced to a Ford dealership owned by Caro-Quintero. Under the watchful eye of the MFJP at the Guadalajara Airport, the FBI forensic team processed the vehicle for any hair, fiber, blood, and/or fingerprint evidence it might contain.

During April 1985, the MFJP informed the DEA that they believed they had located the residence where SA Camarena and Captain Zavala had been held. The FBI forensic team was immediately dispatched to Guadalajara; however, they were not allowed to proceed to the residence, located at 881 Lope De Vega, until an MFJP forensic team had processed the residence and had removed all of the obvious evidence. The DEA was also informed that since the abduction of SA Camarena, all of the interior walls had been painted, the entire residence had recently been cleaned, and that a group of MFJP officers were presently occupying, and thereby contaminating, the residence.

On the first day after the arrival of the FBI forensic team, they surveyed and began a crime scene search of the residence and surrounding grounds. [See Figure 1.] The residence consists of a large, two-story structure with a swimming pool, covered patio, aviary, and tennis court surrounded by a common wall. The most logical place to hold a prisoner at this location would be in the small outbuilding located to the rear of the main residence. This outbuilding,

designated as the "guest house," consisted of a small room, carpeted by a beige rug, with an adjoining bathroom. The entire room and bathroom were processed for hairs, fibers, and latent fingerprints. The single door into this room was made of steel and reinforced by iron bars. It was ultimately determined by means of testimony and forensic evidence that several individuals interrogated and tortured SA Camarena in this room. In addition, a locked bedroom, located on the second floor of the main house, was also processed, and the bed linens were removed from a single bed. Known carpet samples were taken from every room in the residence.

A beige VW Atlantic, which fit the general description of the smaller vehicle noted by the person who witnessed SA Camarena's abduction, was parked under a carport at the rear of the residence. The VW Atlantic was also processed for hairs, fibers, and fingerprints.

On the second day, a thorough grounds search was conducted. As FBI forensic team members were walking around the tennis court, they caught a glimpse of something blue in one of the drains. Upon closer inspection, it appeared to be a folded license plate, at the bottom of the drain. However, a heavy iron grate covered the drain and prevented the plate's immediate retrieval.

When one of the FBI Agents returned to the main house to ask the MFJP officers for a crowbar, they became extremely curious and followed the Agent as he returned, empty handed, to the tennis court. By this time, a second Agent had managed to remove the grate by using a heavy-wire coat hanger. The license plate was retrieved, unfolded and photographed. The MFJP officers, all of whom were now at the tennis court, became upset at this discovery, and one of them immediately contacted his superior at MFJP headquarters, who ordered them to secure the license plate until the

FIGURE 1 Diagram of the 881 Lope De Vega grounds. Camarena was held prisoner in the guest house.

Assistant Primer Comandante arrived on the scene. After his arrival approximately 20 minutes later, he seized the license plate and would not allow the Americans to conduct any further searches.

However, by this time, five very large plastic bags of evidence had been recovered and were placed in the rear of a DEA truck. The evidence was quickly transported to the DEA vault in the U.S. Consulate.

After negotiations between the United States and Mexico, the MFJP did allow a second, final search of the residence. On June 24, 1985, a forensic team returned and processed the four remaining rooms on the first floor of the main house.

By this point in the investigation, an associate of Rafael Caro-Quintero had been arrested and interrogated by the MFJP. He stated that the bodies of two Americans, Albert Radelat and John Walker, who had been abducted and killed by Mexican drug traffickers, were buried on the south side of La Primavera Park, a large, primitive park west of Guadalajara. The bodies of Radelat and Walker were located and recovered. Soil samples taken from the surface of an area near their graves were similar in most respects to the soil recovered earlier from the bodies of SA Camarena and Captain Zavala.

In September 1985, DEA personnel went to La Primavera Park and sampled an area approximately 2 feet below the surface near the same site. This sample matched the soil samples from SA Camarena and Captain Zavala almost grain for grain, indicating that this site was almost certainly their burial site before they were relocated to the Bravo ranch.

Later that fall, after further negotiations between the U.S. and the Mexican governments, permission was finally granted for an FBI forensic team to process the

evidence seized by the MFJP forensic team from 881 Lope De Vega the previous April. The evidence consisted of small samples the MFJP had taken of SA Camarena's burial sheet, a piece of rope used to bind SA Camarena, a portion of a pillowcase removed from bedroom number 3, a piece of unsoiled rope removed from the covered patio, and a laboratory report prepared by the MFJP Crime Laboratory. The remainder of the evidence had been destroyed for "health reasons."

In January 1986, a drug trafficker named Rene Verdugo, who was considered to be a high-ranking member of the Caro-Quintero gang, was apprehended and taken to San Diego, where he was arrested by the DEA. He was then transported to Washington, D.C., where hair samples were taken. He refused to testify before a federal grand jury investigating the Camarena case. Later that year, DEA personnel obtained hair samples in Mexico City from Sergio Espino-Verdin, a former federal comandante, who is believed to have been SA Camarena's primary interrogator during his ordeal at 881 Lope De Vega.

The Trial

In July 1988, the main trial of the murder, interrogation, and abduction of SA Camarena began in U.S. District Court in Los Angeles, CA. The forensic evidence presented in this trial identified 881 Lope De Vega as the site where SA Camarena had been held. The evidence also strongly associated two Mexican citizens, Rene Verdugo and Sergio Espino-Verdin, with the "guest house" at 881 Lope De Vega. Several types of forensic evidence were used to associate SA Camarena with 881 Lope De Vega: forcibly removed head hairs, found in the "guest house" and bedroom number 4, in the VW Atlantic and in the Mercury Gran Marquis, and two types of polyester rug fibers, a dark, rose-

FIGURE 2 Trial chart showing hair comparisons between known Camarena hairs and hairs recovered from 881 Lope De Vega.

FIGURE 3 Trial chart showing hair comparisons between known Camarena hairs and hairs recovered from the Mercury Gran Marquis.

FIGURE 4   A model of 881 Lope De Vega prepared as a trial exhibit.

colored fiber and a light-colored fiber. [See Figures 2 and 3.] Fabric evidence was also presented, which demonstrated the similarities of color, composition, construction, and design between SA Camarena's burial sheet and the two pillowcases recovered from bedrooms number 3 and 5.

Based on this evidence associating SA Camarena and 881 Lope De Vega, the FBI Laboratory examiner was able to testify that SA Camarena was at this residence, as well as in the VW Atlantic and the Mercury Gran Marquis, and that he had been in a position such that his head hairs were forcibly removed. Captain Alfredo Zavala was also found to be associated with the "guest house" at 881 Lope De Vega. Light-colored nylon rug fibers, found on samples of his clothing taken at the second autopsy, matched the fibers from the "guest house" carpet.

A detailed model of the residence at 881 Lope De Vega was prepared by the Special Projects Section of the FBI Laboratory for the trial. [See Figure 4.]

Over 20 trial charts were also prepared to explain the various types of forensic evidence. These charts proved invaluable in clarifying the complicated techniques and characteristics used in the examination of the hair, fiber, fabric, and cordage evidence. [See Figure 5.]

Conclusion

The forensic pitfalls and problems in this case (i.e., destruction of evidence, contamination of crime scenes) were eventually resolved. In some cases, certain routine procedures had to be ignored or unconventional methods employed. However, in many instances, detailed trial testimony overcame the limitations of certain evidence, and eventually, almost all of the evidence introduced at the trial made a tremendous impact on the outcome of this proceeding. After an 8-week trial, conducted under tight security and involving hundreds of witnesses, all of the defendants were found guilty, convicted on all counts, and are currently serving lengthy sentences.

CATEGORIES OF FORENSIC EVIDENCE
IN CAMARENA CASE

TYPE OF EVIDENCE						
LOCATION	Hair	Carpet Fibers	Fabric Match	Cordage Match	Tape Match	Misc.
Mercury	**Camarena Head Hair**					Blood on Floor Mat
VW Atlantic	**Camarena Head Hair**					Blood on Tissue
Guest House	**Camarena Head Hair**	Zavala Clothes Nylon				
Bedroom #3		Camarena Blindfold Polyester	Pillow Case Camarena Burial Sheet			
Bedroom #4	**Camarena Head Hair**	Camarena Blindfold & Burial Sheet Polyester				
Bedroom #5			Pillow Case Camarena Burial Sheet			
Tennis Court						License Plate VW/Merc.
Camarena Burial Sheet	**Camarena Head Hair**	Bedroom #4 Polyester	Pillow Case Bedrooms #3 and #5			Soil La Primavera
Source − Blindfold/ Rope	**Camarena Head Hair**	Bedrooms #3 and #4 Polyester			Camarena Blindfold Tape	
Camarena Burial Cordage				Burial Rope from Covered Patio		
Zavala Clothing	**Zavala Head Hair**	Guest House Nylon				Soil La Primavera

FIGURE 5 Trial chart used to show the association of Camarena and Zavala with various locations.

The Green River Killer

This case takes its name from the Green River, which flows through Washington State and empties into Puget Sound in Seattle. Within a six-month span in 1982, the bodies of five females were discovered in or near the river. Most of the victims were known prostitutes who were strangled and apparently raped. As police focused their attention on an area known as Sea-Tac Strip, a haven for prostitutes, girls mysteriously disappeared with increasing frequency. By the end of 1986, the body count in the Seattle region rose to forty; all were believed to have been murdered by the Green River Killer.

As the investigation pressed on into 1987, the police renewed their interest in one suspect, Gary Ridgway, a local truck painter. Ridgway had been known to frequent the Sea-Tac Strip. Interestingly, in 1984 Ridgway actually had passed a lie detector test regarding the Green River killings. Now with a search warrant in hand, police searched Ridgway's residence and also obtained hair and saliva samples from him. Again, insufficient evidence caused Ridgway to be released from custody.

With the exception of one killing in 1998, the murder spree stopped in 1990, and the case remained dormant for nearly ten years. However, the advent of DNA testing brought renewed vigor to the investigation. In 2001, semen samples collected from three early victims of the Green River Killer were compared to saliva that had been collected from Ridgway in 1987. The DNA profiles matched and the police had their man. An added forensic link to Ridgway was made by the location of minute amounts of spray paint on the clothing of six victims that compared to paints collected from Ridgway's workplace. Ridgway ultimately avoided the death penalty by confessing to the murders of forty-eight women.

Physical Evidence

It would be impossible to list all the objects that could conceivably be important to a crime; every crime scene obviously has to be treated on an individual basis, having its own peculiar history, circumstances, and problems. It is practical, however, to list items whose scientific examination is likely to yield significant results in ascertaining the nature and circumstances of a crime. The investigator who is thoroughly familiar with the recognition, collection, and analysis of these items, as well as with laboratory procedures and capabilities, can make logical decisions when the uncommon and unexpected are encountered at the crime scene. Just as important, a qualified evidence collector cannot rely on collection procedures memorized from a pamphlet but must be able to make innovative, on-the-spot decisions at the crime scene.

Common Types of Physical Evidence

Blood, semen, and saliva All suspected blood, semen, or saliva—liquid or dried, animal or human—present in a form that suggests a relation to the offense or people involved in a crime. This category includes blood or semen dried onto fabrics or other objects, as well as cigarette butts that may contain saliva residues. These substances are subjected to serological and biochemical analysis to determine identity and possible origin.

Documents Any handwriting and typewriting submitted so that authenticity or source can be determined. Related items include paper, ink, indented writings, obliterations, and burned or charred documents.

Drugs Any substance seized in violation of laws regulating the sale, manufacture, distribution, and use of drugs.

Explosives Any device containing an explosive charge, as well as all objects removed from the scene of an explosion that are suspected to contain the residues of an explosive.

Fibers Any natural or synthetic fiber whose transfer may be useful in establishing a relationship between objects and/or people.

Fingerprints   All prints of this nature, hidden (latent) and visible.

Firearms and ammunition   Any firearm, as well as discharged or intact ammunition, suspected of being involved in a criminal offense.

Glass   Any glass particle or fragment that may have been transferred to a person or object involved in a crime. Windowpanes containing holes made by a bullet or other projectile are included in this category.

Hair   Any animal or human hair present that could link a person with a crime.

Impressions   Tire markings, shoe prints, depressions in soft soils, and all other forms of tracks. Glove and other fabric impressions, as well as bite marks in skin or foodstuffs, are also included.

Organs and physiological fluids   Body organs and fluids are submitted for analysis to detect the possible existence of drugs and poisons. This category includes blood to be analyzed for the presence of alcohol and other drugs.

Paint   Any paint, liquid or dried, that may have been transferred from the surface of one object to another during the commission of a crime. A common example is the transfer of paint from one vehicle to another during an automobile collision.

Petroleum products   Any petroleum product removed from a suspect or recovered from a crime scene. The most common examples are gasoline residues removed from the scene of an arson, or grease and oil stains whose presence may suggest involvement in a crime.

Plastic bags   A disposable polyethylene bag such as a garbage bag may be evidential in a homicide or drug case. Examinations are conducted to associate a bag with a similar bag in the possession of a suspect.

Plastic, rubber, and other polymers   Remnants of these manufactured materials recovered at crime scenes may be linked to objects recovered in the possession of a criminal suspect.

Powder residues   Any item suspected of containing powder residues resulting from the discharge of a firearm.

Serial numbers   This category includes all stolen property submitted to the laboratory for the restoration of erased identification numbers.

Soil and minerals   All items containing soil or minerals that could link a person or object to a particular location. Common examples are soil imbedded in shoes and insulation found on garments.

Tool marks   This category includes any object suspected of containing the impression of another object that served as a tool in a crime. For example, a screwdriver or crowbar could produce tool marks by being impressed into or scraped along a surface of a wall.

Vehicle lights   Examination of vehicle headlights and taillights is normally conducted to determine whether a light was on or off at the time of impact.

Wood and other vegetative matter   Any fragments of wood, sawdust, shavings, or vegetative matter discovered on clothing, shoes, or tools that could link a person or object to a crime location.

Key Points

- Biological crime-scene evidence includes blood, saliva, semen, DNA, hair, organs, and physiological fluids.

- Impression crime-scene evidence includes tire markings, shoe prints, depressions in soft soils, all other forms of tracks, glove and other fabric impressions, tool marks, and bite marks.

- Manufactured items considered common items of crime-scene evidence include firearms, ammunition, fibers, paint, glass, petroleum products, plastic bags, rubber, polymers, and vehicle headlights.

The Examination of Physical Evidence

Physical evidence is usually examined by a forensic scientist for identification or comparison.

Identification

identification

The process of determining a substance's physical or chemical identity.

Identification has as its purpose the determination of the physical or chemical identity of a substance with as near absolute certainty as existing analytical techniques will permit. For example, the crime laboratory is frequently asked to identify the chemical composition of preparations that may contain illicit drugs such as heroin, cocaine, or barbiturates. It may be asked to identify gasoline in residues recovered from the debris of a fire, or it may have to identify the nature of explosive residues—for example, dynamite or TNT. Also, the identification of blood, semen, hair, or wood would, as a matter of routine, include a determination for species origin. For example, did a bloodstain originate from a human as opposed to a dog or cat? Each of these requests requires the analysis and ultimate identification of a specific physical or chemical substance to the exclusion of all other possible substances.

The process of identification first requires the adoption of testing procedures that give characteristic results for specific standard materials. Once these test results have been established, they may be permanently recorded and used repeatedly to prove the identity of suspect materials. For example, to ascertain that a particular suspect powder is heroin, the test results on the powder must be identical to those that have been previously obtained from a known heroin sample.

Second, identification requires that the number and type of tests needed to identify a substance be sufficient to exclude all other substances. This means that the examiner must devise a specific analytical scheme that will eliminate all but one substance from consideration. Hence, if the examiner concludes that a white powder contains heroin, the test results must have been comprehensive enough to have excluded all other drugs—or, for that matter, all other substances—from consideration.

Simple rules cannot be devised for defining what constitutes a thorough and foolproof analytical scheme. Each type of evidence obviously requires different tests, and each test has a different degree of specificity. Thus, one substance could conceivably be identified by one test, whereas another may require the combination of five or six different tests to arrive at an identification. In a science in which the practitioner has little or no control over the quality and quantity of the specimens received, a standard series of tests cannot encompass all possible problems and pitfalls. So the forensic scientist must determine at what point the analysis can be concluded and the criteria for positive identification satisfied; for this, he or she must rely on knowledge gained through education and experience. Ultimately, the conclusion will have to be substantiated beyond any reasonable doubt in a court of law.

Comparison

A comparison analysis subjects a suspect specimen and a standard/ reference specimen to the same tests and examinations for the ultimate purpose of determining whether they have a common origin. For example, the forensic scientist may place a suspect at a particular location by noting the similarities of a hair found at the crime scene to hairs removed from a suspect's head (Figure 3–1). Or a paint chip found on a hit-and-run victim's garment may be compared with paint removed from a vehicle suspected of being involved in the incident.

The forensic comparison is actually a two-step procedure. First, combinations of select properties are chosen from the suspect and the standard/ reference specimen for comparison. The question of which and how many properties are selected obviously depends on the type of materials being examined. (This subject will receive a good deal of discussion in forthcoming chapters.) The overriding consideration must be the ultimate evidential value of the conclusion.

This brings us to the second objective. Once the examination has been completed, the forensic scientist must draw a conclusion about the origins of the specimens. Do they or do they not come from the same source? Certainly if one or more of the properties selected for comparison do not

comparison
The process of ascertaining whether two or more objects have a common origin.

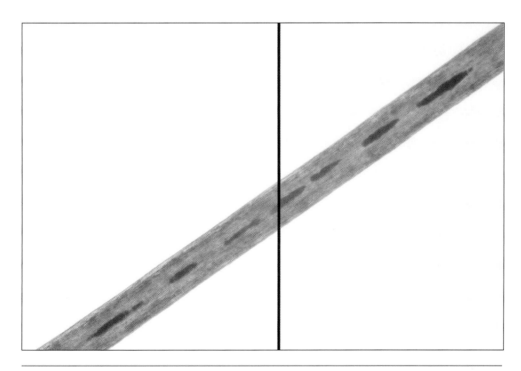

FIGURE 3–1 **Side-by-side comparison of hairs.** *Courtesy Chris Palenik, Microtrace, Elgin, IL., www.microtracescientific.com*

agree, the analyst will conclude that the specimens are not the same and hence could not have originated from the same source. Suppose, on the other hand, that all the properties do compare and the specimens, as far as the examiner can determine, are indistinguishable. Does it logically follow that they come from the same source? Not necessarily so.

To comprehend the evidential value of a comparison, one must appreciate the role that probability has in ascertaining the origins of two or more specimens. Simply defined, *probability* is the frequency of occurrence of an event. If a coin is flipped hundred times, in theory we can expect heads to come up fifty times. Hence, the probability of the event (heads) occurring is 50 in 100. In other words, probability defines the odds that a certain event will occur.

individual characteristics
Properties of evidence that can be attributed to a common source with an extremely high degree of certainty.

Individual Characteristics   Evidence that can be associated with a common source with an extremely high degree of probability is said to possess individual characteristics. Examples of such associations are the matching ridge characteristics of two fingerprints, the comparison of random striations (markings) on bullets or tool marks, the comparison of irregular and random wear patterns in tire or footwear impressions, the comparison of handwriting characteristics, the fitting together of the irregular edges of broken objects in the manner of a jigsaw puzzle (see Figure 3–2), or matching sequentially made plastic bags by striation marks running across the bags (see Figure 3–3).

FIGURE 3–2   The body of a woman was found with evidence of beating about the head and a stablike wound in the neck. Her husband was charged with the murder. The pathologist found a knife blade tip in the wound in the neck. The knife blade tip was compared with the broken blade of a penknife found in the trousers pocket of the accused. Note that in addition to the fit of the indentations on the edges, the scratch marks running across the blade tip correspond in detail to those on the broken blade. *Courtesy Centre of Forensic Sciences, Toronto, Canada*

FIGURE 3–3 **The bound body of a young woman was recovered from a river. Her head was covered with a black polyethylene trash bag (shown on the right). Among the items recovered from one of several suspects was a black polyethylene trash bag (shown on the left). A side-by-side comparison of the two bags' extrusion marks and pigment bands showed them to be consecutively manufactured. This information allowed investigators to focus their attention on one suspect, who ultimately was convicted of the homicide.** *Courtesy George W. Neighbor, New Jersey State Police*

In all of these cases, it is not possible to state with mathematical exactness the probability that the specimens are of common origin; it can only be concluded that this probability is so high as to defy mathematical calculations or human comprehension. Furthermore, the conclusion of common origin must be substantiated by the practical experience of the examiner. For example, the French scientist Victor Balthazard has mathematically determined that the probability of two individuals having the same fingerprints is one out of 1×10^{60}, or 1 followed by sixty zeros. This probability is so small as to exclude the possibility of any two individuals having the same fingerprints. This contention is also supported by the experience of fingerprint examiners who, after classifying millions of prints over the past hundred years, have never found any two to be exactly alike.

Class Characteristics   One disappointment awaiting the investigator unfamiliar with the limitations of forensic science is the frequent inability of the laboratory to relate physical evidence to a common origin with a high degree of certainty. Evidence is said to possess class characteristics when it can be associated only with a group and never with a single source. Here again, probability is a determining factor. For example, if we compare two single-layer automobile paint chips of a similar color, their chance of originating from the same car is not nearly as great as when we compare two paint chips with seven similar layers of paint, not all of which were part of the car's original color. The former will have class characteristics and could be associated at best only with one car model (which may number in the thousands), whereas the latter may be judged to have individual characteristics and to have a high probability of originating from one specific car.

Blood offers another good example of evidence that can have class characteristics. For example, suppose that two blood specimens are compared and both are found to be of human origin, type A. The frequency of occurrence in the population of type A blood is 26 percent—hardly offering a basis for establishing the common origin of the stains. However, if other blood factors are also determined and are found to compare, the probability that the two bloods originated from a common source increases.

class characteristics
Properties of evidence that can be associated only with a group and never with a single source.

product rule
A formula for determining how frequently a certain combination of characteristics occurs in a population. The product rule states that one must first determine the probability of each characteristic occurring separately, then multiply together the frequencies of all independently occurring characteristics. The result is the overall frequency of occurrence for that particular combination of characteristics.

Thus, if one uses a series of blood factors that occur independently of each other than one can apply the product rule to calculate the overall frequency of occurrence of the blood in a population. In this case, the product rule states that multiplying together the frequency of each factor present in a blood sample will determine how common blood containing that combination of factors is in the general population.

For example, in the O. J. Simpson murder case, a bloodstain located at the crime scene was found to contain a number of factors that compared to O. J.'s blood:

Blood Factors	Frequency
A	26%
EsD	85%
PGM 2+2−	2%

The product of all the frequencies shown in the table determines the probability that any one individual possesses such a combination of blood factors. In this instance, applying the product rule, $0.26 \times 0.85 \times 0.02$ equals 0.0044. Thus, only 0.44 percent, or less than 1 in 200 people, would be expected to have this particular combination of blood factors. These bloodstain factors did not match either of the two victims, Nicole Brown Simpson or Ronald Goldman, thus eliminating them as possible sources of the blood. Although the forensic scientist has still not individualized the bloodstains to one person (in this case, O. J. Simpson), data have been provided that will permit investigators and the courts to better assess the evidential value of the crime-scene stain.

As we will learn in Chapter 9, the product rule is used to determine the frequency of occurrence of DNA profiles typically determined from blood and other biological materials. Importantly, modern DNA technology provides enough factors to allow an analyst to individualize blood, semen, and other biological materials to a single person.

Key Points

- Two methods used by forensic scientists when examining physical evidence are identification and comparison.

- Identification is the process of determining a substance's chemical or physical identity to the exclusion of all other substances; e.g., drugs, explosives, petroleum products, blood, semen, and hair species.

- A comparison analysis determines whether a suspect specimen and a standard/reference specimen have a common origin.

- Evidence that can be associated with a common source with an extremely high degree of probability is said to possess individual characteristics.

- Evidence associated with only a group is said to have class characteristics.

- The overall frequency of occurrence of an event can be obtained by multiplying the frequencies of all independently occurring instances related to that event. This is known as the *product rule*.

The Significance
of Physical Evidence

One of the current weaknesses of forensic science is the inability of the examiner to assign exact or even approximate probability values to the comparison of most class physical evidence. For example, what is the probability that a nylon fiber originated from a particular sweater, or that a hair came from a particular person's head, or that a paint chip came from a car suspected to have been involved in a hit-and-run accident? Very few statistical data are available from which to derive this information, and in a society that is increasingly dependent on mass-produced products, the gathering of such data is becoming an increasingly elusive goal.

One of the primary endeavors of forensic scientists must be to create and update statistical databases for evaluating the significance of class physical evidence. Of course, when such information—for example, the population frequency of blood factors—is available, it is used; but for the most part, the forensic scientist must rely on personal experience when interpreting the significance of class physical evidence.

People who are unfamiliar with the realities of modern criminalistics are often disappointed to learn that most items of physical evidence retrieved at crime scenes cannot be linked definitively to a single person or object. Although investigators always try to uncover physical evidence with individual characteristics—such as fingerprints, tool marks, and bullets—the chances of finding class physical evidence are far greater. To deny or belittle the value of such evidence is to reject the potential role that criminalistics can play in a criminal investigation.

In practice, criminal cases are fashioned for the courtroom around a collection of diverse elements, each pointing to the guilt or involvement of a party in a criminal act. Often, most of the evidence gathered is subjective, prone to human error and bias. The believability of eyewitness accounts, confessions, and informant testimony can all be disputed, maligned, and subjected to severe attack and skepticism in the courtroom. Under these circumstances, errors in human judgment are often magnified to detract from the credibility of the witness.

Assessing the Value of Evidence

The value of class physical evidence lies in its ability to corroborate events with data in a manner that is, as nearly as possible, free of human error and bias. It is the thread that binds together other investigative findings that are more dependent on human judgments and, therefore, more prone to human failings. The fact that scientists have not yet learned to individualize many kinds of physical evidence means that criminal investigators should not abdicate or falter in their pursuit of all investigative leads. However, the ability of scientists to achieve a high degree of success in evaluating class physical evidence means that criminal investigators can pursue their work with a much greater chance of success.

Admittedly, defining the significance of an item of class evidence in exact mathematical terms is usually a difficult if not impossible goal. While class evidence is by its very nature not unique, meaningful items of physical evidence, such as those listed at the beginning of this chapter, are extremely diverse in our environment. Select, for example, a colored fiber from an article of clothing and try to locate the exact same color on the clothing of random individuals you meet, or select a car color and try to

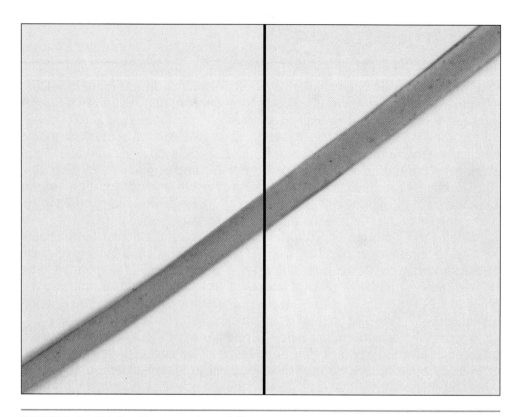

FIGURE 3–4   Side-by-side comparison of fibers. *Courtesy Chris Palenik, Microtrace, Elgin, IL., www.microtracescientific.com*

match it to other automobiles you see on local streets. Furthermore, keep in mind that a forensic comparison goes beyond a mere color comparison and involves examining and comparing a variety of chemical and/or physical properties (Figure 3–4). The chances are low of encountering two indistinguishable items of physical evidence at a crime scene that actually originated from different sources. Obviously, given these circumstances, only objects that exhibit significant diversity are appropriate for classification as physical evidence.

In the same way, when one is dealing with more than one type of class evidence, their collective presence may lead to an extremely high certainty that they originated from the same source. As the number of different objects linking an individual to a crime increases, the probability of involvement increases dramatically. A classic example of this situation can be found in the evidence presented at the trial of Wayne Williams (see the case reading at the end of this chapter). Wayne Williams was charged with the murders of two individuals in the Atlanta, Georgia, metropolitan area; he was also linked to the murders of ten other boys and young men. An essential element of the state's case involved the association of Williams with the victims through a variety of fiber evidence. Actually, twenty-eight different types of fibers linked Williams to the murder victims, evidence that the forensic examiner characterized as "overwhelming."

Cautions and Limitations in Dealing with Physical Evidence

In further evaluating the contribution of physical evidence, one cannot overlook one important reality in the courtroom: The weight or significance accorded physical evidence is a determination left entirely to the trier of fact, usually a jury of laypeople. Given the high esteem in which scientists are generally held by society and the infallible image created for forensic science by books and television, scientifically evaluated evidence often takes on an aura of special reliability and trustworthiness in the courtroom. Often physical evidence, whether individual or class, is accorded great weight during jury deliberations and becomes a primary factor in reinforcing or overcoming lingering doubts about guilt or innocence. In fact, a number of jurists have already cautioned against giving carte blanche approval to admitting scientific testimony without first considering its relevance to the case. Given the potential weight of scientific evidence, failure to take proper safeguards may unfairly prejudice a case against the accused.

Physical evidence may also serve to exclude or exonerate a person from suspicion. For instance, if type A blood is linked to the suspect, all individuals who have types B, AB, and O blood can be eliminated from consideration. Because it is not possible to assess at the crime scene what value, if any, the scientist will find in the evidence collected, or what significance such findings will ultimately have to a jury, thorough collection and scientific evaluation of physical evidence must become a routine part of all criminal investigations.

Just when an item of physical evidence crosses the line that distinguishes class from individual is a difficult question to answer and is often the source of heated debate and honest disagreement among forensic scientists. How many striations are necessary to individualize a mark to a single tool and no other? How many color layers individualize a paint chip to a single car? How many ridge characteristics individualize a fingerprint, and how many handwriting characteristics tie a person to a signature? These questions defy simple answers. The task of the forensic scientist is to find as many characteristics as possible to compare one substance with another. The significance attached to the findings is decided by the quality and composition of the evidence, the case history, and the examiner's experience. Ultimately, the conclusion can range from mere speculation to near certainty.

There are practical limits to the properties and characteristics the forensic scientist can select for comparison. Carried to the extreme, no two things in this world are alike in every detail. Modern analytical techniques have become so sophisticated and sensitive that the criminalist must define the limits of natural variation among materials when interpreting the data gathered from a comparative analysis. For example, we will learn in the next chapter that two properties, density and refractive index, are best suited for comparing two pieces of glass. But the latest techniques that have been developed to measure these properties are so sensitive that they can even distinguish glass originating from a single pane of glass. Certainly this goes beyond the desires of a criminalist trying to determine only whether two glass particles originated from the same window. Similarly, if the surface of a paint chip is magnified 1,600 times with a powerful scanning electron microscope, it is apparent that the fine details that are revealed could not be duplicated in any other paint chip. Under these circumstances, no two paint chips, even those coming from the same surface, could ever compare in the true sense of the word. Therefore, practicality dictates that such examinations be conducted at a less revealing, but more meaningful, magnification (see Figure 3–5).

Distinguishing evidential variations from natural variations is not always an easy task. Learning how to use the microscope and all the other modern instruments in a crime laboratory properly is one thing; gaining the proficiency needed to interpret the observations and data is another. As new

(a)

(b)

FIGURE 3–5 (a) Two-layer paint chip magnified 244 times with a scanning electron microscope. (b) The same paint chip viewed at a magnification of 1,600 times. *Courtesy Jeff Albright*

crime laboratories are created and others expand to meet the requirements of the law enforcement community, many individuals are starting new careers in forensic science. They must be cautioned that merely reading relevant textbooks and journals is no substitute for experience in this most practical of sciences.

- The value of class physical evidence lies in its ability to corroborate events with data in a manner that is, as nearly as possible, free of human error and bias.

- As the number of different objects linking an individual to a crime scene increases, so does the likelihood of that individual's involvement with the crime.

- A person may be exonerated or excluded from suspicion if physical evidence collected at a crime scene is found to be different from standard/reference samples collected from that subject.

Forensic Databases

In a criminal investigation, the ultimate contribution a criminalist can make is to link a suspect to a crime through comparative analysis. This comparison defines the unique role of the criminalist in a criminal investigation. Of course, a one-on-one comparison requires a suspect. Little or nothing of evidential value can be accomplished if crime-scene investigators acquire fingerprints, hairs, fibers, paint, blood, and semen without the ability to link these items to a suspect. In this respect, computer technology has dramatically altered the role of the crime laboratory in the investigative process.

No longer is the crime laboratory a passive bystander waiting for investigators to uncover clues about who may have committed a crime. Today, the crime laboratory is on the forefront of the investigation seeking to identify perpetrators. This dramatic enhancement of the role of forensic science in criminal investigation has come about through the creation of computerized databases that not only link all fifty states, but tie together police agencies throughout the world.

Fingerprint Databases

The premier model of all forensic database systems is the *Integrated Automated Fingerprint Identification System* (IAFIS), a national fingerprint and criminal history system maintained by the FBI and launched in 1999. IAFIS contains fingerprints and corresponding criminal history information for nearly 50 million subjects (or 500 million fingerprint images), which are submitted voluntarily to the FBI by state, local, and federal law enforcement agencies.

A crime-scene fingerprint or latent fingerprint is a dramatic find for the criminal investigator. Once the quality of the print has been deemed suitable for the IAFIS search, the latent-print examiner creates a digital image of the print with either a digital camera or a scanner. Next, the examiner, with the aid of a coder, marks points on the print to guide the computerized search. The print is then electronically submitted to IAFIS and within minutes the search is completed against all fingerprint images in IAFIS; the examiner may receive a list of potential candidates and their corresponding fingerprints for comparison and verification (see Figure 3–6).

Many countries throughout the world have created *National Automated Fingerprint Identification Systems* that are comparable to the FBI's model. For example, a computerized fingerprint database containing nearly nine million ten-print records connects the Home Office and forty-three police forces throughout England and Wales.

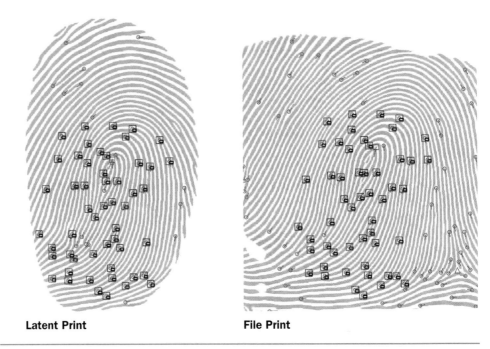

Latent Print   **File Print**

FIGURE 3–6 **The computerized search of a fingerprint database first requires that selected ridge characteristics be designated by a coder. The positions of these ridge characteristics serve as a basis for comparing the print against file fingerprints.** *Courtesy Sirchie Finger Print Laboratories, Inc., Youngsville, N.C., www.sirchie.com*

Forensic Brief

In 1975, police found Gerald Wallace's body on his living room couch. He had been savagely beaten, his hands bound with an electric cord. Detectives searched his ransacked house, cataloging every piece of evidence they could find. None of it led to the murderer. They had no witnesses. Sixteen years after the fact, a lone fingerprint, lifted from a cigarette pack found in Wallace's house and kept for sixteen years in the police files, was entered into the Pennsylvania State Police AFIS database. Within minutes, it hit a match. That print, police say, gave investigators the identity of a man who had been at the house the night of the murder. Police talked to him. He led them to other witnesses, who led them to the man police ultimately charged with the murder of Gerald Wallace.

DNA Databases

In 1998, the FBI's *Combined DNA Index System* (CODIS) became fully operational. CODIS enables federal, state, and local crime laboratories to electronically exchange and compare DNA profiles, thereby linking crimes to each other and to convicted offenders. All fifty states have enacted legislation to establish a data bank containing DNA profiles of individuals convicted of felony sexual offenses (and other crimes, depending on each state's statute).

CODIS creates investigative leads from two sources: the *forensic index* and the *offender index*. The forensic index currently contains about 110,000 profiles from unsolved crime-scene evidence. Based on a match, police in multiple jurisdictions can identify serial crimes, allowing coordination of investigations and sharing of leads developed independently. The offender

Forensic Brief

Fort Collins, Colorado, and Philadelphia, Pennsylvania, are separated by nearly 1,800 miles, but in 2001 they were tragically linked though DNA. Troy Graves left the Philadelphia area in 1999, joined the Air Force, and settled down with his wife in Colorado. A frenzied string of eight sexual assaults around the Colorado University campus set off a manhunt that ultimately resulted in the arrest of Graves. However, his DNA profile inextricably identified him as Philadelphia's notorious "Center City rapist." This assailant attacked four women in 1997 and brutally murdered Shannon Schieber, a Wharton School graduate student, in 1998. His last known attack in Philadelphia was the rape of an 18-year-old student in August 1999, shortly before he left the city. In 2002 Graves was returned to Philadelphia, where he was sentenced to life in prison without parole.

index contains the profiles of nearly three million convicted or arrested individuals. (Unfortunately, hundreds of thousands of samples are back-logged, still awaiting DNA analysis and entry into the offender index.) Law enforcement agencies search this index against DNA profiles recovered from biological evidence found at unsolved crime scenes. This approach has been tremendously successful in identifying perpetrators because most crimes involving biological evidence are committed by repeat offenders.

Several countries throughout the world have initiated national DNA data banks. The United Kingdom's *National DNA Database*, established in 1995, was the world's first national database. Currently it holds about three million profiles, and DNA can be taken for entry into the database from anyone arrested for an offense likely to involve a prison term. In a typical month, matches are found linking suspects to 26 murders; 57 rapes and other sexual offenses; and 3,000 motor vehicle, property and drug crimes.

Other Databases

The *National Integrated Ballistics Information Network* (NIBIN) maintained by the Bureau of Alcohol, Tobacco, Firearms and Explosives, allows firearms analysts to acquire, digitize, and compare markings made by a firearm on bullets and cartridge casings recovered from crime scenes. The NIBIN program currently has 236 sites that are electronically joined to sixteen multistate regions.

The heart of NIBIN is the *Integrated Ballistic Identification System* (IBIS), comprising a microscope and a computer unit that can capture an image of a bullet or cartridge casing. The images are then forwarded to a regional server, where they are stored and correlated against other images in the regional database. IBIS does not positively match bullets or casings fired from the same weapon; this must be done by a firearms examiner. IBIS does, however, facilitate the work of the firearms examiner by producing a short list of candidates for the examiner to manually compare. Nearly 900,000 pieces of crime-scene evidence have been entered in NIBIN and more than 10,000 "hits" have been recorded, many of them yielding investigative information not obtainable by other means.

The *International Forensic Automotive Paint Data Query* (PDQ) database contains chemical and color information pertaining to original automotive paints. This database, developed and is maintained by the Forensic

Forensic Brief

After a series of armed robberies in which suspects fired shots, the sheriff's office of Broward County, Florida, entered the cartridge casings from the crime scenes into NIBIN. Through NIBIN, four of the armed robberies were linked to the same 40-caliber handgun. A short time later, sheriff's deputies noticed suspicious activity around a local business. When they attempted to interview the suspects, the suspects fled in a vehicle. During the chase, the suspects attempted to dispose of a handgun; deputies recovered the gun after making the arrests. The gun was test-fired and the resulting evidence entered into NIBIN, which indicated a possible link between this handgun and the four previous armed robberies. Firearms examiners confirmed the link by examining the original evidence. The suspects were arrested and charged with four prior armed robbery offenses.

Laboratory Services of the Royal Canadian Mounted Police (RCMP), contains information about make, model, year, and assembly plant on more than 13,000 vehicles, with a library of more than 50,000 layers of paint. Contributors to the PDQ include the RCMP and forensic laboratories in Ontario and Quebec, as well as forty U.S. forensic laboratories and police agencies in twenty-one other countries. Accredited users of PDQ are required to submit sixty new automotive paint samples per year for addition to the database. The PDQ database has found its greatest utility in the investigation of hit-and-runs by providing police with possible make, model, and year information to aid in the search for the unknown vehicle.

The previously described databases are maintained and controlled by government agencies. There is one exception: a commercially available computer retrieval system for comparing and identifying crime-scene shoe prints known as *SICAR (shoeprint image capture and retrieval).*[1] SICAR's pattern-coding system enables an analyst to create a simple description of a shoe print by assigning codes to individual pattern features (see Figure 3–7). Shoe print images can be entered into SICAR by either a scanner or a digital camera. This product has a comprehensive shoe sole database that includes more than three hundred manufacturers of shoes with more than eight thousand different sole patterns, providing investigators with a means for linking a crime-scene footwear impression to a particular shoe manufacturer.

Key Points

- The creation of computerized databases for fingerprints, criminal histories, DNA profiles, markings on bullets and cartridges, automotive paints, and shoe prints has dramatically enhanced the role of forensic science in criminal investigation.

- IAFIS is the Integrated Automated Fingerprint Identification System, a national fingerprint and criminal history database maintained by the FBI. IAFIS allows criminal investigators to compare fingerprints at a crime scene to an index of 500 million known prints. CODIS is the FBI's Combined DNA Index System. It enables federal, state, and local crime laboratories to electronically exchange and compare DNA profiles, linking crimes to each other and to convicted offenders.

FIGURE 3–7 **The crime-scene footwear print on the right is being searched against eight thousand sole patterns to determine its make and model.** *Courtesy Foster & Freeman Limited, Worcestershire, U.K., www.fosterfreeman.co.uk*

Crime-Scene Reconstruction

Previous discussions of identification and comparison have stressed laboratory work routinely performed by forensic scientists. However, there is another dimension to the role of forensic scientists in a criminal investigation: working as a team to reconstruct events before, during, and after the commission of a crime.

Reconstructing the circumstances of a crime scene entails a collaborative effort that includes experienced law enforcement personnel, medical examiners, and criminalists. All of the professionals contribute a unique perspective to develop the crime-scene reconstruction. Was more than one person involved? How was the victim killed? Were actions taken to cover up what actually took place? To answer these questions, everyone involved with the investigation must pay careful attention and apply logical thinking.

Principles of Crime-Scene Reconstruction

The physical evidence left behind at a crime scene plays a crucial role in reconstructing the events that took place surrounding the crime. Although the evidence alone does not describe everything that happened, it can support or contradict accounts given by witnesses and/or suspects. Information obtained from physical evidence can also generate leads and confirm the reconstruction of a crime to a jury. The collection and documentation of physical evidence is the foundation of a reconstruction. Reconstruction supports a likely sequence of events by observing and evaluating physical evidence and statements made by witnesses and those involved with the incident.

reconstruction
The method used to support a likely sequence of events at a crime scene by observing and evaluating physical evidence and statements made by those involved with the incident.

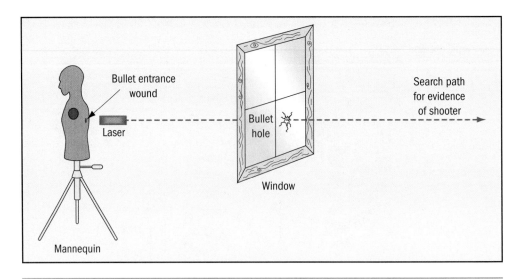

FIGURE 3–8   A laser beam is used to determine the search area for the position of a shooter who has fired a bullet through a window and wounded a victim. The bullet path is determined by lining up the victim's bullet wound with the bullet hole in the glass pane.

Law enforcement personnel must take the proper actions to enhance all aspects of the crime-scene search so as to optimize the crime-scene reconstruction. First, and most important, is securing and protecting the crime scene. Protecting the scene is a continuous endeavor from the beginning to the end of the search. Evidence that can be invaluable to reconstructing the crime can be unknowingly altered or destroyed by people trampling through the scene, rendering the evidence useless. The issue of possible contamination of evidence will certainly be attacked during the litigation process and could make the difference between a guilty and not-guilty verdict.

Before processing the crime scene for physical evidence, the investigator should make a preliminary examination of the scene as it was left by the perpetrator. Each crime scene presents its own set of circumstances. The investigator's experience and the presence or absence of physical evidence become critical factors in reconstructing a crime.

The investigator captures the nature of the scene as a whole by performing an initial walk-through of the crime scene and contemplating the events that took place. Using the physical evidence available to the naked eye, he or she can hypothesize about what occurred, where it occurred, and when it occurred. During the walk-through, the investigator must document observations and formulate how the scene should ultimately be processed.

As the collection of physical evidence begins, any and all observations should be recorded through photographs, sketches, and notes. By carefully collecting physical evidence and thoroughly documenting the crime scene, the investigator can begin to unravel the sequence of events that took place during the commission of the crime.

Personnel Involved in Reconstruction

Often reconstruction requires the involvement of a medical examiner or a criminalist. For example, a trained medical examiner might determine whether a corpse has been moved after death by evaluating the livor distribution within the body. If livor has developed in areas other than those closest to the ground, the medical examiner can reason that the victim was probably moved after death. Likewise, the examiner can determine whether

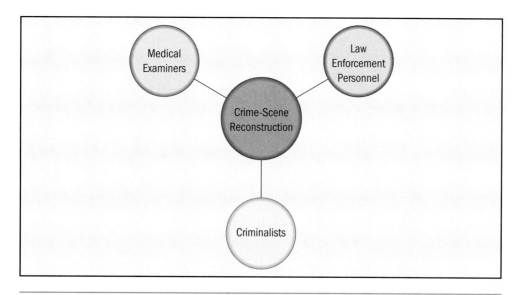

FIGURE 3–9 **Crime-scene reconstruction relies on the combined efforts of medical examiners, criminalists, and law enforcement personnel to recover physical evidence and to sort out the events surrounding the occurrence of a crime.**

the victim was clothed after death, because livor will not develop within areas of the body that are restricted by clothing. Such determinations can often reveal pertinent information that will aid the investigation.

A criminalist or trained crime-scene investigator can also bring special skills to the reconstruction of events that occurred during the commission of a crime. For example, a criminalist using a laser beam to plot the approximate bullet path in trajectory analysis can help determine the probable position of the shooter relative to that of the victim (see Figure 3–8). Other skills that a criminalist may employ during a crime-scene reconstruction analysis include blood spatter analysis (discussed more fully in Chapter 8), determining the direction of impact of projectiles penetrating glass objects (Chapter 4), locating gunshot residues deposited on the victim's clothing to estimate the distance of a shooter from a target, and searching for primer residues deposited on the hands of a suspect shooter (both covered in Chapter 15).

Reconstruction is a team effort that involves putting together many different pieces of a puzzle (see Figure 3–9). The right connections must be made among all the parts involved so as to portray the relationship among the victim, the suspect, and the crime scene. If successful, reconstruction can play a vital role in helping a jury arrive at an appropriate verdict.

Key Points

- Crime-scene reconstruction relies on the combined efforts of medical examiners, criminalists, and law enforcement personnel to recover physical evidence and to sort out the events surrounding the occurrence of a crime.

- Examples of crime scene reconstruction include determining whether a body was moved after death, determining whether a victim was clothed after death, analyzing bullet trajectory, analyzing blood spatter, determining the direction from which projectiles penetrated glass objects, estimating the distance of a shooter from a target, and locating primer residue on suspects.

Chapter Summary

Physical evidence is usually examined by a forensic scientist for identification or comparison. The object of identification is to determine the physical or chemical identity with as near absolute certainty as existing analytical techniques will permit. Identification first requires the adoption of testing procedures that give characteristic results for specific standard/reference materials. Once this is done, the examiner uses an appropriate number of tests to identify a substance and exclude all other substances from consideration. The identification process is normally used in crime laboratories to identify drugs, explosives, and petroleum products. Also, evidence such as blood, semen, or hair is routinely identified in a crime laboratory. Normally these identifications include a determination for species origin (such as human blood or rabbit hair).

A comparative analysis has the important role of determining whether a suspect specimen and a standard/reference specimen have a common origin. Both the standard/reference and the suspect specimen are subject to the same tests. Evidence that can be associated with a common source with an extremely high degree of probability is said to possess individual characteristics. Evidence associated only with a group is said to have class characteristics. Nevertheless, the high diversity of class evidence in our environment makes their comparison very significant in the context of a criminal investigation. As the number of different objects linking an individual to a crime scene increases, so does the likelihood of that individual's involvement with the crime. Importantly, a person may be exonerated or excluded from suspicion if physical evidence collected at a crime scene is found to be different from standard/reference samples collected from that subject.

A dramatic enhancement of the role of forensic science in criminal investigation has come about through the creation of computerized databases. The Integrated Automated Fingerprint Identification System (IAFIS), a national fingerprint and criminal history system, is maintained by the FBI. The FBI's Combined DNA Index System (CODIS) enables federal, state, and local crime laboratories to electronically exchange and compare DNA profiles, thereby linking crimes to each other and to convicted offenders. The National Integrated Ballistics Information Network (NIBIN), maintained by the Bureau of Alcohol, Tobacco, Firearms and Explosives, allows firearms analysts to acquire, digitize, and compare markings made by a firearm on bullets and cartridge casings recovered from crime scenes. The International Forensic Automotive Paint Data Query (PDQ) database contains chemical and color information pertaining to original automotive paints. SICAR (shoeprint image capture and retrieval) has a comprehensive shoe sole database.

Physical evidence left behind at a crime scene, properly handled and preserved, plays a crucial role in reconstructing the events that took place surrounding the crime. Crime-scene reconstruction relies on the combined efforts of medical examiners, criminalists, and law enforcement personnel to recover physical evidence and to sort out the events surrounding the occurrence of a crime.

Review Questions

Facts and Concepts

1. List five examples of each of the following types of physical evidence: biological materials, impressions, and manufactured items.

2. What is the purpose of identification? What are the two main requirements for identification?

3. List three reasons why it is not possible to define a simple analytical scheme that can be applied to all types of evidence.

4. What is a comparison analysis? What are the two steps in comparison?

5. Define *individual characteristics* and give two examples.

6. Define *class characteristics* and give two examples.

7. State the product rule and explain how it applies to the comparison of physical evidence.

8. Explain how the product rule is relevant to the murder conviction of Wayne Williams.

9. What is the greatest weakness of class physical evidence? What is the main reason for this weakness?

10. What is the greatest value of class physical evidence?

11. Who ultimately determines the significance of physical evidence in a trial?
    a. the judge
    b. expert witnesses
    c. the Supreme Court
    d. the jury

12. State two reasons why it is important to consider the relevance of scientific evidence before allowing it to be introduced into a criminal case.

13. Why does a forensic scientist often opt not to use the most sensitive analytical techniques when comparing suspect substances?

14. What is a forensic database and how are such databases useful to criminalists?

15. Name three forensic databases and describe the type of information stored in each.

16. Describe the difference between the forensic and offender indexes in the CODIS database.

17. What is crime-scene reconstruction?

18. In which of the following ways can physical evidence aid in crime-scene reconstruction? (You may choose more than one response.)
    a. by supporting or contradicting statements given by witnesses and/or suspects
    b. by describing exactly what happened at the crime scene
    c. by confirming the accuracy of a crime-scene reconstruction to a jury
    d. by distinguishing between individual and class characteristics
    e. by generating leads that may help investigators solve the case

19. What is the first and most important step in crime-scene reconstruction?

20. Give at least three examples of a specialized task a criminalist might perform in crime-scene reconstruction.

Application and Critical Thinking

1. Arrange the following tasks in order from the one that would require the least extensive testing procedure to the one that would require the most extensive. Explain your answer.

   a. determining whether an unknown substance contains an illicit drug
   b. determining the composition of an unknown substance
   c. determining whether an unknown substance contains heroin

2. The following are three possible combinations of DNA characteristics that might be found in an individual's genetic profile. Using the probability rule, rank each of these combinations of DNA characteristics from most common to least common. The number after each characteristic indicates its percentage distribution in the population.

   a. FGA 24,24 (3.6%), TH01 6,8 (8.1%), and D16S539 11, 12 (8.9%)
   b. vWA 14,19 (6.2%), D21S11 30,30 (3.9%), and D13S317 12,12 (8.5%)
   c. CSF1PO 9,10 (11.2%), D18S51 14,17 (2.8%), and D8S1179 17,18 (6.7%)

3. For each piece of evidence listed below, indicate whether the item is more likely to possess class or individual characteristics and explain your answers:

   a. an impression from a new automobile tire
   b. a fingerprint
   c. a spent bullet cartridge
   d. a mass-produced synthetic fiber
   e. pieces of a shredded document
   f. commercial potting soil
   g. skin and hair scrapings
   h. fragments of a multi-layer custom automobile paint

4. Which of the forensic databases described in the text contain information that relates primarily to evidence exhibiting class characteristics? Which ones contain information that relates primarily to evidence exhibiting individual characteristics? Explain your answers.

Case Analysis

In 1982, the state of Georgia convicted Wayne Williams of murdering several boys and young men in the Atlanta area. The case featured unique uses of fiber evidence that proved crucial to establishing Williams's guilt. The case also highlighted the effectiveness of statistical probability for establishing links between evidence found at multiple crime scenes.

1. In what respects did the use of fiber evidence in the Williams case differ significantly from its use in previous cases?

2. What did investigators hope to learn from their initial examination of fibers found on the bodies of several murder victims found in the Atlanta area from July 1979 to May 1981? What steps did they take to gather this information? What did they learn from their investigations? What was the significance of this information?

3. How could information on the source of the fibers be helpful to investigators? Explain how investigators might use information about the source of a fiber to help them locate the perpetrator.

4. What pieces of information did investigators collect from the West Point Pepperell Corporation that led them to conclude that the fibers found on Nathaniel Carter's body came from the carpeting in Wayne Williams's house? Explain the importance of each of these pieces of information for connecting Williams to Carter's murder.

5. Describe how investigators used the concepts of statistical probability to tie Williams to Nathaniel Carter as well as to his other victims.

Web Resources

An Introduction to Criminalistics and Physical Evidence (Article providing a brief introduction to concepts and principles of physical evidence)
faculty.ncwc.edu/toconnor/315/315lect02.htm

Evidence Dynamics: Locard's Exchange Principle & Crime Reconstruction (Online article from the *Journal of Behavioral Profiling* discussing crime-scene reconstruction and integrity of physical evidence)
www.profiling.org/journal/vol1_no1/jbp_ed_january2000_1-1.html

Houck, M. M., "Statistics and Trace Evidence: The Tyranny of Numbers," *Forensic Science Communications,* 1, no. 3 (1999)
www.fbi.gov/hq/lab/fsc/backissu/oct1999/houck.htm

Endnotes

1. Foster & Freeman Limited, Worcestershire, U.K., www.fosterfreeman.co.uk.

Case Reading

Fiber Evidence and the Wayne Williams Trial

Harold A. Deadman
Special Agent, Microscopic Analysis Unit, Laboratory Division Federal Bureau of Investigation, Washington, D.C.

On February 26, 1982, a Fulton County, Ga., Superior Court jury returned a verdict of "guilty as charged" on two counts of murder brought against Wayne Bertram Williams by a Fulton County grand jury in July 1981. Williams had been on trial since December 28, 1981, for the asphyxial murders of Nathaniel Cater and Jimmy Payne in April and May of 1981. During the 8-week trial, evidence linking Williams to those murders and to the murders of 10 other boys or young men was introduced.

An essential part of this case, presented by the Fulton County District Attorney's Office, involved the association of fibrous debris removed from the bodies of 12 murder victims with objects from the everyday environment of Williams.

Fiber evidence has often been an important part of criminal cases, but the Williams trial differed from other cases in several respects. Fiber evidence has not played a significant role in any case involving a large number of murder victims. The victims whose deaths were charged to Williams were 2 of 30 black children and black young men who were reported missing or who had died under suspicious circumstances in the Atlanta area over a 22-month period beginning in July 1979. During the trial, fiber evidence was used to associate Williams with 12 of those victims.

Fiber evidence is often used to corroborate other evidence in a case—it is used to support other testimony and validate other evidence presented at a trial. This was not the situation in the Williams trial. Other

Wayne Williams is shown talking to police outside his home. *Courtesy Corbis Bettmann*

Reprinted in part from *FBI Law Enforcement Bulletin,* March and May 1984.

evidence and other aspects of the trial were important but were used to support and complement the fiber evidence, not the usual order of things. The "hair and fiber matches" between Williams's environment and 11 of the 12 murder victims discussed at the trial were so significant that, in the author's opinion, these victims were positively linked to both the residence and automobiles that were a major part of the world of Wayne Williams.

Another difference between this case and most other cases was the extremely large amount of publicity surrounding both the investigation of the missing and murdered children and the arrest and subsequent trial of Williams. Few other murder trials have received the attention that the Williams case received. . . .

It is often difficult to get an accurate picture from press reports of the physical evidence introduced at a trial and the significance of that evidence. This article will also set forth in some detail the fiber evidence that linked Williams to the murder victims.

By discussing only the fiber evidence introduced at the trial, many other aspects of the case against Williams are being neglected. Additional evidence dealing with Williams's motivations—his character and behavior, his association with several of the victims by eyewitness accounts, and his link to a victim recovered from a river in Atlanta—was also essential to the case. . . .

Development of Williams as a Murder Suspect

Before Wayne Williams became a suspect in the Nathaniel Cater murder case, the Georgia State Crime Laboratory located a number of yellowish-green nylon fibers and some violet acetate fibers on the bodies

and clothing of the murder victims whose bodies had been recovered during the period of July 1979 to May 1981. The names of those victims were included on the list of missing and murdered children that was compiled by the Atlanta Task Force (a large group of investigators from law enforcement agencies in the Atlanta area). The yellowish-green nylon fibers were generally similar to each other in appearance and properties and were considered to have originated from a single source. This was also true of the violet acetate fibers. Although there were many other similarities that would link these murders together, the fiber linkage was notable since the possibility existed that a source of these fibers might be located in the future.

Initially, the major concern with these yellowish-green nylon fibers was determining what type of object could have been their source. This information could provide avenues of investigative activity. The fibers were very coarse and had a lobed cross-sectional appearance, tending to indicate that they originated from a carpet or a rug. The lobed cross-sectional shape of these fibers, however, was unique, and initially, the manufacturer of these fibers could not be determined. Photomicrographs of the fibers were prepared for display to contacts within the textile industry. On one occasion, these photomicrographs were distributed among several chemists attending a meeting at the research facilities of a large fiber producer. The chemists concurred that the yellowish-green nylon fiber was very unusual in cross-sectional shape and was consistent with being a carpet fiber, but again, the manufacturer of this fiber could not be determined. Contacts with other textile producers and textile chemists likewise did not result in an identification of the manufacturer.

In February 1981, an Atlanta newspaper article publicized that several different fiber types had been found on two murder victims. Following the publication of this article, bodies recovered from rivers in the Atlanta metropolitan area were either nude or clothed only in undershorts. It appeared possible that the victims were being disposed of in this undressed state and in rivers in order to eliminate fibers from being found on their bodies.[1]

On May 22, 1981, a four-man surveillance team of personnel from the Atlanta Police Department and the Atlanta Office of the FBI was situated under and at both ends of the James Jackson Parkway Bridge over the Chattahoochee River in northwest Atlanta. Around 2 a.m., a loud splash alerted the surveillance team to the presence of an automobile being driven slowly off the bridge. The driver was stopped and identified as Wayne Bertram Williams.

Two days after Williams's presence on the bridge, the nude body of Nathaniel Cater was pulled from the Chattahoochee River, approximately 1 mile downstream from the James Jackson Parkway Bridge. A yellowish-green nylon carpet-type fiber, similar to the nylon fibers discussed above, was recovered from the head hair of Nathaniel Cater. When details of Williams's reason for being on the bridge at 2 a.m. could not be confirmed, search warrants for Williams's home and automobile were obtained and were served on the afternoon of June 3, 1981. During the late evening hours of the same day, the initial associations of fibers from Cater and other murder victims were made with a green carpet in the home of Williams. Associations with a bedspread from Williams's bed and with [Williams's] family dog were also made at that time.

An apparent source of the yellowish-green nylon fibers had been found. It now became important to completely characterize these fibers in order to verify the associations and determine the strength of the associations resulting from the fiber matches. Because of the unusual cross-sectional appearance of the nylon fiber and the difficulty in determining the manufacturer, it was believed that this was a relatively rare fiber type, and therefore, would not be present in large amounts (or in a large number of carpets).

[Williams's] Carpet

Shortly after Williams was developed as a suspect, it was determined the yellowish-green nylon fibers were manufactured by the Wellman Corporation. The next step was to ascertain, if possible, how much carpet like Williams's bedroom carpet had been sold in the Atlanta area—carpet composed of the Wellman fiber and dyed with the same dye formulation as [Williams's] carpet. Names of Wellman Corporation customers who had purchased this fiber type, technical information about the fiber, and data concerning when and how much of this fiber type had been manufactured were obtained.

It was confirmed that the Wellman Corporation had, in fact, manufactured the fiber in Williams's carpet and that no other fiber manufacturer was known to have made a fiber with a similar cross section. It was also determined that fibers having this cross-sectional shape were manufactured and sold during the years 1967 through 1974. Prior to 1967, this company manufactured only a round cross section; after 1974, the unusual trilobal cross section seen in Williams's carpet was modified to a more regular trilobal cross-sectional shape. A list of sales of that fiber type during the period 1967 through 1974 was compiled. . . .

Through numerous contacts with yarn spinners and carpet manufacturers, it was determined that the West Point Pepperell Corporation of Dalton, Ga., had manufactured a line of carpet called "Luxaire," which was constructed in the same manner as [Williams's] carpet. One of the colors offered in the "Luxaire" line was called "English Olive," and this color was the same as that of [Williams's] carpet (both visually and by the use of discriminating chemical and instrumental tests). It was learned that the West Point Pepperell Corporation had manufactured the "Luxaire" line for a five-year period from December 1970 through 1975; however, it had only purchased Wellman 181B fiber for this line during 1970 and 1971. In December 1971, the West Point Pepperell Corporation changed the fiber composition of the "Luxaire" line to a different nylon fiber, one that was dissimilar to the Wellman 181B fiber in appearance. Accordingly, "Luxaire" carpet, like [Williams's] carpet, was only manufactured for a 1-year period. This change of carpet fiber after only 1 year in production was yet another factor that made [Williams's] carpet unusual.

It is interesting to speculate on the course the investigation would have taken if the James Jackson Parkway Bridge had not been covered by the surveillance team. The identification of the manufacturer of the nylon fibers showing up on the bodies could still have occurred and the same list of purchasers of the Wellman fiber could have been obtained. The same contacts with the yarn and carpet manufacturers could have been made; however, there would not have been an actual carpet sample to display. It is believed that eventually the carpet manufacturer could have been determined. With a sample of carpet supplied by West Point Pepperell—which they had retained in their files for over 10 years—it would have been possible to conduct a house-by-house search of the Atlanta area in an attempt to

find a similar carpet. Whether this very difficult task would have been attempted, of course, will never be known. A search of that type, however, would have accurately answered an important question that was discussed at the trial—the question of how many other homes in the Atlanta area had a carpet like [Williams's] carpet. An estimation, to be discussed later, based on sales records provided by the West Point Pepperell Corporation indicated that there was a very low chance (1/7792) of finding a carpet like Williams's carpet by randomly selecting occupied residences in the Atlanta area.

Only the West Point Pepperell Corporation was found to have manufactured a carpet exactly like [Williams's] carpet. Even though several manufacturers had gone out of business and could not be located, it was believed that, considering the many variables that exist in the manufacture of carpet and the probable uniqueness of each carpet manufacturer's dye formulations, it would be extremely unlikely for two unrelated companies to construct a carpet or dye the carpet fibers in exactly the same way. A large number of other green fibers, visually similar in color to Williams's carpet, were examined. None was found to be consistent with fibers from [Williams's] carpet.

Probability Determinations

To convey the unusual nature of [Williams's] residential carpet, an attempt was made to develop a numerical probability—something never before done in connection with textile materials used as evidence in a criminal trial.[2] The following information was gathered from the West Point Pepperell Corporation:

1. West Point Pepperell reported purchases of Wellman 181B fiber for the "Luxaire" line during a 1-year

period. The Wellman 181B fiber was used to manufacture "Luxaire" carpet from December 1970 until December 1971, at which time a new fiber type replaced that Wellman fiber.

2. In 1971, West Point Pepperell sold 5,710 square yards of English Olive "Luxaire" and "Dreamer" carpet to Region C (10 southeastern states which include Georgia). "Dreamer" was a line of carpet similar to "Luxaire" but contained a less dense pile. In order to account for the carpet manufactured during 1971, but sold after that time, all of the "Luxaire" English Olive carpet sold during 1972 to Region C (10,687 square yards) was added to the 1971 sales. Therefore, it was estimated that a total of 16,397 square yards of carpet containing the Wellman 181B fiber and dyed English Olive in color was sold by the West Point Pepperell Corporation to retailers in 10 southeastern states during 1971 and 1972. (In 1979, existing residential carpeted floor space in the United States was estimated at 6.7 billion square yards.)[3]

3. By assuming that this carpet was installed in one room, averaging 12 feet by 15 feet in size, per house, and also assuming that the total sales of carpet were divided equally among the 10 southeastern states, then approximately 82 rooms with this carpet could be found in the state of Georgia.

4. Information from the Atlanta Regional Commission showed that there were 638,995 occupied housing units in the Atlanta metropolitan area in November 1981.[4] Using this figure, the chance of randomly selecting an occupied housing unit in metropolitan Atlanta and finding a house with a room having carpet like Williams's carpet was determined to be 1 chance in 7,792—a very low chance. To the degree that the assumptions used in calculating the above probability number are reasonable, we can be confident in arriving at a valid probability number. . . .

The probability figures illustrate clearly that [Williams's] carpet is, in fact, very uncommon. To enhance the figures even further, it is important to emphasize that these figures are based on the assumption that none of the carpet of concern had been discarded during the past 11 years. In fact, carpet of this type, often used in commercial settings, such as apartment houses, would probably have had a normal life span of only 4 or 5 years. . . .[5]

The Williams Trial

To any experienced forensic fiber examiner, the fiber evidence linking Williams to the murder victims was overwhelming. But regardless of the apparent validity of the fiber findings, it was during the trial that its true weight would be determined. Unless it could be conveyed meaningfully to a jury, its effect would be lost. Because of this, considerable time was spent determining what should be done to convey the full significance of the fiber evidence. Juries are not usually composed of individuals with a scientific background, and therefore, it was necessary to "educate" the jury in what procedures were followed and the significance of the fiber results. In the Williams case, over 40 charts with over 350 photographs were prepared to illustrate exactly what the crime laboratory examiners had observed. . . .

Representatives of the textile fiber industry, including technical representatives from the Wellman and West Point Pepperell Corporations, were involved in educating the jury regarding textile fibers in general and helped lay the foundation for the conclusions of the forensic fiber examiners. The jury also was told about fiber analysis in the crime laboratory.

The trial, as it developed, can be divided into two parts. Initially, testimony was given concerning the murders of Nathaniel Cater and Jimmy Ray Payne, the two victims included in the indictment drawn against Williams in July 1981. Testimony was then given concerning Williams's association with 10 other murder victims.

The fiber matches made between fibers in Williams's environment and fibers from victims Payne and Cater were discussed. The items from Williams's environment that were linked to either or both of the victims are shown in the center of the chart. (See Figure 1.) Not only is Payne linked to Williams's environment by seven items and Cater linked by six items, but

both of the victims are linked strongly to each other based on the fiber matches and circumstances surrounding their deaths.

In discussing the significance or strength of an association based on textile fibers, it was emphasized that the more uncommon the fibers, the stronger the association. None of the fiber types from the items in Williams's environment shown in the center of Figure 1 is by definition a "common" fiber type. Several of the fiber types would be termed "uncommon."

One of the fibers linking the body of Jimmy Ray Payne to the carpet in the 1970 station wagon driven by Williams was a small rayon fiber fragment recovered from Payne's shorts. Data were obtained from the station wagon's manufacturer concerning which automobile models produced prior to 1973 contained carpet made of this fiber type. These data were coupled with additional information from Georgia concerning the number of these models registered in the Atlanta metropolitan

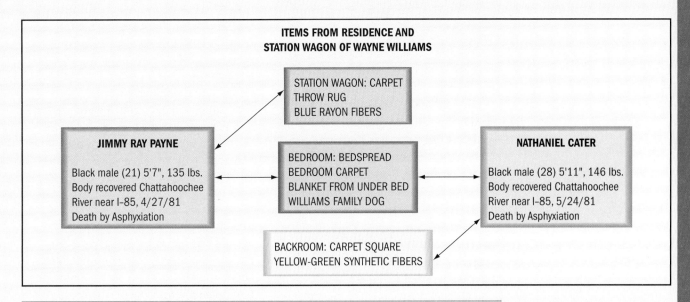

FIGURE 1 Items from residence and station wagon of Wayne Williams that were found on Jimmy Ray Payne and Nathaniel Cater.

area during 1981. This allowed a calculation to be made relating to the probability of randomly selecting an automobile having carpet like that in the 1970 Chevrolet station wagon from the 2,373,512 cars registered in the Atlanta metropolitan area. This probability is 1 chance in 3,828, a very low probability representing a significant association.

Another factor to consider when assessing the significance of fiber evidence is the increased strength of the association when multiple fiber matches become the basis of the association. This is true if different fiber types from more than one object are found and each fiber type either links two people together or links an individual with a particular environment. As the number of different objects increases, the strength of an association increases dramatically. That is, the chance of randomly finding several particular fiber types in a certain location is much smaller than the chance of finding one particular fiber type.

The following example can be used to illustrate the significance of multiple fiber matches linking two items together. If one were to throw a single die one time, the chance or probability of throwing a particular number would be one chance in six. The probability of throwing a second die and getting that same number also would be one chance in six. However, the probability of getting 2 of the same numbers on 2 dice thrown simultaneously is only 1 in every 36 double throws—a much smaller chance than with either of the single throws. This number is a result of the product rule of probability theory. That is, the probability of the joint occurrence of a number of mutually independent events equals the product of the individual probabilities of each of the events (in this example—$\frac{1}{6} \times \frac{1}{6} = \frac{1}{36}$). Since numerous fiber types are in

existence, the chance of finding one particular fiber type, other than a common type, in a specific randomly selected location is small. The chance then of finding several fiber types together in a specific location is the product of several small probabilities, resulting in an extremely small chance. . . .

However, no attempt was made to use the product rule and multiply the individual probability numbers together to get an approximation of the probability of finding carpets like Williams's residential carpet and Williams's automobile carpet in the same household. The probability numbers were used only to show that the individual fiber types involved in these associations were very uncommon. . . .[6]

In addition to the two probability numbers already discussed (bedroom and station wagon carpets), each of the other fiber types linking Williams to both Cater and Payne has a probability of being found in a particular location. The chance of finding all of the fiber types indicated on the chart [Figure 1] in one location (seven types on Payne's body and six types on Cater's body) would be extremely small. Although an actual probability number for those findings could not be determined, it is believed that the multiple fiber associations shown on this chart are proof that Williams is linked to the bodies of these two victims, even though each fiber match by itself does not show a positive association with Williams's environment.

Studies have been conducted in England that show that transferred fibers are usually lost rapidly as people go about their daily routine.[7] Therefore, the foreign fibers present on a person are most often from recent surroundings. The fibrous debris found on a murder victim reflects the body's more recent surroundings, especially important if the body was moved after the killing. Accordingly, the victims' bodies in this particular case are not only associated with Williams but are apparently associated with Williams shortly before or after their deaths. It was also pointed out during the trial that the locations of the fibers—on Payne's shorts and in Cater's head hairs and pubic hairs—were not those where one would expect to find fibrous debris transferred from an automobile or a house to victims who had been fully clothed.

Although from these findings it would appear that the victims were in the residence of Williams, there was one other location that contained many of the same fibers as those in the composition of various objects in his residence—Williams's station wagon. The environment of a family automobile might be expected to reflect, to some extent, fibers from objects located within the residence. This was true of the 1970 station wagon. With one exception, all of the fiber types removed from Payne and Cater, consistent with originating from items shown in the center of Figure 1, were present in debris removed by vacuuming the station wagon. The automobile would be the most logical source of the foreign fibers found on both Payne and Cater if they were associated with Williams shortly before or after their deaths. It should also be pointed out that two objects, the bedspread and the blanket, were portable and could have at one time been present inside the station wagon.

Both Payne and Cater were recovered from the Chattahoochee River. Their bodies had been in the water for several days. Some of the fibers found on these victims were like fibers in the compositions of the bedroom carpet and bedspread except for color intensity. They appeared to have been bleached. By subjecting various known fibers to small amounts of

Chattahoochee River water for different periods of time, it was found that bleaching did occur. This was especially true with the carpet and bedspread fibers from Williams's bedroom.

Two crime laboratory examiners testified during the closing stages of the first part of the trial about Williams's association with Payne and Cater. They concluded that it was highly unlikely that any environment other than that present in Wayne Williams's house and car could have resulted in the combination of fibers and hairs found on the victims and that it would be virtually impossible to have matched so many fibers found on Cater and Payne to items in Williams's house and car unless the victims were in contact with or in some way associated with the environment of Wayne Williams.

After testimony was presented concerning the Payne and Cater cases, the Fulton County District Attorney's Office asked the court to be allowed to introduce evidence in the cases of 10 other victims whose murders were similar in many respects. Georgia law allows evidence of another crime to be introduced ". . . if some logical connection can be shown between the two from which it can be said that proof of the one tends to establish the other as relevant to some fact other than general bad character."[8] There need be no conviction for the other crime in order for details about that crime to be admissible.

It was ruled that evidence concerning other murders could be introduced in an attempt to prove a "pattern or scheme" of killing that included the two murders with which Williams was charged. The additional evidence in these cases was to be used to help the jury ". . . decide whether Williams had committed the two murders with which he is charged."[9]

There were similarities between these additional victims and Payne and Cater (See Figure 2.) Although some differences can also be seen on this chart, the prosecution considered these differences to fit within the "pattern of killing" of which Payne and Cater were a part. The most important similarities between these additional victims were the fiber matches that linked 9 of the 10 victims to Williams's environment. The fiber findings discussed during the trial and used to associate Williams to the 12 victims were illustrated during the trial. (See Figure 3.)

The 12 victims were listed in chronological order based on the dates their bodies were recovered. The time period covered by this chart, approximately 22 months, is from July 1979 until May 1981. During that time period, the Williams family had access to a large number of automobiles, including a number of rental cars. Three of these automobiles are listed at the top of Figure 3. If one or more of the cars was in the possession of the Williams family at the time a victim was found to be missing, the space under that car(s) and after the particular victim's name is shaded.

Four objects (including the dog) from Williams's residence are listed horizontally across the top of Figure 3, along with objects from three of his automobiles. An

VICTIM'S NAME	DATE VICTIM MISSING	DAYS MISSING	BODY RECOVERY AREA	CAUSE OF DEATH	AGE	WEIGHT	HEIGHT
EVANS	7/25/79	3	WOODED AREA S.W. ATLANTA	PROBABLE ASPHYXIATION/ STRANGULATION	13	87 LBS.	5'4"
MIDDLEBROOKS	5/18/80	1	NEAR STREET S.E. ATLANTA	BLUNT TRAUMA TO HEAD	14	88 LBS.	4'10"
STEPHENS	10/9/80	1	NEAR STREET S.E. ATLANTA	ASPHYXIATION	10	120 LBS.	5'0"
GETER	1/3/81	33	WOODED AREA FULTON COUNTY	MANUAL STRANGULATION	14	130 LBS.	5'4"
PUE	1/22/81	1	NEAR HIGHWAY ROCKDALE CO.	LIGATURE STRANGULATION	15	105 LBS.	5'5"
BALTAZAR	2/6/81	7	NEAR HIGHWAY DEKALB CO.	LIGATURE STRANGULATION	12	125 LBS.	5'4"
BELL	3/2/81	31	SOUTH RIVER DEKALB CO.	ASPHYXIATION	16	100 LBS.	5'2"
ROGERS	3/30/81	10	NEAR STREET N.W. ATLANTA	ASPHYXIATION/ STRANGULATION	20	110 LBS.	5'3"
PORTER	4/10/81	1	NEAR STREET S.W. ATLANTA	STABBING	28	123 LBS.	5'7"
PAYNE	4/22/81	5	CHATTAHOOCHEE RIVER FULTON COUNTY	ASPHYXIATION	21	135 LBS.	5'7"
BARRETT	5/11/81	1	NEAR STREET DEKALB CO.	LIGATURE STRANGULATION (3 PUNCTURE WOUNDS)	17	125 LBS.	5'4"
CATER	5/21/81	3	CHATTAHOOCHEE RIVER FULTON COUNTY	ASPHYXIATION/ STRANGULATION	28	146 LBS.	5'11"

FIGURE 2 **Chart used during the trial to show similarities between Payne and Cater and 10 other murder victims.**

NAME OF VICTIM	VIOLET-GREEN BEDSPREAD WILLIAMS' BEDROOM	GREEN CARPET WILLIAMS' BEDROOM	DOG HAIRS WILLIAMS' DOG	YELLOW BLANKET WILLIAMS' BEDROOM	BLUE RAYON FIBERS, DEBRIS FROM WILLIAMS' HOME	TRUNK LINER 1978 PLYMOUTH	CARPET 1979 FORD	CARPET 1970 CHEVROLET	ADDITIONAL ITEMS FROM WILLIAMS' HOME, AUTOMOBILES OR PERSON
Alfred Evans	X	X	X			X			
Eric Middlebrooks	X		X				X		YELLOW NYLON FORD TRUNK LINER
Charles Stephens	X	X	X		X				YELLOW NYLON WHITE POLYESTER BACKROOM CARPET FORD TRUNK LINER
Lubie Geter	X	X	X					X	KITCHEN CARPET
Terry Pue	X	X	X						WHITE POLYESTER BACKROOM CARPET
Patrick Baltazar	X	X	X	X				X	YELLOW NYLON WHITE POLYESTER HEAD HAIR GLOVE JACKET PIGMENTED POLYPROPYLENE
Joseph Bell	X			X					
Larry Rogers	X	X	X	X				X	YELLOW NYLON PORCH BEDSPREAD
John Porter	X	X	X	X	X			X	PORCH BEDSPREAD
Jimmy Payne	X	X	X	X	X			X	BLUE THROW RUG
William Barrett	X	X	X	X	X			X	GLOVE
Nathaniel Cater	X	X	X	X					BACKROOM CARPET YELLOW-GREEN SYNTHETIC

FIGURE 3 **Fiber findings discussed during the trial and used to associate Williams with the 12 victims.**

"X" on the chart indicates an apparent transfer of textile fibers from the listed object to a victim. Other objects from Williams's environment which were linked to various victims by an apparent fiber transfer are listed on the right side of the chart. Fiber types from objects (never actually located) that were matched to fiber types from one or more victims are also listed either at the top or on the right side of the chart. Fourteen specific objects and five fiber types (probably from five other objects) listed on this chart are linked to one or more of the victims. More than 28 different fiber types, along with the dog hairs, were used to link up to 19 objects from Williams's environment to 1 or more

of the victims. Of the more than 28 fiber types from Williams's environment, 14 of these originated from a rug or carpet.

The combination of more than 28 different fiber types would not be considered so significant if they were primarily common fiber types. In fact, there is only 1 light green cotton fiber of the 28 that might be considered common. This cotton fiber was blended with acetate fibers in Williams's bedspread. Light green cotton fibers removed from many victims were not considered or compared unless they were physically intermingled with violet acetate fibers which were consistent with originating from the bedspread. It should be noted that a combination of cotton and acetate fibers blended together in a single textile material, as in the bedspread, is in itself uncommon. . . .

The previous discussion concerning the significance of multiple fiber matches can be applied to the associations made in the cases of all the victims except Bell, but especially to the association of Patrick Baltazar to Williams's environment. Fibers and animal hairs consistent with having originated from 10 sources were removed from Baltazar's body. These 10 sources include the uncommon bedroom carpet and station wagon carpet. In addition to the fiber (and animal hair) linkage, two head hairs of Negroid origin were removed from Baltazar's body that were consistent with originating from the scalp area of Williams. Head hair matches were also very significant in linking Williams to Baltazar's body. In the opinion of the author, the association based upon the hair and fiber analyses is a positive association.

Another important aspect of the fiber linkage between Williams and these victims is the correspondence between the fiber findings and the time periods during which Williams had access to the three automobiles listed on the chart. Nine victims are linked to automobiles used by the Williams family. When Williams did not have access to a particular car, no fibers were recovered that were consistent with having originated from that automobile. Trunk liner fibers of the type used in the trunks of many late-model Ford Motor Company automobiles were also recovered from the bodies of two victims.

One final point should be made concerning Williams's bedroom and station wagon carpets where probability numbers had

been determined. Fibers consistent with having originated from both of these "unusual" carpets were recovered from Payne's body. Of the 9 victims who were killed during the time period when Williams had access to the 1970 station wagon, fibers consistent with having originated from both the station wagon carpet and the bedroom carpet were recovered from 6 of these victims.

The apparent bleaching of several fibers removed from the bodies of Payne and Cater was consistent with having been caused by river water. Several fibers similar to those from Payne and Cater were removed from many of the victims whose bodies were recovered on land. Consistent with the bleaching argument, none of the fibers from the victims found on land showed any apparent bleaching. The finding of many of the same fiber types on the remaining victims, who were recovered from many different locations, refutes the possibility that Payne's and Cater's bodies picked up foreign fibers from the river.

The fact that many of the victims were involved with so many of the same fiber types, all of which linked the victims to Williams's environment, is the basis for arguing conclusively against these fibers originating from a source other than Williams's environment.

It is hoped that this article has provided valuable insight concerning the use of fiber evidence in a criminal trial, has provided answers to questions from those in the law enforcement community about textile fiber evidence in general, and has presented convincing arguments to establish Wayne Williams's association with the bodies of the murder victims.

Endnotes

1. Prior to the publication of the February 11, 1981, newspaper article, one victim from the task force list, who was fully clothed, had been recovered from a river in the Atlanta area. In the $2\frac{1}{2}$-month period after publication, the nude or nearly nude bodies of 7 of the 9 victims added to the task force list were recovered from rivers in the Atlanta area.

2. J. Mitchell and D. Holland, "An Unusual Case of Identification of Transferred Fibers," *Journal of the Forensic Science Society,* vol. 19, 1979, p. 23. This article describes a case in which carpet fibers transferred to a murder victim's body in England were traced back to the carpet manufacturer and finally to an automobile owned by the person who eventually confessed to the murder.

3. This information was taken from a study by E. I. du Pont de Nemours & Co. concerned with the existing residential floor space with carpet in the United States. This study was reported in a marketing survey conducted by the Marketing Corporation of America, Westport, Conn.

4. Information regarding the number of housing units in the Atlanta metropolitan area was obtained from a report provided by the Atlanta Regional Commission. The report, dated November 11, 1981, contained population and housing counts for counties, super districts, and census tracts in the Atlanta metropolitan area.

5. Information about carpet similar to Williams's carpet was developed through contacts with carpet manufacturers and carpet salesmen in Georgia. It was determined that this type carpet was often installed in commercial settings, such as apartments, and in those settings, had an average life span of 4 to 5 years.

6. Joseph L. Peterson, ed., *Forensic Science* (New York: AMS Press, 1975), pp. 181–225. This collection of articles, dealing with various aspects of forensic science, contains five papers concerned with using statistics to interpret the meaning of physical evidence. It is a good discussion of probability theory and reviews cases where probability theory has been used in trial situations.

7. C. A. Pounds and K. W. Smalldon, "The Transfer of Fibers between Clothing Materials During Simulated Contacts and Their Persistence During Wear," *Journal of the Forensic Science Society,* vol. 15, 1975, pp. 29–37.

8. *Encyclopedia of Georgia Law,* vol. 11A (The Harrison Company, 1979), p. 70.

9. *The Atlanta Constitution,* "Williams Jury Told of Other Slayings," Sec. 1=A, 1/26/82, p. 25.

Murder and the Horse Chestnut Tree

Roger Severs was the son of a wealthy English couple, Eileen and Derek Severs, who were reported missing in 1983. Police investigators were greeted at the Severs home by Roger, who at first explained that his parents had decided to spend some time in London. Suspicion of foul play quickly arose when investigators located traces of blood in the residence. More blood was found in Derek's car and signs of blood spatter were on the garage door. Curiously, a number of green fibers were located throughout the house, as well as in the trunk of Derek's car.

A thorough geological examination of soil and vegetation caked onto Severs's car wheel rims seemed to indicate that the car had been in a location at the edge of a wooded area. Closer examination of the debris also revealed the presence of horse chestnut pollen. Horse chestnut is an exceptionally rare tree in the region of the Severs residence.

Using land maps, a geologist located possible areas where horse chestnut pollen might be found. In one of the locations, investigators found a shallow grave that contained the bludgeoned bodies of the elder Severses. Not surprisingly, they were wrapped in a green blanket. A jury rejected Roger's defense of diminished capacity and found him guilty of murder.

chapter 4

Properties of Matter and the Analysis of Glass

Key Terms

amorphous solid	laser
atom	liquid
Becke line	mass
birefringence	matter
Celsius scale	periodic table
chemical property	phase
compound	photon
concentric fracture	physical property
crystalline solid	physical state
density	radial fracture
dispersion	refraction
electromagnetic spectrum	refractive index
element	solid
Fahrenheit scale	sublimation
frequency	tempered glass
gas	visible light
intensive property	wavelength
	weight
laminated glass	X-ray

Learning Objectives

After studying this chapter you should be able to:

- Define and distinguish the physical and chemical properties of matter

- Understand how to use the basic units of the metric system

- Define and distinguish elements and compounds

- Contrast the differences between a solid, liquid, and gas

- Understand the differences between the wave and particle theories of light

- Understand and explain the dispersion of light through a prism

- Describe the electromagnetic spectrum

- Define and understand the properties of density and refractive index

- List and explain forensic methods for comparing glass fragments

- Understand how to examine glass fractures to determine the direction of impact for a projectile

- Describe the proper collection of glass evidence

Properties of Matter

The forensic scientist must constantly determine the properties that impart distinguishing characteristics to matter, giving it a unique identity. The continuing search for distinctive properties ends only when the scientist has completely individualized a substance to one correct source. Properties are the identifying characteristics of substances. In this and succeeding chapters, we will examine properties that are most useful for characterizing soil, glass, and other physical evidence. However, before we begin, we can simplify our understanding of the nature of properties by classifying them into two broad categories: physical and chemical.

physical property
A property that describes the behavior of a substance without reference to any other substance.

chemical property
A property that describes the behavior of a substance when it reacts or combines with another substance.

Physical properties describe a substance without reference to any other substance. For example, weight, volume, color, boiling point, and melting point are typical physical properties that can be measured for a particular substance without altering the material's composition through a chemical reaction; they are associated only with the physical existence of that substance. A chemical property describes the behavior of a substance when it reacts or combines with another substance. For example, when wood burns, it chemically combines with oxygen in the air to form new substances; this transformation describes a chemical property of wood. In the crime laboratory, a routine procedure for determining the presence of heroin in a suspect specimen is to react it with a chemical reagent known as the Marquis reagent, which turns purple in the presence of heroin. This color transformation becomes a chemical property of heroin and provides a convenient test for its identification.

Which physical and chemical properties the forensic scientist ultimately chooses to observe and measure depends on the type of material that is being examined. Logic requires, however, that if the property can be assigned a numerical value, it must relate to a standard system of measurement accepted throughout the scientific community. That standard system is called the metric system.

Closer Analysis

The Metric System

Although scientists, including forensic scientists, throughout the world have been using the metric system of measurement for more than a century, the United States still uses the cumbersome "English system" to express length in inches, feet, or yards; weight in ounces or pounds; and volume in pints or quarts. The inherent difficulty of this system is that no simple numerical relationship exists between the various units of measurement. For example, to convert inches to feet one must know that 1 foot is equal to 12 inches; the conversion of ounces to pounds requires the knowledge that 16 ounces is equivalent to 1 pound.

In 1791, the French Academy of Science devised the simple system of measurement known as the metric system. This system uses a simple decimal relationship so that a unit of length, volume, or mass can be converted into a subunit by simply multiplying or dividing by a multiple of 10—for example, 10, 100, or 1,000. Even though the United States has not yet adopted the metric system, its system of currency is decimal and, hence, is analogous to the metric system. The basic unit of currency is the dollar. A dollar is divided into 10 equal units called dimes, and each dime is further divided into 10 equal units of cents.

The metric system has basic units of measurement for length, mass, and volume: the meter, gram, and liter, respectively. These three basic units can be converted into subunits that are decimal multiples of the basic unit by simply attaching a prefix to the unit name. The following are common prefixes and their equivalent decimal value:

Prefix	Equivalent Value
deci-	1/10 or 0.1
centi-	1/100 or 0.01
milli-	1/1000 or 0.001
micro-	1/1,000,000 or 0.000001
nano-	1/1,000,000,000 or 0.000000001
kilo-	1000
mega-	1,000,000

Hence, 1/10 or 0.1 gram (g) is the same as a decigram (dg), 1/100 or 0.01 meter is equal to a centimeter (cm), and 1/1000 liter (0.001) is a milliliter (mL). A metric conversion is carried out simply by moving the decimal point to the right or left and inserting the proper prefix to show the direction and number of places that the decimal point has been moved. For example, if the weight of a powder is 0.0165 gram, it may be more convenient to multiply this value by 100 and express it as 1.65 centigrams or by 1,000 to show it as its equivalent value of 16.5 milligrams. Similarly, an object that weighs 264,450 grams may be expressed as 264.45 kilograms simply by dividing it by 1,000. It is important to remember that in any of these conversions, the value of the measurement has not changed; 0.0165 gram is still equivalent to 1.65 centigrams, just as one dollar is still equal to 100 cents. We have simply adjusted the position of the decimal and shown the extent of the adjustment with a prefix.

One interesting aspect of the metric system is that volume can be defined in terms of length. A liter by definition is the volume of a cube with sides of length 10 centimeters. One liter is therefore equivalent to a volume of $(10 \text{ cm})^3$, or 1,000 cubic centimeters (cc). Thus, 1/1,000 liter or 1 milliliter (mL) is equal to 1 cubic centimeter (cc) (see Figure 1). Scientists commonly use the subunits mL and cc interchangeably to express volume.

At times, it may be necessary to convert units from the metric system into the English system, or vice versa (see Figure 2). To accomplish this, we must consult

(*continued*)

Closer Analysis

The Metric System (*continued*)

FIGURE 1   Volume equivalencies in the metric system.

FIGURE 2   Comparison of the metric and English systems of length measurement; 2.54 centimeters = 1 inch.

references that list English units and their metric equivalents. Some of the more useful equivalents follow:

1 inch = 2.54 centimeters
1 meter = 39.37 inches
1 pound = 453.6 grams
1 liter = 1.06 quarts
1 kilogram = 2.2 pounds

The general mathematical procedures for converting from one system to another can be illustrated by converting 12 inches into centimeters. To change inches into centimeters, we need to know that there are 2.54 centimeters per inch. Hence, if we multiply 12 inches by 2.54 centimeters per inch (12 in. × 2.54 cm/in.), the unit of inches will cancel out, leaving the product 30.48 cm. Similarly, converting grams to pounds, 227 grams is equivalent to 227 g × 1 lb/453.6 g or 0.5 lb.

The Nature of Matter

Before examining physical and chemical properties that are important to the forensic scientist, it is important to understand the basic nature of matter, which comprises all substances. **Matter** is anything that has mass and occupies space.

matter
Anything that has mass and occupies space.

Elements and Compounds

As we examine the world that surrounds us and consider the countless variety of materials that we encounter, we must consider one of humankind's most remarkable accomplishments, the discovery of the concept of the atom, to explain the composition of all matter. This search had its earliest contribution from the ancient Greek philosophers, who suggested air, water, fire, and earth as matter's fundamental building blocks. It culminated with the development of the atomic theory and the discovery of matter's simplest identity, the element.

Table 4–1 List of Elements with Their Symbols and Atomic Masses

Element	Symbol	Atomic Mass[a] (amu)	Element	Symbol	Atomic Mass[a] (amu)
Actinum	Ac	(227)	Gold	Au	196.9665
Aluminum	Al	26.9815	Hafnium	Hf	178.49
Americium	Am	(243)	Hassium	Hs	(265)
Antimony	Sb	121.75	Helium	He	4.00260
Argon	Ar	39.948	Holmium	Ho	164.9303
Arsenic	As	74.9216	Hydrogen	H	1.0080
Astatine	At	(210)	Indium	In	114.82
Barium	Ba	137.34	Iodine	I	126.9045
Berkelium	Bk	(247)	Iridium	Ir	192.22
Beryllium	Be	9.01218	Iron	Fe	55.847
Bismuth	Bi	208.9806	Krypton	Kr	83.80
Bohrium	Bh	(262)	Lanthanum	La	138.9055
Boron	B	10.81	Lawrencium	Lr	(257)
Bromine	Br	79.904	Lead	Pb	207.2
Cadmium	Cd	112.40	Lithium	Li	6.941
Calcium	Ca	40.08	Lutetium	Lu	174.97
Californium	Cf	(251)	Magnesium	Mg	24.305
Carbon	C	12.011	Manganese	Mn	54.9380
Cerium	Ce	140.12	Meitnerium	Mt	(266)
Cesium	Cs	132.9055	Mendelevium	Md	(256)
Chlorine	Cl	35.453	Mercury	Hg	200.59
Chromium	Cr	51.996	Molybdenum	Mo	95.94
Cobalt	Co	58.9332	Neodymium	Nd	144.24
Copper	Cu	63.546	Neon	Ne	20.179
Curium	Cm	(247)	Neptunium	Np	237.0482
Darmstadtium	Ds	(271)	Nickel	Ni	58.71
Dubnium	Db	(260)	Niobium	Nb	92.9064
Dysprosium	Dy	162.50	Nitrogen	N	14.0067
Einsteinium	Es	(254)	Nobelium	No	(254)
Erbium	Er	167.26	Osmium	Os	190.2
Europium	Eu	151.96	Oxygen	O	15.9994
Fermium	Fm	(253)	Palladium	Pd	106.4
Fluorine	F	18.9984	Phosphorus	P	30.9738
Francium	Fr	(223)	Platinum	Pt	195.09
Gadolinium	Gd	157.25	Plutonium	Pu	(244)
Gallium	Ga	69.72	Polonium	Po	(209)
Germanium	Ge	72.59	Potassium	K	39.102

(continued)

Table 4–1 (*continued*)

Element	Symbol	Atomic Mass[a] (amu)	Element	Symbol	Atomic Mass[a] (amu)
Praseodymium	Pr	140.9077	Thallium	Tl	204.37
Promethium	Pm	(145)	Terbium	Tb	158.9254
Protactinium	Pa	231.0359	Tellurium	Te	127.60
Radium	Ra	226.0254	Thorium	Th	232.0381
Radon	Rn	(222)	Thulium	Tm	168.9342
Rhenium	Re	186.2	Tin	Sn	118.69
Rhodium	Rh	102.9055	Titanium	Ti	47.90
Roentgenium	Rg	(272)	Tungsten	W	183.85
Rubidium	Rb	85.4678	Ununbium	Uub	(285)
Ruthenium	Ru	101.07	Ununhexium	Uuh	(292)
Rutherfordium	Rf	(257)	Ununoctium	Uuo	(?)
Samarium	Sm	105.4	Ununpentium	Uup	(288)
Scandium	Sc	44.9559	Ununquadium	Uuq	(289)
Seaborgium	Sg	(263)	Ununseptium	Uus	(?)
Selenium	Se	78.96	Ununtrium	Uut	(284)
Silicon	Si	28.086	Uranium	U	238.029
Silver	Ag	107.868	Vanadium	V	50.9414
Sodium	Na	22.9898	Xenon	Xe	131.3
Strontium	Sr	87.62	Ytterbium	Yb	173.04
Sulfur	S	32.06	Yttrium	Y	88.9059
Tantalum	Ta	180.9479	Zinc	Zn	65.57
Technetium	Tc	98.9062	Zirconium	Zr	91.22

[a]Based on the assigned relative atomic mass of C = exactly 12; parentheses denote the mass number of the isotope with the longest half-life.

element
A fundamental particle of matter that cannot be broken down into simpler substances by chemical means.

periodic table
A chart of all the known elements arranged in a systematic fashion.

atom
The smallest unit of an element that can exist and still retain its identity as that element.

An **element** is a fundamental particle of matter that cannot be broken down into simpler substances by chemical means. Elements provide the building blocks from which all matter is composed. At present, 118 elements have been identified (see Table 4–1); of these, 89 occur naturally on the earth, and the remainder have been created in the laboratory.

Figure 4–1 shows the **periodic table**, a chart of all the known elements arranged in a systematic fashion. This table is most useful to chemists because it arranges elements with similar chemical properties in the same vertical or horizontal rows. Vertical rows of elements in the table are called groups or families; horizontal rows are called series. Elements in the same group have similar properties (for example, atomic mass or density) and exhibit a clear trend in properties as one moves down the group. As a result, groups are considered the most important way of classifying the elements. In some parts of the table, however, similarities in properties of the elements in the same row makes the series a more useful method for classification.

For convenience, chemists have chosen letter symbols to represent the elements. Many of these symbols come from the first letter of the element's English name—for example, carbon (C), hydrogen (H), and oxygen (O). Others are two-letter abbreviations of the English name—calcium (Ca) and zinc (Zn). Some symbols are derived from the first letters of Latin or Greek names. Thus, the symbol for silver, Ag, comes from the Latin name *argentum;* copper, Cu, from the Latin *cuprum;* and helium, He, from the Greek name *helios.*

The smallest particle of an element that can exist and still retain its identity as that element is the **atom.** When we write the symbol C we mean one atom of carbon; the chemical symbol for carbon dioxide, CO_2, signifies

Group Period	IA	IIA	IIIB	IVB	VB	VIB	VIIB		VIII		IB	IIB	IIIA	IVA	VA	VIA	VIIA	0
1	1 H																	2 He
2	3 Li	4 Be											5 B	6 C	7 N	8 O	9 F	10 Ne
3	11 Na	12 Mg											13 Al	14 Si	15 P	16 S	17 Cl	18 Ar
4	19 K	20 Ca	21 Sc	22 Ti	23 V	24 Cr	25 Mn	26 Fe	27 Co	28 Ni	29 Cu	30 Zn	31 Ga	32 Ge	33 As	34 Se	35 Br	36 Kr
5	37 Rb	38 Sr	39 Y	40 Zr	41 Nb	42 Mo	43 Tc	44 Ru	45 Rh	46 Pd	47 Ag	48 Cd	49 In	50 Sn	51 Sb	52 Te	53 I	54 Xe
6	55 Cs	56 Ba	57 La a	72 Hf	73 Ta	74 W	75 Re	76 Os	77 Ir	78 Pt	79 Au	80 Hg	81 Tl	82 Pb	83 Bi	84 Po	85 At	86 Rn
7	87 Fr	88 Ra	89 Ac b	104 Rf	105 Db	106 Sg	107 Bh	108 Hs	109 Mt	110 Ps	111 Rg	112 Uub	113 Uut	114 Uuq	115 Uup	116 Uuh	117 Uus	118 Uuo

aLanthanide series	58 Ce	59 Pr	60 Nd	61 Pm	62 Sm	63 Eu	64 Gd	65 Tb	66 Dy	67 Ho	68 Er	69 Tm	70 Yb	71 Lu
bActinide series	90 Th	91 Pa	92 U	93 Np	94 Pu	95 Am	96 Cm	97 Bk	98 Cf	99 Es	100 Fm	101 Md	102 No	103 Lr

FIGURE 4–1   The periodic table.

one atom of carbon combined with two atoms of oxygen. When two or more elements are combined, as with carbon dioxide, a new substance is created, different in its physical and chemical properties from its elemental components. This new material is called a compound. Compounds contain at least two elements. Considering that there are eighty-nine natural elements, it is easy to imagine the large number of possible elemental combinations that may form compounds. Not surprisingly, more than 16 million known compounds have already been identified.

Just as the atom is the basic unit of an element, the molecule is the smallest unit of a compound. Thus, a molecule of carbon dioxide is represented by the symbol CO_2, and a molecule of table salt is symbolized by NaCl, representing the combination of one atom of the element sodium (Na) with one atom of the element chlorine (Cl).

States of Matter

As we look around us and view the materials that make up the earth, it becomes an awesome task even to attempt to estimate the number of different kinds of matter. A much more logical approach is to classify matter according to the physical form it takes. These forms are called physical states. There are three such states: solid, liquid, and gas (vapor).

In the solid state, molecules of matter are held closely together by strong attractive forces. This tightly packed molecular arrangement makes solid matter rigid and gives it a definite shape and volume. In a liquid, the attractive forces between molecules are weaker. The molecules are in contact with one another, but are not held as rigidly in place. Like a solid, a liquid also occupies a specific volume, but its fluidity causes it to take the

compound
A pure substance composed of two or more elements.

physical state
The physical form taken by matter: solid, liquid, or gas.

solid
A state of matter in which molecules are held closely together by strong attractive forces.

liquid
A state of matter in which the attractive forces are strong enough to allow molecules to be in contact with one another but too weak to hold them rigidly in place.

gas (vapor)
A state of matter in which the attractive forces between molecules are weak enough to permit them to move with complete freedom.

sublimation
A change of state from a solid directly into a gas.

phase
A uniform substance separated from other substances by definite visible boundaries.

shape of the container in which it resides. The attractive forces between molecules in a gas are much weaker still, allowing them to move freely. Thus, gaseous matter has neither a definite shape nor volume, and it will completely fill any container into which it is placed.

Changes of State Substances can change from one state to another. For example, as water is heated, it is converted from a liquid form into a vapor. At a high enough temperature (100°C), water boils and rapidly changes into steam. Similarly, at 0°C, water solidifies or freezes into ice. Under certain conditions, some solids can be converted directly into a gaseous state. For instance, a piece of dry ice (solid carbon dioxide) left standing at room temperature quickly forms carbon dioxide vapor and disappears. This change of state from a solid to a gas is called sublimation.

In each of these examples, no new chemical species are formed; matter simply changes from one physical state to another. Water, whether in the form of liquid, ice, or steam, remains chemically H_2O. Simply, what has been altered are the attractive forces between the water molecules. In a solid, these forces are very strong, and the molecules are held closely together in a rigid state. In a liquid, the attractive forces are not as strong, and the molecules have more mobility. Finally, in the vapor state, appreciable attractive forces no longer exist between the molecules; thus, they may move in any direction at will.

Phases Chemists are forever combining different substances, no matter whether they are in the solid, liquid, or gaseous states, hoping to create new and useful products. Not all attempts at mixing matter are productive. For instance, oil spills demonstrate that oil and water do not mix. Whenever substances can be distinguished by a visible boundary, different phases are said to exist.

Oil floating on water is an example of a two-phase system. The oil and water each constitute a separate liquid phase, clearly distinct from each other. Similarly, when sugar is first added to water, it will not dissolve, and two distinctly different phases exist: the solid sugar and the liquid water. However, after stirring, all the sugar dissolves, leaving just one liquid phase. As we shall see, forensic scientists use the existence of different phases to identify and classify evidence found at a crime scene.

Key Points

• Physical properties such as weight, volume, color, boiling point, and melting point describe a substance without reference to any other substance. A chemical property describes the behavior of a substance when it reacts or combines with another substance.

• Matter is anything that has mass and occupies space. An element is a fundamental particle of matter that cannot be broken down into simpler substances by chemical means.

• The smallest particle of an element that can exist and still retain its identity as that element is the atom.

• A compound is a pure substance composed of two or more elements. The smallest unit of a compound is a molecule.

• The three states of matter are solid, liquid, and gas.

• Sublimation is a change of state from a solid to a gas.

• A phase is a uniform body of matter distinguished from other matter by definite visible boundaries.

Theory of Light

As with matter, knowledge of the nature and behavior of light is fundamental to understanding physical properties important to the examination of forensic evidence. Two simple models explain light's behavior. The first model describes light as a continuous wave; the second depicts it as a stream of discrete energy particles. Together, these two very different descriptions explain all of the observed properties of light, but by itself, no one model can explain all the facets of the behavior of light.

Light as a Wave

The wave concept depicts light as having an up-and-down motion of a continuous wave, as shown in Figure 4–2. Such a wave can be characterized by two distinct properties: wavelength and frequency. The distance between two consecutive crests (high points) or troughs (low points) of a wave is called the wavelength; it is designated by the Greek letter *lambda* (λ) and is typically measured in nanometers (nm), or millionths of a meter. The number of crests (or troughs) passing any one given point in a unit of time is defined as the frequency of the wave. Frequency is normally designated by the letter f and is expressed in cycles per second (cps). Frequency and wavelength are inversely proportional to one another, as shown by the relationship expressed in Equation 4–1:

$$F = c / \lambda \qquad \textbf{(4–1)}$$

In the equation, c represents the speed of light.

wavelength
The distance between crests of adjacent waves.

frequency
The number of waves that pass a given point per unit of time.

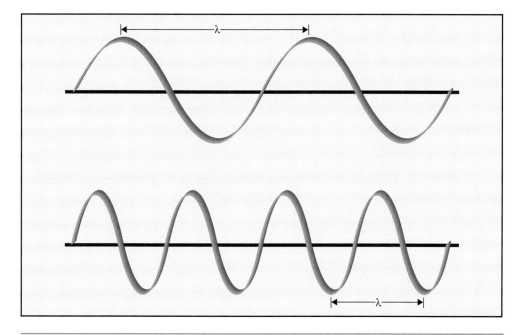

FIGURE 4–2   The frequency of the lower wave is twice that of the upper wave.

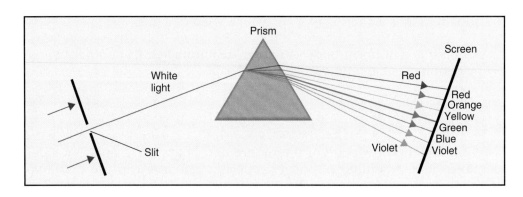

FIGURE 4–3   Representation of the dispersion of light by a glass prism.

Many of us have held a glass prism up toward the sunlight and watched it transform light into the colors of the rainbow. The process of separating light into its component colors is called dispersion. Visible light usually travels at a constant velocity of nearly 300 million meters per second. However, on passing through the glass of a prism, each color component of light is slowed to a speed slightly different from those of the others, causing each component to bend at a different angle as it emerges from the prism (see Figure 4–3). This bending of light waves because of a change in velocity is called refraction.

The observation that a substance has a color is consistent with this description of white light. For example, when light passes through a red glass, the glass absorbs all the component colors of light except red, which passes through or is transmitted by the glass. Likewise, one can determine the color of an opaque object by observing its ability to absorb some of the component colors of light while reflecting others back to the eye. Color is thus a visual indication that objects absorb certain portions of visible light and transmit or reflect others. Scientists have long recognized this phenomenon and have learned to characterize different chemical substances by the type and quantity of light they absorb. This has important applications for the identification and classification of forensic evidence.

The Electromagnetic Spectrum   Visible light is only a small part of a large family of radiation waves known as the electromagnetic spectrum (see Figure 4–4). All electromagnetic waves travel at the speed of light (c) and are distinguishable from one another only by their different wavelengths or frequencies. Hence, the only property that distinguishes X-rays from radio waves is the different frequencies the two types of waves possess.

Similarly, the range of colors that make up the visible spectrum can be correlated with frequency. For instance, the lowest frequencies of visible light are red; waves with a lower frequency fall into the invisible infrared (IR) region. The highest frequencies of visible light are violet; waves with a higher frequency extend into the invisible ultraviolet (UV) region. No definite boundaries exist between any colors or regions of the electromagnetic spectrum; instead, each region is composed of a continuous range of frequencies, each blending into the other.

Ordinarily, light in any region of the electromagnetic spectrum is a collection of waves possessing a range of wavelengths. Under normal circumstances, this light comprises waves that are all out of step with each other (incoherent light). However, scientists can produce light that has all its waves

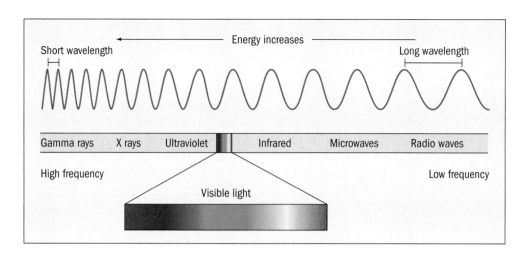

FIGURE 4–4 The electromagnetic spectrum.

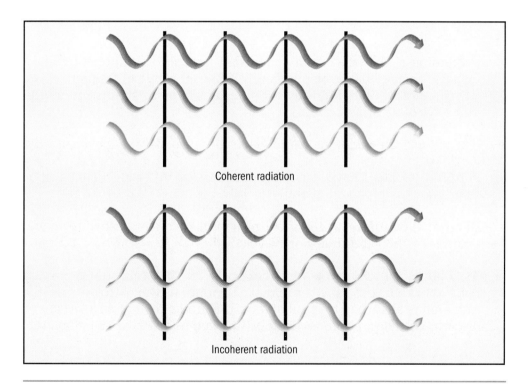

FIGURE 4–5 Coherent and incoherent radiation.

pulsating in unison (see Figure 4–5). This is called a laser (*l*ight *a*mplification by *s*timulated *e*mission of *r*adiation). Light in this form is very intense and can be focused on a very small area. Laser beams can be focused to pinpoints that are so intense that they can zap microscopic holes in a diamond.

Light as a Particle

As long as electromagnetic radiation is moving through space, its behavior can be described as that of a continuous wave. However, once radiation is absorbed by a substance, the model of light as a stream of discrete particles must be invoked to describe its behavior. Here, light is depicted as consisting of energy particles that are known as photons. Each photon

laser
An acronym for light amplification by stimulated emission of radiation; light that has all its waves pulsating in unison.

photon
A discrete particle of electromagnetic radiation.

has a definite amount of energy associated with its behavior. This energy is related to the frequency of light, as shown by Equation (4–2):

$$E = hf \tag{4–2}$$

where E specifies the energy of the photon, f is the frequency of radiation, and h is a universal constant called Planck's constant. As shown by Equation (4–2), the energy of a photon is directly proportional to its frequency. Therefore, the photons of ultraviolet light will be more energetic than the photons of visible or infrared light, and exposure to the more energetic photons of X-rays presents more danger to human health than exposure to the photons of radio waves.

Just as a substance can absorb visible light to produce color, many of the invisible radiations of the electromagnetic spectrum are likewise absorbed. This absorption phenomenon is the basis for spectrophotometry, an analytical technique that measures the quantity of radiation that a particular material absorbs as a function of wavelength or frequency. We will examine spectrophotometry in more detail when we discuss the forensic analysis of drugs in Chapter 5.

Key Points

- Dispersion is the process of separating light into component colors. Because each color corresponds to a different range of frequencies or wavelengths of light, light rays of one color bend to a different degree than rays of all other colors.

- Refraction is the bending of light waves because of a change in velocity.

- Forensic scientists have learned to characterize different chemical substances by the type and quantity of light they absorb.

- Different types of electromagnetic radiation are distinguished from one another by their frequency or wavelength.

- As long as electromagnetic radiation is moving through space, its behavior can be described as that of a continuous wave. However, once radiation is absorbed by a substance, the model of light as a stream of discrete particles (photons) must be invoked to describe its behavior.

Physical Properties of Matter

Temperature

Determining the physical properties of any material often requires measuring its temperature. For instance, the temperatures at which a substance melts or boils are readily determinable characteristics that will help identify it. Temperature is a measure of heat intensity, or the amount of heat in a substance. Temperature is usually measured by placing a thermometer in contact with a substance. The familiar mercury-in-glass thermometer functions because mercury expands more than glass when heated and contracts more than glass when cooled. Thus, the length of the mercury column in the glass tube measures the surrounding environment's temperature.

The construction of a temperature scale requires two reference points and a choice of units. The reference points most conveniently chosen

Celsius   Fahrenheit

FIGURE 4–6   Comparison of the Celsius and Fahrenheit temperature scales.

---

are the freezing point and boiling point of water. The two most common temperature scales used are the Fahrenheit and Celsius (formerly called *centigrade*) scales (see Figure 4–6).

The Fahrenheit scale is based on the assignment of the value 32°F to the freezing point of water and 212°F to its boiling point. The difference between the two points is evenly divided into 180 units. Thus, a degree Fahrenheit is 1/180 of the temperature change between the freezing point and boiling point of water. The Celsius scale is derived by assigning the freezing point of water a value of 0°C and its boiling point a value of 100°C. A degree Celsius is thus 1/100 of the temperature change between the two reference points. Scientists in most countries use the Celsius scale to measure temperature.

Weight and Mass

The force with which gravity attracts a body is called weight. If your weight is 180 pounds, this means that the earth's gravity is pulling you down with a force of 180 pounds; on the moon, where the force of gravity is one-sixth that of the earth, your weight would be 30 pounds.

Fahrenheit scale
The temperature scale that defines the melting point of ice as 32° and the boiling point of water as 212°, with 180 equal divisions or degrees between.

Celsius scale
The temperature scale that defines the melting point of ice as 0° and the boiling point of water as 100°, with 100 equal divisions or degrees between.

weight
The force with which gravity attracts a body.

mass

A constant property that refers to the amount of matter an object contains.

Mass differs from weight because it refers to the amount of matter an object contains and is independent of its location on the earth or any other place in the universe. The mathematical relationship between weight (w) and mass (m) is shown in Equation (4–3), where g is the acceleration imparted to a body by the force of gravity.

$$w = mg \qquad\qquad (4\text{–}3)$$

The weight of a body is seen to be directly proportional to its mass; hence, a large mass weighs more than a small mass.

In the metric system, the mass of an object is always specified, rather than its weight. The basic unit of mass is the gram. An object that has a mass of 40 grams on the earth will have a mass of 40 grams anywhere else in the universe. Normally, however, the terms *mass* and *weight* are used interchangeably, and we often speak of the weight of an object when we really mean its mass.

The mass of an object is determined by comparing it against the known mass of standard objects. The comparison is confusingly called *weighing,* and the standard objects are called *weights* (*masses* would be a more correct term). The comparison is performed on a balance. The simplest type of balance for weighing is the equal-arm balance shown in Figure 4–7. The object to be weighed is placed on the left pan, and the standard weights are placed on the right pan; when the pointer between the two pans is at the center mark, the total mass on the right pan is equal to the mass of the object on the left pan.

The modern laboratory has progressed beyond the simple equal-arm balance, and either the top-loading balance or the single-pan analytical balance (see Figure 4–8) is now likely to be used. The choice depends on the accuracy required and the amount of material being weighed. Each works on the same counterbalancing principle as the simple equal-arm balance, but the second pan, the one on which the standard weights are placed, is hidden from view within the balance's housing. Once the object whose weight is to be determined is placed on the visible pan, the operator selects the proper standard weights (also contained with the housing) by manually

FIGURE 4–7 **The measurement of mass.**

(a)

FIGURE 4–8   **(a) Top-loading balance. (b) Single-pan
analytical balance.** *Courtesy Superior Scale, Deptford, N.J.,
www.superiorscale.com, and Sirchie Finger Print Laboratories, Inc.,
Youngsville, N.C., www.sirchie.com*

(b)

turning a set of knobs located on the front side of the balance. At the point
of balance, the weights selected are automatically recorded on digital and
optical readout scales. Other versions of single-pan balances rely on an
electromagnetic field to generate a current to balance the force pressing
down on the pan from the sample being weighed. When the scale is properly calibrated, the amount of current needed to keep the pan balanced is
used to determine the weight of the sample. The strength of the current is
converted to a digitized signal for a readout. The top-loading balance can
accurately weigh an object to the nearest 1 milligram or 0.001 gram; the
analytical balance is even more accurate, weighing to the nearest tenth of a
milligram or 0.0001 gram.

Density

An important physical property of matter with respect to the analysis of
certain kinds of physical evidence is **density**. Density is defined as mass
per unit volume [see Equation (4–4)].

$$\text{Density} = \frac{\text{mass}}{\text{volume}} \qquad \textbf{(4–4)}$$

Density is an **intensive property** of matter—that is, it remains the same
regardless of the size of an object; thus, it is a characteristic property of a
substance and can be used in identification. Solids tend to be more dense
than liquids, and liquids more dense than gases. The densities of some
common substances are shown in Table 4–2.

A simple procedure for determining the density of a solid is illustrated
in Figure 4–9. First, the solid is weighed on a balance against known
standard gram weights to determine its mass. The solid's volume is then
determined from the volume of water it displaces. This is easily measured
by filling a cylinder with a known volume of water (V_1), adding the object,
and measuring the new water level (V_2). The difference ($V_2 - V_1$) in milliliters

density
A physical property of matter
that is equivalent to the mass
per unit volume of a
substance.

intensive property
A property that is not
dependent on the size of an
object.

Table 4–2 Densities of Select Materials (at 20°C unless otherwise stated)	
Substance	Density (g/mL)
Solids	
Silver	10.5
Lead	11.5
Iron	7.8
Aluminum	2.7
Window glass	2.47–2.54
Ice (0°C)	0.92
Liquids	
Mercury	13.6
Benzene	0.88
Ethyl alcohol	0.79
Gasoline	0.69
Water at 4°C	1.00
Water at 20°C	0.998
Gases	
Air (0°C)	0.0013
Chlorine (0°C)	0.0032
Oxygen (0°C)	0.0014
Carbon dioxide (0°C)	0.0020

Mass = 20 g

$$\text{Density} = \frac{\text{Mass}}{\text{Volume } (v_2 - v_1)}$$

$$\text{Density} = \frac{75g}{(50ml - 40ml)}$$

$$\text{Density} = \frac{75g}{10ml} = 7.5g/ml$$

Volume

FIGURE 4–9 A simple procedure for determining the density of a solid is to first weigh it and then measure its volume by noting the volume of water it displaces.

is equal to the volume of the solid. Density can now be calculated from Equation (4–4) in grams per milliliter.

The volumes of gases and liquids vary considerably with temperature; hence, when determining density, it is important to control and record the temperature at which the measurements are made. For example, 1 gram of water occupies a volume of 1 milliliter at 4°C and thus has a density of 1.0 g/mL. However, as the temperature of water increases, its volume expands. Therefore, at 20°C (room temperature), 1 gram of water occupies a volume of 1.002 mL and has a density of 0.998 g/mL.

The observation that a solid object either sinks, floats, or remains suspended when immersed in a liquid can be accounted for by the property of density. For instance, if the density of a solid is greater than that of the liquid in which it is immersed, the object sinks; if the solid's density is less than that of the liquid, it floats; and when the solid and liquid have equal densities, the solid remains suspended in the liquid medium. As we will see shortly, these observations provide a convenient technique for comparing the densities of solid objects.

Refractive Index

As we noted earlier, the bending of a light wave because of a change in velocity is called refraction. The phenomenon of refraction is apparent when we view an object that is immersed in a transparent medium such as water; because we are accustomed to thinking that light travels in a straight line, we often forget to account for refraction. For instance, suppose a ball is observed at the bottom of a swimming pool; the light rays reflected from the ball travel through the water and into the air to reach the eye. As the rays leave the water and enter the air, their velocity suddenly increases, causing them to be refracted. However, because of our assumption that light travels in a straight line, our eyes deceive us and make us think we see an object lying at a higher point than is actually the case. This phenomenon is illustrated in Figure 4–10.

The ratio of the velocity of light in a vacuum to its speed in any medium determines the refractive index of that medium and is expressed as follows:

refractive index
The ratio of the speed of light in a vacuum to its speed in a given medium.

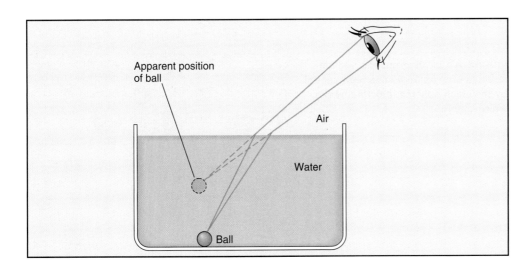

FIGURE 4–10 **Light is refracted when it travels obliquely from one medium to another.**

$$\text{Refractive index} = \frac{\text{velocity of light in vacuum}}{\text{velocity of light in medium}} \qquad \textbf{(4–5)}$$

For example, at 25°C the refractive index of water is 1.333. This means that light travels 1.333 times as fast in a vacuum as it does in water at this temperature.

Like density, the refractive index is an intensive physical property of matter and characterizes a substance. However, any procedure used to determine a substance's refractive index must be performed under carefully controlled temperature and lighting conditions, because the refractive index of a substance varies with its temperature and the wavelength of light passing through it. Nearly all tabulated refractive indices are determined at a standard wavelength, usually 589.3 nanometers; this is the predominant wavelength emitted by sodium light and is commonly known as the sodium D light.

When a transparent solid is immersed in a liquid with a similar refractive index, light is not refracted as it passes from the liquid into the solid. For this reason, the eye cannot distinguish the liquid–solid boundary, and the solid seems to disappear from view. This observation, as we will see, offers the forensic scientist a rather simple method for comparing the refractive indices of transparent solids.

Normally, we expect a solid or a liquid to exhibit only one refractive index value for each wavelength of light; however, many crystalline solids have two refractive indices whose values depend in part on the direction from which the light enters the crystal with respect to the crystal axis. Crystalline solids have definite geometric forms because of the orderly arrangement of the fundamental particle of a solid, the atom.

In any type of crystal, the relative locations and distances between its atoms repeat throughout the solid. Figure 4–11 shows the crystalline structure of sodium chloride, or ordinary table salt. Sodium chloride is an example of a cubic crystal in which each sodium atom is surrounded by six chlorine atoms and each chlorine atom by six sodium atoms, except at the crystal surface. Not all solids are crystalline; some, such as glass, have their atoms arranged randomly throughout the solid; these materials are known as amorphous solids.

Most crystals, excluding those that have cubic configurations, refract a beam of light into two different light-ray components. This phenomenon, known as *double refraction*, can be observed by studying the behavior of

crystalline solid
A solid in which the constituent atoms have a regular arrangement.

amorphous solid
A solid in which the constituent atoms or molecules are arranged in random or disordered positions.

FIGURE 4–11 Diagram of a sodium chloride crystal. Sodium is represented by the black spheres, chlorine by the white spheres.

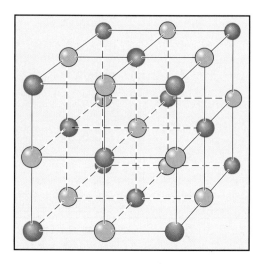

the crystal calcite. When the calcite is laid on a printed page, the observer sees not one but two images of each word covered. The two light rays that create the double image are refracted at different angles, and each has a different refractive index value. The indices of refraction for calcite are 1.486 and 1.658, and subtracting the two values yields a difference of 0.172; this difference is known as birefringence. Thus, the optical properties of crystals provide points of identification that help characterize them.

Now that we have investigated various chemical and physical properties of objects, we are ready to apply some of these properties to the characterization of glass, an item of evidence frequently retrieved at crime scenes and often sent to the crime laboratory for examination.

birefringence
A difference in the two indices of refraction exhibited by most crystalline materials.

Key Points

- Temperature is a measure of heat intensity, or the amount of heat in a substance.

- In science, the most commonly used temperature scale is the Celsius scale, which is derived by assigning the freezing point of water a value of 0°C and its boiling point a value of 100°C.

- Weight is the force with which gravity attracts a body. Mass is a constant property of matter that reflects the amount of material present.

- The formula for calculating the density of an object is mass per unit volume.

- The ratio of the velocity of light in a vacuum to its speed in any medium determines the refractive index of that medium.

- Crystalline solids have definite geometric forms because of the orderly arrangement of their atoms.

- Crystalline solids refract a beam of light in two different light-ray components, resulting in double refraction. Birefringence is the numerical difference between these two refractive indices.

Forensic Analysis of Glass

Glass that is broken and shattered into fragments and minute particles during the commission of a crime can be used to place a suspect at the crime scene. For example, chips of broken glass from a window may lodge in a suspect's shoes or garments during a burglary; particles of headlight glass found at the scene of a hit-and-run accident may confirm the identity of a suspect vehicle. All of these possibilities require the comparison of glass fragments found on the suspect, whether a person or vehicle, with the shattered glass remaining at the crime scene.

Composition of Glass

Glass is a hard, brittle, amorphous substance composed of sand (silicon oxides) mixed with various metal oxides. When sand is mixed with other metal oxides, melted at high temperatures, and then cooled to a rigid condition without crystallization, the product is glass. Soda (sodium carbonate) is normally added to the sand to lower its melting point and make it

FIGURE 4–12 **When tempered glass breaks, it usually holds together without splintering.**
Courtesy Robert Ilewellyn, Alamy Images

easier to work with. Another necessary ingredient is lime (calcium oxide), which is added to prevent the "soda-lime" glass from dissolving in water. The forensic scientist is often asked to analyze soda-lime glass, which is used for manufacturing most window and bottle glass. Usually the molten glass is cooled on top of a bath of molten tin. This manufacturing process produces flat glass typically used for windows. This type of glass is called *float glass.*

The common metal oxides found in soda-lime glass are sodium, calcium, magnesium, and aluminum. In addition, a wide variety of special glasses can be made by substituting in whole or in part other metal oxides for the silica, sodium, and calcium oxides. For example, automobile headlights and heat-resistant glass, such as Pyrex, are manufactured by adding boron oxide to the oxide mix. These glasses are therefore known as *borosilicates.*

tempered glass
Glass to which strength is added by introducing stress through rapid heating and cooling of the glass surfaces.

Another type of glass that the reader may be familiar with is tempered glass. This glass is made stronger than ordinary window glass by introducing stress through rapid heating and cooling of the glass surfaces. When tempered glass breaks, it does not shatter but rather fragments or "dices" into small squares with little splintering (see Figure 4–12). Because of this safety feature, tempered glass is used in the side and rear windows of automobiles sold in the United States. The windshields of all cars manufactured in the United States are constructed from laminated glass. This glass derives its strength by sandwiching one layer of plastic between two pieces of ordinary window glass.

laminated glass
Two sheets of ordinary glass bonded together with a plastic film.

Comparing Glass Fragments

For the forensic scientist, comparing glass consists of finding and measuring the properties that will associate one glass fragment with another while minimizing or eliminating the possible existence of other sources. Considering the prevalence of glass in our society, it is easy to appreciate

FIGURE 4–13 Match of broken glass. Note the physical fit of the edges.
Courtesy Sirchie Finger Print Laboratories, Inc., Youngsville, N.C., www.sirchie.com

the magnitude of this analytical problem. Obviously, glass possesses its greatest evidential value when it can be individualized to one source. Such a determination, however, can be made only when the suspect and crime-scene fragments are assembled and physically fitted together. Comparisons of this type require piecing together irregular edges of broken glass as well as matching all irregularities and striations on the broken surfaces (see Figure 4–13). The possibility that two pieces of glass originating from different sources will fit together exactly is so unlikely as to exclude all other sources from practical consideration.

Unfortunately, most glass evidence is either too fragmentary or too minute to permit a comparison of this type. In such instances, the search for individual properties has proven fruitless. For example, the general chemical composition of various window glasses within the capability of current analytical methods has so far been found to be relatively uniform among various manufacturers and thus offers no basis for individualization. However, as more sensitive analytical techniques are developed, trace elements present in glass may prove to be distinctive and measurable characteristics.

The physical properties of density and refractive index are used most successfully for characterizing glass particles. However, these properties are class characteristics, which cannot provide the sole criteria for individualizing glass to a common source. They do, however, give the analyst sufficient data to evaluate the significance of a glass comparison, and the absence of comparable density and refractive index values will certainly exclude glass fragments that originate from different sources.

Measuring and Comparing Density

Recall that a solid particle will either float, sink, or remain suspended in a liquid, depending on its density relative to the liquid medium. This knowledge gives the criminalist a rather precise and rapid method for comparing densities of glass.

In a method known as *flotation,* a standard/reference glass particle is immersed in a liquid; a mixture of bromoform and bromobenzene may be used. The composition of the liquid is carefully adjusted by adding small amounts of bromoform or bromobenzene until the glass chip remains suspended in the liquid medium. At this point, the standard/reference glass and liquid each have the same density. Glass chips of approximately the same size and shape as the standard/reference are now added to the liquid for comparison. If both the unknown and the standard/reference particles remain suspended in the liquid, their densities are equal to each other and to that of the liquid.[1] Particles of different densities either sink or float, depending on whether they are more or less dense than the liquid.

The density of a single sheet of window glass is not completely homogeneous throughout. It has a range of values that can differ by as much as 0.0003 g/mL. Therefore, in order to distinguish between the normal internal density variations of a single sheet of glass and those of glasses of different origins, it is advisable to let the comparative density approach but not exceed a sensitivity value of 0.0003g/mL. The flotation method meets this requirement and can adequately distinguish glass particles that differ in density by 0.001 g/mL.

Determining and Comparing Refractive Index

Once glass has been distinguished by a density determination, different origins are immediately concluded. Comparable density results, however, require the added comparison of refractive indices. This determination is best accomplished by the *immersion method*. For this, glass particles are immersed in a liquid medium whose refractive index is adjusted until it equals that of the glass particles. At this point, known as the *match point*, the observer notes the disappearance of the Becke line, indicating minimum contrast between the glass and liquid medium. The Becke line is a bright halo observed near the border of a particle that is immersed in a liquid of a different refractive index. This halo disappears when the medium and fragment have similar refractive indices.

Becke line
A bright halo observed near the border of a particle immersed in a liquid of a different refractive index.

FIGURE 4–14 Hot-stage microscope. *Courtesy Chris Palenik, Microtrace, Elgin, IL, www.microstracescientific.com*

The refractive index of an immersion fluid is best adjusted by changing the temperature of the liquid. Temperature control is, of course, critical to the success of the procedure. One approach is to heat the liquid in a special apparatus known as a *hot stage* (see Figure 4–14). The glass is immersed in a boiling liquid, usually a silicone oil, and heated at the rate of 0.2°C per minute until the match point is reached. The examiner then observes the disappearance of the Becke line on minute glass particles that are illuminated with sodium D light or at other wavelengths of light. If all the glass fragments examined have similar match points, it can be concluded that they have comparable refractive indices (see Figure 4–15). Furthermore, the examiner can determine the refractive index value of the immersion fluid as it changes with temperature. With this information, the exact numerical value of the glass refractive index can be calculated at the match point temperature.[2]

(a)

(b)

(c)

(d)

FIGURE 4–15 **Determining the refractive index of glass. (a) Glass particles are immersed in a liquid of a much higher refractive index at a temperature of 77°C. (b) At 87°C the liquid still has a higher refractive index than the glass. (c) The refractive index of the liquid is closest to that of the glass at 97°C, as shown by the disappearance of the glass and the Becke lines. (d) At the higher temperature of 117°C, the liquid has a much lower index than the glass, and the glass is plainly visible.** *Courtesy Walter C. McCrone*

As with density, glass fragments removed from a single sheet of plate glass may not have a uniform refractive index value; instead, their values may vary by as much as 0.0002. Hence, for comparison purposes, the difference in refractive index between a standard/reference and questioned glass must exceed this value. This allows the examiner to differentiate between the normal internal variations present in a sheet of glass and those present in glasses that originated from completely different sources.

Closer Analysis

GRIM 3

An automated approach for measuring the refractive index of glass fragments by temperature control using the immersion method with a hot stage is with the instrument known as GRIM 3 (Glass Refractive Index Measurement)[*] (see Figure 1). The GRIM 3 is a personal computer/video system designed to automate the measurements of the match temperature and refractive index for glass fragments. This instrument uses a video camera to view the glass fragments as they are being heated. As the immersion oil is heated or cooled, the contrast of the video image is measured continually until a minimum, the match point, is detected (see Figure 2). The match point temperature is then converted to a refractive index using stored calibration data.

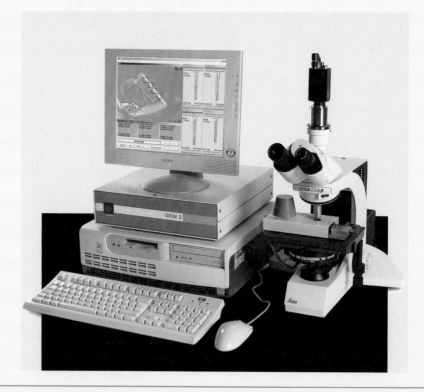

FIGURE 1   An automated system for glass fragment identification. *Courtesy Foster & Freeman Limited, Worcestershire, U.K., www.fosterfreeman.co.uk*

[*]Foster and Freeman Limited, 25 Swan Lane, Evesham, Worcestershire WRII 4PE, U.K.

FIGURE 2 GRIM 3 identifies the refraction match point by monitoring a video image of the glass fragment immersed in an oil. As the immersion oil is heated or cooled, the contrast of the image is measured continuously until a minimum, the match point, is detected. *Courtesy Foster & Freeman Limited, Worcestershire, U.K., www.fosterfreeman.co.uk*

Classification of Glass Samples

A significant difference in either density or refractive index proves that the glasses examined do not have a common origin. But what if two pieces of glass exhibit comparable densities and comparable refractive indices? How certain can one be that they did, indeed, come from the same source? After all, there are untold millions of windows and other glass objects in this world.

To provide a reasonable answer to this question, the FBI Laboratory has collected density and refractive indices values from glass submitted to it for examination. What has emerged is a data bank correlating these values to their frequency of occurrence in the glass population of the United States. This collection is available to all forensic laboratories in the United States. This means that once a criminalist has completed a comparison of glass fragments, he or she can correlate their density and refractive index values to their frequency of occurrence and assess the probability that the fragments came from the same source.

Figure 4–16 shows the distribution of refractive index values (measured with sodium D light) for approximately two thousand glasses analyzed by the FBI. The wide distribution of values clearly demonstrates that the refractive index is a highly distinctive property of glass and is thus useful for defining its frequency of occurrence and hence its evidential value. For example, a glass fragment with a refractive index value of 1.5290 is found in approximately only 1 out of 2,000 specimens, while glass with a value of 1.5180 occurs approximately in 22 glasses out of 2,000.

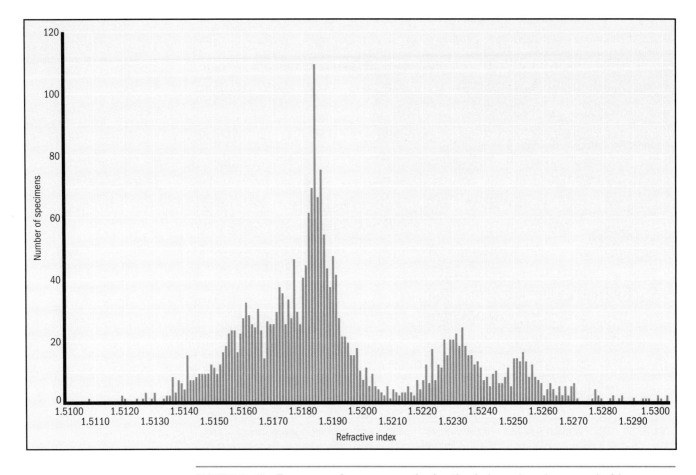

FIGURE 4–16 Frequency of occurrence of refractive index values (measured with sodium D light) for approximately two thousand flat glass specimens received by the FBI Laboratory. *Courtesy FBI Laboratory, Washington, D.C.*

The distinction between tempered and nontempered glass particles can be made by slowly heating and then cooling the glass (a process known as *annealing*). The change in the refractive index value for tempered glass upon annealing is significantly greater when compared to nontempered glass and thus serves as a point of distinction.[3]

Glass Fractures

Glass bends in response to any force that is exerted on any one of its surfaces; when the limit of its elasticity is reached, the glass fractures. Frequently, fractured window glass reveals information about the force and direction of an impact; such knowledge may be useful for reconstructing events at a crime-scene investigation.

The penetration of ordinary window glass by a projectile, whether a bullet or a stone, produces a familiar fracture pattern in which cracks both radiate outward and encircle the hole, as shown in Figure 4–17. The radiating lines are appropriately known as radial fractures, and the circular lines are termed concentric fractures.

Often it is difficult to determine just from the size and shape of a hole in glass whether it was made by a bullet or by some other projectile. For instance, a small stone thrown at a comparatively high speed against a pane of glass often produces a hole very similar to that produced by a bullet. On the other hand, a large stone can completely shatter a pane of glass in a manner closely resembling the result of a close-range shot. However,

radial fracture
A crack in a glass that extends outward like the spoke of a wheel from the point at which the glass was struck.

concentric fracture
A crack in a glass that forms a rough circle around the point of impact.

FIGURE 4–17 Radial and concentric fracture lines in a sheet of glass. *Courtesy Sirchie Finger Print Laboratories, Inc., Youngsville, N.C., www.sirchie.com*

FIGURE 4–18 Crater-shaped hole made by a pellet passing through glass. The upper surface is the exit side of the projectile. *Courtesy New Jersey State Police*

in the latter instance, the presence of gunpowder deposits on the shattered glass fragments points to damage caused by a firearm.

When it penetrates glass, a high-velocity projectile such as a bullet often leaves a round, crater-shaped hole surrounded by a nearly symmetrical pattern of radial and concentric cracks. The hole is inevitably wider on the exit side (see Figure 4–18), and hence examining it is an important step in determining the direction of impact. However, as the velocity of the penetrating projectile decreases, the irregularity of the shape of the hole and of its surrounding cracks increases, so that at some point the hole shape will not help determine the direction of impact. At this point, examining the radial and concentric fracture lines may help determine the direction of impact.

When a force pushes on one side of a pane of glass, the elasticity of the glass permits it to bend in the direction of the force applied. Once the elastic limit is exceeded, the glass begins to crack. As shown in Figure 4–19, the first fractures form on the surface opposite that of the penetrating force and develop into radial lines. The continued motion of the force places tension on the front surface of the glass, resulting in the formation of concentric cracks. An examination of the edges of the radial and concentric cracks frequently reveals stress markings whose shape can be related to the side on which the window first cracked.

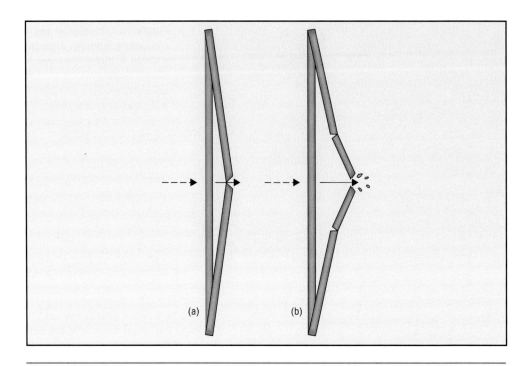

FIGURE 4–19 **Production of radial and concentric fractures in glass. (a) Radial cracks are formed first, beginning on the side of the glass opposite to the destructive force. (b) Concentric cracks occur afterward, starting on the same side as the force.**

Stress marks, shown in Figure 4–20, are shaped like arches that are perpendicular to one glass surface and curved nearly parallel to the opposite surface. The importance of stress marks stems from the observation that the perpendicular edge always faces the surface on which the crack originated. Thus, in examining the stress marks on the edge of a radial crack near the point of impact, the perpendicular end is always found opposite the side from which the force of impact was applied. For a concentric fracture, the perpendicular end always faces the surface on which the force originated. A convenient way for remembering these observations is the 3R rule—*Radial* cracks form a *Right* angle on the *Reverse* side of the force. These facts enable the examiner to determine the side on which a window was broken. Unfortunately, the absence of radial or concentric fracture lines prevents these observations from being applied to broken tempered glass.

When there have been successive penetrations of glass, it is frequently possible to determine the sequence of impact by observing the existing fracture lines and their points of termination. A fracture always terminates at an existing line of fracture. In Figure 4–21, the fracture on the left preceded that on the right; we know this because the latter's radial fracture lines terminate at the cracks of the former.

Collection and Preservation of Glass Evidence

The gathering of glass evidence at the crime scene and from the suspect must be thorough if the examiner is to have any chance to individualize the fragments to a common source. If even the remotest possibility exists that fragments may be pieced together, every effort must be made to collect all the glass found. For example, evidence collection at hit-and-run scenes must include all the broken parts of the headlight and reflector lenses. This evidence may ultimately prove invaluable in placing a suspect vehicle at the accident scene by matching the fragments with glass remaining in the

FIGURE 4–20 **Stress marks on the edge of a radial glass fracture. Arrow indicates direction of force.** *Courtesy New Jersey State Police*

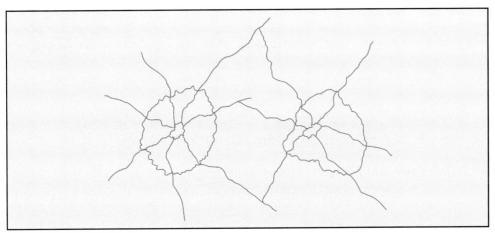

FIGURE 4–21 **Two bullet holes in a piece of glass. The left hole preceded the right hole.**

headlight or reflector shell of the suspect vehicle. In addition, examining the headlight's filaments may reveal whether an automobile's headlights were on or off before the impact (see Figure 4–22).

When an individual fit is improbable, the evidence collector must submit all glass evidence found in the possession of the suspect along with a sample of broken glass remaining at the crime scene. This standard/reference glass should always be taken from any remaining glass in the window or door frames, as close as possible to the point of breakage. About one square inch of sample is usually adequate for this purpose. The glass fragments should be packaged in solid containers to avoid further breakage. If the suspect's shoes and/or clothing are to be examined for the presence of glass fragments, they should be individually wrapped in paper and transmitted to the laboratory. The field investigator should avoid removing such evidence from garments unless absolutely necessary for its preservation.

When a determination of the direction of impact is desired, all broken glass must be recovered and submitted for analysis. Wherever possible, the exterior and interior surfaces of the glass must be indicated. When this is not immediately apparent, the presence of dirt, paint, grease, or putty may indicate the exterior surface of the glass.

FIGURE 4–22 The presence of black tungsten oxide on the upper filament indicates that the filament was on when it was exposed to air. The lower filament was off, but its surface was coated with a yellow/white tungsten oxide, which was vaporized from the upper ("on") filament and condensed onto the lower filament. *Courtesy New Jersey State Police*

Key Points

- To compare glass fragments, a forensic scientist evaluates two important physical properties: density and refractive index.

- The immersion method is used to determine a glass fragment's refractive index. It involves immersing a glass particle in a liquid medium whose refractive index is adjusted by varying its temperature. At the refractive index match point the contrast between the glass and liquid is at a minimum.

- The flotation method is used to determine a glass fragment's density. It involves immersing a glass particle in a liquid whose density is carefully adjusted by adding small amounts of an appropriate liquid until the glass chip remains suspended in the liquid medium.

- By analyzing the radial and concentric fracture patterns in glass, the forensic scientist can determine the direction of impact by applying the 3R Rule: *R*adial cracks form a *R*ight angle on the *R*everse side of the force.

Chapter Summary

The forensic scientist must constantly determine the properties that impart distinguishing characteristics to matter, giving it a unique identity. Physical properties such as weight, volume, color, boiling point, and melting point describe a substance without reference to any other substance. A chemical property describes the behavior of a substance when it reacts or combines with another substance.

Scientists throughout the world use the metric system of measurement. The metric system has basic units of measurement for length, mass, and volume: the meter, gram, and liter, respectively.

Matter is anything that has mass and occupies space. An element is a fundamental particle of matter that cannot be broken down into simpler substances by chemical means. The smallest particle of an element that can exist and still retain its identity as that element is the atom. The periodic table is a chart of all the known elements arranged in a systematic fashion. When two or more elements are combined the new material created is called a compound. Matter can exist in one of three states: solid, liquid, or gas (vapor).

Light can behave either as a continuous wave or as a stream of discrete energy particles known as photons. Waves are characterized by two distinct properties: wavelength and frequency. Visible light consists of light of all colors; the process of separating light into component colors is called dispersion. Upon passing through the glass of a prism, each color component of light is slowed to a speed slightly different from the others, thus causing each component to bend at a different angle as it emerges from the prism. This bending of light waves because of a change in velocity is called refraction. Visible light is part of a large family of radiation waves known as the electromagnetic spectrum. All electromagnetic waves travel at the speed of light and are distinguishable from one another only by their different wavelengths or frequencies.

Temperature is a measure of heat intensity, or the amount of heat in a substance. In science, the most commonly used temperature scale is the Celsius scale. This scale is derived by assigning the freezing point of water a value of 0°C and its boiling point a value of 100°C.

To compare glass fragments, a forensic scientist evaluates two important physical properties: density and refractive index. Density is defined as the mass per unit volume. Refractive index is the ratio of the velocity of light in a vacuum to that in the medium under examination.

Crystalline solids have definite geometric forms because of the orderly arrangement of their atoms. These solids refract a beam of light in two different light-ray components. This results in double refraction. Birefringence is the numerical difference between these two refractive indices. Not all solids are crystalline in nature. For example, glass has a random arrangement of atoms to form an amorphous or noncrystalline solid.

The flotation and immersion methods are best used to determine a glass fragment's density and refractive index, respectively. In the flotation method, a glass particle is immersed in a liquid. The density of the liquid is carefully adjusted by adding small amounts of an appropriate liquid until the glass chip remains suspended in the liquid medium. At this point, the glass has the same density as the liquid medium and can be compared to other relevant pieces of glass. The immersion method involves immersing a glass particle in a liquid medium whose refractive index is adjusted until it equals that of the glass particle. At this point, known as the match point, minimum contrast between liquid and particle is observed.

By analyzing the radial and concentric fracture patterns in glass, the forensic scientist can determine the direction of impact. This can be accomplished by applying the 3R Rule: *R*adial cracks form a *R*ight angle on the *R*everse side of the force.

Review Questions

Facts and Concepts

1. What is the difference between a physical property and a chemical property?

2. Define *matter* and *element*. How are matter and elements related?

3. What is the smallest particle of an element that can exist and still retain its identity?

4. What is a compound? Name three common compounds and give the chemical symbol for each.

5. What is the smallest unit of a compound?

6. Name the three states of matter. What chemical property of a substance determines its state?

7. Give two examples of a substance undergoing a change in state.

8. What is sublimation?

9. Are changes of state physical or chemical changes? Explain your answer.

10. What is a phase? Give an example of a two-phase system.

11. Wavelength is
    a. the distance between crests of adjacent waves.
    b. the speed of a wave.
    c. the distance from the crest of a wave to the trough.
    d. the number of waves that pass a given point in a second.

12. Define *dispersion* and explain how it is related to wavelength and frequency.

13. What is refraction?

14. Explain how color is related to the behavior of light. How do forensic scientists use this knowledge in their work?

15. What property distinguishes different types of electromagnetic radiation from one another?

16. When must the particle theory be invoked to explain the behavior of light?

17. Define *temperature* and name the two most common temperature scales.

18. What is weight? How does weight differ from mass?

19. How is the mass of an object determined? List three devices used for comparing the masses of different objects.

20. What is the formula for calculating the density of an object?

21. What is an intensive property? Name three intensive properties of matter.

22. Refractive index measures the speed of light in a vacuum to its speed in
    a. air.
    b. water.
    c. glass.
    d. any given substance.

23. What is the main ingredient in ordinary glass?

24. What kind of glass is used commonly in bottles and windows? How did this type of glass acquire its name?

25. What are tempered glass and laminated glass? On what part of an automobile is each type typically used?

26. What is the only way to individualize glass fragments found at a crime scene to a single source?

27. What physical properties are used most often to characterize glass particles? What is the main drawback of using these properties to characterize glass?

28. Define *flotation* and describe how it works.

29. Describe how a forensic scientist determines the refractive indices of suspect glass fragments.

30. Why should tests for density and refractive index not exceed a certain level of sensitivity?

31. What is annealing and how is it useful to the analysis of glass?

32. What is the 3R rule and what does it tell an investigator examining glass evidence?

33. How might a forensic scientist tell which of two fractures on a piece of glass was created earlier?

Application and Critical Thinking

1. Use metric conversions to answer the following questions:
   a. Who is taller—someone who measures 6 feet, 3 inches, or someone who measures 1.9 meters?
   b. Which is heavier—a package that weighs 210 pounds or one that weighs 90 kilograms?
   c. Which holds more water—a 2-gallon bottle or an 8-liter bottle?

2. The following table shows the force of gravity on other planets relative to the force of gravity on the earth. For example, the force of gravity on the moon is only 0.166 (about one-sixth) that of the earth.

Table 1	The Force of Gravity On Other Planets
PLANET	Gravity Relative to Earth
Mercury	0.378
Venus	0.907
Moon	0.166
Earth	1.000
Mars	0.377
Jupiter	2.533
Saturn	1.064
Uranus	0.889
Neptune	1.125
Pluto	0.067

Using this information, along with your knowledge of the difference between mass and weight, answer the following questions:

   a. Which weighs more—a 100-pound Great Dane on Pluto or a 25-pound terrier on Mars?

   b. Which weighs more—a quarter-pound hamburger on Jupiter or a 12-ounce steak on Venus?

   c. Which has a greater mass—a 300-pound football player on Saturn or an 800-pound gorilla on Mercury?

   d. If a car has a mass of 4,500 pounds on the earth, how much will it weigh on Neptune?

3. An accident investigator arrives at the scene of a hit-and-run collision. The driver who remained at the scene reports that the windshield or a side window of the car that struck him shattered on impact. The investigator searches the accident site and collects a large number of fragments of tempered glass. This is the only type of glass recovered from the scene. How can the glass evidence help the investigator locate the vehicle that fled the scene?

4. Indicate the order in which the bullet holes were made in the glass depicted in the figure at left below. Explain the reason for your answer.

5. The figure at right below depicts stress marks on the edge of a glass fracture caused by the application of force. If this is a radial fracture, from which side of the glass (left or right) was the force applied? From which side was force applied if it is a concentric fracture? Explain the reason for your answers.

Web Resources

U.S. Metric Association (Links to websites, articles, and FAQs about the metric system)
lamar.colostate.edu/~hillger

Mass and Weight Conversion (Online application that converts units to and from metric, English, and eleven other measuring systems)
www.convert-me.com/en/convert/weight

Matter/Mass/Atoms/Molecules (Links to Web sites, online lessons, and online activities about the properties of matter)
edtech.kennesaw.edu/web/matter.html

The Pictorial Periodic Table (Interactive periodic table containing information about each element; searchable by various properties)
chemlab.pc.maricopa.edu/periodic/periodic.html

States of Matter (Brief animated explanation of behavior of molecules in various states of matter)
www.chem.purdue.edu/gchelp/atoms/states.html

Demonstrations of Physical Properties (Online lab suggestions for demonstrating temperature effects, measuring density, explaining refractive index; page also contains additional forensics lab exercises)
intro.chem.okstate.edu/ChemSource/Forensic/forechem8.htm

Electromagnetic Spectrum (Article on basic principles of the spectrum with examples of various types of radiation and hyperlinked glossary of terms)
imagine.gsfc.nasa.gov/docs/science/know_l1/emspectrum.html

Physical Properties of Glass and Soil (Online slideshow covering important points in chapter)
www.stfrancis.edu/ns/diab/ForensicCoursePPT/Ch4webGlass&Soil.htm

Endnotes

1. As an added step, the analyst can determine the exact numerical density value of the particles of glass by transferring the liquid to a density meter, which will electrically measure and calculate the liquid's density. See A. P. Beveridge and C. Semen, "Glass Density Measurement Using a Calculating Digital Density Meter," *Canadian Society of Forensic Science Journal* 12 (1979): 113.
2. A. R. Cassista and P. M. L. Sandercock, "Precision of Glass Refractive Index Measurements: Temperature Variation and Double Variation Methods, and the Value of Dispersion," *Canadian Society of Forensic Science Journal* 27 (1994): 203.
3. G. Edmondstone, "The Identification of Heat Strengthened Glass in Windshields," *Canadian Society of Forensic Science Journal* 30 (1997): 181.

Pablo Escobar, Drug Lord

In 1989, *Forbes* magazine listed Pablo Escobar as the seventh richest man in the world. Escobar began his climb to wealth as a teenage car thief in the streets of Medellin, Colombia, and eventually moved into the cocaine-smuggling business. At the peak of his power in the mid-1980s, he was shipping as much as eleven tons of cocaine per flight in jetliners to the United States. Law enforcement officials estimate that the Medellin cartel controlled 80 percent of the world's cocaine market and was taking in about $25 billion annually.

Escobar ruthlessly ruled by the gun: murdering, assassinating, and kidnapping. He was responsible for killing three presidential candidates in Colombia, as well as the storming of the Colombian Supreme Court, which resulted in the murder of half the justices. All the while, Escobar curried favor with the Colombian general public by cultivating a Robin Hood image and distributing money to the poor.

In 1991, hoping to avoid extradition to the United States, Escobar turned himself in to the Colombian government and agreed to be sent to prison. However, the prison compound could easily be mistaken for a country club. There he continued his high-flying lifestyle, trafficking by telephone and even murdering a few associates. When the Colombian government attempted to move Escobar to another jail, he escaped, again fearing extradition to the United States.

Pressured by the U.S. government, Colombia organized a task force dedicated to apprehending Escobar. The manhunt for Escobar ended on December 2, 1993, when he was cornered on the roof of one of his hideouts. A shootout ensued and Escobar was fatally wounded by a bullet behind his ear.

chapter 5

Drugs

Key Terms

anabolic steroids

analgesic

chromatography

confirmation

depressant

fluoresce

hallucinogen

infrared

ion

microcrystalline test

monochromatic light

monochromator

narcotic

physical dependence

psychological dependence

screening test

spectrophotometry

stimulant

ultraviolet

A *drug* can be defined as a natural or synthetic substance that is used to produce physiological or psychological effects in humans or other animals. However, criminalists are concerned primarily with a small number of drugs—many of them illicit—that are commonly used for their intoxicating effects. These include marijuana, the most widely used illicit drug in the United States, and alcohol, which is consumed regularly by 90 million Americans. Drug abuse has grown from a problem generally associated with members of the lower end of the socioeconomic ladder to one that cuts across all social and ethnic classes of society. Today, approximately 23 million people in the United States use illicit drugs.

Because of the epidemic proportions of illegal drug use, more than 75 percent of the evidence evaluated by crime laboratories in the United States is drug related (see Figure 5–1). The deluge of drug specimens has forced the expansion of existing crime laboratories and the creation of new ones. For many concerned forensic scientists, the crime laboratory's preoccupation with drug evidence represents a serious distraction from time that could be devoted to evaluating evidence related to homicides and other types of serious crimes. However, the increasing caseloads associated with drug evidence have justified the expansion of forensic laboratory services. This expansion has increased the overall analytical capabilities of crime laboratories.

Drug Dependence

In assessing the potential danger of drugs, society has become particularly conscious of their effects on human behavior. In fact, the first drugs to be regulated by law in the early years of the twentieth century were those deemed to have "habit-forming" properties. The early laws were aimed primarily at controlling opium and its derivatives, cocaine, and later marijuana. The ability of a drug to induce dependence after repeated use is submerged in a complex array of physiological and social factors.

Dependence on drugs exists in numerous patterns and in all degrees of intensity, depending on the nature of the drug, the route of administration, the dose, the frequency of administration, and the individual's rate of metabolism. Furthermore, nondrug factors play an equally

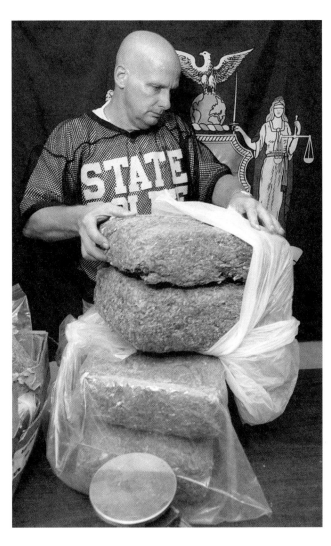

FIGURE 5–1 Drug bust.
Courtesy Syracuse Newspapers/The Image Works

crucial role in determining the behavioral patterns associated with drug use. The personal characteristics of the user, his or her expectations about the drug experience, society's attitudes and possible responses, and the setting in which the drug is used are all major determinants of drug dependence.

The question of how to define and measure a drug's influence on the individual and its danger to society is difficult to assess. The nature and significance of drug dependence must be considered from two overlapping points of view: the interaction of the drug with the individual, and the drug's impact on society. It will be useful to approach the problem from two distinctly different aspects of human behavior—psychological dependence and physical dependence.

Psychological Dependence

The common denominator that characterizes all types of repeated drug use is the creation of a psychological dependence for continued use of the drug. It is important to discard the unrealistic image that all drug users are hopeless "addicts" who are social dropouts. Most users present quite a normal appearance and remain both socially and economically integrated in the life of the community.

The reasons why some people abstain from drugs while others become moderately or heavily involved are difficult if not impossible to

psychological dependence
The conditioned use of a drug caused by underlying emotional needs.

physical dependence
Physiological need for a drug brought about by its regular use and characterized by withdrawal sickness when administration of the drug is abruptly stopped.

delineate. Psychological needs arise from numerous personal and social factors that inevitably stem from the individual's desire to create a sense of well-being and to escape from reality. In some cases, the individual may seek relief from personal problems or stressful situations, or may be trying to sustain a physical and emotional state that permits an improved level of performance. Whatever the reasons, the underlying psychological needs and the desire to fulfill them create a conditioned pattern of drug abuse (see Figure 5–2).

The intensity of the psychological dependence associated with a drug's use is difficult to define and largely, depends on the nature of the drug used. For drugs such as alcohol, heroin, amphetamines, barbiturates, and cocaine, continued use will likely result in a high degree of involvement. Other drugs, such as marijuana and codeine, appear to have a considerably lower potential for the development of psychological dependence. However, this does not imply that repeated abuse of drugs deemed to have a low potential for psychological dependence is safe or will always produce low psychological dependence. We have no precise way to measure or predict the impact of drug abuse on the individual. Even if a system could be devised for controlling the many possible variables affecting a user's response, the unpredictability of the human personality would still have to be considered.

Our general knowledge of alcohol consumption should warn us of the fallacy of generalizing when attempting to describe the danger of drug abuse. Obviously, not all alcohol drinkers are psychologically addicted to the drug; most are "social" drinkers who drink in reasonable amounts and on an irregular basis. Many people have progressed beyond this stage and consider alcohol a necessary crutch for dealing with life's stresses and anxieties. However, a wide range of behavioral patterns exists

FIGURE 5–2 Young people drinking. *Courtesy Daytona Beach News-Journal/Jim Tiller*

among alcohol abusers, and to a large extent the determination of the degree of psychological dependence must be made on an individual basis. Likewise, it would be fallacious to generalize that all users of marijuana can at worst develop a low degree of dependence on the drug. A wide range of factors also influence marijuana's effect, and heavy users of the drug expose themselves to the danger of developing a high degree of psychological dependence.

Physical Dependence

Although emotional well-being is the primary motive leading to repeated and intensive use of a drug, certain drugs, taken in sufficient dose and frequency, can produce physiological changes that encourage their continued use. Once the user abstains from such a drug, severe physical illness follows. The desire to avoid this *withdrawal sickness*, or *abstinence syndrome*, ultimately causes physical dependence, or addiction. Hence, for the addict who is accustomed to receiving large doses of heroin, the thought of abstaining and encountering body chills, vomiting, stomach cramps, convulsions, insomnia, pain, and hallucinations is a powerful inducement for continued drug use.

Interestingly, some of the more widely abused drugs have little or no potential for creating physical dependence. Drugs such as marijuana, LSD, and cocaine create strong anxieties when their repeated use is discontinued; however, no medical evidence attributes these discomforts to physiological reactions that accompany withdrawal sickness. On the other hand, use of alcohol, heroin, and barbiturates can result in development of physical dependence.

Physical dependence develops only when the drug user adheres to a regular schedule of drug intake; that is, the interval between doses must be short enough so that the effects of the drug never wear off completely. For example, the interval between injections of heroin for the drug addict probably does not exceed six to eight hours. Beyond this time the addict begins to experience the uncomfortable symptoms of withdrawal. Many users of heroin avoid taking the drug on a regular basis for fear of becoming physically addicted to its use. Similarly, the risk of developing physical dependence on alcohol becomes greatest when the consumption is characterized by a continuing pattern of daily use in large quantities.

Table 5–1 categorizes some of the more commonly abused drugs according to their effect on the body and summarizes their tendency to produce psychological dependence and to induce physical dependence with repeated use.

Societal Aspects of Drug Use

The social impact of drug dependence is directly related to the extent to which the user has become preoccupied with the drug. Here, the most important element is the extent to which drug use has become interwoven in the fabric of the user's life. The more frequently the drug satisfies the person's need, the greater the likelihood that he or she will become preoccupied with its use, with a consequent neglect of individual and social responsibilities. Personal health, economic relationships, and family obligations may all suffer as the drug-seeking behavior increases in frequency and intensity and dominates the individual's life. The extreme of drug

Table 5–1 The Potential of Some Commonly Abused Drugs to Produce Dependence with Regular Use

Drug	Psychological Dependence	Physical Dependence
Narcotics		
Morphine	High	Yes
Heroin	High	Yes
Methadone	High	Yes
Codeine	Low	Yes
Depressants		
Barbiturates (short-acting)	High	Yes
Barbiturates (long-acting)	Low	Yes
Alcohol	High	Yes
Methaqualone (Quaalude)	High	Yes
Meprobamate (Miltown, Equanil)	Moderate	Yes
Diazepam (Valium)	Moderate	Yes
Chlordiazepoxide (Librium)	Moderate	Yes
Stimulants		
Amphetamines	High	?
Cocaine	High	No
Caffeine	Low	No
Nicotine	High	Yes
Hallucinogens		
Marijuana	Low	No
LSD	Low	No
Phencyclidine (PCP)	High	No

dependence may lead to behavior that has serious implications for the public's safety, health, and welfare.

Drug dependence in its broadest sense involves much of the world's population. As a result, a complex array of individual, social, cultural, legal, and medical factors ultimately influence society's decision to prohibit or impose strict controls on a drug's distribution and use. Invariably, society must weigh the beneficial aspects of the drug against the ultimate harm its abuse will do to the individual and to society as a whole. Obviously, many forms of drug dependence do not carry sufficient adverse social consequences to warrant their prohibition, as illustrated by the widespread use of such drug-containing substances as tobacco and coffee. Although the heavy and prolonged use of these drugs may eventually damage body organs and injure an individual's health, there is no evidence that they result in antisocial behavior, even with prolonged or excessive use. Hence, society is willing to accept the widespread use of these substances.

We are certainly all aware of the disastrous failure in the United States to prohibit the use of alcohol during the 1920s and the current debate on whether marijuana should be legalized. Each of these issues emphasizes the delicate balance between individual desires and needs and society's concern with the consequences of drug abuse; moreover, this balance is continuously subject to change and reevaluation.

Key Points

- A drug is a natural or synthetic substance that is used to produce physiological or psychological effects in humans or other animals.

- Nondrug factors that play a part in drug dependence include the personal characteristics of the user, his or her expectations about the drug experience, society's attitudes and possible responses, and the setting in which the drug is used.

- Physical dependence is defined as the physiological need for a drug that has been brought about by its regular use. Psychological dependence is the conditioned use of a drug caused by underlying emotional needs.

Types of Drugs

Narcotic Drugs

The term narcotic is derived from the Greek word *narkotikos*, meaning numbness or deadening. Although pharmacologists classify narcotic drugs as substances that relieve pain and produce sleep, the term *narcotic* has become popularly associated with any drug that is socially unacceptable. As a consequence of this incorrect usage, many drugs are improperly called narcotics.

> **narcotic**
> A drug that induces sleep and depresses vital body functions such as blood pressure, pulse rate, and breathing rate.

This confusion has produced legal definitions that differ from the pharmacological actions of many drugs. For example, until the early 1970s, most drug laws in the United States incorrectly designated marijuana as a narcotic. Even today, federal law classifies cocaine as a narcotic drug, although pharmacologically, cocaine is actually a powerful central nervous system stimulant, possessing properties opposite those normally associated with the depressant effects of a narcotic.

Opiates   Medical professionals apply the term *opiate* to most of the drugs properly classified as narcotics. Opiates behave pharmacologically like morphine, a painkiller derived from opium—a gummy, milky juice exuded through a cut made in the unripe pod of the Asian poppy *(Papaver somniferum)*. Although morphine is readily extracted from opium, the most commonly used opium-based drug is heroin, which is produced by reacting morphine with acetic anhydride or acetyl chloride (see Figure 5–3). Heroin's high solubility in water makes its street preparation for intravenous administration rather simple, for only by injection are heroin's effects felt almost instantaneously and with maximum sensitivity. To prepare the drug for injection, the addict frequently dissolves it in a small quantity of water in a spoon. The process can be speeded up by heating the spoon over a candle or several matches. The solution is then drawn into a syringe or eyedropper for injection under the skin (see Figure 5–4).

Heroin and other narcotic drugs are analgesics—that is, they relieve pain by depressing the central nervous system. Besides being a powerful analgesic, heroin produces a "high" that is accompanied by drowsiness and a deep sense of well-being. The effect is short, generally lasting only three to four hours. Regular use of heroin—or any other narcotic drug—invariably leads to physical dependence, with all its dire consequences.

> **analgesic**
> A substance that lessens or eliminates pain.

FIGURE 5–3 The opium poppy and its derivatives. Shown are the poppy plant, crude and smoking opium, codeine, heroin, and morphine. *Courtesy Drug Enforcement Administration, Washington, D.C.*

FIGURE 5–4 Heroin paraphernalia. *Courtesy Drug Enforcement Administration, Washington, D.C.*

Codeine is also present in opium, but it is usually prepared synthetically from morphine. It is commonly used as a cough suppressant in prescription cough syrup. Codeine, only one-sixth as strong as morphine, is not an attractive street drug for addicts.

Synthetic Opiates A number of narcotic drugs are not naturally derived from opium. However, because they have similar physiological effects on the body as the opium narcotics, they are also commonly referred to as opiates.

Methadone is perhaps the best known synthetic opiate. In the 1960s, scientists discovered that a person who received periodic doses of methadone would not get high if he or she then took heroin or morphine. Although

Closer Analysis

What's in That Bag?

The content of a typical heroin bag is an excellent example of the uncertainty attached to buying illicit drugs. For many years into the 1960s and early 1970s, the average bag contained 15 to 20 percent heroin. Currently, the average purity of heroin obtained in the illicit U.S. market is approximately 35 percent. The addict rarely knows or cares what comprises the other 65 percent or so of the material. Traditionally, quinine has been the most common diluent of heroin. Like heroin, it has a bitter taste and was probably originally used to obscure the actual potency of a heroin preparation from those who wished to taste-test the material before buying it. Other diluents commonly added to heroin are starch, lactose, procaine (Novocain), and mannitol.

methadone is pharmacologically related to heroin, its administration appears to eliminate the addict's desire for heroin, with minimal side effects. These discoveries led to the establishment of controversial methadone maintenance programs in which heroin addicts receive methadone to reduce or prevent future heroin use. Physicians increasingly prescribe methadone for pain relief. Unfortunately the wide availability of methadone for legitimate medical purposes has recently led to greater quantities of the drug being diverted into the illicit market.

In 1995, the U.S. Food and Drug Administration (FDA) approved for use the pain-killing drug *OxyContin*. The active ingredient in OxyContin is oxycodone, a synthetic closely related to morphine and heroin in its chemical structure. OxyContin is an analgesic narcotic that has effects similar to those of heroin. It is prescribed to a million patients for treatment of chronic pain with doctors writing close to seven million OxyContin prescriptions each year. The drug is compounded with a time-release formulation that the manufacturer initially believed would reduce the risk of abuse and addiction. This has not turned out to be the case. It is estimated that close to a quarter of a million individuals abuse the drug.

Because it is a legal drug that is diverted from legitimate sources, OxyContin is obtained very differently from illegal drugs. Pharmacy robberies, forged prescriptions, and theft of the drug from patients with a legitimate prescription are ways in which abusers access OxyContin. Some abusers visit numerous doctors and receive prescriptions even though their medical condition may not warrant it.

Hallucinogens

Hallucinogens are drugs that can cause marked alterations in normal thought processes, perceptions, and moods. Perhaps the most popular and controversial member of this class of drugs is marijuana.

Marijuana   Marijuana is the popular name of the plant *Cannabis sativa*, a weed that grows wild under most climatic conditions. The *Cannabis* plant contains a chemical known as *tetrahydrocannabinol*, or THC, which produces the psychoactive effects experienced by users. The THC content of *Cannabis* varies in different parts of the plant. The greatest concentration is usually found in a sticky resin produced by the plant, known as *hashish*.

hallucinogen
A substance that induces changes in normal thought processes, perceptions, and moods.

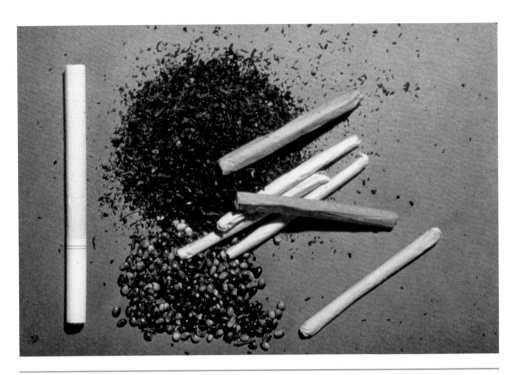

FIGURE 5–5 **Several rolled marijuana cigarettes lie on a pile of crushed dried marijuana leaves next to a tobacco cigarette.** *Courtesy Drug Enforcement Administration, Washington, D.C.*

Declining concentrations are typically found in the flowers and leaves, respectively. Little THC is found in the stem, roots, or seeds of the plant. The potency and resulting effect of the drug fluctuate, depending on the relative proportion of these plant parts in the marijuana mixture consumed by the user. The most common method of administration is by smoking either the dried flowers and leaves, or various preparations of hashish (see Figure 5–5). Marijuana is also occasionally taken orally, typically baked in sweets such as brownies or cookies.

Any study of marijuana's effect on humans must consider the potency of the marijuana preparation. An interesting insight into the relationship between dosage level and marijuana's pharmacological effect was presented in the first report of the National Commission on Marijuana and Drug Abuse:

> At low, usual "social" doses the user may experience an increased sense of well-being; initial restlessness and hilarity followed by a dreamy, carefree state of relaxation; alteration of sensory perceptions including expansion of space and time; a more vivid sense of touch, sight, smell, taste and sound; a feeling of hunger, especially a craving for sweets; and subtle changes in thought formation and expression. To an unknowing observer, an individual in this state of consciousness would not appear noticeably different from his normal state.
>
> At higher, moderate doses these same reactions are intensified but the changes in the individual would still be scarcely noticeable to an observer. At very high doses, psychotomimetic phenomena may be experienced. These include distortion of body image, loss of personal identity, sensory and mental illusions, fantasies and hallucinations.[1]

Closer Analysis

Marijuana and Hashish

Marijuana is a weed that grows wild under most climatic conditions. The plant grows to a height of 5 to 15 feet and is characterized by an odd number of leaflets on each leaf. Normally each leaf contains five to nine leaflets, all with serrated or saw-tooth edges.

The potency of marijuana depends on its form. Marijuana in the form of loose vegetation has an average THC content of about 3–4.5 percent (see Figure 1). The more potent sinsemilla form averages about 6–12 percent in THC content. Sinsemilla is made from the unfertilized flowering tops of the female *Cannabis* plants, acquired by removing all male plants from the growing field at the first sign of their appearance. Production of sinsemilla requires a great deal of attention and care, and the plant is therefore cultivated on small plots.

FIGURE 2   Blocks of hashish in front of leaves and flowering tops of the marijuana plant. *Courtesy James King-Holmes, Photo Researchers, Inc.*

Hashish preparations average about 2–8 percent THC. On the illicit drug market, hashish usually appears in the form of compressed vegetation containing a high percentage of resin (see Figure 2). A particularly potent form of hashish is known as *liquid hashish* or *hashish oil*. Hashish in this form is normally a viscous substance, dark green with a tarry consistency. Liquid hashish is produced by efficiently extracting the THC-rich resin from the marijuana plant with an appropriate solvent, such as alcohol. Liquid hashish typically varies between 8 and 22 percent in THC content. Because of its extraordinary potency, one drop of the material can produce a "high."

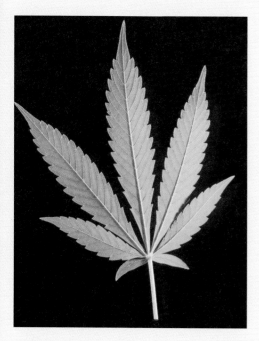

FIGURE 1   The marijuana leaf. *Courtesy Drug Enforcement Administration, Washington, D.C.*

Marijuana easily qualifies as the most widely used illicit drug in the United States. For instance, more than 43 million Americans have tried marijuana, according to the latest surveys, and almost half that number may be regular users. In addition to its widespread illegal use, accumulating evidence suggests that marijuana has potential medical uses. Two promising areas of research are marijuana's reduction of excessive eye pressure in glaucoma and the lessening of nausea caused by powerful anticancer drugs. Marijuana may also be useful as a muscle relaxant.

No current evidence suggests that experimental or intermittent use causes physical or psychological harm. Marijuana does not cause physical dependence. However, the risk of harm lies instead in heavy, long-term use, particularly of the more potent preparations. Heavy users can develop a strong psychological dependence on the drug. Some effects of marijuana use include increased heart rate, dry mouth, reddened eyes, impaired motor skills and concentration, and frequently hunger and an increased desire for sweets.

Other Hallucinogens A substantial number of other substances with widely varying chemical compositions are also used recreationally because of their hallucinogenic properties. These include both naturally occurring substances such as mescaline and psilocybin and synthetically created drugs including lysergic acid diethylamide (LSD) and phencyclidine (PCP).

Closer Analysis

A Brief History of Marijuana

Marijuana and its related products have been in use legally and illegally for almost three thousand years. The first reference to medical use of marijuana is in a pharmacy book written about 2737 B.C. by the Chinese emperor Shen Nung, who recommended it for "female weakness, gout, rheumatism, malaria, beriberi, constipation and absent-mindedness." In China, at that time and even today, the marijuana or hemp plant was also a major source of fiber for rope production. Marijuana's mood-altering powers probably did not receive wide attention until about 1000 B.C., when it became an integral part of Hindu culture in India. After A.D. 500, marijuana began creeping westward, and references to it began to appear in Persian and Arabian literature.

The plant was probably brought to Europe by Napoleon's soldiers when they returned from Egypt in the early nineteenth century. In Europe, the drug excited the interest of many physicians who foresaw its application for treating a wide range of ailments. At this time, it also found some use as a painkiller and mild sedative. In later years, these applications were either forgotten or ignored.

Marijuana was first introduced into the United States around 1920. The weed was smuggled by Mexican laborers across the border into Texas. American soldiers also brought the plant in from the ports of Havana, Tampico, and Veracruz. Although its use was confined to a small segment of the population, its popularity quickly spread from the border and Gulf states into most major U.S. cities. By 1937, forty six states and the federal government had laws prohibiting the use or possession of marijuana. Under most of these laws, marijuana was subject to the same rigorous penalties applicable to morphine, heroin, and cocaine and was often erroneously designated a narcotic.

LSD is synthesized from lysergic acid, a substance derived from ergot, which is a type of fungus that attacks certain grasses and grains. The drug appears in a variety of forms—as a pill, added to a cube of sugar, or absorbed onto a small piece of paper—and is taken orally. Its hallucinogenic effects were first described by the Swiss chemist Albert Hofmann after he accidentally ingested some of the material in his laboratory in 1943. LSD produces marked changes in mood, leading to laughing or crying at the slightest provocation. Feelings of anxiety and tension almost always accompany LSD use. LSD is very potent; as little as 25 micrograms is enough to start vivid visual hallucinations that can last for about twelve hours. Although physical dependence does not develop with continued use, the individual user may be prone to flashbacks and psychotic reactions even after use is discontinued.

Abuse of the hallucinogen phencyclidine, commonly called PCP, has recently grown to alarming proportions. Because this drug can be synthesized by simple chemical processes, it is manufactured surreptitiously for the illicit market in so-called clandestine laboratories (see Figure 5–6). These laboratories range from large, sophisticated operations to small labs located in a garage or bathroom. Small-time operators normally have little or no training in chemistry and employ "cookbook" methods to synthesize the drug. Some of the more knowledgeable and experienced operators have been able to achieve clandestine production levels that approach a commercial level of operation.

Phencyclidine is often mixed with other drugs, such as LSD or amphetamine, and is sold as a powder ("angel dust"), capsule, or tablet, or as a liquid sprayed on plant leaves. The drug is smoked, ingested, or sniffed. Following oral intake of moderate doses (1–6 milligrams), the user first experiences feelings of strength and invulnerability, along with a dreamy sense of detachment. However, the user soon becomes unresponsive, confused, and agitated. Depression, irritability, feelings of isolation, audio and

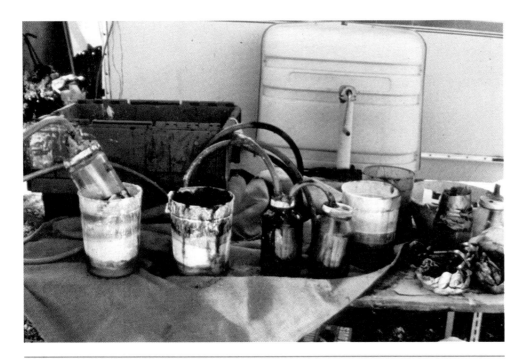

FIGURE 5–6 **Scene from a clandestine drug laboratory.** *Courtesy Drug Enforcement Administration, Washington, D.C.*

visual hallucinations, and sometimes paranoia accompany PCP use. Severe depression, tendencies toward violence, and suicide accompany long-term daily use of the drug. In some cases, the PCP user experiences sudden schizophrenic behavior days after the drug has been taken.

Depressants

Depressants are drugs that slow down, or depress, the central nervous system. Several types of drugs fall under this category, including the most widely used drug in the United States—alcohol.

depressant
A substance that slows down, or depresses, the functions of the central nervous system.

Alcohol (Ethyl Alcohol)   Many people overlook the fact that alcohol is a drug, however, it exerts a powerful depressant action on the central nervous system. When alcohol enters the bloodstream, it quickly travels to the brain, where it suppresses the brain's control of thought processes and muscle coordination. Low doses of alcohol tend to inhibit the mental processes of judgment, memory, and concentration. The drinker's personality becomes expansive, and he or she exudes confidence. When taken in moderate doses, alcohol reduces coordination substantially, inhibits orderly thought processes and speech patterns, and slows reaction times. Under these conditions, the ability to walk or drive becomes noticeably impaired. Higher doses of alcohol may cause the user to become highly irritable and emotional; displays of anger and crying are not uncommon. Extremely high doses may cause an individual to lapse into unconsciousness or even a comatose state that may precede a fatal depression of circulatory and respiratory functions. The behavioral patterns of alcohol intoxication vary and depend partly on such factors as social setting, amount consumed, and the personal expectation of the individual with regard to alcohol.

In the United States, the alcohol industry annually produces more than one billion gallons of spirits, wine, and beer for which 90 million consumers

FIGURE 5–7   Rows of alcohol bottles behind a bar. *Courtesy Jeremy Liebman/Stone/Getty Images*

pay nearly $40 billion. Unquestionably, these and other statistics support the fact that alcohol is the most widely used and abused drug (see Figure 5–7).

Barbiturates   Barbiturates are derivatives of barbituric acid, a substance first synthesized by a German chemist, Adolf Von Bayer, more than a hundred years ago. They are commonly referred to as "downers" because they relax the user, create a feeling of well-being, and produce sleep. Like alcohol, barbiturates suppress the vital functions of the central nervous system. Twenty-five barbiturate derivatives are currently used in medical practice in the United States; however, five—amobarbital, secobarbital, phenobarbital, pentobarbital, and butabarbital—tend to be used for most medical applications.

Normally, barbiturate users take these drugs orally. The average sedative dose is about 10–70 milligrams. When taken in this fashion, the drug enters the blood through the walls of the small intestine. Some barbiturates, such as phenobarbital, are classified as long-acting barbiturates. They are absorbed into the bloodstream more slowly than others and therefore produce less pronounced effects than faster-acting barbiturates. The slow action of phenobarbital accounts for its low incidence of abuse. Apparently, barbiturate abusers prefer the faster-acting varieties—secobarbital, pentobarbital, and amobarbital.

Since the early 1970s, a nonbarbiturate depressant, methaqualone (Quaalude), has appeared on the illicit-drug scene. Methaqualone is a powerful sedative and muscle relaxant that possesses many of the depressant properties of barbiturates. When taken in prescribed amounts, barbiturates are relatively safe, but in instances of extensive and prolonged use, physical dependence can develop.

Antipsychotics and Antianxiety Drugs   Although these drugs can be considered depressants, they differ from barbiturates in the extent of their actions on the central nervous system. Generally, these drugs produce a relaxing tranquility without impairing high-thinking faculties or inducing sleep. Antipsychotics such as reserpine and chlorpromazine have been used to reduce the anxieties and tensions of mental patients. Antianxiety drugs are commonly prescribed to deal with the everyday tensions of many healthy people. These drugs include meprobamate (Miltown), chlordiazepoxide (Librium), and diazepam (Valium).

In the past thirty five years, the use of these drugs—particularly antianxiety drugs—has grown dramatically. Medical evidence shows that these drugs produce psychological and physical dependence with repeated and high levels of usage. For this reason, the widespread prescribing of antianxiety drugs to overcome the pressures and tensions of life has worried many who fear the creation of a legalized drug culture.

"Huffing"   Since the early 1960s, "huffing," the practice of sniffing materials containing volatile solvents (airplane glue or model cement, for example), has grown in popularity. Another dimension has recently been added to the problem with the increasing number of incidents involving the sniffing of aerosol gas propellants such as freon. All materials abused by huffing contain volatile or gaseous substances that are primarily central nervous system depressants. Although toluene (a solvent used in airplane glue) seems to be the most popular solvent to sniff, others can produce comparable physiological effects. These chemicals include naphtha, methyl ethyl ketone (antifreeze), gasoline, and trichloroethylene (dry-cleaning solvent).

The usual immediate effects of huffing are a feeling of exhilaration and euphoria combined with slurred speech, impaired judgment, and double vision. Finally, the user may experience drowsiness and stupor, with these depressant effects slowly wearing off as the user returns to a normal state. Most experts believe that users become physiologically dependent on the effects achieved by huffing. However, little evidence suggests that solvent inhalation is addictive. But huffers expose themselves to the danger of liver, heart, and brain damage from the chemicals they have inhaled. Even worse, sniffing of some solvents, particularly halogenated hydrocarbons such as freon and related gases, is accompanied by a significant risk of death.

Stimulants

stimulant

A substance that speeds up, or stimulates, the central nervous system.

The term stimulants refers to a range of drugs that stimulate, or speed up, the central nervous system.

Amphetamines   Amphetamines are a group of synthetic stimulants that share a similar chemical structure and are commonly referred to in the terminology of the drug culture as "uppers" or "speed." They are typically taken either orally or via intravenous injection, and provide a feeling of well-being and increased alertness that is followed by a decrease in fatigue and a loss of appetite. However, these apparent benefits of the drug are accompanied by restlessness and instability or apprehension, and once the stimulant effect wears off, depression may set in.

In the United States, the most serious form of amphetamine abuse stems from intravenous injection of amphetamine or its chemical derivative, methamphetamine (see Figure 5–8). The desire for a more intense amphetamine experience is the primary motive for this route of administration. The initial sensation of a "flash" or "rush," followed by an intense feeling of pleasure, constitutes the principal appeal of the intravenous route for the user. During a "speed binge," the individual may inject amphetamines every two to three hours. Users have reported experiencing a euphoria that produces hyperactivity, with a feeling of clarity of vision as well as hallucinations.

FIGURE 5–8   Granular amphetamine beside a razor blade. *Courtesy Cordelia Molloy, Photo Researchers, Inc.*

As the effect of the amphetamines wears off, the individual lapses into a period of exhaustion and may sleep continuously for one or two days. Following this, the user often experiences a prolonged period of severe depression, lasting from days to weeks.

A smokable form of methamphetamine known as "ice" is reportedly in heavy demand in some areas of the United States. Ice is prepared by slowly evaporating a methamphetamine solution to produce large, crystal-clear "rocks." Like crack cocaine (discussed next), ice is smoked and produces effects similar to those of crack cocaine, but the effects last longer. Once the effects of ice wear off, users often become depressed and may sleep for days. Chronic users exhibit violent destructive behavior and acute psychosis similar to paranoid schizophrenia. Repeated use of amphetamines leads to a strong psychological dependence, which encourages their continued administration.

Cocaine Between 1884 and 1887, pioneering psychologist Sigmund Freud created something of a sensation in European medical circles by describing his experiments with a new drug. He reported a substance of seemingly limitless potential as a source of "exhilaration and lasting euphoria" that permitted "intensive mental or physical work [to be] performed without fatigue. . . . It is as though the need for food and sleep was completely banished."

The object of Freud's enthusiasm was cocaine, a stimulant extracted from the leaves of *Erythroxylon coca*, a plant grown in the Andes mountains of South America as well as in tropical Asia (see Figure 5–9). Most commonly, cocaine is sniffed or "snorted" and is absorbed into the body through the mucous membranes of the nose, although it is sometimes injected. Cocaine is a powerful stimulant to the central nervous system, and its effects resemble those caused by amphetamines—namely, increased alertness and vigor, accompanied by suppression of hunger, fatigue, and boredom. Cocaine produces a feeling of euphoria by stimulating a pleasure center in the base of the brain, in an area connected to nerves that are responsible for emotions. It stimulates this pleasure center to a far greater degree than it

FIGURE 5–9 Coca leaves and illicit forms of cocaine. *Courtesy Drug Enforcement Administration, Washington, D.C.*

would ever normally be stimulated. Some regular users of cocaine report accompanying feelings of restlessness, irritability, and anxiety. Cocaine used chronically or at high doses can have toxic effects. Cocaine-related deaths result from cardiac arrest or seizures followed by respiratory arrest.

A particularly potent form of cocaine known as "crack" can be produced by mixing cocaine with baking soda and water and then heating the resulting solution. This material is then dried and broken into tiny chunks that dealers sell as crack "rocks" that are sufficiently volatile to be smoked. The faster the cocaine level rises in the brain, the greater the euphoria, and the surest way to obtain a fast rise in the brain's cocaine level is to smoke crack. Inhaling the cocaine vapor delivers the drug to the brain in less than fifteen seconds—about as fast as injecting it and much faster than snorting it. The dark side of crack, however, is that the euphoria fades quickly as cocaine levels drop, leaving the user feeling depressed, anxious, and pleasureless. The desire to return to a euphoric feeling is so intense that crack users quickly develop a habit for the drug that is almost impossible to overcome. Only a small percentage of crack abusers will ever be cured of this drug habit.

In the United States, cocaine abuse is on the rise. Many people are apparently using cocaine to improve their ability to work and to keep going when tired. While there is no evidence of physical dependency accompanying cocaine's repeated use, abstention from cocaine after prolonged use brings on severe bouts of mental depression, which produce a very strong compulsion to resume using the drug. In fact, laboratory experiments with animals have demonstrated that of all the commonly abused drugs, cocaine produces the strongest psychological compulsions for continued use.

The United States spends millions of dollars annually in attempting to control cultivation of the coca leaf in various South American countries and to prevent cocaine trafficking into the United States. Three-quarters of the cocaine smuggled into the United States is refined in clandestine laboratories in Colombia. The profits are astronomical. Peruvian farmers may be paid $200 for enough coca leaves to make one pound of cocaine. The refined cocaine is worth $1,000 when it leaves Colombia and sells at retail in the United States for up to $20,000.

Club Drugs

The term *club drugs* refers to synthetic drugs that are often used at nightclubs, bars, and raves (all-night dance parties). Substances that are used as club drugs include, but are not limited to, MDMA (Ecstasy, see Figure 5–10), GHB (gamma hydroxybutyrate), Rohypnol ("Roofies"), ketamine, and methamphetamine. These drugs have become popular at the dance scene as a way to stimulate the rave experience. A high incidence of use has been found among teens and young adults.

GHB and Rohypnol are central nervous system depressants that are often connected with drug-facilitated sexual assault, rape, and robbery. Effects accompanying the use of GHB include dizziness, sedation, headache, and nausea. Recreational users have reported euphoria, relaxation, disinhibition, and increased libido (sex drive). Rohypnol causes muscle relaxation, loss of consciousness, and an inability to remember what happened during the hours after ingesting the drug. This is particularly a concern in a sexual assault because victims are physically unable to resist the attack. Unsuspecting victims become drowsy or dizzy. Effects are even stronger when the drug is combined with alcohol because the user experiences memory loss, blackouts, and disinhibition. Drugs such as Rohypnol and

FIGURE 5–10 **Ecstasy, a popular club drug.** *Courtesy Rusty Kennedy, AP Wide World Photos*

GHB are odorless, colorless, and tasteless, and thus remain undetected when slipped into a drink.

Methylenedioxymethamphetamine, also known as MDMA or Ecstasy, is a synthetic, mind-altering drug that exhibits many hallucinogenic and amphetamine-like effects. Ecstasy was originally patented as an appetite suppressant and was later discovered to induce feelings of happiness and relaxation. Recreational drug users find that Ecstasy enhances self-awareness and decreases inhibitions. However, seizures, muscle breakdown, stroke, kidney failure, and cardiovascular system failure often accompany chronic abuse of Ecstasy. In addition, chronic use of Ecstasy leads to serious damage to the areas of the brain responsible for thought and memory. Ecstasy increases heart rate and blood pressure; produces muscle tension, teeth grinding, and nausea; and causes psychological difficulties such as confusion, severe anxiety, and paranoia. The drug can cause significant increases in body temperature from the combination of the drug's stimulant effect with the often hot, crowded atmosphere of a rave club.

Ketamine is primarily used in veterinary medicine as an animal anesthetic. When used by humans, the drug can cause euphoria and feelings of unreality accompanied by visual hallucinations. Ketamine can also cause impaired motor function, high blood pressure, amnesia, and mild respiratory depression.

Anabolic Steroids

Anabolic steroids are synthetic compounds that are chemically related to the male sex hormone testosterone. Testosterone has two different effects on the body. It promotes the development of secondary male characteristics (androgenic effects), and it accelerates muscle growth (anabolic effects). Efforts to promote muscle growth and to minimize the hormone's androgenic effects have led to the synthesis of numerous anabolic steroids. However, a steroid free of the accompanying harmful side effects of an androgen drug has not yet been developed.

anabolic steroids Synthetic compounds chemically related to the male sex hormone testosterone that are used to promote muscle growth.

Incidence of steroid abuse first received widespread public attention when both amateur and professional athletes were discovered using these substances to enhance their performance. Interestingly, current research on male athletes given anabolic steroids has generally found little or, at best, marginal evidence of enhanced strength or performance. While the full extent of anabolic steroid abuse by the general public is not fully known, the U.S. government is sufficiently concerned to regulate the availability of these drugs to the general population and to severely punish individuals for illegal possession and distribution of anabolic steroids. In 1991, anabolic steroids were classified as controlled dangerous substances, and the Drug Enforcement Administration was given enforcement power to prevent their illegal use and distribution.

Anabolic steroids are usually taken by individuals who are unfamiliar with the harmful medical side effects. Liver cancer and other liver malfunctions have been linked to steroid use. These drugs also cause masculinizing effects in females, infertility, and diminished sex drive in males. For teenagers, anabolic steroids result in premature halting of bone growth. Anabolic steroids can also cause unpredictable effects on mood and personality, leading to unprovoked acts of anger and destructive behavior. Depression is also a frequent side effect of anabolic steroid abuse.

Key Points

- Narcotic drugs are analgesics, meaning they relieve pain by depressing the central nervous system.

- The most common source for narcotic drugs is opium. Morphine is extracted from opium and used to synthesize heroin.

- Opiates are not derived from opium or morphine, but they have the same physiological effects on the body. Examples of opiates include methadone and OxyContin (oxycodone).

- Hallucinogens cause marked changes in normal thought processes, perceptions, and moods. Marijuana is the most well-known drug in this class. Other hallucinogens include LSD, mescaline, PCP, psilocybin, and MDMA (Ecstasy).

- Depressants decrease the activity of the central nervous system, calm irritability and excitability, and produce sleep. Depressants include alcohol (ethanol), barbiturates, tranquilizers, and various substances that can be sniffed, such as airplane glue or model cement.

- Stimulants increase the activity of the central nervous system and are taken to increase alertness and activity. Stimulants include amphetamines, sometimes known as "uppers" or "speed," and cocaine, which in its freebase form is known as *crack*.

- Club drugs are synthetic drugs that are used at nightclubs, bars, and raves (all-night dance parties). Some club drugs act as stimulants; others have depressant effects.

- Anabolic steroids are synthetic compounds that are chemically related to the male sex hormone testosterone. Anabolic steroids are often abused by individuals who are interested in accelerating muscle growth.

Drug-Control Laws

The provisions of drug laws are of particular interest to the criminalist, for they may impose specific analytical requirements on drug analysis. For example, the severity of a penalty associated with the manufacture, distribution, possession, and use of a drug may depend on the weight of the drug or its concentration in a mixture. In such cases, the chemist's report must contain all information that is needed to properly charge a suspect under the provisions of the existing law.

The provisions of any drug-control law are an outgrowth of national and local law enforcement requirements and customs, as well as the result of moral and political philosophies. These factors have produced a wide spectrum of national and local drug-control laws. Although their detailed discussion is beyond the intended scope of this book, a brief description of the U.S. federal law known as the Controlled Substances Act will illustrate a legal drug classification system that has been created to prevent and control drug abuse. Many states have modeled their own drug-control laws after this act, an important step in establishing uniform drug-control laws throughout the United States.

Closer Analysis

Controlled Substances Act

The federal law establishes five schedules of classification for controlled dangerous substances on the basis of a drug's potential for abuse, potential for physical and psychological dependence, and medical value. This classification system is extremely flexible in that the U.S. attorney general has the authority to add, delete, or reschedule a drug as more information becomes available.

Schedule I. Schedule I drugs have a high potential for abuse, have no currently accepted medical use in the United States, and/or lack accepted safety for use in treatment under medical supervision. Drugs controlled under this schedule include heroin, marijuana, methaqualone, and LSD.

Schedule II. Schedule II drugs have a high potential for abuse, a currently accepted medical use or a medical use with severe restrictions, and a potential for severe psychological or physical dependence. Schedule II drugs include opium and its derivatives not listed in schedule I, cocaine, methadone, phencyclidine (PCP), most amphetamine preparations, and most barbiturate preparations containing amobarbital, secobarbital, and pentobarbital. Dronabinol, the synthetic equivalent of the active ingredient in marijuana, has been placed in schedule II in recognition of its growing medical uses in treating glaucoma and chemotherapy patients.

Schedule III. Schedule III drugs have less potential for abuse than those in schedules I and II, a currently accepted medical use in the United States, and a potential for low or moderate physical dependence or high psychological dependence. Schedule III controls, among other substances, all barbiturate preparations (except phenobarbital) not covered under schedule II and certain codeine preparations. Anabolic steroids were added to this schedule in 1991.

Schedule IV. Schedule IV drugs have a low potential for abuse relative to schedule III drugs and have a current medical

(*continued*)

Closer Analysis

Controlled Substances Act (*continued*)

Schedule	Registration	Record Keeping	Manufacturing Quotas	Distribution Restrictions	Dispensing Limits
Table 5–2	**Control Mechanisms of the Controlled Substances Act**				
I	Required	Separate	Yes	Order forms	Research use only
II	Required	Separate	Yes	Order forms	Rx: written; no Refills
III	Required	Readily retrievable	No, but some drugs limited by schedule II quotas	Records required	Rx: written or oral; with medical authorization refills up to 5 times in 6 months
IV	Required	Readily retrievable	No, but some drugs limited by schedule II quotas	Records required	Rx: written or oral; with medical authorization refills up to 5 times in 6 months
V	Required	Readily retrievable	No, but some drugs limited by schedule II quotas	Records required	Over-the-counter (Rx drugs limited to MD's order) refills up to 5 times

Source: Drug Enforcement Administration, Washington, D.C.

use in the United States; their abuse may lead to limited dependence relative to schedule III drugs. Drugs controlled in this schedule include propoxyphene (Darvon), phenobarbital, and tranquilizers such as meprobamate (Miltown), diazepam (Valium), and chlordiazepoxide (Librium).

Schedule V. Schedule V drugs must show low abuse potential, have medical use in the United States, and have less potential for producing dependence than schedule IV drugs. Schedule V controls certain opiate drug mixtures that contain nonnarcotic medicinal ingredients.

Controlled dangerous substances listed in schedules I and II are subject to manufacturing quotas set by the attorney general. For example, eight billion doses of amphetamines were manufactured in the United States in 1971. In 1972, production quotas were established reducing amphetamine production approximately 80 percent below 1971 levels.

The criminal penalties for unauthorized manufacture, sale, or possession of controlled dangerous substances are related to the schedules as well. The most severe penalties are associated with drugs listed in schedules I and II. For example, for drugs included in schedules I and II, a first offense is punishable by up to twenty years in prison and/or a fine of up to $1 million for an individual or up to $5 million for other than individuals. Table 5–2 summarizes the control mechanisms and penalties for each schedule of the Controlled Substances Act.

The Controlled Substances Act also stipulates that an offense involving a controlled substance analog, a chemical substance substantially similar in chemical structure to a controlled substance, triggers penalties as if it were a controlled substance listed in schedule I. This section is designed to combat the proliferation of so-called *designer drugs*—substances that are chemically related to some controlled drugs and are pharmacologically very potent. These substances are manufactured by skilled individuals in clandestine laboratories, with the knowledge that their products will not be covered by the schedules of the Controlled

Import–Export		Security	Manufacturer/Distributor Reports to Drug Enforcement Administration	Criminal Penalties for Individual Trafficking (First Offense)
Narcotic	Nonnarcotic			
Permit	Permit	Vault/safe	Yes	0–20 years/$1 million
Permit	Permit	Vault/safe	Yes	0–20 years/$1 million
Permit	Declaration	Secure storage area	Yes, narcotic No, nonnarcotic	0–5 years/$250,000
Permit	Declaration	Secure storage area	Manufacturer only, narcotic No, nonnarcotic	0–3 years/$250,000
Permit to import; declaration to export	Declaration	Secure storage area	Manufacturer only, narcotic No, nonnarcotic	0–1 year/$100,000

Substances Act. For instance, fentanyl is a powerful narcotic that is commercially marketed for medical use and is also listed as a controlled dangerous substance. This drug is about one hundred times as potent as morphine. A number of substances chemically related to fentanyl have been synthesized by underground chemists and sold on the street. The first such substance encountered was sold under the street name China White. These drugs have been responsible for more than a hundred overdose deaths in California and nearly twenty deaths in western Pennsylvania. As designer drugs, such as China White, are identified and linked to drug abuse, they are placed in appropriate schedules.

The Controlled Substances Act also reflects an effort to decrease the prevalence of clandestine drug laboratories designed to manufacture controlled substances. The act regulates the manufacture and distribution of precursors, the chemical compounds used by clandestine drug laboratories to synthesize abused drugs. Targeted precursor chemicals are listed in the definition section of the Controlled Substances Act. Severe penalties are provided for a person who possesses a listed precursor chemical with the intent to manufacture a controlled substance or who possesses or distributes a listed chemical knowing, or having reasonable cause to believe, that the listed chemical will be used to manufacture a controlled substance. In addition, precursors to PCP, amphetamines, and methamphetamines are enumerated specifically in schedule II, making them subject to regulation in the same manner as other schedule II substances.

Key Points

- Federal law establishes five schedules of classification for controlled dangerous substances on the basis of a drug's potential for abuse, potential for physical and psychological dependence, and medical value.

Forensic Drug Analysis

One only has to look into the evidence vaults of crime laboratories to appreciate the assortment of drug specimens that confront the criminalist. The presence of a huge array of powders, tablets, capsules, vegetable matter, liquids, pipes, cigarettes, cookers, and syringes is testimony to the vitality and sophistication of the illicit-drug market. If outward appearance is not evidence enough of the difficult analytical chore facing the forensic chemist, consider the complexity of the drug preparations themselves. Usually these contain active drug ingredients of unknown origin and identity, as well as additives—for example, sugar, starch, and quinine—that dilute their potency and stretch their value on the illicit-drug market. Do not forget that illicit-drug dealers are not hampered by government regulations that ensure the quality and consistency of a product.

When a forensic chemist picks up a drug specimen for analysis, he or she can expect to find just about anything, so all contingencies must be prepared for. The analysis must leave no room for error, because its results will have a direct bearing on the process of determining the guilt or innocence of a defendant. There is no middle ground in drug identification—either the specimen is a specific drug or it is not—and once a positive conclusion is drawn, the chemist must be prepared to support and defend the validity of the results in a court of law.

Screening and Confirmation

The challenge or difficulty of forensic drug identification comes in selecting analytical procedures that will ensure a specific identification of a drug. Presented with a substance of unknown origin and composition, the forensic chemist must develop a plan of action that will ultimately yield the drug's identity. This plan, or scheme of analysis, is divided into two phases.

screening test
A preliminary test used to reduce the number of possible identities of an unknown substance.

First, faced with the prospect that the unknown substance may be any one of a thousand or more commonly encountered drugs, the analyst must employ screening tests to reduce these possibilities to a small and manageable number. This objective is often accomplished by subjecting the material to a series of color tests that produce characteristic colors for the more commonly encountered illicit drugs. Even if these tests produce negative results, their value lies in having excluded certain drugs from further consideration.

Once the number of possibilities has been reduced substantially, the second phase of the analysis must be devoted to pinpointing and confirming the drug's identity. In an era in which crime laboratories receive voluminous quantities of drug evidence, it is impractical to subject a drug to all the chemical and instrumental tests available. Indeed, it is more realistic to look on these techniques as constituting a large analytical arsenal. The chemist, aided by training and experience, must choose tests that will most conveniently identify a particular drug.

confirmation
A single test that specifically identifies a substance.

Forensic chemists often use a specific test to identify a drug substance to the exclusion of all other known chemical substances. A single test that identifies a substance is known as a confirmation. The analytical scheme sometimes consists of a series of nonspecific or presumptive tests. Each test in itself is insufficient to prove the drug's identity; however, the proper analytical scheme encompasses a combination of test results that characterize one and only one chemical substance—the drug under investigation. Furthermore, experimental evidence must confirm that the probability of any other substance responding in an identical manner to the scheme selected is so small as to be beyond any reasonable scientific certainty.

Another consideration in selecting an analytical technique is the need for either a *qualitative* or a *quantitative* determination. The former relates just to the identity of the material, whereas the latter refers to the percentage combination of the components of a mixture. Hence, a qualitative identification of a powder may reveal the presence of heroin and quinine, whereas a quantitative analysis may conclude the presence of 10 percent heroin and 90 percent quinine.

Obviously, a qualitative identification must precede any attempt at quantitation, for little value is served by attempting to quantitate a material without first determining its identity. Essentially, a qualitative analysis of a material requires the determination of numerous properties using a variety of analytical techniques. On the other hand, a quantitative measurement is usually accomplished by precise measurement of a single property of the material.

Forensic chemists normally rely on several tests for a routine drug-identification scheme: color tests, microcrystalline tests, chromatography, spectrophotometry, and mass spectrometry.

Color Tests

Many drugs yield characteristic colors when brought into contact with specific chemical reagents. Not only do these tests provide a useful indicator of a drug's presence, but they are also used by investigators in the field to examine materials suspected of containing a drug (see Figure 5–11).[2] However, color tests are useful for screening purposes only and are never taken as conclusive identification of unknown drugs.

Five primary color test reagents are as follows:

1. *Marquis.* The reagent turns purple in the presence of heroin and morphine and most opium derivatives. Marquis also becomes orange-brown when mixed with amphetamines and methamphetamines.

2. *Dillie-Koppanyi.* This is a valuable screening test for barbiturates, in whose presence the reagent turns violet-blue in color.

FIGURE 5–11 **A field color test kit for cocaine. The suspect drug is placed in the plastic pouch. Tubes containing chemicals are broken open and the color of the chemical reaction is oberved.** *Courtesy Tri-Tech, Inc., Southport, N.C., www.tritechusa.com*

3. *Duquenois-Levine.* This is a valuable color test for marijuana, performed by adding a series of chemical solutions, to the suspect vegetation. A positive result is shown by a purple color when chloroform is added.

4. *Van Urk.* The reagent turns blue-purple in the presence of LSD. However, owing to the extremely small quantities of LSD in illicit preparations, this test is difficult to conduct under field conditions.

5. *Scott Test.* This is a color test for cocaine. A powder containing cocaine turns a cobalt thiocyanate solution blue. Upon addition of hydrochloric acid, the blue color is transformed to a clear pink color. Upon addition of chloroform, if cocaine is present, the blue color reappears in the chloroform layer.

Key Points

- Analysts use screening tests to determine the identity of drugs present in a sample. These tests reduce the number of possible drugs to a small and manageable number.

- A series of color tests produce characteristic colors for the more commonly encountered illicit drugs. In a microcrystalline test, a drop of a chemical reagent added to a small quantity of drug on a microscope slide produces crystals highly characteristic of a drug.

- After preliminary testing, forensic chemists use more specific tests to identify a drug substance to the exclusion of all other known chemical substances.

Microcrystalline Tests

microcrystalline test
A test that identifies a specific substance based on the color and shape of crystals formed when the substance is mixed with specific reagents.

A technique considerably more specific than color tests is the microcrystalline test. A drop of a chemical reagent is added to a small quantity of the drug on a microscopic slide. After a short time, a chemical reaction ensues, producing a crystalline precipitate. The size and shape of the crystals, under microscope examination, are highly characteristic of the drug. Crystal tests for cocaine and methamphetamine are illustrated in Figure 5–12.

(a)

(b)

FIGURE 5–12 **(a) A photomicrograph of a cocaine crystal formed in platinum chloride (400×). (b) A photomicrograph of a methamphetamine crystal formed in gold chloride (400×).** *Courtesy David P. Blackburn, San Bernardino County Sheriff's Department, San Bernardino, Calif.*

Over the years, analysts have developed hundreds of crystal tests to characterize the most commonly abused drugs. These tests are rapid and often do not require the isolation of a drug from its diluents; however, because diluents can sometimes alter or modify the shape of the crystal, the examiner must develop experience in interpreting the results of the test.

Most color and crystal tests are largely empirical—that is, scientists do not fully understand why they produce the results that they do. From the forensic chemist's point of view, this is not important. When the tests are properly chosen and used in proper combination, their results constitute an analytical scheme that is characteristic for one and only one drug.

Chromatography

Chromatography is a means of separating and tentatively identifying the components of a mixture. It is particularly useful for analyzing drug specimens, which may be diluted with practically any material in order to increase the quantity of the product available to prospective customers. The task of identifying an illicit-drug preparation would be arduous without the aid of chromatographic methods to first separate the mixture into its components.

chromatography
Any of several analytical techniques for separating organic mixtures into their components by attraction to a stationary phase while being propelled by a moving phase.

Theory of Chromatography   The theory of chromatography is based on the fact that chemical substances tend to partially escape into the surrounding environment when dissolved in a liquid or when absorbed on a solid surface. For example, if a beaker of water is covered with a bell jar, as shown in Figure 5–13, gas molecules (represented by green balls) escape from the water into the surrounding enclosed air. The molecules that remain are said to be in the liquid phase; the molecules that have escaped into the air are said to be in the gas phase.

As the gas molecules escape into the surrounding air, they accumulate above the water; random motion carries some of them back into the water. Eventually, a point is reached at which the number of molecules leaving the water equals the number returning. At this time, the liquid and gas phases are in *equilibrium*.

If the temperature of the water is increased, the equilibrium state readjusts itself to a point at which more gas molecules move into the gas phase.

This behavior was first observed in 1803 by British chemist William Henry. His explanation of this phenomenon, known appropriately as Henry's law, may be stated as follows: **When a volatile chemical compound is dissolved in a liquid and is brought to equilibrium with air,**

FIGURE 5–13   **Evaporation of a liquid.**

there is a fixed ratio between the concentration of the volatile compound in air and its concentration in the liquid, and this ratio remains constant for a given temperature.

The distribution of a gas between the liquid and gas phases is determined by the solubility of the gas; that is, how easily the gas dissolves in the liquid. The higher its solubility, the greater the tendency of the gas molecules to remain in the liquid phase. If two different gases are simultaneously dissolved in the same liquid, each reaches a state of equilibrium with the surrounding air independently of the other. For example, as shown in Figure 5–14, gas A (green balls) and gas B (blue balls) are both dissolved in water. At equilibrium, gas A has a greater number of molecules dissolved in the water than does gas B. This is so because gas A is more soluble in water than gas B.

Thin-Layer Chromatography   Thin-layer chromatography (TLC) uses a solid stationary phase and a moving liquid phase to separate the constituents of a mixture. Thin-layer chromatography is a powerful tool for solving many of the analytical problems presented to the forensic scientist. The method

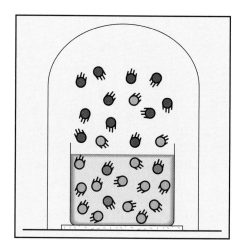

FIGURE 5–14   At equilibrium, there are more gas A molecules (green balls) than gas B molecules (blue balls) in the liquid phase.

Closer Analysis

The Chromatographic Process

In Figures 5–13 and 5–14, both phases—liquid and gas—were kept stationary; that is, they were not moving. During a chromatographic process, however, this is not the case. Instead, one phase is always made to move continuously in one direction over a stationary or fixed phase. For example, in Figure 5–14, chromatography will occur only when the air is forced to move continuously in one direction over the water. Because gas B (blue balls) has a greater percentage of its molecules in the moving phase than does gas A (green balls), the molecules of gas B will travel over the liquid at a faster pace than those of gas A. Eventually, when the moving phase has advanced a reasonable

distance, the molecules of gas B will become entirely separated from those of gas A, and the chromatographic process will be complete. This process is illustrated in Figure 1.

Simply, we can think of chromatography as being analogous to a race between chemical compounds. At the starting line, all the participating substances are mixed together; however, as the race progresses, materials that prefer the moving phase slowly pull ahead of those substances that prefer to remain in the stationary phase. Finally, at the end of the race, all the participants are separated, each crossing the finish line at different times.

FIGURE 1 In this illustration of chromatography, the molecules represented by the blue balls have a greater affinity for the upper phase and hence will be pushed along at a faster rate by the moving air. Eventually, the two sets of molecules will seperate from each other, completing the chromatograohic process.

The different types of chromatographic systems are as varied as the number of stationary and moving-phase combinations that can be devised. However, two chromatographic processes—gas chromatography and thin-layer chromatography—are most applicable for solving many analytical problems in the crime laboratory.

is both rapid and sensitive; moreover, less than 100 micrograms of suspect material are required for the analysis. In addition, the equipment necessary for TLC work has minimal cost and space requirements. Importantly, numerous samples can be analyzed simultaneously on one thin-layer plate. This technique is principally used to detect and identify components in complex mixtures.

Theory of thin-layer chromatography In TLC, the components of a suspect mixture are separated as they travel up a glass plate, eventually appearing as a series of dark or colored spots on the plate. This action is then compared to a standard sample separation of a specific drug, such as heroin. If both the standard and the suspect substance travel the same distance up the plate, they can tentatively be identified as being produced by the same substance.

Figure 5–15 shows a sample suspected of containing heroin and quinine that has been chromatographed alongside known heroin and quinine standards. The distance the unknown material migrated up the suspect plate is compared to the distances that heroin and quinine migrated up a standard sample plate. If the distances are the same, a tentative identification can be made. However, such an identification cannot be considered definitive, for numerous other substances can migrate the same distance up the plate when chromatographed under similar conditions. Thus, thin-layer chromatography alone cannot provide an absolute identification; it must be used in conjunction with other testing procedures to prove absolute identity.

TLC in practice.   A thin-layer plate is prepared by coating a glass plate or plastic backing with a thin film of a granular material, usually silica gel or aluminum oxide. This granular material serves as the solid stationary phase and is usually held in place on the plate with a binding agent such as plaster of Paris. If the sample to be analyzed is a solid, it must first be dissolved in a suitable solvent and a few microliters of the solution spotted with a capillary tube onto the granular surface near the lower edge of the plate. A liquid sample may be applied directly to the plate in the same manner. The plate is then placed upright into a closed chamber that contains a selected liquid, with care that the liquid does not touch the sample spot.

FIGURE 5–15   Chromatograms of known heroin (1) and quinine (2) standards alongside suspect sample (3).

The liquid slowly rises up the plate by capillary action. This rising liquid is the moving phase in thin-layer chromatography. As the liquid moves past the sample spot, the components of the sample become distributed between the stationary solid phase and the moving liquid phase. The components with the greatest affinity for the moving phase travel up the plate faster than those that have greater affinity for the stationary phase. When the liquid front has moved a sufficient distance (usually 10 cm), the development is complete, and the plate is removed from the chamber and dried (see Figure 5–16). An example of the chromatographic separation of ink is shown in Figure 5–17.

Because most compounds are colorless, no separation will be noticed after development unless the materials are *visualized*. To accomplish this, the plates are placed under ultraviolet light, revealing fluorescent materials (those that emit visible light when exposed to light of a shorter wavelength) as bright spots on a dark background. When a fluorescent dye has been incorporated into the solid phase, nonfluorescent substances

fluoresce
To emit visible light when exposed to light of a shorter wavelength—that is, ultraviolet light.

FIGURE 5–16 **(a) In thin-layer chromatography, a liquid sample is spotted onto the granular surface of a gel-coated plate. (b) The plate is placed into a closed chamber that contains a liquid. As the liquid rises up the plate, the components of the sample distribute themselves between the coating and the moving liquid. The mixture is separated, with substances with a greater affinity for the moving liquid traveling up the plate at a faster speed.**

(a)   (b)   (c)

FIGURE 5–17 **(a) The liquid phase begins to move up the stationary phase. (b) Liquid moves past the ink spot carrying the ink components up the stationary phase. (c) The moving liquid has separated the ink into its several components.**

FIGURE 5–18 **Thin-layer chromatogram of a marijuana extract.** *Courtesy Sirchie Finger Print Laboratories, Inc., Youngsville, N.C., www.sirchie.com*

appear as dark spots against a fluorescent background when exposed to the ultraviolet light. In a second method of visualization, the plate is sprayed with a chemical reagent that reacts with the separated substances and causes them to form colored spots. Figure 5–18 shows the chromatogram of a marijuana extract that has been separated into its components by TLC and visualized by having been sprayed with a chemical reagent.

The distance a spot has traveled up a thin-layer plate can be assigned a numerical value known as the R_f value. This value is defined as the distance traveled by the component divided by the distance traveled by the moving liquid phase. For example, in Figure 5–15 the moving phase traveled 10 centimeters up the plate before the plate was removed from the tank. After visualization, the heroin spot moved 8 centimeters, for an R_f value of 0.8; the quinine migrated 4 centimeters, for an R_f value of 0.4.

Gas Chromatography (GC)   Gas chromatography (GC) separates mixtures based on their distribution between a stationary liquid phase and a moving gas phase. In gas chromatography, the moving phase is called the *carrier gas,* which flows through a column constructed of stainless steel or glass. The stationary phase is a thin film of liquid within the column.

Two types of columns used: the *packed column* and the *capillary column.* With the packed column, the stationary phase is a thin film of liquid fixed onto small granular particles packed into the column. This column, usually constructed of stainless steel or glass, is 2 to 6 meters long and about 3 millimeters in diameter. Capillary columns are composed of glass and are much longer than packed columns—15 to 60 meters in length. These types of columns are very narrow, ranging from 0.25 to 0.75 millimeter in diameter. Capillary columns can be made narrower than packed columns because their stationary liquid phase is actually coated as a very thin film directly onto the column's inner wall.

As the carrier gas flows through the packed or capillary column, it carries with it the components of a mixture that have been injected into the column. Components with a greater affinity for the moving gas phase travel through the column more quickly than those with a greater affinity for the stationary liquid phase. Eventually, after the mixture has traversed the length of the column, it emerges separated into its components.

The time required for a component to emerge from the column from the time of its injection into the column is known as the *retention time,* which is a useful identifying characteristic of a material. Figure 5–20(a) shows the chromatogram of two barbiturates; each barbiturate has tentatively been identified by comparing its retention time to those of known barbiturates, shown in Figure 5–20(b). However, because other substances may have comparable retention times under similar chromatographic conditions, gas chromatography cannot be considered an absolute means of identification. Conclusions derived from this technique must be confirmed by other testing procedures.

Gas chromatography is widely used because of its ability to resolve a highly complex mixture into its components, usually within minutes. It has an added advantage in that it is extremely sensitive and can yield quantitative results. Gas chromatography has sufficient sensitivity to detect and quantitate materials at the nanogram (0.000000001 gram or 1×10^{-9} gram) level.[3]

WebExtra 5.1

Watch Animated Depictions of Thin-Layer Chromatography and Gas Chromatography
www.prenhall.com/hsforensics

WebExtra 5.2

Watch the Gas Chromatograph at Work
www.prenhall.com/hsforensics

Spectrophotometry

The technique of chromatography is particularly suited for analyzing illicit drugs, because it can separate a drug from other substances that may be present in the drug preparation. However, chromatography has the drawback of not being able to specifically identify the material under investigation. For this reason, other analytical tools are frequently used to identify drugs. These include the technique of spectrophotometry, which can identify a substance by exposing it to a specific type of electromagnetic radiation.

Closer Analysis

The Gas Chromatograph

A simplified scheme of the gas chromatograph is shown in Figure 5–19. The operation of the instrument can be summed up briefly as follows: The carrier gas is fed into the column at a constant rate. The carrier gas is chemically inert and is generally nitrogen or helium. The sample under investigation is injected as a liquid into a heated injection port with a syringe, where it is immediately vaporized and swept into the column by the carrier gas. The column itself is heated in an oven in order to keep the sample in a vapor state as it travels through the column. In the column, the components of the sample travel in the direction of the carrier gas flow at speeds that are determined by their distribution between the stationary and moving phases. If the analyst has selected the proper liquid phase and has made the column long enough, the components of the sample will be completely separated as they emerge from the column.

As each component emerges from the column, it enters a detector. One type of detector uses a flame to ionize the emerging chemical substance, thus generating an electrical signal. The signal is recorded on a strip-chart recorder as a function of time. This written record of the separation is called a chromatogram. A gas chromatogram is a plot of the recorder response (vertical axis) versus time (horizontal axis). A typical chromatogram shows a series of peaks, each peak corresponding to one component of the mixture.

1. **Sample**
2. **Injector**
3. **Carrier gas**
4. **Column**
5. **Detector**
6. **Power supply**
7. **Recorder**
8. **Chromatogram**

FIGURE 5–19 **Basic gas chromatography. Gas chromatography permits rapid separation of complex mixtures into individual compounds and allows identification and quantitative determination of each compound. As shown, a sample is introduced by a syringe (1) into a heated injection chamber (2). A constant stream of nitrogen gas (3) flows through the injector, carrying the sample into the column (4), which contains a thin film of liquid. The sample is separated in the column, and the carrier gas and separated components emerge from the column and enter the detector (5). Signals developed by the detector activate the recorder (7), which makes a permanent record of the separation by tracing a series of peaks on the chromatograph (8). The time of elution identifies the component present, and the peak area identifies the concentration.** *Courtesy Varian Inc., Palo Alto, Calif.*

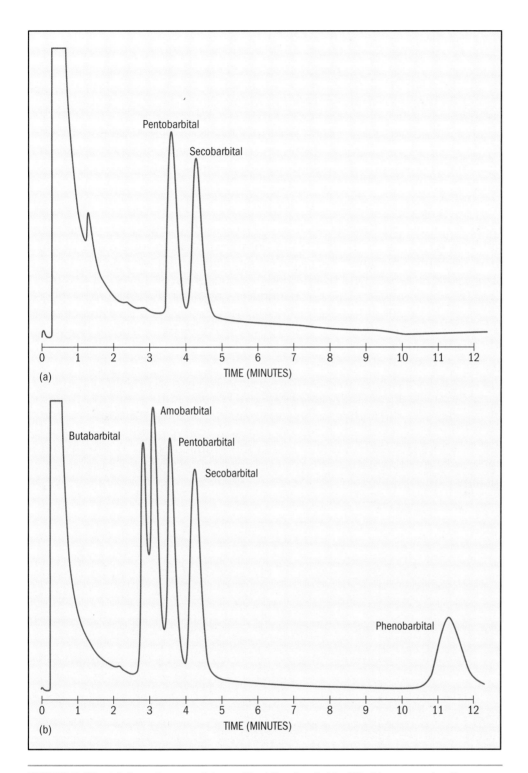

FIGURE 5–20 **(a) An unknown mixture of barbiturates is identified by comparing its retention times to (b), a known mixture of barbiturates.** *Courtesy Varian Inc., Palo Alto, Calif.*

Theory of Spectrophotometry   We have already observed in the description of color that an object does not absorb all the visible light it is exposed to; instead, it selectively absorbs some frequencies and reflects or transmits others. Simlarly, the absorption of other types of electromagnetic radiation by chemical substances is also selective. Selective absorption of a

spectrophotometry
An analytical method for identifying a substance by its selective absorption of different wavelengths of light.

substance is measured by an instrument called a *spectrophotometer,* which produces a graph or *absorption spectrum* that depicts the absorption of light as a function of wavelength or frequency. The absorption of ultraviolet (UV), visible, and infrared (IR) radiation is particularly applicable for obtaining qualitative data pertaining to the identification of drugs.

Absorption at a single wavelength or frequency of light is not 100 percent complete—some radiation is transmitted or reflected by the material. Just how much radiation a substance absorbs is defined by a fundamental relationship known as Beer's law, shown in Equation (5–1):

$$A = kc \qquad\qquad (5\text{–}1)$$

Here, A symbolizes the absorption or the quantity of light taken up at a single frequency, c is the concentration of the absorbing material, and k is a proportionality constant. This relationship shows that the quantity of light absorbed at any frequency is directly proportional to the concentration of the absorbing species; the more material you have, the more radiation it will absorb. By defining the relationship between absorbance and concentration, Beer's law permits spectrophotometry to be used as a technique for quantification.

ultraviolet
Invisible long frequencies of light beyond violet in the visible spectrum.

Ultraviolet and Visible Spectrophotometry   Ultraviolet (UV) and visible spectrophotometry measure the absorbance of UV and visible light as a function of wavelength or frequency. For example, the UV absorption spectrum of heroin shows a maximum absorption band at a wavelength of 278 nanometers (see Figure 5–21). This shows that the simplicity of a UV spectrum facilitates its use as a tool for determining a material's probable identity. For instance, a white powder may have a UV spectrum comparable to heroin

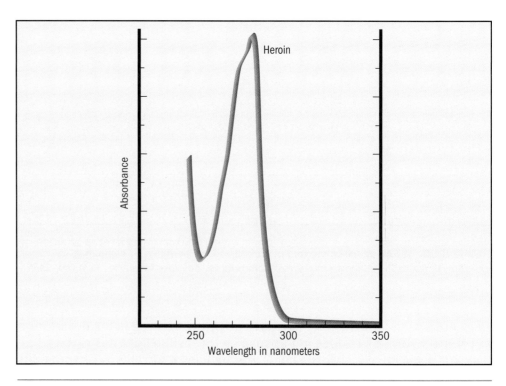

FIGURE 5–21   Ultraviolet spectrum of heroin.

and therefore may be tentatively identified as such. (Fortunately, sugar and starch, common diluents of heroin, do not absorb UV light.)

This technique, however, does not provide a definitive result; other drugs or materials may have a UV absorption spectrum similar to that of heroin. Nevertheless, UV spectrophotometry is often useful in establishing the *probable* identity of a drug. For example, if an unknown substance yields a UV spectrum that resembles that of amphetamine (see Figure 5–22), thousands of substances are immediately eliminated from consideration, and the analyst can begin to identify the material from a relatively small number of possibilities. A comprehensive collection of UV drug spectra provides an index that can rapidly be searched in order to tentatively identify a drug or, failing that, at least to exclude certain drugs from consideration.

Infrared Spectrophotometry In contrast to the simplicity of a UV spectrum, absorption in the infrared region provides a far more complex pattern. Figure 5–23 depicts the IR spectra of heroin and secobarbital. Here, the absorption bands are so numerous that each spectrum can provide enough characteristics to identify a substance specifically. **Different materials always have distinctively different infrared spectra; each IR spectrum is therefore equivalent to a "fingerprint" of that substance and no other.** This technique is one of the few tests available to the forensic scientist that can be considered specific in itself for identification. The IR spectra of thousands of organic compounds have been collected, indexed, and cataloged as invaluable references for identifying organic substances. The selective absorption of light by drugs in the UV and IR regions of the electromagnetic spectrum provides a valuable technique for characterizing drugs.

infrared
Invisible short frequencies of light before red in the visible spectrum.

WebExtra 5.3
See How a Spectrophotometer Works
www.prenhall.com/hsforensics

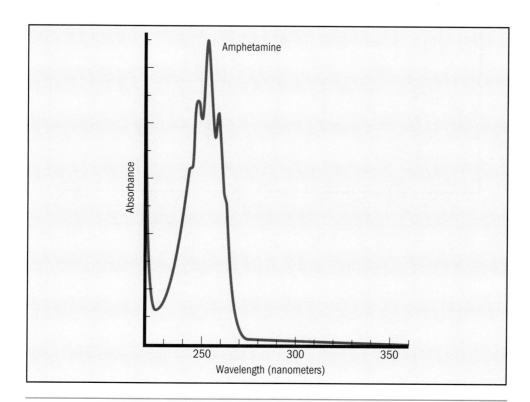

FIGURE 5–22 Ultraviolet spectrum of amphetamine.

(a)

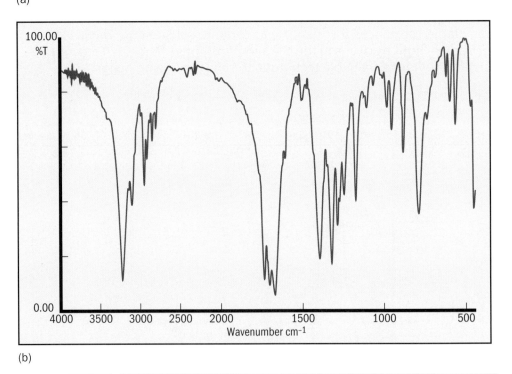

(b)

FIGURE 5–23 (a) Infrared spectrum of heroin. (b) Infrared spectrum of secobarbital.

Closer Analysis

The Spectrophotometer

The spectrophotometer measures and records the absorption spectrum of a chemical. The basic components of a simple spectrophotometer are the same regardless of whether it is designed to measure the absorption of UV, visible, or IR radiation. These components are illustrated diagrammatically in the figure. They include (1) a radiation source, (2) a monochromator or frequency selector, (3) a sample holder, (4) a detector to convert electromagnetic radiation into an electrical signal, and (5) a recorder to produce a record of the signal.

The choice of source varies with the type of radiation desired. For visible radiation, an ordinary tungsten bulb provides a convenient source of radiation. In the UV region, a hydrogen or deuterium discharge lamp is normally used, and a heated molded rod containing a mixture of rare-earth oxides is a good source of IR light.

The function of the **monochromator** is to select a single wavelength or frequency of light from the source—**monochromatic light.** Some inexpensive spectrophotometers pass the light through colored glass filters to remove all radiation from the beam except for a desired range of wavelengths.

More precise spectrophotometers may use a prism or diffraction grating to disperse radiation into its component wavelengths or frequencies. A diffraction grating is made by scratching thousands of parallel lines on a transparent surface such as glass. As light passes through the narrow spacings between the lines, it spreads out and produces a spectrum similar to that formed by a prism. The desired wavelength is obtained when the dispersed radiation is focused onto a narrow slit that permits only selected wavelengths to pass through.

Most laboratory infrared spectrophotometers use Fourier transform analysis to measure the wavelengths of light at which a material absorbs in the infrared spectrum. This approach does not use any dispersive elements that select single wavelengths or frequencies of light emitted from a source; instead, the heart of a Fourier transform infrared (FT-IR) spectrometer is the Michelson interferometer. The interferometer uses a beam-splitting prism and two mirrors, one movable and one stationary, to direct light toward a sample. As the wavelengths pass through the sample and reach a detector, they are all measured simultaneously. A mathematical operation, the Fourier transform method, is used to decode the measured signals and record the wavelength data. These Fourier calculations are rapidly carried out by a computer. In a matter of seconds, a computer-operated FT-IR instrument can produce an infrared absorption pattern compatible to one generated by a prism instrument.

monochromator
A device for isolating individual wavelengths or frequencies of light.

monochromatic light
Light having a single wavelength or frequency.

Prism disperses radiation into component wavelengths

Radiation source   Monochromator   Prism   Slit

Sample cell

Detector   Recorder

(a)

(*continued*)

Closer Analysis

The Spectrophotometer (*continued*)

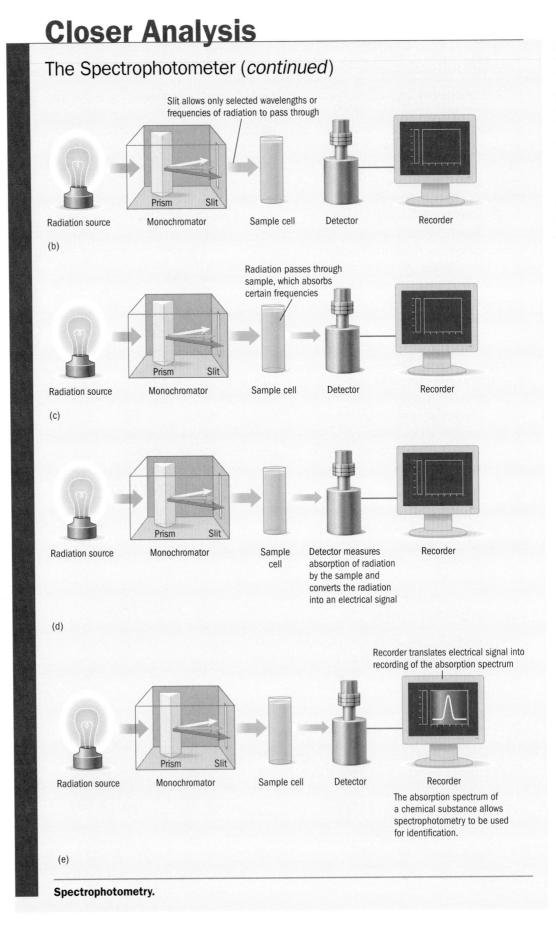

Slit allows only selected wavelengths or frequencies of radiation to pass through

Radiation source   Monochromator   Sample cell   Detector   Recorder

Prism   Slit

(b)

Radiation passes through sample, which absorbs certain frequencies

Radiation source   Monochromator   Sample cell   Detector   Recorder

Prism   Slit

(c)

Radiation source   Monochromator   Sample cell   Recorder

Prism   Slit

Detector measures absorption of radiation by the sample and converts the radiation into an electrical signal

(d)

Recorder translates electrical signal into recording of the absorption spectrum

Radiation source   Monochromator   Sample cell   Detector   Recorder

Prism   Slit

The absorption spectrum of a chemical substance allows spectrophotometry to be used for identification.

(e)

Spectrophotometry.

Sample preparation varies with the type of radiation being studied. Absorption spectra in the UV and visible regions are usually obtained from samples that have been dissolved in an appropriate solvent. Because the cells holding the solution must be transparent to the light being measured, glass cells are used in the visible region and quartz cells in the ultraviolet region. Practically all substances absorb in some region of the IR spectrum, so sampling techniques must be modified to measure absorption in this spectral region; special cells made out of sodium chloride or potassium bromide are commonly used because they do not absorb light over a wide range of the IR portion of the electromagnetic spectrum.

The detector measures the quantity of radiation that passes through the sample by converting it to an electrical signal. UV and visible spectrophotometers use photoelectric tube detectors. A signal is generated when the photons strike the tube surface to produce a current that is directly proportional to the intensity of the light transmitted through the sample. When this signal is compared to the intensity of light that is transmitted to the detector in the absence of an absorbing material, the absorbance of a substance can be determined at each wavelength or frequency of light selected. The signal from the detection system is then fed into a recorder, which plots absorbance as a function of wavelength or frequency. Modern spectrophotometers are designed to trace an entire absorption spectrum automatically.

Mass Spectrometry

A previous section discussed the operation of the gas chromatograph. This instrument is one of the most important tools in a crime laboratory. Its ability to separate the components of a complex mixture is unsurpassed. However, gas chromatography has one important drawback— its inability to produce specific identification. A forensic chemist cannot unequivocally state the identification of a substance based solely on a retention time as determined by the gas chromatograph. Fortunately, by coupling the gas chromatograph to a mass spectrometer this problem has largely been overcome.

A mixture's components are first separated on the gas chromatograph. A direct connection between the gas chromatograph column and the mass spectrometer then allows each component to flow into the spectrometer as it emerges from the gas chromatograph. In the mass spectrometer, the material enters a high-vacuum chamber where a beam of high-energy electrons is aimed at the sample molecules. The electrons collide with the molecules, causing them to lose electrons and to acquire a positive charge. These positively charged molecules, or **ions**, are very unstable or are formed with excess energy and almost instantaneously decompose into numerous smaller fragments. The fragments then pass through an electric or magnetic field, where they are separated according to their masses. The unique feature of mass spectrometry is that under carefully controlled conditions, no two substances produce the same fragmentation pattern. In essence, one can think of this pattern as a "fingerprint" of the substance being examined (see Figure 5–24).

ion
An atom or molecule bearing a positive or negative charge.

FIGURE 5–24 How GC/MS works. Left to right, the sample is separated into its components by the gas chromatograph, and then the components are ionized and identified by characteristic fragmentation patterns of the spectra produced by the mass spectrometer. *Courtesy Agilent Technologies, Inc., Palo Alto, Calif.*

The technique thus provides a specific means for identifying a chemical structure. It is also sensitive to minute concentrations. Mass spectrometry is mostly widely used to identify drugs; however, further research is expected to yield significant applications to identifying other types of physical evidence. Figure 5–25 illustrates the mass spectra of heroin and cocaine; here, each line represents a fragment of a different mass (actually the ratio of mass to charge), and the line height reflects the relative abundance of each fragment. Note how different the fragmentation patterns of heroin and cocaine are. Each mass spectrum is unique to each drug and therefore provides a specific test for identifying that substance.

The combination of the gas chromatograph and mass spectrometer (GC/MS) is further enhanced when a computer is added to the system. The integrated gas chromatograph/mass spectrometer/computer system provides the ultimate in speed, accuracy, and sensitivity. With the ability to record and store in its memory several hundred mass spectra, such a system can detect and identify substances present in only one-millionth-of-a-gram quantities. Furthermore, the computer can be programmed to compare an unknown spectrum against a comprehensive library of mass spectra stored in its memory. The advent of personal computers and microcircuitry has made it possible to design mass spectrometer systems that can fit on a small table. Such a unit is pictured in Figure 5–26. With data obtained from a GC/MS determination, a forensic analyst can, with one instrument, separate the components of a complex drug mixture and then unequivocally identify each substance present in the mixture.

WebExtra 5.4

Watch the Gas Chromatograph/Mass Spectrometer at Work

www.prenhall.com/hsforensics

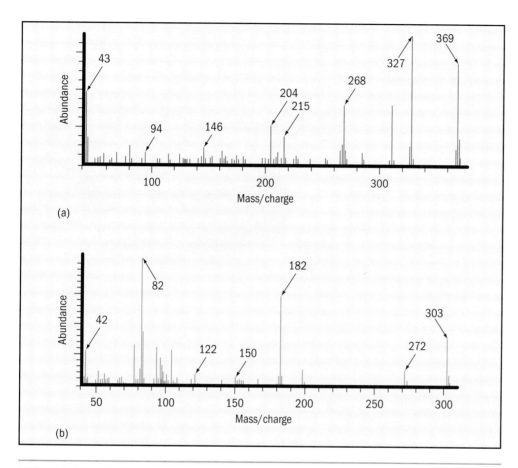

FIGURE 5–25   **(a) Mass spectrum of heroin. (b) Mass spectrum of cocaine.**

FIGURE 5–26   **A tabletop mass spectrometer. (1) The sample is injected into a heated inlet port, and a carrier gas sweeps it into the column. (2) The GC column separates the mixture into its components. (3) In the ion source, a filament wire emits electrons that strike the sample molecules, causing them to fragment as they leave the GC column. (4) The quadrupole, consisting of four rods, separates the fragments according to their mass. (5) The detector counts the fragments passing through the quadrupole. The signal is small and must be amplified. (6) The data system is responsible for total control of the entire GC/MS system. It detects and measures the abundance of each fragment and displays the mass spectrum.** *Courtesy Agilent Technologies, Inc., Palo Alto, Calif.*

FIGURE 5–27 **A scientist injecting a sample into a research-grade mass spectrometer.** *Courtesy Geoff Tompkinson/Science Photo Library*

Research-grade mass spectrometers are found in laboratories as larger floor-model units (see Figure 5–27).

Key Points

- Chromatography is a means of separating and tentatively identifying the components of a mixture.

- TLC uses a solid stationary phase, usually coated onto a glass plate, and a mobile liquid phase to separate the components of the mixture.

- Gas chromatography (GC) separates mixtures on the basis of their distribution between a stationary liquid phase and a mobile gas phase.

- Spectrophotometry is the study of the absorption of light by chemical substances.

- Most forensic laboratories use ultraviolet (UV) and infrared (IR) spectrophotometers to characterize chemical compounds.

- IR spectrophotometry provides a far more complex pattern than UV spectrophotometry. Because different materials have distinctively different infrared spectra, each IR spectrum is equivalent to a "fingerprint" of that substance.

- Mass spectrometry characterizes organic molecules by observing their fragmentation pattern after their collision with a beam of high-energy electrons.

- Infrared spectrophotometry and mass spectrophotometry typically are used to specifically identify a drug substance.

Collection and Preservation of Drug Evidence

Preparation of drug evidence for submission to the crime laboratory is normally relatively simple, accomplished with minimal precautions in the field. The field investigator must ensure that the evidence is properly packaged and labeled for delivery to the laboratory. Considering the countless forms and varieties of drug evidence seized, it is not practical to prescribe any single packaging procedure for fulfilling these requirements. Generally, common sense is the best guide in such situations, keeping in mind that the package must prevent loss and/or cross-contamination of the contents. Often, the original container in which the drug was seized will suffice to meet these requirements. Specimens suspected of containing volatile solvents, such as those involved in glue-sniffing cases, must be packaged in an airtight container to prevent evaporation of the solvent. All packages must be marked with sufficient information to ensure identification by the officer in future legal proceedings and to establish the chain of custody.

To aid the drug analyst, the investigator should supply any background information that may relate to a drug's identity. Analysis time can be markedly reduced when the chemist has this information. For the same reason, the results of drug-screening tests used in the field must also be transmitted to the laboratory. However, although these tests may indicate the presence of a drug and may help the officer establish probable cause to search and arrest a suspect, they do not offer conclusive evidence of a drug's identity.

Chapter Summary

A drug can be defined as a natural or synthetic substance that is used to produce physiological or psychological effects in humans or other animals. Narcotic drugs are analgesics, meaning they relieve pain by depressing the central nervous system. Regular use of a narcotic drug leads to physical dependence. The most common source of narcotic drugs is opium. Morphine is readily extracted from opium and is used to synthesize heroin. Opiates, which include methadone and OxyContin (oxycodone), are not derived from opium or morphine, but they have the same physiological effects on the body as opium narcotics.

Another class of drugs is hallucinogens; marijuana is the most well-known member of this class. Hallucinogens cause marked changes in thought processes, perceptions, and moods. Marijuana is the most controversial drug in this class because its long-term effects on health are still largely unknown. Other hallucinogens include LSD, mescaline, PCP, psilocybin, and MDMA (Ecstasy).

Depressants are drugs that slow the central nervous system. These include alcohol (ethanol), barbiturates, tranquilizers, and various substances that can be sniffed, such as airplane glue and model cement. Stimulants have the opposite effect; they increase the activity of the central nervous system. Stimulants include amphetamines, sometimes known as "uppers" or "speed," and cocaine, which in its freebase form is known as crack.

The term *club drugs* refers to synthetic drugs that are used at nightclubs, bars, and raves (all-night dance parties). Substances that are often used as club drugs include, but are not limited to, MDMA (Ecstasy), GHB (gamma hydroxybutyrate), Rohypnol ("Roofies"), ketamine, and methamphetamine.

Anabolic steroids are synthetic compounds that are chemically related to the male sex hormone testosterone. Anabolic steroids are often abused by individuals who want to accelerate muscle growth.

Federal law establishes five schedules of classification for controlled dangerous substances on the basis of a drug's potential for abuse, potential for physical and psychological dependence, and medical value.

Analysts use screening tests to determine whether a sample contains one or more commonly encountered illicit drugs. These tests include color tests that produce characteristic colors for certain drugs. Once this preliminary analysis is completed, a forensic scientist performs a confirmation test to identify a drug substance to the exclusion of all other known chemical substances.

Chromatography, spectrophotometry, and mass spectrometry are all readily used by forensic scientists to identify illicit drugs. Chromatography is a means of separating and tentatively identifying the components of a mixture. Gas chromatography (GC) separates mixtures based on their distribution between a stationary liquid phase and a mobile gas phase. Thin-layer chromatography (TLC) uses a solid stationary phase, usually coated onto a glass plate, and a mobile liquid phase to separate the components of the mixture. Spectrophotometry is the study of the absorption of light by chemical substances. Mass spectrometry characterizes organic molecules by observing their fragmentation pattern after their collision with a beam of high-energy electrons. By connecting a GC to a mass spectrometer, the forensic scientist can capture a unique "fingerprint" of the substance being examined.

Most forensic laboratories use ultraviolet (UV) or infrared (IR) spectrophotometers to characterize chemical compounds. Absorption in the infrared region provides a far more complex pattern than absorption in the UV spectrum. Different materials always have distinctively different infrared spectra; each IR spectrum is therefore equivalent to a "fingerprint" of that substance.

Review Questions

Facts and Concepts

1. What is a drug? How has drug use affected the growth of crime laboratories in the United States?

2. Name three nondrug factors that play a part in drug dependence.

3. Define *physical dependence* and *psychological dependence.*

4. Physical dependence develops only when the drug user
   a. takes large doses of a drug.
   b. takes one drug to the exclusion of all others.
   c. uses a drug on a regular schedule.
   d. has used a drug for at least six months.

5. What is the most important factor to consider when evaluating the social impact of drug dependence on an individual?

6. What is the pharmacological definition of a narcotic?

7. What is the source of most narcotic analgesics? Name two popular drugs prepared from this substance.

8. Name two synthetic opiates and describe the purpose for which each typically is used.

9. What is a hallucinogen? Name three commonly used hallucinogens.

10. What is the most widely used illicit drug in the United States? What is the active ingredient in this drug?

11. Arrange the following parts or products of the *Cannabis* plant in order of THC content, from highest to lowest concentration of THC: flowers, leaves, resin, seeds, stem.

12. List three potential medical uses of marijuana.

13. What is angel dust and what are the negative consequences of long-term use?

14. What is the most widely abused drug in the United States?

15. In what class of drugs do alcohol and barbiturates belong? What is the main physiological effect of such drugs?

16. What is huffing?

17. What is a stimulant? Name two widely used stimulants.

18. Name two potent forms of methamphetamine. How is each of these drugs typically taken into the body?

19. What popular stimulant is derived from a plant that grows in the Andes mountains of South America?

20. What is crack and how is it produced?

21. Name club drugs belonging to three different classes of drugs, and indicate the class to which each belongs.

22. What are anabolic steroids and why were they developed?

23. What are the two phases in a forensic scientist's analytical scheme?

24. What is the difference between a screening test and a confirmation test?

25. Name two types of empirical tests used to identify drugs. Why are these tests referred to as empirical?

26. What is the difference between a qualitative evaluation and a quantitative evaluation?

27. Why is chromatography particularly well suited to the needs of a drug analyst?

28. In chromatography, the distribution of a gas between the liquid and gas phases is determined by
    a. the density of the gas relative to the liquid.
    b. the volume of the gas in the container.
    c. the solubility of the gas in the liquid.
    d. the mass of the gas relative to the liquid.

29. Explain how chromatography is like a race between chemical compounds.

30. Name three distinct advantages of gas chromatography in the identification of drugs.

31. What is the main drawback of gas chromatography in the identification of drugs?

32. What phenomenon forms the basis of spectrophotometry?

33. What is the main advantage of infrared spectrophotometry over ultraviolet or visible-light spectrophotometry?

34. With what analytical device is a gas chromatograph often connected to analyze drug mixtures, and why?

Application and Critical Thinking

1. An individual who has been using a drug for an extended period of time suddenly finds himself unable to secure more of the drug. He acts nervous and irritable and is hyperactive. He seems almost desperate to find more of the drug, but experiences no sickness, pain, or other outward physical discomfort. Based on his behavior, what drugs might he possibly have been using? Explain your answer.

2. Following are descriptions of behavior that are characteristic among users of certain classes of drugs. For each description, indicate the class of drug (narcotics, stimulants, and so on) for which the behavior is most characteristic. For each description, also name at least one drug that produces the described effects.
   a. slurred speech, slow reaction time, impaired judgment, reduced coordination
   b. intense emotional responses, anxiety, altered sensory perceptions
   c. alertness, feelings of strength and confidence, rapid speech and movement, decreased appetite
   d. drowsiness, intense feeling of well-being, relief from pain

3. Following are descriptions of four hypothetical drugs. According to the Controlled Substances Act, under which drug schedule would each substance be classified?
   a. This drug has a high potential for psychological dependence, it currently has accepted medical uses in the United States, and the distributor is not required to report to the U.S. Drug Enforcement Administration.
   b. This drug has medical use in the United States, is not limited by manufacturing quotas, and may be exported without a permit.
   c. This drug must be stored in a vault or safe, requires separate record keeping, and may be distributed with a prescription.
   d. This drug may not be imported or exported without a permit, is subject to manufacturing quotas, and currently has no medical use in the United States.

4. A police officer stops a motorist who is driving erratically and notices a bag of white powder on the front seat of the car that he suspects contains heroin. The officer brings the bag to you, a forensic scientist in the local crime lab. Name one screening test that you might perform to determine the presence of heroin. Assuming the powder tests positive for heroin, what should you do next?

5. The figure on page 198 shows a chromatogram of a known mixture of barbiturates. Based on this figure, answer the following questions:
   a. What barbiturate detected by the chromatogram had the longest retention time?
   b. Which barbiturate had the shortest retention time?
   c. What is the approximate retention time of amobarbital?

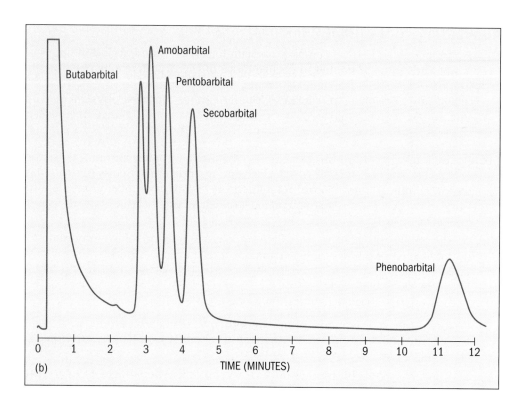

Butabarbital

Amobarbital

Pentobarbital

Secobarbital

Phenobarbital

(b)

TIME (MINUTES)

Web Resources

Drugs.com (Extensive database of information about the use and effects of 24,000 different drugs)
www.drugs.com

National Institute on Drug Abuse (Division of the National Institute of Health with links to information about effects of and studies about legal and illicit drugs)
www.nida.nih.gov

General Alcohol Information (Fact sheet on impact of alcohol use on accidents, injuries, violence, unwanted pregnancy, and other areas of public health and welfare)
www.cdc.gov/alcohol/factsheets/general_information.htm

Impaired Driving Facts (Statistics compiled by the National Center for Injury Prevention and Control)
www.cdc.gov/ncipc/factsheets/drving.htm

Neuroscience for Kids (Information about the history, production, use, effects, and detection of the drugs discussed in the text)
faculty.washington.edu/chudler/introb.html#drug

Drugs of Abuse (A publication of the Drug Enforcement Administration decribing illicit drugs)
www.dea.gov/pubs/abuse/index.htm

StreetDrugs.org (Extensive information about the history and effects of hundreds of different legal and illicit drugs)
www.streetdrugs.org

Drug Schedules (List of substances classified under each section of the U.S. federal narcotics laws)
www.mspta.com/dre/pdf/Drug_Schedules.pdf

Chromatography (Simple description of chromatographic processes with diagrams)
antoine.frostburg.edu/chem/senese/101/matter/chromatography.shtml

Basic Principles of Spectrophotometry (Online simulation of a spectrophotometer)
www.chm.davidson.edu/ChemistryApplets/spectrophotometry/Spectrophotometry.html

Beer's Law (Online experiment applying Beer's law using spectrophotometer simulation)
www.chm.davidson.edu/ChemistryApplets/spectrophotometry/BeersLaw.html

Endnotes

1. *Marijuana—A Signal of Misunderstanding* (Washington, D.C.: U.S. Government Printing Office, 1972), p. 56.
2. Field-test color kits for drugs can be purchased from various commercial manufacturers.
3. Powers of 10 are quite useful and simple for handling large or small numbers. The exponent expresses the number of places the decimal point must be moved. If it is positive, the decimal point is moved to the right; if it is negative, the decimal point is moved to the left. Thus, to express 1×10^{-9} as a number, the decimal point is simply moved nine places to the left of 1.

Harold Shipman, Dr. Death

Kathleen Grundy's sudden death in 1998 was shocking news to her daughter, Angela Woodruff. Mrs. Grundy, an 81-year-old widow, was believed to be in good health when her physician, Dr. Harold Shipman, visited her a few hours before her demise. Some hours later, when friends came to her home to check on her whereabouts, they found Mrs. Grundy lying on a sofa fully dressed and dead.

Dr. Shipman pronounced her dead and informed her daughter that an autopsy was not necessary. A few days later, Mrs. Woodruff was surprised to learn that a will had surfaced leaving all of Mrs. Grundy's money to Dr. Shipman. The will was immediately recognized as a forgery and led to the exhumation of Mrs. Grundy's body. A toxicological analysis of the remains revealed a lethal quantity of morphine.

In retrospect, there was good reason to suspect that Dr. Shipman was capable of foul play. In the 1970s, he was asked to leave a medical practice because of a drug abuse problem and charges that he obtained drugs by forgery and deception. However, Dr. Shipman was quickly back to practicing medicine. By 1998, local undertakers became suspicious at the number of his patients who were dying. What is more, they all seemed to be elderly women who were found sitting in a chair or lying fully clothed on a bed. As police investigated, the horror of Dr. Shipman's deeds became apparent. One clinical audit estimated that Dr. Shipman killed at least 236 of his patients over a twenty four-year period. Most of the deaths were attributed to fatal doses of heroin or morphine. Toxicological analysis on seven exhumed bodies clearly showed significant quantities of morphine. Convicted of murder, Dr. Shipman hanged himself in his jail cell in 2004.

Forensic Toxicology

chapter 6

Key Terms

absorption

acid

alveoli

anticoagulant

artery

base

capillary

catalyst

excretion

fuel cell detector

metabolism

oxidation

pH scale

preservative

toxicologist

vein

Learning Objectives

After studying this chapter you should be able to:

- Explain how alcohol is absorbed into the bloodstream, transported throughout the body, and eliminated by oxidation and excretion

- Understand the process by which alcohol is excreted in the breath via the lungs

- Understand the concepts of infrared and fuel cell breath-testing devices for alcohol testing

- Describe commonly employed field sobriety tests to assess alcohol impairment

- List and contrast laboratory procedures for measuring the concentration of alcohol in the blood

- Relate the precautions to be taken to properly preserve blood in order to analyze its alcohol content

- Understand the significance of implied-consent laws and the *Schmerber* v. *California* case to traffic enforcement

- Describe techniques that forensic toxicologists use to isolate and identify drugs and poisons

- Appreciate the significance of finding of a drug in human tissues and organs to assessing impairment

The Role of Forensic Toxicology

toxicologist

An individual whose job is to detect and identify drugs and poisons in body fluids, tissues, and organs.

Because the uncontrolled use of drugs has become a worldwide problem affecting all segments of society, the role of the toxicologist has taken on new and added significance. Toxicologists detect and identify drugs and poisons in body fluids, tissues, and organs. Their services are required not only in such legal institutions as crime laboratories and medical examiners' offices; they also reach into hospital laboratories—where identifying a drug overdose may represent the difference between life and death—and into various health facilities that monitor the intake of drugs and other toxic substances. Primary examples include performing blood tests on children exposed to leaded paints and analyzing the urine of addicts enrolled in methadone maintenance programs.

The role of the forensic toxicologist is limited to matters that pertain to violations of criminal law. However, responsibility for performing toxicological services in a criminal justice system varies considerably throughout the United States. In systems with a crime laboratory independent of the medical examiner, this responsibility may reside with one or the other or may be shared by both. Some systems, however, take advantage of the expertise of government health department laboratories and assign this role to them. Nevertheless, whatever facility handles this work, its caseload will reflect the prevailing popularity of the drugs that are abused in the community. In most cases, this means that the forensic toxicologist handles numerous requests to determine the presence of alcohol in the body.

All of the statistical and medical evidence shows that ethyl alcohol—a legal, over-the-counter substance—is the most heavily abused drug in Western countries. Forty percent of all traffic deaths in the United States, nearly 17,500 fatalities per year, are alcohol related, along with more than 2 million injuries each year requiring hospital treatment. This highway death toll, as well as the untold damage to life, limb, and property, shows the dangerous consequences of alcohol abuse. Because of the prevalence of alcohol in the toxicologist's work, we will begin by taking a closer look at how the body processes and responds to alcohol.

Key Points

- Forensic toxicologists detect and identify drugs and poisons in body fluids, tissues, and organs in matters that pertain to violations of criminal laws.

- Ethyl alcohol is the most heavily abused drug in Western countries.

Toxicology of Alcohol

The subject of the analysis of alcohol immediately confronts us with the primary objective of forensic toxicology—detecting and isolating drugs in the body to determine their influence on human behavior. Knowing how the body metabolizes alcohol provides the key to understanding its effects on human behavior. This knowledge has also made possible the development of instruments that measure the presence and concentration of alcohol in individuals suspected of driving under the influence.

The Metabolism of Alcohol

All chemicals that enter the body are eventually broken down by chemicals in the body and transformed into other chemicals that are easier to eliminate. This process of transformation, called metabolism, consists of three basic steps: absorption, distribution, and elimination.

metabolism
The transformation of a chemical in the body to other chemicals to facilitate its elimination from the body.

Absorption and Distribution   Alcohol, or ethyl alcohol, is a colorless liquid normally diluted with water and consumed as a beverage. Alcohol appears in the blood within minutes after it has been consumed and slowly increases in concentration while it is being absorbed from the stomach and the small intestine into the bloodstream. During the absorption phase, alcohol slowly enters the body's bloodstream and is carried to all parts of the body. When the absorption period is completed, the alcohol becomes distributed uniformly throughout the watery portions of the body—that is, throughout about two-thirds of the body volume. Fat, bones, and hair are low in water content and therefore contain little alcohol, whereas alcohol concentration in the rest of the body is fairly uniform. After absorption is completed, a maximum alcohol level is reached in the blood, and the postabsorption period begins. Then the alcohol concentration slowly decreases until a zero level is again reached.

absorption
Passage of alcohol across the wall of the stomach and small intestine into the bloodstream.

Many factors determine the rate at which alcohol is absorbed into the bloodstream, including the total time taken to consume the drink, the alcohol content of the beverage, the amount consumed, and the quantity and type of food present in the stomach at the time of drinking. With so many variables, it is difficult to predict just how long the absorption process will require. For example, beer is absorbed more slowly than an equivalent concentration of alcohol in water, apparently because of the carbohydrates in beer. Also, alcohol consumed on an empty stomach is absorbed faster than an equivalent amount of alcohol taken when there is food in the stomach (see Figure 6–1).

oxidation
The combination of oxygen with other substances to produce new products.

Elimination   As the alcohol is circulated by the bloodstream, the body begins to eliminate it. Alcohol is eliminated through two mechanisms—oxidation and excretion. Nearly all of the alcohol (95–98 percent) consumed is eventually oxidized to carbon dioxide and water. Oxidation takes place almost entirely in the liver. Here, in the presence of the enzyme

excretion
Elimination of alcohol from the body in an unchanged state; alcohol is normally excreted in breath and urine.

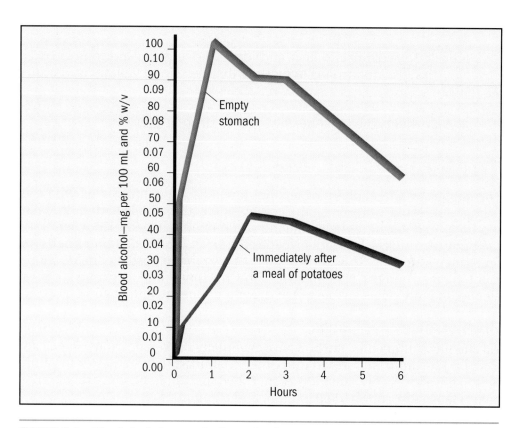

FIGURE 6–1 **Blood-alcohol concentrations after ingestion of 2 ounces of pure alcohol mixed in 8 ounces of water (equivalent to about 5 ounces of 80-proof vodka).** *Courtesy U.S. Department of Transportation, Washington, D.C.*

alcohol dehydrogenase, the alcohol is converted into acetaldehyde and then to acetic acid. The acetic acid is subsequently oxidized in practically all parts of the body to carbon dioxide and water.

The remaining alcohol is excreted unchanged in the breath, urine, and perspiration. Most significantly, the amount of alcohol exhaled in the breath is in direct proportion to the concentration of alcohol in the blood. This observation has had a tremendous impact on the technology and procedures used for blood-alcohol testing. The development of instruments to reliably measure breath for its alcohol content has made possible the testing of millions of people in a rapid, safe, and convenient manner.

The fate of alcohol in the body is therefore relatively simple—namely, absorption into the bloodstream, distribution throughout the body's water, and finally, elimination by oxidation and excretion. The elimination or "burn-off" rate of alcohol varies in different individuals; 0.015 percent w/v (weight per volume) per hour seems to be an average value once the absorption process is complete.[1] However, this figure is an average that varies by as much as 30 percent among individuals.

Blood-Alcohol Concentration   Logically, the most obvious measure of intoxication would be the amount of liquor a person has consumed. Unfortunately, most arrests are made after the fact, when such information is not available to legal authorities; furthermore, even if these data could be collected, numerous related factors, such as body weight and the rate of alcohol's absorption into the body, are so variable that it would be impossible to prescribe uniform standards that would yield reliable alcohol intoxication levels for all individuals.

Theoretically, for a true determination of the quantity of alcohol impairing an individual's normal body functions, it would be best to remove a portion of brain tissue and analyze it for alcohol content. For obvious reasons, this cannot be done on living subjects. Consequently, toxicologists concentrate on the blood, which provides the medium for circulating alcohol throughout the body, carrying it to all tissues, including the brain. Fortunately, experimental evidence supports this approach and shows blood-alcohol concentration to be directly proportional to the concentration of alcohol in the brain. From the medicolegal point of view, blood-alcohol levels have become the accepted standard for relating alcohol intake to its effect on the body.

The longer the total time required for complete absorption to occur, the lower the peak alcohol concentration in the blood. Depending on a combination of factors, maximum blood-alcohol concentration may not be reached until two or three hours have elapsed from the time of consumption. However, under normal social drinking conditions, it takes anywhere from thirty to ninety minutes from the time of the final drink until the absorption process is completed.

As noted earlier, alcohol becomes concentrated evenly throughout the watery portions of the body. This knowledge can be useful for the toxicologist analyzing a body for the presence of alcohol. If blood is not available, as in some postmortem situations, a medical examiner can select a water-rich organ or fluid—for example, the brain, cerebrospinal fluid, or vitreous humor—to determine the body's alcohol content to a reasonable degree of accuracy.

Alcohol in the Circulatory System

The extent to which an individual may be under the influence of alcohol is usually determined by measuring the quantity of alcohol present in the blood system. Normally, this is accomplished in one of two ways: (1) by analyzing the blood for its alcohol content or (2) by measuring the alcohol content of the breath. In either case, the significance and meaning of the results can better be understood when the movement of alcohol through the circulatory system is studied.

Humans, like all vertebrates, have a closed circulatory system, which consists basically of a heart and numerous arteries, capillaries, and veins. An artery is a blood vessel carrying blood away from the heart, and a vein is a vessel carrying blood back toward the heart. Capillaries are tiny blood vessels that connect the arteries with the veins. The exchange of materials between the blood and the other tissues takes place across the thin walls of the capillaries. A schematic diagram of the circulatory system is shown in Figure 6–2.

Ingestion and Distribution Let us now trace the movement of alcohol through the human circulatory system. After alcohol is ingested, it moves down the esophagus into the stomach. About 20 percent of the alcohol is absorbed through the stomach walls into the portal vein of the blood system. The remaining alcohol passes into the blood through the walls of the small intestine. Once in the blood, the alcohol is carried to the liver, where enzymes begin to break it down.

As the blood (still carrying the alcohol) leaves the liver, it moves up to the heart. The blood enters the upper right chamber of the heart, called the right atrium (or auricle), and is forced into the lower right chamber of the heart, known as the right ventricle. Having returned to the heart from its

artery
A blood vessel that carries blood away from the heart.

vein
A blood vessel that carries blood toward the heart.

capillary
A tiny blood vessel that receives blood from arteries and carries it to veins, and across whose walls exchange of materials between the blood and the tissues takes place.

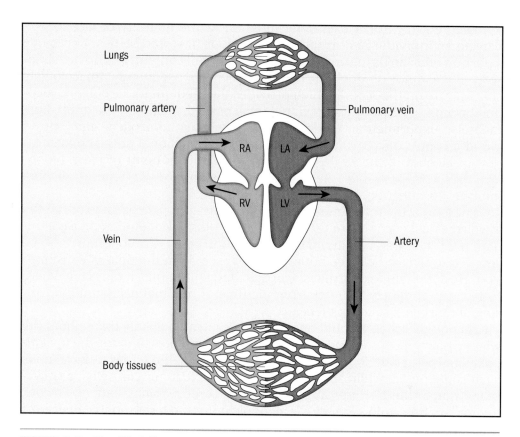

FIGURE 6–2 **Simplified diagram of the human circulatory system. Dark vessels contain oxygenated blood; light vessels contain deoxygenated blood.**

circulation through the tissues, the blood at this time contains very little oxygen and much carbon dioxide. Consequently, the blood must be pumped up to the lungs, through the pulmonary artery, to be replenished with oxygen.

Aeration   In the lungs, the respiratory system bridges with the circulatory system so that oxygen can enter the blood and carbon dioxide can leave it. As shown in Figure 6–3, the pulmonary artery branches into capillaries lying close to tiny pear-shaped sacs called alveoli. The lungs contain about 250 million alveoli, all located at the ends of the bronchial tubes. The bronchial tubes connect to the windpipe (trachea), which leads up to the mouth and nose (see Figure 6–4). At the surface of the alveolar sacs, blood flowing through the capillaries comes in contact with fresh oxygenated air in the sacs.

A rapid exchange now takes place between the fresh air in the sacs and the spent air in the blood. Oxygen passes through the walls of the alveoli into the blood while carbon dioxide is discharged from the blood into the air. If, during this exchange, alcohol or any other volatile substance is in the blood, it too will pass into the alveoli. During breathing, the carbon dioxide and alcohol are expelled through the nose and mouth, and the alveoli sacs are replenished with fresh oxygenated air breathed into the lungs, allowing the process to begin all over again.

The distribution of alcohol between the blood and alveolar air is similar to the example of a gas dissolved in an enclosed beaker of water, as described in Chapter 5. Here again, one can use Henry's law (see pp. 175–176) to explain how the alcohol will divide itself between the air and blood. Henry's Law may now be restated as follows: **When a volatile chemical**

alveoli

Small sacs in the lungs through whose walls air and other gases are exchanged between the breath and the blood.

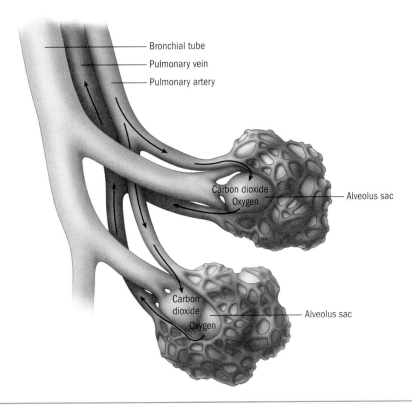

FIGURE 6–3 **Gas exchange in the lungs. Blood flows from the pulmonary artery into vessels that lie close to the walls of the alveoli sacs. Here the blood gives up its carbon dioxide and absorbs oxygen. The oxygenated blood leaves the lungs via the pulmonary vein and returns to the heart.**

(alcohol) is dissolved in a liquid (blood) and is brought to equilibrium with air (alveolar breath), there is a fixed ratio between the concentration of the volatile compound (alcohol) in air (alveolar breath) and its concentration in the liquid (blood), and this ratio is constant for a given temperature.

The temperature at which the breath leaves the mouth is normally 34°C. At this temperature, the ratio of alcohol in the blood to alcohol in alveolar air is approximately 2,100 to 1. In other words, 1 milliliter of blood contains nearly the same amount of alcohol as 2,100 milliliters of alveolar breath. Henry's law thus becomes a basis for relating breath to blood-alcohol concentration.

Recirculation and Absorption   Now let's return to the circulating blood. After emerging from the lungs, the oxygenated blood is rushed back to the upper left chamber of the heart (left atrium) by the pulmonary vein. When the left atrium contracts, it forces the blood through a valve into the left ventricle, which is the lower left chamber of the heart. The left ventricle then pumps the freshly oxygenated blood into the arteries, which carry the blood to all parts of the body. Each of these arteries, in turn, branches into smaller arteries, which eventually connect with the numerous tiny capillaries embedded in the tissues. Here the alcohol moves out of the blood and into the tissues. The blood then runs from the capillaries into tiny veins that fuse to form larger veins. These veins eventually lead back to the heart to complete the circuit.

During absorption, the concentration of alcohol in the arterial blood is considerably higher than the concentration of alcohol in the venous

FIGURE 6–4 **The respiratory system. The trachea connects the nose and mouth to the bronchial tubes. The bronchial tubes divide into numerous branches that terminate in the alveoli sacs in the lungs.**

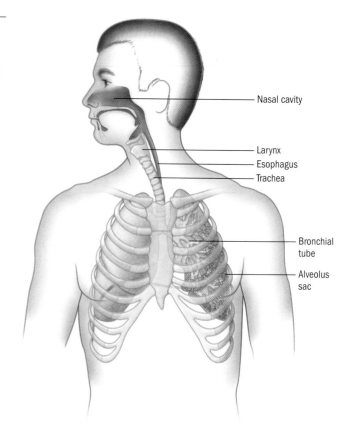

Nasal cavity

Larynx
Esophagus
Trachea

Bronchial tube

Alveolus sac

blood. One typical study revealed a subject's arterial blood-alcohol level to be 41 percent higher than the venous level thirty minutes after the last drink.[2] This difference is thought to exist because of the rapid diffusion of alcohol into the body tissues from venous blood during the early phases of absorption. Because the administration of a blood test requires drawing venous blood from the arm, this test is clearly to the advantage of a subject who may still be in the absorption stage. However, once absorption is complete, the alcohol becomes equally distributed throughout the blood system.

Key Points

- Alcohol appears in the blood within minutes after it has been taken by mouth. It slowly increases in concentration while it is being absorbed from the stomach and the small intestine into the bloodstream.

- When all the alcohol has been absorbed, a maximum alcohol level is reached in the blood, and the postabsorption period begins. During postabsorption, the alcohol concentration slowly decreases until a zero level is reached.

- Elimination of alcohol throughout the body is accomplished through oxidation and excretion. Oxidation takes place almost entirely in the liver, while alcohol is excreted unchanged in the breath, urine, and perspiration.

- Breath-testing devices operate on the principle that the ratio between the concentration of alcohol in alveolar breath and its concentration in blood is fixed.

Testing for Intoxication

From a practical point of view, the idea of drawing blood from a vein to test motorists suspected of being under the influence of alcohol simply does not provide a convenient method for monitoring drivers. The need to transport the suspect to a location where a medically qualified person can draw blood would be costly and time consuming, considering the hundreds of tests that the average police department must conduct every year. The methods used must be designed to test hundreds of thousands of motorists annually without causing them undue physical harm or unreasonable inconvenience, while providing a reliable diagnosis that can be supported and defended within the framework of the legal system. This means that toxicologists have had to devise rapid and specific procedures for measuring a driver's degree of alcohol intoxication that can be easily administered in the field.

Breath Testing for Alcohol

The most widespread method for rapidly determining alcohol intoxication is breath testing. A breath tester is simply a device for collecting and measuring the alcohol content of alveolar breath. As we saw earlier, alcohol is expelled unchanged in the breath of a person who has been drinking. A breath test measures the alcohol concentration in the pulmonary artery by measuring its concentration in alveolar breath. Thus, breath analysis provides an easily obtainable specimen along with a rapid and accurate result.

Breath-test results obtained during the absorption phase may be higher than results obtained from a simultaneous analysis of venous blood. However, the former are more reflective of the concentration of alcohol reaching the brain and therefore more accurately reflect the effects of alcohol on the subject. Again, once absorption is complete, the difference between a blood test and a breath test should be minimal.

Breath-Test Instruments   The first widely used instrument for measuring the alcohol content of alveolar breath was the *Breathalyzer*, developed in 1954 by R. F. Borkenstein, who was a captain in the Indiana State Police. Although the Breathalyzer has undergone several modifications since its development, the basic theory and design of the instrument have not changed. The "Closer Analysis" feature on the Breathalyzer explains the working of the device in greater detail.

Closer Analysis

The Breathalyzer

The Breathalyzer is a device for collecting and measuring the alcohol content of alveolar breath (see figure). The subject blows into a mouthpiece that leads into a metal cylinder. The last portion of breath (alveolar breath) is trapped in the cylinder. The amount of breath collected in this manner is 52.5 milliliters, or 1/40 of 2,100 milliliters.[*] We have already seen that the amount of alcohol in 2,100 milliliters of alveolar breath approximates that in 1 milliliter of blood. Hence, in essence, the Breathalyzer is designed to measure the alcohol concentration present in 1/40 of a milliliter of blood.

(continued)

Closer Analysis

The Breathalyzer (*continued*)

*Actually, the collection cylinder is designed to hold 56.5 milliliters of breath. This is because, having left the mouth at 34°C, the breath will expand when heated to 50°C in the cylinder. Furthermore, added breath is needed to compensate for the air that remains in the delivery tube leading to the test ampoule.

The quantity of alcohol in the trapped breath is measured by passing the breath into a glass ampoule containing potassium dichromate, sulfuric acid, and water. Any alcohol in the breath immediately dissolves in the dichromate

Schematic diagram of a Breathalyzer. *Courtesy Draeger Safety, Inc., Breathalyzer Division, Durango, Colo.*

solution and is oxidized to acetic acid. In the oxidation process, potassium dichromate is also destroyed. The extent of this destruction is measured by the Breathalyzer and is related to the quantity of alcohol passed into the ampoule.

Basically, the Breathalyzer is a spectrophotometer (see Chapter 5) designed to measure the absorption of light passing through the potassium dichromate solution at a single wavelength. To better understand its operation, let's examine what is happening in the ampoule when alcohol is converted to acetic acid. Whenever a chemical reaction occurs between two or more substances, chemists use a chemical equation as a shorthand method to describe the changes taking place. The equation serves two purposes: it identifies the participants, and it describes the quantitative aspects of the reaction.

The following equation depicts the chemical reaction taking place in the ampoule:

$$2K_2Cr_2O_7 + 3C_2H_5OH + 8H_2SO_4 \longrightarrow$$

potassium dichromate   ethyl alcohol   sulfuric acid   yields

$$2Cr_2(SO_4)_3 + 2K_2SO_4 + 3CH_3COOH + 11H_2O$$

chromium sulfate   potassium sulfate   acetic acid   water

From this chemical equation, we can see that there is always a fixed relationship between the number of potassium dichromate molecules reacting with the alcohol. Two molecules of potassium dichromate always combine with three molecules of ethyl alcohol. Hence, determining the amount of potassium dichromate consumed is an indirect way to determine the quantity of alcohol originally present. Silver nitrate is also present in the Breathalyzer ampoule; however, this substance acts only as a catalyst to speed up the rate of reaction between potassium dichromate and ethyl alcohol. As a **catalyst**, silver nitrate undergoes no net change itself during the reaction.

catalyst
A substance that accelerates the rate of a chemical reaction but is not itself permanently changed by the reaction.

Starting in the 1970s, the Breathalyzer was phased out and replaced by other instruments for measuring the alcoholic content of alveolar breath. Like the Breathalyzer, they assume that the ratio of alcohol in the blood to alcohol in alveolar breath is 2,100 to 1 at a mouth temperature of 34°C. Unlike the Breathalyzer, modern breath testers are free of chemicals. These devices include infrared light absorption devices (described in the following "Closer Analysis" feature) and fuel cell detectors.

Infrared and fuel-cell-based breath testers are microprocessor controlled so that all an operator has to do is press a start button and the instrument automatically moves through a sequence of steps that produce a readout of the subject's test results. These instruments also perform self-diagnostic tests to ascertain whether the instrument is in proper operating condition.

fuel cell detector
A detector in which a chemical reaction involving alcohol produces electricity.

Considerations in Breath Testing   The key to the accuracy of a breath-testing device is to ensure that the unit captures the alcohol in the alveolar (deep-lung) breath of the subject. This is typically accomplished by programming the unit to accept no less than 1.1 to 1.5 liters of breath from the subject. Also, the subject must blow for a minimum time (such as 6 seconds) with a minimum breath flow rate (such as 3 liters per minute).

The breath-test instruments just described feature a *slope detector,* which ensures that the breath sample is alveolar or deep-lung breath. As the subject blows into the instrument, the breath alcohol concentration is continuously monitored. The instrument accepts a breath sample only when consecutive measurements fall within a predetermined rate of change. This approach

Closer Analysis

Infrared Light Absorption

(a)   (b)

FIGURE 1   (a) An infrared breath-testing instrument—the Data Master DMT. (b) A subject blowing into the DMT breath tester. *Courtesy National Patent Analytical Systems, Inc., Mansfield, Ohio, www.npas.com*

In principle, infrared instruments operate no differently from the spectrophotometers described in Chapter 5. An evidential testing instrument that incorporates the principle of infrared light absorption is shown in Figure 1. Any alcohol present in the subject's breath flows into the instrument's breath chamber. As shown in Figure 2, a beam of infrared light is aimed through the chamber. A filter is used to select a wavelength of infrared light at which alcohol will absorb. As the infrared light passes through the chamber, it interacts with the alcohol and causes the light to decrease in intensity. The decrease in light intensity is measured by a photoelectric detector that gives a signal proportional to the concentration of alcohol present in the breath sample. This information is processed by an electronic microprocessor, and the percent blood-alcohol concentration is displayed on a digital readout. Also, the blood-alcohol level is printed on a card to produce a permanent record of the test result. Most infrared breath testers aim a second infrared beam into the same chamber to check for acetone or other chemical interferences on the breath. If the instrument detects differences in the relative response of the two infrared beams that does not conform to ethyl alcohol, the operator is immediately informed of the presence of an "interferant."

Breath inlet   Breath outlet   Breath flows into chamber

Infrared radiation source   Sample chamber   Filter   Detector

(a)

FIGURE 2   Schematic diagram of an infrared breath-testing instrument.

Closer Analysis

The Fuel Cell

A fuel cell converts energy arising from a chemical reaction into electrochemical energy. A typical fuel cell consists of two platinum electrodes separated by an acid- or base-containing porous membrane. A platinum wire connects the electrodes and allows a current to flow between them. In the alcohol fuel cell, one of the electrodes is positioned to come in contact with a subject's breath sample. If alcohol is present in the breath, a reaction at the electrode's surface converts the alcohol to acetic acid. One by-product of this conversion is free electrons, which flow through the connecting wire to the opposite electrode, where they interact with atmospheric oxygen to form water (see figure). The fuel cell also requires the migration of hydrogen ions across the acidic porous membrane to complete the circuit. The strength of the current flow between the two electrodes is proportional to the concentration of alcohol in the breath.

Schematic diagram of a fuel cell using alcohol as a fuel.

ensures that the sample measurement is deep-lung breath and closely relates to the true blood-alcohol concentration of the subject being tested.

A breath-test operator must take other steps to ensure that the breath-test result truly reflects the actual blood-alcohol concentration of the subject. A major consideration is to avoid measuring "mouth alcohol" resulting from regurgitation, belching, or recent intake of an alcoholic beverage. Also, the recent gargling of an alcohol-containing mouthwash can lead to the presence of mouth alcohol. As a result, the alcohol concentration detected in the exhaled breath is higher than the concentration in the alveolar breath. To avoid this possibility, the operator must not allow the subject to take any foreign material into his/her mouth for at least fifteen to twenty minutes before the breath test. Likewise, the subject should be observed not to have belched or regurgitated during this period. Mouth alcohol has been shown to dissipate after fifteen to twenty minutes from its inception.

Independent measurement of duplicate breath samples taken within a few minutes of each other is another extremely important check of the integrity of the breath test. Acceptable agreement between the two tests taken minutes apart significantly reduces the possibility of errors arising from the operator, mouth alcohol, instrument component failures, and spurious electric signals.

Field Sobriety Testing

A police officer who suspects that an individual is under the influence of alcohol usually conducts a series of preliminary tests before ordering the suspect to submit to an evidential breath or blood test. These preliminary, or

(a)   (b)

FIGURE 6–5   (a) The Alco-Sensor FST. (b) A subject blowing into the roadside tester
device. *Courtesy Intoximeters, Inc., St. Louis, Mo., www.intox.com*

field sobriety, tests are normally performed to ascertain the degree of the
suspect's physical impairment and whether an evidential test is justified.

Field sobriety tests usually consist of a series of psychophysical tests
and a preliminary breath test (if such devices are authorized and available
for use). A portable handheld, roadside breath tester is shown in Figure 6–5.
This device, about the size of a pack of cigarettes, weighs 5 ounces and uses
a fuel cell to measure the alcohol content of a breath sample. The fuel cell
absorbs the alcohol from the breath sample, oxidizes it, and produces an
electrical current proportional to the breath-alcohol content. This instrument can typically perform for three to five years before the fuel cell needs
to be replaced. Breath-test results obtained with devices such as those
shown in Figure 6–6 must be considered preliminary and nonevidential.
They should only establish probable cause for requiring an individual to
submit to a more thorough breath or blood test.

Horizontal-gaze nystagmus, walk and turn, and the one-leg stand constitute a series of reliable and effective psychophysical tests. Horizontal-
gaze nystagmus is an involuntary jerking of the eye as it moves to the side.
A person experiencing nystagmus is usually unaware that the jerking is
happening and is unable to stop or control it. The subject being tested is
asked to follow a penlight or some other object with his or her eye as far
to the side as the eye can go. The more intoxicated the person is, the less
the eye has to move toward the side before jerking or nystagmus begins.
Usually, when a person's blood-alcohol concentration is in the range of
0.10 percent, the jerking begins before the eyeball has moved 45 degrees
to the side (see Figure 6–7). Higher blood-alcohol concentration causes
jerking at smaller angles. Also, if the suspect has taken a drug that also
causes nystagmus (such as phencyclidine, barbiturates, and other depressants), the nystagmus onset angle may occur much earlier than would be
expected from alcohol alone.

Walk and turn and the one-leg stand are divided-attention tasks, testing the subject's ability to comprehend and execute two or more simple
instructions at one time. The ability to understand and simultaneously
carry out more than two instructions is significantly affected by increasing
blood-alcohol levels. Walk and turn requires the suspect to maintain balance while standing heel-to-toe and at the same time listening to and comprehending the test instructions. During the walking stage, the suspect

FIGURE 6–6 When a person's blood-alcohol level is in the range of 0.10 percent, jerking of the eye during the horizontal-gaze nystagmus test begins before the eyeball has moved 45 degrees to the side.

must walk a straight line, touching heel-to-toe for nine steps, then turn around on the line and repeat the process. The one-leg stand requires the suspect to maintain balance while standing with heels together listening to the instructions. During the balancing stage, the suspect must stand on one foot while holding the other foot several inches off the ground for 30 seconds; simultaneously, the suspect must count out loud during the 30-second time period.

Key Points

- Modern breath testers are free of chemicals. They include infrared light absorption devices and fuel cell detectors.

- The key to the accuracy of a breath-testing device is to ensure that the unit captures the alcohol in the alveolar (deep-lung) breath of the subject.

- Many breath testers collect a set volume of breath and expose it to infrared light. The instrument measures alcohol concentration in breath by measuring the degree of the interaction of the light with alcohol in the collected breath sample.

- Law enforcement officers use field sobriety tests to estimate a motorist's degree of physical impairment by alcohol and to determine whether an evidential test for alcohol is justified.

- The horizontal-gaze nystagmus test, walk and turn, and the one-leg stand are all considered reliable and effective psychophysical tests for alcohol impairment.

The Analysis of Blood for Alcohol

Gas chromatography offers the toxicologist the most widely used approach for determining alcohol levels in blood. Under proper gas chromatographic conditions, alcohol can be separated from other volatiles in the blood. By comparing the resultant alcohol peak area to ones obtained with known blood-alcohol standards, the investigator can calculate the alcohol level with a high degree of accuracy (see Figure 6–7).

Another procedure for alcohol analysis involves the oxidation of alcohol to acetaldehyde. This reaction is carried out in the presence of the enzyme

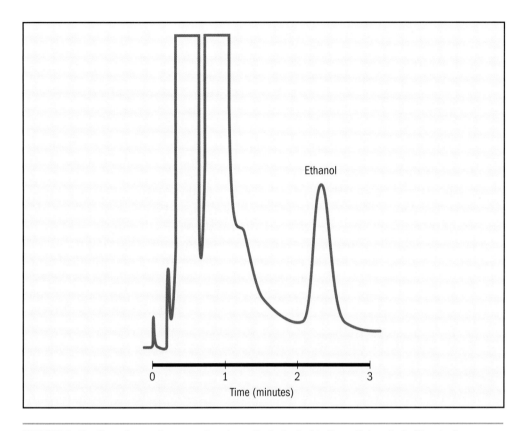

FIGURE 6–7 **Gas chromatogram showing ethyl alcohol (ethanol) in whole blood.** *Courtesy Varian Inc., Palo Alto, Calif.*

alcohol dehydrogenase and the coenzyme nicotin-amide-adenine dinucleotide (NAD). As the oxidation proceeds, NAD is converted into another chemical species, NADH. The extent of this conversion is measured by a spectrophotometer and is related to alcohol concentration. This approach to blood-alcohol testing is normally associated with instruments used in a clinical or hospital setting. On the other hand, forensic laboratories normally use gas chromatography for determining blood-alcohol content.

Collection and Preservation of Blood

Blood must always be drawn under medically accepted conditions by a qualified individual. It is important to apply a nonalcoholic disinfectant before the suspect's skin is penetrated with a sterile needle or lancet. It is important to negate any argument that an alcoholic disinfectant may have inadvertently contributed to a falsely high blood-alcohol result. Nonalcoholic disinfectants such as aqueous benzalkonium chloride (Zepiran), aqueous mercuric chloride, or povidone-iodine (Betadine) are recommended for this purpose.

Once blood is removed from an individual, it is best preserved sealed in an airtight container after adding an anticoagulant and a preservative. The blood should be stored in a refrigerator until delivery to the toxicology laboratory. The addition of an anticoagulant, such as EDTA or potassium oxalate, prevents clotting; a preservative, such as sodium fluoride, inhibits the growth of microorganisms capable of destroying alcohol.

One study performed to determine the stability of alcohol in blood removed from living individuals found that the most significant factors affecting alcohol's stability in blood are storage temperature, the presence of

anticoagulant
A substance that prevents coagulation or clotting of blood.

preservative
A substance that stops the growth of microorganisms in blood.

a preservative, and the time of storage.[3] Not a single blood specimen examined showed an increase in alcohol level with time. Failure to keep the blood refrigerated or to add sodium fluoride resulted in a substantial decline in alcohol concentration. Longer storage times also reduced blood-alcohol levels. Hence, failure to adhere to any of the proper preservation requirements for blood works to the benefit of the suspect and to the detriment of society.

The collection of postmortem blood samples for alcohol determination requires added precautions as compared to collection from living subjects. Ethyl alcohol may be generated in a deceased individual as a result of bacterial action. Therefore, it is best to collect a number of blood samples from different body sites. For example, blood may be removed from the heart and from the femoral (leg) and cubital (arm) veins. Each sample should be placed in a clean, airtight container containing an anticoagulant and sodium fluoride preservative and should be refrigerated. Blood-alcohol levels attributed solely to alcohol consumption should result in nearly similar results for all blood samples collected from the same person. Alternatively, collection of vitreous humor and urine is recommended. Vitreous humor and urine usually do not suffer from postmortem ethyl alcohol production to any significant extent.

Key Points

- Gas chromatography is the most widely used approach for determining blood-alcohol levels in forensic laboratories.

- An anticoagulant should be added to a blood sample to prevent clotting; a preservative should be added to inhibit the growth of microorganisms capable of destroying alcohol.

Alcohol and the Law

Constitutionally, every state in the United States must establish and administer statutes regulating the operation of motor vehicles. Although such an arrangement might encourage diverse laws defining permissible blood-alcohol levels, this has not been the case. Since the 1930s, both the American Medical Association and the National Safety Council have exerted considerable influence in persuading the states to establish uniform and reasonable blood-alcohol standards.

Blood-Alcohol Laws

The American Medical Association and the National Safety Council initially recommended that a person with a blood-alcohol concentration in excess of 0.15 percent w/v was to be considered under the influence of alcohol.[4] However, continued experimental studies showed a clear correlation between drinking and driving impairment at blood-alcohol levels much below 0.15 percent w/v. These findings eventually led to a lowering of the blood-concentration standard for intoxication from 0.15 percent w/v to its current 0.08 percent w/v.

In 1992, the U.S. Department of Transportation (DOT) recommended that states adopt 0.08 percent blood-alcohol concentration as the legal measure of drunk driving. This recommendation was enacted into federal law in 2000. All fifty states have now established *per se laws*, meaning that any individual meeting or exceeding a defined blood-alcohol level (usually 0.08 percent) shall be deemed intoxicated. No other proof of alcohol impairment is necessary. Starting in 2003, states that had not adopted the 0.08 percent per se level stood to lose part of their federal funds for highway construction. The 0.08 percent level applies only to noncommercial drivers, as the federal government has set the maximum allowable blood-alcohol concentration for commercial truck and bus drivers at 0.04 percent.

Several Western countries have also set 0.08 percent w/v as the blood-alcohol level above which it is an offense to drive a motor vehicle, including Canada, Italy, Switzerland, and the United Kingdom. Finland, France, Germany, Ireland, Japan, the Netherlands, and Norway have a 0.05 percent limit. Australian states have adopted a 0.05 percent blood-alcohol concentration level. Sweden has lowered its blood-alcohol concentration limit to 0.02 percent.

As shown in Figure 6–8, one is about four times as likely to become involved in an automobile accident at the 0.08 percent level as compared to a sober individual. At the 0.15 percent level, the chances are twenty-five times as much for involvement in an automobile accident as compared to a sober driver. The reader can estimate the relationship of blood-alcohol levels to body weight and the quantity of 80-proof liquor consumed by referring to Figure 6–9.

Constitutional Issues

The Fifth Amendment to the U.S. Constitution guarantees all citizens protection against *self-incrimination*—that is, against being forced to make an admission that would prove one's own guilt in a legal matter. Because consenting to a breath test for alcohol might be considered a form of self-incrimination, the National Highway Traffic Safety Administration recommended an *implied-consent law* to prevent a person from refusing to take

WebExtra 6.1
Calculate Your Blood Alcohol Level
www.prenhall.com/hsforensics

WebExtra 6.2
See How Alcohol Affects Your Behavior
www.prenhall.com/hsforensics

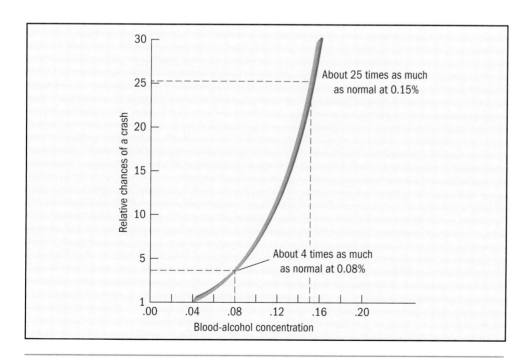

FIGURE 6–8 Diagram of increased driving risk in relation to blood-alcohol concentration.
Courtesy U.S. Department of Transportation, Washington, D.C.

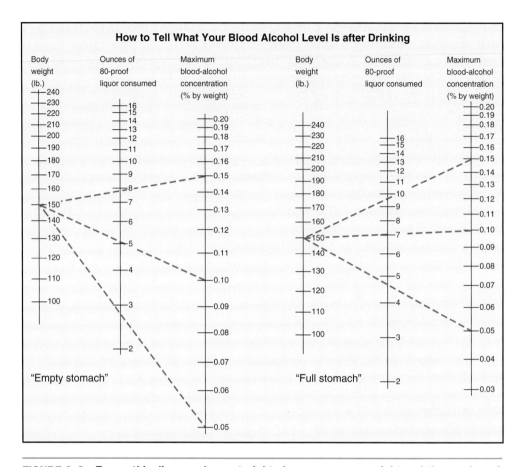

How to Tell What Your Blood Alcohol Level Is after Drinking

FIGURE 6–9 **To use this diagram, lay a straightedge across your weight and the number of ounces of liquor you've consumed on an empty or full stomach. The point where the edge hits the right-hand column is your maximum blood-alcohol level. The rate of elimination of alcohol from the bloodstream is approximately 0.015 percent per hour. Therefore, to calculate your actual blood-alcohol level, subtract 0.015 from the number in the right-hand column for each hour from the start of drinking.**

a test on those constitutional grounds. This law states that the operator of a motor vehicle on a public highway must either consent to a test for alcohol intoxication, if requested, or lose his or her license for some designated period—usually six months to one year.

The leading case relating to the constitutionality of collecting a blood specimen for alcohol testing, as well as for obtaining other types of physical evidence from a suspect without consent, is *Schmerber* v. *California*.[5] While being treated at a Los Angeles hospital for injuries sustained in an automobile collision, Schmerber was arrested for driving under the influence of alcohol. Despite Schmerber's objections, a physician took a blood sample from him at the direction of the police. Schmerber was convicted of driving while intoxicated and he subsequently appealed the decision. The case eventually reached the U.S. Supreme Court, where Schmerber argued that his privilege against self-incrimination had been violated by the introduction of the results of the blood test at his trial. The Court ruled against him, reasoning that the Fifth Amendment prohibits only compelling a suspect to give *testimonial* evidence that may prove to be self-incriminating; being compelled to furnish *physical* evidence, such as fingerprints, photographs, measurements, and blood samples, the Court ruled, was not protected by the Fifth Amendment.

The Court also addressed the question of whether the police violated Schmerber's Fourth Amendment protection against unreasonable search and seizure by taking a blood specimen from him without a search warrant. The Court upheld the constitutionality of the blood removal, reasoning in this case that the police were confronted with an emergency situation. By the time police officials would have obtained a warrant, Schmerber's blood-alcohol levels would have declined significantly as a result of natural body elimination processes. In effect, the evidence would have been destroyed. The Court also emphasized that the blood specimen was taken in a medically accepted manner and without unreasonable force. This opinion in no way condones warrantless taking of blood for alcohol or drug testing under all circumstances. The reasonableness of actions a police officer may take to compel an individual to yield evidence can be judged only on a case-by-case basis.

Key Points

* The current legal measure of drunk driving in the United States is a blood-alcohol concentration of 0.08 percent, or 0.08 grams of alcohol per 100 milliliters of blood.

* An implied-consent law states that the operator of a motor vehicle on a public highway must either consent to a test for alcohol intoxication, if requested, or lose his or her license for some designated period—usually six months to one year.

The Role of the Toxicologist

Once the forensic toxicologist ventures beyond the analysis of alcohol, he or she encounters an encyclopedic maze of drugs and poisons. Even a cursory discussion of the problems and handicaps imposed on toxicologists is enough to develop a sense of appreciation for their accomplishments and ingenuity.

Challenges Facing the Toxicologist

The toxicologist is presented with body fluids and/or organs and asked to examine them for drugs and poisons. If he or she is fortunate, which is not often, some clue as to the type of toxic substance present may develop from the victim's symptoms, a postmortem pathological examination, an examination of the victim's personal effects, or the nearby presence of empty drug containers or household chemicals. Without such supportive information, the toxicologist must use general screening procedures with the hope of narrowing thousands of possibilities to one.

If this task does not seem monumental, consider that the toxicologist is not dealing with drugs at the concentration levels found in powders and pills. By the time a drug specimen reaches the toxicology laboratory, it has been dissipated and distributed throughout the body. The drug analyst may have gram or milligram quantities of material to work with, but the toxicologist must be satisfied with nanogram or at best microgram amounts, acquired only after careful extraction from body fluids and organs.

Furthermore, the body is an active chemistry laboratory, and no one can appreciate this observation more than a toxicologist. Few substances enter and completely leave the body in the same chemical state. The drug

FIGURE 6–10 Scientist analyzing blood samples.
Courtesy Risto Bozovic, AP Wide World Photos

that is injected is not always the substance extracted from the body tissues. Therefore, a thorough understanding of how the body alters or metabolizes the chemical structure of a drug is essential in detecting its presence.

It would, for example, be futile and frustrating to search exhaustively for heroin in the human body. This drug is almost immediately metabolized to morphine on entering the bloodstream. Even with this information, the search may still prove impossible unless the examiner also knows that only a small percentage of morphine is excreted unchanged in urine. For the most part, morphine becomes chemically bonded to body carbohydrates before elimination in urine. Thus, successful detection of morphine requires that its extraction be planned in accordance with a knowledge of its chemical fate in the body.

Last, when and if the toxicologist has surmounted all of these obstacles and has finally detected, identified, and quantitated a drug or poison, he or she must assess the substance's toxicity. Fortunately, there is published information relating to the toxic levels of most drugs. However, even when such data are available, their interpretation must assume that the victim's physiological behavior agrees with that of subjects of previous studies. Such an assumption may not be entirely valid without knowing the subject's case history. No experienced toxicologist would be surprised to find an individual tolerating a toxic level of a drug that would have killed most other people.

Collection and Preservation of Toxicological Evidence

The toxicologist's capabilities depend directly on input from the attending physician, medical examiner, and police investigator. It is a tribute to

Case Study

Death by Tylenol

Tylenol® on the pharmacy shelf. *Courtesy UPI, Corbis/Bettmann*

In 1982, two firefighters from a Chicago suburb were casually discussing four bizarre deaths that had recently taken place in a neighboring area. As they discussed the circumstances of the deaths, they realized that each of the victims had taken Tylenol. Their suspicions were immediately reported to police investigators. Tragically, before the general public could be alerted, three more victims died after taking poison-laced Tylenol capsules. Seven individuals, all in the Chicago area, were the first victims to die from what has become known as *product tampering*.

A forensic chemical analysis of Tylenol capsules recovered from the victims' residences showed that the capsules were filled with potassium cyanide in a quantity ten thousand times what was needed to kill an average person. It was quickly determined that the cyanide was not introduced into the bottles at the factory. Instead, the perpetrator methodically emptied each of twenty to thirty capsules and then refilled them with potassium cyanide. The tampered capsules were rebottled, carefully repackaged, and placed on the shelves of six different stores. The case of the Tylenol murders remains unsolved, and the $100,000 reward offered by Tylenol's manufacturer remains unclaimed.

forensic toxicologists, who must often labor under conditions that do not afford such cooperation, that they can achieve the high level of proficiency that they do.

Generally, with a deceased person, the medical examiner decides what biological specimens must be shipped to the toxicology laboratory for analysis. However, a living person suspected of being under the influence of a drug presents a completely different problem, and few options are available. When possible, both blood and urine are taken from any suspected drug user. The entire urine void (sample) is collected and submitted for toxicological analysis. Preferably, two consecutive voids should be collected in separate specimen containers.

When a licensed physician or registered nurse is available, a sample of blood should also be collected. The amount of blood taken depends on the type of examination to be conducted. Comprehensive toxicological tests for drugs and poisons can conveniently be carried out on a minimum of 10 milliliters of blood. A determination solely for the presence of alcohol will require much less—approximately 5 milliliters of blood. However, many therapeutic drugs, such as tranquilizers and barbiturates, taken in combination with a small, nonintoxicating amount of alcohol, produce behavioral patterns resembling alcohol intoxication. For this reason, the toxicologist must be given enough blood to perform a comprehensive analysis for drugs in cases of low alcohol concentrations.

Techniques Used in Toxicology

For the toxicologist, the upsurge in drug use and abuse has meant that the overwhelming majority of fatal and nonfatal toxic agents are drugs. Not surprisingly, a relatively small number of drugs—namely, those discussed in Chapter 5—comprise nearly all the toxic agents encountered. Of these, alcohol, marijuana, and cocaine account for 90 percent or more of the drugs encountered in a typical toxicology laboratory.

Like the drug analyst, the toxicologist must devise an analytical scheme to detect, isolate, and identify a toxic substance. The first chore is to remove and isolate drugs and other toxic agents from the biological materials submitted as evidence. Because drugs constitute a large portion of the toxic materials found, a good deal of effort must be devoted to their extraction and detection. Many different procedures are used, and a useful description of them would be too detailed for this text. We can best understand the underlying principle of drug extraction by observing that many drugs fall into the categories of acids and bases.

Acids and Bases   Although several definitions exist for these two classes, a simple one states that an acid is a compound capable of donating a hydrogen ion (or a hydrogen atom minus its electron) to another compound with reasonable ease. Conversely, a base is a molecule capable of accepting a hydrogen ion shed by an acid. The idea of acidity and basicity can be expressed in terms of a simple numerical value that relates to the concentration of the hydrogen ion (H^+) in a liquid medium such as water. Chemists use the pH scale to do this. This scale runs from 0 to 14:

$$\text{PH} = 0 \quad 1 \quad 2 \quad 3 \quad 4 \quad 5 \quad 6 \quad 7 \quad 8 \quad 9 \quad 10 \quad 11 \quad 12 \quad 13 \quad 14$$

Increasing acidity   Neutral   Increasing basicity

Normally, water is neither acid nor basic—in other words, it is neutral, with a pH of 7. However, when an acidic substance—for example, sulfuric acid or hydrochloric acid—is added to the water, it adds excess hydrogen ions, and the pH value becomes less than 7. The lower the number, the more acidic the water. Similarly, when a basic substance—for example, sodium hydroxide or ammonium hydroxide—is added to water, it removes hydrogen ions, thus making water basic. The more basic the water, the higher its pH value.

By controlling the pH of a water solution into which blood, urine, or tissues are dissolved, the toxicologist can control the type of drug that is recovered. For example, acid drugs are easily extracted from an acidified water solution (pH less than 7) with organic solvents such as chloroform. Similarly, basic drugs are readily removed from a basic water solution (pH greater than 7) with organic solvents. This simple approach gives the toxicologist a general technique for extracting and categorizing drugs. Some of the more commonly encountered drugs may be classified as follows:

acid
A compound capable of donating a hydrogen ion (H^+) to another compound.

base
A compound capable of accepting a hydrogen ion (H^+).

pH scale
A scale used to express the basicity or acidity of a substance. A pH of 7 is neutral; lower values are acidic and higher values basic.

Acid Drugs	Basic Drugs
Barbiturates	Phencyclidine
Acetylsalicylic acid (aspirin)	Methadone
	Amphetamines
	Cocaine

Screening and Confirmation   Once the specimen has been extracted and divided into acidic and basic fractions, the toxicologist can identify the drugs present. The strategy for identifying abused drugs entails a two-step approach: *screening* and *confirmation* (see Figure 6–11). A screening test normally gives quick insight into the likelihood that a specimen contains a drug substance. This test allows a toxicologist to examine a large number of specimens within a short period of time for a wide range of drugs. Any positive results from a screening test are tentative at best and must be verified with a confirmation test.

Screening Tests.   The three most widely used screening tests are thin-layer chromatography (TLC), gas chromatography (GC), and immunoassay. The techniques of GC and TLC were described in Chapter 5. The third technique, immunoassay, has proven to be a useful screening tool in toxicology laboratories. Its principles are very different from any of the analytical techniques we have discussed so far. Basically, immunoassay is based on specific drug antibody reactions. We will learn about this concept in Chapter 8. The primary advantage of immunoassay is its ability to detect small concentrations of drugs in body fluids and organs. In fact, this technique provides the best approach for detecting the low drug levels normally associated with smoking marijuana.

Confirmation Tests.   A positive screening test may be due to a substance's close chemical structure to an abused drug. For this reason, the toxicologist must follow up any positive screening test with a confirmation test. Because of the potential impact of the results of a drug finding on an individual, only the most conclusive confirmation procedures should be used.

Gas chromatography/mass spectrometry is generally accepted as the confirmation test of choice. As we learned in Chapter 5, the combination of gas chromatography and mass spectrometry provides a one-step

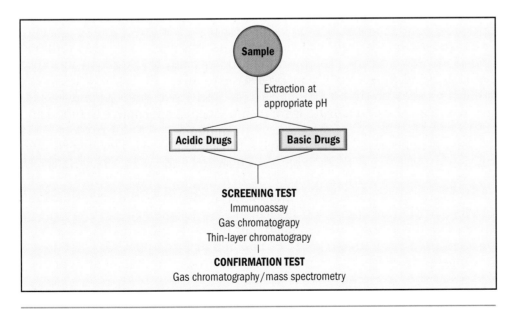

FIGURE 6–11   Biological fluids and tissues are extracted for acidic and basic drugs by controlling the pH of a water solution in which they are dissolved. Once this is accomplished, the toxicologist analyzes for drugs by using screening and confirmation test procedures.

FIGURE 6–12 The combination of the gas chromatograph and the mass spectrometer enables forensic toxicologists to separate the components of a drug mixture and provides specific identification of a drug substance.

confirmation test of unequaled sensitivity and specificity. Figure 6–12 illustrates the process. After being introduced to the gas chromatograph, the sample is separated into its components. When the separated sample component leaves the column of the gas chromatograph, it enters the mass spectrometer, where it is bombarded with high-energy electrons. This bombardment causes the sample to break up into fragments, producing a fragmentation pattern or mass spectrum for each sample. For most compounds, the mass spectrum represents a unique "fingerprint" pattern that can be used for identification.

There is tremendous interest in drug-testing programs conducted not only in criminal matters but for industry and government as well. Urine testing for drugs is becoming common for job applicants and employees in the workplace. Likewise, the U.S. military has an extensive drug urine-testing program for its members. Many urine-testing programs rely on private laboratories to perform the required analyses. In any case, when the test results form the basis for taking action against an individual, both a screening and confirmation test must be incorporated into the testing protocol to ensure the integrity of the laboratory's conclusions.

Detecting Drugs in Hair When a forensic toxicological examination on a living person is required, practicality limits available specimens to blood and urine. Most drugs remain in the bloodstream for about twenty-four hours; in urine, they normally are present up to seventy-two hours. However, it may be necessary to go further back in time to ascertain whether a subject has been abusing a drug. If so, the only viable alternative to blood and urine is head hair.

Hair is nourished by blood flowing through capillaries located close to the hair root. Drugs present in blood diffuse through the capillary walls into the base of the hair and become permanently entrapped in the hair's hardening protein structure. As the hair continues to grow, the drug's location on the hair shaft becomes a historical marker for delineating drug intake. Given that the average human head hair grows at the rate of 1 centimeter per month, analyzing segments of hair for drug content may define the timeline for drug use, dating it back over a period of weeks, months, or even years, depending on the hair's length.

However, caution is required in interpreting the timeline. The chronology of drug intake may be distorted by drugs penetrating the hair's surface as a result of environmental exposure, or drugs may enter the hair's surface through sweat. Nevertheless, drug hair analysis is the only viable approach for measuring long-term abuse of a drug.

Detecting Nondrug Poisons   Although forensic toxicologists devote most of their efforts to detecting drugs, they also test for a wide variety of other toxic substances. Some of these are rare elements, not widely or commercially available. Others are so common that virtually everyone is exposed to nontoxic amounts of them every day.

Heavy Metals.   One group of poisons once commonly encountered in criminal cases of murder are known as *heavy metals*. They include arsenic, bismuth, antimony, mercury, and thallium. These days, however, the forensic toxicologist only occasionally encounters heavy metals because severe environmental protection regulations restrict their availability to the general public. Nevertheless, as the following case study makes clear, their use is by no means only a historical curiosity.

To screen for many of these metals, the investigator may dissolve the suspect body fluid or tissue in a hydrochloric acid solution and insert a copper strip into the solution. This process is known as the Reinsch test. The appearance of a silvery or dark coating on the copper indicates the presence of a heavy metal. Such a finding must be confirmed by analytical techniques suitable for inorganic analysis—namely, emission spectroscopy, or X-ray diffraction. These procedures are discussed in more detail in Chapters 11 and 13.

Case Study

Joann Curley: Caught by a Hair

A vibrant young woman named Joann Curley rushed to the Wilkes-Barre (Pennsylvania) General Hospital—her husband, Bobby, was having an attack and required immediate medical attention. Bobby was experiencing a burning sensation in his feet, numbness in his hands, a flushed face, and intense sweating. He was diagnosed with Guillain-Barré syndrome, an acute inflammation of the nervous system that accounted for all of Bobby's symptoms. After being discharged, Bobby experienced another bout of debilitating pain and numbness. He was admitted to another hospital, the larger and more capable Hershey Medical Center in Hershey, Pennsylvania. There doctors observed extreme alopecia, or hair loss.

Test results of Bobby's urine showed high levels of the heavy metal thallium in his body. Thallium, a rare and highly toxic metal that was used decades ago in substances such as rat poison and to treat ringworm and gout, was found in sufficient quantities to cause Bobby's sickness. The use of thallium was banned in the United States in 1984. Now, at least, Bobby could be treated. However,

before Bobby's doctors could treat him for thallium poisoning, he experienced cardiac arrest and slipped into a coma. Joann Curley made the difficult decision to remove her husband of thirteen months from life support equipment. He died shortly thereafter.

Bobby Curley was an electrician and, for five months before his death, he worked in the chemistry department at nearby Wilkes University. Authorities suspected that Bobby had been accidentally exposed to thallium there among old chemicals and laboratory equipment. The laboratory was searched and several old bottles of powdered thallium salts were discovered in a storage closet. After testing the air and surfaces, these were eliminated as possible sources for exposure. This finding was supported by the discovery that none of Bobby's co-workers had any thallium in their systems. The next most logical route of exposure was in the home; thus, the Curley kitchen was sampled. Of the hundreds of items tested, three thermoses were found to contain traces of thallium.

(*continued*)

Case Study

Joann Curley: Caught by a Hair (*continued*)

Investigators also learned that Bobby had changed his life insurance to list his wife, Joann, as the beneficiary of his $300,000 policy. Based on this information, police consulted a forensic toxicologist in an effort to glean as much from the physical evidence in Bobby Curley's body as possible. The toxicologist conducted segmental analysis of Bobby's hair, an analytical method based on the predictable rate of hair growth on the human scalp: an average of 1 centimeter per month. Bobby had approximately 5 inches (12.5 centimeters) of hair, which represents almost twelve months of hair growth. Each section tested represented a specific period of time in Bobby's final year of his life.

The hair analysis proved that Bobby Curley was poisoned with thallium long before he began working at Wilkes University. The first few doses were small, which probably barely made him sick at the time. Gradually, over a year or more, Bobby was receiving more doses of thallium until he finally succumbed to a massive dose three or four days before his death. After careful scrutiny of the timeline, investigators concluded that only Joann Curley had access to Bobby during each of these intervals. She also had motive, in the amount of $300,000.

Presented with the timeline and the solid toxicological evidence against her, Joann Curley pleaded guilty to murder. As part of her plea agreement, she provided a forty-page written confession of how she haphazardly dosed Bobby with some rat poison she found in her basement. She admitted that she murdered him for the money she would receive from Bobby's life insurance policy.

Carbon Monoxide. Unlike heavy metals, *carbon monoxide* still represents one of the most common poisons encountered in a forensic laboratory. Inhaling the carbon monoxide from automobile exhaust fumes is a relatively common way to commit suicide. The victim typically uses a garden or vacuum cleaner hose to connect the tailpipe with the vehicle's interior, or allows the engine to run in a closed garage. A level of carbon monoxide sufficient to cause death accumulates in five to ten minutes in a closed single-car garage.

When carbon monoxide enters the human body, it is primarily absorbed by the red blood cells, where it combines with hemoglobin to form carboxyhemoglobin. An average red blood cell contains about 280 million molecules of hemoglobin. Oxygen normally combines with hemoglobin, which transports the oxygen throughout the body. However, if a high percentage of the hemoglobin combines with carbon monoxide, not enough is left to carry sufficient oxygen to the tissues, and death by asphyxiation quickly follows.

There are two basic methods for measuring the concentration of carbon monoxide in the blood. Spectrophotometric methods examine the visible spectrum of blood to determine the amount of carboxyhemoglobin relative to oxyhemoglobin or total hemoglobin; or a volume of blood can be treated with a reagent to liberate the carbon monoxide, which is then measured by gas chromatography.

The amount of carbon monoxide in blood is generally expressed as *percent saturation*. This represents the extent to which the available hemoglobin has been converted to carboxyhemoglobin. The transition from normal or occupational levels of carbon monoxide to toxic levels is not sharply defined. It depends, among other things, on the age, health, and general fitness of each individual. In a healthy middle-aged individual, a carbon monoxide blood saturation greater than 50 to 60 percent is considered fatal. However, in combination with alcohol or other depressants, fatal levels may be significantly lower. For instance, a carbon monoxide saturation of 35 to 40 percent may prove fatal in the presence of a blood-alcohol concentration of 0.20 percent w/v. Interestingly, chain smokers may have a constant carbon monoxide level of 8 to 10 percent from the carbon monoxide in cigarette smoke.

The level of carbon monoxide in the blood of a victim found dead at the scene of a fire can help ascertain whether foul play has occurred. High levels of carbon monoxide in the blood prove that the victim breathed the combustion products of the fire and was therefore alive when the fire began. By contrast, low levels of carbon monoxide indicate that the victim was likely dead before the fire started, and may have been deliberately placed at the scene in order to destroy the body. Many attempts at covering up a murder by setting fire to a victim's house or car have been uncovered in this manner.

The Significance of Toxicological Findings

Once a drug is found and identified, the toxicologist assesses its influence on the behavior of the individual. Interpreting the results of a toxicology finding is one of the toxicologist's more difficult chores. Recall that many countries have designated a specific blood-alcohol level at which an individual is deemed under the influence of alcohol. These levels were established as a result of numerous studies conducted over several years to measure the effects of alcohol levels on driving performance. However, no such legal guidelines are available to the toxicologist who must judge how a drug other than alcohol affects an individual's performance or physical state.

For many drugs, blood concentration levels are readily determined and can be used to estimate the pharmacological effects of the drug on the individual. Often, when dealing with a living person, the toxicologist has the added benefit of knowing what a police officer may have observed about an individual's behavior and motor skills. For a deceased person, drug levels in various body organs and tissues provide additional information about the individual's state at the time of death. However, before drawing conclusions about drug-induced behavior, the analyst must consider other factors, including the age, physical condition, and tolerance of the drug user.

With prolonged use of a drug, an individual may become less responsive to a drug's effects and tolerate blood-drug concentrations that would kill a casual drug user. Therefore, knowledge of an individual's history of drug use is important in evaluating drug concentrations. Another consideration is additive or synergistic effects of the interaction of two or more drugs, which may produce a highly intoxicated or comatose state even though none of the drugs alone is present at high or toxic levels. The combination of alcohol with barbiturates or narcotics is a common example of a potentially lethal drug combination.

The concentration of a drug present in urine is a poor indicator of how extensively an individual's behavior or state is influenced by the drug. Urine is formed outside the body's circulatory system, and consequently drug levels can build up in it over a relatively long period of time. Some drugs are found in the urine one to three days after they have been taken and long after their effects on the user have disappeared. Nevertheless, the value of this information should not be discounted. Urine drug levels, like blood levels, are best used by law enforcement authorities and the courts to corroborate other investigative and medical findings regarding an individual's condition. Hence, for an individual arrested for suspicion of being under the influence of a drug, a toxicologist's determinations supplement the observations of the arresting officer, including the results of field sobriety tests performed at the time of apprehension.

For a deceased person, the medical examiner or coroner must establish a cause of death. However, before a conclusive determination is made, the examining physician depends on the forensic toxicologist to demonstrate the presence or absence of a drug or poison in the tissues or body fluids of the deceased. Only through the combined efforts of the toxicologist and the medical examiner (or coroner) can society be assured that death investigations achieve high professional and legal standards.

While recognizing alcohol-impaired performance is an expertise generally accorded to police officers by the courts, recognizing drug-induced intoxication is much more difficult and generally not part of police training. During the 1970s, the Los Angeles Police Department developed and tested a series of clinical and psychophysical examinations that a trained police officer could use to identify and differentiate between types of drug impairment. This program has evolved into a national program to train police as *drug recognition experts*. Normally, a three- to five-month training program is required to certify an officer as a drug recognition expert (DRE).

Key Points

- The forensic toxicologist must devise an analytical scheme to detect, isolate, and identify toxic drug substances extracted from biological fluids, tissues, and organs.

- A screening test gives quick insight into the likelihood that a specimen contains a drug substance. Positive results arising from a screening test are tentative at best and must be verified with a confirmation test.

- The most widely used screening tests are thin-layer chromatography, gas chromatography, and immunoassay. Gas chromatography/mass spectrometry is generally accepted as the confirmation test of choice.

- Once a drug is extracted and identified, a toxicologist may be required to judge the drug's effect on an individual's natural performance or physical state.

Chapter Summary

Toxicologists detect and identify drugs and poisons in body fluids, tissues, and organs. A major branch of forensic toxicology deals with the measurement of alcohol in the body for matters that pertain to violations of criminal law.

Alcohol appears in the blood within minutes after it has been taken by mouth and slowly increases in concentration while it is being absorbed from the stomach and the small intestine into the bloodstream. When all the alcohol has been absorbed, a maximum alcohol level is reached in the blood and the postabsorption period begins. Then the alcohol concentration slowly decreases until a zero level is again reached. Alcohol is eliminated from the body through oxidation and excretion. Oxidation takes place almost entirely in the liver, while alcohol is excreted unchanged in the breath, urine, and perspiration.

The extent to which an individual is under the influence of alcohol is usually determined by measuring the quantity of alcohol present in the blood or the breath. Breath testers that operate on the principle of infrared light absorption are becoming increasingly popular within the law enforcement community.

Many types of breath testers capture a set volume of breath. The captured breath is exposed to infrared light. The degree of interaction of the light with alcohol in the breath sample allows the instrument to measure blood-alcohol concentration in the breath. These breath-testing devices operate on the principle that the ratio between the concentration of alcohol in deep-lung or alveolar breath and its concentration in blood is fixed.

Law enforcement officers typically use field sobriety tests to estimate a motorist's degree of physical impairment by alcohol and whether an evidential test for alcohol is justified. The horizontal-gaze nystagmus test, walk and turn, and the one-leg stand are all reliable and effective psychophysical tests.

Gas chromatography is the most widely used approach for determining alcohol levels in blood. Blood must always be drawn under medically accepted conditions by a qualified individual. A nonalcoholic disinfectant must be applied before the suspect's skin is penetrated with a sterile needle or lancet. Once blood is removed from an individual, it is best preserved sealed in an airtight container after adding an anticoagulant and a preservative.

The forensic toxicologist must devise an analytical scheme to detect, isolate, and identify toxic drug substances. Once the drug has been extracted from appropriate biological fluids, tissues, and organs, the forensic toxicologist can identify the drug substance. The strategy for identifying abused drugs entails a two-step approach: screening and confirmation. A screening test gives quick insight into the likelihood that a specimen contains a drug substance. Positive results from a screening test are tentative at best and must be verified with a confirmation test. The most widely used screening tests are thin-layer chromatography, gas chromatography, and immunoassay. Gas chromatography/mass spectrometry is generally accepted as the confirmation test of choice. Once the drug is extracted and identified, the toxicologist may be required to judge the drug's effect on an individual's natural performance or physical state.

Review Questions

Facts and Concepts

1. What is a toxicologist? Name three settings in which a toxicologist often works.

2. What is the most widely abused drug in Western countries?

3. Define *metabolism*.

4. List and describe the three stages of alcohol's fate in the human body.

5. In what parts of the body does alcohol tend to accumulate? Why does it accumulate in these places?

6. Name at least three factors that influence the rate at which alcohol is absorbed into the bloodstream.

7. About 95–98 percent of alcohol is oxidized to what two substances?
   a. carbon dioxide and dehydrogenase
   b. water and acetic acid
   c. acetaldehyde and acetic acid
   d. water and carbon dioxide

8. Alcohol that is not oxidized is expelled unchanged in what bodily excretions?

9. The amount of alcohol exhaled in the breath is in direct proportion to what?

10. From the medicolegal point of view, what is the accepted standard for relating alcohol intake to its effect on the body?

11. For a longer total time required for complete absorption, will the peak blood-alcohol concentration be higher or lower?

12. List and describe the functions of the three types of blood vessels in the circulatory system.

13. Through the walls of which organ is most alcohol absorbed into the bloodstream? In what other organ does the remainder of absorption occur?

14. When the blood enters the lung region from the heart, what are the relative levels of oxygen and carbon dioxide?

15. What are alveoli and what role do they play in circulation?

16. What is the most widespread method for rapidly determining alcohol intoxication?

17. What scientific observation forms the theoretical basis for breath testing?

18. Briefly describe how a fuel cell detector measures blood-alcohol concentration.

19. What is the key to the accuracy of a breath test? How is this typically accomplished?

20. What is a slope detector and how does it work?

21. What is mouth alcohol and how does it affect the accuracy of a breath test? Name three potential sources of mouth alcohol.

22. What is a field sobriety test? What two general types of test are included in a field sobriety test?

23. Name and describe two divided-attention tasks administered during a field sobriety text.

24. What analytical technique is the most widely used approach for determining alcohol levels in blood?

25. What type of disinfectant must be applied to a subject's skin before drawing blood? Why must such a disinfectant be applied?

26. What type of container best ensures the preservation of blood samples?

27. What two substances should be added to a blood sample after collection and why?

28. How do each of the following factors affect alcohol's stability in blood: storage temperature, the presence of a preservative, and the time of storage?

29. When collecting postmortem blood samples for alcohol determination, why is it best to collect a number of blood samples from different body sites?

30. What blood-alcohol concentration is the current legal measure of drunk driving in the United States, as established by the National Highway Traffic Safety Administration?

31. What is a per se law?

32. What is an implied-consent law? Why were such laws implemented?

33. Describe two challenges toxicologists face in detecting drugs and determining their toxicity.

34. What bodily fluids should be collected from any suspected drug user?

35. What three drugs account for 90 percent or more of the drugs encountered in a typical toxicology laboratory?

36. What is the first task of a forensic toxicologist when establishing an analytical scheme to detect and identify drugs?

37. What are acids and bases? How are they used to extract and categorize drugs?

38. What is the difference between a screening test and a confirmation test?

39. What are the three screening tests most widely used by forensic toxicologists? What is the confirmation test of choice?

40. Which of the following is not classified as a heavy metal?
    a. lead
    b. arsenic
    c. mercury
    d. thallium

41. Explain how inhaling carbon monoxide can cause death.

42. Name at least three factors in addition to blood concentration levels that must be considered before drawing conclusions about a subject's drug-induced behavior.

43. Why is the concentration of a drug present in urine a poor indicator of how extensively an individual's behavior or state is influenced by the drug?

Application and Critical Thinking

1. Answer the following questions about driving risk associated with drinking and blood alcohol concentration:
    a. Randy is just barely legally intoxicated. How much more likely is he to have an accident than someone who is sober?
    b. Marissa, who has been drinking, is fifteen times as likely to have an accident as her sober friend, Christine. What is Marissa's approximate blood-alcohol concentration?

c. After several drinks, Charles is ten times as likely to have an accident as a sober person. Is he more or less intoxicated than James, whose blood alcohol level is 0.10?

d. Under the original blood-alcohol standards recommended by NHTSA, a person considered just barely legally intoxicated was how much more likely to have an accident than a sober individual?

2. Following is a description of four individuals who have been drinking. Rank them from highest to lowest blood-alcohol concentration:

a. John, who weighs 200 pounds and has consumed eight 8-ounce drinks on a full stomach

b. Frank, who weighs 170 pounds and has consumed four 8-ounce drinks on an empty stomach

c. Gary, who weighs 240 pounds and has consumed six 8-ounce drinks on an empty stomach

d. Stephen, who weighs 180 pounds and has consumed six 8-ounce drinks on a full stomach

3. Following is a description of four individuals who have been drinking. In which (if any) of the following countries would each be considered legally drunk: the United States, Australia, Sweden?

a. Bill, who weighs 150 pounds and has consumed three 8-ounce drinks on an empty stomach

b. Sally, who weighs 110 pounds and has consumed three 8-ounce drinks on a full stomach

c. Rich, who weighs 200 pounds and has consumed six 8-ounce drinks on an empty stomach

d. Carrie, who weighs 140 pounds and has consumed four 8-ounce drinks on a full stomach

4. You are a forensic scientist who has been asked to test two blood samples. You know that one sample is suspected of containing barbiturates and the other contains no drugs; however, you cannot tell the two samples apart. Describe how you would use the concept of pH to determine which sample contains barbiturates. Explain your reasoning.

5. You are investigating an arson scene and you find a corpse in the rubble, but you suspect that the victim did not die as a result of the fire. Instead, you suspect that the victim was murdered earlier, and that the blaze was started to cover up the murder. How would you go about determining whether the victim died before the fire?

Web Resources

About Alcohol (Describes the absorption, excretion, metabolism and circulation of alcohol in the body)
www.intox.com/about_alcohol.asp

Alcohol Metabolism Effects (Describes the chemical breakdown of alcohol and the effects of the by-products of alcohol consumption)
www.elmhurst.edu/~chm/vchembook/642alcoholmet.html

Couper, F. J., and B. K. Logan, *Drugs and Human Performance*. Washington, D.C.: National Highway Traffic Safety Administration, 2004
www.nhtsa.dot.gov/people/injury/research/job185drugs/technical-page.htm

Forensic Toxicology—A Review
faculty.ncwc.edu/toconnor/425/425lect14.htm

Forensic Toxicology Slide Show
www.stfrancis.edu/ns/diab/Forensic1/Toxicology1_files/frame.htm

How Breathalyzers Work (Layperson's guide to understanding how Breathalyzers
detect alcohol levels)
www.howstuffworks.com/breathalyzer.htm

Impaired Driving Factsheet (Statistics compiled by the National Center for Injury
Prevention and Control)
www.cdc.gov/ncipc/factsheets/drving.htm

Endnotes

1. In the United States, laws that define blood-alcohol levels almost exclusively use
   the unit *percent weight per volume*—% w/v. Hence, 0.015 percent w/v is
   equivalent to 0.015 grams of alcohol per 100 milliliters of blood, or 15 milligrams
   of alcohol per 100 milliliters.

2. R. B. Forney et al., "Alcohol Distribution in the Vascular System: Concentrations
   of Orally Administered Alcohol in Blood from Various Points in the Vascular
   System and in Rebreathed Air during Absorption," *Quarterly Journal of Studies
   on Alcohol* 25 (1964): 205.

3. G. A. Brown et al., "The Stability of Ethanol in Stored Blood," *Analytica Chemica
   Acta* 66 (1973): 271.

4. 0.15 percent w/v is equivalent to 0.15 grams of alcohol per 100 milliliters of blood,
   or 150 milligrams per 100 milliliters.

5. 384 U.S. 757 (1966).

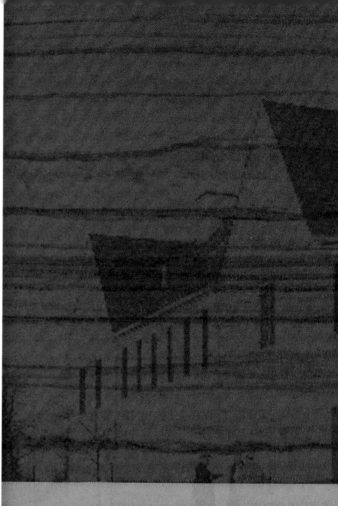

The Lindbergh Baby Case

On the evening of March 1, 1932, a kidnapper crept up his homemade ladder and stole the baby of Charles and Anne Lindbergh directly from the second-floor nursery of their house in Hopewell, New Jersey. The only evidence of his coming was a ransom note, the ladder, a chisel, and the tragic absence of the infant.
A couple of months later, although the $50,000 ransom had been paid, the baby turned up dead in the woods a mile away. There was no additional sign of the killer. Fortunately, when finally studied by wood technologist Arthur Koehler, the abandoned ladder yielded some important investigative clues (see Case Reading on page 258).

By studying the types of wood used and the cutter marks on the wood,

Koehler ascertained where the materials might have come from and what specific equipment was used to create them. Koehler traced the wood from a South Carolina mill to a lumberyard in the Bronx, New York. Unfortunately the trail went cold, as the lumberyard did not keep sales records of purchases. The break in the case came in 1934, when Bruno Richard Hauptmann paid for gasoline with a bill that matched a serial number on the ransom money. Koehler showed that microscopic markings on the wood were made by a tool in Hauptmann's possession. Ultimately, handwriting analysis of the ransom note clearly showed it to be written by Hauptmann.

The Microscope

Learning Objectives

After studying this chapter you should be able to:

- List and understand the parts of the compound microscope

- Define *magnification, field of view, working distance,* and *depth of focus*

- Contrast the comparison and compound microscopes

- Understand the theory and utility of the stereoscopic microscope

- Appreciate how a polarizing microscope is designed to characterize polarized light

- Appreciate how a microspectrophotometer can be used to examine trace physical evidence

- Compare and contrast the image formation mechanism of a light microscope to that of a scanning electron microscope

- Outline some forensic applications of the scanning electron microscope

A microscope is an optical instrument that uses a lens or a combination of lenses to magnify and resolve the fine details of an object. The earliest methods for examining physical evidence in crime laboratories relied almost solely on the microscope to study the structure and composition of matter. Even the advent of modern analytical instrumentation and techniques has done little to diminish the usefulness of the microscope for forensic analysis. If anything, the development of the powerful scanning electron microscope promises to add a new dimension to forensic science heretofore unattainable within the limits of the ordinary light microscope.

Basics of the Microscope

virtual image
An image that cannot be seen directly, but can be seen only by a viewer looking through a lens.

real image
An image that can be seen directly with the naked eye.

The earliest and simplest microscope was the single lens commonly referred to as a *magnifying glass*. The handheld magnifying glass makes things appear larger than they are because of the way light rays are refracted, or bent, in passing from the air into the glass and back into the air. The magnified image is observed by looking through the lens, as shown in Figure 7–1. Such an image is known as a virtual image; it can be seen only by looking through a lens and cannot be viewed directly. This is distinguished from a real image, which can be seen directly, like the image that is projected onto a motion picture screen.

FIGURE 7–1   The passage of light through a lens, showing how magnification is obtained.

The ordinary magnifying glass can achieve a magnification of about 5 to 10 times. Higher magnifying power is obtainable only with a *compound microscope,* constructed of two lenses mounted at each end of a hollow tube. The object to be magnified is placed under the lower lens, called the objective lens, and the magnified image is viewed through the upper lens, known as the eyepiece lens. As shown in Figure 7–2, the objective lens forms a real, inverted, magnified image of the object. The eyepiece, acting just like a simple magnifying glass, further magnifies this image into a virtual image, which is seen by the eye. The combined magnifying power of both lenses can produce an image magnified up to 1,500 times.

The optical principles of the compound microscope are incorporated into the basic design of different types of light microscopes. The microscopes most applicable for examining forensic specimens are as follows:

- the compound microscope
- the comparison microscope
- the stereoscopic microscope
- the polarizing microscope
- the microspectrophotometer

After describing these five microscopes, we will talk about a completely different approach to microscopy, the scanning electron microscope (SEM). This instrument focuses a beam of electrons, instead of visible light, onto the specimen to produce a magnified image. The principle and design of this microscope permit magnifying powers as high as 100,000 times.

objective lens
The lower lens of a compound microscope; it is positioned directly over the specimen.

eyepiece lens
The upper lens of a compound microscope, into which the viewer looks.

FIGURE 7–2 The principle of the compound microscope. The passage of light through two lenses forms the virtual image of the object seen by the eye.

Key Points

- A microscope is an optical instrument that uses a lens or a combination of lenses to magnify and resolve the fine details of an object.

- Two types of images are virtual images and real images. A real image can be seen directly with the naked eye; a virtual image can be seen only by a viewer looking through a lens.

- The eyepiece lens is the upper lens through which the viewer looks. The objective lens is the lower lens that is positioned directly over the specimen.

The Compound Microscope

The parts of the compound microscope are illustrated in Figure 7–3. Basically, this microscope consists of a mechanical system, which supports the microscope, and an optical system. The optical system illuminates the object under investigation and passes the light through a series of lenses to form an image of the specimen on the retina of the eye. The optical path of light through a compound microscope is shown in Figure 7–4.

FIGURE 7–3 **Parts of the compound microscope: (1) base, (2) arm, (3) stage, (4) body tube, (5) coarse adjust, (6) fine adjust, (7) illuminator, (8) condenser, (9) objective lens, and (10) eyepiece lens.** *Courtesy Leica Microsystems, Buffalo, N.Y., www.leica-microsystems.com*

FIGURE 7–4 **Optics of the compound microscope.** *Courtesy Leica Microsystems, Buffalo, N.Y., www.leica-microsystems.com*

Construction of the Compound Microscope

The mechanical system of the compound microscope is composed of six parts:

Base. The support on which the instrument rests.

Arm. A C-shaped upright structure, hinged to the base, that supports the microscope and acts as a handle for carrying.

Stage. The horizontal plate on which the specimens are placed for study. The specimens are normally mounted on glass slides that are held firmly in place on the stage by spring clips.

Body tube. A cylindrical hollow tube on which the objective and eyepiece lenses are mounted at opposite ends. This tube is merely a corridor through which light passes from one lens to another.

Coarse adjustment. This knob focuses the microscope lenses on the specimen by raising and lowering the body tube.

Fine adjustment. The movements effected by this knob are similar to those of the coarse adjustment but are of a much smaller magnitude.

The optical system is made up of four parts:

Illuminator. Most modern microscopes use artificial light supplied by a lightbulb to illuminate the specimen being examined. If the specimen is transparent, the light is directed up toward and through the specimen stage from an illuminator built into the base of the microscope. This is known as transmitted illumination. When the object is opaque—that is,

transmitted illumination
Light that passes up from the condenser and through the specimen; it is used to examine transparent specimens.

vertical or reflected illumination
Illumination of a specimen from above; it is used to examine opaque specimens.

condenser
The lens system under the microscope stage that collects light rays from the base illuminator and focuses them onto the specimen.

parfocal
Describes a microscope such that when an image is focused with one objective in position, the other objective can be rotated into place and the field will remain in focus.

monocular
Describes a microscope with one eyepiece.

binocular
Describes a microscope with two eyepieces.

WebExtra 7.1
Explore the Concept of Magnification with a Compound Microscope
www.prenhall.com/hsforensics

WebExtra 7.2
Scan a Sample under the Compound Microscope
www.prenhall.com/hsforensics

WebExtra 7.3
Observe the Concept of Depth of Focus
www.prenhall.com/hsforensics

field of view
The area of the specimen that can be seen after it is magnified.

depth of focus
The thickness of a specimen that is entirely in focus under a microscope.

not transparent—the light source must be placed above the specimen so that it can reflect off the specimen's surface and into the lens system of the microscope. This type of illumination is known as vertical or reflected illumination.

Condenser. The condenser is a lens system under the microscope stage that collects light rays from the base illuminator and focuses them on the specimen. The simplest condenser is known as the *Abbé condenser*. It consists of two lenses held together in a metal mount. The condenser also includes an iris diaphragm that can be opened or closed to control the amount of light passing into the condenser.

Objective lens. This is the lens positioned closest to the specimen. To facilitate changing from one objective lens to another, several objectives are mounted on a revolving nosepiece or turret located above the specimen. Most microscopes are parfocal, meaning that when the microscope is focused with one objective in position, the other objective can be rotated into place by revolving the nosepiece while the specimen remains very nearly in correct focus.

Eyepiece or ocular lens. This is the lens closest to the eye. A microscope with only one eyepiece is monocular; one constructed with two eyepieces (one for each eye) is binocular.

Magnification and Resolution

Each microscope lens is inscribed with a number signifying its magnifying power. The image viewed by the microscopist will have a total magnification equal to the product of the magnifying power of the objective and eyepiece lenses. For example, an eyepiece lens with a magnification of 10 times ($10\times$) used in combination with an objective lens of 10 times has a total magnification power of 100 times ($100\times$). Most forensic work requires a $10\times$ eyepiece in combination with either a $4\times$, $10\times$, $20\times$, or $45\times$ objective. The respective magnifications will be $40\times$, $100\times$, $200\times$, and $450\times$.

In addition, each objective lens is inscribed with its numerical aperture (N.A.). The ability of an objective lens to resolve details into separate images instead of one blurred image is directly proportional to the numerical aperture value of the objective lens. For example, an objective lens of N.A. 1.30 can separate details at half the distance of a lens with an N.A. of 0.65. The maximum useful magnification of a compound microscope is approximately 1,000 times the N.A. of the objective being used. This magnification is sufficient to permit the eye to see all the detail that can be resolved. Any effort to increase the total magnification beyond this figure will yield no additional detail and is referred to as *empty magnification*.

Although a new student of the microscope may be tempted to immediately choose the highest magnifying power available to view a specimen, the experienced microscopist weighs a number of important factors before choosing a magnifying power. A first consideration must be the size of the specimen area, or the field of view, that the examiner wishes to study. As magnifying power increases, the field of view decreases. Thus, it is best to first select a low magnification in which a good general overall view of the specimen is seen and to switch later to a higher power in which a smaller portion of the specimen can be viewed in more detail.

The depth of focus is also a function of magnifying power. After a focus has been achieved on a specimen, the depth of focus defines the thickness of that specimen. Areas above and below this region will be blurred and can be viewed only when the focus is readjusted. Depth of focus decreases as magnifying power increases.

Key Points

- Transparent illumination is light directed up toward and through a specimen from an illuminator built into the base of the microscope. It is used to view transparent specimens. Vertical or reflected illumination is light from a source above the specimen that reflects off the specimen's surface and into the lens system of the microscope. It is used to view opaque specimens.

- A condenser is a lens system under the microscope stage that collects light rays from the base illuminator and focuses them on the specimen.

- A monocular microscope has one eyepiece; a binocular microscope has two eyepieces.

- One determines the total magnification of a compound microscope by multiplying the magnifying power of the eyepiece lens by the magnifying power of the objective lens.

- When you increase a compound microscope's magnification, its field of view and depth of focus decrease.

The Comparison Microscope

Forensic microscopy often requires a side-by-side comparison of specimens. This kind of examination can best be performed with a comparison microscope, such as the one pictured in Figure 7–5.

Basically, the comparison microscope is two compound microscopes combined into one unit. The unique feature of its design is that it uses a bridge incorporating a series of mirrors and lenses to join two independent objective lenses into a single binocular unit. A viewer looking through the eyepiece lenses of the comparison microscope observes a circular field, equally divided into two parts by a fine line. The specimen mounted under the left-hand objective appears in the left half of the field, and the specimen under the right-hand objective appears in the right half of the field. It is important to closely match the optical characteristics of the objective lenses to ensure that both specimens are seen at equal magnification and with minimal but identical lens distortions. Comparison microscopes designed to compare opaque objects, such as bullets and cartridges, are equipped with vertical or reflected illumination. Comparison microscopes used to compare hairs or fibers use transmitted illumination.

Figure 7–6 shows the striation markings on two bullets that have been placed under the objective lenses of a comparison microscope. Modern firearms examination began with the introduction of the comparison microscope, with its ability to give the firearms examiner a side-by-side magnified view of bullets. Bullets that are fired through the same rifle barrel display comparable rifling markings on their surfaces. Matching the majority of striations present on each bullet justifies a conclusion that both bullets traveled through the same barrel.

WebExtra 7.4
Practice Matching Bullets with the Aid of a 3D Interactive Illustration
www.prenhall.com/hsforensics

FIGURE 7–6 Photomicrograph taken through a comparison microscope. On the right are the striation markings on the test-fired bullet, fired through the suspect weapon. On the left are the markings of the crime-scene bullet. *Courtesy Getty Images Inc.—Hulton Archive*

Key Points

- The comparison microscope consists of two independent objective lenses joined by an optical bridge to a common eyepiece lens. A viewer looking through the eyepiece lens observes the objects under investigation side-by-side in a circular field that is equally divided into two parts.

- Modern firearms examination began with the introduction of the comparison microscope, which gives the examiner a side-by-side magnified view of bullets.

The Stereoscopic Microscope

The details that characterize the structures of many types of physical evidence do not always require examination under very high magnifications. For such specimens, the stereoscopic microscope has proven quite adequate, providing magnifying powers from 10× to 125×. This microscope has the advantage of presenting a distinctive three-dimensional image of an object. Also, whereas the image formed by the compound microscope is inverted and reversed (upside-down and backward), the stereoscopic microscope is more convenient because prisms in its light path create a right-side-up image.

The stereoscopic microscope, shown in Figure 7–7, is actually two monocular compound microscopes properly spaced and aligned to present

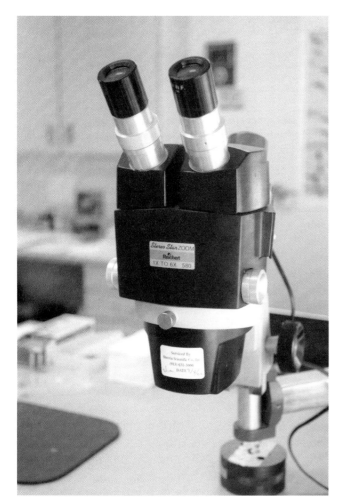

FIGURE 7–7 A stereoscopic microscope. *Courtesy Mikael Karlsson, Arresting Images*

FIGURE 7–8 Schematic diagram of a stereoscopic microscope. This microscope is actually two separate monocular microscopes, each with its own set of lenses except for the lowest objective lens, which is common to both microscopes.

a three-dimensional image of a specimen to the viewer, who looks through both eyepiece lenses. The light path of a stereoscopic microscope is shown in Figure 7–8.

The stereoscopic microscope is undoubtedly the most frequently used and versatile microscope found in the crime laboratory. Its wide field of view and great depth of focus make it an ideal instrument for locating trace evidence in debris, garments, weapons, and tools. Furthermore, its potentially large *working distance* (the distance between the objective lens and the specimen) makes it ideal for microscopic examination of big, bulky items. When fitted with vertical illumination, the stereoscopic microscope becomes the primary tool for characterizing physical evidence as diverse as paint, soil, gunpowder residues, and marijuana.

WebExtra 7.5
Explore the Stereoscopic Microscope
www.prenhall.com/hsforensics

Key Points

- The stereoscopic microscope consists of two monocular compound microscopes properly spaced and aligned to present a three-dimensional image of a specimen to the viewer, who looks through both eyepiece lenses.

- The large working distance of the stereoscopic microscope makes it ideal for microscopic examination of big, bulky items.

The Polarizing Microscope

Recall from Chapter 5 that light's wavelike motion in space can be invoked to explain many facets of its behavior. The waves that compose a beam of light can be pictured as vibrating in all directions perpendicular to the direction in which the light is traveling. However, when a beam of light passes through certain types of specially fabricated crystalline substances, it emerges vibrating in only one plane. Light that is confined to a single plane of vibration is said to be plane-polarized. The device that polarizes light in this manner is called a polarizer. A common example of this phenomenon is the passage of sunlight through polarized sunglasses. By transmitting light vibrating in the vertical plane only, these sunglasses eliminate or reduce light glare. Most glare consists of partially polarized light that has been reflected off horizontal surfaces and thus is vibrating in a horizontal plane.

Because polarized light appears no different to the eye from ordinary light, special means must be devised for detecting it. This is accomplished simply by placing a second polarizing crystal, called an *analyzer*, in the path of the polarized beam. As shown in Figure 7–9, if the polarizer and analyzer are aligned parallel to each other, the polarized light passes through and is seen by the eye. If, on the other hand, the polarizer and analyzer are set perpendicular to one another, or are "crossed," no light penetrates, and the result is total darkness or *extinction*.

In this manner, a compound or stereoscopic microscope can be outfitted with a polarizer and analyzer to allow the viewer to detect polarized light. Such a microscope is known as a *polarizing microscope*. Essentially, the polarizer is placed between the light source and the sample stage to polarize the light before it passes through the specimen. The polarized light penetrating the specimen must then pass through an analyzer before it reaches the eyepiece and finally the eye. Normally the polarizer and analyzer are "crossed" so that when no specimen is in place, the field appears dark. However, introducing a specimen that polarizes light reorients the polarized light, allowing it to pass through the analyzer. This result produces vivid colors and intensity contrasts that make the specimen readily distinguishable.

The most obvious and important applications of this microscope relate to studying materials that polarize light. For example, as we learned in

plane-polarized light
Light confined to a single plane of vibration.

polarizer
A device that permits the passage of light waves vibrating in only one plane.

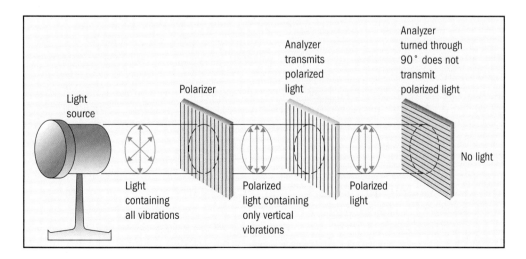

FIGURE 7–9   Polarization of light.

Chapter 4, many crystalline substances are birefringent; that is, they split a beam of light into two light-ray components of different refractive index values. What makes this observation particularly relevant to our discussion of the polarizing microscope is that the light beams are polarized at right angles to each other. Thus, polarizing microscopy has found wide application for the examination of birefringent minerals present in soil.

By using the immersion method and selecting the proper immersion liquids, a refractive index corresponding to each plane of polarized light can be determined. Thus, when a mineral is viewed under polarized light in a liquid that matches one of its refractive indices, the Becke line will no longer be visible. This information, plus observations on crystal color, form, and so on, makes it possible for the microscopist to identify the mineral. Similarly, criminalists use the fact that many synthetic fibers are birefringent to characterize them with a polarizing microscope.

Key Points

- Light that is confined to a single plane of vibration is said to be plane-polarized.

- The polarizing microscope made possible the examination of the interaction of plane-polarized light with matter.

- Polarizing microscopy is used to study birefringent materials, that is, materials that have a double refraction. Refractive index data provide information that helps identify minerals present in a soil sample or the identity of a synthetic fiber.

The Microspectrophotometer

Few instruments in a crime laboratory can match the versatility of the microscope. The microscope's magnifying power is indispensable for finding minute traces of physical evidence. Many items of physical evidence can be characterized by a microscopic examination of their morphological features. Likewise, the microscope can be used to study how light interacts with the material under investigation, or it can be used to observe the effects that other chemical substances have on such evidence. Each of these features allows an examiner to better characterize and identify physical evidence. Recently, linking the microscope to a computerized spectrophotometer has added a new dimension to its capability. This combination has given rise to a new instrument called the microspectrophotometer. In many respects, this is an ideal marriage from the forensic scientist's viewpoint.

In Chapter 5, we saw how a chemist can use selective absorption of light by materials to characterize them. In particular, light in the ultraviolet, visible, and infrared regions of the electromagnetic spectrum is most helpful for this purpose. Unfortunately, in the past, forensic chemists were unable to take full advantage of the capabilities of spectrophotometry for examining trace evidence, because most spectrophotometers are not well suited for examining the very small particles frequently encountered as evidence.

With the development of the microspectrophotometer, a forensic analyst can view a particle under a microscope while a beam of light is directed at the particle to obtain its absorption spectrum. Depending on the

WebExtra 7.6

Explore the Polarizing Microscope—I
www.prenhall.com/hsforensics

WebExtra 7.7

Explore the Polarizing Microscope—II
www.prenhall.com/hsforensics

microspectrophotometer
An instrument that links a microscope to a spectrophotometer.

FIGURE 7–10   A visible-light microspectrophotometer. *Courtesy Craig Technologies Inc., Altadena, Calif., www.microspectra.com*

type of light employed, an examiner can acquire either a visible or an IR spectral pattern of the substance being viewed under the microscope. The obvious advantage of this approach is to provide added information to characterize trace quantities of evidence. A microspectrophotometer designed to measure the uptake of visible light by materials is shown in Figure 7–10.

Visual comparison of color is usually one of the first steps in examining paint, fiber, and ink evidence. Such comparisons are easily obtained using a comparison microscope. A forensic scientist can use the microspectrophotometer to compare the color of materials visually while plotting an absorption spectrum for each item under examination. This displays the exact wavelengths at which each item absorbs in the visible-light spectrum. Occasionally colors that appear similar by visual examination show significant differences in their absorption spectra. An example of this approach is shown in Figure 7–11, in which the microspectrophotometer is used to distinguish counterfeit and authentic currency by comparing the spectral patterns of inked lines on the paper.

Another emerging technique in forensic science is the use of the infrared microspectrophotometer to examine fibers and paints. The "fingerprint" IR spectrum (see p. 185) is unique for each chemical substance. Therefore, obtaining such a spectrum from either a fiber or a paint chip allows the analyst to better identify and compare the type of chemicals from which these materials are manufactured. With a microspectrophotometer, a forensic analyst can view a substance through the microscope and at the same time have the instrument plot the infrared absorption spectrum for that material.

FIGURE 7–11 Two $50 bills are shown at top; one is genuine and the other is counterfeit. Below each bill is a microphotograph of an inked line present on each bill. Each line was examined under a visible-light microspectrophotometer. As shown, the visible absorption spectrum of each line is readily differentiated, thus allowing the examiner to distinguish a counterfeit bill from genuine currency. *Courtesy Peter W. Pfefferli, forensic scientist, Lausanne, Switzerland*

- The microspectrophotometer is a spectrophotometer coupled with a light microscope. The device allows an examiner studying a specimen under the microscope to obtain the visible-light or IR spectrum of the material.

The Scanning Electron Microscope (SEM)

All the microscopes described thus far use light coming off the specimen to produce a magnified image. The scanning electron microscope is, however, a special case in the family of microscopes (see Figure 7–12). The image is formed by aiming a beam of electrons onto the specimen and studying electron emissions on a closed TV circuit.

In the SEM, a hot tungsten filament emits a beam of electrons, which is focused by electromagnets onto the surface of the specimen. This primary electron beam causes the elements that make up the upper layers of the specimen to emit electrons known as secondary electrons. About 20 to 30 percent of the primary electrons rebound off the surface of the specimen. These electrons are known as *backscattered electrons*. The emitted electrons (both secondary and backscattered) are collected and the amplified signal is displayed on a cathode-ray or TV tube. By scanning the primary

FIGURE 7–12 **A scanning electron microscope.** *Courtesy Jeol USA Inc., Peabody, Mass., www.jeolusa.com*

FIGURE 7–13 **The cystolithic hairs of the marijuana leaf, as viewed with a scanning electron microscope (800×).** *Courtesy Jeff Albright*

electron beam across the specimen's surface in synchronization with the cathode-ray tube, the SEM converts the emitted electrons into an image of the specimen for display on the cathode-ray tube.

The major attractions of the SEM image are its high magnification, high resolution, and great depth of focus. In its usual mode, the SEM has a magnification that ranges from 10× to 100,000×. Its depth of focus is some 300 times better than optical systems at similar magnifications, and the resultant picture is almost stereoscopic in appearance. Its great depth of field and magnification are exemplified by the magnification of cystolithic hair on the marijuana leaf, as shown in Figure 7–13. An SEM image of a vehicle's headlight filaments may reveal whether the headlights were on or off at the time of a collision (see Figures 7–14 and 7–15).

Another facet of scanning electron microscopy has been the use of X-ray production to determine the elemental composition of a specimen. X-rays are generated when the electron beam of the scanning electron microscope strikes a target. When the SEM is coupled to an X-ray analyzer, the emitted X-rays can be sorted according to their energy values and used to build a picture of the elemental distribution in the specimen. Because each element emits X-rays of characteristic energy values, the X-ray analyzer can identify the elements present in a specimen. Furthermore, the element's concentration can be determined by measuring the intensity of the X-ray emission.

One application of scanning electron microscopy has been to determine whether a suspect has recently fired a gun. In this case, an attempt is made to remove any gunshot particles that remain on a shooter's hands

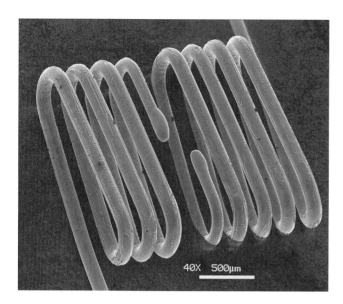

FIGURE 7–14 **The melted ends of a hot filament break indicate that the headlights were on when an accident occurred.** *Courtesy Jeol USA Inc., Peabody, Mass., www.jeolusa.com*

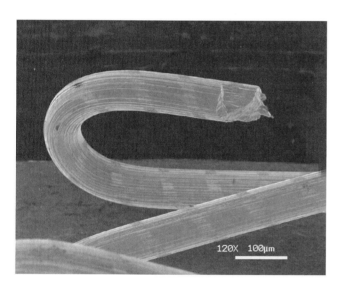

FIGURE 7–15 **The sharp ends of a cold filament break indicate that the headlights were off when an accident occurred.** *Courtesy Jeol USA Inc., Peabody, Mass., www.jeolusa.com*

by lifting them off with a piece of adhesive tape. The tape is then examined under the SEM for the presence of particles that may have originated from the bullet primer. These particles can be characterized by their size, shape, and elemental composition. As shown in Figure 7–16, when the sample of gunshot residue is exposed to a beam of electrons from the scanning electron microscope, X-rays are emitted. These X-rays are passed into a detector, where they are converted into electrical signals. These signals are sorted and displayed according to the energies of the emitted X-rays. Through the use of this technique, the elements lead, antimony, and barium, frequently found in most primers, can be rapidly detected and identified.

WebExtra 7.8
Explore the Scanning Electron Microscope
www.prenhall.com/hsforensics

Key Points

- The scanning electron microscope (SEM) bombards a specimen with a beam of electrons instead of light to produce a highly magnified image. This produces X-ray emissions that can be used to characterize elements present in the material.

FIGURE 7–16 **A schematic diagram of a scanning electron microscope displaying the image of a gunshot residue particle. Simultaneously, an X-ray analyzer detects and displays X-ray emissions from the elements lead (Pb), antimony (Sb), and barium (Ba) present in the particle.** *Courtesy Aerospace Corp., El Segundo, Calif.*

Chapter Summary

A microscope is an optical instrument that uses a lens or a combination of lenses to magnify and resolve the fine details of an object. Various types of microscopes are used to analyze forensic specimens. In the basic compound microscope, the object to be magnified is placed under the lower lens, called the objective lens, and the magnified image is viewed through the upper lens, known as the eyepiece lens.

Forensic microscopy often requires side-by-side comparison of specimens. The comparison microscope consists of two independent objective lenses joined by an optical bridge to a common eyepiece lens. A viewer looking through the eyepiece lens of the comparison microscope observes the objects under investigation side-by-side in a circular field that is equally divided into two parts.

Modern firearms examination began with the introduction of the comparison microscope, with its ability to give the firearms examiner a side-by-side magnified view of bullets. The stereoscopic microscope is actually two monocular compound microscopes properly spaced and aligned to present a three-dimensional image of a specimen to the viewer, who looks through both eyepiece lenses. Its large working distance makes it ideal for microscopic examination of big, bulky items.

Light that is confined to a single plane of vibration is said to be plane-polarized. The examination of the interaction of plane-polarized light with matter is made possible with the polarizing microscope. Polarizing microscopy has found wide applications for the study of birefringent materials, that is, materials that have a double refraction. These refractive index data help identify minerals present in a soil sample or the identity of a synthetic fiber.

The microspectrophotometer is a spectrophotometer coupled with a light microscope. The examiner studying a specimen under a microscope can simultaneously obtain the visible-light or IR spectrum of the material.

The scanning electron microscope (SEM) bombards a specimen with a beam of electrons instead of light to produce a highly magnified image from 10× to 100,000×. The bombardment of the specimen's surface with electrons normally produces X-ray emissions that can be used to characterize elements present in the material.

Review Questions

Facts and Concepts

1. Name two types of images and explain the difference between them.

2. List and define the two types of lenses in an ordinary microscope.

3. Name two types of illumination and explain the difference between them. What types of specimens are viewed under each type of illumination?

4. What is a condenser? Name and describe the simplest type of condenser.

5. Define *parfocal*.

6. What is the difference between a monocular and a binocular microscope?

7. How does one determine the total magnification of a compound microsope?

8. What does numerical aperture describe?

9. What is the maximum useful magnification for a compound microscope? Why?

10. What happens to a compound microscope's field of view field when you increase its magnification? How does this affect the way a microscopist views specimens under a compound microscope?

11. What is a comparison microscope? How is the image viewed through a comparison microscope different from one viewed through an ordinary or compound microscope?

12. When using a comparison microscope, why is it important to closely match the optical characteristics of the objective lenses?

13. What is the most frequently used and versatile microscope found in the crime laboratory? List three reasons why this type of microscope is so widely used.

14. What is plane-polarized light?

15. Name two types of physical evidence that are often characterized using a polarizing microscope.

16. What is a microspectrophotometer? What advantage does it enjoy over the spectrophotometer for analyzing physical evidence?

17. Briefly explain how a scanning electron microscope (SEM) produces an image.

18. What are the three major attractions of the SEM?

19. What device can be coupled to an SEM to produce a picture of the elemental distribution of a specimen? Briefly describe how this combination of devices can be used to determine whether a suspect has recently fired a gun.

Application and Critical Thinking

1. A compound microscope has eyepiece lenses of 10×, 15×, and 20× magnification and objective lenses with 4×, 10×, 25×, 50×, and 100× magnifications. Determine the total magnification power of every possible combination of lenses. Which combinations of lenses would a forensic scientist be unlikely to use and why?

2. What type of microscope would a forensic scientist most likely use in each of the following situations? Explain your answers.
   a. examining two bullets to see if they were fired by the same gun
   b. determining the chemical composition of paint chips
   c. identifying birefringent minerals present in soil
   d. examining a large specimen, such as a tool or piece of clothing
   e. examining extremely tiny specimens that require very high magnification

Case Analysis

In the 1930s, the Lindbergh kidnapping case became the latest "trial of the century," marked by sensationalism and continuous media coverage. The key piece of evidence was a homemade ladder left at the scene by the kidnapper. Forensic investigation of the ladder by Arthur Koehler, a wood technologist with the U.S. Forest Products Laboratory, eventually tied the accused kidnapper, Bruno Hauptmann, to the ladder and helped secure his conviction for the crime.

1. What aspects of the ladder rail did Koehler note that helped him determine the source of the wood used to make it? How did Koehler interpret each of these pieces of information to arrive at his conclusions?

2. How did Koehler determine that a belt-driven planer had been used to finish the wood? How did this information help pinpoint the location where the wood was purchased?

3. The wood used to make the rails was very common and used widely throughout the United States. Why did Koehler believe it was milled in the same general area where the kidnapping occurred? How did this information help the investigation?

4. What additional discoveries allowed Koehler to link the wood used in the ladder to Bruno Hauptmann?

Web Resources

Basic Concepts in Optical Microscopy
micro.magnet.fsu.edu/primer/anatomy/anatomy.html

Microscope Lab (Extensive lists of links to many different topics in microscopy)
microscopelab.com/microscope/

Microscopes at Nobelprize.org (A discussion of different types of microscopes and their uses; includes simulation of a scanning electron microscope)
nobelprize.org/physics/educational/microscopes/1.html

Scanning Electron Microscope (Explanation of the workings of an SEM, with a link to images produced by SEMs)
www.unl.edu/CMRAcfem/semoptic.htm

Types of Microscopes (Side-by-side comparison of types of microscopes, with links to additional information and images)
www.cas.muohio.edu/~mbi-ws/microscopes/types.html

Case Reading

Microscopic Trace Evidence: The Overlooked Clue
Arthur Koehler: Wood Detective

Skip Palenik
Walter C. McCrone Associates Inc.

. . . Arthur Koehler . . . wood technologist and chief of the division of silvicultural relations at the U.S. Forest Products Laboratory in Madison, Wisconsin, . . . was born on June 4, 1885, in Mishicot, Wisconsin. His father was a carpenter and young Koehler grew up on a farm with a love of both wood and fine tools. This love naturally led him into forestry and he received a B.S. degree in the subject from the University of Michigan in 1911. . . . Upon graduation he went to work for the U.S. Forest Service in Washington, D.C., and three years later obtained a post at the U.S. Forest Products Laboratory where he served in various capacities until his retirement.

Although his primary responsibilities lay in wood identification and the correlation of microscopic wood structure and end use, Koehler also began to build a reputation as a wood detective after his success in obtaining evidence from wood fragments which were submitted to the laboratory in several cases of local importance. . . . The case which thrust Koehler into the limelight of international publicity, however, was the Lindbergh kidnapping case in which he, by the most painstaking work, traced the kidnap ladder back to the lumberyard from which its constituent parts had been purchased.

Sometime between the hours of 8 and 10 p.m. on the night of March 1, 1932, a kidnapper climbed into the nursery of the newly completed home of Charles and Anne Lindbergh in Hopewell, New Jersey, and abducted their infant son. The only clues left behind were a few indistinct muddy footprints, a ransom note in the nursery, a homemade ladder and a chisel found a short distance from the house. Scarcely two months later, on May 12, the dead body of the child was found, half buried in the woods, about a mile from the Lindbergh home. One of the most intensive manhunts in U.S. history ensued, but failed to uncover any trace of the kidnapper or the ransom money which had been paid.[1]

Shortly after the news of the kidnapping broke in the press Koehler wrote a letter to Colonel Lindbergh offering his services to help with the investigation of the ladder. He never received a reply (which was not surprising considering the flood of mail which arrived at the Lindbergh home in the weeks following the kidnapping). He was not entirely surprised though when his boss, Carlyle P. Winslow, placed before him some slivers of the ladder with the request that the wood be accurately identified.[2] This Koehler did, noting in his report the presence of golden brown, white and black wool fibers which he speculated might be from clothing worn by the kidnapper. That was the last he heard about the ladder for almost a year. During this time it was carried around the country (carefully wrapped in a wool blanket) to various experts including specialists at the National Bureau of Standards.[3] However, after a year of investigation the authorities were no closer to arresting a suspect than they were the day after the crime.

It was almost a year after the kidnapping when Koehler was asked by the head of the U.S. Forest Service, Major Robert Y. Stuart, to travel to Trenton to give the ladder an in-depth examination. Discussions between Colonel Norman Schwarzkopf, who headed the New Jersey State Police (and the kidnap investigation), and Major Stuart had convinced Colonel Schwarzkopf that the ladder might still yield clues about its maker if Koehler were given a chance to examine it thoroughly. Schwarzkopf wasn't too certain about Koehler's ability ("Wasn't he the one who identified the blanket fibers on the wood we sent him?" he asked) but felt he had nothing to lose.

For the first time, Koehler saw the ladder (Figure 1). He was immediately struck by the fact that, although it was cleverly contrived, it was shamefully constructed. Instead of rungs it had cleats, which had been carelessly mortised with a dull chisel. A dull hand plane had been used needlessly in some places and a handsaw had been drawn carelessly across some of the boards.

Alone for four days, Koehler studied the ladder in the police training school in Wilburtha. He then returned to the Forest Products Laboratory with the ladder and closed himself up in a private laboratory with the best optical equipment available.[4] He began by completely dissecting the ladder into its component parts. Each piece was numbered. The cleats were labeled 1 (bottom) through 11 (top). The rails were numbered starting from 12 (bottom left) to 17 (right-hand top). . . . Each mark was noted and indexed. After probing with microscopes, calipers and a variety of lighting and photographic techniques, the ladder slowly began to give up its secrets.

The sheer number of observations, facts and deductions about the origin of the ladder (and its producer) made by Koehler are truly staggering. We are concerned here only with those facts and observations which (1) allowed the parts to be traced and (2) described the carpenter and the previous environment of the ladder. The results were presented not as the subject of a single report but of

FIGURE 1   The ladder used in the kidnapping of the Lindbergh baby.

daily letters to the director of the laboratory. As certain aspects were revealed they were pursued until the object could be traced no further. The most pertinent observations and deductions are listed and described below.

1. Microscopical examination showed four types of wood were used (Table 1). North Carolina pine is a trade name for wood from the southern yellow pine group which grows in commercial stands in the

Table 1	Woods Used in Kidnap Ladder
Cleats	
1–10	**Ponderosa pine** Thirteen 6-inch boards ripped lengthwise into strips 2¾ inches wide to make cleats.
11	**Douglas fir** Grain matched bottom of rail 15.
Side Rails	
12, 13	**North Carolina pine** Second growth. Cut from one board originally 14 feet long. Dressed to 3¾ inches in width. Both dressed on same planer.
14, 15	**Douglas fir** Dressed on two different planers.
16	**North Carolina pine** Narrowed from a wider board as indicated by handsaw and hand-planer marks on edges.
17	**Douglas fir** Dressed on different planers than 14 and 15.
Dowel Pins	
All	**Birch**

Southern U.S. along the Gulf of Mexico and along the Eastern Seaboard up into New Jersey and southern New York.[5] Douglas fir and ponderosa pine grow in the Western U.S. and birch is found throughout the country.[6]

2. Rails 12 and 13 showed faint marks which gave information about the planer in the mill where the wood was dressed. . . . Figure 2 shows the operation of a mill planer in diagrammatic form. Defects in the cutters allowed the number of knives in the cutters to be determined by counting cutter marks between defect marks. Eight cutter heads dressed the wide surface and six heads the edges. . . .

The lumber went through the planer at a rate of 0.93 inches per complete revolution of the top and bottom cutter heads and 0.86 inches per revolution of the cutter heads that dressed the edges. This was determined by the distance of identical cuts made by a defective knife on each surface. . . .[7] Using the

FIGURE 2   Detail of a cutter head illustrating how a defect allowed the number of knives to be determined.

fact that the cutters in mill planers are usually driven at 3600 revolutions per minute it was possible to calculate the speed at which the wood passed into the planer as 258 feet per minute for the edge and 279 feet per minute for the board surfaces. The difference in the speed of the horizontal and vertical heads indicated that the planer was belt driven.

3. Rail 16 had four nail holes made by old fashioned square cut 8-penny nails. The holes had no connection with the construction of the ladder and therefore indicated prior use. The nail holes were clean and free from rust indicating inside use. This was confirmed by the general appearance of the rail which, although sapwood, showed no sign of exposure to the weather for any length of time since it was bright and unchecked. Therefore, it must have been nailed down indoors. Since it was low-grade lumber it would not have been used for finish purposes, but for rough construction. The spacing of the nails at 16 and 32 inches was considered significant and the suggestion was made that the rail came from the interior of a barn, garage or attic.

After an initial, futile attempt to trace the birch dowels, Koehler set out to try and trace the North Carolina rails (numbers 12 and 13). Although North Carolina pine grew in a large region it would not be profitable to ship it far, and since the ladder had turned up in New Jersey he felt certain that it had been milled somewhere in the Atlantic States. Using the Southern Lumberman's Directory, a list of 1598 planing mills from Alabama to New York was compiled. A confidential letter from Colonel Schwarzkopf and a two-page description written by Koehler were sent off to all of the mills on the list.

Of all the letters sent, only 25 mills reported having planers which matched the specifications outlined in the letter. Two were immediately excluded since they didn't dress lumber of the requisite size. Samples of 1- × 4-inch wood were requested from each of the remaining 23 mills. A sample received from the M. G. and J. J. Dorn mill of McCormick, South Carolina, showed exactly the marks Koehler was looking for.

A visit to the mill showed that the particular spacing was due to a pulley which had been purchased in September of 1929. The records of the mill showed that forty-six carloads of 1 × 4 had been shipped north of the Potomac River in the time between the purchases of the pulley and the kidnapping. . . . After personally visiting the final destination of each of the shipments, Koehler and Detective Bornmann finally arrived at a Bronx firm, the National Lumber and Millwork Company. Although the entire shipment had long before been sold, the foreman remembered that some storage bins had been built from some of the wood. The wood matched that from the ladder perfectly (Figures 3 and 4). Examination of wood from shipments before and after the Bronx carload showed that the belt on the planer had been changed and the knife sharpened. This meant that this shipment was the only one from which the two particular rails from the attic could have come. Whoever built the ladder had purchased part of the wood here! Koehler was unprepared for the foreman's answer to his request to see the sales records. They had none. They had started selling cash and carry sometime before the Dorn shipment arrived and had no records. Although he had failed to come up with the carpenter's name, the authorities at least now knew the region where the kidnapper lived and bought his wood for the ladder.

FIGURE 3 Comparison of knife marks from mill planer on edges of 1- × 4-inch pine from two shipments from the Dorn mill and a ladder rail.

FIGURE 4 Comparison of knife marks on upper surface of ladder rail and North Carolina pine board located in shipment to the National Lumber and Millwork Company.

Koehler went back to his laboratory and, undaunted, started tracing the Douglas fir rails. At the time a suspect was arrested, he had succeeded in tracing one of the boards to a mill in Bend, Oregon, and another to Spokane, Washington. With the arrest of Richard Hauptmann on September 19, 1934, . . . his role in the case changed from an investigative to a comparative one. In Hauptmann's garage a variety of tools were found whose markings could be compared with those from the ladder. Comparative micrographs of marks made with Hauptmann's plane and plane marks on the ladder showed that his plane was used to plane the cleats (Figure 5). Finally, one of the investigators searching the attic of the suspect's home found that a board had been sawed out of the floor (Figure 6). Koehler's examination showed that the nail holes in the floor joists and the ladder rail (No. 16) aligned perfectly. A detailed analysis of the grain and wood itself showed that rail 16 and the section of board remaining in the attic were originally all one piece (Figure 7 and Figure 8).

FIGURE 5 **Comparison of defect marks in Hauptmann's hand-plane with marks on cleats (runs) from the ladder.**

FIGURE 6 **Rail 16 fitted into its original position in Hauptmann's attic.**

FIGURE 7 Composite photograph by Koehler showing comparison of end grain (growth rings) in board from attic and rail 16.

FIGURE 8 Construction by Koehler showing probable grain pattern of missing piece between attic board and rail 16.

Richard Bruno Hauptmann was convicted and sentenced to death in a sensational trial. Although, in retrospect, there may have been many errors and a good deal of prejudice in the trial itself, the professionalism and objectiveness of Arthur Koehler still stand as an example of science at its best in the service of the law. . . .

Endnotes

1. Waller, George. *Kidnap: The Story of the Lindbergh Case*. Dial Press, New York, 1961.

2. Koehler, Arthur. "Who Made That Ladder?" as told to Boyden Sparkes. *The Saturday Evening Post*, 297, p. 10, April 20, 1935.

3. Saylor, Charles Proffer. "Optical Microscopy as Used in Unorthodox Ways," *SPIE*, 104, Multi-disciplinary Microscopy, 31–33, 1977.

4. Koehler, Arthur. *The Saturday Evening Post*, 297, p. 84, April 20, 1935.

5. Isenberg, Irving. *Pulpwoods of the United States and Canada*. Institute of Paper Chemistry, Appleton, Wisc., pp. 19–22, 1951.

6. Christensen, Donna. *Wood Technology and the Lindbergh Kidnap Case*. Report, May 1971.

7. Koehler, Arthur. "Techniques Used in Tracing the Lindbergh Kidnapping Ladder," *Am. J. Police Science*, 27, 5 (1937).

Acknowledgment
The author gratefully acknowledges the invaluable assistance of Dr. Regis Miller and Donna Christensen of the Forest Products Laboratory in Madison, Wisconsin, for making available documents and photographs which were necessary to this article. Additional thanks are due Jame Gerakaris of McCrone Associates for preparing the drawings of the ladder and mill planer.

The Sam Sheppard Case—A Trail of Blood

Convicted in 1954 of bludgeoning his wife to death, Dr. Sam Sheppard achieved celebrity status when the storyline of TV's *The Fugitive* was apparently modeled on his efforts to seek vindication for the crime he professed not to have committed. Dr. Sheppard, a physician, claimed he was dozing on his living room couch when his pregnant wife, Marilyn, was attacked. Sheppard's story was that he quickly ran upstairs to stop the carnage, but was knocked unconscious briefly by the intruder. The suspicion that fell on Dr. Sheppard was fueled by the revelation that he was having an adulterous affair. At trial, the local coroner testified that a pool of blood on Marilyn's pillow contained the impression of a "surgical instrument." After Sheppard had been imprisoned for ten years, the U.S Supreme Court set aside his conviction due to the "massive, pervasive, and prejudicial publicity" that had attended his trial.

In 1966, the second Sheppard trial commenced. This time, the same coroner was forced to back off from his insistence that the bloody outline of a surgical instrument was present on Marilyn's pillow. However, a medical technician from the coroner's office now testified that blood on Dr. Sheppard's watch was from blood spatter, indicating that Dr. Sheppard was wearing the watch in the presence of the battering of his wife. The defense countered with the expert testimony of eminent criminalist Dr. Paul Kirk. Dr. Kirk concluded that blood spatter marks in the bedroom showed the killer to be left-handed. Dr. Sheppard was right-handed.

Dr. Kirk further testified that Sheppard stained his watch while attempting to obtain a pulse reading. After less than twelve hours of deliberation, the jury failed to convict Sheppard. But the ordeal had taken its toll. Four years later Sheppard died, a victim of drug and alcohol abuse.

chapter 8

Forensic Serology

Key Terms

acid phosphatase
agglutination
allele
antibody
antigen
antiserum
aspermia
chromosome
deoxyribonucleic acid (DNA)
egg
enzyme
erythrocyte
gene
genotype
hemoglobin
heterozygous
homozygous
hybridoma cells
locus
luminol/monoclonal
  antibodies
oligospermia
phenotype
plasma
polyclonal antibodies
precipitin
serology
serum
sperm
X chromosome
Y chromosome
zygote

Learning Objectives

After studying this chapter you should be able to:

- List the A-B-O antigens and antibodies found in the blood for each of the four blood types: A, B, AB, and O

- Understand and describe how whole blood is typed

- List and describe forensic tests used to characterize a stain as blood

- Understand the concept of antigen–antibody interactions and how it is applied to species identification and drug identification

- Contrast chromosomes and genes

- Learn how the Punnett square is used to determine the genotypes and phenotypes of offspring

- List the laboratory tests necessary to characterize seminal stains

- Explain how suspect blood and semen stains are properly preserved for laboratory examination

- Describe the proper collection of physical evidence in a rape investigation

In 1901, Karl Landsteiner announced one of the most significant discoveries of the twentieth century—the typing of blood—a finding that twenty nine years later earned him a Nobel Prize. For years physicians had attempted to transfuse blood from one individual to another. Their efforts often ended in failure because the transfused blood tended to coagulate, or clot, in the body of the recipient, causing instantaneous death. Landsteiner was the first to recognize that all human blood was not the same; instead, he found that blood is distinguishable by its group or type.

Out of Landsteiner's work came the classification system that we call the *A-B-O system*. Now physicians had the key for properly matching the blood of a donor to that of a recipient. One blood type cannot be mixed with a different blood type without disastrous consequences. This discovery, of course, had important implications for blood transfusion and the millions of lives it has since saved.

Meanwhile, Landsteiner's findings opened a new field of research in the biological sciences. Others began to pursue the identification of additional characteristics that could further differentiate blood. By 1937, the Rh factor in blood had been demonstrated and, shortly thereafter, numerous blood factors or groups were discovered. More than 100 different blood factors have been identified. However, the ones in the A-B-O system are still the most important for properly matching a donor and recipient for a transfusion.

Until the early 1990s, forensic scientists focused on blood factors, such as A-B-O, as offering the best means for linking blood to an individual. What made these factors so attractive was that in theory no two individuals, except for identical twins, could be expected to have the same combination of blood factors. In other words, blood factors are controlled genetically and have the potential of being a highly distinctive feature for personal identification. What makes this observation so relevant is the great frequency of bloodstains at crime scenes, especially crimes of the most serious nature—homicides, assaults, and rapes. Consider, for example, a transfer of blood between the victim and assailant during a struggle; that is, the victim's blood is transferred to the suspect's garment or vice versa. If the criminalist could individualize human blood by identifying all of its known factors, the result would be strong evidence for linking the suspect to the crime.

The advent of DNA technology has dramatically altered the approach of forensic scientists toward individualization of bloodstains and other biological evidence. The search for genetically controlled blood factors in bloodstains has been abandoned in favor of characterizing biological evidence by select regions of our deoxyribonucleic acid (DNA), which carries the body's genetic information. As a result, the individualization of dried blood and other biological evidence has become a reality and has significantly altered the role that crime laboratories play in criminal investigations. In fact, as we will learn in the next chapter, the high sensitivity of DNA analysis has even altered the types of materials collected from crime scenes in the search for DNA.

The next chapter is devoted to discussing recent breakthroughs in associating blood and semen stains with a single individual through characterization of DNA. This chapter focuses on underlying biological concepts that forensic scientists historically relied on as they sought to characterize and individualize biological evidence prior to the dawning of the age of DNA.

deoxyribonucleic acid (DNA)
The molecules that carry the body's genetic information.

The Nature of Blood

The word *blood* refers to a highly complex mixture of cells, enzymes, proteins, and inorganic substances. The fluid portion of blood is called plasma; it is composed principally of water and accounts for 55 percent of blood content. Suspended in the plasma are solid materials consisting chiefly of several types of cells—red blood cells (erythrocytes), white blood cells (leukocytes), and platelets. The solid portion of blood accounts for 45 percent of its content. Blood clots when a protein in the plasma known as *fibrin* traps and enmeshes the red blood cells. If the clotted material were removed, a pale yellowish liquid known as serum would be left.

Obviously, considering the complexity of blood, any discussion of its function and chemistry would have to be extensive, extending beyond the scope of this text. It is certainly far more relevant at this point to concentrate our discussion on the blood components that are directly pertinent to the forensic aspects of blood identification—the red blood cells and the blood serum.

plasma
The fluid portion of unclotted blood.

erythrocyte
A red blood cell.

serum
The liquid that separates from the blood when a clot is formed.

Antigens and Antibodies

Red blood cells transport oxygen from the lungs to the body tissues and remove carbon dioxide from tissues by transporting it back to the lungs, where it is exhaled. However, for reasons unrelated to the red blood cell's transporting mission, on the surface of each cell are millions of characteristic chemical structures called antigens. Antigens impart specific characteristics to the red blood cells. Blood antigens are grouped into systems depending on their relationship to one another. More than fifteen blood antigen systems have been identified to date; of these, the A-B-O and Rh systems are the most important.

If an individual is type A, this simply indicates that each red blood cell has A antigens on its surface; similarly, all type B individuals have B antigens, and the red blood cells of type AB individuals contain both A and B antigens. Type O individuals have neither A nor B antigens on their cells. Hence, the presence or absence of A and B antigens on the red blood cells determines a person's blood type in the A-B-O system.

Another important blood antigen has been designated as the *Rh factor*, or D antigen. Those people having the D antigen are said to be *Rh positive*;

antigen
A substance, usually a protein, that stimulates the body to produce antibodies against it.

those without this antigen are *Rh negative*. In routine blood banking, the presence or absence of the three antigens—A, B, and D—must be determined in testing compatibility of the donor and recipient.

Serum is important because it contains proteins known as antibodies. The fundamental principle of blood typing is that for every antigen, there exists a specific antibody. Each antibody symbol contains the prefix *anti-*, followed by the name of the antigen for which it is specific. Hence, anti-A is specific only for A antigen, anti-B for B antigen, and anti-D for D antigen. The serum-containing antibody is referred to as the antiserum, meaning a serum that reacts against something (antigens).

An antibody reacts only with its specific antigen and no other. Thus, if serum containing anti-B is added to red blood cells carrying the B antigen, the two will combine, causing the antibody to attach itself to the cell. Antibodies are normally *bivalent*—that is, they have two reactive sites. This means that each antibody can simultaneously be attached to antigens located on two different red blood cells. This creates a vast network of cross-linked cells usually seen as clumping or agglutination (see Figure 8–1).

antibody
A protein in the blood serum that destroys or inactivates a specific antigen.

antiserum
Blood serum that contains specific antibodies.

agglutination
The clumping together of red blood cells by the action of an antibody.

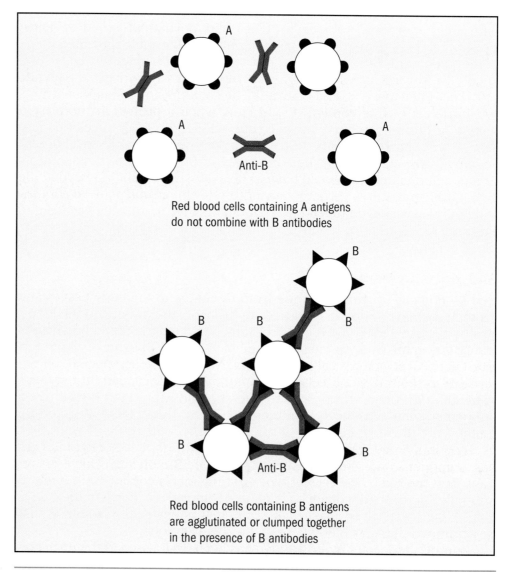

Red blood cells containing A antigens do not combine with B antibodies

Red blood cells containing B antigens are agglutinated or clumped together in the presence of B antibodies

FIGURE 8–1

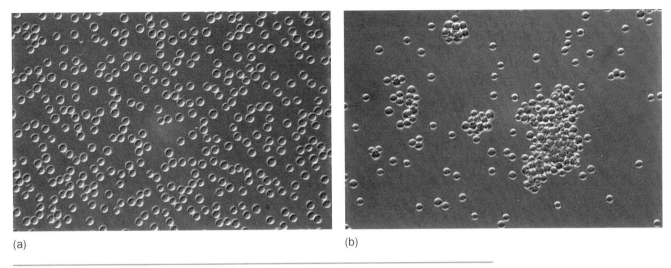

(a)   (b)

FIGURE 8–2   (a) Microscopic view of normal and red blood cells (500×). (b) Microscopic view of agglutinated red blood cells (500×). *Courtesy J. C. Revy, Phototake NYC*

Let's look a little more closely at this phenomenon. In normal blood, shown in Figure 8–2(a), antigens on red blood cells and antibodies coexist without destroying each other because the antibodies present are not specific toward any of the antigens. However, suppose a foreign serum added to the blood introduces a new antibody. This results in a specific antigen–antibody reaction that immediately causes the red blood cells to link together, or agglutinate, as shown in Figure 8–2(b).

Evidently, nature has taken this situation into account, for when we examine the serum of type A blood, we find anti-B and no anti-A. Similarly, type B blood contains only anti-A, type O blood has both anti-A and anti-B, and type AB blood contains neither anti-A nor anti-B. The antigen and antibody components of normal blood are summarized in the following table:

Blood Type	Antigens on Red Blood Cells	Antibodies in Serum
A	A	Anti-B
B	B	Anti-A
AB	AB	Neither anti-A nor anti-B
O	Neither A nor B	Both anti-A and anti-B

The reasons for the fatal consequences of mixing incompatible blood during a transfusion should now be quite obvious. For example, the transfusion of type A blood into a type B patient will cause the natural anti-A in the blood of the type B patient to react promptly with the incoming A antigens, resulting in agglutination. In addition, the incoming anti-B of the donor will react with the B antigens of the patient.

Blood Typing

The term serology describes a broad scope of laboratory tests that use specific antigen and serum antibody reactions. The most widespread application of serology is the typing of whole blood for its A-B-O identity. In determining the A-B-O blood type, only two antiserums are needed—anti-A and anti-B. For routine blood typing, both of these antiserums are commercially available.

Table 8–1 summarizes how the identity of each of the four blood groups is established when the blood is tested with anti-A and anti-B serum. Type A blood is agglutinated by anti-A serum; type B blood is agglutinated

serology
The study of antigen–antibody reactions.

by anti-B serum; type AB blood is agglutinated by both anti-A and anti-B; and type O blood is not agglutinated by either the anti-A or anti-B serum.

The identification of natural antibodies present in blood offers another way to determine blood type. Testing blood for the presence of anti-A and anti-B requires using red blood cells that have known antigens. Again, these cells are commercially available. Hence, when A cells are added to a blood specimen, agglutination occurs only in the presence of anti-A. Similarly, B cells agglutinate only in the presence of anti-B. All four A-B-O types can be identified in this manner by testing blood with known A and B cells, as summarized in Table 8–2.

The population distribution of blood types varies with location and race throughout the world. In the United States, a typical distribution is as follows:

O	A	B	AB
43%	42%	12%	3%

Key Points

- Serology involves a broad scope of laboratory tests that use specific antigen and serum antibody reactions.

- An antibody reacts or agglutinates only with its specific antigen. The concept of specific antigen–antibody reactions has been applied to techniques for detecting abused drugs in blood and urine.

- Every red blood cell contains either an A antigen, a B antigen, or no antigen (this is called type O). The type of antigen on one's red blood cells determines one's A-B-O blood type. People with type A blood have A antigens on their red blood cells, those with type B blood have B antigens, and those with type O blood have no antigens on their red blood cells.

Table 8–1 Identification of Blood with Known Antiserum

Anti-A Serum + Whole Blood	Anti-B Serum + Whole Blood	Antigen Present	Blood Type
+	−	A	A
−	+	B	B
+	+	A and B	AB
−	−	Neither A nor B	O

Note: + shows agglutination; − shows absence of agglutination.

Table 8–2 Identification of Blood with Known Cells

A Cells + Blood	B Cells + Blood	Antibody Present	Blood Type
+	−	Anti-A	B
−	+	Anti-B	A
+	+	Both anti-A and anti-B	O
−	−	Neither anti-A nor anti-B	AB

Note: + shows agglutination; − shows absence of agglutination.

Immunoassay Techniques

The concept of a specific antigen–antibody reaction is finding application in other areas unrelated to blood typing. Most significantly, this approach has been extended to the detection of drugs in blood and urine. Antibodies that react with drugs do not exist naturally; however, they can be produced in animals such as rabbits by first combining the drug with a protein and injecting this combination into the animal. This drug–protein complex acts as an antigen stimulating the animal to produce antibodies (see Figure 8–3). The recovered blood serum of the animal now contains antibodies that are specific or nearly specific to the drug.

Currently, each day, thousands of individuals are voluntarily being subjected to urinalysis tests for the presence of drug-of-abuse. These individuals include military personnel, transportation industry employees, police and correction personnel, and subjects requiring pre-employment drug screening. Immunoassay testing for drugs has proven quite suitable for handling the large volume of specimens that must be rapidly analyzed on a daily basis for drug content. Testing laboratories have available to them a variety of commercially prepared sera arising from animals being injected with any one of a variety of drugs. Once a particular serum is added to a urine specimen, it's designed to interact with either opiates, cannabinoids, cocaine, amphetamines, phencyclidine, barbiturates, methadone, or other drugs. A word of caution: immunoassay is only presumptive in nature and its result must be confirmed by additional testing.

Radioimmunoassay (RIA)

Although EMIT is currently a popular immunoassay technique in forensic laboratories, other immunoassay procedures are commercially available. For example, *radioimmunoassay (RIA)* uses drugs labeled with radioactive

Drug Protein carrier Drug antibodies

FIGURE 8–3 Stimulating production of drug antibodies.

Closer Analysis

Enzyme-Multiplied Immunoassay Technique (EMIT)

Several immunological assay techniques are commercially available for detecting drugs through an antigen–antibody reaction. One such technique, the *enzyme-multiplied immunoassay technique (EMIT)*, has gained widespread popularity among toxicologists because of its speed and high sensitivity for detecting drugs in urine.

A typical EMIT analysis begins by adding to a subject's urine antibodies that bind to a particular type or class of drug being looked for. This is followed by adding to the urine a chemically-labeled version of the drug. As shown in the figure, a competition will ensue between the labeled and unlabeled drug (if it's present in the subject's urine) to

(*continued*)

Closer Analysis

Enzyme-Multiplied Immunoassay Technique (EMIT) (*continued*)

bind with the antibody. If this competition does occur in a person's urine, it signifies that that the urine screen test was positive for the drug being tested. For example, to check someone's urine for methadone, the analyst would add methadone antibodies and chemically-labeled methadone to the urine. Any methadone present in the urine immediately competes with the labeled methadone to bind with the methadone antibodies. The quantity of chemically-labeled methadone left uncombined is then measured, and this value is related to the concentration of methadone originally present in the urine.

One of the most frequent uses of EMIT in forensic laboratories has been for screening the urine of suspected marijuana users. The primary pharmacologically active agent in marijuana is tetrahydrocannabinol, or THC. To facilitate the elimination of THC, the body converts it to a series of substances called *metabolites* that are more readily excreted. The major THC metabolite found in urine is a substance called *THC-9-carboxylic acid*. Antibodies against this metabolite are prepared for EMIT testing. Normally the urine of marijuana users contains a very small quantity of THC-9-carboxylic acid (less than one-millionth of a gram); however, this level is readily detected by EMIT.

The greatest problem with detecting marijuana in urine is interpretation of the test results. Although marijuana use results in the detection of THC metabolites, it is very difficult to determine when the individual actually used marijuana. In individuals who use marijuana frequently, detection is possible within two to five days after the last use of the drug. However, some individuals may yield positive results up to ten days after the last use of marijuana.

In the **EMIT assay, a drug that may be present in a urine specimen will compete with added labeled drug for a limited number of antibody binding sites. The labeled drugs are indicated by an asterisk. Once the competition for antibody sites is completed, the number of remaining unbound labeled drug is proportional to the drug's concentration in urine.**

tags. Whether using an enzyme tag as in EMIT or a radioactive tag as in RIA, the analyst must be cautious because immunoassay techniques are not totally specific for any drug. Substances with a chemical structure similar to the drug in question may cross-react with the antibody to give a false-positive reaction. Hence, positive immunoassay tests must always be confirmed by another reliable analytical procedure. The issue of specificity, along with other questions relating to the reliability of RIA, was raised during the murder trial of Dr. Mario E. Jascalevich, which is described in detail in the Case Reading at the end of Chapter 1.

Closer Analysis

Polyclonal and Monoclonal Antibodies

As we have seen in the previous section, when an animal such as a rabbit or mouse is injected with an antigen, the animal responds by producing antibodies designed to bind to the invading antigen. However, the process of producing antibodies designed to respond to foreign antigens is complex. For instance, an antigen typically has structurally different sites to which an antibody may bind. Thus, in the presence of a specific antigen, an animal produces many different antibodies, all of which are designed to attack some particular site on the antigen of interest. These antibodies are known as **polyclonal antibodies**. However, the disadvantage of polyclonal antibodies is that an animal can produce antibodies that

polyclonal antibodies
Antibodies produced by injecting animals with a specific antigen. A series of antobodies are produced responding to a variety of different sites on the antigen.

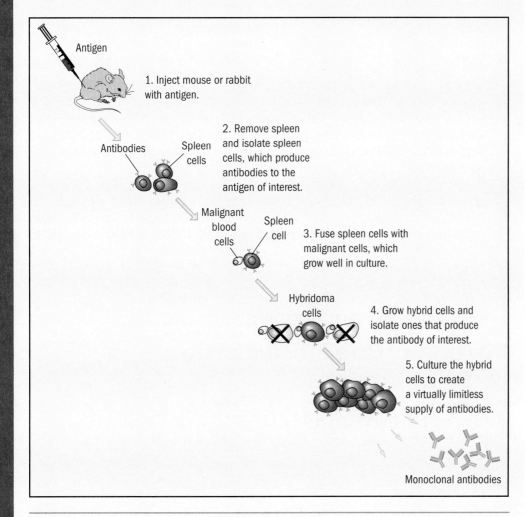

Steps required to produce monoclonal antibodies.

(continued)

Closer Analysis

Polyclonal and Monoclonal Antibodies (*continued*)

vary in composition over time. As a result, different batches of polyclonals may vary in their specificity and their ability to bind to a particular antigen site.

Modern forensic technologies occasionally require antibodies that are more uniform in their composition and attack power than the traditional polyclonals. Forensic scientists thus need a way to produce antibodies designed to attack one and only one site on an antigen. Such antibodies are known as **monoclonal antibodies.** How can such monoclonals be produced?

The process begins by injecting a mouse with the antigen of interest. In response, the mouse's spleen cells produce antibodies to fight off the invading antigen. The spleen cells are removed from the animal and are fused to fast-growing blood cancer cells to produce **hybridoma cells.** The hybridoma cells are then allowed to multiply and are screened for their specific antibody activity. Hybridoma cells bearing the antibody activity of interest are then selected and cultured. The rapidly multiplying cancer cells linked to the selected antibody cells produce identical monoclonal antibodies in a limitless supply (see figure).

Monoclonal antibodies are being incorporated into commercial forensic test kits with increasing frequency. Many immunoassay test kits for abused drugs are being formulated with monoclonal antibodies. Also, a recently introduced test for semen that incorporates a monoclonal antibody has found wide popularity in crime laboratories.

monoclonal antibodies
A collection of identical antibodies that interact with a single antigen site.

hybridoma cells
Fused spleen and tumor cells. Used to produce identical monoclonal antibodies in a limitless supply.

Key Points

- To produce antibodies capable of reacting with drugs, the analyst combines a specific drug with a protein and injects this combination into an animal such as a rabbit. This drug–protein complex acts as an antigen, stimulating the animal to produce antibodies. The recovered blood serum of the animal now contains antibodies that are specific or nearly specific to the drug.

- When an animal is injected with an antigen, its body produces a series of different antibodies, all of which are designed to attack some particular site on the antigen of interest. These antibodies are known as polyclonal antibodies.

- A more uniform and specific collection of antibodies designed to combine with a single antigen site can be manufactured. Such antibodies are known as monoclonal antibodies.

Forensic Characterization of Bloodstains

The criminalist must answer the following questions when examining dried blood: (1) Is it blood? (2) From what species did the blood originate? (3) If the blood is human, how closely can it be associated with a particular individual?

Color Tests

The determination of blood is best made by means of a preliminary color test. For many years, the most common test was the *benzidine color test.*

However, because benzidine has been identified as a known carcinogen, its use has generally been discontinued, and the chemical phenolphthalein is usually substituted in its place (this test is also known as the *Kastle-Meyer color test*).[1]

Both the benzidine and Kastle-Meyer color tests are based on the observation that blood hemoglobin possesses peroxidase-like activity. Peroxidases are enzymes that accelerate the oxidation of several classes of organic compounds when combined with peroxides. For example, when a bloodstain, phenolphthalein reagent, and hydrogen peroxide are mixed together, oxidation of the hemoglobin in the blood produces a deep pink color.

The Kastle-Meyer test is not a specific test for blood; some vegetable materials, for instance, may turn Kastle-Meyer pink. These substances include potatoes and horseradish. However, such materials will probably not be encountered in criminal situations, and thus from a practical point of view, a positive Kastle-Meyer test is highly indicative of blood. Field investigators have found Hemastix strips a useful presumptive field test for blood. Designed as a urine dipstick test for blood, the strip can be moistened with distilled water and placed in contact with a suspect bloodstain. The appearance of a green color indicates blood.

hemoglobin
A red blood cell protein that transports oxygen in the bloodstream; it is responsible for the red color of blood.

Luminol

Another important presumptive identification test for blood is the luminol test.[2] Unlike the benzidine and Kastle-Meyer tests, the reaction of luminol with blood produces light rather than color. After spraying luminol reagent onto suspect items, agents darken the room; any bloodstains produce a faint blue glow, known as *luminescence*. Using luminol, investigators can quickly screen large areas for bloodstains.

The luminol test is extremely sensitive, capable of detecting bloodstains diluted up to 300,000 times. For this reason, spraying large areas such as carpets, walls, flooring, or the interior of a vehicle may reveal blood traces or patterns that would have gone unnoticed under normal lighting conditions (see Figure 8–4). Luminol does not interfere with any subsequent DNA testing.[3]

luminol
The most sensitive chemical test that is capable of presumptively detecting bloodstains diluted up to 300,000 times. Its reaction with blood emits light and thus requires the result to be observed in a darkened area.

Microcrystalline Tests

The identification of blood can be made more specific if microcrystalline tests are performed on the material. Several tests are available; the two most popular ones are the *Takayama* and *Teichmann tests*. Both depend on the addition of specific chemicals to the blood to form characteristic crystals containing hemoglobin derivatives. Crystal tests are far less sensitive than color tests for blood identification and are more susceptible to interference from contaminants that may be present in the stain.

Precipitin Test

Once the stain has been characterized as blood, the serologist determines whether the blood is of human or animal origin. The standard test is the precipitin test. Precipitin tests are based on the fact that when animals (usually rabbits) are injected with human blood, antibodies form that react with the invading human blood to neutralize its presence. The investigator can recover these antibodies by bleeding the animal and isolating the blood serum, which contains antibodies that specifically react with human

precipitin
An antibody that reacts with its corresponding antigen to form a precipitate.

(a)

(b)

FIGURE 8–4 **(a) A section of a linoleum floor photographed under normal light. This floor was located in the residence of a missing person. (b) Same section of the floor shown in (a) after spraying with luminol. A circular pattern was revealed. Investigators concluded that the circular blood pattern was left by the bottom of a bucket carried about during the cleaning up of the blood. A small clump of sponge, blood, and hair was found near where this photograph was taken.** *Courtesy North Carolina State Bureau of Investigation*

antigens. For this reason, the serum is known as *human antiserum.* In the same manner, by injecting rabbits with the blood of other known animals, virtually any kind of animal antiserum can be produced. Antiserums are commercially available for humans and for a variety of commonly encountered animals—for example, dogs, cats, and deer.

Several techniques have been devised for performing precipitin tests on bloodstains. The classic method is to layer an extract of the bloodstain on top of the human antiserum in a capillary tube. Human blood, or for that matter, any protein of human origin in the extract, reacts specifically with antibodies present in the antiserum, as indicated by the formation of a cloudy ring or band at the interface of the two liquids (see Figure 8–5).

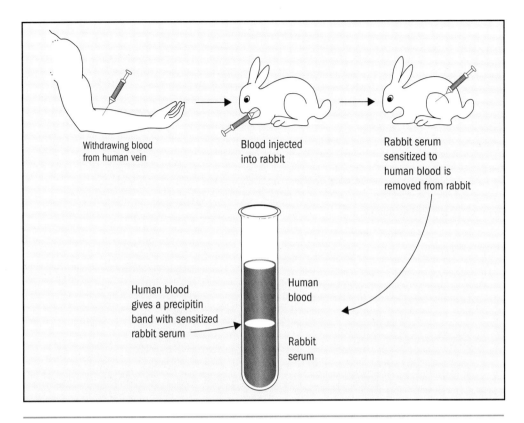

FIGURE 8–5   The precipitin test.

Gel Diffusion

Another method, called *gel diffusion,* takes advantage of the fact that antibodies and antigens diffuse or move toward one another on a plate coated with a gel medium made from a natural polymer called agar. The extracted bloodstain and the human antiserum are placed in separate holes opposite each other on the gel. If the blood is human, a line of precipitation forms where the antigens and antibodies meet.

Similarly, the antigens and antibodies can be induced to move toward one another under the influence of an electrical field. In the *electrophoretic method* (examined in detail in Chapter 9), an electrical potential is applied to the gel medium; a specific antigen–antibody reaction is denoted by a line of precipitation formed between the hole containing the blood extract and the hole containing the human antiserum (see Figure 8–6).

The precipitin test is very sensitive and requires only a small amount of blood for testing. Human bloodstains dried for ten to fifteen years and longer may still give a positive precipitin reaction. Even extracts of tissue from mummies four to five thousand years old have given positive reactions with this test. Furthermore, human bloodstains diluted by washing in water and left with only a faint color may still yield a positive precipitin reaction (see Figure 8–7).

Once it has been determined that the bloodstain is human, an effort must be made to associate or disassociate the stain with a particular individual. Until the mid-1990s, routine characterization of bloodstains included the determination of A-B-O types; however, the widespread use of DNA profiling or typing has relegated this subject to one of historical interest only.

FIGURE 8–6   Gel diffusion.

FIGURE 8–7   Results of the precipitin test of dilutions of human serum up to 1 in 4,096 against a human antiserum. A reaction is visible for blood dilutions up to 1 in 256. *Courtesy Millipore Biomedica, Acton, Mass*

Key Points

- The criminalist must answer the following questions when examining dried blood: (1) Is it blood? (2) From what species did the blood originate? (3) If the blood is human, how closely can it be associated with a particular individual?

- The determination of blood is best made with a preliminary color test. A positive result from the Kastle-Meyer color test is highly indicative of blood.

- The luminol test is used to find trace amounts of blood at crime scenes.

- The precipitin test uses antisera normally derived from rabbits that have been injected with the blood of a known animal to determine the species origin of a questioned bloodstain.

- Materials undergoing electrophoresis are forced to move across a gel-coated plate under the influence of an electrical potential. Antigens and antibodies can be induced to move toward one another under the influence of an electrical field.

Bloodstain Patterns

The location, distribution, and appearance of bloodstains and spatters may be useful for interpreting and reconstructing the events that produced the bleeding. A thorough analysis of the significance of the position and shape of blood patterns with respect to their origin and trajectory is exceedingly complex and requires the services of an examiner who is experienced in such determinations. Most important, the interpretation of bloodstain patterns necessitates carefully planned control experiments using surface materials comparable to those found at the crime scene.

A number of observations and conclusions have important implications for any investigator who seeks to trace the direction, dropping distance, and angle of impact of a bloodstain. Some of them can be summarized as follows:

1. Surface texture is very important in the interpretation of bloodstain patterns, and correlations between standards and unknowns are valid only if identical surfaces are used. In general, the harder and less porous the surface, the less spatter. The effect of surface is shown in Figure 8–8.

2. The direction of travel of blood striking an object may be discerned by the stain's shape. The pointed end of a bloodstain always faces its direction of travel. In Figure 8–9, the bloodstain pattern was produced by several droplets of blood that were traveling from left to right before striking a flat level surface.

3. It is possible to determine the impact angle of blood on a flat surface by measuring the degree of circular distortion of the stain. A drop of blood striking a surface at right angles produces a nearly circular stain; as the angle decreases, the stain elongates. This progressive elongation is evident in Figure 8–10.

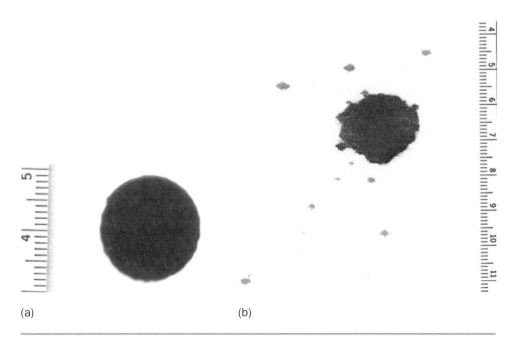

(a) (b)

FIGURE 8–8 **(a) Bloodstain from a single drop of blood that struck a glass surface after falling 24 inches. (b) Bloodstain from a single drop of blood that struck a cotton muslin sheet after falling 24 inches.** *Courtesy A. Y. Wonder*

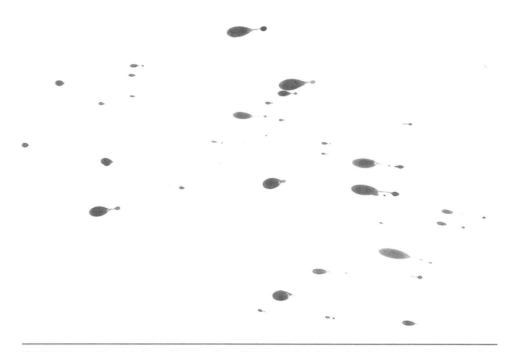

FIGURE 8–9   Bloodstain pattern produced by droplets of blood that were traveling from left to right. *Courtesy A. Y. Wonder*

FIGURE 8–10   The higher pattern is of a single drop of human blood that fell 24 inches and struck hard, smooth cardboard at 50 degrees. The lower pattern is of a single drop of human blood that fell 24 inches and struck hard, smooth cardboard at 15 degrees. *Courtesy A. Y. Wonder*

4. The origin of a blood spatter in a two-dimensional configuration can be established by drawing straight lines through the long axis of several individual bloodstains. The intersection or area of convergence of the lines represents the area from which the blood emanated (see Figure 8–11).

An example of the utility of blood spatter formations in performing crime-scene reconstruction is illustrated in Figures 8–12 through 8–14. This case relates to an elderly male who was found lying dead on his living room floor. He had been beaten about the face and head, then stabbed in the chest and robbed. The reconstruction of bloodstains found on the interior front door and the adjacent wall documented that the victim was beaten about the face with a fist and struck on the back of the head with his cane. A suspect was apprehended three days later, and he was found to have an acute fracture of the right hand. When he was confronted with the bloodstain evidence, the suspect admitted striking the victim, first with his fist, then with a cane, and finally stabbing him with a kitchen knife. The suspect pleaded guilty to three first-degree felonies.

WebExtra 8.1

See How Bloodstain Spatter Patterns Are Formed
www.prenhall.com/hsforensics

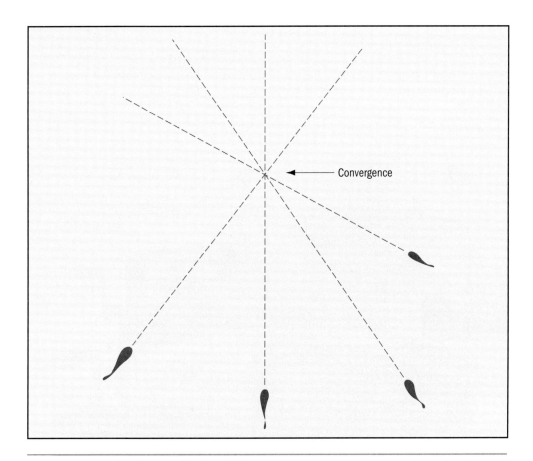

FIGURE 8–11   Illustration of stain convergence on a two-dimensional plane. Convergence represents the area from which the stains emanated. *Courtesy Judith Bunker, J. L. Bunker & Assoc., Ocoee, Fla.*

FIGURE 8–12a **Three-dimensional diagram illustrating bloodstain patterns that were located, documented, and reconstructed.** *Courtesy Judith Bunker, J. L. Bunker & Assoc., Ocoee, Fla.*

FIGURE 8–12b **Crime-scene photograph of bloodstained areas.** *Courtesy Sarasota County (Fla.) Sheriff's Department*

FIGURE 8–12c   Detail photograph of bloodstains on the wall next to the interior door. Positions of impact spatter from blows that were inflicted to the victim's face are indicated in Figure 8–14(a). Arrow 1 points to the cast-off pattern directed left to right as blood was flung from the perpetrator's fist while inflicting blows. Arrow 2 points to three repetitive transfer impression patterns directed left to right as the perpetrator's bloodstained hand contacted the wall as the fist blows were being inflicted on the victim. Arrow 3 points to blood flow from the victim's wounds as he slumped against the wall. *Courtesy Judith Bunker, J. L. Bunker & Assoc., Ocoee, Fla.*

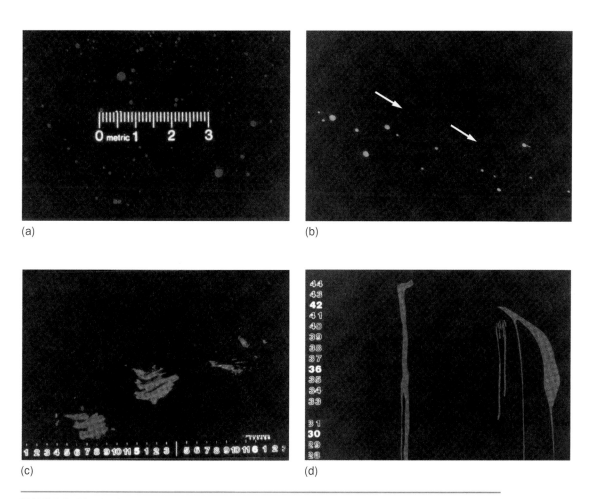

(a)

(b)

(c)

(d)

FIGURE 8–13   (a) Laboratory test pattern showing an impact spatter. The size and shape of the stains demonstrate a forceful impact 90 degrees to the target. (b) Laboratory test pattern illustrating a cast-off pattern directed left to right from a right overhead swing. (c) Laboratory test pattern showing a repetitive transfer impression pattern produced by a bloodstained hand moving left to right across the target. (d) Laboratory test patterns illustrating vertical flow patterns. The left pattern represents a stationary source; the right pattern was produced by left-to-right motion. *Courtesy Judith Bunker, J. L. Bunker & Assoc., Ocoee, Fla.*

(a)   (b)   (c)

FIGURE 8–14 (a) Convergence of impact spatter patterns associated with beating by fist. (b) Convergence of impact spatter associated with the victim falling to the floor while bleeding from the nose. (c) Convergence of impact spatter associated with the victim while face down at the door, being struck with a cane. *Courtesy Judith Bunker, J. L. Bunker & Assoc., Ocoee, Fla.*

Forensic Brief

Stephen Scher banged on the door of a cabin in the woods outside Montrose, Pennsylvania. According to Scher, his friend, Marty Dillon, had just shot himself while chasing after a porcupine. The two had been skeet shooting at Scher's cabin, enjoying a friendly sporting weekend, when Dillon spotted a porcupine and took off out of sight. Scher heard a single shot and waited to hear his friend's voice. After a few moments, he chased after Dillon and found him lying on the ground near a tree stump, bleeding from a wound in his chest. Scher administered CPR after locating his dying friend, but he was unable to save Dillon, who later died from his injuries. Police found that Dillon's untied boot had been the cause of his shotgun wound. They determined that he had tripped while running with his loaded gun and shot himself. The grief-stricken Scher aroused no suspicion, so the shooting was ruled an accident.

Shortly thereafter, Scher moved from the area, divorced his wife, and married Dillon's widow. This was too suspicious to be ignored; police reopened the case and decides to reconstruct the crime scene.

The reconstruction provided investigators with several pieces of blood evidence that pointed to Scher as Dillon's murderer.

Police noticed that Scher's boots bore the unmistakable spray of high-velocity impact bloodspatter, evidence that he was standing within an arm's length of Dillon when Dillon was shot. This pattern of bloodstains can not be created while administering CPR, as Scher claimed had happened. The spatter pattern also clearly refuted Scher's claim that he did not witness the incident. In addition, the tree stump near Dillon's body bore the same type of blood spatter, in a pattern that indicated that Dillon was *seated on the stump* and not running when he was shot. Finally, Dillon's ears were free of the high-velocity blood spatter that covered his face, but blood was on his hearing protectors found nearby. This is a clear indication that he was wearing his hearing protectors when he was shot and they were removed before investigators arrived. This and other evidence resulted in Scher's conviction for the murder of his longtime friend Marty Dillon.

Key Points

- The location, distribution, and appearance of bloodstains and spatters may be useful for interpreting and reconstructing the events that produced bleeding.

- Surface texture and the stain's shape, size, and location must be considered when determining the direction, dropping distance, and angle of impact of a bloodstain.

- In general, the harder and less porous the surface, the less spatter.

- The direction of travel of blood striking an object may be discerned by the stain's shape. The pointed end of a bloodstain always faces its direction of travel.

Principles of Heredity

All of the antigens and polymorphic enzymes and proteins that have been described in previous sections are genetically controlled traits. That is, they are inherited from parents and become a permanent feature of a person's biological makeup from the moment he or she is conceived. Determining the identity of these traits, then, not only provides us with a picture of how one individual compares to or differs from another, but also gives us an insight into the basic biological substances that determine our overall makeup as human beings and the mechanism by which those substances are transmitted from one generation to the next.

Genes and Chromosomes

Hereditary material is transmitted via microscopic units called genes. The gene is the basic unit of heredity. Each gene by itself or in concert with other genes controls the development of a specific characteristic in the new individual; the genes determine the nature and growth of virtually every body structure.

The genes are positioned on chromosomes, threadlike bodies that appear in the nucleus of every body cell (see Figure 8–15). Almost all human cells contain forty six chromosomes, mated in twenty three pairs. The only exceptions are the human reproductive cells, the egg and sperm, which contain twenty three unmated chromosomes. During fertilization, a sperm and egg combine so that each contributes twenty three chromosomes to form the new cell (zygote). Hence, the new individual begins life properly with twenty three mated chromosome pairs. Because the genes are positioned on the chromosomes, the new individual inherits genetic material from each parent.

Actually, two dissimilar chromosomes are involved in the determination of sex. The egg cell always contains a long chromosome known as the X chromosome; the sperm cell may contain either a long X chromosome or a short Y chromosome. When an X-carrying sperm fertilizes an egg, the new cell is XX and develops into a female. A Y-carrying sperm produces an XY fertilized egg and develops into a male. Because the sperm cell determines the nature of the chromosome pair, we can say that the father biologically determines the sex of the child.

Alleles Just as chromosomes come together in pairs, so do the genes they bear. The position a gene occupies on a chromosome is its locus. Genes that

gene
The basic unit of heredity, consisting of a DNA segment located on a chromosome.

chromosome
A threadlike structure in the cell nucleus, along which the genes are located.

egg
The female reproductive cell.

sperm
The male reproductive cell.

zygote
The cell arising from the union of an egg and a sperm cell.

X chromosome
The female sex chromosome.

Y chromosome
The male sex chromosome.

locus
The physical location of a gene on a chromosome.

FIGURE 8–15 **Computer-enhanced photomicrograph image of human chromosomes.**
Courtesy Alfred Pasieka, Science Photo Library

WebExtra 8.2

**Learn about the Structure
of Our Genes**
www.prenhall.com/hsforensics

allele
Any of several alternative forms
of a gene located at the same
point on a particular pair of
chromosomes.

homozygous
Having two identical allelic
genes on two corresponding
positions of a pair of
chromosomes.

heterozygous
Having two different allelic
genes on two corresponding
positions of a pair of
chromosomes.

WebExtra 8.3

**Learn about the
Chromosomes Present in
Our Cells**
www.prenhall.com/hsforensics

govern a given characteristic are similarly positioned on the chromosomes inherited from the mother and father. Thus, a gene for eye color on the mother's chromosome will be aligned with a gene for eye color on the corresponding chromosome inherited from the father. Alternative forms of genes that influence a given characteristic and are aligned with one another on a chromosome pair are known as alleles.

Inheritance of blood type offers a simple example of allele genes in humans. An individual's blood type is determined by three genes, designated A, B, and O. A gene pair made up of two similar alleles—for example, AA and BB—is said to be homozygous. For example, if the chromosome inherited from the father carries the A gene and the chromosome inherited from the mother carries the same gene, the offspring will have an AA combination. Thus, when an individual inherits two similar genes from his or her parents, there is no problem in determining the blood type of that person. An individual with an AA combination will always be type A, a BB will be type B, and an OO will be type O.

A gene pair made up of two different alleles—AO, for example—is said to be heterozygous. For example, if the chromosome from one parent carries the A gene and the chromosome from the other parent carries the O gene, the genetic makeup of the offspring will be AO. When two different genes are inherited, one gene will be *dominant*—that is, the characteristic coded for by that gene is expressed. The other gene will be *recessive*—that is, its characteristics remain hidden. In the case of blood types, A and B genes are dominant and the O gene is recessive. Thus, with an AO combination, A is always dominant over O, and the individual is typed as A. Similarly, a BO combination is typed as B. In the case of AB, the genes are

WebExtra 8.4
See How Genes Position Themselves on a Chromosome Pair
www.prenhall.com/hsforensics

genotype
The particular combination of genes present in the cells of an individual.

phenotype
The physical manifestation of a genetic trait such as shape, color, or blood type.

codominant, and the individual's blood type will be AB. The recessive characteristics of O appear only when both recessive genes are present in combination OO, which is typed simply as O.

Genotypes and Phenotypes A pair of allele genes together constitutes the genotype of the individual. However, no known laboratory test can determine an individual's A-B-O genotype. For example, a person's outward characteristic, or phenotype, may be type A, but this does not tell us whether the genotype is AA or AO. The genotype can be determined only by studying the family history of the individual. If the genotypes of both parents are known, that of their possible offspring can be forecast.

An easy way to determine an individual's genotype is to construct a *Punnett square*. To do this, write along a horizontal line the two genes of the male parent, and in the vertical column write the two kinds of female genes present, as shown. In our example, we assume the male parent is type O and therefore has to be an OO genotype; the female parent is type AB and can be only an AB genotype:

```
              Father's
              genotype

              O      O
          A  ┌──────┬──────┐
Mother's     │      │      │
genotype  B  ├──────┼──────┤
             │      │      │
             └──────┴──────┘
```

Next, write in each box the corresponding gene contributed from the female and then from the male. The squares will contain all the possible genotype combinations that the parents can produce in their offspring:

```
        O      O
   A  ┌─────┬─────┐
      │ AO  │ AO  │
   B  ├─────┼─────┤
      │ BO  │ BO  │
      └─────┴─────┘
```

In this case, 50 percent of the offspring are likely to be AO and the other 50 percent BO. These are the only genotypes possible from this combination. Because O is recessive, 50 percent of the offspring will probably be type A and 50 percent type B. From this example, we can see that no blood group gene can appear in a child unless it is present in at least one of the parents.

WebExtra 8.5
See How Genes Define Our Genetic Makeup
www.prenhall.com/hsforensics

Paternity Testing

Although the genotyping of blood factors has useful applications for studying the transmission of blood characteristics from one generation to the next, it has no direct relevance to criminal investigations. It does, however, have important implications in disputed-paternity cases, which are normally encountered in civil, not criminal, courts.

Many cases of disputed paternity can be resolved by comparing the blood group genotypes of the suspected parents and offspring. For instance, suppose the male in the preceding Punnett square example is suspected of fathering a child by the female. If the child has type AB blood, the suspected father will be cleared because a type O father and a type AB mother cannot have a type AB child. On the other hand, if the child has type A or type B, the most that can be said is that the suspect may be the father. This does not mean that he *is* the father, just that he is not excluded based on blood typing. Obviously, many other males also have type O blood. Of course, the more blood group systems that are tested, the better the chances of excluding an innocent male from involvement. Conversely, if no discrepancies are found between the offspring and the suspect father, the more certain one can be that the suspect is indeed the father.

In fact, routine paternity testing involves characterizing blood factors other than A-B-O. For example, the HLA (human leukocyte antigen) test relies on identifying a complex system of antigens on white blood cells. If this test cannot exclude a suspect as the father of a child, the chances are better than 90 percent that he is the father. Paternity-testing laboratories have implemented DNA test procedures that can raise the odds of establishing paternity beyond 99 percent.

Key Points

- The gene is the basic unit of heredity. A chromosome is a threadlike structure in the cell nucleus, along which the genes are located.

- Most human cells contain forty six chromosomes, arranged in twenty-three mated pairs. The only exceptions are the human reproductive cells, the egg and sperm, which contain twenty three unmated chromosomes.

- During fertilization, a sperm and egg combine so that each contributes twenty three chromosomes to form the new cell, or zygote, that develops into the offspring.

- An allele is any of several alternative forms of genes that influence a given characteristic and that are aligned with one another on a chromosome pair.

- A heterozygous gene pair is made up of two different alleles; a homozygous gene pair is made up of two similar alleles.

- When two different genes are inherited, the characteristic coded for by a dominant gene is expressed. The characteristic coded for by a recessive gene remains hidden.

- A genotype is the particular combination of genes present in the cells of an individual. A phenotype is the physical manifestation of a genetic trait.

Forensic Characterization of Semen

Many cases received in a forensic laboratory involve sexual offenses, making it necessary to examine exhibits for the presence of seminal stains. The forensic examination of articles for seminal stains can actually be considered a two-step process. First, before any tests can be conducted, the stain must be located. Considering the number and soiled condition of outergarments, undergarments, and possible bedclothing submitted for examination, this may prove to be an arduous task. Once located, the stain must be subjected to tests that will prove its identity. It may even be tested for the blood type of the individual from whom it originated.

Testing for Seminal Stains

Often seminal stains are visible on a fabric because they exhibit a stiff, crusty appearance. However, reliance on such appearance for locating the stain is unreliable, and is useful only when the stain is in an obvious area. If the fabric has been washed or contains only minute quantities of semen, visual examination offers little chance of detecting the stain. The best way to locate and at the same time characterize a seminal stain is to perform the *acid phosphatase color test.*

Acid Phosphatase Test   Acid phosphatase is an enzyme that is secreted by the prostate gland into seminal fluid. Its concentrations in seminal fluid are up to 400 times those found in any other body fluid. Its presence can easily be detected when it comes in contact with an acidic solution of sodium alpha naphthylphosphate and Fast Blue B dye. Also, 4-methyl umbelliferyl phosphate (MUP) will fluoresces (emit light) under UV light when it comes in contact with acid phosphatase.

acid phosphatase
An enzyme found in high concentration in semen.

enzyme
A protein that acts as a catalyst for certain specific reactions.

The utility of the acid phosphatase test is apparent when it becomes necessary to search many garments or large fabric areas for seminal stains. Simply moistening a filter paper with water and rubbing it lightly over the suspect area transfers any acid phosphatase present to the filter paper. Placing a drop or two of the sodium alpha naphthylphosphate and Fast Blue B solution on the paper produces a purple color that indicates the acid phosphatase enzyme. In this manner, any fabric or surface can be systematically searched for seminal stains.

If it is necessary to search extremely large areas—for example, a bedsheet or carpet—the article can be tested in sections, narrowing the location of the stain with each successive test. Alternatively, the garment can be pressed against a suitably sized piece of moistened filter paper. The paper is then sprayed with MUP solution. Semen stains appear as strongly fluorescent areas under UV light. A negative reaction can be interpreted as absence of semen. Although some vegetable and fruit juices (such as cauliflower and watermelon), fungi, contraceptive creams, and vaginal secretions give a positive response to the acid phosphatase test, none of these substances normally reacts with the speed of seminal fluid. A reaction time of less than 30 seconds is considered a strong indication of semen.

Microscopic Examination of Semen   Semen can be unequivocally identified by the presence of spermatozoa. When spermatozoa are located through a microscope examination, the stain is definitely identified as having been derived from semen. *Spermatozoa* are slender, elongated structures 50–70 microns long, each with a head and a thin flagellate tail (see Figure 8–16). The criminalist can normally locate them by immersing the stained material in a small volume of water. Rapidly stirring the liquid transfers a small percentage of the spermatozoa present into the

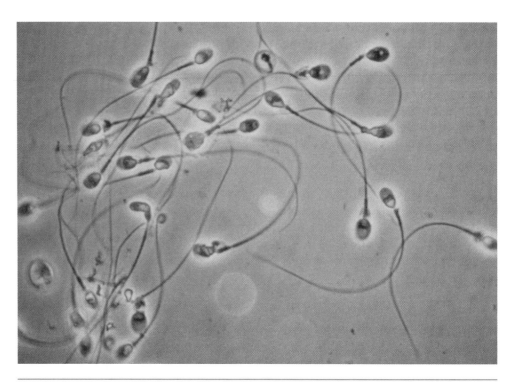

FIGURE 8–16   Photomicrograph of human spermatozoa (300×). *Courtesy John Walsh*

water. A drop of the water is dried onto a microscope slide, then stained and examined under a compound microscope at a magnification of approximately 400×.[4]

Considering the extremely large number of spermatozoa found in seminal fluid (the normal male releases 250–600 million spermatozoa during ejaculation), the chance of locating one should be very good; however, this is not always true. One reason is that spermatozoa bind tightly to cloth materials.[5] Also, spermatozoa are extremely brittle when dry and easily disintegrate if the stain is washed or when the stain is rubbed against another object, as happens frequently in the handling and packaging of this type of evidence. Furthermore, sexual crimes may involve males who have an abnormally low sperm count, a condition known as oligospermia, or who have no spermatozoa at all in their seminal fluid (aspermia). Significantly, aspermatic individuals are increasing in numbers due to the growing popularity of vasectomies.

oligospermia
An abnormally low sperm count.

aspermia
The absence of sperm; sterility in males.

Prostate Specific Antigen (PSA)   Analysts often examine stains or swabs that they suspect contain semen (because of the presence of acid phosphatase), but that yield no detectable spermatozoa. How, then, can one unequivocally prove the presence of semen? The solution to this problem came with the discovery in the 1970s of a protein called *p30* or *prostate specific antigen (PSA)*. Under the analytical conditions employed in forensic laboratories, p30 is unique to seminal plasma.

When p30 is isolated and injected into a rabbit, it stimulates the production of polyclonal antibodies (anti-p30). The serum collected from these immunized rabbits can then be used to test suspected semen stains. As shown in Figure 8–17, the stain extract is placed in one well of an electrophoretic plate and the anti-p30 in an opposite well. When an electric potential is applied, the antigens and antibodies move toward each other. The formation of a visible line midway between the two wells shows the presence of p30 in the stain and proves that the stain was seminal.

A more elegant approach to identifying PSA (p30) is shown in Figure 8–18. First, a monoclonal PSA antibody is attached to a dye and placed on a porous membrane. Next, an extract from a sample suspected of containing PSA is placed on the membrane. If PSA is present in the extract, it combines with the monoclonal PSA antibody to form a PSA antigen–monoclonal PSA antibody complex. This complex migrates along the membrane, where it interacts with a polyclonal PSA antibody imbedded in the membrane. The antibody–antigen–antibody "sandwich" that forms is apparent by the presence of a colored line (see Figure 8–18). This monoclonal antibody technique is about 100 times as sensitive as the electrophoretic method for detecting PSA.[6]

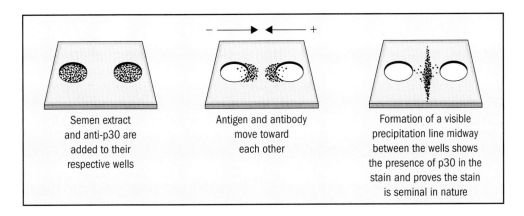

FIGURE 8–17   PSA testing by electrophoresis.

FIGURE 8–18   An antibody–antigen–antibody sandwich or complex is seen as a colored band. This signifies the presence of PSA in the extract of a stain and positively identifies human semen.

Once the material is proven to be semen, the next task is to associate the semen as closely as possible with an individual. As we will learn in Chapter 9, forensic scientists can link seminal material to one individual with DNA technology. Just as important is the knowledge that this technology can exonerate many of those wrongfully accused of sexual assault.

Key Points

- The best way to locate and characterize a seminal stain is to perform the acid phosphatase color test.

- The presence of spermatozoa, or of the protein called prostate specific antigen (PSA), also known as p30, proves that a sample stain contains semen.

- Forensic scientists can link seminal material to an individual by DNA typing.

Collection of Rape Evidence

Seminal constituents on a rape victim are important evidence that sexual intercourse has taken place, but their absence does not necessarily mean that a rape did not occur. Physical injuries such as bruises and bleeding tend to confirm that a violent assault occurred. Furthermore, the forceful physical contact between victim and assailant may result in a transfer of physical evidence—blood, semen, hairs, and fibers. The presence of such evidence helps forge a vital link in the chain of circumstances surrounding a sexual crime.

To protect this kind of evidence, all the outer garments and undergarments from the people involved should be carefully removed and packaged separately in paper (not plastic) bags. Place a clean bedsheet on the floor and lay a clean paper sheet over it. The victim must remove her shoes before standing on the paper. Have the person disrobe while standing on the paper in order to collect any loose foreign material falling from the clothing. Collect each piece of clothing as it is removed and place in separate paper bags to avoid cross-contamination. Carefully fold the paper sheet so that all foreign materials are contained inside. If appropriate, bedding or the object on which the assault took place should be submitted to the laboratory for processing.

Items suspected of containing seminal stains must be handled carefully. Folding an article through the stain may cause it to flake off, as will rubbing the stained area against the surface of the packaging material. If, under unusual circumstances, it is not possible to transport the stained article to the laboratory, the stained area should be cut out and submitted with an unstained piece as a substrate control.

In the laboratory, analysts try to link seminal material to a donor(s) using DNA typing. Because an individual may transfer his or her DNA types to a stain through perspiration, investigators must handle stained articles with care, minimizing direct personal contact. The evidence collector must wear disposable latex gloves when such evidence must be touched.

The rape victim must undergo a medical examination as soon as possible after the assault. At this time, the appropriate items of physical evidence are collected by trained personnel. Evidence collectors should have an evidence-collection kit from the local crime laboratory (see Figure 8–19).

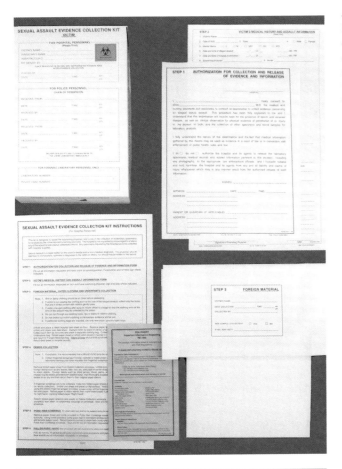

FIGURE 8–19a Victim rape collection kit showing the kit envelope, kit instructions, medical history and assault information forms, and foreign materials collection bag. *Courtesy Tri-Tech, Inc., Southport, N.C., www.tritechusa.com*

FIGURE 8–19b Victim rape collection kit showing collection bags for outer clothing, underpants, debris, pubic hair combings, pubic hair standard/reference samples, vaginal swabs, and rectal swabs. *Courtesy Tri-Tech, Inc., Southport, N.C., www.tritechusa.com*

FIGURE 8–19c Victim rape collection kit showing collection bags for oral swabs and smear, pulled head hair standard/ reference, known saliva sample, known blood samples, and anatomical drawings. *Courtesy Tri-Tech, Inc., Southport, N.C., www.tritechusa.com*

The following items of physical evidence are to be collected:

1. *Pubic combings.* Place a paper towel under the buttocks and comb the pubic area for loose or foreign hairs.

2. *Pubic hair standard/reference samples.* Cut fifteen to twenty full-length hairs from the pubic area at the skin line.

3. *External genital dry-skin areas.* Swab with at least one dry swab and one moistening swab.

4. *Vaginal swabs and smear.* Using two swabs simultaneously, carefully swab the vaginal area and let the swabs air-dry before packaging. Using two additional swabs, repeat the swabbing procedure and smear the swabs onto separate microscope slides, allowing them to air-dry before packaging.

5. *Cervix swabs.* Using two swabs simultaneously, carefully swab the cervix area and let the swabs air-dry before packaging.

6. *Rectal swabs and smear.* To be taken when warranted by case history. Using two swabs simultaneously, swab the rectal canal, smearing one of the swabs onto a microscope slide. Allow both samples to air-dry before packaging.

7. *Oral swabs and smear.* To be taken if oral–genital contact occurred. Use two swabs simultaneously to swab the cheek area and gum line. Using both swabs, prepare one smear slide. Allow both swabs and the smear to air-dry before packaging.

8. *Head hairs.* Cut at the skin line a minimum of five full-length hairs from each of the following scalp locations: center, front, back, left side, and

right side. A total of at least fifty hairs should be cut and submitted to the laboratory.

9. **Blood sample.** Collect at least 7 milliliters in a vacuum tube containing the preservative EDTA. The blood sample can be used for DNA typing as well as for toxicological analysis if required.

10. **Fingernail scrapings.** Scrape the undersurface of the nails with a dull object over a piece of clean paper to collect debris. Use separate paper, one for each hand.

11. **All clothing.** Package as described earlier.

12. **Urine specimen.** Collect 30 milliliters or more of urine from the victim for analysis for Rohypnol, GHB, and other substances associated with drug-facilitated sexual assaults (see pp. 166–167).

Often during the investigation of a sexual assault, the victim reports that a perpetrator engaged in biting, sucking, or licking of areas of the victim's body. As we will learn in the next chapter, the tremendous sensitivity associated with DNA technology offers investigators the opportunity to identify a perpetuator's DNA types from saliva residues collected off the skin. The most efficient way to recover saliva residues from the skin is to first swab the suspect area with a rotating motion using a cotton swab moistened with distilled water. A second, dry swab is then rotated over the skin to recover the moist remains on the skin's surface from the wet swab. The swabs are air-dried and packaged together as a single sample.[7]

If a suspect is apprehended, the following items are routinely collected:

1. *All clothing* and any other items believed to have been worn at the time of assault.

2. *Pubic hair combings.*

3. *Pulled head and pubic hair standard/reference samples.*

4. A *penile swab* taken within twenty four hours of the assault, when appropriate to the case history.

5. A blood sample or buccal swab (see p. 341) for DNA typing purposes.

The advent of DNA profiling has forced investigators to rethink what items are evidential in a sexual assault. As we will learn in Chapter 9, DNA levels in the range of one-billionth of a gram are now routinely characterized in crime laboratories. In the past, scant attention was paid to the underwear recovered from a male who was suspected of being involved in a sexual assault; seminal constituents on a man's underwear had little or no investigative value. Today, the sensitivity of DNA analysis has created new areas of investigation. It is possible to link between a victim and an assailant by analyzing biological material recovered from the interior front surface of a male suspect's underwear. This is especially important when investigations have failed to yield the presence of suspect's DNA on exhibits recovered from the victim.

The persistence of seminal constituents in the vagina may help determine the time of an alleged sexual attack. While spermatozoa in the vaginal cavity provide evidence of intercourse, important information regarding the time of sexual activity can be obtained from the knowledge that motile (living) sperm generally survive for up to four to six hours in the vaginal

Forensic Brief

A common mode of DNA transfer occurs when skin cells from the walls of the victim's vagina are transferred onto the suspect during intercourse. Subsequent penile contact with the inner surface of the suspect's underwear often leads to the recovery of the female victim's DNA from the underwear's inner surface. The power of DNA is illustrated in a case in which the female victim of a rape had consensual sexual intercourse with a male partner before being assaulted by a different male. DNA extracted from the inside front area of the suspect's underwear revealed a female DNA profile matching that of the victim. The added bonus in this case was finding male DNA on the same underwear that matched that of the consensual partner.

Source: Gary G. Verret, "Sexual Assault Cases with No Primary Transfer of Biological Material from Suspect to Victim: Evidence of Secondary and Tertiary Transfer of Biological Material from Victim to Suspect's Undergarments," *Proceedings of the Canadian Society of Forensic Science,* Toronto, Ontario, November 2001.

cavity of a living female. However, a successful search for motile sperm requires a microscopic examination of a vaginal smear immediately after it is taken from the victim.

A more extensive examination of vaginal collections is later made at a forensic laboratory. Nonmotile sperm may be found in a living female for up to three days after intercourse and occasionally up to six days later. However, intact sperm (sperm with tails) are not normally found sixteen hours after intercourse but have been found as late as seventy two hours after intercourse. The likelihood of finding seminal acid phosphatase in the vaginal cavity markedly decreases with time following intercourse, with little chance of identifying this substance forty eight hours after intercourse.[8] Hence, with the possibility of prolonged persistence of both spermatozoa and acid phosphatase in the vaginal cavity after intercourse, investigators should determine when and if voluntary sexual activity last occurred before the sexual assault. This information will help in evaluating the significance of finding these seminal constituents in a female victim. Blood or buccal swabs for DNA analysis should be taken from any consensual partner who had sex with the victim within seventy two hours of the assault.

Another significant indicator of recent sexual activity is p30. This semen marker normally is not detected in the vaginal cavity beyond twenty four hours following intercourse.[9]

Key Points

- A rape victim must undergo a medical examination as soon as possible after the assault. At that time clothing, hairs, and vaginal and rectal swabs can be collected for subsequent laboratory examination.

Chapter Summary

The term *serology* describes a broad scope of laboratory tests that use specific antigen and serum antibody reactions. An antibody reacts or agglutinates only with its specific antigen. The identity of each of the four A-B-O blood groups can be established by testing the blood with anti-A and anti-B sera.

The concept of specific antigen–antibody reactions has been applied to immunoassay techniques for detecting abused drugs in blood and urine. When an animal is injected with an antigen, its body produces a series of different antibodies, all of which are designed to attack some particular site on the antigen of interest. These antibodies are known as polyclonal antibodies. Alternatively, a more uniform and specific collection of antibodies designed to combine with a single antigen site can be manufactured. Such antibodies are known as monoclonal antibodies.

The criminalist must answer the following questions when examining dried blood: (1) Is it blood? (2) From what species did the blood originate? (3) If the blood is human, how closely can it be associated with a particular individual? The determination of blood is best made by means of a preliminary color test. A positive result from the Kastle-Meyer color test is highly indicative of blood. Alternatively, the luminol test is used to find trace amounts of blood at crime scenes. The precipitin test uses antisera normally derived from rabbits that have been injected with the blood of a known animal to determine the species origin of a questioned bloodstain. Before the advent of DNA typing, bloodstains were linked, in part, to a source by A-B-O typing. This approach has now been supplanted by DNA technology.

The location, distribution, and appearance of bloodstains and spatters may be useful for interpreting and reconstructing the events that produced the bleeding. Surface texture and the stain's shape, size, and location must be considered when determining the direction, dropping distance, and angle of impact of a bloodstain.

Many cases sent to a forensic laboratory involve sexual offenses, making it necessary to examine exhibits for seminal stains. The best way to locate and characterize a seminal stain is to perform the acid phosphatase color test. Semen can be unequivocally identified by the presence of either spermatozoa or p30, a protein unique to seminal plasma. Forensic scientists can link seminal material to an individual by DNA typing. The rape victim must undergo a medical examination as soon as possible after the assault. At that time clothing, hairs, and vaginal and rectal swabs can be collected for subsequent laboratory examination. If a suspect is apprehended within twenty four hours of the assault, it may be possible to detect the victim's DNA on the male's underwear or on a penile swab of the suspect.

Review Questions

Facts and Concepts

1. Who discovered that blood is distinguishable by its group or type?

2. What blood factors are the most important for properly matching a donor and recipient for a transfusion?

3. What technique supplanted blood typing for associating bloodstain evidence with a particular individual?

4. What is plasma? What percentage of blood content does plasma account for?

5. Which of the following types of cells are not contained in plasma?
   a. phagocytes
   b. leukocytes
   c. erythrocytes
   d. platelets

6. What are antigens and antibodies? What part of the blood contains antibodies?

7. Describe how antibodies and antigens determine one's A-B-O blood type.

8. What is the fourth important antigen other than A, B, and O?

9. What happens when serum containing B antibodies is added to red blood cells carrying the B antigen? Will the same thing happen if serum containing B antibodies is added to red blood cells carrying the A antigen? Explain your answer.

10. What is serology and what is its most widespread application? In what other areas related to forensic science is it finding application?

11. Briefly describe how antibodies capable of reacting with drugs are produced in animals.

12. What immunoassay technique has gained widespread popularity among toxicologists because of its speed and high sensitivity for detecting drugs in urine? What drug is this technique frequently used to screen for?

13. What is the greatest problem associated with detecting marijuana in urine?

14. What is the difference between monoclonal and polyclonal antibodies?

15. What three questions must the criminalist answer when examining dried blood?

16. Name the most common color test for blood and briefly describe how it identifies bloodstains.

17. Briefly describe how luminol is used to detect bloodstains.

18. Name two reasons why color tests are superior to microcrystalline tests for identifying blood.

19. What is the standard test used to determine whether blood is of human or animal origin? Briefly state the principle underlying the test.

20. Which technique takes advantage of the fact that antibodies and antigens move toward one another on a plate coated with medium made from a natural polymer called agar?

21. In what technique can antigens and antibodies be induced to move toward one another under the influence of an electrical field?

22. How do the hardness and porosity of a surface affect blood spattering on that surface?

23. How does a blood spatter analyst determine the direction of travel of blood striking an object?

24. A drop of blood striking a surface at right angles produces a stain of what shape? As the angle decreases, what happens to the shape of the stain?

25. When examining a blood spatter in a two-dimensional configuration, how does an analyst determine the area from which the blood emanated?

26. Define *gene* and *chromosome*.

27. How many chromosomes do most human cells contain and how are chromosomes arranged in the cell? What cells are the exception to this rule? How are these cells different from all other cells?

28. Describe how genetic material is transferred from parents to offspring.

29. What is an allele?

30. What is the difference between a heterozygous gene pair and a homozygous gene pair?

31. What is the difference between a dominant and a recessive gene?

32. Define *genotype* and *phenotype*. What is the only way to determine an individual's genotype?

33. In what type of noncriminal cases does blood typing have important implications?

34. The best way to locate and characterize a seminal stain is to perform what test? In what situation is this test particularly useful?

35. Define *ogliospermia* and *aspermia*.

36. The presence of what protein proves that a sample stain contains semen? What two techniques are used to detect this protein?

37. Why must a rape victim stand on a sheet of paper while disrobing for forensic analysis?

38. Besides swabbing for semen constituents, what other bodily fluids should be collected from a rape victim during a medical examination?

39. What items should be collected from the suspected perpetrator of a sexual assault?

40. How long do motile sperm generally survive in the vaginal cavity of a living female? How long do nonmotile sperm generally survive in the vaginal cavity of a living female?

Application and Critical Thinking

1. After looking at the bloodstains in the figure, answer the following questions:

   a. Which three drops struck the surface closest to a 90-degree angle? Explain your answer.

   b. Which three drops struck the surface farthest from a 90-degree angle? Explain your answer.

   c. In what direction were drops 2 and 7 traveling when they struck the surface? Explain your answer.

2. Complete the following Punnett squares and answer the questions that follow.

   Subject: Greg

Subject: Dale

Subject: Maura

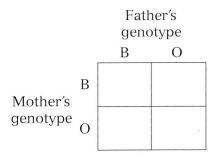

a. Among this group of people, which blood type(s) is most likely to be expressed? Which blood type is least likely to be expressed? Explain your answers.

b. What blood type is Greg most likely to have? Explain your answer.

c. Which person is least likely to have type B blood? Explain your answer.

d. In which, if any, of these people may a recessive gene express itself? Explain your answer.

3. Suppose that Greg and Maura have a child. Construct all of the possible Punnett squares for that child and answer the following questions:

a. What blood type(s) is the child most likely to have?

b. What genotype(s) is the child most likely to have?

c. If Maura and Greg have the same genotype, what blood type is the child most likely to have? What are the chances that the child will have type O blood? Explain your answers.

4. Police investigating the scene of a sexual assault recover a large blanket that they believe may contain useful physical evidence. They take it to the laboratory of forensic serologist Scott Alden, asking him to test it for the presence of semen. Noticing faint pink stains on the blanket, Scott asks the investigating detective if he is aware of anything that might recently have been spilled on the blanket. The detective reports that an overturned bowl of grapes and watermelon was found at the scene, as well as a broken glass that had contained wine. After the detective departs, Scott chooses and administers what he considers the best test for analyzing the piece of evidence in his possession. Three minutes after completion of the test, the blanket shows a positive reaction. What test did Scott choose and what was his conclusion? Explain your answer.

5. Criminalist Cathy Richards is collecting evidence from the victim of a sexual assault. She places a sheet on the floor, asks the victim to disrobe, and places the clothing in a paper bag. After collecting pubic combings and pubic hair samples, she takes two vaginal swabs, which she allows to air-dry before packaging. Finally, Cathy collects blood, urine, and scalp hair samples from the victim. What mistakes, if any, did she make in collecting this evidence?

WebExtra 8.6
Virtual Crime Scene 8.1
www.prenhall.com/hsforensics

WebExtra 8.7
Virtual Crime Scene 8.2
www.prenhall.com/hsforensics

Virtual Crime Scenes

Crime Scene 8.1
Step into the role of the first responding officer at a sexual assault scene
www.prenhall.com/hsforensics

Crime Scene 8.2
Assume the duties of an evidence-collection technician at a sexual assault scene
www.prenhall.com/hsforensics

Web Resources

Animated Blood Types (Discusses blood factors, blood typing, antibodies, and antigens using both text and animated sequences)
waynesword.palomar.edu/aniblood.htm

Blood Typing Game (Interactive application teaches about blood types and factors by having the user analyze a patient's blood and determine the right type of blood to give in a transfusion)
nobelprize.org/educational_games/medicine/landsteiner/

Bloodstains as Investigative Evidence (Discussion of characteristics of blood; shape, persistence, and age of bloodstains; procedures for processing blood evidence; and lab analysis of blood evidence)
www.pimall.com/nais/nl/n.bloodstains.html

Bloodstain Pattern Analysis Tutorial (Illustrated guide to bloodstain analysis includes examples of different types of bloodstains, blood spatter patterns and directionality, and impact angle determination)
www.bloodspatter.com/BPATutorial.htm

Forensic Serology
faculty.ncwc.edu/toconnor/425/425lect13.htm

How Luminol Works
www.howstuffworks.com/luminol.htm

Human Heredity (Online slide show covering basic principles of heredity and gene interactions)
www.bsd405.org/teachers/suttonk/Inheritance/Powerpoint1/humheredity/humanheredity/index.htm

Endnotes

1. M. Cox, "A Study of the Sensitivity and Specificity of Four Presumptive Tests for Blood," *Journal of Forensic Sciences* 36 (1991): 1503.
2. The luminol reagent is prepared by mixing 0.1 grams 3-amino-phthalhydrazide and 5.0 grams sodium carbonate in 100 milliliters distilled water. Before use, 0.7 grams sodium perborate is added to the solution.
3. A. M. Gross et al., "The Effect of Luminol on Presumptive Tests and DNA Analysis Using the Polymerase Chain Reaction," *Journal of Forensic Sciences* 44 (1999): 837.
4. J. P. Allery et al., "Cytological Detection of Spermatozoa: Comparison of Three Staining Methods," *Journal of Forensic Sciences* 46 (2001): 349.
5. In one study, only a maximum of 4 sperm cells out of 1,000 could be extracted from a cotton patch and observed under the microscope. Edwin Jones (Ventura County Sheriff's Department, Ventura, Calif.), personal communication.

6. J. Kearsey, H. Louie, and H. Poon, "Validation Study of the Onestep ABAcard® PSA Test Kit for RCMP Casework," *Canadian Society of Forensic Science Journal* 34 (2001): 63.

7. D. Sweet et al., "An Improved Method to Recover Saliva from Human Skin: The Double Swab Technique," *Journal of Forensic Sciences* 42 (1997): 320.

8. Anne Davies and Elizabeth Wilson, "The Persistence of Seminal Constituents in the Human Vagina," *Forensic Science* 3 (1974): 45.

9. J. Kearsey, H. Louie, and H. Poon, "Validation Study of the Onestep ABAcard® PSA Test Kit for RCMP Casework," *Canadian Society of Forensic Science Journal* 34 (2001): 63.

O. J. Simpson—A Mountain of Evidence

On June 12, 1994, police arrived at the home of Nicole Simpson only to view a horrific scene. The bodies of O. J. Simpson's estranged wife and her friend Ron Goldman were found on the path leading to the front door of Nicole's home. Both bodies were covered in blood and had received deep knife wounds. Nicole's head was nearly severed from her body. This was not a well-planned murder. A trail of blood led away from the murder scene. Blood was found in O. J. Simpson's Bronco. Blood drops were on O. J.'s driveway and in the foyer of his home. A blood-soaked sock was located in O. J. Simpson's bedroom, and a bloodstained glove rested outside his residence.

As DNA was extracted and profiled from each bloodstained article, a picture emerged that seemed to irrefutably link Simpson to the murders. A trail of DNA leaving the crime scene was consistent with O. J.'s profile, as was the DNA found entering Simpson's home. Simpson's DNA profile was found in the Bronco along with that of both victims. The glove contained the DNA profiles of Nicole and Ron, and the sock had Nicole's DNA profile. At trial, the defense team valiantly fought back. Miscues in evidence collection were craftily exploited. The defense strategy was to paint a picture of not only an incompetent investigation, but one that was tinged with dishonest police planting evidence. The strategy worked. O. J. Simpson was acquitted of murder.

chapter 9

DNA The Indispensable Forensic Science Tool

Key Terms

amelogenin gene
amino acids
buccal cells
chromosome
complementary base pairing
deoxyribonucleic acid (DNA)
electrophoresis
epithelial cells
human genome
hybridization
low copy number
mitochondria
multiplexing
nucleotide
picogram
polymer
polymerase chain reaction (PCR)
primer
proteins
replication
restriction enzymes
restriction fragment length
  polymorphisms (RFLPs)
sequencing
short tandem repeat (STR)
substrate control
tandem repeat
Y-STRs

Learning Objectives

After studying this chapter you should be able to:

- Name the parts of a nucleotide and explain how they are linked to form DNA

- Understand the concept of base pairing as it relates to the double-helix structure of DNA

- Contrast DNA strands that code for the production of proteins with strands that contain repeating base sequences

- Explain the technology of polymerase chain reaction (PCR) and how it applies to forensic DNA typing

- Contrast the newest DNA-typing technique, short tandem repeats (STRs), with previous DNA-typing technologies

- Describe the difference between nuclear and mitochondrial DNA

- Understand the use of DNA computerized databases in criminal investigation

- List the necessary procedures for proper preservation of biological evidence for laboratory DNA analysis

Understanding DNA

deoxyribonucleic acid (DNA)

Deoxyribonucleic acid—the molecules that carry the body's genetic information.

The discovery of deoxyribonucleic acid (DNA), the deciphering of its structure, and the decoding of its genetic information were turning points in our understanding of the underlying concepts of inheritance. Now, with incredible speed, as molecular biologists unravel the basic structure of genes, we can create new products through genetic engineering and develop diagnostic tools and treatments for genetic disorders.

For a number of years, these developments were of seemingly peripheral interest to forensic scientists. All that changed when, in 1985, what started out as a more or less routine investigation into the structure of a human gene led to the discovery that portions of the DNA structure of certain genes are as unique to each individual as fingerprints. Alec Jeffreys and his colleagues at Leicester University, England, who were responsible for these revelations, named the process for isolating and reading these DNA markers *DNA fingerprinting*. As researchers uncovered new approaches and variations to the original Jeffreys technique, the terms *DNA profiling* and *DNA typing* came to be applied to describe this relatively new technology.

This discovery caught the imagination of the forensic science community, for forensic scientists have long searched for ways to definitively link biological evidence such as blood, semen, hair, and tissue to a single individual. Although conventional testing procedures had gone a long way toward narrowing the source of biological materials, individualization remained an elusive goal. DNA typing has allowed forensic scientists to accomplish this goal. Although the technique is still relatively new, DNA typing has become routine in public crime laboratories. It also has been made available to interested parties through the services of a number of skilled private laboratories. In the United States, courts have overwhelmingly admitted DNA evidence and accepted the reliability of its scientific underpinnings.

What Is DNA?

chromosome

A threadlike structure in the cell nucleus composed of DNA, along which the genes are located.

Inside each of 60 trillion cells in the human body are strands of genetic material called chromosomes. Arranged along the chromosomes, like beads on a thread, are nearly 25,000 genes. The gene is the fundamental unit of heredity. It instructs body cells to make proteins that determine everything from hair color to susceptibility to diseases. Each gene is composed of DNA designed to carry out a single body function.

Although DNA was first discovered in 1868, scientists were slow to understand and appreciate its fundamental role in inheritance. Painstakingly, researchers developed evidence that DNA was probably the substance by which genetic instructions are passed from one generation to the next. However, the first major breakthrough in comprehending how DNA works did not occur until the early 1950s, when two researchers, James Watson and Francis Crick, deduced the structure of DNA. It turns out that DNA is an extraordinary molecule skillfully designed to control the genetic traits of all living cells, plant and animal.

The Structure of DNA Before examining the implications of Watson and Crick's discovery, let's see how DNA is constructed. DNA is a polymer. A polymer is a very large molecule made by linking a series of repeating units, or monomers. In this case, the units are known as nucleotides.

Nucleotides. A nucleotide is composed of a sugar molecule, a phosphorus atom surrounded by four oxygen atoms, and a nitrogen-containing molecule called a *base*. Figure 9–1 shows how nucleotides can be strung together to form a DNA strand. In this figure, S designates the sugar component, which is joined with a phosphate group to form the backbone of the DNA strand. Projecting from the backbone are the bases.

The key to understanding how DNA works is to appreciate the fact that only four types of bases are associated with DNA: adenine, cytosine, guanine, and thymine. To simplify our discussion of DNA, we will designate each of these bases by the first letter of their names. Hence, *A* will stand for adenine, *C* for cytosine, *G* for guanine, and *T* for thymine.

polymer
A substance composed of a large number of atoms. These atoms are usually arranged in repeating units, or monomers.

nucleotide
A repeating unit of DNA consisting of one of four bases—adenine, guanine, cytosine, or thymine—attached to a phosphate-sugar group.

FIGURE 9–1 **How nucleotides can be linked to form a DNA strand. S designates the sugar component, which is joined with phosphate groups (P) to form the backbone of DNA. Projecting from the backbone are four bases: *A*, adenine; *G*, guanine; *T*, thymine; and *C*, cytosine.**

Again, notice in Figure 9–1 how the bases project from the backbone of DNA. Also, although this figure shows a DNA strand of four bases, keep in mind that in theory there is no limit to the length of the DNA strand; a DNA strand can be composed of a long chain with millions of bases. This information was well known to Watson and Crick by the time they set about to detail the structure of DNA. Their efforts led them to discover that the DNA molecule is composed of two DNA strands coiled into a *double helix*. This can be thought of as resembling two wires twisted around each other.

As Watson and Crick manipulated scale models of DNA strands, they realized that the only way the bases on each strand could be properly aligned with each other in a double-helix configuration was to place base *A* opposite *T* and *G* opposite *C*. Watson and Crick had solved the puzzle of the double helix and presented the world with a simple but elegant picture of DNA (see Figure 9–2).

complementary base pairing

The specific pairing of base *A* with *T* and base *C* with *G* in double-stranded DNA.

Complementary Base Pairing. The only arrangement possible in the double-helix configuration is the pairing of bases *A* to *T* and *G* to *C*, a concept that has become known as complementary base pairing. Although *A–T* and *G–C* pairs are always required, there are no restrictions on how the bases are sequenced on a DNA strand. Thus, one can observe the

FIGURE 9–2 A representation of a DNA double helix. Notice how bases *G* and *C* pair with each other, as do bases *A* and *T*. This is the only arrangement in which two DNA strands can align with each other in a double-helix configuration.

sequences *T–A–T–T* or *G–T–A–A* or *G–T–C–A*. When these sequences are joined with their complements in a double-helix configuration, they pair as follows:

```
TATT   GTAA   GTCA
||||   ||||   ||||
ATAA   CATT   CAGT
```

Any base can follow another on a DNA strand, which means that the possible number of different sequence combinations is staggering. Consider that the average human chromosome has DNA containing 100 million base pairs. All of the human chromosomes taken together contain about three billion base pairs. From these numbers, we can begin to appreciate the diversity of DNA and hence the diversity of living organisms. DNA is like a book of instructions. The alphabet used to create the book is simple enough: *A, T, G,* and *C.* The order in which these letters are arranged defines the role and function of a DNA molecule.

DNA at Work   The inheritable traits that are controlled by DNA arise out of its ability to direct the production of complex molecules called proteins. Proteins are actually made by linking a combination of amino acids. Although thousands of proteins exist, they can all be derived from a combination of up to twenty known amino acids. The sequence of amino acids in a protein chain determines the shape and function of the protein.

Let's look at one example: The protein hemoglobin is found in our red blood cells. It carries oxygen to our body cells and removes carbon dioxide from these cells. One of the four amino acid chains of "normal" hemoglobin is shown in Figure 9–3(a). Studies of individuals who have sickle-cell anemia show that this inheritable disorder arises from the presence of

WebExtra 9.1
What Is DNA?
www.prenhall.com/hsforensics

proteins
Polymers of amino acids that play basic roles in the structure and function of living things.

amino acids
The building blocks of proteins.

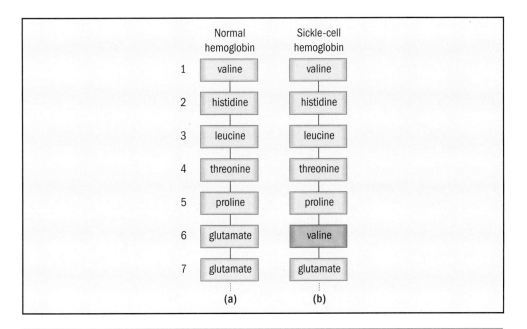

FIGURE 9–3 **(a) A string of amino acids composes one of the protein chains of hemoglobin. (b) Substitution of just one amino acid for another in the protein chain results in sickle-cell hemoglobin.**

"abnormal" hemoglobin in their red blood cells. An amino acid chain for "abnormal" hemoglobin is shown in Figure 9–3(b). Note that the sole difference between "normal" and "abnormal" or sickle-cell hemoglobin arises from the substitution of one amino acid for another in the protein chain.

The genetic information that determines the amino acid sequence for every protein manufactured in the human body is stored in DNA in a genetic code that relies on the sequence of bases along the DNA strand. The alphabet of DNA is simple—*A, T, G,* and *C*—but the key to deciphering the genetic code is to know that each amino acid is coded by a sequence of three bases. Thus, the amino acid alanine is coded by the combination *C–G–T;* the amino acid aspartate is coded by the combination *C–T–A;* and the amino acid phenylalanine is coded by the combination *A–A–A.* With this code in hand, we can now see how the amino acid sequence in a protein chain is determined by the structure of DNA. Consider the DNA segment

   –C–G–T–C–T–A–A–A–A–C–G–T–

The triplet code in this segment translates into

   [C–G–T] – [C–T–A] – [A–A–A] – [C–G–T]

or the protein chain

Interestingly, this code is not restricted to humans. Almost all living cells studied to date use the same genetic code as the language of protein synthesis.[1]

If we look at the difference between "normal" and sickle-cell hemoglobin (see Figure 9–3), we see that the latter is formed by substituting one amino acid (valine) for another (glutamate). Within the DNA segment that codes for the production of normal hemoglobin, the letter sequence is

   –[C–C–T] – [G–A–G] – [G–A–G]–
   proline   glutamate glutamate

Individuals with sickle-cell disease carry the sequence

   –[C–C–T] – [G–T–G] – [G–A–G]–
   proline   valine   glutamate

Thus, we see that a single base or letter change (*T* has been substituted for *A* in valine) is the underlying cause of sickle-cell anemia, demonstrating the delicate chemical balance between health and disease in the human body.

As scientists unravel the base sequences of DNA, they obtain a greater appreciation for the roles of proteins in the chemistry of life. Already the genes responsible for hemophilia, Duchenne muscular dystrophy, and Huntington's disease have been located. Once scientists have isolated a disease-causing gene, they can determine the protein that the gene has directed the cell to manufacture. By studying these proteins—or the absence of them—scientists will be able to devise a treatment for genetic disorders.

A thirteen-year project to determine the order of bases on all twenty-three pairs of human chromosomes (also called the **human genome**) is now

human genome
The order of bases on all twenty-three pairs of human chromosomes.

complete. Knowing the location on a specific chromosome at which DNA codes for production of a particular protein is useful for diagnosing and treating genetic diseases. This information is also crucial for understanding the underlying causes of cancer. Also, comparing the human genome with that of other organisms will help us understand the role and implications of evolution.

Key Points

- The gene is the fundamental unit of heredity. Each gene is composed of DNA specifically designed to control the genetic traits of our cells.

- DNA is constructed as a very large molecule made by linking a series of repeating units called nucleotides.

- Four types of bases are associated with the DNA structure: adenine (*A*), guanine (*G*), cytosine (*C*), and thymine (*T*).

- The bases on each strand of DNA are aligned in a double-helix configuration so that adenine pairs with thymine and guanine pairs with cytosine. This concept is known as complimentary base pairing.

- The order in which the base pairs are arranged defines the role and function of a DNA molecule.

Replication of DNA

Once the double-helix structure of DNA was discovered, how DNA duplicated itself prior to cell division became apparent. The concept of base pairing in DNA suggests the analogy of positive and negative photographic film. Each strand of DNA in the double helix has the same information; one can make a positive print from a negative or a negative from a positive.

The Process of Replication

DNA replication—the synthesis of new DNA from existing DNA—begins with the unwinding of the DNA strands in the double helix. Each strand is then exposed to a collection of free nucleotides. Letter by letter, the double helix is re-created as the nucleotides are assembled in the proper order, as dictated by the principle of base pairing (*A* with *T* and *G* with *C*). The result is the emergence of two identical copies of DNA where before there was only one (see Figure 9–4). A cell can now pass on its genetic identity when it divides.

replication
The synthesis of new DNA from existing DNA.

Many enzymes and proteins are involved in unwinding the DNA strands, keeping the two DNA strands apart, and assembling the new DNA strands. For example, DNA *polymerases* are enzymes that assemble a new DNA strand in the proper base sequence determined by the original or parent DNA strand. DNA polymerases also "proofread" the growing DNA double helices for mismatched base pairs, which are replaced with correct bases.

Polymerase Chain Reaction

Until recently, the phenomenon of DNA replication appeared to be only of academic interest to forensic scientists interested in DNA for identification.

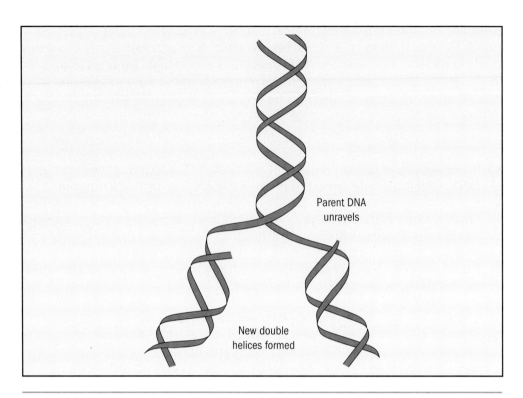

FIGURE 9–4 **Replication of DNA. The strands of the original DNA molecule are separated, and two new strands are assembled.**

polymerase chain reaction (PCR)

A technique for replicating or copying a portion of a DNA strand outside a living cell.

However, this changed when researchers perfected the technology of using DNA polymerases to copy a DNA strand located outside a living cell. This relatively new laboratory technique is known as polymerase chain reaction (PCR).

In PCR, small quantities of DNA or broken pieces of DNA found in crime-scene evidence can be copied with the aid of a DNA polymerase. The copying process can be accomplished in an automated fashion using a DNA Thermal Cycler (see Figure 9–5). Each cycle of the PCR technique results in a doubling of the DNA, as shown in Figure 9–4. Within a few hours, thirty cycles can multiply DNA a billionfold. Once DNA copies are in hand, they can be analyzed by any of the methods of modern molecular biology. The ability to multiply small bits of DNA opens new and exciting avenues for forensic scientists to explore. It means that sample size is no longer a limitation in characterizing DNA recovered from crime-scene evidence.

Key Points

- DNA replication begins with the unwinding of the DNA strands in the double helix. The double helix is re-created as the nucleotides are assembled in the proper order (*A* with *T* and *G* with *C*). Two identical copies of DNA emerge from the process.

- PCR (polymerase chain reaction) is a technique for replicating or copying a portion of a DNA strand outside a living cell.

- Recombinant DNA is a process by which the DNA of an organism is altered by inserting into it fragments of DNA from another organism.

FIGURE 9–5 The DNA Thermal Cycler, an instrument that automates the rapid and precise temperature changes required to copy a DNA strand. Within a matter of hours, DNA can be multiplied a billionfold. *Courtesy Applied Biosystems, Foster City, Calif.*

Closer Analysis

Recombinant DNA

The relationship between the base letters on a DNA strand and the type of protein specified for manufacture by the sequence of these letters is called the *genetic code.* Once a particular DNA site has been identified as controlling the production of a certain protein, molecular biologists can take advantage of the natural chemical-producing abilities of the DNA site. This undertaking has given rise to the technology known as *recombinant DNA.*

Recombinant DNA relies on the ability of certain chemicals, known as restriction enzymes, to cut DNA into fragments that can later be incorporated into another DNA strand. Restriction enzymes can be thought of as highly specialized scissors that cut a DNA molecule when they recognize a specific sequence of bases. At present, more than 150 restriction enzymes are commercially available. Thus, molecular biologists have a great deal of flexibility in choosing the portion of a DNA strand they wish to cut out.

Once a portion of the DNA strand has been cut out with the aid of a restriction enzyme, the next step in the recombinant DNA process is to insert the isolated DNA segment into a foreign DNA strand (normally, bacterium DNA is selected). Many types of bacteria contain DNA shaped in a circle. A restriction enzyme is used to cut open the circular DNA; then the foreign DNA is spliced in to re-form the circle (see figure). The newly fashioned DNA is reintroduced into the bacterial cells. As the bacteria multiply rapidly in their usual fashion, copies of altered DNA are passed on to all descendants.

The commercial implications of recombinant DNA technology are enormous. For example, the gene that produces human growth hormone has been introduced into goldfish and carp, and the gene that produces growth hormone in rainbow trout has been introduced into carp. In each case, the gene-altered fish have grown significantly faster and larger than their natural relatives. If altered bacteria are infused with the DNA segment that makes human insulin, for example, the bacteria make

(continued)

Closer Analysis

Recombinant DNA (*continued*)

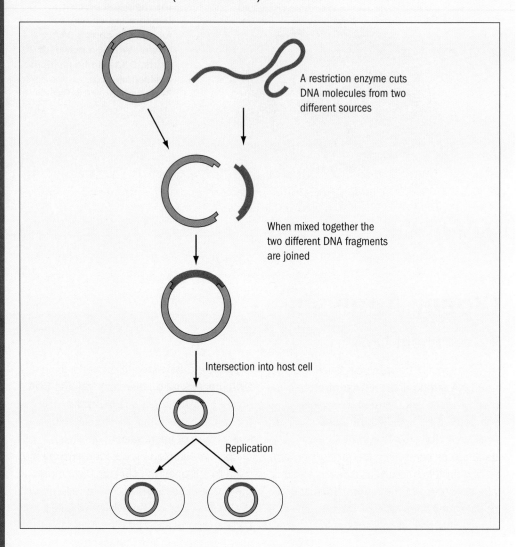

A restriction enzyme cuts DNA molecules from two different sources

When mixed together the two different DNA fragments are joined

Intersection into host cell

Replication

The joining of DNA from two different sources via recombinant DNA technology.

human insulin. Because bacteria multiply so rapidly, it is not long before significant amounts of insulin can be recovered and used to treat diabetes. In this manner, other naturally occurring substances can be produced in commercial quantities for the treatment of human ailments. Likewise, plant genetic engineering holds promise for increasing global food production.

DNA Typing with Tandem Repeats

Geneticists have discovered that portions of the DNA molecule contain sequences of letters that are repeated numerous times. In fact, more than thirty percent of the human genome is composed of repeating segments of DNA. These repeating sequences, or tandem repeats, seem to act as filler or spacers between the coding regions of DNA. Although these repeating segments do not seem to affect our outward appearance or control any other basic genetic function, they are nevertheless part of our genetic makeup, inherited from our parents in the manner illustrated by the Punnett

tandem repeat
Region of a chromosome that contains multiple copies of a core DNA sequence arranged in a repeating fashion.

square (p. 289). The origin and significance of these tandem repeats is a mystery, but to forensic scientists they offer a means of distinguishing one individual from another through DNA typing.

Restriction Fragment Length Polymorphisms

Forensic scientists first began applying DNA technology to human identity in 1985. From the beginning, attention has focused on the tandem repeats of the genome. These repeats can be visualized as a string of connected boxes with each box having the same core sequence of DNA bases (see Figure 9–6). All humans have the same type of repeats, but there is tremendous variation in the number of repeats that each of us has.

Until the mid-1990s, the forensic community aimed its efforts at characterizing repeat segments known as restriction fragment length polymorphisms (RFLPs). These repeats are cut out of the DNA double helix by a restriction enzyme that acts like a pair of scissors. The forensic science community selected a number of different RFLPs for performing DNA typing. Typically a core sequence is fifteen to thirty-five bases long and repeats itself up to a thousand times.

Let's examine some DNA strands with regions of repeating base sequences to see how this process works. Figure 9–7 illustrates a portion of a pair of chromosomes. Note that each chromosome is composed of two DNA strands wrapped in a double-helix configuration. Each chromosome has a region that contains repeating bases. For the sake of simplicity in illustrating the RFLP method, we assume that the core repeat is only three bases long with a sequence of *T–A–G*.

Note an important distinction between the two chromosomes: the chromosome on the left has three repeating sequences of *T–A–G,* while the one on the right has two repeating sequences of *T–A–G*. As with any genetic trait, these repeating sequences were inherited from the parents. In this example, one parent contributed the chromosome containing the three repeating sequences, and the other parent passed on the chromosome containing the two repeating sequences.

The key to understanding DNA typing lies in the knowledge that, within the world's population, numerous possibilities exist for the number of times a particular sequence of base letters can repeat itself on a DNA strand. The possibilities become even greater when one deals with two chromosomes, each containing different lengths of repeating sequences. During RFLP typing, restriction enzymes cut up chromosomes into hundreds of fragments, some containing repeating sequences from the DNA molecule. In our example, shown in Figure 9–7, the chromosome pair, when cut, will yield two different fragment lengths of *T–A–G*.

Electrophoresis The length differences associated with DNA strands or RFLPs allow forensic scientists to distinguish one person from another. In

restriction fragment length polymorphisms (RFLP)
Different fragment lengths of base pairs that result from cutting a DNA molecule with restriction enzymes.

restriction enzyme
Chemical that acts as scissors to cut DNA molecules at specific locations.

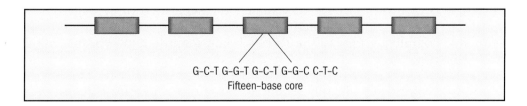

G-C-T G-G-T G-C-T G-G-C C-T-C
Fifteen–base core

FIGURE 9–6 A DNA segment consisting of a series of repeating DNA units. In this illustration, the fifteen-base core can repeat itself hundreds of times. The entire DNA segment is typically hundreds to thousands of bases long.

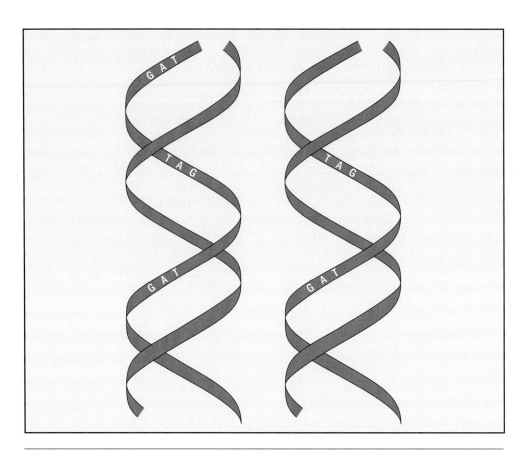

FIGURE 9–7 **Intertwined strands of DNA representing segments of two chromosomes.**
Note that the chromosome segment on the left contains three repeating sequences of
T–A–G, while the chromosome segment on the right has two repeating sequences of T–A–G.

actuality, these strands are relatively long, often consisting of thousands of bases. Once the DNA molecules have been cut up by the restriction enzyme, the resulting fragments must be sorted out. This is accomplished by separating the fragments by electrophoresis.

During the electrophoretic process, DNA from various sources, cut up by restriction enzymes, is placed on a plate coated with a gel medium. When the gel is subjected to an electric potential the DNA fragments migrate across the plate. Because smaller DNA fragments move faster along the plate than do larger fragments, the process separates the fragments according to size.

Hybridization   Once the electrophoresis process is completed, the double-stranded fragments of DNA are chemically treated so that the strands separate from each other. The fragments are then transferred to a nylon membrane in much the same way as one would transfer an ink line onto a blotter. This transfer process is called *Southern blotting,* named after its developer, Edward Southern. To visualize the separated RFLPs, the nylon sheet is treated with radioactively labeled probes containing a base sequence complementary to the RFLPs being identified (a process called hybridization).

DNA Typing with RFLP   In our example, we aim to identify RFLPs composed of a repeating string of letters spelling *T–A–G.* Hence, the appropriate probes would have the complementary letter sequence *A–T–C,* as shown in the following diagram, so that the probes can specifically bind to the desired RFLP. (Note: The asterisk designates a radioactive label.)

electrophoresis
A technique for separating molecules through their migration on a support medium under the influence of an electrical potential.

WebExtra 9.2

An Animated Demonstration of Gel Electrophoresis
www.prenhall.com/hsforensics

hybridization
The process of joining two complementary strands of DNA to form a double-stranded molecule.

Next, the nylon sheet is placed against X-ray film and exposed for several days. The radioactive decay products strike the film. When the film is processed, bands appear where the radioactive probes stuck to the fragments on the nylon sheet. The length of each fragment is determined by running known DNA fragment lengths alongside the test specimens and comparing the distances they migrated across the plate. The entire DNA typing process is depicted in Figure 9–8.

A typical DNA fragment pattern shows two bands (one RFLP from each chromosome). When comparing the DNA fragment patterns of two

DNA is cut into fragments by a restriction enzyme

DNA fragments are separated into bands by electrophoresis; three rows of bands are shown to represent blood or semen samples from three sources

Gel
Membrane

The DNA band pattern on the electrophoretic gel is transferred to a nylon membrane

Nylon membrane with DNA fragments positioned exactly as they were on the gel

A radioactive DNA probe is added to the membrane where it binds to specific fragments

X-ray film
Membrane

X-ray film is placed next to the membrane to detect the radioactive pattern

Developed X-ray film showing DNA fragments that combined with the radioactive probe

FIGURE 9–8   The DNA RFLP typing process.

Closer Analysis

Electrophoresis

Electrophoresis is somewhat related to thin-layer chromatography (discussed in Chapter 5) in that it separates materials according to their migration rates on a stationary solid phase. However, electrophoresis does not use a moving liquid phase to move the material; instead, an electrical potential is placed across the stationary medium.

The nature of the medium can vary; most forensic applications call for a starch or agar gel coated onto a glass plate. Under these conditions, only substances that possess an electrical charge migrate across the stationary phase (see Figure 1). Because many substances in blood carry an electrical charge, they can be separated and identified by electrophoresis. The technique is particularly useful for separating and identifying complex biochemical mixtures. In forensic science, electrophoresis is most useful for characterizing proteins and DNA in dried blood (see Figure 2).

Forensic serologists have developed several electrophoretic procedures for characterizing DNA in dried blood. Mixtures of DNA fragments can be separated by gel electrophoresis by taking advantage of the fact that the rate of movement of DNA across a gel-coated plate depends on the

(a)

(b)

(c)

FIGURE 1

molecule's size. Smaller DNA fragments move faster along the plate than larger DNA fragments. After completing the electrophoresis run, the separated DNA is stained with a suitable developing agent for visual observation.

FIGURE 2   DNA fragments separated by gel electrophoresis are visualized under a UV light. *Courtesy Cytographics, Visuals Unlimited*

or more specimens, one merely looks for a match between the band sets. For example, in Figure 9–9, DNA extracted from a crime-scene stain matches the DNA recovered from one of three suspects. Although only a limited number of people in a population would have the same DNA fragment pattern as the suspect, this test in itself cannot be used to individualize the stain to the suspect. However, by using additional DNA probes, each of which recognizes different repeating DNA segments (other than T–A–G), a high degree of discrimination or even near individualization can be achieved. For example, if each probe selected yielded a DNA type having a frequency of occurrence of one in a hundred in a population, then four different probes would have a combined frequency of one in 100 million (1/100 × 1/100 × 1/100 × 1/100).

FIGURE 9–9   A DNA profile pattern of a suspect and its match to crime-scene DNA. From left to right, lane 1 is a DNA standard marker; lane 2 is the crime-scene DNA; and lanes 3 to 5 are control samples from suspects 1, 2, and 3, respectively. Crime-scene DNA matches suspect 2. *Courtesy Edvotek, The Biotechnology Education Company*

RFLP DNA typing has the distinction of being the first scientifically accepted protocol in the United States used for forensic characterization of DNA. However, its utility has been short lived. New technology incorporating polymerase chain reaction (PCR) has supplanted RFLP. In its short history, perhaps RFLP's most startling impact related to the impeachment trial of President Bill Clinton. The whole complexion of the investigation regarding the relationship of the president with a White House intern, Monica Lewinsky, changed when it was revealed that Ms. Lewinsky possessed a dress that she claimed was stained with the president's semen. The FBI Laboratory was asked to compare the DNA extracted from the

---

FEDERAL BUREAU OF INVESTIGATION
WASHINGTON, D. C. 20535

Report of Examination

Examiner Name:	▉▉▉▉▉▉▉▉	Date: 08/17/98
Unit: DNA Analysis 1		Phone No.: 202-324-4409
FBI File No.: 29D-OIC-LR-35063		Lab No.: 980730002 S BO
		980803100 S BO

Results of Examinations:

Deoxyribonucleic acid (DNA) profiles for the genetic loci D2S44, D17S79, D1S7, D4S139, D10S28, D5S110 and D7S467 were developed from HaeIII-digested high molecular weight DNA extracted from specimens K39 and Q3243-1(a semen stain removed from specimen Q3243). Based on the results of these seven genetic loci, specimen K39 (CLINTON) is the source of the DNA obtained from specimen Q3243-1, to a reasonable degree of scientific certainty.

No DNA-RFLP examinations were conducted on specimen Q3243-2 (a semen stain removed from specimen Q3243).

BLACK — 1,440,000,000,000
CAUC — 7,870,000,000,000
SEH — 3,140,000,000,000
SEH — 943,000,000,000

DNAU1 - Page 1 of 1

Q3243

FIGURE 9–10 The dress and the FBI Report of Examination for a semen stain located on the dress.

dress stain with that of the president. A seven-probe RFLP match was obtained between the president's DNA and the stain. The combined frequency of occurrence for the seven DNA types found was nearly one in eight trillion, an undeniable link. The dress and a copy of the FBI DNA report are shown in Figure 9–10.

Key Points

- Portions of the DNA molecule contain sequences of bases that are repeated numerous times. These tandem repeats offer a means of distinguishing one individual from another through DNA typing.

- Length differences associated with relatively long repeating DNA strands—called restriction fragment length polymorphisms (RFLPs)—formed the basis for one of the first DNA-typing procedures.

- In the laboratory, DNA molecules are cut up by a restriction enzyme and the resulting fragments are sorted out by electrophoresis.

- Materials undergoing electrophoresis are forced to move across a gel-coated plate under the influence of an electrical potential. Substances such as DNA can be separated and characterized using electrophoresis.

- A typical DNA fragment pattern shows two bands (one RFLP from each chromosome).

Polymerase Chain Reaction (PCR)

For nearly a decade, RFLP was the dominant DNA-typing procedure in the United States. However, its utility quickly ended by the mid-1990s. What caused this change? The answer is quite simple: the emergence of a revolutionary and elegant technique known as polymerase chain reaction, or PCR. Put simply, PCR is a technique designed to copy or multiply DNA strands. For the forensic scientist, who is often presented with minute quantities of materials, the opportunity to multiply the quantity of sample available for analysis was too good to pass up.

The PCR Process

PCR is the outgrowth of knowledge gained from an understanding of how DNA strands naturally replicate within a cell. The most important feature of PCR is the knowledge that an enzyme called *DNA polymerase* can be directed to synthesize a specific region of DNA. In a relatively straightforward manner, PCR can be used to repeatedly duplicate or amplify a strand of DNA millions of times. As an example, let's consider a segment of DNA that we want to duplicate by PCR:

*–G–T–C–T–C–A–G–C–T–T–**C**–**C**–**A**–**G**–*
*–**C**–**A**–**G**–A–G–T–C–G–A–A–G–G–T–C–*

To perform PCR on this DNA segment, short sequences of DNA on each side of the region of interest must be identified. In the example shown here, the short sequences are designated by boldface letters in the DNA segment. These short DNA segments must be available in a pure form known as a primer if the PCR technique is going to work.

primer
A short strand of DNA used to target a region of DNA for replication by PCR.

The first step in PCR is to heat the DNA strands to about 94°C. At this temperature, the double-stranded DNA molecules separate completely:

–G–T–C–T–C–A–G–C–T–T–C–C–A–G–

–C–A–G–A–G–T–C–G–A–A–G–G–T–C–

WebExtra 9.3

Polymerase Chain Reaction
www.prenhall.com/hsforensics

The second step is to add the primers to the separated strands and allow the primers to combine, or hybridize, with the strands by lowering the test-tube temperature to about 60°C.

–G–T–C–T–C–A–G–C–T–T–C–C–A–G–
C–A–G–A

C–C–A–G
–C–A–G–A–G–T–C–G–A–A–G–G–T–C–

The third step is to add the DNA polymerase and a mixture of free nucleotides (*A, C, G, T*) to the separated strands. When the test tube is heated to 72°C, the polymerase enzyme directs the rebuilding of a double-stranded DNA molecule, extending the primers by adding the appropriate bases, one at a time, resulting in the production of two complete pairs of double-stranded DNA segments:

–G–T–C–T–C–A–G–C–T–T–C–C–A–G–
C–A–G–A–G–T–C–G–A–A–G–G–T–C–

–G–T–C–T–C–A–G–C–T–T–C–C–A–G
–C–A–G–A–G–T–C–G–A–A–G–G–T–C–

This completes the first cycle of the PCR technique, which results in a doubling of the number of DNA strands from one to two. The cycle of heating, cooling, and strand rebuilding is then repeated, resulting in a further doubling of the DNA strands. On completion of the second cycle, four double-stranded DNA molecules have been created from the original double-stranded DNA sample. Typically, twenty-eight to thirty-two cycles are carried out to yield more than one billion copies of the original DNA molecule. Each cycle takes less than two minutes.

Advantages of PCR

Why couldn't the PCR technology be applied to RFLP DNA typing? Simply put, the RFLP strands are too long, often containing thousands of bases. PCR is best used with DNA strands that are no longer than a couple of hundred bases. The obvious solution to this problem is to characterize DNA strands that are much shorter than RFLPs.

Another advantage in moving to shorter DNA strands is that they would be expected to be more stable and less subject to degradation brought about by adverse environmental conditions. The long RFLP strands tend to break apart under adverse conditions not uncommon at crime scenes.

From the forensic scientist's viewpoint, PCR offers a third distinct advantage in that it can amplify minute quantities of DNA, thus overcoming the limited-sample-size problem often associated with crime-scene evidence. With PCR, less than one-billionth of a gram of DNA is required for analysis. Consequently, PCR can characterize DNA extracted from small quantities of blood, semen, and saliva. The extraordinary sensitivity of PCR allows forensic analysts to characterize small quantities of DNA that could never be detected by RFLP. For instance, PCR has been applied to the identification of saliva residues found on envelopes, stamps, soda cans, and cigarette butts.

Key Points

- Polymerase chain reaction (PCR) can amplify minute quantities of DNA. The technique evolved from an understanding of how DNA strands naturally replicate within a cell.

- PCR technology cannot be applied to RFLP DNA typing because RFLP strands are too long, often numbering in the thousands of bases. PCR is best used with DNA strands that are no longer than a couple of hundred bases.

- Long RFLP strands tend to break apart under the adverse conditions at many crime scenes. The shorter DNA strands used in PCR are more stable and less subject to degradation caused by adverse environmental conditions.

Short Tandem Repeats (STRs)

The latest method of DNA typing, short tandem repeat (STR) analysis, has emerged as the most successful and widely used DNA-profiling procedure. STRs are locations (loci) on the chromosome that contain short sequence elements that repeat themselves within the DNA molecule. They serve as helpful markers for identification because they are found in great abundance throughout the human genome.

short tandem repeat (STR)
A region of a DNA molecule that contains short segments of three to seven repeating base pairs.

STRs normally consist of repeating sequences of three to seven bases; the entire strand of an STR is also very short, less than 450 bases long. These strands are significantly shorter than those encountered in the RFLP procedure. This means that STRs are much less susceptible to degradation and are often recovered from bodies or stains that have been subject to extreme decomposition. Also, because of their shortness, STRs are an ideal candidate for multiplication by PCR, thus overcoming the limited-sample-size problem often associated with crime-scene evidence. Only one-billionth of a gram or less of DNA is required—1/50 to 1/100 the amount normally required for RFLP analysis.

To understand the utility of STRs in forensic science, let's look at one commonly used STR known as TH01. This DNA segment contains the repeating sequence A–A–T–G. Seven TH01 variants have been identified in the human genome. These variants contain five to eleven repeats of A–A–T–G. Figure 9–11 illustrates two such TH01 variants, one containing six repeats and the other containing eight repeats of A–A–T–G.

During a forensic examination, TH01 is extracted from biological materials and amplified by PCR as described earlier. The ability to copy an STR means that extremely small amounts of the molecule can be detected and analyzed. Once the STRs have been copied or amplified, they are separated by electrophoresis. By examining the distance the STR has migrated on the electrophoretic plate, one can determine the number of A–A–T–G repeats in the STR. Every person has two STR types for TH01, one inherited from each parent. Thus, for example, one may find in a semen stain TH01 with six repeats and eight repeats. This combination of TH01 is found in approximately 3.5 percent of the population.

FIGURE 9–11 Variants of the short tandem repeat TH01. The upper DNA strand contains six repeats of the sequence *A–A–T–G;* the lower DNA strand contains eight repeats of the sequence *A–A–T–G.* This DNA type is known as TH01 6, 8.

Multiplexing

What makes STRs so attractive to forensic scientists is that hundreds of different types of STRs are found in human genes. The more STRs one can characterize, the smaller the percentage of the population from which these STRs can emanate. This gives rise to the concept of **multiplexing**. Using PCR technology, one can simultaneously extract and amplify a combination of different STRs.

One STR system on the commercial market is the STR Blue Kit.[2] This kit provides the necessary materials for amplifying and detecting three STRs (a process called *triplexing*)—D3S1358, vWA, and FGA. The design of the system ensures that the size of the STRs does not overlap, thereby allowing each marker to be viewed clearly on an electrophoretic gel, as shown in Figure 9–12. In the United States, the forensic science community has standardized on thirteen STRs for entry into a national database known as the Combined DNA Index System (CODIS).

When an STR is selected for analysis, not only must the identity and number of core repeats be defined, but the sequence of bases flanking the repeats must also be known. This knowledge allows commercial manufacturers of STR-typing kits to prepare the correct primers to delineate the STR segment to be amplified by PCR. Figure 9–13 illustrates how appropriate primers are used to define the region of DNA to be amplified. Also, a mix of different primers aimed at different STRs will be used to simultaneously amplify a multitude of STRs (multiplexing). In fact, one STR kit on the commercial market can simultaneously make copies of fifteen different STRs.

DNA Typing with STRs

The thirteen CODIS STRs are listed in Table 9–1 along with their probabilities of identity. The probability of identity is a measure of the likelihood that two individuals selected at random will have an identical STR type.

multiplexing
A technique that simultaneously detects more than one DNA marker in a single analysis.

WebExtra 9.4
See the 13 CODIS STRs and Their Chromosomal Positions
www.prenhall.com/hsforensics

FIGURE 9–12   Triplex system containing three loci: FGA, vWA, and D3S1358, indicating a match between the questioned and the standard/reference stains.

FIGURE 9–13   Appropriate primers flanking the repeat units of a DNA segment must be selected and put in place to initiate the PCR process.

The smaller the value of this probability, the more discriminating the STR. A high degree of discrimination and even individualization can be attained by analyzing a combination of STRs (multiplexing). Because STRs occur independently of each other, the probability of biological evidence having a particular combination of STR types is determined by the product of their frequency of occurrence in a population. Hence, the greater the number of STRs characterized, the smaller the frequency of occurrence of the analyzed sample in the general population.

The combination of the first three STRs shown in Table 9–1 typically produces a frequency of occurrence of about 1 in 5,000. A combination of the first six STRs typically yields a frequency of occurrence in the range of 1 in two million for the Caucasian population, and if the top nine STRs are

Table 9–1 The Thirteen CODIS STRs and Their Probability of Identities

STR	African-American	U.S. Caucasian
D3S1358	0.094	0.075
vWA	0.063	0.062
FGA	0.033	0.036
TH01	0.109	0.081
TPOX	0.090	0.195
CSF1PO	0.081	0.112
D5S818	0.112	0.158
D13S317	0.136	0.085
D7S820	0.080	0.065
D8S1179	0.082	0.067
D21S11	0.034	0.039
D18S51	0.029	0.028
D16S539	0.070	0.089

Source: *The Future of Forensic DNA Testing: Predictions of the Research and Development Working Group.* Washington, D.C.: National Institute of Justice, Department of Justice, 2000, p. 41.

WebExtra 9.5

Calculate the Frequency of Occurrence of a DNA Profile
www.prenhall.com/hsforensics

determined in combination, this frequency declines to about 1 in one billion. The combination of all thirteen STRs shown in Table 9–1 typically produces frequencies of occurrence that measure in the range of 1 in 575 trillion for Caucasian Americans and 1 in 900 trillion for African-Americans. Importantly, several commercially available kits allow forensic scientists to profile STRs in the kinds of combinations cited here.

Capillary Electrophoresis

The separation of STRs can typically be carried out on a flat gel-coated electrophoretic plate, as described earlier. However, the need to reduce analysis time and to automate sampling and data collection has led to the emergence of *capillary electrophoresis* as the preferred technology for characterization of STRs. Capillary electrophoresis is carried out in a thin glass column rather than on the surface of a coated-glass plate.

WebExtra 9.6

Understand the Operational Principles of Capillary Electrophoresis
www.prenhall.com/hsforensics

As illustrated in Figure 9–14, each end of the column is immersed in a reservoir of buffer liquid that also holds electrodes (coated with platinum) to supply high-voltage energy. The column is coated with a gel polymer, and the DNA-containing sample solution is injected into one end of the column with a syringe. The STR fragments then move through the column under the influence of an electrical potential at a speed that is related to the length of the STR fragments. The other end of the column is connected to a detector that tracks the separated STRs as they emerge from the column. As the DNA peaks pass through the detector, they are recorded on a display known as an *electropherogram*.

WebExtra 9.7

See the Electopherogram Record from One Individual's DNA
www.prenhall.com/hsforensics

Sex Identification Using STRs

Manufacturers of commercial STR kits typically used by crime laboratories provide one additional piece of useful information along with STR types: the sex of the DNA contributor. The focus of attention here is the amelogenin gene located on both the X and Y chromosomes. This gene,

amelogenin gene
A genetic locus useful for determining gender.

(a)

(b)

FIGURE 9–14 Capillary electrophoresis technology has evolved from the traditional flat gel electrophoresis approach. The separation of DNA segments is carried out on the interior wall of a glass capillary tube coated with a gel polymer and kept at a constant voltage. The size of the DNA fragments determines the speed at which they move through the column. This figure illustrates the separation of three sets of STRs (triplexing).

which is actually the gene for tooth pulp, has an interesting characteristic in that it is shorter by six bases in the X chromosome than in the Y chromosome. Hence, when the amelogenin gene is amplified by PCR and separated by electrophoresis, males, who have an X and a Y chromosome, show two bands; females, who have two X chromosomes, have just one band. Typically, these results are obtained in conjunction with STR types.

Another tool in the arsenal of the DNA analyst is the ability to type STRs located on the Y chromosome. The Y chromosome is male specific and is always paired with the X chromosome. More than twenty different Y-STR markers have been identified, and a commercial kit allows for the characterization of seventeen Y chromosome STRs. When can it be advantageous to seek out Y-STR types? Generally, Y-STRs are useful for analyzing blood, saliva, or a vaginal swab that is a mix originating from more than one male. For example, Y-STRs prove useful when multiple males are involved in a sexual assault.

Keep in mind that STR types derived from the Y chromosome originate only from this single male chromosome. A female subject, or one with an XX chromosome pattern, does not contribute any DNA information. Also, unlike a conventional STR analysis that is derived from two chromosomes and typically shows two bands or peaks, a Y-STR has only one band or peak for each STR type.

For example, the traditional STR DNA pattern may prove to be overly complex in the case of a vaginal swab containing the semen of two males. Each STR type would be expected to show four bands, two from each male. Also complicating the appearance of the DNA profile may be the presence of DNA from skin cells emanating from the walls of the vagina. In this circumstance, homing in on the Y chromosome greatly simplifies the appearance and interpretation of the DNA profile. Thus, when presented with a DNA mixture of two males and one female, each STR type would be expected to show six bands. However, the same mixture subjected to Y-STR analysis would show only two bands (one band for each male) for each Y-STR type.

Significance of DNA Typing

STR DNA typing has become an essential and basic investigative tool in the law enforcement community. The technology has progressed at a rapid rate and in only a few years has surmounted numerous legal challenges to become vital evidence for resolving violent crimes and sex offenses. DNA evidence is impartial, implicating the guilty and exonerating the innocent.

Significantly, about 25 percent of the DNA examinations conducted by the FBI Laboratory since 1989 have excluded suspects identified by police as the source of DNA evidence collected from the crime scene. In a number of well-publicized cases, DNA evidence has exonerated individuals who have been wrongly convicted and imprisoned (see Figure 9–15). The importance of DNA analyses in criminal investigations has also placed added burdens on crime laboratories to improve their quality-assurance procedures and to ensure the correctness of their results. In several well-publicized instances, the accuracy of DNA tests conducted by government-funded laboratories has been called into question.

Key Points

- STRs are locations on the chromosome that contain short sequences that repeat themselves within the DNA molecule. They serve as useful

Y-STRs
Short tandem repeats located on the human Y chromosome.

WebExtra 9.8
An Animation Depicting Y-STRs
www.prenhall.com/hsforensics

markers for identification because they are found in great abundance throughout the human genome.

- The entire strand of an STR is very short, less than 450 bases long. This makes STRs much less susceptible to degradation and they are often recovered from bodies or stains that have been subjected to extreme decomposition.

- The more STRs one can characterize, the smaller the percentage of the population from which a particular combination of STRs can emanate. This gives rise to the concept of multiplexing, in which the forensic scientist can simultaneously extract and amplify a combination of different STRs.

- With STR, as little as 125 picograms of DNA is required for analysis— 1/100 the amount normally required for RFLP analysis.

Mitochondrial DNA

Typically, when one describes DNA in the context of a criminal investigation, the subject is assumed to be the DNA in the nucleus of a cell. Actually, a human cell contains two types of DNA—nuclear and mitochondrial. The first constitutes the twenty three pairs of chromosomes in the nuclei of our cells. Each parent contributes to the genetic makeup of these chromosomes. Mitochondrial DNA (mtDNA), on the other hand, is found outside the nucleus of the cell and is inherited solely from the mother.

Mitochondria are cell structures found in all human cells. They are the power plants of the body, providing about 90 percent of the energy that the body needs to function. A single mitochondrion contains several loops of DNA, all of which are involved in energy generation. Further, because each cell in our bodies contains hundreds to thousands of mitochondria, there are hundreds to thousands of mtDNA copies in a human cell. This compares to just one set of nuclear DNA located in that same cell.

Forensic scientists rely on mtDNA to identify a subject when nuclear DNA is significantly degraded, such as in charred remains, or when nuclear DNA may be present in only very small quantities (such as in a hair shaft). Interestingly, when authorities cannot obtain a reference sample from an individual who may be long deceased or missing, an mtDNA reference sample can be obtained from any maternally related relative. However, all individuals of the same maternal lineage will be indistinguishable by mtDNA analysis.

Although mtDNA analysis is significantly more sensitive than nuclear DNA profiling, forensic analysis of mtDNA is more rigorous, time consuming, and costly than nuclear DNA profiling. For this reason, only a handful of public and private forensic laboratories receive evidence for mtDNA determination. The FBI Laboratory strictly limits the types of cases in which it will apply mtDNA technology.

As was previously discussed, nuclear DNA is composed of a continuous linear strand of nucleotides (A, C, G, and T). By contrast, mtDNA is constructed in a circular or loop configuration. Each loop contains enough A, C, G, and T (approximately 16,569 total nucleotides) to make up thirty-seven genes involved in mitochondrial energy generation.

mitochondria
Small structures outside the nucleus that supply energy to the cell.

After 24 Years in Prison, Man Has a Reason to Smile

By SHAILA DEWAN

MARIETTA, Ga., Dec. 7—It is rare to see a prison inmate with a life sentence who cannot stop grinning. Thus, when presented with a DNA mixture of two males and one female, each STR type would be expected to show six bands. However, the same mixture subjected to Y-STR analysis would show only two bands (one band for each male) for each Y-STR type.

But that was Robert Clark Jr. on Wednesday, the day before his conviction for rape, robbery and kidnapping was expected to be vacated on the strength of a DNA test that showed he was not the rapist.

After 24 years in prison—one of the longest incarcerations served by the 164 people who have been exonerated by DNA testing—Mr. Clark, 45, was buoyant at the prospect of seeing his siblings, children and the five grandchildren he did not have when he was sentenced in 1982.

"I still got a little life in me," he said.

Though wrenching, Mr. Clark's story is not so different from that of others who were wrongfully convicted. What is stunning about it is the fact that the man who the authorities now believe was the real rapist, Floyd Antonio Arnold, was in early reach of the police at the time.

The DNA test that exonerated Mr. Clark started a chain reaction that revealed not just Mr. Clark's innocence, but a series of law-enforcement bungles. Those missteps allowed Mr. Arnold to commit violent crimes repeatedly and, very nearly, to walk out of prison, where he is serving time for cruelty to children, at the end of January, despite the fact that his DNA matches that found in Mr. Clark's case and two other previously unsolved rapes.

"This is the worst case of tunnel vision that we've seen in the history of the Innocence Project," said Peter J. Neufeld, a co-founder of the project, which has been instrumental in DNA exonerations and which is handling Mr. Clark's case.

At 21, Mr. Clark was living with his mother and 5-year-old son in southwestern Atlanta. He worked as a roofer and had no criminal record, save a juvenile burglary charge. One day an acquaintance, Mr. Arnold, lent him a car. Because the car was not hotwired and Mr. Arnold had the keys, Mr. Clark said, he did not think the car was stolen.

But the car had belonged to Patricia J. Tucker, 29, who had been getting into the driver's seat in a Kentucky Fried Chicken parking lot where she was carjacked, kidnapped, taken to the woods and raped three times. At Mr. Clark's trial, the sole defense witness identified Mr. Arnold in the courtroom and testified she had seen him driving the car before Mr. Clark was arrested with it.

But Ms. Tucker testified that Mr. Clark had been her attacker, even though she had initially described him as 5-foot-7 and Mr. Clark was 6-foot-1. The detective in the case told the jury that he never investigated Mr. Arnold because Mr. Clark had initially lied to officers about where he had gotten the car, then switched his story. The judge sentenced Mr. Clark to life.

When Mr. Clark heard that, he interrupted, saying: "Your Honor, they had Tony here. I can't put him on the stand. He'll tell you I didn't do nothing but drive the car two weeks later. Y'all got him right here."

"Mr. Clark, you have had your trial," the jury admonished. "Just remain silent."

Mr. Arnold went on to commit a string of felonies, including burglary, gun possession and sodomy. In 2001, he was charged with multiple counts of child molesting in a case prosecutors say involved a 13-year-old female relative. He pleaded guilty to a lesser charge, cruelty to children, for which he is now serving time.

Meanwhile, Mr. Clark wrote birthday cards to his children and letters to anyone he thought might be able to help with his case.

When his mother came to visit, he would lay his head in her lap and sleep. When her kidneys failed, he asked to be locked up in solitary confinement so he could be alone to grieve. She died last year, before he gained his freedom. "She knew I got the court order I needed," Mr. Clark said, smiling again.

Finally, the Innocence Project took his case, and a DNA test was done on the evidence. In November, the results showed that the attacker was not Mr. Clark. The district attorney in Cobb County, Pat Head, ran the DNA profile against the criminal offender database. A match came back: Mr. Arnold.

But there was more, said Ted Staples, the manager of forensic biology for the Georgia Bureau of Investigation. The printout showed that in 2003, when Mr. Arnold's DNA was first added to the database, it matched that in two other rapes, in Fulton and DeKalb Counties.

No action was taken against Mr. Arnold, who will finish his current sentence on Jan. 31.

Mr. Staples said the police in those jurisdictions were notified at the time by phone and letter. But a spokesman for the Fulton County Police Department said it did not know of the match until last week. It has put a hold on Mr. Arnold so he cannot be released.

In DeKalb, Detective Sgt. K. D. Johnson, of the DeKalb County Police Department's youth and sex crimes unit, acknowledged that the department was notified in 2003, but said that the information had slipped through the cracks. "It had gone through several different detectives who have since been transferred to other departments," Sergeant Johnson said. "We're trying to figure out who had it and when."

For his part, Mr. Clark stands to get some restitution from the state, which has paid $1.5 million to two other exonerated men. But, he said, he is thinking more about his 5-year-old granddaughter, Alexis, than how much he might be owed. "They owe me an apology," he said. "They done messed my life up." And he smiled.

Two regions of mtDNA have been found to be highly variable in the human population. These two regions have been designated hypervariable region I (HV1) and hypervariable region II (HV2), as shown in Figure 9–16. As indicated previously, the process for analyzing HV1 and HV2 is tedious. It involves generating many copies of these DNA hypervariable regions by PCR and then determining the order of the *A–T–C–G* bases constituting the hypervariable regions. This process is known as sequencing. The FBI Laboratory, the Armed Forces DNA Identification Laboratory, and other laboratories have collaborated to compile an mtDNA population database containing the base sequences from HV1 and HV2.

Once the sequences of the hypervariable regions from a case sample are obtained, most laboratories simply report the number of times these sequences appear in the mtDNA database maintained by the FBI. The mtDNA database contains about five thousand sequences. This approach permits an assessment of how common or rare an observed mtDNA sequence is in the database.

Interestingly, many of the sequences that have been determined in case work are unique to the existing database, and many types are present at frequencies of no greater than 1 percent in the database. Thus it is often possible to demonstrate how uncommon a particular mtDNA sequence is. However, even under the best circumstances, mtDNA typing does not approach STR analysis in its discrimination power. Thus, mtDNA analysis is best reserved for samples for which nuclear DNA typing is simply not possible.

The first time mtDNA was admitted as evidence in a U.S. court was in 1996 in the case of *State of Tennessee* v. *Paul Ware*. Here, mtDNA was used to link two hairs recovered from the crime scene to the defendant. Interestingly, in this case, blood and semen evidence was absent. Mitochondrial DNA analysis also plays a key role in the identification of human remains. An abundant amount of mtDNA is generally found in skeletal remains. Importantly, mtDNA reference samples are available from family members sharing the same mother, grandmother, great-grandmother, and so on.

One of the most publicized cases performed on human remains was the identification of the individual buried in the tomb of the Vietnam War's unknown soldier. The remains lying in the tomb were believed to belong to First Lt. Michael J. Blassie, whose A-37 warplane was shot down near An Loc, South Vietnam, in 1972. In 1984, the U.S. Army Central Identification Laboratory failed to identify the remains by physical characteristics, personal artifacts, or blood-typing results from hairs. The remains were subsequently placed in the tomb. In 1998, at the insistence of the Blassie family, the remains were disinterred for mtDNA analysis and the results were compared to references from seven families thought to be associated with the case. The remains in the tomb were subsequently analyzed and confirmed to be consistent with DNA from Lt. Blassie's family.

sequencing
A procedure used to determine the order of the base pairs that constitute DNA.

WebExtra 9.9
See How We Inherit Our Mitochondrial DNA
www.prenhall.com/hsforensics

WebExtra 9.10
Look into the Structure of Mitochondrial DNA and See How It's Used for DNA Typing
www.prenhall.com/hsforensics

Key Points

- Mitochondrial DNA is located outside the cell's nucleus and is inherited from the mother.

- Two regions of mitochondrial DNA, HV1 and HV2, are sequenced for forensic typing purposes.

- Mitochondrial DNA typing does not approach STR analysis in its discrimination power and thus is best reserved for samples, such as hair, for which STR analysis may not be possible.

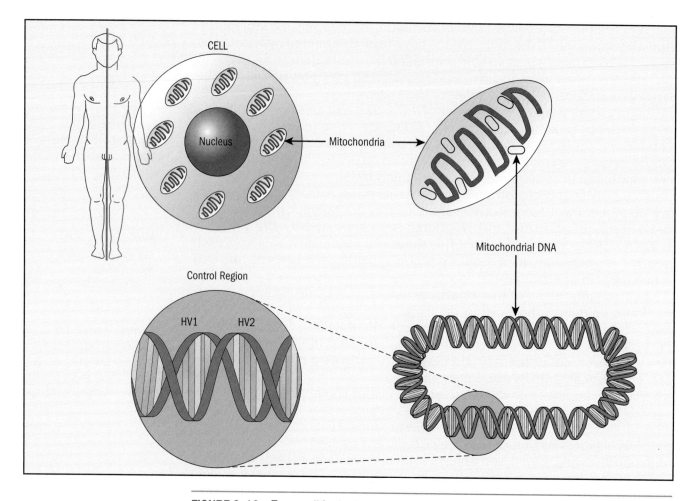

FIGURE 9–16 Every cell in the body contains hundreds of mitochondria, which provide energy to the cell. Each mitochondrion contains numerous copies of DNA shaped in the form of a loop. Distinctive differences between individuals in their mitochondrial DNA makeup are found in two specific segments of the control region on the DNA loop known as HV1 and HV2.

Forensics at Work

Outrage: The O. J. Simpson Verdict

To distill this case down to its irreducible minimum (and temporarily ignoring all the other evidence pointing inexorably to Simpson's guilt), if your blood is found at the murder scene, as Simpson's was conclusively proved to be by DNA tests, that's really the end of the ball game. There is nothing more to say. (And in this case, not only was Simpson's blood found at the murder scene, but the victims' blood was found inside his car and home.) I mean, to deny guilt when your blood is at the murder scene is the equivalent of a man being caught by his wife *in flagrante* with another woman and saying to her (quoting comedian

Richard Pryor), "Who are you going to believe? Me or your lying eyes?"

At the crime scene there were five blood drops leading away from the slain bodies of Nicole Brown Simpson and Ronald Goldman toward the rear alley, four of which were immediately to the *left* of bloody size-12 shoe prints (Simpson's shoe size). This indicated, of course, that the killer had been wounded on the left side of his body. And the morning after the murders, Simpson was observed by the police to be wearing a bandage on his left middle finger. When the bandage was removed that afternoon, it was seen that he had a deep cut on the knuckle of the finger.

DNA (deoxyribonucleic acid) is the genetic material found in all human cells that carries the coded messages of heredity unique (with the exception of identical twins) to each individual. DNA, then, is our genetic fingerprint. Each of the approximately 100 trillion cells in a human body contains twenty-three pairs of chromosomes—one of each pair coming from one's father, the other from the mother—which contain DNA molecules. In criminal cases, DNA can be extracted from samples of blood, semen, saliva, skin, or hair follicles found at a crime scene and then compared to DNA drawn from a suspect to determine if there is a "match." DNA testing is a new forensic science, first used in Great Britain in 1985 and in the United States in 1987.

DNA tests on all five blood drops and on three bloodstains found on the rear gate at the crime scene showed that all of this blood belonged to Simpson. Two DNA tests were used: PCR (polymerase chain reaction) and RFLP (restrictive fragment length polymorphism). The PCR test is less precise than the RFLP, but can be conducted on much smaller blood samples as well as samples that have degenerated ("degraded") because of bacteria and/or exposure to the elements. PCR tests were conducted on four out of the five blood drops. Three showed that only one out of 240,000 people had DNA with the markers found in the sample. (A marker is a gene that makes up one portion of the DNA molecule, and the more markers in the sample, the more comparison tests can be conducted, and hence the greater the exclusion of other humans.) The fourth blood drop had markers which one out of 5200 people could have. Simpson was one of these people. The fifth blood drop had sufficient markers for an RFLP test, and showed that only one out of 170 million people had DNA with those markers. Again, Simpson's blood did.

The richest sample was on the rear gate, and an RFLP test showed that only one out of 57 billion people had those markers. Simpson was one of them. In other words, just on the blood evidence alone, there's only a one out of 57 billion chance that Simpson is innocent. Fifty-seven billion is approximately ten times the current population of the entire world.

Now I realize that Igor in Kiev, Gino in Naples, Colin down Johannesburg way, and Kartac on Pluto might have the same DNA as O. J. Simpson. If you're a skeptic I wouldn't blame you if you checked to see if Igor, Gino, Colin, or Kartac was in Brentwood on the night of the murders, used to beat Nicole within an inch of her life, had blood all over his car, driveway, and home on the night of the murders, had no alibi, and, if charged with the murders, would refuse to take the witness stand to defend himself. Who knows—maybe Simpson isn't the murderer after all. Maybe Igor or one of the others is. You should definitely check this out. And while you're checking it out, someone should be checking you into the nearest mental ward.

To elaborate on the irreducible minimum mentioned earlier, there are only three possible explanations other than guilt for one's blood being found at the murder scene, and all three are preposterous on their face. One is that Simpson left his blood there on an earlier occasion. When Simpson was interrogated by LAPD detectives on the afternoon after these murders, he said he had not cut himself the last time he was at the Bundy address a week earlier. But even without that, how can one believe that on some prior occasion Simpson bled, not just on the Bundy premises, but at the precise point on the premises where the murders occurred? In fact, so farfetched is this possibility that even the defense attorneys, whose stock-in-trade during the trial was absurdity, never proffered it to the jury.

(continued)

Forensics at Work

Outrage: The O. J. Simpson Verdict (*continued*)

And here, not only was Simpson's blood found at the murder scene, but there were the four drops of Simpson's blood found just to the left of the killer's bloody shoe prints leaving the murder scene. If there is someone who isn't satisfied even by this, I would suggest that this book is perhaps not for you, that you think about pursuing more appropriate intellectual pursuits, such as comic strips. When I was a kid, one of my favorites was *Mandrake the Magician.* You might check to see if Mandrake is still doing his thing.

The second possibility is that Simpson cut himself while killing Ron Goldman and Nicole Brown in self-defense—that is, either Ron or Nicole or both together unleashed a deadly assault on Simpson, and he either took out a knife he had on his own person or wrestled Ron's or Nicole's knife away, and stabbed the two of them to death. This, of course, is just too insane to talk about. Again, even the defense attorneys, who apparently possess the gonads of ten thousand elephants, never suggested this possibility. It should be added parenthetically that if such a situation had occurred, Simpson wouldn't have had any reason to worry, since self-defense is a justifiable homicide, a complete defense to murder.

The third and final possibility is that the LAPD detectives planted Simpson's blood not just at the murder scene but to the left of the bloody shoe prints leaving the scene. This is not as insane a proposition as the first two, but only because there are degrees of everything in life. It is still an insane possibility, and if any reader is silly enough to believe that the LAPD detectives decided to frame someone they believed to be innocent of these murders (Simpson) and actually planted his blood all over the murder scene (and, of course, planted the victims' blood in Simpson's car and home), again, this book is probably not for that reader. This book is for people who are very angry that a brutal murderer is among us—with a smile on his face, no less—and want to know how this terrible miscarriage of justice could have occurred. . . .

Let me point out to those who believe in the "possible" existence of either of the aforementioned three innocent possibilities for Simpson's blood being found at the murder scene, that the prosecution only has the burden of proving guilt beyond a *reasonable* doubt, not beyond all possible doubt. So it isn't necessary to have all possible doubts of guilt removed from one's mind in order to reach a conclusion of guilt. Only reasonable doubts of guilt have to be removed. Of course, in this case, *no* doubt remains of Simpson's guilt. . . .

Source: Vincent Bugliosi, *OUTRAGE: The Five Reasons Why O. J. Simpson Got Away with Murder.* Copyright © 1996 by Vincent Bugliosi. Reprinted by permission of W. W. Norton & Company, Inc.

The Combined DNA Index System (CODIS)

Perhaps the most significant investigative tool to arise from a DNA-typing program is CODIS (Combined DNA Index System), a computer software program developed by the FBI that maintains local, state, and national databases of DNA profiles from convicted offenders, unsolved crime-scene

Forensic Brief

In the fall of 1979, a 61-year-old patient wandered away from a U.S. Department of Veterans Affairs medical facility. Despite an extensive search, authorities never located the missing man. More than ten years later, a dog discovered a human skull in a wooded area near the facility. DNA Analysis Unit II of the FBI Laboratory received the case in the winter of 1999.

The laboratory determined that the mitochondrial DNA profile from the missing patient's brother matched the mitochondrial DNA profile from the recovered skull and provided the information to the local medical examiner. Subsequently, the remains were declared to be those of the missing patient and returned to the family for burial.

Source: *FBI Law Enforcement Bulletin* 78 (2002): 21.

evidence, and profiles of missing people. CODIS allows crime laboratories to compare DNA types recovered from crime-scene evidence to those of convicted sex offenders and other convicted criminals.

Thousands of CODIS matches have linked serial crimes to each other and have solved crimes by allowing investigators to match crime-scene evidence to known convicted offenders. This capability is of tremendous value to investigators in cases in which the police have not been able to identify a suspect. The CODIS concept has already had a significant impact on police investigations in various states, as shown by the following brief.

Key Points

- CODIS is a computer software program developed by the FBI that maintains local, state, and national databases of DNA profiles from convicted offenders, unsolved crime-scene evidence, and profiles of missing people.

Collection and Preservation of Biological Evidence for DNA Analysis

Since the early 1990s, the advent of DNA profiling has vaulted biological crime-scene evidence to a stature of importance that is eclipsed only by the fingerprint. In fact, the high sensitivity of DNA determinations has even changed the way police investigators define biological evidence.

Just how sensitive is STR profiling? Forensic analysts using currently accepted protocols can reach sensitivity levels as low as 125 picograms. Interestingly, a human cell has an estimated 7 picograms of DNA, which means that only eighteen DNA-bearing cells are needed to obtain an STR profile. However, modifications in the technology can readily extend the level of detection down to eighteen or even nine cells. A quantity of DNA that is below the normal level of detection is defined as a low copy number.

picogram
One-trillionth of a gram, or 0.000000000001 gram.

low copy number
Fewer than eighteen DNA-bearing cells.

Forensic Brief

In 1990, a series of attacks on elderly victims were committed in Goldsboro, North Carolina, by an unknown individual dubbed the Night Stalker. During one such attack in March, an elderly woman was brutally raped and almost murdered. Her daughter's early arrival home saved the woman's life. The suspect fled, leaving behind materials intended to burn the residence and the victim in an attempt to conceal the crime.

In July 1990, another elderly woman was raped and murdered in her home. Three months later, a third elderly woman was raped and stabbed to death. Her husband was also murdered. Although their house was set alight in an attempt to cover up the crime, fire and rescue personnel pulled the bodies from the house before it was engulfed in flames. DNA analysis of biological evidence collected from vaginal swabs from the three rape victims enabled authorities to conclude that the same perpetrator had committed all three crimes. However, there was no suspect.

More than ten years after these crimes were committed, law enforcement authorities retested the biological evidence from all three cases using newer DNA technology and entered the DNA profiles into North Carolina's DNA database. The DNA profile developed from the crime-scene evidence was compared to thousands of convicted-offender profiles already in the database.

In April 2001, a "cold hit" was made with an individual in the convicted-offender DNA database. The perpetrator had been convicted of shooting into an occupied dwelling, an offense that requires inclusion in the North Carolina DNA database. The suspect was brought into custody for questioning and was served with a search warrant to obtain a sample of his blood. That sample was analyzed and compared to the crime-scene evidence, confirming the DNA database match. When confronted with the DNA evidence, the suspect confessed to all three crimes.

Source: National Institute of Justice, "Using DNA to Solve Cold Cases," NIJ special report, 2002, *http://www.ojp.usdoj.gov/nij/pubs_sum/194197.htm.*

---

epithelial cells
The outer layer of skin cells.

With this technology in hand, the horizon of the criminal investigator extends beyond the traditional dried blood or semen stain to include stamps and envelopes licked with saliva, a cup or can that has touched a person's lips, chewing gum, the sweat band of a hat, or a bedsheet containing dead skin cells. Likewise, skin or epithelial cells transferred onto the surface of a weapon, the interior of a glove, or a pen have yielded DNA results.[3]

The ultimate sensitivity goal in forensic DNA analysis is profiling DNA extracted from one human cell. Such an accomplishment seems close to fruition. Researchers have reported obtaining STR profiles from one or two cells and have profiled DNA from single dermal ridge fingerprints.[4] While it's premature to imply that this technology, or a comparable one, is eligible for admission in criminal trials, one cannot exclude its use in criminal and forensic intelligence investigations. Table 9–2 illustrates the power of DNA as a creator of physical evidence.

Collection of Biological Evidence

Before investigators become enamored with the wonders of DNA, they should first realize that the crime scene must be treated in the traditional

Table 9–2 Location and Sources of DNA at Crime Scenes

Evidence	Possible Location of DNA on the Evidence	Source of DNA
baseball bat or similar weapon	handle, end	sweat, skin, blood, tissue
hat, bandanna or mask	inside	sweat, hair, dandruff
eyeglasses	nose or ear pieces, lens	sweat, skin
facial tissue, cotton swab	surface area	mucus, blood, sweat, semen, ear wax
dirty laundry	surface area	blood, sweat, semen
toothpick	tips	saliva
used cigarette	cigarette butt	saliva
stamp or envelope	licked area	saliva
tape or ligature	inside/outside surface	skin, sweat
bottle, can, or glass	sides, mouthpiece	saliva, sweat
used condom	inside/outside surface	semen, vaginal or rectal cells
blanket, pillow, sheet	surface area	sweat, hair, semen, urine, saliva
"through and through" bullet	outside surface	blood, tissue
bite mark	person's skin or clothing	saliva
fingernail, partial fingernail	scrapings	blood, sweat, tissue

Source: National Institute of Justice, U.S. Department of Justice.

manner. Before the collection of evidence begins, biological evidence should be photographed close up and its location relative to the entire crime scene recorded through notes, sketches, and photographs. If the shape and position of bloodstains may provide information about the circumstances of the crime, an expert must immediately evaluate the blood evidence. The significance of the position and shape of bloodstains can best be ascertained when the expert has an on-site overview of the entire crime scene and can better reconstruct the movement of the individuals involved. The blood pattern should not be disturbed before this phase of the investigation is completed.

The evidence collector must handle all body fluids and biologically stained materials with a minimum of personal contact. All body fluids must be assumed to be infectious; hence, wearing disposable latex gloves while handling the evidence is required. Latex gloves also significantly reduce the possibility that the evidence collector will contaminate the evidence. These gloves should be changed frequently during the evidence-collection phase of the investigation. Safety considerations and avoidance of contamination also call for the wearing of face masks, shoe covers, and possibly coveralls.

Blood has great evidential value when a transfer between a victim and suspect can be demonstrated. For this reason, all clothing from both victim and suspect should be collected and sent to the laboratory for examination. This procedure must be followed even when the presence of blood on a garment does not appear obvious to the investigator. Laboratory search procedures are far more revealing and sensitive than any that can be conducted at the crime scene. In addition, blood should also be searched for in less-than-obvious places. For example, the criminal may have wiped his or her hands on materials not readily apparent to the investigator. Investigators should look for towels, handkerchiefs, or rags that may have been used and then hidden, and should also examine floor cracks or other crevices that may have trapped blood.

Packaging of Biological Evidence

Biological evidence should not be packaged in plastic or airtight containers, because accumulation of residual moisture could contribute to the growth of DNA-destroying bacteria and fungi. Each stained article should be packaged separately in a paper bag or a well-ventilated box. If feasible, the entire stained article should be packaged and submitted for examination. If this is not possible, dried blood is best removed from a surface with a sterile cotton-tipped swab lightly moistened with distilled water from a dropper bottle.

A portion of the unstained surface material near the recovered stain must likewise be removed or swabbed and placed in a separate package. This is known as a substrate control. The forensic examiner might use the substrate swab to confirm that the results of the tests performed were brought about by the stain and not by the material on which it was deposited. However, this practice is normally not necessary when DNA determinations are carried out in the laboratory. One point is critical, and that is that the collected swabs must not be packaged in a wet state. After collection, the swab must be air-dried for approximately five to ten minutes. Then it is best to place it in a swab box (see Figure 9–17), which has a circular hole to allow air circulation. The swab box can then be placed in a paper or manila envelope.

All packages containing biological evidence should be refrigerated or stored in a cool location out of direct sunlight until delivery to the laboratory. However, one common exception is blood mixed with soil. Microbes present in soil rapidly degrade DNA. Therefore, blood in soil

substrate control
An unstained object adjacent to an area on which biological material has been deposited.

FIGURE 9–17 Air-dried swabs are placed in a swab box for delivery to the forensic laboratory. *Courtesy Tri-Tech, Inc., Southport, N.C., www.tritechusa.com*

must be stored in a clean glass or plastic container and immediately frozen.

Obtaining DNA Reference Specimens

Biological evidence attains its full forensic value only when an analyst can compare each of its DNA types to known DNA samples collected from victims and suspects. For this purpose, at least 7 milliliters of whole blood should be drawn from individuals by a qualified medical person. The blood sample should be collected in a sterile vacuum tube containing the preservative EDTA (ethylenediamine tetraacetic acid). In addition to serving as a preservative, EDTA inhibits the activity of enzymes that degrade DNA. The tubes must be kept refrigerated (not frozen) while awaiting transportation to the laboratory.

In addition to blood, other options exist for obtaining standard/reference DNA specimens. The least intrusive method for obtaining a DNA standard/reference, one that nonmedical personnel can readily use, is the *buccal swab*. Cotton swabs are placed in the subject's mouth and the inside of the cheek is vigorously swabbed, resulting in the transfer of buccal cells onto the swab (see Figure 9–18).

buccal cells
Cells from the inner cheek lining.

If an individual is not available to give a DNA standard/reference sample, some interesting alternatives are available, including a toothbrush, combs and hairbrushes, a razor, soiled laundry, used cigarette butts, and earplugs. Any of these items may contain a sufficient quantity of DNA for typing. Interestingly, as investigators worked to identify the remains of victims of the World Trade Center attack on September 11, 2001, the families of the missing were asked to supply the New York City DNA Laboratory with these types of items in an effort to match recovered DNA with human remains.

Contamination of DNA Evidence

One key concern during the collection of a DNA-containing specimen is contamination. Contamination can occur by introducing foreign DNA through coughing or sneezing onto a stain during the collection process, or there can be a transfer of DNA when items of evidence are incorrectly placed in contact with each other during packaging. Fortunately, an examination of DNA band patterns in the laboratory readily reveals the presence of contamination. For example, with an STR, one will expect to see a two-band pattern. More than two bands suggests a mixture of DNA from more than one source.

Crime-scene investigators can take some relatively simple steps to minimize contamination of biological evidence:

1. Change gloves before handling each new piece of evidence.

2. Collect a substrate control for possible subsequent laboratory examination.

3. Pick up small items of evidence such as cigarette butts and stamps with clean forceps. Disposable forceps are to be used so that they can be discarded after a single evidence collection.

4. Always package each item of evidence in its own well-ventilated container.

A common occurrence at crime scenes is to suspect the presence of blood, but not be able to observe any with the naked eye. In these situations, the common test of choice is luminol (discussed in Chapter 8).

(a)

(b)

(c)

FIGURE 9–18 A buccal swab collection kit is designed for use by nonmedical personnel. The cotton-tipped swabs are placed in the subject's mouth and the inside of the cheek is vigorously swabbed, resulting in the transfer of buccal cells onto the cotton bulb of the swab. The kit is then delivered to the forensic laboratory. *Courtesy Tri-Tech, Inc., Southport, N.C., www.tritechusa.com*

Interestingly, luminol does not inhibit the ability to detect and characterize STRs.[5] Therefore, luminol can be used to locate traces of blood and areas that have been washed nearly free of blood without compromising the potential for DNA typing.

WebExtra 9.11

DNA Forensics
www.prenhall.com/hsforensics

Key Points

- Biological evidence should not be packaged in plastic or airtight containers because the accumulation of residual moisture could contribute to the growth of blood-destroying bacteria and fungi. Each article should be packaged separately in a paper bag or in a well-ventilated box.

- The least intrusive method for obtaining a DNA standard/reference is the buccal swab. In this procedure, cotton swabs are placed in the subject's mouth and the inside of the cheek is vigorously swabbed, resulting in the transfer of cells from the inner cheek lining onto the swab.

Forensic Brief

A woman alleged that she had been held against her will and sexually assaulted by a male friend in an apartment. During the course of the assault, a contact lens was knocked from the victim's eye. After the assault, she escaped, but due to fear from threats made by her attacker, she did not report the assault to the police for three days. When the police examined the apartment, they noted that it had been thoroughly cleaned. A vacuum cleaner bag was seized for examination and several pieces of material resembling fragments of a contact lens were discovered within the bag.

In the laboratory, approximately 20 nanograms of human DNA was recovered from the contact lens fragments. Cells from both the eyeball and the interior of the eyelids are naturally replaced every six to twenty-four hours. As such, both are potential sources for the DNA found. The DNA profile originating from the fragments matched the victim, thus corroborating the victim's account of the crime. The estimated population frequency of occurrence for the nine matching STRs are approximately 1 in 850 million. The suspect subsequently pleaded guilty to the offense.

STR Locus	Victim's DNA Type	Contact Lens
D3S1358	15,18	15,18
FGA	24,25	24,25
vWA	17,17	17,17
THO1	6,7	6,7
F13A1	5,6	5,6
fes/fps	11,12	11,12
D5S818	11,12	11,12
D13S317	11,12	11,12
D7S820	10,12	10,12

Source: R. A. Wickenheiser and R. M. Jobin, "Comparison of DNA Recovered from a Contact Lens Using PCR DNA Typing," *Canadian Society of Forensic Science Journal* 32 (1999): 67.

Chapter Summary

The gene is the fundamental unit of heredity. Each gene is composed of DNA specifically designed to control the genetic traits of our cells. Portions of the DNA structure are as unique to each individual as fingerprints.

DNA is constructed as a very large molecule made by linking a series of repeating units called nucleotides. Four types of bases are associated with the DNA structure: adenine (A), guanine (G), cytosine (C), and thymine (T). The bases on each strand are properly aligned in a double-helix configuration. As a result, adenine pairs with thymine and guanine pairs with cytosine. This concept is known as base pairing. The order of the bases is what distinguishes different DNA strands.

Portions of the DNA molecule contain sequences of bases that are repeated numerous times. To a forensic scientist, these tandem repeats offer a means of distinguishing one individual from another through DNA typing. Length differences associated with relatively long repeating DNA strands are called restriction fragment length polymorphisms (RFLPs) and form the basis for one of the first DNA-typing procedures.

Polymerase chain reaction (PCR) is the outgrowth of knowledge gained from an understanding of how DNA strands naturally replicate within a cell. PCR offers a distinct advantage in that it can amplify minute quantities of DNA. PCR technology cannot be applied to RFLP DNA typing. The RFLP strands are too long, often numbering in the thousands of bases. PCR is best used with DNA strands that are no longer than a couple of hundred bases. Shorter DNA strands are expected to be more stable and less subject to degradation brought about by adverse environmental conditions. By contrast, the long RFLP strands tend to break apart under the adverse conditions common at crime scenes.

The latest method of DNA typing, short tandem repeat (STR) analysis, has emerged as the most successful and widely used DNA-profiling procedure. STRs are locations on the chromosome that contain short sequences that repeat themselves within the DNA molecule. They serve as useful markers for identification because they are found in great abundance throughout the human genome.

STRs normally consist of repeating sequences three to seven bases long, and the entire strand of an STR is also very short, less than 450 bases long. This means that STRs are much less susceptible to degradation and may often be recovered from bodies or stains that have been subjected to extreme decomposition. Also, because of their shortness, STRs are ideal candidates for multiplication by PCR, thus overcoming the limited-sample-size problem often associated with crime-scene evidence.

What makes STRs so attractive to forensic scientists is that hundreds of different types of STRs are found in human genes. The more STRs one can characterize, the smaller the percentage of the population from which a particular combination of STRs can emanate. This gives rise to the concept of multiplexing. Using PCR technology, one can simultaneously extract and amplify a combination of different STRs. U.S. crime laboratories have standardized on thirteen STRs. With STR, as little as 125 picograms of DNA is required for analysis. This is 1/100 the amount normally required for RFLP analysis.

Another type of DNA used for individual characterization is mitochondrial DNA. Mitochondrial DNA is located outside the cell's nucleus and is inherited from the mother. However, mitochondrial DNA typing does not approach STR analysis in its discrimination power and thus is best reserved for samples, such as hair, for which STR analysis may not be possible.

Biological evidence should not be packaged in plastic or airtight containers because accumulation of residual moisture could contribute to the growth of blood-destroying bacteria and fungi. Each article should be packaged separately in a paper bag or in a well-ventilated box.

Review Questions

Facts and Concepts

1. What is DNA and why is it important to forensic scientists?

2. What are genes and what is their function? Of what are genes composed and where are they located?

3. With what discovery are James Watson and Francis Crick credited?

4. DNA is a large molecule created by linking a series of repeating units. What is this type of molecule called? What are the repeating units known as?

5. Describe the basic structure of the DNA molecule. What is the name given to this type of structure?

6. Name the four bases associated with DNA. How are these bases paired on the DNA molecule?

7. What aspect of DNA defines the role and function of a DNA molecule?

8. DNA controls inheritable traits by producing complex molecules called
   a. amino acids.
   b. nucleotides.
   c. chromosomes.
   d. proteins.

9. How are proteins made? What determines the shape and function of a protein molecule?

10. What is the human genome? Name two medical applications of information about the human genome.

11. Briefly describe the process of DNA replication.

12. What is PCR? Why is it useful to forensic scientists?

13. What is recombinant DNA? How is recombinant DNA technology used to treat diabetes?

14. What are tandem repeats? How are they useful to forensic scientists?

15. What was the dominant DNA-typing procedure in the United States until the mid-1990s?

16. What is a short tandem repeat (STR)? Why are STRs so attractive to forensic scientists?

17. How does the number of STRs characterized relate to the frequency of occurrence of the analyzed sample in the general population?

18. Name two processes by which a forensic scientist can separate STRs for characterization. Which process is preferred and why?

19. What gene is often used to determine the sex of a DNA contributor? What characteristic of the gene allows forensic scientists to make this determination?

20. List two differences between nuclear DNA and mitochondrial DNA.

21. Name one advantage and three disadvantages of mtDNA analysis compared to nuclear DNA profiling.

22. What is CODIS? How is CODIS useful to forensic scientists?

23. Approximately how many DNA-bearing cells are needed to obtain an STR profile? What term is used to describe a quantity of DNA that is below this normal level of detection?

24. What type of gloves should an evidence collector wear when handling biological evidence? Name two reasons he or she should wear this type of glove.

25. What type of packaging should not be used for biological evidence? Why? What type of packaging should be used instead for articles containing biological evidence?

26. How should packages containing biological evidence be stored until they are delivered to a laboratory? Name one common exception and describe how it should be stored.

27. What substance should be added to blood samples collected from a crime scene? Name two reasons for adding this substance to blood evidence.

28. Name and describe the least intrusive method for obtaining a DNA standard/reference.

29. List four ways to minimize contamination of biological evidence.

Application and Critical Thinking

1. The following sequence of bases is located on one strand of a DNA molecule:

   C–G–A–A–T–C–G–C–A–A–T–C–G–A–C–C–T–G

   List the sequence of bases that will form complementary pairs on the other strand of the DNA molecule.

2. A woman reports being mugged by a masked assailant, whom she scratched on the arm during a brief struggle. The victim gives the police a good description of her attacker, but she is not sure if the attacker was male or female. Describe the steps and procedures you would use to determine the sex of the attacker. How will you know whether the attacker is male or female?

3. Police discover a badly decomposed body buried in an area where a man disappeared some years before. The case was never solved, nor was the victim's body ever recovered. As the lead investigator, you suspect that the newly discovered body is that of the victim. What is your main challenge in using DNA typing to determine whether your suspicion is correct? How would you go about using DNA technology to test your theory?

4. You are a forensic scientist performing DNA typing on a blood sample sent to your laboratory. While performing an STR analysis on the sample, you notice a four-band pattern. What conclusion should you draw? Why?

Virtual Crime Scenes

Crime Scene 9.1
Step into the role of the first responding officer at a burglary scene
www.prenhall.com/hsforensics

Crime Scene 9.2
Assume the duties of an evidence collection technician at a burglary scene
www.prenhall.com/hsforensics

WebExtra 9.12
Virtual Crime Scene 9.1
www.prenhall.com/hsforensics

WebExtra 9.13
Virtual Crime Scene 9.2
www.prenhall.com/hsforensics

Web Resources

Principles of Forensic DNA for Officers of the Court
www.dna.gov/training/otc/

Using DNA to Solve Cold Cases: Special Report
www.ncjrs.gov/pdffiles1/nij/194197.pdf

Convicted by Juries, Exonerated by Science: Case Studies in the Use of DNA Evidence to Establish Innocence after Trial
www.ncjrs.gov/pdffiles/dnaevid.pdf

DNA Evidence: What Law Enforcement Officers Should Know
www.ncjrs.gov/pdffiles1/jr000249c.pdf

DNA from the Beginning (An animated primer on the basics of DNA, genes, and heredity; features a series of animated flash tutorials on genetics and DNA)
www.dnaftb.org/dnaftb/

DNA Structure (Animated online tutorials about the basics of DNA; Includes a lesson plan for instructors teaching about DNA and review questions for students)
molvis.sdsc.edu/dna/index.htm

DNA Testing: An Introduction for Non-Scientists: An Illustrated Explanation (Illustrated article that explains in simplified language the theory and process behind various types of DNA testing, including STR and RFLP, and discusses PCR contamination)
www.scientific.org/tutorials/articles/riley/riley.html

DNA Typing and Identification—Lecture Notes
faculty.ncwc.edu/toconnor/425/425lect15.htm

DNA Workshop (Overview of basics of DNA including replication and protein synthesis; Features an interactive presentation on replication and synthesis)
www.pbs.org/wgbh/aso/tryit/dna/index.html#

Short Tandem Repeat DNA Internet Database
www.cstl.nist.gov/biotech/strbase/

How DNA Works
http://science.howstuffworks.com/dna-evidence.htm

Endnotes

1. Instructions for assembling proteins are actually carried from DNA to another region of the cell by ribonucleic acid (RNA). RNA is directly involved in the assembly of the protein, using the genetic code it received from DNA.
2. Applied Biosystems, 850 Lincoln Centre Drive, Foster City, Calif. 94404.

3. R. A. Wickenheiser, "Trace DNA: A Review, Discussion of Theory, and Application of the Transfer of Trace Quantities through Skin Contact," *Journal of Forensic Sciences* 47 (2002): 442.

4. E. K. Hanson and J. Ballantyne, "Whole Genome Amplification Strategy for Forensic Genetic Analysis Using Single or Few Cell Equivalents of Genomic DNA," *Analytical Biochemistry* 346 (2005): 246.

5. A. M. Gross et al., "The Effect of Luminol on Presumptive Tests and DNA Analysis Using the Polymerase Chain Reaction," *Journal of Forensic Sciences* 44 (1999): 837.

Case Reading

The Forensic Community's Response to September 11

On September 11, Brion Smith was home in Frederick, Md., enjoying a vacation day when the news flashed across his television screen—the World Trade Center (WTC) buildings had been struck by two hijacked airplanes. Minutes later, a third plane struck the Pentagon while a fourth later crashed in a field in Somerset County, Pa. Acting on impulse, Smith, chief deputy medical examiner for the DNA Division of the Office of the Armed Forces Medical Examiner (OAFME), immediately gathered his things and headed in to work. "Your first inclination, of course, is to go to the crash site," he says, "however, a DNA person has little utility outside of the laboratory." . . .

World Trade Center

Marie Samples, an assistant director in the Department of Forensic Biology in the Office of Chief Medical Examiner (OCME) in New York, was sitting in a management meeting when a co-worker poked his head in and delivered the horrific news. "When someone tells you that the WTCs have just collapsed, you don't ever fathom that happening," says Samples. "I don't think it sunk in with me until I got home."

Overseeing mass tragedies is nothing new to the OCME. In 1990, the lab handled the Happy Land Social Club fire in which 87 people died; then in 1993, they handled the *Golden Venture* tragedy in which 286 Chinese immigrants drowned when their boat went aground off the coast of New Jersey. The OCME has about 90 experienced technicians on staff who

perform various tasks, including examining physical evidence; conducting DNA extractions; and overseeing DNA quantitation, amplification, and finally, DNA typing.

"Our first thought was that we would be able to handle the samples in-house," says Samples. But as the estimates of the number of bodies at the WTC site continued to pile up—initial reports were as high as 7000—those plans quickly changed. "We've handled big disasters in the past, but this was nothing like we've ever seen," exclaims Samples. Although the OCME has the largest DNA analysis lab in the country, the thought of tackling a project with that many unknown and presumed dead presented other problems for Samples and her lab. "We had two big responsibilities that were clashing," she says, "our commitment to serve the criminal justice system in New York for the cases we normally handle—sexual

Wilder Damian Smith
Staff editor for *Analytical Chemistry*

United Flight 175, hijacked by terrorists, crashes into 2 World Trade Center.
Courtesy Aurora & Quanta Productions Inc.

assaults, homicides, etc.—and our role as a support lab for the medical examiners in determining the cause of death." She goes on to say, "We knew we couldn't do both of them well at the same time, so we decided to contract out the DNA typing work."

As the search and rescue mission for the victims of the WTC collapse became a recovery mission, more problems faced the forensic community. At Ground Zero—the name given to the site of the collapsed WTC buildings—literally millions of human remains were lying scattered deep beneath the tons of twisted metal and shattered cement. "We have to remember that when those towers fell, they turned into giant shredders," says Kevin McElfresh, a senior scientist with BODE Technologies. The smoldering fires, the exposure to the outside weather, and the estimated amount of time it would take to remove the debris—a year, by some calculations—also presented problems for the chemists. "At least in the [1999] Swiss Air crash, the remains were in the water at the bottom of the ocean in four degree water; even though they were down there for three months, we were still able to extract DNA to generate full profiles," says Benoit Leclair, senior scientist with Myriad Genetics. . . .

Some 7 months later, remains were still being collected and taken to Fresh Kills, an abandoned 3000-acre landfill on Staten Island, N.Y., that has been reincarnated as the country's largest "rake-and-sift" DNA lab. There, workers meticulously pick through bits of concrete, rocks, and other rubble in search of the tiniest remnants of human tissue, teeth, and even hair to aid in the identification process. The OCME extracts the DNA from each of the remains recovered, and those extracts are then shipped off to the respective companies for DNA typing and profiling.

To handle the profiling, the OCME contracted the services of three companies: Myriad Genetics, Celera Genomics, and BODE Technologies. Blood and tissue samples recovered from the site are being sent to Myriad Genetics, based in Salt Lake City, Utah. The company is using the technique of short tandem repeats (STR) on the recovered tissues. "I would refer to this as data mining," says Leclair. STR is a technique that focuses on 13 loci found over the 23 pairs of chromosomes that make up a human's genome. After polymerase chain reaction (PCR) amplification, the newly formed DNA fragments are separated by capillary electrophoresis. Myriad had worked with the New York State Police prior to September 11, performing similar analysis on New York's rape kits.

When blood and tissue samples are not available from the WTC site for DNA typing,

Courtesy AP/Wide World Photos

forensic scientists often have to turn to another source: bones. BODE Technical Group, a Virginia-based company, is overseeing the bone analysis of the victims. Its lab has about 70 employees, and one of its two specialized units is devoted to forensic analysis. The company participated in the forensic identification of the 88 victims in the Alaska Air crash in 2000. Currently, it has received over 7000 samples from the WTC site.

When the tissue samples are severely burned or degraded, a process called mitochondrial DNA (mtDNA) analysis often has to be done; because this was the case with some of the recovered remains from Ground Zero, the OCME contracted the Rockville, Md., company Celera Genomics to oversee the mtDNA analyses of the WTC victims. However, Celera, a business under the Applera Corp., was an unusual choice. "Unlike BODE and Myriad," says Heather Kowalski, Celera's director of corporate communications, "[Celera] didn't have a forensic part to our business before this tragedy occurred." Celera is known mainly for its work on the Human Genome Project and as a high-throughput sequencing company.

In preparation for the incoming samples, Celera built four new forensic laboratories in the span of two months and hired Rhonda Roby to oversee the forensics program. Before that, Roby worked as a forensic scientist for Applied Biosystems (AB), which is also a business unit of Applera, and which has a Human Identification Group and experience working with the forensic community. Despite the novelty of the project, Roby wasn't intimidated. "As scientists, we knew we had something to offer, and Applera wanted to do it right," says Roby. "Celera offers expertise in high-throughput sequencing and bioinformatics capabilities,

and Applied Biosystems offers expertise as the inventors of the sequencing chemistry, software and instruments, and a team of forensic scientists from the Human Identification Group."

Quality Control

After DNA profiles are obtained, the results are then shipped back to the New York State Police Laboratory in Albany, N.Y. There, the information is stored in a specially modified version of the FBI's Combined DNA Index System (CODIS) database.

The original CODIS database stores the DNA information of convicted felons and is used to match that information in prosecution cases. This new version of the database uses the same DNA comparison software, but only for purposes of matching the September 11 DNA profiles to those of the recovered victims' blood samples submitted by their relatives, and to the DNA information obtained from the victims' toothbrushes, hair, soiled laundry, and used cigarette butts. Also, as part of the OCME's quality control efforts, BODE is also repeating 5% of the mtDNA analysis that Celera conducts.

Sample Analysis

Medical and legal issues have to be considered when determining how much of a sample is needed to yield identifying information. The condition of the recovered body parts determines which type of analysis—nuclear (nucDNA) or mtDNA—is performed.

NucDNA analysis is the most commonly used because it's faster, the genome is found in the cell's nucleus, and the DNA has alleles from each parent. In nucDNA analysis, the DNA fragments are analyzed and amplified using PCR. The profile from the nucDNA is then obtained and used to match and verify a victim. However, this type of analysis usually requires a lot of sample. "The problem," says Smith, "is that despite having a large amount of sample, sometimes there are only three grams of usable tissue available for analysis; and that is often totally exhausted during analysis."

MtDNA analysis is somewhat different. Mitochondria are abundant in the cell's cytoplasm, but the mtDNA only comes from the mother. The high number of mtDNA genomes in the cell increases the likelihood of successful PCR amplification. However, mtDNA analysis is more difficult to perform than nucDNA, more time consuming, and very expensive.

The second issue facing analysts is more humanitarian. "We can't tell someone, 'The good news was that it was him; the bad news is that he's all gone'," says Smith. Most families would rather have some remains of their loved one to take home, even if it is just a small piece. "There isn't one of our people that doesn't understand that there is a family in dire need to know what happened to their loved one," says McElfresh. The scientists use every piece of information they can to find answers. "What gets to me the most is that when it's late and you have a set of records in front of you and what you are looking at is the reconstruction of a person's life through the eyes and the contributions of their family," he says. The resolve of the scientists, says Smith, is evident every day. "With this project, I've seen people so driven that they are standing with their eyes shut and you have to tell them to go home," he says.

The Pentagon and Somerset

Civilian plane crashes are normally assigned to the Federal Aviation Administration (FAA) and the National Transportation Safety Board (NTSB).

However, the DNA Division of the OAFME—a federal lab based in Rockville, Md., with two forensic facilities—handled the remains from the Pentagon and the Somerset County, Pa., sites. "We [NTSB] don't have DNA analysis capability," says Frank Ciaccio, chief of forensic sciences and a forensic anthropologist for the NTSB.

In 1996, the NTSB established a memorandum of understanding with the Department of Defense that recommends to local coroners that they use the services of the Armed Forces DNA Identification Laboratory (AFDIL)—the first facility of the OAFME—for DNA analysis. Under the terms of that agreement, the Armed Forces Institute of Pathology (AFIP) simply had to be invited to perform the DNA identifications of the crash victims by the local coroner, and that is what happened in the Pentagon and Somerset cases.

Previously, the AFDIL had performed DNA casework on the victims of the 1999 Egypt Air and the 2000 Alaska Air plane crashes. The AFDIL has 30 technicians divided into 6 teams that specialize in mtDNA analysis and a smaller group that handles all the nucDNA casework. The mtDNA section of the AFDIL was created in 1991 and has been instrumental in the identification of the recovered remains of American servicemen from the Korean War. To date, the AFDIL has received over 2000 samples for typing from the Pentagon and Somerset crashes.

The second OAFME facility, called the Armed Forces Repository of Specimen Samples for the Identification of Remains, houses blood-stained cards for all active duty, reserve, and National Guard military personnel. These filter paper cards are refrigerated and contain each person's name, social security number, date of birth, and two quarter-size spots of blood. In the Pentagon and Somerset crashes, about 50 of the victims were active duty American servicemen.

Were They Prepared?

"We have the largest DNA lab in the country, and even we couldn't handle [the WTC] caseload," says Samples. "It's hard for a lab to try to prepare for something along the lines of New York when it isn't likely to happen." (Sample's lab also had 12 new lab technicians start work on September 10.)

Learning from previous crashes, Smith's lab implemented a few critical changes. "We found that by having a DNA collection team [at the crash site], they could collect the tissue sample after it has been taken from the body and tag it with a number and bar code onsite before it gets back to the lab," he says. Creating better software in the chain of custody was also important. "For the Pentagon and Somerset crashes we set up two computer systems, one at the Dover Air Force Base and the other in Somerset County for the Pennsylvania crash."

Smith believes experience is the best teacher. "The thing we were missing in the Egypt and Alaska Air crashes was how to compare hundreds of DNA profiles obtained from the evidence with hundreds of DNA reference profiles," he says. "The hardest part of the project was sorting, comparing, matching, and reporting the data, so there was clearly a role for automation."

Need for New Technology

Although forensic technology has advanced, Leclair believes it still is always a step behind the last disaster. "We have the DNA typing tools to tackle a disaster such as Swiss Air only as a result of the TWA 800 disaster," states Leclair. Back in the late 1980s, DNA analysis was all done using a variable number of tandem repeats or restriction fragment-length polymorphisms, which required an enormous amount of sample and analysis time.

Today, most labs are using PCR to analyze DNA. "PCR has been the biggest addition to forensic technology," says McElfresh. "I can't imagine dealing with something the magnitude of this [WTC buildings and Pentagon] with that old technology."

But the tragedies of September 11, say some forensic scientists, should be a wake-up call to the community. "Considering the magnitude of the New York disaster, one can readily see the need for powerful bioinformatics tools," states Leclair.

Roby believes that robotics and more advanced automation are the technologies of the future for forensics. "What may come out of [September 11] is that we are using robotic systems and automation, and we may be able to advance forensic sciences with the scientific technology that is available in other areas with these systems," she says. Samples agrees. "We had thought about using the robotics system before, but our caseload had never justified using them."

Justifying new technology, and finding the time to develop it, seem to be the biggest obstacles. "I think the forensic community could have handled the caseload of the WTC buildings without robotics and automation," says Roby, "but the question is how long would it have taken?"

Jeffrey MacDonald: Fatal Vision

The grisly murder scene that confronted police on February 17, 1970, is one that cannot be wiped from memory. Summoned to the Fort Bragg residence of Captain Jeffrey MacDonald, a physician, police found the bludgeoned body of MacDonald's wife. She had been repeatedly knifed and her face was smashed to a pulp. MacDonald's two children, ages 2 and 5, had been brutally and repeatedly knifed and battered to death.

Suspicion quickly fell on MacDonald. To the eyes of investigators, the murder scene had a staged appearance. MacDonald described a frantic effort to subdue four intruders who had slashed at him with an ice pick. However, the confrontation left MacDonald with minor wounds and no apparent defensive wounds on his arms. MacDonald then described how he had covered his slashed wife with his blue pajama top. Interestingly, when the body was removed, blue threads were observed under the body. In fact, blue threads matching the

pajama top turned up throughout the house—nineteen in one child's bedroom, including one beneath her fingernail, and two in the other child's bedroom. Eighty-one blue fibers were recovered from the master bedroom, and two were located on a bloodstained piece of wood outside the house.

Later forensic examination showed that the forty-eight ice pick holes in the pajama top were smooth and cylindrical, a sign that the top was stationary when it was slashed. Also, folding the pajama top demonstrated that the forty-eight holes actually could have been made by twenty-one thrusts of an ice pick. This coincided with the number of wounds that MacDonald's wife sustained. As described in the book *Fatal Vision*, which chronicled the murder investigation, when MacDonald was confronted with adulterous conduct, he replied, "You guys are more thorough than I thought." MacDonald is currently serving three consecutive life sentences.

chapter 10

Trace Evidence I
Hairs and
Fibers

Key Terms

anagen phase

catagen phase

cortex

cuticle

follicular tag

macromolecule

manufactured fibers

medulla

mitochondrial DNA

molecule

monomer

natural fibers

nuclear DNA

polymer

telogen phase

Learning Objectives

After studying this chapter you should be able to:

- Recognize and understand the cuticle, cortex, and medulla areas of hair

- List the three phases of hair growth

- Appreciate the distinction between animal and human hairs

- List hair features that are useful for microscopic comparison of human hairs

- Explain proper collection of forensic hair evidence

- Describe and understand the role of DNA typing in hair comparisons

- Understand the differences between natural and manufactured fibers

- List the properties of fibers that are most useful for forensic comparisons

- Describe proper collection of fiber evidence

The trace evidence transferred between individuals and objects during the commission of a crime, if recovered, often corroborates other evidence developed during the course of an investigation. Although in most cases physical evidence cannot by itself positively identify a suspect, laboratory examination may narrow the origin of such evidence to a group that includes the suspect. Using many of the instruments and techniques we have already examined, the crime laboratory has developed a variety of procedures for comparing and tracing the origins of physical evidence. This and the forthcoming chapters discuss how to apply these techniques to the analysis of the types of physical evidence most often encountered at crime scenes. We begin with a discussion of hairs and fibers.

Forensic Examination of Hair

Hair is encountered as physical evidence in a wide variety of crimes. However, any review of the forensic aspects of hair examination must start with the observation that it is not yet possible to individualize a human hair to any single head or body through its morphology, or structural characteristics. Over the years, criminalists have tried to isolate the physical and chemical properties of hair that could serve as individual characteristics of identity. Partial success has finally been achieved by isolating and characterizing the DNA present in hair.

The importance of hair as physical evidence cannot be overemphasized. Its removal from the body often denotes physical contact between a victim and perpetrator and hence a crime of a serious or violent nature. When hair is properly collected at the crime scene and submitted to the laboratory along with enough standard/reference samples, it can provide strong corroborative evidence for placing an individual at a crime site. The first step in the forensic examination of hair logically starts with its color and structure, or morphology, and, if warranted, progresses to the more detailed DNA extraction, isolation, and characterization.

FIGURE 10–1   Cross section of skin showing hair growing out of a tubelike structure called the follicle.

Morphology of Hair

Hair is an appendage of the skin that grows out of an organ known as the *hair follicle*. The length of a hair extends from its root or bulb embedded in the follicle, continues into the shaft, and terminates at the tip end. The shaft, which is composed of three layers—the cuticle, cortex, and medulla—is most intensely examined by the forensic scientist (see Figure 10–1).

The Cuticle   Two features that make hair a good subject for establishing individual identity are its resistance to chemical decomposition and its ability to retain structural features over a long period of time. Much of this resistance and stability is attributed to the cuticle, a scale structure covering the exterior of the hair. The cuticle is formed by overlapping scales that always point toward the tip end of each hair. The scales form from specialized cells that have hardened *(keratinized)* and flattened in progressing from the follicle.

Although the scale pattern is not a useful characteristic for individualizing human hair, the variety of patterns formed by animal hair makes it an important feature for species identification. Figure 10–2 shows the scale patterns of some animal hairs and of a human hair as viewed by the scanning electron microscope. Another method of studying the scale pattern of hair is to make a cast of its surface. This is done by embedding the hair in a soft medium, such as clear nail polish or softened vinyl. When the medium has hardened, the hair is removed, leaving a clear, distinct impression of the hair's cuticle, ideal for examination with a compound microscope.

The Cortex   Contained within the protective layer of the cuticle is the cortex, the main body of the hair shaft. The cortex is made up of spindle-shaped cortical cells aligned in a regular array, parallel to the length of the

cuticle
The scale structure covering the exterior of the hair.

cortex
The main body of the hair shaft.

medulla
A cellular column running through the center of the hair.

(a) (b) (c)

(d) (e) (f)

FIGURE 10–2 **Scale patterns of various types of hair. (a) Human head hair (600×), (b) dog (1250×), (c) deer (120×), (d) rabbit (300×), (e) cat (2000×), and (f) horse (450×).** *Courtesy International Scientific Instruments, Mountain View, Calif., and New Jersey State Police*

hair. The cortex derives its major forensic importance from the fact that it is embedded with the pigment granules that give hair its color. The color, shape, and distribution of these granules provide important points of comparison among the hairs of different individuals.

The structural features of the cortex are examined microscopically after the hair has been mounted in a liquid medium with a refractive index close to that of the hair. Under these conditions, the amount of light reflected off the hair's surface is minimized, and the amount of light penetrating the hair is optimized.

The Medulla   The medulla is a collection of cells that looks like a central canal running through a hair. In many animals, this canal is a predominant feature, occupying more than half of the hair's diameter. The *medullary index* measures the diameter of the medulla relative to the diameter of the hair shaft and is normally expressed as a fraction. For humans, the index is generally less than one-third; for most other animals, the index is one-half or greater.

The presence and appearance of the medulla vary from individual to individual and even among the hairs of a given individual. Not all hairs

WebExtra 10.1

Test Your Skills as a Forensic Hair Examiner

www.prenhall.com/hsforensics

Continuous   Interrupted   Fragmented

FIGURE 10–3 Medulla patterns.

have medullae, and when they do exist, the degree of medullation can vary. In this respect, medullae may be classified as being either continuous, interrupted, fragmented, or absent (see Figure 10–3). Human head hairs generally exhibit no medullae or have fragmented ones; they rarely show continuous medullation. One noted exception is the Mongoloid race, whose members usually have head hairs with continuous medullae. Also, most animals have medullae that are either continuous or interrupted.

Another interesting feature of the medulla is its shape. Humans, as well as many animals, have medullae that give a nearly cylindrical appearance. Other animals exhibit medullae that have a patterned shape. For example, the medulla of a cat can best be described as resembling a string of pearls, whereas members of the deer family show a medullary structure consisting of spherical cells occupying the entire hair shaft. Figure 10–4 illustrates medullary sizes and forms for a number of common animal hairs and a human head hair.

A searchable database on CD-ROM of the thirty-five most common animal hairs encountered in forensic casework is commercially available.[1] This database allows an examiner to rapidly search for animal hairs based on scale patterns and/or medulla type using a PC. A typical screen presentation arising from such a data search is shown in Figure 10–5.

The Root   The root and other surrounding cells within the hair follicle provide the tools necessary to produce hair and continue its growth. Human head hair grows in three developmental stages, and the shape and size of the hair root is determined by the hair's current growth phase. The three phases of hair growth are the anagen, catagen, and telogen phases.

In the anagen phase (the initial growth phase), which may last up to six years, the root is attached to the follicle for continued growth, giving the root bulb a flame-shaped appearance [Figure 10–6(a)]. When pulled from the root, some hairs in the anagen phase have a follicular tag. With the advent of DNA analysis, this follicular tag is important for individualizing hair.

Hair continues to grow, but at a decreasing rate, during the catagen phase, which can last anywhere from two to three weeks. In the catagen phase, roots typically take on an elongated appearance [Figure 10–6(b)] as the root bulb shrinks and is pushed out of the hair follicle. Once hair growth ends, the telogen phase begins and the root takes on a club-shaped appearance [Figure 10–6(c)]. Over two to six months, the hair is pushed out of the follicle, causing the hair to be naturally shed.

Identification and Comparison of Hair

Most often the prime purpose for examining hair evidence in a crime laboratory is to establish whether the hair is human or animal in origin, or to determine whether human hair retrieved at a crime scene compares with hair from a particular individual. A careful microscopic examination of hair reveals morphological features that can distinguish human hair from

anagen phase
The initial growth phase during which the hair follicle actively produces hair.

catagen phase
A transition stage between the anagen and telogen phases of hair growth.

telogen phase
The final growth phase in which hair naturally falls out of the skin.

follicular tag
A translucent piece of tissue surrounding the hair's shaft near the root that contains the richest source of DNA associated with hair.

FIGURE 10–4 **Medulla patterns for various types of hair. (a) Human head hair (400×),** **(b) dog (400×), (c) deer (500×), (d) rabbit (450×), (e) cat (400×), and (f) mouse (500×).**

animal hair. The hair of various animals also differs enough in structure that the examiner can often identify the species. Before reaching such a conclusion, however, the examiner must have access to a comprehensive collection of reference standards and the accumulated experience of hundreds of prior hair examinations. Scale structure, medullary index, and medullary shape are particularly important in hair identification.

The most common request when hair is used as forensic evidence is to determine whether hair recovered at the crime scene compares to hair removed from a suspect. In most cases, such a comparison relates to hair obtained from the scalp or pubic area. Ultimately, the evidential value of the comparison depends on the degree of probability with which the examiner can associate the hair in question with a particular individual.

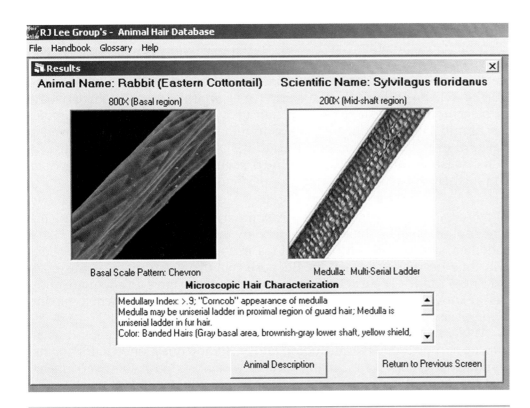

FIGURE 10–5 **Information on rabbit hair contained within the _Forensic Animal Hair Atlas._**
Courtesy RJ Lee Group, Inc. Monroeville, Pa.

(a)

(b)

(c)

FIGURE 10–6 **Hair roots in the (a) anagen phase, (b) catagen phase, and (c) telogen phase (100×).** *Courtesy Charles A. Linch*

Factors in Comparison of Hair Although animal hair normally can be distinguished from human hair with little difficulty, human hair comparisons must be undertaken with extreme caution. Hair tends to exhibit variable morphological characteristics, not only from one person to another but also within a single individual. In comparing hair, the criminalist is particularly interested in matching the color, length, and diameter. Other important features are the presence or absence of a medulla and the distribution, shape, and color intensity of the pigment granules in the cortex. A microscopic examination may also distinguish dyed or bleached hair from natural hair.

A dyed color is often present in the cuticle as well as throughout the cortex. Bleaching, on the other hand, tends to remove pigment from the hair and gives it a yellowish tint.

If hair has grown since it was last bleached or dyed, the natural-end portion will be quite distinct in color. An estimate of the time since dyeing or bleaching can be made because hair grows approximately 1 centimeter per month. Other significant but less frequent features may be observed in hair. For example, morphological abnormalities may be present due to certain diseases or deficiencies. Also, the presence of fungal and nit infections can further link a hair specimen to a particular individual.

Microscopic Examination of Hair   A comparison microscope is an invaluable tool that allows the examiner to view the questioned and known hair together, side by side. Any variations in the microscopic characteristics will thus be readily observed. Because hair from any part of the body exhibits a range of characteristics, it is necessary to have an adequate number of known hairs that are representative of all its features when making a comparison.

While microscopic comparison of hairs has long been accepted as an appropriate approach for including and excluding questioned hairs against standard/reference hairs, many forensic scientists have long recognized that this approach is very subjective and is highly dependent on the skills and integrity of the analyst, as well as the hair morphology being examined. However, until the advent of DNA analysis, the forensic science community had no choice but to rely on the microscope to carry out hair comparisons.

Any lingering doubts about the necessity of augmenting microscopic hair examinations with DNA analysis evaporated with the publication of an FBI study describing significant error rates associated with microscopic comparison of hairs.[2] Hair evidence submitted to the FBI for DNA analysis between 1996 and 2000 was examined both microscopically and by DNA analysis. Approximately 11 percent of the hairs (9 out of 80) in which FBI hair examiners found a positive microscopic match between questioned and standard/reference hairs were found to be nonmatches when they were later subjected to DNA analysis. The course of events is clear; microscopic hair comparisons must be regarded by police and courts as presumptive in nature and all positive microscopic hair comparisons must be confirmed by DNA determinations.

Questions about Hair Examination   A number of questions may be asked to further ascertain the present status of forensic hair examinations. The answers to these questions can be of great significance to the investigator working with hair evidence.

Can the Body Area from Which a Hair Originated Be Determined?
Normally it is easy to determine the body area from which a hair came. For example, scalp hairs generally show little diameter variation and have a more uniform distribution of pigment when compared to other body hairs. Pubic hairs are short and curly, with wide variations in shaft diameter, and usually have continuous medullae. Beard hairs are coarse, are normally triangular in cross-section, and have blunt tips acquired from cutting or shaving.

Can the Racial Origin of Hair Be Determined?
In many instances, the examiner can distinguish hair originating from members of different races; this is especially true of Caucasian and Negroid head hair. Negroid

Case Study

The Central Park Jogger Case Revisited

Battery Park at night. *Courtesy Hans Deumling, Getty Images Inc. Image Bank*

On April 19, 1989, a young woman left her apartment around nine p.m. to jog in New York's Central Park. Nearly five hours later, she was found comatose lying in a puddle of mud in the park. She had been raped, her skull was fractured, and she had lost 75 percent of her blood. When the woman recovered, she had no memory of what happened to her. The brutality of the crime sent shock waves through the city and seemed to fuel a national perception that crime was running rampant and unchecked through the streets of New York.

Already in custody at the station house of the Central Park Precinct was a group of 14- and 15-year-old boys who had been rounded up leaving the park earlier in the night by police who suspected that they had been involved in a series of random attacks. Over the next two days, four of the teenagers gave videotaped statements, which they later recanted, admitting to participating in the attack. Ultimately, five of the teenagers were charged with the crime.

Interestingly, none of the semen collected from the victim could be linked to any of the defendants. However, according to the testimony of a forensic analyst, two head hairs collected from the clothing of one of the defendants microscopically compared to those of the victim, and a third hair collected from the same defendant's T-shirt microscopically compared to the victim's pubic hair. Besides these three hairs, a fourth hair was found microscopically similar to the victim's. This hair was recovered from the clothing of Steven Lopez, who was originally charged with rape but not prosecuted for the crime.

Hairs were the only pieces of physical evidence offered by the district attorney to directly link any of the teenagers to the crime. The hairs were cited by the district attorney as proof for the jury that the videotaped confessions of the teenagers were reliable. The five defendants were convicted and ultimately served from nine to thirteen years.

In August 1989, more than three months after the jogger attack, New York Police arrested a man named Matias Reyes, who pleaded guilty to murdering a pregnant woman, raping three others, and committing a robbery. Reyes was sentenced to thirty-three years to life for these crimes. In January 2002, Reyes also confessed to the Central Park attack. Follow-up tests revealed that Reyes's DNA compared to semen recovered from the jogger's body and her sock. Other DNA tests showed that the hairs offered into evidence at the original trial did not come from the victim, and so could not be used to link the teenagers to the crime as the district attorney had argued. After an eleven-month reinvestigation of the original charges, a New York State Supreme Court judge dismissed all the convictions against the five teenage suspects in the Central Park jogger case.

hairs are normally kinky, containing dense, unevenly distributed pigments. Caucasian hairs are usually straight or wavy, with very fine to coarse pigments that are more evenly distributed when compared to Negroid hair.

Sometimes a cross-sectional examination of hair may help identify race. Cross-sections of hair from Caucasians are oval to round in shape, whereas cross-sections of Negroid hair are flat to oval in shape. However, all of these observations are general, with many possible exceptions. The criminalist must approach the determination of race from hair with caution and a good deal of experience.

Can the Age and Sex of an Individual Be Determined from a Hair Sample? The age of an individual cannot be learned from a hair examination with any degree of certainty except with infant hair. Infant hairs are fine and short and have fine pigmentation. Although the presence of dye or bleach on the hair may offer some clue to sex, present hairstyles make these characteristics less valuable than they were in the past. The recovery of nuclear DNA either from tissue adhering to hair or from the root structure of the hair will allow a determination of whether the hair originated from a male or female (see p. 328).

Is It Possible to Determine Whether Hair Was Forcibly Removed from the Body? A microscopic examination of the hair root may establish whether the hair fell out or was pulled out of the skin. A hair root with follicular tissue (root sheath cells) adhering to it, as shown in Figure 10–7, indicates a hair that has been pulled out either by a person or by brushing or combing. Hair naturally falling off the body has a bulbous-shaped root free of any adhering tissue.

The absence of sheath cells cannot always be relied on for correctly judging whether hair has been forcibly pulled from the body. In some cases the root of a hair is devoid of any adhering tissue even when it has been pulled from the body. Apparently, an important consideration is how quickly the hair is pulled out of the head. Hairs pulled quickly from the head are much more likely to have sheath cells compared to hairs that have been removed slowly from the scalp.[3]

nuclear DNA
DNA that is present in the nucleus of a cell and that is inherited from both parents.

Are Efforts Being Made to Individualize Human Hair? As we saw in Chapter 9, forensic scientists routinely isolate and characterize individual variations in DNA. Forensic hair examiners can link human hair to a particular individual by characterizing the nuclear DNA in the hair root or

FIGURE 10–7 Forcibly removed head hair, with follicular tissue attached. *Courtesy New Jersey State Police*

in follicular tissue adhering to the root (see Figure 10–7). Recall that the follicular tag is the richest source of DNA associated with hair. In the absence of follicular tissue, an examiner must extract DNA from the hair root.

The growth phase of hair (see p. 359) is a useful predictor of the likelihood of successfully typing DNA in human hair.[4] Examiners have a higher success rate in extracting DNA from hair roots in the anagen phase or from anagen-phase hairs entering the catagen phase of growth. Telogen-phase hairs have an inadequate amount of DNA for typing. Because most hairs are naturally shed and are expected to be in the telogen stage, these observations do not portend well for hairs collected at crime scenes. However, some crime scenes are populated with forcibly removed hairs that are expected to be rich sources for nuclear DNA.

When a questioned hair does not have adhering tissue or a root structure amenable to isolation of nuclear DNA, there is an alternative—mitochondrial DNA. Unlike the nuclear DNA described earlier, which is located in the nuclei of practically every cell in our body, mitochondrial DNA is found in cellular material outside the nucleus. Interestingly, unlike nuclear DNA, which is passed down to us from both parents, mitochondrial DNA is transmitted only from mother to child. Importantly, many more copies of mitochondrial DNA are located in our cells as compared to nuclear DNA. For this reason, the success rate of finding and typing mitochondrial DNA is much greater from samples, such as hair, that have limited quantities of nuclear DNA. Hairs 1–2 centimeters long can be subjected to mitochondrial analysis with extremely high odds of success. This subject is discussed in greater detail in Chapter 9.

mitochondrial DNA
DNA present in small structures (mitochondria) outside the nucleus of a cell. Mitochondria supply energy to the cell. This form of DNA is inherited maternally (from the mother).

Can DNA Individualize a Human Hair?   In some cases, the answer is yes. As we learned in Chapter 9, nuclear DNA produces frequencies of occurrence as low as one in billions or trillions. On the other hand, mitochondrial DNA cannot individualize human hair, but its diversity within the human population often permits exclusion of a significant portion of a population as potential contributors of a hair sample. Ideally, the combination of a positive microscopic comparison and an association through nuclear or mitochondrial DNA analysis strongly links a questioned hair and standard/reference hairs. However, a word of caution: mitochondrial DNA cannot distinguish microscopically similar hairs from different individuals who are maternally related.

Collection and Preservation of Hair Evidence

When questioned hairs are submitted to a forensic laboratory for examination, they must always be accompanied by an adequate number of standard/reference samples from the victim of the crime and from individuals suspected of having deposited hair at the crime scene. We have learned that hair from different parts of the body varies significantly in its physical characteristics. Likewise, hair from any one area of the body can also have a wide range of characteristics. For this reason, the questioned and standard/reference hairs must come from the same area of the body; one cannot, for instance, compare head hair to pubic hair. It is also important that the collection of standard/reference hair be carried out in a way to ensure a representative sampling of hair from any one area of the body.

Forensic hair comparisons generally involve either head hair or pubic hair. Collecting fifty full-length hairs from all areas of the scalp normally ensures a representative sampling of head hair. Likewise, a minimum collection of twenty-four full-length pubic hairs should cover the range of characteristics present in this type of hair. In rape cases, care must first be

Forensic Brief

Bill Cosby and his son Ennis Cosby. *Courtesy Andrea Mohin, The New York Times*

The murder of Ennis Cosby, son of entertainer Bill Cosby, at first appeared unsolvable. It was a random act. When his car tire went flat, Ennis pulled off the road and called a friend on his cellular phone to ask for assistance. Shortly thereafter, an assailant demanded money and, when

Cosby didn't respond quickly enough, shot him once in the temple. Acting on a tip from a friend of the assailant, police investigators later found a .38-caliber revolver wrapped in a blue cap miles from the crime scene. Mikail Markhasev was arrested and charged with murder.

At trial, the district attorney introduced firearms evidence to show that the recovered gun had fired the bullet aimed at Cosby. However, a single hair also recovered from the hat dramatically linked Markhasev to the crime. Los Angeles Police Department forensic analyst Harry Klann identified six DNA markers from the follicular tissue adhering to the hair root that matched Markhasev's DNA. This particular DNA profile is found in one out of 15,500 members of the general population. Upon hearing all the evidence, the jury deliberated and convicted Markhasev of murder.

taken to comb the pubic area with a clean comb to remove all loose foreign hair present before the victim is sampled for standard/reference hair. The comb should then be packaged in a separate envelope.

Because a hair may vary in color and other morphological features over its entire length, the entire hair is collected. This requirement is best accomplished by either pulling the hair out of the skin or clipping it at the skin line. During an autopsy, hair samples are routinely collected from a victim of suspicious death. Because the autopsy may occur early in an investigation, the need for hair standard/reference samples may not always be apparent. However, one should never rule out the possible involvement of hair evidence in subsequent investigative findings. Failure to make this simple collection may result in complicated legal problems later.

Key Points

- The hair shaft is composed of three layers called the cuticle, cortex, and medulla and is most intensely examined by the forensic scientist.

- When comparing strands of hair, the criminalist is particularly interested in matching the color, length, and diameter. Other important features for comparing hair are the presence or absence of a medulla and the distribution, shape, and color intensity of pigment granules in the cortex.

- The probability of detecting DNA in hair roots is more likely for hair being examined in its anagen or early growth phase as opposed to its catagen or telogen phases.

- The follicular tag, a translucent piece of tissue surrounding the hair's shaft near the root, is a rich source of DNA associated with hair. Mitochondrial DNA can also be extracted from the hair shaft.

- All positive microscopic hair comparisons must be confirmed by DNA analysis.

Forensic Examination of Fibers

Just as hair left at a crime scene can serve as identification, the same logic can reasonably be extended to the fibers that compose our fabrics and garments. Fibers may become important evidence in incidents that involve personal contact—such as homicide, assault, and sexual offenses—in which cross-transfers may occur between the clothing of suspect and victim. Similarly, the force of impact between a hit-and-run victim and a vehicle often leaves fibers, threads, or even whole pieces of clothing adhering to parts of the vehicle. Fibers may also become fixed in screens or glass broken in the course of a breaking-and-entering attempt.

Regardless of where and under what conditions fibers are recovered, their ultimate value as forensic evidence depends on the criminalist's ability to narrow their origin to a limited number of sources or even to a single source. Unfortunately, mass production of garments and fabrics has limited the value of fiber evidence in this respect, and only rarely do fibers recovered at a crime scene provide individual identification with a high degree of certainty.

Types of Fibers

For centuries, humans depended on fibers derived from natural sources such as plants and animals. However, early in the twentieth century, the first manufactured fiber—rayon—became a practical reality, followed in the 1920s by the introduction of cellulose acetate. Since the late 1930s, scientists have produced dozens of new fibers. In fact, the development of fibers, fabrics, finishes, and other textile-processing techniques has made greater advances since 1900 than in the preceding five thousand years of recorded history. Today, such varied items as clothing, carpeting, drapes, wigs, and even artificial turf attest to the predominant role that manufactured fibers have come to play in our culture and environment. When discussing forensic examination of fibers, it is convenient to classify them into two broad groups: *natural* and *manufactured*.

Natural Fibers Natural fibers are wholly derived from animal or plant sources. Animal fibers comprise most natural fibers encountered in crime laboratory examinations. These include hair coverings from such animals as sheep (wool), goats (mohair, cashmere), camels, llamas, alpacas, and vicuñas. Fur fibers include those obtained from animals such as mink, rabbit, beaver, and muskrat.

Forensic examination of animal fibers uses the same procedures discussed in the previous section for the forensic examination of animal hairs.

natural fibers
Fibers derived entirely from animal or plant sources.

Identification and comparison of such fibers relies solely on a microscopic examination of color and morphological characteristics. Again, a sufficient number of standard/reference specimens must be examined to establish the range of fiber characteristics that comprise the suspect fabric.

By far the most prevalent plant fiber is cotton. The wide use of undyed white cotton fibers in clothing and other fabrics has made its evidential value almost meaningless, although the presence of dyed cotton in a combination of colors has, in some cases, enhanced its evidential significance. The microscopic view of cotton fiber shown in Figure 10–8 reveals its most distinguishing feature—a ribbonlike shape with twists at irregular intervals.

manufactured fibers
Fibers derived from either natural or synthetic polymers.

Manufactured Fibers   Beginning with the introduction of rayon in 1911 and the development of nylon in 1939, manufactured fibers have increasingly replaced natural fibers in garments and fabrics. Such fibers are marketed under hundreds of different trade names. To reduce consumer confusion, the U.S. Federal Trade Commission has approved "generic" or family names for the grouping of all manufactured fibers. Many of these generic classes are produced by several manufacturers and are sold under a confusing variety of trade names. For example, in the United States, polyesters are marketed under names that include Dacron, Fortrel, and Kodel. In England, polyesters are called Terylene. Table 10–1 lists major generic fibers, along with common trade names and their characteristics and applications.

The first machine-made fibers were manufactured from raw materials derived from cotton or wood pulp. These materials are processed, and pure cellulose is extracted from them. Depending on the type of fiber desired, the cellulose may be chemically treated and dissolved in an appropriate solvent

FIGURE 10–8   Photomicrograph of cotton fiber (450×).

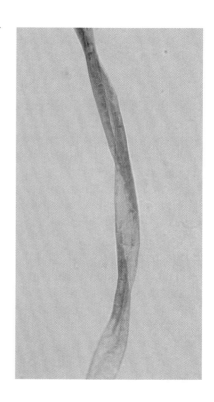

Table 10–1 Major Generic Fibers

Major Generic Fiber	Characteristics	Major Domestic and Industrial Uses
Acetate	• Luxurious feel and appearance • Wide range of colors and lusters • Excellent drapability and softness • Relatively fast-drying • Shrink-, moth-, and mildew-resistant	*Apparel:* Blouses, dresses, foundation garments, lingerie, linings, shirts, slacks, sportswear *Fabrics:* Brocade, crepe, double knits, faille, knitted jerseys, lace, satin, taffeta, tricot *Home Furnishings:* Draperies, upholstery *Other:* Cigarette filters, fiberfill for pillows, quilted products
Acrylic	• Soft and warm • Wool-like • Retains shape • Resilient • Quick-drying • Resistant to moths, sunlight, oil, and chemicals	*Apparel:* Dresses, infant wear, knitted garments, skiwear, socks, sportswear, sweaters *Fabrics:* Fleece and pile fabrics, face fabrics in bonded fabrics, simulated furs, jerseys *Home Furnishings:* Blankets carpets, draperies, upholstery *Other:* Auto tops, awnings, hand-knitting and craft yarns, industrial and geotextile fabrics
Aramid	• Does not melt • Highly flame-resistant • Great strength • Great resistance to stretch • Maintains shape and form at high temperatures	Hot-gas filtration fabrics, protective clothing, military helmets, protective vests, structural composites for aircraft and boats, sailcloth, tires, ropes and cables, mechanical rubber goods, marine and sporting goods
Bicomponent	• Thermal bonding • Self bulking • Very fine fibers • Unique cross-sections • The functionality of special polymers or additives at reduced cost	Uniform distribution of adhesive; fiber remains a part of structure and adds integrity; customized sheath materials to bond various materials; wide range of bonding temperatures; cleaner, environmentally friendly (*no effluent*); recyclable; lamination/molding/densification of composites
Lyocell	• Soft, strong, absorbent • Good dyeability • Fibrillates during wet processing to produce special textures	Dresses, slacks, and coats
Melamine	• White and dyeable • Flame resistance and low thermal conductivity • High-heat dimensional stability • Processable on standard textile equipment	*Fire-Blocking Fabrics:* Aircraft seating, fire blockers for upholstered furniture in high-risk occupancies (e.g., to meet California TB 133 requirements) *Protective Clothing:* Firefighters' turnout gear, insulating thermal liners, knit hoods, molten metal splash apparel, heat-resistant gloves *Filter Media:* High-capacity, high-efficiency, high-temperature baghouse air filters
Modacrylic	• Soft • Resilient • Abrasion- and flame-resistant • Quick-drying • Resists acids and alkalies • Retains shape	*Apparel:* Deep-pile coats, trims, linings, simulated fur, wigs and hairpieces *Fabrics:* Fleece fabrics, industrial fabrics, knit-pile fabric backings, nonwoven fabrics *Home Furnishings:* Awnings, blankets, carpets, flame-resistant draperies and curtains, scatter rugs *Other:* Filters, paint rollers, stuffed toys

(continued)

Table 10–1 Major Generic Fibers (*continued*)

Major Generic Fiber	Characteristics	Major Domestic and Industrial Uses
Nylon	• Exceptionally strong • Supple • Abrasion-resistant • Lustrous • Easy to wash • Resists damage from oil and many chemicals • Resilient • Low in moisture absorbency	*Apparel:* Blouses, dresses, foundation garments, hosiery, lingerie and underwear, raincoats, ski and snow apparel, suits, windbreakers *Home Furnishings:* Bedspreads, carpets, draperies, curtains, upholstery *Other:* Air hoses, conveyor and seat belts, parachutes, racket strings, ropes and nets, sleeping bags, tarpaulins, tents, thread, tire cord, geotextiles
Olefin	• Unique wicking properties that make it very comfortable • Abrasion-resistant • Quick-drying • Resistant to deterioration from chemicals, mildew, perspiration, rot, and weather • Sensitive to heat • Soil resistant • Strong; very lightweight • Excellent colorfastness	*Apparel:* Pantyhose, underwear, knitted sports shirts, men's half-hose, men's knitted sportswear, sweaters *Home Furnishings:* Carpet and carpet backing, slipcovers, upholstery *Other:* Dye nets, filter fabrics, laundry and sandbags, geotextiles, automotive interiors, cordage, doll hair, industrial sewing thread
Polyester	• Strong • Resistant to stretching and shrinking • Resistant to most chemicals • Quick-drying • Crisp and resilient when wet or dry • Wrinkle- and abrasion-resistant • Retains heat-set pleats and creases • Easy to wash	*Apparel:* Blouses, shirts, career apparel, children's wear, dresses, half-hose, insulated garments, ties, lingerie and underwear, permanent press garments, slacks, suits *Home Furnishings:* Carpets, curtains, draperies, sheets and pillowcases *Other:* Fiberfill for various products, fire hose, power belting, ropes and nets, tire cord, sail, V-belts
PBI	• Extremely flame-resistant • Outstanding comfort factor combined with thermal and chemical stability properties • Will not burn or melt • Low shrinkage when exposed to flame	Suitable for high-performance protective apparel such as firefighters' turnout coats, astronaut space suits, and applications in which fire resistance is important
Rayon	• Highly absorbent • Soft and comfortable • Easy to dye • Versatile • Good drapability	*Apparel:* Blouses, coats, dresses, jackets, lingerie, linings, millinery, rainwear, slacks, sports shirts, sportswear, suits, ties, work clothes *Home Furnishings:* Bedspreads, blankets, carpets, curtains, draperies, sheets, slipcovers, tablecloths, upholstery *Other:* Industrial products, medical-surgical products, nonwoven products, tire cord
Spandex	• Can be stretched 500 percent without breaking • Can be stretched repeatedly and recover original length • Lightweight • Stronger and more durable than rubber • Resistant to body oils	*Articles* (in which stretch is desired): Athletic apparel, bathing suits, delicate laces, foundation garments, golf jackets, ski pants, slacks, support and surgical hose

Source: American Fiber Manufacturers Assoc. Inc., Washington, D.C., *http://www.fingersource.com/f-tutor/q-guide.htm.*

before it is forced through the small holes of a spinning jet, or spinneret, to produce the fiber. Fibers manufactured from natural raw materials in this manner are classified as *regenerated fibers* and commonly include rayon, acetate, and triacetate, all of which are produced from regenerated cellulose.

Most of the fibers currently manufactured are produced solely from synthetic chemicals and are therefore classified as *synthetic fibers.* These include nylons, polyesters, and acrylics. The creation of synthetic fibers became a reality only when scientists developed a method of synthesizing long-chained molecules called polymers.

In 1930, chemists discovered an unusual characteristic of one of the polymers under investigation. When a glass rod in contact with viscous material in a beaker was slowly pulled away, the substance adhered to the rod and formed a fine filament that hardened as soon as it entered the cool air. Furthermore, the cold filaments could be stretched several times their extended length to produce a flexible, strong, and attractive fiber. This first synthetic fiber was improved and then marketed as nylon. Since then, fiber chemists have successfully synthesized new polymers and have developed more efficient methods for manufacturing them. These efforts have produced a multitude of synthetic fibers.

Polymers   The polymer is the basic chemical substance of all synthetic fibers. Indeed, an almost unbelievable array of household, industrial, and recreational products is manufactured from polymers; these include plastics, paints, adhesives, and synthetic rubber. Polymers exist in countless forms and varieties and with the proper treatment can be made to assume different chemical and physical properties.

As we have already observed, chemical substances are composed of basic structural units called molecules. The molecules of most materials are composed of just a few atoms; for example, water, H_2O, has 2 atoms of hydrogen and 1 atom of oxygen. The heroin molecule, $C_{21}H_{23}O_5N$, contains 21 atoms of carbon, 23 atoms of hydrogen, 5 atoms of oxygen, and 1 atom of nitrogen. Polymers, on the other hand, are formed by linking a large number of molecules, so that a polymer often contains thousands or even millions of atoms. This is why polymers are often referred to as macromolecules, or "big" molecules.

Simply, a polymer can be pictured as resembling a long, repeating chain, with each link representing the basic structure of the polymer (see Figure 10–9). The repeating molecular units in the polymer, called monomers, are joined end to end, so that thousands link to form a long chain. What makes polymer chemistry so fascinating is the countless possibilities for linking different molecules. By simply varying the chemical

polymer
A substance composed of a large number of atoms that are usually arranged in repeating units.

molecule
Two or more atoms held together by chemical bonds.

macromolecule
A molecule with a high molecular mass.

monomer
The basic unit of structure from which a polymer is constructed.

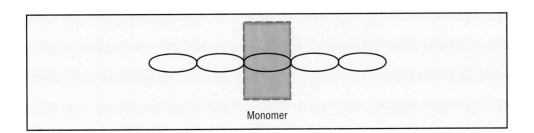

Monomer

FIGURE 10–9   The chain-link model of a segment of a polymer molecule. The molecule may contain as many as several million monomer units or links.

structure of the monomers, and by devising numerous ways to weave them together, chemists have created polymers that exhibit different properties. This versatility enables polymer chemists to synthesize glues, plastics, paints, and fibers.

Not all polymers are synthesized in the chemical laboratory; nature has produced polymers that humans have not yet been able to copy. For example, the proteins that form the basic structure of animal hairs, as well as of all living matter, are polymers, composed of thousands of amino acids linked in a highly organized arrangement and sequence. Similarly, cellulose (the basic ingredient of wood and cotton) and starch are both natural polymers built by the combination of several thousand carbohydrate monomers, as shown in Figure 10–10. Hence, the synthesis of manufactured fibers merely represents an extension of chemical principles that nature has used to produce hair and vegetable fibers.

Identification and Comparison of Manufactured Fibers

The evidential value of fibers lies in the criminalist's ability to trace their origin. Obviously, if the examiner is presented with fabrics that can be exactly fitted together at their torn edges, the fabrics must be of common origin. Such a fit is demonstrated in Figure 10–11 for a piece of fabric that was removed from a vehicle suspected of involvement in a hit-and-run fatality. The exact fit with the remains of the victim's trousers directly implicated the car's driver in the incident.

More often, however, the criminalist obtains a limited number of fibers for identification and comparison. Generally, in these situations obtaining a physical match is unlikely, and the examiner must resort to a side-by-side comparison of the standard/reference and crime-scene fibers.

Microscopic Examination of Fibers   The first and most important step in the examination is a microscopic comparison for color and diameter using a comparison microscope. Unless these two characteristics agree, there is little reason to suspect a match. Other morphological features that may aid in the comparison are lengthwise striations (lined markings) on the surface of some fibers and the pitting of the fiber's surface with delustering particles (usually titanium dioxide) added in the manufacturing process to reduce shine (see Figure 10–12).

The cross-sectional shape of a fiber may also help characterize the fiber.[5] In the Wayne Williams case (see the case reading at the end of

FIGURE 10–10   Starch and cellulose are natural carbohydrate polymers consisting of a large number of repeating units or monomers.

FIGURE 10–11 **A piece of fabric found on a suspect hit-and-run vehicle inserted into the torn trousers of the victim.** *Courtesy New Jersey State Police*

(a)   (b)

FIGURE 10–12 **Photomicrographs of synthetic fibers: (a) cellulose triacetate (450×) and (b) olefin fiber embedded with titanium dioxide particles (450×).**

Chapter 3), unusually shaped yellow-green fibers discovered on a number of the murder victims were linked to a carpet in the Williams home. This fiber was a key element in proving Williams's guilt. A photomicrograph of this unusually shaped fiber is shown in Figure 10–13.

Although two fibers may seem to have the same color when viewed under the microscope, compositional differences may actually exist in the

FIGURE 10–13   **A scanning electron photomicrograph of the cross-section of a nylon fiber removed from a sheet used to transport the body of a murder victim. The fiber, associated with a carpet in Wayne Williams's home, was manufactured in 1971 in relatively small quantities.** *Courtesy Federal Bureau of Investigation, Washington, D.C.*

dyes that were applied to them during their manufacture. In fact, most textile fibers are impregnated with a mixture of dyes selected to obtain a desired shade or color. The significance of a fiber comparison is enhanced when the forensic examiner can show that the questioned and standard/reference fibers have the same dye composition.

Analytical Techniques Used in Fiber Examination   The visible-light microspectrophotometer (pp. 248–249) is a convenient way for analysts to compare the colors of fibers through spectral patterns. This technique is not limited by sample size—a fiber as small as 1 millimeter long or less can be examined by this type of microscope. The examination is nondestructive and is carried out on fibers simply mounted on a microscope slide.

A more detailed analysis of the fiber's dye composition can be obtained through a chromatographic separation of the dye constituents. To accomplish this, small strands of fibers are compared for dye content by first extracting the dye off each fiber with a suitable solvent and then spotting the dye solution onto a thin-layer chromatography plate. The dye components of the questioned and standard/reference fibers are separated on the thin-layer plate and compared side by side for similarity.[6]

Chemical Composition.   Once this phase of the analysis is complete, and before any conclusion can be reached that two or more fibers compare, they must be shown to have the same chemical composition. In this respect, tests are performed to confirm that all of the fibers involved belong to the same broad generic class. Additionally, the comparison will be substantially enhanced if it can be demonstrated that all of the fibers belong to the same subclassification within their generic class. For example, at least four different types of nylon are available in commercial and consumer markets, including nylon 6, nylon 6–10, nylon 11, and nylon 6–6. Although all types of nylon have many properties in common, each may differ in physical shape, appearance, and dyeability because of modifications in basic chemical structure. Similarly, a study of more than two hundred different samples of acrylic fibers revealed that they could actually be divided into twenty-four distinguishable groups on the basis of their polymeric structure and microscopic characteristics.[7]

Textile chemists have devised numerous tests for determining the class of a fiber. However, unlike the textile chemist, the criminalist frequently does not have the luxury of having a substantial quantity of fabric to work with and must therefore select tests that will yield the most information with the least amount of material. Only a single fiber may be available for analysis, and often this may amount to no more than a minute strand recovered from a fingernail scraping of a homicide or rape victim.

Birefringence. A useful physical property of fibers is that many manufactured fibers exhibit double refraction or birefringence (discussed in Chapter 4). Synthetic fibers are manufactured by melting a polymeric substance or dissolving it in a solvent and then forcing it through the very fine holes of a spinneret. The polymer emerges as a very fine filament, with its molecules aligned parallel to the length of the filament (see Figure 10–14). Just as the regular arrangement of atoms produces a crystal, so will the regular arrangement of the fiber's polymers cause crystallinity in the finished fiber. This crystallinity makes a fiber stiff and strong and gives it the optical property of double refraction.

Polarized white light passing through a synthetic fiber is split into two rays that are perpendicular to each other, causing the fiber to display polarization or interference colors when viewed under a polarizing microscope (see Figure 10–15). Depending on the class of fiber, each polarized plane of light has a characteristic index of refraction. This value can be determined by immersing the fiber in a fluid with a comparable refractive index and observing the disappearance of the Becke line under a polarizing microscope. Table 10–2 lists the two refractive indices of some common classes of fibers, along with their birefringence. The virtue of this technique is that a single microscopic fiber can be analyzed in a nondestructive manner.

Infrared Absorption. The polymers that compose a manufactured fiber, just as in any other organic substance, selectively absorb infrared light in a characteristic pattern. Infrared spectrophotometry thus provides a rapid and reliable method for identifying the generic class, and in some cases the subclasses, of fibers. The infrared microspectrophotometer combines a microscope with an infrared spectrophotometer (see p. 249). Such a combination makes possible the infrared analysis of a small single-strand fiber while it is being viewed under a microscope.[8]

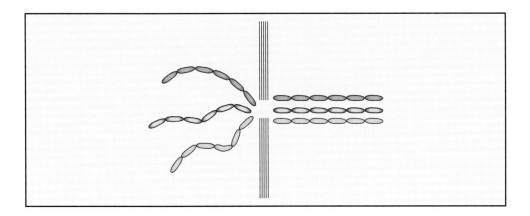

FIGURE 10–14 In the production of manufactured fibers, the bulk polymer is forced through small holes to form a filament in which all the polymers are aligned in the same direction.

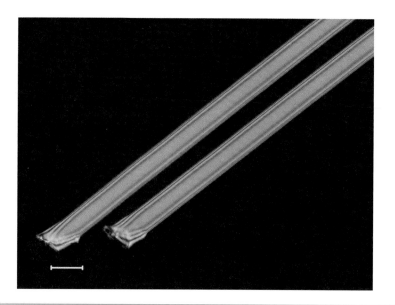

FIGURE 10–15 **A photomicrograph of nylon fibers displaying interference colors when observed between the crossed polars of a polarizing microscope (50×).** *Courtesy William Randle, Missouri State Highway Patrol crime laboratory, Jefferson City, Mo.*

Table 10–2	Refractive Indices of Common Textile Fibers		
	Refractive Index		
Fiber	Parallel	Perpendicular	Birefringence
Acetate	1.478	1.477	0.001
Triacetate	1.472	1.471	0.001
Acrylic	1.524	1.520	0.004
Nylon			
Nylon 6	1.568	1.515	0.053
Nylon 6–6	1.582	1.519	0.063
Polyester			
Dacron	1.710	1.535	0.175
Kodel	1.642	1.540	0.102
Modacrylic	1.536	1.531	0.005
Rayon			
Cuprammonium rayon	1.552	1.520	0.032
Viscose rayon	1.544	1.520	0.024

Note: The listed values are for specific fibers, which explains the precise values given. In identification work, such precision is not practical; values within 0.02 or 0.03 of those listed will suffice.

Significance of Fiber Evidence

Once a fiber match has been determined, the question of the significance of such a finding is bound to be raised. In reality, no analytical technique permits the criminalist to associate a fiber strand definitively to any single garment. Furthermore, except in the most unusual circumstances, no statistical databases are available for determining the probability of a fiber's origin. Considering the mass distribution of synthetic fibers and the constantly changing fashion tastes of our society, it is highly unlikely that such data will be available in the foreseeable future.

Despite these limitations, one should not discount or minimize the significance of a fiber association. An enormous variety of fibers exists in our

Forensics at Work

Fatal Vision Revisited

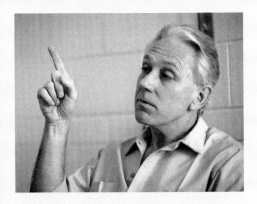

Jeffrey MacDonald in 1995 at Sheridan, Oregon, Federal Correctional Institution.
Courtesy AP Wide World Photos

Dr. Jeffrey MacDonald was convicted in 1979 of murdering his wife and two young daughters. The events surrounding the crime and the subsequent trial were recounted in Joe McGinniss's best-selling book *Fatal Vision*. The focus of MacDonald's defense was that intruders entered his home and committed these violent acts. Eleven years after this conviction, MacDonald's attorneys filed a petition for a new trial, claiming the existence of "critical new" evidence.

The defense asserted that wig fibers found on a hairbrush in the MacDonald residence were evidence that an intruder dressed in a wig entered the MacDonald home on the day of the murder. Subsequent examination of this claim by the FBI

FIGURE 1   A fiber comparison made with an infrared spectrophotometer. The infrared spectrum of a fiber from Mrs. MacDonald's fall compares to a fiber recovered from a hairbrush in the MacDonald home. These fibers were identified as modacrylics, the most common type of synthetic fiber used in the manufacture of human hair goods.
Courtesy SA Michael Malone, FBI Laboratory, Washington, D.C.

Source: B. M. Murtagh and M. P. Malone, "Fatal Vision Revisited," *Police Chief* (June 1993): 15.

(*continued*)

Forensics at Work

Fatal Vision Revisited (*continued*)

Laboratory focused on a blond fall (a type of artificial hair extension) frequently worn by MacDonald's wife. Fibers removed from the fall were shown to clearly match fibers on the hairbrush. The examination included the use of infrared microspectrophotometry to demonstrate that the suspect wig fibers were chemically identical to fibers found in the composition of the MacDonald fall (see Figure 1). Hence, although wig fibers were found at the crime scene, the source of these fibers could be accounted for—they came from Mrs. MacDonald's fall.

Another piece of evidence cited by MacDonald's lawyers was a bluish-black woolen fiber found on the body of Mrs. MacDonald. They claimed that this fiber compared to a bluish-black woolen fiber recovered from the club used to assault her. These wool fibers were central to MacDonald's defense that the "intruders" wore dark-colored clothing. Initial examination showed that the fibers were microscopically indistinguishable. However, the FBI also compared the two wool fibers by visible-light microspectrophotometry. Comparison of their spectra clearly showed that their dye compositions differed, providing no evidence of outside intruders (see Figure 2). Ultimately, the U.S. Supreme Court denied the merits of MacDonald's petition for a new trial.

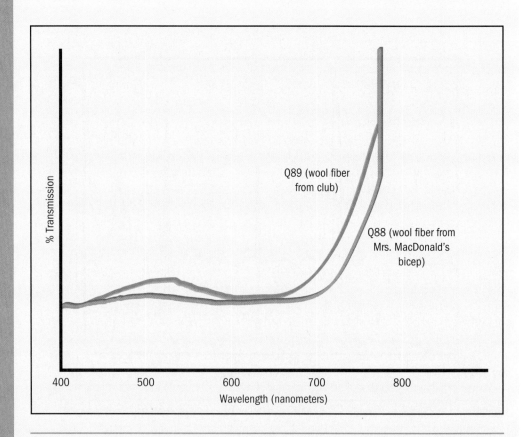

FIGURE 2 **The visible-light spectrum for the woolen fiber recovered from Mrs. MacDonald's body is clearly different from that of the fiber recovered from the club used to assault her.**
Courtesy SA Michael Malone, FBI Laboratory, Washington, D.C.

society. By simply looking at the random individuals we meet every day, we can see how unlikely it is to find two different people wearing identically colored fabrics (with the exception of blue denims or white cottons). There are thousands of different-colored fibers in our environment. Combine this with the fact that forensic scientists compare not only the color of fibers but also their size, shape, microscopic appearance, chemical composition, and dye content, and one can now begin to appreciate how unlikely it is to find two indistinguishable colored fibers emanating from randomly selected sources.

Furthermore, the significance of a fiber association increases dramatically if the analyst can link two or more distinctly different fibers to the same object. Likewise, the associative value of fiber evidence is dramatically enhanced if it is accompanied by other types of physical evidence linking a person or object to a crime. As with most class evidence, the significance of a fiber comparison is dictated by the circumstances of the case; by the location, number, and nature of the fibers examined; and, most important, by the judgment of an experienced examiner.

Collection and Preservation of Fiber Evidence

As criminal investigators have become more aware of the potential contribution of trace physical evidence to the success of their investigations, they have placed greater emphasis on conducting thorough crime-scene searches for evidence of forensic value. Their skill and determination at carrying out these tasks is tested in the collection of fiber-related evidence. Fiber evidence can be associated with virtually any type of crime. It usually cannot be seen with the naked eye and thus easily can be overlooked by someone not specifically searching for it.

An investigator committed to optimizing the laboratory's chances for locating minute strands of fibers identifies and preserves potential "carriers" of fiber evidence. Relevant articles of clothing should be packaged carefully in paper bags. Each article must be placed in a separate bag to avoid cross-contamination of evidence. Scrupulous care must be taken to prevent articles of clothing from different people or from different locations from coming into contact. Such articles must not even be placed on the same surface prior to packaging. Likewise, carpets, rugs, and bedding are to be folded carefully to protect areas suspected of containing fibers. Car seats should be carefully covered with polyethylene sheets to protect fiber evidence, and knife blades should be covered to protect adhering fibers. If a body is thought to have been wrapped at one time in a blanket or carpet, adhesive tape lifts of exposed body areas may reveal fiber strands.

Occasionally the field investigator may need to remove a fiber from an object, particularly if loosely adhering fibrous material may be lost in transit to the laboratory. These fibers must be removed with a clean forceps and placed in a small sheet of paper, which, after folding and labeling, can be placed inside another container. Again, scrupulous care must be taken to prevent contact between fibers collected from different objects or from different locations.

In the laboratory, the search for fiber evidence on clothing and other relevant objects, as well as in debris, is time consuming and tedious, and will test the skill and patience of the examiner. The crime-scene investigator can manage this task by collecting only relevant items for examination. The crime-scene investigator must pinpoint areas where a likely transfer of fiber evidence occurred and then ensure proper collection and preservation of these materials.

Key Points

- Fibers may be classified into two broad groups: *natural* and *manufactured*.

- Most fibers currently manufactured are produced solely from synthetic chemicals and are therefore classified as *synthetic fibers*. They include nylons, polyesters, and acrylics.

- Microscopic comparisons between questioned and standard/reference fibers are initially undertaken for color and diameter characteristics. Other features that could be important in comparing fibers are striations on the surface of the fiber, the presence of delustering particles, and the cross-sectional shape of the fiber.

- The visible-light microspectrophotometer is a convenient way for analysts to compare the colors of fibers through spectral patterns.

- Infrared spectrophotometry and the polarizing microscope are reliable methods for identifying the chemical composition of fibers.

- Fiber evidence collected at each location should be placed in separate containers to avoid cross-contamination. Care must be taken to prevent articles of clothing from different people or from different locations from coming into contact.

Case Study

The Telltale Rabbit

On a cold winter's day . . . a female was found in the alleyway of an East Harlem tenement. Close to the body was a California florist flower box and a plastic liner. The victim was identified as a member of a well-known church who had been selling church literature in the buildings that surround the alley in which the body was discovered.

The detectives investigating the case forwarded the flower box, the plastic liner, and the victim's clothing to the forensic science laboratory. On the box and liner were found tan wool fibers, red acrylic fibers, and navy blue wool fibers (all identified by polarized light microscopy). The three types of questioned fibers were compared microscopically with the vicitm's clothing. All three were found to be consistent in all respects to the textile fibers composing the victim's clothing (tan wool overcoat, navy blue wool/polyester blend slacks, and red acrylic sweater), thereby associating the woman with the flower box and liner.

In addition, light blue nylon rug fibers and several brown rabbit hairs were found on the box and liner. Similar light blue nylon rug fibers and rabbit hairs, as well as red nylon rug fibers, were found on the victim's tan wool overcoat. Neither the rabbit hairs nor the nylon rug fibers could be associated with the victim's environment (her clothing or residence). All of this information was conveyed to the field investigators.

Upon further inquiry in the neighborhood, investigators learned the identity of a man who had, the day after the body was discovered, sold a full-length brown rabbit hair coat to a local man. The investigators obtained the rabbit hair coat from the purchaser. The hair composing the coat was compared microscopically to the questioned rabbit hairs found on the victim's wool coat and the flower box liner. The specimens of questioned rabbit hair were found to be consistent in all physical and microscopic characteristics to the rabbit hair composing the suspect's coat. Armed with this information, the police now had probable cause to obtain a search warrant for the suspect's apartment.

In the suspect's apartment two rugs were found. One was light blue and the other was red, both rugs were composed of nylon fibers. Samples of each rug were collected by the crime-scene unit and forwarded to the forensic science laboratory for comparison with the questioned rug fibers found on the victim's clothing, the flower box, and the plastic liner. The questioned and known rug fibers were found to be consistent in all respects. The presence of light blue nylon rug fibers, red nylon rug fibers, and

brown-colored rabbit hairs on the flower box, plastic liner, and woman's clothing enabled the author to make associations between the woman, flower box, and liner found in the alleyway with the suspect and his apartment. . . .

The investigating officers made further inquiries in the neighborhood about the suspect. They located a witness who stated that he saw the suspect carrying a large California flower box a day or two before the body was discovered.

From the evidence, investigators theorized that the woman was killed in the suspect's apartment, placed in the flower box, brought up to the roof of the building in which the defendant resided, and thrown off the building into the alley below. On the basis of all of this evidence, the suspect was arrested, indicted, and tried for second-degree murder. After two trials, at which the author gave extensive testimony (three days) about the trace evidence, the defendant was found guilty of second-degree murder and subsequently sentenced to life imprisonment.

Source: Reprinted in part by permission of the American Society of Testing and Materials from N. Petraco, "Trace Evidence—The Invisible Witness," *Journal of Forensic Sciences* 31 (1986): 321. Copyright 1986.

Chapter Summary

Hair is an appendage of the skin that grows out of an organ known as the hair follicle. The length of a hair extends from its root or bulb embedded in the follicle, continues into a shaft, and terminates at a tip end. The shaft, which is composed of three layers—the cuticle, cortex, and medulla—is most intensely examined by the forensic scientist. The comparison microscope is an indispensable tool for comparing these morphological characteristics.

When comparing strands of hair, the criminalist is particularly interested in matching the color, length, and diameter. A careful microscopic examination of hair reveals morphological features that can distinguish human hair from animal hair. Scale structure, medullary index, and medullary shape are particularly important in hair identification. Other important features for comparing hair are the presence or absence of a medulla and the distribution, shape, and color intensity of pigment granules in the cortex. Microscopic hair examinations tend to be subjective and highly dependent on the skills and integrity of the analyst.

Recent breakthroughs in DNA profiling have extended this technology to the individualization of human hair. The probability of detecting DNA in hair roots is more likely for hair being examined in its anagen or early growth phase as opposed to its catagen or telogen phases. Often when hair is forcibly removed a follicular tag, a translucent piece of tissue surrounding the hair's shaft near the root, may be present. This is a rich source of DNA associated with hair. Also, mitochondrial DNA can be extracted from the hair shaft. All positive microscopic hair comparisons must be confirmed by DNA analysis.

The quality of fiber evidence depends on the ability of the criminalist to identify the origin of the fiber or at least to narrow the possibilities to a limited number of sources. Microscopic comparisons between questioned and standard/reference fibers are initially undertaken for color and diameter characteristics. Other morphological features that could be important in comparing fibers are striations on the surface of the fiber, the presence of delustering particles, and the cross-sectional shape of the fiber.

The visible-light microspectrophotometer provides a convenient way to compare the colors of fibers through spectral patterns. Infrared spectrophotometry is a rapid and reliable tool for identifying the generic class of fibers, as is the polarizing microscope.

Review Questions

Facts and Concepts

1. What is hair and what organ produces it?

2. Name and briefly define the three layers of the hair shaft.

3. What two features make hair a good subject for establishing individual identity? To which layer of the hair shaft are much of these features attributed?

4. The scale pattern of the cuticle is an important feature for characterizing _____ hair.

5. What is the main forensic importance of the cortex?

6. What is the difference between the medullae of human and animal hairs? Name one exception to this among humans.

7. Name the three phases of hair growth. A criminalist is more likely to collect DNA from hairs in which stage of growth? Why?

8. Why must microscopic human hair comparisons be undertaken with extreme caution?

9. In comparing hairs, what aspects of the hair is the criminalist particularly interested in matching? Name at least one other important feature that the criminalist might compare.

10. Which of the following questions cannot be answered with a microscopic examination of hair?
    a. whether a hair came from a 25-year-old or an infant
    b. whether a hair is from a man or a woman
    c. whether a hair is from a scalp or a beard
    d. whether the hair is consistent with Caucasian or Negroid hair

11. What types of hairs found at a crime scene are most likely to provide useful DNA evidence? Why?

12. Why must questioned hairs and standard/reference hairs being compared come from the same area of the body?

13. Hairs from which parts of the body are most often used for hair comparisons?

14. Why should the entire hair be collected when performing a hair comparison?

15. Define *polymer* and *monomer*. Why are polymers sometimes known as macromolecules?

16. Which of the following is not an example of a natural polymer?
    a. starch
    b. cellulose
    c. sugar
    d. proteins

17. What two morphological characteristics does a criminalist first compare when examining fibers with a microscope? What other features might be important in such a comparison?

18. Name two physical characteristics that frequently are used to identify fibers.

19. What analytical technique does a criminalist use to analyze the composition of the dye in a fiber?

20. Describe three analytical techniques for comparing the color of two fibers.

Application and Critical Thinking

1. Indicate the phase of growth of each of the following hairs:
    a. the root is club-shaped
    b. the hair has a follicular tag
    c. the root bulb is flame-shaped
    d. the root is elongated

2. A criminalist studying a dyed sample hair notices that the dyed color ends about 1.5 centimeters from the tip of the hair. Approximately how many weeks before the examination was the hair dyed? Explain your answer.

3. Following are descriptions of several hairs; based on these descriptions, indicate the likely race of the person from whom the hair originated:
   a. evenly distributed, fine pigmentation
   b. continuous medullation
   c. dense, uneven pigmentation
   d. wavy with a round cross-section

4. Criminalist Pete Evett is collecting fiber evidence from a murder scene. He notices fibers on the victim's shirt and trousers, so he places both of these items of clothing in a plastic bag. He also sees fibers on a sheet near the victim, so he balls up the sheet and places it in separate plastic bag. Noticing fibers adhering to the windowsill from which the attacker gained entrance, Pete carefully removes it with his fingers and places it in a regular envelope. What mistakes, if any, did Pete make while collecting this evidence?

Virtual Crime Scenes

WebExtra 10.2
Virtual Crime Scene 10.1
www.prenhall.com/hsforensics

WebExtra 10.3
Virtual Crime Scene 10.2
www.prenhall.com/hsforensics

Crime Scene 10.1
Step into the role of the first officer responding to a violent crime scene
www.prenhall.com/hsforensics

Crime Scene 10.2
Assume the duties of an evidence-collection technician at a violent crime scene
www.prenhall.com/hsforensics

Web Resources

Deedrick, D. W., "Hairs, Fibers, Crime, and Evidence," *Forensic Science Communications* 2, no. 3, (2000)
www.fbi.gov/hq/lab/fsc/backissu/july2000/deedrick.htm

Deedrick, D. W., and S. L. Koch, "Microscopy of Hair Part I: A Practical Guide and Manual for Human Hairs," *Forensic Science Communications* 6, no. 1 (2004)
www.fbi.gov/hq/lab/fsc/backissu/jan2004/research/2004_01_research01b.htm

Deedrick, D. W., and S. L. Koch, "Microscopy of Hair Part II: A Practical Guide and Manual for Animal Hairs," *Forensic Science Communications* 6, no. 3 (2004)
www.fbi.gov/hq/lab/fsc/backissu/july2004/research/2004_03_research02.htm

Exline, D. L., "That's Not My Hair," *Forensic Echo* 4, no. 1 (2000)
echo.forensicpanel.com/2000/10/12/thatsnot.html

Partin, K. D., A Microscopical Study of Exotic Animal Hair: Part l
www.modernmicroscopy.com/main.asp?article=24&page=1

Trace Evidence (Online article discussing the analysis of hair and fiber evidence based on true crime stories)
www.crimelibrary.com/forensics/trace/

Endnotes

1. J. D. Baker and D. L. Exline, *Forensic Animal Hair Atlas: A Searchable Database on CD-ROM*. RJ Lee Group, Inc., 350 Hochberg Rd., Monroeville, Pa. 15146.

2. M. M. Houk and B. Budowle, "Correlation of Microscopic and Mitochondrial DNA Hair Comparisons," *Journal of Forensic Sciences* 47 (2002): 964.

3. L. A. King, R. Wigmore, and J. M. Twibell, "The Morphology and Occurrence of Human Hair Sheath Cells," *Journal of the Forensic Science Society* 22 (1982): 267.

4. C. A. Linch et al., "Evaluation of the Human Hair Root for DNA Typing Subsequent to Microscopic Comparison," *Journal of Forensic Sciences* 43 (1998): 305.

5. S. Palenki and C. Fitzsimons, "Fiber Cross-Sections: Part I," *Microscope* 38 (1990): 187.

6. D. K. Laing et al., "The Standardisation of Thin-Layer Chromatographic Systems for Comparisons of Fibre Dyes," *Journal of the Forensic Science Society* 30 (1990): 299.

7. M. C. Grieve, "Another Look at the Classification of Acrylic Fibres, Using FTIR Microscopy," *Science & Justice* 35 (1995): 179.

8. M. W. Tungol et al., "Analysis of Single Polymer Fibers by Fourier Transform Infrared Microscopy: The Results of Case Studies," *Journal of Forensic Sciences* 36 (1992): 1027.

What Killed Napoleon?

Napoleon I, emperor of France, was sent into exile on the remote island of St. Helena by the British after his defeat at the Battle of Waterloo in 1815. St. Helena was hot, unsanitary, and rampant with disease. There, Napoleon was confined to a large reconstructed agricultural building known as Longwood House. Boredom and unhealthy living conditions gradually took their toll on Napoleon's mental and physical state. He began suffering from severe abdominal pains and experienced swelling of the ankles and general weakness of his limbs. From the fall of 1820, Napoleon's health began to deteriorate rapidly until death arrived on May 5, 1821. An autopsy concluded the cause of death to be stomach cancer.

It was inevitable that dying under British control, as Napoleon did, would bring with it numerous conspiratorial theories to account for his death. One of the more fascinating inquiries was conducted by a Swedish dentist, Sven Forshufvud, who systematically correlated the clinical symptoms of Napoleon's last days to those of arsenic poisoning. For Forshufvud, the key to unlocking the cause of Napoleon's death rested with Napoleon's hair. Forshufvud arranged to have Napoleon's hair measured for arsenic content by neutron activation analysis and found it consistent with arsenic poisoning over a lengthy period of time. Nevertheless, the cause of Napoleon's demise is still a matter for debate and speculation. Other Napoleon hairs have been examined and found to be low in arsenic content. Some question whether Napoleon even had clinical symptoms associated with arsenic poisoning. In truth, forensic science may never be able to answer the question—what killed Napoleon?

chapter 11

Trace Evidence II
Metals, Paint, and Soil

Key Terms

alpha ray

atomic mass

atomic number

beta ray

continuous spectrum

density-gradient tube

electron

electron orbital

emission spectrum

excited state

gamma ray

isotope

line spectrum

mineral

neutron

nucleus

proton

pyrolysis

radioactivity

Learning Objectives

After studying this chapter you should be able to:

- Describe the usefulness of trace elements for forensic comparison of various types of physical evidence

- Define and distinguish protons, neutrons, and electrons

- Define and distinguish atomic number and atomic mass number

- Explain the concept of an isotope

- Understand how elements can be made radioactive

- List the most useful examinations for performing a forensic comparison of paint

- Distinguish continuous and line emission spectra

- Understand the parts of a simple emission spectrograph

- Appreciate the phenomenon of how an atom absorbs and releases energy in the form of light

- Describe proper collection and preservation of forensic paint evidence

- List the important forensic properties of soil

- Describe proper collection of soil evidence

Considering that most materials originate from the earth's crust, it is not surprising that they are rarely obtained in pure form; instead, they include numerous elemental impurities that usually must be eliminated through industrial processing. However, it is usually not economically feasible to completely exclude all such minor impurities, especially if their presence has no effect on the appearance or performance of the final product. For this reason, many manufactured products, and even most natural materials, contain small quantities of elements present in concentrations of less than 1 percent, which are known as *trace elements*.

Forensic Analysis of Metals

For the criminalist, the presence of trace elements is particularly useful because they provide "invisible" markers that may establish the source of a material or at least provide additional points for comparison. For example, comparison of trace elements present in two metallic specimens may provide data on their source or origin. Table 11–1 illustrates how two types of brass alloys can readily be distinguished by their elemental composition.

Forensic investigators have examined the evidential value of trace elements present in metallic objects as well as paint, soil, glass, and fibers. One example is the examination of the bullet and bullet fragments recovered after the assassination of President John F. Kennedy.

Evidence in the Assassination of President Kennedy

Ever since President Kennedy was killed in 1963, questions have lingered about whether Lee Harvey Oswald was part of a conspiracy to assassinate the president, or a lone assassin. The Warren Commission, the official government body appointed to investigate the shooting, concluded that Oswald acted alone. This conclusion was criticized widely at the time it was reported, and has been a source of controversy since that day.

Reconstructing the Assassination   In arriving at its conclusions, the Warren Commission reconstructed the crime as follows: From a hidden position on the sixth floor of the Texas School Book Depository building, Oswald fired three shots from behind the president. The president was struck by two bullets, with one bullet totally missing the president's limousine. One

Table 11–1 Elemental Analysis of Brass Alloys

	High-Tensile Brass (percentage)	Manganese Brass Element (percentage)
Copper	57.0	58.6
Aluminum	2.8	1.7
Zinc	35.0	33.8
Manganese	2.13	1.06
Iron	1.32	0.90
Nickel	0.48	1.02
Tin	0.64	1.70
Lead	0.17	0.72
Silicon	0.08	Nil

Source: R. L. Williams, "An Evaluation of the SEM with X-Ray Microanalyzer Accessory for Forensic Work," in *Scanning Electron Microscopy/1971*, O. Johari and I. Corvin, eds. (Chicago: IIT Research Institute, 1971), p. 541.

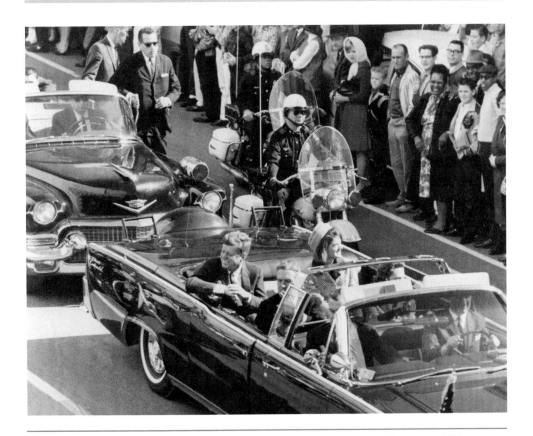

FIGURE 11–1   President John F. Kennedy, Governor John Connally of Texas, and Mrs. Jacqueline Kennedy ride through Dallas moments before the assassination. *Courtesy Corbis/Bettmann*

bullet hit the president in the back, exited his throat, and went on to strike Texas Governor John Connally, who was sitting in a jump seat in front of the president. The bullet hit Connally in his back, exited his chest, struck his right wrist, and temporarily lodged in his left thigh. This bullet was later found on the governor's stretcher at the hospital. A second bullet in the skull fatally wounded the president.

In a room at the Texas School Book Depository, a 6.5-millimeter Mannlicher-Carcano military rifle was found with Oswald's palm print on it. Also found were three spent 6.5-millimeter Western Cartridge Co./Mannlicher-Carcano (WCC/MC) cartridge cases. Oswald, an employee of the depository, had been seen there that morning and also a few minutes after the assassination, disappearing soon thereafter. He was apprehended a few miles from the depository nearly two hours after the shooting.

Questions and Criticisms Critics of the Warren Commission have long argued that evidence proves that Oswald did not act alone. Eyewitness accounts and acoustical data interpreted by some experts have been used to contend that a second shooter fired at the president from a region in front of the limousine (the so-called grassy knoll). Furthermore, critics argue that the Warren Commission's reconstruction of the crime assumed that only one bullet caused both the president's throat wound and Governor Connally's back wound. Critics contend that such damage would have deformed and mutilated a bullet. Instead, the recovered bullet showed some flattening, no deformity, and only about 1 percent weight loss.

In 1977 the U.S. House of Representatives Select Committee on Assassinations requested that the bullet taken from Connally's stretcher—along with bullet fragments recovered from the car and various wound areas—be examined for trace element levels. Because lead alloys used to manufacture bullets contain an assortment of trace elements, analysis of those trace elements provides a possible means for characterizing lead bullets. For example, antimony is often added to lead as a hardening agent; copper, bismuth, and silver are other trace elements commonly found in bullet lead.

Investigators compared the antimony and silver content of the bullet and bullet fragments recovered after the assassination. Previous studies had amply demonstrated that the levels of these two elements are particularly important for characterizing WCC/MC bullets. Bullet lead from this type of ammunition ranges in antimony concentration from 20 to 1,200 parts per million (ppm) and 5 to 15 ppm in silver content.

As can be seen in Table 11–2, the samples designated Q1 (the Connally stretcher bullet) and Q9 (bullet fragments from Connally's wrist) are indistinguishable from one another in antimony and silver content. The samples

Table 11–2	Antimony and Silver Concentrations in the Kennedy Assassination Bullets		
Sample	Silver (parts per million)[a]	Antimony (parts per million)	Sample Description
Q1	8.8 ± 0.5	833 ± 9	Connally stretcher bullet
Q9	9.8 ± 0.5	797 ± 7	Fragments from Connally's wrist
Q2	8.1 ± 0.6	602 ± 4	Large fragment from car
Q4, 5	7.9 ± 0.3	621 ± 4	Fragments from Kennedy's brain
Q14	8.2 ± 0.4	642 ± 6	Small fragments found in car

[a]One part per million equals 0.0001 percent.

Source: Reprinted with permission from V. P. Guinn, "JFK Assassination: Bullet Analyses," *Analytical Chemistry* 51 (1979): 484 A. Copyright 1979, American Chemical Society.

designated Q4 and Q5 (fragments from Kennedy's brain) are indistinguishable in antimony and silver content from samples Q2 and Q14 (fragments recovered from two different areas in the car). However, all four of those samples are different from Q1 and Q9.

Conclusions From studying these results we can derive the following conclusions:

1. There is evidence of only two bullets—one composed of 815 ppm antimony and 9.3 ppm silver, the other composed of 622 ppm antimony and 8.1 ppm silver.

2. Both bullets have a composition highly consistent with WCC/MC bullet lead, although other sources cannot be ruled out entirely.

3. The bullet found on the Connally stretcher also damaged Connally's wrist. The absence of bullet fragments from the back wounds of Kennedy and Connally prevented any effort at linking these wounds to the stretcher bullet.

None of these conclusions can verify absolutely the Warren Commission's reconstruction of the assassination, but the results are at least consistent with the commission's findings. The analyses on the Kennedy assassination bullets used a method known as *neutron activation analysis,* one of several forensic techniques we will examine in this chapter.

Atomic Structure

To understand the principle behind neutron activation analysis, one must first understand the fundamental structure of the atom. Each atom is composed of elementary particles that are collectively known as *subatomic particles.* The most important subatomic particles are the proton, electron, and neutron.

The properties of the proton, neutron, and electron are summarized in the following table:

Particle	Symbol	Relative Mass	Electrical Charge
Proton	P	1	+
Neutron	n	1	0
Electron	e	1/1837	−

As you can see, the masses of the proton and neutron are each about 1,837 times the mass of an electron. The proton has a positive electrical charge; the electron has a negative charge equal in magnitude to that of the proton; and the neutron is a neutral particle with neither a positive nor a negative charge.

A popular descriptive model of the atom, and the one that will be adopted for the purpose of this discussion, pictures an atom as consisting of electrons orbiting a central nucleus composed of protons and neutrons—an image that is analogous to our solar system, in which the planets revolve around the sun.[1] To maintain a zero net electrical charge, the number of protons in the nucleus must always equal the number of electrons in orbit around the nucleus.

With this knowledge, we can describe the atomic structure of the elements. For example, hydrogen has a nucleus consisting of one proton and no neutrons, and it has one orbiting electron. Helium has a nucleus comprising two protons and two neutrons, with two electrons in orbit around the nucleus (see Figure 11–2).

proton
A positively charged particle that is one of the basic structures in the nucleus of an atom.

electron
A negatively charged particle that is one of the fundamental structural units of the atom.

neutron
A particle with no electrical charge that is one of the basic structures in the nucleus of an atom.

nucleus
The core of an atom, consisting of protons and neutrons.

FIGURE 11–2   The atomic structures of hydrogen and helium.

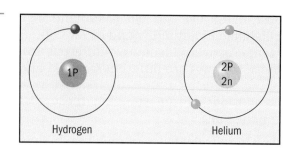

The behavior and properties that distinguish one element from another must be related to the differences in the atomic structure of each element. One such distinction is that each element possesses a different number of protons. This number is called the atomic number of the element. As we look back at the periodic table on p. 119, we see that the elements are numbered consecutively. Those numbers represent the atomic number or number of protons associated with each element. An element is therefore a collection of atoms that all have the same number of protons. Thus, each atom of hydrogen has one and only one proton, each atom of helium has 2 protons, each atom of silver has 47 protons, and each atom of lead has 82 protons in its nucleus.

Isotopes and Radioactivity

Although the atoms of a single element must have the same number of protons, nothing prevents them from having different numbers of neutrons. The total number of protons and neutrons in a nucleus is known as the atomic mass number. Atoms with the same number of protons but differing solely in the number of neutrons are called isotopes.

For example, hydrogen consists of three isotopes: ordinary hydrogen, which has one proton and no neutrons in its nucleus, and two other isotopes called deuterium and tritium. Deuterium (or heavy hydrogen) also has one proton, but contains one neutron as well. Tritium has one proton and two neutrons in its nucleus.

Therefore, all the isotopes of hydrogen have an atomic number of 1 but differ in their atomic mass numbers. Hydrogen has an atomic mass of 1, deuterium a mass of 2, and tritium a mass of 3. Ordinary hydrogen makes up 99.98 percent of all the hydrogen atoms found in nature. The atomic structures of these isotopes are shown in Figure 11–3.

Like hydrogen, most elements have two or more isotopes. Tin, for example, has ten isotopes. Many of these isotopes are quite stable, and the isotopes of any one element have indistinguishable properties. Others, however, are not as stable and decompose over time by a process known as *radioactive decay*. Radioactivity is the emission of high-energy

atomic number
The number of protons in the nucleus of an atom.

atomic mass
The sum of the number of protons and neutrons in the nucleus of an atom.

isotope
An atom differing from another atom of the same element in the number of neutrons it has in its nucleus.

radioactivity
The emission of high-energy subatomic particles that accompanies the spontaneous disintegration of unstable nuclei.

FIGURE 11–3   Isotopes of hydrogen.

subatomic particles that accompanies the spontaneous disintegration of unstable nuclei.

Radioactivity is composed of three types of radiation: alpha rays, beta rays, and gamma rays. Alpha rays are helium atoms stripped of their orbiting electrons; thus, they are positively charged particles. Each alpha ray particle has a mass approximately four times that of a hydrogen atom. Beta rays are electrons, and gamma rays are a form of electromagnetic radiation similar to X-rays (discussed in Chapter 4), but of a higher frequency and energy. Fortunately, most naturally occurring isotopes are not radioactive, and those that are—radium, uranium, and thorium—are found in such small quantities in the earth's crust that their radioactivity presents no hazard to human survival.

When an atom is bombarded with neutrons, some neutrons are captured to form new isotopes. This is what happens in a nuclear reactor. A nuclear reactor is simply a source of neutrons that bombard the atoms of a specimen, thereby creating radioactive isotopes. The nucleus of an atom that has captured one or more neutrons is said to be activated, and it often begins to decompose immediately, emitting radioactivity.

Neutron Activation Analysis

Forensic chemists can characterize the trace elements in a specimen by bombarding it with neutrons and measuring the energy of the gamma rays emitted by the activated isotopes. The gamma rays of each element are associated with characteristic energy values, and thus exhibit unique levels of energy. This technique, known as neutron activation analysis, is depicted in Figure 11–4. Once an element has been identified, its concentration can be measured by the intensity of its gamma-ray radiation; the intensity of the radiation is directly proportional to the concentration of the element in a specimen.

The major advantage of neutron activation analysis is that it provides a nondestructive method for identifying and quantitating trace elements. A median detection sensitivity of one-billionth of a gram (1 nanogram) makes

alpha ray
Radiation composed of helium atoms minus their orbiting electrons.

beta ray
Radiation composed of electrons.

gamma ray
A high-energy form of electromagnetic radiation.

Neutrons bombard specimen

Gamma Rays

Neutron Atom Neutron Atom

Gamma Rays

Intensity

Energy

Intensity

Energy

Atom Detector measures the energies and intensities of the gamma rays Multichannel analyzer

Intensity

Energy

Each element is associated with a characteristic energy value. Intensity indicates the element concentration in the specimen

FIGURE 11–4 The neutron activation process requires the capture of a neutron by the nucleus of an atom. The new atom is now radioactive and emits gamma rays. A detector permits identification of the radioactive atoms present by measuring the energies and intensities of the gamma rays emitted.

Table 11–3 Concentration of Trace Elements in Copper Wire				
	Selenium	Gold	Antimony	Silver
Control Wire				
A_1	2.4	0.047	0.16	12.7
A_2	3.5	0.064	0.27	17.2
A_3	2.6	0.050	0.20	13.3
A_4	1.9	0.034	0.21	12.6
Suspect Wire				
B	2.3	0.042	0.15	13.0

Note: Average concentration measured in parts per million.

Source: R. K. H. Chan, "Identification of Single-Stranded Copper Wires by Nondestructive Neutron Activation Analysis." *Journal of Forensic Sciences* 17 (1972): 93. Reprinted by permission of the American Society for Testing and Materials, copyright 1972.

neutron activation analysis one of the most sensitive methods available for quantitative detection of many elements. Further, neutron activation can simultaneously analyze twenty to thirty elements. A major drawback to the technique is its expense. Only a handful of crime laboratories have access to a nuclear reactor; in addition, sophisticated analyzers are needed to detect and discriminate gamma-ray emissions.

Neutron activation has been used to characterize trace elements in metals, drugs, paint, soil, gunpowder residues, and hair. A typical illustration of its application occurred during the investigation of a theft of copper telegraphic wires in Canada. Four lengths of copper wire (A_1, A_2, A_3, A_4) found at the scene of the theft were compared by neutron activation with a length of copper wire (B) seized at a scrap yard and suspected of being stolen. All were bare, single-strand wire with the same general physical appearance and a diameter of 0.28 centimeter.

Prior experiments had revealed that significant variations could be expected in the concentration levels of the trace elements selenium, gold, antimony, and silver for wires originating from different sources. Analysts compared these elements present in the wire involved in the theft. After exposing the wires to neutrons in a nuclear reactor, neutron activation analysis revealed a match between A_1 and B that was well within experimental error (see Table 11–3). The findings suggested a common origin of the control and suspect wires.

Key Points

- Trace elements are small quantities of elements present in concentrations of less than 1 percent. They provide "invisible" markers that may establish the source of a material or provide additional points for comparison.

- The three most important subatomic particles are the proton, neutron, and electron. The proton has a positive electrical charge, the neutron has no electrical charge, and the electron has a negative electrical charge.

- Atomic number indicates the number of protons in the nucleus of an atom. Atomic mass refers to the total number of protons and neutrons in a nucleus.

- An isotope is an atom differing from other atoms of the same element in the number of neutrons in its nucleus.

- Radioactivity is the emission of high-energy subatomic particles that accompanies the spontaneous disintegration of the nuclei of unstable isotopes. The three types of radiation are alpha rays, beta rays, and gamma rays.

- In neutron activation analysis, a sample is bombarded with neutrons and the energy of the gamma rays emitted by the activated isotopes is measured. The gamma rays of each element are associated with characteristic energy values that helps identify the specific element that produces them.

Forensic Examination of Paint

Our environment contains millions of objects whose surfaces are painted. Thus paint, in one form or another, is one of the most prevalent types of physical evidence received by the crime laboratory.

Paint as physical evidence is perhaps most frequently encountered in hit-and-run and burglary cases. For example, a chip of dried paint or a paint smear may be transferred to the clothing of a hit-and-run victim on impact with an automobile, or paint smears could be transferred onto a tool during a burglary. Obviously, in many situations a transfer of paint from one surface to another could impart an object with an identifiable forensic characteristic.

In most circumstances, the criminalist must compare two or more paints to establish their common origin. For example, such a comparison may associate an individual or a vehicle with the crime site. However, the criminalist need not be confined to comparisons alone. Crime laboratories often help identify the color, make, and model of an automobile by examining small quantities of paint recovered at an accident scene. Such requests, normally made in hit-and-run cases, can lead to the apprehension of the responsible vehicle.

Composition of Paint

Paint is composed of a binder and pigments, as well as other additives, all dissolved or dispersed in a suitable solvent. Pigments impart color and hiding (or opacity) to paint and are usually mixtures of different inorganic and organic compounds added to the paint by the manufacturer to produce specific colors and properties. The binder is a polymeric substance that provides the support medium for the pigments and additives. After paint has been applied to a surface, the solvent evaporates, leaving behind a hard polymeric binder and any pigments that are suspended in it.

One of the most common types of paint examined in the crime laboratory is finishes from automobiles. Manufacturers apply a variety of coatings to the body of an automobile; this adds significant diversity to automobile paint and contributes to the forensic significance of automobile paint comparisons. The automotive finishing system for steel usually consists of at least four organic coatings:

Electrocoat Primer   The first layer applied to the steel body of a car is the electrocoat primer. The primer, consisting of epoxy-based resins, is electroplated onto the steel body of the automobile to provide corrosion resistance. The resulting coating is uniform in appearance and thickness. The color of these primers ranges from black to gray.

Primer Surfacer Originally responsible for corrosion control, the surfacer usually follows the electrocoat layer and is applied before the basecoat. Primer surfacers are epoxy-modified polyesters or urethanes. The function of this layer is to completely smooth out and hide any seams or imperfections, because the basecoat will be applied on this surface. This layer is highly pigmented. Color pigments are used to minimize color contrast between primer and topcoats. For example, a light gray primer may be used under pastel shades of a colored topcoat; a red oxide may be used under a dark-colored topcoat.

Basecoat The next layer of paint on a car is the basecoat or colorcoat. This layer provides the color and aesthetics of the finish and represents the "eye appeal" of the finished automobile. The integrity of this layer depends on its ability to resist weather, UV radiation, and acid rain. Most commonly, an acrylic-based polymer comprises the binder system of basecoats. Interestingly, the choice of automotive pigments is dictated by toxic and environmental concerns. Thus, the use of lead, chrome, and other heavy-metal pigments has been abandoned in favor of organic-based pigments. There is also a growing trend toward pearl luster or mica pigments. Mica pigments are coated with layers of metal oxide to generate interference colors. Also, the addition of aluminum flakes to automotive paint imparts a metallic look to the paint's finish.

Clearcoat An unpigmented clearcoat is applied to improve gloss, durability, and appearance. Most clearcoats are acrylic based, but polyurethane clearcoats are increasing in popularity. These topcoats provide outstanding etch resistance and appearance.

Microscopic Examination of Paint

The microscope has traditionally been and remains the most important instrument for locating and comparing paint specimens. Considering the thousands of paint colors and shades, it is quite understandable why color, more than any other property, imparts paint with its most distinctive forensic characteristics. Questioned and known specimens are best compared side by side under a stereoscopic microscope for color, surface texture, and color layer sequence (see Figure 11–5).

The importance of layer structure for evaluating the evidential significance of paint evidence cannot be overemphasized. When paint specimens possess colored layers that match in number and sequence of colors, the examiner can begin to relate the paints to a common origin. How many layers must be matched before the criminalist can conclude that the paints come from the same source? There is no one accepted criterion. Much depends on the uniqueness of each layer's color and texture, as well as the frequency with which the particular combination of colors under investigation is observed. Because no books or journals have compiled this type of information, the criminalist is left to his or her own experience and knowledge when making this decision.

Unfortunately, most paint specimens do not have a layer structure of sufficient complexity to allow them to be individualized to a single source, nor is it common to have paint chips that can be physically fitted together to prove common origin, as shown in Figure 11–6. However, the diverse chemical composition of modern paints provides additional points of comparison

FIGURE 11–5 **A stereoscopic microscope comparison of two automotive paints. The questioned paint on the left has a layer structure consistent with the contol paint on the right.** *Courtesy Leica Microsystems, Inc., Buffalo, N.Y., www.leica-microsystems.com*

FIGURE 11–6 **Paint chip 1 was recovered from the scene of a hit-and-run. Paint chip 2 was obtained from the suspect vehicle.** *Courtesy New Jersey State Police*

between specimens. Specifically, a thorough comparison of paint must include a chemical analysis of the paint's pigments, its binder composition, or both.

Analytical Techniques Used in Paint Comparison

The wide variation in binder formulations in automobile finishes provides significant information. More important, paint manufacturers make automobile finishes in hundreds of varieties; this knowledge is most helpful to the criminalist who is trying to associate a paint chip with one car as distinguished from the thousands of similar models that have been produced in any one year. For instance, there are more than a hundred automobile production plants in the United States and Canada. Each can use one paint supplier for a particular color or vary suppliers during a model year. Although a paint supplier must maintain strict quality control over a paint's color, the batch formulation of any paint binder can vary, depending on the availability and cost of basic ingredients.

Characterization of Paint Binders   An important extension of the application of gas chromatography to forensic science is the technique of pyrolysis *gas chromatography*. Many solid materials commonly encountered as physical evidence—for example, paint chips, fibers, and plastics—cannot be readily dissolved in a solvent for injection into the gas chromatograph. Thus, under normal conditions these substances cannot be subjected to gas chromatographic analysis. However, materials such as these can be heated, or *pyrolyzed*, to high temperatures (500–1000°C) so that they will decompose into numerous gaseous products. Pyrolyzers permit these gaseous products to enter the carrier gas stream, where they flow into and through the GC column. The pyrolyzed material can then be characterized by the pattern produced by its chromatogram, or *pyrogram*.

Pyrolysis gas chromatography is particularly invaluable for distinguishing most paint formulations. In this process, paint chips as small as 20 micrograms are decomposed by heat into numerous gaseous products and are sent through a gas chromatograph.

As shown in Figure 11–7, the polymer chain is decomposed by a heated filament, and the resultant products are swept into and through a gas chromatograph column. The separated decomposition products of the polymer emerge and are recorded. The pattern of this chromatogram or "pyrogram" distinguishes one polymer from another. The result is a pyrogram that is

pyrolysis
The decomposition of organic matter by heat.

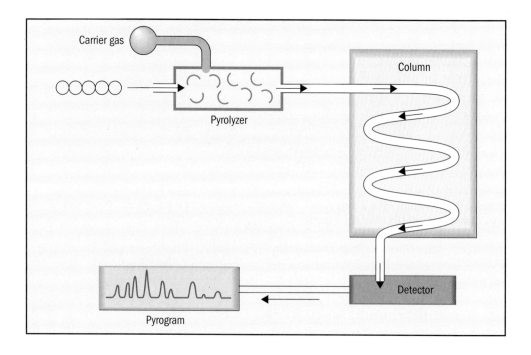

FIGURE 11–7   Schematic diagram of pyrolysis gas chromatography.

sufficiently detailed to reflect the chemical makeup of the binder. Figure 11–8 illustrates how the patterns produced by paint pyrograms can differentiate acrylic enamel paints removed from two different automobiles.

Infrared spectrophotometry is still another analytical technique that provides information about the binder composition of paint.[2] Binders selectively absorb infrared radiation to yield a spectrum that is highly characteristic of a paint specimen.

Characterization of Paint Pigments The elements that constitute the inorganic pigments of paints can be identified by a variety of techniques:

emission spectroscopy, neutron activation analysis, and X-ray spectroscopy (pp. 252–253). The emission spectrograph for example, can simultaneously detect fifteen to twenty elements in most automobile paints. Some of these elements are relatively common to all paints and have little forensic value; others are less frequently encountered and provide excellent points of comparison between paint specimens.

We saw in Chapter 5 that organic compounds can be characterized by selective absorption of ultraviolet, visible, or infrared radiation. Equally significant to the forensic chemist is the knowledge that elements also selectively emit and absorb light. These observations form the basis of emission spectroscopy.

When sunlight or the light from an incandescent bulb is passed through a prism, a range of rainbow colors is produced. The resulting display of colors is called an emission spectrum. This type of emission spectrum is called a continuous spectrum because all the colors merge or blend into one another to form a continuous band.

Not all light sources, however, produce a continuous spectrum. For example, if the light from a sodium lamp, a mercury arc lamp, or a neon light is passed through a prism, the resultant spectrum consists not of a continuous band, but of several individual colored lines separated by dark spaces. Here, each line represents a definite wavelength or frequency of light that is separate and distinct from all others in the spectrum. This type of spectrum is called a line spectrum. Figure 11–9 shows the line spectra of three elements. If a solid or liquid is vaporized and "excited" by exposure to high temperature, each element that is present emits light composed of select frequencies that are characteristic of the element. This spectrum is in essence a "fingerprint" of an element and offers a practical method of identification for liquid media such as paint. Sodium vapor, for example, always shows the same line spectrum, which differs from the spectrum of all other elements.

emission spectrum
Light emitted from a source and separated into its component colors or frequencies.

continuous spectrum
A type of emission spectrum showing a continuous band of colors all blending into one another.

line spectrum
A type of emission spectrum showing a series of lines separated by black areas. Each line represents a definite wavelength or frequency.

FIGURE 11–9 Some characteristic emission spectra.

Closer Analysis

The Carbon Arc Emission Spectrograph

An *emission spectrograph* is an instrument used to obtain and record the line spectra of elements. This instrument requires a means for vaporizing and exciting the atoms of elements so that they emit light, a means for separating this light into its component frequencies, and a means of recording the resultant spectrum. A simple emission spectrograph is depicted in Figure 1.

The specimen under investigation is inserted between two carbon electrodes through which a direct current arc is passed. The arc produces enough heat to vaporize and excite the specimen's atoms. A lens collects the light emitted by the excited atoms and focuses it onto a prism that disperses it into component frequencies.

The separated frequencies of light are then directed toward a photographic plate, where they are recorded as line images. Normally, a specimen consists of numerous elements; hence, the typical emission spectrum contains many lines.

Each element in the spectrum can be identified when it is compared to a standard chart that shows the position of the principal spectral lines of all the elements. However, forensic analysis usually requires a rapid comparison of the elemental composition of two or more specimens. This is easily accomplished by comparing the emission spectra line for line, as illustrated in Figure 2, in which the emission spectra of two paint chips are shown to be comparable.

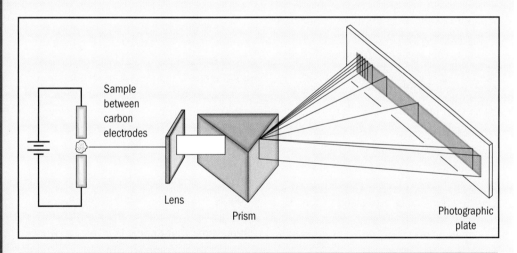

FIGURE 1   Parts of a simple emission spectrograph.

FIGURE 2   A comparison of paint chips 1 and 2 by emission spectrographic analysis. A line-for-line comparison shows that the paints have the same elemental composition.

Closer Analysis

The Origin of Emission Spectra

electron orbital
The path of electrons as they move around the nuclei of atoms; each orbital is associated with a particular electronic energy level.

excited state
The state in which an atom absorbs energy and an electron moves from a lower to a higher energy level.

To explain the origin of atomic spectra, we must focus on the *electron orbitals* of the atom. As electrons move around the nucleus, they are confined to a path from which they cannot stray. This orbital path is associated with a definite amount of energy and is therefore called an *energy level*. Each element has its own set of characteristic energy levels at varying distances from the nucleus. Some levels are occupied by electrons; others are empty.

An atom is in its most stable state when all of its electrons are positioned in their lowest possible energy orbitals. When an atom absorbs energy, such as heat or light, its electrons are pushed into higher-energy orbitals. In this condition, the atom is in an *excited state*. However, because energy levels have fixed values, only a definite amount of energy can be absorbed in moving an electron from one level to another. This is an important observation; atoms absorb only a definite value of energy, and all other energy values are excluded, as shown in the figure.

A specific frequency of light is required to cause this transition, and its energy must correspond to the exact energy difference between the two orbitals involved. This energy difference is expressed by the relationship $E = hf$, where E represents the energy difference between the two orbitals, f is the frequency of absorbed light, and h is a universal constant called Planck's constant. Any energy value that is more or less than

this difference will not produce the transition. Hence, an element is selective in the frequency of light it will absorb, and this selectivity is determined by the electron energy levels each element possesses.

In the same manner, if atoms are exposed to intense heat, enough energy will be generated to push electrons into unoccupied higher-energy orbitals. Normally the electron does not remain in this excited state for long, and it quickly falls back to its original energy level. As the electron falls back, it releases energy. An emission spectrum shows that this energy loss comes about in the form of light emission (see figure). The frequency of light emitted is again determined by the relationship $E = hf$, where E is the energy difference between the upper and lower energy levels and f is the frequency of emitted light. Because each element has its own characteristic set of energy levels, each emits a unique set of frequency values. The emission spectrum thus provides a "picture" of the energy levels that surround the nucleus of each element.

Thus, we see that as far as atoms are concerned, energy is a two-way street. Energy can be put into the atom at the same time that energy is given off; what goes in must come out. The chemist can study the atom using either approach.

**(a) The absorption of light by an atom, causing an electron to jump into a higher orbital.
(b) The emission of light by an atom, caused by an electron falling back to a lower orbital.**

(a) (b)

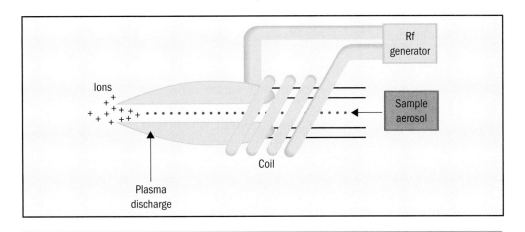

FIGURE 11–10   The creation of charged particles in the torch of an ICP discharge.

Inductively Coupled Plasma Emission Spectrometry (ICP)   Recently, inductively coupled plasma (ICP) emission spectrometry has supplanted carbon arc emission spectroscopy for most applications. Like emission spectroscopy, ICP identifies and measures elements through light energy emitted by excited atoms. However, instead of using an electrical arc, the atoms are excited by placing the sample in a hot plasma torch. The torch is designed as three concentric quartz tubes through which argon gas flows (see Figure 11–10). A radio-frequency (RF) coil that carries a current is wrapped around the tubes. The RF current creates an intense magnetic field.

The process begins when a high-voltage spark is applied to the argon gas flowing through the torch. This strips some electrons from their argon atoms. These electrons are then caught and accelerated in the magnetic field such that they collide with other argon atoms, stripping off still more electrons. The collision of electrons and argon atoms continues in a chain reaction, breaking down the gas into argon atoms, argon ions, and electrons, forming an *inductively coupled plasma discharge*. The discharge is sustained by RF energy that is continuously transferred to it from the coil.

The plasma discharge acts like a very intense continuous flame generating temperatures in the range of 7,000–10,000°C. The sample, in aerosol form, is then introduced into the hot plasma, where it collides with the energetic argon electrons and generates charged particles (ions). The ions emit light of characteristic wavelengths that correspond to the identity of the elements in the sample.

The Significance of Paint Evidence

Once a paint comparison is completed, the task of assessing the significance of the finding begins. How certain can one be that two similar paints came from the same surface? For instance, a casual observer sees countless identically colored automobiles on our roads and streets. If this is the case, what value is a comparison of a paint chip from a hit-and-run scene to paint removed from a suspect car?

From previous discussions it should be apparent that far more is involved in paint comparison than matching surface paint colors. Paint layers beneath a surface layer offer valuable points of comparison. Furthermore, forensic analysts can detect subtle differences in paint binder

Closer Analysis

ICP Analysis of Bullets

Mutilated bullets often are not suitable for traditional microscopic comparisons against an exemplar test-fired bullet. In such situations, ICP has been used to obtain an elemental profile of the questioned bullet fragment for comparison against an unfired bullet generally found in the possession of the suspect.

For a number of years forensic scientists have been aware of significant compositional differences among lead sources for the manufacture of lead-based bullets. Knowledge of these differences can be valuable when comparing bullets that are too mutilated to analyze with a microscope. Compositional differences in trace elements are typically reflected in the copper, arsenic, silver, antimony, bismuth, cadmium, and tin profiles of lead bullets.

When two or more bullets have comparable elemental compositions, evidence of their similarity may be offered in a court of law. In this respect, the comparison of lead bullets faces the same quandry as most common types of class physical evidence. The forensic analyst must convince a jury that the test results are meaningful to a criminal inquiry in the absence of any supporting statistical or probability data. Furthermore, creating meaningful databases to define the statistical significance of bullets compared by elemental profiles is currently an unrealistic undertaking.

Nevertheless, the significant diversity of bullet lead compositions in our population, like other class evidence such as fibers, hairs, paint, plastics, and glass, makes their chance occurrence at a crime scene and subsequent link to a defendant highly unlikely. However, care must be taken to avoid giving the impression that elemental profiles constitute a definitive match. Given the millions of bullets produced each year, one cannot conclusively rule out the possibility of a coincidental match with a non-case-related bullet.

formulations, as well as major or minor differences in the elemental composition of paint. Obviously, these properties cannot be discerned by the naked eye.

The significance of a paint comparison was convincingly demonstrated from data gathered at the Centre of Forensic Science, Toronto, Canada.[3] Paint chips randomly taken from 260 vehicles located in a local wreck yard were compared by color, layer structure, and, when required, by infrared spectroscopy. All were distinguishable except for one pair. In statistical terms, these results signify that if a crime-scene paint sample and a paint standard/reference sample removed from a suspect car compare by the previously discussed tests, the odds against the crime-scene paint originating from another randomly chosen vehicle are approximately 33,000 to one. Obviously, this type of evidence is bound to forge a strong link between the suspect car and the crime scene.

Crime laboratories are often asked to identify the make and model of a car from a very small amount of paint left behind at a crime scene. Such information is frequently of use in a search for an unknown car involved in a hit-and-run incident. Often the questioned paint can be identified when its color is compared to color chips representing the various makes and models of manufactured cars. However, in many cases it is not possible to state the exact make or model of the car in question, because any one paint color can be found on more than one car model. For instance, General Motors may have used the same paint color for several production years on cars in its Cadillac, Buick, Pontiac, and Chevrolet lines.

Color charts for automobile finishes are available from various paint manufacturers and refinishers (see Figure 11–11). Since 1975, the Royal Canadian Mounted Police Forensic Laboratories have been systematically gathering color and chemical information on automotive paints. This computerized database, known as PDQ (Paint Data Query), allows an analyst to obtain information on paints related to automobile make, model, and year. The database contains such parameters as automotive paint layer colors, primer colors, and binder composition (see Figure 11–12). A number of U.S. laboratories have access to PDQ.[4] Also, some crime laboratories maintain an in-house collection of automotive paints associated with various makes and models, as shown in Figure 11–13.

Collection and Preservation of Paint Evidence

As has already been noted, paint chips are most likely to be found on or near people or objects involved in hit-and-run incidents. The recovery of loose paint chips from a garment or from the road surface must be done with the utmost care to keep the paint chip intact. Paint chips may be

FIGURE 11–11 Automotive color chart of various car models. *Courtesy Damian Dovanganes, AP Wide World Photos*

FIGURE 11–12 **(a) Home screen for PDQ database. (b) Partial list of autopaints contained in the PDQ database.** *Courtesy Royal Canadian Mounted Police*

picked up with a tweezers or scooped up with a piece of paper. Paper druggist folds and glass or plastic vials make excellent containers for paint. If the paint is smeared on or embedded in garments or objects, the investigator should not attempt to remove it; instead, it is best to package the whole item carefully and send it to the laboratory for examination.

When a transfer of paint occurs in hit-and-run situations (such as to the clothing of a pedestrian victim), uncontaminated standard/reference

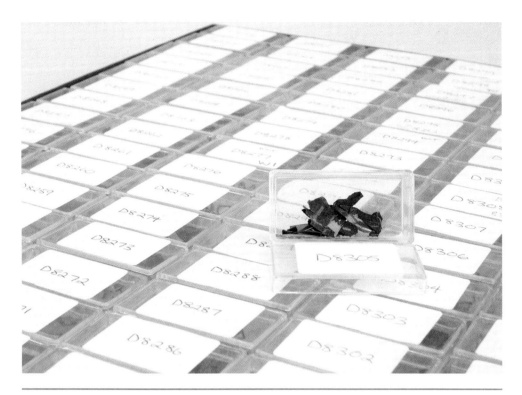

FIGURE 11–13   A crime laboratory's automotive paint library. Paints were collected at an automobile impound yard and then cataloged for rapid retrieval and examination. *Courtesy Gavin Edmonstone, Centre for Forensic Sciences, Toronto, Canada*

paint must always be collected from an undamaged area of the vehicle for comparison in the laboratory. The collected paint must be close to the area of the car that is suspected of being in contact with the victim. This is necessary because other portions of the car may have faded or been repainted.

Standard/reference samples are always removed so as to include all the paint layers down to the bare metal. This is best accomplished by removing a painted section with a clean scalpel or knife blade. Samples 1/4 inch square are sufficient for laboratory examination. Each paint sample should be separately packaged and marked with the exact location of its recovery.

When a cross-transfer of paint occurs between two vehicles, again all of the layers, including the foreign as well as the underlying original paints, must be removed from each vehicle. A standard/reference sample from an adjacent undamaged area of each vehicle must also be taken in such cases. Carefully wipe the blade of any knife or scraping tool used before collecting each sample, to avoid cross-contamination of paints.

Case Study

The Predator

September in Arizona is hot and dry, much like the rest of the year—but September 1984 was a little different. Unusually heavy rains fell for two days, which must have seemed fitting for the friends and family of 8-year-old Vicki Lynn Hoskinson. Vicki went missing on September 17 of that year, and her disappearance was investigated as a kidnapping. A school-teacher who knew Vicki remembered a suspicious vehicle loitering near the school that day, and he happened to jot down the license plate number. This

(continued)

Case Study

The Predator (*continued*)

crucial tip led police to 28-year-old Frank Atwood, recently paroled from a California prison. Police soon learned that Atwood had been convicted for committing sex offenses and for kidnapping a boy. This galvanized the investigators, who realized Vicki could be at the mercy of a dangerous and perverse man.

The only evidence the police had to work with was Vicki's bike, which was found abandoned in the middle of the street a few blocks from her home. Police found scrapes from her bike pedal on the underside of the gravel pan on Atwood's car, as well as pink paint apparently transferred from Vicki's bike to Atwood's front bumper. The police believed that Atwood deliberately struck Vicki while she was riding her bicycle, knocking her to the ground.

The pink paint on Atwood's bumper was first looked at microscopically and then examined by pyrolysis gas chromatography, which entails heating the paint sample to extremely high temperature to vaporize and fragment the components of the paint. The pyrolyzed sample, in the form of a gas, is then pushed through a gas chromatographic column. By the time the paint components have reached the end of the column, they have separated and each chemical constituent is recorded. This technique provides investigators with a "fingerprint" pattern of the paint sample, enabling them to compare this paint to any other paint evidence. In this case, the pink paint on Atwood's bumper matched the paint from Vicki's bicycle.

Further evidence proving Atwood's involvement in the crime came when a gouge on the surface of Vicki's bicycle was checked for its elemental composition with the aid of a scanning electron microscope (SEM) in combination with an X-ray analyzer. Traces of nickel were found on the gouge's surface. The bumper of Atwood's car was coated with a thin film of nickel, providing solid evidence of the cross-transfer of paint and metal between the bumper of Frank Atwood's car and Vicki Lynn's bicycle.

Vicki's skeletal remains were discovered in the desert, several miles away from her home, in the spring of 1985. Positive identification was made using dental records, but investigators wanted to see if the remains could help them determine how long she had been dead. Atwood was jailed on an unrelated charge three days after Vicki disappeared, so the approximate date of death was very important to proving his guilt.

Investigators found adipocere, a white, fatty residue produced during decomposition, inside Vicki's skull. This provided evidence that moisture was present around Vicki's body after her death, which does not make sense considering she was found in the Arizona desert! A check of the weather revealed that there had been an unusual amount of rainfall at only one time since Vicki was last seen alive: a mere forty-eight hours after her disappearance. This put Vicki's death squarely within Frank Atwood's three-day window of opportunity between her disappearance and his arrest. Frank Atwood was sentenced to death in 1987 for the murder of Vicki Lynn Hoskinson. He remains on death row awaiting execution.

Key Points

- Paint spread onto a surface dries into a hard film that is best described as consisting of pigments and additives suspended in the binder.

- Questioned and known paint specimens are best compared side by side under a stereoscopic microscope for color, surface texture, and color layer sequence.

- Pyrolysis gas chromatography and infrared spectrophotometry are used to distinguish most paint binder formulations.

- Emission spectroscopy and inductively coupled plasma are techniques available for determining the elemental composition of paint pigments.

- PDQ (Paint Data Query) is a computerized database that allows an analyst to obtain information on paints related to automobile make, model, and year.

Forensic Analysis of Soil

There are many definitions for the term *soil;* however, for forensic purposes, soil may be thought of as any disintegrated surface material, natural or and artificial, that lies on or near the earth's surface. Therefore, forensic examination of soil not only is concerned with analysis of naturally occurring rocks, minerals, vegetation, and animal matter; it also encompasses detection of such manufactured objects as glass, paint chips, asphalt, brick fragments, and cinders, whose presence may impart soil with characteristics that make it unique to a particular location. When this material is collected accidentally or deliberately in a manner that associates it with a crime under investigation, it becomes valuable physical evidence.[5]

The Significance of Soil Evidence

The value of soil as evidence rests with its prevalence at crime scenes and its transferability between the scene and the criminal. Thus, soil or dried mud found adhering to a suspect's clothing or shoes or to an automobile, when compared to soil samples collected at the crime site, may link a suspect or object to the crime scene. As with most types of physical evidence, forensic soil analysis is comparative in nature; soil found in the possession of the suspect must be carefully collected to be compared to soil samplings from the crime scene and its vicinity.

However, one should not rule out the value of soil even if the site of the crime has not been ascertained. For instance, small amounts of soil may be found on a person or object far from the actual site of a crime. A geologist who knows the local geology may be able to use geological maps to direct police to the general vicinity where the soil was originally picked up and the crime committed.

Forensic Examination of Soil

Most soils can be differentiated by their gross appearance. A side-by-side visual comparison of the color and texture of soil specimens is easy to perform and provides a sensitive property for distinguishing soils that originate from different locations. Soil is darker when it is wet; therefore, color comparisons must always be made when all the samples are dried under identical laboratory conditions. It is estimated that there are nearly 1,100 distinguishable soil colors; hence, color offers a logical first step in a forensic soil comparison.

Microscopic Examination of Soil   Low-power microscopic examination of soil reveals the presence of plant and animal materials as well as of artificial debris. Further high-power microscopic examination helps characterize minerals and rocks in earth materials. Although this approach to forensic soil identification requires the expertise of an investigator trained in geology, it can provide the most varied and significant points of comparison between soil samples. Only by carefully examining and comparing the minerals and rocks naturally present in soil can one take advantage of the large number of variations between soils and thus add to the evidential value of a positive comparison.[6]

A mineral is a naturally occurring crystal, and like any other crystal, its physical properties—for example, color, geometric shape, density, and refractive index or birefringence—are useful for identification. More than 2,200 minerals exist; however, most are so rare that forensic geologists usually encounter only about twenty of the more common ones. Rocks are composed of a combination of minerals and therefore exist in thousands of varieties on the earth's surface. They are usually identified by characterizing their mineral content and grain size (see Figure 11–14).

Considering the vast variety of minerals and rocks and the possible presence of artificial debris in soil, the forensic geologist is presented with many points of comparison between two or more specimens. The number of comparative points and their frequency of occurrence must be considered before concluding similarity between specimens and judging the probability of common origin.

Rocks and minerals not only are present in earth materials but are also used to manufacture a wide variety of industrial and commercial products. For example, the tools and garments of an individual suspected of breaking into a safe often contain traces of safe insulation. Safe insulation may be made from a wide combination of mineral mixtures that provide significant points of identification. Similarly, building materials such as brick, plaster, and concrete blocks are combinations of minerals and rocks that can easily be recognized and compared microscopically to similar minerals found on the breaking-and-entering suspect.

mineral
A naturally occurring crystalline solid.

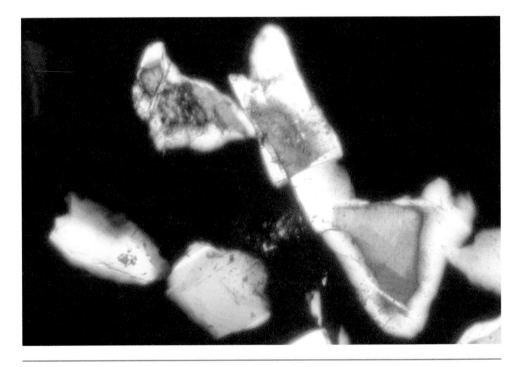

FIGURE 11–14   A mineral viewed under a microscope. *Courtesy Chris Palenik, Ph. D., Microtrace, Elgin, IL., www.microtracescientific.com*

Density-Gradient Tube   Some forensic laboratories utilize the density-gradient tube technique to compare soil specimens. Typically, glass tubes 6–10 millimeters in diameter and 25–40 centimeters long are filled with layers of two liquids mixed in varying proportions so that each layer has a different density value. For example, tetrabromoethane (density 2.96 g/mL) and ethanol (density 0.789 g/mL) may be mixed so that each successive layer has a lower density than the preceding one, from the bottom to the top of the tube. The simplest gradient tube may have from six to ten layers, in which the bottom layer is pure tetrabromoethane and the top layer is pure ethanol, with corresponding variations of concentration in the layers between these two extremes.

When soil is added to the density-gradient tube, its particles sink to the portion of the tube that has a density of equal value; the particles remain suspended in the liquid at this point. In this way, a density distribution pattern of soil particles can be obtained and compared to other specimens treated in a similar manner (see Figure 11–15).

Only a few crime laboratories use this procedure to compare soil evidence. There is evidence that the test is far from definitive, because many soils collected from different locations yield similar density distribution patterns.[7] At best, the density-gradient test is useful for comparing soils when it is used in combination with other tests.

> **density-gradient tube**
> A glass tube filled from bottom to top with liquids of successively lighter densities; used to determine the density distribution of soil.

Variations in Soil

The ultimate forensic value of soil evidence depends on its variation at the crime scene. If, for example, soil is indistinguishable for miles surrounding the location of a crime, it will have limited value in associating soil found on the suspect with that particular site. Significant conclusions relating a suspect to a particular location through a soil comparison may be made when variations in soil composition occur every 10–100 yards from the crime site. However, even when such variations do exist, the forensic geologist usually cannot individualize soil to any one location unless an unusual combination of rare minerals, rocks, or artificial debris can be located.

FIGURE 11–15   A soil comparison by density gradient tubes.
Courtesy Philadelphia Police Department Laboratory

No statistically valid forensic studies have examined the variability of soil evidence. A study conducted in southern Ontario, Canada, seems to indicate that soil in that part of Canada shows extensive diversity. It estimated a probability of less than 1 in 50 of finding two soils that are indistinguishable in both color and mineral properties but originate in two different locations separated by a distance of 1,000 feet. Based on these preliminary results, similar diversity may be expected in the northern United States, Canada, northern Europe, and eastern Europe. However, such probability values can only generally indicate the variation of soil within these geographical areas. Each crime scene must be evaluated separately to establish its own soil variation probabilities.

Collection and Preservation of Soil Evidence

When gathering soil specimens, the evidence collector must give primary consideration to establishing the variation of soil at the crime-scene area. For this reason, standard/reference soils should be collected at various intervals within a 100-yard radius of the crime scene, as well as at the site of the crime, for comparison to the questioned soil. Soil specimens also should be collected at all possible alibi locations that the suspect may claim.

All specimens gathered should be representative of the soil that was removed by the suspect. In most cases, only the top layer of soil is picked up during the commission of a crime. Thus, standard/reference specimens must be removed from the surface without digging too deeply into the unrepresentative subsurface layers. Approximately a tablespoon or two of soil is all the laboratory needs for a thorough comparative analysis. All specimens collected should be packaged in individual containers, such as plastic vials. Each vial should be marked to indicate the location at which the sampling was made.

Soil found on a suspect must be carefully preserved for analysis. If it is found adhering to an object, as in the case of soil on a shoe, the investigator must not remove it. Instead, each object should be individually wrapped in paper, with the soil intact, and transmitted to the laboratory. Similarly, loose soil adhering to garments should not be removed; these items should be carefully and individually wrapped in paper bags and sent to the laboratory for analysis. Care must be taken that particles that may accidentally fall off the garment during transportation will remain in the paper bag.

When a lump of soil is found, it should be collected and preserved intact. For example, an automobile tends to collect and build up layers of soil under the fenders, body, and so on. The impact of an automobile with another object may jar some of this soil loose. Once the suspect car has been apprehended, a comparison of the soil left at the scene with soil remaining on the automobile may help establish that the car was present at the accident scene. In these situations, separate samples are collected from under all the fender and frame areas of the vehicle; care is taken to remove the soil in lump form in order to preserve the order in which the soil adhered to the car. Undoubtedly, during the normal use of an automobile, soil will be picked up from numerous locations over a period of months and years. This layering effect may impart soil with greater variation, and hence greater evidential value, than that normally associated with loose soil.

Key Points

- A side-by-side visual comparison of the color and texture of soil specimens provides a way to distinguish soils that originate from different locations.

- Minerals are naturally occurring crystalline solids found in soil. Their physical properties—for example, color, geometric shape, density, and refractive index or birefringence—are useful for characterizing soils.

- Some crime laboratories compare soils by using density-gradient tubes filled with layers of liquids with different density values.

Forensic Brief

Soil: The Silent Witness

Alice Redmond was reported missing by her husband on a Monday night in 1983. Police learned that she had been seen with a co-worker, Mark Miller, after work that evening. When police questioned Miller, he stated that the two just "drove around" after work and then she dropped him off at home. Despite his statement, Miller was the prime suspect because he had a criminal record for burglary and theft.

Alice's car was recovered in town the following morning. The wheel wells were thickly coated in mud, which investigators hoped might provide a good lead. These hopes were dampened when police learned that Alice and her husband had attended a motorcycle race on Sunday, where her car was driven through deep mud.

After careful scrutiny, analysts found two colors of soil on the undercarriage of Alice's car. The thickest soil was brown; on top of the brown layer was a reddish soil that looked unlike anything in the county. Investigators hoped the reddish soil, which had to have been deposited sometime after the Sunday night motorcycle event and before the vehicle was discovered on Tuesday morning, could link the vehicle to the location of Alice Redmond.

An interview with Mark Miller's sister provided a break in the case. She told police that Mark had visited her on Monday evening. During that visit, he confessed that he had driven Alice in her car across the Alabama state line into Georgia, killed her, and buried her in a remote location. Now that investigators had a better idea where to look for Alice, forensic analysts took soil samples that would prove or disprove Miller's sister's story.

Each field sample was dried and compared for color and texture by eye and stereomicroscopy to the reddish-colored soil gathered from the car. Next, soils that compared to the car were passed through a series of mesh filters, each of a finer gauge than the last. In this way, the components of the soil samples were physically separated by size. Finally, each fraction was analyzed and compared for mineral composition with the aid of a polarizing light microscope.

Only samples collected from areas across the Alabama state line near the suspected dump site were consistent with the topmost reddish soil recovered from Alice's car. This finding supported Miller's sister's story and was instrumental in Mark Miller's being charged with murder and kidnapping. After pleading guilty, the defendant led the authorities to where he had buried the body. The burial site was within a half mile of the location where forensic analysts had collected a soil sample consistent with the soil removed from Alice's vehicle.

Source: T. J. Hopen, "The Value of Soil Evidence," in *Trace Evidence Analysis: More Cases in Mute Witnesses*, M. M. Houck, ed. (Elsevier Academic Press, Burlington, Mass.:, 2004), pp. 105–122.

Chapter Summary

For the criminalist, the presence of trace elements is particularly useful, because they provide "invisible" markers that may establish the source of a material or at least provide additional points for comparison.

A popular descriptive model of the atom pictures an atom as consisting of electrons orbiting a central nucleus. The nucleus is composed of positively charged protons and neutrons that have no charge. Because the atom has no net electrical charge, the number of protons must always equal the number of electrons in orbit around the nucleus.

One method used to identify trace elements in metals is neutron activation analysis, which measures the gamma-ray frequencies of specimens that have been bombarded with neutrons. The nucleus of an atom captures one or more neutrons and forms an isotope and often decomposes, emitting radioactivity in the form of gamma-ray frequencies. This method provides a highly sensitive and nondestructive analysis for simultaneously identifying and quantitating twenty to thirty trace elements. Because this technique requires access to a nuclear reactor, however, it has limited value to forensic analysis.

Paint spread onto a surface dries into a hard film consisting of pigments and additives suspended in the binder. One of the most common types of paint examined in the crime laboratory is finishes from automobiles. Manufacturers apply a variety of coatings to the body of an automobile. Hence, the wide diversity of automotive paint contributes to the forensic significance of an automobile paint comparison.

Questioned and known paint specimens are best compared side by side under a stereoscopic microscope for color, surface texture, and color layer sequence. Pyrolysis gas chromatography and infrared spectrophotometry are invaluable for distinguishing most paint formulations, adding further significance to a forensic paint comparison.

Emission spectroscopy and inductively coupled plasma are two techniques available to forensic scientists for determining the elemental composition of paint and other substances. An emission spectrograph vaporizes and heats samples to a high temperature so that the atoms in the material achieve an "excited" state. Under these circumstances, the excited atoms emit light. If the light is separated into its components, one observes a line spectrum. Each element in the spectrum can be identified by its characteristic line frequencies. In inductively coupled plasma, the sample, in the form of an aerosol, is introduced into a hot plasma, creating charged particles that emit light of characteristic wavelengths corresponding to the identity of the elements present.

The value of soil as evidence rests with its prevalence at crime scenes and its transferability between the scene and the criminal. Most soils can be differentiated by their gross appearance. A side-by-side visual comparison of the color and texture of soil specimens is easy to perform and provides a sensitive property for distinguishing soils that originate from different locations. In many forensic laboratories, forensic geologists characterize and compare the mineral content of soils. Some crime laboratories use density-gradient tubes to compare soils. These tubes are typically filled with layers of liquids that have different density values.

Review Questions

Facts and Concepts

1. What are trace elements and how are they useful to forensic scientists?

2. Forensic analysis of the bullets recovered after the assassination of President John F. Kennedy focused on the concentration of what two trace elements?

3. Which of the following conclusions can be drawn from the forensic analysis of the bullets recovered after the assassination of President John F. Kennedy?
   a. The analysis absolutely verified the findings of the Warren Commission.
   b. The analysis cast doubt on the findings of the Warren Commission.
   c. The analysis generally supported the findings of the Warren Commission.
   d. The analysis absolutely disproved the findings of the Warren Commission.

4. Name the three most important subatomic particles and their electrical charges, and indicate where each is located in the atom.

5. How does atomic number differ from atomic mass?

6. What is an isotope?

7. What is radioactivity? What are the three types of radiation?

8. Briefly describe the process of neutron activation analysis.

9. Name two advantages and two drawbacks of neutron activation analysis.

10. In what types of criminal cases is paint evidence most frequently encountered?

11. Describe the basic composition of paint. What component of paint evaporates after paint is applied to a surface?

12. What aspect of the automotive painting process is helpful in forensic characterization of automobile paint? How is it helpful?

13. What is the best way to make a microscopic comparison of paint chips?

14. What characteristics does a criminalist look for when comparing paint chips under a microscope? Which of these characteristics is most important in evaluating the significance of paint evidence?

15. A thorough comparison of paint must include a chemical analysis of what two properties?

16. What chromatographic process has proven to be particularly invaluable for distinguishing most paint formulations? Why is it so useful in the comparison of paint?

17. Briefly describe the process of emission spectroscopy.

18. What technique has largely supplanted carbon arc emission spectroscopy for most applications? What is the main difference between the two techniques?

19. What is PDQ and how is it helpful to forensic scientists?

20. Why must paint collected from a vehicle involved in a hit-and-run accident be taken from the area of the car suspected of being in contact with the victim?

21. How should the investigator handle the collection of trace paint evidence left on a tool?

22. What is the first step in a forensic soil comparison?

23. What is a mineral? How are minerals useful in forensic soil analysis?

24. Briefly describe how soil is separated in a density-gradient tube.

25. From what areas should standard/reference soils be collected when gathering soil evidence?

26. How should soil evidence adhering to shoes and clothing be collected and packaged?

27. How should lumps of soil be collected and preserved? Why?

Application and Critical Thinking

1. Using the periodic table shown in Chapter 4, determine the atomic numbers for antimony, tin, barium, and lead. Which do you think has the largest atomic mass? Which do you think has the smallest atomic mass? Explain your answers.

2. You are investigating a hit-and-run accident and have identified a suspect vehicle. Describe how you would collect paint to determine whether the suspect vehicle was involved in the accident. Be sure to indicate the tools you would use and the steps you would take to prevent cross contamination.

3. Criminalist Jared Heath responds to the scene of an assault on an unpaved lane in a rural neighborhood. Rain had fallen steadily the night before, making the area quite muddy. A suspect with very muddy shoes was apprehended nearby, but claimed to have picked up the mud either from his garden or from the unpaved parking lot of a local restaurant. Jared uses a spade to remove several samples of soil, each about 2 inches deep, from the immediate crime scene, and places each in a separate plastic vial. He collects the muddy shoes and wraps them in plastic as well. At the laboratory, he unpackages the soil samples and examines them carefully, one at a time. He then analyzes the soil on the shoes to see if it matches the soil from the crime scene. What mistakes, if any, did Jared make in his investigation?

Case Analysis

In the case of the CBS Murders, police suspected that the female victim had been moved from the location where she was murdered. Although an eyewitness placed a woman at the scene of the shooting, trace evidence ultimately was the key to solving the case.

1. What was the primary challenge facing the investigators in this case?

2. What items of evidence directly linked the victim to the suspect? Which items indirectly linked the two?

3. How was paint evidence used to show that the female victim was shot at the garage?

Web Resources

Forensic Paint Analysis and Comparison Guidelines (Article from the July 1999 issue of the online FBI journal *Forensic Science Communications*)
www.fbi.gov/hq/lab/fsc/backissu/july1999/painta.htm

Collecting Crime Evidence from Earth (Online article by forensic geologist Raymond C. Murray that includes a discussion of soil analysis)
www.forensicgeology.net/science.htm

Forensic Examination of Soil Evidence (Online report from Interpol about methods/advances in soil examination)
www.interpol.int/Public/Forensic/IFSS/meeting13/Reviews/Soil.pdf

The Atom Builder (Interactive exercise that explains fundamentals of atomic structure and allows users to try to construct stable atoms from subatomic particles)
www.pbs.org/wgbh/aso/tryit/atom/#

The Atom and Electromagnetic Radiation (Discussion of nuclear structure and electromagnetic radiation with practice problems)
chemed.chem.purdue.edu/genchem/topicreview/bp/ch6/atom_emrframe.html

Intro to Quantum Mechanics (Layperson's explanation of basic concepts of quantum theory)
www.hi.is/~hj/QuantumMechanics/quantum.html

Endnotes

1. Actually, the electrons are moving so rapidly around the nucleus that they are best visualized as an electron cloud spread out over the surface of the atom.

2. P. G. Rodgers et al., "The Classification of Automobile Paint by Diamond Window Infrared Spectrophotometry, Part I: Binders and Pigments," *Canadian Society of Forensic Science Journal* 9 (1976): 1; T. J. Allen, "Paint Sample Presentation for Fourier Transform Infrared Microscopy," *Vibration Spectroscopy* 3 (1992): 217.

3. G. Edmondstone, J. Hellman, K. Legate, G. L. Vardy, and E. Lindsay, "An Assessment of the Evidential Value of Automotive Paint Comparisons," *Canadian Society of Forensic Science Journal* 37 (2004): 147.

4. J. L. Buckle et al., "PDQ—Paint Data Queries: The History and Technology behind the Development of the Royal Canadian Mounted Police Laboratory Services Automotive Paint Database," *Canadian Society of Forensic Science Journal* 30 (1997): 199. An excellent discussion of the PDQ database is also available in A. Beveridge, T. Fung, and D. MacDougall, "Use of Infrared Spectroscopy for the Characterisation of Paint Fragments," in B. Caddy, ed., *Forensic Examination of Glass and Paint* (New York: Taylor & Francis, 2001), pp. 222–233.

5. E. P. Junger, "Assessing the Unique Characteristics of Close-Proximity Soil Samples: Just How Useful Is Soil Evidence?" *Journal of Forensic Sciences* 41 (1996), 27.

6. W. J. Graves, "A Mineralogical Soil Classification Technique for the Forensic Scientist," *Journal of Forensic Sciences* 24 (1979): 323; M. J. McVicar and W. J. Graves, "The Forensic Comparison of Soil by Automated Scanning Electron Microscopy," *Canadian Society of Forensic Science Journal* 30 (1997): 241.

7. K. Chaperlin and P. S. Howarth, "Soil Comparison by the Density Gradient Method—A Review and Evaluation," *Forensic Science International* 23 (1983): 161–177.

Case Reading

The CBS Murders*

In the early morning hours . . . atop a lonely roof garage on the west side of Manhattan, three men [all employed by CBS-TV] were found murdered. Each man had been shot once in the back of the head. A light-colored van was seen speeding away from the scene. Hours later, in a secluded alley street on the lower east side of Manhattan, the body of a fully clothed woman was found lying face down by two dog walkers. The woman had been killed in the same manner as the men on the roof garage. The condition of the woman's body, and other evidence, made it apparent that she had been shot at the garage, and then transported to the alley.

An eyewitness to the incident stated that he saw a man shoot a woman and place her in a light-colored van. The gunman then chased down the three men who were coming to the woman's aid, and shot each one of them. Days later, the prime suspect to the killings was arrested in Kentucky, in a black-colored van.

Numerous items of evidence (over 100) were collected from the van, and forwarded to the New York City police laboratory for examination. Among the items of evidence forwarded were three sets of vacuum sweepings from the van's interior.

An autopsy of the woman produced several items of trace evidence that were removed from the victim and forwarded to the author for microscopic examination. The woman's clothing was also received by the author for trace analysis.

A prime question that arose during the investigation was: could the woman's body, which had been placed in a light-colored van at the garage, and later left in an alley on the lower east side, be associated with the black van recovered over 1000 km (600 miles) away from the scene? Microscopic analysis and comparison of the trace evidential materials found on the victim and inside the van made this association possible.

Listed in Table 1 are all the items of similar trace materials that both the victim and the van had in common.

Microscopic comparisons of the questioned human head hair present on the victim's clothing were made with known samples. Ten of the brown-colored and gray-colored Caucasian head hairs from the victim's blazer were consistent in microscopic characteristics to the defendant's known head hair sample. One chemically treated head hair found on the victim was consistent in microscopic characteristics to the known head hair sample obtained from the defendant's wife. One forcibly removed, brown-colored, Caucasian head hair that was found on the rear door of the van's interior by the Kentucky state police was found to be consistent in all characteristics with the decedent's known head hair sample.

Microscopic comparisons of the white- and brown/white-colored dog hair from the victim's clothing, and the van's interior, were made with known samples of dog hair obtained from a dog owned by the defendant's nephew, the van's previous owner. The questioned dog hairs were found to be consistent with the hair from the nephew's dog.

Source: Reprinted by permission of the American Society of Testing and Materials from N. Petraco, "Trace Evidence—The Invisible Witness," *Journal of Forensic Science* 31 (1986), 321. Copyright 1986.

* This case takes its title from the fact that the three victims were employees of CBS-TV.

Table 1 Items of Similar Trace Evidence That Were Recovered from Both the Victim and the Van's Interior

| | Source | |
Trace Evidence	Victim	Van
White seed	mouth	sweepings
Paint chips	hair and wool	sweepings
gray/metallic/	blazer	and floor
black		
Sawdust	hair, blazer, and sheet	sweepings and misc. items
Glass fragments	wool blazer and	sweepings and
clear	sheet	misc. items
amber		
green		
Cellophane	wool blazer	floor
Urethane foam	wool blazer	sweepings, misc.
foam mattress		items, and foam mattress
Blue olefin	skirt	floor
plastic		
Dog hair	wool blazer	sweepings and misc.
brown/white		items
white		
Human hair	wool blazer	hairbrush, sweepings,
brown		and misc. items
gray		

The white seed that was recovered from the victim's mouth by the medical examiner, and the white seed that was found in the van's sweepings by the author, were forwarded to an internationally known botanist for identification and comparison. During the trial, the botanist testified that the two seeds were identical in all respects, and that although he could not identify the seed, both were either from the same species of plant, if not the same plant, probably a rare wild flower.

Sixteen gray metallic/black-colored paint chips from the victim and her clothing were compared to the gray metallic/black-colored paint removed from the van. Samples from the questioned and known sources were examined and compared by microscopic, chemical, and instrumental means. All of the paint specimens from the van and from the victim were found to be similar in all respects.

The remaining items of trace evidence from the victim and the van were examined and compared microscopically, and where necessary, by chemical and instrumental methods. Each of the remaining types of trace evidence from the victim was found to be similar to its counterpart from the van.

Blue- and black-colored flakes of acrylic paint were found in the van's sweepings, and on the suspect's sneakers. No blue- or black-colored paint flakes were found on the victim and her clothing. During a crime scene search of the defendant's residence in New Jersey, a large quantity of blue- and black-colored acrylic paint was found in the garage. It was apparent from the evidence present in the defendant's garage that a large rectangular shaped object had recently been painted with blue- and black-colored paint. The blue and black paint flakes from all the sources and the known blue (undercoat) and black (topcoat) paint from the van were compared by microscopic, chemical, and instrumental means. All the samples of paint were found to be consistent in every respect.

At the trial, extensive testimony concerning the collection, examination, identification, and comparison of the trace evidence from the victim and the van was given by the author, over a two-day period. When questioned about the source of the trace evidence found on the victim and her clothing, the author stated unequivocally that the trace evidence on the victim was from the defendant's van. On the basis of this evidence and other circumstantial evidence, the defendant was found guilty of all charges and sentenced to 100 years in prison.

Debora Green—Poisoning the American Dream

On the face of it, the Farrar family had it all. Dr. Debora Green, a nonpracticing oncologist, and her husband, Dr. Michael Farrar, had an opulent home in an exclusive Kansas City suburb. Michael, a cardiologist, had a successful practice that enabled Debora to stay home to raise their three loving children, Tim, Kate, and Kelly.

In late 1995, Michael Farrar was hospitalized for a mysterious illness. Michael entered a revolving door of excruciating stomach pain and recovery, framed in the context of his failing marriage. Unknown to outsiders, Michael had initially asked Debora for a divorce in 1994.

Michael's suspicion of foul play was aroused when he found a large number of castor bean packets in Debora's purse. She had used the castor beans to poison Michael's food; they contain ricin, a deadly poison.

On the night of October 24, 1995, the Green house became engulfed in flames and was destroyed. Michael Farrar was sleeping elsewhere while the couple were beginning a legal separation preceding their divorce. Their daughter Kate, then 10 years old, escaped the fire by exiting her bedroom window, scaling the garage roof, and jumping to safety into the arms of her mother, who was standing outside the house. Their son Tim, 13, and daughter Kelly, 6, were killed in the blaze that consumed their home.

Fire investigators quickly realized that they were confronting a criminal case of arson. Unconnected fires had occurred in various rooms of the house. Throughout the first floor of the house, pour patterns were obvious where someone had spread accelerants—flammable substances used to spread the fire more quickly—on the floors. Heavy soaking of the carpet on the stairways leading to the children's rooms would have created a wall of fire effectively blocking the children's escape route. This arsonist was also a murderer.

Police arrested Debora and charged her with two counts of first-degree murder and aggravated arson. Psychological evaluation of the defendant concluded that she had a schizoid personality that was masked by a high degree of intelligence. Debora Green is currently serving a life sentence in a Missouri prison. Her psychotic behavior became the subject of Ann Rule's novel *Bitter Harvest*.

chapter 12

Forensic Aspects of Fire Investigation

Key Terms

accelerant

combustion

endothermic reaction

energy

exothermic reaction

flammable range

flash point

glowing combustion

heat of combustion

hydrocarbon

ignition temperature

modus operandi

oxidation

pyrolysis

spontaneous combustion

Learning Objectives

After studying this chapter you should be able to:

- List the conditions necessary to initiate and sustain combustion

- Understand the three mechanisms of heat transfer

- Recognize the telltale signs of an accelerant-initiated fire

- Describe how to collect physical evidence at the scene of a suspected arson

- Describe laboratory procedures used to detect and identify hydrocarbon residues

Forensic Investigation of Arson

Arson often presents complex and difficult circumstances to investigate. Normally these incidents are committed at the convenience of a perpetrator who has thoroughly planned the criminal act and has left the crime scene long before any official investigation is launched. Furthermore, proving commission of the offense is more difficult because of the extensive destruction that frequently dominates the crime scene. The contribution of the criminalist is only one aspect of a comprehensive and difficult investigative process that must establish a motive, the modus operandi, and a suspect.

modus operandi
An offender's pattern of operation.

The criminalist's function is limited; usually he or she is expected only to detect and identify relevant chemical materials collected at the scene and to reconstruct and identify igniters. Although a chemist can identify trace amounts of gasoline or kerosene in debris, no scientific test can determine whether an arsonist has used a pile of rubbish or paper to start a fire. Furthermore, a fire can have many accidental causes, including faulty wiring, overheated electric motors, improperly cleaned and regulated heating systems, and cigarette smoking—which usually leave no chemical traces. Thus, the final determination of the cause of a fire must consider numerous factors and requires an extensive on-site investigation. The ultimate determination must be made by an investigator whose training and knowledge have been augmented by the practical experiences of fire investigation.

The Chemistry of Fire

Humankind's early search to explain the physical concepts underlying the behavior of matter always bestowed a central and fundamental role on fire. To ancient Greek philosophers, fire was one of the four basic elements from which all matter was derived. The medieval alchemist thought of fire as an instrument of transformation, capable of changing one element into another. One ancient recipe expresses its mystical power as follows: "Now the substance of cinnabar is such that the more it is heated, the more exquisite are its sublimations. Cinnabar will become mercury, and passing through a series of other sublimations, it is again turned into cinnabar, and thus it enables man to enjoy eternal life."

oxidation
The combination of oxygen with other substances to produce new substances.

Today, we know of fire not as an element of matter but as a transformation process during which oxygen is united with some other substance to produce noticeable quantities of heat and light (a flame). Therefore, any insight into why and how a fire is initiated and sustained must begin with the knowledge of the fundamental chemical reaction of fire—oxidation.

Oxidation

In a simple description of oxidation, oxygen combines with other substances to produce new products. Thus, we may write the chemical equation for the burning of methane gas, a major component of natural gas, as follows:

$$CH_4 + 2O_2 \longrightarrow CO_2 + 2H_2O$$

methane   oxygen   yields   carbon dioxide   water

However, not all oxidation proceeds in the manner that one associates with fire. For example, oxygen combines with many metals to form oxides. Thus, iron forms a red-brown iron oxide, or rust, as follows (see Figure 12–1):

$$4Fe + 3O_2 \longrightarrow 2Fe_2O_3$$

iron   oxygen   yields   iron oxide

Yet chemical equations do not give us a complete insight into the oxidation process. We must consider other factors to understand all of the implications of oxidation or, for that matter, any other chemical reaction. Methane burns when it unites with oxygen, but merely mixing methane and oxygen does not produce a fire. Nor, for example, does gasoline burn when it is simply exposed to air. However, lighting a match in the presence of any one of these fuel–air mixtures (assuming proper proportions) produces an instant fire.

What are the reasons behind these differences? Why do some oxidations proceed with the outward appearances that we associate with a fire while others do not? Why do we need a match to initiate some oxidations

FIGURE 12–1 Rust forming on iron is an example of oxidation. *Courtesy Nichola Gissing–Debut Art, Getty Images–Digital Vision*

while others proceed at room temperature? The explanation lies in a fundamental but abstract concept—energy.

Energy

Energy can be defined as the ability or potential of a system or material to do work. Energy takes many forms, such as heat energy, electrical energy, mechanical energy, nuclear energy, light energy, and chemical energy. For example, when methane is burned, the stored chemical energy in methane is converted to energy in the form of heat and light. This heat may be used to boil water or to provide high-pressure steam to turn a turbine. This is an example of converting chemical energy to heat energy to mechanical energy. The turbine can then be used to generate electricity, transforming mechanical energy to electrical energy. Electrical energy may then be used to turn a motor. In other words, energy can enable work to be done; heat is energy.

The quantity of heat from a chemical reaction comes from the breaking and formation of chemical bonds. Methane is a molecule composed of one carbon atom bonded with four hydrogen atoms:

$$
\begin{array}{c}
\text{H} \\
| \\
\text{H—C—H} \\
| \\
\text{H}
\end{array}
$$

An oxygen molecule forms when two atoms of the element oxygen bond:

$$O = O$$

In chemical changes, atoms are not lost but merely redistributed during the chemical reaction; thus, the products of methane's oxidation will be carbon dioxide:

$$O = C = O$$

and water:

$$H—O—H$$

This rearrangement, however, means that the chemical bonds holding the atoms together must be broken and new bonds formed. We now have arrived at a fundamental observation in our dissection of a chemical reaction—that molecules must absorb energy to break apart their chemical bonds, and that they liberate energy when their bonds are re-formed.

The amount of energy needed to break a bond and the amount of energy liberated when a bond is formed are characteristic of the type of chemical bond involved. Hence, a chemical reaction involves a change in energy content; energy is going in and energy is given off. The quantities of energies involved are different for each reaction and are determined by the participants in the chemical reaction.

Combustion

All oxidation reactions, including the combustion of methane, are examples of reactions in which more energy is liberated than is required to break the chemical bonds between atoms. Such reactions are said to be exothermic. The excess energy is liberated as heat, and often as light, and is known as the heat of combustion. Table 12–1 summarizes the heats of combustion of some important fuels in fire investigation.

Although we will not be concerned with them, some reactions require more energy than they eventually liberate. These reactions are known as endothermic reactions.

Table 12–1   Heats of Combustion of Fuels

Fuel	Heat of Combustion[a]
Crude oil	19,650 Btu/gal
Diesel fuel	19,550 Btu/lb
Gasoline	19,250 Btu/lb
Methane	995 Btu/cu ft
Natural gas	128–1,868 Btu/cu ft
Octane	121,300 Btu/gal
Wood	7,500 Btu/lb
Coal, bituminous	11,000–14,000 Btu/lb
Anthracite	13,351 Btu/lb

[a]Btu (British thermal unit) is defined as the quantity of heat required to raise the temperature of 1 pound of water 1°F at or near its point of maximum density.

Source: John D. DeHaan, *Kirk's Fire Investigation*, 2nd ed. Upper Saddle River, N.J.: Prentice Hall, 1983.

FIGURE 12–2   An energy barrier must be hurdled before reactants such as methane and oxygen can combine with one another to form the products of carbon dioxide and water.

Thus, all reactions require an energy input to start them. We can think of this requirement as an invisible energy barrier between the reactants and the products of a reaction (see Figure 12–2). The higher this barrier, the more energy required to initiate the reaction. Where does this initial energy come from? There are many sources of energy; however, for the purpose of this discussion we need to look at only one—heat.

Heat   The energy barrier in the conversion of iron to rust is relatively small, and it can be surmounted with the help of heat energy in the surrounding environment at normal outdoor temperatures. Not so for methane or gasoline; these energy barriers are quite high, and a high temperature must be applied to start the oxidation of these fuels. Hence, before any fire can result, the temperature of these fuels must be raised enough to exceed the energy barrier. Table 12–2 shows that this temperature, known as the ignition temperature, is quite high for common fuels.

Once combustion starts, enough heat is liberated to keep the reaction going by itself. In essence, the fire becomes a chain reaction, absorbing a portion of its own liberated heat to generate even more heat. The fire burns until either the oxygen or the fuel is exhausted.

Normally, a lighted match provides a convenient igniter of fuels. However, the fire investigator must also consider other potential sources

ignition temperature
The minimum temperature at which a fuel spontaneously ignites.

Table 12–2 Ignition Temperatures of Some Common Fuels

Fuel	Ignition Temperature, °F
Acetone	869
Benzene	928
Fuel oil #2	495
Gasoline (low octane)	536
Kerosene (fuel oil #1)	410
n-Octane	428
Petroleum ether	550
Turpentine	488

Source: John D. DeHaan, *Kirk's Fire Investigation*, 4th ed. Upper Saddle River, N.J.: Prentice Hall, 1997.

of ignition—for example, electrical discharges, sparks, and chemicals—while reconstructing the initiation of a fire. All of these sources have temperatures higher than the ignition temperature of most fuels.

Speed of Reaction   Although the liberation of energy explains many important features of oxidation, it does not explain all characteristics of the reaction. Obviously, although all oxidations liberate energy, not all are accompanied by a flame; witness the oxidation of iron to rust. Therefore, one other important consideration will make our understanding of oxidation and fire complete: the rate or speed at which the reaction takes place.

A chemical reaction, such as oxidation, takes place when molecules combine or collide with one another. The faster the molecules move, the greater the number of collisions between them and the faster the rate of reaction. Many factors influence the rate of these collisions. In our description of fire and oxidation, we consider only two: the physical state of the fuel and the temperature.

Physical State of Fuel   A fuel achieves a reaction rate with oxygen sufficient to produce a flame only when it is in the gaseous state, for only in this state molecules can collide frequently enough to support a flaming fire. This remains true whether the fuel is a solid such as wood, paper, cloth, or plastic, or a liquid such as gasoline or kerosene.

For example, the conversion of iron to rust proceeds slowly because the iron atoms cannot achieve a gaseous state. The combination of oxygen with iron is thus restricted to the surface area of the metal exposed to air, a limitation that severely reduces the rate of reaction. On the other hand, the reaction of methane and oxygen proceeds rapidly because all the reactants are in the gaseous state. The speed of the reaction is reflected by the production of noticeable quantities of heat and light (a flame).

Fuel Temperature   How then does a liquid or solid maintain a gaseous reaction? In the case of a liquid fuel, the temperature must be high enough to vaporize the fuel. The vapor that forms burns when it mixes with oxygen and combusts as a flame. The flash point is the *lowest* temperature at which a liquid gives off sufficient vapor to form a mixture with air that will support combustion. Once the flash point is reached, the fuel can be ignited by some outside source of temperature to start a fire. The ignition temperature of a fuel is always considerably higher than the flash point.

flash point
The minimum temperature at which a liquid fuel produces enough vapor to burn.

For example, gasoline has a flash point of −50°F; however, an ignition temperature of 495°F is needed to start a gasoline fire.

With a solid fuel such as wood, the process of generating vapor is more complex. A solid fuel burns only when exposed to heat intense enough to decompose the solid into gaseous products. This chemical breakdown of solid material is known as pyrolysis. The gaseous products of pyrolysis combine with oxygen to produce a fire (see Figure 12–3). Here again, fire can be described as a chain reaction. A match or other source of heat initiates the pyrolysis of the solid fuel, the gaseous products react with oxygen in the air to produce heat and light, and this heat in turn pyrolyzes more solid fuel into volatile gases.

Typically, the rate of a chemical reaction increases when the temperature is raised. The magnitude of the increase varies from one reaction to another and also from one temperature range to another. For most reactions, a 10°C (18°F) rise in temperature doubles or triples the reaction rate. This observation explains in part why burning is so rapid. As the fire spreads, it raises the temperature of the fuel–air mixture, thus increasing the rate of reaction; this in turn generates more heat, again increasing the rate of reaction. Only when the fuel or oxygen is depleted does this vicious cycle come to a halt.

pyrolysis
The decomposition of solid organic matter by heat.

The Fuel–Air Mix   As we have seen from our discussion about gaseous fuel, air (oxygen) and sufficient heat are the basic ingredients of a flaming fire. There is also one other consideration—the gas fuel–air mix. A mixture of gaseous fuel and air burns only if its composition lies within certain limits. If the fuel concentration is too low (lean) or too great (rich), combustion

FIGURE 12–3   Intense heat causes solid fuels such as wood to decompose into gaseous products, a process called *pyrolysis*. *Courtesy David Trood/Image Bank/Getty Images*

flammable range
The entire range of possible gas or vapor fuel concentrations in air that are capable of burning.

does not occur. The concentration range between the upper and lower limits is called the flammable range. For example, the flammable range for gasoline is 1.3–6.0 percent. Thus, in order for a gasoline–air mix to burn, gasoline must make up at least 1.3 percent, and no more than 6 percent, of the mixture.

Glowing Combustion Although a flaming fire can be supported only by a gaseous fuel, in some instances a fuel can burn without a flame. Witness a burning cigarette or the red glow of hot charcoals (see Figure 12–4). These are examples of glowing combustion or *smoldering*. Here combustion occurs on the surface of a solid fuel in the absence of heat high enough to pyrolyze the fuel. Interestingly, this phenomenon generally ensues long after the flames have gone out. Wood, for example, tends to burn with a flame until all of its pyrolyzable components have been expended; however, wood's carbonaceous residue continues to smolder long after the flame has extinguished itself.

glowing combustion
Combustion on the surface of a solid fuel in the absence of heat high enough to pyrolyze the fuel.

spontaneous combustion
A fire caused by a natural heat-producing process in the presence of sufficient air and fuel.

Spontaneous Combustion One interesting phenomenon often invoked by arson suspects as the cause of a fire is spontaneous combustion. Actually, the conditions under which spontaneous combustion can develop are rather limited and rarely account for the cause of a fire. Spontaneous combustion is the result of a natural heat-producing process in poorly ventilated containers or areas. For example, hay stored in barns provides an excellent growing medium for bacteria whose activities generate heat. If the hay is not properly ventilated, the heat builds to a level that supports other types of heat-producing chemical reactions in the hay. Eventually, as the heat rises, the ignition temperature of hay is reached, spontaneously setting off a fire.

FIGURE 12–4   Red-hot charcoals are an example of glowing combustion. *Courtesy Paul Sisul/Stone/Getty Images*

Another example of spontaneous combustion involves the ignition of improperly ventilated containers containing rags soaked with certain types of highly unsaturated oils, such as linseed oil. Heat can build up to the point of ignition as a result of a slow heat-producing chemical oxidation between the air and the oil. Of course, storage conditions must encourage the accumulation of the heat over a prolonged period of time. However, spontaneous combustion does not occur with hydrocarbon lubricating oils, and it is not expected to occur with most household fats and oils.

In summary, three requirements must be satisfied to initiate and sustain combustion:

1. **A fuel must be present.**

2. **Oxygen must be available in sufficient quantity to combine with the fuel.**

3. **Heat must be applied to initiate the combustion, and sufficient heat must be generated to sustain the reaction.**

Heat Transfer

Consider how a structural fire begins. The typical scenario starts with heat ignition at a single location. It may be an arsonist lighting a gasoline-soaked rag, a malfunctioning electric appliance sparking, or an individual falling asleep while smoking a cigarette in bed. How does a flame initially confined to a single location spread to engulf an entire structure? Understanding the anatomy of a fire begins with comprehending how heat travels through a burning structure.

The previous section stressed the importance of the role of heat in generating sufficient fuel vapors to support combustion, as well as the requirement that the heat source be hot enough to ignite the fuel's vapor. Once the fire begins, the heat generated by the fuel's reaction with air is fed back into the fuel–air mix to keep the chemical reaction going.

As a fire progresses, the heat created by the combustion process tends to move from a high-temperature region to one at a lower temperature. Understanding heat transfer from one location to another is important for reconstructing the origin of a fire, as well as for understanding why and how fire spreads through a structure. The three mechanisms of heat transfer are conduction, radiation, and convection.

Conduction Movement of heat through a solid object is caused by a process called *conduction*, in which electrons and atoms within the heated object collide with one another. Heat always travels from hot areas of a solid to cold ones by conduction. Solids whose atoms or molecules have loosely held electrons are good conductors of heat. Metals have the most loosely held electrons and are therefore excellent conductors of heat. Thus, when you insert one end of a metal object into an open flame, the entire object quickly becomes hot to the touch.

Materials that have electrons firmly attached to their molecules are poor conductors of heat. Poor conductors are called insulators. Wood is a good insulator; for that reason, metal objects that are subject to intense heat (such as skillets and saucepans) often have wooden handles (see Figure 12–5).

In reconstructing a fire scene, it's important to keep in mind that heat may be transported through metals such as beams, nails, fasteners, bolts, and other good conductors to a location far from the initial heat source. Any fuel in contact with the conductor may be ignited, creating a new fire location. On the other hand, the conductivity of wood, plastic, and paper are

FIGURE 12–5 **The wooden handle on this saucepan is a poor conductor of heat.** *Courtesy Topham, The Image Works*

very low, meaning that heat emanating from these surfaces does not spread well and does not cause ignitions far from the initial heat source.

Radiation *Radiation* is the transfer of heat energy from a heated surface to a cooler surface by electromagnetic radiation. A hot surface emits electromagnetic radiation of various wavelengths, and in a fire scene the electromagnetic radiation moves in a straight line from one surface to another. Radiant heat plays a key role in understanding how fire spreads throughout a structure. For example, all surfaces that face the fire are exposed to radiant heat and burst into flames when the surface reaches their ignition temperature. In very large fires, nearby structures and vehicles are often ignited at a distance by radiant heat.

Convection *Convection* is the transfer of heat energy by movement of molecules within a liquid or gas. Water being heated on a stove illustrates the concept of convection. As the water molecules on the bottom of the pot move faster they spread apart and become less dense, causing them to move upward. Denser, cooler water molecules then migrate to the bottom of the pot. In this way convection currents keep the fluid stirred up as warmer fluid moves away from the heat source and cooler fluid moves toward the heat source. Likewise, warm air expands, becoming less dense and causing it to rise and move toward the cooler surrounding air.

In a structural fire, the gaseous hot products of combustion expand, and convection moves the hot gases to the upper portions of the structure (see Figure 12–6). The convected hot gases become a source of heat, radiating heat energy downward onto all the surfaces below them. The hot surfaces of the exposed objects often pyrolyze or break down, releasing gaseous molecules. The phenomenon known as *flashover* occurs when all the combustible fuels simultaneously ignite, engulfing the entire structure in flame.

FIGURE 12–6 **Convection causes flames to rise to the upper floor of a burning structure.** *Courtesy Dave Frazier, Danita Delimont Photography*

Key Points

• Oxidation is the combination of oxygen with other substances to produce new substances.

• Combustion is rapid combination of oxygen with another substance, accompanied by production of noticeable heat and light.

• In an exothermic reaction, heat energy is liberated. In an endothermic reaction, heat energy is absorbed from the surroundings.

• Pyrolysis is the chemical breakdown of solid organic matter by heat. The gaseous products of pyrolysis combine with oxygen to produce a fire.

• Spontaneous combustion is fire caused by a natural heat-producing process in the presence of sufficient air and fuel.

• To initiate and sustain combustion, (1) a fuel must be present, (2) oxygen must be available in sufficient quantity to combine with the fuel, and (3) heat must be applied to initiate the combustion, and sufficient heat must be generated to sustain the reaction.

• The three mechanisms of heat transfer are conduction, radiation, and convection. Conduction is the movement of heat through a solid object. Radiation is the transfer of heat energy from a heated surface to a cooler surface by electromagnetic radiation. Convection is the transfer of heat energy by the movement of molecules within a liquid or gas.

Searching the Fire Scene

The arson investigator should begin examining a fire scene for signs of arson as soon as the fire has been extinguished. Most arsons are started with petroleum-based **accelerants** such as gasoline or kerosene. Thus, the presence of containers capable of holding an accelerant arouse suspicions of arson. Discovery of an ignition device ranging in sophistication from a candle to a time-delay device is another indication of possible arson. A common telltale sign of arson may be an irregularly shaped pattern on a floor or on the ground (see Figure 12–7) resulting from pouring an accelerant onto the surface. In addition to these visual indicators, investigators should look for signs of breaking and entering and theft, and they should begin interviewing any eyewitnesses to the fire.

accelerant
Any material used to start or sustain a fire.

Timeliness of Investigation

Time constantly works against the arson investigator. Any accelerant residues that remain after a fire is extinguished may evaporate within a few days or even hours. Furthermore, safety and health conditions may necessitate that cleanup and salvage operations begin as quickly as possible. Once this occurs, a meaningful investigation of the fire scene is impossible. Accelerants in soil and vegetation can be rapidly degraded by bacterial action. Freezing samples containing soil or vegetation is an effective way to prevent this degradation.

The need to begin an *immediate* investigation of the circumstances surrounding a fire even takes precedence over the requirement to obtain a search warrant to enter and search the premises. The Supreme Court, explaining its position on this issue, stated in part:

> . . . Fire officials are charged not only with extinguishing fires, but with finding their causes. Prompt determination of the fire's origin may be necessary to prevent its recurrence, as through the detection of continuing dangers such as faulty wiring or a defective furnace. Immediate investigation may also be necessary to preserve

FIGURE 12–7 Irregularly shaped pattern on the ground resulting from a poured ignitable liquid. *Courtesy Franklin County Crime Scene Unit, North Carolina*

evidence from intentional or accidental destruction. And, of course, the sooner the officials complete their duties, the less will be their subsequent interference with the privacy and the recovery efforts of the victims. For these reasons, officials need no warrant to remain in a building for a reasonable time to investigate the cause of a blaze after it has been extinguished. And if the warrantless entry to put out the fire and determine its cause is constitutional, the warrantless seizure of evidence while inspecting the premises for these purposes also is constitutional. . . .

In determining what constitutes a reasonable time to investigate, appropriate recognition must be given to the exigencies that confront officials serving under these conditions, as well as to individuals' reasonable expectations of privacy.[1]

Locating the Fire's Origin

A search of the fire scene must focus on finding the fire's origin, which will prove most productive in any search for an accelerant or ignition device. In searching for a fire's specific point of origin, the investigator may uncover telltale signs of arson such as evidence of separate and unconnected fires or the use of "streamers" to spread the fire from one area to another. For example, the arsonist may have spread a trail of gasoline or paper to cause the fire to move rapidly from one room to another.

There are no fast and simple rules for identifying a fire's origin. Normally a fire tends to move upward, and thus the probable origin is most likely closest to the lowest point that shows the most intense characteristics of burning. Sometimes as the fire burns upward, a V-shaped pattern forms against a vertical wall, as shown in Figure 12–8. Because flammable liquids always flow to the lowest point, more severe burning found on the floor than on the ceiling may indicate the presence of an accelerant. If a flammable liquid was used, charring is expected to be more intense on the bottom of furniture, shelves, and other items rather than the top.

FIGURE 12–8 **Typical V patterns illustrating upward movement of the fire.** *Courtesy John Lentini*

However, many factors can contribute to the deviation of a fire from normal behavior. Prevailing drafts and winds; secondary fires due to collapsing floors and roofs; the physical arrangement of the burning structure; stairways and elevator shafts; holes in the floor, wall, or roof; and the effects of the firefighter in suppressing the fire are all factors that the fire investigator must consider before determining conclusive findings.

Once located, the point of origin should be protected to permit careful investigation. As at any crime scene, nothing should be touched or moved before notes, sketches, and photographs are taken. An examination must also be made for possible accidental causes, as well as for evidence of arson. The most common materials used by an arsonist to ensure the rapid spread and intensity of a fire are gasoline and kerosene or, for that matter, any volatile flammable liquid.

Searching for Accelerants

Fortunately, only under the most ideal conditions will combustible liquids be entirely consumed during a fire. When the liquid is poured over a large area, a portion of it will likely seep into a porous surface, such as cracks in the floor, upholstery, rags, plaster, wallboards, or carpet. Enough of the liquid may remain unchanged to permit its detection in the crime laboratory. In addition, when a fire is extinguished with water, the evaporation rate of volatile fluids may be slowed, because water cools and covers materials through which the combustible liquid may have soaked. Fortunately, water does not interfere with laboratory methods used to detect and characterize flammable liquid residues.

The search for traces of flammable liquid residues may be aided by the use of a sensitive portable vapor detector or "sniffer" (see Figure 12–9). This device can rapidly screen suspect materials for volatile residues by sucking in the air surrounding the questioned sample. The air is passed over a heated filament; if a combustible vapor is present, it oxidizes and immediately increases the temperature of the filament. The rise in filament temperature is then registered as a deflection on the detector's meter.

Of course, such a device is not a conclusive test for a flammable vapor, but it is an excellent screening device for checking suspect samples at the fire scene. Another approach is to use dogs that have been trained to recognize the odor of hydrocarbon accelerants.

FIGURE 12–9 Portable hydrocarbon detector. *Courtesy Sirchie Finger Print Laboratories, Inc., Youngsville, N.C., www.sirchie.com*

Collection and Preservation of Arson Evidence

Two to 3 quarts of ash and soot debris must be collected at the point of origin of a fire when arson is suspected. The collection should include all porous materials and all other substances thought likely to contain flammable residues. These include such things as wood flooring, rugs, upholstery, and rags.

Packaging and Preservation of Evidence

Specimens should be packaged immediately in airtight containers so possible residues are not lost through evaporation. New, clean paint cans with friction lids are good containers because they are low cost, airtight, unbreakable, and available in a variety of sizes (see Figure 12–10). Wide-mouthed glass jars are also useful for packaging suspect specimens, provided that they have airtight lids. Cans and jars should be filled one-half to two-thirds full, leaving an air space in the container above the debris.

Large bulky samples should be cut to size at the scene as needed so that they will fit into available containers. Plastic polyethylene bags are not suitable for packaging specimens because they react with hydrocarbons and permit volatile hydrocarbon vapors to be depleted. Fluids found in open bottles or cans must be collected and sealed. Even when such containers appear empty, the investigator is wise to seal and preserve them in case they contain trace amounts of liquids or vapors.

Substrate Control

The collection of all materials suspected of containing volatile liquids must be accompanied by a thorough sampling of similar but uncontaminated control specimens from another area of the fire scene. This is known as *substrate control*. For example, if an investigator collects carpeting at the point of origin, he or she must sample the same carpet from another part of the room, where it can be reasonably assumed that no flammable substance was placed.

In the laboratory, the criminalist checks the substrate control to be sure that it is free of any flammables. This procedure reduces the possibility (and subsequent argument) that the carpet was exposed to

FIGURE 12–10 Various sizes of paint cans suitable for collecting debris at fire scenes. *Courtesy Sirchie Finger Print Laboratories, Inc., Youngsville, N.C., www.sirchie.com*

a flammable liquid such as a cleaning solution during normal maintenance. In addition, laboratory tests on the unburned control material may
help analyze the breakdown products from the material's exposure to
intense heat during the fire. Common materials such as plastic floor tiles,
carpet, linoleum, and adhesives can produce volatile hydrocarbons when
they are burned. These breakdown products can sometimes be mistaken
for an accelerant.

Igniters and Other Evidence

The scene should also be thoroughly searched for igniters. The most common igniter is a match. Normally the match is completely consumed during a fire and is impossible to locate. However, there have been cases in
which, by force of habit, matches have been extinguished and tossed aside
only to be recovered later by the investigator. This evidence may prove
valuable if the criminalist can fit the match to a book found in the possession of a suspect, as shown in Figure 12–11.

Arsonists can construct many other types of devices to start a fire.
These include burning cigarettes, firearms, ammunition, a mechanical
match striker, electrical sparking devices, and a "Molotov cocktail"—a
glass bottle containing flammable liquid with a cloth rag stuffed into it and
lit as a fuse. Relatively complex mechanical devices are much more likely to
survive the fire for later discovery. The broken glass and wick of the Molotov
cocktail, if recovered, must be preserved as well.

One important piece of evidence is the clothing of the suspect perpetrator. If this individual is arrested within a few hours of initiating the fire,
residual quantities of the accelerant may still be present in the clothing.
As we will see in the next section, the forensic laboratory can detect
extremely small quantities of accelerants, making the examination of

**FIGURE 12–11 Three matches (Spec. 3, 4, 5) discarded at the scene of an arson are each
shown to fit into a matchbook (Spec. 1) found in the suspect's possession. Such evidence
strongly links the crime scene and the suspect.** *Courtesy New Jersey State Police*

a suspect's clothing a feasible investigative approach. Each item of clothing should be placed in a separate airtight container, preferably a new, clean paint can.

Key Points

• Telltale signs of arson include evidence of separate and unconnected fires, the use of "streamers" to spread the fire from one area to another, and evidence of severe burning found on the floor as opposed to the ceiling of a structure.

• Other common signs of arson at a fire scene are the presence of accelerants and the discovery of an ignition device.

• Porous materials, at the suspected point of origin of a fire should be collected and stored in airtight containers.

Analysis of Flammable Residues

Criminalists are nearly unanimous in judging the gas chromatograph to be the most sensitive and reliable instrument for detecting and characterizing flammable residues. Most arsons are initiated by petroleum distillates, such as gasoline and kerosene, that are composed of a complex mixture of hydrocarbons. The gas chromatograph separates the hydrocarbon components of these liquids and produces a chromatographic pattern characteristic of a particular petroleum product.

hydrocarbon
Any compound consisting of only carbon and hydrogen.

The Headspace Technique

Before accelerant residues can be analyzed, they first must be recovered from the debris collected at the scene. The easiest way to recover accelerant residues from fire-scene debris is to heat the airtight container in which the sample is sent to the laboratory. When the container is heated, any volatile residue in the debris is driven off and trapped in the container's enclosed airspace. The vapor or *headspace* is then removed with a syringe, as shown in Figure 12–12.

When the vapor is injected into the gas chromatograph, it is separated into its components, and each peak is recorded on the chromatogram. The identity of the volatile residue is determined when the pattern of the resultant chromatogram is compared to patterns produced by known petroleum products. For example, in Figure 12–13, a gas chromatographic analysis of debris recovered from a fire site shows a chromatogram similar to a known gasoline standard, thus proving the presence of gasoline.

In the absence of any recognizable pattern, the individual peaks can be identified when the investigator compares their retention times to known hydrocarbon standards (such as hexane, benzene, toluene, and xylenes). The brand name of a gasoline sample cannot currently by determined by gas chromatography or any other technique. Fluctuating gasoline markets and exchange agreements among the various oil companies preclude this possibility.

Vapor Concentration

One major disadvantage of the headspace technique is that the size of the syringe limits the volume of vapor that can be removed from the container and injected into the gas chromatograph. To overcome this deficiency,

FIGURE 12–12   Removal of vapor from an enclosed container for gas chromatographic analysis. *Courtesy New Jersey State Police*

many crime laboratories augment the headspace technique with a method called *vapor concentration*. One setup for this analysis is shown in Figure 12–14.

A charcoal-coated strip, similar to that used in environmental monitoring badges, is placed within the container holding the debris that has been collected from the fire scene.[2] The container is then heated to about 60°C for about one hour. At this temperature, a significant quantity of accelerant vaporizes into the container airspace. The charcoal absorbs the accelerant vapor with which it comes into contact. In this manner, over a short period of time a significant quantity of the accelerant will be trapped and concentrated onto the charcoal strip.

Once the heating procedure is complete, the analyst removes the charcoal strip from the container and recovers the accelerant from the strip by washing it with a small volume of solvent (carbon disulfide). The solvent is then injected into the gas chromatograph for analysis. The major advantage of using vapor concentration with gas chromatography is its sensitivity. By absorbing the accelerant into a charcoal strip, the forensic analyst can increase the sensitivity of accelerant detection at least a hundredfold over the conventional headspace technique.

An examination of Figure 12–13 shows that identifying an accelerant such as gasoline by gas chromatography is an exercise in pattern recognition. Typically a forensic analyst compares the pattern generated by the sample to chromatograms from accelerant standards obtained under the same conditions. The pattern of gasoline, as with many other accelerants, can easily be placed in a searchable library.

Gas Chromatography/Mass Spectrometry

On occasion, discernible patterns are not attainable by gas chromatography. This may be due to a combination of accelerants, or to the mixing of accelerant residue with heat-generated breakdown products of materials burning at the fire scene. Under such conditions, a gas chromatographic pattern can be difficult if not impossible to interpret. In these cases, gas chromatography combined with mass spectrometry (discussed in Chapter 5)

FIGURE 12–13 (*top*) **Gas chromatograph of vapor from a genuine gasoline sample.** (*bottom*) **Gas chromatograph of vapor from debris recovered at a fire site. Note the similarity of the known gasoline to vapor removed from the debris.** *Courtesy New Jersey State Police*

has proven valuable for solving difficult problems in the detection of accelerant residues.

Complex chromatographic patterns can be simplified by passing the separated components emerging from the gas chromatographic column through a mass spectrometer. As each component enters the mass spectrometer, it is fragmented into a collection of ions. The analyst can then control which ions will be detected and which will go unnoticed. In

FIGURE 12–14 Apparatus for accelerant recovery by vapor concentration. The vapor in the enclosed container is exposed to charcoal, a chemical absorbent, where it is trapped for later analysis.

FIGURE 12–15 Chromatogram of a residue sample collected at a fire scene (a) shows a pattern somewhat like that of gasoline (b). However, a definitive conclusion that the unknown contained gasoline could be obtained only after extraneous peaks were eliminated from the unknown by the use of GC/MS (c).

essence, the mass spectrometer acts as a filter allowing the analyst to see only the peaks associated with the ions selected for a particular accelerant. In this manner, the chromatographic pattern can be simplified by eliminating extraneous peaks that may obliterate the pattern.[3] The process is illustrated in Figure 12–15.

- Most arsons are initiated by petroleum distillates such as gasoline and kerosene.

- The gas chromatograph is the most sensitive and reliable instrument for detecting and characterizing flammable residues. A gas chromatograph separates the hydrocarbon components and produces a chromatographic pattern characteristic of a particular petroleum product.

- By comparing select gas chromatographic peaks recovered from fire-scene debris to known flammable liquids, a forensic analyst may be able to identify the accelerant used to initiate the fire.

- Complex chromatographic patterns can be simplified by passing the separated components emerging from the gas chromatographic column through a mass spectrometer.

Chapter Summary

When a fire occurs, oxygen combines with a fuel to produce noticeable quantities of heat and light (flames). Three requirements must be satisfied to initiate and sustain combustion: (1) a fuel must be present; (2) oxygen must be available in sufficient quantity to combine with the fuel; and (3) sufficient heat must be applied to initiate the combustion and generated to sustain the reaction. A fuel achieves a reaction rate with oxygen sufficient to sustain a fire only when it is in the gaseous state.

As a fire progresses, the heat created by the combustion process tends to move from a high-temperature region to one at a lower temperature. Heat transfer during a fire can occur in a number of ways. Conduction is movement of heat through an object caused by electrons and atoms colliding within the heated object. Radiation is the transfer of heat energy from a heated surface to a cooler surface by electromagnetic radiation. Convection is the transfer of heat energy by movement of molecules within a liquid or gas.

The arson investigator must begin examining a fire scene for signs of arson as soon as the fire has been extinguished. Some telltale signs of arson include evidence of separate and unconnected fires, the use of "streamers" to spread the fire from one area to another, and evidence of severe burning found on the floor as opposed to the ceiling of a structure.

The search of the fire scene must focus on finding the fire's origin. There are no fast and simple rules for identifying a fire's origin. Normally a fire tends to move upward, and thus the probable origin is most likely closest to the lowest point that shows the most intense characteristics of burning. Sometimes as the fire burns upward, a V-shaped pattern forms against a vertical wall. At the suspect point of origin of a fire, porous materials should be collected and stored in airtight containers.

In the laboratory, the gas chromatograph is the most sensitive and reliable instrument for detecting and characterizing flammable residues. Most arsons are initiated by petroleum distillates such as gasoline and kerosene. The gas chromatograph separates the hydrocarbon components and produces a chromatographic pattern characteristic of a particular petroleum product. By comparing select gas chromatographic peaks recovered from fire-scene debris to known flammable liquids, a forensic analyst may be able to identify the accelerant used to initiate the fire.

Review Questions

Facts and Concepts

1. What is oxidation?

2. The quantity of heat from a chemical reaction comes from
   a. the breaking and formation of chemical bonds.
   b. the presence of oxygen in the reaction.
   c. the emission of radiation.
   d. the composition of the fuel–air mix.

3. Molecules must absorb energy to _____, and they liberate energy when _____.

4. What is combustion? Why is rusting not accompanied by combustion?

5. How does an exothermic reaction differ from an endothermic reaction?

6. A fire will burn until either of which two components is exhausted?

7. Name two factors that influence the speed of reaction of a fire.

8. In what physical state must a fuel exist in order to produce combustion when it reacts with oxygen? Why must it be in this state?

9. How high must the temperature of a liquid fuel be before the fuel will burn? What is the term for the lowest temperature at which this occurs?

10. What is pyrolysis? How does pyrolysis produce fire?

11. How does the fuel–air mix affect combustion?

12. Define and give two examples of glowing combustion.

13. Define *spontaneous combustion* and give two examples of conditions under which it may occur.

14. What three requirements must be satisfied to initiate and sustain combustion?

15. As a fire progresses, toward what region does the heat created by combustion tend to move?

16. List and define the three mechanisms of heat transfer.

17. What is an insulator? Give an example of a good insulator.

18. List three common signs of arson at a fire scene.

19. Name three reasons why arson investigators must work quickly to collect evidence at a fire scene.

20. A search of the fire scene must focus on finding
    a. traces of accelerant.
    b. ignition devices.
    c. human remains.
    d. the fire's point of origin.

21. What are streamers? What does evidence of their presence at a fire scene suggest?

22. Why should fire evidence be packaged in airtight containers?

23. What instrument do most criminalists consider the most sensitive and reliable for detecting and characterizing flammable residues?

24. What is headspace? How is it recovered?

25. What is the main advantage of vapor concentration over the headspace technique?

Application and Critical Thinking

1. Indicate which method of heat transfer is most likely to be responsible for each of the following:

   a. ignition of papers in the room where a fire starts
   b. ignition of electrical wiring in a room adjoining the fire's point or origin
   c. ignition of roof timbers
   d. ignition of a neighboring house

2. It is late August in Houston, Texas, and you are investigating a fire that occurred at a facility that stores motor oils and other lubricating oils. A witness points out a man who allegedly ran from the structure about the same time that the fire started. You question the man, who turns out to be the owner of the facility. He tells you that he was checking his inventory when barrels of waste motor oil stored in an unventilated back room spontaneously burst into flames. The owner claims that the fire spread so rapidly that he had to flee the building before he could call 911. After speaking with several employees, you learn that the building has no air conditioning and that the oil had been stored for almost a year in the cramped back room. You also learn from a detective assisting on the case that the owner increased his insurance coverage on the facility within the past three months. Should you believe the owner's story, or should you suspect arson? Upon what do you base your conclusion?

3. Criminalist Mick Mickelson is collecting evidence from a fire scene. He gathers about a quart of ash and soot debris collected from several rooms surrounding the point of origin. He stored the debris in a new, clean paint can, filled about three-quarters full. Seeing several pieces of timber that he believes may contain accelerant residues, he cuts them and places them in airtight plastic bags. A short time later, a suspect is arrested and Mick searches him for any signs of an igniter or accelerants. He finds a cigarette lighter on the suspect and seizes it for evidence before turning the suspect over to the police. What mistakes, if any, did Mick make in collecting evidence?

Web Resources

An Introduction of Fire and Arson Evidence (Article outlining the basics of arson investigation, collection and preservation of evidence, common myths about arson, and common mistakes made by arson investigators)
www.jwharbert.com/arsonge20033.htm

Arson Investigation (Article about the process of arson investigation)
www.crimeandclues.com/arson.htm

Is It an Accidental Fire or Arson?
www.tcforensic.com.au/docs/article3.html

Fire and Arson Scene Evidence: A Guide for Public Safety Personnel
www.ncjrs.gov/pdffiles1/nij/181584.pdf

Endnotes

1. *Michigan* v. *Tyler,* 436 U.S. 499 (1978).
2. R. T. Newman et al., "The Use of Activated Charcoal Strips for Fire Debris Extractions by Passive Diffusion. Part 1: The Effects of Time, Temperature, Strip Size, and Sample Concentration," *Journal of Forensic Sciences* 41 (1996): 361.
3. M. W. Gilbert, "The Use of Individual Extracted Ion Profiles versus Summed Extracted Ion Profiles in Fire Debris Analysis," *Journal of Forensic Sciences* 43 (1998): 871.

The Oklahoma City Bombing

It was the biggest act of mass murder in U.S. history. On a sunny spring morning in April 1995, a Ryder rental truck pulled into the parking area of the Alfred P. Murrah federal building in Oklahoma City. The driver stepped down from the truck's cab and casually walked away. Minutes later, the truck exploded into a fireball, unleashing enough energy to destroy the building and kill 168 people, including 19 children and infants in the building's day care center.

Later that morning, an Oklahoma Highway Patrol officer pulled over a beat-up 1977 Mercury Marquis being driven without a license plate. On further investigation, the driver, Timothy McVeigh, was found to be in possession of a loaded firearm and charged with transporting a firearm. At the explosion site, remnants of the Ryder truck were located and the truck was quickly traced to a renter—Robert Kling, an alias for Timothy McVeigh. Coincidentally, the rental agreement and McVeigh's driver's license both used the address of McVeigh's friend, Terry Nichols.

Investigators later recovered McVeigh's fingerprint on a receipt for 2,000 pounds of ammonium nitrate, a basic explosive ingredient. Forensic analysts also located PETN residues on the clothing McVeigh wore on the day of his arrest. PETN is a component of detonating cord. After three days of deliberation, a jury declared McVeigh guilty of the bombing and sentenced him to die by lethal injection.

chapter 13

Forensic
Investigation of
Explosions

Key Terms

black powder

deflagration

detonating cord

detonation

explosion

high explosive

low explosive

oxidizing agent

primary explosive

safety fuse

secondary explosive

smokeless powder
(double-base)

smokeless powder
(single-base)

X-ray diffraction

Learning Objectives

After studying this chapter you should be able to:

- Understand how explosives are classified

- List some common commercial, homemade, and military explosives

- Describe how to collect physical evidence at the scene of an explosion

- Describe laboratory procedures used to detect and identify explosive residues.

Explosions and Explosives

The ready accessibility of potentially explosive laboratory chemicals, dynamite, and, in some countries, an assortment of military explosives has provided the criminal element of society with a lethal weapon. Unfortunately for society, explosives have become an attractive weapon to criminals bent on revenge, destruction of commercial operations, or just plain mischief.

Although politically motivated bombings have received considerable publicity worldwide, in the United States most bombing incidents are perpetrated by isolated individuals rather than by organized terrorists. These incidents typically involve homemade explosives and incendiary devices. The design of such weapons is limited only by the imagination and ingenuity of the bomber.

Like arson investigation, bomb investigation requires close cooperation of a group of highly specialized individuals trained and experienced in bomb disposal, bomb-site investigation, forensic analysis, and criminal investigation. The criminalist must detect and identify explosive chemicals recovered from the crime scene as well as identify the detonating mechanisms. This special responsibility concerns us for the remainder of this chapter.

The Chemistry of Explosions

explosion
A chemical or mechanical action caused by combustion, accompanied by creation of heat and rapid expansion of gases.

Like fire, an explosion is the product of combustion accompanied by the creation of gases and heat. However, the distinguishing characteristic of an explosion is the rapid rate of the reaction. The sudden buildup of expanding gas pressure at the origin of the explosion produces the violent physical disruption of the surrounding environment.

Our previous discussion of the chemistry of fire referred only to oxidation reactions that rely on air as the sole source of oxygen. However, we need not restrict ourselves to this type of situation. For example, explosives are substances that undergo a rapid exothermic oxidation reaction, producing large quantities of gases. This sudden buildup of gas pressure constitutes an explosion. Detonation occurs so rapidly that oxygen in the air cannot participate in the reaction; thus, many explosives must have their own source of oxygen.

oxidizing agent
A substance that supplies oxygen to a chemical reaction.

Chemicals that supply oxygen are known as oxidizing agents. One such agent is found in black powder, a *low explosive*, which is composed of a mixture of the following chemical ingredients:

75 percent potassium nitrate (KNO_3)

15 percent charcoal (C)

10 percent sulfur (S)

In this combination, oxygen containing potassium nitrate acts as an oxidizing agent for the charcoal and sulfur fuels. As heat is applied to black powder, oxygen is liberated from potassium nitrate and simultaneously combines with charcoal and sulfur to produce heat and gases (symbolized by ↑), as represented in the following chemical equation:

$$3C \quad + \quad S \quad + \quad 2KNO_3 \qquad \rightarrow$$

carbon   sulfur   potassium nitrate   yields

$$3CO_2{\uparrow} \quad + \quad N_2{\uparrow} \quad + \quad K_2S$$

carbon dioxide   nitrogen   potassium sulfide

Some explosives have their oxygen and fuel components combined within one molecule. For example, the chemical structure of nitroglycerin, the major constituent of dynamite, combines carbon, hydrogen, nitrogen, and oxygen:

$$
\begin{array}{ccc}
H & H & H \\
| & | & | \\
\end{array}
$$
$$ H-C-C-C-H $$
$$
\begin{array}{ccc}
| & | & | \\
NO_2 & NO_2 & NO_2 \\
\end{array}
$$

When nitroglycerin detonates, large quantities of energy are released as the molecule decomposes, and the oxygen recombines to produce large volumes of carbon dioxide, nitrogen, and water.

Consider, for example, the effect of confining an explosive charge to a relatively small, closed container. On detonation, the explosive almost instantaneously produces large volumes of gases that exert enormously high pressures on the interior walls of the container. In addition, the heat energy released by the explosion expands the gases, causing them to push on the walls with an even greater force. If we could observe the effects of an exploding lead pipe in slow motion, we would first see the pipe's walls stretch and balloon under pressures as high as several hundred tons per square inch. Finally, the walls would fragment and fly outward in all directions. This flying debris or shrapnel constitutes a great danger to life and limb in the immediate vicinity.

On release from confinement, the gaseous products of the explosion suddenly expand and compress layers of surrounding air as they move outward from the origin of the explosion. This blast effect, or outward rush of gases, at a rate that may be as high as 7,000 miles per hour creates an artificial gale that can overthrow walls, collapse roofs, and disturb any object in its path. If a bomb is sufficiently powerful, more serious damage will be inflicted by the blast effect than by fragmentation debris (see Figure 13–1).

Types of Explosives

The speed at which explosives decompose varies greatly from one to another and permits their classification as *high* and *low explosives*. In a low explosive, this speed is called the speed of deflagration (burning). It is characterized by very rapid oxidation that produces heat, light, and a subsonic pressure wave. In a high explosive, it is called the speed of detonation. Detonation refers to the creation of a supersonic shock wave within the explosive charge. This shock wave breaks the chemical bonds of the

deflagration
A very rapid oxidation reaction accompanied by the generation of a low-intensity pressure wave that can disrupt the surroundings.

detonation
An extremely rapid oxidation reaction accompanied by a violent disruptive effect and an intense, high-speed shock wave.

FIGURE 13–1 A violent explosion.

explosive charge, leading to the new instantaneous buildup of heat and gases.

low explosive
An explosive with a velocity of detonation less than 1,000 meters per second.

black powder
Normally, a mixture of potassium nitrate, carbon, and sulfur in the ratio 75/15/10.

safety fuse
A cord containing a core of black powder, used to carry a flame at a uniform rate to an explosive charge.

smokeless powder (single-base)
An explosive consisting of nitrocellulose.

smokeless powder (double-base)
An explosive consisting of a mixture of nitrocellulose and nitroglycerin.

Low Explosives Low explosives, such as black and smokeless powders, decompose relatively slowly at rates up to 1,000 meters per second. Because of their slow burning rates, they produce a propelling or throwing action that makes them suitable as propellants for ammunition or skyrockets. However, the danger of this group of explosives must not be underestimated, because when any one of them is confined to a relatively small container, it can explode with a force as lethal as that of any known explosive.

Black Powder and Smokeless Powder The most widely used explosives in the low-explosive group are black powder and smokeless powder. The popularity of these two explosives is enhanced by their accessibility to the public. Both are available in any gun store, and black powder can easily be made from ingredients purchased at any chemical supply house as well.

Black powder is a relatively stable mixture of potassium nitrate or sodium nitrate, charcoal, and sulfur. Unconfined, it merely burns; thus it commonly is used in safety fuses that carry a flame to an explosive charge. A safety fuse usually consists of black powder wrapped in a fabric or plastic casing. When ignited, a sufficient length of fuse will burn at a rate slow enough to allow a person adequate time to leave the site of the pending explosion. Black powder, like any other low explosive, becomes explosive and lethal only when it is confined.

The safest and most powerful low explosive is smokeless powder. This explosive usually consists of nitrated cotton or nitrocellulose (single-base powder) or nitroglycerin mixed with nitrocellulose (double-base powder). The powder is manufactured in a variety of grain sizes and shapes, depending on the desired application (see Figure 13–2).

FIGURE 13–2 Samples of smokeless powders. *Courtesy Bureau of Alcohol, Tobacco, Firearms and Explosives*

Chlorate Mixtures The only ingredients required for a low explosive are fuel and a good oxidizing agent. The oxidizing agent potassium chlorate, for example, when mixed with sugar, produces a popular and accessible explosive mix. When confined to a small container—for example, a pipe—and ignited, this mixture can explode with a force equivalent to a stick of 40 percent dynamite.

Some other commonly encountered ingredients that may be combined with chlorate to produce an explosive are carbon, sulfur, starch, phosphorus, and magnesium filings. Chlorate mixtures may also be ignited by the heat generated from a chemical reaction. For instance, sufficient heat can be generated to initiate combustion when concentrated sulfuric acid comes in contact with a sugar–chlorate mix.

Gas-Air Mixtures Another form of low explosive is created when a considerable quantity of natural gas escapes into a confined area and mixes with a sufficient amount of air. If ignited, this mixture results in simultaneous combustion and sudden production of large volumes of gases and heat. In a building, walls are forced outward by the expanding gases, causing the roof to fall into the interiors, and objects are thrown outward and scattered in erratic directions with no semblance of pattern.

Mixtures of air and a gaseous fuel explode or burn only within a limited concentration range. For example, the concentration limits for methane in air range from 5.3 to 13.9 percent. In the presence of too much air, the fuel becomes too diluted and does not ignite. On the other hand, if the fuel becomes too concentrated, ignition is prevented because there is not enough oxygen to support the combustion.

Mixtures at or near the upper concentration limit ("rich" mixtures) explode; however, some gas remains unconsumed because there is not enough oxygen to complete the combustion. As air rushes back into the origin of the explosion, it combines with the residual hot gas, producing a fire that is characterized by a *whoosh* sound. This fire is often more destructive than the explosion that preceded it. Mixtures near the lower end of the limit ("lean" mixtures) generally cause an explosion without accompanying damage due to fire.

High Explosives High explosives include dynamite, TNT, PETN, and RDX. They detonate almost instantaneously at rates of 1,000–8,500 meters per second, producing a smashing or shattering effect on their target. High explosives are classified into two groups—primary and secondary explosives—based on their sensitivity to heat, shock, or friction.

high explosive
An explosive with a velocity of detonation greater than 1,000 meters per second.

primary explosive
A high explosive that is easily detonated by heat, shock, or friction.

secondary explosive
A high explosive that is relatively insensitive to heat, shock, or friction.

Primary explosives are ultrasensitive to heat, shock, or friction, and under normal conditions detonate violently instead of burning. For this reason, they are used to detonate other explosives through a chain reaction and are often referred to as *primers*. Primary explosives provide the major ingredients of blasting caps and include lead azide, lead styphnate, and diazodinitrophenol (see Figure 13–3). Because of their extreme sensitivity, these explosives are rarely used as the main charge of a homemade bomb.

Secondary explosives are relatively insensitive to heat, shock, or friction, and normally burn rather than detonate when ignited in small quantities in open air. This group comprises most high explosives used for commercial and military blasting. Some common examples of secondary explosives are dynamite, TNT (trinitrotoluene), PETN (pentaerythritol tetranitrate), RDX (cyclotrimethylenetrinitramine), and tetryl (2,4,6-trinitrophenylmethylnitramine).

Dynamite It is an irony of history that the prize most symbolic of humanity's search for peace—the Nobel Peace Prize—should bear the name of the developer of one of our most lethal discoveries—dynamite. In 1867, the Swedish chemist Alfred Nobel, searching for a method to desensitize nitroglycerin, found that when kieselguhr, a variety of diatomaceous earth,

FIGURE 13–3 Blasting caps. The left and center caps are initiated by an electrical current; the right cap is initiated by a safety fuse.

absorbed a large portion of nitroglycerin, it became far less sensitive but still retained its explosive force. Nobel later decided to use pulp as an absorbent because kieselguhr was a heat-absorbing material.

This so-called pulp dynamite was the beginning of what is now known as the straight dynamite series. These dynamites are used when a quick shattering action is desired. In addition to nitroglycerine and pulp, present-day straight dynamites also include sodium nitrate (which furnishes oxygen for complete combustion) and a small percentage of a stabilizer, such as calcium carbonate.

All straight dynamite is rated by strength; the strength rating is determined by the weight percentage of nitroglycerin in the formula. Thus, a 40 percent straight dynamite contains 40 percent nitroglycerin, a 60 percent grade contains 60 percent nitroglycerin, and so forth. However, the relative blasting power of different strengths of dynamite is not directly proportional to their strength ratings. A 60 percent straight dynamite, rather than being three times as strong as a 20 percent, is only one and one-half times as strong (see Figure 13–4).

Ammonium Nitrate Explosives   In recent years, nitroglycerin-based dynamite has all but disappeared from the industrial explosives market. Commercially, these explosives have been replaced mainly by ammonium nitrate–based explosives, that is, water gels, emulsions, and ANFO explosives. These explosives mix oxygen-rich ammonium nitrate with a fuel to form a low-cost and very stable explosive.

Typically, water gels have a consistency resembling that of set gelatin or gel-type toothpaste. They are characterized by their water-resistant nature and are employed for all types of blasting under wet conditions. These explosives are based on formulations of ammonium nitrate and

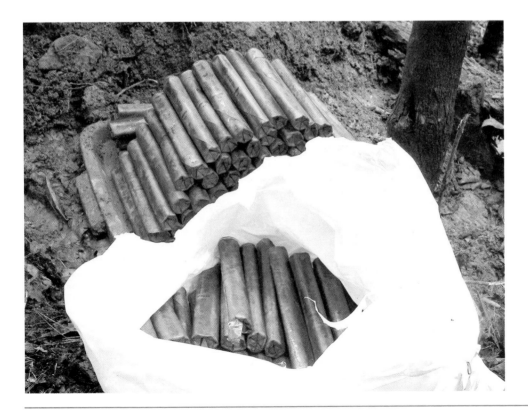

FIGURE 13–4   **Sticks of dynamite.** *Courtesy AP Wide World Photos*

sodium nitrate gelled with a natural polysaccharide such as guar gum. Commonly, a combustible material such as aluminum is mixed into the gel to serve as the explosive's fuel.

Emulsion explosives differ from gels in that they consist of two distinct phases, an oil phase and a water phase. In these emulsions, a droplet of a supersaturated solution of ammonium nitrate is surrounded by a hydrocarbon serving as a fuel. A typical emulsion consists of water, one or more inorganic nitrate oxidizers, oil, and emulsifying agents. Commonly, emulsions contain micron-sized glass, resin, or ceramic spheres known as *microspheres* or *microballoons*. The size of these spheres controls the explosive's sensitivity and detonation velocity.

Ammonium nitrate soaked in fuel oil is an explosive known as *ANFO*. Such commercial explosives are inexpensive and safe to handle and have found wide applications in blasting operations in the mining industry. Ammonium nitrate in the form of fertilizer makes a readily obtainable ingredient for homemade explosives. Indeed, in an incident related to the 1993 bombing of New York City's World Trade Center, the FBI arrested five men during a raid on their hideout in New York City, where they were mixing a "witches' brew" of fuel oil and an ammonium nitrate–based fertilizer.

TATP *Triacetone triperoxide* (TATP) is a homemade explosive that has been used as an improvised explosive by terrorist organizations in Israel and other Middle Eastern countries. It is prepared by reacting the common ingredients of acetone and hydrogen peroxide in the presence of an acid catalyst such as hydrochloric acid.

TATP is a friction- and impact-sensitive explosive that is extremely potent when confined in a container such as a pipe. The 2005 London transit bombings were caused by TATP-based explosives and provide ample evidence that terrorist cells have moved TATP outside the Middle East. A London bus destroyed by one of the TATP bombs is shown in Figure 13–5.

A plot to blow up ten international plane flights leaving Britain for the United States with a "liquid explosive" apparently involved plans to smuggle the peroxide-based TATP explosive onto the planes. This plot has prompted authorities to prohibit airline passengers from carrying liquids and gels onto planes.

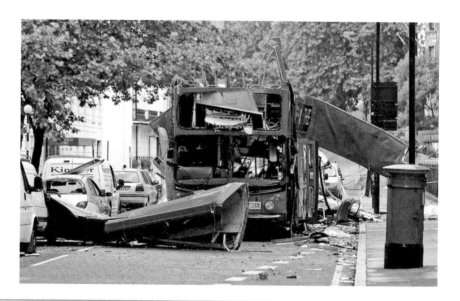

FIGURE 13–5   A London bus destroyed by a TATP-based bomb. *Courtesy AP Wide World Photos*

Forensics at Work

Liquid Explosives

Of the hundreds of types of explosives, most are solid. Only about a dozen are liquid. But some of those liquid explosives can be readily purchased and others can be made from hundreds of different kinds of chemicals that are not difficult to obtain. A memo issued by federal security officials about the plot to blow up ten international planes highlighted a type of liquid explosive based on peroxide.

The most common peroxide explosive is triacetone triperoxide, or TATP, which is made from two liquids: acetone, the primary ingredient of most nail polish removers, and hydrogen peroxide, commonly used in diluted form as an antiseptic. TATP, which can be used as a detonator or a primary explosive, has been used in Qaeda-related bomb plots and by Palestinian suicide bombers.

TATP itself is a white powder made up of crystals that form when acetone and hydrogen peroxide are mixed together, usually with a catalyst added to speed the chemical reactions. But there is no need to wait for the crystals. Acetone and peroxide form is an "exceedingly reactive mixture" that can be easily detonated by an electrical spark, said Neal Langerman, president of Advanced Chemical Safety, a consulting company in San Diego.

Acetone is easy to obtain; hydrogen peroxide is somewhat more difficult to obtain. The hydrogen peroxide solution sold in pharmacies is too dilute—only 3 percent—to be used in an explosive. Stronger hydrogen peroxide of 30 percent concentration can be ordered from chemical supply companies, but concentrations strong enough to generate a powerful explosion—about 70 percent—are not readily available, Dr. Langerman said.

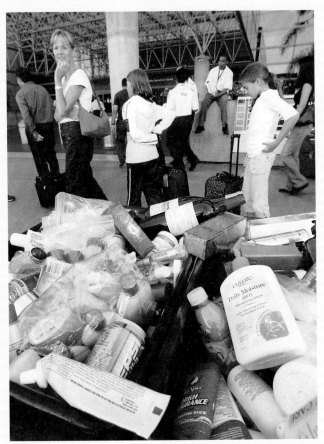

Liquids and gels discarded by airline passengers before boarding. *Stefano Paltera, AP Wide World Photos*

(*continued*)

Forensics at Work

Liquid Explosives (*continued*)

But Dr. Langerman added that acetone mixed with a 30 percent peroxide solution could still set off a fire that might burn through the aluminum skin of an airliner and cause it to crash. "All of them are highly energetic," he said of the various chemical combinations. "It doesn't take much to punch a hole in the side of a plane, and if you punch a hole in the side of a plane, the plane comes down."

In theory, scientists know how to detect peroxide based explosives. The challenge will be to design machines that can perform the scans quickly and efficiently on thousands of passengers passing through security checks. "It will not be easy as the swab tests we are using for nitrogen compounds right now," Dr. Langerman said. Other common liquid explosives, such as nitroglycerine and nitromethane (the fuel of dragster race cars) contain nitrogen compounds, so it may be possible to adjust current scanning machines to detect them.

Robert M. Blitzer, a former FBI terrorism official now at ICF International in Fairfax, Virginia, said the Bureau had worried for more than 15 years about the possibility of liquid explosives on airliners. "We were very concerned about any form of explosive material, including liquids and gels," he said. But after the September 11 attacks worries about solid explosives became the main concern. It is therefore not surprising that terrorists turned to liquids in this latest plot, said Jimmie C. Oxley, an expert on the chemistry of explosives at the University of Rhode Island who has advised federal officials.

"It was not seen as the threat," she said. "Now that the terrorists have staked out our vulnerabilities, that's where the threat has gone, and we'll have to respond." But, once new equipment gets into airports to reduce the threat of liquid explosives, Dr. Oxley said, terrorists will "look for the next vulnerability."

Source: Kenneth Chang and William J. Broad, "Lethal and Wet: It's Not Hard to Use Fluids to Cause an Explosion on a Plane, Chemists Say, "*New York Times*, August 11, 2006. Copyright © 2006 by the New York Times Company. Reprinted by permission.

Military High Explosives   No discussion of high explosives would be complete without a mention of military high explosives. In many countries outside the United States, the accessibility of high explosives to terrorist organizations makes them very common constituents of homemade bombs. RDX, the most popular and powerful military explosive, is often encountered in the form of a pliable plastic of doughlike consistency known as *composition C–4* (a U.S. military designation).

TNT was produced and used on an enormous scale during World War II and may be considered the most important military bursting charge explosive. Alone or in combination with other explosives, it has found wide application in shells, bombs, grenades, demolition explosives, and propellant compositions (see Figure 13–6). Interestingly, military "dynamite" contains no nitroglycerin but is actually composed of a mixture of RDX and TNT. Like other military explosives, TNT is rarely encountered in bombings in the United States.

FIGURE 13–6   Military explosives in combat use. *Courtesy Getty Images/Time Life Pictures*

PETN is used by the military in TNT mixtures for small-caliber projectiles and grenades. Commercially, the chemical is used as the explosive core in a **detonating cord** or *primacord*. Instead of the slower-burning safety fuse, a detonating cord is often used to connect a series of explosive charges so that they will detonate simultaneously.

Detonators   Unlike low explosives, bombs made of high explosives must be detonated by an initiating explosion. In most cases, detonators are blasting caps composed of copper or aluminum cases filled with lead azide as an initiating charge and PETN or RDX as a detonating charge. Blasting caps can be initiated by means of a burning safety fuse or by an electrical current.

Homemade bombs camouflaged in packages, suitcases, and the like are usually initiated with an electrical blasting cap wired to a battery. An unlimited number of switching-mechanism designs have been devised for setting off these devices; clocks and mercury switches are favored. Bombers sometimes prefer to employ outside electrical sources. For instance, most automobile bombs are detonated when the ignition switch of a car is turned on.

detonating cord
A cordlike explosive containing a core of high-explosive material, usually PETN; also called primacord.

Key Points

- Explosives are substances that undergo a rapid oxidation reaction with the production of large quantities of gases. The sudden buildup of gas pressure leads to the explosion.

- The speed at which an explosive decomposes determines whether it is classified as a high or low explosive.

- The most widely used low explosives are black powder and smokeless powder. Common high explosives include ammonium nitrate–based explosives (water gels, emulsions, and ANFO explosives).

- Among the high explosives, primary explosives are ultrasensitive to heat, shock, or friction and provide the major ingredients found in blasting caps. Secondary explosives normally constitute the main charge of a high explosive.

Collection and Analysis of Evidence of Explosives

The most important step in the detection and analysis of explosive residues is the collection of appropriate samples from the explosion scene. Invariably, undetonated residues of the explosive remain at the site of the explosion. The detection and identification of these explosives in the laboratory depends on the bomb-scene investigator's skill and ability to recognize and sample the areas most likely to contain such materials.

Detecting and Recovering Evidence of Explosives

The most obvious characteristic of a high or contained low explosive is the presence of a crater at the origin of the blast. Once the crater has been located, all loose soil and other debris must immediately be removed from the interior of the hole and preserved for laboratory analysis. Other good sources of explosive residues are objects located near the origin of detonation. Wood, insulation, rubber, and other soft materials that are readily penetrated often collect traces of the explosive. However, nonporous objects near the blast must not be overlooked. For instance, residues can be found on the surfaces of metal objects near the site of an explosion. Material blown away from the blast's origin should also be recovered because it, too, may retain explosive residues.

The entire area must be systematically searched, with great care given to recovering any trace of a detonating mechanism or any other item foreign to the explosion site. Wire-mesh screens are best used for sifting through debris. All personnel involved in searching the bomb scene must take appropriate measures to avoid contaminating the scene, including dressing in disposable gloves, shoe covers, and overalls.

Ion Mobility Spectrometer   In pipe-bomb explosions, particles of the explosive are frequently found adhering to the pipe cap or to the pipe threads, as a result of either being impacted into the metal by the force of the explosion or being deposited in the threads during the construction of the bomb. One approach for screening objects for the presence of explosive residues in the field or the laboratory is the ion mobility spectrometer (IMS).[1] A portable IMS is shown in Figure 13–7.

This handheld detector uses a vacuum to collect explosive residues from suspect surfaces. Alternatively, the surface suspected of containing explosive residues is wiped down with a Teflon-coated fiberglass disc and the collected residues are then drawn into the spectrometer off the disc. Once in the IMS, the explosive residues are vaporized by the application of heat. These vaporized substances are exposed to a beam of electrons or beta rays emitted by radioactive nickel and converted into electrically charged molecules or ions. The ions are then allowed to move through a tube (drift region) under the influence of an electric field. A schematic diagram of an IMS is shown in Figure 13–8.

FIGURE 13–7 A portable ion mobility spectrometer used to rapidly detect and tentatively identify trace quantities of explosives. *Courtesy GE Ion Track, Wilmington, Mass. 01887*

The preliminary identification of an explosive residue can be made by noting the time it takes the explosive to move through the tube. Because ions move at different speeds depending on their size and structure, they can be characterized by the speed at which they pass through the tube. Used as a screening tool, this method rapidly detects a full range of explosives, even at low detection levels. However, all results need to be verified through confirmatory tests.

The IMS can detect plastic explosives as well as commercial and military explosives. More than 10,000 portable and full-size IMS units are currently used at airport security checkpoints, and more than 50,000 handheld IMS analyzers have been deployed for chemical-weapons monitoring in various armed forces.

Collection and Packaging All materials collected for examination by the laboratory must be placed in airtight sealed containers and labeled with all pertinent information. Soil and other soft loose materials are best stored in metal airtight containers such as clean paint cans. Debris and articles collected from different areas are to be packaged in separate airtight containers. Plastic bags should not be used to store evidence suspected of containing explosive residues. Some explosives can actually escape through the plastic. Sharp-edged objects should not be allowed to pierce the sides of a plastic bag. It is best to place these types of items in metal containers.

Key Points

- The entire bomb site must be systematically searched to recover any trace of a detonating mechanism or any other item foreign to the explosion site. Objects located at or near the origin of the explosion must be collected for laboratory examination.

(a)

(b)

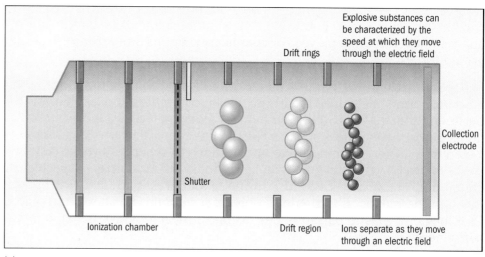

(c)

FIGURE 13–8 Schematic diagram of an ion mobility spectrometer. A sample is introduced into an ionization chamber, where bombardment with radioactive particles emitted by an isotope of nickel converts the sample to ions. The ions move into a drift region where ion separation occurs based on the speed of the ions as they move through an electric field.

- The most obvious characteristic of a high or contained low explosive is the presence of a crater at the origin of the blast.

- A device widely used to screen objects for the presence of explosive residues is the ion mobility spectrometer.

- All materials collected at bombing scenes must be placed in airtight containers such as clean paint cans.

Analysis of Evidence of Explosives

When the bomb-scene debris and other materials arrive at the laboratory, everything is first examined microscopically to detect particles of unconsumed explosive. Portions of the recovered debris and detonating mechanism, if found, are carefully viewed under a low-power stereoscopic microscope in a painstaking effort to locate particles of the explosive. Black powder and smokeless powder are relatively easy to locate in debris because of their characteristic shapes and colors (see Figure 13–2). However, dynamite and other high explosives present the microscopist with a much more difficult task and often must be detected by other means.

Following microscopic examination, the recovered debris is thoroughly rinsed with acetone. The high solubility of most explosives in acetone ensures their quick removal from the debris. When a water-gel explosive containing ammonium nitrate or a low explosive is suspected, the debris should be rinsed with water so that water-soluble substances (such as nitrates and chlorates) will be extracted. Table 13–1 lists a number of simple color tests the examiner can perform on the acetone and water extracts to screen for the presence of organic and inorganic explosives, respectively.

Screening and Confirmation Tests Once collected, the acetone extract is concentrated and analyzed using color spot tests, thin-layer chromatography (TLC), and gas chromatography/mass spectrometry. The presence of an explosive is indicated by a well-defined spot on a TLC plate with an R_f value corresponding to a known explosive—for example, nitroglycerin, RDX, or PETN.

When sufficient quantities of explosives are recoverable, confirmatory tests may be performed by either infrared spectrophotometry or X-ray diffraction. The former produces a unique "fingerprint" pattern for an organic explosive, as shown by the IR spectrum of RDX in Figure 13–9. The latter provides a unique diffraction pattern for inorganic substances such as potassium nitrate and potassium chlorate.

Taggants An explosive "taggant" program has been proposed to further enhance a bomb-scene investigator's chances of recovering useful evidence at a postexplosion scene. Under this proposal, tiny color-coded chips the size of sand grains would be added to commercial explosives during their manufacture. Some of these chips would be expected to survive an explosion and be capable of recovery at explosion scenes. To aid in their recovery, the chips are made both fluorescent and magnetic sensitive. Hence, investigators can search for taggants at the explosion site with magnetic tools and ultraviolet light.

Table 13–1 Color Spot Tests for Common Explosives

Substance	Reagent		
	Griess[a]	Diphenylamine[b]	Alcoholic KOH[c]
Chlorate	No color	Blue	No color
Nitrate	Pink to red	Blue	No color
Nitrocellulose	Pink	Blue-black	No color
Nitroglycerin	Pink to red	Blue	No color
PETN	Pink to red	Blue	No color
RDX	Pink to red	Blue	No color
TNT	No color	No color	Red
Tetryl	Pink to red	Blue	Red-violet

[a]Griess reagent: Solution 1—Dissolve 1 g sulfanilic acid in 100 mL 30% acetic acid. Solution 2—Dissolve 0.5 g *N*-(1-napthyl) ethylenediamine in 100 mL methyl alcohol. Add solutions 1 and 2 and a few milligrams of zinc dust to the suspect extract.
[b]Diphenylamine reagent: Dissolve 1 g diphenylamine in 100 mL concentrated sulfuric acid.
[c]Alcoholic KOH reagent: Dissolve 10 g of potassium hydroxide in 100 mL absolute alcohol.

The taggant chip is arranged in a color sequence that indicates where the explosive was made and when it was produced (see Figure 13–10). With this knowledge, the explosive can be traced through its distribution chain to its final legal possessor. The taggant colors are readily observed and are read with the aid of a low-power microscope.

There are no plans to institute a taggant program for commercial explosives in the United States. In Europe, only Switzerland has adopted a taggant program; thus, it is extremely doubtful that taggants will be found in any significant number of bombing incidents in the foreseeable future. Interestingly, the International Civil Aviation Organization has mandated that a volatile taggant be added to plastic explosives during their manufacture in order to facilitate the detection of these explosives. Programs are now under way to tag commercial C–4 with the volatile chemical known as DMNB (2,3-dimethyl-2,3-dinitrobutane).

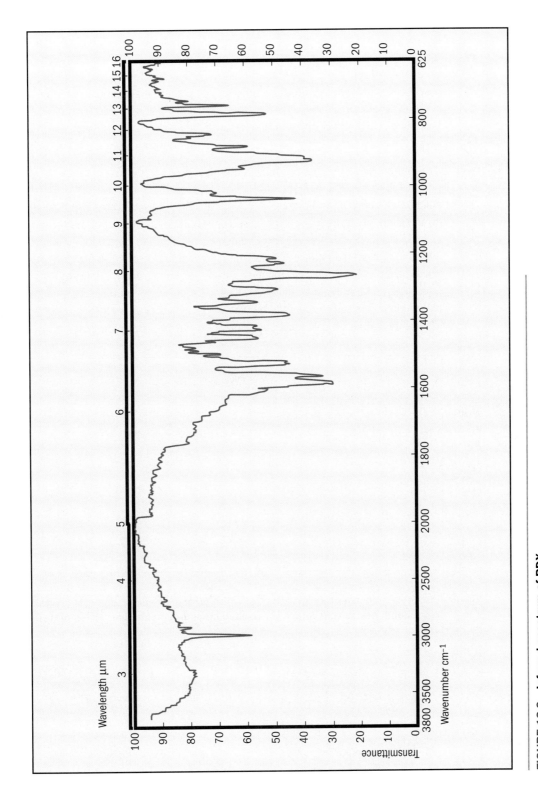

FIGURE 13-9 Infrared spectrum of RDX.

Closer Analysis

X-Ray Diffraction

x-ray diffraction
An analytical technique for identifying crystalline materials.

One way to elicit information about how elements have combined to constitute the makeup of a particular substance is to aim a beam of X-rays at the material and study how the X-rays interact with the atoms that compose the substance under investigation. This technique is known as **X-ray diffraction**.

X-ray diffraction can be applied only to the study of solid, crystalline materials—that is, solids with a definite and orderly arrangement of atoms. For example, sodium chloride (common table salt) is crystalline. Fortunately, many substances, including 95 percent of all inorganic compounds, are crystalline and are thus identifiable by X-ray diffraction analysis. The atoms in a crystal may be thought of as being composed of a

series of parallel planes. As the X-rays penetrate the crystal, a portion of the beam is reflected by each of the atomic planes. As the reflected beams leave the crystal's planes, they combine with one another to form a series of light and dark bands known as a *diffraction pattern*. Every compound produces a unique diffraction pattern, thus giving analysts a means for "fingerprinting" compounds.

Figure 1 illustrates the X-ray diffraction process. Diffraction patterns for potassium nitrate and potassium chlorate, two common constituents of homemade explosives, are shown in Figure 2. Comparing a questioned specimen with a known X-ray pattern is a rapid and specific way to prove chemical identity.

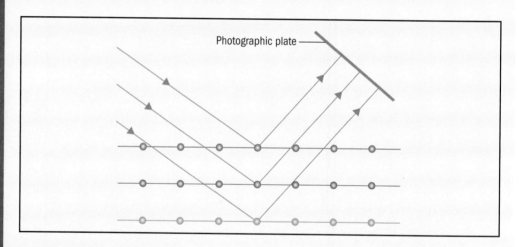

Photographic plate

FIGURE 1 **A beam of X-rays being reflected off the atomic planes of a crystal. The diffraction patterns that form are recorded on photographic film. These patterns are unique for each crystalline substance.**

(a)

(b)

FIGURE 2 **X-ray diffraction patterns for (a) potassium nitrate and (b) potassium chlorate.**

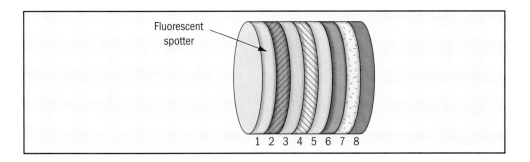

Fluorescent spotter

1 2 3 4 5 6 7 8

FIGURE 13–10   Cross-section of a taggant. The color sequence of the recovered taggant is observed with the aid of a low-power microscope. The colors are then matched to a color code to yield information about the plant of manufacture, production lot, and purchasers of the explosive material.

Forensics at Work

The Crash of TWA Flight 800

Although the crash of TWA Flight 800 was ultimately not proven to be an act of terrorism, the initial investigation revealed the difficulties investigators can expect to encounter in recovering explosive residues at bombing scenes. For example, in spite of the large quantities of explosive used, investigators encountered extreme difficulties in recovering explosive residues at both the World Trade Center (1993) and Oklahoma federal building bombing sites.

The Search: The TWA Plane Crash

Three weeks after the Atlantic Ocean swallowed a flaming Boeing 747, investigators continue to explore a prevailing theory that the downfall of Trans World Airlines Flight 800 was caused by a bomb. But their complicated mission is made all the more complex by the very water in which much of the plane rests.

Investigators say they are still concerned that the extended submersion in saltwater

FBI agents and New York State Police guard the reconstruction of TWA Flight 800. *Courtesy Mark Lennihan, AP Wide World Photos*

(continued)

Forensics at Work

The Crash of TWA Flight 800 (*continued*)

might have an effect on telltale chemical traces that a bomb would have left on airplane aluminum, plastic containers, luggage—and anything else from the jumbo jet's front end, where, investigators theorize, the explosion that downed the aircraft took place. More than 80 percent of the airplane remains scattered on the ocean floor, 120 feet down.

Their worry has heightened the sense of urgency in recovering debris from the water, said Joseph Cantamessa Jr., an F.B.I. special agent in charge. "It's the reason we have been so impatient about getting the evidence in the lab for testing."

Christopher Ronay, the former head of the Federal Bureau of Investigation's explosives unit and now president of the Institute of Makers of Explosives in Washington, D.C., said investigators have cause for concern. "Your explosive residue," he said, "adheres to all sorts of materials—to carpet fibers and upholstery and plastics, and it can be trapped in the surface material through all sorts of means. And certainly water washes away some kinds of residues."

But the July 17 explosion of Flight 800, which killed all 230 people on board, remains a puzzle in many pieces. As Mr. Ronay and others point out, the airplane may or may not have been brought down by a bomb. And if a bomb was the cause, the explosive material could have been one of several kinds. And depending on the kind of explosive, ocean water could either wash away the chemical residue or have little effect.

Dr. Jesse L. Beauchamp, a chemistry professor at the California Institute of Technology in Pasadena, said: "It goes without saying that any traces of explosives that were present on wreckage would likely be partially removed—not entirely removed—by continued exposure to saltwater. But it depends on the type of explosives."

Mr. Ronay, who helped coordinate the bureau's successful investigation into the fatal explosion of Pan Am Flight 103 over Lockerbie, Scotland in 1988, expressed confidence in the F.B.I. laboratory's sophisticated equipment and in Tom Thurman, his successor as chief of the explosives unit and the case agent in the Lockerbie investigation.

Mr. Thurman and his team of forensic specialists have been examining the recovered airplane debris at a hangar in Calverton, L.I. In general they are concentrating on two avenues of inquiry: finding any explosive's chemical residue, and searching for pockmarks, tearing and other signs found on items that were near the explosion, often called "witness material."

In an explosion, a chemical reaction transforms the explosive material into gas. But some of that material is merely scattered, albeit in microscopic fragments. And that is what the forensic investigator seeks.

"There's almost always some residue," said Dr. Jimmie Oxley, a professor of chemistry at the University of Rhode Island. "And you look for something abnormal in the chemical analysis, something that shouldn't be there."

Dr. Oxley, who is a consultant to the F.B.I. and the Bureau of Alcohol, Tobacco and Firearms, said that investigators undoubtedly are rinsing airplane parts with an organic solvent to see if there is organic material that would not normally be present. "If you found traces of a military explosive such as RDX, which is not water soluble, it would have no reason for possibly being there," she said. "So now you have positive evidence."

But the ocean presents another variable. "On the other hand, if you never find anything at all, you can't draw any conclusions," Dr. Oxley said. "Now you've got to look at a lot of other things. There are explosive materials that could have been used that are water soluble. There is ammonium nitrate fuel oil, which is water soluble except for the oil. And this stuff has been bathing down there for a long time."

Even in the case of ammonium nitrate fuel oil, or ANFO, the material used in last year's deadly bombing of a Federal building in Oklahoma City, the investigators would expect to find traces of insoluble materials used to detonate the mixture.

Investigators in Calverton are using tools such as a gas chromatograph, which separates organic components, and a mass spectrometer, which identifies each component by its molecular weight. But Mr. Ronay said that more in-depth analysis is being done at the F.B.I. laboratory in Washington where, he said, there are specific instruments to use on specific explosives.

"Their equipment is so sensitive that it can track material in parts per trillion," he said. "I don't think a shark can smell blood in the water to that degree."

Still, Mr. Ronay acknowledged the difficulty that his former colleagues face. "It's such a big, big project," he said. "And you might never find the right piece."

That would force investigators to focus on the other avenue of inquiry—the hunt for a specific kind of tear in metal, or the pitting in a piece of luggage that might have been near the source of an explosion.

"If they never find the residue, the experts will probably characterize the damage and make some estimates regarding the kind of explosive that was used," Mr. Ronay said. "But if you find residue, you don't need to guess."

Source: Dan Barry, "Saltwater's Ill Effects Depend on Bomb Type," *New York Times*, August 7, 1996, p. B-5. Copyright © 1996 by the New York Times Company. Reprinted with permission.

Key Points

- Debris collected at explosion scenes is examined microscopically for unconsumed explosive particles.

- Recovered debris may be thoroughly rinsed with organic solvents and analyzed by testing procedures that include color spot tests, thin-layer chromatography, and gas chromatography/mass spectrometry.

- Unconsumed explosives are identified by either infrared spectrophotometry or X-ray diffraction.

Chapter Summary

Explosives are substances that undergo a rapid oxidation reaction with the production of large quantities of gases. This sudden buildup of gas pressure constitutes an explosion. The speed at which explosives decompose permits their classification as high or low explosives.

The most widely used low explosives are black powder and smokeless powder. Among the high explosives, primary explosives are ultrasensitive to heat, shock, or friction and provide the major ingredients found in blasting caps. Secondary explosives normally constitute the main charge of a high explosive.

Among the high explosives, nitroglycerin-based dynamite has all but disappeared from the industrial explosives market and has been replaced by ammonium nitrate–based explosives (such as water gels, emulsions, and ANFO explosives). In many countries outside the United States, the accessibility of military high explosives to terrorist organizations makes them very common constituents of homemade bombs. RDX is the most popular and powerful of the military explosives.

The entire bomb site must be systematically searched with great care given to recovering any trace of a detonating mechanism or any other item foreign to the explosion site. Objects located at or near the origin of the explosion must be collected for laboratory examination.

Typically, in the laboratory, debris collected at explosion scenes is examined microscopically for unconsumed explosive particles. Recovered debris may also be thoroughly rinsed with organic solvents and analyzed by testing procedures that include color spot tests, thin-layer chromatography, high-performance liquid chromatography, and gas chromatography/mass spectrometry.

Review Questions

Facts and Concepts

1. What produces the violent physical disruption associated with an explosion?

2. What is the difference between deflagration and detonation?

3. What is the difference between low explosives and high explosives?

4. What are the most widely used low explosives?

5. What is a safety fuse and what is it used for?

6. What ingredients are required to create a low explosive?

7. What are the two classes of high explosives? What is the difference between the two classes?

8. What are the main ingredients in straight dynamite? What other substances also are included in modern straight dynamites and what purpose do they serve?

9. What types of explosives largely have replaced dynamite for industrial uses? What are the advantages of these types of explosives?

10. What is ANFO?

11. Name three military high explosives. Which is the most powerful and popular of these explosives?

12. What is a detonator? What is the composition of most detonators?

13. What is the most obvious post-explosion characteristic of a high or contained low explosive?

14. What device is widely used to screen objects for the presence of explosive residues?

15. How are soil and other soft loose materials collected at the scene of an explosion best stored?

16. What is the first procedure typically used to analyze bomb-scene debris that arrives in the laboratory?

17. What does the forensic scientist do to explosive debris following microscopic examination? Why?

18. List three procedures commonly used as screening tests for explosive residues.

19. Name two confirmatory tests for the presence of intact explosives located in debris.

20. What is a taggant? What purpose do taggants serve?

Application and Critical Thinking

1. The following pieces of evidence were found at separate explosion sites. For each item, indicate whether the explosion was more likely caused by low or high explosives, and explain your answer:

   a. lead azide residues
   b. nitrocellulose residues
   c. ammonium nitrate residues
   d. scraps of primacord
   e. potassium chlorate residues

2. Which color test or tests would you run first on a suspect sample to test for evidence of each of the following explosives? Explain your answers.

   a. tetryl
   b. TNT
   c. chlorate
   d. nitrocellulose

3. Criminalist Matt Weir is collecting evidence from the site of an explosion. Arriving on the scene, he immediately proceeds to look for the crater caused by the blast. After finding the crater, he picks through the debris at the site by hand, looking for evidence of detonators or foreign materials. Matt collects loose soil and debris from the immediate area, placing the smaller bits in paper folded into a druggist fold. Larger items he stores in plastic bags for transportation to the laboratory. What mistakes, if any, did Matt make in collecting and storing this evidence?

Web Resources

A Guide for Explosion and Bombing Scene Investigation (Adobe Acrobat publication from the U.S. Department of Justice outlining federal procedures for investigation of explosions)
www.bombsecurity.com/downloads2/nij_181869.pdf

Arson and Explosives (Article that discusses principles of combustion, types of explosives, and investigation of explosion sites; includes brief list of links to other sites about arson and explosives)
faculty.ncwc.edu/toconnor/425/425lect07.htm

Pyrotechnics, Explosives, & Fireworks (Detailed article on the workings and types of explosives; has good material about low explosives, high explosives, and taggants)
www.faqs.org/docs/air/ttpyro.html

Endnotes

1. T. Keller et al., "Application of Ion Mobility Spectrometry in Cases of Forensic Interest," *Forensic Science International, 161* (2006):130.

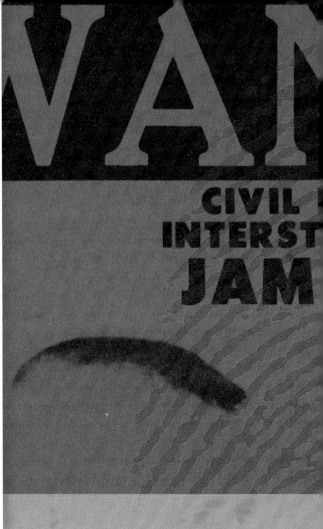

James Earl Ray: Conspirator or Lone Gunman?

Since his arrest in 1968 for the assassination of Dr. Martin Luther King, Jr., endless speculation has swirled around the motives and connections of James Earl Ray. Ray was a career criminal who was serving time for armed robbery when he escaped from the Missouri State Prison almost one year before the assassination. On April 3, 1968, Ray arrived in Memphis, Tennessee. The next day he rented a room at Bessie Brewer's Rooming House, across the street from the Lorraine Motel where Dr. King was staying.

At 6:00 p.m., Dr. King left his second-story motel room and stepped onto the balcony. As King turned toward his room, a shot rang out, striking the civil rights activist. Nothing could be done to revive him and Dr. King was pronounced dead at 7:05 p.m. As the assailant ran on foot from

Bessie Brewer's, he left a blanket-covered package in front of a nearby building and then drove off in a white Mustang. The package contained a high-powered rifle equipped with a scope, a radio, some clothes, a pair of binoculars, a couple of beer cans, and a receipt for the binoculars. Almost a week after the shooting, the white Mustang was found abandoned in Atlanta, Georgia.

Fingerprints later identified as James Earl Ray's were found in the Mustang, on the rifle, on the binoculars, and on a beer can. In 1969, Ray entered a guilty plea in return for a sentence of ninety-nine years. While a variety of conspiracy theories surround this crime, the indisputable fact is that a fingerprint put the rifle that killed Martin Luther King, Jr., in the hands of James Earl Ray.

Fingerprints

Photograph

History of Fingerprinting

Since the beginnings of criminal investigation, police have sought an infallible means of human identification. The first systematic attempt at personal identification was devised and introduced by a French police expert, Alphonse Bertillon, in 1883. The Bertillon system relied on a detailed description (portrait parlé) of the subject, combined with full-length and profile photographs and a system of precise body measurements known as anthropometry.

The use of anthropometry as a method of identification rested on the premise that the dimensions of the human bone system remained fixed from age 20 until death. Skeleton sizes were thought to be so extremely diverse that no two individuals could have exactly the same measurements. Bertillon recommended routine taking of eleven measurements of the human anatomy, including height, reach, width of head, and length of the left foot (see Figure 1–1).

For two decades, this system was considered the most accurate method of identification. But in the early years of the twentieth century, police began to appreciate and accept a system of identification based on the classification of finger ridge patterns known as *fingerprints*. Today, the fingerprint is the pillar of modern criminal identification.

Early Use of Fingerprints

The Chinese used fingerprints to sign legal documents as far back as three thousand years ago. Whether this practice was performed for ceremonial custom or as a means of personal identity remains a point of conjecture lost to history. In any case, the examples of fingerprinting in ancient history are ambiguous, and the few that exist did not contribute to the development of fingerprinting techniques as we know them today.

Several years before Bertillon began work on his system, William Herschel, an English civil servant stationed in India, started requiring natives to sign contracts with the imprint of their right hand, which was pressed against a stamp pad for the purpose. The motives for Herschel's requirement remain unclear; he may have envisioned fingerprinting as a means of personal identification or just as a form of the Hindu custom that a trace of bodily contact was more binding than a signature on a contract. In any case, he did not publish anything about his activities until after a Scottish physician, Henry Fauld, working in a hospital in Japan, published his views on the potential application of fingerprinting to personal identification.

portrait parlé
A verbal description of a perpetrator's physical characteristics and dress provided by an eyewitness.

anthropometry
A system of identification of individuals by measurement of parts of the body, developed by Alphonse Bertillon.

In 1880, Fauld suggested that skin ridge patterns could be important for the identification of criminals. He told about a thief who left his fingerprint on a whitewashed wall, and how in comparing these prints with those of a suspect, he found that they were quite different. A few days later another suspect was found whose fingerprints compared with those on the wall. When confronted with this evidence, the individual confessed to the crime.

Fauld was convinced that fingerprints furnished infallible proof of identification. He even offered to set up at his own expense a fingerprint bureau at Scotland Yard to test the practicality of the method. But his offer was rejected in favor of the Bertillon system. This decision was reversed less than two decades later.

Early Classification of Fingerprints

The extensive research into fingerprinting conducted by another Englishman, Francis Galton, provided the needed impetus that made police agencies aware of its potential application. In 1892, Galton published his classic textbook *Finger Prints,* the first book of its kind on the subject. In his book, Galton discussed the anatomy of fingerprints and suggested methods for recording them. He also proposed assigning fingerprints to three pattern types—loops, arches, and whorls. Most important, the book demonstrated that no two prints are identical and that an individual's prints remain unchanged from year to year. At Galton's insistence, the British government adopted fingerprinting as a supplement to the Bertillon system.

The next step in the development of fingerprint technology was the creation of classification systems capable of filing thousands of prints in a logical and searchable sequence. Dr. Juan Vucetich, an Argentinian police officer fascinated by Galton's work, devised a workable concept in 1891. His classification system has been refined over the years and is still widely used today in most Spanish-speaking countries. In 1897, another classification system was proposed by an Englishman, Sir Edward Richard Henry. Four years later, Henry's system was adopted by Scotland Yard. Today, most English-speaking countries, including the United States, use some version of Henry's classification system to file fingerprints.

Adoption of Fingerprinting

Early in the twentieth century, Bertillon's measurement system began to fall into disfavor. Its results were highly susceptible to error, particularly when the measurements were taken by people who were not thoroughly trained. The method was dealt its most severe and notable setback in 1903 when a convict, Will West, arrived at Fort Leavenworth prison. A routine check of the prison files startlingly revealed that a William West, already in the prison, could not be distinguished from the new prisoner by body measurements or even by photographs. In fact, the two men looked just like twins, and their measurements were practically the same. Subsequently, fingerprints of the prisoners clearly distinguished them.

In the United States, the first systematic and official use of fingerprints for personal identification was adopted by the New York City Civil Service Commission in 1901. The method was used for certifying all civil service applications. Several American police officials received instruction in fingerprint identification at the 1904 World's Fair in St. Louis from representatives of Scotland Yard. After the fair and the Will West incident, fingerprinting began to be used in earnest in all major cities of the United States.

In 1924, the fingerprint records of the Bureau of Investigation and Leavenworth were merged to form the nucleus of the identification records of the new Federal Bureau of Investigation. The FBI has the largest collection of fingerprints in the world. By the beginning of World War I, England and practically all of Europe had adopted fingerprinting as their primary method of identifying criminals.

Fundamental Principles of Fingerprints

Since Galton's time, and as a result of his efforts, fingerprints have become an integral part of policing and forensic science. The principal reason for this is that fingerprints constitute a unique and unchanging means of personal identification. In fact, fingerprint analysts have formulated three basic principles of fingerprints that encompass these notions of the uniqueness and stability of fingerprint identification.

First Principle: A Fingerprint Is an Individual Characteristic; No Two Fingers Have Yet Been Found to Possess Identical Ridge Characteristics

The acceptance of fingerprint evidence by the courts has always been predicated on the assumption that no two individuals have identical fingerprints. Early fingerprint experts consistently referred to Galton's calculation, showing the possible existence of 64 billion different fingerprints, to support this contention. Later, researchers questioned the validity of Galton's figures and attempted to devise mathematical models to better approximate this value. However, no matter what mathematical model one refers to, the conclusions are always the same: The probability for the existence of two identical fingerprint patterns in the world's population is extremely small.

Not only is this principle supported by theoretical calculations, but just as important, it is verified by the millions of individuals who have had their prints classified during the past 110 years—no two have ever been found to be identical. The FBI has nearly 50 million fingerprint records in its computer database and has yet to find an identical image belonging to two different people.

ridge characteristics (minutiae)
Ridge endings, bifurcations, enclosures, and other ridge details, which must match in two fingerprints to establish their common origin.

The individuality of a fingerprint is not determined by its general shape or pattern but by a careful study of its ridge characteristics (also known as minutiae). The identity, number, and relative location of characteristics such as those illustrated in Figure 14–1 impart individuality to a fingerprint. If two prints are to match, they must reveal characteristics that not only are identical but have the same relative location to one another in a print. In a judicial proceeding, a point-by-point comparison must be demonstrated by the expert, using charts similar to the one shown in Figure 14–2, in order to prove the identity of an individual.

An expert can easily compare the characteristics of the complete fingerprint; the average fingerprint has as many as 150 individual ridge characteristics. However, most prints recovered at crime scenes are partial impressions, showing only a segment of the entire print. Under these

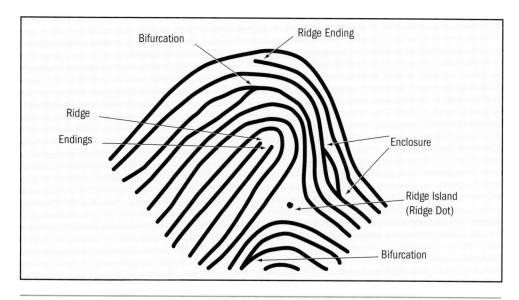

FIGURE 14–1 **Fingerprint ridge characteristics.** *Courtesy Sirchie Finger Print Laboratories, Inc., Youngsville, N.C., www.sirchie.com*

1. Bifurcation	5. Bifurcation	9. Ridge ending
2. Ridge ending	6. Bifurcation	10. Short ridge
3. Enclosure	7. Bifurcation	11. Bifurcation
4. Ridge ending	8. Ridge ending	12. Ridge ending

FIGURE 14–2 **A fingerprint exhibit illustrating the matching ridge characteristics between the crime-scene print and an inked impression of one of the suspect's fingers.** *Courtesy New Jersey State Police*

circumstances, the expert can compare only a small number of ridge characteristics from the recovered print to a known recorded print.

For years, experts have debated how many ridge comparisons are necessary to identify two fingerprints as the same. Numbers that range from eight to sixteen have been suggested as being sufficient to meet the criteria of individuality. However, the difficulty in establishing such a minimum is that no comprehensive statistical study has ever determined the frequency of occurrence of different ridge characteristics and their relative locations. Until such a study is undertaken and completed, no meaningful guidelines can be established for defining the uniqueness of a fingerprint.

In 1973, the International Association for Identification, after a three-year study of this question, concluded that "no valid basis exists for requiring a predetermined minimum number of friction ridge characters which must be present in two impressions in order to establish positive identification." Hence, the final determination must be based on the experience and knowledge of the expert, with the understanding that others may profess honest differences of opinion on the uniqueness of a fingerprint if the question of minimal number of ridge characteristics exists. In 1995, members of the international fingerprint community at a conference in Israel issued the Ne'urim Declaration, which supported the 1973 International Association for Identification resolution.

Second Principle: A Fingerprint Remains Unchanged During an Individual's Lifetime

Fingerprints are a reproduction of friction skin ridges found on the palm side of the fingers and thumbs. Similar friction skin can also be found on the surface of the palms and soles of the feet. Apparently, these skin surfaces have been designed by nature to provide our bodies with a firmer grasp and a resistance to slippage. A visual inspection of friction skin reveals a series of lines corresponding to hills (ridges) and valleys (grooves). The shape and form of the skin ridges are what one sees as the black lines of an inked fingerprint impression.

Actually, skin is composed of layers of cells. Those nearest the surface make up the outer portion of the skin known as the *epidermis,* and the inner skin is known as the *dermis.* A cross-section of skin (see Figure 14–3)

Ridge island
Sweat pores
Epidermis
Papillae
Dermis
Duct of sweat gland
Sweat gland
Nerves of touch

FIGURE 14–3   Cross-section of human skin.

reveals a boundary of cells separating the epidermis and dermis. The shape of this boundary, made up of *dermal papillae*, determines the form and pattern of the ridges on the surface of the skin. Once the dermal papillae develop in the human fetus, the ridge patterns remain unchanged throughout life except to enlarge during growth.

Each skin ridge is populated by a single row of pores that are the openings for ducts leading from the sweat glands. Through these pores, perspiration is discharged and deposited on the surface of the skin. Once the finger touches a surface, perspiration, along with oils that may have been picked up by touching the hairy portions of the body, is transferred onto that surface, thereby leaving an impression of the finger's ridge pattern (a fingerprint). Prints deposited in this manner are invisible to the eye and are commonly referred to as latent fingerprints.

Although it is impossible to change one's fingerprints, some criminals have tried to obscure them. If an injury reaches deeply enough into the skin and damages the dermal papillae, a permanent scar forms. However, for this to happen, such a wound would have to penetrate 1 to 2 millimeters beneath the skin's surface. Indeed, efforts at intentionally scarring the skin can only be self-defeating, for it is totally impossible to obliterate all of the ridge characteristics on the hand, and the presence of permanent scars merely provides new characteristics for identification.

Perhaps the most publicized attempt at obliteration was that of the notorious gangster John Dillinger, who tried to destroy his own fingerprints by applying a corrosive acid to them. Prints taken at the morgue after he was shot to death, compared with fingerprints recorded at the time of a previous arrest, proved that his efforts had been fruitless (see Figure 14–4).

Third Principle: Fingerprints Have General Ridge Patterns That Permit Them to Be Systematically Classified

All fingerprints are divided into three classes on the basis of their general pattern: loops, whorls, and arches. Sixty to 65 percent of the population have loops, 30–35 percent have whorls, and about 5 percent have arches. These three classes form the basis for all ten-finger classification systems presently in use.

latent fingerprint
A fingerprint made by the deposit of oils and/or perspiration; it is invisible to the naked eye.

loop
A class of fingerprints characterized by ridge lines that enter from one side of the pattern and curve around to exit from the same side of the pattern.

whorl
A class of fingerprints that includes ridge patterns that are generally rounded or circular and have two deltas.

arch
A class of fingerprints characterized by ridge lines that enter the print from one side and flow out the other side.

FIGURE 14–4 **The right index finger impression of John Dillinger, before scarification on the left and afterward on the right. Comparison is proved by the fourteen matching ridge characteristics.** *Courtesy Institute of Applied Science, Youngsville, S.C.*

A loop must have one or more ridges entering from one side of the print, recurving, and exiting from the same side. If the loop opens toward the little finger, it is called an *ulnar loop;* if it opens toward the thumb, it is a *radial loop.* The pattern area of the loop is surrounded by two diverging ridges known as *type lines.* The ridge point at or nearest the type-line divergence and located at or directly in front of the point of divergence is known as the *delta.* To many, a fingerprint delta resembles the silt formation that builds up as a river flows into the entrance of a lake—hence, the analogy to the geological formation known as a delta. All loops must have one delta. The *core,* as the name suggests, is the approximate center of the pattern. A typical loop pattern is illustrated in Figure 14–5.

Whorls are actually divided into four distinct groups, as shown in Figure 14–6: plain, central pocket loop, double loop, and accidental. All whorl patterns must have type lines and at least two deltas. A plain whorl and a central pocket loop have at least one ridge that makes a complete circuit. This ridge may be in the form of a spiral, oval, or any variant of a circle. If an imaginary line drawn between the two deltas contained within these two patterns touches any one of the spiral ridges, the pattern is a plain whorl. If no such ridge is touched, the pattern is a central pocket loop.

As the name implies, the double loop is made up of two loops combined into one fingerprint. Any whorl classified as an accidental either contains two or more patterns (not including the plain arch) or is a pattern not covered by other categories. Hence, an accidental may consist of a combination loop and plain whorl or loop and tented arch.

Arches, the least common of the three general patterns, are subdivided into two distinct groups: plain arches and tented arches, as shown in Figure 14–7. The plain arch is the simplest of all fingerprint patterns; it is formed by ridges entering from one side of the print and exiting on the

FIGURE 14–5   Loop pattern.

Plain whorl   Central pocket   Double loop   Accidental
                         loop

FIGURE 14–6   Whorl patterns.

Plain Tented

FIGURE 14–7 **Arch patterns.**

opposite side. Generally, these ridges tend to rise in the center of the pattern, forming a wavelike pattern. The tented arch is similar to the plain arch except that instead of rising smoothly at the center, there is a sharp upthrust or spike, or the ridges meet at an angle that is less than 90 degrees.[1] Arches do not have type lines, deltas, or cores.

Key Points

- Fingerprints are a reproduction of friction skin ridges found on the palm side of the fingers and thumbs.

- The basic principles underlying the use of fingerprints in criminal investigations are as follows: (1) A fingerprint is an individual characteristic because no two fingers have yet been found to possess identical ridge characteristics; (2) a fingerprint remains unchanged during an individual's lifetime; and (3) fingerprints have general ridge patterns that permit them to be systematically classified.

- All fingerprints are divided into three classes on the basis of their general pattern: loops, whorls, and arches.

- The individuality of a fingerprint is determined not by its general shape or pattern, but by a careful study of its ridge characteristics. The expert must demonstrate a point-by-point comparison in order to prove the identity of an individual.

- When the finger touches a surface, perspiration and oils are transferred onto that surface, leaving a fingerprint. Prints deposited in this manner are invisible to the eye and are commonly referred to as latent or invisible fingerprints.

Classification of Fingerprints

The original Henry system, as adopted by Scotland Yard in 1901, converted ridge patterns on all ten fingers into a series of letters and numbers arranged in the form of a fraction. However, the system as it was originally designed could accommodate files of up to only 100,000 sets of prints. Thus, as collections grew in size, it became necessary to expand the capacity of the classification system. In the United States, the FBI, faced with the problem of filing ever-increasing numbers of prints, expanded its classification capacity by modifying the original Henry system and adding additional extensions. These modifications are collectively known as the *FBI system* and are used by most agencies in the United States today. Although we will not discuss all of the different divisions of the FBI system, a description of just one part, the primary classification, will provide an interesting insight into the process of fingerprint classification.

The primary classification is part of the original Henry system and provides the first classification step in the FBI system. Using this classification alone, all of the fingerprint cards in the world could be divided into 1,024 groups. The first step in obtaining the primary classification is to pair up fingers, placing one finger in the numerator of a fraction, the other in the denominator. The fingers are paired in the following sequence:

R. Index	R. Ring	L. Thumb	L. Middle	L. Little
R. Thumb	R. Middle	R. Little	L. Index	L. Ring

The presence or absence of the whorl pattern is the basis for determination of the primary classification. If a whorl pattern is found on any finger of the first pair, it is assigned a value of 16; on the second pair, a value of 8; on the third pair, a value of 4; on the fourth pair, a value of 2; and on the last pair, a value of 1. Any finger with an arch or loop pattern is assigned a value of 0. Approximately 25 percent of the population falls into the 1/1 category; that is, all their fingers have either loops or arches.

After values for all ten fingers are obtained in this manner, they are totaled, and 1 is added to both the numerator and denominator. The fraction thus obtained is the primary classification. For example, if the right index and right middle fingers are whorls and all the others are loops, the primary classification is

$$\frac{16 + 0 + 0 + 0 + 0 + 1}{0 + 8 + 0 + 0 + 0 + 1} = \frac{17}{8}$$

A fingerprint classification system cannot in itself unequivocally identify an individual; it merely provides the fingerprint examiner with a number of candidates, all of whom have an indistinguishable set of prints in the system's file. The identification must always be made by a final visual comparison of the suspect print's and file print's ridge characteristics; only these features can impart individuality to a fingerprint. Although ridge patterns impart class characteristics to the print, the type and position of ridge characteristics give it its individual character.

Key Points

• The primary classification is the first step in classifying fingerprints under the FBI system. The presence or absence of the whorl pattern is the basis for determination of the primary classification.

Automated Fingerprint Identification Systems

The Henry system and its subclassifications have proven to be a cumbersome system for storing, retrieving, and searching for fingerprints, particularly as fingerprint collections grow in size. Nevertheless, until the emergence of fingerprint computer technology, this manual approach was the only viable method for maintaining fingerprint collections. Since 1970, technological advances have made possible the classification and retrieval of fingerprints by computers. Automated Fingerprint Identification Systems (AFISs) have proliferated throughout the law enforcement community.

In 1999, the FBI initiated full operation of the Integrated Automated Fingerprint Identification System (IAFIS), the largest AFIS in the United States, which links state AFIS computers with the FBI database. This database contains nearly 50 million fingerprint records. However, an AFIS can come in all sizes ranging from the FBI's to independent systems operated by cities, counties, and other agencies of local government. Unfortunately, these local systems often cannot be linked to the state's AFIS system because of differences in software configurations.

How AFIS Works

The heart of AFIS technology is the ability of a computer to scan and digitally encode fingerprints so that they can be subject to high-speed computer processing. The AFIS uses automatic scanning devices that convert the image of a fingerprint into digital minutiae that contain data showing ridges at their points of termination (ridge endings) and the branching of ridges into two ridges (bifurcations). The relative position and orientation of the minutiae are also determined, allowing the computer to store each fingerprint in the form of a digitally recorded geometric pattern.

The computer's search algorithm determines the degree of correlation between the location and relationship of the minutiae for both the search and file prints. In this manner, a computer can make thousands of fingerprint comparisons in a second. For example, a set of ten fingerprints can be searched against a file of 500,000 ten-finger prints (ten-prints) in about eight-tenths of a second. During the search for a match, the computer uses a scoring system that assigns prints to each of the criteria set by an operator. When the search is complete, the computer produces a list of file prints that have the closest correlation to the search prints. All of the selected prints are then examined by a fingerprint expert, who makes the final verification of the print's identity. Thus, the AFIS makes no final decisions on the identity of a fingerprint, leaving this function to the eyes of a trained examiner.

The speed and accuracy of ten-print processing by AFIS have made possible the search of single latent crime-scene fingerprints against an entire file's print collection. Before AFIS, police were usually restricted to comparing crime-scene fingerprints against those of known suspects. The impact of the AFIS on no-suspect cases has been dramatic. In its first year of operation, San Francisco's AFIS computer conducted 5,514 latent fingerprint searches and achieved 1,001 identifications—a hit rate of 18 percent. This compares to the previous year's average of 8 percent for manual latent-print searches.

As an example of how an AFIS computer operates, one system has been designed to automatically filter out imperfections in a latent print, enhance its image, and create a graphic representation of the fingerprint's ridge endings and bifurcations and their direction. The print is then computer searched against file prints. The image of the latent print and a matching file print are then displayed side by side on a high-resolution video monitor as shown in Figure 14–8. The matching latent

Forensic Brief

The Night Stalker

Richard Ramirez committed his first murder in June 1984. His victim was a 79-year-old woman who was stabbed repeatedly and sexually assaulted, and then had her throat slashed. It would be eight months before Ramirez murdered again. In the spring, Ramirez began a murderous rampage that resulted in thirteen additional killings and five rapes.

His modus operandi was to enter a home through an open window, shoot the male residents, and savagely rape his female victims. He scribed a pentagram on the wall of one of his victims and the words "Jack the Knife," and was reported by another to force her to "swear to Satan" during the assault. His identity still unknown, the news media dubbed him the "Night Stalker." As the body count continued to rise, public hysteria and a media frenzy prevailed.

The break in the case came when the license plate of what seemed to be a suspicious car relating to a sighting of the Night Stalker was reported to the police. The police determined that the car had been stolen and eventually located it, abandoned in a parking lot. After processing the car for prints, police found one usable partial fingerprint. This fingerprint was entered into the Los Angeles Police Department's brand-new AFIS computerized fingerprint system.

Without AFIS, it would have taken a single technician, manually searching the Los Angeles' 1.7 million print cards, sixty-

Richard Ramirez, the Night Stalker.
© *Bettmann/CORBIS. All Rights Reserved.*

seven years to come up with the perpetrator's prints. Thanks to AFIS, it took only a few seconds to locate and identify them. The Night Stalker was identified as Richard Ramirez, who had been fingerprinted following a traffic violation some years before. Police searching the home of one of his friends found the gun used to commit the murders, and jewelry belonging to his victims was found in the possession of Ramirez's sister. Ramirez was convicted of murder and sentenced to death in 1989. He still remains on death row.

and file prints are then verified and charted by a fingerprint examiner at a video workstation.

The stereotypical image of a booking officer rolling inked fingers onto a standard ten-print card for ultimate transmission to a database has, for the most part, been replaced with digital-capture devices (**livescan**) that eliminate ink and paper (see Figure 14–9). The livescan captures the image on each finger and the palms as they are lightly pressed against a glass platen. These livescan images can then be sent to the AFIS database electronically, so that within minutes the booking agency can enter the fingerprint record

livescan
An inkless device that captures digital images of fingerprints and palm prints and electronically transmits them to an AFIS.

FIGURE 14–8   A side-by-side comparison of a latent print against a file fingerprint is conducted in seconds and their similarity rating (SIM) is displayed on the upper-left portion of the screen. *Courtesy Sirchie Finger Print Laboratories, Inc., Youngsville, N.C., www.sirchie.com*

into the AFIS database and search the database for previous entries of the same individual.

Considerations with AFIS

AFIS has fundamentally changed the way criminal investigators operate, allowing them to spend less time developing suspect lists and more time investigating the suspects generated by the computer. However, investigators must be cautioned against overreliance on a computer. Sometimes a latent print does not make a hit because of the poor quality of the file print. To avoid these potential problems, investigators must still print all known suspects in a case and manually search these prints against the crime-scene prints.

AFIS computers are available from several different suppliers. Each system scans fingerprint images and detects and records information about minutiae (ridge endings and bifurcations); however, they do not all incorporate exactly the same features, coordinate systems, or units of measure to record fingerprint information. These software incompatibilities often mean that although state systems can communicate with the FBI's IAFIS, they do not communicate with each other directly. Likewise, local and state systems frequently cannot share information with each other. Many of these technical problems will be resolved as more agencies follow transmission standards developed by the National Institute of Standards and Technology and the FBI.

FIGURE 14–9 Livescan technology enables law enforcement personnel to print and compare a subject's fingerprints rapidly, without inking the fingerprints. *Courtesy Printrac International*

Forensic Brief

The Mayfield Affair

On March 11, 2004, a series of ten explosions at four sites occurred on commuter trains traveling to or near the Atocha train station in Madrid, Spain. The death toll from these explosions was nearly 200, with more than 1,500 injured. On the day of the attack, a plastic bag was found in a van previously reported as stolen. The bag contained copper detonators like those used on the train bombs.

On March 17 the FBI received electronic images of latent fingerprints that were recovered from the plastic bag, and a search was initiated on the FBI's IAFIS. A senior fingerprint examiner encoded seven minutiae points from the high-resolution image of one suspect latent fingerprint and initiated an IAFIS search matching the print to Brandon Mayfield. Mayfield's prints were in the FBI's central database because they had been taken when he joined the

Forensic Brief

military, where he served for eight years before being honorably discharged as a second lieutenant.

After a visual comparison of the suspect and file prints, the examiner concluded a "100 percent match." The identification was verified by a retired FBI fingerprint examiner with more than thirty years of experience who was under working contract with the bureau, as well as by a court-appointed independent fingerprint examiner (see figure).

Mayfield, age 37, a Muslim convert, was arrested on May 6 on a material witness warrant. The U.S. Attorney's Office came up with a list of Mayfield's potential ties to Muslim terrorists, which they included in the affidavit they presented to the federal judge who ordered his arrest and detention. The document also said that while no travel records were found for Mayfield, "It is believed that Mayfield may have traveled under a false or fictitious name." On May 24, after the Spaniards had linked the print from the plastic bag to

an Algerian national, Mayfield's case was thrown out. The FBI issued him a highly unusual official apology, and his ordeal became a stunning embarrassment to the U.S. government.

As part of its corrective-action process, the FBI formed an international committee of distinguished latent-print examiners and forensic experts. Their task was to review the analysis performed by the FBI Laboratory and make recommendations that would help prevent this type of error in the future. The committee came up with some startling findings and observations (available at www.fbi.gov/ hq/lab/fsc/backissu/jan2005/ special_report/2005_special_report.htm).

The committee members agreed that "the quality of the images that were used to make the erroneous identification was not a factor. . . . The identification is filled with dissimilarities that were easily observed when a detailed analysis of the latent print was conducted." They further stated, the power of the IAFIS match,

(a)

(b)

(a) Questioned print recovered in connection with the Madrid bombing Investigation.
(b) File print of Brandon Mayfield. *(a) Courtesy www.onin.com/fp/problemidents.html/ madrid*

(continued)

Forensic Brief

The Mayfield Affair (*continued*)

coupled with the inherent pressure of working an extremely high-profile case, was thought to have influenced the initial examiner's judgment and subsequent examination. . . . The apparent mind-set of the initial examiner after reviewing the results of the IAFIS search was that a match did exist; therefore, it would be reasonable to assume that the other characteristics must match as well. In the absence of a detailed analysis of the print, it can be a short distance from finding only seven characteristics sufficient for plotting, prior to the automated search, to the position of 12 or 13 matching characteristics once the mind-set of identification has become dominant. . . .

Once the mind-set occurred with the initial examiner, the subsequent examinations were tainted. . . . Because of the inherent pressure of such a high-profile case, the power of an IAFIS match in conjunction with the similarities in the candidate's print, and the knowledge of the previous examiners' conclusions (especially since the initial examiner was a highly respected supervisor with many years of experience), it was concluded that subsequent examinations were incomplete and inaccurate. To disagree was not an expected response. . . . When the individualization had been made by the examiner, it became

increasingly difficult for others in the agency to disagree.

The committee went on to make a number of quality-assurance recommendations to help avoid a recurrence of this type of error.

The Mayfield incident has also been the subject of an investigation by the Office of the Inspector General (OIG), U.S. Department of Justice (www.usdoj.gov/oig/special/s0601/final.pdf). The OIG investigation concluded that a "series of systemic issues" in the FBI Laboratory contributed to the Mayfield misidentification. The report noted that the FBI has made significant procedural modifications to help prevent similar errors in the future, and strongly supported the FBI's decision to develop more objective standards for fingerprint identification. An internal review of the FBI Latent Print Unit conducted in the aftermath of the Mayfield affair has resulted in the implementation of revisions in training, as well as in the decision-making process when determining the comparative value of a latent print, along with more stringent verification policies and procedures [Smrz, M. A., et al., *Journal of Forensic Identification* 56 (2006): 402–434].

The impact of the Mayfield affair on fingerprint technology as currently practiced and the weight courts will assign to fingerprint matches remain open questions.

Key Points

- The FBI fingerprint database known as AFIS converts the image of a fingerprint into digital minutiae that contain data showing ridges at their points of termination (ridge endings) and their branching into two ridges (bifurcations).

- Livescan is an inkless device that captures digital images of fingerprints and palm prints and electronically transmits them to an AFIS.

Methods of Detecting Fingerprints

Through common usage, the term *latent fingerprint* has come to be associated with any fingerprint discovered at a crime scene. Sometimes, however, prints found at the scene of a crime are quite visible to the eye, and the word *latent* is a misnomer.

Actually, there are three kinds of crime-scene prints. Visible prints are made by fingers touching a surface after the ridges have been in contact with a colored material such as blood, paint, grease, or ink; plastic prints are ridge impressions left on a soft material such as putty, wax, soap, or dust; and *latent* or *invisible prints* are impressions caused by the transfer of body perspiration or oils present on finger ridges to the surface of an object.

Locating Fingerprints

Locating visible or plastic prints at the crime scene normally presents little problem to the investigator, because these prints are usually distinct and visible to the eye. Locating latent or invisible prints is obviously much more difficult and requires the use of techniques to make the print visible. Although the investigator can choose from several methods for visualizing a latent print, the choice depends on the type of surface being examined.

Hard and nonabsorbent surfaces (such as glass, mirror, tile, and painted wood) require different development procedures from surfaces that are soft and porous (such as papers, cardboard, and cloth). Prints on the former are preferably developed by the application of a powder or treatment with Super Glue, whereas prints on the latter generally require treatment with one or more chemicals.

Sometimes the most difficult aspect of fingerprint examination is the location of prints. Recent advances in fingerprint technology have led to the development of an ultraviolet image converter for the purpose of detecting latent fingerprints. This device, called the Reflected Ultraviolet Imaging System (RUVIS), can locate prints on most nonabsorbent surfaces without the aid of chemical or powder treatments (see Figure 14–10).

RUVIS detects the print in its natural state by aiming UV light at the surface suspected of containing prints. When the UV light strikes the

visible print
A fingerprint made when the finger deposits a visible material such as ink, dirt, or blood onto a surface.

plastic print
A fingerprint impressed in a soft surface.

FIGURE 14–10   A Reflected Ultraviolet Imaging System allows an investigator to directly view surfaces for the presence of untreated latent fingerprints. *Courtesy Sirchie Finger Print Laboratories, Inc., Youngsville, N.C., www.sirchie.com*

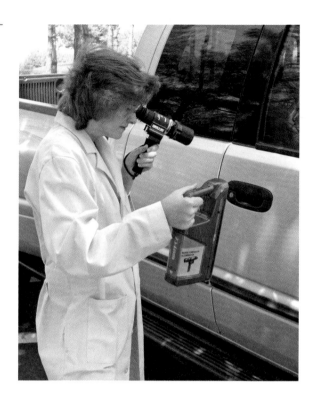

FIGURE 14–11 Using a Reflected Ultraviolet Imaging System with the aid of a UV lamp to search for latent fingerprints. *Courtesy Sirchie Finger Print Laboratories, Inc., Youngsville, N.C., www.sirchie.com*

fingerprint, the light is reflected back to the viewer, differentiating the print from its background surface. The transmitted UV light is then converted into visible light by an image intensifier. Once the print is located in this manner, the crime-scene investigator can develop it in the most appropriate fashion (see Figure 14–11).

Developing Latent Prints

Several techniques are available to the criminalist to develop latent prints on a variety of surfaces. These range from chemical methods such as powders and iodine fuming to the use of laser light.

Fingerprint Powders   Fingerprint powders are commercially available in a variety of compositions and colors. These powders, when applied lightly to a nonabsorbent surface with a camel's-hair or fiberglass brush, readily adhere to perspiration residues and/or deposits of body oils left on the surface (see Figure 14–12).

Experienced examiners find that gray and black powders are adequate for most latent-print work; the examiner selects the powder that affords the best color contrast with the surface being dusted. Hence, the gray powder, composed of an aluminum dust, is used on dark-colored surfaces. It is also applied to mirrors and metal surfaces that are polished to a mirrorlike finish, because these surfaces photograph as black. The black powder, composed basically of black carbon or charcoal, is applied to white or light-colored surfaces.

Other types of powders are available for developing latent prints. A magnetic-sensitive powder can be spread over a surface with a magnet in the form of a Magna Brush. A Magna Brush does not have any bristles to come in contact with the surface, so there is less chance that the print will be destroyed or damaged. The magnetic-sensitive powder comes in

FIGURE 14–12 Developing a latent fingerprint on a surface by applying a fingerprint powder with a fiberglass brush. *Courtesy Sirchie Finger Print Laboratories, Inc., Youngsville, N.C., www.sirchie.com*

black and gray and is especially useful on such items as finished leather and rough plastics, on which the minute texture of the surface tends to hold particles of ordinary powder. Fluorescent powders are also used to develop latent fingerprints. These powders fluoresce under ultraviolet light. By photographing the fluorescence pattern of the developing print under UV light, it is possible to avoid having the color of the surface obscure the print.

Iodine Fuming   Of the several chemical methods used for visualizing latent prints, iodine fuming is the oldest. Iodine is a solid crystal that, when heated, is transformed into a vapor without passing through a liquid phase; such a transformation is called sublimation. Most often, the suspect material is placed in an enclosed cabinet along with iodine crystals (see Figure 14–13). As the crystals are heated, the resultant vapors fill the chamber and combine with constituents of the latent print to make it visible.

Unfortunately, iodine prints are not permanent and begin to fade once the fuming process is stopped. Therefore, the examiner must photograph the prints immediately on development in order to retain a permanent record. Also, iodine-developed prints can be fixed with a 1 percent solution of starch in water, applied by spraying. The print turns blue and lasts for several weeks to several months.

The reasons why latent prints are visualized by iodine vapors are not yet fully understood. Many believe that the iodine fumes combine with fatty oils; however, there is also convincing evidence that the iodine may actually interact with residual water left on a print from perspiration.[2]

Ninhydrin   Another chemical used for visualizing latent prints is ninhydrin. The development of latent prints with ninhydrin depends on its chemical reaction to form a purple-blue color with amino acids present in trace amounts in perspiration. Ninhydrin (triketohydrindene hydrate) is commonly sprayed onto the porous surface from an aerosol can. A solution is prepared by mixing the ninhydrin powder with a suitable solvent, such as acetone or ethyl alcohol; a 0.6 percent solution appears to be effective for most applications.

iodine fuming
A technique for visualizing latent fingerprints by exposing them to iodine vapors.

sublimation
A physical change from the solid directly into the gaseous state.

ninhydrin
A chemical reagent used to develop latent fingerprints on porous materials by reacting with amino acids in perspiration.

FIGURE 14–13   A heated fuming cabinet. *Courtesy Sirchie Finger Print Laboratories, Inc., Youngsville, N.C., www.sirchie.com*

Generally, prints begin to appear within an hour or two after ninhydrin application; however, weaker prints may be visualized after twenty-four to forty-eight hours. The development can be hastened if the treated specimen is heated in an oven or on a hot plate at a temperature of 80–100°C. The ninhydrin method has developed latent prints on paper as old as fifteen years.

Physical Developer
A silver nitrate–based reagent formulated to develop latent fingerprints on porous surfaces.

Physical Developer   Physical Developer is a third chemical mixture used for visualizing latent prints. Physical Developer is a silver nitrate–based liquid reagent. This method has gained wide acceptance by fingerprint examiners, who have found it effective for visualizing latent prints that remain undetected by the previously described methods. Also, this technique is very effective for developing latent fingerprints on porous articles that may have been wet at one time.

For most fingerprint examiners, the chemical method of choice is ninhydrin. Its extreme sensitivity and ease of application have all but eliminated the use of iodine for latent-print visualization. However, when ninhydrin fails, development with Physical Developer may provide identifiable results. Application of Physical Developer washes away any traces of proteins from an object's surface; hence, if one wishes to use all of the previously mentioned chemical development methods on the same surface, it is necessary to first fume with iodine, follow this treatment with ninhydrin, and then apply Physical Developer to the object.

Super Glue fuming
A technique for visualizing latent fingerprints on nonporous surfaces by exposing them to cyanoacrylate vapors; named for the commercial product Super Glue.

Super Glue Fuming   In the past, chemical treatment for fingerprint development was reserved for porous surfaces such as paper and cardboard. However, since 1982, a chemical technique known as Super Glue fuming has

FIGURE 14–14 **Super Glue fuming a nonporous metallic surface in the search for latent fingerprints.**
Courtesy Sirchie Finger Print Laboratories, Inc., Youngsville, N.C., www.sirchie.com

gained wide popularity for developing latent prints on nonporous surfaces such as metals, electrical tape, leather, and plastic bags.[3] See Figure 14–14.

Super Glue is approximately 98–99 percent cyanoacrylate ester, a chemical that interacts with and visualizes a latent fingerprint. Cyanoacrylate ester fumes can be created when Super Glue is placed on absorbent cotton treated with sodium hydroxide. The fumes can also be created by heating the glue. The fumes and the evidential object are contained within an enclosed chamber for up to six hours. Development occurs when fumes from the glue adhere to the latent print, usually producing a white-appearing latent print. Interestingly, small enclosed areas, such as the interior of an automobile, have been successfully processed for latent prints with fumes from Super Glue.

Through the use of a small handheld wand, cyanoacrylate fuming is now easily done at a crime scene or in a laboratory setting. The wand heats a small cartridge containing cyanoacrylate. Once heated, the cyanoacrylate vaporizes, allowing the operator to direct the fumes onto the suspect area (see Figure 14–15).

Other Techniques for Visualization In recent years, researchers have explored a variety of new processes applicable to the visualization of latent fingerprints. However, for many years progress in this field was minimal. Fingerprint specialists traditionally relied on three chemical techniques— iodine, ninhydrin, and silver nitrate—to reveal a hidden fingerprint. Then, Super Glue fuming extended chemical development to prints deposited on nonporous surfaces.

Another hint of things to come emerged with the discovery that latent fingerprints could be visualized by exposure to laser light. This laser method took advantage of the fact that perspiration contains a variety of components that fluoresce when illuminated by laser light.

fluoresce
To emit visible light when exposed to light of a shorter wavelength.

(a)   (b)

FIGURE 14–15   (a) A handheld fuming wand uses disposable cartridges containing cyanoacrylate. The wand is used to develop prints at the crime scene and (b) in the laboratory. *Courtesy Sirchie Finger Print Laboratories, Inc., Youngsville, N.C., www.sirchie.com*

The next advancement in latent-fingerprint development occurred with the discovery that fingerprints could be treated with chemicals that would induce fluorescence when exposed to laser illumination. For example, application of zinc chloride after ninhydrin treatment or application of the dye rhodamine 6G after Super Glue fuming caused fluorescence and increased the sensitivity of detection on exposure to laser illumination. The discovery of numerous chemical developers for visualizing fingerprints through fluorescence quickly followed. This knowledge set the stage for the next advance in latent-fingerprint development—the *alternate light source*.

With the advent of chemically induced fluorescence, lasers were no longer needed to induce fingerprints to fluoresce through perspiration residues. High-intensity light sources or alternate light sources have proliferated and all but replaced laser lights (see Figure 14–16). High-intensity quartz halogen or xenon-arc light sources can be focused on a suspect area through a fiber-optic cable. This light can be passed through several filters, giving the user more flexibility in selecting the wavelength of light to be aimed at the latent print. Alternatively, lightweight, portable alternate light sources that use light-emitting diodes (LEDs) are also commercially available (see Figure 14–17).

In most cases, these light sources have proven to be as effective as laser light in developing latent prints, and they are commercially available at costs significantly below those of laser illuminators. Furthermore, these light sources are portable and can be readily taken to any crime scene.

Many chemical treatment processes are available to the fingerprint examiner (see Figure 14–18), and the field is in a constant state of flux. Selection of an appropriate procedure is best left to technicians who have developed their skills through casework experience. Newer chemical processes include a substitute for ninhydrin called DFO (1,8-diazafluoren-9-one). This chemical visualizes latent prints on porous materials when exposed to an alternate light source. DFO has been shown to develop 2.5 times more latent prints on paper than ninhydrin.

FIGURE 14–16   An alternate light source system incorporating a high-intensity light source. *Courtesy Foster & Freeman Limited, Worcestershire, U.K., www.fosterfreeman.co.uk*

FIGURE 14–17   Lightweight handheld alternate light source that uses an LED light source.
Courtesy Foster & Freeman Limited, Worcestershire, U.K., www.fosterfreeman.co.uk

(a)

(b)

(c)

(d)

FIGURE 14–18 (a) Latent fingerprint visualized by cyanoacrylate fuming. (b) Fingerprint treated with cyanoacrylate and a blue/green fluorescent dye. (c) Fingerprint treated with cyanoacrylate and rhodamine 6G fluorescent dye. (d) Fingerprint treated with cyanoacrylate and the fluorescent dye combination RAM. (e) Fingerprint visualized by the fluorescent chemical DFO. (f) Fingerprint visualized by Redwop fluorescent fingerprint powder. (g) A bloody fingerprint detected by laser light without any chemical treatment. (h) A bloody fingerprint detected by laser light after spraying with merbromin and hydrogen peroxide. *(a) Courtesy North Carolina State Bureau of Investigation, Raleigh, N.C. (b) Courtesy 3M Corp., Austin, Texas (f) Courtesy Melles Griot Inc., Carlsbad, Calif.*

(e)

(f)

(g)

(h)

FIGURE 14.18 (*continued*)

Closer Analysis

Fluorescence

Fluorescence occurs when a substance absorbs light and reemits the light in wavelengths longer than that of the illuminating source. Importantly, substances that emit light or fluoresce are more readily seen either with the naked eye or through photography than are non-light-emitting materials. The high sensitivity of fluorescence serves as the underlying principle of many of the new chemical techniques used to visualize latent fingerprints.

The earliest use of fluorescence to visualize fingerprints came with the direct illumination of a fingerprint with argon–ion lasers. This laser type was chosen because its blue-green light output induced some of the perspiration components of a fingerprint to fluoresce (see figure). The major drawback of this approach is that the perspiration components of a fingerprint are often present in quantities too minute to observe even with the aid of fluorescence.

The fingerprint examiner, wearing safety goggles containing optical filters, visually examines the specimen being exposed to the laser light. The filters absorb the laser light and permit the wavelengths at which latent-print residues fluoresce to pass through to the eyes of the wearer. The filter also protects the operator

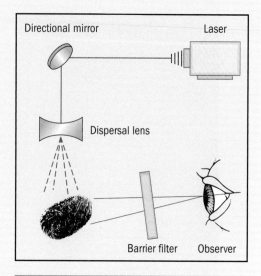

Schematic depicting latent-print detection with the aid of a laser. A fingerprint examiner, wearing safety goggles containing optical filters, examines the specimen being exposed to the laser light. The filter absorbs the laser light and permits the wavelengths at which latent-print residues fluoresce to pass through to the eyes of the wearer. *Courtesy Federal Bureau of Investigation, Washington, D.C.*

against eye damage from scattered or reflected laser light. Likewise, latent-print residue producing sufficient fluorescence can be photographed by placing this same filter across the lens of the camera. Examination of specimens and photography of the fluorescing latent prints are carried out in a darkened room.

Studies have demonstrated that common fingerprint-developing agents do not interfere with DNA-testing methods used for characterizing bloodstains.[4] Nonetheless, in cases involving items with material adhering to their surfaces and/or items that will require further laboratory examinations, fingerprint processing should not be performed at the crime scene. Rather, the items should be submitted to the laboratory, where they can be processed for fingerprints in conjunction with other necessary examinations.

- Visible prints are made when fingers touch a surface after the ridges have been in contact with a colored material such as blood, paint, grease, or ink.

- Plastic prints are ridge impressions left on a soft material, such as putty, wax, soap, or dust.

- Latent prints deposited on hard and nonabsorbent surfaces (such as glass, mirror, tile, and painted wood) are usually developed by the application of a powder, whereas prints on porous surfaces (such as papers and cardboard) generally require treatment with a chemical.

- Examiners use various chemical methods to visualize latent prints, such as iodine fuming, ninhydrin, and Physical Developer.

- Super Glue fuming develops latent prints on nonporous surfaces.

- Latent fingerprints can also be treated with chemicals that induce fluorescence when exposed to a high-intensity light or an alternate light source.

Preservation of Developed Prints

Once the latent print has been visualized, it must be permanently preserved for future comparison and possible use in court as evidence. A photograph must be taken before any further attempts at preservation. Any camera equipped with a close-up lens will do; however, many investigators prefer to use a camera specially designed for fingerprint photography. Such a camera comes equipped with a fixed focus to take photographs on a 1:1 scale when the camera's open eye is held exactly flush against the print's surface (see Figure 14–19). In addition, photographs must be taken to provide an overall view of the print's location with respect to other evidential items at the crime scene.

Once photographs have been secured, one of two procedures is to be followed. If the object is small enough to be transported without destroying the print, it should be preserved in its entirety. The print should be covered with cellophane so it will be protected from damage. On the other hand, prints on large immovable objects that have been developed with a powder can best be preserved by "lifting." The most popular type of lifter is a broad adhesive tape similar to Scotch tape. Fingerprint powder is applied to the print, and the surface containing the print is covered with the adhesive side of the tape. When the tape is pulled up, the powder is transferred to the tape. Then the tape is placed on a properly labeled card that provides a good background contrast with the powder.

A variation of this procedure is the use of an adhesive-backed clear plastic sheet attached to a colored cardboard backing. Before it is applied to the print, a celluloid separator is peeled from the plastic sheet to expose the adhesive lifting surface. The tape is then pressed evenly and firmly over the powdered print and pulled up (see Figure 14–20). The sheet containing the adhering powder is now pressed against the cardboard backing to provide a permanent record of the fingerprint.

FIGURE 14–19 **Camera fitted with an adapter designed to give an approximate 1:1 photograph of a fingerprint.** *Courtesy Sirchie Finger Print Laboratories, Inc., Youngsville, N.C., www.sirchie.com*

FIGURE 14–20 **"Lifting" a fingerprint.** *Courtesy Sirchie Finger Print Laboratories, Inc., Youngsville, N.C., www.sirchie.com*

Digital Imaging for Fingerprint Enhancement

When fingerprints are lifted from a crime scene, they are not usually in perfect condition, making the analysis that much more difficult. Computers have advanced technology in most fields, and fingerprint identification has not been left behind. With the help of digital imaging software, fingerprints can now be enhanced for the most accurate and comprehensive analysis.

Digital imaging is the process by which a picture is converted into a digital file. The image produced from this digital file is composed of numerous square electronic dots called pixels. Images composed of only black and white elements are referred to as *grayscale images*. Each pixel is assigned a number according to its intensity. The grayscale image is made from the set of numbers to which a pixel may be assigned, ranging from 0 (black) to 255 (white). Once an image is digitally stored, it is manipulated by computer software that changes the numerical value of each pixel, thus altering the image as directed by the user. Resolution reveals the degree of detail that can be seen in an image. It is defined in terms of dimensions, such as 800×600 pixels. The larger the numbers, the more closely the digital image resembles the real-world image.

The input of pictures into a digital imaging system is usually done through the use of scanners, digital cameras, and video cameras. After the picture is changed to its digital image, several methods can be employed to enhance the image. The overall brightness of an image, as well as the contrast between the image and the background, can be adjusted through contrast-enhancement methods.

Color interferences can pose a problem when analyzing an image. For example, a latent fingerprint found on paper currency or a check may be difficult to analyze because of the distracting colored background. With the imaging software, the colored background can simply be removed to make the image stand out (see Figure 14–21). If the image itself is a particular color, such as a ninhydrin-developed print, the color can be isolated and enhanced to distinguish it from the background.

Digital imaging software also provides functions in which portions of the image can be examined individually. With a scaling and resizing tool,

digital imaging
A process through which a picture is converted into a series of square electronic dots known as pixels.

pixel
A square electronic dot that is used to compose a digital image.

FIGURE 14–21 **A fingerprint being enhanced in Adobe Photoshop. In this example, on the left is the original scan of an inked fingerprint on a check. On the right is the same image after using Adobe Photoshop's Channel Mixer to eliminate the green security background.**
Courtesy Imaging Forensics, Fountain Valley, Calif., www.imagingforensics.com

the user can select a part of an image and resize it for a closer look. This function operates much like a magnifying glass, helping the examiner view fine details of an image.

An important and useful tool, especially for fingerprint identification, is the compare function. This specialized feature places two images side by side and allows the examiner to chart the common features on both images simultaneously (see Figure 14–22). The zoom function is used in conjunction with the compare tool. As the examiner zooms into a portion of one image, the software automatically zooms into the second image for comparison.

Although digital imaging is undoubtedly an effective tool for enhancing and analyzing images, it is only as useful as the images it has to work with. If the details do not exist on the original images, the enhancement procedures are not going to work. The benefits of digital enhancement methods are apparent when weak images are made more distinguishable.

Key Points

• Once a latent print has been visualized, it must be permanently preserved for future comparison and for possible use as court evidence. A photograph must be taken before any further attempts at preservation are made.

Case # 05-01234

Latent Print
Inside of bathroom window

John Smith
Finger #7

FIGURE 14–22 Current imaging software allows fingerprint analysts to prepare a fingerprint comparison chart. The fingerprint examiner can compare prints side by side and display important features that are consistent between the fingerprints. The time needed to create a display of this sort digitally is about thirty to sixty minutes. *Courtesy Imaging Forensics, Fountain Valley, Calif., www.imagingforensics.com*

- A common method for preserving prints developed with a powder is lifting the print with an adhesive tape.

- Digital imaging is a process through which a picture is converted into a series of square electronic dots known as pixels. By using digital imaging, fingerprints can be enhanced.

Chapter Summary

Fingerprints are a reproduction of friction skin ridges found on the palm side of the fingers and thumbs. The basic principles underlying the use of fingerprints in criminal investigations are that (1) a fingerprint is an individual characteristic because no two fingers have yet been found to possess identical ridge characteristics; (2) a fingerprint remains unchanged during an individual's lifetime; and (3) fingerprints have general ridge patterns that permit them to be systematically classified.

All fingerprints are divided into three classes on the basis of their general pattern: loops, whorls, and arches. Fingerprint classification systems are based on knowledge of fingerprint pattern classes. The individuality of a fingerprint is not determined by its general shape or pattern, but by a careful study of its ridge characteristics. The expert must demonstrate a point-by-point comparison in order to prove the identity of an individual. AFIS aids this process by converting the image of a fingerprint into digital minutiae that contain data showing ridges at their points of termination (ridge endings) and their branching into two ridges (bifurcations). A single fingerprint can be searched against the FBI AFIS digital database of 50 million fingerprint records in a matter of minutes.

Once the finger touches a surface, perspiration, along with oils that may have been picked up by touching the hairy portions of the body, is transferred onto that surface, thereby leaving an impression of the finger's ridge pattern (a fingerprint). Prints deposited in this manner are invisible to the eye and are commonly referred to as latent or invisible fingerprints.

Visible prints are made when fingers touch a surface after the ridges have been in contact with a colored material such as blood, paint, grease, or ink. Plastic prints are ridge impressions left on a soft material, such as putty, wax, soap, or dust.

Latent prints deposited on hard and nonabsorbent surfaces (such as glass, mirror, tile, and painted wood) are preferably developed by application of a powder; prints on porous surfaces (such as paper and cardboard) generally require treatment with a chemical. Examiners use various chemical methods to visualize latent prints, such as iodine fuming, ninhydrin, and Physical Developer. Super Glue fuming develops latent prints on nonporous surfaces, such as metals, electrical tape, leather, and plastic bags. Development occurs when fumes from the glue adhere to the print, usually producing a white latent print.

The high sensitivity of fluorescence serves as the underlying principle of many of the new chemical techniques used to visualize latent fingerprints. Fingerprints are treated with chemicals that induce fluorescence when exposed to a high-intensity light or an alternate light source.

Once the latent print has been visualized, it must be permanently preserved for future comparison and for possible use as court evidence. A photograph must be taken before any further attempts at preservation are made. If the object is small enough to be transported without destroying the print, it should be preserved in its entirety. Prints on large immovable objects that have been developed with a powder are best preserved by "lifting" with a broad adhesive tape.

Review Questions

Facts and Concepts

1. What are fingerprints?

2. What is the first fundamental principle of fingerprints?

3. What imparts individuality to a fingerprint?

4. What are ridge characteristics? What is another name for ridge characteristics?

5. What is the second fundamental principle of fingerprints?

6. What are dermal papillae and how are they related to fingerprints?

7. What is a latent fingerprint? Briefly describe how a latent fingerprint is formed.

8. Why is it pointless to try to obscure or obliterate one's fingerprints by scarring or otherwise damaging the skin?

9. What is the third fundamental principle of fingerprints?

10. What are the three types of fingerprint patterns? Which is most common?

11. Which class of fingerprints includes ridge patterns that are generally rounded or circular and have two deltas?

12. Which type of fingerprint pattern must have at least one delta?

13. Which is the simplest of all fingerprint patterns, formed by ridges entering from one side of the print and exiting on the opposite side?

14. What is the primary classification? What is the basis for this classification?

15. What is an AFIS? What is the heart of AFIS technology?

16. When using AFIS, who makes the final verification of a print's identity?

17. What is livescan? What procedure has livescan largely replaced?

18. Name two main drawbacks to using AFIS.

19. Name the three kinds of crime-scene fingerprints.

20. How are prints from hard and nonabsorbent surfaces preferably developed? How are soft and porous surfaces generally treated?

21. What is RUVIS and how does it work?

22. Name four common chemical methods for visualizing latent prints.

23. Explain how latent prints can be visualized when illuminated by laser light.

24. Name three reasons why alternate light sources have replaced lasers for visualizing latent prints.

25. What is the first thing that the criminalist must do after visualizing a print but before making any further attempts at preserving it?

26. Briefly describe how the criminalist should handle prints on small objects.

27. Describe the basic process used to "lift" a fingerprint. When should this procedure be used?

28. What is digital imaging? How is it useful for analyzing fingerprints?

29. Under what conditions is digital imaging not effective in enhancing latent fingerprints?

(1). _____

(2). _____

(3). _____

(4). _____

(5). _____

(6). _____

Application and Critical Thinking

1. Classify each of the following prints as loop, whorl, or arch.

2. Following is a description of the types of prints from the fingers of a criminal suspect. Using the FBI system, determine the primary classification of this individual.

Finger	Right Hand	Left Hand
Thumb	Whorl	Whorl
Index	Loop	Whorl
Middle	Whorl	Arch
Ring	Whorl	Whorl
Little	Arch	Whorl

3. While searching a murder scene, you find the following items that you believe may contain latent fingerprints. Indicate whether prints on each item should be developed using fingerprint powder or chemicals.
   a. a leather sofa
   b. a mirror
   c. a painted wooden knife handle
   d. blood-soaked newspapers
   e. a revolver

4. Criminalist Frank Mortimer is using digital imaging to enhance latent fingerprints. Indicate which features of digital imaging he would most likely use for each of the following tasks:
   a. isolating part of a print and enlarging it for closer examination
   b. increasing the contrast between a print and the background surface on which it is located
   c. examining two prints that overlap one another

Web Resources

Averbeck, R., "Super Glue to the Rescue"
www.detectoprint.com/article.htm

The Detection and Enhancement of Latent Fingerprints (Adobe Acrobat article from the 2001 Interpol Forensic Science Symposium)
www.interpol.int/Public/Forensic/IFSS/meeting13/SpecialPresentation.pdf

Fingerprint Patterns (Online article discussing the various types of fingerprint patterns, accompanied by extensive illustrations)
www.policensw.com/info/fingerprints/finger07.html

The Fingerprint System (Online article that traces the history of fingerprinting and discusses the elements of the standard fingerprinting system used by law enforcement)
www.criminaljustice.state.ny.us/ojis/history/fp_sys.htm

Frequently Asked Questions about Fingerprints
www.onin.com/fp/lpfaq.html

The History of Fingerprints (Article that traces the history of the use of fingerprints in crime solving)
www.onin.com/fp/fphistory.html

IAFIS Home Page (FBI Web site for the Integrated Automated Fingerprint Identification System; describes the functions and organization of IAFIS and the fingerprint identification services it provides)
www.fbi.gov/hq/cjisd/iafis.htm

Is Fingerprint Identification a "Science"? (Article written by a fingerprinting expert that examines the criteria that validate the science of fingerprinting; also includes a large list of links to identification evidence)
www.forensic-evidence.com/site/ID/ID00004_2.html

Ridges and Furrows (Site that presents information on fingerprinting history, the anatomy of skin, friction ridge identification, latent print development, AFIS, and more)
www.ridgesandfurrows.homestead.com

Taking Legible Fingerprints (Information from the FBI outlining proper procedures for lifting fingerprints)
www.fbi.gov/hq/cjisd/takingfps.html

Endnotes

1. A tented arch is also any pattern that resembles a loop but lacks one of the essential requirements for classification as a loop.
2. J. Almag, Y. Sasson, and A. Anati, "Chemical Reagents for the Development of Latent Fingerprints II: Controlled Addition of Water Vapor to Iodine Fumes—A Solution to the Aging Problem," *Journal of Forensic Sciences* 24 (1979): 431.
3. F. G. Kendall and B. W. Rehn, "Rapid Method of Super Glue Fuming Application for the Development of Latent Fingerprints," *Journal of Forensic Sciences* 28 (1983): 777.
4. C. Roux et al., "A Further Study to Investigate the Effect of Fingerprint Enhancement Techniques on the DNA Analysis of Bloodstains," *Journal of Forensic Identification* 49 (1999): 357; C. J. Frégeau et al., "Fingerprint Enhancement Revisited and the Effects of Blood Enhancement Chemicals on Subsequent Profiler Plus™ Fluorescent Short Tandem Repeat DNA Analysis of Fresh and Aged Bloody Fingerprints," *Journal of Forensic Sciences* 45 (2000): 354; P. Grubwieser et al., "Systematic Study on STR Profiling on Blood and Saliva Traces after Visualization of Fingerprints," *Journal of Forensic Sciences* 48 (2003): 733.

The Beltway Snipers

During a three-week period in October 2002, ten people were killed and three others wounded as two snipers terrorized the region in and around the Baltimore–Washington metropolitan area. The arrest of John Allen Muhammad, 41, and Lee Boyd Malvo, 17, ended the ordeal. The semiautomatic .223-caliber rifle seized from them was ultimately linked by ballistics tests to eight of the ten killings. The car that Muhammad and Malvo were driving had been specially configured with one hole in the trunk through which a rifle barrel could protrude, so that a sniper could shoot from inside a slightly ajar trunk.

The major break in the case came when a friend of Muhammad's called police suggesting that Muhammad and his friend Malvo were the likely snipers. Muhammad's automobile records revealed numerous traffic stops in the Beltway area during the time of the shootings. Another break in the case came when Malvo called a priest to boast of a killing weeks before in Montgomery, Alabama. Investigators traced the claim to a recent liquor store holdup that left one person dead. Fortunately, the perpetrator of this crime left a latent fingerprint at the murder scene. Authorities quickly tracked the print to Malvo, a Jamaican citizen, through his fingerprints on file with the Immigration and Naturalization Service. A description of Muhammad's car was released to the media, leading to tips from alert citizens who noticed the car parked in a rest area with both occupants asleep.

The motive for the shooting spree was believed to be a plot to extort $10 million from local and state governments. Muhammad was sentenced to death and Malvo is currently serving life imprisonment without parole.

chapter 15

Firearms, Tool Marks, and Other Impressions

Key Terms

bore

breechblock

caliber

choke

distance determination

ejector

extractor

firearms identification

gauge

Greiss test

grooves

lands

rifling

Learning Objectives

After studying this chapter you should be able to:

- Describe techniques for rifling a barrel

- Recognize the class and individual characteristics of bullets and cartridge cases

- Understand the use of the comparison microscope to compare bullets and cartridge cases

- Explain the concept of the NIBIN database

- Explain the procedure for determining how far a weapon was fired from a target

- Identify the laboratory tests for determining whether an individual has fired a weapon

- Explain the forensic significance of class and individual characteristics to the comparison of tool mark, footwear, and tire impressions

- List some common field reagents used to enhance bloody footprints

Just as natural variations in skin ridge patterns and characteristics provide a key to human identification, minute random markings on surfaces can impart individuality to inanimate objects. Structural variations and irregularities caused by scratches, nicks, breaks, and wear permit the criminalist to relate a bullet to a gun; a scratch or abrasion mark to a single tool; or a tire track to a particular automobile. Individualization, so vigorously pursued in all other areas of criminalistics, is frequently attainable in firearms and tool mark examination.

Although a portion of this chapter will be devoted to the comparison of surface features for the purposes of bullet identification, a complete description of the services and capabilities of the modern forensic firearms laboratory cannot be restricted to just this one subject, important as it may be. The high frequency of shooting cases means that the science of firearms identification must extend beyond mere comparison of bullets to include knowledge of the operation of all types of weapons, restoration of obliterated serial numbers on weapons, detection and characterization of gunpowder residues on garments and around wounds, estimation of muzzle-to-target distances, and detection of powder residues on hands. Each of these functions will be covered in this chapter.

firearms identification
A discipline mainly concerned with determining whether a bullet or cartridge was fired by a particular weapon.

Bullet and Cartridge Comparisons

The inner surface of the barrel of a gun leaves its markings on a bullet passing through it. These markings are peculiar to each gun. Hence, if one bullet found at the scene of a crime and another test-fired from a suspect's gun show the same markings, the suspect is linked to the crime. Because these inner surface markings, or striations, are so important for bullet comparison, it is important to know why and how they originate.

The Gun Barrel

The gun barrel is produced from a solid bar of steel that has been hollowed out by drilling. The microscopic drill marks left on the barrel's inner surface are randomly irregular and in themselves impart a uniqueness to each barrel. However, the manufacture of a barrel requires the additional step of impressing its inner surface with spiral grooves, a step known as

grooves
The cut or low-lying portions between the lands in a rifled bore.

rifling. The surfaces of the original bore remaining between the grooves are called lands (see Figure 15–1).

As a fired bullet travels through a barrel, it engages the rifling grooves. These grooves then guide the bullet through the barrel, giving it a rapid spin. This is done because a spinning bullet does not tumble end over end on leaving the barrel, but remains instead on a true and accurate course.

The diameter of the gun barrel, sketched in Figure 15–2, measured between opposite lands, is known as the caliber of the weapon. Caliber is normally recorded in hundredths of an inch or in millimeters—for example, .22 caliber and 9 mm. Actually, the term *caliber,* as it is commonly applied, is not an exact measurement of the barrel's diameter; for example, a .38-caliber weapon might actually have a bore diameter that ranges from 0.345 to 0.365 inch.

Rifling Methods   Before 1940, barrels were rifled by having one or two grooves at a time cut into the surface with steel hook cutters. The cutting tool was rotated as it passed down the barrel, so that the final results were grooves spiraling to either the right or left. However, as the need for increased speed in weapons manufacture became apparent, newer techniques were developed that were far more suitable for the mass production of weapons.

The broach cutter, shown in Figure 15–3, consists of a series of concentric steel rings, with each ring slightly larger than the preceding one. As the broach passes through the barrel, it simultaneously cuts all grooves

rifling
The spiral grooves formed in the bore of a firearm barrel that impart spin to the projectile when it is fired.

bore
The interior of a firearm barrel.

lands
The raised portion between the grooves in a rifled bore.

caliber
The diameter of the bore of a rifled firearm, usually expressed in hundredths of an inch or millimeters—for example, .22 caliber and 9 mm.

FIGURE 15–1   Interior view of a gun barrel, showing the presence of lands and grooves.

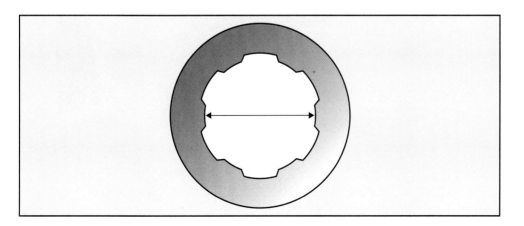

FIGURE 15–2   Cross-section of a barrel with six grooves. The diameter of the bore is the caliber.

into the barrel at the required depth. The broach rotates as it passes through the barrel, giving the grooves their desired direction and rate of twist.

In contrast to the broach, the button process involves no cuttings. A steel plug or "button" impressed with the desired number of grooves is forced under extremely high pressure through the barrel. A single pass of the button down the barrel compresses the metal to create lands and grooves on the barrel walls that are negative forms of those on the button. The button rotates to produce the desired direction and rate of twist (see Figure 15–4).

Like the button process, the mandrel rifling hammer forging process involves no cutting of metal. A mandrel is a rod of hardened steel machined

FIGURE 15–3 **A segment of a broach cutter.** *Courtesy New Jersey State Police*

FIGURE 15–4 (*top*) **Cross-section of a .22-caliber rifled barrel.** (*bottom*) **A button used to produce the lands and grooves in the barrel.** *Courtesy New Jersey State Police*

so its form is the reverse impression of the rifling it is intended to produce. The mandrel is inserted into a slightly oversized bore, and the barrel is compressed with hammering or heavy rollers into the mandrel's form.

Every firearms manufacturer chooses a rifling process that is best suited to meet the production standards and requirements of its product. Once the choice is made, however, the class characteristics of the weapon's barrel remain consistent; each has the same number of lands and grooves, with the same approximate width and direction of twist. For example, .32 caliber Smith & Wesson revolvers have five lands and grooves twisting to the right. On the other hand, Colt .32-caliber revolvers exhibit six lands and grooves twisting to the left. Although these class characteristics permit the examiner to distinguish one type or brand name of weapon from another, they do not impart individuality to any one barrel; no class characteristic can do this.

If one could cut a barrel open lengthwise, careful examination of the interior would reveal the existence of fine lines, or *striations,* many running the length of the barrel's lands and grooves. These striations are impressed into the metal as the negatives of minute imperfections found on the rifling cutter's surface, or they are produced by minute chips of steel pushed against the barrel's inner surface by a moving broach cutter. The random distribution and irregularities of these markings are impossible to duplicate exactly in any two barrels. No two rifled barrels, even those manufactured in succession, have identical striation markings. These striations form the individual characteristics of the barrel.

Comparing Bullet Markings As the bullet passes through the barrel, its surface is impressed with the rifled markings of the barrel. The bullet emerges from the barrel carrying the impressions of the bore's interior surface (see Figure 15–5). Because there is no practical way to directly compare the markings on the fired bullet and those within a barrel, the examiner must obtain test bullets fired through the suspect barrel for comparison. To prevent damage to the test bullet's markings and to facilitate the bullet's recovery, test firings are normally made into a recovery box filled with cotton or into a water tank.

The number of lands and grooves, and their direction of twist, are obvious points of comparison during the initial stages of the examination. Any differences in these class characteristics immediately eliminate the possibility that both bullets traveled through the same barrel. A bullet with five lands and grooves could not possibly have been fired from a weapon of like caliber with six lands and grooves, nor could one having a right twist have come through a barrel impressed with a left twist. If both bullets carry the same class characteristics, the analyst must begin to match the striated markings on both bullets. This can be done only with the assistance of the comparison microscope (see Chapter 7).

Modern firearms identification began with the development and use of the comparison microscope. This instrument is the firearms examiner's most important tool. The test and evidence bullets are mounted on cylindrical adjustable holders beneath the objective lenses of the microscope, each pointing in the same direction (see Figure 15–6). Both bullets are observed simultaneously within the same field of view, and the examiner rotates one bullet until a well-defined land or groove comes into view.

Once the striation markings are located, the other bullet is rotated until a matching region is found. Not only must the lands and grooves of the

FIGURE 15–5 A bullet is impressed with the rifling markings of the barrel when it emerges from the weapon.
Courtesy New Jersey State Police

test and evidence bullet have identical widths, but the longitudinal striations on each must coincide. When a matching area is located, the two bullets are simultaneously rotated to obtain additional matching areas around the periphery of the bullets. Figure 15–7 shows a typical photomicrograph of a bullet match as viewed under a comparison microscope.

Considerations in Bullet Comparison   Unfortunately, the firearms examiner rarely encounters a perfect match all around the bullet's periphery. The presence of grit and rust can alter the markings on bullets fired through the same barrel. More commonly, recovered evidence bullets become so mutilated and distorted on impact that they yield only a small area with intact markings.

Furthermore, striation markings on a barrel are not permanent structures; they are subject to continuing alteration through wear as succeeding bullets traverse the length of the barrel. Fortunately these changes are usually not dramatic and do not prevent the matching of two bullets fired by the same weapon. As with fingerprint comparison, there are no hard-and-fast rules governing the minimum number of points required for a bullet comparison. The final opinion must be based on the judgment, experience, and knowledge of the expert.

Frequently the firearms examiner receives a spent bullet without an accompanying suspect weapon and is asked to determine the caliber and

FIGURE 15–6 A bullet holder beneath the objective lens of a comparison microscope. *Courtesy Leica Microsystems, Buffalo, N.Y., www.leica-microsystems.com*

possible make of the weapon. If a bullet appears not to have lost its metal, its weight may be one factor in determining its caliber. In some instances, the number of lands and grooves, the direction of twist, and the widths of lands and grooves are useful class characteristics for eliminating certain makes of weapons from consideration. For example, a bullet that has five lands and grooves and twists to the right could not come from a weapon manufactured by Colt, because Colts are not manufactured with these class characteristics.

Sometimes a bullet has rifling marks that set it apart from most other manufactured weapons, as in the case of Marlin rifles. These weapons are rifled by a technique known as *microgrooving* and may have eight to twenty-four grooves impressed into their barrels; few other weapons are manufactured in this fashion. In this respect, the FBI maintains a record known as the General Rifling Characteristics File. This file contains listings of class characteristics, such as land and groove width dimensions, for known weapons. It is periodically updated and distributed to the law enforcement community to help identify rifled weapons from retrieved bullets.

Unlike rifled firearms, a shotgun has a smooth barrel, so projectiles passing through a shotgun barrel are not impressed with any characteristic markings that can later be related back to the weapon. Shotguns generally fire small lead balls or pellets contained within a shotgun shell

FIGURE 15–7 **Photomicrograph of two bullets through a comparison microscope. The test bullet is on the right; the questioned bullet is on the left.** *Courtesy Philadelphia Police Department Laboratory*

Case Study

Sacco and Vanzetti

Courtesy Corbis/Bettmann

In 1920, two security guards were viciously gunned down by unidentified assailants. The security guards were transporting shoe factory payroll, nearly $16,000 in cash, at the time of the robbery-murder. Eyewitnesses described the assailants as "Italian-looking," one with a full handlebar moustache. The robbers had used two

firearms, leaving behind three different brands of shells.

Two suspects were identified and arrested—Nicola Sacco and his friend, the amply mustachioed Bartolomeo Vanzetti. After denying owning any firearms, each was found to be in possession of a loaded pistol. In fact, Sacco's pistol was .32 caliber, the same caliber as the crime-scene bullets. In Sacco's pockets were found twenty-three bullets matching the brands of the empty shells found at the murder scene.

This case coincided with the "Red Scare," a politically turbulent time in post–World War I America. Citizens feared socialist zealots, and the media played up these emotions. Political maneuvering and the use of the media muddied the waters surrounding the case, and the fact that both suspects belonged to anarchist political groups that advocated

Case Study

revolutionary violence against the government only incited public animosity toward them. Sympathetic socialist organizations attempted to turn Sacco and Vanzetti into martyrs, calling their prosecution a "witch hunt."

The outcome of the trial ultimately depended on whether the prosecution could prove that Sacco's pistol fired the bullets that killed the two security guards. At trial, the ballistics experts testified that the bullets used were no longer in production and they could not find similar ammunition to use in test firings—aside from the unused cartridges found in Sacco's pockets. A forensics expert for the prosecution concluded that a visual examination showed that the bullets matched, leading the jury to return a

verdict of guilty. Sacco and Vanzetti were sentenced to death.

Because of continued public protests, a committee was appointed in 1927 to review the case. Around this time, Calvin Goddard, at the Bureau of Forensic Ballistics in New York, perfected the comparison microscope for use in forensic firearms investigations. With this instrument, two bullets are viewed side by side to compare the striations imparted to a bullet's surface as it travels through the gun's barrel. The committee asked Goddard to examine the bullets in question. A test-fired bullet from Sacco's weapon was matched conclusively by Goddard to one of the crime scene bullets. The fates of Sacco and Vanzetti were sealed and they were put to death in 1927.

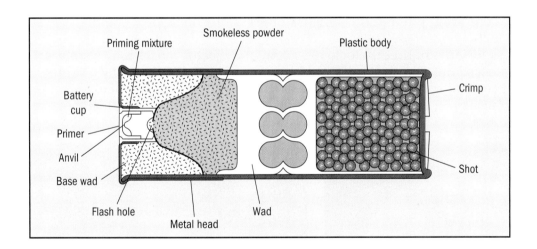

FIGURE 15–8 **Cross-section of a loaded shotgun shell.**

(see Figure 15–8). A paper or plastic wad pushes the pellets through the barrel on ignition of the cartridge's powder charge. By weighing and measuring the diameter of the shot recovered at a crime scene, the examiner can usually determine the size of shot used in the shell. The size and shape of the recovered wad may also reveal the gauge of the shotgun used and, in some instances, may indicate the manufacturer of the fired shell.

The diameter of the shotgun barrel is expressed by the term gauge.[1] The higher the gauge number, the smaller the barrel's diameter. For example, a 12-gauge shotgun has a bore diameter of 0.730 inch as contrasted

WebExtra 15.2
3-D Shotgun Shell Illustrations
www.prenhall.com/hsforensics

gauge
Size designation of a shotgun, originally the number of lead balls with the same diameter as the barrel that would make a pound. The only exception is the .410 shotgun, in which bore size is 0.41 inch.

to 0.670 inch for a 16-gauge shotgun. The exception to this rule is the .410-gauge shotgun, which refers to a barrel 0.41 inch in diameter.

Cartridge Cases

The act of pulling a trigger releases the weapon's firing pin, causing it to strike the primer, which in turn ignites the powder. The expanding gases generated by the burning gunpowder propel the bullet forward through the barrel, simultaneously pushing the spent cartridge case or shell back with equal force against the breechblock. As the bullet is marked by its passage through the barrel, the shell is also impressed with markings by its contact with the metal surfaces of the weapon's firing and loading mechanisms. As with bullets, these markings can be reproduced in test-fired cartridges to provide distinctive points of comparison for individualizing a spent shell to a rifled weapon or shotgun.

The shape of the firing pin is impressed into the relatively soft metal of the primer on the cartridge case, revealing the minute distortions of the firing pin. These imperfections may be sufficiently random to individualize the pin impression to a single weapon. Similarly, the cartridge case, in its rearward thrust, is impressed with the surface markings of the breechblock. The breechblock, like any machined surface, is populated with random striation markings that become a highly distinctive signature for individualizing its surface.

Other distinctive markings that may appear on the shell as a result of metal-to-metal contact are caused by the extractor and ejector mechanism and the magazine or clip, as well as by imperfections on the firing chamber walls. The photomicrographs in Figure 15–9 reveal a comparison of the firing pin and breechblock impressions on evidence and test-fired shells.

Firing pin, breechblock, extractor, and ejector marks may also be impressed onto the surface of the brass portion of shells fired by a shotgun. These impressions provide points for individualizing the shell to a weapon that are just as valuable as cartridge cases discharged from a rifled firearm.

(a) (b)

FIGURE 15.9 **Comparison microscope photomicrograph showing a match between (a) firing pin impressions and (b) the breechblock markings on two shells.** *Courtesy Ronald Welsh, Bureau of Forensic Services, Central Valley Laboratory, Ripon, Calif*

Furthermore, in the absence of a suspect weapon, the size and shape of a firing pin impression and/or the position of ejector marks in relationship to extractor and other markings may provide some clue to the type or make of the weapon that fired the questioned shell, or at least eliminate a large number of possibilities.

WebExtra 15.6
View Animations to Illustrate the Firing Process and the Extraction/Ejection Process of a Semiautomatic Pistol
www.prenhall.com/hsforensics

Key Points

- The manufacture of a gun barrel requires impressing its inner surface with spiral grooves, a step known as rifling. Rifling imparts spin to the projectile when it is fired, which keeps it on an accurate course.

- No two rifled barrels have identical striation markings. These striations form the individual characteristics of the barrel. The inner surface of the barrel of a gun leaves its striation markings on a bullet passing through it.

- The class characteristics of a rifled barrel include the number of lands and grooves and the width and direction of twist.

- The comparison microscope is a firearms examiner's most important tool because it allows two bullets to be observed and compared simultaneously.

- The firing pin, breechblock, and ejector and extractor mechanism also offer a highly distinctive signature for individualization of cartridge cases.

- Unlike handguns, a shotgun is not rifled—it has a smooth barrel. Because of this, shotgun shells are not impressed with any characteristic markings that can be used to compare two shotgun shells to determine whether they were fired from the same weapon.

Automated Firearms Search Systems

The use of firearms, especially semiautomatic weapons, during the commission of a crime has significantly increased throughout the United States. Because of the expense of such firearms, the likelihood that a specific weapon will be used in multiple crimes has risen. The advent of computerized imaging technology has made possible the storage of bullet and cartridge surface characteristics in a manner analogous to the storage of automated fingerprint files (see pp. 480–483). Using this concept, crime laboratories can be networked, allowing them to share information on bullets and cartridges retrieved from several jurisdictions.

Early Systems

The effort to build a national computerized database for firearms evidence in the United States had a rather confusing and inefficient start in the early 1990s. Two major federal law enforcement agencies, the FBI and the Bureau of Alcohol, Tobacco, Firearms and Explosives (ATF), offered the law enforcement community competing and incompatible computerized systems.

The automated search system developed for the FBI was known as *DRUGFIRE*. This system emphasized the examination of unique markings on the cartridge casings expended by the weapon. The specimen was analyzed through a microscope attached to a video camera. The magnification allowed for a close-up view to identify individual characteristics. The image was captured by a video camera, digitized, and stored in a database. Although DRUGFIRE emphasized cartridge-case imagery, the images of highly characteristic bullet striations could also be stored in a like manner for comparisons.

The *Integrated Ballistic Identification System (IBIS),* developed for the Bureau of Alcohol, Tobacco, Firearms and Explosives, processed digital microscopic images of identifying features found on both expended bullets and cartridge casings. IBIS incorporated two software programs: Bulletproof, a bullet-analyzing module, and Brasscatcher, a cartridge-case-analyzing module. A schematic diagram of Bulletproof's operation is depicted in Figure 15–10.[2]

FIGURE 15–10 **Bulletproof configuration. The sample is mounted on the specimen manipulator and illuminated by the light source from a microscope. The image is captured by a video camera and digitized. This digital image is then stored in a database, available for retrieval and comparison. The search for a match includes analyzing the width of land and groove impressions along with both rifling and individual characteristics. The Brasscatcher software uses the same system configuration but emphasizes the analysis of expended cartridge casings rather than the expended bullets.** *Courtesy Forensic Technology (WAI) Inc., Côte St-Luc, Quebec, Canada*

NIBIN   In 1999, members of the FBI and ATF joined forces to introduce the *National Integrated Ballistics Information Network (NIBIN)* program to the discipline of firearms examination. The new unified system incorporates both DRUGFIRE and IBIS technologies available in prior years. ATF has overall responsibility for the system sites, while the FBI is responsible for the communications network.

Agencies using the new NIBIN technology produce database files from bullets and cartridge casings retrieved from crime scenes or test fires from retrieved firearms. More than two hundred law enforcement agencies worldwide have adapted to this technology. The success of the system has been proven with more than 800,000 images compiled; nationwide, law enforcement agencies have connected more than 11,000 bullets and casings to more than one crime (see Figure 15–11).

FIGURE 15–11   Bullets A, B, C, and D were acquired in the IBIS database at different times from different crime scenes. D is a fragmented bullet that had only three land impressions available for acquisition. Upon the entry of bullet D, IBIS found a potential matching candidate in the database: B. On the far right, bullet D is compared to bullet B using the IBIS imaging software. Finally, a forensic firearms examiner using the actual evidence under a conventional comparison microscope will confirm the match between B and **D.** *Courtesy Forensic Technology (WAI) Inc., Côte St-Luc, Quebec, Canada*

For example, in a recent case, a Houston security guard was shot and killed during a botched armed robbery. A bullet and .40-caliber Smith & Wesson cartridge casing were recovered and imaged into NIBIN. Earlier that day, a robbery-turned-double-homicide left two store clerks dead. Again, two bullets and two .40-caliber Smith & Wesson cartridge casings were recovered. Once they were processed into NIBIN, a correlation was found with the murder of the security officer and a separate aggravated robbery that occurred two weeks earlier. All three crimes were linked with a firearm believed to be a .40-caliber Smith & Wesson pistol.

Further investigation into the use of a victim's credit card helped police locate two suspects. In the possession of one suspect was a .40-caliber Smith & Wesson pistol. The gun was test-fired and imaged into NIBIN. The casing from the test-fired weapon matched the evidence obtained in the robbery and the aggravated robbery-homicides. A firearms examiner verified the associations by traditional comparisons. Before this computerized technology was developed, it would have taken years, or may have been impossible, to link all of these shootings to a single firearm.

In another example, the ATF laboratory in Rockville, Maryland, received 1,466 cartridge casings from the Ovcara mass burial site in Bosnia. After processing and imaging profiles for all casings, the examiners determined that eighteen different firearms were used at the site. With the help of NIBIN technology and competent examiners, jurists were able to try and convict an individual for war crimes.

NIBIN serves only as a screening tool for firearms evidence. A computerized system does not replace the skills of the firearms examiner. NIBIN can screen hundreds of unsolved firearms cases and may narrow the possibilities to several firearms. However, the final comparison will be made by a forensic examiner through traditional microscopic methods.

Ballistic Fingerprinting

Participating crime laboratories in the United States are building databases of bullet and cartridge cases found at crime scenes and those fired in tests of guns seized from criminals. As these databases come online and prove their usefulness in solving crimes, law enforcement officials and the political community are scrutinizing the feasibility of scaling this concept up to create a system of *ballistic fingerprinting*. This system would entail the capture and storage of appropriate markings on bullets and cartridges test-fired from handguns and rifles before they are sold to the public. Questions regarding who will be responsible for collecting the images and details of how will they be stored are but two of many issues to be determined. The concept of ballistic fingerprinting is an intriguing one for the law enforcement community and promises to be explored and debated intensely in the future.

Key Points

- The advent of computerized imaging technology has made possible the storage of bullet and cartridge surface characteristics in a manner analogous to automated fingerprint files.

- Two automated firearms search systems are DRUGFIRE, developed by the FBI, and IBIS, developed by the ATF.

- NIBIN is the National Integrated Ballistics Information Network, a unified firearms search system that incorporates both DRUGFIRE and IBIS technologies.

Gunpowder Residues

Modern ammunition is propelled toward a target by the expanding gases created by the ignition of smokeless powder or nitrocellulose in a cartridge. Under ideal circumstances, all of the powder is consumed in the process and converted into the rapidly expanding gases. However, in practice the powder is never totally burned. When a firearm is discharged, unburned and partially burned particles of gunpowder in addition to smoke are propelled out of the barrel along with the bullet toward the target. If the muzzle of the weapon is sufficiently close, these products are deposited onto the target. The distribution of gunpowder particles and other discharge residues around the bullet hole permits a distance determination, an assessment of the distance from which a handgun or rifle was fired.

distance determination
The process of determining the distance between the firearm and a target, usually based on the distribution of powder patterns or the spread of a shot pattern.

Distance Determination

In incidents involving gunshot wounds, it is often necessary to determine the distance from which the weapon was fired. For example, in incidents involving a shooting death, the suspect often pleads self-defense as the motive for the attack. Such claims are fertile grounds for distance determinations, because finding the proximity of the people involved is necessary to establish the facts of the incident. Similarly, careful examination of the wounds of suicide victims usually reveals characteristics associated with a very close-range gunshot wound. The absence of such characteristics strongly indicates that the wound was not self-inflicted and signals the possibility of foul play.

The accuracy of a distance determination varies according to the circumstances of the case. When the investigator is unable to recover a suspect weapon, the best that the examiner can do is to state whether a shot could have been fired within some distance from the target. More exact opinions are possible only when the examiner has the suspect weapon in hand and has knowledge of the type of ammunition used in the shooting.

Handguns and Rifles   The precise distance from which a handgun or rifle has been fired must be determined by carefully comparing the powder residue pattern on the victim's clothing or skin to test patterns made when the suspect weapon is fired at varying distances from a target. A white cloth or a fabric comparable to the victim's clothing may be used as a test target (see Figure 15–12). Because the spread and density of the residue pattern vary widely between weapons and ammunition, such a comparison is significant only when it is made with the suspect weapon and suspect ammunition, or with ammunition of the same type and make. By comparing the test and evidence patterns, the examiner may find enough similarity in shape and density on which to judge the distance from which the shot was fired.

Without the weapon, the examiner is restricted to looking for recognizable characteristics around the bullet hole. Such findings are at best approximations made as a result of general observations and the examiner's experience. However, some noticeable characteristics should be sought. For instance, when the weapon is held in contact with or less than 1 inch from the target, a heavy concentration of smokelike vaporous lead usually surrounds the bullet entrance hole. Often loose fibers surrounding a contact hole show scorch marks from the flame discharge of the weapon, and some synthetic fibers may show signs of being melted as a result of the heat from the discharge. Furthermore, the blowback of muzzle gases may

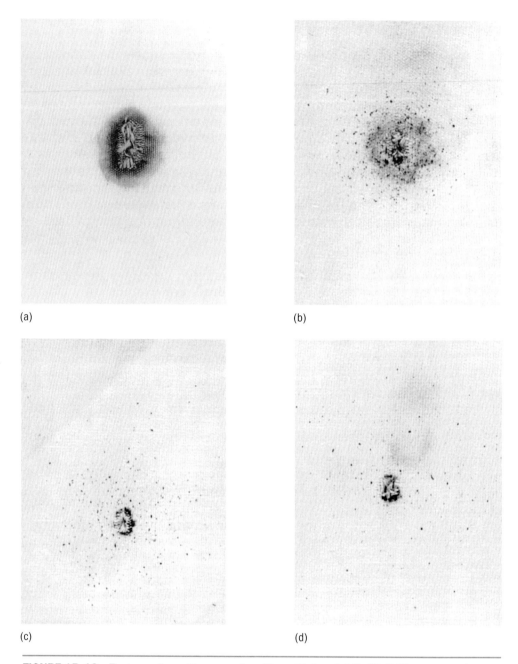

(a)

(b)

(c)

(d)

FIGURE 15–12 **Test powder patterns made with a .38 Special Smith & Wesson revolver fired at the following distances from the target: (a) contact, (b) 6 inches, (c) 12 inches, and (d) 18 inches.** *Courtesy New Jersey State Police*

produce a stellate (star-shape) tear pattern around the hole. Such a hole is invariably surrounded by a rim of a smokelike deposit of vaporous lead (see Figure 15–13).

A halo of vaporous lead (smoke) deposited around a bullet hole normally indicates a discharge 12–18 inches or less from the target. The presence of scattered specks of unburned and partially burned powder grains without any accompanying soot can often be observed at distances up to approximately 25 inches. Occasionally, however, scattered gunpowder particles are noted at a firing distance as far out as 36 inches. With ball powder ammunition, this distance may be extended to 6–8 feet.

FIGURE 15–13 A contact shot. *Courtesy New Jersey State Police*

Finally, a weapon that has been fired more than 3 feet from a target usually does not deposit any powder residues on the target's surface. In these cases, the only visual indication that the hole was made by a bullet is a dark ring, known as *bullet wipe,* around the perimeter of the entrance hole. Bullet wipe consists of a mixture of carbon, dirt, lubricant, primer residue, and lead wiped off the bullet's surface as it passes through the target. Again, in the absence of a suspect weapon, these observations are general guidelines for estimating target distances. Numerous factors— barrel length, caliber, type of ammunition, and type and condition of the weapon fired—influence the amount of gunpowder residue deposited on a target.

Shotguns   The determination of firing distances involving shotguns must also be related to test firings performed with the suspect weapon, using the same type of ammunition known to be used in the crime. In the absence of a weapon, the muzzle-to-target distance can be estimated by measuring the spread of the discharged shot. With close-range shots varying in distance up to 4–5 feet, the shot charge enters the target as a concentrated mass, producing a hole somewhat larger than the bore of the barrel. As the distance increases, the pellets progressively separate and spread out. Generally speaking, the spread in the pattern made by a 12-gauge shotgun increases 1 inch for each yard of distance. Thus, a 10-inch pattern would be produced at approximately 10 yards. Of course, this is only a rule of thumb; normally, many variables can affect the shot pattern.

Other factors include the barrel length, the size and quantity of the pellets fired, the quantity of powder charge used to propel the pellets, and the choke of the gun under examination. **Choke** is the degree of constriction placed at the muzzle end of the barrel. The greater the choke, the narrower the shotgun pattern and the faster and farther the pellets will travel.

choke

An interior constriction placed at or near the muzzle end of a shotgun's barrel to control shot dispersion.

Powder Residues on Garments

When garments or other evidence relevant to a shooting are received in the crime laboratory, the surfaces of all items are first examined micro-scopically for gunpowder residue. These particles may be identifiable by their characteristic colors, sizes, and shapes. However, the absence of vi-sual indications does not preclude the possibility that gunpowder residue is present. Sometimes the lack of color contrast between the powder and garment or the presence of heavily encrusted deposits of blood can ob-scure the visual detection of gunpowder. Often, an infrared photograph of the suspect area overcomes the problem. Such a photograph may enhance the contrast, thus revealing vaporous lead and powder particles deposited around the hole (see Figure 15–14). In other situations, this may not help, and the analyst must use chemical tests to detect gunpowder residues.

Nitrites are one type of chemical product that results from the incom-plete combustion of smokeless (nitrocellulose) powder. One test method for locating powder residues involves transferring particles embedded on the target surface to chemically treated gelatin-coated photographic pa-per. This procedure is known as the Greiss test. The examiner presses the photographic paper onto the target with a hot iron; once the nitrite parti-cles are on the paper, they are made easily visible by chemical treatment.[3] In addition, comparing the developed nitrite pattern to nitrite patterns ob-tained from test firings at known distances can be useful in determining the shooting distance from the target. A second chemical test is then per-formed to detect any trace of lead residue around the bullet hole. The ques-tioned surface is sprayed with a solution of sodium rhodizonate, followed by a series of oversprays with acid solutions. This treatment turns lead par-ticles pink, followed by blue-violet.

Greiss test
A chemical test used to develop patterns of gunpowder residues around bullet holes.

 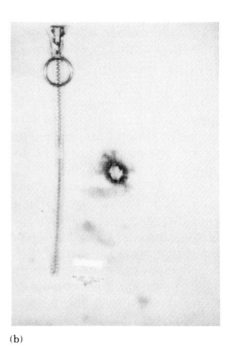

(a)   (b)

FIGURE 15–14 **(a) A shirt bearing a powder stain, photographed under normal light. (b) Infrared photograph of the same shirt.** *Courtesy New Jersey State Police*

Key Points

- The distribution of gunpowder particles and other discharge residues around a bullet hole permits an assessment of the distance from which a handgun or rifle was fired.

- The precise distance from which a handgun or rifle is determined by carefully comparing the powder residue pattern on the victim's clothing to test patterns made when the suspect weapon is fired at varying distances from a target.

- The Greiss test is a chemical test used to develop patterns of gunpowder residues around bullet holes. It tests for the presence of nitrates.

Primer Residues on the Hands

The firing of a weapon not only propels residues toward the target, but also blows gunpowder and primer residues back toward the shooter (see Figure 15–15). As a result, traces of these residues are often deposited on the firing hand of the shooter, and their detection can provide valuable information as to whether an individual has recently fired a weapon.

Detecting Primer Residues

Early efforts at demonstrating powder residues on the hands centered on chemical tests that could detect unburned gunpowder or nitrates. For many years, the *dermal nitrate test* was popular. It required the application of hot paraffin or wax to the suspect's hand with a paintbrush. After

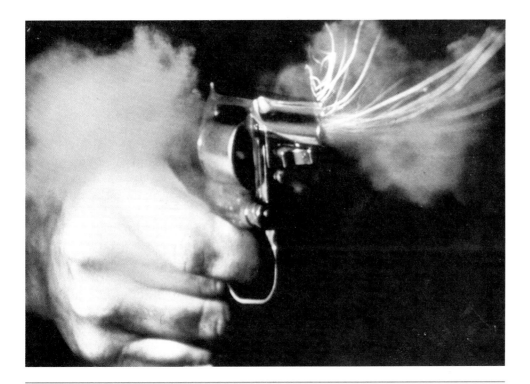

FIGURE 15–15 **When a handgun is fired, gunpowder and primer residues are normally blown back toward the hand of the shooter.** *Courtesy Centre of Forensic Sciences, Toronto, Canada*

drying into a solid crust, the paraffin was removed and tested with diphenylamine. A blue color indicated a positive reaction for nitrates. However, the dermal nitrate test has fallen into disfavor with law enforcement agencies, owing mainly to its lack of specificity. Common materials such as fertilizers, cosmetics, urine, and tobacco all give positive reactions that are indistinguishable from that obtained for gunpowder by this test.

Efforts to identify a shooter now center on the detection of primer residues deposited on the hand of a shooter at the time of firing. With the exception of most .22-caliber ammunition, primers currently manufactured contain a blend of lead styphnate, barium nitrate, and antimony sulfide. Residues from these materials are most likely to be deposited on the thumb web and the back of the firing hand of a shooter, because these areas are closest to gases escaping along the side or back of the gun during discharge. In addition, individuals who handle a gun without firing it may have primer residues deposited on the palm of the hand coming in contact with the weapon.

However, with the handling of a used firearm, the passage of time, and the resumption of normal activities following a shooting, gunshot residues from the back of the hand are frequently redistributed to other areas, including the palms. Therefore, it is not unusual to find higher levels of barium and antimony on the palms than on the backs of the hands of known shooters. Another possibility is the deposition of significant levels of barium and antimony on the hands of an individual who is near a firearm when it is discharged.

Tests for Primer Residues

Determination of whether a person has fired or handled a weapon or has been near a discharged firearm is normally made by measuring the presence and possibly the amount of barium and antimony on the relevant portions of the suspect's hands. A variety of materials and techniques are used for removing these residues. The most popular approach, and certainly the most convenient for the field investigator, is to apply an adhesive tape or adhesive to the hand's surface in order to remove any adhering residue particles.

Swabbing Another approach is to remove any residues present by swabbing both the firing and nonfiring hands with cotton that has been moistened with 5 percent nitric acid. The front and back of each hand are separately swabbed. All four swabs, along with a moistened control, are then forwarded to the crime laboratory for analysis.

In any case, once the hands are treated for the collection of barium and antimony, the collection medium must be analyzed for the presence of these elements. High barium and antimony levels on the suspect's hand(s) strongly indicate that the person fired or handled a weapon or was near a firearm when it was discharged. Because these elements are normally present in small quantities (less than 10 micrograms) after a firing, only the most sensitive analytical techniques can be used to detect them.

Unfortunately, even though most specimens submitted for this type of analysis have been from individuals strongly suspected of having fired a gun, there has been a low rate of positive findings. The major difficulty appears to be the short time that primer residues remain on the hands. These residues are readily removed by intentional or unintentional washing, rubbing, or wiping of the hands. In fact, one study demonstrated that it is very difficult to detect primer residues on cotton hand swabs taken as soon as two hours after firing a weapon.[4] Hence, some laboratories do not accept cotton hand swabs taken from living people six or more hours after a firing has occurred.

In cases that involve suicide victims, a higher rate of positives for the presence of gunshot residue is obtained when the hand swabbing is conducted before the person's body is moved or when the hands are protected by paper bags.[5] However, hand swabbing or the application of an adhesive cannot be used to detect firings with most .22-caliber rim-fire ammunition. Such ammunition may contain only barium or neither barium nor antimony in its primer composition.

SEM Testing   Most laboratories that can detect gunshot residue require application of an adhesive to the shooter's hands.[6] Microscopic primer and gunpowder particles on the adhesive are then found with a scanning electron microscope (SEM). The characteristic size and shape of these particles distinguishes them from other contaminants on the hands (see Figure 15–16). When the SEM is linked to an X-ray analyzer (see pp. 251–253), an elemental analysis of the particles can be conducted. A finding of a select combination of elements (lead, barium, and antimony) confirms that the particles were indeed primer residue (see Figure 15–17).

The major advantage of the SEM approach for primer residue detection is its enhanced specificity over hand swabbing. The SEM characterizes primer particles by their size and shape as well as by their chemical composition. Unfortunately, the excessive operator time required to find and characterize gunshot residue has deterred this technique's use. The availability of automated particle search and identification systems for use with scanning electron microscopes may overcome this problem. Results of work performed with automated systems show it to be significantly faster than a manual approach for finding gunshot residue particles.[7]

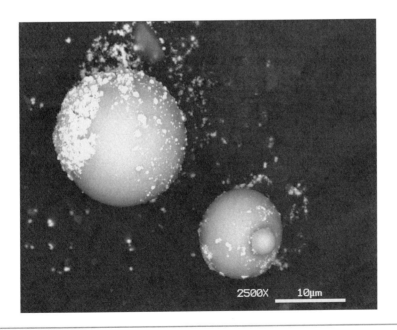

FIGURE 15–16   An SEM view of gunshot residue particles. *Courtesy Jeol USA Inc., Peabody, Mass., www.jeolusa.com*

Other Primer Residue Tests Neutron activation analysis and flameless atomic absorption spectrophotometry are analytical methods sensitive enough to detect barium and antimony in gunshot residues in hand swabs. However, the need for access to a neutron source, expensive counting equipment, and extensive regulatory requirements limit neutron activation analysis technology to a small number of crime laboratories. On the other hand, flameless atomic absorption spectrophotometry can be purchased at a cost well within the budgets of most crime laboratories, and a number of laboratories use this instrument to detect barium and antimony on a shooter's hands.

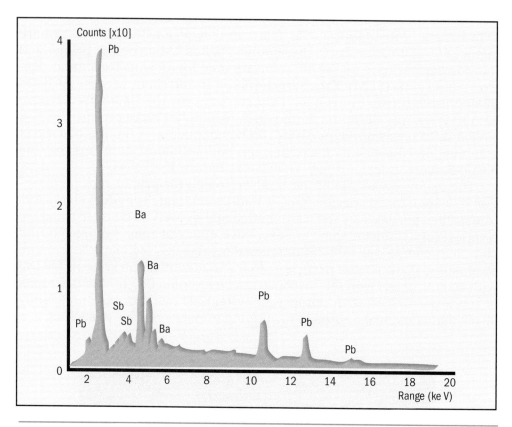

FIGURE 15–17 **Spectrum showing the presence of lead, barium, and antimony in gunshot residue.** *Courtesy Jeol USA Inc., Peabody, Mass., www.jeolusa.com*

Closer Analysis

Atomic Absorption Spectrophotometry

When an atom is vaporized, it absorbs many of the same frequencies of light that it emits in an excited state. Selective absorption of light by atoms is the basis for a technique known as *atomic absorption spectrophotometry*. A simple atomic absorption spectrophotometer is illustrated in the figure.

In atomic absorption spectrophotometry, the specimen is heated to a temperature that is hot enough to vaporize its atoms while leaving a substantial number of atoms in an unexcited state. Normally the specimen is inserted into an air-acetylene flame to achieve this temperature. The vaporized atoms are then exposed to

Parts of a simple flame atomic absorption spectrophotometer.

radiation emitted from a light source. The technique achieves great specificity by using as its radiation source a discharge tube made of the same element being analyzed in the specimen.

When the discharge lamp is turned on, it emits only the frequencies of light that are present in the emission spectrum of the element. Likewise, the sample absorbs these frequencies only when it contains the same element. Therefore, to determine the presence of antimony in a specimen, the atomic absorption spectrophotometer must be fitted with a discharge lamp that is constructed of antimony. Under these conditions, the sample absorbs light only if it contains antimony.

Once the radiation has passed through the sample, a monochromator, consisting of a prism or a diffraction grating and a slit, isolates the desired radiation frequency and transmits it to a detector. The detector converts the light into an electrical signal, the intensity of which is recorded on a strip-chart recorder.

Atomic absorption spectrophotometry measures the absorption of light by the element of interest. The concentration of the absorbing element is directly proportional to the quantity of the light absorbed. The higher the concentration of the element, the more light is absorbed. For this reason, atomic absorption spectroscopy is most useful for accurately determining an element's concentration in a sample. Furthermore, the technique is sufficiently sensitive to find wide application in detecting and quantitating elements that are present in trace levels. However, one drawback is that the analyst can determine only one element at a time, each time having to select the proper lamp to match the element under investigation.

Although atomic absorption spectrophotometry has been used for chemical analysis since 1955, it has not yet found wide application for solving forensic problems. However, a modification in the design of the instrument may change this situation. By substituting a heated graphite furnace or a heated strip of metal (tantalum) for the flame, analysts have achieved a more efficient means of atomic volatilization and as a result have

(*continued*)

Closer Analysis

Atomic Absorption Spectrophotometry *(continued)*

substantially increased the sensitivity of the technique. Many elements can now be detected at levels that approach one-trillionth of a gram.

The high sensitivity of "flameless" atomic absorption now equals or surpasses that of most known analytical procedures. Considering the relative simplicity and low cost of the technique, atomic absorption spectrophotometry has become an attractive method for detecting and measuring the smallest levels of trace elements in physical evidence.

As far as atoms are concerned, energy is a two-way street. Energy can be put into the atom at the same time that energy is given off; what goes in must come out. The chemist can study the atom using either approach. Atomic absorption spectrophotometry carefully measures the value and amount of light energy going into the atom; emission spectroscopy (see pp. 401–402) collects and measures the various light energies given off. The result is the same: atoms are identified by the existence of characteristic energy levels.

Key Points

- Firing a weapon propels residues toward the target and blows gunpowder and primer residues back toward the shooter. Traces of these residues are often deposited on the firing hand of the shooter, providing valuable information as to whether an individual has recently fired a weapon.

- Examiners measure the amount of barium and antimony on the relevant portion of the suspect's hands or characterize the morphology of particles containing these elements to determine whether a person has fired or handled a weapon or was near a discharged firearm.

Serial Number Restoration

Today, many manufactured items, including automobile engine blocks and firearms, are impressed with a serial number for identification. Increasingly the criminalist must restore such a number when it has been removed or obliterated by grinding, rifling, or punching.

Serial numbers are usually stamped on a metal body or frame, or on a plate, with hard steel dies. These dies strike the metal surface with a force that allows each digit to sink into the metal at a prescribed depth. Serial numbers can be restored because the metal crystals in the stamped zone are placed under a permanent strain that extends a short distance beneath the original numbers. When a suitable etching agent is applied, the strained area dissolves faster than the unaltered metal, thus revealing the etched pattern in the form of the original numbers. However, if the zone of strain has been removed, or if the area has been impressed with a different strain pattern, the number usually cannot be restored.

Before any treatment with the etching reagent, the obliterated surface must be thoroughly cleaned of dirt and oil and polished to a mirrorlike finish. The reagent is swabbed onto the surface with a cotton ball. The choice of etching reagent depends on the type of metal surface being worked on. A solution of hydrochloric acid (120 milliliters), copper chloride (90 grams), and water (100 milliliters) generally works well for steel surfaces.

Collection and Preservation of Firearms Evidence

Firearms

The Hollywood image of an investigator picking up a weapon by its barrel with a pencil or stick in order to protect fingerprints must be avoided. This practice only disturbs powder deposits, rust, or dirt lodged in the barrel, and consequently may alter the striation markings on test-fired bullets. If recovery of latent fingerprints is a primary concern, hold the weapon by the edge of the trigger guard or by the checkered portion of the grip, which usually does not retain identifiable fingerprints.

The most important consideration in handling a weapon is safety. Before any weapon is sent to the laboratory, all precautions must be taken to prevent an accidental discharge of a loaded weapon in transit. In most cases, it will be necessary to unload the weapon. If this is done, a record should first be made of the weapon's hammer and safety position; likewise, the location of all fired and unfired ammunition in the weapon must be recorded.

When a revolver is recovered, the chamber position in line with the barrel should be indicated by a scratch mark on the cylinder. Each chamber is designated with a number on a diagram, and as each cartridge or casing is removed, it should be marked to correspond to the numbered chambers in the diagram. Knowledge of the cylinder position of a cartridge casing may be useful for later determination of the sequence of events, particularly in shooting cases, when more than one shot was fired. Place each round in a separate box or envelope. If the weapon is an automatic, the magazine must be removed and checked for prints and the chamber then emptied.

As with any other type of physical evidence recovered at a crime scene, firearms evidence must be marked for identification and a chain of custody must be established. Therefore, when a firearm is recovered, an identification tag should be attached to the trigger guard. The tag should be marked to show appropriate identifying data, including the weapon's serial number, make, and model and the investigator's initials. The firearm itself may be further identified by being marked directly with a sharp-pointed scriber in an inconspicuous area of the weapon—for example, the inside of the trigger guard. This practice will avoid any permanent defacement of the weapon.

When a weapon is recovered from an underwater location, no effort must be made to dry or clean it. Instead, the firearm should be transported to the laboratory in a receptacle containing enough of the same water necessary to keep it submerged. This procedure prevents rust from developing during transport.

Ammunition

Protection of class and individual markings on bullets and cartridge cases must be the primary concern of the field investigator. Thus, extreme caution is needed when removing a lodged bullet from a wall or other object. If the bullet's surface is accidentally scratched during this operation, valuable striation markings could be obliterated. It is best to free bullets from their target by carefully breaking away the surrounding support material while avoiding direct contact with the projectile.

Bullets recovered at the crime scene should be scribed with the investigator's initials, on either the base or the nose of the bullet (see Figure 15–18). Again, obliteration of any striation markings on the bullet must be scrupulously avoided. If the bullet is badly deformed and there is no apparent place for identification, it should just be placed in a container that is appropriately marked for identification. In any case, the investigator must protect the bullet by wrapping it in tissue paper before placing it in a pillbox or an envelope for shipment to the crime laboratory.

Minute traces of evidence such as paint and fibers may be adhering to the bullet; the investigator must take care to leave these trace materials intact. Similarly, a fired casing must be identified so as to avoid destroying marks impressed on it from the weapon. The investigator's initials should be placed near the outside or inside mouth of the shell (see Figure 15–19).

FIGURE 15–18 Discharged evidence bullets should be marked on the base or nose. When there is more than one bullet, a number should accompany the initials. *Never* mark bullets on the side.

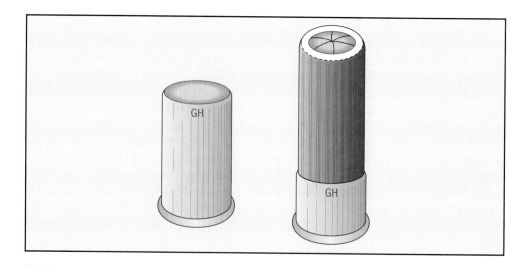

FIGURE 15–19 Discharged evidence shells should be marked on the outside or inside, as close as possible to the mouth of the shell. Discharged shotgun shells should be marked on the brass, close to the paper or plastic. *Never* mark the shells where the firing pin strikes the primer.

Discharged shells from shotguns are initialed with ink or indelible pencil on the paper or plastic tube remaining on the shell or on the metal nearest the mouth of the shell. In incidents involving shotguns, any wads recovered should also be packaged and sent to the laboratory. An examination of the size and composition of the wad may reveal information about the type of ammunition used and the gauge of the shotgun.

When semiautomatic or automatic weapons have been fired, the ejection pattern of the casings can help establish the relationship of the suspect to his or her victim. For this reason, the investigator must note the exact location where a shell casing was recovered.

Gunpowder Deposits

The clothing of a firearms victim must be carefully preserved to prevent damage or disruption to powder residues deposited around a bullet or shell hole. Cutting or tearing of clothing in the area of the holes must be avoided when removing the clothing. All wet clothing should be air-dried out of direct sunlight and then folded carefully so as not to disrupt the area around the bullet hole. Each item should be placed in a separate paper bag.

Key Points

- Criminalists can restore serial numbers removed or obliterated by grinding, rifling, or punching.

- Because the metal crystals in the stamped zone are placed under a permanent strain that extends a short distance beneath the original numbers, the serial number can be restored through chemical etching.

- A suspect firearm should never be picked up by inserting an object into its barrel because this practice may alter the striation markings on test-fired bullets.

- Before unloading a suspect weapon, the weapon's hammer and safety position should be recorded, as well as the location of all fired and unfired ammunition in the weapon.

- Protection of class and individual markings on bullets and cartridge cases is the primary concern of the field investigator when recovering bullets and cartridge casings.

Tool Marks

A *tool mark* is any impression, cut, gouge, or abrasion caused by a tool coming into contact with another object. Most often, tool marks are encountered at burglary scenes that involve forcible entry into a building or safe. Generally, these marks occur as indented impressions into a softer surface or as abrasion marks caused by the tool cutting or sliding against another object.

Comparing Tool Marks

Typically, an indented impression is left on the frame of a door or window as a result of the prying action of a screwdriver or crowbar. Careful examination of these impressions can reveal important class characteristics—that is,

FIGURE 15–20 A comparison of a tool mark with a suspect screwdriver. Note how the presence of nicks and breaks on the tool's edge helps individualize the tool to the mark.
Courtesy New Jersey State Police

the size and shape of the tool. However, they rarely reveal any significant individual characteristics that could permit the examiner to individualize the mark to a single tool. Such characteristics, when they do exist, usually take the form of discernible random nicks and breaks that the tool has acquired through wear and use (Figure 15–20).

Just as the machined surfaces of a firearm are impressed with random striations during its manufacture, the edges of a pry bar, chisel, screwdriver, knife, or cutting tool likewise display a series of microscopic irregularities that look like ridges and valleys. Such markings are left as a result of the machining processes used to cut and finish tools. The shape and pattern of such minute imperfections are further modified by damage and wear during the life of the tool. Considering the variety of patterns that the hills and valleys can assume, it is highly unlikely that any two tools will be identical. Hence, these minute imperfections impart individuality to each tool.

If the edge of a tool is scraped against a softer surface, it may cut a series of striated lines that reflect the pattern of the tool's edge. Markings left in this manner are compared in the laboratory through a comparison microscope with test tool marks made from the suspect tool. The result can be a positive comparison, and hence a definitive association of the tool with the evidence mark, when a sufficient quantity of striations match between the evidence and test markings.

A major problem of tool mark comparisons is the difficulty in duplicating in the laboratory the tool mark left at the crime scene. A thorough comparison requires preparing a series of test marks by applying the suspect tool at various angles and pressures to a soft metal surface (lead is commonly used). This approach gives the examiner ample opportunity to duplicate many of the details of the original evidence marking. A photomicrograph of a typical tool mark comparison is illustrated in Figure 15–21.

Collecting Tool Mark Evidence

Whenever practical, the entire object or the part of the object bearing a tool mark should be submitted to the crime laboratory for examination. When removal of the tool mark is impractical, the only recourse is to photograph the marked area to scale and make a cast of the mark. Liquid silicone casting material is best for reproducing most of the fine details of the mark (see Figure 15–22). However, even under the best conditions, the clarity of many

FIGURE 15–21 **A photograph of a tool mark comparison seen under a comparison microscope.** *Courtesy Leica Microsystems, Buffalo, N.Y., www.leica-microsystems.com*

(a)   (b)

FIGURE 15–22 **(a) Casting a tool mark impression with a silicone-based putty.**
(b) Impression alongside suspect tool. *Courtesy Sirchie Finger Print Laboratories, Inc., Youngsville, N.C., www.sirchie.com*

of the tool mark's minute details will be lost or obscured in a photograph or cast. Of course, this will reduce the chance of individualizing the mark to a single tool.

The crime-scene investigator must never attempt to fit the suspect tool into the tool mark. Any contact between the tool and the marked surface may alter the mark and will, at the least, raise serious questions about the integrity of the evidence. The suspect tool and mark must be packaged in separate containers, with every precaution taken to avoid contact between the tool or mark and another hard surface. Failure to protect the tool or mark from damage could result in the destruction of its individual characteristics.

Furthermore, the tool or its impression may contain valuable trace evidence. Chips of paint adhering to the mark or tool provide perhaps the best example of how the transfer of trace physical evidence can occur as a result of using a tool to gain forcible entry into a building. Obviously, the presence of trace evidence greatly enhances the evidential value of the tool or its mark and requires special care in handling and packaging the evidence to avoid losing or destroying these items.

Key Points

- The presence of minute imperfections on a tool imparts individuality to that tool. The shape and pattern of such imperfections are further modified by damage and wear during the life of the tool.

- The comparison microscope is used to compare crime-scene tool marks with test impressions made with the suspect tool.

Other Impressions

From time to time, other types of impressions are left at a crime scene. This evidence may take the form of a shoe, tire, or fabric impression. It may be as varied as a shoe impression left on a piece of paper at the scene of a burglary (Figure 15–23), a hit-and-run victim's garment that has come into violent contact with an automobile (Figure 15–24), or the impression of a bloody shoe print left on a floor or carpet at a homicide scene (Figure 15–25).

Preserving Impressions

The primary consideration in collecting impressions at the crime scene is the preservation of the impression or its reproduction for later examination in the crime laboratory. Before any impression is moved or otherwise handled, it must be photographed (a scale should be included in the picture) to show all the observable details of the impression. Several shots should be taken directly over the impression as well as at various angles around the impression. Skillful use of side lighting for illumination will help highlight many ridge details that might otherwise remain obscured. Photographs should also be taken to show the position of the questioned impression in relation to the overall crime scene.

Although photography is an important first step in preserving an impression, it must be considered merely a backup procedure that is available to the examiner if the impression is damaged before reaching the crime laboratory. Naturally, the examiner prefers to receive the original

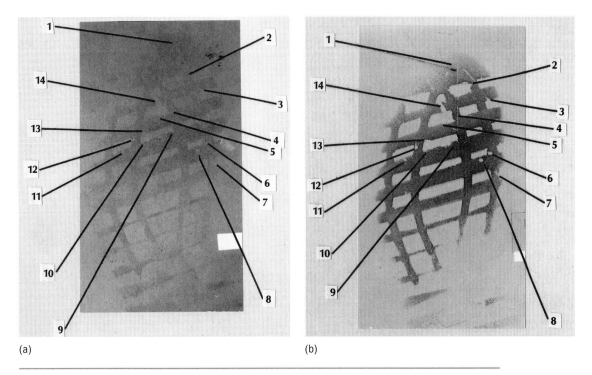

(a)   (b)

FIGURE 15–23   (a) Impression of shoe found at a crime scene. (b) Test impression made with suspect shoe. A sufficient number of points of comparison exist to support the conclusion that the suspect shoe left the impression at the crime scene.

FIGURE 15–24   A small child was found dead at the edge of a rural road near a railroad crossing, the victim of a hit-and-run driver. A local resident was suspected, but he denied any knowledge of the incident. The investigating officer noted what appeared to be a fabric imprint on the bumper of the suspect's automobile. The weave pattern of the clothing of the deceased was compared with the imprint on the bumper and was found to match. When the suspect was confronted with this information, he admitted his guilt.

(a)

(b)

FIGURE 15-25 **A bloody imprint of a shoe was found on the carpet in the home of a homicide victim. (b) The suspect's shoe, shown in (a), made the impression. Note the distinctive impression of the hole present in the shoe's sole.** *Courtesy Dade County Crime Lab, Miami, Fla.*

impression for comparison to the suspect shoe, tire, garment, and so forth. In most cases when the impression is on a readily recoverable item, such as glass, paper, or floor tile, the evidence is easily transported intact to the laboratory.

Lifting Impressions

If an impression is encountered on a surface that cannot be submitted to the laboratory, the investigator may be able to preserve the print in a manner that is analogous to lifting a fingerprint. This is especially true of impressions made in light deposits of dust or dirt. A lifting material large enough to lift the entire impression should be used. Carefully place the lifting material over the entire impression. Use a fingerprint roller to eliminate any air pockets before lifting the impression off the surface.

A more exotic approach to lifting and preserving dust impressions involves the use of a portable electrostatic lifting device.[8] The principle is similar to that of creating an electrostatic charge on a comb and using the comb to lift small pieces of tissue paper. A sheet of mylar film is placed on top of the dust mark, and the film is pressed against the impression with the aid of a roller. The high-voltage electrode of the electrostatic unit is then placed in contact with the film while the unit's earth electrodes are placed against a metal plate (earth plate) (see Figure 15–26). A charge difference develops between the mylar film and the surface below the dust mark so that the dust is attached to the lifting film. In this manner, dust prints on chairs, walls, floors, and the like can be transferred to the mylar film. Floor surfaces up to 40 feet long can be covered with a mylar sheet and searched for dust impressions. The electrostatic lifting technique

FIGURE 15–26 **Electrostatic lifting of a dust impression off a floor using an electrostatic unit.** *Courtesy Sirchie Finger Print Laboratories, Inc., Youngsville, N.C., www.sirchie.com*

is particularly helpful in recovering barely visible dust prints on colored surfaces. Dust impressions can also be enhanced through chemical development (see Figure 15–27).[9]

Casting Impressions

Shoe and tire marks impressed into soft earth at a crime scene are best preserved by photography and casting.[10] Class I dental stone, a form of gypsum, is widely recommended for making casts of shoe and tire impressions. A series of photographs clearly illustrating the steps in casting an impression may be found at www.sccja.org/csr-cast.htm. The cast should be allowed to air-dry for twenty-four to forty-eight hours before it is shipped to the forensic science laboratory for examination. Figure 15–28 illustrates a cast made from a shoe print in mud. The cast compares to the suspect shoe.

An aerosol product known as Snow Impression Wax is available for casting snow impressions.[11] The recommended procedure is to spray three light coats of the wax at an interval of one to two minutes between layers, and then let it dry for ten minutes. A viscous mixture of Class I dental stone is then poured onto the wax-coated impression. After the casting material has hardened, the cast can be removed.

Several chemicals can be used to develop and enhance footwear impressions made with blood. In areas where a bloody footwear impression is very faint or where the subject has tracked through blood leaving a trail of bloody impressions, chemical enhancement can visualize latent or nearly invisible blood impressions (see Figure 15–29).

Several blood enhancement chemicals have been examined for their impact on STR DNA typing. None of the chemicals examined had a deleterious effect, on a short-term basis, on the ability to carry out STR DNA typing on the blood.[12]

Comparing Impressions

Whatever the circumstances, the laboratory procedures used to examine any type of impression remain the same. Of course, a comparison is possible only when an item suspected of having made the impression is recovered. Test

(a)

(b)

FIGURE 15–27 **(a) A dust impression of a shoe print on cardboard before enhancement. (b) Shoe print after chemical enhancement with Bromophenol Blue and exposure to water vapor.** *Courtesy Division of Identification and Forensic Science, Israel Police Headquarters, Jerusalem, Israel*

impressions may be necessary to compare the characteristics of the suspect item with the evidence impression.

The evidential value of the impression is determined by the number of class and individual characteristics that the examiner finds. Agreement with respect to size, shape, or design may permit the conclusion that the impression could have been made by a particular shoe, tire, or garment; however, one cannot entirely exclude other possible sources from having the same class characteristics. More significant is the existence of individual characteristics arising out of wear, cuts, gouges, or other damage. A sufficient number or the uniqueness of such points of comparison support a finding that both the evidence and test impressions originated from one and only one source.

When tire tread impressions are left at a crime scene, the laboratory can examine the design of the impression and possibly determine the style

(a)   (b)   (c)

FIGURE 15–28   (a) Shoe impression in mud. (b) Cast of shoe impression. (c) Shoe suspected of leaving muddy impression. *Courtesy Sirchie Finger Print Laboratories, Inc., Youngsville, N.C., www.sirchie.com*

and/or manufacturer of the tire. This may be particularly helpful to investigators when a suspect tire has not yet been located.

New computer software may help the forensic scientist compare shoe prints. For example, an automated shoe print identification system developed in England, called Shoeprint Image Capture and Retrieval (SICAR), incorporates multiple databases to search known and unknown footwear files for comparison against footwear specimens. Using the system, an impression from a crime scene can be compared to a reference database to find out what type of shoe caused the imprint. That same impression can also be searched in the suspect and crime databases to reveal whether that shoe print matches the shoes of a person who has been in custody or the shoe prints left behind at another crime scene. When matches are made during the searching process, the images are displayed side by side on the computer screen.

An excellent resource for shoe print and tire impression examiners is a Web site that has been assembled by the Chesapeake area shoe print and tire track examiners at members.aol.com/varfee/mastssite/. The Web site's goal is to "enable examiners to enhance their footwear or tire track impression examinations by providing references, databases, and links to manufacturers, experts, vendors, trade associations, and professional societies connected to these forensic disciplines."

Human bite mark impressions on skin and foodstuffs have proven to be important items of evidence for convicting defendants in a number of homicide and rape cases in recent years. If a sufficient number of points of similarity between test and suspect marks are present, a forensic

(a)

(b)

(c)

(d)

FIGURE 15–29 **(a) Bloody footprint on cardboard treated with amido black. (b) Bloody footprint treated with Hungarian Red dye. (c) Bloody footprint visualized with leucocrystal violet. (d) Bloody footprint enhanced with patent blue.** *(a) Courtesy Dwane S. Hilderbrand and David P. Coy, Scottsdale Police Crime Laboratory, Scottsdale, Ariz. (b) Courtesy ODV Inc., South Paris, Maine. (c–h) Courtesy William Bodziak, FBI Laboratory*

(e)

(f)

(g)

(h)

FIGURE 15–29 *(continued)* **(e) Bloody foot impression treated with amido black. (f) Bloody footprint visualized with fushin acid dye. (g) Bloody foot impression visualized with tartrazine. (h) Bloody footprint treated with diaminobenzidine.**

Case Study

The O. J. Simpson Trial—Who Left the Impressions at the Crime Scene?

On the night of June 12, 1994, Nicole Brown—ex-wife of football star O. J. Simpson—and her friend Ron Goldman were brutally murdered on the grounds outside her home in Brentwood, California. O. J. Simpson was arrested for their murders, but professed his innocence. At the crime scene, investigators found bloody shoe impressions along the concrete walkway leading up to the front door of Brown's condominium. These shoe impressions were of extremely high quality and of intricate detail. The news media broadcast countless images of these bloody shoe prints on television, making it obvious to the killer that those shoes would surely link him to the crime.

Famed FBI shoe print examiner William J. Bodziak investigated the footwear evidence from the scene. His first task was to identify the brand of shoe that made the marks. Because the pattern was very clear and distinct, with complete toe-to-heel detail, this seemed a simple task at first. Bodziak compared this pattern to the thousands of sole patterns in the FBI's database. None matched. He then went to his reference collection of books and trade show brochures, again with no success.

Bodziak's experience told him that these were expensive, Italian-made casual dress shoes with a sole made from synthetic material. Using this knowledge, he shopped the high-end stores for a similar tread pattern, but still was unable to identify the shoes. He then drew a composite sketch of the sole and faxed the image to law enforcement agencies and shoe manufacturers and distributors worldwide. The owner of the American distributing company for Bruno Magli shoes was the only one to respond.

Further exhaustive investigation revealed that these were extremely rare shoes. There were two styles of shoe bearing this exact sole design. They were available for only two years, and from a mere forty stores in the United States and Puerto Rico. The Lorenzo style shoe had a bootlike upper that came to the ankle. The Lyon style shoe had the lower, more typical dress shoe cut. The impressions were made by a size 12 shoe, and it was later determined that only 299 pairs of size 12 with this tread pattern were sold in the United States.

Simpson flatly denied ever owning these shoes, adding that he would never wear anything so ugly. However, he was known to wear a size 12, and photographs taken almost nine months before the murders show Simpson wearing a pair of black leather Bruno Magli Lorenzo shoes. These shoes were available in several colors, so this narrows the number of shoes matching Simpson's pair of Lorenzos (this size, color, and style) sold in the United States to twenty-nine pairs.

Proving that Simpson owned a pair of shoes that had the exact pattern found printed in blood at the crime scene was an essential component of the case, but it was not done in time to be used during the criminal prosecution. The photographs of Simpson in his Bruno Magli shoes were released after the culmination of the criminal trial, so the jury never heard the direct evidence that Simpson owned these shoes. However, this proved to be an important link uniting Simpson with the crime scene in the civil trial. Although O. J. Simpson was acquitted of the murders of Nicole Brown and Ron Goldman in the criminal trial, he was judged responsible for their murders in the civil court case.

(a)

(b)

FIGURE 15–30   **(a) Bite mark impression on the victim's forearm. (b) Upper dental model from the teeth of the suspect matches the individual teeth characteristics of the bite marks.** *Courtesy Haskin Askin, D.D.S., Chief Forensic Odontologist, City of Philadelphia, Pa*

odontologist may conclude that a bite mark was made by one particular individual (see Figure 15–30).

WebExtra 15.7

Casting a Footwear Impression
www.prenhall.com/hsforensics

Key Points

- Shoe and tire marks impressed into soft earth at a crime scene are best preserved by photography and casting.

- The electrostatic lifting technique is particularly helpful in recovering barely visible dust prints on floor surfaces.

- In areas where a bloody footwear impression is very faint or where the subject has tracked through blood, leaving a trail of bloody impressions, chemical enhancement can visualize latent or nearly invisible blood impressions.

Chapter Summary

Structural variations and irregularities caused by scratches, nicks, breaks, and wear permit the criminalist to relate a bullet to a gun; a scratch or abrasion mark to a single tool; or a tire track to a particular automobile.

The manufacture of a barrel requires impressing its inner surface with spiral grooves, a step known as rifling. The surfaces of the original bore remaining between the grooves are called lands. No two rifled barrels, even those manufactured in succession, have identical striation markings. These striations form the individual characteristics of the barrel. The inner surface of the barrel of a gun leaves its striation markings on a bullet passing through it.

The number of lands and grooves and their direction of twist are obvious points of comparison during the initial stages of an examination. Any differences in these class characteristics immediately eliminate the possibility that both bullets traveled through the same barrel. Not only must the lands and grooves of the test and evidence bullet have identical widths, but the longitudinal striations on each must coincide. The firing pin, breechblock, and ejector and extractor mechanism also offer a highly distinctive signature for individualization of cartridge cases.

The comparison microscope is a firearms examiner's most important tool. Two bullets can be observed and compared simultaneously within the same field of view. The advent of computerized imaging technology has made possible the storage of bullet and cartridge surface characteristics in a manner analogous to automated fingerprint files. However, the forensic examiner makes the final comparison through traditional methods.

The distribution of gunpowder particles and other discharge residues around a bullet hole permits an assessment of the distance from which a handgun or rifle was fired. The firing of a weapon not only propels residues toward the target, but also blows gunpowder and primer residues back toward the shooter. As a result, traces of these residues are often deposited on the firing hand of the shooter, and their detection can provide valuable information as to whether an individual has recently fired a weapon. Examiners measure the amount of barium and antimony on the relevant portion of the suspect's hands or characterize the morphology of particles containing these elements to determine whether a person has fired or handled a weapon, or was near a discharged firearm.

Increasingly the criminalist must restore a serial number that has been obliterated by grinding, rifling, or punching. Restoration of serial numbers is possible through chemical etching because the metal crystals in the stamped zone are placed under a permanent strain that extends a short distance beneath the original numbers.

A tool mark is any impression, cut, gouge, or abrasion caused by a tool coming into contact with another object. Any minute imperfections on a tool impart individuality to that tool. The shape and pattern of such imperfections are further modified by damage and wear during the life of the tool. The comparison microscope is used to compare crime-scene tool marks with test impressions made with the suspect tool.

Shoe and tire marks impressed into soft earth at a crime scene are best preserved by photography and casting. In areas where a bloody footwear impression is very faint or where the subject has tracked through blood, leaving a trail of bloody impressions, chemical enhancement can visualize latent or nearly invisible blood impressions. A sufficient number of points of comparison or the uniqueness of such points support a finding that both the questioned and test impressions originated from one and only one source.

Review Questions

Facts and Concepts

1. What is rifling and what is its purpose?

2. What are grooves and lands?

3. What is caliber?

4. Which of the following rifling methods is no longer in use?
   a. the button method
   b. the hook cutter method
   c. the mandrel method
   d. the broach cutter method

5. List the class characteristics of a rifled barrel.

6. What are striations? How are they produced?

7. How are striations useful for comparing bullets?

8. What is the firearms examiner's most important tool and why is it so important?

9. Name three factors that can prevent a firearms examiner from obtaining a perfect match of striation markings around the periphery of two bullets.

10. How does a shotgun barrel differ from the barrel of a handgun? How does this difference affect the ability of a firearms examiner to compare shotgun shells?

11. Describe the relationship between a shotgun's gauge and the diameter of its barrel.

12. Briefly describe the sequence of events that occur from the time the trigger of a firearm is pulled to the time the bullet is fired.

13. What parts of a firearm leave impressions on a cartridge case that constitute individual characteristics of that weapon?

14. Name two automated firearms search systems and indicate which federal agency developed each.

15. What is NIBIN?

16. Which of the following makes the final determination about whether two bullets were fired by the same gun?
    a. IBIS
    b. a comparison microscope
    c. NIBIN
    d. a trained firearms examiner

17. What is distance determination and upon what is it based?

18. Briefly describe how a firearms examiner makes a distance determination for a handgun or rifle shot.

19. What is bullet wipe? Of what does it consist?

20. Name five factors that influence the amount of gunpowder residue deposited on a target.

21. How does a firearms examiner estimate a distance determination for a shooting involving a shotgun?

22. As the distance to the target of a shotgun blast increases, what do the pellets do?

23. What is choke? How is it related to the speed, range, and spread pattern of shotgun pellets?

24. What is the Greiss test? What substance is being tested for in this procedure?

25. On what portions of a shooter's hands are powder and primer residues most likely to be deposited just after a weapon is fired, and why?

26. Name and briefly describe two popular approaches for collecting gunshot residue from a suspect's hands.

27. What device is often used to locate primer and gunpowder particles by their characteristic size and shape?

28. What is the major advantage of the SEM approach for primer residue detection? What is its major drawback?

29. Name two analytical methods besides SEM testing for detecting gunshot residues in hand swabs.

30. Why is it possible to restore an obliterated serial number? Name two situations in which an obliterated serial number usually cannot be restored.

31. Why should a suspect firearm never be picked up by inserting an object into its barrel?

32. What information should be recorded before unloading a suspect weapon?

33. How should a suspect weapon discovered underwater be transported to the laboratory and why?

34. What is the primary concern of the field investigator when recovering bullets and cartridge casings?

35. What typically imparts individual characteristics to a tool mark?

36. How does the criminalist record a tool mark for comparison when removal of the original tool mark is impractical?

37. Why must the crime-scene investigator never attempt to fit a suspect tool into a tool mark?

38. What is the first step that must be taken before moving or handling an impression at a crime scene?

39. Name two procedures used to preserve impressions that cannot be submitted to the laboratory.

40. What is SICAR and how is it useful in comparing impressions?

Application and Critical Thinking

1. From each of the following descriptions of bullet holes, estimate the distance from the shooter to the target.

   a. a few widely scattered gunpowder particles with no soot around the entrance hole
   b. a dark ring around the bullet hole, but no soot or gunpowder particles
   c. a halo of soot surrounding the entrance hole along with scattered specks of powder grains
   d. scorch marks and melted fibers surrounding the entrance hole

2. You are investigating a shooting involving a 12-gauge shotgun with a moderately high choke. The spread of the pattern made by the pellets measures 12 inches. In your opinion, which of the following is probably closest to the distance from the target to the shooter? Explain your answer and explain why the other answers are likely to be incorrect.

   a. 18 yards
   b. 12 yards
   c. 6 yards
   d. 30 yards

3. Criminalist Ben Baldanza is collecting evidence from the scene of a shooting. After locating the revolver suspected of firing the shots, Ben picks the gun up by the grip, unloads it, and places the ammunition in an envelope. He then attaches an identification tag to the grip. Searching the scene, Ben finds a bullet lodged in the wall. He uses pliers to grab the bullet and pull it from the wall, then inscribes the bullet with his initials and places it in an envelope. What mistakes, if any, did Ben make in collecting this evidence?

4. How would you go about collecting impressions in each of the following situations?

   a. You discover a shoe print in dry dirt.
   b. You discover a tool mark on a windowsill.
   c. You discover tire marks in soft earth.
   d. You discover a shoe print on a loose piece of tile.
   e. You discover a very faint shoe print in dust on a colored linoleum floor.

Web Resources

Ballistics Slide Presentation
www.stfrancis.edu/ns/diab/Forensic1/Ballistics1_files/frame.htm

FirearmsID.com (Contains information about firearms identification, ballistics, distance determination, history of firearms identification, and case studies)
www.firearmsid.com/new_index.htm

Firearms Identification and Ballistics (Article that covers bullet and cartridge identification, ballistics, gunshot residue analysis, tool marks, and other impressions, and includes a small list of links)
www.faculty.ncwc.edu/toconnor/425/425lect06.htm

Firearms Identification (Comprehensive article about firearms identification and examination, tool mark identification, and collection and analysis of evidence)
www.fbi.gov/hq/lab/fsc/backissu/april2000/schehl1.htm#FirearmsID

Firearms Tutorial (Covers many aspects of firearms identification including history, ballistics, tissue injury, gunshot residue, and laboratory methods)
www.medstat.med.utah.edu/WebPath/TUTORIAL/GUNS/GUNINTRO.html

Footwear, The Missed Evidence (Article about collection and interpretation of footprint evidence)
www.crimeandclues.com/footwear.htm

Footwear and Tire Impression Evidence
www.members.aol.com/varfee/mastssite/index.html

Forensic Dentistry: Issues in Animal and Human Bite Mark Analysis
www.forensic.to/webhome/bitemarks/

Handwriting, Typewriting, Shoeprints, and Tire Treads: FBI Laboratory's Questioned Documents Unit (FBI article that includes sections on identification of shoeprints and tire treads)
www.fbi.gov/hq/lab/fsc/backissu/april2001/held.htm

Endnotes

1. Originally, the number of lead balls with the same diameter as the barrel would make a pound. For example, a 20-gauge shotgun has an inside diameter equal to the diameter of a lead ball that weighs 1/20 of a pound.
2. R. E. Tontarski, Jr., and R. M. Thompson, "Automated Firearms Evidence Comparison: A Forensic Tool for Firearms Identification—An Update," *Journal of Forensic Sciences* 43 (1998): 641.
3. P. C. Maiti, "Powder Patterns around Bullet Holes in Bloodstained Articles," *Journal of the Forensic Science Society* 13 (1973): 197.
4. J. W. Kilty, "Activity after Shooting and Its Effect on the Retention of Primer Residues," *Journal of Forensic Sciences* 20 (1975): 219.
5. G. E. Reed et al., "Analysis of Gunshot Residue Test Results in 112 Suicides," *Journal of Forensic Sciences* 35 (1990): 62.
6. G. M. Woiten et al., "Particle Analysis for the Detection of Gunshot Residue, I: Scanning Electron Microscopy/Energy Dispersive X-Ray Characterization of Hand Deposits from Firing," *Journal of Forensic Sciences* 24 (1979): 409.
7. R. S. White and A. D. Owens, "Automation of Gunshot Residue Detection and Analysis by Scanning Electron Microscopy/Energy Dispersive X-Ray Analysis (SEM/EDX)," *Journal of Forensic Sciences* 32 (1987): 1595; W. L. Tillman, "Automated Gunshot Residue Particle Search and Characterization," *Journal of Forensic Sciences* 32 (1987): 62.
8. See R. Milne, "Electrostatic Lifting of Marks at Crime Scenes and the Development of Pathfinder," *Science & Justice* 38 (1998): 135.

9. B. Glattstein, Y. Shor, N. Levin, and A. Zeichner, "pH Indicators as Chemical Reagents for the Enhancement of Footwear Marks," *Journal of Forensic Sciences* 41 (1996): 23.

10. D. S. Hilderbrand and M. Miller, "Casting Materials—Which One to Use?" *Journal of Forensic Identification* 45 (1995): 618.

11. Available from Sirchie Finger Print Laboratories, Inc., Youngsville, N.C.

12. C. J. Frégeau et al., "Fingerprint Enhancement Revisited and the Effects of Blood Enhancement Chemicals on Subsequent Profiler Plus™ Fluorescent Short Tandem Repeat DNA Analysis of Fresh and Aged Bloody Fingerprints," *Journal of Forensic Sciences* 45 (2000): 354.

The Unabomber

In 1978, a parcel addressed to a Northwestern University professor exploded as it was being opened by a campus security officer. This was the start of a series of bomb-containing packages that typically were sent to universities and airlines. Considering the intended victims, the perpetrator was dubbed UN (university) A (airlines) BOM; hence, *the Unabomber*.

The explosives were usually housed in a pipe within a wooden box. The explosive ingredients generally were black powder, smokeless powder, or an ammonium nitrate mix. The box was filled with metal objects to create a shrapnel effect on explosion. The device typically had the initials "FC" punched into it.

The first Unabomber fatality came in 1985, when a computer store owner was killed after picking up a package left outside his business. The Unabomber emerged again in 1993 after a six-year hiatus by mailing bombs to two university professors. Their injuries were not fatal, but his next two attacks did result in fatalities.

In 1995, the case took an unexpected turn when the Unabomber promised to end his mad spree if his 35,000-word typewritten "Manifesto," sent to the *New York Times* and the *Washington Post* were published. The manifesto proved to be a long, rambling rant against technology, but it offered valuable clues that broke the case. David Kaczynski realized that the manifesto's writing style and the philosophy it espoused closely resembled that of his brother, Ted. His suspicions were confirmed by linguistics experts, who carefully pored over the manifesto's content. Ted Kaczynski was arrested in Montana in 1996. Inside his ramshackle cabin were writings similar to the manifesto, three manual typewriters, and bomb-making materials. Forensic document examiners were able to match the typewritten manifesto to one of the typewriters recovered from the cabin.

chapter 16

Document
Examination

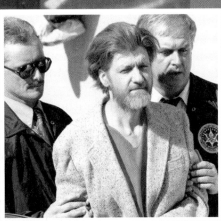

Key Terms

charred document

erasure

exemplar

indented writings

infrared luminescence

natural variations

obliteration

questioned document

The Document Examiner

Ordinarily, the work of the document examiner involves examining handwriting and typescript to ascertain the source or authenticity of a questioned document. However, document examination is not restricted to a mere visual comparison of words and letters. The document examiner must know how to use microscopy, photography, and even such analytical methods as chromatography to uncover all efforts, both brazen and subtle, to change the content or meaning of a document.

Alterations of documents through overwriting, erasures, or the more obvious crossing out of words must be recognized and characterized as efforts to alter or obscure the original meaning of a document. The document examiner identifies such efforts and recovers the original contents of the writing. An examiner may even reconstruct writing on charred or burned papers, or uncover the meaning of indented writings found on a paper pad after the top sheet has been removed.

questioned document
Any document about which some issue has been raised or that is the subject of an investigation.

Any object that contains handwritten or typewritten markings whose source or authenticity is in doubt may be referred to as a questioned document. Such a broad definition covers all of the written and printed materials we normally encounter in our daily activities. Letters, checks, driver's licenses, contracts, wills, voter registrations, passports, petitions, and even lottery tickets are commonly examined in crime laboratories. However, we need not restrict our examples to paper documents. Questioned documents may include writings or other markings found on walls, windows, doors, or any other objects.

Document examiners possess no mystical powers or scientific formulas for identifying the authors of writings. They apply knowledge gathered through years of training and experience to recognize and compare the individual characteristics of questioned and known authentic writings. For this purpose, gathering documents of known authorship or origin is critical to the outcome of the examination. Collecting known writings may entail considerable time and effort and may be further hampered by uncooperative or missing witnesses. However, the uniqueness of handwriting makes this type of physical evidence, like fingerprints, one of few definitive individual characteristics available to the investigator, a fact that certainly justifies an extensive investigative effort.

Handwriting Comparisons

Document experts continually testify that no two individuals write exactly alike. This is not to say that there cannot be marked resemblances between two individuals' handwritings, because many factors make up the total character of a person's writing.

General Style

Perhaps the most obvious feature of handwriting to the layperson is its general style. As children we all learn to write by attempting to copy letters that match a standard form or style shown to us by our teachers. The style of writing acquired by the learner is that which is fashionable for the particular time and locale. In the United States, for example, the two most widely used systems are the Palmer method, first introduced in 1880, and the Zaner-Bloser method, introduced in about 1895 (see Figure 16–1). To some extent, both of these systems are taught in nearly all fifty states.

The early stages of learning and practicing handwriting are characterized by a conscious effort by the student to copy standard letter forms. Many pupils in a handwriting class tend at first to have writing styles that are similar to one another, with minor differences attributable to skill in copying. However, as initial writing skills improve, a child normally reaches the stage at which the nerve and motor responses associated with the act of writing become subconscious. The individual's writing now begins to take on innumerable habitual shapes and patterns that distinguish it from all others. The document examiner looks for these unique writing traits.

Variations in Handwriting

The unconscious handwriting of two different individuals can never be identical. Individual variations associated with mechanical, physical, and mental functions make it extremely unlikely that all of these factors can be exactly reproduced by any two people. Thus, variations are expected in angularity, slope, speed, pressure, letter and word spacings, relative dimensions of letters, connections, pen movement, writing skill, and finger dexterity.

Furthermore, many other factors besides pure handwriting characteristics should be considered. The arrangement of the writing on the paper may be as distinctive as the writing itself. Margins, spacings, crowding, insertions, and alignment are all results of personal habits. Spelling, punctuation, phraseology, and grammar can be personal and, if so, combine to individualize the writer.

In a problem involving the authorship of handwriting, all characteristics of both the known and questioned documents must be considered and compared. Dissimilarities between the two writings strongly indicate two writers, unless these differences can logically be accounted for by the facts surrounding the preparation of the documents. Because any single characteristic, even the most distinctive one, may be found in the handwriting of other individuals, no single handwriting characteristic can by itself be taken as the basis for a positive comparison. The final conclusion must be based on a sufficient number of common characteristics between the known and questioned writings to effectively preclude their having originated from two different sources.

What constitutes a sufficient number of personal characteristics? Here again, there are no hard-and-fast rules for making such a determination.

FIGURE 16–1 **(top) Example of Zaner-Bloser handwriting; (bottom) Example of Palmer handwriting.** *Courtesy Robert J. Phillips, Document Examiner, Audubon, New Jersey*

The expert examiner can make this judgment only in the context of each particular case.

Challenges to Handwriting Comparison

When the examiner receives a reasonable amount of known handwriting for comparison, sufficient evidence to determine the source of a questioned document is usually easy to find. Frequently, however, circumstances prevent a positive conclusion or permit only the expression of a qualified opinion. Such situations usually develop when an insufficient number of known writings are available for comparison. Although nothing may be found that definitely points to the questioned and known handwriting being of different origin, not enough personal characteristics may be present in the known writings that are consistent with the questioned materials.

Difficulties may also arise when the examiner receives questioned writings containing only a few words, all deliberately written in a crude, unnatural form or all very carefully written and thought out so as to disguise the writer's natural style—a situation usually encountered with threatening or obscene letters. It is extremely difficult to compare handwriting that has been very carefully prepared to a document written with such little thought for structural details that it contains only the subconscious writing habits of the writer. However, although one's writing habits may be relatively easy to change for a few words or sentences, maintaining such an effort grows more difficult with each additional word.

When an adequate amount of writing is available, the attempt at total disguise may fail. This was illustrated by Clifford Irving's attempt to forge letters in the name of the late industrialist Howard Hughes in order to obtain lucrative publishing contracts for Hughes's life story. Figure 16–2 shows forged signatures of Howard Hughes along with Clifford Irving's known writings. By comparing these signatures, document examiner R. A. Cabbane of the U.S. Postal Inspection Service detected many examples of Irving's personal characteristics in the forged signatures.

For example, note the formation of the letter *r* in the word *Howard* on lines 1 and 3, as compared with the composite on line 6. Observe the

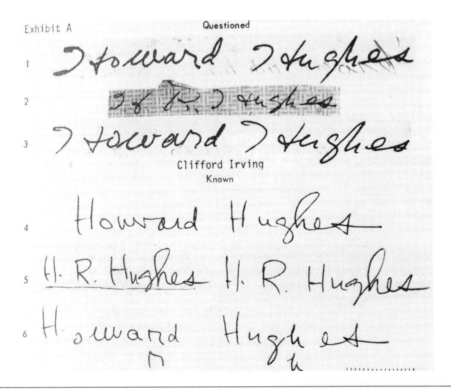

FIGURE 16–2   Forged signatures of Howard Hughes and examples of Clifford Irving's writing. *Reprinted by permission of the American Society for Testing and Materials from the Journal of Forensic Sciences, copyright 1975*

manner in which the terminal stroke of the letter *r* tends to terminate with a little curve at the baseline of Irving's writing and the forgery. Notice the way the bridge of the *w* drops in line 1 and also in line 6. Also, observe the similarity in the formation of the letter *g* as it appears on line 1 as compared with the second signature on line 5.

The document examiner must also be aware that writing habits may be altered beyond recognition by the influence of drugs or alcohol. Under these circumstances, it may be impossible to obtain known writings of a suspect written under conditions comparable to those at the time the questioned document was prepared.

Collection of Handwriting Exemplars

exemplar
An authentic sample used for comparison purposes, such as handwriting.

Collection of an adequate number of known writings (exemplars) is critical for determining the outcome of a comparison. Generally, known writings of the suspect furnished to the examiner should be as similar as possible to the questioned document. This is especially true with respect to the writing implement and paper. Styles and habits may be somewhat altered if a person switches from a pencil to a ballpoint pen or to a fountain pen. The way the paper is ruled, or the fact that it is unruled, may also affect the handwriting of a person who has become particularly accustomed

Forensics at Work

Hitler's Diaries

In 1981 a spectacular manuscript attributed to Adolf Hitler was disclosed by the brother of an East German general. These documents included Hitler's twenty-seven-volume diary and an unknown third volume of his autobiography, *Mein Kampf*. The existence of these works was both culturally and politically significant to the millions who were affected by World War II.

Authentication of the diaries was undertaken by two world-renowned experts, one Swiss and one American. Both declared that the handwritten manuscripts were identical to the known samples of Adolf Hitler's handwriting that they were given. Bidding wars began for publishing rights, and a major national newspaper in the United States won with a price near $4 million.

The publishing company that originally released the documents to the world market undertook its own investigation, which ultimately revealed a clever but devious plot. The paper on which the diaries were written contained a whitener that didn't exist until 1954, long after Hitler committed suicide. The manuscript binding threads contained viscose and polyester, neither of which was available until after World War II. Further, the inks used in the manuscript were all inconsistent with those in use during the year these pages were allegedly written.

Moreover, the exemplars sent to the Swiss and American experts as purportedly known examples of Hitler's handwriting were actually from the same source as the diaries. Thus, the experts were justified in proclaiming the documents were authentic because they *were* written by the same hand—it just wasn't Hitler's. Chemical analysis of the inks later determined that the "Hitler diaries" were in fact less than one year old—spectacular, but fake!

to one type or the other. Known writings should also contain some of the words and combinations of letters present in the questioned document.

The known writings must be adequate in number to show the examiner the range of natural variations in a suspect's writing characteristics. No two specimens of writing prepared by one person are ever identical in every detail. Variation is an inherent part of natural writing. In fact, a signature forged by tracing an authentic signature can often be detected even if the original and tracing coincide exactly, because no one ever signs two signatures exactly alike (see Figure 16–3).

Many sources are available to the investigator for establishing the authenticity of the writings of a suspect. An important consideration in selecting sample writings is the age of the genuine document relative to the questioned one. It is important to try to find standards that date closely in time to the questioned document. For most typical adults, basic writing changes are comparatively slow. Therefore, material written within two or

natural variations
Normal deviations found between repeated specimens of an individual's handwriting.

FIGURE 16–3 **Examples of handwriting from the same individual over an extended period of time.** *Courtesy Robert J. Phillips, Document Examiner, Audubon, New Jersey* three years of the disputed writing is usually satisfactory for comparison; as the age difference between the genuine and unknown specimens becomes greater, the standard tends to become less representative.

Despite the many potential sources of handwriting exemplars, obtaining an adequate set of collected standards may be difficult or impossible. In these situations, handwriting may have to be obtained voluntarily or under court order from the suspect. Ample case law supports the constitutionality of taking handwriting specimens. In *Gilbert* v. *California*,[1] the Supreme Court upheld the taking of handwriting exemplars before the appointment of counsel. The Court also reasoned that handwriting samples are identifying physical characteristics that lie outside the protection privileges of the Fifth Amendment. Furthermore, in *United States* v. *Mara*,[2] the Supreme Court ruled that taking a handwriting sample did not constitute an unreasonable search and seizure of a person and hence did not violate Fourth Amendment rights.

As opposed to nonrequested specimens (written without the thought that they may someday be used in a police investigation), requested writing samples may be consciously altered by the writer. However, the investigator can take certain steps to minimize attempts at deception. The requirement of several pages of writing normally provides enough material that is free of nervousness or attempts at deliberate disguise for a valid comparison. In addition, the writing of dictation yields exemplars that best represent the suspect's subconscious style and characteristics.

Other steps that can be taken to minimize a conscious writing effort, as well as to ensure conditions approximating those of the questioned writing, can be summarized as follows:

1. The writer should be allowed to write sitting comfortably at a desk or table and without distraction.

2. The suspect should not under any conditions be shown the questioned document or be told how to spell certain words or what punctuation to use.

3. The suspect should be furnished a pen and paper similar to those used in the questioned document.

4. The dictated text should be the same as the contents of the questioned document, or at least should contain many of the same words, phrases, and letter combinations found in the document. In handprinting cases, the suspect must not be told whether to use uppercase (capital) or lowercase (small) lettering. If, after writing several pages, the writer fails to use the desired type of lettering, he or she can then be instructed to include it. Altogether, the text must be no shorter than a page.

5. Dictation of the text should take place at least three times. If the writer is trying to disguise the writing, noticeable variations should appear among the three repetitions. Discovering this, the investigator must insist on continued repetitive dictation of the text.

6. Signature exemplars can best be obtained when the suspect is required to combine other writings with a signature. For example, instead of compiling a set of signatures alone, the writer might be asked to fill out completely twenty to thirty separate checks or receipts, each of which includes a signature.

7. Before requested exemplars are taken from the suspect, a document examiner should be consulted and shown the questioned specimens.

Key Points

- Any object with handwriting or print whose source or authenticity is in doubt may be referred to as a questioned document.

- Document examiners gather documents of known authorship or origin and compare them to the individual characteristics of questioned writings.

- Collecting an adequate number of known writings is critical for determining the outcome of a handwriting comparison. Known writing should contain some of the words and combinations of letters in the questioned document.

- The unconscious handwriting of two different individuals can never be identical. However, the writing style of an individual may be altered beyond recognition by the influence of drugs or alcohol.

Typescript Comparisons

The document examiner analyzes not only handwritten documents, but machine-created ones as well. This includes a wide variety of devices including computer printers, photocopiers, fax machines, and typewriters.

Photocopier, Printer, and Fax Examination

With the emergence of digital technology, document examiners are confronted with a new array of machines capable of creating documents subject to alteration or fraudulent use. Personal computers use daisy wheel, dot-matrix, ink-jet, and laser printers. More and more, the document examiner encounters problems involving these machines, which often produce typed copies that have only inconspicuous defects.

In the cases of photocopiers, fax machines, and computer printers, an examiner may need to identify the make and model of a machine that may have been used in printing a document. Alternatively, the examiner may need to compare a questioned document with test samples printed from a suspect machine. Typically, the examiner generates approximately ten samples through each machine to obtain a sufficient representation of a machine's characteristics. A side-by-side comparison is then made between the questioned document and the printed exemplars to compare markings produced by the machine.

Photocopiers   Transitory defect marks originating from random debris on the glass platen, inner cover, or mechanical portions of a copier produce images. These images are often irregularly shaped and sometimes form distinctive patterns. Thus, they become points of comparison as the document examiner attempts to link the document to suspect copiers. The gradual change, shift, or duplication of these marks may help the examiner date the document.

Fax Machines   Fax machines print a header known as the *transmitting terminal identifier* (*TTI*) at the top of each fax page. For the document examiner, the TTI is a very important point of comparison (see Figure 16–4). The header and the document's text should have different type styles.

FIGURE 16–4 A fax page showing a transmitting terminal identifier (TTI).

TTIs can be fraudulently prepared and placed in the appropriate position on a fax copy. However, a microscopic examination of the TTI's print quickly reveals significant characteristics that distinguish it from a genuine TTI.

In determining the fax machine's model type, the examiner usually begins by analyzing the TTI type style. The fonts of that line are determined by the sending machine. The number of characters, their style, and their position in the header are best evaluated through a collection of TTI fonts organized into a useful database. One such database is maintained by the American Society of Questioned Document Examiners.

Computer Printers Computer printer model determination requires extensive analysis of the specific printer technology and type of ink used. Visual and microscopic techniques help determine the technology and toner used. Generally printers are categorized as *impact* and *nonimpact* printers by the mechanism of their toner application. Nonimpact printers, such as ink-jet and laser printers, and impact printers, such as thermal and dot-matrix printers, all have characteristic ways of printing documents. Character shapes, toner differentiation, and toner application methods are easily determined with a low-power microscope and help the examiner narrow the possibilities of model type.

In analyzing computer printouts and faxes, examiners use the same approach for comparing the markings on a questioned document to exemplar documents generated by a suspect machine. These markings include all possible transitory patterns arising from debris and other extraneous materials. When the suspect machine is not available, the examiner may need to analyze the document's class characteristics to identify the make and model of the machine. It is important to identify the printing technology, the type of paper, the type of toner or ink used, the chemical composition of the toner, and the type of toner-to-paper fusing method used in producing the document.

Examination of the toner usually involves microscopic analysis to characterize its surface morphology, followed by identification of the inorganic and organic components of the toner. These results separate model types into categories based on their mechanical and printing characteristics. Typically, document examiners access databases to help identify the model type of machine used to prepare a questioned document. The resulting list of possibilities produced by the database hopefully reduces the number of potential machines to a manageable number. Obviously, once a suspect machine is identified, the examiner must perform a side-by-side comparison of questioned and exemplar printouts as described previously.

Typewriters   Although typewriters are not used as widely as they were at one time, document examiners still analyze typescripts. Examiners are most often asked the following two questions about typewriters: (1) Can the make and model of the typewriter used to type the questioned document be identified? (2) Can a particular suspect typewriter be identified as having prepared the questioned document?

To answer the first question, the examiner must have access to a complete reference collection of past and present typefaces used by typewriter manufacturers. The two most popular typeface sizes are pica (ten letters to the inch) and elite (twelve letters to the inch). Although a dozen manufacturers may use a pica or an elite typeface, many of these are distinguishable when the individual type character's style, shape, and size are compared.

As is true for any mechanical device, use of a typewriter will result in wear and damage to the machine's moving parts. These changes occur both randomly and irregularly, thereby imparting individual characteristics to the typewriter. Variations in vertical and horizontal alignment (characters are too high or low or too far left or right of their correct position) and perpendicular misalignment of characters (characters leaning to the left or to the right), as well as defects in each typeface, are valuable for proving the identity of a typewriter (see Figure 16–5).

Associating a particular typewriter with a typewritten document requires comparing questioned document to exemplars prepared from the suspect typewriter. As with handwriting, collection of proper standards is the foundation of such comparisons. In this respect, it is best if the document examiner has the questioned typewriter, allowing the examiner to prepare an adequate number of exemplars and examine the machine's

FIGURE 16–5   A portion of a typewriting comparison points to the conclusion that the same machine typed both specimens. Besides the similarity in the design and size of type, note the light impression consistently made by the letter _M_. Also, the letter _E_ slants to the right, almost touching _D_ in the word _USED_ in both specimens. *Courtesy New Jersey State Police*

typefaces. If the investigator must prepare standards from the questioned machine, a minimum of one copy in full word-for-word order of the questioned typewriting must be obtained.

Another area of investigation relates to the ribbon. An examination of the type impressions left on a ribbon may reveal the portion of the ribbon on which a particular text was typed.

When the suspect typewriter is not available for examination, the investigator must gather known writings that have been typed on the suspect machine. Ideally, material should be selected that contains many of the same combinations of letters and words found on the questioned document. The individual defects that characterize a typewriter develop and change as the machine is used; some may have changed between the preparation of the questioned and standard material. Hence, if many specimens are available, those prepared near the time of the disputed document should be collected.

Key Points

- The examiner compares the individual type character's style, shape, and size to a complete reference collection of past and present typefaces.

- Use of a printing device results in wear and damage to the machine's moving parts in a way that is both random and irregular, thereby imparting individual characteristics to it.

- Transitory defect marks originating from random debris on the glass platen, inner cover, or mechanical portions of a copier produce irregularly shaped images that may serve as points of comparison.

- A TTI, or transmitting terminal identifier, is a header at the top of each page of a fax document. It is useful in document comparison because it serves as a way to distinguish between a real and a fraudulently prepared fax document.

- Variations in vertical and horizontal alignment and perpendicular misalignment of characters, as well as defects in each typeface, are valuable for proving the identity of a typewriter.

Alterations, Erasures, and Obliterations

Documents are often altered or changed after preparation, to hide their original intent or to perpetrate a forgery. Documents can be changed in several ways, and for each way, the application of a special discovery technique is necessary.

One of the most common ways to alter a document is to try to erase parts of it, using an India rubber eraser, sandpaper, a razor blade, or a knife to remove writing or type by abrading or scratching the paper's surface. All such attempts at erasure disturb the upper fibers of the paper. These changes are apparent when the suspect area is examined under a microscope using direct light or by allowing the light to strike the paper obliquely from one side (side lighting). Although microscopy may reveal whether an erasure has been made, it does not necessarily indicate the original letters or words present. Sometimes so much of the paper has been removed that identifying the original contents is impossible.

In addition to abrading the paper, the perpetrator may also obliterate words with chemicals. In this case, strong oxidizing agents are placed over the ink, producing a colorless reaction product. Although such an attempt may not be noticeable to the naked eye, examination under the microscope reveals discoloration on the treated area of the paper. Sometimes examination of the document under ultraviolet or infrared lighting reveals the chemically treated portion of the paper. Interestingly, examination of documents under ultraviolet light may also reveal fluorescent ink markings that go unnoticed in room light, as seen in Figure 16–6.

Some inks, when exposed to blue-green light, absorb the radiation and reradiate infrared light. This phenomenon is known as infrared luminescence. Thus, alteration of a document with ink differing from the original can sometimes be detected by illuminating the document with blue-green light and using infrared-sensitive film to record the light emanating from the document's surface. In this fashion, any differences in the luminescent properties of the inks are observed (see Figure 16–7). Infrared

erasure
The removal of writing, typewriting, or printing from a document, normally accomplished by either chemical means or an abrasive instrument.

infrared luminescence
A property exhibited by some dyes that emit infrared light when exposed to blue-green light.

(a)

(b)

FIGURE 16–6 (a) A twenty-dollar bill as it appears under room light. (b) The bill illuminated with ultraviolet light reveals ink writing. *Courtesy Sirchie Finger Print Laboratories, Inc., Youngsville, N.C., www.sirchie.com*

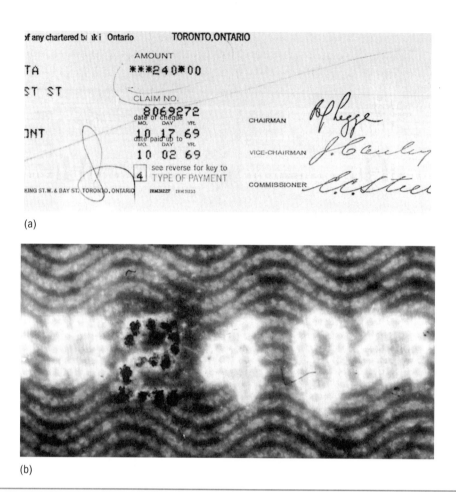

(a)

(b)

FIGURE 16–7 Part of a check stolen from a government agency as it appears to the naked eye is shown in (a). An infrared luminescence photograph was prepared of the amount figures at a magnification of 10× in (b). This clearly shows that the number 2 was added with a different ink. The accused pleaded guilty. *Courtesy Centre of Forensic Sciences, Toronto, Canada*

luminescence has also revealed writing that has been erased. Such writings may be recorded by invisible residues of the original ink that remain embedded in the paper even after an erasure.

Another important application of infrared photography arises from the observation that inks differ in their ability to absorb infrared light. Thus, illuminating a document with infrared light and recording the light reflected off the document's surface with infrared-sensitive film enables the examiner to differentiate inks of a dissimilar chemical composition (see Figure 16–8).

obliteration
Blotting out or smearing over writing or printing to make the original unreadable.

Intentional obliteration of writing by overwriting or crossing out is seldom used for fraudulent purposes because of its obviousness. Nevertheless, such cases may be encountered in all types of documents. Success at permanently hiding the original writing depends on the material used to cover the writing. If it is done with the same ink as was used to write the original material, recovery will be difficult if not impossible. However, if the two inks are of a different chemical composition, photography with infrared-sensitive film may reveal the original writing. Infrared radiation may pass through the upper layer of writing while being absorbed by the underlying area (see Figure 16–9).

Close examination of a questioned document sometimes reveals crossing strokes or strokes across folds of perforations in the paper that are not

(a) (b)

FIGURE 16–8   (a) This photograph, taken under normal illumination, shows the owner of an American Express check to be "Freda C. Brightly Jones." Actually, this signature was altered. The check initially bore the signature "Fred C. Brightly Jr." (b) This photograph taken under infrared illumination, using infrared-sensitive film, clearly shows that the check was altered by adding *a* to *Fred* and *ones* to *Jr.* The ink used to commit these changes is distinguishable because it absorbs infrared light, whereas the original ink does not.
Courtesy New Jersey State Police

in a sequence that is consistent with the natural preparation of the document. Again, these differences can be shown by microscopic or photographic scrutiny.

Infrared photography sometimes reveals the contents of a document that has been accidentally or purposely charred in a fire. Another way to decipher charred documents involves reflecting light off the paper's surface at different angles in order to contrast the writing against the charred background (see Figure 16–10).

Digital image processing is the method by which the visual quality of digital pictures is improved or enhanced. *Digitizing* is the process by which the image is stored in memory. This is commonly done by scanning an image with a flatbed scanner or a digital camera and converting the image by computer into an array of digital intensity values called *pixels,* or picture elements (see p. 499). Once the image has been digitized, an image-editing program such as Adobe Photoshop is used to adjust the image. An image may be enhanced through lightening, darkening, and color and contrast controls. An example of how the technology is applied to forensic document examination is shown in Figures 16–11 and 16–12.

charred document
Any document that has become darkened and brittle through exposure to fire or excessive heat.

Other Document Problems

Document examiners encounter other challenges when analyzing questioned documents, including visualizing writing pressed or indented into a surface and analyzing the inks and paper used in suspect documents.

Indented Writings

Indented writings are the partially visible depressions on a sheet of paper underneath the one on which the visible writing was done. Such depressions are due to the application of pressure on the writing instrument and would

indented writings
Impressions left on paper positioned under a piece of paper that has been written on.

(a)

(b)

FIGURE 16–9   (a) A photograph showing an area of a document that has been blacked out with a heavy layer of ink overwriting. (b) In this photograph, the covering ink has been penetrated by infrared photography to reveal the original writing. *Courtesy Centre of Forensic Sciences, Toronto, Canada*

appear as a carbon copy of a sheet if carbon paper had been inserted between the pages.

Indented writings have proved to be valuable evidence. For example, the top sheet of a bookmaker's records may have been removed and destroyed, but it still may be possible to determine the writing by the impressions left on the pad. These impressions may contain incriminating evidence supporting the charge of illegal gambling activities. When paper

FIGURE 16–10   Decipherment of charred papers seized in the raid of a suspected bookmaking establishment. The charred documents were photographed with reflected light.
Courtesy New Jersey State Police

is studied under oblique or side lighting, its indented impressions are often readable (see Figure 16–13).

An innovative approach to visualizing indented writings has been developed at the London College of Printing in close consultation with the Metropolitan Police Forensic Science Laboratory.[3] The method involves applying an electrostatic charge to the surface of a polymer film that has been placed in contact with a questioned document, as shown in Figure 16–14. Indented impressions on the document are revealed by applying a toner powder to the charged film. For many documents examined by this process, clearly readable images have been produced from impressions that could not be seen or were barely visible under

ORIGINAL

EXCLUSION

LEVELS

CURVES

SCREEN

REPLACE COLOR

FIGURE 16–11 **This composite demonstrates the various changes that can be applied to a digitized image in order to reveal information that has been obscured. Using a photo editor (Adobe Photoshop), the original was duplicated and pasted as a second layer. Colors were changed in selected areas of the image using the "screen" and "exclusion" options. "Replace color" allows the user to choose a specific color or range of colors and lighten, darken, or change the hue of the colors selected. "Level" and "curves" tools can adjust the lightest and darkest color ranges and optimize contrast, highlights, and shadow detail of the image for additional clarity.** *Courtesy Lt. Robert J. Garrett, Middlesex County Prosecutor's Office, N.J.*

normal illumination. An instrument that develops indented writings by electrostatic detection is commercially available and is routinely used by document examiners.

Ink and Paper Comparisons

A study of the chemical composition of writing ink present on documents may verify whether known and questioned documents were prepared by the same pen. A nondestructive approach to comparing ink lines is accomplished

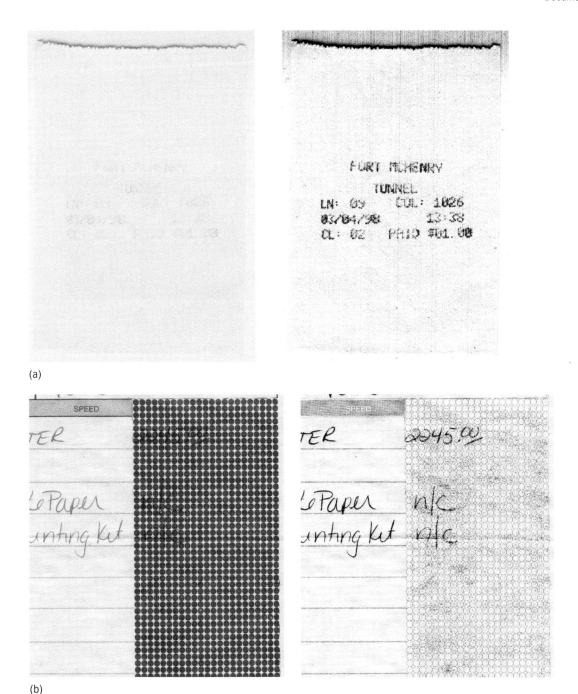

(a)

(b)

FIGURE 16–12 (a) Receipts have been used in investigations to establish a victim's whereabouts, provide suspects with alibis, and substantiate a host of personal conduct. Unfortunately, due to wear, age, or poor printing at the register, the receipt is often unreadable. This can be corrected using photo-editing software. In this example, the original toll receipt was scanned at the highest color resolution, which allows more than 16 million colors to be reproduced. The image was then manipulated, revealing the printed details, by adjusting the lightest and darkest levels and the color content of the image. (b) Invoices may contain details about a transaction that are important to an investigation. The copy that ships with the merchandise may have that information blocked out. This information may be recovered using digital imaging. The left figure shows the original shipping ticket. The right figure shows the information revealed after replacing the color of the blocking pattern. *Courtesy Lt. Robert J. Garrett, Middlesex County Prosecutor's Office, N.J.*

(a)

(b)

FIGURE 16–13 A suspected forger was arrested. In his car, police found written lists of the victims he intended to defraud. Some of these writings are shown in (a). A writing pad found in his house had indentations on the top page of the pad shown in (b). These indentations corresponded to the writings found in the car, further linking the suspect to the writings. *Courtesy Centre of Forensic Sciences, Toronto, Canada*

FIGURE 16–14 An electrostatic detection apparatus (ESDA) works by applying an electrostatic charge to a document suspected of containing indented writings. The indentations are then visualized by the application of charge-sensitive toner. *Courtesy Foster & Freeman Limited, Worcestershire, U.K., www.fosterfreeman.co.uk*

with a visible microspectrophotometer (see pp. 248–251).[4] A case example illustrating the application of this approach to ink analysis appears in Figure 7–11, on p. 250. Thin-layer chromatography is also suitable for ink comparisons. Most commercial inks, especially ballpoint inks, are actually mixtures of several organic dyes. These dyes can be separated on a properly developed thin-layer chromatographic plate. The separation pattern of the component dyes is distinctly different for inks with different dye compositions and thus provides many points of comparison between a known and a questioned ink.

Ink can be removed from paper with a hypodermic needle with a blunted point to punch out a small sample from a written line. About ten plugs or microdots of ink are sufficient for chromatographic analysis. The United States Secret Service and the Internal Revenue Service jointly maintain the United States International Ink Library. This collection includes more than 8,500 inks, which date back to the 1920s. Each year new pen and ink formulations are added to the reference collection. These inks have been systematically cataloged according to dye patterns developed by thin-layer chromatography (TLC; see Figure 16–15). On several occasions, this approach has been used to prove that a document has been fraudulently backdated. For example, in one instance, it was possible to establish that a document dated 1958 was backdated because a dye identified in the questioned ink had not been synthesized until 1959.

To further aid forensic chemists in ink-dating matters, several ink manufacturers, at the request of the U.S. Treasury Department, voluntarily tag their inks during the manufacturing process. The tagging program allows inks to be dated to the exact year of manufacture by changing the tags annually.

Another area of inquiry for the document examiner is the paper on which a document is written or printed. Paper is often made from cellulose fibers found in wood and fibers recovered from recycled paper products. The most common features associated with a paper examination are general appearance, color, weight, and watermarks. Other areas of examination include fiber identification and the characterization of additives, fillers, and pigments present in the paper product.

Key Points

- Document examiners deal with evidence that has been changed in several ways, such as through alterations, erasures, and obliterations.

- Infrared luminescence can be used to detect alterations to a document made with ink differing from the original. Infrared luminescence can also reveal writing that has been erased.

- A digitized image can be lightened, darkened, and color and contrast adjusted with appropriate software.

- It may be possible to read indented writing—the impressions left on a paper pad—by applying an electrostatic charge to the surface of a polymer film that has been placed in contact with a questioned document.

- Studying the chemical composition of writing ink present on documents may verify whether known and questioned documents were prepared by the same pen.

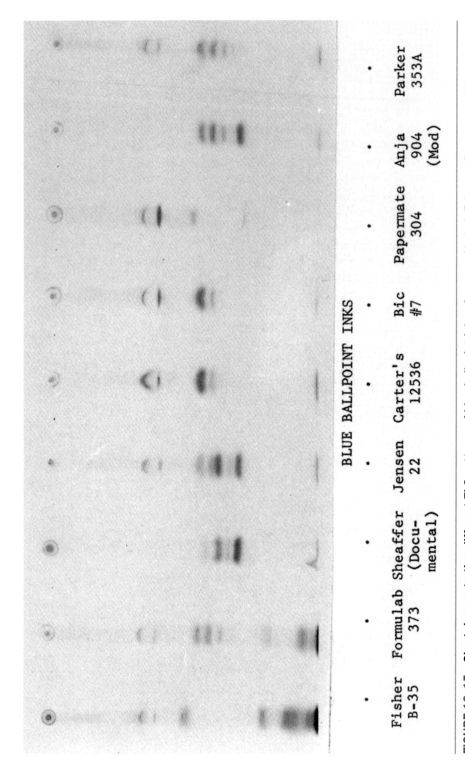

BLUE BALLPOINT INKS

| Fisher
B-35 | Formulab
373 | Sheaffer
(Docu-
mental) | Jensen
22 | Carter's
12536 | Bic
#7 | Papermate
304 | Anja
904
(Mod) | Parker
353A |

FIGURE 16–15 Chart demonstrating different TLC patterns of blue ballpoint inks. *Courtesy Alcohol, Tobacco, Firearms and Explosives Laboratory, U.S. Department of Justice, Washington, D.C.*

Chapter Summary

Any object with handwriting or print whose source or authenticity is in doubt may be referred to as a questioned document. Document examiners apply knowledge gathered through years of training and experience to recognize and compare the individual characteristics of questioned and known authentic writings. For this purpose, gathering documents of known authorship or origin is critical to the outcome of the examination.

Many factors compose the total character of a person's writing. The unconscious handwriting of two different individuals can never be identical. Furthermore, the writing style of one individual may be altered beyond recognition by the influence of drugs or alcohol. Collecting an adequate number of known writings is critical for determining the outcome of a handwriting comparison. Known writing should contain some of the words and combinations of letters present in the questioned document.

The two requests most often made of the examiner in connection with the examination of typewriters and printing devices are to identify the make and model of the typewriter and printing devices used to prepare the questioned document and to determine whether a particular suspect typewriter or printing device prepared the questioned document. The individual type character's style, shape, and size are compared to a complete reference collection of past and present typefaces. As is true for any mechanical device, use of a printing device results in wear and damage to the machine's moving parts. These changes occur both randomly and irregularly, thereby imparting individual characteristics to the printing device. The document examiner deals with problems involving business and personal computers, which often produce printed copies that have only subtle defects.

Document examiners deal with evidence that has been changed in several ways, such as through alterations, erasures, and obliterations. Indented writings have proved to be valuable evidence. It may be possible to determine what was written by the impressions left on a paper pad. Applying an electrostatic charge to the surface of a polymer film that has been placed in contact with a questioned document visualizes indented writings. A study of the chemical composition of writing ink on documents may verify whether known and questioned documents were prepared by the same pen.

Review Questions

Facts and Concepts

1. What is a questioned document?

2. Name at least five characteristics of handwriting in which one might expect to encounter variations between individuals.

3. Name at least five factors besides handwriting characteristics that can impart individual variations to writing.

4. Describe two situations in which a document examiner may be prevented from coming to a positive conclusion about a questioned document.

5. What are exemplars? Why are they important for document examination?

6. What are natural variations? How can they be useful for detecting forgeries?

7. When comparing sample writing to a suspect document, the age difference between the documents should be no more than
   a. six to twelve months.
   b. twelve to eighteen months.
   c. two to three years.
   d. five to seven years.

8. What constitutional principle did the Supreme Court address in *Gilbert* v. *California*, and how did the court rule?

9. What constitutional principle did the Supreme Court address in the case of *United States* v. *Mara*, and how did the court rule?

10. What distinguishing marks serve as points of comparison on documents produced by a photocopier?

11. What is a TTI? Name two ways in which it is useful in document comparison.

12. Name the two general categories of printers and list two examples of each type.

13. Name five important characteristics of a printer, photocopier, or fax machine that a document examiner must identify when analyzing a document in a situation where the suspect machine is not available.

14. What two processes typically are involved in examination of toner?

15. What two questions are document examiners most often asked about typewriters?

16. What individual characteristics of a typewriter are valuable for proving its identity?

17. Name two ways in which infrared luminescence is useful in examining documents.

18. Describe two methods for visualizing indented writing.

19. Name two analytical techniques used to analyze writing inks.

20. List the most common features associated with a paper examination.

Application and Critical Thinking

1. Criminalist Julie Sandel is investigating a series of threatening notes written in pencil and sent to a local politician. A suspect is arrested and Julie directs the suspect to prepare writing samples to compare to the writing on the notes. She has the suspect sit at a desk in an empty office and gives him a pen and a piece of paper. She begins to read one of the notes and asks the suspect to write the words she dictates. After reading about half a page, she stops, then dictates the same part of the note a second time for the suspect. At one point, the suspect indicates that he does not know how to spell one of the words, so Julie spells it for him. After completing the task, Julie takes the original notes and the dictated writing from the suspect to a document examiner. What mistakes, if any, did Julie make?

2. In each of the following situations, indicate how you would go about recovering original writing that is not visible to the naked eye.

   a. The original words have been obliterated with a different ink than was used to compose the original.
   b. The original words have been obliterated by chemical erasure.
   c. The original writing was made with fluorescent ink.
   d. The original documents have been charred or burned.

3. You have been asked to determine whether a handwritten will, supposedly prepared thirty years ago, is authentic or a modern forgery. What aspects of the document would you examine to make this determination? Explain how you would use thin-layer chromatography to help you come to your conclusion.

Web Resources

Emily J. DeWill, Certified Document Examiner (Page with articles on history, theory, and applications of document examination)
www.qdewill.com

Forgery Finder (Site that discusses handwriting identification and offers examples of altered documents, obliterations, ink identification, graffiti, and anonymous letters)
www.forgeryfinder.com

Guidelines for Forensic Document Examination (Article that discusses procedures for collecting, handling, and examining questioned documents)
www.fbi.gov/hq/lab/fsc/backissu/april2000/swgdoc1.htm

Handwriting, Typewriting, Shoeprints, and Tire Treads: FBI Laboratory's Questioned Documents Unit (Article that includes sections on analysis of questioned handwriting and typewriting samples)
www.fbi.gov/hq/lab/fsc/backissu/april2001/held.htm

Obtaining Handwriting Specimens (Article on sources of and methods for obtaining and submitting handwriting samples)
www.fdeservices.com/Exemplars.htm

Questioned Document Examination (Discusses the history, techniques, and court use of document examination; includes a brief list of links to document examination sites)
www.faculty.ncwc.edu/toconnor/425/425lect05.htm

Endnotes

1. 388 U.S. 263 (1967).
2. 410 U.S. 19 (1973).
3. D. M. Ellen, D. J. Foster, and D. J. Morantz, "The Use of Electrostatic Imaging in the Detection of Indented Impressions," *Forensic Science International* 15 (1980): 53.
4. P. W. Pfefferli, "Application of Microspectrophotometry in Document Examination," *Forensic Science International* 23 (1983): 129.

Bill Thomas Killman
1684 S. Oldmanor
Wichita, KS. 67218

The Wichita Eagle &
Pub. Co. Inc.
825 E. Douglas
Wichita, KS. 67202

The BTK Killer

Dennis Rader was arrested in February 2005 and charged with committing ten murders since 1974 in the Wichita, Kansas, area. The killer, whose nickname stands for "bind, torture, kill," hadn't murdered since 1991, but he resurfaced in early 2004 by sending a letter to a local newspaper taking credit for a 1986 slaying. Included with the letter were a photocopy of the victim's driver's license and three photos of her body. The BTK killer was back to his old habit of taunting the police.

Three months later another letter surfaced. This letter detailed some of the events surrounding BTK's first murder victims. In 1974, he strangled Joseph and Julie Otero along with two of their children. Shortly after those murders, BTK sent a letter to a local newspaper in which he gave himself the name BTK. In December 2004, a package found in a park contained the driver's license of another BTK victim along with a doll covered with a plastic bag, its hands bound with pantyhose.

The major break in the case came when BTK sent a message on a floppy disk to a local TV station. "Erased" information on the disk was recovered and restored by forensic computer specialists, and the disk was traced to the Christ Lutheran Church in Wichita. The disk was then quickly linked to Dennis Rader, the church council president. The long odyssey of the BTK killer was finally over.

chapter 17

Computer
Forensics

Andrew W. Donofrio

Key Terms

bit

byte

central processing unit
(CPU)

cluster

file slack

hard disk drive (HDD)

hardware

latent data

Message Digest 5
(MD5)/Secure Hash
Algorithm (SHA)

motherboard

operating system (OS)

partition

RAM slack

random-access memory
(RAM)

sector

software

swap file

temporary files

unallocated space

visible data

Learning Objectives

After studying this chapter you should be able to:

- List and describe the hardware and software components of a computer

- Understand the difference between read-only memory and random-access memory

- Describe how a hard disk drive is partitioned

- Describe the proper procedure for preserving computer evidence at a crime scene

- Understand the difference between and location of visible and latent data

- List the areas of the computer that will be examined to retrieve forensic data

Since the 1990s, few fields have progressed as rapidly as computer technology. Computers are no longer a luxury, nor are they in the hands of just a select few. Technology and electronic data are a part of everyday life and permeate all aspects of society. Consequently, computers have become increasingly important as sources of evidence in an ever-widening spectrum of criminal activities.

Investigators frequently encounter computers and other digital devices in all types of cases. As homicide investigators sift for clues they may inquire whether the method for a murder was researched on the Internet, whether signs of an extramarital affair can be found in e-mail or remnants of instant messages (which might provide motive for a spouse killing or murder for hire), or whether an obsessed stalker threatened the victim before a murder. Arson investigators want to know whether financial records on a computer might provide a motive in an arson-for-profit fire. A burglary investigation would certainly be aided if law enforcement determined that the proceeds from a theft were being sold online—perhaps through eBay or a similar online auction site.

Accessibility to children and the perception of anonymity has given sexual predators a way to seek out child victims online. The vulnerability of computers to hacker attacks is a constant reminder of security issues surrounding digitally stored data. Finally, the fact that computers control most of our critical infrastructure makes technology an appetizing target for would-be terrorists.

Computer forensics involves preserving, acquiring, extracting, analyzing, and interpreting computer data. Although this is a simple definition, it gets a bit more complicated. Part of this complication arises from technology itself. More and more devices are capable of storing electronic data: cell phones, personal digital assistants (PDAs), iPods, digital cameras, flash memory cards, smart cards, jump drives, and many others. Each method for extracting data from these devices presents unique challenges.

Andrew W. Donofrio is a detective sergeant with the prosecutor's office in Bergen County, New Jersey, and is a leading computer forensics examiner for Bergen County, with more than eighteen years experience in law enforcement. He has conducted more than five hundred forensic examinations of computer evidence and frequently lectures on the subject throughout the state, as well as teaching multiday courses on computer forensics and investigative topics at police academies and colleges in New Jersey. Detective Sergeant Donofrio writes regularly on Internet-related and computer forensics issues for a number of law enforcement publications and has appeared as a guest expert on Internet-related stories on MSNBC.

However, sound forensic practices apply to all these devices. The most logical place to start to examine these practices is with the most common form of electronic data: the personal computer.

From Input to Output: How Does the Computer Work?

Hardware versus Software

Before we get into the nuts and bolts of computers, we must establish the important distinction between hardware and software. Hardware comprises the physical components of the computer: the computer chassis, monitor, keyboard, mouse, hard disk drive, random-access memory (RAM), central processing unit (CPU), and so on (see Figure 17–1). The list is much more extensive but, generally speaking, if it is a computer component or peripheral that you can see, feel, and touch, it is hardware.

Software, conversely, is a set of instructions compiled into a program that performs a particular task. Software consists of programs and applications that carry out a set of instructions on the hardware. Operating systems (Windows, Mac OS, Linux, Unix), word-processing programs (Microsoft Word, WordPerfect), web-browsing applications (Internet Explorer, Netscape Navigator, Firefox), and accounting applications (Quicken, QuickBooks, Microsoft Money) are all examples of software.

hardware
The physical components of a computer: case, keyboard, monitor, motherboard, RAM, HDD, mouse, and so on. Generally speaking, if it is a computer component you can touch, it is hardware.

software
A set of instructions compiled into a program that performs a particular task.

FIGURE 17–1   **Cutaway diagram of a personal computer.** *Courtesy Tim Downs*

It is important not to confuse software with the physical media that it comes on. When you buy an application such as Microsoft Office, it comes on a compact disc (CD). The CD containing this suite of applications is typically referred to as software, but this is technically wrong. The CD is external computer media that contains the software; it is a container for and a medium to load the set of instructions onto the hard disk drive (the hardware).

Hardware Components

Motherboard   The main circuit board in a computer (or other electronic devices) is referred to as the motherboard. Motherboards contain sockets for chips (such as the CPU and ROM, discussed shortly) and slots for add-on cards. Examples of add-on cards are a video card to connect the computer to the monitor, a network card or modem to connect to an internal network or the Internet, and a sound card to connect to speakers.

Sockets on the motherboard typically accept things such as random-access memory (RAM) or the central processing unit (CPU). The keyboard, mouse, CD-ROM drives, floppy disk drives, monitor, and other peripherals or components connect to the motherboard in one way or another.

System Bus   Contained on the motherboard, the system bus is a vast complex network of wires that carries data from one hardware device to another. This network is analogous to a complex highway. Data is sent along the bus in the form of ones and zeros (or, more appropriately stated, as electrical impulses representing an "on" or "off" state—this two-state computing is also known as *binary computing*.

Central Processing Unit (CPU)   The central processing unit (CPU), also referred to as a processor, is the brain of the computer; it is the part of the computer that actually computes. It is the main (and typically the largest) chip that plugs into a socket on the motherboard. Basically, all operations performed by the computer are run through the CPU. The CPU carries out the program steps to perform the requested task. That task can range from opening and working in a Microsoft Word document to performing advanced mathematical algorithms.

Read-Only Memory (ROM)   This rather generic term describes special chips on the motherboard. ROM chips store programs called *firmware*, used to start the boot process (in which the computer starts up before the system is fully functioning) and configure a computer's components. This technology is referred to as the BIOS, for *basic input-output system*. The operation of the BIOS is relevant to several computer forensics procedures, particularly the boot sequence. As will become clear later, it is important not to boot the actual computer under investigation to the original hard disk drive. This would cause changes to the data, thus compromising the integrity of evidence. The BIOS allows investigators to control the boot process to some degree.

Random-Access Memory (RAM)   Random-access memory (RAM) stores software programs and instructions while the computer is turned on; it takes the physical form of chips that plug into the motherboard. Most of the data on a computer is stored on the hard disk drive (HDD). However, if the computer had to access the HDD each time it wanted data, it would run slowly and inefficiently. Instead, the computer, aware that it may need certain data at a moment's notice, stores the data in RAM. This takes the burden off the computer's processor and hard disk drive (HDD). RAM is referred to as

---

motherboard
The main system board of a computer (and many other electronic devices) that delivers power, data, and instructions to the computer's components.

central processing unit (CPU)
The main chip within the computer; also referred to as the brain of the computer. This microprocessor chip handles most of the operations (code and instructions) of the computer.

random-access memory (RAM)
The volatile memory of the computer; when power is turned off, its contents are lost. Programs and instructions are loaded into RAM while they are in use.

volatile memory because it is not permanent; its contents undergo constant change and are forever lost once power is taken away from the computer.

Hard Disk Drive (HDD)   Generally speaking, the hard disk drive (HDD) is the primary component of storage in the personal computer (see Figure 17–2). It typically stores the operating system, programs, and data files created by the user, such as documents, spreadsheets, accounting information, or a company database. Unlike RAM, the HDD is permanent storage and retains its information even after the power is turned off. HDDs work off a controller that is typically part of the motherboard, but sometimes takes the form of an add-on (expansion) card plugged into the motherboard.

hard disk drive (HDD)
Typically the main storage location within the computer, consisting of magnetic platters contained in a case.

Input Devices   Input devices are used to get data into the computer or to give the computer instructions. Input devices constitute part of the "user" side of the computer. Examples include the keyboard, mouse, joystick, and scanner.

Output Devices   Output devices are equipment through which data is obtained from the computer. Output devices are also part of the "user" side of the computer, and provide the results of the user's tasks. They include the monitor, printer, and speakers.

Key Points

- Computer forensics involves preserving, acquiring, extracting, and interpreting computer data.

- Software programs are applications that carry out a set of instructions.

- The central processing unit (CPU) is the brain of the computer—the main chip responsible for doing the actual computing.

- The motherboard is the main circuit board within a computer.

FIGURE 17–2   An inside view of the platter and read/write head of a hard disk drive.
Courtesy Corbis RF

- Read-only memory (ROM) chips store programs that control the boot (startup) process and configure a computer's components.

- Random-access memory (RAM) is volatile memory, which is lost when power is turned off. Programs are loaded into RAM because of its faster read speed.

- The hard disk drive (HDD) is typically the primary location of data storage within the computer.

Storing and Retrieving Data

operating system (OS)
Software that allows the user to interact with the hardware and manages the file system and applications.

As mentioned earlier, most of the data in a computer is stored on the hard disk drive (HDD). However, before beginning to understand how data is stored on the HDD, it is first important to understand the role of the operating system (OS). An OS is the bridge between the human user and the computer's electronic components. It provides the user with a working environment and facilitates interaction with the system's components. Each OS supports certain types of file systems that store data in different ways, but some support the methods of others.

Formatting and Partitioning the HDD

partition
A contiguous set of blocks that are defined and treated as an independent disk.

Generally speaking, before an OS can store data on a HDD, the HDD must first be formatted, or prepared to accept the data in its current form. Before the HDD can be formatted, a partition must be defined. A partition is nothing more than a contiguous set of blocks (physical areas on the HDD in which data can be stored) that are defined and treated as an independent disk. Thus, a hard disk drive can hold several partitions, making a single HDD appear as several disks.

Partitioning a drive can be thought of as dividing a container that begins as nothing more than four sides with empty space on the inside. Imagine that we then cut a hole in the front of the container and place inside two drawers containing the hardware to open and close the drawers. We have just created a two-drawer filing cabinet and defined each drawer as a contiguous block of storage. A partitioning program then defines the partitions that will later hold the data on the HDD. Just as the style, size, and shape of a filing cabinet drawer can vary, so too can partitions.

sector
The smallest unit of data addressable by a hard disk drive, generally consisting of 512 bytes.

byte
A group of eight bits.

bit
Short for *binary digit*; taking the form of either a one or a zero, it is the smallest unit of information on a machine.

After a hard drive is partitioned, it is typically formatted. The formatting process *initializes* portions of the HDD, so that they can store data, and creates the structure of the file system. There are various types of file systems—methods for storing and organizing computer files and data so they are easier to locate and access. Each has a different way of storing, retrieving, and allocating data.

At the conclusion of these processes, we say that the drive is *logically defined*. The term *logically* is used because no real divisions are made. If you were to crack open the HDD before or after partitioning and formatting, to the naked eye the platters would look the same.

cluster
A group of sectors in multiples of two; typically the minimum space allocated to a file.

Mapping the HDD

As shown in Figure 17–3, disks are logically divided into sectors, clusters, tracks, and cylinders. A sector is the smallest unit of data that a hard drive can address; sectors are typically 512 bytes in size (a byte is eight bits; a bit is a single one or zero).[1] A cluster usually is the minimum space allocated

Closer Analysis

Other Common Storage Devices

Although the HDD is the most common storage device for the personal computer, many others exist. Methods for storing data and the layout of that data can vary from device to device. A CD-ROM, for example, uses a different technology and format for writing data than a floppy disk or USB thumb drive. Fortunately, regardless of the differences among devices, the same basic forensic principles apply for acquiring the data. Common storage devices include the following:

CDs and DVDs

Compact discs (CDs) and digital versatile discs (DVDs) are two of the most common forms of storing all sorts of external data, including music, video, and data files. Both types of media consist of plastic discs with an aluminum layer containing the data that is read by a beam of laser light in the CD/DVD reader. Different CDs are encoded in different ways, which makes forensic examination of such discs difficult at times.

Floppy Disks

Although "floppies" are not as common as they once were, forensic examiners still encounter the 3.5-inch floppy disk. Floppy disks can be used to boot an operating system or to store data. They are constructed of hard plastic with a thin plastic disk on the inside. That thin plastic disk is coated with a magnetic iron oxide material. The disk stores data in a similar fashion to the hard disk drive. By today's standards, floppy disks don't hold much data.

Zip Disks

Similar in structure to floppy disks, Zip disks hold a much larger amount of data.

They come in several storage capacities, each with their own drive.

USB Thumb Drives and Smart Media Cards

These devices, which can store a large amount of data, are known as *solid-state storage devices* because they have no moving parts. Smart media cards are typically found in digital cameras and PDAs, while USB thumb drives come in many shapes, sizes, and storage capacities.

Tapes

Tapes come in many different formats and storage capacities. Each typically comes with its own hardware reader and sometimes a proprietary application to read and write its contents. Tapes are typically used for backup purposes and consequently have great forensic potential.

Network Interface Card (NIC)

Very rarely do we find a computer today that doesn't have a NIC. Whether they are on a local network or the Internet, when computers need to communicate with each other, they typically do so through a NIC. NICs come in many different forms: add-on cards that plug into the motherboard, hard-wired devices on the motherboard, add-on cards (PCMCIA) for laptops, and universal serial bus (USB) plug-in cards, to name a few. Some are wired cards, meaning they need a physical wired connection to participate on the network, and others are wireless, meaning they receive their data via radio waves.

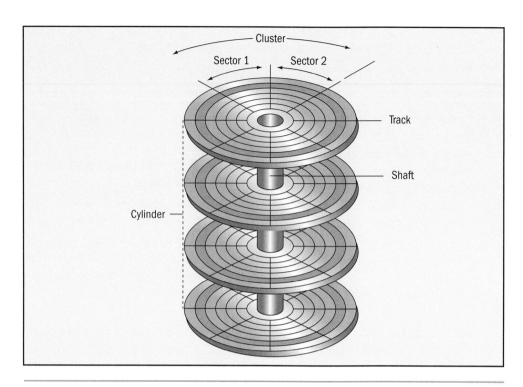

FIGURE 17–3 Partitions of a hard disk drive.

to a file. Clusters are groups of sectors; their size is defined by the file system, but they are always in multiples of two. A cluster, therefore, consists of two, four, six, or eight sectors, and so on. (With modern file systems, the user can exercise some control over the number of sectors per cluster.) *Tracks* are concentric circles that are defined around the platter. *Cylinders* are groups of tracks that reside directly above and below each other.

Additionally, the HDD has a file system table (map) of the layout of the defined space in that partition. FAT file systems use a *file allocation table* (which is where the acronym *FAT* comes from) to track the location of files and folders (data) on the HDD, while NTFS file systems use, among other things, *a master file table (MFT)*. Each file system table tracks data in different ways, and forensic computer examiners should be versed in the technical nuances of the HDDs they examine. It is sufficient for our purposes here, however, to merely visualize the file system table as a map to where the data is located. This map numbers sectors, clusters, tracks, and cylinders to keep track of the data.

One way to envision a partition and file system is as a room full of safe-deposit boxes. The room itself symbolizes the entire partition and the boxes with their contents represent clusters of data. In order to determine who rented which box, and subsequently where each depositor's property is, a central database is needed. This is especially true if a person rented two boxes located in opposite ends of the room. A similar situation often arises when storing data on a computer, because not all the data in a particular file or program is always stored in contiguous (adjacent) clusters on the HDD. Thus, a database tracking the locations of the safe-deposit boxes is much like a file system table tracking the location of data within the clusters.

This example is also useful to understand the concept of reformatting a HDD, which involves changing the way the disk stores data. If the database managing the locations of the safe-deposit boxes were wiped out, the property in them would still remain; we just wouldn't know what was where. So too with the hard disk drive. If a user were to wipe the file system table clean—for example, by reformatting it—the data itself would not be gone. Both the database tracking the locations of the safe-deposit boxes and the file system table tracking the location of the data in the cluster are maps—not the actual contents.

Key Points

- The computer's operating system (OS) is the bridge between the human user and the computer's electronic components. It provides the user with a working environment and facilitates interaction with the system's components.

- Formatting is the process of preparing a hard disk drive to store and retrieve data in its current form.

- A sector is the smallest unit of data that a hard drive can address. A cluster usually is the minimum space allocated to a file. Clusters are groups of sectors.

- A FAT is a file allocation table. It tracks the location of files and folders on the hard disk drive.

Putting It All Together

Let's now see how all of the parts of a computer come together to allow a user to access and manipulate data. When a person presses the power button, the power supply wakes up and delivers power to the motherboard and all of the hardware connected to the computer. At this point the flash ROM chip on the motherboard (the one that contains the BIOS) conducts a power-on self test (POST) to make sure everything is working properly.

The flash ROM polls the motherboard to check to see that the hardware that is attached, then reads from itself the boot order, thus determining from what device it should boot. Typically the boot device is the HDD, but it can also be a floppy disk, CD, or USB drive.

If the boot device is the HDD, the HDD is then sent control. It locates the first sector of its disk (known as the *master boot record*), determines its layout (partition(s)), and boots an operating system (Windows, Mac OS, Linux, Unix). The user is then presented with a computer work environment, commonly referred to as a *desktop*.

Now ready to work, the user double-clicks an icon on the desktop, such as a Microsoft Word shortcut, to open the program and begin to type a document. The CPU processes this request, locates the Microsoft Word program on the HDD (using a predefined map of the drive called a *file system table*), and carries out the programming instructions associated with the application. The CPU also loads Microsoft Word into RAM via the system bus and sends the output to the monitor by way of the video controller, which is either located on or attached to the motherboard.

As the user types, data from the keyboard is loaded into RAM. When the user is finished, he or she might print the document or simply save it to the HDD for later retrieval. If printed, the data is copied from RAM, processed by the CPU, placed in a format suitable for printing, and sent through the system bus to a printer. If the document is saved, the data is copied from RAM, processed by the CPU, passed to the HDD controller by way of the system bus, and written to a portion of the HDD. The HDD's file system table is updated so it knows where to retrieve that data later. This is a very simplistic overview of the boot process. Forensic examiners must possess a much more in-depth understanding of the boot process.

The preceding example illustrates how three components of the computer perform most of the work: the CPU, RAM, and system bus. The example can get even more complicated as the user opens more applications and performs multiple tasks simultaneously (multitasking). Several tasks can be loaded into RAM at once, and the CPU is capable of juggling them all. This allows for the multitasking environment and the ability to switch back and forth between applications. (To further enhance this ability, RAM can use a portion of the HDD as virtual memory, which can be very forensically valuable—but more on this later.) All of this is orchestrated by the operating system and is written in the language of the computer—ones and zeros.

Processing the Electronic Crime Scene

Processing the electronic crime scene has a lot in common with processing a traditional crime scene. The investigator must first ensure that the proper legal requirements (search warrant, consent, and so on) have been met so that the scene can be searched and the evidence seized. The investigator should then devise a plan of approach based on the facts of the case and the physical location.

Documenting the Scene

The scene should be documented in as much detail as possible before disturbing any evidence, and before the investigator lays a finger on any computer components. Of course there are circumstances in which an investigator might have to act quickly and pull a plug before documenting the scene, such as when data is in the process of being deleted.

Crime-scene documentation is accomplished through two actions: sketching and photographing. The electronic crime scene is no different. The scene should be sketched in a floor plan fashion (see Figure 17–4) and then overall photographs of the location taken. In a case in which several computers are connected together in a network, a technical network sketch should also be included if possible (covered in greater detail in the next chapter).

After investigators photograph the overall layout, close-up photographs should be shot. A close-up photograph of any running computer monitor should be taken. All the connections to the main system unit, such as peripheral devices (keyboard, monitor, speakers, mouse, and so on), should be photographed. If necessary, system units should be moved delicately and carefully to facilitate the connections photograph (see Figure 17–5). Close-up photographs of equipment serial numbers should be taken if practical.

At this point, investigators must decide whether to perform a live acquisition of the data, perform a system shutdown (as in the case of server equipment), pull the plug from the back of the computer,[2] or a combination thereof. Several factors influence this decision. For example, if encryption is being used and pulling the plug will encrypt the data, rendering it unreadable without a password or key, pulling the plug would not be

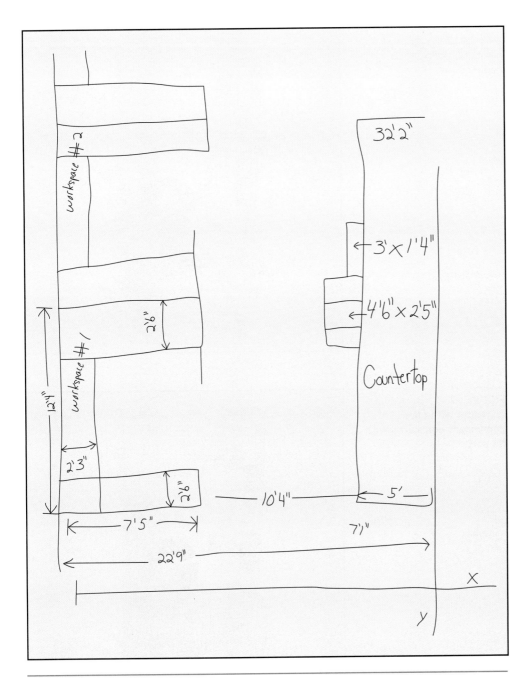

FIGURE 17–4 Rough sketch made at a crime scene, with necessary measurements included.

prudent. Similarly, any data that exists in RAM and has not been saved to the HDD will be lost if power to the system is discontinued. Regardless of how investigators decide to proceed, the equipment most likely will be seized. Exceptions exist in the corporate environment, where servers are fundamental to business operations.

After the photographs and sketches are complete, but before disconnecting the peripherals from the computer, a label should be placed on the cord of each peripheral, with a corresponding label placed on the port to which it is connected. A numbering scheme should be devised to identify the system unit if several computers are at the scene (Figure 17–6). The combination of sketching, photographing, and labeling should adequately

FIGURE 17–5 Back of a computer showing all connections.

FIGURE 17–6 Back of a computer with each component correlated with its port.

document the scene, prevent confusion of which component went with which system unit, and facilitate reconstruction if necessary for lab or courtroom purposes.

Forensic Image Acquisition

Once a computer has been seized, the data it contains must be obtained for analysis. The number of electronic items that potentially store evidentiary data are too vast to cover in this section. The hard disk drive will be used as an example, but the same "best practices" principles apply for other electronic devices as well.

The goal in obtaining data from a HDD is to do so without altering even one bit of data. Thus, throughout the entire process, the forensic computer examiner must use the least intrusive method to retrieve data. Because booting a HDD to its operating system changes many files and could potentially destroy evidentiary data, obtaining data is generally accomplished by removing the HDD from the system and placing it in a laboratory forensic computer so that a *forensic image* can be created. However, the BIOS of the seized computer sometimes interprets the geometry of the HDD differently than the forensic computer does. *Geometry* refers to the functional dimensions of a drive, including the number of heads, cylinders, and sector per track. In these instances, the image of the HDD must be obtained using the seized computer.

Regardless of the computer in which the HDD is placed, the examiner must ensure that, when creating the forensic image, the drive to be analyzed is in a "write-blocked" read-only state in which no new data can be added to the drive. Furthermore, the examiner needs to be able to prove that the forensic image he or she obtained includes every bit of data and caused no changes (writes) to the HDD.

To this end, a sort of fingerprint of the drive is taken before and after imaging through the use of a Message Digest 5 (MD5), Secure Hash Algorithm (SHA), or similar algorithm. Before imaging the drive, the algorithm is run and a thirty-two-character alphanumeric string is produced based on the drive's contents. The algorithm is then run against the resulting forensic image. If nothing changed, the same alphanumeric string is produced, thus demonstrating that the image is all-inclusive of the original contents and that nothing was altered in the process.

A forensic image of the data on a hard disk drive (or any type of storage medium) is merely an exact duplicate of the entire contents of that medium. In other words, all portions of a hard disk drive—even blank portions—are copied from the first bit (one or zero) to the last. Why would investigators want to copy what appears to be blank or unused portions of the HDD? The answer is simple: to preserve *latent data*, discussed later in the chapter. Data exists in areas of the drive that are, generally speaking, unknown and inaccessible to most end users. This data can be valuable as evidence. Therefore, a forensic image—one that copies every single bit of information on the drive—is necessary.[3] A forensic image differs from a backup or standard copy in that it takes the entire contents, not only data the operating system is aware of.

Many forensic software packages come equipped with a method to obtain a forensic image. The most popular software forensic tools—EnCase, Forensic Toolkit (FTK), Forensic Autopsy (Linux-based freeware), and SMART (Linux-based software by ASR Data)—all include a method to obtain a forensic image. All produce self-contained image files that can then be interpreted and analyzed. They also allow image compression to conserve storage. The fact that self-contained, compressed files are the result of forensic imaging allows many images from different cases to be stored on the same forensic storage drive. This makes case management and storage much easier (see Figure 17–7).

Message Digest 5 (MD5)/Secure Hash Algorithm (SHA)
A software algorithm used to "fingerprint" a file or contents of a disk; used to verify the integrity of data. In forensic analysis it is typically used to verify that an acquired image of suspect data was not altered during the process of imaging.

Key Points

- Aspects of a computer that should be photographed close up at an electronic crime scene include (1) the screen of any running computer monitor, (2) all the connections to the main system unit, such as peripheral

FIGURE 17–7 **Screen shot of EnCase Software.** *Courtesy EnCase, www.encase.com*

devices (keyboard, monitor, speakers, mouse, and so on), and (3) equipment serial numbers.

- Two situations in which an investigator would not unplug a computer at an electronic crime scene are (1) if encryption is being used and pulling the plug will encrypt the data, rendering it unreadable without a password or key, and (2) if data exists in RAM that has not been saved to the HDD, and will thus be lost if power to the system is discontinued.

- The primary goal in obtaining data from a HDD is to do so without altering even one bit of data. To this end, a Message Digest 5 (MD5)/ Secure Hash Algorithm (SHA) takes a "fingerprint" of a hard disk drive (HDD) before and after forensic imaging.

Analysis of Electronic Data

Analysis of electronic data is virtually limitless and bound only to the level of skill of the examiner. The more familiar an examiner is with computers, operating systems, application software, data storage, and a host of other disciplines, the more prepared he or she will be to look for evidentiary data.

Because computers are vast and complex, discussing each area, file, directory, log, or computer process that could potentially contain evidentiary data is beyond the scope of one chapter—and may be beyond the scope of an entire book. What follows are some of the more common areas of analysis. While reading this section, reflect on your own knowledge of computers and consider what other data might be of evidentiary value and where it might be found.

Visible Data

The category of visible data includes all information that the operating system is presently aware of, and thus is readily accessible to the user. Here we present several common types of visible data considered in many investigations. This list is by no means exhaustive and can include any information that has value as evidence.

Data/Work Product Files   One place to find evidence is in documents or files produced by the suspect. This category is extremely broad and can include data from just about any software program. Microsoft Word and WordPerfect word-processing programs typically produce text-based files such as typed documents and correspondence. These programs, and a host of other word-processing programs, have replaced the typewriter. They are common sources of evidence in criminal cases, particularly those involving white-collar crime.

Also relevant in white-collar crime and similar financial investigations are any data related to personal and business finance. Programs such as QuickBooks and Peachtree accounting packages can run the entire financial portion of a small to midsize business. Similarly, personal bank account records in the computer are often managed with personal finance software such as Microsoft Money and Quicken. Moreover, criminals sometimes use these programs as well as spreadsheet applications to track bank accounts stolen from unsuspecting victims. Forensic computer examiners should familiarize themselves with these programs, the ways in which they store data, and methods for extracting and reading the data.

Advances in printer technology have made high-quality color printing both affordable and common in many homes. While this is a huge benefit for home office workers and those interested in graphic arts, the technology has been used for criminal gain. Counterfeiting and check and document fraud are easily perpetrated by most home computer users. All that is required is a decent ink-jet printer and a scanner. Including the computer, a criminal could set up a counterfeiting operation for less than $1500. Examiners must learn the graphics and photo-editing applications used for such nefarious purposes. Being able to recognize the data produced by these applications and knowing how to display the images is key to identifying the evidence.

Swap File Data   When an application is running, the program and the data being accessed are loaded into RAM. A computer's RAM can read data much faster than the hard disk drive, which is why the programs are loaded here. RAM, however, has its limits. Some computers have 256 MB of RAM, others 512 MB, and still others as much as a gigabyte or two. Regardless of the amount, though, most operating systems (Windows, Linux, and so on) are programmed to conserve RAM when possible. This is where the *swap file* comes in. The operating system attempts to keep only data and applications that are presently being used in RAM. Other applications that were started, but are currently waiting for user attention, may be swapped out of RAM and written to the swap file on the hard disk drive.[4]

For example, a manager of a retail store may want to type a quarterly report based on sales. The manager starts Microsoft Word and begins his report. Needing to incorporate sales figure data from a particular spreadsheet, he opens Microsoft Excel. Depending on what is running on the computer, the original Word document may be swapped from RAM to the swap space on the HDD to free up space for Excel. As the manager goes

visible data
All data that the operating system is presently aware of, and thus is readily accessible to the user.

swap file
A file or defined space on the HDD to which data is written, or swapped, to free RAM for applications that are in use.

back and forth between the programs (and maybe checks his e-mail in between) this swapping continues. Data that is swapped back and forth is sometimes left behind in the swap space. Even as this area is constantly changed, some of the data is orphaned in unallocated space, an area of the HDD discussed later in this chapter.

Swap file can be defined as a particular file or even a separate HDD partition, depending on the operating system and file system type. Data in the swap space can be read by examining the HDD through forensic software or a utility that provides a binary view, such as Norton Disk Editor or WinHex (see Figure 17–8).

temporary files

Files temporarily written by an application to perform a function.

Temporary Files   Any user who has suffered a sudden loss of power in the middle of typing a document can attest to the value of a temporary file. Most programs automatically save a copy of the file being worked on in a temporary file. After typing a document, working on a spreadsheet, or working on a slide presentation, the user can save the changes, thus promoting the temporary copy to an actual file. This is done as a sort of backup on the fly. If the computer experiences a sudden loss of power or other catastrophic failure, the temporary file can be recovered, limiting the amount of data lost. The loss is limited because the temporary file is not updated in real time. Rather, it is updated periodically (typically defaulted to every ten minutes in most programs), depending on the application's settings.

Temporary files can sometimes be recovered during a forensic examination. Some of the data that may have been orphaned from a previous version may be recoverable, if not the complete file. This is true even when a document has been typed and printed, but never saved. The creation of the temporary file makes it possible for some of this "unsaved" data to be recovered during analysis.

Another type of temporary file valuable to the computer investigator is the *print spool file*. When a print job is sent to the printer, a spooling process delays the sending of the data so the application can continue to work while the printing takes place in the background. To facilitate this, a temporary print spool file is created; this file typically includes the data to

FIGURE 17–8   As user switches between applications and performs multiple tasks, data is swapped back and forth between RAM and the computer's hard drive. This area on the hard drive is referred to as *swap space*.

be printed and information specific to the printer. There are different methods for accomplishing this, and thus the files created as a result of this process vary. It is sometimes possible to view the data in a readable format from the files created during the spooling process.

Latent Data

The term latent data includes data that are blocked (not necessarily intentionally) from a user's view. It includes areas of files and disks that typically are not apparent to the computer user, but contain data nonetheless. Latent data are one of the reasons a forensic image of the media is created. If a standard copy were all that was produced, only the logical data (that which the operating system is aware of) would be captured. Getting every bit of data ensures that potentially valuable evidence in latent data is not missed.

Once the all-inclusive forensic image is produced, how are the latent data viewed? Utilities that allow a user to examine a hard disk drive on a binary level (ones and zeros) are the answer. Applications such as Norton Disk Editor and WinHex provide this type of access to a hard disk drive or other computer media. Thus these applications, sometimes also referred to as *hex editors* (for the hexadecimal shorthand of computer language), allow all data to be read on the binary level independent of the operating system's file system table. Utilities such as these can write to the media under examination, thus changing data. Consequently, a software or hardware write-blocker should be used.

A more common option in data forensics is to use specialized forensic examination software. EnCase and Forensic Toolkit for Windows and SMART and Forensic Autopsy for Linux are examples of forensic software. Each allows a search for evidence on the binary level and provides automated tools for performing common forensic processing techniques. Examiners should be cautious, however, about relying too heavily on automated tools. Merely using an automated tool without understanding what is happening in the background and why evidentiary data might exist in particular locations would severely impede the ability to testify to the findings.

Slack Space   Slack space is empty space on a hard disk drive created because of the way the HDD stores files. Recall that although the smallest unit of data measure is one bit (either a one or a zero), a HDD cannot address or deal with such a small unit. In fact, not even a byte (eight bits) can be addressed. Rather, the smallest unit of addressable space by a HDD is the sector. HDDs typically group sectors in 512-byte increments, while CD-ROMs allocate 2048 bytes per sector.

If the minimum addressable unit of the HDD is 512 bytes, what happens if the file is only 100 bytes? In this instance there are 412 bytes of slack space. It does not end here, however, because of the minimum cluster requirement. As you may recall, clusters are groups of sectors used to store files and folders. The cluster is the minimum storage unit defined and used by the logical partition. It is because of the minimum addressable sector of the HDD and the minimum unit of storage requirement of the volume that we have slack space.

Minimum cluster allocation must be defined in a sector multiple of two. Thus a cluster must be a minimum of two, four, six, or eight sectors, and so on. Returning to our initial example of the 100-byte file, suppose an HDD has a two-sector-per-cluster volume requirement. This means that the HDD will isolate a minimum of two 512-byte sectors (a total of 1024 bytes)

latent data
Areas of files and disks that are typically not apparent to the computer user (and often not to the operating system), but contain data nonetheless.

FIGURE 17–9 Slack space illustrated in a two-sector cluster. Cluster sizes are typically greater than two sectors, but two sectors are displayed here for simplicity.

of storage space for that 100-byte file. The remaining 924 bytes would be slack space (see Figure 17–9).

To illustrate this point, let us expand on the previous example of safe-deposit boxes. The bank offers safe-deposit boxes of a particular size. This is the equivalent of the HDD's clusters. A person wanting to place only a deed to a house in the box gets the same size box as a person who wants to stuff it full of cash. The former would have empty space should he or she desire to place additional items in the box. This empty space is the equivalent of slack space. But what if the box becomes full and the person needs more space? That person must then get a second box. Similarly, if a file grows to fill one cluster and beyond, a second cluster (and subsequent clusters as needed) is allocated. The remaining space in the second cluster is slack space. This continues as more and more clusters are allocated depending on file size and file growth.

This example is a bit of an oversimplification because there are actually two types of slack space: RAM slack and file slack. RAM slack occupies the space from where the actual (logical) data portion of the file ends to where the first allocated sector in the cluster terminates. File slack, therefore, occupies the remaining space of the cluster.

Let us go back to the 100-byte file with the two-sector-per-cluster minimum requirement. Following the end of the logical data (the end of the 100 bytes), the remaining 412 bytes of that sector is RAM slack; the additional 512 bytes completing the cluster is then file slack. See Figure 17–10 for a visual depiction. The question now becomes: What can I expect to find in slack space and why is this important? The answer: junk—valuable junk.

RAM slack is a concept that was more relevant in older operating systems. Remember that the minimum amount of space the HDD can address is the 512-byte sector. Therefore if the file size is only 100 bytes, the remaining space must be padded. Some operating systems pad this area with data contained in RAM. This could include Web pages, passwords, data files, or other data that existed in RAM when the file was written. Modern Windows operating systems pad this space with zeros, but some examinations may still yield valuable data in this area.

RAM slack

The area beginning at the end of the logical file and terminating at the end of that sector. In some older operating systems this area is padded with information in RAM.

file slack

The area that begins at the end of the last sector that contains logical data and terminates at the end of the cluster.

FIGURE 17–10   File slack.

File slack, on the other hand, can contain a lot of old, orphaned data. To illustrate this point, let's take the 100-byte file example a bit further. Let's say that prior to the 100-byte file being written to the HDD and occupying one cluster (two sectors totaling 1024 bytes), a 1,000-byte file occupied this space but was deleted by the user. When a file is "deleted" the data still remains behind, so it is probably a safe bet that data from the original 1000-byte file remains in the slack space of the new 100-byte file now occupying this cluster. This is just one example of why data exists in file slack and why it might be valuable as evidence.

In one final attempt to illustrate this point, let us again build on our safe-deposit box analogy. Suppose a person rents two safe-deposit boxes, each box representing a sector and the two combined representing a cluster. If that person places the deed to his house in the first box, the remaining space in that box would be analogous to RAM slack. The space in the second box would be the equivalent of file slack. The only difference is that unlike the empty spaces of the safe-deposit box, the slack space of the file most likely contains data that might be valuable as evidence.

The data contained in RAM and file slack is not really the concern of the operating system. As far as the OS is concerned, this space is empty and therefore ready to be used. Until that happens, however, an examination with one of the aforementioned tools will allow a look into these areas, thus revealing the orphaned data. The same is true for unallocated space.

Unallocated Space   Latent evidentiary data also resides in unallocated space. What is unallocated space, how does data get in there, and what is done to access this space?

If we have an 80-GB hard drive and only half of the hard drive is filled with data, then the other half, or 40 GB, is unallocated space (see Figure 17–11.) Returning to our safe-deposit box analogy, if the entire bank of safe-deposit boxes contains 100 boxes, but only 50 are currently in use, then the other 50 would be the equivalent of unallocated space. The HDD's unallocated space typically contains a lot of useful data. The constant shuffling of

unallocated space
The area of the HDD that the operating system (file system table) sees as empty (containing no logical files) and ready for data. Simply stated, it is the unused portion of the HDD, but is not necessarily empty.

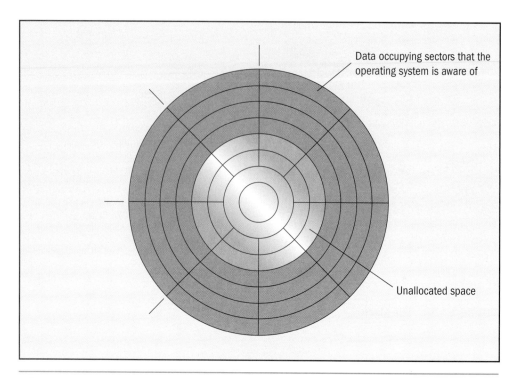

Data occupying sectors that the operating system is aware of

Unallocated space

FIGURE 17–11 **Simplistic view of a hard drive platter demonstrating the concept of unallocated space.**

files on the HDD causes data to become orphaned in unallocated space as the logical portion of the file is rewritten to other places. Some examples of how data is orphaned may help.

Defragmenting Defragmenting a HDD involves moving noncontiguous data back together. Remember that the HDD has minimum space reservation requirements. Again, if a file requires only 100 bytes of space, the operating system might allocate much more than that for use. If the file grows past what has been allocated for it, another cluster is required. If, however, a different file occupies the next cluster in line, then the operating system will have to find another place for that first file on the drive. In this scenario, the file is said to be *fragmented* because data for the same file is contained in noncontiguous clusters. In the case of the HDD, the shuffling of files causes data to be orphaned in unallocated space.

Ultimately, fragmentation of numerous files can degrade the performance of a HDD, causing the read/write heads to have to traverse the platters to locate the data. Defragmenting the HDD takes noncontiguous data and rearranges it so it is in contiguous clusters. Building yet again on our safe-deposit box analogy, if a renter eventually needs to store more property than his original box can hold, the bank will rent him a second box. If, however, all the boxes around his are occupied and the only free one is in another section of the room, then his property is "fragmented. " The bank would have to "defrag" the safe-deposit boxes to get the property of users with more than one box into adjacent boxes.

Swap File/Swap Space Recall that a computer uses the HDD to maximize the amount of RAM by constantly swapping data in and out of RAM to a predetermined location on the HDD, thus freeing valuable RAM. The constant read and write operations of RAM cause a constant change in the swap file or swap space. Data can become orphaned in unallocated space from this constant swapping to and from the HDD.

Deleted Files The deletion of files is another way that data becomes orphaned in unallocated space. Data from deleted files can manifest itself in different ways during a forensic examination. The actions that occur when a file is deleted vary among file systems. However, generally speaking, the data is not gone. For example, consider what happens when a user or program deletes a file in a Windows operating system with a FAT file system. When a file is deleted the first character in the file's directory entry (its name) is replaced with the Greek letter sigma. When the sigma replaces the first character, the file is no longer viewable through conventional methods and the operating system views the space previously occupied by the file as available. The data, however, is still there.

This example doesn't account for the actions of the Windows Recycle Bin. When the Windows operating system is set up to merely place the deleted file in the Recycle Bin, the original directory entry is deleted and one is created in the Recycle folder for that particular user. The new Recycle folder entry is linked to another file, the *info* or *info2* file, which includes some additional data, such as the location of the file prior to its deletion should the user wish to restore it to that location. Detailed discussions of the function of the Recycle Bin are beyond the scope of this chapter, but suffice it to say that, even when the Recycle Bin is emptied, the data usually remains behind until overwritten. Moreover, Windows NTFS partitions and Linux EXT partitions handle deleted files differently, but in both cases data typically remains.

What if a new file writes data to the location of the original file? Generally speaking, the data is gone. This is, of course, unless the new file only partially overwrites the original. In this instance we return to the unallocated space orphaned data scenario. If a file that occupied two clusters is deleted, and a new file overwrites one of the clusters, then the data in the second cluster is orphaned in unallocated space. Of course yet a third file can overwrite the second cluster entirely, but until then the data remains in unallocated space.

Let us once again look to our safe-deposit box analogy. If, for example, the owner of two safe-deposit boxes stopped renting them, the bank would list them as available. If the owner didn't clean them out, the contents would remain unchanged. If a new owner rented one of the boxes, the contents from the former owner would be replaced with the new owner's possessions. The second box would therefore still contain orphaned contents from its previous owner. The contents would remain in this "unallocated box" space until another renter occupies it.

Key Points

- The types of computer evidence can be grouped under two major subheadings: visible and latent data.

- Visible data is data that the operating system is aware of, and thus easily accessible to the user. It includes any type of user-created data, such as word-processing documents, spreadsheets, accounting records, databases, and pictures.

- Temporary files created by programs as a sort of backup on the fly can prove valuable as evidence. Data in the swap space (used to conserve the valuable RAM within the computer system) can also yield evidentiary data.

- Latent data is data that the operating system is not aware of. The constant shuffling of data through deletion, defragmentation, swapping, and so on is one of the ways data is stored in latent areas.

- Latent data can exist in both RAM slack and file slack. RAM slack is the area from the end of the logical file to the end of the sector. File slack is the remaining area from the end of the final sector containing data to the end of the cluster.

- Latent data might be found in unallocated space—space on a HDD that the operating system sees as empty and ready for data.

- When a user deletes files the data typically remains behind, so deleted files are another source of latent data.

Chapter Summary

Computers have permeated society and are used in countless ways with innumerable applications. Similarly, the role of electronic data in investigative work has realized exponential growth in the last decade. Users of computers and other electronic data storage devices leave footprints and data trails behind. Computer forensics involves preserving, acquiring, extracting, analyzing, and interpreting computer data. In today's world of technology, many devices are capable of storing data and could thus be grouped into the field of computer forensics.

The central processing unit (CPU) is the brain of the computer—the main chip responsible for doing the actual computing. Random-access memory (RAM) is volatile memory containing data that is forever lost when the power is turned off. Programs are loaded into RAM because of its faster read speed. The hard disk drive (HDD) is typically the primary location of data storage within the computer. Different operating systems map out HDDs differently and examiners must be familiar with the file system they are examining. Evidence exists in many different locations and in numerous forms on a HDD. This evidence can be grouped into two major categories: visible and latent data.

Visible data is data that the operating system is aware of, and consequently is easily accessible to the user. From an evidentiary standpoint, it can encompass any type of user-created data, such as word-processing documents, spreadsheets, accounting records, databases, and pictures. Temporary files created by programs as a sort of backup on the fly can also prove valuable as evidence. Finally, data in the swap space (used to conserve the valuable RAM within the computer system) can yield evidentiary visible data.

Latent data, on the other hand, is data that the operating system, typically is not aware of. Evidentiary latent data can exist in both RAM slack and file slack. RAM slack is the area from the end of the logical file to the end of the sector. File slack is the remaining area from the end of the final sector containing logical data to the end of the cluster. Another area where latent data might be found is in unallocated space. Unallocated space is space on a HDD that the operating system sees as empty and ready for data. The constant shuffling of data through deletion, defragmentation, and swapping is one of the ways data is orphaned in latent areas. Finally, when a user deletes files the data typically remains behind. Deleted files are therefore another source of latent data to be examined during forensic analysis.

Computer file systems and data structures are vast and complex. Therefore, areas of forensic analysis are almost limitless and constrained only by the knowledge and skill of the examiner. With a working knowledge of how computers function, how they are used, and how they store data, an examiner is on his or her way to begin to locate the evidentiary data.

Review Questions

Facts and Concepts

1. What is the difference between hardware and software?

2. What are CDs, DVDs, and other containers for programs that are loaded into the memory of a computer referred to as?

3. What is a computer's motherboard?

4. Which of the following carries data from one hardware device to another?
   a. system bus
   b. central processing unit (CPU)
   c. random-access memory (RAM)
   d. network interface card (NIC)

5. What part of a computer actually does the computing?

6. What type of memory stores software programs and instructions while the computer is turned on? Because it is not permanent, and its contents are forever lost once power is taken away from the computer, what is it also referred to as?

7. What is firmware? What is another name for firmware? Why is it important to forensic computer investigation?

8. What is the role of the computer's operating system (OS)?

9. What is the primary storage device on most computers?

10. What is formatting? Why must a hard disk drive be formatted?

11. What are sectors and clusters? How are they related to one another?

12. What is the smallest unit of information on a computer? What do eight of them constitute?

13. What is a FAT and what purpose does it serve?

14. What aspects of a computer should be photographed close up at an electronic crime scene?

15. Name two situations in which an investigator would not immediately unplug a computer at an electronic crime scene?

16. What is the primary goal in obtaining data from a HDD?

17. What is the purpose of a Message Digest 5 (MD5)/Secure Hash Algorithm (SHA)? Why would a forensic computer examiner run such an algorithm?

18. Why would investigators want to copy blank or unused portions of the HDD?

19. List and define the two main types of evidentiary computer data.

20. What is swap space?

21. In which of the following places would a computer forensic investigator not look for latent data?
    a. RAM slack
    b. file slack
    c. unallocated space
    d. temporary files

22. What is slack space?

23. What is fragmentation? What effect does fragmentation have on a hard disk drive (HDD)?

Application and Critical Thinking

1. If a file system defines a cluster as six sectors, how many bits of information can be stored on each cluster? Explain your answer.

2. Criminalist Tom Parauda is investigating the scene of a crime involving a computer. After he arrives, he photographs the overall scene and takes close-up shots of all the connections to the single computer involved, as well as photos of the serial numbers of the computer and all peripheral devices. Tom then labels the cord to each peripheral device, then disconnects them from the computer. After making sure that all data in RAM has been saved to the hard disk drive, he unplugs the computer from the wall. What mistakes, if any, did Tom make?

3. You are investigating a case in which an accountant is accused of keeping fraudulent books for a firm. Upon examining his computer, you notice that the suspect uses two different accounting programs that are capable of reading the same types of files. Given this information, where would you probably begin to search for latent data on the computer and why?

Case Analysis 1

Suspicious circumstances surrounding the death of Ms. Smith in a home fire led the police to suspect her husband of murder. Evidence later recovered from Mr. Smith's computer proved key in solving the case.

1. What did police hope to prove by examining the Microsoft Word files on Mr. Smith's computer? Why did they believe this would implicate him in his wife's murder?

2. How were the documents titled *insurance1.doc* and *WRL1604.tmp* important to tying Mr. Smith to his wife's death?

Case Analysis 2

When police seized a laptop from a van parked suspiciously outside a local shopping mall, they discovered a counterfeiting ring that employed modern technology to perpetrate this age-old crime.

1. What physical evidence most strongly implicated the driver of the van in a currency counterfeiting operation? What aspect of this evidence confirmed these suspicions?

2. What files located on the suspect's computer indicated that the suspects were producing more than counterfeit currency? What conclusion did the investigators draw from the existence of these files?

Web Resources

Computer Forensics, Cybercrime and Steganography Resources (Links to books, articles, Web sites, and other resources dealing with computer forensics)
www.forensics.nl

Digital Evidence (Links to articles on computer and Internet forensics)
www.crimeandclues.com/digital.htm

Digital Evidence Collection and Handling (Article about dealing with computer information seized at a crime scene)
www.faculty.ncwc.edu/toconnor/426/426lect06.htm

Computer Forensics World (Online community of computer forensics professionals, with links to articles and other resources on computer forensics)
www.computerforensicsworld.com

The Electronic Evidence Information Center (Links to articles and audio/video presentations on topics in computer forensics)
www.e-evidence.info/biblio.html

Do's and Don'ts of Forensic Computer Investigations (Basic advice on conducting computer forensics)
www.eweek.com/article2/0,1759,1646899,00.asp

Recovering and Examining Computer Forensic Evidence (Article that discusses the process and techniques of computer forensics)
www.fbi.gov/hq/lab/fsc/backissu/oct2000/computer.htm

Endnotes

1. One million bytes is referred to as a megabyte (MB), while 1 billion bytes is termed a gigabyte (GB).
2. Pulling the plug should always be done by removing the plug from the back of the computer. If the plug is removed from the wall and a battery backup (UPS) is in place, the UPS might cause an alert to the system and keep the unit powered on.
3. In this instance, *bit* is both metaphorical and literal. Every bit of information is needed, so we must get it all. So too every bit, as in the smallest unit of data storage—a one or a zero—must be imaged.
4. Actually, the more appropriate term is probably *paging* as opposed to swapping. This is because entire programs are typically not swapped in and out of memory to the swap space; rather, *pages* of memory are placed there.

Case Reading 1

Computer Forensic Analysis Answers the Question "Arson or Accident?"

Courtesy Peter Arnold, Inc.

Brief

The home of John Smith was destroyed by a fire, which was later determined to be the result of arson. During the fire, Smith's wife, Jane, died. Investigators learned that insurance policies taken against both the home and the life of Jane Smith were recently increased, so Smith stands to receive a very large monetary settlement. This fact, and problems with his purported alibi at the time of the fire, makes him the primary suspect. Smith has steadfastly denied the existence of the insurance policies and offers that his wife must have recently changed the policies.

Further investigation discloses that the couple did not possess a home computer but that Smith uses a computer at work. After applying for and receiving a search warrant for Smith's workplace, the arson investigator seizes the computer system unit from underneath Smith's desk, which he found in a powered-off condition. During execution of the search warrant, the company's computer administrator tells investigators that the computer was used only by Smith. The computer system unit is submitted for forensic analysis.

Analysis Request

Locate any incriminating or exculpatory evidentiary data with respect to Smith's knowledge of changes in his insurance policy. Locate any evidentiary data with respect to motive for the crimes of arson and/or homicide.

Forensic Image Acquisition

1. The computer system was documented and its chassis was opened and a single IDE/ATA hard disk drive (HDD) was located and documented. The HDD was removed from the system and the computer system unit was booted to the BIOS setup program. The system date and time were verified.

2. The HDD was then placed in a forensic workstation, connected to the system using a hardware write-blocking device to ensure that the suspect HDD was not altered in any way.

3. A forensic image of the HDD was acquired using EnCase Version 5. The integrity of this image was verified using the MD5 algorithm inherent in the EnCase program. A date and time analysis was done on all the files, revealing no dates later than the date of the execution of the search warrant.

Analysis

1. Deleted files were recovered.

2. A file signature analysis was run.

3. All files, including dates and times, logical and physical sizes, and complete location path, were documented by the EnCase program.

4. User accounts were documented: two default accounts (*Administrator* and *Guest*, SID 500 and 501 respectively) and one user account (*jsmith*).

5. The operating system and file system type were documented: Windows 2000 using an NTFS partition.

6. Keyword text searches, derived from the text of letters received by the insurance company, were conducted.

7. All Microsoft Word documents were examined.

8. All text documents were examined.

9. Print spool files were examined.

Findings

1. A file titled *insurance1.doc* was located in the directory *C:\Documents and Settings\jsmith\junk*. The directory structure *C:\Documents and Settings\jsmith* coincides with a default directory for the user name *jsmith,* which would have been established with that account. The subdirectory *junk* was then added by a user of the *jsmith* account. The text in this file is the same as the one received by the insurance company requesting an increase in homeowner's insurance.

2. Text found in unallocated space matches sections of text in a second letter received by the insurance company requesting an increase in life insurance for Jane Smith.

3. A file titled *WRL1604.tmp* was found in the directory *C:\Documents and Settings\jsmith\junk*. The file matches that of a temporary Microsoft Word file and contains text matching sections of text in the letter received by the insurance company requesting an increase in life insurance for Jane Smith.

4. A file titled *46127a.SPL* was located in the directory *C:\windows\ system32\spool\printers*. This file appears to be a print spool file. This file, when viewed as an Enhanced Meta File (EMF), reveals a document exact in composition and similar in layout to the letter received by the insurance company requesting an increase in life insurance for Jane Smith. An EMF is a type of spool file created during the printing process and can be viewed as a Windows picture file in the forensic software.

Conclusion

Based on the forensic examination of the computer data submitted in this case, it can be stated within a reasonable degree of scientific certainty that a user of this computer had knowledgeable interaction with letters very similar in content, composition, and structure to the evidentiary letters submitted as reference for analysis.

Case Reading 2

Counterfeiting and Fraud: A Forensic Computer Investigation

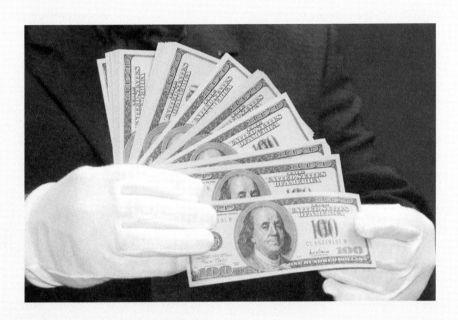

Courtesy Getty Images, Inc.

Brief

A detective submits a laptop computer for examination and explains that it was seized in connection with a case of counterfeiting and fraud. According to the detective, patrol officers happened upon a large sport-utility vehicle, occupied by one male driver, parked in the lot of a local mall. According to the officers, the driver and the circumstances appeared suspicious.

After investigating further, the officers located a laptop computer, color printer, and scanner in the rear of the vehicle. All equipment was hooked up and running. Additionally, the officers located gift certificates for one of the stores within the mall, which apparently were printed inside the vehicle. Finally, two $100 bills bearing exactly the same serial number were located in the driver's wallet. In response to questioning, the driver admitted using the system to print bogus gift certificates and counterfeit cash,

which he then redeemed inside the mall. Prior to submission at the computer forensics laboratory, the equipment was processed for fingerprints at the state Bureau of Criminal Identification (BCI).

Analysis Request

Locate any evidentiary data with respect to the crimes of counterfeiting and fraud. Demonstrate any connection between the recovered printed documents and the electronic equipment seized from the vehicle.

Forensic Image Acquisition

1. The computer system was documented and its case was opened and a single IDE hard disk drive (HDD) was located and documented. The HDD was removed from the system and the computer system unit was booted to the BIOS setup program. The system date and time were verified.

2. The HDD was then placed in a forensic workstation, connected to the system using a hardware write-blocking device to ensure that the suspect HDD was not altered in any way.

3. A forensic image of the HDD was acquired using EnCase Version 5. The integrity of this image was verified using the MD5 algorithm inherent in the EnCase program. A date and time analysis was done on all the files, revealing no dates later than the date of the execution of the search warrant.

Analysis

1. Deleted files were recovered.

2. A file signature analysis was run.

3. All files, including dates and times, logical and physical sizes, and complete location path, were documented by the EnCase program.

4. The operating system and file system type were documented: Windows XP using an NTFS file system.

5. All graphics files were viewed, including ones previously deleted.

6. A graphics finder script was run against unallocated space. The script searched this area to locate file signatures of known graphics files.

7. All print spool files were located and examined.

Findings

1. A file titled *100front.jpg* was located in the directory *C:\Documents and Settings\user1\My Documents*. This file is an image of the front of a $100 bill. The serial number on this image matched the serial number of the suspected counterfeit $100 bills found on the suspect.

2. A file titled *100back.jpg* was located in the directory *C:\Documents and Settings\user1\My Documents*. This file is an image of the back of a $100 bill.

3. A file titled *GapGiftCert1.jpg* was located in the directory *C:\Documents and Settings\user1\My Documents*. This file is an image of the front of a gift certificate for The Gap, a retail store.

4. A file titled *GapGiftCert2.jpg* was located in the directory *C:\Documents and Settings\user1\My Documents*. This file is an image of the back of a gift certificate for The Gap, a retail store.

5. A file titled *thumbs.db.* was located in the directory *C:\Documents and Settings\user1\My Documents*. This file, when viewed as a compound file, displayed several images, namely the images in items 1–4.

6. In the folder *C:\Documents and Settings\User1\My Recent Documents,* link files were found to the following:

   a. *C:\Documents and Settings\user1\My Documents\100front.jpg*

   b. *C:\Documents and Settings\user1\My Documents\100back.jpg*

   c. *C:\Documents and Settings\user1\My Documents\GapGiftCert1.jpg*

   d. *C:\Documents and Settings\user1\My Documents\GapGiftCert2.jpg*

7. The submitted scanner and printer were connected to a laboratory computer system and the aforementioned evidentiary files were copied onto the HDD of that system. Several printouts of the images were made. Additionally, test items were

scanned and printed. All exemplars produced from the laboratory computer system were submitted to the state Bureau of Criminal Identification. The original counterfeit currency and gift certificates were also submitted to BCI for comparison to the exemplars. BCI was asked to locate any distinguishing characteristics produced by the printer and scanner submitted in this case.

Conclusion

Based on the forensic examination of the computer data submitted in this case, it can be stated within a reasonable degree of scientific certainty that a user of this computer knowingly produced counterfeit currency and counterfeit gift certificates.

Scott Peterson: A Case of Circumstantial Evidence

On the surface, Scott Peterson and his wife, Laci, appeared to live a happy and contented lifestyle in Modesto, California. The 30-year-old Peterson and his 27-year-old former college sweetheart, a substitute teacher, were expecting their first child in about one month when Laci suddenly disappeared. Scott Peterson told investigators that he had last seen his wife on December 24, 2002, at 9:30 a.m. when he left home for a fishing trip off San Francisco Bay.

In April 2003, Laci's decomposed remains washed ashore not far from where Scott said he had gone fishing on the day she vanished. Peterson claimed that Laci was dressed in a white top and black pants when he last saw her, but when her body was found she was wearing khaki pants. Scott's sister recalled that Laci was wearing khaki pants the night before her disappearance.

When questioned, Peterson claimed that he had gone fishing for sturgeon or striped bass. However, the police investigation revealed that he failed to bring the appropriate fishing rod and lines to catch such fish. Further revelations surfaced when it became known that Scott was having an affair with another woman. A search of Scott's warehouse led to the recovery of a black hair on a pair of pliers resting in Scott's boat. A mitochondrial DNA profile of the hair was consistent with Laci's DNA. Scott Peterson was charged with murder and convicted and currently awaits his fate on death row.

Visit WebExtra 18.1 to view the evidence that prosecutors presented to convict Scott Peterson.

chapter 18

Forensic Science and the Internet

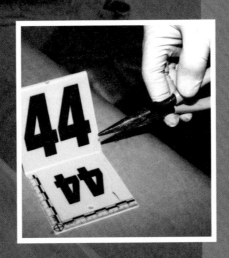

Andrew W. Donofrio
Richard Saferstein

Key Terms

bookmark
broadband
browser
cookies
domain
download
e-mail
firewall
hacking
hypertext
Internet cache
Internet history
Internet protocol
Internet service provider (ISP)
mailing list
modem
newsgroups
router
search engine
uniform resource locator (URL)
VoIP (Voice over Internet Protocol)
Wi-Fi

Learning Objectives

After studying this chapter you should be able to:

- Understand how the Internet is structured

- Know how to search for information on the Internet

- Describe information retrieval sources, such as mailing lists and newsgroups, available through the Internet

- Learn how to retrieve information about forensic science on the Internet

- Relate various areas found on the computer where a user's Internet activities can be investigated

- Describe how e-mails, chat, and instant messages on the Internet can be traced and recovered

- List and describe three locations where investigators may pinpoint the origin of a hacker

WebExtra 18.1

The Scott Peterson Case
www.prenhall.com/hsforensics

Today, one cannot read a newspaper or turn on the television without seeing some reference to the Internet. The Internet, often referred to as the "information superhighway," is a medium for people to communicate with others and to access millions of pieces of information on computers located anywhere on the globe. No subject or profession remains untouched by the Internet, including forensic science. Every week many new pages of information are added to the Internet on the subject of forensic science, providing instant access to updated forensic science news and information. The Internet brings together forensic scientists from all parts of the world, linking them into one common electronic community.

What Is the Internet?

The Internet can be defined as a "network of networks." A single network consists of two or more computers that are connected in some fashion to share information; the Internet connects thousands of these networks so information can be exchanged worldwide.

Closer Analysis

Building the Internet

The Internet was developed in 1969 by the U.S. Department of Defense to connect computers in different locations. The project, called ARPANET, originated from a group of scientists and engineers funded by the Pentagon's Advanced Research Projects Agency (ARPA). Their idea was based on the premise that the network would still operate even if part of the connection failed.

The first successful link was established between computers housed at UCLA and Stanford Research Institute. Shortly thereafter, USC–Santa Barbara and University of Utah computers were added to the system. In 1972, more than twenty sites were connected on the system when the first electronic mail (e-mail) message was sent.

In the 1980s, this network of interconnected computers grew with the establishment of the National Science Foundation Network (NSFNet), which encompassed five supercomputing centers across the United States. At about the same time, regional networks were formed around the United States for the purpose of accessing NSFNet. By 1989, ARPANET had closed down and NSFNet, along with its regional networks, began to mushroom into a worldwide network known as the Internet.[1]

Connecting to the Internet

Connections are sometimes made through a modem, a device that allows computers to exchange and transmit information through telephone lines. A modem passes digital information through a series of steps to convert it to analog signals that can be passed over a telephone line. The process is reversed when the modem converts analog signals coming in from the phone line.

Modems transfer information at a rate measured in bits per second (bps). Recall from the previous chapter that a bit is a single unit of digital data. Obviously, a modem with high-speed capabilities will ensure a faster connection on the Internet. Currently, a modem that transmits at 56,000 bits (or 56 kilobits) per second is recommended for convenience and reasonable connection speed. This speed is roughly equivalent to transmitting 1,000 to 2,000 words per second.

The trend, however, is to offer Internet users even higher-speed broadband connections to Web sites. Digital subscriber line (DSL) service is available from phone companies in many regions. DSL carries digital information on your regular telephone line without disturbing voice traffic. These lines can carry up to 1.1 megabits per second. Alternatively, one may opt to transmit over a TV cable line. Cable modems offer speeds comparable to DSL.

Once your computer is hooked into a DSL or cable line you now have an additional option to link other computers in your home or office, through either a network wire (typically Ethernet) or high-frequency radio waves via a wireless or Wi-Fi connection. A device called a router serves as a sort of splitter, designed to link computers and manage traffic between them. The router, whether wired or wireless, allows computers to share a connection to the Internet. The advantage of Wi-Fi technology is that it avoids messy wires. Once you have positioned a router in your home or office, another option awaits you—voice over Internet protocol (VoIP). The IP (Internet Protocol) portion of VoIP is the bloodline of the Internet—but more on that later.

A broadband Internet connection can send and receive the human voice in a manner indistinguishable from a traditional telephone line. If you're in the range of a router, your Wi-Fi phone can operate like a traditional cell phone.

It is quite astonishing to think that there is no overriding network controlling the Internet. Rather, various larger, higher-level networks are connected through *network access points*. Many large Internet service providers (ISPs) (such as Verizon, AOL, and Yahoo) connect to each other through these network access points. The ISP's customers can then connect to the network by connecting to the bank of modems or the cable/DSL-connected routers located at the Internet service provider location and thus be connected to all the other networks. Because this places many individual computers on the network, an address system is needed so that all the data traveling on the network can get to its intended location.

Internet Addressing

With all of the different computer manufacturers and software developers, some rules are necessary for computers to communicate on a global network. Just as any human language needs rules for people to communicate successfully, so does the language of computers. Computers that participate on the Internet, therefore, must be provided with an address known as an

modem
A device that connects a computer to another computer through a phone line.

broadband
Describes any kind of Internet connection with a download speed of more than 56 kilobits per second.

Wi-Fi
Technology that uses high-frequency radio signals to transmit and receive data over the Internet. Allows for a wireless connection to the Internet.

router
A device that manages traffic between computers belonging to a network, enabling them to share a connection to the Internet.

VoIP (voice over internet protocol)
Transmission of the human voice over the Internet, usually through a telephone.

Internet service provider (ISP)
A company that provides connections to the Internet.

Internet protocol
The set of rules used to transmit packets of data over the Internet and route them to their destination.

domain
A human-readable name and abbreviation for a Web site.

Internet protocol (IP) address from the Internet service provider to which they connect.

IP addresses take the form ###.###.###.###, in which, generally speaking, ### can be any number from 0 to 255. A typical IP address might look like this: 66.94.234.13. Not only do these IP addresses provide the means by which data can be routed to the appropriate location, but they also provide the means by which most Internet investigations are conducted (see Figure 18–1).

Of course, having to remember strings of numbers is a very inefficient and inconvenient way to access sites on the Internet. For this reason, every IP address also is assigned a domain name. Domains are human-readable names assigned to IP addresses. A domain name usually consists of two or more labels separated by dots. For example, www.nytimes.com is the registered domain name for the *New York Times*.

The rightmost label in a domain name is the *top-level domain*. Following are the most common abbreviations by which a top-level domain name is identified on the Internet:

.gov—government

.mil—military

.edu—educational institution

.com—commercial providers

.org—nonprofit organizations

To the left of the top-level domain is the *subdomain;* thus, nytimes is a subdomain of the .com domain. For the purpose of e-mail, the name of an individual at the *New York Times* may be added before the subdomain, with the @ sign used to separate them. An example of such an e-mail address might be Johndoe@nytimes.com.

At this point you may be wondering: If everything on the Internet uses an IP address to route data to the correct location, how can we use Web addresses and e-mail addresses to access Web sites and send e-mail? The answer, although technically complex, is quite simple. Understanding the

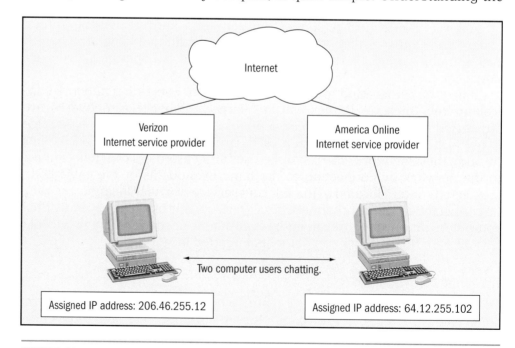

FIGURE 18–1   Two computers communicating by sending data to each other's IP address via the Internet. An IP address is assigned to each computer by their respective Internet service providers (ISPs).

apparent limitations of the human mind to remember numbers, developers created the concept of the domain name system (DNS). *Domain name systems* are essentially large databases distributed over the Internet that relate the names of networks to their actual IP address.

For instance, a person who wants to go to the *New York Times* online needs to know only the domain name. Even if the user is unsure of the actual address, the most logical place to start would obviously be www.newyorktimes.com or www.nytimes.com (both of which work, by the way). In actuality, however, the address is 199.239.136.245. This can be verified by typing that IP address directly into your Web browser where you would normally type the Web address. Domain name systems make it much easier for us to navigate the Web, but for investigative purposes it is important to realize that no names exist on the Internet; rather it's all about the IP address (see Figure 18–2).

Key Points

- A single network consists of two or more computers that are connected to share information. The Internet can be defined as a "network of networks"—it connects thousands of networks so information can be exchanged worldwide.

- Connection to the Internet can be made through a modem, a device that allows computers to exchange and transmit information through telephone lines. Higher-speed broadband connections are available through cable lines or through DSL telephone lines. Computers can be linked or networked through wired or wireless (Wi-Fi) connections.

- Computers that participate in the Internet have a unique numerical Internet protocol (IP) address and usually a name.

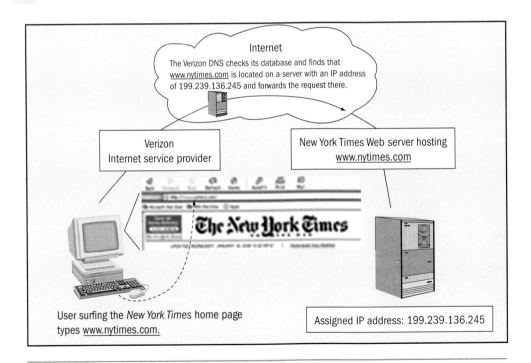

FIGURE 18–2 **A user wishing to visit the *New York Times* Web site types the user-friendly URL (uniform resource locator) www.nytimes.com. Because all traffic on the Internet is routed by IP address, the URL needs to be resolved to the IP address. This is done by the user's ISP's domain name system (DNS).**

The World Wide Web

The most popular area of the Internet is the World Wide Web. Also known as WWW, W3, or the Web, it is a collection of documents called *Web pages* that are stored in the computers connected to the Internet throughout the world. Web browsers, such as Netscape Navigator and Microsoft Internet Explorer, are programs that allow the user to explore information stored on the Web and to retrieve Web pages the viewer wishes to read. Web browsers permit the downloading and capture of documents, as well as printing of selected portions of Web sites.

Each Web page is stored in a specific Web site that has a unique Web address that indicates where the document is actually located. The Web address is called the uniform resource locator (URL). The URL designates the site at which information is stored on the Internet. You can access a page by directly entering the URL into your browser. For example, the FBI has a Web site that can be accessed by typing in its URL: www.fbi.gov. The URL for the FBI consists of the following components:

> *http://*—Hypertext Transfer Protocol is the programming language the browser uses to locate and read web pages.
> *www.*—Denotes the World Wide Web, the place on the Internet where the information is located.
> *fbi.*—Designates the subdomain or server in this case, for the Federal Bureau of Investigation.
> *gov*—Designates the domain name.

The Internet has made browsing or exploring the Web easy through the existence of hypertext. Hypertext is usually easy to find because it is highlighted with a different color within the Web page. When clicked, hypertext enables the user to jump to another Web page related to the subject at hand.

For example, a user interested in examining the FBI's *Law Enforcement Bulletin* Web page would merely go to the FBI's home page and search for the term *Law Enforcement Bulletin*. The user is immediately transferred to a hypertext page where, with a click of the mouse, he or she is taken to the Web site. This Web site has the URL www.fbi.gov/publications/leb/leb.htm, where *leb.htm* designates a document on the FBI Web site. Another FBI publication available online is *Forensic Science Communications*. This quarterly online forensic science journal presents technical articles, technical notes, case reports, and review articles in a paperless format.

The advantage of using hypertext is that the user can quickly switch back and forth between related Web pages without having to retype the URL or start over at the beginning of the search. Hypertext makes the Internet user-friendly and has given rise to the expressions *browsing* and *surfing the Net*. Users can navigate from one Web site to another, browsing at leisure through a succession of documents. Another quick way to reach a site is to designate it as a bookmark or favorite place. Most browsers allow the user to customize a list of favorite Web sites for easy access with one click (see Figure 18–3).

Hundreds of new sites are added every day, providing Internet users with a staggering amount of information. You may wish to explore popular web site locations by using the list of the Top 100 Classic Websites compiled by *PC Magazine* (www.pcmag.com) (see Table 18–1). The *PC Magazine* Top 100 Classic Websites list includes sites related to business and finance,

browser
A program that allows a computer user to access Web sites.

uniform resource locator (URL)
A standard method by which Internet sites are addressed.

hypertext
Highlighted text or graphics on a Web page that, when clicked, links to other Web sites.

bookmark
A feature that allows the user to designate favorite Web sites for fast and easy access.

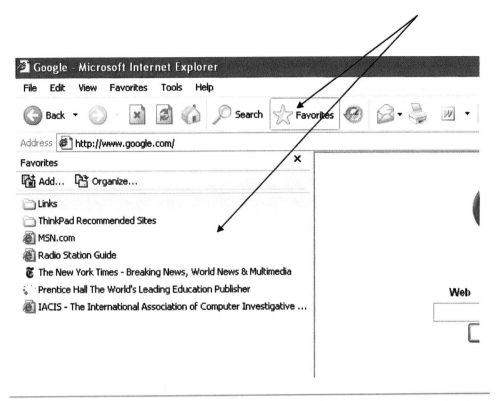

FIGURE 18–3 Bookmarks or favorite places can be saved for quick access in most Web browsers.

Table 18–1 PC Magazine's Top 100 Classic Web Sites

AAPS: PC and Mobile
AvantGo
www.avantgo.com

Homestead
www.homestead.com

Mailblocks
www.mailblocks.com

MSN Hotmail
www.hotmail.com

Shutterfly
www.shutterfly.com

Vindigo
www.vindigo.com

WebEx
www.webex.com

Yahoo! Groups
groups.yahoo.com

Business and Finance
Bloomberg.com
www.bloomberg.com

Internal Revenue Service
www.irs.gov

MSN Money
www.moneycentral.msn.com

SmartMoney.com
www.smartmoney.com

The Motley Fool
www.fool.com

TheStreet.com
www.thestreet.com

U.S. Securities and Exchange Commission
www.sec.gov

Careers
Dice.com
www.dice.com

Monster.com
www.monster.com

Yahoo! HotJobs
hotjobs.yahoo.com

Computing
Annoyances.org
www.annoyances.org

Answers that Work
www.answersthatwork.com

Digital Photography Review
www.dpreview.com

EarthWeb
www.earthweb.com

eWeek
www.eweek.com

ExtremeTech
www.extremetech.com

Java Technology
www.java.sun.com

PalmGear.com
www.palmgear.com

PC Magazine
www.pcmag.com

Slashdot
slashdot.org

Technology Review
www.technologyreview.com

W3Schools
www.w3schools.com

Webopedia
www.webopedia.com

Current Events and News You Can Use
Electronic Privacy Information Center
www.epic.org

(*continued*)

Table 18–1 PC Magazine's Top 100 Classic Web Sites *(continued)*

IEEE Virtual Museum
www.ieee-virtual-museum.org

NASA
www.nasa.gov

Project Vote Smart
www.vote-smart.org

World Health Organization
www.who.int

Lifestyle and Fun
Citysearch
www.citysearch.com

Discovery Kids
kids.discovery.com

Epicurious
www.epicurious.com

HowStuffWorks
www.howstuffworks.com

ifilm
www.ifilm.com

National Geographic Society
www.nationalgeographic.com

Nickelodeon Online
www.nick.com

Pogo
www.pogo.com

Smithsonian Institution
www.si.edu

Yahoo! Games
games.yahoo.com

News and Entertainment
AMG All Music Guide
www.allmusic.com

BBC News
www.bbc.co.uk

CNN
www.cnn.com

E! Online
www.eonline.com

ESPN.com
www.espn.com

Internet Archive
www.archive.org

Internet Movie Database
(IMDb)
www.imdb.com

Slate
www.slate.com

The New York Times on the Web
www.nytimes.com

NPR
www.npr.org

The Onion
www.theonion.com

RollingStone.com
www.rollingstone.com

Salon.com
www.salon.com

ScienceDaily
www.sciencedaily.com

Television Without Pity
www.televisionwithoutpity.com

Wired News
www.wired.com

Security and the Net
Broadbandreports.com
dslreports.com

CERT Coordination Center
www.cert.org

GetNetWise
www.getnetwise.org

Gibson Research Corp.
www.grc.com

Internet Traffic Report
www.internettrafficreport.com

Netcraft
news.netcraft.com

SecurityFocus
www.securityfocus.com

TrendMicro
www.trendmicro.com

Search, Reference, and Portals
About.com
www.about.com

Centers for Disease
Control and Prevention
www.cdc.gov

Dictionary.com
dictionary.reference.com

Encyclopaedia Britannica
www.britannica.com

FedStats
www.fedstats.gov

FirstGov.gov
www.firstgov.gov

Google
www.google.com

iVillage.com
www.ivillage.com

Librarians' Internet Index
www.lii.org

The Library of Congress
www.loc.gov

MSN Encarta
encarta.msn.com

Nolo.com
www.nolo.com

WebMD
www.webmd.com

Yahoo!
www.yahoo.com

Shopping
Amazon.com
www.amazon.com

CarsDirect.com
www.carsdirect.com

ConsumerReview.com
www.consumerreview.com

eBay
www.ebay.com

Netflix
www.netflix.com

Overstock.com
www.overstock.com

PriceGrabber.com
www.pricegrabber.com

Shopping.com
www.shopping.com

Surprise.com
www.surprise.com

Techbargains.com
www.techbargains.com

Travel
Expedia
www.expedia.com

Fodors
www.fodors.com

Frommers.com
www.frommers.com

Lonely Planet
www.lonelyplanet.com

Orbitz
www.orbitz.com

Travelocity
www.travelocity.com

computing, news, entertainment, online shopping, and reference sources. This list opens a gateway to exploring the diversity of the World Wide Web. For example, you can easily visit Expedia.com, a popular travel information site. Through this site you can book flights, hotel rooms, and cruises and plan most any type of vacation. The Amazon.com web site provides the largest bookstore on the Internet. Here the user can search by keyword, author, subject, or title to locate or purchase books on any topic imaginable. You can even ask Amazon.com to e-mail you when books related to your personal interests come in stock.

A favorite site of the author is Switchboard (www.switchboard.com). This site is devoted to helping users locate long-lost friends or relatives. A database of names, phone numbers, addresses, and e-mail addresses can easily be searched with a variety of options. Another interesting web site is MapQuest (www.mapquest.com). The user designates a location and the site generates a map, accompanied by written directions. A fun site is Blue-Mountain (www.bluemountain.com), where the user can compose, personalize, and send greeting cards for all sorts of occasions.

Search Engines

Sifting through the enormous amount of information on the World Wide Web can often resemble looking for a needle in a haystack. As the Internet grows, so does the need for automated search tools. Several directories and indexes known as **search engines** help users search the Internet for a particular topic. Through search engines, the user can locate relevant Web pages containing a particular piece of information on the Internet. When the user types in keywords and phrases related to the needed information, the search engine searches its database and lists all the pages involving the keyword selection. Most search engines contain tools called *spiders* or *crawlers* that search the Web seeking titles, subjects, and keywords to index the contents of individual Web pages.

search engine
A Web site devoted to searching for information on the Internet using keywords.

The number of search engines continues to change with new technology, as faster, newer tools are adopted and slower, older ones are phased out. Interestingly, search engines have taken on a new look, becoming *portals* offering a wide variety of Internet services in addition to their traditional search functions. Some of the more popular search engines, along with their URLs, are listed here:

Search Engine	URL
Yahoo!	www.yahoo.com
Google	www.google.com
MSN	www.msn.com
Dogpile	www.dogpile.com
Lycos	www.lycos.com

The reader can also find a multitude of search engines at www.easysearcher.com/index.html. Because each search engine has different capabilities, it is recommended that multiple search engines be used when researching a subject. Automated search tools called *meta-engines* load a query into several of the Net's leading search engines to compile a single list of results. One example of a meta-engine is MetaCrawler (www.metacrawler.com).

Electronic Mail and Mailing Lists

e-mail
Electronic mail.

The service that is most commonly used in conjunction with the Internet is electronic mail. Also called e-mail, this communication system can transport messages across the world in a matter of seconds. In order to use e-mail, users must acquire an e-mail address, usually through an Internet service provider or a free e-mail server. Like regular postal mail, you will need an address to receive mail, and you will need to know a recipient's address to send messages. These messages are stored in an individualized mailbox that can be opened electronically at your convenience.

download
The transfer of a file through an Internet connection from a remote computer to a user's computer.

Another interesting feature is that one can attach a file to an e-mail so that the recipient can download the attached file. The file can then be saved and stored on the recipient's computer. A file may consist of text, pictures, music, or video. For example, a text file can be viewed and modified by means of a word-processing program.

mailing list
A list of people with a common interest who receive all the e-mails sent to the list.

Also, having an e-mail account provides the opportunity to receive information through mailing lists. A mailing list is a discussion group for a selected topic in which related messages are sent directly to your mailbox through e-mail. For example, Forens-L is a mailing list dedicated to the discussion of forensic medicine and forensic science that provides a quick, useful way to exchange ideas or share information about forensics with people of similar interests around the world. To subscribe to the Forens-L mailing list, go to www.geradts.com/mailman/listinfo/forens-geradts.com for instructions.

Newsgroups

newsgroups
Large bulletin board systems that consist of several thousand specialized discussion groups. Messages are posted to a bulletin board for others to read.

Another service much like mailing lists involves newsgroups. Like a mailing list, a newsgroup is devoted to a particular topic. Whereas a mailing list, however, is usually managed by a single site, a newsgroup networks many sites that are set up by local Internet service providers. The result is that a newsgroup joins together a significantly larger audience compared to a mailing list. A newsgroup is analogous to a bulletin board where subscribers post articles or messages. When you connect to a newsgroup, you can quickly scan through a list of article titles, selecting only those that interest you.

To find a newsgroup of interest, you can explore Usenet, an index of the available newsgroups. The index can be located through search engines such as Google. Usenet can be searched through keywords in the same manner in which the World Wide Web is explored. For example, entering the keyword *law enforcement* into Usenet produces a list of articles from any of the newsgroups containing that keyword. The articles are hypertext so that with a click of the mouse, you can read the article instantaneously. The useful Google Groups Web site (groups.google.com) lists newsgroups in hypertext so that the newsgroup can be accessed directly from the World Wide Web. Commercial services such as AOL allow the user to subscribe to a newsgroup and provide the program that will keep track of how many articles are available, which ones you have read, and which ones you have not read.

Key Points

- Web browsers allow the user to explore information stored on the Web and to retrieve Web pages the viewer wishes to read.

- Hypertext is highlighted text or graphics on a Web page that, when clicked, links to other Web sites. Hypertext has given rise to the expressions *browsing* and *surfing the Net*.

- Several directories and indexes on the Internet, known as search engines, help users find information on a particular topic from the hundreds of thousands of Web sites located on the Internet.

- The service that is most commonly used in conjunction with the Internet is electronic mail (e-mail), a communication system that can transport messages across the world in a matter of seconds.

- Besides Web pages, three ways for a computer user to receive information via the Internet are e-mail, mailing lists, and newsgroups.

Exploring Forensic Science on the World Wide Web

There are no limits to the amount or type of information that can be found on the Internet. The fields of law enforcement and forensic science have not been left behind by advancing computer technology. Extensive information about forensic science is available on the Internet. The types of Web pages range from simple explanations of the different fields of forensics to intricate details of crime-scene reconstruction. You can also find information on which colleges offer programs for degrees in forensics or pages posted by law enforcement agencies that detail their activities, as well as possible employment opportunities.

General Forensics Sites

Reddy's Forensic Home Page (www.forensicpage.com) is a valuable starting point. This site is a collection of forensic Web pages listed under categories such as new links in forensics; general forensic information sources; associations, colleges, and societies; literature and journals; forensic laboratories; general Web pages; forensic-related mailing lists and newsgroups; universities; conferences; and various forensic fields of expertise.

Another Web site offering a multitude of information related to forensic science is Zeno's Forensic Science Site (forensic.to/forensic.html). Here you can find links to forensic education and expert consultation, as well as a wealth of information concerning specific fields of forensic science.

A comprehensive and useful Web site for those interested in law enforcement is Officer.com (www.officer.com). This comprehensive collection of criminal justice resources is organized into easy-to-read subdirectories that relate to topics such as law enforcement agencies, police association and organization sites, criminal justice organizations, law research pages, and police mailing-list directories.

Web Sites on Specific Topics

An Introduction to Forensic Firearm Identification (www.firearmsid.com)
This Web site contains an extensive collection of information relating to the identification of firearms. An individual can explore in detail how to examine bullets, cartridge cases, and clothing for gunshot residues and suspect shooters' hands for primer residues. Information on the latest technology involving the automated firearms search system IBIS can also be found on this site.

Carpenter's Forensic Science Resources (www.tncrimlaw.com/forensic/)
This site provides a bibliography with hypertext references pertaining to

WebExtra 18.2

An Introduction to Forensic
Firearms Identification
www.prenhall.com/hsforensics

different aspects of criminal investigations involving forensic evidence. For example, the user can find references about DNA, fingerprints, hairs, fibers, and questioned documents as they relate to crime scenes and assist investigations. This Web site is an excellent place to start a research project in forensic science.

Crime Scene Investigation (www.crime-scene-investigator.net/index.html) For those who are interested in learning the process of crime-scene investigation, this site provides detailed guidelines and information regarding crime-scene response and collection and preservation of evidence. For example, information concerning packaging and analysis of bloodstains, seminal fluids, hairs, fibers, paint, glass, firearms, documents, and fingerprints can be found through this Web site. This Web site explains the importance of inspecting the crime scene and the impact forensic evidence has on the investigation.

Crime and Clues (www.crimeandclues.com) Users interested in learning about the forensic aspects of fingerprinting will find this a useful and informative Web site. The site covers the history of fingerprints, as well as subjects pertaining to the development of latent fingerprints. The user will also find links to other Web sites covering a variety of subjects pertaining to crime-scene investigation, documentation of the crime scene, and expert testimony.

Interactive Investigator—Détective Interactif (www.virtualmuseum.ca/Exhibitions/ Myst) At this outstanding site, visitors can obtain general information and an introduction to the main aspects of forensic science from a database on the subject. They can also explore actual evidence gathered from notorious crime scenes. Users will be able to employ deductive skills and forensic knowledge while playing an interactive game in which they must help Detective Wilson and Detective Marlow solve a gruesome murder.

The Chemical Detective (caligula.bcs.deakin.edu.au/bcs_courses/forensic/ Chemical%20Detective/index.htm) This site offers descriptions of relevant forensic science disciplines. Topics such as fingerprint, fire and arson, and DNA analysis are described in informative layperson's terms. Case histories describe the application of forensic evidence to criminal investigations. Emphasis is placed on securing and documenting the crime scene. The site directs the reader to other important forensic links.

Contact a Document Examiner (www.qdewill.com) This basic, informative Web page answers frequently asked questions concerning document examination, explains the application of typical document examinations, and details the basic facts and theory of handwriting and signatures. There are also links to noted document examination cases for the user to read and recognize the real-life application of forensic document examination.

Table 18–2 lists a number of additional Web sites available in the forensic science field.

Forensic Analysis of Internet Data

It's important from the investigative standpoint to be familiar with the evidence left behind from a user's Internet activity. A forensic examination of a computer system reveals quite a bit of data about a user's Internet activity. The data described next would be accessed and examined using the forensic techniques outlined in Chapter 17.

Table 18–2 Forensic Science Web Sites

American Academy of Forensic Sciences—Professional society dedicated to the application of science to the law and committed to the promotion of education in the forensic sciences.

American Board of Forensic Entomology—Provides information about the field's history, case studies, and professional status.

American Board of Forensic Toxicology Inc.—Establishes and revises as necessary standards of qualification for those who practice forensic toxicology.

American College of Forensic Examiners (ACFE)—Dedicated to members of the forensic community. Also provides links to help people find expert witnesses in the forensic field.

American Society of Crime Laboratory Directors (ASCLD)—Nonprofit professional society devoted to the improvement of crime laboratory operations through sound management practices.

American Society of Questioned Document Examiners—Online references, technical notes on handwriting identification, and other areas of professional interest to the forensic document analyst.

ASCLD: Laboratory Accreditation Board—Offers the general public and users of laboratory services a means of identifying laboratories that have demonstrated that they meet established standards.

Association for Crime Scene Reconstruction (ACSR)—Members are law enforcement investigators, forensic experts, and educators.

Association of Firearm and Tool Mark Examiners—Defines standards and ethics for individual workers in the field of firearms and toolmark examination.

California Association of Criminalists—Membership is offered to individuals currently employed as laboratory scientists and professionally engaged in one or more fields directly related to the forensic sciences.

Canadian Society of Forensic Science—Includes journal abstracts, history, and meeting information.

European Association for Forensic Entomology—Created in May 2002 in Rosny Sous Bois, France, to promote forensic entomology in Europe.

Forensic Science Service—Source for training, consultancy, and scientific support.

Forensic Science Society—Provides information on careers, conferences, and publications.

International Association for Identification—Professional association for those engaged in forensic identification, investigation, and scientific examination.

International Association of Bloodstain Pattern Analysis—Organization of forensic experts promoting education, establishing training standards, and encouraging research in the field of bloodstain pattern analysis.

(continued)

Table 18–2 Forensic Science Web Sites (*continued*)

International Association of Forensic Toxicologists—Promotes cooperation and coordination of efforts among members.

International Organisation on Electronic Evidence (IOCE)—Formed to develop international principles for the procedures relating to digital evidence.

National Forensic Science Technology Center—Dedicated to supporting forensic science laboratories to achieve the highest possible quality of operations.

Natural Resources DNA Profiling and Forensic Centre—Undertakes research on natural populations of animals and plants for the purpose of providing information to managers charged with conserving biodiversity and ensuring the sustainable use of Canada's biological resources.

Society of Forensic Toxicologists—Promotes and develops field of forensic toxicology.

Southern Association of Forensic Scientists—Organization of professional forensic scientists.

Southern California Association of Fingerprint Officers—An association for scientific investigation and identification.

U.S. Department of Justice: National Commission on the Future of DNA Evidence—Working to maximize the value of forensic DNA evidence in the criminal justice system.

Vidocq Society—Forensic experts who meet in the shadow of Independence Hall to investigate and solve unsolved homicides.

Websites are hypertexted at http://dir.yahoo.com/Science/Forensics/Organizations/?o=a.

Internet Cache

When a user accesses a Web site, such as the *New York Times* home page, data is transferred from the server at that site to the user's computer. If the user is accessing the Internet via a dial-up connection, the transfer may take a while, because the data transfer rate and capabilities (bandwidth) of the telephone system are limited. Even with the high-speed access of a DSL line or cable connection, conservation of bandwidth is always a consideration.

Internet cache
Portions of visited Web pages placed on the local hard disk drive to facilitate quicker retrieval once revisited.

To expedite web browsing and make it more efficient, most Web browsers use an Internet cache that stores, or caches, portions of the pages visited on the local hard disk drive. This way, if the page is revisited, portions of it can be reconstructed more quickly from this saved data, rather than having to pull it yet again from the Internet and use precious bandwidth.

The Internet cache is a potential source of evidence for the computer investigator. Portions of, and in some cases, entire visited Web pages can be reconstructed from data in the cache. Even if deleted, these cached files can often be recovered (see the section on deleted data in Chapter 17). Investigators must know how to search for this data within the particular Web browser used by a suspect.

cookies
Files placed on a computer from a visited Web site; they are used to track visits and usage of that site.

Cookies

Internet cookies are another area where potential evidence can be found. Cookies are placed on the local hard disk drive by Web sites the user has visited, if the user's Web browser is set to allow this to happen. The Web site uses cookies to track certain information about its visitors. This information can be anything from history of visits and purchasing habits to passwords and personal information used to recognize the user for later visits.

Consider a user who registers for an account at a Web site, and then returns to the same site from the same computer a few days later. The site often displays a banner reading "Welcome, *Your User Name.*" Data about the user is retrieved from the cookie file placed on the user's hard disk drive by the Web site during the initial visit and registration with the site. It is helpful to think of cookies as a "Caller ID" for Web sites. The site recognizes visitors and retrieves information about them, just as you recognize the name of a caller when answering a phone equipped with a Caller ID display.

Cookie files can be a valuable source of evidence. In Internet Explorer they take the form of plain text files, which can typically be opened with a standard text viewer or word-processing program, revealing part of the data. The existence of the files themselves, regardless of the information contained within, can be of evidentiary value to show a history of Web visits.

A typical cookie may resemble the following: rsaferstein@ forensicscience. txt. From this we can surmise that someone using the local computer login *rsaferstein* accessed the forensic science Web site. It is possible that the cookie was placed there by an annoying pop-up ad, but considered against other evidence in the computer data, the presence of this cookie may be of corroborative value.

Internet History

Most Web browsers track the history of Web page visits for the computer user. Like the "recent calls" list on a cell phone, the Internet history provides an accounting of sites most recently visited, sometimes storing weeks' worth of visits. Users can go back and access sites they recently visited just by going through the browser's history. Most Web browsers store this information in one particular file; Internet Explorer uses the *index.dat* file. On a Windows system, an *index.dat* file is created for each login user name on the computer.

The history file can be located and read with most popular computer forensic software packages. It displays the uniform resource locator (URL) of each Web site, along with the date and time the site was accessed. An investigation involving Internet use almost always includes an examination of Internet history data.

In some respects, the term *"Internet* history" is inaccurate because it doesn't encompass all of the functions of this utility. Some browsers store other valuable evidence independent of Internet access. Files accessed over a network are often listed in the history. Similarly, files accessed on external media, such as floppy disks, CDs, or thumb drives, may also appear in the history. Regardless, the Internet history data is a valuable source of evidence worthy of examination (see Figure 18–4).

Internet history
An accounting of Web sites visited. Different browsers store this information in different ways.

Bookmarks and Favorite Places

Another way users can access Web sites quickly is to store them in their bookmarks or "favorite places." Like a preset radio station, Web browsers allow users to bookmark Web sites for future visits. Much can be learned from a user's bookmarked sites. You might learn what online news a person is interested in, or what type of hobbies he or she has. You may also see that person's favorite child pornography or computer hacking sites bookmarked.

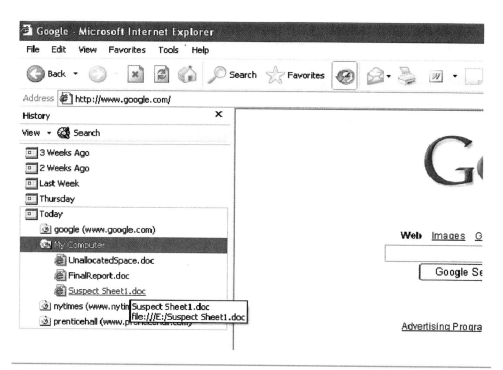

FIGURE 18–4 **The Internet history displays more than just Web browsing activity. Here we see Microsoft Word documents and a picture accessed on the current day.**

Key Points

- Places where a forensic computer examiner might look to determine what Web sites a computer user has visited recently are the Internet cache, cookies, and the Internet history.

Forensic Investigation of Internet Communications

Computer investigations often begin with or are centered on Internet communication. Whether it is a chat conversation among many people, an instant message conversation between two individuals, or the back-and-forth of an e-mail exchange, human communication has long been a source of evidentiary material. Regardless of the type, investigators are typically interested in communication.

The Role of the IP

Recall that in order to communicate on the Internet, a device needs to be assigned an Internet protocol (IP) address. The IP address is provided by the Internet service provider from which the device accesses the Internet. Thus, the IP address may lead to the identity of a real person. If an IP address is the link to the identity of a real person, then it is quite obviously valuable for identifying someone on the Internet.

To illustrate, let's assume that a user of the Internet, fictitiously named John Smith, connects to the Internet from his home by way of a Verizon DSL connection. Verizon in this case would provide Smith's IP address. Verizon owns a bank of IP addresses to service its customers; these addresses were issued by a regulatory body designed to track the usage of IP addresses, so no two addresses are ever used at the same time.

Suppose that Smith, while connected to the Internet, decides to threaten an ex-girlfriend by sending her an e-mail telling her he is going to kill her. That e-mail must first pass through the computers of Smith's Internet service provider—in this case Verizon—on its way to its destination, Smith's girlfriend. The e-mail would be stamped by the servers that it passes through, and this stamp would include the IP address given to Smith by Verizon for his session on the Internet.

An investigator tracking the e-mail would locate the originating IP address stamped in the e-mail header. That IP address could be researched using one of many Internet sites (such as www.samspade.org or www.arin.net) to determine which Internet service provider was given this IP as part of a block to service its customers (see Figure 18–5). The investigator then files a subpoena with the Internet service provider (Verizon) asking which of its customers was using that IP address on that date and time.

IP addresses are located in different places for different methods of Internet communications. E-mail has the IP address in the header portion of the mail. This may not be readily apparent and may require a bit of configuration to reveal. Each e-mail client is different and needs to be evaluated on a case-by-case basis. For an instant message or chat session, the service provider making the chat mechanism available would be contacted to provide the user's IP address.

E-mail, Chat, and Instant Messaging

E-mail can be read by a number of software programs called *clients*. Two of the most popular ways to access, read, and store e-mail in today's Internet environment, however, are Microsoft Outlook and Web-based clients. Some people even use a combination of the two.

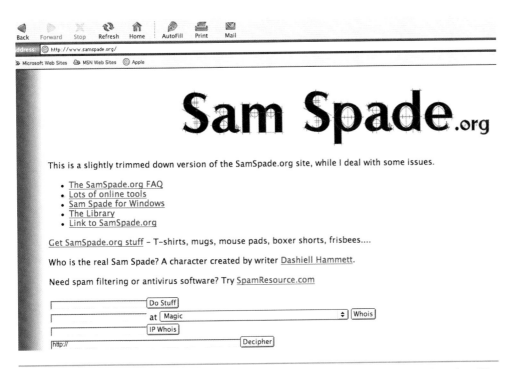

FIGURE 18–5 **Sites such as www.samspade.org can be used to track the origins of an IP address.** *Courtesy Word to the Wise*

If an e-mail account is linked through Microsoft Outlook, the e-mail is stored in a compound file (a file with several layers). Typically, a compound file exists for received, sent, and deleted e-mail. Users can also create new categories under which to save e-mail. Most forensic computer software applications can view these compound files so that the e-mail, including any file attachments, can be seen. These files can also be imported into a copy of Microsoft Outlook that is not attached to an e-mail account and the e-mail can be viewed there. Investigators must also be aware that in a computer network environment, the user's Outlook files may not reside on his or her workstation computer, but rather on a central mail or file server.

Most accounts offer the ability to access e-mail through a Web-based interface as well. This way, users can access their e-mail remotely from other computers. For e-mail accessed through a Web browser, the information presented earlier on Internet-based evidence applies. The Web interface converts the e-mail into a document suitable for reading in a Web browser. Consequently, Web-based e-mail is often found in the Internet cache. This is particularly true of free Internet e-mail accounts such as Hotmail and Yahoo.

Much of the evidence from Internet communication is also derived from chat and instant message technology. This is particularly true in the world of child sexual exploitation over the Internet. Various technologies provide chat and instant message services. Most chat and instant message conversations are not saved by the parties involved. Although most of the software does allow for conversation archiving, it is typically turned off by default. Therefore, conversations of this nature typically exist in the volatile memory space of random-access memory (RAM).

Recall from Chapter 17 that RAM is termed volatile because it holds data only if it has power. Unplugging the computer causes the data located in RAM to be lost. If, however, chat or instant message conversations are relevant as evidence and the computer was turned off, thus erasing the data in RAM, all might not be lost. Remember that there is an interaction between the computer system's RAM and the hard disk drive. RAM is a commodity, and the computer's operating system conserves it as much as possible by swapping/paging that information back and forth into the swap space/paging file. Therefore remnants of chat conversations are often found in the swap space/paging file during a forensic examination of the hard disk drive. These remnants, however, are typically fragmented, disconnected, and incomplete. Therefore if the chat or instant message is still present on the screen (and thus probably still in RAM) the investigator needs a method by which to preserve and collect it.

A detailed discussion of capturing volatile data from RAM is beyond the scope of this chapter. Suffice it to say that many commercial forensic software packages can capture this data. Similarly, Linux-based tools can accomplish this as well. The examiner may even be able to export the data remotely to another device. Regardless of the method, the data needs to be acquired.

Furthermore, many programs such as America Online Instant Messenger, Yahoo Messenger, and IRC (Internet Relay Chat) create files regarding the rooms or channels a user chatted in or the screen names with which a user exchanged instant messages. Each application needs to be researched and the forensic computer examination guided by an understanding of how it functions.

Hacking

hacking

Slang term for an unauthorized computer or network intrusion.

Unauthorized computer intrusion, more commonly referred to as **hacking**, is the concern of every computer administrator. Hackers penetrate computer systems for a number of reasons. Sometimes the motive is corporate espionage; other times it is merely for bragging rights within the hacker community. Most commonly, though, a rogue or disgruntled employee with some knowledge of the computer network is looking to cause damage. Whatever the motivation, corporate America frequently turns to law enforcement to investigate and prosecute these cases.

Generally speaking, when investigating an unauthorized computer intrusion, investigators concentrate their efforts in three locations: *log files, volatile memory*, and *network traffic*. Log files typically document the IP address of the computer that made the connection. Logs can be located in several locations on a computer network. Most servers on the Internet track connections made to them through the use of logs. Additionally the router (the device responsible for directing data) may contain log files detailing connections.

Similarly, devices known as firewalls may contain log files listing computers that were allowed access to the network or an individual system. Firewalls are devices (either hardware or software) that permit only requested traffic to enter a computer network. In other words, if a user didn't send out a request for Internet traffic from a specific system, the firewall should block its entry. If the log files captured the IP address of the intruder, then revealing the user behind the IP is the same process as for e-mail. Investigating a computer intrusion, however, gets a bit more complicated than this.

firewall
Hardware or software designed to protect against intrusions into a computer network.

Frequently, in cases of unlawful access to a computer network, the perpetrator attempts to cover the tracks of his or her IP address. In these instances, advanced investigative techniques might be necessary to discover the hacker's true identity. When an intrusion is in progress, the investigator may have to capture volatile data (data in RAM). The data in RAM at the time of an intrusion may provide valuable clues into the identity of the intruder, or at the very least his or her method of attack. As in the case of the instant message or chat conversation, the data in RAM needs to be acquired.

Another standard tactic for investigating intrusion cases is to document all programs installed and running on a system, in order to discover malicious software installed by the perpetrator to facilitate entry. The investigator uses specialized software to document running processes, registry entries, open ports, and any installed files.

Additionally, the investigator may want to capture live network traffic as part of the evidence collection and investigation process. Traffic that travels the network does so in the form of data packets. In addition to data, these packets also contain source and destination IP addresses. If the attack requires two-way communication, as in the case of a hacker stealing data, then data needs to be transmitted back to the hacker's computer using the destination IP address. Once this is learned, the investigation can focus on that system. Moreover, the type of data that is being transmitted on the network may be a clue as to what type of attack is being launched, whether any important data is being stolen, or what types of malicious software, if any, are involved in the attack.

Key Points

- An investigator tracking the origin of an e-mail seeks out the sender's IP address in the e-mail's header. Chat and instant messages are typically located in a computer's random-access memory (RAM).

- Tracking the origin of unauthorized computer intrusions (hacking) requires investigating a computer's log file, RAM, and network traffic.

- A firewall is a device designed to protect against intrusions into a computer network.

Chapter Summary

The Internet, often referred to as the "information superhighway," is a medium for people to communicate and to access millions of pieces of information from computers located anywhere on the globe. No subject or profession remains untouched by the Internet, including forensic science. The Internet brings together forensic scientists from all parts of the world, linking them into one common electronic community.

The Internet can be defined as a "network of networks." A single network consists of two or more computers that are connected to share information; the Internet connects thousands of these networks so all of the information can be exchanged worldwide. Connections can be made through a modem, a device that allows computers to exchange and transmit information through telephone lines. Higher-speed broadband connections are available through cable lines or through DSL telephone lines. Computers can be linked or networked through wired or wireless (Wi-Fi) connections.

Computers on the Internet have a unique numerical Internet protocol (IP) address and usually a name. Commercial Internet service providers connect computers to the Internet while offering the user an array of options. The most popular area of the Internet is the World Wide Web, a collection of pages stored in computers connected to the Internet throughout the world.

Web browsers allow users to explore information stored on the Web and to retrieve Web pages they wish to read. Several directories and indexes on the Internet, known as search engines, help users locate information on a particular topic from the hundreds of thousands of Web sites on the Internet. A keyword or phrase entered into a search engine locates Web sites that are relevant to that subject.

The service that is most commonly used in conjunction with the Internet is electronic mail (e-mail). This communication system can transport messages across the world in a matter of seconds. Extensive information relating to forensic science is available on the Internet. The types of Web pages range from simple explanations of the different fields of forensics to intricate details of forensic science specialties.

Investigators seeking a history of an Internet user's destinations can take advantage of the fact that computers store or cache portions of Web pages visited, and Web sites often create cookies to track certain information about Web site visitors. An investigator tracking the origin of an e-mail seeks out the sender's IP address in the e-mail's header. Chat and instant messages are typically located in a computer's random-access memory (RAM). Finding the origin of unauthorized computer intrusions (hacking) requires investigation of a computer's log file, RAM, and network traffic, among other things.

Review Questions

Facts and Concepts

1. Why is the Internet referred to as "a network of networks?"

2. Name three ways a computer can be connected to the Internet.

3. Which of the following manages traffic between computers on a network?
   a. an Internet protocol (IP)
   b. a router
   c. an Internet service provider (ISP)
   d. a domain

4. What is a company that provides connections to the Internet called?

5. What is an IP address? What form do addresses typically take?

6. What is a human-readable name assigned to an IP address called?

7. What is a browser?

8. Which of the following is not a utility for quickly accessing Web pages a user has visited previously?
   a. bookmarks
   b. Internet history
   c. a search engine
   d. a favorites file

9. What is hypertext? What expressions did the existence of hypertext give rise to?

10. Besides Web pages, name three ways for a computer user to receive information via the Internet.

11. What is the purpose of an Internet cache?

12. List three places where a forensic computer examiner might look to determine what Web sites a computer user has visited recently.

13. Why is an IP important to forensic computer examination?

14. Where are chat and instant messages typically stored on a computer?

15. What is hacking? Who most commonly engages in hacking, and for what purpose?

16. What is a firewall and how does it work?

Application and Critical Thinking

1. List the top-level domain most likely to be assigned to each of the following Web sites:
   a. an online car dealership
   b. the official Web site of the U.S. Coast Guard
   c. a local humane society
   d. the Web site of the U.S. Department of Justice
   e. your school's Web site

2. You are examining two computers to determine the IP address from which several threatening e-mails were sent. The first computer uses Microsoft Outlook as an e-mail client and the second uses a Web-based e-mail client. Where would you probably look first for the IP addresses in each of these computers?

Endnotes

1. An excellent history of the Internet is found in Katie Hefner and Matthew Lyon, *Where Wizards Stay Up Late: The Origins of the Internet* (New York: Simon & Schuster, 1996).

CRIME SCE
DO NOT CR

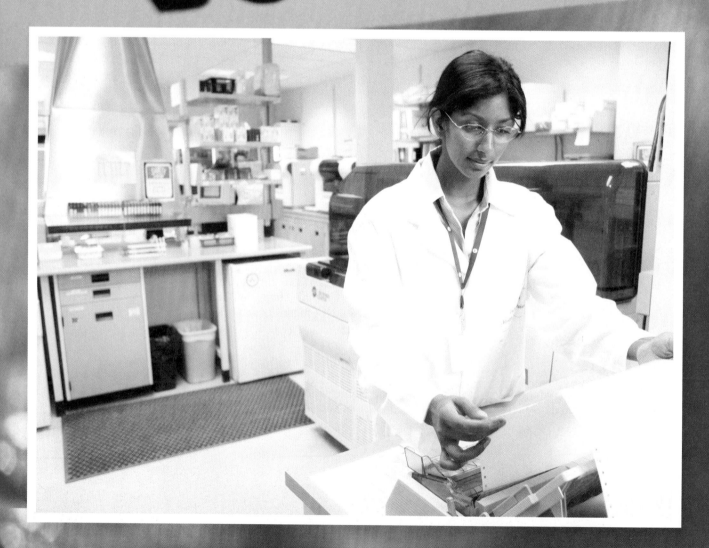

chapter 19

Careers in Forensic Science

In previous chapters we have encountered some of the many disciplines within forensic science—pathology, toxicology, anthropology, archaeology, and entomology, to name a few. However, the profession of forensic science encompasses an even wider range of activities, with work taking place in the field, the laboratory, and the courtroom. In this chapter, we will explore some of the various careers within forensic science and discuss the kind of training necessary to pursue each.

Disciplines in Forensic Science

The wide variety of activities comprising forensic science is reflected in the structure of the American Academy of Forensic Sciences (AAFS), the largest forensic science organization in the world. Each of the five-thousand scientists who are members of the AAFS belongs to one of the academy's ten divisions: Criminalistics, Engineering Sciences, General, Jurisprudence, Odontology, Pathology/Biology, Physical Anthropology, Psychiatry & Behavioral Science, Questioned Documents, and Toxicology.

Criminalistics

As we have seen throughout this text, the criminalist works primarily with physical evidence—analyzing, comparing, identifying, and interpreting items that may help solve a crime. The criminalist applies techniques from the physical and natural sciences to the examination of physical evidence. However, examining, testing, and interpreting results are only part of the responsibilities of the criminalist. He or she must also effectively communicate technical details and scientific findings to nonspecialist members of the law enforcement community.

The extent and depth of versatility expected of the forensic scientist are usually determined by the size of the crime laboratory's staff. Scientists in smaller laboratories are often expected to be generalists, performing a wide variety of tasks in order to fulfill the varied objectives of the laboratory. Their counterparts in larger facilities enjoy the luxury of working in specialized areas, relying on a teamwork approach to provide the spectrum of scientific skills needed for the comparison or identification of physical evidence. Currently there is a huge demand for forensic DNA analysts. Generally these positions require a graduate degree in biochemistry or forensic science.

In addition to his or her technical responsibilities, the newly trained criminalist must discover and master the role of the expert witness. A good courtroom demeanor and the ability to communicate thoughts and ideas in clear, concise terms are absolutely essential if the scientist's examination and conclusions are to be properly and effectively presented at a hearing or in court.

Education and Training The minimum educational requirement is a bachelor's degree in a science such as chemistry, biology, physics, or molecular biology. Coursework must include mathematics, chemistry, and/or biology. Many government criminalist positions have either local or national civil service educational and work experience requirements. Interested job applicants should inquire with appropriate civil service authorities to determine these requirements for a particular jurisdiction. The criminalist also participates in continuing education courses throughout his or her career to remain current with the ever-changing technology and procedures in the field. The American Board of Criminalistics (www.criminalistics.com/ABC) offers certification for trained criminalists who pass a rigorous examination.

Career Opportunities Criminalists work in a wide array of settings, including forensic laboratories in local, regional, and state police and sheriff's departments and district attorneys' offices. They may also serve federal agencies such as the U.S. military; Drug Enforcement Administration (DEA); Alcohol, Tobacco, Firearms and Explosives (ATF&E); Federal Bureau of Investigation (FBI); Department of Justice (DOJ); U.S. Postal Service (USPS); Secret Service (SS); Central Intelligence Agency (CIA); and U.S. Fish and Wildlife Services. Trained criminalists also may teach at community colleges and universities.

Forensic Engineering

Forensic engineers apply principles of engineering to resolve legal issues, primarily in civil, rather than criminal cases. However, a forensic engineer may also assist in criminal matters or cases involving violation of government regulations. These areas of activity cover investigations into structural failure; reconstruction of automobile accidents; exploring the causes of fires or explosions; and evaluation of construction, manufacturing, or maintenance procedures. The forensic engineer's work applies in personal-injury suits, construction claims, contract or warranty disputes, patent or copyright infringements, and criminal and regulatory matters. Certification in the forensic engineering sciences is available from the International Institute of Forensic Engineering Sciences. (www.iifes.org).

Education and Training The minimum educational requirement for a forensic engineer is a bachelor's degree in engineering or an allied science. However, an advanced degree is desirable, as is registration in a professional engineering society. Because of the wide range of engineering disciplines, a forensic engineer should have professional experience in the particular field(s) of engineering that are the subject of his or her investigation.

Career Opportunities Although some forensic engineers work for sizable corporations or government agencies, most are either self-employed or employed by small firms. Some forensic engineers hold a full-time job in another field (such as engineering consulting or teaching) and perform forensic services on a part-time or contract basis.

Forensic Odontology

As we saw in previous chapters, forensic odontology applies the principles of dental science to law. This includes such activities as identifying human remains through dental analysis as well as comparing bite marks, using both physical and biological dental evidence. Forensic odontologists frequently are called upon after catastrophic events involving large numbers of casualties for which identification from other physical remains is difficult or impossible. Another important area of forensic dentistry is bite mark analysis in cases of assault, rape, and/or homicide. Bite mark analysis may involve collecting saliva for DNA profiling and matching.

Education and Training The forensic odontologist must of course possess a Doctor of Dental Science (D.D.S.) degree, but this basic education by itself is not sufficient to function in this field. Courses in forensic science and medico-legal death investigation are strongly recommended. Additional courses and advanced training in approved forensic techniques and procedures are required to prepare a forensic odontologist to conduct proper crime-scene investigations. Several professional organizations, including the American Board of Forensic Odontology, the American Society of Forensic Odontology, the New York Society of Forensic Dentistry, and the New York County Dental Society, offer advanced training in this field. The American Board of Forensic Odontology (www.abfo.org) serves as a highly regarded credentialing body for forensic dentists.

Career Opportunities Most forensic odontologists are engaged in private dental practice. They typically have either formal appointments or consulting relationships with coroners, medical examiners' offices, state and local government agencies, and branches of the military. They also often offer private consultations for insurance companies and law firms. Qualified forensic odontologists frequently provide expert testimony in criminal and civil cases involving personal injuries, worker's compensation, malpractice suits, potential violations of the dentist–patient relationship, and identification of bite marks in criminal cases. Once a commitment is made to enter this field, the dental investigator needs to be current in the most accurate methods available, be aware of ethical values and conflicts, and possess the dedication to render assistance in a timely and professional manner.

Forensic Pathology

Forensic pathology is the application of the principles of pathology—and medicine in general—to the legal process. Forensic pathologists perform autopsies to determine the causes of an individual's death and the circumstances surrounding the death. Understanding the circumstances of a person's death allows the pathologist to determine whether the death was the result of natural causes, an accident, suicide, or homicide. Forensic pathologists also identify remains using medical information, dental records, and other peculiarities of an individual. Forensic pathologists help public health officials recognize and control epidemic diseases. Clinical forensic pathologists study patterns of injury in living people to help law investigations into crimes such as child and elder abuse. The principal professional organization for forensic pathologists is the National Association of Medical Examiners (www.thename.org).

Education and Training Forensic pathologists undergo the same training and education as any medical doctor: four years of college, followed by four years of medical school, then a residency in pathology. After college, medical school, internship, and residency, an additional one- or two-year fellowship in forensic pathology must be completed. This is then followed by certification in pathology or one of its subspecialties from the American Board of Pathology.

Career Opportunities Forensic pathologists are usually employed by city, county, or state medical examiners' offices and hospitals. Some federal government agencies, such as the Centers for Disease Control (CDC) and the Armed Forces Institute of Pathology (AFIP), also employ forensic pathologists.

Forensic Anthropology

Forensic anthropologists are trained in the study of human skeletal biology, and they typically use this training to identify deceased individuals when skeletal remains are the only useful evidence. They also determine whether recovered bones are human or nonhuman and determine sex based on skeletal structure. Forensic pathologists may estimate the cause and time of death when remains are unsuitable for examination by a pathologist.

Education and Training   Forensic anthropologists usually earn a Ph.D. in anthropology with an emphasis on human osteology (the study of bones) and anatomy. Practical experience in forensic anthropology typically is required before a court accepts an individual as an expert witness in the field. The American Board of Forensic Anthropology (ABFA) (www.csuchico.edu/anth/ABFA/) provides professional certification for experts in the field of forensic anthropology. To earn certification, an individual must submit case reports for review that demonstrate practical experience in the field. The applicant must also pass both a written and a practical examination.

Career Opportunities   Most forensic anthropologists work out of laboratories at major research institutions or universities. In addition, various state and local medical examiner offices use forensic anthropologists as medical investigators or administrators. The federal government employs forensic anthropologists at the U.S. Army Central Identification Laboratory and the Armed Forces Institute of Pathology. State and federal law enforcement agencies also hire physical anthropologists to act as special agents and laboratory personnel. The largest group of forensic anthropologists works for the military in the U.S. Army's Central Identification Laboratory in Hawaii (www.jpac.pacom.mil/CIL/CIL_Home.htm). A major professional organization in this field is the American Association of Physical Anthropologists (www.physanth.org).

Forensic Psychology and Psychiatry

The forensic psychologist or psychiatrist deals with issues of human behavior and mental illness as they relate to matters of civil and criminal law. This involves such activities as determining an individual's competence to stand trial, testify, or waive legal representation, and determining whether mental illness mitigates a suspect's responsibility for his or her actions. For example, the forensic psychiatrist often gives an opinion about whether a defendant might be innocent by reason of mental illness or defect. Other areas in which such expertise is applied includes cases of involuntary psychiatric hospitalization, a patient's right to refuse treatment, and competency to participate in do-not-resuscitate decisions. Forensic psychology includes psychological evaluation and expert testimony regarding such criminal forensic issues as trial competency and forensic behavioral analysis.

Education and Training   Forensic psychiatrists are medical doctors who complete a course of study similar to that of forensic pathologists. This includes four years of college followed by medical school and residency training in psychiatry. Some forensic psychiatrists take an additional year or two of post-residency training in psychiatry and the law, and many continue independent study and on-the-job training after completing their formal education. The American Board of Psychiatry and Neurology offers certification in forensic psychiatry for those who pass special examinations. Forensic psychologists usually obtain a Ph.D. degree and are licensed by a state board, and may be board certified by the American Board of Professional Psychology (www.abpp.org).

Career Opportunities   As with other professionals in the psychiatric profession, forensic psychiatrists and forensic psychologists may be employed in private practice, by hospitals, or by city, county, state, or federal government agencies. They often work in a prison or state hospital setting. The major professional organization for forensic psychiatrists is the American Academy of Psychiatry and the Law (www.aapl.org).

Document Examiners

As we saw in Chapter 16, the document examiner analyzes questioned documents and related material, such as ink, paper, toner from a copier or fax, and computer printers. Detecting forged documents and counterfeit currency is a large part of the document examiner's work.

Education and Training   Document examiners should possess at least a bachelor's degree, preferably in a scientific field. Several colleges and universities offer questioned-document or related courses as part of criminal justice, forensic science, or criminalistics degree programs, although no document examination degree programs currently exist. In addition to a college education, the prospective document examiner must complete an apprenticeship program lasting approximately two years under the direct supervision of a full member or fellow of the questioned-documents section of the AAFS, a member of the American Society of Questioned Document Examiners, or a diplomate of the American Board of Forensic Document Examiners (www.asqde.org/abfde.htm).

Career Opportunities   Forensic document examiners are often consultants working in private practice, but many large police organizations, as well as most state and federal law enforcement agencies, also employ forensic document experts.

Forensic Toxicology

Forensic toxicology deals with the effects of drugs and chemicals on the human body and the application of that knowledge to questions of law. Forensic toxicologists perform a wide range of activities, including determining whether an individual has consumed illegal drugs and identifying the substances involved. Forensic toxicologists are often called upon to determine whether an individual was driving under the influence of alcohol or drugs. They may be involved in postmortem toxicology, which involves determining the contribution drugs or chemicals make to the circumstances of a death. The forensic toxicologist investigates cases as varied as animal poisoning, the use of drugs in sexual assault, and drug use and doping in human and animal sports. Currently, many forensic toxicologists are employed by private laboratories engaged in conducting workplace drug testing and forensic urine testing on employees of organizations and industries associated with the public's safety or engaged in performing hazardous work.

Education and Training   Training for a career in forensic toxicology requires a bachelor's degree in a physical science, ideally including a solid background in chemistry and coursework in pharmacology. Several colleges and universities offer graduate coursework in forensic toxicology at the master's or Ph.D. level. Membership in the forensic toxicology section of AAFS requires at least one year of additional experience and further requirements of scholarly work or advanced study. The American Board of Forensic Toxicology and the Forensic Toxicologist Certification Board offer professional certification to scientists with work experience in forensic toxicology. A major forensic toxicology organization is the Society of Forensic Toxicologists (www.soft-tox.org).

Career Opportunities   Many forensic toxicologists work in police laboratories, medical examiners' offices, and workplace drug-testing laboratories. Other career opportunities for forensic toxicologists exist in hospitals, universities, corporations, and agencies that monitor drug use in sports.

College Courses in Forensic Science

Degree Programs in Forensic Science

It is something of an irony that, although most of the careers discussed previously require at least a bachelor's degree, few colleges and universities in the United States offer undergraduate or graduate degrees in forensic science. As of early 2006, there were only eleven programs in forensic science accredited by the Forensic Science Education Programs Accreditation Commission (FEPAC). Institutions offering FEPAC accredited undergraduate and graduate programs include the following:

Arcadia University, Glenside, Pa.: Accreditation for the Master of Science Degree in Forensic Science.

Cedar Crest College, Allentown, Pa.: Accreditation for the Bachelor of Science Degree in Chemistry, Biochemistry, Biology, and Genetic Engineering with a concentration in Forensic Science.

Eastern Kentucky University, Richmond, Ky.: Accreditation for the Bachelor of Science Degree Program in Forensic Science.

Florida International University, Miami, Fla.: Accreditation for both the Certificate Programs in conjunction with the Bachelor of Science Degree in a natural science such as chemistry or biology and the Master of Science in Forensic Science.

Marshall University, Huntington, W.V.: Accreditation for the Master of Science Degree in Forensic Science.

Metropolitan State College of Denver, Denver, Colo.: Accreditation for the Bachelor of Science Degree Program in Chemistry with a concentration in Criminalistics.

Michigan State University, East Lansing, Mich.: Accreditation for the Master of Science Degree Program (biology and chemistry tracks).

Ohio University, Athens, Ohio: Accreditation for the Bachelor of Science in Forensic Chemistry Program.

Virginia Commonwealth University, Richmond, Va.: Accreditation for the Master of Science in Forensic Science Program.

West Chester University, West Chester, Pa.: Accreditation for the Bachelor of Science Degree in Forensic and Toxicological Chemistry.

West Virginia University, Morgantown, W.V.: Accreditation for the Bachelor of Science–Forensic and Investigative Science Program.

This is not to suggest, however, that course and degree programs in forensic sciences are not available at other colleges and universities. In fact, more than a hundred schools offer associate's, bachelor's, and master's degrees in some area of forensic science, and others provide seminars and courses in forensic specialties such as DNA typing and profiling. Although most of these programs have not been accredited by the FEPAC, most working forensic scientists obtained their education and degrees from non-FEPAC-accredited schools. A complete list of undergraduate and graduate programs in forensic science in the United States and abroad can be found at the AAFS Web site, www.aafs.org.

A small number of schools have initiated programs and courses in computer forensics. Interested students should search out schools on the AAFS Web site for these programs.

Required College Courses

Certain natural science courses are required for any student in forensic science. Unlike other criminal justice professionals, a forensic scientist requires a foundation in chemistry, biology, physics, and mathematics. The minimum general core requirements recommended for undergraduate forensic science programs include the following:

- General chemistry I and II and lab for science majors (eight credit hours).
- Organic chemistry I and II and lab (eight credit hours).
- Biology I and II for science majors (four to eight credit hours). (Classes with laboratory components are preferable, if available.)
- Physics I and II for science majors and lab (eight credit hours).
- Calculus (three credit hours).
- Statistics for science majors (three credit hours).

An undergraduate degree in forensic science is expected to be an interdisciplinary degree that includes substantial laboratory work and an emphasis on advanced coursework in chemistry or biology. Students can use these additional courses to begin to specialize along a forensic science discipline track, such as forensic biology or forensic chemistry. Specialized science courses may be selected from any of the following:

- Biochemistry
- Molecular biology
- Genetics
- Population genetics
- Inorganic chemistry
- Analytical/quantitative chemistry
- Physical chemistry
- Instrumental analysis
- Cell biology
- Pharmacology
- Calculus II
- Microbiology

As you can see, the path to becoming a forensic scientist is neither brief nor easy. It begins with rigorous college coursework, typically followed by additional training and certification in the specific area of forensic science one chooses to pursue. It involves lifelong learning and the dedication to seek out the newest and best methods to gather, analyze, and interpret data needed to solve all types of crimes.

Despite these hurdles, forensic science is a fascinating profession that challenges one's scientific knowledge, powers of observation, critical-thinking skills, deductive and inductive reasoning, and ability to think creatively and imagine various possible scenarios when presented with facts and physical evidence. Hopefully, this text will provide both a spark of interest and the basic information that will spur you to take the first steps toward pursuing a career in this challenging and ever-evolving field.

FORENSIC CASES

The "Bobby Joe" Long Serial Murder Case
A Study in Cooperation

Capt. Gary Terry
Hillsborough County Sheriff's Office, Tampa, Florida

SA Michael P. Malone, M. S.
Hairs and Fiber Unit, Laboratory Division, Federal Bureau of Investigation, Washington, DC

On May 13, 1984, the Hillsborough County Sheriff's Office (HCSO) responded to the scene of a homicide in southern Hillsborough County, where the body of a nude female had been discovered. This was the beginning of an intensive, 8-month investigation into the abduction, rape, and murder of at least 10 women in 3 jurisdictions in the Tampa Bay area. This investigation would ultimately involve personnel from the HCSO, the Federal Bureau of Investigation (FBI), the Tampa Police Department (TPD), the Pasco County Sheriff's Office (PCSO), and the Florida Department of Law Enforcement (FDLE).

Never before had the HCSO been involved in a serial murder case of this magnitude. During one period of time in the 8 months, the killer was averaging a murder every other week. This series of grisly killings would eventually end due to the efforts of the homicide detectives who pored over each crime scene striving to find any and all physical evidence, the expertise and skill of the examiners in the FBI Laboratory who analyzed this evidence, the close cooperation and continuous exchange of information between the law enforcement agencies involved, and the fact that the killer released one of his victims alive, yielding physical evidence that would ultimately tie all of the cases together.

The first body, nude and bound, of a young Asian female was discovered by young boys late in the afternoon, in a remote area of southern Hillsborough County. This victim was identified as Lana Long, a 20-year-old Laotian female. She was employed as an exotic dancer at a lounge located on Nebraska Avenue in the city of Tampa. She normally worked the evening shift and was known to use alcohol and drugs. Long was last seen in the apartment complex where she lived. This was in an area near the University of South Florida, where many of the residents were transient. She had been missing for approximately 3 days.

Long had been dead for approximately 48 to 72 hours. She was lying face down with her hands tied behind her back with rope and fabric. A rope was also observed around her neck which had a "leash-like" extension approximately 14 inches in length. It was noted that the ropes around the wrists and neck were different in nature.[1] Under the victim's face was a piece of fabric which may have been used as a gag. The victim's feet were spread apart to a distance of over 5 feet, and it appeared as if the body had been deliberately "displayed" in this manner. The victim's clothing and personal belongings were never found. During the autopsy a large open wound was discovered on the victim's face. Decomposition was extensive in this area, but the cause of death was determined to be strangulation. Tire impressions were found on the roadway leading to the body. It appeared that three of the tires were of different brands and all were worn.

Reprinted in part from FBI Law Enforcement Bulletin, November/December, 1987.

[1] Ropes and cordages were found in 7 of the 10 homicide cases. All of these were compared with one another. Even though cordages found in one case were sometimes found to be of the same type, there were no instances in which cordages from two or more different cases were found to be similar. However, these cordages and knots did provide a "link" in the patterns which would associate these cases together.

Hillsborough County had been averaging about 30 to 35 homicides per year, and while some prior victims had been bound, none had been bound in this manner. Prior to the death of Long, the HCSO had completed a difficult homicide investigation in which the forensic work had been done by the FBI Laboratory. The close cooperation between the HCSO and the FBI Laboratory resulted in the successful conclusion of the case and the conviction of the individual who had committed the murder. Thus, the decision was made to fly the evidence in the Long murder to the FBI Laboratory in Washington, D.C., accompanied by an HCSO homicide detective.

The hairs that were removed from the evidence were examined and found to be either the victim's hairs or unsuitable for comparison. The serology examinations were also negative due to the decomposition of the body. The knots in the ropes were examined and were identified; however, these knots were extremely common and not unique to any particular profession or occupation. The tire casts of the tire tread impressions were examined and photographs of these impressions were kept for future reference.

The fibers which were removed from the items in this case were also examined, and this evidence would provide the first important lead in the case. Eventually, it would prove to be the most critical evidence of the entire case. The equipment used for the fiber examinations consisted of a stereoscopic microscope, a comparison microscope, a polarized light microscope, a microspectrophotometer, a melting point apparatus, and eventually, an infrared spectrophotometer. A single lustrous red trilobal nylon fiber was found on a piece of fabric found near the victim. Because of the size, type, and cross-sectional shape of this fiber, it was determined that this fiber was probably a carpet fiber. Because the body had been exposed to the elements for a substantial period of time, and fibers which have been transferred are very transient in nature,[2] it was surmised that most of the carpet fibers which had originally been transferred to the victim's body had been lost. Since the victim's body was found in a remote area, she had probably been transported in a vehicle, and the carpeting of this vehicle was probably the last item she had been in contact with. Furthermore, since there is normally a transference of trace materials (i.e., fibers) when two objects come into close contact, it was also surmised that the killer was probably driving a vehicle with a red carpet. Vehicular carpets readily shed their fibers, and these types of fibers are commonly found on the bodies of victims at crime scenes. These fibers could then provide a critical "link" in determining whether a serial murderer was operating in the Tampa Bay area.

The above information was provided to the HCSO, with the caution that the fiber information should be kept confidential. Experience has shown that if the existence of fiber evidence is publicized, serial killers might change their pattern and start disposing of the bodies in such a manner that this fiber evidence is either lost or destroyed. The most famous example of this is the Wayne Williams case. [See pp. 87–97.] The possibility also existed that if the killer knew of the existence of the red carpet fibers, he would probably get rid of the vehicle that was the source of this evidence.

Two weeks later, on May 27, 1984, at approximately 11:30 A.M., the body of a young white female was discovered in an isolated area of eastern Hillsborough County. The victim was found nude, with

---

[2] C. A. Pounds and K. W. Smalldon, "The Transfer of Fibers between Clothing Materials during Simulated Contacts and Their Persistence during Wear," *Journal of the Forensic Science Society, 15* (1975), 29.

clothing near the body. The victim was on her back, with her hands bound at the waist and a ligature around the neck. Her throat had been cut, and she had sustained multiple blunt trauma injuries to the head. The victim had been at the scene for approximately 8 to 10 hours. The victim's hands were bound to her sides with a clothesline type of rope. The ligature at the neck was made of the same type of rope and was tied in a type of hangman's noose. There was a 3- to 4-foot length of rope extending from the noose. The victim also had what appeared to be a man's green T-shirt binding her upper arms. Hair and fiber evidence were collected from the victim's body.

Several tire tread impressions were located in a dirt roadway that passed approximately 8 feet from the victim's body. These impressions appeared to have been caused by a vehicle turning around in the area next to the victim's location.

The responding homicide detectives believed this homicide was related to the Long case. Since the victim was unidentified, a composite drawing of the victim was made and released to the media. It was through this effort that the victim was identified as Michelle Denise Simms, 22 years old and a native of California. She was last seen the previous night talking with two white males near Kennedy Boulevard in an area that is popular for working prostitutes. Simms had previously worked as a prostitute.

The evidence collected from where Simms was found was immediately flown to the FBI Laboratory. Since this had been a "fresh" site, the chances of recovering significant evidence would be tremendously improved. The tire casts were examined and one of the impressions from the right rear area was identified as being from a Goodyear Viva tire, with the white wall facing inward. The tire impression from the left rear area could not be immediately identified, as it was not in the FBI Laboratory reference files.

However, the HCSO was provided with the name of an individual in Akron, Ohio, who was a tire expert, and the tire casts were flown to Akron, where the tire impression was identified as being made by a Vogue tire, an expensive tire that comes only on Cadillacs. A Vogue tire was obtained and photographed in detail.

The fibers removed from the evidence revealed red lustrous trilobal nylon fibers, which matched the Long fiber. In addition, a second type of fiber, a red trilobal delustered fiber, was found, indicating that the killer was driving a vehicle containing two different types of carpet fibers.

Grouping tests conducted on semen stains identified on the clothing of Michelle Simms disclosed the presence of the "B" and "H" blood group substances.

The hairs from the body and clothing of Michelle Simms were examined. Brown, medium-length Caucasian head hairs were found that could have originated from the killer. Human hair is valuable evidence, and in addition to providing information on race, body area, artificial treatment, or other unusual characteristics, it can be strongly associated with a particular individual when matched with a known hair sample from the individual. With this information, the HCSO was able to build a "physical evidence" profile of the killer, which was distributed to other law enforcement agencies; however, the information on the carpet fibers and cordage was kept confidential.

On June 24, 1984, the body of another young white female was found, the third victim in this series of homicides, although this would not be known for a few months. The victim was found in an orange grove in southeastern Hillsborough County. The victim was found fully clothed, and the body was in an advanced stage of decomposition. The total body weight of the victim, including her clothes, was only 25 pounds. There were no ligatures present, and the victim was not found near an interstate as the first two victims had been. During the initial stages of the investigation, the victim's boyfriend failed a polygraph examination and appeared to be an excellent suspect. Evidence from the case was sent to the FBI Laboratory; however, no request was made for this evidence to be compared to the evidence from the previous two homicides until much later.

The victim was identified as Elizabeth B. Loudenback, 22, of Tampa. Loudenback was employed as an assembly line worker and was last seen at approximately 7:00 P.M. on June 8, 1984. She was known to frequent the area of Nebraska Avenue and Skipper Road in northern Hillsborough County, but had no criminal history.

The hairs from the Loudenback case were examined with negative results. Serology examinations were also negative due to the extensive decomposition of the body. The fibers, examined later, were determined to be both types of the red carpet fibers evidenced in the two previous cases. If this examination had been done initially, it would have been immediately known that Loudenback was, in fact, the third victim. When the evidence arrived at the FBI Laboratory, it was not assigned to the examiner who had worked the first two homicides. One of the most important aspects of handling a serial murder investigation is to have the same crime scene technician at all crime scenes and the same forensic examiners at the laboratory, so that one individual can become totally familiar with the forensic portion of the investigation, in order to recognize patterns and associations which might be present.

On October 7, 1984, the nude body of a young black female was discovered near the Pasco/Hillsborough County line, lying next to the dirt entrance road of a cattle ranch. The victim's clothing, except for her bra, was found next to the body. The bra had been tied in a knot and was found hanging from the entrance gate. The head area was in an advanced state of decomposition, much more so than the remainder of the body. The autopsy revealed a puncture wound to the back of the neck, but a gunshot wound to the neck was the cause of death.

The victim was identified as Chanel Devon Williams, an 18-year-old black female. The victim had been previously arrested for prostitution. She was known to frequent a gay bar on Kennedy Boulevard in Tampa. She had been last seen on the night of September 30, 1984, by another prostitute with whom she had been working. The pair were working the area of Nebraska Avenue when Williams' companion was solicited by a "john." They were approximately two-tenths of a mile from the motel where they were conducting their "business." Williams' companion rode back to the motel in the "john's" car, and Williams was instructed to slowly walk back to the motel in order to check on her companion. Williams never made it back to the motel.

The homicide detectives who responded to the place Williams was found began looking for similarities to the previous homicides. Other than the fact that the victim was found nude in a rural area and that Williams was a prostitute, there were no other apparent similarities.

At this point in the investigation, the HCSO requested a criminal personality profile be done by the FBI on the Long, Simms, and Williams cases, and one other homicide in which another female had been shot. A profile was returned (see Figure R1–1) indicating strong similarities between the Long case and the Simms case. However, due to various differences (race, lack of ligatures, and cause of death), it was believed that the Williams case and the other above-mentioned cases were not related.

The evidence from the Williams case was sent to the FBI Laboratory a second time, and both types of the red nylon carpet fibers were found on various articles of her clothing. A brown Caucasian pubic hair,

FIGURE R1–1 FBI criminal personality profile.

Race	Caucasian
Age	Mid 20s
Personality	"Macho" Image Assaultive
Employment	Difficulty in Holding Job
Marriage	Probably Divorced
Vehicle	"Flashy Car"
Weapons	Likely to Carry Weapons
Personality	Inclined to Mentally and Physically Taunt and Torture
Victims	Randomly Selected Susceptible to Approach
Geographics	Confine Activity to Given Geographic Region

which would ultimately be associated with Robert Long, was also discovered on the victim's sweater. Grouping tests conducted on semen stains identified on Williams' clothing disclosed the presence of the "A" and "H" blood group substances. This was inconsistent with the grouping results found in the Simms case; however, this could be due to their working as prostitutes.

On the morning of October 14, 1984, the body of a white female, nude from the waist down, was discovered in an unpopulated area of northeastern Hillsborough County. The body was found in an orange grove approximately 30 feet from a dirt road, apparently dragged from the roadway. The body had been placed on a gold-colored bedspread, and a blue jogging suit was tied outside the blanket. The bedspread had been tied at both ends with common white string. The victim's hands were bound in front with a red and white handkerchief. Her right wrist and legs were bound with another white string. The victim's feet were bound with a drawstring, and there were ligature marks on the victim's throat. She had been struck on the forehead and strangled.

The victim was identified as Karen Beth Dinsfriend, a 28-year-old cocaine user and prostitute. Dinsfriend had been working the area of Nebraska and Hillsborough Avenues and was last seen during the early morning hours of October 14, 1984.

Upon arriving at the scene, the detectives strongly suspected that Dinsfriend's death was related to the previous homicides. The ligatures were almost a "signature" of the offender. Red fibers were found when the body was examined at the medical examiner's office.

By this time, all homicide detectives of the HCSO were assigned to the case. Other assaults, suicides, and unrelated homicides were assigned to property detectives. Six tactical deputies were assigned to do night surveillance in the suspect's "hunting grounds," the area of Nebraska Avenue and West Kennedy Boulevard in North Tampa. The patrol divisions were again given alerts and were continually sending in field interrogation reports (FIR), which were checked. A personal computer was purchased specifically for this investigation and was used to record information on vehicles, vehicular tags, information gathered from talking to prostitutes, and information derived from the FIRs. At this point, the HCSO again went "public" to warn the community about these related homicides. However, the fiber information was kept confidential.

The evidence from the Dinsfriend disposal site was sent directly to the FBI Laboratory, and it yielded valuable evidence. The knots in the ligatures were similar to the knots from the previous cases; a brown Caucasian pubic hair, eventually associated with Robert Long, was found on the bedspread; and semen was found on the bedspread and sweatshirt and tests again disclosed the "A" and "H" blood group substances. The bedspread was tested and found to be composed of gold delustered acrylic fibers. These fibers would also provide a link to Long's vehicle.

Both types of red nylon carpet fibers were again found on most of the items and were microscopically compared to the previous carpet fibers. The color produced by the dyes from the red carpet fibers was also compared using the microspectrophotometer. The microspectrophotometer is one of the most discriminating techniques which can be used in the comparison of fibers. Since these carpet fibers both microscopically and optically matched the red carpet fibers from the previous five cases, it was strongly believed that all of these fibers were consistent with having originated from the same source, and therefore, all of the cases were related.

On October 30, 1984, the nude mummified remains of a white female were discovered near Highway 301 in northern Hillsborough County just south of the Pasco County line. No clothing, ligatures, or any other type of physical evidence were found at the scene. Due to the amount of time the body was exposed to the elements and the fact that the victim was nude, no foreign hairs, fibers, semen, or any other type of evidence were

discovered. This victim would not be identified until after the arrest of the suspect, Robert Long, who referred to the victim by her street name, "Sugar." Using this information, the HCSO was able to identify the victim as Kimberly Kyle Hopps, a 22-year-old white female, last seen by her boyfriend getting into a 1977–78 maroon Chrysler Cordoba. Hopps would eventually be associated with Long's vehicle through a comparison of her head hairs with hairs found in his vehicle.

On November 6, 1984, the remains of a female were discovered near Morris Bridge Road in Pasco County just north of the Hillsborough County line. The bones of the victim were scattered about a large area; however, a ligature was found. Another ligature was discovered on an arm bone. A shirt, a pair of panties, and some jewelry were also found. Human head hairs, presumed to be from the victim, were also recovered.

On learning of the discovery of this body, the Hillsborough homicide detectives met with the Pasco County detectives, and because of the ligatures, believed that this case was related to their homicides. The two agencies worked together to identify the victim, Virginia Lee Johnson, an 18-year-old white female originally from Connecticut. It was learned that she split her time between Connecticut and the North Tampa area, working as a prostitute in the North Nebraska Avenue area in Hillsborough County.

The evidence from the Johnson site was sent by the PCSO to the FBI Laboratory. Again, due to the extensive decomposition, the body yielded very little physical evidence; however, in the victim's head hair from the crime scene a single red lustrous carpet fiber was found, relating this case to the others. Eventually, Virginia Johnson would also be associated with Robert Long's vehicle through a transfer of her head hairs.

On November 24, 1984, the nude body of a young white female was found on an incline off of North Orient Road in the City of Tampa, involving yet a third jurisdiction in the homicides. The victim had been at the scene less than 24 hours. A wadded pair of blue jeans and a blue flowered top were near the body. The victim was wearing knee high nylons; the body was face down with the head at the lower portion of the incline. Faint tire impressions were observed in the grass next to the roadway, and a piece of wood with possible tire impressions was found. It appeared that the killer had pulled off the road and had thrown the body over the edge and onto the incline. Examination of the body revealed that fecal matter was present on the inside of the victim's legs and on the exterior of the clothing. The body had a pronounced ligature mark on the front portion of the neck. There were also ligature marks on both wrists and on both arms; however, no ligatures were found.

This victim was identified as Kim Marie Swann, a 21-year-old female narcotics user, who worked as a nude dancer. She was last seen walking out of a convenience store near her parents' home at approximately 3:00 P.M. on November 11, 1984.

When the Tampa Police Department responded and noted the ligature marks on the victim, they immediately called the HCSO and requested that they also respond. This homicide was also believed to be related to the previous seven homicides.

The evidence from the Swann disposal site was sent to the FBI Laboratory. The tire tread impressions on the board bore limited design similarities to the tire impressions from the Lana Long and Michelle Simms homicides. Again, red nylon carpet fibers were found on the victim's clothing. The head hair of the victim was examined and would eventually be associated with the suspect's vehicle.

Even though the three jurisdictions now directly involved in the eight homicides

continued to work separately on their own cases, there was continual exchange of information among these agencies, which enabled the HCSO to learn that the Tampa Police Department sex crimes detectives were working on an abduction and rape of a 17-year-old white female. This exchange of information would ultimately lead to the big "break" in the case, a case which had completely captivated the attention of the Tampa Bay area and one which was beginning to attract national attention as well.

On November 3, 1984, a young girl, Lisa McVey, was leaving a doughnut shop in northern Tampa when she was abducted. The offender took her to an unknown apartment and sexually assaulted her for 26 hours before releasing her. The HCSO urged the Tampa Police Department to send their rape evidence to the FBI Laboratory, and on November 13, 1984, the FBI Laboratory called with the biggest break yet in the serial murder case; they found the same red fibers on McVey's clothes as had been found on the homicide victims.

After the rape case had been linked to the murders, a task force was formed the next day, consisting of the Hillsborough County Sheriff's Office, the Tampa Police Department, the Florida Department of Law Enforcement, the Pasco County Sheriff's Office, and the Federal Bureau of Investigation. The rape victim, McVey, was extensively interviewed and recalled that after leaving the apartment where she was held, the suspect stopped at a "24-hour teller machine" to withdraw some money at approximately 3:00 A.M. She described the suspect's vehicle as being red with a red interior and red carpet, with the word "Magnum" on the dash. En route to the release site, the victim recalled peeking out from under the blindfold and seeing a Howard Johnson's motel as they drove up on the interstate.

At this time, there were approximately 30 officers assigned to the task force.

They immediately flooded the North Tampa area searching for the apartment and vehicle (only a 1978 Dodge Magnum has the word "Magnum" on the dash). A task force member was flown to the State capital and returned with a list of every Dodge Magnum registered in Hillsborough County. An examination of the computer printout of these registrations revealed Robert Joe Long's name as a listed owner of a Dodge Magnum.

Each team of detectives was assigned certain areas to search, and as one team drove to their area, they noticed a red Dodge Magnum driving down Nebraska Avenue in North Tampa. The vehicle was stopped, and the driver was told that they were looking for a robbery suspect. The driver, identified as Robert Joe Long, was photographed and a field interrogation report was written.

During the same time period, bank records for all bank machines in North Tampa were being subpoenaed. These bank records revealed that Robert Long had used the 24-hour teller machine close to his apartment at approximately 3:00 A.M. on the morning the rape victim was released. The rape victim identified Long as her assailant from a photo selection. Based on McVey's statements, both an arrest warrant and a search warrant were drawn up and approved by a circuit court judge.

Robert Long was located at his apartment approximately 2 hours after being stopped by the task force members. They began a 24-hour surveillance of Long, also using aircraft to minimize the chances that Long would spot the surveillance teams.

The task force then consulted the Behavioral Science Unit at the FBI Academy for guidelines to use when interviewing the suspect. A Special Agent from the FBI Laboratory in Washington was flown to Tampa for an immediate comparison of fibers from the suspect's apartment and vehicle and to assist in the crime scene searches. An aircraft was standing by so that after the arrest this

Agent could be flown immediately to the closest FDLE laboratory which had the special microscope required for comparison of the fiber samples.

The following teams were organized from the task force:

1. Arrest team selected to physically arrest Long. Two of these officers were selected to interview Long at the office after the arrest.

2. Search and seizure team for the vehicle.

3. Search team for the residence.

4. Neighborhood survey team to interview Long's neighbors in his apartment complex after the arrest and before any information was released to the media.

After all task force teams were at their assigned locations, the signal to effect the arrest was given. By this time, Long was in a movie theater; as Long walked out of the theater, he was arrested. This arrest occurred only 36 hours after the task force was formed.

Long was returned to his apartment where approximately 10 to 15 detectives were waiting. In this jurisdiction (Hillsborough County), it is preferred to serve a search warrant while the owner of the property is there to witness the search. In this case, an embarrassed Long refused to exit the police vehicle and witness the search. Long was then taken to the HCSO operations center for interrogation. The interview was begun after the interviewing officers had consulted with the FBI Agent present who had prepared the criminal personality profile. The Agent advised that this suspect would most likely cooperate if the officers displayed both their authority and a thorough knowledge of the case.

The officers opened the interview by carefully talking only about the McVey rape and abduction until the suspect confessed to the McVey case. Then, the detectives began going into the other homicide cases. Long denied any involvement in the homicides initially.

Meanwhile, the suspect's vehicle had been brought to the Sheriff's office where it was being searched. The vehicle was found to have the Vogue tire and the Goodyear Viva tire, all with the white wall inverted and in the exact location on the vehicle as had been suspected. A sample of the carpet was removed from the vehicle, and the FBI fiber expert was immediately flown with this sample and previous fiber samples to the FDLE lab in Sanford, Florida, which had a comparison microscope. A short time later, the Agent telephoned the HCSO confirming that the fibers from Long's vehicle matched the red carpet fibers found previously on the victims. Long continued to deny committing the murders until the fibers were matched. The interviewing detectives then explained the physical evidence to the suspect. They also explained the significance of the matched fibers and what other comparisons would be done, i.e., hair, blood, etc. At this time, the suspect confessed.

The suspect gave a brief description of each homicide. He admitted killing Loudenback (victim #3) and using her money card. In each case, Long had talked the victims into his vehicle, immediately gaining control of them with a knife and gun. He then bound them and took them to various areas where he sexually assaulted and then murdered them. The suspect also drew a map showing where he had placed victim number nine. This victim had been abducted from the City of Tampa during an earlier part of the investigation, and the Tampa Police Department had informed the HCSO of this fact. They believed she fit the "victim profile" but she remained missing until Long told them where to find the body.

Eventually, a total of 10 homicides which had occurred in and around the Tampa Bay area over a period of approximately 8 months were attributed to Long (see Table R1–1). The victims ranged from 18 to 28 years in age, and the majority of the victims were prostitutes. Most victims were strangled and/or asphyxiated; however, one was shot and one died of a cut throat. . . .

As a result of laboratory examinations, numerous associations were made between the various crime scenes, the suspect, the victims, and the suspect's vehicle. (See Table R1–2.) The probative value of these associations was explained to the prosecutors from the Hillsborough County State Attorney's Office and the Pasco County State Attorney's Office. The importance of the fiber evidence was apparent from the beginning, as 8 of the 10 victims were associated with Long's vehicle through fiber comparisons. The importance of the hair evidence also began to emerge as all of the forensic examinations were completed. Six of the victims were associated to Long's vehicle through hair transfers, even though Long had thoroughly vacuumed his Dodge Magnum the day before he was arrested. Two of the 10 victims were associated directly to Long by transfer of his hairs to these victims. The significance of the ligatures and knots should not be overlooked as these provided a valuable link between cases. The tire tread evidence provided many leads and would associate Long's vehicle directly to the crime scene in two of the cases. The importance of the criminal personality profile should also be noted (see Figure R1–2). In addition to providing valuable leads, it can also "guide" a case. It cannot, however, take the place of a thorough and competent investigation.

The first trial of Robert Long was held in Dade City, Florida (Pasco County), on April 22, 1985. This was the trial for the murder of Virginia Johnson. The strongest evidence presented at this trial was the hair and fiber associations, as well as the confession of Long. The trial lasted a week and received a great deal of media coverage. Long was found guilty of the murder of Virginia Johnson and was sentenced to die in the electric chair.

Table R1–1

Victim's Name	Date Victim Found	Date Victim Missing	Body Recovery Area	Cause of Death	Age	Occupation
Lana Long	5/13/84	5/10/84	Isolated Area Southern Hillsborough Co.	Asphyxiation	20	Exotic Dancer
Michelle Simms	5/27/84	5/25/84	Isolated Area Eastern Hillsborough Co.	Blunt Force, Cut Throat	22	Prostitute
Elizabeth Loudenback	6/24/84	6/8/84	Orange Grove Southeast Hillsborough Co.	Unknown	22	Factory Worker
Chanel Williams	10/7/84	10/1/84	Isolated Area Northern Hillsborough Co.	Gunshot Wound to Head	18	Prostitute
Karen Dinsfriend	10/14/84	10/13/84	Isolated Area Northeast Hillsborough Co.	Asphyxiation	28	Prostitute
Kimberly Hopps	10/30/84	9/31/84	Isolated Area Northern Hillsborough Co.	Unknown	20s	Prostitute
Juvenile Female	11/4/84	11/3/84	—	—	17	Doughnut Shop Worker
Virginia Johnson	11/6/84	10/15/84	Isolated Area Pasco Co. near County Line	Strangulation	18	Waitress (Prostitute)
Kim Swann	11/24/84	11/11/84	Tampa Near Rt. 60	Strangulation	21	Student (Part-Time Exotic Dancer)
Vicky Elliot	11/16/84	9/7/84	Isolated Area Northern Hillsborough Co.	Strangulation	21	Waitress
Artis Wick	11/22/84	3/28/84	Isolated Area Southern Hillsborough Co.	Unknown	18	

It was decided that the first case that would be tried in Hillsborough County would be the Michelle Simms case. This case was picked due to the brutal nature in which she had been killed and the fact that it contained the strongest forensic evidence. The second case to be tried would be the Karen Dinsfriend case. As a result of discussions between the Hillsborough County State Attorney's Office and the Public Defender's Office of Hillsborough County, a plea bargain was agreed upon for 8 of the homicides and the abduction and rape of Lisa McVey.

Long pled guilty on September 24, 1985, to all of these crimes, receiving 26 life sentences (24 concurrent and 2 to run consecutively to the first 24) and 7 life sentences (no parole for 25 years). In addition, the State retained the option to seek the death penalty for the murder of Michelle Simms. In July of 1986, the penalty phase of the Michelle Simms trial was held in Tampa. It lasted 1 week and again received great media attention. Long was found guilty and was again sentenced to die in Florida's electric chair.

Table R1–2

Name of Victim	Red Delustered Trilobal Nylon Fibers	Red Lustrous Trilobal Nylon Fibers	Yellow Delustered Acrylic Fibers	Hair Transfer Long's → Victim	Hair Transfer Victim → Long's Car	Semen	Tire Tread	Cordage/Knots	Misc.
Lana Long	Neg.	Yes	—	Neg.	Head Hair	Neg.	Similar Design and Size	Yes	Partially Decomposed—3 Days
Michelle Simms	Yes	Yes	—	Neg.	Head Hair	"B" & "H"	Similar Design and Size	Yes	Intact Body—2 Days
Elizabeth Loudenback	Yes	Yes	—	Neg.	Neg.	—	—	No	Badly Decomposed—16 Days
Chanel Williams	Yes	Yes	—	Pubic Hair—Sweater	Neg.	"A" & "H"	—	Yes	Badly Decomposed—6 Days
Karen Dinsfriend	Yes	Yes	Blanket to Trunk	Pubic Hair—Blanket	Head Hair	"A" & "H"	Neg.	Yes	Intact Body—1 Day
Kimberly Hopps	Neg.	Neg.	—	Neg.	Head Hair	Neg.	—	No	Skeletonized—1 mo.
Juvenile Female	Yes	Yes	—	Head Hair—Shirt	Neg.	Neg.	—	Yes	Head Hairs Like Victim in Long's Apartment
Virginia Johnson	Neg.	Yes	—	Neg.	Head Hair	—	—	Yes	Skeletonized—3 wks.
Kim Swann	Yes	Yes	—	Neg.	Head Hair	Neg.	Limited Design	No	Intact Body—3 Days
Vicky Elliot	Yes	Yes	—	Neg.	Neg.	Neg.	—	Yes	Skeletonized—60 Days
Artis Wick	Neg.	Neg.	—	Neg.	Neg.	Neg.	—	Yes	Skeletonized—6 mos.

Race	Caucasian	Caucasian
Age	Mid 20s	31
Personality	"Macho" Image Assaultive with Weaker Individuals	On Probation for Assault/ Lifted Weights/Transferred from S.O. to State Penn.
Employment	Difficulty in Holding Job	Fired from Prev. Job Currently Unemployed
Marriage	Probably Divorced	Divorced
Vehicle	"Flashy Car"	Red Dodge Magnum
Weapons	Likely to Carry Weapons	Carried Gun and Knife
Personality	Inclined to Mentally and Physically Taunt and Torture	Tied "Leash" to Some Victims
Victims	Randomly Selected Susceptible to Approach	
Geographics	Confine Activity to Given Geographic Region	Tampa Bay Area

FIGURE R1–2 FBI criminal personality profile compared against Robert Long.

The Attempted Assassination of Archbishop Makarios
A Forensic Science Case Study

At about 7:05 a.m. on the morning of Sunday, March 8, 1970, the President of the Republic of Cyprus, Archbishop Makarios, boarded his personal helicopter in the courtyard of the archbishop's palace in Nicosia, in order to fly to Macheras Monastery to officiate at a memorial service. He sat on the left of the pilot, Major Zacharias Papadoyiannis. The helicopter took off, and when it had attained the height of the Archbishopric, it made a turn of 150 degrees, still climbing. At a point about 10 metres above the roof of the Archbishopric (Figure R2–1), a shot was heard from the left and rear, and a burst of machine-gun fire came from the same direction. The Archbishop was not hit, but his pilot sustained a severe wound in the abdomen. With great difficulty in view of his wound, the damage caused to the helicopter and the proximity of buildings and electric cables, the pilot managed to land on an open space on the corner of two neighbouring streets, out of range of the firing (Figure R2–2). The Archbishop and pilot dismounted from the helicopter and ran away from it, having in mind the

Julius Grant, MSc, Ph.D., FRIC

Reprinted by permission from the *Medico-Legal Journal*, Vol. 40, Part 2, 1972.

FIGURE R2–1

FIGURE R2–2

possibility of an explosion. However, the pilot collapsed and was taken to a hospital where, after a critical illness, he eventually recovered.

The Presidential Guard at the Archbishopric was conscious that the firing came from the roof of the Pancyprian Gymnasium opposite the Archbishop's palace, and they fired in that direction (see Figure R2–1). Shortly after the firing occurred, early risers in Thysseos and Othellos Streets, which adjoin the high side wall of the Pancyprian Gymnasium, saw four men climbing over the wall of the school into Thysseos Street. One spectator asked what was happening, but received no reply; he called out to the men to stop or he would shoot them. One then held his hands to his face, and turned back and said to one of the others who was coming up behind him and was holding a pistol, "They are shooting at us." All four then

(a)   (b)

(c)   (d)

FIGURE R2–3

turned into Othellos Street. The spectator and other onlookers then saw the four men board a car waiting nearby and drive off. The first spectator telephoned the police and subsequently identified the car by appearance, although he was unable to note the number. Other spectators were able to provide confirmatory evidence regarding the car, although the evidence of identification of the four persons was weak. However, eventually it seems to have been established that the car was of a light blue colour with a white line and was a Fiat, Model 850, registration number ZDR 320. In the meantime the police had been informed of the incident. They entered the Pancyprian Gymnasium, and took possession of the firearms and other exhibits found on the roof.

In another part of Nicosia, at a distance of about a mile from the scene of the attempt, a merchant opening his shop at about 8:30 in the morning noticed a self-drive car having the above description. As this had not been moved by 11:30 a.m. he telephoned the police. On Sunday, March

8, the day of the attempt, at 8:30 in the morning, one G. A. Taliadoros went to the Larnaca Road police station and reported that the car which he had hired on February 12 had been stolen from a parking place. His agitated condition and confused replies to questions aroused suspicion, and he was questioned about the circumstances of the theft of his car as well as about his own movements. In due course two associates of Taliadoros were also detained. They were questioned as to their whereabouts at the relevant time, and as their answers were deemed to be unsatisfactory, they were held in custody. Further arrests were made subsequently, and six persons, as follows, were ultimately detained, namely (Figure R2–3):

Adamos Haritonos, 23, student; and associate of Taliadoros
Georghios Alexandrou Taliadoros, 33, estate agent
Antonakis Prokopi Solomonodos, 32, former inspector of police
Antonakis Petrou Yenagritis, 28, police constable

Costas Polykarpou Ioannides, 32, newspaper editor
Polikarpos Antoni Polykarpou, 32, police constable

Monday, March 9, was a holiday and when on Tuesday, the 10th, Maria Constantinou, a cleaner of the Pancyprian school unlocked the toilets, she found below an aperture in the wall two dirty blankets in a heap. One was light grey in colour and the other a darker colour, rather brownish. These also were taken by the police for examination.

The police force acted with great promptitude and efficiency under the direction of Chief Supt. G. Hadjiloizou of the C.I.D. They took possession of the weapons found on the roof of the Pancyprian school and a number of other articles from the school roof, and also the blankets referred to above. At about the same time a shepherd found a cache of arms, also wrapped in two blankets, hidden in a ditch near Nicosia; and these were taken by the Police. They were similar to the arms found on the roof of the Gymnasium and fingerprints were obtainable from them.

Shortly after the above events, I received a telephone call from the High Commissioner for Cyprus in London asking me if I could fly to Cyprus at once; he hinted at the reason. A few days later I attended a Cabinet meeting at the Presidential Palace, where I met the President, and I was formally invited to be responsible for the forensic investigation of the assassination attempt. The resources of the police force and Government Analyst were placed at my disposal, and I take pleasure in paying tribute to the assistance and hospitality I received.

The activities of the police had resulted in the following list of articles of potential importance to be investigated:

From the school: weapons; two blankets; cigarette ends; button; fecal matter.
From the arms cache: weapons; two blankets.

From the car: dust from the floor; dust from boot; fingerprints; cigarette ends. From the persons detained: all outer clothing; also some 50 articles of other miscellaneous clothing; dust from a car and blankets from the homes of the persons detained. Miscellaneous: revolver holster; newspapers; car cover; etc.

The forensic examination of the above is now dealt with in order of importance. The jacket worn by Taliadoros, when he was arrested, bore a smear of white dust on the right shoulder approximately 3×2 cm in dimensions, and similar in colour to that of the whitewashed walls of the school. Taliadoros said that he picked it up while sitting on a bench and leaning against the wall of the police station where he was originally detained. The police had assiduously taken samples of plaster from the walls of the school along the escape route of the gunmen from the roof to the wall of Thysseos Street, but it was apparent that the mark on the jacket was a surface rubbing, and was a top coat of whitewash and not plaster. In view of the importance of this smear and the lack of wholly positive other forensic evidence concerning Taliadoros, I thought it advisable to make a fresh examination of the scene. Surface rubbings were, therefore, first taken from the areas from which the plaster had been removed. An attempt was then made to reconstruct the early stages of the escape after the shots had been fired.

It will be seen from Figure R2–1 that the gunmen must have climbed down from the flat roof where they had fired at the President on to an open air passage flanked on the right by the high whitewashed wall shown in Figure R2–4. Free passage down the area was prevented on the left by the pitched skylights (four in number) which serve the classroom below and which are apparent in the photograph. It was found that the most convenient way of travelling along this passage in a hurry was to pass between the wall and the skylight, a

FIGURE R2–4

distance of only 40 cm. This is too small to accommodate a man facing the direction in which he was running. Indeed there was a natural instinct, I found, to half-turn to the left, i.e., away from the wall, on passing between the narrow gaps. If this was done, the right shoulder did not necessarily touch the wall but, as a runner emerged from the gap, there was a distinct probability that his right shoulder would rub against the square-section vertical drainpipes from the roof, which project from the wall to the extent of about 10 cm. When this happened, a smear could be produced on the shoulder of the same size and type and in the same location as that found on Taliadoros's jacket.

A surface rubbing was, therefore, taken from one of the drainpipes at shoulder level, and it was found that the superficial coating was apparently unlike ordinary whitewash but was consistent with a mixture of whitewash and a white emulsion paint. A likely explanation of this is that it had been found that the whitewash would not cover the metal drainpipe, as well as on the actual wall, and a topcoating of emulsion paint had, therefore, been applied over it. The claim that the smear had come from the police station was

easily disposed of, because the bench on which Taliadoros had sat had a wooden back separating the sitter from the wall; and moreover, the whitewash on the wall was not pure white but a pale yellow colour. Table R2–1 shows the spectroscopic analysis of all the powders collected, from which it will be seen that the powder from the coat and that from the drainpipe matched perfectly; moreover they have no counterpart in any of the other samples, which are characteristic of an ordinary lime wash. The presence of both calcium and titanium is consistent with the use of a paint of good covering power, with the limewash on the pipe; and this occurs also on the coat.

In the course of the hearing the defense pointed out that in Nicosia all the drainpipes of the houses are of this rectangular type, so that the rubbing could have come from one of hundreds in the town. Having foreseen this argument I had spent nearly two hours roaming the streets of the town and rubbing my jacket against drainpipes—often to the mystification of passersby! Out of many in various parts of the town I found that about 60% were whitewashed; with the whitewash often partly rubbed off, and the remainder were

Table R2–1

Sample	J	1	2	3	4	5
Aluminum	Minor	Absent	Trace	Minor	Trace	Minor
Barium	Minor	Major	Trace	Minor	Trace	Major
Calcium	Major	Major	Major	Major	Major	Major
Chromium	Trace	Trace	Trace	Trace	Trace	Trace
Iron	Trace	Minor	Trace	Trace	Trace	Trace
Magnesium	Minor	Major	Major	Minor	Major	Major
Silicon	Major	Minor	Trace	Major	Trace	Minor
Titanium	Major	Absent	Absent	Major	Absent	Absent
Zinc	Absent	Minor	Absent	Absent	Trace	Trace

Key
J—Taliadoros's jacket.
1—Landing outside classroom door.
2—Lavatory outside wall.
3—Drainpipe on roof.
4—Lavatory wall where blankets were found.
5—Column at foot of staircase near classroom.

painted with a gloss paint which could not be rubbed off. I did not find one which had the appearance or effect of the drainpipes in the roof corridor at the school. The Court regarded this as significant, according to the Presiding Judge in his summing-up.

Coming now to the two blankets found by the lavatories, these consisted of a grey blanket, torn, with bloodstains and dark stains resembling grease. There was also a brown blanket with several holes, also with dark stains resembling grease. The majority of the fibres comprising it were of wool, and were of a rather unusual shade of brown. The grease stains were extracted, and it was possible to show that the substance present was similar to a type of greasy lubricant in the stores of the Police Department; and that both were similar to the grease on the weapons, which doubtless was used to prevent them from rusting. Infrared spectroscopy was used for this purpose. There was nothing characteristic about this grease, and this evidence, though contributory, was not in itself conclusive. However, an interesting fact noted was that the grease stains on the blanket and the grease on the weapons, while alike, were completely

dissimilar from four other types of oil or grease also kept in the police store. Thus, although the weapons were not police weapons, the grease on them could have come from the police store.

It has been mentioned that bloodstains were found on the grey blanket. These were of human blood. It was thought at first that they were associated with the observation that one of the fugitives seen climbing over the wall had his hand against his face. However, none of the men arrested had any wounds, and examination of the bloodstains showed that they were of the drop rather than of the smear type to be expected from a wound. Medical examination showed no evidence of recent nose-bleeding from any of the men detained. As the stains were old, it was not possible to carry out a grouping test. It was felt that they could have been produced before the relevant date, and this aspect of the evidence was not pursued further.

So far as the weapons found on the scene were concerned, these are shown in Figure R2–1. They comprised a Bren gun, a Lee Enfield rifle, and an M6 rifle; 39 spent cartridges were found, and there were about the same number unused. The only features of importance were the grease referred to above, and fingerprints in the grease. On the weapons were found two prints each having 13 points of diagnostic identity with the right forefinger of Haritonos; one was on the magazine of the Bren gun. On some ammunition was found a print which had 16 points of diagnostic identity with the print from the right forefinger of Yenagritis. On other ammunition was found a print which had 16 points of identity with a print from the left thumb of Solomonodos. On further items of ammunition was found a print which had 16 points of diagnostic identity with a print from the left thumb of Yenagritis. Other prints were found, but were not produced in evidence. On the loaded Bren gun magazine and ammunition found on the roof of the Gymnasium were two prints having 16 points of diagnostic identity with a print from the right thumb of Solomonodos. Other fingerprint evidence attributable to Taliadoros, Haritonos, and Yenagritis was found on the car. Some of these were found near the top edge and on the outside of one of the windows, indicating that the door had been pulled shut, using the partly opened window, by the owner of the print who was sitting inside.

In England 16 points of identity are taken as conclusive evidence of the identity of origin of two fingerprints. In Cyprus, in general the courts accept the same standards as in this country. It will be seen that except in one case the requisite 16 points were obtained. In the case of Haritonos only 13 such points per print were obtained, but points from different parts of more than one print from the same finger can be added together to make the necessary 16. It could be claimed that the lack of further points of identity was due to the poor character of the prints found on the scene in this instance and that there were no dissimilarities between the two prints which could not be accounted for in the

same way. Solomonodos, who had been a police officer, accepted that the prints found could have been his. Both he and Yenagritis were in the National Guard in 1963–67, and they stated that they had been in the habit of handling arms and ammunition. In mid-1969 the police authorized the collection of arms surrounded by civilians. Yenagritis and Solomonodos claimed to have been involved in this operation; no Bren guns were among the arms then collected. Haritonos was in the National Guard in 1968 and said that he had handled Bren guns within nine months of the assassination attempt.

This gave rise to a lively controversy as to the age of the fingerprints, which is always difficult to determine with certainty. Supt. Dekatris, the capable fingerprint expert of the Cyprus C.I.D., held the view that the sharpness of the prints indicated recent origin. This was contested by the defence, but I felt that I could support the prosecution's argument because the prints were made in grease, which in the hot climate of Cyprus tends to run; and under these conditions fingerprints become blurred rapidly. An experiment in which prints made in grease on metal were kept at 20°C and 30°C (the summer temperature in Cyprus) for a few days showed a distinct difference in sharpness when developed.

The defence called an expert, formerly of the Greek police force, but he was unable to convince the Court that the fingerprints were old or that the blurring on aging theory was untenable, especially bearing in mind that at least nine months had elapsed since the alleged handling of the weapons and the discovery of the arms. In any case this referred only to the presence of the fingerprints of Solomonodos and Yenagritis, and not to those of their associates.

Fingerprint evidence was also sought from the cigarette ends. These were found on the scene, in the car, and in the police station after detention. Practically all were of the same make and had been smoked in the same way, i.e., to the extent of two-thirds of their length. They were then stubbed out in a similar way by being bent almost at right-angles. It was hoped that the stubbing-out operation would have left a fingerprint on the cigarette paper, but unfortunately nothing that could be satisfactorily used as evidence was found when we used the ninhydrin test. On the other hand, experiments in which we produced similar stubs did leave fingerprints. The reason for this difference may have been the greater heat of burning in the case of the cigarette ends believed to have been associated with the accused; or because the smoker was one of the few people whose fingerprints do not respond to the ninhydrin test. It would have been interesting to have tested the fingerprints of the six men on paper to check this. A saliva grouping test on the cigarette ends might also have been helpful, but facilities were not available.

Much of the forensic work concerned fibres. The objective was to link the fibres from one or more blankets with one or more of the accused. This applied both to the fibres of which the blankets were made and to adventitious fibres found on the blankets. To this end a large collection from the wardrobes of the six men was seized and thoroughly examined, including the pocket linings—since the latest style in trousers can apparently contain as many as seven pockets! In all some 60 outer garments, including shoes, were tested; also included were contents of cars and blankets from the homes of the accused, which the defence alleged were the source of certain of the fibres found. This was extremely laborious work but was fully justified. The connecting links in the evidence were small in number but important. In my evidence on this aspect I thought it advisable to make clear the significance and limitation of evidence based on fibres. This disarmed some anticipated cross-examination.

In making a comparison between fibres found on a suspect and fibres found at the scene of a crime or on an article associated with it, there are three principal criteria to be taken into account, namely:

a. the material of which the fibre is made;
b. the colour of the fibre;
c. its dimensions, i.e., shape and size.

1. Now, if one has two single fibres, one from the scene and one from the suspect, and they are alike in all the three above respects, then one can say that the fibres could have come from the same source, but that there is no certainty that they did so.

2. On the other hand if the fibres being compared are unusual in some respect as well as being alike, then the chance that they come from the same source is greater.

3. Finally, if one is examining groups of fibres, i.e., tufts of fibres of different kinds and different colours, then if the two groups contain the same fibres in the same proportions, then the possibility that they come from the same source is very high indeed; but one still cannot say with absolute certainty that they did so.

On the jacket belonging to Taliadoros, which had the white smear referred to above, I found a number of fibres which were not part of the composition of the jacket, i.e., extraneous fibres. On the left shoulder of the jacket was such a brown fibre, which matched closely the principal fibres of the brown blanket found at the scene of the assassination attempt. Since this was an unusual fibre, I placed it in category 2 above. This could not be regarded as conclusive evidence because the brown fibre could have come from some other source. However, as stated, the shade of the colour was unusual and it is interesting to note that although some hundreds of fibres from various items of clothing, car dust, etc. were examined, in no case did a brown fibre similar to that from the blanket occur except on the left shoulder of Taliadoros's jacket. It should be added that the police took a multicoloured blanket from the home of Taliadoros. It contained brown fibres, which were said to have accounted for the fibre on his jacket; there was a superficial resemblance, but microscopical methods showed the fibres to be quite different.

In the right-hand pocket of the trousers of Taliadoros I found a tuft of fibres which was similar to the fibres comprising one of the blankets used to wrap the weapons. Since this consisted of no less than four fibres of different colours and types in each case, I placed this in the third category, representing the strongest possibility of identity.

On a pullover belonging to Yenagritis I found a human hair which was similar to a human hair which I found on one of the blankets from the school lavatory. It is impossible to say with complete certainty that two human hairs are or are not identical. However, these were alike in colour; they were both relatively long, too long for a male hair, even in these days; and I felt that the possibility that they came from the same source was strong. This was another link between Yenagritis and the blanket.

On the left arm of the jacket of Polykarpou I also found a tuft of fibres similar to those of one of the blankets, and the nature of these was such as to put them in the third category, of the strongest possibility. I also examined debris I collected from the body and boot of the car of Solomonodos and here I found a tuft of fibres similar to those of one of the blankets presumably used to wrap the guns. Here again the nature and the proportions of the fibres placed them in the category of maximum possibility.

The forensic evidence established links as follows:

Linking:
Arms to blankets—grease.
Arms to accused—fingerprints.
Blanket to accused—fibres.
Scene to accused—white smears (Taliadoros).
Car to accused—fingerprints and fibres.

The preliminary enquiry was heard in Nicosia starting April 15, 1970, with Mr. A. Frangos, Senior Counsel of the Republic, for the prosecution. Ninety-five witnesses were called by the prosecution; cross-examination was reserved.

The subsequent trial was held in the assize court room of Nicosia in October 1970. The prosecution was conducted by Mr. Talarides, Senior Counsel, and Mr. Frangos. In Cyprus legal procedure resembles that of England except that there is no jury, the verdict resting with the three presiding Judges. In a small country such as Cyprus this is regarded as a more desirable procedure. Apart from the prosecution's forensic evidence, testimony was largely concerned with the actions, behaviour, and alleged alibis of the accused. The Defence sought to establish alibis and to prove reasonable doubt as to the forensic evidence, but the combined effect of the latter apparently convinced the Judges. The charge against Polykarpou was withdrawn at the first hearing due to lack of evidence; only that from the fibres being available. Ioannides was acquitted owing to insufficient evidence; he was expelled from Cyprus. The remaining four were sentenced to 14 years imprisonment in Nicosia and, according to the press, they subsequently confessed that theirs was one of several plots which were due to take place at the time of the attempted assassination and which undoubtedly would have done so had it not been for the prompt action of the authorities. The accused instructed their respective Counsel not to place any factors in mitigation before the Court; Haritonos stated that he did not pray for leniency.

The author is indebted to the Government of Cyprus for permission to reproduce the illustrations; and to Chief Supt. Hadjiloizou for his cooperation in the preparation of this paper.

Teamwork in the Forensic Sciences
Report of a Case

L. W. Bradford and A. A. Biasotti

Director and Supervising Criminalist, respectively, Laboratory of Criminalistics, San José, California

The scene in which the following events occurred is a single story dwelling in a quiet residential neighborhood where the victim lived. The victim was a 45-year-old woman who lived in the second house on a particular cul-de-sac street next to a red house on the corner (which is of later significance). A streetlight is situated here.

The investigative events began with the discovery of the victim lying face up over the foot of her bed with the top of her head completely blown off. Tissue debris covered both walls and the ceiling surrounding the victim. The gruesome discovery was made and reported immediately at 2:30 a.m. by an elderly male boarder who rented one bedroom in the victim's house. The boarder had entered the house, using his key, at about 1:15 a.m. after working as a bartender since 4 p.m. the previous day. He went directly to his bedroom and read for about an hour. When ready to retire, he noticed lights in the victim's bedroom and kitchen. Investigating, he discovered the victim. The first patrol unit arrived at the scene within minutes. The patrol officer found no weapon and, after a quick search for a possible intruder on the premises, called for assistance.

The detective team arrived at the scene within ten minutes and was followed within the hour by a team of four investigators who were immediately deployed to interview neighbors for possible leads. A more detailed search of the scene revealed that:

1. All doors were locked and there were no signs of forced entry.

2. The victim's clothing was neatly arranged on a chair next to her bed.

3. There was no indication of a struggle prior to the fatal shot.

4. Valuables appeared to be intact and undisturbed.

After photographing the victim and the scene, the body was removed; and a search was made for the projectile which caused the extensive trauma to the victim. A high-velocity weapon was assumed to be the cause of death.

The major portion of a 150 grain, military type, jacketed bullet was recovered in the wall space in back of the headboard of the victim's bed. A projection of the bullet path through the mattress, headboard, and wall, in conjunction with the position of the body, an apparent "defense" type wound on the lower right wrist of the victim, and the lack of powder residues indicated that the victim was shot while sitting on the end of the bed, leaning back at about a 30-degree angle, and holding her right arm in defensive fashion over her face. Class characteristics of the rifle impressed on the .30 caliber bullet indicated the possibility of Remington Rifles, Model numbers 721 to 760.

This fatal bullet was destined to be the vital link in connecting the suspect with the victim, but in a very unusual manner. The second vital link, discovered later in the investigation, was a cancelled check, which will be discussed separately.

Canvassing of the immediate neighbors developed several witnesses who on the evening before:

1. Heard a loud "bang" or "back fire" between 10:15 p.m. and 10:30 p.m.

2. Saw a red station wagon with white top, round taillights, and loud muffler start

Reprinted by permission of the American Society for Testing and Materials from *Journal of Forensic Sciences*.

up and drive out of cul-de-sac within a few minutes after hearing the "loud bang." The license number was not obtained.

3. Described the driver of the vehicle as a male—without further details.

It was also learned from persons in the neighborhood that a vehicle similar to the described station wagon had been parked near the scene on several occasions.

Careful and methodical interrogation of all the neighbors, known friends, and former husband (amicably separated) of the victim continued until such time that a conference was called by the detective-in-charge to summarize and evaluate the information assembled. Logical suspects, including the boarder, the former husband, and several known acquaintances, were quickly eliminated because alibis were confirmed by investigation. One lead, however, needed to be followed. It was learned from friends that the victim frequented a local commercial dance studio. Questioning of persons present during Wednesday afternoon at the dance studio indicated that most of the victim's dancing lessons had been with a part-time instructor who would be in a position to give more information about the victim's acquaintances and habits than anyone else.

Through further leads and contacts, the address of this man was found to be an apartment in an adjacent city. The instructor was 23 years old and married with two children. Two detectives, upon arriving at the suspect's apartment, noted a red and white 1955 Ford station wagon parked in the stall of the apartment. Upon knocking and identifying themselves they were invited into the living room by the instructor. While questioning him about the victim, her acquaintances, and his actions the night of the murder, the detectives noted a marble-topped coffee table, end table, and lamp which fitted the description of furniture taken in a burglary of the victim's residence several months prior. When asked about this furniture, the instructor said that he had purchased it

somewhere at a department store. He later changed his story indicating that it was given to him by a friend. The suspect further stated that he had visited the victim the previous week to borrow $50; but instead he sold her a painting for $140. He denied any knowledge of the murder or of owning a .30 caliber rifle.

He had a good alibi for the night of the murder. He had taken his wife (a waitress) to work early Wednesday evening, taking their children (girl, age 5; boy, age 3) with them and returned home to baby-sit, clean house, and watch TV until about 12:30 a.m. when he departed, leaving the children at home alone, to pick up his wife at work.

As the result of this initial questioning, during which the suspect had changed some of his story, and considering the presence of the stolen furniture, the investigators asked the suspect to go to police headquarters for further questioning, which he did willingly. Further interrogation of the suspect at headquarters, and interrogation of his wife, separately, strengthened the investigators' suspicions that the suspect was not telling the truth and knew more about the murder than he had admitted. At the conclusion of these interviews, the man and wife accepted the police opinion that the furniture was stolen property and allowed it to be taken from their apartment. The man was released at this time after agreeing to a polygraph examination the following day.

Shortly after midnight when the investigators arrived at the suspect's apartment to recover the furniture, they learned from a neighbor adjacent to the suspect's apartment that their apartment had been burglarized about three weeks earlier while she and her husband were away for that weekend. This burglary had been investigated and revealed a forced entry by cutting a screen over the bathroom window and entry through an unlocked window. Reported stolen were a Remington .30-'06 Model 760 Gamemaster rifle and

$10 in cash. With this information in hand, a warrant to search the suspect's apartment and station wagon was obtained and executed on Friday afternoon, the second day following the murder.

The search of the suspect's apartment brought forth the following:

1. A paper target with bullet holes which appeared to be about .30 caliber.

2. One fired caliber .30-'06 cartridge case (established by laboratory examination to be not connected with the stolen rifle).

3. A caliber .22 rifle, a .410 gauge shotgun, and a caliber .25 pistol.

4. An electric shaver identified as belonging to the boarder living in the victim's house and reported stolen in a burglary.

5. A pair of stained trousers (lab examination revealed no blood or human tissue on these trousers).

The search of the suspect's station wagon developed the following:

1. Cuff links identified as taken with the electric shaver found in the apartment.

2. A large "gunshot" penetration from interior to exterior at about a 45 degree angle in the right side with the entry in line with the top of the rear-seat cushion.

The "gunshot" hole in the suspect's vehicle was an unexplained event which later developed into yet another interesting speculative aspect of this case. From an examination of the penetration, powder, pattern, and lead pellets found in the vehicle, it was determined that this hole was consistent with the firing of a .410 gauge shotgun. It was found that this single shot, bolt action Mossberg, Model 173 A, .410 gauge shotgun found in the suspect's apartment would fire when dropped on its butt with the thumb safety in the "fire" position. This information at the time did little more than add mystery to the investigation. About 19 days after the murder, however, this event assumed new significance when one of the investigators in checking out the neighborhood near the scene observed what appeared to be a pellet pattern on the sidewalk next to the curb in front of the house on the corner next to the victim's residence. This was the area in which the red and white station wagon had been observed parked on previous occasions. Examination of the pattern in conjunction with the hole in the vehicle indicated that the pattern, size, shape, shot imprints, and angle were all consistent with the hypothesis that the suspect's .410 shotgun discharged through the right side while parked at the curb. No statements had been given by the suspect to the point of this evidence.

When again questioned about the items recovered in the search and his alibis, the suspect refused to answer most questions without his attorney. He did, however, attempt to explain the target with the caliber .30 bullet holes by saying that he had recently been to a local outdoor shooting ranch where he was shooting a "large caliber rifle" which he described as "more than a .22 and smaller than a cannon." This statement, which must have been an inadvertent "slip" by the suspect, provided a useful clue.

All information thus far obtained pointed to a connection between the suspect and the victim, the burglaries, and possibly the murder; but a direct link with the crime was not a matter of established fact. Based upon these tenuous developments and on the advice of the District Attorney of Santa Clara County, the suspect was arrested and charged with Burglary, Receiving Stolen Property, and Murder. After the arrest the chief detective found a key in the personal property taken from the suspect at the time of booking which appeared to be identical with the house key to the victim's residence. The suspect when questioned about the key said that it was for a prior residence in the area and gave an address. A check of this alibi address revealed that the suspect and his wife had lived at that address. The locks had not been changed after they had moved, and the key taken from the suspect and matching the victim's key did not open any of the locks at the alibi address; but it did open the entrance door to the victim's house. How or when the suspect obtained this key has never been determined, but it was known that the victim stored her wraps and purse in the cloak room at dancing periods when the suspect was present. Consequently, he had an opportunity to make a duplicate.

At this point, a service station attendant was located who tentatively identified the suspect as one who had stopped at his gas station in the vicinity of the death scene on the night of the murder.

The suspect, when faced with all of the apparent contradictions to his alibis, accused the police of lying and attempting to falsely implicate him and refused to answer further questions. When the time for an agreed polygraph examination arrived, he refused to undergo the examination. From this point on no further information was obtained directly from the suspect which would aid in the solution of the case.

Two days after the murder, the police were faced with an array of alibis, contradictions, and facts which appeared to be pieces of a puzzle, but which defied fitting together in any logical way. It was again time for reflection and contemplation before planning the next move. A review of the progress to date indicated that the next two main lines of investigation should be:

1. To contact the neighbors of the suspect who resided in the apartment adjacent to the suspect to determine whether any fired components from the caliber .30-'06 Remington Model 760 rifle were available from the period prior to the time of the burglary in which the rifle was taken.

2. To investigate the shooting range for spent bullets where the suspect indicated that he may have fired a rifle.

The neighbors were contacted first, and three fired .30-'06 cartridge cases were obtained which had been fired from the rifle before it was stolen. When asked when and where the rifle had last been fired, the neighbor replied that it had been at a pine tree during the recent fall deer hunting season in the Sierra Nevada mountains located about 150 miles from his apartment. This occurred while he was hunting with a friend and a nephew. The neighbor had his .30-'06 Remington Model 760 rifle; the friend had a .30-'06 Springfield Model 1903 rifle; and his nephew had a .30-30 Winchester Model 94 rifle. He said that he and his nephew had sighted in their rifles with targets placed against a large pine tree at a distance of about 150 feet from a clearing near a road. Several shots were fired. He thought that he could locate the tree. Four days after the murder, the neighbor guided investigators to a pine tree approximately 100 feet tall and about 30-in. in diameter. A small section surrounding one apparent bullet hole was cut out, and a jacketed bullet was recovered and returned to the laboratory in San Jose for examination. This bullet was found to be from a caliber .30 weapon of six right-hand riflings with a land width consistent with the Model 94 Winchester used by the neighbor's nephew. A second trip to the pine tree was made; and with permission and assistance of the U.S. Forest Service, the tree was felled. A five-foot section of the trunk was returned to Santa Clara County where it was split and dissected. With the aid of X-ray equipment, a second bullet was recovered. The bullet was fully mushroomed, leading to a cover over the rifling marks which had preserved the class and individual characteristics on the base portion of the metal jacket. The bullet proved to be a soft point fired from a caliber .30 weapon with class characteristics consistent with a Remington Model 760 rifle. These class characteristics were the same as those of the fatal bullet. Further study revealed a

FIGURE R3–1 Bullets used to link the fatal bullet with the missing murder rifle. The fatal bullet and the two range bullets are metal-jacketed, spitzer, 150 grain M2 ball (U.S. Army) military type. The bullet from the tree is a 180 grain soft point corresponding to ammunition possessed by the owner of the stolen rifle. The two tests were not fired by the murder weapon and are included solely for the purpose of illustrating bullet type and class characteristics of rifling marks.

significant similarity of individual characteristics between the fatal bullet and the bullet from the tree indicating that both had been fired by the neighbor's stolen rifle (Figures R3–1 and R3–2).

The next phase of the investigation proceeded to the shooting range where it was believed that the suspect may have fired a rifle prior to the murder. Nine days after the murder the range master of the Sunnyvale Rod and Gun Club was contacted, and it was determined that the range had opened about a month prior to the murder after renovating the sandstone-shale embankment which served as a

FIGURE R3–2 Comparison photomicrographs demonstrating the identification between the bullets shown in Figure R3–1.

backstop at 100 yards from the firing point. The range had been closed for about three months while the embankment was scraped and cleared. When shown a photo of the suspect and asked if he recognized the person, the range master stated that the photo resembled a person using the range during the past month who was shooting a .30-'06 Remington Model Gamemaster "pump-action" rifle. Entries on the sign-in register required for all persons using the range were hastily searched for the name and address of the suspect. None being found, the list was submitted to the Laboratory of Criminalistics for a handwriting examination to determine whether or not the suspect could have signed the register using an assumed name.

When the register was examined at the Laboratory, the only immediately available authentic specimen of handwriting of the suspect was his endorsement of a $140 check which he had earlier mentioned in connection with the purported sale of a painting to the victim. An examination of the complete range record revealed the name of the suspect one week later than the date first indicated by the range master. This name was identified with the writing on the check endorsement. There was further examination of the check which will be discussed separately. The signature on the range record was dated three days prior to the murder. The register indicated that he was assigned to firing Point #29. Point #30 was the last firing position. A man and his son assigned lanes 27 and 28 and another person assigned lane 30 were immediately contacted and questioned. Lanes 29 and 30 were customarily the only targets used for high velocity weapons.

The man and his son from shooting lanes 27 and 28 identified the suspect from a photograph and said he was firing a .30-'06 Remington Model 742 or 760 in lane 29. Also that he was firing military type ammunition and when asked if they could have his brass, the suspect replied that he was saving it for a friend. They further noted that a girl, about 5, and a boy, about 3, accompanied the suspect at the range. Based upon this information the embankment covering targets #28, 29, and 30 was searched with the aid of a screen. Several buckets of metal jacket fragments were recovered. The buckets of projectiles were taken to the laboratory where rapid sorting based on gross class characteristics eliminated all but a few jackets and jacket fragments with class characteristics similar to the fatal bullet (see Figure R3–1).

A detailed comparison microscope examination was now begun which revealed that two bullet jackets from the range had class and individual characteristics that established an identity between the .30 caliber bullet from the tree and the fatal bullet (see Figures R3–1 and R3–2). Thus, about three weeks after the murder, the two bullets from the range provided the needed missing link between the stolen rifle and the fatal bullet. Without this evidence a connection between the stolen rifle and the fatal bullet would never have been established because the rifle had not been found. The physical evidence had now provided a link between the murder weapon and the suspect and the fatal bullet. To strengthen this link further, a third trip was made to the area from which the neighbor had fired at the pine tree. With the aid of a metal detector, three fired .30-'06 cartridge cases were found. Microscopic comparisons of breech bolt marks on these cases led to an identification with the three fired cases previously obtained from the neighbor (Figure R3–3).

Returning to the subject of the $140 check, the endorsement was of interest as an exemplar of the defendant's signature for the purpose of comparison with the range record. Much to the surprise of the investigators during the preliminary examination of this document at the laboratory, it was discovered that the entire face of the check was traced. It was further determined that the payer signature was traced from an authentic victim's signature and the remainder of the check was traced

(a) (b)

FIGURE R3–3 Comparison photomicrographs demonstrating the identification between cartridge cases recovered near tree to cases from the owner of stolen rifle.

from authentic writing of the suspect, including his own name as payee.

The document examiner, upon this finding, asked the detectives to obtain the victim's check stubs for the period involved with the $140 check.

It was found that the traced check was numbered in a sequence different from those covering the period of her stubs. The traced check was number 330. A new group of five personalized checkbooks had recently been received from the bank by mail. Four of these were found by the detectives in an opened bank envelope on the victim's desk. The fifth book containing checks No. 325 through 349 was missing. Speculate now as to the reason that check No. 330 was cashed by the defendant rather than Nos. 325, 326, 327, 328, and 329.

The prosecutor charged first degree murder. The defendant was found guilty and was sentenced to life. The prosecutor used the following lines of argument following the presentation of all the evidence:

1. The victim was a lonely woman who had spent several thousand dollars for dancing lessons over a period of years as a form of recreation.

2. The defendant gained a knowledge of the victim's habits, address, and situation through frequent association as a dance instructor.

3. Through access to the defendant's wraps and purse while at dancing sessions, the defendant gained possession of a key by either replication or theft.

4. Using this illicit key, the defendant had made visits to the victim's home while she was attending dance sessions in other areas. He had taken property from this home on several occasions. This included the furniture, boarder's cuff links, and checkbook.

5. The defendant had burglarized his neighbor's apartment and had taken the .30-'06 rifle. When entering the victim's home, he was armed, first with the .410

gauge shotgun, later with the .30-'06 rifle. The long-barreled weapons were concealed by placing them on the floor behind the driver's seat of the vehicle. On one of these occasions, while the vehicle was parked near the victim's home, the shotgun was accidentally discharged while in the act of placing or removing it from this position.

6. The defendant traced the victim's signature on check No. 325, using the technique of carbon paper; however, when he covered the tracing with ink, it was a different color than his freehand writing on the remainder of the check face. He continued practicing the forgery until he learned that tracing the entire check face was the only method of avoiding a difference in appearance of the ink color between the payer line and remaining entries. In this way he used up checks Nos. 325, 326, 327, 328, and 329, and finally perfected the forgery on check No. 330.

7. After cashing the check, the defendant waited until the day that he thought cancelled checks through the mail would arrive at the victim's house, at which time he again entered the home armed with the rifle intending to remove the cancelled check No. 330 and destroy it in order to conceal the forgery; he unexpectedly encountered the victim and killed her.

The case is bizarre for several reasons:

1. The connection of the fatal bullet with the suspect without the rifle is exceptionally uncommon.

2. The fact of a defendant tracing his own name is very peculiar.

3. The good fortune of finding exemplar bullets in examinable condition from the tree and range under the circumstances described is unlikely.

It is to the credit of the investigators, examiners, and prosecutors that they recognized the value and significance of all the facets of the evidence and were able to communicate with each other in a manner which made the most effective use of all of it.

APPENDIX

Guides to the Collection
of Physical Evidence—FBI

Specimen	Amount Desired		Send By
	Standard	Evidence	
Abrasives	Not less than one ounce.	All	Registered mail or equivalent
Ammunition (Live Cartridges)			Live ammunition must be shipped via Federal Express. The following guidelines must be followed to comply with U.S. Department of Transportation regulations. Pack ammunition in a cardboard container. Label invoices FEDERAL EXPRESS. The shipper's certification for restricted articles must be included. The outside of the container must be labeled ORMD AIR, CARTRIDGES SMALL ARMS. The shipping papers must also include the weight in grams
Anonymous tion Letters, and Bank Robbery Notes		Documentary evidence condition in which it was found. It should not be folded, torn, marked, soiled, stamped, written on, or handled unnecessarily. Protect the evidence from inadvertent indented writing. Mark documents unobtrusively by writing the collector's initials, date, and other information with a pencil. Whenever possible, submit the original evidence to the Laboratory. The lack of detail in photocopies makes examinations difficult. Copies are sufficient for reference file searches.	Registered mail or equivalent
Bullets (projector without cartridge) (Live Cartridges)		All found.	Same as Ammunition
Cartridge Cases (shells only)		All	Same as Ammunition

Source: Courtesy of the Federal Bureau of Investigation, Washington, D.C.

Identification	Wrapping and Packing	Remarks
Outside container: type of material, date obtained, investigator's name or initials.	Submit abrasives in heat-sealed or resealable plastic bags or paint cans. Avoid using paper or glass containers.	Abrasives settle in oil and fuel. Submit the oil and fuel from the engine sump and/or filters. Abrasives embed in bearings and other parts. Submit the bearings and other parts.
Same as above.	Ammunition components such as bullets, cartridge cases and shotshell casings can be sent via registered mail through the U.S. Postal Service. Evidence should be packaged separately and identified by date, time, location, collector's name, case number, and evidence number.	Unless specific examination of the cartridge is essential, do not submit.
Initial and date each document, if advisable.	Use proper enclosure. Place in envelope and seal with "Evidence" tape or transparent cellophane tape. Flap side of envelope should show: (1) wording "Enclosure(s) to FBI from (name of submitting office)," (2) title of case, (3) brief description of contents, (4) file number, if known. Staple to original letter of transmittal.	Do not handle with bare hands. Advise if evidence should be treated for latent fingerprints. Whenever possible, submit the original evidence to the laboratory. The lack of detail in photocopies makes examinations difficult. Copies are sufficient for reference file searches.
Do not mark bullets, cartridges and cartridge cases, and shotshells and shotshell casings. The date, time, location, collector's name, case number, and evidence number should be on the container.	Pack tightly in cotton or soft paper in pill, match, or powder box. Place in box. Label outside of box as to contents.	Unnecessary handling obliterates marks.
Same as above.	Same as above.	Spent cartridge cases.

Specimen	Amount Desired		Send By
	Standard	Evidence	
Casts (Dental or Die Stone Casts of Tire Treads and Shoe Prints)	Send in suspect's shoes and tires. Photographs and sample impressions are usually not suitable for comparison.	All shoe prints and entire circumference of tires.	Registered mail or equivalent
Checks (fraudulent)		See Anonymous Letter (p. 674)	Registered mail or equivalent
Check Protector, Rubber Stamp, and/or Date Stamp Known Standards (if possible, send actual device)	Obtain several copies in full word-for-word order of each questioned check-writer impression. If unable to forward rubber stamps, prepare numerous samples with different degrees of pressure.		Registered mail or equivalent
Clothing		All	Registered mail or equivalent
DNA Examinations (see pp. 686–688)			
Documents (charred or burned)		All	Registered mail or equivalent
Drugs: 1. Liquids		All	Registered mail or equivalent
2. Powders, Pills, and Solids		All to 30 g.	Registered mail or equivalent
EXPLOSIVES: Detonators, Blasting Caps, Detonating Cord, Black Powder, Smokeless Powder, Explosives, and Accessories, call FBI Laboratory, for shipping instructions.			
Fibers	Entire garment or other cloth item.	All	Registered mail or equivalent
Firearms (unloaded weapons)		Firearms must be packaged and shipped separately from live ammunition. All firearms must be unloaded.	Firearms and ammunition components such as bullets, cartridge cases, and shotshell casings can be sent via registered mail through the U.S. Postal Service. Evidence must be packaged separately and identified by date, time, location, collector's name, case number, and evidence number.

Identification	Wrapping and Packing	Remarks
On back of cast before it hardens, write location and date taken, and investigator's name or initials.	Wrap in paper and cover with suitable packing material to prevent breakage Label "Fragile." Plaster of Paris is no longer recommended.	For shoeprint and tire tread file searches, submit quality photographs of the impressions. If photographs are not available, submit casts, lifts, or the original evidence. Detailed sketches or photocopies are acceptable.
See Anonymous Letters on p. 674.	See Anonymous Letters on p. 674.	Advise what parts are questioned or known. Furnish physical description of subject.
Place name or initials, date, name of make and model, etc., on sample impressions.	See Anonymous Letters on p. 674.	Do not disturb inking mechanisms on printing devices.
Mark directly on garment or use string tag indicating type of evidence, date obtained, investigator's name or initials.	Wrap each article individually. Place in strong container with identification written on outside of package.	Do not cut out stains, leave clothing whole. If wet, hang in room to dry before packing.
Outside container: indicate if fragile, date obtained, investigator's name or initials.	Pack in rigid container between layers of cotton.	If moisture is added use atomizer, otherwise, not recommended.
Affix label to bottle in which found, including date it was found and investigator's name or initials.	Make sure container does not leak. Seal with tape to prevent any loss.	Mark "Fragile." If possible, use heat-seal plastic bags.
Outside of pillbox: affix label with date found and investigator's name or initials.	Seal with tape to prevent any loss.	If powder, pills, or solids are found in paper bags, place them in plastic bags to prevent any loss. Do not submit used drug field test kits with evidence.
Outside container or on the object fibers are adhering, include date and investigator's name or initials.	Use folder paper or pillbox. Seal edges and openings with tape.	Do not place loose in an envelope.
Do not mark the firearm. Firearms should be identified with a tag containing the caliber, make, model, and serial number. The date, time, owner(s)' name(s), location, collector's name, case number, and evidence number should be on the container.	Wrap in paper and identify contents of packages. Place in cardboard box or wooden box.	The firearm should be handled minimally to avoid loss or destruction of evidence. Do not allow objects to enter or contact the firearm's barrel, chamber, or other operating surface.

Specimen	Amount Desired		Send By
	Standard	Evidence	
Flash Paper	One sheet	All to 5 sheets.	Call FBI Laboratory.
Gasoline	10 ml	All to 10 ml	Call Chemistry-Toxicology Unit for instructions.
General Unknown:			
1. Solids (nonhazardous)	10 gm	All to 10 gm	Registered mail or equivalent
2. Liquids (non-hazardous)	10 ml	All to 10 ml	Registered mail or equivalent
Glass Fractures		All	Registered mail or equivalent
Glass Particles	Submit the victim(s)'and suspect's air-dried clothing. each item must be packaged separately in a paper bag. Search for particles in the victim(s)' and Suspect(s)' hair, skin, and wounds. Submit particles in leakproof containers such as film canisters or plastic pill bottles. Do not use paper or glass containers Search for particles in vehicles by vacuuming each section of the vehicle separately. Do not use tape for covering glass particles. Submit vacuum sweepings in leakproof containers. Do not use paper or glass containers.	All	Registered mail or equivalent

Identification	Wrapping and Packing	Remarks
Outside container: label indicating date and investigator's name or initials.	Flash paper is a hazardous material. Do not store flash paper near combustible materials. Seal flash paper in polyethylene envelopes and refrigerate.	
Outside container: label indicating type of material, date, and investigator's name or initials.	Use an all-metal container packed in wooden box.	An all-metal container should be used for its fireproof qualities.
Outside container: label indicating date and investigator's name or initials.	Same as Drugs (see p. 676).	Call Chemistry-Toxicology Unit for instructions.
Same as Liquid Drugs (see p. 676).	Same as Liquid Drugs (see p. 676).	Same as above.
Label the sides of the glass in the frame INSIDE and OUTSIDE. Label the glass where it was removed in the frame such as TOP, BOTTOM, LEFT, and RIGHT.	Wrap each piece separately in cotton. Pack in sturdy container to prevent shifting and breakage. Identify contents.	Submit all glass pieces so that the pieces can be fitted together to identify the radial cracks near and at the point(s) of impact and to increase the probability of matching edges. Pack all glass separately and securely to avoid shifting and breaking during transport.
Outside container: label indicating date and investigator's name or initials.	Place in film canister or plastic vial. Seal and protect against breakage.	Submit samples of glass from each broken window or source in leakproof containers such as film canisters or plastic pill bottles. Avoid using paper or glass containers.

Specimen	Amount Desired		Send By
	Standard	Evidence	
Gunshot Residues The Laboratory provides gunshot residue examinations to assist FBI field office investigations only.		Usually gunshot residue examinations will only be performed when samples are collected from living person's hands. Gunshot residue evidence must be collected within five hours of exposure to the discharge of a firearm.	
On cloth only to determine weapon to target distance.		All	Clothing submitted for gunshot residue examination should be handled carefully, air dried, and wrapped separately in paper. Clothing with blood must be air dried and labeled BIOHAZARD on the inner and outer containers. The date, time, location, collector's name, case number, and evidence number should be on the container.
Hair	Twenty-five full-length hairs from different parts of head and/ or pubic region.	All	Registered mail or equivalent
Handwriting and Hand Printing Known Standards			Registered mail or equivalent
Insulation **1.** Glass Wool	1″ mass from each suspect area.	All	Registered mail or equivalent
2. Safe	Sample all damaged areas.	All	Registered mail or equivalent
Matches	One to two books of paper. One full box of wood.	All	Federal Express, UPS, or equivalent
Obliterated, Eradicated, or Indented Writing		Same as Anonymous Letters (see p. 674).	Registered mail or equivalent

Identification	Wrapping and Packing	Remarks
		Collecting gunshot residue samples requires five adhesive lifts suitable for scanning electron microscopic analysis. Dab the adhesive side of the stub against the surface (right palm, back of right hand, left palm, back of left hand). Use one stub per sampling surface. The remaining stub will be used as a control. Label each sampling surface stub (e.g., RIGHT PALM, BACK OF RIGHT HAND). Cap and seal the stubs in separate, resealable plastic bags.
Outside container: Indicate date, obtained from whom, description, name or initials.	Dry and package individually in **unused** brown wrapping paper or brown grocery bag.	The deposition of gunshot residue on evidence such as clothing varies with the distance from the muzzle of the firearm to the target. Patterns of gunshot residue can be duplicated using a questioned firearm and ammunition combination fired into test materials at known distances. These patterns serve as a basis for estimating muzzle-to-garment distances.
Outside container: Type of material, date, and investigator's name or initials.	Folded paper or pillbox. Seal edges and openings with tape.	Do not place loose in envelope.
Indicate from whom obtained, voluntary statement included in appropriate place, date obtained, and investigator's name or initials.	Same as Anonymous Letters (see p. 674).	Same as Anonymous Letters (see p. 674).
Outside container: type of material, date, name or initials.	Use pillbox or plastic vial. Seal to prevent any loss.	Submit known and questioned debris in leakproof containers such as film canisters or plastic pill bottles. Avoid using paper or glass containers. Pack to keep lumps intact.
Same as above.	Safe insulation can adhere to persons, clothing, tools, bags, and loot and can transfer to vehicles. If possible, submit the evidence to the Laboratory for examiners to remove the debris. Package each item of evidence in a separate paper bag. Do not process tools for latent prints.	
Outside container: label indicating type of material, date, and investigator's name or initials.	Pack in metal container and in larger package to prevent shifting. Pack matches in box or metal container to prevent friction between matches.	Keep and label: "Keep away from fire."
Same as Anonymous Letters (see p. 674).	Same as Anonymous Letters (see p. 674).	Advise whether bleaching or staining methods may be used. Avoid folding.

	Amount Desired		
Specimen	Standard	Evidence	Send By
Organs of the Body		200 g of each organ.	Call Chemistry-Toxicology Unit for instructions.
Paint:			
1. Liquid	Original unopened container up to 1/4 pint, if possible.	All to 1/4 pint.	Registered mail or equivalent
2. Solid (paint chips or scrapings)	At least 1/2 sq. in. of solid, with all layers represented.	Standard: Control paint chips must be collected from the suspected source of the evidentiary paint. Controls must be taken from an area close to, but not in, any damaged area. If no damage is obvious, controls should be taken from several areas of the suspect substrate. Each layer can be a point of comparison. Controls must have all of the layers of paint to the substrate.	Registered mail or equivalent
Rope, Twine, and Cordage	One yard or amount available.	Submit the entire rope or cord. If the rope or cord must be cut, specify which end was cut during evidence collection. Label the known and questioned samples. Handle the sections of rope or cord carefully to prevent loss of trace material or contamination.	Registered mail or equivalent
Saliva Samples	1.5″ diameter stain in center of filter paper.	All	Registered mail or equivalent
Shoe Print Lifts (impressions on hard surfaces)	Photograph before making lift of dust impression.	For shoeprint and tire tread comparisons, submit original evidence whenever possible (shoes, tires, photographic negatives, casts, lifts).	Registered mail or equivalent
Soils and Minerals	Samples from areas near pertinent spot.	Collect soil samples from the immediate crime scene area and from the logical access and/or escape route(s). Collect soil samples at a depth that is consistent with the depth from which the questioned soil may have originated. If possile, collect soil samples from alibi areas such as the yard or work area of the suspect(s).	Registered mail

Identification	Wrapping and Packing	Remarks
Each biological specimen must be placed in a separate, labeled, sealed glass tube, plastic cup, or heat-sealed or resealable plastic bag. Affix BIOHAZARD labels to the inside and outside containers.	To avoid deterioration, biological specimens must be refrigerated or frozen during storage and shipping. Pack so that no breakage, leakage, or contamination occurs.	Submit a copy of the autopsy or incident report. Describe the symptoms of the suspect(s) or victim(s) at the time of the crime or prior to the death. List any known or questioned drugs consumed by or prescribed for the suspect(s) or victim(s). Describe any known or questioned environmental exposure to toxic substances by the suspect(s) or victim(s).
Outside container: Type of material, origin if known, date, investigator's name or initials.	Use friction-top paint can or large-mouth, screw-top jar. If glass, pack to prevent breakage. Use heavy corrugated paper or wooden box.	Protect spray can nozzles to keep them from going off. Avoid contact w/adhesive materials. Wrap to protect paint smears. Do not use envelopes, paper/plastic bags, or glass vials.
Same as above.	Package paint specimens in leakproof containers such as vials or pillboxes. Do not stick paint particles on adhesive tape. Do not use plastic bags, cotton, or envelopes to package paint specimens.	Avoid contact with adhesive materials. Wrap so as to protect smear. If *small amount:* seal round pillbox, film cannister, or plastic vial to protect against leakage/breakage.
On tag or container: Type of material, date, investigator's name or initials.	Submit in heat-sealed or resealable plastic or paper bags.	
Outside envelope and on filter paper: Type of sample, name of donor, date of collection, and collector's initials or name.	Seal in envelope.	Stain should be circled in pencil for identification. Filter paper available from hospitals and drugstores. Allow to dry.
On lifting tape or paper attached to tape: date, investigator's name or initials.	Prints in dust are easily damaged. Fasten print or lift to bottom of box so that nothing will rub against it.	Always secure crime-scene area until shoe prints or tire treads are located and preserved.
Outside container: Type of material, date, investigator's name or initials.	Do not remove soil adhering to shoes, clothing, and tools. Do not process tools for latent prints. Air-dry the soil and the clothing and package separately in paper bags. Carefully remove soil adhering to vehicles. Air-dry the soil and package separately in paper bags.	Ship known and questioned debris separately to avoid contamination. Submit known and questioned soil in leakproof containers such as film canisters or plastic pill bottles. Do not use paper envelopes or glass containers. Pack to keep lumps intact.

| Specimen | Amount Desired | | Send By |
	Standard	Evidence	
Tape (Adhesive Tape)	Recovered roll.	All	Registered mail or equivalent
Tools/Toolmarks	Send in the tool. If impractical, make several impressions on similar materials as evidence using entire marking area of tool.	If it is not possible to submit the tool-marked evidence, submit a cast of the toolmark.	Registered mail or equivalent
Typewriting, known standards	See Anonymous Letters (p. 612).		Registered mail or equivalent
Wire	3 ft. (Do not kink.)	All (Do not kink.)	Registered mail or equivalent
Wood	One foot or amount available.	All	Registered mail or equivalent

Identification	Wrapping and Packing	Remarks
Same as above.	Place on waxed paper, cellophane, or plastic.	Do not cut, wad, distort, or separate tapes that are stuck together.
On object or on tag attached to an opposite end from where toolmarks appear: date recovered and investigator's name or initials.	After marks have been protected with soft paper, wrap in strong wrapping paper, place in strong box, and pack to prevent shifting.	Photographs locate tool-marks but are of no value for identification purposes. Obtain samples of any material deposited on the tools. To avoid contamination, do not place the tool against the toolmarked evidence. Submit the tool rather than making test cuts or impressions. Mark the ends of the evidence and specify which end was cut during evidence collection.
On specimens: serial number, brand, model, etc., date recovered, and investigator's name or initials.	Same as Anonymous Letters (p. 674).	Examine ribbon for evidence of questioned message.
On label or tab: describe type of material, date, investigator's name or initials.	Wrap securely.	Do not kink wire.
Same as above.	Submit wood in heat-sealed or resealable plastic of paper bags.	

DNA Examinations

Deoxyribonucleic acid (DNA) is analyzed in body fluids, stains, and other biological tissues recovered from evidence. The results of DNA analysis of questioned biological samples are compared with the results of DNA analysis of known samples. This analysis can associate victim(s) and/or suspect(s) with each other or with a crime scene.

There are two sources of DNA used in forensic analyses. Nuclear DNA (nDNA) is typically analyzed in evidence containing blood, semen, saliva, body tissues, and hairs that have tissue at their root ends. Mithochondrial DNA (mtDNA) is typically analyzed in evidence containing naturally shed hairs, hair fragments, bones, and teeth.

If DNA evidence is not properly documented, collected, packaged, and preserved, it will not meet the legal and scientific requirements for admissibility in a court of law.

- If it is not properly documented, its origin can be questioned.
- If it is not properly collected, biological activity can be lost.
- If it is not properly packaged, contamination can occur.
- If it is not properly preserved, decomposition and deterioration can occur.

When DNA evidence is transferred by direct or secondary (indirect) means, it remains on surfaces by absorption or adherence. In general, liquid biological evidence is absorbed into surfaces, and solid biological evidence adheres to surfaces. Collecting, packaging, and preserving DNA evidence depends on the liquid or solid state and the condition of the evidence.

The more that evidence retains its original integrity until it reaches the Laboratory, the greater the possibility of conducting useful examinations. It may be necessary to use a variety of techniques to collect suspected body fluid evidence.

Blood Examinations

Examinations can determine the presence or absence of blood in stains. Examinations can also determine whether blood is human or not. Blood examinations cannot determine the age or the race of a person. Conventional serological techniques are not adequately informative to positively identify a person as the source of a stain.

Collecting Known Samples

Blood
- Only qualified medical personnel should collect blood samples from a person.
- Collect at least two 5-ml tubes of blood in purple-top tubes with EDTA as an anticoagulant for DNA analysis. Collect drug- or alcohol-testing samples in gray-top tubes with NaF (sodium fluoride).
- Identify each tube with the date, time, subject's name, location, collector's name, case number, and evidence number.
- Refrigerate, do not freeze blood samples. Use cold packs, not dry ice, during shipping.
- Pack liquid blood tubes individually in Styrofoam or cylindrical tubes with absorbent material surrounding the tubes.
- Label the outer container KEEP IN A COOL DRY PLACE, REFRIGERATE ON ARRIVAL, and BIOHAZARD.
- Submit to the Laboratory as soon as possible.

Blood on a Person
- Absorb suspected **liquid blood** onto a clean cotton cloth or swab. Leave a portion of the cloth or swab unstained as a control. Air-dry the cloth or swab and pack in clean paper or an envelope with sealed corners. Do not use plastic containers.
- Absorb suspected **dried blood** onto a clean cotton cloth or swab moistened with distilled water. Leave a portion of the cloth or swab unstained as a control. Air-dry the cloth or swab and pack in clean paper or an envelope with sealed corners. Do not use plastic containers.

Blood on Surfaces or in Snow or Water
- Absorb suspected **liquid blood or blood clots** onto a clean cotton cloth or swab. Leave a portion of the cloth or swab unstained as a control. Air-dry the cloth or swab and pack in clean paper or an envelope with sealed corners. Do not use plastic containers.

- Collect suspected **blood in snow or water** immediately to avoid further dilution. Eliminate as much snow as possible. Place in a clean airtight container. Freeze the evidence and submit as soon as possible to the Laboratory.

Bloodstains

- Air-dry **wet bloodstained garments.** Wrap **dried bloodstained garments** in clean paper. Do not place wet or dried garments in plastic or airtight containers. Place all debris or residue from the garments in clean paper or an envelope with sealed corners.

- Air-dry small suspected **wet bloodstained objects** and submit the objects to the Laboratory. Preserve bloodstain patterns. Avoid creating additional stain patterns during drying and packaging. Pack to prevent stain removal by abrasive action during shipping. Pack in clean paper. Do not use plastic containers.

- When possible, cut a large sample of suspected **bloodstains from immovable objects** with a clean, sharp instrument. Collect an unstained control sample. Pack to prevent strain removal by abrasive action during shipping. Pack in clean paper. Do not use plastic containers.

- Absorb suspected **dried bloodstains on immovable objects** onto a clean cotton cloth or swab moistened with distilled water. Leave a portion of the cloth or swab unstained as a control. Air-dry the cloth or swab and pack in clean paper or an envelope with sealed corners. Do not use plastic containers.

Blood Examination Request Letter

A blood examination request letter must contain the following information:

- A brief statement of facts relating to the case.

- Claims made by the suspect(s) regarding the source of the blood.

- Whether animal blood is present.

- Whether the stains were laundered or diluted with other body fluids.

- Information regarding the victim(s)' and suspect(s)' health such as AIDS, hepatitis, or tuberculosis.

Semen and Semen Stains

- Absorb suspected **liquid semen** onto a clean cotton cloth or swab. Leave a portion of the cloth or swab unstained as a control. Air-dry the cloth or swab and pack in clean paper or an envelope with sealed corners. Do not use plastic containers.

- Submit small suspected **dry semen-stained objects** to the Laboratory. Pack to prevent stain removal by abrasive action during shipping. Pack in clean paper. Do not use plastic containers.

- When possible, cut a large sample of suspected **seman stains from immovable objects** with a clean, sharp instrument. Collect an unstained control sample. Pack to prevent stain removal by abrasive action during shipping. Pack in clean paper. Do not use plastic containers.

- Absorb suspected **dried semen stains on immovable objects** onto a clean cotton cloth or swab moistened with distilled water. Leave a portion of the cloth or swab unstained as a control. Air-dry the swab or cloth and place in clean paper or an envelope with sealed corners. Do not use plastic containers.

Seminal Evidence From Sexual Assault Victim(s)

- Sexual assault victim(s) must be medically examined in a hospital or a physician's office using a standard sexual assault evidence kit to collect vaginal, oral, and anal evidence.

- Refrigerate and submit the evidence as soon as possible to the Laboratory.

Buccal (Oral) Swabs

- Use clean cotton swabs to collect buccal (oral) samples. Rub the inside surfaces of the cheeks thoroughly.

- Air-dry the swabs and place in clean paper or an envelope with sealed corners. Do not use plastic containers.

- Identify each sample with the date, time subject's name, location, collector's name, case number, and evidence number.

- Buccal samples do not need to be refrigerated.

Saliva and Urine

- Absorb suspected **liquid saliva or urine** onto a clean cotton cloth or swab. Leave a portion of the cloth unstained as a control. Air-dry the cloth or swab and pack in clean paper or an envelope with sealed corners. Do not use plastic containers.

- Submit suspected small, **dry saliva- or urine-stained objects** to the Laboratory. Pack to prevent stain removal by abrasive action during shipping. Pack in clean paper or an envelope with sealed corners. Do not use plastic containers.

- When possible, cut a large sample of suspected **saliva or urine stains from immovable objects** with a clean, sharp instrument. Collect an unstained control sample. Pack to prevent stain removal by abrasive action during shipping. Pack in clean paper. Do not use plastic containers.

- Pick up **cigarette butts** with gloved hands or clean forceps. Do not submit ashes. Air-dry and place the cigarette butts from the same location (e.g., ashtray) in clean paper or an envelope with sealed corners. Do not submit the ashtray unless a latent print examination is requested. Package the ashtray separately. Do not use plastic containers.

- Pick up **chewing gum** with gloved hands or clean forceps. Air-dry and place in clean paper or an envelope with sealed corners. Do not use plastic containers.

- Pick up **envelops and stamps** with gloved hands or clean forceps and place in a clean envelope. Do not use plastic containers.

Hair

- Pick up hair carefully with clean forceps to prevent damaging the root tissue.
- Air-dry hair mixed with suspected body fluids.
- Package each group of hair separately in clean paper or an envelope with sealed corners. Do not use plastic containers.
- Refrigerate and submit as soon as possible to the Laboratory.

Tissues, Bones, and Teeth

- Pick up suspected tissues, bones, and teeth with gloved hands or clean forceps.
- Collect 1–2 cubic inches of red skeletal muscle.
- Collect 3–5 inches of long bone such as the fibula or femur.
- Collect teeth in the following order:
    1. nonrestored molar.
    2. nonrestored premolar.
    3. nonrestored canine.
    4. nonrestored front tooth.
    5. restored molar.
    6. restored premolar.
    7. restored canine.
    8. restored front tooth.
- Place tissue samples in a clean, airtight plastic container without formalin or formaldehyde. Place teeth and bone samples in clean paper or an envelope with sealed corners.
- Freeze the evidence, place in Styrofoam containers, and ship overnight on dry ice.

Answers to Review Questions

Chapter 1
Facts and Concepts

1. Forensic science is the application of science to law.

2. The first system of personal identification was called *anthropometry*. It distinguished one individual from another based on a series of body measurements.

3. Francis Henry Galton undertook the first definitive study of fingerprints and developed a methodology of classifying them for filing.

4. Mathieu Orfila is known as "the father of forensic toxicology" because he published the first scientific treatise on the detection of poisons and their effects on animals, a work that established forensic toxicology as a legitimate scientific endeavor.

5. Hans Gross wrote the first treatise describing the application of scientific disciplines to the field of criminal investigation. He also introduced the forensic journal *Archiv für Kriminal Anthropologie und Kriminalistik*, which still reports improved methods of scientific crime detection.

6. b

7. Karl Landsteiner and Louis Lattes are associated with blood typing.

8. Edmond Locard first applied the principles of forensic science to a working crime laboratory.

9. Locard's exchange principle states that when two objects come into contact with each other, a cross-transfer of materials occurs.

10. Walter C. McCrone made significant contributions to forensic science using the microscope.

11. Los Angeles boasts the oldest forensic laboratory in the United States.

12. The world's largest forensic laboratory is the FBI Laboratory.

13. Four major reasons for the increase in the number of crime laboratories in the United States since the 1960s are as follows: (1) the fact that the requirement to advise criminal suspects of their constitutional rights and their right of immediate access to counsel has all but eliminated confessions as a routine investigative tool; (2) the staggering increase in crime rates in the United States; (3) the fact that all illicit-drug seizures must be sent to a forensic laboratory for confirmatory chemical analysis before the case can be adjudicated in court; and (4) the advent of DNA profiling.

14. Demand for DNA analysis is expected to lead to a dramatic increase in the number of crime lab personnel.

15. Four government agencies that offer forensic services at the federal level are the FBI; the Drug Enforcement Administration; the Bureau of Alcohol, Tobacco, Firearms and Explosives; and the U.S. Postal Inspection Service.

16. c

17. Three advantages of having regional laboratories operating as part of a statewide system are (1) increasing the accessibility of local law enforcement agencies to a crime laboratory; (2) minimizing duplication of services; and (3) ensuring maximum interlaboratory cooperation through sharing of expertise and equipment.

18. The United States features a variety of independent laboratories, precluding the creation of a national system. By contrast, Great Britain has developed a national system of regional laboratories under the direction of the government's Home Office.

19. b

20. The toxicology unit examines body fluids and organs for drugs and poisons.

21. The firearms unit examines and compares tool marks.

22. Forensic odontologists identify victims by studying the teeth. Teeth are particularly useful for identification because they are composed of enamel, which is the hardest substance in the body. Thus, teeth outlast tissues and organs as decomposition begins.

23. The three basic functions of a forensic scientist are (1) analysis of physical evidence; (2) providing expert testimony; and (3) furnishing training in the proper recognition, collection, and preservation of physical evidence.

24. In *Frye* v. *United States*, the court ruled that in order to be admitted as evidence at trial, a questioned procedure, technique, or principle must be "generally accepted" by a meaningful segment of the relevant scientific community.

25. The Federal Rules of Evidence is an alternative to the *Frye* standard.

26. In *Daubert* v. *Merrell Dow Pharmaceuticals, Inc.*, the U.S. Supreme Court charged the trial judge with ensuring that an expert's testimony rests on a reliable foundation and is relevant to the case.

27. d

28. An expert witness is an individual whom the court determines to possess knowledge relevant to the trial that is not expected of the average layperson.

29. The ordinary or lay witness must give testimony that does not contain the personal opinions of the witness. On the other hand, the expert witness may express his or her personal opinion as to the significance of specific findings.

Application and Critical Thinking

1. There are a range of possible answers to this question. Under the British fee-for-service model, government budgets might limit the number and type of laboratory tests police and prosecutors may request. On the other hand, if they must pay fees for crime lab services, police

and prosecutors may be more careful about the types of evidence they submit. The fact that the U.S. model allows investigators to submit a theoretically unlimited amount of evidence for examination means that it might encourage police to spend more time and resources than are necessary to investigate a case. Under a fee-for-service model, police must be more efficient in their investigations. However, this can be a drawback in cases in which initial tests prove inconclusive and more extensive methods of examination are needed.

2. The note would be examined by the document examination unit; the revolver would be examined by both the firearms unit and the latent fingerprint unit; the traces of skin and blood would be examined by the biology unit.

3. Again, this question could have several answers, which might include greater expertise in crime-scene investigation, using the skills of experts in several areas of criminalistics, and reducing the workload on patrol officers.

4. On appeal, the defense raised the question of whether a new test that has not been generally accepted by the scientific community is admissible as evidence in court. The court rejected the appeal, arguing that "general acceptance," as stated in *Frye v. United States,* is not an absolute prerequisite to the admissibility of scientific evidence.

Case Analysis

1. The main legal issue was the validity of the scientific procedures the state used as evidence to show that Dr. Jascalevitch had murdered patients by administering the poison curare. The defense contended that the results of tests using those procedures should not be admitted as evidence because the procedures were relatively new and because there was no precedent of their use in previous court cases. The prosecution argued that the procedures were standard methods used widely in the field of toxicology and that there was thus no reason to regard them as invalid.

2. The court ruled that the results of the procedures could be allowed as evidence. Arguments in support of the decision include the following: (a) the fact that a procedure is new does not necessarily mean it is invalid or unreliable for use as evidence; and (b) lack of precedent should not bar a certain type of evidence from being admitted; doing so would prevent all new developments and discoveries from ever being used as evidence.

3. The primary scientific issue was whether the procedures cited as evidence by the prosecution could reliably and definitively determine whether curare was present in the victims' bodies. The defense challenged the evidence on two main points: (a) that the corpses had been subjected to environmental conditions that would have destroyed any traces of curare that might have been once been present, and therefore the presence of curare in the body of Nancy Savino hints of evidence planting; and (b) that the test results were not specific enough to prove the presence of curare in the other victims.

Chapter 2
Facts and Concepts

1. Physical evidence encompasses any and all objects that can establish that a crime has been committed or can link a crime and its victim or its perpetrator. Examples (others are acceptable) include hair, skin, fibers, fingerprints, blood, DNA, weapons, soil, glass, and documents.

2. The first step in processing a crime scene is to secure and isolate the scene.

3. It is important to exclude onlookers from a crime scene because every individual who enters the scene has the potential to destroy physical evidence.

4. Three methods for recording a crime scene are as follows:
    a. Photography. Advantage: unsurpassed in the definition of detail it provides.
    b. Sketches. Advantage: record precise distances between important points in the crime scene.
    c. Notes. Advantage: provide a source of detailed information about the scene for future reference.

5. The most important prerequisite for photographing a crime scene is for it to be unaltered.

6. c

7. The areas photographed should include the location in which the crime actually took place and all adjacent areas where important acts occurred immediately before or after the commission of the crime.

8. A rough sketch is a draft representation of all essential information and measurements, and is drawn at the crime scene. A finished sketch is a precise rendering of the crime scene, usually drawn to scale.

9. Notes taken at a crime scene must include a detailed written description of the scene with the location of items of physical evidence recovered; the time an item of physical evidence was discovered; by whom, how, and by whom it was packaged and marked; and the disposition of the item after it was collected.

10. How an investigator conducts a crime-scene search depends on the locale, the size of the area, and the actions of the suspect(s) and victim(s) at the scene.

11. Evidence from a murder scene that should be collected and sent to the forensic laboratory includes the victim's clothing; fingernail scrapings; head and pubic hairs; blood (for DNA typing); vaginal, anal, and oral swabs (in sex-related crimes); recovered bullets from the body; and hand swabs from shooting victims (for gunshot residue analysis). These items must be collected at the autopsy because once the body is buried, efforts at obtaining them may prove difficult or futile. Also, a lengthy delay in obtaining many of these items will diminish or destroy their forensic value.

12. Physical evidence must be handled and processed in a way that prevents any change from taking place between the time it is removed from the crime scene and the time it is received by the crime laboratory.

13. The integrity of evidence is best maintained when the item is kept in its original condition as found at the crime site.

14. Trace evidence should not normally be removed from articles at a crime scene. Instead, the entire object should

be sent to the laboratory for processing. If evidence is adhering to an object in a precarious manner, however, it should be removed and packaged. If evidence is found adhering to a large structure, such as a door, wall, or floor, it should be removed with a forceps or other appropriate tool.

15. A "druggist fold" consists of folding one end of a piece of paper over one-third, then folding the other end (one-third) over that, and repeating the process from the other two sides. After the paper is folded in this manner, the outside two edges are tucked into each other to produce a closed container that keeps the specimen from falling out. The "druggist fold" is a better way to store evidence than an ordinary mailing envelope because powders and fine particles will leak out of the corners of an envelope.

16. All items of evidence should be placed in separate containers to prevent damage through contact and cross-contamination.

17. Charred debris recovered from the scene of a suspicious fire must be sealed in an airtight container to prevent evaporation of volatile petroleum residues. Items of clothing found at a crime scene should be air-dried and placed individually in separate paper bags to ensure constant circulation of air through them and thus prevent the formation of mold and mildew.

18. Chain of custody is a list of all people who came into possession of an item of evidence. Failure to substantiate the evidence's chain of custody may lead to serious questions regarding the authenticity and integrity of the evidence and the examinations of it.

19. A standard/reference sample is an item of physical evidence whose origin is known, such as blood or hair from a suspect, that can be compared to crime-scene evidence. The quality and quantity of standard/reference specimens often determine the evidential value of crime-scene evidence.

20. A substrate control is uncontaminated surface material close to an area where physical evidence has been deposited. This sample is used to ensure that the surface on which a sample has been deposited does not interfere with laboratory tests.

21. b

22. An autopsy is normally performed if the cause of death is suspicious or unexplained.

23. Rigor mortis is a medical condition that occurs after death and results in the stiffening of body parts in the position they are in when death occurs. Livor mortis is a medical condition that occurs after death and results in the settling of blood in areas of the body closest to the ground. Algor mortis refers to postmortem changes that cause a body to lose heat. They are important to the forensic pathologist because they offer several ways to approximate the time of death.

24. c

25. Forensic anthropology is concerned primarily with identifying and examining human skeletal remains. A forensic anthropologist might identify a victim by examining bones for specific characteristics, such as sex, age, race, or traces of injury. A forensic anthropologist

might also identify a victim by creating a facial reconstruction.

26. A forensic entomologist studies the development of insect larvae in a body to estimate time of death. These determinations are not always straightforward because the rate at which the larvae develop is affected by environmental influences such as geographical location, climate, and weather conditions.

Application and Critical Thinking

1. There can be a wide range of correct answers to this question. These might include objects being broken or trampled by onlookers; blood or other fluids being obliterated or contaminated by contact; fibers, hairs, and other items from onlookers being left at the scene; onlookers who obliterate fingerprints or leave their own fingerprints; or intentional removal of an item of evidence.

2. Missing elements are the time, a description of the type of crime, and measurements of the scene.

3. An investigator would likely collect standard/reference samples of hair, fibers, and blood because these items are most likely to have been transferred from the perpetrator to the victim, and vice versa, during a long struggle.

4. Rigor mortis would be unsuitable if the victim has been dead longer than thirty-six hours because the condition disappears after this time. Livor mortis ceases twelve hours after death, so it would be of limited value in estimating time of death after this period had elapsed. Algor mortis would not be an accurate method for estimating time of death if the body was stored in a particularly hot or cold environment, because this would affect the rate at which the body lost heat.

5. a. a forensic entomologist
   b. a forensic odontologist
   c. a forensic anthropologist

Case Analysis

1. The first challenge investigators faced was destruction of evidence. Mexican authorities autopsied the bodies twice before the corpses had been inspected, which likely destroyed potentially helpful evidence. Authorities also prevented forensic scientists from examining the corpses until the bodies had decomposed significantly. Mexican police removed all of the obvious evidence from the residence where the victims were held before allowing the FBI forensic team to enter the scene. Mexican authorities later seized a license plate found hidden at the scene and would not allow FBI agents to examine it or to conduct any further searches of the property. In addition, Mexican authorities destroyed much of the evidence that had been collected from the crime scene for "health reasons." The second main challenge was contamination of crime scenes linked to the murders. The location where the bodies were discovered was not sealed by police, thus allowing both police officers and onlookers to contaminate the scene. Also, the residence at 881 Lope De Vega—where the victims were believed to have been killed—was cleaned and painted before forensics experts had a chance to

examine it. In addition, Mexican federal police officers had been living in the residence since shortly after the time of the murders, further contaminating the scene.

2. Investigators collected reference samples of carpeting from the victims' bodies as well as bits of the victims' clothing and the sheets in which the bodies were buried. The carpet samples matched samples taken from the residence at 881 Lope De Vega, where investigators suspected the victims were killed. The samples of burial sheet matched pillowcases found at the residence, and bits of clothing matching that worn by the victims were also found at the residence. In addition, hair and blood samples matching those of the victims were found in the residence at 881 Lope De Vega.

3. Investigators found that soil samples from the victims' bodies did not match the soil from the area where the bodies were found. They also found no significant bodily fluids in the area where the bodies were found. This evidence suggested that the bodies originally had been buried elsewhere and later transported to the location where they were found. Investigators later compared soil samples from the victims' bodies to samples taken from a park where the bodies of two Americans killed by drug traffickers had been discovered. Soil samples from the bodies of Camarena and Zavala exactly matched the soil found at the location where the Americans' bodies were found.

Chapter 3
Facts and Concepts

1. Biological materials include blood, saliva, semen, DNA, hair, organs, and physiological fluids. Impressions include tire markings, shoe prints, depressions in soft soils, all other forms of tracks, glove and other fabric impressions, tool marks, and bite marks. Manufactured items include firearms, ammunition, fibers, paint, glass, petroleum products, plastic bags, rubber, polymers, and vehicle headlights.

2. The purpose of identification is to determine the physical or chemical identity of a substance with as near absolute certainty as existing analytical techniques will permit. Identification first requires the adoption of testing procedures that give characteristic results for specific standard materials. Identification also requires that the number and type of tests needed to identify a substance be sufficient to exclude all other substances.

3. It is not possible to define a simple analytical scheme that can be applied to all types of evidence because (1) each type of evidence obviously requires different tests; (2) each test has a different degree of specificity; and (3) the practitioner has little or no control over the quality and quantity of the specimens received.

4. A comparison analysis subjects a suspect specimen and a standard/reference specimen to the same tests and examinations to determine whether they have a common origin. The first step in comparison is to choose specific combinations of properties from the suspect and the standard/reference specimen for comparison. The second

step is for the forensic scientist to render a conclusion about whether the specimens come from the same source.

5. Individual characteristics are properties of evidence that can be attributed to a common source with an extremely high degree of certainty. Examples include the ridge characteristics of fingerprints, random striations (markings) on bullets or tools, irregular and random wear patterns in tire or footwear impressions, handwriting characteristics, and the irregular edges of broken objects fitted together in the manner of a jigsaw puzzle.

6. Class characteristics are properties of evidence that can be associated only with a group and never with a single source. Examples include paint chips, random glass fragments, blood, and artificial fibers.

7. The product rule states that multiplying together the frequencies of independently occurring factors allows one to determine an overall frequency of occurrence for that combination of factors. The product rule can be used to show the likelihood of two pieces of evidence containing the exact same set of characteristics.

8. The product rule suggests that, as the number of different objects linking an individual to a crime increases, the probability of that person being involved increases dramatically. In the case of Wayne Williams, twenty-eight different types of fibers linked Williams to several murder victims, making it extremely likely that Williams was responsible for the killings.

9. The greatest weakness of class physical evidence is that it cannot relate physical evidence to a common origin with a high degree of certainty. Evidence possessing class characteristics can be associated only with a group and never with a single source.

10. The value of class physical evidence lies in its ability to corroborate events with data in a manner that is, as nearly as possible, free of human error and bias.

11. d

12. It is important to consider the relevance of scientific evidence before allowing it to be introduced into a criminal case because physical evidence is accorded great weight during jury deliberations. In addition, failure to take proper safeguards when determining the relevance of evidence may unfairly prejudice a case against the accused.

13. A forensic scientist often opts not to use the most sensitive analytical techniques when comparing suspect substances because, carried to the extreme, no two things in this world are alike in every detail. Measurements that are extremely sensitive may show differences between two samples that suggest the samples came from difference sources even though they actually came from the same source.

14. A forensic database is a computerized archive of information relating to a specific type of physical evidence. Such databases make it much easier for a forensic scientist to link a suspect to the commission of a crime through comparative analysis of evidence.

15. Forensic databases include the Integrated Automated Fingerprint Identification System (IAFIS), a national fingerprint and criminal history system maintained by the FBI; the Combined DNA Index System (CODIS), which

stores DNA profiles; the National Integrated Ballistics Information Network (NIBIN), which contains records of markings made by firearms on bullets and cartridge casings recovered from crime scenes; the International Forensic Automotive Paint Data Query (PDQ) database, which contains chemical and color information pertaining to original automotive paints; and SICAR (shoeprint image capture and retrieval) contains a comprehensive shoe sole database that includes more than three hundred manufacturers of shoes with more than eight thousand different sole patterns.

16. The forensic index contains DNA profiles from unsolved crime-scene evidence. The offender index contains the profiles of convicted or arrested individuals.

17. Crime-scene reconstruction is the method used to support a likely sequence of events by observing and evaluating physical evidence, as well as statements made by those involved with the incident.

18. a, c, and e

19. The first and most important step in crime-scene reconstruction is securing and protecting the crime scene.

20. Examples of specialized tasks a criminalist might perform as part of crime-scene reconstruction are (1) using a laser beam to plot the approximate bullet path; (2) blood spatter analysis; (3) determining the direction of impact of projectiles penetrating glass objects; (4) locating gunshot residues deposited on the victim's clothing to estimate the distance of a shooter from a target; and (5) searching for primer residues deposited on the hands of a suspect shooter.

Application and Critical Thinking

1. Determining whether an unknown substance contains heroin would require the least extensive testing, because the investigator can select only procedures that are designed to identify the presence of heroin. Determining whether an unknown substance contains an illicit drug would require the next most extensive testing regime, because the investigator must select as many procedures as necessary to test for all types of illicit drugs. Determining the composition of an unknown substance would likely require the most extensive testing, because of the extremely large number of possible substances to test for.

2. From most common to least common, the order would be a, c, and b.

3. a. class characteristic
   b. individual characteristic
   c. individual characteristic
   d. class characteristic
   e. individual characteristic
   f. class characteristic
   g. individual characteristic
   h. individual characteristic

4. PDQ and SICAR contain information that relates primarily to evidence exhibiting class characteristics. The paint finishes and sole prints in these databases can identify the manufacturer of a shoe or paint mixture, but cannot determine the exact source of evidence that matches the samples stored in the database. CODIS, IAFIS, and NIBIN, on the other hand, contain information that relates primarily to evidence exhibiting individual characteristics. The DNA profiles, fingerprints, and striation markings stored in these databases are unique, and thus can be used to link specific individuals or weapons with a crime scene.

Case Analysis

1. The Williams case was notable for the fact that fiber evidence was used to tie a large number of murder victims to a single suspect. Also, fiber evidence is typically used to support other evidence and testimony in court. In the Williams trial, the fiber evidence was the centerpiece of the state's case, and other testimony was used to support the fiber evidence.

2. Investigators hoped to learn the source of the fibers. To do this, they studied the fibers under a microscope and photographed the fibers' cross-sectional shape. The investigators then showed the photographs to chemists and textiles experts to see if they could identify the likely source of the fibers. The investigators learned that a yellowish-green fiber was probably from a carpet, but that its shape was not common. The fact that the fiber was relatively rare meant that it probably was not widely used. This significantly reduced the number of possible locations where the murders could have occurred, making it easier for investigators to focus their search for a suspect.

3. Information about the source of the fiber could help investigators determine where the crime might have occurred, which could lead them to a suspect. If investigators know who produced the item from which the fibers came, they can contact the manufacturer and get a list of local stores or individuals who purchased the item before the crime occurred. Interviews with the purchasers may provide investigators with leads to suspects or other information that can help them solve the case.

4. Investigators found that the company produced a carpet using the same rare type of fiber in the same color as that found on Cater's body and in Williams's home. This meant that there was at least a probable connection between Williams and Cater. Investigators also learned that the company used that type of fiber in their carpets for only one year. This significantly narrowed the number of places where such carpeting might be found. During the year the carpet was manufactured using the rare fiber, only a small amount was sold in the southeastern United States. This further narrowed the possible number of rooms in Georgia in which the carpet could have been installed. The extremely small number of possible locations where the carpet could be found in the Atlanta area meant that there could be very few likely suspects besides Williams.

5. The investigators used probability to connect the fibers found on Nathaniel Cater's body and Williams's home. By demonstrating that there was an extremely low probability that the fibers came from any place but

Williams's home and car, prosecutors were able to tie Williams to Cater's murder. Investigators also used probability to tie fibers and hairs found on other Atlanta-area murder victims to Williams. Prosecutors showed that each of the victims' bodies contained traces of fibers matching those found in Williams's home and cars and/or hair belonging to Williams's dog. They pointed out that there was an extremely low probability of finding so many matching fibers and hairs on several different individuals. The only reasonable explanation, they argued, was that all the victims had contact with a common source of the fibers and hairs, namely Williams.

Chapter 4
Facts and Concepts

1. A physical property describes a substance without reference to any other substance. A chemical property describes the behavior of a substance when it reacts or combines with another substance.

2. Matter is anything that has mass and occupies space. An element is a fundamental particle of matter that cannot be broken down into simpler substances by chemical means. Elements provide the building blocks from which all matter is composed.

3. The smallest particle of an element that can exist and still retain its identity as that element is the atom.

4. A compound is a pure substance composed of two or more elements. Three common compounds are water (H_2O), carbon dioxide (CO_2), and salt ($NaCl$).

5. The smallest unit of a compound is a molecule.

6. The three states of matter are solid, liquid, and gas. The state in which matter exists is determined by the strength of the attractive forces between its molecules.

7. Examples of change in state include liquid water turning into steam when heated; liquid water turning into ice when chilled; ice turning into water when heated; and dry ice turning into carbon dioxide vapor when stored at room temperature.

8. Sublimation is a change of state from a solid to a gas.

9. Changes of state are physical changes. When a substance changes state, the only thing that has been altered are the attractive forces between among its molecules. The substance retains the same chemical identity.

10. A phase is a uniform body of matter distinguished from other matter by definite visible boundaries. Oil floating on water is an example of a two-phase system.

11. a

12. Dispersion is the process of separating light into component colors. Because each color corresponds to a different range of frequencies or wavelengths of light, light rays of one color bend to a different degree than rays of all other colors.

13. Refraction is the bending of light waves because of a change in velocity.

14. Color is a visual indication of the fact that objects absorb certain portions of visible light and transmit or reflect others. Forensic scientists have learned to characterize

different chemical substances by the type and quantity of light they absorb.

15. Different types of electromagnetic radiation are distinguished from one another by their frequency.

16. The particle theory of light must be invoked to describe its behavior when radiation is absorbed by a substance.

17. Temperature is a measure of heat intensity, or the amount of heat in a substance. The two most common temperature scales are the Fahrenheit and Celsius scales.

18. Weight is the force with which gravity attracts a body. Mass is a constant property of matter that reflects the amount of material present. The mass of an object remains the same everywhere, while weight can vary depending on the force of gravity at a particular location.

19. The mass of an object is determined by comparing it against the known mass of standard objects. Three devices used for comparing the masses of different objects are the equal-arm balance, the top-loading balance, and the single-pan analytical balance.

20. The formula for calculating the density of an object is mass per unit volume.

21. An intensive property is a property that remains the same regardless of the size of a substance. Intensive properties of matter include mass, density, and refractive index.

22. d

23. The main ingredient in ordinary glass is sand.

24. Soda-lime glass is used commonly in bottles and windows. The name comes from the fact that soda and lime are added to the glass to make it easier to work and to prevent it from dissolving in water.

25. Tempered glass is glass made stronger by introducing stress through rapid heating and cooling of the glass surfaces. When tempered glass breaks, it does not shatter but rather fragments or "dices" into small squares with little splintering. It is used in the side and rear windows of U.S.-built cars. Laminated glass is created by sandwiching one layer of plastic between two pieces of ordinary window glass. It is used in the windshields of U.S.-built cars.

26. The only way to individualize glass fragments at a crime scene to a single source is to assemble the fragments and physically fit them together like a jigsaw puzzle.

27. The physical properties of density and refractive index are used most successfully for characterizing glass particles. The main drawback of using these properties to characterize glass is that they are class characteristics and as such will not provide the sole criteria for individualizing glass to a common source.

28. Flotation is a method for measuring the density of glass. In flotation, a standard/reference glass particle is immersed in a liquid whose composition is carefully adjusted until the object remains suspended in the liquid medium. At this point, the standard/reference glass and the liquid have the same density. Glass chips of approximately the same size and shape as the standard/reference glass are now added to the liquid for comparison. If both the unknown and the standard/reference particles remain suspended in the

2. Alcohol is the most widely abused drug in Western countries.

3. Metabolism is the transformation of a chemical in the body to other chemicals to facilitate its elimination from the body.

4. The three stages are absorption, distribution, and elimination. During absorption, a chemical substance enters the bloodstream. During distribution, the blood carries the substance to all watery parts of the body. During elimination, the substance is excreted from the body.

5. Alcohol does not concentrate in the fat, bones, and hair, because these parts of the body contain little water and alcohol tends to be distributed throughout the watery parts of the body.

6. Factors that influence the rate at which alcohol is absorbed include the total time taken to consume the drink, the alcohol content of the beverage, the amount consumed, and the quantity and type of food present in the stomach at the time of drinking.

7. d

8. Alcohol that is not oxidized is expelled unchanged in breath, perspiration, and urine.

9. The amount of alcohol exhaled in the breath is in direct proportion to the concentration of alcohol in the blood.

10. Blood-alcohol level is the accepted standard for relating alcohol intake to its effect on the body.

11. For a longer total time required for complete absorption, the peak blood-alcohol concentration will be lower.

12. The three types of blood vessels are arteries, veins, and capillaries. Arteries carry blood away from the heart, veins carry blood toward the heart, and capillaries connect the arteries with the veins.

13. Most alcohol is absorbed into the bloodstream through the walls of the small intestine. The remainder is absorbed through the stomach walls.

14. When the blood enters the lungs, it contains very little oxygen and a great deal of carbon dioxide.

15. Alveoli are small sacs in the lungs through whose walls air and other gases are exchanged between the breath and the blood. At the surface of the alveolar sacs, blood flowing through the capillaries comes in contact with fresh oxygenated air in the sacs. Oxygen passes through the walls of the alveoli into the blood while carbon dioxide is discharged from the blood into the air.

16. The most widespread method for rapidly determining alcohol intoxication is breath testing.

17. Breath testing is based on the observation that there is a fixed ratio between the concentration of alcohol in alveolar breath and the concentration of alcohol in the blood.

18. A fuel cell detector converts alcohol in alveolar breath into acetic acid, generating an electrical current that is proportional to the quantity of alcohol present in the breath. The stronger the current, the greater the concentration of alcohol in the subject's breath.

19. The key to the accuracy of a breath-testing device is to ensure that the unit captures the alcohol in the alveolar breath (deep-lung breath) of the subject. This is typically accomplished by programming the unit to accept approximately 1.5 liters of breath from the subject. Also, the subject must blow for a minimum time with a minimum breath flow rate.

20. A slope detector is a device attached to a breath tester to ensure that the breath sample being measured is alveolar or deep-lung breath. As the subject blows into the instrument, the slope detector continuously monitors breath-alcohol concentration. The instrument accepts a breath sample only when consecutive measurements fall within a predetermined rate of change.

21. Mouth alcohol is alcohol present in a breath-test subject's mouth. The presence of mouth alcohol can cause the alcohol concentration detected in exhaled breath to be higher than the actual concentration in the blood. Potential sources of mouth alcohol include regurgitation, belching, recent intake of an alcoholic beverage, and recent gargling of an alcohol-containing mouthwash.

22. Field sobriety tests are normally performed to ascertain the degree of a suspect's physical impairment and whether an evidential test is justified. They include psychophysical tests and a breath test.

23. Walk and turn and the one-leg stand are divided-attention tasks. Walk and turn requires the suspect to maintain balance while standing heel-to-toe and at the same time listening to and comprehending the test instructions. During the walking stage, the suspect must walk a straight line, touching heel-to-toe for nine steps, then turn around on the line and repeat the process. The one-leg stand requires the suspect to maintain balance while standing with heels together listening to the instructions. During the balancing stage, the suspect must stand on one foot while holding the other foot several inches off the ground for 30 seconds; simultaneously, the suspect must count out loud during the 30-second time period.

24. Gas chromatography is the most widely used approach for determining alcohol levels in blood.

25. A nonalcoholic disinfectant must be applied to a subject's skin before drawing blood, to negate any argument that an alcoholic disinfectant may have inadvertently contributed to a falsely high blood-alcohol result.

26. An airtight container best ensures the preservation of blood samples.

27. An anticoagulant should be added to the blood sample to prevent clotting; a preservative should be added to inhibit the growth of microorganisms capable of destroying alcohol.

28. Failure to keep the blood refrigerated or to add a preservative may result in a substantial decline in alcohol concentration. Longer storage times may also reduce alcohol concentration.

29. It is best to collect a number of blood samples from different body sites because alcohol may be generated in a deceased individual as a result of bacterial action. Blood-alcohol levels attributed solely to alcohol consumption should result in nearly similar results for all blood samples collected from the same person.

30. The current legal measure of drunk driving in the United States is a blood-alcohol concentration of 0.08 percent

weight/volume, or 0.08 grams of alcohol per 100 milliliters of blood.

31. A per se law states that any individual meeting or exceeding a defined blood-alcohol level (usually 0.08 percent) shall be deemed intoxicated, and no other proof of alcohol impairment is necessary.

32. An implied-consent law states that the operator of a motor vehicle on a public highway must either consent to a test for alcohol intoxication, if requested, or lose his or her license for some designated period—usually six months to one year. Implied-consent laws were implemented to prevent drivers from refusing to take a breath test on grounds of self-incrimination.

33. Challenges facing the toxicologist include the following: (1) The toxicologist is not dealing with drugs at the concentration levels found in powders and pills. By the time a drug specimen reaches the toxicology laboratory, it has been dissipated and distributed throughout the body. (2) Few substances enter and completely leave the body in the same chemical state.

34. Blood and urine should be collected from any suspected drug user.

35. Alcohol, marijuana, and cocaine account for 90 percent or more of the drugs encountered in a typical toxicology laboratory.

36. The first task of a forensic toxicologist when establishing an analytical scheme to detect and identify drugs is to remove and isolate drugs and other toxic agents from the biological materials submitted as evidence.

37. An acid is a compound capable of donating a hydrogen ion (H^+) to another compound. A base is a compound capable of accepting a hydrogen ion (H^+). By controlling the acidity or basicity of a water solution into which blood, urine, or tissues are dissolved, a toxicologist can control the type of drug that will be recovered. Acid drugs are easily extracted from an acidified water solution with organic solvents, while basic drugs are readily removed from a basic water solution with organic solvents.

38. A screening test gives quick insight into the likelihood that a specimen contains a drug substance. It allows a toxicologist to examine a large number of specimens within a short period of time for a wide range of drugs. A confirmation test identifies a specific drug or drugs.

39. The three most widely used screening tests are thin-layer chromatography (TLC), gas chromatography (GC), and immunoassay. Gas chromatography/mass spectrometry is generally accepted as the confirmation test of choice.

40. a

41. Oxygen normally combines with hemoglobin, which transports the oxygen throughout the body. However, carbon monoxide in the bloodstream also combines with hemoglobin, reducing the amount of hemoglobin left to carry oxygen. If enough hemoglobin combines with carbon monoxide, not enough is left to carry sufficient oxygen to the tissues, and death by asphyxiation follows.

42. Factors in addition to blood concentration levels that must be considered before drawing conclusions about a subject's drug-induced behavior include age, physical condition, the tolerance of the drug user, and the additive or synergistic effects caused by the interaction of two or more drugs.

43. The concentration of a drug present in urine is a poor indicator of how extensively an individual's behavior or state is influenced by the drug because urine is formed outside the body's circulatory system, and consequently drug levels can build up in it over a relatively long period of time.

Application and Critical Thinking

1. a. Randy is four times as likely to have an accident as a sober person.

   b. Marissa's blood-alcohol concentration is approximately 0.13.

   c. Charles is more intoxicated; his blood-alcohol concentration is approximately 0.11.

   d. At the original NHTSA standard of 0.15, an individual is about twenty-five times as likely to have an accident as a sober person.

2. John, Gary, Frank, Stephen

3. Bill and Carrie are both legally drunk in Australia and Sweden. Sally is legally drunk in Sweden. Rich is legally drunk in all three countries.

4. Barbiturates are acidic drugs, which means they have a pH less than 7. You can use this knowledge to devise a simple test to determine which blood sample contains barbiturates. First, you would dissolve blood from each sample into separate containers of water. To each container you would add an acidic substance such as hydrochloric acid (to make the water more acidic). Then you would add an organic solvent such as chloroform to the water in each container. The blood sample containing barbiturates will be easily identified, because acidic drugs are readily removed from a acidic solution with an organic solvent.

5. To determine whether the victim died before or as a result of the fire, you would measure the level of carbon monoxide in the victim's blood. High levels of carbon monoxide in the victim's blood would indicate that he or she breathed the combustion products of the fire and was therefore alive when the fire started. Low levels of carbon monoxide would indicate that the victim did not breathe the combustion products of the fire and was therefore dead before the fire started.

Chapter 7
Facts and Concepts

1. Two types of images are virtual images and real images. A real image can be seen directly with the naked eye; a virtual image can be seen only by a viewer looking through a lens.

2. The eyepiece lens is the upper lens through which the viewer looks. The objective lens is the lower lens that is positioned directly over the specimen.

3. Transparent illumination is light directed up toward and through a specimen from an illuminator built into the base of the microscope. It is used to view transparent

specimens. Vertical or reflected illumination is light from a source above the specimen that reflects off the specimen's surface and into the lens system of the microscope. It is used to view opaque specimens.

4. A condenser is a lens system under the microscope stage that collects light rays from the base illuminator and focuses them on the specimen. The simplest condenser is the Abbé condenser, which consists of two lenses held together in a metal mount.

5. Parfocal describes a microscope such that when an image is focused with one objective in position, the other objective can be rotated into place by revolving the nosepiece and the field will remain in focus.

6. A monocular microscope has one eyepiece; a binocular microscope has two eyepieces.

7. One determines the total magnification of a compound microscope by multiplying the magnifying power of the eyepiece lens by the magnifying power of the objective lens.

8. Numerical aperture describes the ability of an objective lens to resolve details into separate images instead of one blurred image.

9. The maximum useful magnification for a compound microscope is approximately 1,000 times the N.A. of the objective lens being used. Any effort to increase the total magnification beyond this figure will yield no additional detail.

10. When you increase a compound microscope's magnification, its field of view decreases. Because of this, the microscopist is likely to begin by selecting a low magnification in which a good general overall view of the specimen is seen and to switch later to a higher power in which a smaller portion of the specimen can be viewed in more detail.

11. A comparison microscope is two compound microscopes combined into one unit. Ordinary and compound microscopes allow the user to view only one specimen at a time; a comparison microscope permits the user to view two separate specimens side-by-side.

12. It is important to closely match the optical characteristics of the objective lenses in a comparison microscope to ensure that both specimens are seen at equal magnification and with minimal but identical lens distortions.

13. The most frequently used and versatile microscope found in the crime laboratory is the stereoscopic microscope. Three reasons why this type of microscope is so widely used are its wide field of view, great depth of focus, and potentially large working distance (the distance between the objective lens and the specimen).

14. Plane-polarized light is light confined to a single plane of vibration.

15. Minerals in soil and synthetic fibers are often characterized using a polarizing microscope.

16. A microspectrophotometer is an instrument that links a microscope to a spectrophotometer. The advantage it enjoys over the spectrophotometer for analyzing physical evidence is that it can examine the very small particles frequently encountered as evidence, whereas the spectrophotometer cannot easily examine such small specimens.

17. In the SEM, a hot tungsten filament emits a beam of electrons, which is focused by electromagnets onto the surface of the specimen. This primary electron beam causes the elements that make up the upper layers of the specimen to emit electrons known as secondary electrons. About 20–30 percent of the primary electrons rebound off the surface of the specimen. These electrons are known as backscattered electrons. The emitted electrons (both secondary and backscattered) are collected, and the amplified signal is displayed on a cathode-ray or TV tube. By scanning the primary electron beam across the specimen's surface in synchronization with the cathode-ray tube, the SEM converts the emitted electrons into an image of the specimen that is displayed on the cathode-ray tube.

18. The three attractions of the SEM image are its high magnification, high resolution, and great depth of focus.

19. An X-ray analyzer can be coupled to an SEM to produce a picture of the elemental distribution of a specimen. Gunshot particles are lifted from the shooter's hands with a piece of adhesive tape, which is then examined under the SEM for the particles that may have originated from the bullet primer. When the gunshot residue is exposed to a beam of electrons from the SEM, X-rays are emitted and passed into a detector, where they are converted into electrical signals. These signals are sorted and displayed according to the energies of the emitted X-rays, which can reveal the presence of lead, antimony, and barium, which are frequently found in most primers.

Application and Critical Thinking

1. Total magnification of each combination is as follows:
   - for the 10× eyepiece: 40×, 100×, 250×, and 1,000×
   - for the 15× eyepiece: 60×, 150×, 375×, and 1,500×
   - for the 20× eyepiece: 80×, 200×, 500×, and 2,000×

   A forensic scientist would be unlikely to use either the 15× or 20× eyepiece in combination with the 100× objective because 1000× is the highest useful total magnification that one can achieve with a compound microscope. Further magnification beyond this figure yields no additional detail.

2. a. A comparison microscope would be used because it allows the forensic scientist to view the images of two separate specimens side-by-side.

   b. A microspectrophotometer would be used because it can produce an infrared "fingerprint" spectrum that reveals the unique chemical composition of the paint chips.

   c. A polarizing microscope would be used because birefringent materials polarize light that strikes them, creating two beams of light with different refractive indices at right angles to one another. The polarizing microscope can help the scientist determine the refractive index of each plane of light, which can then be used to identify the mineral(s) present.

   d. A stereoscopic microscope would be used because its large working distance allows the user to view the entire object being studied.

   e. A scanning electron microscope (SEM) would be used because it can magnify specimens up to 100,000 times.

Case Analysis

1. The main aspects of the rail noted by Koehler were the presence of nail holes, the general condition of the wood, and the quality of the lumber used to make the rail. The nail holes were not made during the construction of the ladder, which indicated that the wood had been used for another purpose before being made into a ladder rail. The fact that the holes were clean and free of rust suggested that the wood was used inside and not exposed to the elements. The spacing of the nail holes suggested that the wood likely was used in a barn, garage, or attic. The wood itself was also in good shape and not weathered, further confirming that it was used inside. The lumber was of a poor quality, meaning it would have been used for rough construction (such as a floor or wall joist) and not finished work (such as a doorframe or decorative trim).

2. Koehler found notches in surfaces and on the edges of the ladder rails that were caused by a defect in the cutting heads of the planer used to finish the wood. By measuring the distance between the notches, Koehler was able to calculate the speed at which the rails passed through the planer. His calculations showed that surfaces and edges of the wood moved through the planer at different speeds. This difference in speed told Koehler that the planer was belt-driven. Information about the speed and type of the planer helped narrow down the number of lumber mills that could possibly have produced the wood.

3. Koehler reasoned that because the wood was inexpensive, it would not be profitable to ship it very far from where it was milled. Because the ladder was found in New Jersey, Koehler believed it must have been milled somewhere in the Atlantic States region. This information helped narrow the number of possible mills to those along the Atlantic coast. When authorities contacted these mills they found only a handful that used planers of the type and speed used to mill the ladder rails. When the investigators asked for samples of wood from these mills, they found a sample that had the same notches as found on the ladder rails. This allowed the investigators to pinpoint the mill that produced the wood.

4. Koehler found marks on the wood that were made by a hand planer. He discovered that these marks were comparable to those made by a hand planer found at Hauptmann's house. In addition, investigators found that a section of board had been sawed out of the floor joists in Hauptmann's attic. The nail holes in the ladder rail aligned perfectly with the nail holes in the floor joists. Also, the grain pattern of the wood used in the rail was an exact match with the grain pattern in the remaining portion of the floor joist that had been cut to make the ladder. These facts clearly connected Hauptmann with the ladder used in the kidnapping.

Chapter 8
Facts and Concepts

1. Karl Landsteiner discovered that blood is distinguishable by its group or type.

2. The blood factors belonging to the A-B-O system are the most important for properly matching a donor and recipient for a transfusion.

3. Characterizing biological evidence by select regions of DNA supplanted blood typing for associating bloodstain evidence with a particular individual.

4. Plasma is the fluid portion of the blood. It accounts for 55 percent of blood content.

5. a

6. An antigen is a substance that stimulates the body to produce antibodies against it. An antibody is a protein in the blood serum that destroys or inactivates a specific antigen. Antibodies are contained in the blood serum.

7. Every red blood cell contains either an A antigen, a B antigen, or no antigen (this is called type O). The type of antigen on one's red blood cells determines one's A-B-O blood type. People with type A blood have A antigens on their red blood cells, those with type B blood have B antigens, and those with type O blood have no antigens on their red blood cells.

8. Rh factor (D antigen) is the fourth important antigen other than A, B, and O.

9. When serum containing B antibodies is added to red blood cells carrying the B antigen, the blood agglutinates, or clots. This does not happen when serum containing B antibodies is added to red blood cells carrying the A antigen because an antibody reacts only with its specific antigen and no other.

10. Serology is the study of antigen and serum antibody reactions. The most widespread application of serology is the typing of whole blood for its A-B-O identity. It is also finding application in the detection of drugs in blood and urine.

11. To produce antibodies capable of reacting with drugs, the analyst first combines a specific drug with a protein and injects this combination into an animal such as a rabbit. This drug–protein complex acts as an antigen, stimulating the animal to produce antibodies. The recovered blood serum of the animal now contains antibodies that are specific or nearly specific to the drug.

12. The enzyme-multiplied immunoassay technique (EMIT) has gained widespread popularity among toxicologists because of its speed and high sensitivity for detecting drugs in urine. It is frequently used to screen the urine of suspected marijuana users.

13. The greatest problem associated with detecting marijuana in urine is that is it is difficult to determine when the individual actually used marijuana.

14. Monoclonal antibodies are designed to attack one and only one site on an antigen. Polyclonal antibodies attack a variety of different sites on an antigen.

15. The criminalist must answer the following questions when examining dried blood: (1) Is it blood? (2) From what species did the blood originate? (3) If the blood is human, how closely can it be associated with a particular individual?

16. The most common color test for bloodstains is the Kastle-Meyer test. This test is based on the fact that enzymes called peroxidases accelerate the oxidation of hemoglobin in the blood. When a bloodstain is subjected to this test, oxidation of the hemoglobin in the blood produces a deep pink color.

17. To detect bloodstains, luminol reagent is sprayed onto suspect items and the room containing the items is darkened. Any bloodstains produce a faint blue glow, known as luminescence.

18. Microcrystalline tests are far less sensitive than color tests for blood identification. They are also more susceptible to interference from contaminants that may be present in the material.

19. The standard test used to determine whether blood is of human or animal origin is the precipitin test. This test is based on the fact that when animals (usually rabbits) are injected with human blood, antibodies are formed that react with the invading human blood to neutralize its presence.

20. Gel diffusion takes advantage of the fact that antibodies and antigens move toward one another on a plate coated with a medium made from a natural polymer called agar.

21. In electrophoresis, antigens and antibodies can be induced to move toward one another under the influence of an electrical field.

22. In general, the harder and less porous the surface, the less spatter.

23. The direction of travel of blood striking an object may be discerned by the stain's shape. The pointed end of a bloodstain always faces its direction of travel.

24. A drop of blood striking a surface at right angles produces a nearly circular stain. As the angle decreases, the stain elongates.

25. The origin of a blood spatter in a two-dimensional configuration can be established by drawing straight lines through the long axis of several individual bloodstains. The intersection or area of convergence of the lines represents the point from which the blood emanated.

26. The gene is the basic unit of heredity. A chromosome is a threadlike structure in the cell nucleus along which the genes are located.

27. Most human cells contain forty-six chromosomes, arranged in twenty-three mated pairs. The only exceptions are the human reproductive cells, the egg and sperm, which contain twenty-three unmated chromosomes.

28. During fertilization, a sperm and egg combine so that each contributes twenty-three chromosomes to form the new cell, or zygote, that develops into the offspring. The chromosomes from a parent carry that parent's genes, so the new individual begins life with twenty-three mated chromosome pairs, each carrying genetic material from one of the parents. In this way, the new individual inherits genetic material from each parent.

29. An allele is any of several alternative forms of genes that influence a given characteristic and that are aligned with one another on a chromosome pair.

30. A heterozygous gene pair is made up of two different alleles; a homozygous gene pair is made up of two similar alleles.

31. When two different genes are inherited, the characteristic coded for by a dominant gene is expressed. The characteristic coded for by a recessive gene remains hidden.

32. A genotype is the particular combination of genes present in the cells of an individual. A phenotype is the physical manifestation of a genetic trait such as shape, color, or blood type. An individual's genotype can be determined only by studying his or her family history.

33. Blood typing has important implications in disputed-paternity cases.

34. The best way to locate and characterize a seminal stain is to perform the acid phosphatase test. The acid phosphates test is particularly useful when it is necessary to search many garments or large fabric areas for seminal stains.

35. Oligospermia is an abnormally low sperm count. Aspermia is the absence of sperm, or sterility in males.

36. The presence of prostate specific antigen (PSA), or p30, proves that a sample stain contains semen. Two techniques used to detect this protein are electrophoresis and monoclonal antibody testing.

37. A rape victim must disrobe while standing on a sheet of paper so that the investigator can collect in the paper any loose foreign material that falls from the clothing.

38. Besides swabs, blood and urine samples should be collected from a rape victim during a medical examination.

39. The following items should be collected from the suspected perpetrator of a sexual assault: all clothing and any other items believed to have been worn at the time of the assault, pubic hair combings, pulled or cut head and pubic hair standard/reference samples, a penile swab (when appropriate to the case history), and a blood sample or buccal swab for DNA typing.

40. Motile sperm generally survive for up to four to six hours in the vaginal cavity of a living female. Nonmotile sperm may be found in a living female for up to three days after intercourse and occasionally up to six days.

Application and Critical Thinking

1. a. Drops 1, 5, and 8 struck the surface closest to a 90-degree angle. This can be determined because they are the most nearly circular of the drops, and a drop of blood striking a surface at right angles produces a nearly circular stain.

    b. Drops 3, 4, and 9 struck the surface farthest from a 90-degree angle. This can be determined because they are the most elongated of the drops, and as the angle at which the drop falls decreases, the stain elongates.

    c. Drop 2 was traveling from right to left when it struck the surface. Drop 7 was traveling from bottom to top. This can be determined because the pointed end of the spatter faces the top, and the pointed end of a bloodstain always faces its direction of travel.

2. a. Types A and B are equally likely to be expressed because four of the twelve possible genotypes in the group will be expressed as type A and four will be expressed as type B. The least likely to be expressed is type O; only one of the possible genotypes will result in an offspring with type O blood.

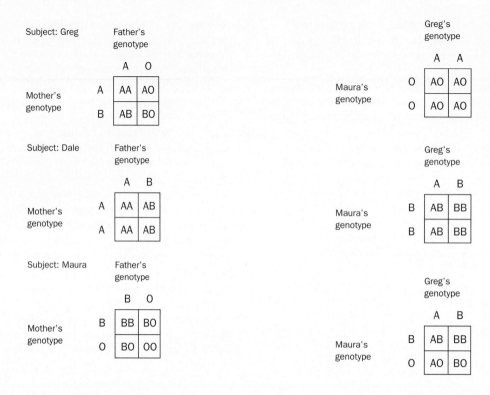

Subject: Greg

Father's genotype

	A	O
A	AA	AO
B	AB	BO

Mother's genotype

Subject: Dale

Father's genotype

	A	B
A	AA	AB
A	AA	AB

Mother's genotype

Subject: Maura

Father's genotype

	B	O
B	BB	BO
O	BO	OO

Mother's genotype

Greg's genotype

	A	A
O	AO	AO
O	AO	AO

Maura's genotype

Greg's genotype

	A	B
B	AB	BB
B	AB	BB

Maura's genotype

Greg's genotype

	A	B
B	AB	BB
O	AO	BO

Maura's genotype

b. Greg is most likely to have type A blood because two of his possible genotypes (AA and AO) are expressed as type A. One (BO) is expressed as type B, and the one (AB) is expressed as AB.

c. Dale is least likely to have type B blood because none of his possible genotypes is expressed as type B. The AA genotypes are expressed as type A, and the AB genotypes are expressed as AB.

d. Only in Maura may a recessive gene be expressed. Because O is the only recessive of these genes, it is expressed only when the genotype is OO. Maura is the only person with that possible genotype.

3. To solve this problem correctly, you must construct Punnett squares for all of the possible genotypes of each parent, based on the information from the previous questions. Greg has four possible genotypes—AA, AB, AO, and BO; Maura has three possible genotypes—BB, BO, and OO. The possible Punnett squares for the child would be as follows:

Greg's genotype

	A	B
O	AO	BO
O	AO	BO

Maura's genotype

Greg's genotype

	A	O
B	AB	BO
B	AB	BO

Maura's genotype

Greg's genotype

	A	A
B	AB	AB
B	AB	AB

Maura's genotype

Greg's genotype

	A	O
B	AB	BO
O	AO	OO

Maura's genotype

Greg's genotype

	A	A
B	AB	AB
O	AO	AO

Maura's genotype

Greg's genotype

	A	O
O	AO	OO
O	AO	OO

Maura's genotype

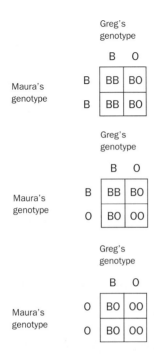

Greg's genotype

	B	O
B	BB	BO
B	BB	BO

Maura's genotype

Greg's genotype

	B	O
B	BB	BO
O	BO	OO

Maura's genotype

Greg's genotype

	B	O
O	BO	OO
O	BO	OO

Maura's genotype

a. The child is most likely to have type B blood.

b. Three genotypes are equally likely: AB, AO, and BO.

c. The only possible genotype that both Maura and Greg share is BO. Thus, to answer the question correctly, you must refer to the Punnett square that shows both parents with BO genotypes. Because the B gene is dominant and the O gene is recessive, the genotypes BB and BO in this square will both result in type B blood. Because three of the four possible genotypes in this Punnett square are either BB or BO, we can see that the child will most likely have type B blood. Because the O gene is recessive, type O blood is expressed only with a genotype of OO. Looking again at the Punnett square, we see that only one of the four boxes contains the genotype OO. Thus, the child has a 1 in 4 chance—25 percent—of having type O blood.

4. Scott chose the acid phosphatase test, because it is extremely useful in searching for semen on large areas of fabric, such as a blanket. He concluded that the blanket did not contain evidence of semen. First of all, he knew that certain fruit juices, including watermelon, can generate a positive reaction with acid phosphatase testing. However, these juices react much more slowly to the test than does semen. A reaction time of less than thirty seconds is considered a strong indication of semen. Because it took three minutes to obtain a positive reaction, Scott concluded that the positive reaction was caused by the watermelon.

5. Cathy made four mistakes in collecting evidence. First, she should have placed a paper sheet over the sheet on which the victim disrobed, in order to collect any loose material that may have fallen from the victim or the clothing. Second, she should have placed each item of clothing in a separate bag, instead of placing all of them in the same bag. Third, she should have taken two additional vaginal swabs, smearing them onto microscope slides. Finally, she failed to collect fingernail scrapings from the victim.

Chapter 9
Facts and Concepts

1. DNA, or deoxyribonucleic acid, is the molecule that carries the body's genetic information. It is important to forensic scientists because portions of the DNA structure of certain genes are as unique to each individual as fingerprints. This allows forensic scientists to link biological evidence such as blood, semen, hair, or tissue to a single individual with certainty.

2. Genes are the fundamental units of heredity. Their function is to instruct cells in the body to make proteins that determine everything from hair color to susceptibility to diseases. Genes are composed of DNA and they are located on chromosomes within the nucleus of each cell.

3. James Watson and Francis Crick are credited with discovering the structure of DNA.

4. DNA is a large molecule called a polymer, created by linking a series of repeating units known as nucleotides.

5. The DNA molecule is composed of two strands of DNA coiled around one another and joined to one another by bases projecting from the DNA strands. This structure is called a double helix.

6. The four bases associated with DNA are adenine, cytosine, guanine, and thymine. They are paired with A opposite T and G opposite C on the DNA molecule.

7. The order in which the base pairs are arranged defines the role and function of a DNA molecule.

8. d

9. Proteins are made by linking a combination of amino acids. The sequence of amino acids in a protein chain determines the shape and function of the protein.

10. The human genome is the order of bases on all twenty-three pairs of human chromosomes. Information about the human genome is useful for diagnosing and treating genetic diseases, as well as for understanding the underlying causes of cancer.

11. DNA replication begins with the unwinding of the DNA strands in the double helix. Each strand is then exposed to a collection of free nucleotides. The double helix is re-created as the nucleotides are assembled in the proper order (A with T and G with C). Two identical copies of DNA emerge from the process.

12. PCR (polymerase chain reaction) is a technique for replicating or copying a portion of a DNA strand outside a living cell. Three advantages of PCR are that (1) PCR can be used with short DNA strands, (2) shorter strands are more stable and less subject to degradation than longer strands, and (3) PCR can amplify minute quantities of DNA, thus overcoming the limited-sample-size problem often associated with crime-scene evidence.

13. Recombinant DNA is a process by which the DNA of an organism is altered by inserting into it fragments of DNA from another organism. Recombinant DNA technology is used to produce insulin, which is used to treat diabetes.

14. Tandem repeats are regions of a chromosome that contain multiple copies of a core DNA sequence arranged in a repeating fashion. They are useful to forensic scientists

because they offer a means of distinguishing one individual from another through DNA typing.

15. Until the mid-1990s, restriction fragment polymorphisms (RFLP) was the dominant DNA typing procedure in the United States.

16. A short tandem repeat (STR) is a region of a DNA molecule that contains short segments consisting of three to seven repeating base pairs. STRs are attractive to forensic scientists because hundreds of different types of STRs are found in human genes. The more STRs one can characterize, the smaller the percentage of the population from which these STRs can emanate, thus making it easier to positively link biological evidence with a particular suspect. Also STRs can be replicated by PCR.

17. The greater the number of STRs characterized, the smaller the frequency of occurrence of the analyzed sample in the general population.

18. The separation of STRs can typically be carried out by electrophoresis using a flat gel-coated plate or by capillary electrophoresis carried out in a thin glass column. Capillary electrophoresis is preferred because it reduces analysis time and automates sampling and data collection.

19. The amelogenin gene is often used to determine the sex of a DNA contributor. Forensic scientists can make this determination because the gene is shorter by six bases in the X chromosome than in the Y chromosome.

20. Nuclear DNA is found in the nucleus of each cell and is inherited from both parents. Mitochondrial DNA (mtDNA), on the other hand, is found outside the nucleus of the cell and is inherited solely from the mother.

21. One advantage of mtDNA analysis is that it is significantly more sensitive than nuclear DNA profiling. The disadvantages are that mtDNA analysis is more time consuming, and more costly than nuclear DNA profiling. Also, mtDNA has far less discriminating power than do STRs.

22. CODIS (Combined DNA Index System) is a computer software program developed by the FBI that maintains local, state, and national databases of DNA profiles from convicted offenders, unsolved crime-scene evidence, and profiles of missing people. CODIS is useful to forensic scientists because it allows them to compare DNA types recovered from crime-scene evidence to those of convicted sex offenders and other convicted criminals.

23. Approximately eighteen DNA-bearing cells are needed to obtain an STR profile. A quantity of DNA that is below this level of detection is referred to as a low copy number.

24. An evidence collector should wear disposable latex gloves when handling biological evidence because (1) all body fluids must be assumed to be infectious, and (2) latex gloves significantly reduce the possibility that the evidence collector will contaminate the evidence.

25. Biological evidence should not be packaged in plastic or airtight containers, because accumulation of residual moisture could contribute to the growth of DNA-destroying bacteria and fungi. Articles containing biological evidence should be packaged separately in a paper bag or in a well-ventilated box.

26. Packages containing biological evidence should be refrigerated or stored in a cool location out of direct sunlight until delivery to the laboratory. One common exception is blood mixed with soil, which must be stored in a clean glass or plastic container and immediately frozen.

27. The preservative EDTA (ethylenediamine tetraacetic acid) should be added to blood samples collected from a crime scene. EDTA serves as a preservative and inhibits the activity of enzymes that degrade DNA.

28. The least intrusive method for obtaining a DNA standard/reference is the buccal swab. In this procedure, cotton swabs are placed in the subject's mouth and the inside of the cheek is vigorously swabbed, resulting in the transfer of cells from the inner cheek lining onto the swab.

29. Four ways to minimize contamination of biological evidence are as follows: (1) Change gloves before handling each new piece of evidence, (2) collect a substrate control for possible subsequent laboratory examination, (3) pick up small items of evidence such as cigarette butts and stamps with clean forceps, and (4) always package each item of evidence in its own well-ventilated container.

Application and Critical Thinking

1. G–C–T–T–A–G–C–G–T–T–A–G–C–T–G–G–A–C

2. You would first collect any blood or skin scrapings under the victim's fingernails, because these may contain DNA. You would then amplify the DNA in the sample using PCR and separate the fragments using electrophoresis. Finally, you would look for the bands of separated DNA that correspond to the amelogenin gene. If the sample contains two bands, the attacker is male; if sample contains only one band, the attacker is female.

3. Investigators use mtDNA to determine whether the body is that of the victim of the unsolved murder. To do so, you would collect mtDNA from one of the victim's maternal relatives and compare it to the mtDNA recovered from the body. If the samples match, the body is that of the victim.

4. With an STR, you should expect to see a two-band pattern. The presence of more than two bands suggests a mixture of DNA from more than one source.

Chapter 10
Facts and Concepts

1. Hair is an appendage of the skin that grows out of an organ known as the hair follicle.

2. The three layers of the hair shaft are the cuticle, cortex, and medulla. The cuticle is the scale structure covering the exterior of the hair. The cortex is the main body of the hair shaft. The medulla is a column of cells running through the center of the hair.

3. Two features that make hair a good subject for establishing individual identity are its resistance to chemical decomposition and its ability to retain structural features over a long period of time. Much of this resistance and stability is attributed to the cuticle.

4. The scale pattern of the cuticle is an important feature for characterizing animal hair.

5. The cortex derives its major forensic importance from the fact that it is embedded with the pigment granules that give hair its color.

6. Most animals have medullae that are either continuous or interrupted. Human head hairs generally exhibit no medullae or have fragmented ones; they rarely show continuous medullation. One exception is the Mongoloid race, whose members usually have head hairs with continuous medullae.

7. The three phases of hair growth are the anagen, catagen, and telogen phases. A criminalist is more likely to collect DNA from hairs in the anagen stage because, when pulled from the root, some hairs in the anagen phase have a follicular tag containing DNA that may be analyzed in order to individualize the hair.

8. Microscopic human hair comparisons must be undertaken with extreme caution because hair tends to exhibit variable morphological characteristics, not only from one person to another but also within a single individual.

9. In comparing hair, the criminalist is particularly interested in matching the color, length, and diameter. Other important features he or she might compare include the presence or absence of a medulla and the distribution, shape, and color intensity of the pigment granules in the cortex.

10. b

11. Forcibly removed hairs are most likely to provide useful DNA evidence because they often bear follicular tags that are rich sources of nuclear DNA.

12. Questioned and standard/reference hairs must come from the same area of the body because hair from different parts of the body varies significantly in its physical characteristics.

13. Forensic hair comparisons generally involve either head hair or pubic hair.

14. The entire hair is collected because a hair may show variation in color and other morphological features over its entire length.

15. A polymer is a substance composed of a large number of atoms that are usually arranged in repeating units. A monomer is the basic unit from which a polymer is constructed. Polymers are often referred to as macromolecules they may contain thousands or even millions of atoms.

16. c

17. A criminalist first compares the color and diameter of the fibers. Other morphological features that may aid in the comparison are lengthwise striations (lined markings) on the surface of some fibers and the pitting of the fiber's surface with delustering particles added in the manufacturing process to reduce shine. The cross-sectional shape of a fiber may also help characterize the fiber.

18. Two physical characteristics that frequently are used to identify fibers are birefringence and their infrared absorption spectrum.

19. A criminalist uses thin-layer chromatography to analyze the composition of the dye in a fiber.

20. The colors of two fibers are first visually compared with a comparison microscope. Confirmation of a color comparison can then be made by comparing the fibers' spectral patterns with a microspectrophotometer. Further analysis of the color dyes constituting the fibers are made by thin-layer chromatography.

Application and Critical Thinking

1. a. telogen phase
   b. anagen phase
   c. anagen phase
   d. catagen phase

2. Because hair grows at a rate of about 1 centimeter per month, the hair was dyed approximately six weeks earlier.

3. a. Caucasian
   b. Mongoloid
   c. Negroid
   d. Caucasian

4. Pete made several mistakes. First, all items of clothing containing fiber evidence should be packaged in paper, not plastic. Second, he placed fibers collected from two separate locations in the same bag, when each individual piece of fiber evidence should be placed in a separate container. Third, he should have carefully folded the sheet before packaging it, rather than simply balling it up. Fourth, he used his fingers, rather than a forceps, to collect fibers from the windowsill. Finally, the fibers from the windowsill should be folded inside a piece of paper and then placed in another container, not put into a regular envelope.

Chapter 11
Facts and Concepts

1. Trace elements are small quantities of elements that are present in most substances in concentrations of less than 1 percent. For the criminalist, the presence of trace elements is particularly useful because they provide "invisible" markers that may establish the source of a material, or at least provide additional points for comparison.

2. Forensic analysis of the bullets recovered after the assassination of President John F. Kennedy focused on the concentration of the trace elements antimony and silver.

3. c

4. The three most important subatomic particles are the proton, neutron, and electron. The proton has a positive electrical charge, the neutron has no electrical charge, and the electron has a negative electrical charge. The proton and the neutron are both located in the nucleus of the atom; the electron orbits the nucleus at a distance.

5. Atomic number indicates the number of protons in the nucleus of an atom. Atomic mass refers to the total number of protons and neutrons in a nucleus.

6. An isotope is an atom differing from other atoms of the same element in the number of neutrons it has in its nucleus.

7. Radioactivity is the emission of high-energy particles and radiation that accompanies the spontaneous disintegration of the nuclei of unstable isotopes. The three types of emissions are alpha rays, beta rays, and gamma rays.

8. In neutron activation analysis, a sample is bombarded with neutrons and the energy of the gamma rays emitted by the activated isotopes is then measured. The gamma rays of each element are associated with characteristic energy values, and thus exhibit unique levels of energy. These appear as distinct bands that identify the specific element that produces them.

9. One major advantage of neutron activation analysis is that it provides a nondestructive method for identifying and quantitating trace elements. Also, neutron activation can simultaneously analyze for twenty to thirty elements. A major drawback to the technique is its expense. Only a handful of crime laboratories have access to a nuclear reactor; in addition, sophisticated analyzers are needed to detect and discriminate gamma-ray emissions.

10. Paint as physical evidence is most frequently encountered in hit-and-run and burglary cases.

11. Paint is composed of a binder and pigments, as well as other additives, dissolved or dispersed in a suitable solvent. After the paint has been applied to a surface, the solvent evaporates.

12. Manufacturers apply a variety of coatings to the body of an automobile. This adds significant diversity to automobile paint and contributes to the forensic significance of automobile paint comparisons.

13. Paint specimens are best compared side by side under a stereoscopic microscope.

14. When comparing paint chips under a microscope, a criminalist looks for color, surface texture, and color layer sequence. Color layer sequence is the most important of these characteristics.

15. A thorough comparison of paint must include a chemical analysis of the paint's pigments and binder composition.

16. Pyrolysis gas chromatography has proven to be particularly invaluable for distinguishing most paint formulations. It is particularly useful in comparing paint because it produces a pattern or "pyrogram" of the polymers that identify the specific chemical makeup of the binder.

17. The specimen is inserted between two carbon electrodes and a direct current arc is then passed through the electrodes to vaporize and excite the specimen's atoms. A lens collects the light emitted by the excited atoms and focuses it onto a prism that disperses it into component frequencies. The separated frequencies of light are then directed toward a photographic plate, where they are recorded as line images. Each element in the spectrum can be identified when it is compared to a standard chart that shows the position of the principal spectral lines of all the elements.

18. Inductively coupled plasma (ICP) emission spectrometry has supplanted carbon arc emission spectroscopy for most applications. The main difference between the two techniques is that in ICP, atoms are excited by placing the sample in a hot plasma torch, rather than using an electrical arc, as in emission spectroscopy.

19. PDQ (Paint Data Query) is a computerized database that allows an analyst to obtain information on paints related to automobile make, model, and year. The database contains such parameters as automotive paint layer colors, primer colors, and binder composition that helps criminalists link a paint chip to a specific make and model of automobile.

20. The collected paint must be close to the area of the car suspected of being in contact with the victim because other portions of the car may have faded or been repainted.

21. The investigator should not try to remove trace paint evidence found on a tool; instead, he or she should package the tool for laboratory examination.

22. The first step in a forensic soil comparison is analysis of the color.

23. A mineral is a naturally occurring crystalline solid found in soil. Its physical properties—for example, color, geometric shape, density, and refractive index or birefringence—are most useful for characterizing soils.

24. Glass tubes are filled with layers of two liquids mixed in varying proportions so that each tube contains several layers of liquid, each with a lower density than the preceding one, from the bottom to the top of the tube. When soil is added to the tube, each particle of soil will sink to the portion of the tube containing the layer of liquid that has a density of equal value; the particles remain suspended in the liquid at this point. In this way, a density distribution pattern of soil particles is obtained and compared to other specimens treated in a similar manner.

25. When gathering soil specimens, standard/reference soils should be collected at various intervals within a 100-yard radius of the crime scene, as well as at the site of the crime. Soil specimens also should be collected at all possible alibi locations that the suspect may claim.

26. If soil is found adhering to an object, the investigator should wrap the object individually in paper, with the soil intact, and transmit it to the laboratory. Garments containing soil evidence should be carefully and individually wrapped in paper bags and sent to the laboratory for analysis. Care must be taken that particles that may accidentally fall off the garment during transportation will remain in the paper bag.

27. When a lump of soil is found, it should be collected and preserved intact. Lumps of soil exhibit a layering effect caused by buildup over time. This layering effect may impart soil with greater variation, and hence greater evidential value, than that which is normally associated with loose soil.

Application and Critical Thinking

1. Antimony (Sb)—51; barium (Ba)—56; lead (Pb)—82; tin (Sn)—50. Lead probably has the largest atomic mass, because it has significantly more protons than the other elements, and atomic mass is equal to the total number of protons and neutrons in the nucleus. Tin, with the fewest protons, probably has the smallest atomic mass.

2. In a hit-and-run situation you would collect from each vehicle standard/reference samples that include all the paint layers down to the bare metal. This is best

accomplished by removing a painted section with a clean scalpel or knife blade. Standard/reference samples should be collected from an undamaged area of each vehicle because other portions of the car may have faded or been repainted. To avoid cross-contamination of paints, carefully wipe the blade of any knife or scraping tool used before collecting each sample.

3. Jared made several mistakes. First, the samples he removed from the scene should have included only the top layer of soil. Second, he failed to collect soil samples from both alibi locations—the garden and the parking lot. Third, he should have packaged the shoes in paper, not plastic. Finally, he should have dried all of the soil samples under identical laboratory conditions before examining any of them.

Case Analysis

1. The primary challenge facing the investigators in this case was linking the female victim's body to the suspect's van. A light-colored van was seen speeding away from the murder scene.

2. Items of evidence that directly linked the victim to the suspect included paint chips, Caucasian head hairs from the victim's blazer that were consistent in microscopic characteristics to the defendant's known head hair sample, and a forcibly removed brown Caucasian head hair that was found to be consistent in all characteristics with the decedent's known head hair sample. Sixteen gray metallic/black-colored paint chips found on the victim's clothing matched similar flakes found in the van's sweepings. Items that indirectly linked the two were the white seeds found in both the victim's mouth and the van, a chemically treated head hair found on the victim that was consistent in microscopic characteristics to the known head hair sample obtained from the defendant's wife, and brown and white dog hair from the victim's clothing and the van's interior that were found to be consistent with the hair from a dog belonging to the suspect's nephew.

3. During a search of the defendant's residence in New Jersey, a large quantity of blue and black acrylic paint was found in the garage. The blue and black paint flakes from all the sources and the known blue (undercoat) and black (topcoat) paint from the van were compared and found to be consistent in every respect. It was apparent that the van had been repainted to hide its original color.

Chapter 12
Facts and Concepts

1. Oxidation is the combination of oxygen with other substances to produce new substances.

2. a

3. break apart their chemical bonds; their bonds are reformed

4. Combustion is the rapid combination of oxygen with another substance, accompanied by the production of noticeable heat and light. Rusting is not accompanied by combustion because iron combines with oxygen too slowly to permit combustion.

5. In an exothermic reaction, heat energy is liberated. In an endothermic reaction, heat energy is absorbed from the surroundings.

6. A fire will burn until either the oxygen or the fuel is exhausted.

7. Two factors that influence the speed of reaction of a fire are the physical state of the fuel and the temperature.

8. A fuel achieves a reaction rate with oxygen sufficient to produce combustion only when it is in the gaseous state, for only in this state molecules can collide frequently enough to support a flaming fire.

9. In order to burn, the temperature of a liquid fuel must be high enough to vaporize the fuel. The flash point is the lowest temperature at which a liquid gives off sufficient vapor to form a mixture with air that will support combustion.

10. Pyrolysis is the chemical breakdown of solid organic matter by heat. The gaseous products of pyrolysis combine with oxygen to produce a fire.

11. If the fuel concentration in the fuel–air mix is too low (lean) or too great (rich), combustion does not occur.

12. Glowing combustion is combustion on the surface of a solid fuel in the absence of heat high enough to pyrolyze the fuel. Two examples are a burning cigarette and red-hot charcoals.

13. Spontaneous combustion is fire caused by a natural heat-producing process in the presence of sufficient air and fuel. Two examples of conditions under which it might occur are hay stored in an improperly ventilated barn and improperly ventilated containers containing rags soaked with highly unsaturated oils.

14. To initiate and sustain combustion, (1) a fuel must be present, (2) oxygen must be available in sufficient quantity to combine with the fuel, and (3) heat must be applied to initiate the combustion, and sufficient heat must be generated to sustain the reaction.

15. As a fire progresses, the heat created by combustion tends to move from a region of higher temperature to a region of lower temperature.

16. The three mechanisms of heat transfer are conduction, radiation, and convection. Conduction is movement of heat through a solid object. Radiation is the transfer of heat energy from a heated surface to a cooler surface by electromagnetic radiation. Convection is the transfer of heat energy by movement of molecules within a liquid or gas.

17. Insulators are materials that are poor conductors of heat. Wood is an example of a good insulator.

18. Common signs of arson at a fire scene include the presence of accelerants, the discovery of an ignition device, irregularly shaped burn patterns on the floor or ground, streamers, and separate and unconnected fires.

19. Arson investigators must work quickly to collect evidence at a fire scene because (1) any accelerant residues may evaporate within a few days or even hours, (2) safety and health conditions may require that cleanup and salvage operations begin as quickly as possible, and (3) accelerants in soil and vegetation can be rapidly degraded by bacterial action.

20. d

21. Streamers are trails of flammable material, such as gasoline or paper, spreading outward from a fire's point or origin in order to cause the fire to move rapidly from one room to another. Evidence of streamers suggests the likelihood of arson.

22. Fire evidence should be packaged in airtight containers so possible accelerant residues are not lost through evaporation.

23. Most criminalists consider the gas chromatograph the most sensible and reliable instrument for detecting and characterizing flammable residues.

24. Headspace is vapor containing volatile residues recovered from debris at a fire scene. It is recovered by heating the airtight container containing the debris, which drives off any volatile residue present and traps it in the container's enclosed airspace. The headspace is then removed with a syringe.

25. Using vapor concentration, a forensic analyst can increase the sensitivity of accelerant detection at least a hundredfold over the conventional headspace technique.

Application and Critical Thinking

1. a. radiation
   b. conduction
   c. convection
   d. radiation

2. You should suspect arson. Although the conditions in which the oil was stored—high heat and lack of ventilation—may lead to spontaneous combustion with some materials, spontaneous combustion does not occur with hydrocarbon lubricating oils such as motor oil. The owner is lying about the oil igniting spontaneously; he may have deliberately set the fire to collect on the increased insurance.

3. Mick made several mistakes. First, he should have used separate containers for each location where debris was collected. Debris should have come from the point of origin of the fire, not from the surrounding rooms. He should not have placed the timbers in plastic bags, which react with hydrocarbons and permit volatile hydrocarbon vapors to be depleted. Finally, Mick should have collected the suspect's clothes to undergo laboratory analysis for the presence of accelerant residues.

Chapter 13
Facts and Concepts

1. The violent physical disruption associated with an explosion is caused by the sudden buildup of expanding gas pressure at the origin of the explosion.

2. Deflagration is characterized by very rapid oxidation that produces heat, light, and a subsonic pressure wave. Detonation is characterized by extremely rapid oxidation that produces a supersonic shock wave.

3. Low explosives detonate relatively slowly (less than 1,000 meters per second), while high explosives detonate very rapidly (from 1,000 to 8,500 meters per second).

4. The most widely used low explosives are black powder and smokeless powder.

5. A safety fuse consists of black powder wrapped in a fabric or plastic casing. It is used to carry a flame at a uniform rate to an explosive charge.

6. The only ingredients required for a low explosive are fuel and a good oxidizing agent.

7. The two classes of high explosives are primary and secondary explosives. Primary explosives are ultrasensitive to heat, shock, or friction, and under normal conditions detonate violently instead of burning. Secondary explosives are relatively insensitive to heat, shock, or friction, and normally burn rather than detonate when ignited in small quantities in open air. Secondary explosives are usually detonated by primary explosives.

8. The main ingredients in straight dynamite are nitroglycerine and pulp. In addition to nitroglycerine and pulp, modern straight dynamites also include sodium nitrate (which furnishes oxygen for complete combustion) and a small percentage of a stabilizer, such as calcium carbonate.

9. Ammonium nitrate–based explosives largely have replaced dynamite for industrial uses. The advantages of these explosives are that they are cheap and very stable.

10. ANFO is an explosive consisting of ammonium nitrate soaked in fuel oil.

11. Three military high explosives are RDX, TNT, and PETN. RDX is the most powerful and popular military explosive.

12. A detonator is a device used to create an explosion needed to ignite a high explosive. In most cases, detonators are blasting caps composed of copper or aluminum cases containing lead azide.

13. The most obvious characteristic of a high or contained low explosive is the presence of a crater at the origin of the blast.

14. A device widely used to screen objects for the presence of explosive residues is the ion mobility spectrometer (IMS).

15. Soil and other soft loose materials collected at the scene of an explosion are best stored in metal containers.

16. When bomb-scene debris and other materials arrive at the laboratory, everything is first examined microscopically to detect particles of unconsumed explosive.

17. Following microscopic examination, the recovered debris is thoroughly rinsed with acetone because the high solubility of most explosives in acetone ensures their quick removal from the debris.

18. Three procedures commonly used as screening tests for explosive residues are color spot tests, thin-layer chromatography (TLC), and gas chromatography/mass spectrometry.

19. Two confirmatory tests for the presence of intact explosives located in debris are infrared spectrophotometry and X-ray diffraction.

20. Taggants are tiny color-coded chips the size of sand that are added to commercial explosives during their manufacture. The taggant chip is arranged in a color sequence that indicates where the explosive was made and when it was

produced. Taggants thus allow an explosive to be traced through its distribution chain to its final legal possessor.

Application and Critical Thinking

1. a. High explosives. Lead azide is a common component of blasting caps, which are used to detonate high explosives.

   b. Low explosives. Nitrocellulose is an ingredient in smokeless powder, one of the most common low explosives.

   c. High explosives. Ammonium nitrate is the main ingredient in a number of high explosives that have replaced dynamite for industrial uses.

   d. High explosives. Primacord is used to as a detonator to ignite several high-explosive charges simultaneously.

   e. Low explosives. Potassium chlorate mixed with sugar is a popular low explosive.

2. a. Alcoholic KOH. Tetryl is the only explosive that produces a red-violet color in response to this test.

   b. Alcoholic KOH. TNT produces a distinctive red color in response to the alcoholic KOH test.

   c. Diphenylamine produces a blue color. No color is produced in response to the Greiss test and to the alcoholic KOH test.

   d. Diphenylamine. Nitrocellulose produces a distinctive blue-black color in response to this test.

3. Matt made several mistakes. First, to avoid contaminating the scene, Matt should have put on disposable gloves, shoe covers, and overalls before beginning his search. Second, he should have used a wire mesh screen to sift through the debris, instead of picking through it by hand. Third, all explosive evidence should be stored in airtight metal containers, not plastic or paper bags. Fourth, Matt should have collected material from not only the immediate area of the blast, but also materials blown away from the blast's origin.

Chapter 14
Facts and Concepts

1. Fingerprints are a reproduction of friction skin ridges found on the palm side of the fingers and thumbs.

2. The first fundamental principle of fingerprints is that a fingerprint is an individual characteristic; no two fingers have yet been found to possess identical ridge characteristics.

3. The identity, number, and relative location of ridge characteristics impart individuality to a fingerprint.

4. Ridge characteristics are ridge endings, bifurcations, enclosures, and other ridge details, which must match in two fingerprints to establish their common origin. They are also known as minutiae.

5. The second fundamental principle of fingerprints is that a fingerprint remains unchanged during an individual's lifetime.

6. Dermal papillae are cells that form a boundary between the outer skin, or epidermis, and the inner skin, or the dermis. The shape of the boundary determines the form and pattern of the ridges on the surface of the skin, and thus the fingerprint pattern.

7. A latent fingerprint is a fingerprint made by the deposit of oils and/or perspiration that is invisible to the naked eye. Latent fingerprints are formed when a finger touches a surface and transfers perspiration, along with oils that may have been picked up by touching the hairy portions of the body, onto that surface, thereby leaving an impression of the finger's ridge pattern.

8. It is pointless to try to obscure or obliterate one's fingerprints by scarring or otherwise damaging the skin because the wound would have to penetrate 1 to 2 millimeters beneath the skin's surface. In addition, the presence of permanent scars caused by the effort to obliterate one's fingerprints merely provides new characteristics for identification.

9. The third fundamental principle of fingerprints is that fingerprints have general ridge patterns that permit them to be systematically classified.

10. The three types of fingerprint patterns are loops, whorls, and arches. Loops are the most common.

11. Whorls include ridge patterns that are generally rounded or circular and have two deltas.

12. A loop must have at least one delta.

13. A plain arch, formed by ridges entering from one side of the print and exiting on the opposite side, is the simplest of all fingerprint patterns.

14. The primary classification is the first step in classifying fingerprints under the FBI system. The presence or absence of the whorl pattern is the basis for determination of the primary classification.

15. An AFIS is an Automated Fingerprint Identification System. The heart of AFIS technology is the ability of a computer to scan and digitally encode fingerprints so that they can be subject to high-speed computer processing.

16. When using AFIS, a fingerprint expert makes the final verification of the print's identity.

17. Livescan is an inkless device that captures digital images of fingerprints and palm prints and electronically transmits them to an AFIS. It has largely replaced the procedure of manually inking fingerprints and rolling the inked fingers onto a standard ten-print card.

18. One drawback to using AFIS is that sometimes a latent print does not make a hit on AFIS because of the poor quality of the file print. The second drawback is that state AFIS systems often do not communicate with each other directly, and thus states frequently cannot share fingerprint information with one another.

19. The three kinds of crime-scene fingerprints are visible prints, latent prints, and plastic prints.

20. Prints from hard and nonabsorbent surfaces are preferably developed by applying fingerprint powder or treating with Super Glue. Soft and porous surfaces are generally treated with one or more chemicals.

21. RUVIS is the Reflected Ultraviolet Imaging System, which can locate prints on most nonabsorbent surfaces without

the aid of chemical or powder treatments. RUVIS detects a print by aiming UV light at the surface suspected of containing prints. When the UV light strikes the fingerprint, the light is reflected back to the viewer, differentiating the print from its background surface. The transmitted UV light is then converted into visible light by an image intensifier.

22. Four common chemical methods for visualizing latent prints are iodine fuming, ninhydrin, Physical Developer, and SuperGlue fuming.

23. Latent fingerprints can be visualized by exposure to laser light because the perspiration in fingerprints contains a variety of components that fluoresce when illuminated by laser light.

24. First, using an alternate light source, light can be passed through several filters, giving the user more flexibility in selecting the wavelength of light to be aimed at the latent print. Second, alternate light sources are commercially available at costs significantly below those of laser illuminators. Third, alternate light sources are portable and can be readily taken to any crime scene.

25. After the latent print has been visualized, a photograph must be taken before any further attempts at preservation.

26. If the object is small enough to be transported without destroying the print, it should be preserved in its entirety. The print should be covered with cellophane so it will be protected from damage.

27. To "lift" a fingerprint, powder is applied to the print, and the surface containing the print is covered with the adhesive side of the tape. When the tape is pulled up, the powder is transferred to the tape. Then the tape is placed on a properly labeled card that provides a good background contrast with the powder. This procedure is used when fingerprints are found on large or immovable objects.

28. Digital imaging is a process through which a picture is converted into a series of square electronic dots known as pixels. By using digital imaging, fingerprints can be enhanced for the most accurate and comprehensive analysis.

29. Digital imaging is not effective in enhancing latent fingerprints if details of the print do not exist on the original images.

Application and Critical Thinking

1. a. Whorl
   b. Arch
   c. Loop
   d. Whorl
   e. Whorl
   f. Arch

2. The primary classification for this individual would be as follows:
$$\frac{0 + 8 + 4 + 0 + 1}{16 + 8 + 0 + 2 + 1}$$

Thus, the classification would be 13/27.

3. a. chemicals
   b. powder
   c. powder
   d. chemicals
   e. chemicals

4. a. scaling and resizing
   b. spatial filtering
   c. frequency analysis, or frequency Fourier transform (FFT)

Chapter 15
Facts and Concepts

1. Rifling refers to the spiral grooves impressed in the bore of a firearm barrel. Rifling imparts spin to the projectile when it is fired, which keeps it on an accurate course.

2. Grooves are the cut or low-lying portions between the lands in a rifled bore. Lands are the raised portion between the grooves in a rifled bore.

3. Caliber is a measure of the diameter of the bore of a rifled firearm.

4. b

5. The class characteristics of a rifled barrel include the number of lands and grooves, and the width and direction of twist.

6. Striations are markings impressed into the metal of a barrel. They are produced as the negatives of minute imperfections found on the rifling cutter's surface, or by minute chips of steel pushed against the barrel's inner surface by a moving broach cutter.

7. No two rifled barrels have identical striations. As the bullet passes through the barrel, its surface is impressed with striations from the lands and grooves of the barrel. A firearms examiner can compare the striations on a bullet recovered at a crime scene to those made on bullets test fired from a suspect gun. If the markings match, this indicates that the recovered bullet was fired by the suspect weapon.

8. The comparison microscope is the firearms examiner's most important tool because it allows two bullets to be observed and compared simultaneously.

9. Three factors that can prevent a firearms examiner from obtaining a perfect match of striation markings around the periphery of two bullets are as follows: (1) The presence of grit and rust can alter the markings on bullets fired through the same barrel; (2) bullets may become so mutilated and distorted on impact as to yield only a small area with intact markings; and (3) striation markings on a barrel are not permanent structures; they are subject to continuing alteration through wear as succeeding bullets traverse the length of the barrel.

10. Unlike handguns, a shotgun is not rifled—it has a smooth barrel. Because of this, shotgun shells are not impressed with any characteristic markings that can be used to compare two shotgun shells to determine if they were fired from the same weapon.

11. The higher a shotgun's gauge, the smaller the diameter of its barrel.

12. Pulling a trigger releases the weapon's firing pin, causing it to strike the primer, which in turn ignites the powder. The expanding gases generated by the burning gunpowder propel the bullet forward through the barrel.

13. The parts of a firearm that leave impressions on a cartridge case that constitute individual characteristics of that weapon are the firing pin, the breechblock, the ejector, and the extractor.

14. Two automated firearms search systems are DRUGFIRE, developed by the FBI, and IBIS, developed by the ATF.

15. NIBIN is the National Integrated Ballistics Information Network, a unified firearms search system that incorporates both DRUGFIRE and IBIS technologies.

16. d

17. Distance determination is the process of determining the distance between the firearm and a target. It is usually based on the distribution of powder patterns or the spread of a shot pattern.

18. The precise distance from which a handgun or rifle is determined by carefully comparing the powder residue pattern on the victim's clothing or skin to test patterns made by firing the suspect weapon at varying distances from a target. By comparing the test and evidence patterns, the examiner may find enough similarity in shape and density on which to judge the distance from which the shot was fired.

19. Bullet wipe is a dark ring formed around the perimeter of an entrance hole that is wiped off the bullet's surface as it passes through the target. Bullet wipe consists of a mixture of carbon, dirt, lubricant, primer residue, and lead.

20. Five factors that influence the amount of gunpowder residue deposited on a target are barrel length, caliber, type of ammunition, the type of weapon fired, and the condition of the weapon.

21. With a shooting involving a shotgun, a distance determination can be estimated by measuring the spread of the discharged shot.

22. As the distance to the target of a shotgun blast increases, the pellets separate and spread out.

23. Choke is an interior constriction placed at the muzzle end of a shotgun barrel. The greater the choke, the narrower the spread pattern of the pellets and the faster and farther the pellets will travel.

24. The Greiss test is a chemical test used to develop patterns of gunpowder residues around bullet holes. It tests for the presence of nitrates.

25. Shortly after a weapon is fired, residues are most likely to be deposited on the thumb web and the back of the firing hand of a shooter, because these areas are closest to gases escaping along the side or back of the gun during discharge.

26. The most popular approach to collecting gunshot residues from a shooter's hands involves applying adhesive tape or adhesive to the hand's surface to remove any adhering residue particles. Another approach is to remove any residues present by swabbing both the firing and nonfiring hands with cotton that has been moistened with 5 percent nitric acid. The front and back of each hand are separately swabbed. All four swabs, along with a moistened control, are then forwarded to the crime laboratory for analysis.

27. The scanning electron microscope (SEM) is often used to locate primer and gunpowder particles by their characteristic size and shape.

28. The major advantage of the SEM approach for primer residue detection is its enhanced specificity over hand swabbing. The major drawback to this approach is the excessive operator time and expense required to find and characterize gunshot residue using the SEM.

29. Neutron activation analysis and flameless atomic absorption spectrophotometry are two analytical methods besides SEM testing for detecting gunshot residues in hand swabs.

30. It is possible to restore an obliterated serial number because the metal crystals in the zone containing the stamped numbers are placed under a permanent strain that extends a short distance beneath the original numbers. If the zone of strain has been removed, or if the area has been impressed with a different strain pattern, the serial number usually cannot be restored.

31. A suspect firearm should never be picked up by inserting an object into its barrel because this practice disturbs powder deposits, rust, or dirt lodged in the barrel, and consequently may alter the striation markings on test-fired bullets.

32. Before unloading a suspect weapon, the weapon's hammer and safety position should be recorded, as well as the location of all fired and unfired ammunition in the weapon.

33. A weapon recovered from underwater should be transported to the laboratory in a receptacle containing enough of the same water in which it was found to keep it submerged. This procedure prevents rust from developing during transport.

34. Protection of class and individual markings on bullets and cartridge cases is the primary concern of the field investigator when recovering bullets and cartridge casings.

35. Discernible random nicks and breaks that the tool has acquired through wear and use typically impart individual characteristics to tool marks.

36. When removal of the original tool mark is impractical, the criminalist photographs the marked area to scale and makes a cast of the mark.

37. The crime-scene investigator must never attempt to fit a suspect tool into a tool mark because any contact between the tool and the marked surface may alter the mark and will, at the least, raise serious questions about the integrity of the evidence.

38. Before any impression is moved or otherwise handled, it must be photographed to show all the observable details of the impression.

39. Two procedures used to preserve impressions that cannot be submitted to the laboratory are lifting and casting.

40. SICAR is Shoeprint Image Capture and Retrieval, an automated shoe print identification system developed in England that incorporates multiple databases to search

known and unknown footwear files for comparison against footwear specimens. Using the system, an impression from a crime scene can be compared to a reference database to find out what type of shoe caused the imprint. That same impression can also be searched in the suspect and crime databases to reveal whether that shoe print matches the shoes of a person who has been in custody or the shoe prints left behind at another crime scene.

Application and Critical Thinking

1. a. 18–36 inches
    b. more than 36 inches
    c. 12–18 inches or less
    d. 1 inch or less

2. The correct answer is (a), 18 yards. A 12-gauge shotgun with no choke would be expected to produce a spread of about 1 inch for each yard from the shooter to the target. Thus, a spread of 12 inches would represent a distance of about 12 yards. A moderately high choke, however, would narrow the spread of the pattern somewhat. This means that at a distance of 12 yards, the spread would be less than 12 inches. At a distance of 6 yards, the spread would be much less than 12 inches. Answers (b) and (c), therefore must be wrong. The distance in answer (d), 30 yards, is probably too far. Although the choke would narrow the spread of the pellets, it would probably not narrow it to such a great extent.

3. Ben made several errors. Before unloading the revolver, Ben should have indicated the chamber position in line with the barrel by scratching a mark on the cylinder. He then should have made a diagram of the gun, designating each chamber with a number. As he removed each cartridge, he should have marked it to correspond to the numbered chambers in the diagram. Ben also should have placed each cartridge in a separate envelope and he should have put the tag on the trigger guard, not the grip. Instead of using pliers to grab the bullet and pull it from the wall, Ben should have carefully broken away the surrounding wall material while avoiding direct contact with the bullet. Finally, he should have wrapped the bullet in tissue paper before placing it in an envelope.

4. a. Photograph the print.
    b. Photograph the tool mark, then make a cast of it.
    c. Photograph the tire marks, then make a cast of them.
    d. Photograph the shoe print, then bring the tile bearing the print to the laboratory.
    e. Photograph the print, then use an electrostatic lifting device to lift it off the surface.

Chapter 16
Facts and Concepts

1. A questioned document is any object that contains handwritten or typewritten markings whose source or authenticity is in doubt.

2. Individual variations may be expected in angularity, slope, speed, pressure, letter and word spacings, relative dimensions of letters, connections, pen movement, writing skill, and finger dexterity.

3. Factors besides handwriting characteristics that can impart individual variations include margins, spacings, crowding, insertions, alignment, spelling, punctuation, phraseology, and grammar.

4. Two situations in which a document examiner may be prevented from making a positive conclusion about a questioned document are (1) when an insufficient number of known writings are made available for comparison, and (2) when the examiner receives questioned writings containing only a few words, all deliberately written so as to disguise the writer's natural style.

5. Exemplars are authentic samples of an individual's writing, used for comparison to suspect handwriting samples. They are important to document examination because collection of an adequate number of exemplars is critical for determining the outcome of a comparison.

6. Natural variations are normal deviations found between repeated specimens of an individual's handwriting. They are useful in detecting forgeries because no two specimens of writing prepared by one person are ever identical in every detail. Thus, a document forged by tracing an authentic sample of writing or a signature can often be detected even if the original and the tracing coincide exactly, because no one ever writes the same words or signs two signatures exactly alike.

7. c

8. In *Gilbert* v. *California,* the Supreme Court addressed the constitutionality of taking handwriting exemplars before the appointment of counsel. The Court ruled that handwriting samples are identifying physical characteristics that lie outside the protection privileges of the Fifth Amendment.

9. In *United States* v. *Mara,* the Supreme Court addressed the constitutionality of taking a handwriting sample without the consent of the suspect. The court ruled that this did not constitute an unreasonable search and seizure of a person and hence did not violate Fourth Amendment rights.

10. Transitory defect marks originating from random debris on the glass platen, inner cover, or mechanical portions of a copier produce irregularly shaped images that may serve as points of comparison.

11. A TTI, or transmitting terminal identifier, is a header at the top of each page of a fax document. It is useful in document comparison because it serves as a way to distinguish between a real and a fraudulently prepared fax document. Investigators also use it to determine the model of fax machine that produced the document.

12. The two general categories of printers are impact and nonimpact printers. Impact printers include thermal and dot-matrix printers. Nonimpact printers include inkjet and laser printers.

13. When the suspect machine is not available, it is important to identify the printing technology, the type of paper, the type of toner or ink used, the chemical composition of the toner, and the type of toner-to-paper fusing method used in producing the document.

14. Examination of toner typically involves microscopic analysis to characterize its surface morphology, followed by identification of the inorganic and organic components of the toner.

15. Examiners are most often asked the following two questions about typewriters: (1) Can the make and model of the typewriter used to type the questioned document be identified? (2) Can a particular suspect typewriter be identified as having prepared the questioned document?

16. Variations in vertical and horizontal alignment (characters are too high or low or too far left or right of their correct position) and perpendicular misalignment of characters (characters leaning to the left or to the right), as well as defects in each typeface, are valuable for proving the identity of a typewriter.

17. Infrared luminescence can be used to detect alterations to a document made with ink differing from the original. Infrared luminescence can also reveal writing that has been erased.

18. Indented writings are often readable when the paper is studied under oblique or side lighting. A second method involves applying an electrostatic charge to the surface of a polymer film that has been placed in contact with a questioned document. Indented impressions on the document are revealed by applying a toner powder to the charged film.

19. Two analytical techniques used to analyze writing inks are microspectrophotometry and thin-layer chromatography.

20. The most common features associated with a paper examination are general appearance, color, weight, and watermarks.

Application and Critical Thinking

1. Julie made several mistakes. She should have given the suspect a pencil, not a pen, because the original notes were written in pencil. She also should have had the suspect prepare at least a full page of writing, and she should have had him write the material at least three times. Also, she should not have spelled any words for the suspect. Finally, Julie should have shown the original threatening notes to a document examiner before taking exemplars from the suspect, not afterward.

2. a. Photograph the document with infrared-sensitive film.
   b. Examine the document under infrared or ultraviolet lighting.
   c. Examine the document under ultraviolet lighting.
   d. Photograph the document with infrared-sensitive film, or reflect light off the paper's surface at different angles in order to contrast the writing against the charred background.

3. The aspects of the document you would examine to determine whether the document was authentic would be the paper and the ink. You would use thin-layer chromatography to characterize the dye used in the ink to determine whether that particular ink was in use when the original document was prepared.

Chapter 17
Facts and Concepts

1. Hardware comprises the physical components of the computer. Software is a set of instructions compiled into a program that performs a particular task.

2. CDs, DVDs, and other containers for programs that are loaded into the memory of a computer are referred to as media.

3. The motherboard is the main system board of a computer that delivers power, data, and instructions to the computer's components.

4. a

5. The central processing unit, or CPU, is the part of the computer that actually computes.

6. Random-access memory (RAM) stores software programs and instructions while the computer is turned on. It is also referred to as volatile memory because it is not permanent; its contents are lost forever once power is taken away from the computer.

7. Firmware consists of programs that are used to start the computer's boot process. Another name for firmware is BIOS (basic input-output system). It is important to forensic computer investigation because it allows investigators to control the boot process to some degree, thus helping preserve evidence located in random-access memory (RAM).

8. The computer's operating system (OS) is the bridge between the human user and the computer's electronic components. It provides the user with a working environment and facilitates interaction with the system's components.

9. The primary storage device on most computers is the hard disk drive (HDD).

10. Formatting is the process of preparing a hard disk drive (HDD) to store and retrieve data in its current form. A HDD must be formatted because each operating system (OS) supports file systems that store data in different ways.

11. A sector is the smallest unit of data that a hard drive can address. A cluster usually is the minimum space allocated to a file. Clusters are groups of sectors.

12. A bit, or a binary digit, is the smallest unit of information on a computer. Eight bits constitute a byte.

13. A FAT is a file allocation table. It tracks the location of files and folders on the hard disk drive (HDD).

14. Aspects of a computer that should be photographed close up at an electronic crime scene include (1) the screen of any running computer monitor, (2) all the connections to the main system unit, such as peripheral devices (keyboard, monitor, speakers, mouse, and so on), and (3) equipment serial numbers.

15. Two situations in which an investigator would not immediately unplug a computer at an electronic crime scene are (1) if encryption is being used and pulling the plug will encrypt the data, rendering it unreadable without a password or key, and (2) if data exists in RAM that has not been saved to the HDD, and will thus be lost if power to the system is discontinued.

16. The primary goal in obtaining data from a HDD is to do so without altering even one bit of data.

17. A Message Digest 5 (MD5)/Secure Hash Algorithm (SHA) takes a "fingerprint" of a hard disk drive (HDD) before and after forensic imaging. A forensic computer examiner would run such an algorithm to demonstrate that the forensic image recovered is all-inclusive of the original contents and that nothing was altered in the process.

18. Investigators would want to copy blank or unused portions of the HDD to preserve latent data—data that exists in areas of the drive that are, generally speaking, unknown and inaccessible to most end users—that can be valuable as evidence.

19. The two main types of evidentiary computer data are visible data and latent data. Visible data includes all information that the operating system is presently aware of, and thus is readily accessible to the user. Latent data includes data that are blocked from a user's view.

20. Swap space is a file or defined space on the HDD to which data is written, or swapped, to free RAM for applications that are in use.

21. d

22. Slack space is empty space on a hard disk drive (HDD) created because of the way the HDD stores files.

23. Fragmentation is a situation in which data for the same file is contained in noncontiguous clusters on the hard disk drive (HDD). Fragmentation can degrade the performance of a HDD, causing the read/write heads to have to traverse the platters to locate the data.

Application and Critical Thinking

1. Because each sector is 512 bytes, a cluster consisting of six sectors would hold 3,072 bytes of data. Because each byte equals 8 bits, each cluster would hold 24,576 bits of data.

2. Tom made several mistakes. When he arrived, he should have sketched the overall layout as well as photographing it. He also should have photographed any running monitors. In addition to labeling the cord of each peripheral, Tom should have placed a corresponding label on the port to which each cord was connected. Before unplugging the computer, he should have checked to ensure that the computer was not using encryption. Finally, he should have removed the plug from the back of the computer, not from the wall.

3. You probably would begin to search for latent data in the swap space on the hard disk drive. If the accountant was keeping fraudulent records, he may well have been transferring data from one accounting program to another. Data from those operations may well be left behind in the swap space, where it later can be retrieved.

Case Analysis 1

1. By examining Mr. Smith's computer, police hoped to prove that he had changed his wife's insurance policy shortly before the fire in which she died. They believed this would implicate him in his wife's murder because the increased insurance settlement Mr. Smith would receive upon his wife's death would serve as a strong motive for murdering her.

2. The documents titled *insurance1.doc* and *WRL1604.tmp* were important to tying Mr. Smith to his wife's death because they proved that he wrote the letter to his insurance company requesting an increase in his wife's life insurance.

Case Analysis 2

1. The physical evidence that most strongly implicated the driver of the van in a counterfeiting operation was the discovery of two $100 bills in his wallet. These suspicions were confirmed by the fact that both bills had identical serial numbers.

2. The documents titled *GapGiftCert1.jpg* and *GapGiftCert2.jpg* indicated that the suspects were producing more than counterfeit currency. From these files, the investigators concluded that the suspects were also producing counterfeit gift certificates to The Gap.

Chapter 18
Facts and Concepts

1. The Internet is referred to as "a network of networks" because it connects computer networks so information can be exchanged worldwide.

2. A computer can be connected to the Internet via a modem, a broadband connection, or a WiFi connection.

3. b

4. A company that provides connections to the Internet is called an Internet service provider (ISP).

5. An IP address is a unique address given to every computer that is connected to the Internet. It typically takes the form ###.###.###.###, in which ### can be any number from 0 to 255.

6. A human-readable name assigned to an IP address is called a domain.

7. A browser is a program that allows a computer user to access Web sites.

8. c

9. Hypertext is highlighted text or graphics on a Web page that, when clicked, links to other Websites. Hypertext has given rise to the expressions *browsing* and *surfing the Net*.

10. Besides Web pages, three ways for a computer user to receive information via the Internet are e-mail, mailing lists, and newsgroups.

11. An Internet cache stores portions of the Web pages a user visits on the local hard disk drive. This way, if the page is revisited, portions of it can be reconstructed more quickly from this saved data, rather than having to pull it yet again from the Internet and use precious bandwidth.

12. Three places where a forensic computer examiner might look to determine what Websites a computer user has visited recently are the Internet cache, cookies, and the Internet history.

13. An IP address is important to forensic computer examination because it may lead to the identity of the

person who was using a particular computer to access the Internet.

14. Chat and instant messages typically are stored in the volatile memory space of random-access memory (RAM).

15. Hacking is a slang term for an unauthorized computer or network intrusion. The individuals who most commonly engage in hacking are rogue or disgruntled employees with some knowledge of a computer network who are looking to cause damage.

16. A firewall is a device designed to protect against intrusions into a computer network. It works by keeping a log of all the computers that are allowed to access a network, and blocking entry to any computer whose address is not contained in the log.

Application and Critical Thinking

1. a. .com
   b. .mil
   c. .org
   d. .gov
   e. .edu

2. On the first computer you probably would look first at the compound files created by Microsoft Outlook. On the second computer you probably would look first in the Internet cache.

Index

Part Opener and Chapter Opener Photo Credits

Chapter 16
Pages 552-553, background: PhotoEdit Inc.
Page 552, left: AP Wide World Photos
Page 553, top: AP Wide World Photos; middle: Getty
  Images, Inc.; bottom: AP Wide World Photos

Chapter 17
Pages 578-579, background: EyeWire Collection, Getty
  Images—Photodisc
Page 578, left: AP Wide World Photos
Page 579, top: EyeWire Collection, Getty Images—
  Photodisc; middle: NewsCom; bottom: © Orjan
  F. Ellingvag/CORBIS. All Rights Reserved

Chapter 18
Pages 610-611, background: AP Wide World Photos
Page 610, left: AP Wide World Photos
Page 611, middle: Ted Benson—Pool, Getty Images,
  Inc.—Liaison; bottom: Al Golub, AP Wide World
  Photos

Chapter 19
Pages 632-633, crime scene tape: Arthur Turner, Alamy
  Images
Page 632, left: © Jim Craigmyle/CORBIS All Rights
  Reserved
Page 633, top: Dr. Jurgen Scriba, Photo Researchers,
  Inc.; middle: Corbis Royalty Free; bottom: AP
  Wide World Photos

Forensic Cases
Page 643: Dr. Jurgen Scriba, Photo Researchers, Inc.

Appendix
Page 673: © Jim Craigmyle/CORBIS All Rights
  Reserved